THIRD EDITION

BUSINESS AND ITS ENVIRONMENT

David P. Baron

Stanford University

Prentice Hall, Upper Saddle River, New Jersey 07458

Senior Editor: Stephanie Johnson
Editorial Assistant: Hersch Doby
Editor-in-Chief: Natalie Anderson
Assistant Editor: Shane Gemza
Editorial Managing Editor: Jennifer Glennon
Marketing Manager: Michael Campbell
Production Manager: Gail Steier de Acevedo
Production Coordinator: Maureen Wilson
Permissions Coordinator: Monica Stipanov
Manufacturing Buyer: Natacha St. Hill Moore
Senior Manufacturing Manager: Vincent Scelta
Cover Design Manager: Pat Smythe
Cover Design: Michael Fruhbeis
Cover Art: Guillermo Wiedemann, Colombian (b. Germany), 1905-69.
"Broken Square 3," 1965. Dilon Canvas, $40^1/_2 \times 35''$. Bequest of
Christina Wiedemann. Copyright Lowe Art Museum, University of Miami,
all rights reserved/Superstock, Inc.
Full Service Composition: Carlisle Publishers Services

Library of Congress Cataloging-in-Publication Data
Baron, David P.
Business and its environment / David P. Baron. — 3rd ed.
p. cm.
Includes bibliographical references and index.
ISBN 0-13-081561-6
1. Social responsibility of business. 2. Industrial policy.
3. Commercial law. 4. Business ethics. I. Title.
HD60.B37 2000
658.4 08—dc21 99-26984
CIP

Prentice-Hall International (UK) Limited, London
Prentice-Hall of Australia Pty. Limited, Sydney
Prentice-Hall Canada, Inc., Toronto
Prentice-Hall Hispanoamericana, S.A., Mexico
Prentice-Hall of India Private Limited, New Delhi
Prentice-Hall of Japan, Inc., Tokyo
Prentice-Hall (Singapore) Pte Ltd.
Editora Prentice-Hall do Brasil, Ltda., Rio de Janeiro

Printed in the United States of America

10 9 8 7 6 5 4 3 2

To Mary

Contents

List of Cases

Preface

The environment of business is composed of market and nonmarket components. The market environment is characterized by the structure of the markets in which a firm operates and the nature of market competition. The nonmarket environment is the legal, political, and social context in which firms are embedded. It is characterized by a set of issues that pose managerial challenges, the interests concerned with those issues, the institutions in whose arenas the issues are addressed, and the information available about the issues, institutions, and interests. In the market environment, firms interact with customers, suppliers, employees, and other firms. In the nonmarket environment firms interact with stakeholders, interest and activist groups, governments, and the public. The market and nonmarket environments are interrelated, and managers are responsible for the performance of their firms in both environments. These environments are not exogenous, but instead are shaped by the actions taken by firms and other interested parties in the arenas of markets and public institutions. These actions not only shape the nonmarket environment, but they also affect the structure of the market environment and the positions of firms in that environment. Similarly, the actions of firms in their market environment generate issues that are addressed in the nonmarket environment. *Business and Its Environment* addresses the interrelationships among the market and nonmarket environments and the effective management of the issues that arise therein.

The third edition of *Business and Its Environment* represents continuity and change. It retains the structure, the subject matter, and the conceptual frameworks of the second edition. It also retains the managerial orientation, including the focus on strategy formulation and implementation, and the normative orientation by focusing both on superior nonmarket strategies and on ethics and corporate responsibility. The book contains cases for each chapter that provide opportunities for students to discuss managerial issues, apply the conceptual material, and learn from class discussion. The third edition retains the integrative cases at the end of each of the five parts of the book. The integrative cases are on the topical subjects of biotechnology, public referenda affecting high technology companies, energy and environmental regulation, globalization, and ethical issues in international supply chains.

A theme retained in the third edition is that of integrated strategy—considering issues that have both market and nonmarket components and emphasizing strategies integrated over those two dimensions. The approach also brings together the disciplines of economics, political science, law, and ethics to provide a deeper understanding of the environment of business and nonmarket issues. For example, the third edition provides an integrated treatment of the economics and politics of antitrust, regulation, environmental protection, and international trade policy. An integrated perspective strengthens the managerial orientation of the book and also enhances the usefulness of the conceptual materials for other parts of the business curriculum.

The principal changes in the third edition include a thorough updating of all the chapters, additional conceptual and analytical material, a strengthened emphasis on nonmarket strategy and its integration with market strategy, new and updated applications, a richer and more complete framework for ethical analysis, and a new chapter and cases on

China, addressing history, culture, political economy, business arrangements, and ethical issues. The third edition contains seventy-three cases, including twenty-seven new cases on companies such as Microsoft, Nike, Federal Express, Shell, Eastman Kodak, and Advanced Technology Laboratories. Many of the new cases are set at the end of the 1990s and address issues in antitrust, biotechnology, regulation of high technology business, globalization, environmental protection, international business, international trade, product safety, and business ethics and responsibility. Twenty-two of the cases concern global and international nonmarket issues and several are on small businesses. Many of the cases are short to engage the reader quickly by providing only the descriptive detail necessary to apply the conceptual material. A number of the cases, such as the antitrust cases on Microsoft and the Staples-Home Depot merger, have richer contextual descriptions. The cases do not necessarily provide exemplary lessons or descriptions of current practice but instead pose a managerial problem that requires analysis and strategy formulation.

In contrast to a public policy or social responsibility perspective, the approach taken in the book is managerial. That is, it takes the perspective of managers, and not of government or the public, and focuses on issues of importance to the performance of their firms. The approach emphasizes analysis and principled reasoning as the foundations for formulating effective and responsible strategies for improving performance.

The book is organized in five parts. Part I introduces the nonmarket environment, the nonmarket issues firms face, and the forces that affect the development of those issues. The focus is on the formulation of strategies for addressing nonmarket issues and the integration of those strategies with market strategies. Part II is concerned with issues addressed in the context of political institutions with an emphasis on legislatures. The substantive focus is on conceptual frameworks for analyzing political issues affecting companies and for formulating strategies for addressing them in an effective manner. The frameworks developed in this part provide a foundation for Parts III and IV. Part III focuses on the interactions between government and markets with an emphasis on antitrust, regulation, liability, and environmental protection. Conceptual frameworks for understanding the political economy of these issues are presented in the context of managerial issues. For example, tradable permits systems for mitigating pollution emissions and global warming are considered to identify the efficient management of environmental externalities, and then the political forces shaping the management of environmental issues are considered. Part IV is explicitly international and provides frameworks for understanding the political economy of countries and the relationships between business and government. Japan, the European Community, and China are considered, and international trade policy is used to bring the policy and strategy issues together. Part V is normative and focuses on issues involving the responsibilities of firms and the guidance that ethics provides. Ethical systems and ethical reasoning about managerial issues are the centerpieces of Part V, and the applications focus on corporate responsibility, the employment relationship, and international business. The complexities involved in operating in developing countries are considered both through conceptual frameworks and cases.

In addition to those who provided encouragement for the first two editions, I would like to thank David Brady, Daniel Diermeier, Daniel Kessler, and Keith Krehbiel for contributing new cases to the third edition. Thanks must also go out to Anthony F. Buono, Bentley College, Hugh Folk, University of Hawaii-Manoa, Wayne Grossman, Kansas State University, Wonsik Lee, Central Connecticut State University, Nancey Nightingale, International College, and Newman Peery, University of the Pacific for their service as reviewers. The Graduate School of Business of Stanford University provided institutional support without which this book could not have been written.

Stanford, California

PART I

Strategy and the Nonmarket Environment

CHAPTER 1

The Market and Nonmarket Environments

Introduction

The environment of business consists of market and nonmarket components. The market environment includes the interactions between firms and other parties that take place through markets or private agreements such as contracts. These interactions typically are voluntary and involve economic transactions and the exchange of property. To succeed, firms must operate effectively in their market environment. They must be efficient in production and responsive to consumer demand. They must anticipate and adapt to change, innovate through research and development, and develop new products and services. Effective management in the market environment is a necessary condition for success, but it is not sufficient.

The performance of a firm, and of its management, also depends on its activities in its nonmarket environment. The nonmarket environment includes the social, political, and legal arrangements that structure interactions outside of, but in conjunction with, markets and private agreements. The nonmarket environment encompasses those interactions between the firm and individuals, interest groups, government entities, and the public that are intermediated by public institutions rather than solely by markets and private agreements. Public institutions differ from markets and private agreements because of characteristics such as majority rule, due process, broad enfranchisement, collective action, and publicness. Activities in the nonmarket environment may be voluntary, as when the firm cooperates with government officials, or involuntary, such as when government regulates an activity or an activist group organizes a boycott of a firm's product. Effective management in the nonmarket environment is a necessary condition for success just as is effective management in the market environment.

The nonmarket environment has increased in importance and complexity over time and commands increased managerial attention. Nonmarket issues high on firms' agendas include environmental protection, health and safety, technology policy, regulation and deregulation, international trade policy, legislative politics, activist pressures, media coverage of business, stakeholder relations, corporate responsibility, and ethics. Although the saliency of particular issues ebbs and flows, nonmarket issues and the forces associated with them have important consequences for managerial and firm performance. Nonmarket issues, the forces that influence their development, and the managerial strategies for addressing them are the focus of the field of business and its environment. The managerial objective is to improve the overall performance of businesses by effectively addressing nonmarket issues and the forces associated with them.

Developments in the nonmarket environment affect performance on a number of dimensions. In the automobile industry, emissions and fuel economy standards affect research and development, design, production, pricing, and marketing. Safety regulation and liability standards have similar broad effects. Import competition and access to international markets affect competitive strategies involving product design, pricing, and capacity planning. Each of these examples has two components—an underlying issue and its impact on firm performance. The fuel economy standards issue, for example, is related to global warming and energy conservation issues and has broad implications for performance. The focus for management in the nonmarket environment is not only on the issue of global warming and the public policy responses to it, but also on how an automobile company can participate both effectively and responsibly in the public processes addressing the issue and the measures proposed to deal with it. Activity in the nonmarket environment is generally organized around specific issues and is motivated by the impacts of those issues. The legislative process, for example, focuses on bills to address a specific issue such as fuel economy standards. Managerial attention thus focuses on specific issues affecting performance and the forces shaping those issues.

The Role of Management

Because of the importance of the nonmarket environment for managerial and organizational performance, nonmarket issues must be the responsibility of managers. As indicated in Figure 1-1, managers operate in both the market and the nonmarket environments. Managers are in the best position to assess the likely impact both of market activities on the firm's nonmarket environment and of developments in the nonmarket environment on market opportunities and performance. Management thus is responsible for formulating and implementing nonmarket, as well as market, strategies.

Firms typically deal with nonmarket issues in proportion to their potential effects on performance. Managers are in the best position to assess those effects and, with the advice of specialists, to formulate strategies to address the underlying issues. The implementation of nonmarket strategies also involves the active participation of managers. They may address the public on issues, communicate with the media, testify in

FIGURE 1-1 The Environment of Business

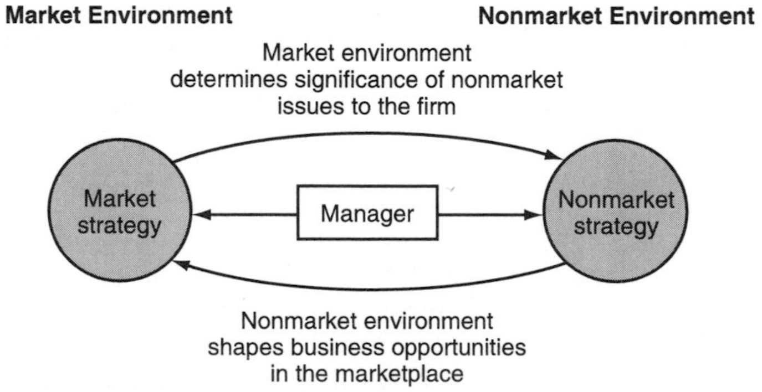
Market Environment
Nonmarket Environment
Market environment determines significance of nonmarket issues to the firm
Market strategy
Manager
Nonmarket strategy
Nonmarket environment shapes business opportunities in the marketplace

Economics (positive, normative)	Disciplinary base	Political science; ethics (positive, normative)

regulatory and antitrust proceedings, lobby government officials, participate in coalitions and associations, serve on government advisory panels, meet with activists, negotiate with interest groups, develop relationships with stakeholders, and participate in constituency programs.

Successful management requires frameworks for analyzing nonmarket issues, principles for reasoning about them, and approaches to formulating strategies to address them. These frameworks, principles, and approaches enable managers to address issues in a systematic manner, allowing them to guide their organizations successfully and responsibly in their nonmarket environments. In formulating nonmarket strategies, managers may draw on the expertise of lawyers, public affairs specialists, Washington representatives, and community relations specialists. Managers, however, ultimately must evaluate the quality of the advice they receive and combine it with their own knowledge of the market and nonmarket environments. Most firms have found that managers must be involved in all stages of a firm's efforts to address nonmarket issues.

The Market and Nonmarket Environments

As illustrated in Figure 1-1, the market and nonmarket environments of business are interrelated. A firm's activities in its market environment can generate nonmarket issues and stimulate actions that change its nonmarket environment. These actions include those of government, such as legislation, regulation, antitrust lawsuits, and international trade agreements. Similarly, the actions of interest groups and activists motivated by moral concerns about a firm's activities may force the firm to change its practices. As an example of the market origins of nonmarket issues, lower real gasoline prices and changing consumer demand resulted in sport utility vehicles (SUVs) and light trucks capturing half the light-vehicle market. This reduced average fuel economy and in conjunction with the global warming issue generated activist pressure to increase fuel economy standards. Moreover, the size and weight of these vehicles raised concerns about the safety of the occupants of automobiles in the event of a collision.

Nonmarket issues and actions also shape the market environment. Higher fuel economy standards would affect virtually all aspects of automobile design and manufacturing. Similarly, political action against Microsoft's alleged abusive practices in the software industry put pressure on the Department of Justice and state attorneys general to file an antitrust lawsuit. The market environment is also shaped directly by the actions of interest groups and the public sentiment for their causes. The Exxon Valdez oil spill increased environmental pressure on firms through liability for damages, more stringent regulations, and direct public pressure.

Both the market and nonmarket environments of business are subject to, and shaped by, competing forces. In the market environment, sales and profits are the result of competition directed by the production, finance, and marketing strategies of firms. In the nonmarket environment, legislation, regulation, administrative decisions, and public pressure are the result of competing nonmarket strategies of individuals, interest groups, firms, and government officials. In the market environment, those strategies are intermediated by markets, whereas in the nonmarket environment, strategies are intermediated by public and private institutions, including legislatures, courts, regulatory agencies, and public sentiment. Just as the market environment of business changes and competitive advantage evolves, the nonmarket environment changes and the issues on a firm's nonmarket agenda evolve.

The nonmarket environment thus should be understood as responsive to the strategies of firms and other interested parties. Moreover, those strategies can shape the market environment and the opportunities for a firm. Robert Galvin (1992), who led Motorola for over three decades, described Motorola's approach to its nonmarket environment as "writing the rules of the game."[1]

> The first step in any defined strategy is writing the rules of the game honorably and fairly in a manner that gives everyone a chance with predictable rules. Our company has started industries. We have helped write standards. We have helped write trade rules. We have helped influence policies. We have helped write national laws of countries where we have engaged, always in a respectful way. We have never taken for granted that the rules of the game would just evolve in a fashion that would make for the greatest opportunity. . . .With the right rules of the game, one's opportunity for success is enhanced.

Galvin's point is not that companies dictate the rules of the game but rather that those rules are shaped by the strategies of interested parties and by governing institutions. Companies such as Motorola and leaders such as Robert Galvin attempt to shape the rules by participating responsibly in the public processes that address those rules.

THE FOUR I'S

The nonmarket environment of a firm or industry is characterized by four I's:

- issues
- interests
- institutions
- information

Issues are the basic unit of analysis and the focus of nonmarket action. Using the agricultural biotechnology industry as an example, the central nonmarket issues in the 1990s were the formulation of regulatory policies for the approval of bioengineered plant and animal foods and the public acceptance of such products. Interests included the individuals and groups with preferences about, or a stake in, an issue. The principal interests were the agricultural biotechnology companies and the interest groups and activists concerned with biotechnology issues. Institutions included government entities such as legislatures and bureaucracies as well as nongovernmental institutions such as the media and public sentiment. The Environmental Protection Agency, the U.S. Department of Agriculture, the Food and Drug Administration, and Congress were the principal government institutions in whose arenas the issues were addressed. Information pertained to what the interested parties knew or believed about the relationship between actions and consequences and about the preferences and capabilities of the parties. For example, information pertaining to the risks associated with individual products and agricultural biotechnology more generally was central to the development of public policy. The issue of the public acceptance of agricultural biotechnology products was also addressed in the institution of public sentiment and was shaped by the information provided by the interests, government institutions, and the media coverage of the issues.[2] The task for management was to formulate and implement strate-

---

[1]See Yoffie (1988) and Chapter 16 for analyses of aspects of this strategy.

[2]Agricultural biotechnology is considered in the Part I integrative case *Calgene, Inc., and Infrastructure Marketing* and the Chapter 4 case *Monsanto and the Synthetic Growth Hormone* in Chapter 4.

gies that effectively addressed the nonmarket issues in the context of institutions in which information plays an important role.

To illustrate this perspective, aspects of the nonmarket environment of the U.S. automobile industry will be described and then characterized in terms of issues, interests, institutions, and information.

The Nonmarket Environment of the Automobile Industry

In the second half of the 1990s the U.S. automobile industry faced a set of complex nonmarket issues. This section identifies selected issues, which will be used to characterize the nonmarket environment of the industry, formulate a nonmarket issue agenda, and introduce a framework for understanding the life cycle of nonmarket issues.

SAFETY

Consumer and safety activists raised concerns about the hazards to occupants of automobiles in accidents with sport utility vehicles (SUVs). Ford's studies indicated that collisions between SUVs and cars resulted in 1,000 deaths that could not be accounted for by the weight difference. The Insurance Institute for Highway Safety, a consortium formed by insurance companies, argued that the frames of SUVs should be lowered and made less rigid to reduce injuries to occupants in cars. Critics, however, argued that such changes would reduce the safety of the occupants of the SUVs.

State Farm Insurance sued Ford to recover claims paid to policyholders for damage done by fires allegedly due to faulty electrical switches. Ford had recalled 8.7 million cars to replace the switches, but State Farm alleged that Ford had withheld data on the switches.

In 1996, on behalf of the National Highway Traffic Safety Administration (NHTSA), the Department of Justice filed suit against Chrysler for refusing to recall 91,000 vehicles for alleged problems with rear seatbelts. No accidents or injuries had been associated with the seatbelts, and the dispute between Chrysler and NHTSA centered on whether NHTSA had followed its own rules in conducting safety tests. The previous year Chrysler had agreed to recall four million minivans to repair a rear door latch.

Repeal of the federal 55 mph speed limit in 1995 led nearly all states to raise their speed limits. Safety activists, such as Advocates for Highway and Auto Safety, opposed the increase and predicted thousands of additional deaths. In 1996 deaths increased only slightly to 41,907 from 41,798, but an initial study by the Insurance Institute for Highway Safety suggested that the higher speed limits had increased deaths but that other factors had reduced deaths by a comparable amount. In 1997 the highway death rate in the United States was at a record low.

A 1998 NHTSA study concluded that cellular telephone use increased the risk of an accident, but NHTSA concluded that more research was needed before regulatory or legislative action was taken.

AIR BAGS

From 1991 to 1996 air bags were reported to have killed 51 children and small adults sitting in the passenger seat. To meet federal standards, air bags inflated at speeds up to 200 miles an hour and could deploy in accidents at speeds as low as 10 miles per hour. The auto industry along with insurance companies and air bag manufacturers formed an ad hoc coalition, the Air Bag Safety Campaign, that urged motorists to seat children under 12 years in the rear seat and children over 20 pounds, who must be in the front seat, in forward-facing child seats with the seat set as far back as possible. In response to public concerns NHTSA announced that automakers would be allowed to install depowered air bags and that motorists would be allowed to install on-off switches for the passenger-side air bag. NHTSA also considered mandating "smart seats" that would sense the size and weight of passengers and automatically adjust the speed at which the air bag deployed. Public Citizen and the Center for Auto Safety, two interest groups in the Ralph Nader network, released a study claiming that air bags that inflated directly at the passenger accounted for all those killed by air bags, whereas air bags that first inflated upward had not resulted in any deaths. The deaths and the additional costs of developing smart air bag systems renewed the debate over whether air bags, which were are mandated primarily because 30 percent of motorists and passengers do not wear seat belts, were warranted. NHTSA estimated that 85 percent of the 9,000 rollover deaths a year were due to not wearing a seat belt.

FUEL ECONOMY

In 1975 Congress enacted Corporate Average Fuel Economy (CAFE) standards, which coupled with high gasoline prices resulted in substantial mileage improvements during the 1970s and 1980s. With falling real gasoline prices and the waning of energy conservation sentiments, motorists turned to larger automobiles, light trucks, and SUVs. The industry was able to avoid further increases in the CAFE standards, and in 1996 Congress enacted a 1-year freeze on CAFE standards for automobiles and extended the freeze the next year. The industry and numerous members of Congress sought a permanent freeze, and some sought elimination of the program.

The fuel efficiency program for light trucks, which included minivans and SUVs, was administered by the Department of Transportation (DOT), and in 1994 DOT proposed large increases in mileage standards over the next decade, but Congress imposed a temporary hold on any increases. In 1998, however, the popularity of large SUVs and larger trucks threatened mileage below the existing 20.7 mpg standard. To avoid fines and the public criticism that would accompany them, General Motors halted production of its largest SUVs in midyear. It also increased the weight of its Suburbans so that they qualified as medium-duty trucks, which were not subject to mileage standards.

ALTERNATIVE FUEL VEHICLES

California had waived its requirement that zero-emissions vehicles account for 2 percent of vehicles sold in the state by 1998, but it had retained its mandate that the vehicles account for 10 percent of sales in 2003. General Motors had introduced its electric-powered EV1 in anticipation of the 1998 mandate, but demand was sluggish.

The industry also showed increased interest in diesel engines which have 30 percent higher mileage. Toyota had introduced the first hybrid electric-gasoline car, which was capable of achieving over 60 mpg. In response, U.S. auto companies announced plans for cars powered by hybrid engines, alternative fuels, and fuel cells.

The big-three auto companies joined with the federal government in the Partnership for New Generation of Vehicles to develop a safe, affordable vehicle capable of attaining 80 mpg. Daimler-Benz and Toyota introduced electric test vehicles powered by fuel cells that produce electricity through chemical reactions, and Ford and Chrysler announced that they were developing vehicles powered by fuel cells. The Canadian government announced that it would subsidize Ballard Power Systems of Vancouver to develop a fuel cell for the Ford vehicle. The Union of Concerned Scientists, an environmental interest group, supported the development of fuel cells for vehicles.

EMISSIONS

Emissions standards for light trucks, minivans, and most SUVs were nearly twice as high as for automobiles. Under the Clean Air Act of 1990 the EPA was prohibited from tightening emissions standards for these vehicles before 2004, and to prepare for that date the EPA began the preliminary stages of its rule-making process. The American Automobile Manufacturers Association argued that oil companies should reduce the sulfur in gasoline to allow catalytic converters to meet more stringent standards, and oil companies argued that the auto companies should design better catalytic converters.

Honda announced that most of its 1998 Accords would meet the 2000 standard of 0.075 grams of nonmethane organic gas emissions per mile. In a 1998 settlement with the Department of Justice, the EPA, and the California Air Resources Board, Honda agreed to pay $17 million in fines for a flaw in its onboard diagnostic system for emissions control.

In 1998 a state science panel in California endorsed an EPA report that soot particles in diesel emissions could cause cancer. The trucking industry labeled the panel's report as "junk science," whereas the Natural Resources Defense Counsel, an environmental interest group, labeled it "a turning point" in the battle to deal with an important health hazard.

In a 1998 settlement with the Department of Justice and the EPA, seven manufacturers of diesel engines agreed to pay $83.4 million in fines and $109 million for pollution reduction and new engine technology programs, and to spend $850 million to reduce emissions in new engines. The issue was the failure to meet emissions standards at cruising rather than laboratory speeds. The manufacturers held that the issue was due to a "precipitous change" in EPA testing procedures and that the EPA was fully aware of the issue. The Sierra Club challenged the settlement arguing that the engines should be recalled immediately.

ACTIVIST PRESSURE

In the early 1990s the Rainforest Action Network (RAN), an environmental activist group, began a boycott of Mitsubishi Motors in an attempt to force Mitsubishi Trading Company, a separate company but also a member of the Mitsubishi *keiretsu,* to stop logging rainforests in Southeast Asia. RAN's activities included picketing dealers, demonstrating at Mitsubishi exhibits at auto shows, and advertising in newspapers urging a boycott of the companies. In 1998 RAN and the two companies signed a memorandum of understanding under which RAN agreed to call off the boycott and Mitsubishi Motors agreed to an environmental review of its operations and to contributions to a program promoting preservation of ancient forests.

MEDIA COVERAGE

An investigation by General Motors revealed that an NBC *Dateline* segment purportedly showing fires caused by side-mounted gasoline tanks on Chevrolet pickup trucks had been faked. GM went public with its evidence, leading NBC to apologize for the incident and retract the story.[3]

In 1996 *Consumer Reports* gave the Isuzu Trooper and the Acura SLX—a Trooper sold with the Acura nameplate—an "unacceptable" rating based on a test that showed that they could tip onto two wheels in quick turns at low speeds. Isuzu Motors replied that the Trooper met all federal safety standards, but that it would examine the test

[3]See the chapter case *GM Like a Rock? (A)*

results In a similar test in Sweden intended to simulate a low-speed maneuver to avoid an elk, Mercedes-Benz's new A-class car, its entry into the small-car segment of the market, rolled over, forcing the company to recall all the vehicles to retrofit them with different tires and an electronic system to control oversteering.

LIABILITY

In the wake of NBC's *Dateline* retraction and a court decision blocking NHTSA from recalling the trucks, plaintiffs alleging injuries due to accidents involving the trucks began to settle their lawsuits with General Motors. In addition to the personal injury lawsuits, a class action lawsuit filed on behalf of the truck owners alleged that the value of their trucks had fallen because of the supposed fire hazard and the publicity surrounding it. After one settlement was thrown out by the courts, a settlement was reached in which GM gave truck owners a certificate for $1,000 for the purchase of a new truck. In 1998 that settlement was thrown out by the courts.

In 1996 the Supreme Court overturned as "grossly excessive" a $2 million punitive damages award in Alabama against BMW for selling a car with a touched-up paint job. The compensatory damages were $4,000. A month later an Alabama jury awarded $50 million in compensatory damages and $100 million in punitive damages to a man who was ejected from his Chevrolet Blazer in a roll-over accident. The plaintiff argued that he was ejected because of a faulty door latch, whereas GM argued that he was ejected through a window when he fell asleep at the wheel after consuming a few beers. The auto industry joined in a campaign for federal legislation to reform the liability system, which was opposed by the Trial Lawyers Association.

TAXES

Automobiles continued to be subject to two special taxes. Under fuel economy regulations a gas guzzler tax of $10 per tenth of a mile was applied to the difference between 22.4 mpg and the car's actual mileage.

In 1997 any car with a price above $36,000 was subject to an 8 percent luxury tax. As a result of nonmarket action by the automobile industry, in 1996 Congress enacted legislation to phase out the tax over 7 years.

GLOBAL WARMING

In 1997 U.S. automobile companies and the coal and oil industries formed a coalition to oppose an international agreement on global warming negotiated in Kyoto, Japan. The American Automobile Manufacturers Association opposed the Kyoto Protocol, arguing that it was too dramatic a response to an unproven problem. Japanese automakers broke ranks with the U.S. companies by refusing to join the coalition. Economists continued to advocate a BTU tax to reduce the use of fossil fuels.

In 1998 the Environmental Protection Agency announced that catalytic converters, which the auto industry had referred to as a "miracle" in reducing emissions of pollutants, were a major contributor to global warming. The converters produce nitrous oxide, which is 360 times more potent than carbon dioxide as a greenhouse gas. The EPA estimated that nitrous oxide accounted for 7.2 percent of greenhouse gases and that catalytic converters produced nearly half that amount. A number of environmentalists called for the industry to move to alternative fuel vehicles.

INTERNATIONAL TRADE

Under strong pressure from the U.S. auto industry, Japan and the United States agreed to a trade accord that would improve access to the Japanese market for U.S. automobiles and parts. The U.S. auto companies then turned their attention to South Korea, pressuring the U.S. Trade Representative to seek removal of import tariffs, discriminatory taxes on vehicles with large engines, and restrictions on auto financing by foreigners. The Association of European Automobile Manufacturers supported the U.S. efforts. Under pressure from U.S. automakers, the United States initiated a Super 301 investigation of Korean trade restraints.[4] Korean government officials called the U.S. actions unfair, and argued that the lagging sales were due to a weak economy. The dispute could be taken to the World Trade Organization.

LABOR RELATIONS

The United Auto Workers (UAW) remained concerned about measures taken by automobile manufacturers to reduce costs and improve competitiveness. The UAW had struck plants, protesting the loss of jobs to Mexico and other countries as a result of globalization and trade agreements such as the North American Free Trade Agreement (NAFTA). In 1998 a strike over productivity and outsourcing idled 160,000 workers in GM's North American operations.

As a result of the merger of Daimler-Benz and Chrysler the UAW obtained one of the three seats on the merged company's supervisory board held by IG Metall, the principal German labor union in the metal-working industry. Under German labor law, labor representatives selected half the members of supervisory boards, and the UAW announced that it would seek to change German law that allowed only German workers to vote for nominees for the supervisory boards.

SEXUAL HARASSMENT

Alleging sexual harassment, 29 employees at Mitsubishi Motor Manufacturing of America filed a lawsuit seeking damages. Jesse Jackson announced a boycott of Mitsubishi, and the National Organization of Women organized demonstrations against the company to attract the news media and generate publicity about the issue. The Equal Employment Opportunity Commission (EEOC) filed a class action sexual harassment lawsuit against Mitsubishi on behalf of female employees. Mitsubishi rejected the allegation, but continued press coverage and criticism led the company to name a former secretary of labor and congresswoman to study sexual harassment, discrimination, and diversity at the plant. The company later settled the EEOC lawsuit, agreeing to pay $34 million and institute a new set of human resources practices.

The Nonmarket Environment and Issue Agenda

This section organizes the nonmarket environment of the automobile industry in terms of the four I's.

ISSUES

A nonmarket issue has consequences, or raises concerns, that cannot be internalized in a private arrangement such as a contract or market transaction. Some nonmarket issues may be localized, as in the case of sexual harassment at a plant, and others may be much

[4]Super 301 refers to a portion of Section 301 of U.S. trade law that provides for investigation of foreign trade barriers that impede U.S. exports. See Chapter 16.

broader, as in the case of global warming. Nonmarket issues can also arise from moral concerns about the manner in which business is conducted, as in the case of the boycott of Mitsubishi or the setting of speed limits. The 14 nonmarket issues identified for the automobile industry are:

1. safety regulation
2. air bag safety
3. liability
4. speed limits
5. fuel economy standards
6. emissions standards
7. alternative fuel vehicles
8. global warming
9. trade policy
10. sexual harassment
11. labor relations
12. activist pressure (e.g., boycotts)
13. luxury, gas guzzlers, and BTU taxes
14. media coverage

Many of these issues are interrelated. Emissions standards and fuel economy standards relate to the global warming issue. Both safety regulation and liability issues center on safety. Similarly, issues may also be related when they are addressed in the same institutional arena or when the same interests are active on those issues. For example, the environmental issues involve the automobile companies and environmental interest groups, and the principal institutions are the EPA and Congress.

INTERESTS

The set of interests includes those who have an economic—or distributive—stake in an issue. U.S. and Japanese automobile companies have interests that are opposed on some issues, such as global warming, but are aligned on others, such as liability reform. Other interest groups with direct stakes in these issues are consumers, employees, insurance companies, and oil companies. On many issues the interests of companies and industries are opposed. The automobile and oil industries are on the opposite sides of the issue of who should be responsible for the next round of emissions reductions. The auto and insurance industries joined together in the Air Bag Safety Campaign but were on the opposite sides of some safety regulation issues. Some interests are organized, as in the case of employees represented by the UAW, and others such as consumers are unorganized.

Interests also include special interest, activist, advocacy, and watchdog groups. Special interest groups pursue issues because of the benefits that accrue to their members, as in the case of the Trial Lawyers Association. Watchdog groups such as Public Citizen and the Center for Auto Safety monitor the activities of firms and call those activities to the attention of the media, government officials, and the public. Advocacy groups, such as Advocates for Highway and Auto Safety, represent the interests of others such as motorists. Activist groups, such as the Rainforest Action Network, often take direct action against firms to force them to change their policies. Public institutions are frequently the arbiters of such conflicts. In the case of air bags, NHTSA allowed on-off switches, but consistent with its command and control approach to regulation, began to consider mandating smart seats.

These interests may be grouped as follows:

ORGANIZED

American Association of Automobile Manufacturers
United Auto Workers
Insurance Institute for Highway Safety
Trial Lawyers Association
Trucking industry

UNORGANIZED
Consumers/motorists
Taxpayers

ACTIVIST, ADVOCACY, AND WATCHDOG GROUPS
Advocates for Highway and Auto Safety
Center for Auto Safety
National Organization of Women
Natural Resources Defense Council
Public Citizen
Rain Forest Action Network
Sierra Club
Union of Concerned Scientists

INSTITUTIONS

As indicated in Figure 1-1, the nonmarket environment includes activities that take place both within and outside public institutions. The principal public institutions are legislatures, the executive branch, the judiciary, administrative agencies, regulatory agencies, and international organizations such as the World Trade Organization. These institutions make decisions and serve as arenas in which competing interests contest issues. The nonmarket environment includes the set of laws and regulations established by these institutions, such as the antitrust, tax, and energy efficiency laws, as well as the set of regulations, such as automobile emissions standards, promulgated by administrative and regulatory agencies. The nonmarket environment also includes the common, or judge-made, law of torts, which governs the liability system.

Institutions can also be established by private means. Such institutions include markets, the insurance system, and mechanisms for private dispute resolution. The nonmarket environment also includes nonpublic institutions such as the news media and public sentiment. As considered in Chapter 3, the news media plays an important role in informing those in the nonmarket environment about issues and the activities of firms.

Institutions serve as arenas in which issues are contested and are not unitary bodies. Congress, for example, is an institution composed of two chambers and 535 members who represent constituencies with varying interests and in which actions are taken by majority rule. Institutions also have internal structures that affect how nonmarket issues are addressed. Congress has an extensive committee system and follows a complex set of procedures for enacting legislation. Understanding the workings of these institutions, their procedures, and the forces that operate within them is essential for effective management in the nonmarket environment. Managers must also be familiar with the mandates, agenda, and procedures of regulatory agencies. The Administrative Procedures Act, for example, imposes procedural requirements on federal regulatory agencies, and those procedural requirements grant important due process rights to individuals and firms.

Public officeholders such as the head of the EPA also may be active on nonmarket issues, and their actions to some extent reflect their personal preferences. Their actions, however, are usually constrained by the mandates, procedures, and policies of the institutions in which they hold office and by the preferences of their political principals. Legislators not only must follow legislative procedures and respect committee jurisdictions, but they must also be attentive to the preferences of their electoral constituents. Regulators must respect the mandates in their enabling legislation and follow a complex set of administrative procedures, both of which provide bases for judicial review. In addition, they must be attentive to their political principals in Congress and the Office of the President. For these reasons institutional officeholders are considered as part of the institution rather than as an interest.[5]

The institutions in whose arenas the nonmarket issues for the automobile industry are addressed can be categorized as follows:

LEGISLATIVE
Congress
State legislatures

REGULATORY AND ADMINISTRATIVE AGENCIES
California Air Resources Board
Environmental Protection Agency
Equal Employment Opportunity Commission
National Highway Traffic Safety Administration/Department of Transportation
Office of the U.S. Trade Representative

JUDICIAL
Federal courts
State courts

INTERNATIONAL
World Trade Organization
Kyoto Protocol on Global Warming
North American Free Trade Association

NONGOVERNMENTAL
Public sentiment
News media

INFORMATION

Information refers to what interests and institutional officeholders know about the issues, the consequences of alternative courses of action, and the preferences of those concerned with an issue. Issues are often contested because interests have different preferences regarding their resolution, but issues can also be contested because interests have different information about the relationship between actions and consequences. Information is frequently at the heart of strategies for addressing issues, and interests often provide information to build support for a particular course of action. Information is the foundation of strategies such as lobbying, which involves providing information to officeholders about the likely consequences of policy alternatives. Information provision is also important in regulatory rule making because agencies are required to develop a record supporting their actions.

Information thus can also be central to the strategies of firms in attempting to affect the outcomes of issues. For example, automobile manufacturers often prefer warn-

[5]The exception is when the jobs of officeholders or the status of the office is at stake.

ings about hazards to costly safety features. The auto companies were successful in having NHTSA choose warnings and instructions to address rollover hazards in SUVs. In 1998 NHTSA strengthened the warnings by using brighter colors and illustrations on safety warnings.

Information can be important to the progress of issues. When NHTSA mandated air bags, it had been warned by General Motors and others that air bags were a risk to small children and could cause severe injuries and death. After deployment of air bags and reports of several deaths in crashes at less than 10 mph, safety officials concluded "that the potential for bad press in these few cases could cause a lot of harm to the public's positive perception and receptiveness to air bags."[6] Five years later the public learned of the fatalities caused by air bags.

Information can also be a means of resolving an issue. The Air Bag Safety Campaign sought to reduce the injuries and deaths caused by air bags by providing information about the seating of children.

Information can also be important to the process of resolving a nonmarket issue. Under pressure from all sides, the EPA allowed lobbyists for a variety of interests, including electric-powered and natural gas-powered vehicle producers and automobile manufacturers, to participate in its negotiations with 12 Northeastern states on their adoption of California's air quality standards. This helped provide information on the technical feasibility of alternate fuel vehicles.

The chapter case *The Nonmarket Environment of McDonald's* provides an opportunity to characterize the issues, interests, institutions, and information in McDonald's nonmarket environment and to consider the likely development of the issues on its agenda.

THE NONMARKET ISSUE AGENDA

Each firm and industry has a set of issues that it must address, and these issues constitute its nonmarket issue agenda. Figure 1-2 shows the organization of the nonmarket issue agenda as a function of the institutional arenas in which the issues will be addressed and the interests likely to be involved.

To illustrate the interplay among issues, interests, institutions, and information, consider the issue of automobile safety. NHTSA is the cognizant regulatory institution, but congressional committees exercise oversight of NHTSA and influence the standards it mandates. The interests involved in the safety issue include auto manufacturers, insurance companies, and safety activists. Through the liability system, automobile safety is also in the domain of the courts, principally the state courts. The interests concerned with the liability dimension include, in addition to those previously identified, the trial lawyers who typically receive a percentage of any award. Information plays two important roles in the automobile safety issue. First, information is at the center of the disagreements among interests about the causes of accidents and injuries, as evidenced by the difference in viewpoints about air bags. Second, information provision is an alternative to mandatory safety standards, as the use of rollover stickers indicates.

A firm's nonmarket issue agenda displays the set of issues the firm must address. Many of these issues require issue-specific strategies, and the purpose of Figure 1-2 is to provide a starting point for analysis and strategy formulation, as developed further in Chapter 2. The remainder of this chapter is concerned with the origin and development of nonmarket issues.

---

[6] *San Francisco Chronicle,* November 21, 1996.

Nonmarket Issues	Congress	State Legislatures	NHTSA DOT	Courts	EPA	California Air Resc. Board	EEOC	USTR	WTO NAFTA	Kyoto Protocol	Public Sentiment	News Media
Safety regulation Air bag safety	● (2) (4) (5)		● (4) (5)	(4) ● (2) (5)								
Liability		● (2) (4)		● (2) (4)								
Speed limits	● (5) (4)	● (5) (4)										
Fuel economy standards	● (1)		● (1)								● (1)	● (1)
Emissions standards					● (1) (4)						● (1)	● (1)
Alternative fuel vehicles					● (1) (4)	● (1) (4)					● (1)	● (1)
Global warming	● (1)				● (1)					● (1) (4)	● (1) (4)	● (1) (4)
Trade policy	● (3) (1)							● (3)	● (3) (1)			
Sexual harassment				● (4)			● (4)					
Labor relations									● (3)			
Activist pressure (boycotts)											● (4)	● (4)
Taxes	● (6)											
Media coverage											● (1) (4)	● (1) (4)

Interests: (1) Environmentalists (2) Trial Lawyers (3) UAW (4) Activists (5) Insurance industry (6) Taxpayers

FIGURE 1–2 Nonmarket Issue Agenda for the Automobile Industry

Change in the Nonmarket Environment

The nonmarket environment changes as issues are resolved, current issues progress, and new issues arise. This section focuses on the origins of issues and the forces that give rise to them, and the following sections address the anticipation of nonmarket issues and their progression and resolution.

Nonmarket issues may originate from external forces or from a firm's actions. Most changes in the tax laws originate in response to ideas that capture a degree of political support. However, the issue of eliminating the investment tax credit, which had been a component of U.S. tax policy for over 20 years, arose in the mid-1980s in part because of political action by service industries that viewed the credit as a subsidy to capital-intensive industries. As indicated in a subsequent section, the issue of automobile safety regulation arose from an automobile accident and articles by two young policy activists. The issue of a possible health risk from the electromagnetic field generated by high-voltage electricity transmission lines arose from a small-scale inferential study linking power lines to leukemia in children, which resulted in sensationalized media coverage. As the varied origins of these issues indicate, managers must be sensitive to the sources of nonmarket issues—even those such as health risks from the electromagnetic field generated by transmission lines—that initially seem remote or even far-fetched.[7]

Nonmarket issues have five basic sources:

- scientific discovery and technological advancement
- new understandings
- institutional change
- interest group activity
- moral concerns

Scientific discoveries and technological advancement can produce fundamental changes in both the market and nonmarket environments. In the market environment, they create opportunities for new products and processes, new applications of existing knowledge, and foundations for future discoveries. They also give rise to nonmarket issues. Measurements suggesting that the earth was warming spawned issues centering on higher fuel economy standards and the deforestation of tropical rain forests. The discovery of an ozone hole above the Antarctic confirmed theories of ozone depletion and propelled a number of nonmarket issues ranging from the elimination of CFCs to measures to reduce the incidence of skin cancer. When the theory of ozone depletion was initially advanced, Du Pont came under pressure to stop production of CFCs. Du Pont argued that there was yet no evidence that CFCs actually caused ozone depletion and pledged in a public advertisement that it would cease production if scientific evidence showed a relationship. When a National Academy of Sciences study concluded that there was a causal link, Du Pont announced the next day that it would cease production earlier than called for by the government.

Nonmarket issues can also arise from technological advancement and an absence of scientific information. The spectacular success of the cellular telephone industry was interrupted one day in 1993 when a man called the "Larry King Live" television talk show and claimed that his wife had died from brain cancer caused by extensive use of a cellular telephone. Earlier in the day a CEO of a major corporation announced that he had brain cancer, and the previous day a CEO of another major corporation had died

---

[7] A 1997 report by the National Academy of Science found no risk from power lines, and a carefully designed 1998 study by the National Cancer Institute and childhood leukemia specialists concluded that there was no risk from the electromagnetic field of power lines.

of brain cancer. The call and speculation that the CEOs might have been heavy users of cellular telephones caused a panic. The stock prices of McCaw Communications, the nation's largest cellular telephone company, and Motorola, the largest manufacturer of cellular telephones, dropped by over 5 percent in a day. Fears were calmed with statements by government officials that there was no scientific evidence linking cellular telephones to cancer. The industry pledged to conduct additional research into whether radio-frequency radiation emitted by the telephones was harmful. The Cellular Telecommunications Industry Association earmarked $25 million for research and established a Scientific Advisory Group on Cellular Telephone Research to oversee the research program. The promise of research to fill the gap in scientific information reassured cellular telephone users, and the growth in usage resumed.

Nonmarket issues also arise from changes in understandings. The environmental movement brought to the attention of the public the damage to the natural environment and the health risks associated with pollution. Renewed confidence in markets and the failure of socialist economic systems spurred a wave of privatization in both developed and developing countries. Increasing confidence in the economic benefits of international trade led not only to further reductions in trade barriers through GATT and the World Trade Organization but also to market integration in North America through NAFTA and in the European Union through the Single European Act. Antitrust policy and enforcement changed substantially during the 1980s as a consequence of new understandings about the objectives of that policy and about how those objectives could be realized. By the late 1990s new economic theory led to more vigorous antitrust enforcement activity by the government. Changes in the membership of the Supreme Court during the 1980s, and the understandings the new members brought with them, resulted in changes in affirmative action policies.

Issues also become salient because groups organize to advance their own interests. Interest groups formed around the issue of extending the period of daylight saving time and worked for nearly a decade to obtain an extension by Congress.[8] As considered in Chapter 7, the growth and developing effectiveness of the American Association of Retired Persons led it to push for congressional enactment of a catastrophic illness insurance plan, only to have a grassroots revolt among its members result in repeal of the act before it had taken effect. Interest groups can also stop change as in the opposition by the auto industry to higher fuel economy standards for light trucks.

Nonmarket issues also arise because of institutional actions. A Supreme Court decision in 1988 supported a new theory of "fraud on the market," under which firms could be held liable if their stock price fell significantly when the firm's projections of future earnings had been favorable. This provided incentives to trial lawyers to file class action lawsuits against high-technology companies when their naturally volatile stock price fell by 10 percent or more. No evidence of fraud was required to file a lawsuit, and filing allowed the lawyers to conduct discovery and to depose company executives. To avoid the costs and disruptions of discovery and depositions, and the subsequent costs of a trial, many companies were willing to settle the lawsuits even if they were certain to win. Settlements totaled nearly $7 billion. Viewing the practice as extortionary and the lawsuits as frivolous, companies backed federal legislation granting a safe harbor for forward-looking projections, and Congress enacted the statute over President Clinton's veto. In response, the trial lawyers brought their cases under state laws, and backed a ballot initiative in California to increase their likelihood of extracting settlements. The high-tech companies and public accounting and other firms subject to the lawsuits then

---

[8]The extension is considered in Chapter 5.

sought new federal legislation to require such cases to be brought in federal courts. The legislation was enacted in 1998.

Change in the nonmarket environment also comes from markets. In the mid-1990s technological advances including the Internet, wireless systems, and integrated services resulted in a restructuring of the telecommunications industry, including several mergers, acquisitions, and strategic alliances. Congress then struggled with legislation to lift the archaic restrictions on competition left over from the era of telecommunications regulation.

Nonmarket issues also arise because of heightened moral concerns. The rapid increase in the participation of women in the labor force, and particularly in management, has not resulted in a corresponding increase in women reaching the top echelons of management. Concerns about a "glass ceiling" raised the issue of internal promotion procedures and implicit discrimination at upper levels of management. Similarly, the increased saliency of personal privacy resulted in a ban on the use of polygraph tests by employers, who responded with a variety of pencil and paper tests, including some designed to test for honesty and loyalty. These tests ultimately became a nonmarket issue. Privacy issues associated with the Internet resulted in calls for new legislation, regulation, and self-restraint on the part of Internet service providers.

Anticipating Nonmarket Issues

The effectiveness with which a firm and its managers address nonmarket issues depends on the approach they take to their nonmarket environment. One approach is to respond to nonmarket issues when they are strong enough to force the firm to act. A second approach emphasizes limiting the extent of the damage once the firm has been challenged by an issue. A third approach is anticipatory and is intended to prepare the firm to take advantage of opportunities as they arise and address issues before they can cause damage. A fourth approach is proactive with the firm and its managers not only anticipating nonmarket issues but also acting to affect which issues arise and how they will be framed. This approach recognizes that nonmarket issues and their development are affected by the way business is conducted. The fourth approach is the most effective, but it requires considerable sensitivity to the sources of nonmarket issues and to how they progress. This section addresses the anticipation of nonmarket issues, and the life cycle of nonmarket issues is considered in the following section.

EXAMPLE

Graduation Cards

Graduation represents an important market for the greeting card industry. In its preparation for the college graduation season, Hallmark Cards was considering the array of cards it would market. Cards could reflect a variety of themes, but two traditionally popular ones were "transition" and "celebration." One transition that seemed particularly salient was the coming of legal drinking age, and Hallmark was considering cards featuring alcoholic beverages. Alcoholic beverages were also associated with celebration, so the cards would draw on two themes. One proposed card had a photo of a Budweiser can with a small cherubic character saying "You're graduating?" Another proposed card portrayed a beer and eggs breakfast on graduation day, and a third suggested a robe large enough to cover two champagne bottles.

Nonmarket issues are apparent once they are on a firm's agenda, but proactive managers attempt to recognize and anticipate potential issues and act to reduce their adverse, or enhance their beneficial, impacts. A fundamental principle for anticipating nonmarket issues is to view the potential issue or business practice from the perspective of others whose interests might be affected by or concerned about it.

Graduation cards are bought by friends and relatives of the graduate, and it is from their perspective that the cards must be considered—for both their market and nonmarket potentials. The proposed cards were intended for the college graduation market, and virtually all those recipients would be of legal drinking age. College students, however, are not the only ones graduating. Nearly twice as many students graduate from high school each year, and virtually none of them is of legal drinking age. Some parents and relatives may well view the cards as promoting alcoholic beverages and contributing to underage drinking and driving, a major cause of accidents and deaths. Parents and others concerned about underage drinking provide the potential for a nonmarket reaction to the cards.

The next step is to assess whether people concerned about the cards are likely to act, other than by not buying the cards. Certainly some parents and relatives will be concerned about the cards, but they are dispersed and most have limited means of generating a nonmarket issue. Some, however, participate in organizations such as the PTA and Mothers Against Drunk Driving (MADD) that are experienced in dealing with nonmarket issues and know how to use the news media to bring an issue to the attention of the public and hence to put it on a firm's agenda. This does not mean that a nonmarket reaction is certain, but it indicates that it is possible.

Hallmark chose to market the cards, and the reaction was swift. MADD activists began to pressure store owners to stop selling the cards, and the media picked up the story. Hallmark quickly agreed to stop producing the cards and to not ship any of those already produced. Hallmark subsequently decided to not produce any graduation cards with a reference to alcoholic beverages.

The Nonmarket Issue Life Cycle

The progression of nonmarket issues can be characterized in terms of a life cycle that relates the stage of their development to their impact on a firm or on business more generally.[9] The nonmarket issue life cycle reflects a pattern, but it is not a theory, as it provides neither an explanation for how or why an issue develops nor a basis for predicting its likely development and impact. In particular, it does not identify the causal factors that govern an issue's development. The life cycle concept is useful, however, because it identifies a pattern and serves as a reminder that issues with simple origins can garner support, propelling them through a series of stages and resulting in significant impacts. This, however, does not mean that issues have a life of their own. To the contrary, the progression of a nonmarket issue is governed by the attention it receives from individuals, the public, firms, interest groups, and government officeholders, and by the institutions in which it is addressed.

Nonmarket issues can pass through a series of stages, although not all issues complete all the stages. The five stages are (1) issue identification, (2) interest group formation, (3) legislation, (4) administration, and (5) enforcement. As an issue progresses through its life cycle, its impact on a firm and its management tends to increase. As the impact increases, management's range of discretion in addressing the issue correspondingly decreases. The impact may take the form of government actions or changes in public sentiment that limit the options available to management.

---

[9] The life cycle concept was originated by Ian Wilson while at General Electric.

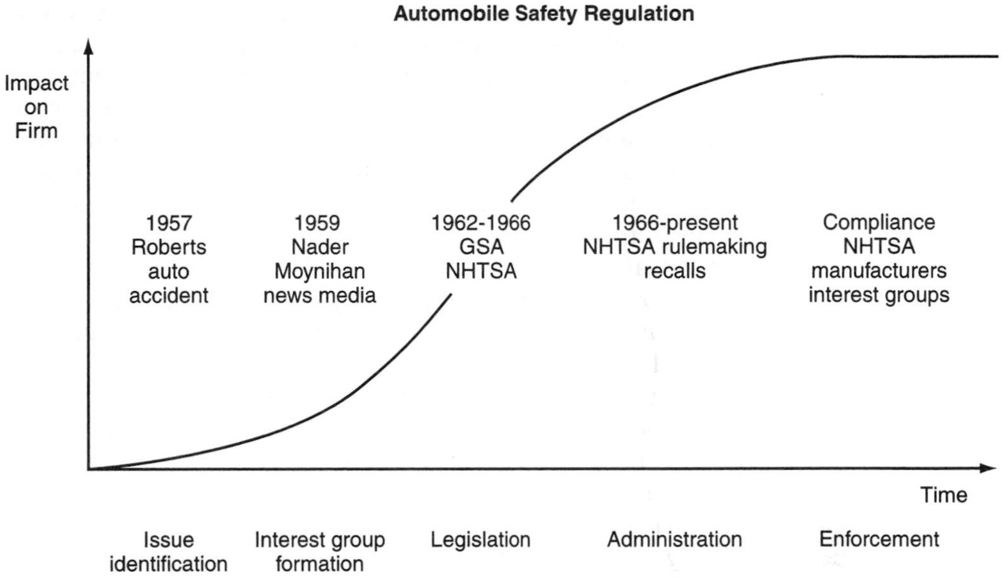

FIGURE 1–3 Nonmarket Issue Life Cycle

To illustrate the origin of an issue and its progression through the stages of the nonmarket life cycle, consider the issue of automobile safety regulation. The progression of the issue is illustrated along the horizontal axis in Figure 1-3, and the vertical axis represents the impact of the issue on firms. Automobile safety has always been a nonmarket issue, but in the 1950s it was viewed as a function of road conditions and the driver's skill. In 1957 as Congressman Kenneth Roberts of Alabama and his wife were returning from their honeymoon, their car was rear-ended. Both were injured, but their well-packaged glass and china wedding presents in the backseat were undamaged. Roberts recognized that an ignored dimension of the auto safety issue was the vehicle itself and how safely it contained its passengers.

Roberts held congressional hearings on the issue, but no action resulted. In 1959 two articles on the issue were published. A young attorney named Ralph Nader published an article on automobile safety that focused on automobile design. A young official in the Department of Labor, Daniel Patrick Moynihan, also published an article arguing for a broader perspective on the automobile safety issue. Interest group activity began to develop, and the media was attracted to the issue, particularly when it was revealed that General Motors had hired a private detective to investigate Nader.

In 1962 the issue entered the legislative phase when the General Services Administration (GSA) issued a standard for brake fluid. Legislation was introduced in Congress and after considerable deliberation and intense politics, the Motor Vehicle Safety Act of 1966 was enacted. The act established NHTSA, which was given administrative rule-making authority to establish mandatory automobile safety standards. In the administrative phase NHTSA has established nearly 40 mandatory standards.

The enforcement phase for auto safety regulation has been multifaceted. Auto manufacturers test their models extensively, not only for compliance with regulations but often to exceed government standards. NHTSA enforces the regulations and can order the recall of vehicles. Interest groups such as the Center for Auto Safety also monitor both the industry and the enforcement activities of NHTSA. Individuals also enforce safety regulation through lawsuits.

Nonmarket issues that complete their life cycles do not always result in more restrictions on business, as evidenced by the case of airline deregulation. Economists who analyzed the performance of airlines regulated by the Civil Aeronautics Board (CAB) concluded that regulation was inducing inefficiencies and increasing costs. The issue attracted attention because of the large difference between the fares of the CAB-regulated airlines and airlines such as Southwest that operated only intrastate routes and hence were not subject to CAB regulation. Regulatory oversight hearings brought additional attention to the issue and planted the seeds of legislative action. These developments coincided with increased public criticism of economic regulation and decreased confidence in government. As congressional and executive branch attention increased, the issue entered the legislative phase. At the same time, economist Alfred Kahn was appointed to head the CAB. Kahn moved quickly to take administrative action to deregulate the industry, which spurred the legislative process. The result was legislation that eliminated the economic regulation of the domestic airline industry. After transferring some of its nonregulatory functions to other government agencies, the CAB ceased to exist. Similar concerns about the economic consequences of surface transportation regulation resulted in the elimination of the Interstate Commerce Commission, the first federal regulatory agency.

Not all nonmarket issues, of course, garner enough support to pass through all five stages, and many do not survive the legislative stage. The fact that an issue does not pass through all the stages does not mean that the environment of business is the same as it was before the issue arose. The attention an issue receives can produce change even in the absence of institutional action. The consumer movement has not progressed as far as its supporters had hoped, and Congress has not passed major consumer legislation since the Magnuson-Moss Warranty Act of 1976. Despite the consumer movement's failure to become broader and more powerful, it has resulted in a variety of significant changes. Furthermore, several interest groups have been formed to advocate consumer interests.

Summary

Firms are embedded in both market and nonmarket environments. The field of business and its environment is concerned with issues in the nonmarket environment that have potentially significant effects on organizational and managerial performance. Managers are in the best position to understand how the firm's market activities give rise to nonmarket issues and to assess the significance of nonmarket issues for market and overall performance. Managers thus have the responsibility for addressing nonmarket issues and for formulating nonmarket as well as market strategies.

The nonmarket environment of a firm is characterized by four I's: issues, interests, institutions, and information. As indicated by the example of the automobile industry, nonmarket issues have important implications for firms and their market and nonmarket performance. Nonmarket issues may be identified externally or by management and may arise from scientific discovery, new understandings, interest group activity, institutional change, and moral concerns. Because these factors change over time, the nonmarket environment and a firm's nonmarket issue agendas evolve.

Management must not only deal effectively with nonmarket issues but must also anticipate issues and take proactive steps to address them. Many nonmarket issues pass through stages—issue identification, interest group formation, legislation, administration, and enforcement—that form a pattern referred to as the nonmarket issue life cycle. It serves as a reminder that issues evolve, that even seemingly minor issues can have substantial effects, and that those effects increase as issues move through the stages of their life cycle. Not all nonmarket issues pass through all five stages, however, and some, such as deregulation, result in fewer rather than more restrictions. The progress of an issue should be viewed as endogenous and shaped by the actions of interests and the characteristics of the institutions in whose arena the issue is addressed.

CASES

General Motors Like a Rock? (A)

In 1992 the General Motors Corporation struggled through rocky management shake-ups and its third consecutive year of red ink. If any silver lining could be found in GM's financial cloud, it was its line of pickup trucks. Large pickups were one of GM's few profitable products among its ailing North American operations. Sales of Chevy and GMC full-size pickups exceeded half a million in 1991. Greater expectations for 1992 and 1993 coincided with a beefed-up marketing campaign centering on the theme "Like a Rock." However, as events unfolded, GM management found itself between a rock and a hard place.

In 1992 the Center for Auto Safety (CAS) petitioned NHTSA to recall some 5 million Chevrolet and GMC full-size pickup trucks. The CAS claimed that more than 300 people had died in side-impact accidents involving the trucks. Unlike most other pickups, GM class C/K pickups built during the years 1973 to 1987 were equipped with twin "side-saddle" gasoline tanks positioned outside the main frame rails. In 1987 GM made a design change in its trucks and brought the tanks inside the frame.

The CAS petition was not the first sign of a potential problem in GM's pickups. For years GM had managed to avoid the eye of the media by fighting on a case-by-case basis as many as 140 fuel tank-related lawsuits. Most were settled out of court with settlements occasionally exceeding $1 million. Throughout these legal proceedings, GM steadfastly defended the overall safety of its trucks. GM regularly pointed out that the NHTSA standard called for crashworthiness at 20 miles per hour, and its pickups easily met that standard. In the 1970s GM regularly tested its trucks with side-impact crashes at 30 miles per hour. In the mid-1980s it increased its internal standard to 50 miles per hour. That fires sometimes broke out in the highest speed tests was not disputed but rather was viewed by GM as evidence that it was pushing its tests to the limit in an effort to make its trucks safer.

Data and interpretations concerning the relative safety of GM trucks were mixed. According to NHTSA, GM's side-saddle trucks were 2.4 times as likely as Ford's to be involved in deadly side-impact crashes. According to the Insurance Institute for Highway Safety—a research group supported by insurance companies—the GM trucks might be slightly more prone to fire than similar models built by Ford and Chrysler, but they could be far safer in certain kinds of accidents. This conclusion, according to GM, suggested a need for a broader and more appropriate criterion of safety—that of overall crashworthiness. At least one large database on accidents indicated that in terms of the overall probability of a fatal accident, GM trucks were marginally safer than their competitors.

In November 1992, NBC's *Dateline* aired a 15-minute segment entitled "Waiting to Explode?" Its focus was the GM series C/K pickup trucks. In preparation for the segment, the NBC news crew hired three "safety consultants" to assist in conducting two crash tests of GM pickups on a rural Indiana road on October 24. Each test simulated a side-impact crash by using a tow truck to push a Chevy Citation along the road into a pickup. The pickup was parked on the road perpendicular to the oncoming car, which slammed into the pickup's passenger side. A minute-long videotape of the tests was aired, and correspondent Michele Gillen stated that the tests were "unscientific." In the first of the tests, Gillen stated that the car was moving at about 40 miles per hour. The truck was jolted significantly, but no fire ensued. In the second test, a fire broke out at a stated speed of 30 miles per hour. In the broadcast one safety consultant described the fire as "a holocaust."

After the nationally televised broadcast that reached approximately 11 million viewers, GM officials examined the NBC test segment in slow motion. Suspicions arose. GM wrote a letter to NBC almost immediately, stating that the show was unfair and requesting NBC's test data. NBC refused to comply. In a follow-up contact, GM asked NBC to allow GM to inspect the pickups. On January 4 the producer of *Dateline* told GM the vehicles were "junked and therefore are no longer available for inspection."

In the meantime, 32-year-old editor Pete Pesterre, of the magazine, *Popular Hot Rodding*, had been pursuing some suspicions of his own. He was intimately familiar with GM trucks. He had owned four of them and once was involved in a side-impact crash from which he emerged unscathed. After Pesterre wrote an editorial criticizing the *Dateline* segment, a reader from Indiana called Pesterre and informed him that he knew a Brownsburg, Indiana, firefighter who was at the scene of the NBC crash tests. When the Brownsburg Fire Department is on assignment, as it was the day NBC staged the crashes, its firefighters customarily videotape the action for subsequent use in training. GM contacted the fire chief, who provided a copy of the tape. Similarly, GM learned that an off-duty sheriff's deputy was on site and had also videotaped the tests. GM also acquired his tape.

To analyze the tapes (including NBC's), GM called on its Hughes Aircraft subsidiary to deploy digital-enhancement techniques for sophisticated frame-by-frame analysis. These investigations revealed that NBC had been less than precise about both the sequence and speeds of the two tests. The first test conducted was the second test aired. The GM/Hughes analysis suggested the actual speed was 39 mph instead of the 30 mph stated in the *Dateline* segment.[1] This test yielded the so-called holocaust. In the other test NBC claimed a speed of 40 mph, but GM/Hughes concluded the speed was 47 mph. No fire occurred in this test.

Another revelation came from the audio portion of the firefighter's tape. After the first test—which, although slower, did produce a fire—the firemen were noticeably unimpressed with the outcome. It was clear that the fire was confined to the grass, short lived, and not life endangering. One fireman laughed, and one said, "So much for that theory."

Meanwhile, GM was able to locate and acquire the two wrecked Citations and the two wrecked pickups. The recovered pickups were sent to GM's plant in Indianapolis where workers discovered a model rocket engine in the bed of one truck. Inspections of the bottom of the truck uncovered flare marks and remnants of duct tape in two places where GM's video analysis had curiously shown both smoke and fire in frames *prior* to impact in the crash. Additional inspection of tapes and photographs fueled suspicions that a detonator or starter device had been wired to the rocket engine.

GM officials wanted to examine the trucks' fuel tanks but they had been stripped from the trucks. GM immediately went to court seeking a restraining order to bar one of the NBC consultants from disposing of the fuel tanks. Days later, through his attorney, GM learned that the consultant had given the tanks to a neighbor. Eventually GM obtained the tanks.

Having obtained the pickups and the tanks, GM identified and contacted the trucks' previous owners. From the owner of the truck that was struck and caught fire, GM learned that the gas cap was nonstandard. The owner had lost gas caps several times and in the last instance obtained one that did not fit correctly. GM also strongly suspected that the tank had been "topped off" with gasoline prior to the test. (Tanks are designed with 5 gallons of excess space to make topping off impossible with properly functioning fuel pumps.) GM sent the gas tank of the truck to an X-ray lab and a metallurgist to test whether, as NBC correspondent Gillen claimed, the tank was punctured and therefore was responsible for the fire. According to the experts, it was not punctured. GM had therefore amassed considerable data that supported a different theory about the crash results and the *Dateline* segment. The pieces of the puzzle were as follows:

- a possibly topped-off tank
- a faulty fuel cap in the truck involved in the fiery accident
- rocket engines that flared prior to impact
- footage indicating that that fire was confined primarily to grass and did not engulf the cab of the pickup
- fuel tanks that, contrary to NBC claims, had not been punctured

Additionally, GM conducted background checks on NBC's "safety experts" and learned the following:

- The consultant referred to by NBC as "vice president of the Institute for Safety Analysis" had no engineering background but was a former stock-car driver with a BA in Asian studies.
- The second consultant worked as a "safety consultant" for trial lawyers and had worked as a consultant for ABC News in seven segments on auto safety. He majored in industrial design but did not complete college.
- The third was hired as an expert from the Institute for Injury Reduction, a nonprofit organization that tests products for plaintiffs' attorneys. He had no college degree but studied Japanese and had a diploma

---

[1]The 9 miles per hour is important because energy is a function of the square of the velocity. To be precise, $e = .5\ MV^2$, where e is kinetic energy, M is mass, and V is velocity.

in Korean from the U.S. Government's Defense Language School.

On Monday February 1, 1993, GM's executive vice president and general counsel, Harry Pearce, presented these findings to GM's board of directors. When asked how the directors responded, Pearce said, "They were shocked."

In January, GM had sent yet another letter to Robert Read, the *Dateline* producer, this time detailing GM's specific findings. Read responded without informing either NBC President Robert Wright or NBC News President Michael Gartner. In a subsequent letter to Read dated February 2, GM carbon-copied Wright and Gartner, finally bringing the case to the attention of top NBC officials. NBC management responded by having its top public relations advisers and NBC General Counsel Richard Cotton draft a letter from Gartner to GM. The letter asserted three separate times that the NBC story was entirely accurate. "NBC does not believe that any statements made . . . were either false or misleading . . . the *Dateline* report was and remains completely factual and accurate."[2]

On February 4, 1993, an Atlanta jury awarded $101 million in punitive damages and $4.2 million in compensatory damages to the parents of a 17-year-old boy killed in a fiery death in a GM C/K pickup. The parents had argued that the placement of the fuel tank outside the frame of the pickup made it vulnerable to puncturing during a collision. GM's defense in the trial had been that the boy had died instantly during the collision which, the GM attorney argued, occurred at such a high speed that the death could not be blamed on the truck's design.

On Friday, February 5—the morning after the verdict in the liability case and a few days before a scheduled press conference by the CAS—GM management had a weekend during which to consider some delicate strategic options. One major option would be for GM to file a defamation suit against NBC. Defamation is the communication (e.g., by journalists) to a third party (e.g., viewers) of an untrue statement of fact that injures the plaintiff (GM).[3] A second major option was to go public with the information it had developed on the *Dateline* segment. With the liability verdict and its aftermath fresh in the news, GM would be taking a significant risk in drawing still more attention to its pickups. Said one Wall Street analyst, "A successful rebuttal won't make anybody go out and buy trucks. The publicity [of an aggressive defense by GM and an attack on GM's critics] can't do anything but harm GM."[4] This perspective reflected the rule-of-thumb that "any news is bad news" when it involves a major company, a less-than-perfectly safe product, and a high level of public sensitivity toward product safety. ■

[2] *The Wall Street Journal*, February 11, 1993.

[3] See Chapter 3 for a discussion of defamation.

[4] *The Wall Street Journal*, February 8, 1993.

This is an abridged version of a case written by Professor Keith Krehbiel. Royal Bryson provided valuable comments.

PREPARATION QUESTIONS

1. From GM's perspective what are the nonmarket issues? What are their sources? Where are they in their life cycles?
2. Should GM fight the *Dateline* issue as a matter of principle? Why or why not?
3. What kind of media coverage should GM anticipate over the next week? Does GM have any control or influence over this situation?
4. Should GM file a defamation suit and/or go public with its findings about the *Dateline* segment?
5. In the position of Mr. Gartner at NBC, what would you do upon receiving GM's letter and findings?

An Emerging Issue: MTBE

The Clean Air Act of 1990 addressed automobile emissions in a novel manner by focusing not only on the automobile and its emissions control system but also on the fuel used. To reduce carbon monoxide emissions which are a principal cause of smog, the act mandated that in ozone nonattainment areas gasoline must contain 15 percent oxygenates or be reformulated to achieve an equivalent reduction in emissions. This reformulated gasoline (RFG) had been required by the Environmental Protection Agency (EPA) in wintertime in several cities and throughout the year in certain areas. The principal substance used by refiners to meet the RFG mandate was methyl tertiary-butyl ether (MTBE), which was produced by combining isobutylene and methanol. The first wintertime RFG program was in 1988 in Denver when gasoline with 15 percent MTBE was used. In 1995, 11 percent MTBE gasoline was used in nonattainment areas, and to meet standards set by the California Air Resources Board, virtually all gasoline sold in California since 1995 contained 11 percent MTBE. This oxygenate was a natural selection by the oil industry because oil companies had been blending 1 to 2 percent MTBE in gasoline since 1979 to increase octane. Using MTBE also solved a waste disposal problem, because it was produced from isobutylene, a by-product of refining.

The EPA estimated that RFG reduced hydrocarbon emissions by at least 15 percent. The California Air Resources Board credited the RFG program with major reductions in emissions equivalent to the elimination of 3.5 million cars. The board claimed to be "oxygenate neutral," however, expressing no preference for MTBE over other oxygenates. Critics, however, argued that the 11 percent mandate served to exclude other oxygenates such as ethanol.

RFG using MTBE had several drawbacks. MTBE cost approximately 20 cents a gallon more than gasoline. It also had less energy content than ordinary gasoline, and hence mileage could be reduced by 2 to 3 percent. MTBE could also make ignition more difficult in cold weather and could affect fuel system seals and hoses, possibly causing fuel leaks. Chevron conducted a 115-vehicle, matched sets study of the effects of MTBE on elastomeric fuel system parts and found a statistically significant higher number of fuel system leaks with gasoline blended with MTBE, particularly in older cars. Chevron posted a warning on its pumps in California.

MTBE also had an odor somewhat different from that of gasoline. Complaints about RFG with MTBE began in 1992 in Alaska, where motorists complained that the fumes made them ill when filling their gas tanks. Research released in 1997 by Timothy Buckley, a professor at the Johns Hopkins School of Public Health, "hypothesized that some MTBE may be retained in respiratory mucous membranes, which may be related to symptoms of lung irritation alleged to be associated with MTBE."[1] The oxygenate mandate had been enacted without substantial research on the oxygenates, and the auto and oil industries had begun a research program on the side effects of clean fuels only in 1990.

MTBE had high water solubility and chemical stability and did not biodegrade, making it a potential groundwater pollutant. In 1996 the city of Santa Monica, California, closed half its drinking water wells because of contamination with MTBE leaking from underground storage tanks at service stations. Both Chevron and Shell agreed to pay at least $5 million in the first year to clean up wells, but obtained the right to cease the cleanup if they found they were not responsible for the contamination. In 1998 Mobil agreed to pay $2.2 million to the city of Santa Monica and could be subject to further cleanup costs.

The EPA had designated MTBE as a "possible," and gasoline as a "probable," carcinogen, so blending MTBE in gasoline could reduce the risk of cancer due to spills. The EPA argued that gasoline with MTBE was less hazardous than conventional gasoline. Some environmentalists and local residents, however, complained about the possible risks, particularly to drinking water.

Several other oxygenates were available, including the alkyl ethers (TAME [tertiary-amyl methyl ether], ETBE [ethyl tertiary-butyl ether], and DIPE [diisopropyl ether]) and alcohols (ethanol, methanol, and TBA [tertiary-butyl alcohol]). Little was known about the health effects of many of these oxygenates.

Ethanol was the second leading oxygenate used in RFG but had only 13 percent of the market. According to Chevron, MTBE was more expensive than the conventional refinery blendstocks and, despite a federal tax subsidy, so was ethanol. Ethanol also had a disadvantage in that it evaporated easily thus adding to smog, and it was difficult to ship by pipeline

[1] Press release, Johns Hopkins University, July 23, 1997.

because the ethanol could separate out. The energy content of ethanol was approximately 66 percent of conventional gasoline, whereas the energy content of MTBE was 81 percent of conventional gasoline. The ethanol industry had worked intensely to preserve the ethanol tax credit through the year 2007. Lobbying for the ethanol industry was conducted by Fuels for the Future, the National Corn Growers Association, and Archer Daniels Midland.[2]

Several organizations were formed to oppose oxygenated fuels. The most active grassroots organization was Oxybusters, founded in 1993 in New Jersey by Barry Grossman. Oxybusters of California was formed by Jodi Walters of Lodi, who complained, "I've experienced short-term memory loss—light-headedness." Oxybusters groups were also established in Connecticut, Maine, Pennsylvania, and Texas. Oxybusters repeated arguments that MTBE reduced carbon monoxide emissions only in older cars and then only by 20 percent. Radio talk show hosts jumped on the campaign opposing RFG.

In 1997 the contamination of the wells in Santa Monica and the activities of Oxybusters resulted in a movement in California to overturn the RFG mandate. One interest group supporting the overturn was CALPIRG, the California Public Interest Research Group with 60,000 members. CALPIRG stated, "Ethanol poses a substantially smaller risk of water pollution. It is readily absorbed into soil, unlike MTBE. It is biodegradable and non-carcinogenic." The Sierra Club and the Natural Resources Defense Council expressed reservations, however, arguing that the use of ethanol could be worse than what it replaces.[3] Environmentalists defending the use of MTBE focused their attention on reducing leaks in gasoline storage tanks.

Tosco Corporation, the third largest refiner in California, broke ranks with the industry in October 1997. In a letter to the California Air Resources Board, Tosco called for the reduction or elimination of MTBE. Citing a 1995 study by the auto and oil industries, Duane Bordvick of Tosco stated, "Theoretically, we can get oxygenates like MTBE down to zero in the new gasoline and still achieve the same goals. Water contamination is what is driving us. This problem is growing every day, and it is going to be very costly to solve. So we think it is better to deal with it now rather than look back and say we should have done something sooner."[4] The 1995 study stated, "No significant differences were observed between California Reformulated Gasoline with and without oxygenate (MTBE)" in emissions and "The addition of an oxygenated (MTBE) had no significant effects on total exhaust toxics."

In October 1997 Governor Pete Wilson of California signed a bill directing the University of California to conduct a study of the health risks of MTBE. Earlier in the year the EPA had written to the American Petroleum Institute identifying research needed on MTBE. Under the Clean Air Act the industry was responsible for research on the health effects of gasoline components.

In December 1997 Senator Barbara Boxer (D-CA) wrote to EPA Administrator Carol Browner asking for safety standards for MTBE in drinking water and for a plan to phase out MTBE. The EPA issued an advisory identifying the levels at which the odor and taste of MTBE could be detected in drinking water. The EPA advisory recommended that MTBE levels not exceed 20 to 40 parts per billion, which is 20,000 to 100,000 times lower than the level at which cancer is observed in animal toxicology studies.[5] The EPA reiterated its conclusion that the benefits of MTBE use "far exceed any known risks from the substance." In January 1998 Senator Diane Feinstein (D-CA) introduced legislation that would preclude the use of RFG in nonattainment areas in California.

In December 1998 Chevron Corporation followed Tosco by asking Congress to eliminate the RFG requirements if clean air goals could be met through other means. "Oxygenates in gasoline do little to reduce smog, but they have raised legitimate environmental concerns about MTBE in groundwater," said Dave O'Reilly, president of Chevron Products Co.[6] Commentators observed that oil companies were becoming increasingly concerned that they would be held liable for cleaning up groundwater contamination.

The MTBE industry had grown to annual sales of $3 billion with 27 companies producing MTBE in the United States. MTBE was also imported from Canada and Argentina. The largest U.S. producer was ARCO Chemical Company, 82.7 percent owned by the Atlantic Richfield Company (ARCO). ARCO Chemical's MTBE capacity was 3,610 million pounds at its Channelview, Texas, plant and 1,140 million pounds at its Corpus Christi, Texas, plant. Ned Griffith of ARCO Chemical and vice chairman of the Oxygenated Fuels Association said, "We're disappointed and don't agree

[2] Chemical Business Newsbase, March 13, 1998.
[3] Copley News Service, March 30, 1998.
[4] *San Francisco Chronicle,* October 30, 1997.
[5] *API Soil & Groundwater Research Bulletin (Summary),* No. 3, March 1998.
[6] Chevron Press Release, December 1, 1997.

with [Tosco's] conclusions. While there has been some water contamination and it needs to be dealt with, there are no cases where people have been directly exposed to MTBE through their water system."[7] Neither Tosco nor Chevron produced MTBE.

In April 1998 Tosco announced that it had begun to sell reformulated gasoline without MTBE in three counties in the San Francisco area. The newly reformulated gasoline was blended with ethanol.

In response to Chevron's announcement, Bill Teaser, a senior scientist with the Environmental Defense Fund, said, "The fact there was a mandate to clean up the air did not justify ignoring potential water-quality problems. The bottom line is that companies need to do a more thorough assessment of all the characteristics of the compounds they put in gasoline."[8] ■

[7] *San Francisco Chronicle,* October 30, 1997.

[8] *San Francisco Chronicle,* December 2, 1997.

PREPARATION QUESTIONS

1. Identify the issues, interests, institutions, and information in the case.
2. Which companies have the strongest interests in the MTBE issue?
3. Are the interests of the oil companies homogeneous or heterogeneous?
4. Are the interests of the environmental interest groups homogeneous or heterogeneous?
5. As an oil company such as Chevron or Tosco, what steps should be taken to advance the campaign to eliminate the RFG mandate?

The Nonmarket Environment of McDonald's

At the beginning of the 1990s, the McDonald's Corporation had over 11,000 restaurants (8,500 in the United States), serving over 22 million customers a day. Because of its success in its market environment, McDonald's was a focal point for a variety of nonmarket issues. Two of the most important concerned health and the environment. McDonald's was one of the country's largest solid waste polluters, and its menu items were under attack by health and nutrition activists. McDonald's nonmarket issue agenda was both immediate and serious.

McDonald's faced criticism for its use of styrofoam in coffee cups and sandwich containers because some of the plastic was foamed with CFCs. The CFCs were being replaced in the foaming process, but McDonald's, which used 50,000 tons of foam packaging each year, remained under attack because of the solid waste problem and the dwindling availability of landfill space. McDonald's was under pressure to use plastic and paper containers that could be recycled, and it had initiated a recycling project for the polystyrene used in styrofoam packaging. Environmental interest groups, however, had attacked the recycling plans because they wanted polystyrene to be eliminated entirely. McDonald's had begun to experiment with onsite incineration, but that experiment had been criticized by the Environmental Defense Fund (EDF).

McDonald's was also under pressure for the volume of paper it used and the timber cut as a consequence. It had begun using recycled paper for its napkins and its Happy Meal boxes, and its annual report was printed on recycled paper. The company took out full-page advertisements pledging to purchase $100 million of recycled materials.

McDonald's environmental strategy changed when the head of the EDF invited McDonald's president to a meeting to discuss waste disposal and environmental protection issues. McDonald's decided to enter into a working arrangement with EDF to study how the use of packaging materials could be reduced and recycled materials increased.[1] In spite of McDonald's efforts, criticism and pressure continued. Ralph Nader said, "Grassroots environmental groups aren't convinced that McDonald's is serious about creating a better environment."[2]

[1] The outcome of this collaboration is discussed in Chapter 12.

[2] *The Wall Street Journal,* August 2, 1990.

On the other front, McDonald's and other fast-food chains had been criticized for the nutritional content of their food. For several years McDonald's had made available in its restaurants a 56-page booklet providing nutritional information on its menu items. Under continuing pressure, it decided to provide nutritional information on its tray liners and on 3-foot-by-3-foot "Did You Know" displays in its restaurants.

McDonald's also was criticized on the grounds that its food harmed its customers. Criticism centered on the fat and cholesterol content. McDonald's promoted its McNuggets by emphasizing that, "they're low in calories, they're 100% tender, delicious, chicken thigh and breast meat cooked in 100% cholesterol-free vegetable oil." Philip Sokolof, a Nebraska businessman, however, took out full-page advertisements in major newspapers charging McDonald's with the "Poisoning of America" because of the fat content of its hamburgers. McDonald's said the advertisements were inaccurate and that it used only lean beef. A spokesperson for the Center for Science in the Public Interest, one of the groups in the Ralph Nader network, commented: "To me, the important part is that the general thrust of the ad was correct. Many of the foods served by McDonald's are loaded with saturated fat and cholesterol."

McDonald's also faced criticism by minority groups because of the company's emphasis on sales in inner-city areas. Inner-city residents tend to be more frequent customers of fast-food restaurants than residents of other areas, and they tend to spend more per visit. In response, fast-food companies had been increasing their advertising targeted to inner-city residents. Some critics argued that McDonald's and other fast-food companies were targeting minorities and endangering their health because of the fat, salt, and cholesterol in their menu items.

McDonald's began to reconsider its menu items, including the fat content of its milk, milkshakes, and beef, and its practice of cooking french fries in beef tallow. It removed the chicken skins from its McNuggets and introduced fat-free, fiber-filled muffins and low-fat, low-sugar cereals for breakfast. Its Big Breakfast, however, contained 1,800 milligrams of sodium, and nearly half its calories came from fat.

On a different dimension of health concerns, restaurant managers faced increased complaints from nonsmokers about second-hand smoke. One alternative was to adopt a no-smoking policy, but that could put McDonald's at a disadvantage relative to restaurants that allowed smoking. McDonald's could implement a no-smoking policy at the 1,400 restaurants it owned in the United States, but it was concerned about whether its franchisees would want to adopt a no-smoking policy.

The fast-food industry and McDonald's in particular had also been criticized by interest groups for not providing health care coverage for part-time, hourly employees. Most of these employees quit within 6 months and providing coverage would be very costly. In the midst of the Clinton administration's effort to reform the nation's health care system, the issue was potentially explosive.

In 1994 McDonald's was sued by a woman who had spilled coffee on herself receiving third-degree burns. A jury awarded her $640,000 in compensatory damages and $2.7 million in punitive damages. The jury was incensed by McDonald's refusal to lower the temperature of its coffee from the 165° to 170° at which it was served despite several lawsuits over the past decade. The judge subsequently reduced the punitive damages to $480,000, but McDonald's planned to appeal the decision.

If McDonald's were to make changes in the United States, it would face the issue of whether it should make similar changes at its restaurants in other countries. Conversely, nonmarket issues from other countries could initiate change in the United States. McDonald's faced waste disposal issues in other countries. In 1994, in a suit filed by two owners of McDonald's restaurants, a German court upheld a municipal ordinance imposing a tax on disposable containers. The tax, which amounted to 30 cents for each paper plate and 6 cents for each disposable spoon, fork, and knife, would likely force major changes in packaging in the fast-food and vending industries if similar ordinances were adopted by other German cities. ■

PREPARATION QUESTIONS

1. Identify the issues on McDonald's nonmarket agenda in the early 1990s. What are the sources of those issues? How might they affect McDonald's performance?
2. In which institutional arenas will these issues be addressed? Which interests will be active on these issues?
3. Where are the issues in their life cycle?
4. How should McDonald's address the issues?

CHAPTER 2

Integrated Strategy

Introduction

A business strategy guides a firm in its market and nonmarket environments and consists of a market component and a nonmarket component. A market strategy is a concerted pattern of actions taken in the market environment to create value by improving the economic performance of a firm, as in the case in which a firm decides to enter a country that has open markets. A nonmarket strategy is a concerted pattern of actions taken in the nonmarket environment to create value by improving overall performance, as in the case in which a firm works through international trade law to open a foreign market. For a business strategy to be effective these two components must be *integrated* and tailored to the firm's market and nonmarket environments as well as to its competencies.[1]

Market and nonmarket strategies focus on the pursuit of opportunity and advantage in the face of market and nonmarket competition, respectively, with the objective of achieving superior performance. In this book, performance is considered at two levels. Initially, performance is assumed to be measured by the value created for the firm's owners. Then in Part V, this objective is examined using concepts of corporate social responsibility and ethics that extend beyond value creation for owners.

This chapter focuses on nonmarket analysis and strategy and their integration with their market counterparts. As illustrated in Figure 2-1, effective management in the nonmarket environment requires conceptual frameworks for (1) analyzing nonmarket issues and the broader environment, (2) formulating effective strategies for addressing those issues, and (3) positioning the firm in its nonmarket environment. The strategy concept is introduced first and then the integration of market and nonmarket analysis and strategy formulation are considered and illustrated through an example involving Microsoft. Nonmarket analysis is then considered, and a framework for analysis is presented and illustrated using an example involving Citibank.

Strategy in the Nonmarket Environment

THE IMPORTANCE OF NONMARKET STRATEGY

The importance of nonmarket issues, and hence of nonmarket strategy, depends on the control of a firm's opportunities. Viewing that control as a continuum, opportunities can be controlled by government at one extreme and markets at the other extreme. Figure 2-2 illustrates the relation between the control of opportunities and the importance of nonmarket strategies. Nonmarket strategies are more important the more opportunities are controlled by government and are less important, but often still important,

[1]This material is adapted from Baron (1995b). Copyright © 1995 by The Board of Regents of the University of California. Reprinted from the *California Management Review*, Vol. 37, No. 2. By permission of The Regents.

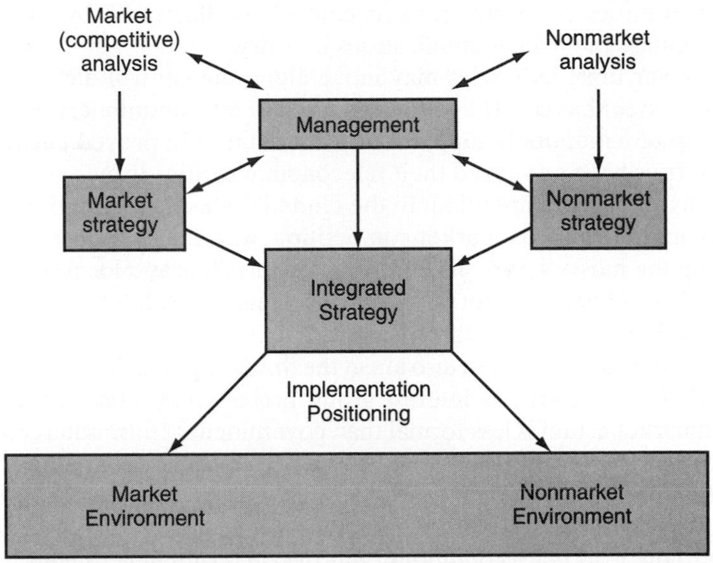

FIGURE 2–1 Management and Integrated Strategy

when opportunities are controlled by markets. In some industries such as consumer electronics and software, government exercises relatively little control over firms and their activities. In contrast, the government exercises considerable control over biotechnology products and local service telecommunications firms. The automobile industry is somewhere in between. One important role of nonmarket strategy is to unlock

FIGURE 2–2 Nonmarket Strategy and Market Control

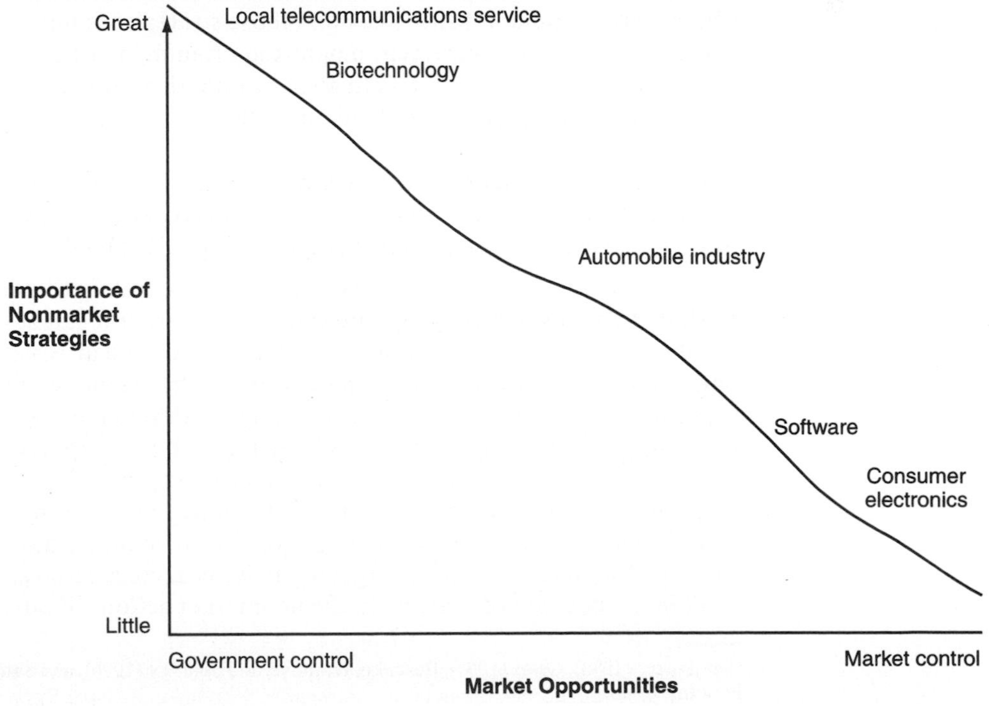

opportunities from government control, as illustrated by the strategies of firms to deregulate the telecommunications industry.

Over time, industries may move along the control dimension. In many countries government has controlled the provision of telecommunications services through ownership of a monopoly supplier. In the pursuit of improved performance many of these countries have privatized their telecommunications firms and replaced ownership with regulation and competition. In the United States the regulation of telecommunications is being replaced by market competition, with long-distance and information services being the most extensively controlled by markets and local service the least.

Two other sets of forces affect opportunities. Behind the government control of opportunities is the public climate in which a firm operates. That climate can give rise to government action, but it can also affect the firm's opportunities directly through private nonmarket action, such as interest group protests, boycotts, and media attention. Private nonmarket action is less formal than government action, but as considered in Chapter 4, it can be important. The second set of forces comes from ethical considerations. These considerations guide firms and their managers in their choice of policies and strategies. For example, based on ethical principles, Levi Strauss & Co. formulated a policy pertaining to the workplace conditions of its overseas suppliers, as considered in Chapter 20.

Market analysis and strategy formulation typically take the nonmarket environment as given and focus on the competitive positions of firms in the industry, the threats from potential entrants and substitutes, and the bargaining power of suppliers and customers.[2] When a firm looks ahead, however, neither the market nor the nonmarket environments can be taken as given. Furthermore, those environments cannot be viewed as changing exogenously because firms and other interested parties employ nonmarket strategies to influence those environments, as the Microsoft example considered in a later section of this chapter indicates.

Firms choose market strategies, but they do not control the outcomes of those strategies. Outcomes are a function of the market strategies of all the participants in the market as well as the structural characteristics of the market. In a similar manner firms choose their nonmarket strategies, and those strategies compete in institutional arenas and shape the nonmarket environment and often the market environment as well. The nonmarket environment thus is to an important degree endogenous, and its characteristics depend on the actions of firms and other interests.

TIMING AND THE NONMARKET ISSUE LIFE CYCLE

The timing of a nonmarket strategy can be crucial to successful performance. Using the life cycle concept from Chapter 1, Figure 2-3 identifies types of strategies as a function of the stage at which a firm begins to address a nonmarket issue. The firm has greater flexibility and a wider range of alternatives the earlier it catches an issue. If an issue is caught at the issue identification stage, strategies can be directed at affecting the development of the issue. The firm may also be able to frame the issue prior to interest groups forming. Levi Strauss was the first company to address the issue of working conditions in its suppliers' factories, and the policies it developed kept it out of the line of attack of activists. If a firm catches the issue once interest groups have formed and the issue is in the legislative stage, the firm has less flexibility and its range of alternatives is narrowed. Nike was late in addressing the issue of working conditions at its suppliers' factories in Asia, and it became a target for activists as considered in Chapter 4. Nike found itself in the position of reacting to the nonmarket actions of others rather than shaping

---

[2]See Porter (1980), Oster (1994), Besanko, Dranove, and Shanley (1996), and Saloner, Shepard, and Podolny (2000).

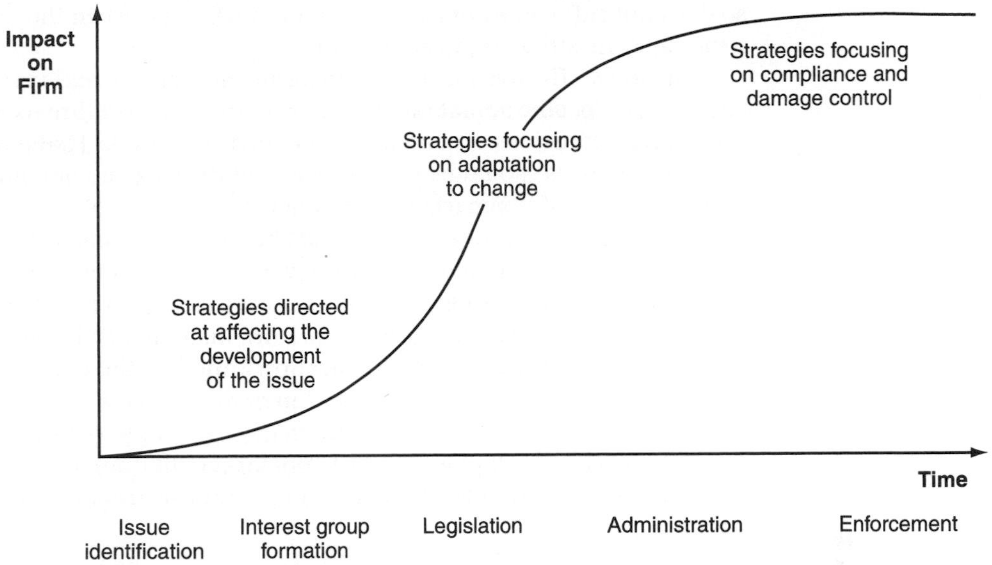

FIGURE 2–3 Nonmarket Issue Life Cycle and Strategy

the development of the issue. Its opportunity to participate in the resolution of the nonmarket issue was largely limited to the enforcement stage. Nike's nonmarket strategy basically focused on damage control.

INTEGRATED STRATEGY

An effective market strategy is necessary for successful performance, but it is not always sufficient. An effective nonmarket strategy is rarely sufficient, but for most firms it is necessary for successful performance. Market strategies serve the objective of superior performance by focusing on identifying opportunities and developing and sustaining the competitive advantage required to pursue those opportunities. Nonmarket strategies also serve the objective of superior performance by participating effectively and responsibly in the public processes that address the control of those opportunities. The performance of a firm depends not only on its environment but also on how well its nonmarket analysis and strategy are integrated with its market analysis and strategy. Because performance is ultimately the responsibility of management, managers are responsible for both market and nonmarket strategies and for their integration, as illustrated in Figure 2-1.

One approach to integrating nonmarket and market analyses is to incorporate them into the market strategy process. For example, regulation pertaining to who may provide services, as in telecommunications, could be incorporated into the analysis of the rivalry among existing firms, potential new entry, and the threat of substitutes. The drawback to this approach is that the institutions in which regulatory policies are set are quite different from the institutions of markets. Moreover, in market institutions only those who transact play a role, whereas in nonmarket institutions other interests are also enfranchised to participate.

Alternatively, nonmarket factors that affect the market environment can be viewed as separate threats and opportunities. Just as market analysis focuses on competitive forces, nonmarket analysis can focus on assessing threats (such as those arising from government, interest groups, and activist pressures) and on unlocking market opportunities. Viewing nonmarket issues as a separate force has considerable merit, but doing so does not sufficiently emphasize the interaction between the market and nonmarket issues and the strategies to address them.[3]

The most effective means of integrating nonmarket and market strategies is to focus both on specific nonmarket issues that affect market threats and opportunities and on nonmarket actions as complements to market actions. That is, both market and nonmarket strategies should be considered in addressing and defending against the forces in the market and nonmarket environments.[4]

Because nonmarket strategies must be tailored to the specific issues, interests, institutions, and information in the nonmarket environment, there is no short list of generic nonmarket strategies to follow. Moreover, the nonmarket agenda of a firm is in part set externally in the environment rather than internally, and strategies must attend to that agenda. Strategy formulation is patterned to the four I's, and it is the focus of much of this book. The chapter case *Envirotest Systems Corporation (A)* provides an opportunity to assess market and nonmarket strategies and the effectiveness of their integration. The developments in the nonmarket environment of Microsoft in 1998 provide a context for consideration of its nonmarket strategy and integration with its market strategy.

Microsoft[5]

Tony Williams, chief of staff for Senator Slade Gorton (R-WA), observed about Microsoft, "They just have not put the same level of brainpower behind politics that they've applied in the world of software production."[6]

Market strategy. Founded in 1975 by Bill Gates and Paul Allen, Microsoft has been one of the greatest successes in the history of business. At the end of 1997 Microsoft had a market value of $200 billion, and Bill Gates had amassed a personal fortune of $50 billion. More importantly, Microsoft had helped make possible the widespread use of personal computers by providing the operating system used in over 90 percent of the PCs shipped. The operating system served as the platform for software developers to offer a dazzling array of products, and Microsoft had begun to dominate the software market by integrating its proprietary software with its Windows operating system.

The rise of the Internet created threats to Microsoft's dominance as well as nearly unlimited opportunities. Microsoft responded to the Internet challenge by introducing Internet Explorer, which served not only as a browser but also as a platform for content and Internet service providers. To ensure standardization and increase the use of Internet Explorer, Microsoft integrated it with its operating system and required PC manufacturers that preload the Windows 95 operating system to incorporate Internet Explorer.

Microsoft's success, however, generated a host of nonmarket challenges. A principal cause of these problems was the spiraling popularity of the Internet and the rapid growth in, and longer-term promise of, electronic commerce. In 1994 Microsoft had become concerned about "shell" screens, which covered the main Windows screen. Microsoft was able to convince PC manufacturers to eliminate the shells, and Windows 95 became the interface with the user. With the rise of the Internet, Microsoft feared that PC makers

---

[3]Gale and Buchholz (1987) discuss the relationship between political strategies and Porter's (1980) five forces. Yoffie (1987) characterizes strategies by the approach to political issues.

[4]Baron (1997)(1999) provides formal models of integrated strategy and a nontechnical analysis in (1996).

[5]

[6]*The Wall Street Journal,* November 11, 1997.

would use a shell or a browser as an alternative to the Windows interface. In response, Microsoft altered its contracts with PC makers to prohibit them from preloading other browsers such as Netscape Navigator.[7] Internet Explorer quickly eroded Netscape's market share, capturing over half the market. A Microsoft executive vice president explained, "It's our product and we get to define what's in it. If PC makers choose to license it, they are not entitled to pick and choose from among the functions."[8]

Microsoft also used its operating system and browser to become a supplier of Internet services and content. For example, it could provide banking, travel, insurance, telecommunications, entertainment, as well as a host of other services. Moreover, Microsoft could bring its services up first on a Windows desktop or an Internet search, giving it a crucial advantage over competitors. For example, clicking the travel button in Internet Explorer brought up Microsoft's Expedia on-line travel service.

Some of the new technologies Microsoft was developing included Windows 98, a significant upgrade of Windows 95, that would further integrate Internet Explorer with the operating system. Microsoft had acquired WebTV and was readying a consumer electronics version of Windows, known as Windows CE, for use with the $200 WebTV box. Microsoft was also developing Auto PC, a voice-activated system that would allow a driver to retrieve e-mail and connect to the Internet. In December 1997 Microsoft acquired Hotmail Corporation which offered e-mail free of charge through the Internet. Hotmail joined MSNBC, Expedia, Sidewalk, CarPoint, and Investor in Microsoft's Interactive Media Group. Windows NT, the operating system for corporate networks, provided Microsoft with the opportunity to penetrate the corporate software and applications market.

The nonmarket environment. Although its meteoric market success was earning it admiration and envy, Microsoft had largely ignored its nonmarket environment. In addressing nonmarket issues Microsoft had relied on the Business Software Alliance and its law firm and did not hire its first in-house specialist to address governmental issues until 1996. This section focuses on nonmarket issues associated with competitive practices. Microsoft also faced several other nonmarket issues such as temporary employee policies, visas for high-tech workers, encryption, and computer privacy.

In 1994 Microsoft encountered what was to become a series of antitrust challenges resulting from its competitive practices. In 1995 it settled an antitrust complaint by entering into a consent decree with the Department of Justice (DOJ) that prohibited Microsoft from tying the sale of one product to another. The consent decree, however, allowed Microsoft to continue selling "integrated" products. Later in 1995 Microsoft attempted to acquire Intuit, Inc. for over $2 billion in stock. The DOJ filed an antitrust lawsuit alleging that the acquisition would give Microsoft dominance over the personal finance software market and provide it with a "springboard" to the emerging electronic commerce market. Three weeks later Microsoft abandoned the acquisition. The consent decree and the blocked acquisition had little apparent effect on Microsoft's growing dominance of the operating system and software markets and its assault on the Internet market.[9]

---

[7]For example, Microsoft sent a "Notice of Intent to Terminate License Agreement" to cut Compaq off from its Windows 95 operating system if Compaq did not reinstate the Microsoft Network and Internet Explorer icons on the desktop of Presario computers. Compaq had planned to create a button to connect to Netscape Navigator.

[8]*The Wall Street Journal,* October 23, 1997.

[9]Microsoft also faced an antitrust suit filed by Caldera Corporation, which had purchased the rights to DR-DOS from Novell Incorporated of Provo, Utah. DR-DOS was an operating system developed as an alternative to Microsoft's DOS operating system. The lawsuit alleged that Microsoft had bundled Windows and DOS to crush DR-DOS. The DOJ had decided to not pursue the DR-DOS case when it agreed to the 1995 consent decree, but Caldera had persisted and the case was scheduled for trial in 1999.

In 1997 Microsoft's spectacular market success began to generate change in its nonmarket environment. The changes came not only from competitors but also from activists and the government. Information providers and service firms, such as travel agencies, became concerned that Microsoft would integrate information services with Windows and Internet Explorer and shut them out of the on-line segment of the market. SABRE, a unit of AMR Corporation and the dominant airline reservation company, joined with Netscape and Sun Microsystems to solicit members of a coalition that would lobby against Microsoft and conduct media activities warning of Microsoft's potential to control on-line services and information.[10]

In 1997 Microsoft released a new version of Internet Explorer integrated with its Windows 95 operating system and planned to further integrate it into its Windows 98 operating system, scheduled for release in mid-1998. Shortly after the release, the DOJ filed a petition in federal court arguing that Microsoft was violating the 1995 consent decree by forcing PC manufacturers to accept the bundling of Internet Explorer and Windows. The petition also asked that users be given instructions on how to remove the Internet Explorer icon from their PC. The DOJ asked for $1 million a day civil contempt charges if Microsoft failed to comply. Scott McNealy, CEO of Sun Microsystems, commented on the DOJ's action, "When the consent decree was signed, I said it was toothless. Now they are trying to enforce something that is toothless. You are not going to gum Microsoft to death."[11]

Microsoft refused to unbundle its browser and contested the suit in court, contending that the consent decree allowed it to provide integrated services. A company vice president explained, "Sometimes you have to take positions in legal cases for a larger purpose, even if it does give you public relations problems. And we have to do a better job of explaining to the court, the industry and the public just how integrated Internet Explorer is into Windows. It's not something you can unbolt." District court judge Thomas Penfield Jackson, a computer novice, however, brought a new PC into the courtroom and personally demonstrated how he was able to remove the browser icon from the screen.[12] In December Judge Jackson issued a preliminary injunction requiring Microsoft to offer Windows without Internet Explorer.

Microsoft was also skewered in *Doonesbury* and on *The Simpsons,* where Microsoft agents broke up Homer's home office start-up company. The sentiment against Microsoft spilled over onto the 22 campuses of the California State University system. The university had entered into an agreement with Microsoft and three other companies to upgrade its telecommunications and computer systems. Some faculty and students protested Microsoft's involvement, and members of the California legislature expressed concerns. At Humboldt State University demonstrating students replaced the university's name on the entrance sign with "Microsoft University."[13]

Ralph Nader also took an interest in Microsoft and in 1997 launched a campaign against Microsoft's dominance of the software industry and its potential control over services and content. Nader visited the Department of Justice urging it to take antitrust action against Microsoft. In full-page newspaper advertisements, Nader and Essential Information, one of the activist organizations in the Nader network, announced a

---

[10]SABRE began as an airline reservation system established by American Airlines, but antitrust concerns about the system bringing up American Airlines flights first on travel agents' screens before the flights of other airlines resulted in it being forced to bring up flights in random order.

[11]*The Wall Street Journal,* October 21, 1997.

[12]The judge, however, was not able to remove the functionality of the browser or its integration with certain software and Internet software.

[13]In April 1998 Microsoft withdrew from the project, stating that it required a greater capital investment than the company was willing to make. General Motors's Hughes Electronics also withdrew for the same reason, and when GTE withdrew, the university dropped the project.

conference on Microsoft under the banner, "We thought we better meet before Microsoft® got a trademark on 'antitrust.'"[14] The well-orchestrated conference held in Washington, DC, was designed for its media appeal, and Nader assembled an array of critics of Microsoft, including Scott McNealy and Roberta Katz, general counsel of Netscape.[15] Nader said, "This is a company whose strategy is to become a tollgate collector at every toll and a choke point at every juncture."[16] Referring to the reluctance of computer manufacturers and other companies with business dealings with Microsoft to attend his conference, Nader commented, "A lot of people are afraid to come. We may have to have an incognito section, with bags over their heads."[17]

Senator Orrin Hatch (R-UT), chairman of the Senate Judiciary Committee, also took an interest in Microsoft, whose rival Novell was located in Utah. Senator Hatch had come under pressure from companies from the telecommunications and media industries that had substantial nonmarket expertise and considerable resources. Senator Hatch held hearings in 1997 during which several witnesses castigated Microsoft. A representative of the American Society of Travel Agents said, "If one firm becomes the gatekeeper... his firm will control where you go first and will distort the entire marketplace." He likened it to turning on a television and an NBC channel came on every time. Senator Hatch expressed "serious concerns about Microsoft's recent efforts to exercise its monopoly power." He also observed that certain companies were fearful of testifying against Microsoft and that in such a climate "innovation will be stifled."[18] The senator also warned that Microsoft was building a "proprietary Internet." He expressed the view that although antitrust authorities should not generally be concerned with a technology monopoly held by a company at a given point in time, they should scrutinize "the transition from one technology to the next," citing the Internet and Sun Microsystems's Java software programming system. The senator announced that further hearings would be held in 1998.

Microsoft belatedly recognized that its rivals were filling the political vacuum it had created by ignoring its nonmarket environment. Microsoft finally responded in late 1997. A company spokesperson explained, "Over the past year, our competitors have been calling all over Washington trying to generate anti-Microsoft activity. We've recognized, perhaps belatedly, that we need to make sure that policy makers hear both sides of the story."[19]

In early 1998 Microsoft changed its position and agreed to offer the latest version of Windows 95 with its browser hidden or partially removed, satisfying the court and ending the DOJ's lawsuit to enforce the 1995 consent decree.

Senator Hatch's second hearing provided a forum both for grilling Bill Gates and for its opponents to criticize Microsoft for its practices and alleged monopoly. Appearing with Gates were two of Microsoft's harshest critics, James Barksdale, CEO of Netscape, and Scott McNealy. At Microsoft's request, also participating in the panel were Michael Dell, founder and CEO of Dell Computers, and Doug Burgum of Great Plains Software, a developer of financial software based on Microsoft's NT platform. McNealy referred to Gates as "the most dangerous and powerful industrialist of our age" and described Windows as "a hairball of software that keeps growing." Barksdale criticized Microsoft for "predatory and exclusionary conduct."

In a spirited defense Gates asked, "Will the United States continue its breathtaking technological advances? I believe the answer is yes—if innovation is not restricted

---

[14]*The New York Times,* October 20, 1997.
[15]See Chapter 4 for a discussion of Nader's strategy in the Microsoft campaign.
[16]*The New York Times,* December 21, 1997.
[17]*Business Week,* November 3, 1997.
[18]*The Wall Street Journal,* November 5, 1997.
[19]*The New York Times,* December 21, 1997.

by government." He pointed to software makers' contribution of $100 billion to the economy and the creation of more than two million jobs. Under persistent questioning by Senator Hatch, Gates admitted that Microsoft did not allow promotion of its rivals' products on its Internet software. Senator Hatch also alleged that Dell refused to sell computers with Netscape products, and Mr. Dell replied that large customers could obtain Netscape products. Senator Hatch then revealed that his staff had made numerous calls to Dell's toll-free number asking for a computer with Netscape's Navigator browser. Senator Hatch said, "[the Dell representatives] told us they couldn't install Netscape because of their agreement with Microsoft. Your people wouldn't even offer a choice of Netscape."[20]

Microsoft responded by emphasizing the benefits to consumers from the innovative products it had developed and would develop in the future. The company pointed to its spending 16 percent of revenue, or $2.5 billion, on research and development and to the benefits to consumers from software developers being able to write their software for a single platform rather than several.

Microsoft's public relations campaign included advertisements in newspapers, tours by senior Microsoft executives including television appearances and a visit to Silicon Valley by Bill Gates, and press releases and op-ed pieces in newspapers. Newspaper ads stated, "At Microsoft the freedom to innovate for our customers is more than a goal, it is a principle worth standing up for." Bill Gates said, "When somebody says we can't innovate, we can't do what's been good for consumers, that's something we have to stand up for. A picture was painted of Microsoft as defiant of a government order. That was not true. I'm humble. I'm respectful."[21] Executive vice president Steve Balmer spoke of the importance of overcoming Microsoft's "harsh" image. "I wouldn't call sensitivity a birth attribute of Microsoft, or even of Microsoft's senior management. In a world in which we are perceived as powerful, I don't think we can make bad business decisions, but there might be ways of being more benevolent."[22]

Microsoft also took its message to activist and advocacy groups such as the Consumer Federation of America. To counter the media effect of Nader's well-publicized conference, Microsoft supported a conference of programmers and installers of Windows and NT systems. Microsoft also hired a political polling firm that reported that by a 4-to-1 ratio Americans believed that the marketplace rather than the government should govern the content of software.

To develop access and maintain relationships with elected officeholders in Washington, Microsoft and its employees had increased their contributions from $105,484 in 1994 to $236,784 in 1996. In the 1997–1998 election cycle Microsoft substantially increased its campaign contributions and its soft money contributions to political parties. From January 1, 1997, through April 30, 1998, Microsoft gave nearly $400,000 to the Democratic and Republican parties.

The companies opposed to Microsoft were also busy and enlisted the services of Robert Dole, former senator and Republican presidential candidate, who began recruiting companies to join in the campaign urging the government to bring a new antitrust suit against Microsoft. The opposition established the Project to Promote Competition and Innovation in the Digital Age, known as ProComp, which included American Airlines, the American Society of Travel Agents, the Software Publishing Association, Sybase, Netscape, Oracle, SABRE, and Sun Microsystems.[23] ProComp

---

[20] *The Wall Street Journal,* March 4, 1998.
[21] *Business Week,* February 9, 1998.
[22] *The Wall Street Journal,* January 1, 1998.
[23] Other members included the Computer & Communications Industry Association, Corel, Preview Travel, and the Air Transport Association.

launched an "educational campaign" with the objective of having the government bring an antitrust case against Microsoft.

In a news conference held by ProComp, former solicitor general and appeals court judge Robert Bork, an antitrust expert who generally supported reliance on market forces rather than government intervention, advocated antitrust action under the Sherman Act. Bork stated, "Microsoft has assembled an overwhelming market share and imposes conditions to exclude rivals. This is a challenge not to Microsoft's size, but to predatory practices." Microsoft responded by accusing Bork and Dole of "putting a new coat of paint on the same dilapidated arguments, calling for unnecessary government regulation of America's most dynamic industry.... [They] are trying to achieve through government regulation what they should be trying to get through making better products."[24]

Gates used his second annual CEOs conference to build a pro-Microsoft group that would counter ProComp. In an attempt to forestall an antitrust case Microsoft enlisted 26 computer industry CEOs, who wrote to the DOJ expressing "our strongest possible concern over the possibility of litigation." Those signing included Michael Dell, Andy Grove of Intel, Eckhard Pfeiffer of Compaq, and Lewis Platt of Hewlett-Packard.

Microsoft also sought to reduce the nonmarket pressure by modifying its contracts to allow PC manufacturers not to display Microsoft's Internet channel bar on the first screen that users see. The channel bar displayed a set of Microsoft-selected entertainment and commerce Web sites on its Internet Explorer desktop, and those sites were those of its partners including Disney, Pointcast, and Warner Brothers. The previous month Microsoft had revised its contracts with Internet access suppliers to remove the prohibition against promoting browsers other than Internet Explorer.

Gateway had been negotiating with Microsoft to ease the screen restrictions imposed by its contract with Microsoft, and when the DOJ learned that Microsoft was opposing the request, it deposed Gateway managers. The DOJ characterized the situation as Gateway wanting to "define its own Internet software and service partners and arrange direct business relationships with them in order to offer its customers additional options." Shortly thereafter, Microsoft relented by allowing Gateway to offer subscribers to its Internet access service the opportunity to use either the Netscape Navigator or Internet Explorer. Ted Watt, chairman of Gateway, said, "Microsoft allowed us to do this, but we don't think we should have to ask permission every time we want to make some minor software modification. Windows is an operating system, not a religion."[25]

The antitrust case. Under pressure from competitors, activists, and Congress, in May 1998 the DOJ and the attorneys general of 19 states filed an antitrust lawsuit against Microsoft alleging violations of the Sherman Act.[26] One antitrust remedy being discussed was breaking Microsoft into separate operating system and software companies, referred to as "Baby Bills."

Several state attorneys general were eager to join the lawsuit. Iowa Attorney General Tom Miller said, "Everyone knew it was high profile; everyone knew it was going to be important. This one was a no-brainer." Texas, which had taken the lead in developing the case against Microsoft, decided at the last moment not to join the lawsuit. A spokesperson explained, "We reacted to input from Texas corporations. They felt the suit would be bad for the computer industry and Texas consumers."[27] The Texas attorney

---

[24] *The Wall Street Journal,* April 21, 1998.
[25] *The New York Times,* May 28, 1998.
[26] See the Chapter 9 case *The Microsoft Antitrust Case.*
[27] *The Wall Street Journal,* May 28, 1998.

general had met with executives from Texas companies, including Michael Dell and representatives from Compaq and Tandy, which owns the Computer City chain.

Microsoft's Windows NT operating system, designed for networking and business use, also was a focus of software developers and providers of network services. The Software Publishers Association (SPA) with 1,200 members, including Microsoft, Oracle, and Novell, was concerned with antitrust issues that extended beyond the government's lawsuit. The SPA focused on Microsoft's drive to dominate the network and server segments of the market using its NT operating system. The SPA issued a report in June 1998 entitled, "Competition in the Network Market: The Microsoft Challenge." The report expressed "serious concerns with Microsoft's leveraging their desktop monopoly to the server." The SPA urged "that the antitrust enforcement officials also examine Microsoft's activities in the NT market."

In July 1998 a federal court of appeals overturned Judge Jackson's order that Microsoft had to offer Windows separately without Internet Explorer. The court ruled that the judge had erred "substantively" in interpreting the antitrust laws. The court noted that "[a]ntitrust scholars have long recognized the undesirability of having courts oversee product design, and any dampening of technological innovation would be at cross-purposes with antitrust law. . . . We recognize here only that the limited competence of courts to evaluate high-tech product designs and the high cost of error should make them wary of second-guessing the claimed benefits of a particular design."[28] Over the next 2 days Microsoft's stock price increased over 9 percent as investors reevaluated the company's prospects for prevailing over the DOJ in the antitrust case.

Also in July 1998 Senator Hatch held another hearing that focused on Microsoft's extension into business applications and its relationships with applications developers. In addition to Larry Ellison of Oracle and Mitchell Kertzman of Sybase, appearing at the hearing was Rob Glaser, a former Microsoft employee who with the backing of Microsoft founded RealNetworks. The company provided streaming technologies that, for example, show video and sound from Internet sites. Glaser demonstrated to the Senate committee how RealNetworks' new software product was disabled when Microsoft's rival product was installed on the computer. Microsoft responded in a press release that it was working "very closely" with RealNetworks to resolve the problem.

Analysis. In the context of Figure 2–2, opportunities in the software market were primarily controlled by markets and not by government or public sentiment. From the perspective of several of its rivals, however, Microsoft increasingly controlled their opportunities.

As with many high-tech companies, Microsoft had ignored its nonmarket environment, concentrating on innovation and creating and seizing opportunities. Its market dominance in the PC operating systems segment of the market gave it a platform from which to extend its dominance to other segments of the market including Internet services and ultimately to content. The Windows NT operating system provided similar opportunities in the business segment of the market. Microsoft had earned a reputation as an aggressive competitor, and the bodies of numerous companies lay strewn along the information superhighway. Microsoft's market strategy continued to be to charge ahead through innovation and pricing intended to broaden and deepen its penetration of an expanding set of markets.

Change in Microsoft's nonmarket environment was caused by technological change and the actions of interests. The principal technological changes were the development of

[28]The court also dismissed the special master appointed by Judge Jackson on the grounds that the appointment gave too much power to someone who was not a judge.

the Internet and electronic commerce and network technologies. They provided tremendous opportunities to Microsoft, creating new applications for software and allowing it to move into service and content provision. This aspect of Microsoft's market strategy substantially broadened the set of interests threatened by Microsoft, bringing into opposition such groups as travel agents, software developers, and American Airlines along with direct rivals including Netscape, Oracle, and Sun Microsystems. These interests formed ProComp to press their complaints against Microsoft. Ralph Nader and his network of activist organizations also became concerned about Microsoft's potential control of information and content.

The nonmarket pressure and the importance of the computer and software industries also attracted the attention of government officials and agencies. More aggressive antitrust enforcement under the Clinton administration increased the scrutiny given to Microsoft's dominant position and to the use, and possible abuse, of its market power.

Microsoft's nonmarket environment thus changed in response to technological developments and its own success. Its disdain for government and for nonmarket action had led it to ignore a set of potential nonmarket issues. Moreover, it had not developed nonmarket competencies nor had it invested in nonmarket assets such as relationships with government officials. Instead, it found itself engaged in a nonmarket competition with opponents with greater nonmarket resources and savvy than it was exhibiting.

In the context of Figure 2–3 Microsoft's rivals caught the nonmarket issue early and were able to affect its development. Microsoft found itself reacting to the actions of others and was forced to adopt a damage control strategy.In terms of the four I's introduced in Chapter 1, the nonmarket issues centered on Microsoft's monopoly, its competitive practices, its entry into service and content provision, and its rapidly increasing share of the networking and business applications markets. The interests concerned included current and future rivals, as well as activist groups. The institutional arenas were the judiciary, where the antitrust lawsuits would be decided, Congress whose members would continue to take an interest in high-tech industries, and public sentiment where Microsoft bashing had become popular. Information centered on the benefits from standardization of platforms and the associated effect on competition and innovation, as well as the likely consequences of alternative remedies to the alleged market domination problems.

Microsoft's focus on its market strategy and the absence of government control of its opportunities had led it to ignore nonmarket strategy. Microsoft belatedly began to lay a foundation for an integrated strategy by developing its nonmarket competencies and assets. Its market position and success gave it access to government officials, and it used that access for lobbying. Microsoft also sought to soften its harsh image by having its top management, including Bill Gates and Steve Balmer, make public appearances, give interviews, and interact with government officials.

As Microsoft expanded its reach into Internet service and content provision, it could have been more attentive to the interests it threatened and their possible nonmarket actions. Enlisting more of those interests as partners or allowing them more flexibility to offer their services might have lessened the nonmarket pressure Microsoft faced. Most PC manufacturers, which were dependent on Microsoft's Windows operating system, were unwilling publicly to oppose Microsoft. Concessions to, or a broader set of partnerships with, service and content providers could also have reduced the nonmarket pressure. In addition, Microsoft could have been more attentive to the desires of PC manufacturers to offer their customers selected services, such as the Internet access service Gateway had sought and the compatibility sought by RealNetworks. These steps would not have eliminated the nonmarket opposition from its rivals, but they might have narrowed the scope of the opposition and possibly avoided the government antitrust suit.

Nonmarket Assets and Competencies

Just as firms create value by developing and deploying market assets, firms employ nonmarket assets to add value. Nonmarket assets take several forms, including expertise in dealing with government, the news media, interest and activist groups, and the public. They include knowledge of the features and functioning of the institutions in whose arenas nonmarket issues are resolved. They include a reputation for responsible behavior earned with government, stakeholders, and the public. To the extent that these nonmarket assets, and the competencies that flow from them, are difficult to replicate, a firm has a nonmarket advantage.[29] Distinctive competencies and firm-specific nonmarket assets thus generate value as a function of how costly it is for market and nonmarket rivals to replicate them and for activists and other interest groups to dissipate them. As the Microsoft example indicates, disregard for the nonmarket environment can provide opportunity and advantage both to market rivals and to interest and activist groups opposed to a firm. Microsoft belatedly began to develop competencies once it came under fire.

Some competencies can either be developed internally or contracted for externally. Firms can hire outside legal counsel, public affairs experts, lobbyists, and political advisors. For example, a firm can hire Washington lobbyists to represent its interests based on their expertise and established relationships. The principal nonmarket competency that cannot be replicated, however, is the knowledge, expertise, and skill of managers in addressing nonmarket issues. Even if a Washington lobbyist is hired, members of Congress are more interested in speaking with the company's CEO and local plant managers than with its lobbyist. The better the CEO and other managers understand the issues, interests, and institutions that comprise the nonmarket environment, the more effective they will be in dealing with nonmarket issues.

The value of a nonmarket competency also depends on the effectiveness of a firm's allies in addressing nonmarket issues. On many issues a firm's market rivals may be its nonmarket allies, as when an issue affects firms in a similar manner. Consequently, industry members frequently work through a trade association or an ad hoc coalition to implement nonmarket strategies. In markets, firms are prohibited by antitrust laws from collusion through their market strategies. In the nonmarket environment, the law generally allows firms to join forces to formulate and implement nonmarket strategies. Netscape, Oracle, and Sun Microsystems thus could form ProComp to oppose Microsoft and urge the government to take antitrust action.

Nonmarket strategies frequently do not involve as extensive a commitment of fixed and nonfungible assets as market strategies. The closest counterpart to a fixed asset is a reputation for responsible actions and principled behavior. In lobbying, for example, providing incorrect or strategically biased information can impair a reputation and decrease the opportunities for, and effectiveness of, lobbying in the future. Nevertheless, many nonmarket strategies are relatively easy to reverse. Microsoft reversed its strategy of reacting to nonmarket developments and began to build relationships with government officials and repair its public image. Firms can also commit themselves by publicly stating a policy. As indicated in Chapter 1, Du Pont publicly pledged in a newspaper advertisement that if CFCs were shown to harm the ozone layer it would voluntarily cease their production, and it followed through on its pledge.

Reputations are thus established, and destroyed, by actions. Many firms invest in their public reputations just as they invest in their market reputations for service or quality. A reputation can be durable if sustained by actions consistent with it, but repu-

[29]See Prahalad and Hamel (1990) for a discussion of core competencies.

tations are fragile and easily lost. A tarnished reputation is difficult to rebuild as Exxon, Drexel Burnham Lambert, Nestlé, and others have learned.

STRATEGIES AND BORDERS

Bartlett and Ghoshal (1989) characterize market strategies as multidomestic [multinational], international, and global. A global market strategy is one in which "products and strategies are developed to exploit an integrated unitary world market." Global market strategies often focus on achieving cost advantages through global-scale operations, as exemplified by Honda's early strategy of selling the same motorcycles in all the markets it entered. In the nonmarket environment, examples of global strategies are (1) working for free trade in every country, (2) building constructive working relationships with governments, (3) applying universal ethical principles, and (4) implementing the same environmental standards in every country. An international strategy centers on transferring the parent's expertise to foreign markets. International strategies are thus specific applications of policy and expertise in other countries.

A global or international nonmarket strategy may not be successful, however, because strategies must take into account the specific nonmarket issues in a country, the institutions in whose context the issues are addressed, the organization of interests in a country, and other country-specific factors. For example, in the United States less than 15 percent of the workforce belongs to a labor union, whereas in Sweden over 90 percent belongs to unions. Applying the same employment practices in the two countries can generate problems as Toys 'R' Us learned. (See the Chapter 14 case *Toys 'R' Us in Sweden.)* Many nonmarket issues thus have a strong domestic component and are more likely than market strategies to require multidomestic strategies. A multidomestic strategy has the property that its successful implementation involves issue-specific action plans tailored to the configuration of institutions and the organization of interests in individual countries. Nonmarket strategies are more likely than market strategies to be multidomestic when issues, institutions, and interests differ across countries.

Nonmarket issues that require a multidomestic approach include legislation, antitrust policies, liability rules, safety regulation, intellectual property rights, and environmental regulation. Although there are common principles, such as information provision as the key to effective lobbying, that underlie the strategies used to address such issues, differences in the institutions can require country-specific, or more appropriately institution-specific, strategies. For example, lobbying must be tailored to the specific institutions and political structure of a country. In the United States, lobbying focuses on Congress and its committees. In Japan, lobbying focuses more on the bureaucracy and political parties and their leaders. In the European Union, lobbying focuses on the Commission and the Directorate Generals as well as on national institutions as a means of influencing the Council of Ministers. In Germany, lobbying occurs through peak associations and their chambers, as well as directly between individual firms and the bureaucracy and political parties.

Analysis of Nonmarket Issues

THE LEVEL OF ANALYSIS

Nonmarket issues may be addressed at three levels: systemic, organizational, and individual.

Systemic Level Systemic issues pertain to societal systems. Examples are demographic changes, global warming, macroeconomic policy, income distribution, and the global competitiveness of nations. These issues are important, but a focus on them and their impact on society seldom yields a basis for action by a firm. Also, analysis of issues at the systemic level often takes the perspective of public policy rather than that of a manager who is responsible for the performance of a firm. The appropriate focus for management is not on generic systemic issues but on specific issues with the potential to affect performance.

Firms and their managers, however, have a responsibility to contribute to the solution of societal problems, usually under the guidance of public policy but also under the guidance of ethical principles and social responsibility. For example, automobile manufacturers have the responsibility to address safety issues not yet covered by NHTSA-mandated standards.

Organizational Level The organizational level centers on the impact of nonmarket issues on the performance of the firm. The emphasis at this level is on specific issues that characterize the firm's nonmarket environment, the impact of those issues on performance, and strategies for addressing the issues in a manner that is both responsible and improves performance. For an automobile manufacturer, relevant issues include emissions controls, fuel economy standards, alternative fuel vehicles, safety, the opening of the Korean market, and employment practices.

Systemic level issues can interact with those at the organizational level. Global warming has implications for the burning of fossil fuels and hence for the oil industry. In anticipation of public and governmental pressures, British Petroleum invested in solar energy technology and became one of the leading suppliers of solar energy systems. It also voluntarily adopted programs to reduce its own CO_2 emissions (see Chapter 20).

Individual Level The individual level pertains to how individuals personally address nonmarket issues, which includes how managers interact with activists, stakeholders, government officials, and other institutional actors. This level may require personal skill development, including lobbying techniques, media training, and skill in bargaining and negotiation. These skills are necessarily intertwined with the individual's personality, preferences, and values. In an organizational setting, however, one's personal preferences and values are rarely dispositive. Because managers serve as agents of their employers, they have only limited latitude to follow the dictates of their personal preferences. Furthermore, managers often share both authority and responsibility, and hence must build consensus, which limits their discretion. Personal values, however, enter into career choices. If one's personal values are incongruent with the requirements of a position, the individual may look for a different position or a different employer. These personal choices are important, and the tension between personal values and managerial responsibilities affects all managers.

Because the focus of nonmarket analysis and strategy is on specific issues that affect the performance of a firm, nonmarket issues are considered primarily at the organizational level. In doing so, it is often necessary to draw on the other two levels. In the case of the automobile or oil industries, managers must understand at the systemic level the institutions that will address the global warming issue and the bases on which alternative policies will be contested. At the organizational level, the focus is on the market and nonmarket strategies an automobile manufacturer or an oil company adopts to address an issue such as higher fuel economy standards or the flaring of natural gas in oil fields. This may include support for alternatives such as a carbon or Btu tax for reducing carbon dioxide emissions or investments in new facilities to capture the natural gas. At the individual level, managers frequently have important roles in implementing strategies, which requires both knowledge and skill development.

DISCIPLINARY FOUNDATIONS OF NONMARKET ANALYSIS

As indicated in Figure 1–1, effective management in the market and nonmarket environments requires disciplinary foundations. Approaches intended to explain and predict behavior and the progress of issues through their life cycles are referred to as positive. Positive approaches are essential to the successful management of nonmarket issues, but they must be combined with normative disciplines pertaining to objectives and standards. The term *normative* has two meanings in management. Its classical meaning pertains to distinguishing between good and bad and right and wrong as embodied in ethical principles (considered in Part V). Its other meaning pertains to improved performance in terms of the objectives the firm pursues, which is the focus in this chapter.

Economics is the principal discipline for analyzing the market environment, and it is also important for issues in the nonmarket environment. As a positive approach, economics helps predict the likely consequences of alternative market strategies. Economics also makes a normative contribution as a basis for analytical methods, such as break-even analysis and capital budgeting, for improving performance. Economics, for example, can provide predictions of the increase in the cost of, and decrease in demand for, a new automobile as a result of more stringent emissions standards.[30] Similarly, economics provides a basis for formulating nonmarket strategies based on the predicted consequences of emissions standards alternatives for the constituents of elected officeholders, as considered in Chapter 6.

Economics is not a sufficient disciplinary base for management in the nonmarket environment and must be supplemented by other social sciences as well as by ethics. Nonmarket behavior is often explicitly collective and involves institutions quite different from markets. Political science is the principal discipline for understanding collective action in the context of nonmarket institutions.[31] Political science makes both a positive and a normative contribution. As a positive discipline, it provides a basis for understanding and predicting the behavior of individuals, interest groups, and government officeholders in the context of nonmarket institutions. In the case of the automobile industry, it provides a basis for predicting which interests will be active on a legislative proposal, for example, to increase fuel economy standards and whether Congress will enact it. From a normative perspective, political science provides a foundation for the formulation of nonmarket strategies and their implementation, for example, through lobbying that emphasizes the consequences of increased fuel economy standards for automobile choice and safety and hence for the constituents of members of Congress.

Ethics makes both a positive and a normative contribution to management in the nonmarket environment. Ethical systems provide managers with a means of assessing how those in the firm's environment are likely to evaluate its activities. Those evaluations often can attract the attention of the news media, the public, and the firm's stakeholders and lead to changes in the market and nonmarket environments. From a normative perspective, ethics provides management with a means of evaluating alternative strategies in terms of their effects on aggregate well-being, their relationship to the rights of individuals, and their fairness to those affected.

A Framework for the Analysis of Nonmarket Issues

Nonmarket issues are typically complex and require conceptual frameworks to guide analysis and strategy formulation. The framework introduced here pertains to specific nonmarket issues and brings together positive and normative approaches. This section

[30]One estimate of the cost increase due to the Clean Air Act of 1990 was $600.

[31]Other social sciences, such as sociology and psychology, can also be useful in positive and normative analysis.

introduces the framework, summarized in Figure 2-4, and in the following section it is applied to a case example. The chapter case *Buffalo Savings Bank (A)* provides an opportunity to consider a nonmarket issue using this framework.

In this framework the unit of analysis is the nonmarket issue. The initial step involves generating strategy alternatives. Managers must exercise creativity in generating alternatives in addition to those that immediately suggest themselves. For example, in addition to opposing higher fuel efficiency standards, General Motors advocated a tax on carbon fuels as a means of addressing the global warming issue, and subsequently the Clinton administration tried, but failed, to have a closely related Btu tax enacted.

Once alternatives have been identified, they are to be evaluated in three stages—screening, analysis, and choice. In the screening stage, alternatives that are contrary to the law, widely shared ethical principles, or a well-evaluated company policy, are eliminated. In the case of the automobile industry, an alternative involving noncompliance with mandatory NHTSA safety standards would be screened out. Several automobile manufacturers, however, routinely pay a fine, as provided for by law, for not meeting fuel efficiency standards.

The alternatives that remain after the screening stage are then analyzed to predict their likely consequences. The analysis stage is based on the positive methods of economics, political science, and other social sciences and focuses on predicting the behavior of interests and the consequences of alternative strategies. For example, automobile manufacturers must predict how successful their opposition to legislation to increase fuel economy standards is likely to be and which other interests will also oppose higher standards. This prediction focuses on interests, institutions and their officeholders, and information and takes into account the likely actions of the other interested parties. The analysis stage is also intended to take into account moral motivations of nonmarket behavior and thus how others will evaluate the firm's actions.

The third stage involves the evaluation of alternatives and the choice among them. On issues that do not involve significant moral concerns, choice is based on the interests of the firm, its shareholders, and its stakeholders such as employees, customers, and the communities in which it operates. The objective is typically value creation, taking into account the impact of alternatives on those stakeholders who are important to long-run

FIGURE 2-4 Framework for the Analysis of Nonmarket Issues

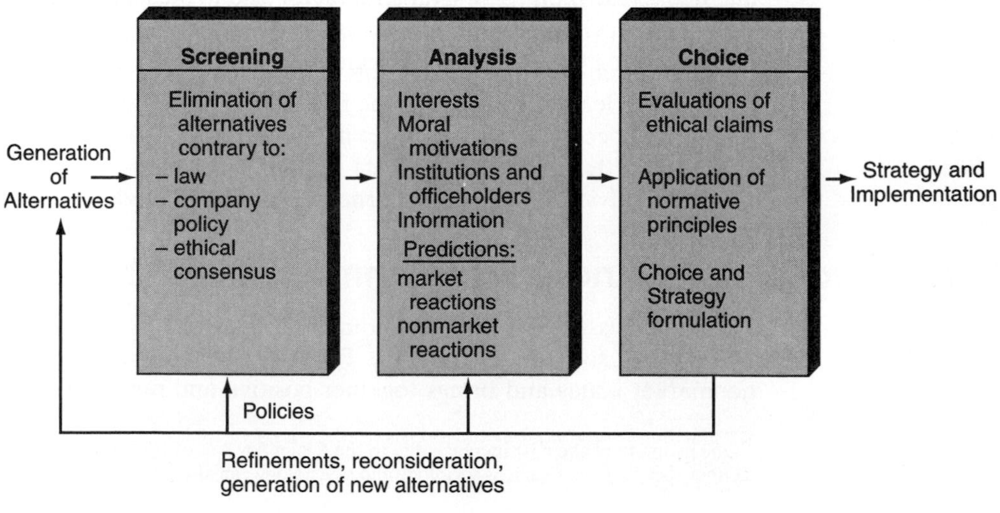

performance. If the issue involves significant moral considerations, ethical reasoning and normative principles pertaining to well-being, rights, and justice are to be applied.

In the nonmarket environment, many moral claims are made about rights. Some rights are "granted" in the sense that the government or ethical consensus has established them and made a clear assignment of the associated duty to respect them. When the duty has not been clearly assigned or the right itself has not been established by the government or through ethical consensus, the right is said to be "claimed." Granted rights are to be taken into account in the screening stage, whereas claimed rights are to be evaluated in the choice stage. For example, there is a general consensus that firms should not exploit children. There may be disagreement about what constitutes exploitation, however, as in the issue of the advertising of children's toys on Saturday morning television.[32] When moral consensus is absent, the claim is to be evaluated in the choice stage of the framework.

The process illustrated in Figure 2-4 yields specific strategies—concerted sets of actions to be taken by identified individuals or units—and policies that guide managers in addressing market and nonmarket issues. Those policies can be stated as rules to be followed or as principles to be used in reasoning about actions to take in particular situations. Policies are to be used in the screening stage to help managers rule out alternatives that are inconsistent with the firm's overall business strategy.

The framework presented in Figure 2-4 is not to be viewed as static but rather as dynamic. The evaluations in the choice stage and the results of choices provide a basis both for learning and for the refinement and reconsideration of policies and strategies. Comparing the consequences of strategies to those that had been anticipated provides a basis for improving analysis and prediction. Similarly, reflection on the results of strategy choices may suggest revisions in the policies used in the screening stage. Learning and reflection are essential to maintaining the usefulness of this or any other approach to the management of nonmarket issues.

Case: Citibank and Credit Cards for Undergraduates

In 1987, Citibank decided to offer VISA and MasterCard credit cards to undergraduate college students. Its objective was to develop an early relationship with individuals likely to be frequent users of the cards once they joined the workforce. To assess the credit rating and future earnings potential of an applicant, Citibank used several indicators. For students who were not employed or worked only on a part-time basis, it planned to use their undergraduate major as one measure of creditworthiness. According to Bill McGuire, a spokesman for Citibank, "using the major [is] a good indicator of future earning potential and of students' ability to pay debt."[33]

APPLICATION OF THE FRAMEWORK

First Stage: Screening

The nonmarket issue is whether Citibank should use students' undergraduate majors in deciding to whom to issue credit cards. The first stage of the framework involves determining whether use of an applicant's undergraduate major is contrary to the law,

---

[32]After years of debate and disagreement, in 1990 Congress passed the Children's Television Act, which limits advertising on children's programs to 12 minutes per hour on weekdays and 10.5 minutes per hour on weekends. Even so, disagreement continued over how to apply those limits to programs such as *GI Joe* that are developed around toys, and programs such as *Sesame Street* that have extensive licensing agreements with toy manufacturers See Hamilton (1998) for a study of the political economy of TV violence and children.

[33]*Peninsula Times Tribune,* March 20, 1988. The following is the application of the framework to the Citibank case and is not Citibank's analysis.

ethical consensus, or company policy. Its use as a predictor of creditworthiness is neither illegal discrimination nor in violation of the Equal Credit Opportunity Act. Similarly, individuals do not have a granted right to have a credit card and using an applicant's undergraduate major was not contrary to widely shared ethical principles. The use of undergraduate major thus passes the screening stage.

Several ethical claims, however, remain to be considered in the subsequent stages of the analysis. As some people claim, should everyone have a right to credit with that right withdrawn only upon failure to make the required payment? If not, which measures are acceptable predictors of creditworthiness? Is it better to use undergraduate major as a predictor, with the result that at least some students receive credit cards, or is it better to offer cards to a smaller number of undergraduates, or even to none at all? Instead of resolving these questions in the first stage, the framework calls for their resolution in the third stage following a positive analysis in the second stage.

Second Stage: Analysis

The second stage of the framework focuses on the consequences not only for Citibank but also for others and on any moral concerns that may motivate action affecting Citibank. The anticipated market consequences were lower losses and higher usage than if Citibank did not use undergraduate major. Although many lower-income people are good credit risks because they match their purchases to their income, people with higher incomes are more likely to have higher credit card usage. Based on similar considerations, Citibank had instituted the "Citidollars" program, which operated like a frequent-flyer program, providing discounts on products as a function of credit card usage.

The possible nonmarket consequences of using undergraduate major are more difficult to quantify than the market consequences, but that does not mean that they are less important or that managers cannot reason about them. Failure to anticipate the consequences of nonmarket behavior is a frequent cause of failed managerial decisions. Citibank's use of undergraduate major is a case in point. An application of the framework might have led Citibank to use other predictors of creditworthiness, thereby avoiding what turned out to be an embarrassing and costly episode.

Proceeding to the positive analysis, the first issue is whether anyone is likely to become aware of Citibank's policy and whether they would be motivated to take action. The law requires that a person denied credit be notified of the reasons for the denial. Those denied will be disappointed, and some will be angry. That anger might be based on self-interest, but some students may be concerned about what they view as the principle underlying Citibank's policy. Some might believe on moral grounds that creditworthiness should be based on credit history and the ability to pay rather than on undergraduate major or likely future earnings. Others may believe that basing creditworthiness on undergraduate major could distort students' choices of majors and ultimately of professions. Some might be concerned that Citibank's practices could induce lying by students who might falsely report their majors to increase their chances of receiving a credit card.

The predictive focus thus is on whether nonmarket action might be expected, what form that action might take, and what impact it might have. Indeed, Citibank contributed directly to the nonmarket action and to the issue becoming public. At the University of California-Berkeley, a Citibank canvasser, who had set up a table at the student union to take applications, was asked by a reporter from the student newspaper if it were true that some students were being rejected as a result of their major. "The canvasser advised her to fill in the credit application by listing business administration or electrical engineering as her major, instead of English."[34]

---

[34]*Peninsula Times Tribune,* March 20, 1988.

The next step is to predict whether the issue will become public. Students have various means of making such an issue public, ranging from bringing it before the student government to complaining to university administrators to organizing demonstrations. The most effective way of calling attention to the issue, however, is to attract the news media. How likely the media is to cover this issue can be assessed using the theory presented in the next chapter. In brief, the media finds claims of discrimination and unfairness to be newsworthy. Furthermore, students know how to make the issue more newsworthy by organizing protests and taking symbolic actions. This analysis does not imply that on all college campuses protests can be expected, but a manager should ask how many protests are necessary to attract the news media. The answer may be "one."

This analysis does not predict that the issue will inevitably become public, but it does indicate that it might. Citibank, however, need not abandon the use of undergraduate major simply because a market issue might develop into a nonmarket issue. Most of the public would never learn of the issue, and many of those who became aware of it might believe that Citibank's policy was appropriate. Those who do not view the use of undergraduate major as appropriate, however, are the principal concern.

Few students had a business relationship with Citibank that they could terminate in protest. Nor, due to the costs of switching banks, were they likely to be able to persuade any significant number of others who do business with Citibank to withdraw their business. The immediate market consequences were thus likely to be small. The effect on future business, however, might be more significant. Some students might choose to not deal with Citibank in the future. Furthermore, Citibank's recruiting on college campuses might be affected, either through boycotts or some other direct action. At Berkeley, student protesters demanded that Citibank be barred from recruiting on campus as a result of the issue. In addition, Citibank's image might be affected by a controversy. Certainly, Citibank management could be embarrassed by any protests or media coverage that might develop.

The Outcome

The issue became public through student protests at Berkeley, and the national media was quickly attracted to the issue. Shortly thereafter, Citibank announced that it would discontinue using a student's undergraduate major. Citibank subsequently developed a new application form for college students that asked only for the name of the college attended, the class, and the expected graduation date, in addition to information on bank accounts, income, and sources of funds.

Had Citibank conducted a positive analysis and been sensitive to the types of concerns—in particular the moral motivations of nonmarket action—that can cause a market issue to become a nonmarket issue, it could have avoided a situation that at a minimum was an embarrassment. In this case, the use of the framework in Figure 2-4 obviates the need for an evaluation in the third stage, since even from a consideration of Citibank's self-interest alone, it was not worthwhile to use undergraduate major.[35] The following Citibank I and II cases suggest that some lessons are not easily learned. As a result of nonmarket action in both cases Citibank made a hasty retreat and retracted its policies.

---

[35]One possible qualification to this conclusion is that the likelihood of the issue becoming public may have been sufficiently low that Citibank's best strategy was to use undergraduate major as a measure of creditworthiness as long as the practice did not draw public attention, and if it did, to discontinue the practice. It is more likely, however, that Citibank did not anticipate a public reaction. Certainly, the canvasser at Berkeley had not been informed about the potential sensitivity of the issue.

CITIBANK I

In early 1983, Citibank decided to service its accounts in New York more efficiently by encouraging account holders to use its automatic teller machines (ATMs). More efficient than human tellers, ATMs can perform most of the services required by account holders. Because small accounts were less profitable than large ones, Citibank decided to bar account holders with deposits under $5,000 from using human tellers.

CITIBANK II

Several weeks later in 1983, Citibank decided to offer investors a 10 percent return, the highest in the nation at the time, on federally insured money market accounts. Citibank was willing to offer this rate only to customers whose accounts did not involve servicing costs. Because customers in New York State received direct and costly services such as free access to ATMs, Citicorp decided to offer the 10 percent return only to those outside the state and to offer residents of New York a rate of 8.6 percent. The accounts were to be offered through a direct mail campaign asking investors to call a toll-free number. Operators servicing the toll-free number were instructed to tell callers from New York that they were not eligible for the 10 percent rate because they received other services from Citibank.

Organization of the Nonmarket Strategy Function

During the 1970s several companies formed strategic planning departments to assist management in developing long-range market strategies. These staff departments were typically attached to, but separate from, top management, which proved to be the cause of many failures. Similarly, several companies formed issues management groups to address nonmarket concerns, but that experiment produced a similar result, particularly when the group focused on societal issues rather than on specific issues impacting the firm's performance. Littlejohn (1986) describes the issues management activities of Monsanto and Gulf Oil during the early 1980s.

Wartick and Rude (1986) analyze the problems experienced by issues management units in eight firms.[36] They identified four conditions necessary for success:

- Top management must support and be involved in the effort.
- Field units and relevant staff departments must be involved.
- The issues management unit must fill a void in the managerial decision-making process.
- Results must come from the effort.

The perspective taken here is that there should be no void for an issues management unit to fill because the responsibility for addressing nonmarket issues should reside with operating managers and not with a separate staff unit.

Management rather than staff now plays the central role in formulating a firm's market strategy, and the same is true for nonmarket strategies. Managers must be centrally involved because they are in the best position to assess the consequences of nonmarket factors for market strategies and overall performance. The nonmarket environment is often more complex than the market environment, however, because public institutions are complex and a larger number of parties are enfranchised to participate. Moreover, successfully addressing a nonmarket issue may require expertise in the law,

[36]Also see Sigman and McDonald (1987).

government institutions, and public affairs. Managers thus should seek the advice of specialists when needed, but to evaluate the advice they receive, managers need to be as knowledgeable about the relevant nonmarket issues as they are about the markets in which the firm operates. Because managers operate continuously in their market environment, but often only on an episodic basis in the nonmarket environment, managers must use conceptual frameworks such as that in Figure 2-4 in developing nonmarket strategies.

Summary

A business strategy must be congruent with the competencies of a firm and the characteristics of its environment—both the market and the nonmarket environments. Just as the environment has two components, a business strategy has both market and nonmarket components, and these components must be integrated. The nonmarket component is of greater importance when the opportunities of a firm are controlled by government, challenged by public pressure, or involve moral concerns. Nonmarket strategies can be directed at competitive forces or at realizing opportunities blocked by the nonmarket environment. Because strategies depend on the issues, interests, institutions, and information that characterize the nonmarket environment, they are more likely to be multidomestic than global. Nonmarket strategies are based on assets such as the knowledge and experience of managers in addressing nonmarket issues and the reputation of the firm for responsible actions in its environment. Nonmarket assets can be developed, and over the long run their development becomes part of a business strategy.

Nonmarket issues may be addressed at the systemic, organizational, or personal level. The organizational level focuses on those issues with a potentially significant effect on performance. Addressing nonmarket issues in an effective manner requires a framework that organizes analysis, reasoning, and strategy formulation. Such a framework should also structure the management process and help bring to bear on issues positive and normative approaches for analyzing issues and guiding strategy formulation. The framework illustrated in Figure 2-4 is composed of three stages: screening, analysis, and choice. The screening stage rules out those alternatives that are contrary to the law, company policy, or ethical consensus. The analysis stage applies positive approaches to the prediction of nonmarket behavior and its likely effect. The choice stage involves evaluating ethical claims and making choices based on those evaluations and on the objectives of the firm. The results of the choice stage are strategies for addressing the issue and policies that can be used to guide managers in the screening stage.

The Part I integrative case *Calgene, Inc. and Infrastructure Marketing* addresses the integration of market and nonmarket strategies, the development of nonmarket assets, and an approach to nonmarket issues in the agricultural biotechnology industry.

CASES

Envirotest Systems Corporation (A)

THE OPPORTUNITY

The Clean Air Act of 1990 called for an average 24 percent reduction in vehicle emissions by the end of the century and directed the Environmental Protection Agency (EPA) to issue revised regulations to expand and enhance state inspection and maintenance (I/M) programs. Not only would additional areas of the country be required to have I/M programs, but the programs currently in place in several states would have to be improved. Nearly all the existing programs were "decentralized" with testing and repairs conducted by service stations and repair shops. In many parts of the country these decentralized systems were believed to be ineffective in attaining clean air standards. Proponents of enhanced emissions testing argued that centralized testing using more sophisticated and costly technology was required to achieve air quality standards. In a centralized system a motorist drives to a test-only facility in which emissions are tested using a dynamometer, a treadmill-like machine that allows emissions to be tested at various speeds rather than at idle as in decentralized testing. Several centralized systems were in operation in 1990.

SEIZING THE OPPORTUNITY

In 1988 Chester Davenport and Slivy Edwards established an investment fund to acquire companies that were expected to benefit from stricter government regulations. Davenport, a lawyer, had worked in several government positions, including serving as assistant secretary of transportation in the Carter administration. He also had practiced law and had successfully invested in several commercial real estate properties in Washington. His experience had brought him a wide set of contacts and considerable expertise in dealing with both government and the financial community. Edwards was an experienced corporate finance specialist who brought financial expertise to the venture.

Recognizing the opportunity created by the Clean Air Act, in 1990 Davenport and Edwards formed Envirotest Systems Corporation to acquire Hamilton Test Systems, Inc. from United Technologies Corporation for $51 million. Hamilton had been founded in 1974 in Arizona to operate the nation's first centralized, contractor-operated emissions testing facility. Envirotest provided test-only facilities and did no repairs, and in 1990 it had four emissions testing contracts in effect. Although it was clear that the demand for emissions testing would increase substantially, there were risks about how large an expansion the EPA would mandate and whether it would recommend the type of testing program Envirotest provided. Davenport was confident about the EPA's recommendations. As he explained, "It was my business to know these things."[1]

The success of Envirotest depended on the forthcoming EPA regulations, and in 1992 Davenport's expectations were realized. The EPA regulations required 182 metropolitan areas in 35 states to have either a basic or an enhanced I/M program. Fifty-three metropolitan areas with 15 million vehicles had no I/M program, and 15 states had either no program or a decentralized program. Envirotest estimated that a total of 59 million vehicles would be required to have an enhanced I/M program.

In addition to the I/M mandate, the EPA concluded that no decentralized program could be as effective as a centralized program. One of the EPA's concerns with decentralized systems was the inherent conflict of interest in a system in which the tester also made the repairs.

This concern was emphasized by proponents of centralized testing such as the Natural Resources Defense Council. A spokesperson said, "Under the old program, mechanics has an incentive to fail cars that should pass and a mechanic had an incentive to pass a car once he worked on it." Studies also showed that a minority of vehicles emitted the majority of emissions. The EPA concluded that a centralized program was superior to a decentralized program and decided that the pollution credits given for implementation of a decentralized program would be 50 percent less than for centralized systems.

The EPA estimated that centralized testing would cost less than decentralized testing and take less of a motorist's time. A test for nitrogen oxide, which was not included in many existing programs, would be added, causing more vehicles to fail. Under the EPA's regula-

---

[1] *The Wall Street Journal,* March 4, 1994.

tions motorists could be required to pay up to $450 for repairs. Existing programs had caps of from $50 to $300.

The EPA required enhanced programs in 83 areas, and in those areas decentralized programs were not permitted unless the jurisdiction demonstrated that a decentralized program was as effective as a centralized program.[2] Under the Clean Air Act, implementation of the National Ambient Air Quality Standards was delegated to the states, and states could choose either a centralized or a decentralized program as well as the test procedures required. The EPA's regulations, however, placed the burden of proof on the states to demonstrate that a decentralized program could be as effective as a centralized program. The EPA, in effect, told the states that they would not be able to demonstrate equivalent effectiveness. If a state failed to adopt an acceptable program by November 1994, the EPA had the authority to ask the Department of Justice and the Department of Transportation to impose penalties on the states. Those penalties included withholding federal highway funds and reducing pollution offset credits that could be used for plant expansions in the state. For Pennsylvania, for example, nearly $1 billion of federal highway funds could be withheld.

Because of the EPA's rule making, in 1992 Envirotest decided to acquire for $83.5 million virtually all of its largest competitor, Systems Control, Inc., renamed ETI, from a unit of Electronic Data Systems, a subsidiary of General Motors.[3] GM was forced to sell because of a conflict of interest between manufacturing and testing vehicles. The acquisition made Envirotest the nation's largest vehicle emissions testing company. Envirotest also formed Ebco-Hamilton Partners for the purpose of operating a sophisticated centralized testing facility in British Columbia.

MARKET STRATEGY

Envirotest's market strategy focused on vehicle testing programs and direct service extensions. Envirotest designed, owned, and operated the test-only facilities and provided complete systems including public education about vehicle emissions testing, in part to avoid conflicts of interests. It was also a marketing advantage because one of the EPA's reasons for favoring centralized programs over decentralized programs was the inherent conflict of interest that arose when the same party did both testing and repairs.

Envirotest had two types of customers: governments and motorists. Emissions testing contracts were let by states and municipalities through a competition typically involving the submission of bids in response to a request for proposals (RFP). Contracts with states extended for 7 years and provided for an exclusive emissions testing operator. Contracts could be terminated at will by a state, but damages could be imposed in that event. Its other customer was the motorist, and Envirotest emphasized customer convenience and user-friendliness. Motorists were also constituents and voters, so states were particularly sensitive to the public reception of emissions testing. Contracts thus required centralized testing facilities to be located within specified distances of the bulk of the population; for example, within 5 miles of all the population in urban areas and within 10 miles of 80 percent of the population in rural areas. Contracts also provided for fines on the operator based on the length of time for completing the tests; for example, if 95 percent of the tests were not completed in 20 minutes or less.

Envirotest formed alliances as part of its bidding strategy. For its successful bid in Colorado, Envirotest formed an alliance with the leader in mechanics hotline services, experts in advanced troubleshooting and vehicle diagnostics, the developer of an onboard diagnostics technology, and a vehicle diagnostic database/expert system company.

To operate testing programs in several states, Envirotest required both long-term capital and short-term financing. Envirotest planned to invest $150 million to purchase land and construct testing facilities in Pennsylvania. In April 1993 it made an initial public offering raising $55 million in equity and $125 million in long-term debt. Envirotest also arranged a $130 million credit facility and project financing of up to $400 million from its investment bank. As important as having the funds available to build and operate several testing systems simultaneously was having the organizational capacity to manage multiple contracts. One benefit of acquiring ETI was obtaining experienced personnel.

A component of Envirotest's market strategy was to have leading-edge technologies, and hence it invested substantially in research and development through its R&D facilities in Tucson. In addition to its centralized testing technologies, in 1993 Envirotest acquired Remote Sensing Technologies (RST)

[2]An association of state air pollution control officials met to review the EPA's regulations and generally concluded that states should switch to centralized testing.

[3]Envirotest sold the name Systems Control and its 50 percent interest in a joint venture in an I/M program in the state of Washington to the joint venture partner Sun Electric Corporation.

from Sun Electric Corporation, which had commercialized a remote sensing device.[4]

Envirotest engaged in a limited set of product extensions. It provided preemissions safety inspections, a quality assurance service, and a referee service. The referee service in Anchorage, Alaska, resolved disputes between motorists and repair shops. The quality assurance program in California provided inspection of the state's 9,300 smog check stations. Its safety inspection services were operated both separately and within its emissions testing facilities.

COMPETITIVE ADVANTAGE AND COMPETENCIES

Envirotest derived a competitive advantage from its experience. Of the 16 centralized testing systems in the United States and British Columbia, Envirotest operated ten systems. Emissions testing had learning curve economies along two dimensions. The first was the usual development of technical sophistication and operational experience. The other pertained to dealing with the public. An advantage of being the largest and most experienced company was that states could have a measure of confidence that Envirotest would effectively manage its interactions with the public.

Envirotest had many distinctive technical, operational, and organizational competencies. It had unparalleled proprietary technologies that it had extended through several strategic alliances. It had two emissions testing technologies, one from Hamilton and the other from ETI, and had acquired a remote testing technology. It had extensive operating experience and a reputation for effective service. It also had the largest number of experienced professionals.

NONMARKET STRATEGY

One foundation of Envirotest's nonmarket strategy was its knowledge of governments in their three roles. Governments created demand (EPA), were customers (states and municipalities), and chose technology through the type of emission testing system they selected (states and municipalities). Envirotest developed relationships with the EPA and was successful in being selected to develop the demonstration facility for the I/M 240 enhanced test required by the EPA for centralized testing facilities. This gave the company a marketing advantage that it could use as evidence that it was the most experienced contractor and had an unparalleled technology. Part of Envirotest's nonmarket strategy with respect to governments as customers was to encourage states to choose centralized testing rather than to attempt to demonstrate that an alternative system could perform as well.

A second foundation of its nonmarket strategy was sensitivity to the concerns of interest groups and the public. An important part of an emissions testing program was public education intended to develop acceptance for the program. Envirotest participated in both the development and implementation of these programs. Envirotest also sought to manage effectively its interactions with "key participant groups," the most important of which were motorists and repair shops. Envirotest was willing to support exemptions for fleet operators, automobile dealers, and government agencies that wished to operate their own testing facilities. The company also sought to develop effective relationships with interest groups at the state level. In Colorado, for example, it interacted with and attempted to be responsive to the concerns of the American Automobile Association, the American Lung Association, the Automobile Service Association, the Colorado Automobile Dealers Association, the Colorado Building and Construction Trades Council, and Coloradans for Clean Air.

As part of its constituency efforts, Envirotest lined up local suppliers and partners. For example, one of its partners was a Colorado firm that manufactured dynamometers. It also pointed to the number of people it would hire in a state and established a Minority/Women Business Enterprise (M/WBE) program for minority and women contractors.

In bidding for state contracts, Envirotest used a three-stage contract award approach in which nonmarket strategies comprised the first of the three stages.[5] The first stage, called Pre-Bid Marketing, was founded on the premise that "participation in the legislative and regulatory authorization process for emissions testing programs [is] an important initial step in marketing its services. With the help of legislative consultants, the Company's marketing staff educates states and municipalities on the environmental and operational benefits associated with contractor-operated centralized programs, and attempts to build support for adoption of such a program among environmental and health organizations." Once legislation had been enacted, "interested parties (including the Company and its competi-

[4]Remote sensing technologies involved portable roadside infrared monitors that examined vehicle emissions and photographed the license plates of vehicles. Vehicles emitting more than allowable levels were sent notices to go to a testing facility or repair shop.

[5]The second stage involved the preparation of proposals/bids, and the final stage involved program implementation.

tors) are often asked to assist the appropriate governmental authority in drafting the technical aspects of a bid request. This effort often includes reviewing bid criteria and recommending specified test programs."[6]

COMPETITIVE ADVANTAGE AND NONMARKET COMPETENCIES

Envirotest's three principal nonmarket competencies were (1) its knowledge of and experience with government, (2) its sensitivity to the concerns of the public and interest groups, and (3) its reputation for dealing effectively with public concerns. Davenport not only had considerable experience and expertise, but he also had a set of relationships with influential members of the federal government and the public. As the company had grown and obtained additional emissions testing contracts, it had hired additional executives to manage its interactions with government.

Its sensitivity to public concerns led Envirotest to develop effective relationships with both organized interest groups, such as repair shops and automobile dealers, and unorganized interests such as motorists. Its educational and outreach programs constituted a competency that could be transferred to other states.

Its reputation for dealing effectively with interests and the public was an important competency, as government officials wanted to avoid a public outcry against emissions testing. A reputation for and experience with these matters provided a degree of reassurance that served Envirotest well in contractor selection.

MARKET THREATS

Envirotest faced a number of threats in its market environment. The centralized testing industry included four rivals: Sun-Systems Control, Gordon-Darby, Allen-MATRA, and Environmental Systems Products. Envirotest operated more testing programs than all the others combined and was the most formidable firm in the industry, but nevertheless it faced competition.

The threat of new entry came both from new firms that might enter the centralized testing business and from states that could choose to provide their own centralized testing facilities. With the pressure on government to become slimmer and the movement toward privatization and outsourcing, however, few states were likely to provide centralized testing themselves.

The threats from substitutes came at two levels. First, states had the authority to achieve air quality standards through a variety of means. For example, they could institute programs to scrap old cars, which accounted for a substantial proportion of the emissions in many states.[7] States could also implement remote testing programs directed at detecting vehicles with excessive emissions. Second, states could choose an alternative emissions testing approach—decentralized or remote testing—provided they demonstrated to the EPA that it would be as effective as centralized testing. Although Envirotest did not have a clear technological advantage in remote testing, it had pursued opportunities for remote testing programs. Remote testing had the advantage of identifying the worst polluting vehicles, including those whose emissions control systems had been tampered with, and requiring them to undergo repair and further testing, while not requiring testing of clean vehicles. California, for example, spent $250 million annually testing clean vehicles and $117 million annually repairing dirty ones.[8] ■

[6]Envirotest Systems Corp. Form 10-K for the fiscal year ended September 30, 1993. Securities and Exchange Commission, Washington, D.C., 1993; pp. 11–13.

[7]Pre-1982 vehicles account for 25 percent of the vehicles on the road.

[8]California Research Bureau. "Motor Vehicle Inspection and Maintenance in California," Sacramento, CA, August 24, 1993.

PREPARATION QUESTIONS

1. What forces gave rise to the opportunity for Davenport and Edwards?
2. Assess the effectiveness of Envirotest's market strategy. Is the company likely to be able to take full advantage of the opportunities presented by the Clean Air Act?
3. How effectively integrated are its market and nonmarket strategies? Are its market and nonmarket competencies complementary?
4. How significant are the threats in its market environment? Is its strategy capable of dealing with those threats?
5. Does it face threats from its nonmarket environment?

Personal Watercraft aka Jet Skis

Personal watercraft, popularly known as water bikes or jet skis, are vessels powered by a jet pump with engines up to 135 horsepower and capable of reaching speeds of over 60 mph. Jet skis skyrocketed in popularity during the 1990s with sales reaching $1.2 billion in 1996, accounting for 37 percent of the boats sold in the United States. The average jet ski cost $6,328 in 1996, and over a million were in operation. The leading producer with nearly half the market was Bombardier, based in Montreal, producer of Sea-Doo personal watercraft. Other producers include Polaris Industries, Kawasaki, and Yamaha. Despite, or perhaps because of, their popularity jet skis were under attack from several quarters.

Safety concerns resulted from the speed of jet skis and from some of their operating characteristics. One characteristic was that they are nearly impossible to control when an operator loses hold of the throttle. A study published in the *Journal of the American Medical Association* reported that injuries associated with personal watercraft increased dramatically with an estimated 12,000 treated in hospital emergency rooms in 1995, including four fatalities. The study also indicated that the accident rate for personal watercraft was substantially greater than for regular motorboats. In California, jet skis accounted for 55 percent of boating injuries but only 18 percent of registered boats. The industry responded that surveys had shown that the average personal watercraft was used more per year than larger boats, making the accident rates "roughly comparable" to water skiing. Kawasaki stated, "More fatalities are routinely recorded for kayaking and canoeing." The National Transportation Safety Board had begun a study of jet ski safety, and a number of states and interest groups were pressuring the U.S. Coast Guard to examine jet ski accidents.

John Donaldson, executive director of the Personal Watercraft Industry Association, said, "This is just a recreational activity—it's fun. It's not a firearm . . . It's not a proven health risk like cigarettes." Pat Hartman of Polaris Industries said that jet skis are "as safe as the driver. It's like a loaded gun. If it's in the wrong hands, it's not safe."

EPA regulations that took effect in 1998 set new hydrocarbon and nitrogen oxide emissions standards for boats, and those standards would become more stringent each year until 2006 when a 75 percent reduction in emissions would have been achieved. The standards were applied on a "corporate average" basis that required that all of a company's certified engines, on average, achieve the standards. This permitted greater flexibility to manufacturers. The Earth Island Institute, an environmental activist group, criticized the EPA regulations as too weak.

The California Air Resources Board had begun a study to determine if jet skis should be regulated for their emissions. Other state and local agencies in California began to examine jet ski operations as a source of MTBE, a gasoline additive that reduced automobile emissions but could contaminate water supplies.[1] The Northern California Marine Association expressed concern about the effect of a boating ban on recreation and the businesses that service boating. Administrative Director Mary Kirwin Veloz said, "Our whole emphasis is on getting the governor to give a waiver to let the oil companies produce gasoline without using MTBE."[2]

Local environmental groups also took up the cause. The Bluewater Network, part of the Earth Island Institute, organized a public demonstration in San Francisco comparing jet skis with two-stroke and four-stroke engines. The two-stroke engine left an oily residue in the water, whereas the four-stroke engine left no apparent residue. Russell Long, director of the Bluewater Network, called jet skis "America's No. 1 water pollution source. . . . We don't want to take away anyone's Jet Ski. Our focus is the new ones that haven't been built yet."[3] Two-stroke engines used gasoline mixed with oil, and critics argued that the fuel did not burn completely. In four-stroke engines the lubricating oil was kept separate from the combustion compartment.[4] Two-stroke engines, however, delivered more power and faster acceleration. Two-stroke engines had been banned in motorcycles because of their emissions. The Tahoe Regional Planning Agency voted to ban two-cycle engines from Lake Tahoe to reduce water pollution. The EPA issued regulations taking effect in 1999 that would require fuel injection, which would substantially reduce pollution.

---

[1]See the Chapter 1 case *An Emerging Issue: MTBE*.
[2]*San Jose Mercury News,* February 14, 1998.
[3]*San Francisco Chronicle,* March 26, 1997.
[4]*The Wall Street Journal,* February 18, 1998.

In addition to water pollution, homeowners and others complained of the noise made by personal watercraft. Mark Desmeules, Director of Maine's Natural Resources Division, referred to jet skis as "the Ninja bikes of the water." He added, "That's why there is such a public outcry—the ability of just one of them to degrade the quality of the natural experience for so many people."[5] Vermont responded by banning water bikes from lakes with less than 300 acres. Legislation introduced in Minnesota would have banned personal watercraft on lakes with less than 200 acres, but opposition by the Jetsporters Association of Minnesota led to defeat of the bill. Jim Medema of the International Jet Sports Boating Association said, "The vote sent a clear message to those that would discriminate against PWC owners. We want to ensure that Minnesotans can continue to ride their PWC safely and responsibly, without any unfair restrictions that do not apply to other boaters."

The National Park Service, an agency of the Department of the Interior, was considering regulations that would allow individual park superintendents to designate personal watercraft usage areas. The regulations were supported by over a hundred conservation organizations, including the American Canoe Association, the National Parks and Conservation Association, and Earth Island Institute. The International Jet Sports Boating Association opposed the regulations. Both sides urged their members to write to the secretary of the interior. Mark Speaks of Yamaha Motors said, "I have not read a study that personal watercraft are particularly annoying to wildlife. I don't know why they would be more annoying to wildlife than any other boat."[6]

Local governments also were addressing personal watercraft issues. For example, the city council of Evanston, Illinois, recommended that PWC operators be charged permit fees twice as high as for other boats. The Illinois Department of Natural Resources notified Evanston that such fees were discriminatory and that it could lose state grants if they were imposed.

The industry adopted several nonmarket strategies to address the issues it faced. Industry members had formed the Personal Watercraft Industry Association (PWIA), which acted on behalf of industry members in public arenas. "Where conflict exists, the PWIA seeks to support resolution through the careful balancing of the interests of all parties, including PWC and other boat operators, swimmers, fishermen, paddlesports enthusiasts, environmentalists, and shoreline residents or recreationists."[7]

At the state level the PWIA developed model legislation intended to make waterways safer and to reduce conflicts. Twenty-six states have enacted regulations based on the model legislation, which included a minimum age requirement of 16 years, defined and restricted unsafe operation, prohibited nighttime operation, required that operators and passengers wear personal flotation devices, required operators of personal watercraft equipped with engine shutoff lanyards to use them, prohibited tow lines, and required safety instruction.[8] Mandatory instruction had been required in Connecticut since 1989 and was credited with keeping accidents down. The PWIA supported state legislation such as that in North Carolina that would prohibit nighttime use and increase the minimum age to 16 unless the person was between 12 and 16 and had an adult onboard or had taken a boat safety course.

Manufacturers' Web sites provided instructions on watercraft safety, rules of the road, and self-tests on operation safety. Jet skis came with a videotape, booklets, and warning labels on the watercraft. Web sites for jet skis also provided an environmental guide, including instructions to fuel and clean watercraft engines away from the water and shore. Operators were also instructed to avoid bird habitats and shallow waters where the watercraft could stir up sediment.

Legislative and regulatory activity took place at the federal, state, and local levels as well as in special jurisdictions such as the Tahoe Regional Planning Agency. The PWIA Web site provided tracking information on legislative and regulatory activity at each of these levels. Manufacturers also encouraged watercraft owners to take political action on issues pertaining to jet skis. Bombardier asked owners to contact their government entities to learn about possible legislative and regulatory action and also provided advice about how to participate effectively in public processes. It recommended that individuals ask their legislators about any restrictions being considered, identify key legislators including committee chairpersons, and ask about hearings schedules. Bombardier also provided guides for effective testimony; for

[5]*San Francisco Chronicle,* December 30, 1997.
[6]*San Francisco Chronicle,* December 30, 1997.

[7]Yamaha Web site, www.yamahausa.com.
[8]Yamaha Web site. Many states, for example, had no age requirement to operate a personal watercraft.

example, "When testifying at the hearing, thank the legislators for the opportunity to make your views known, and state your position on the issue in a clear and concise manner. Be prepared to answer questions, and do not be confrontational or react defensively."

In response to the criticisms, manufacturers made changes in their watercraft in an attempt to reduce the complaints and regulatory pressure. Bombardier announced that all its 1999 Sea-Doo models would include sound reduction technologies adapted from the automotive industry. The technologies included a new muffler, new composite parts that reduced noise levels, and a resonator that suppressed certain frequencies. Bombardier announced that the sound pressure level had been reduced by 50 percent on one of its models.

One strategy of the industry was to lend jet skis to government agencies, and in 1997 nearly 2,000 were loaned to game wardens, search and rescue teams, firefighters, and police and sheriff departments. Mary Ann Anderson, who had led the fight against jet skis in the San Juan Islands in Washington, said, "What they are doing is very ironic—producing a machine that needs to be highly regulated because of the way it is built and the power involved in it. Then they give this product to law enforcement agencies, which is supposed to be policing them. It's ridiculous."[9]

The issues faced by jet skis were similar in some regards to those of snowmobiles in the 1970s. Bombardier and Polaris also manufactured snowmobiles and along with other manufacturers had taken measures, such as developing trails, to defuse criticism by landowners. Bombardier credited the strategy of loaning snowmobiles to law enforcement agencies and search and rescue teams as helping gain their acceptance. As public acceptance increased, the market for snowmobiles continued to grow. ■

[9] *San Francisco Chronicle,* December 30, 1997.

PREPARATION QUESTIONS

1. Identify the issues, interests, institutions, and information dimensions centering on jet skis.
2. How have the jet ski manufacturers used market and nonmarket strategies to address the issues they face?
3. Should the jet ski manufacturers join the National Marine Manufacturers Association, which represents power boat manufacturers?
4. Should the jet ski industry seek to be included in the same regulatory category as power boats or should it seek to have its own regulatory category, for example, with respect to no-wake zones?
5. What nonmarket strategy should a company such as Bombardier adopt? How should it be integrated with its market strategy?
6. Can the jet ski industry overcome its critics and achieve the same continuing success achieved by the snowmobile industry?

Buffalo Savings Bank (A)

In September 1981 the Buffalo Savings Bank, a mutual savings bank located in Buffalo, New York, faced a dilemma. Although it was the largest mortgage lender in the area with $2.95 billion in assets and over 40,000 mortgages outstanding, the bank had a $10.3 million net operating loss during the first 6 months of the year. Gains from the sale of securities and other investments had resulted in a small profit, however.

The operating loss incurred by the bank was typical of the losses being incurred by other thrift institutions as a result of the high cost of short-term funds and the low yield on their long-term loan portfolios. In addition, the nation was in a recession. One opportunity for reducing the bank's operating losses was to call 900 "renegotiable rate mortgages," which because of the state usury law had been made at an 8.5 percent interest rate in 1975 and 1976 even though lenders in other states were receiving 10.5 to 11 percent on the mortgages they were extending.[1] To justify issuing mortgages at below-market rates, the bank had made the mortgages callable in 5 years to protect itself in the event of further increases in interest rates. As bank president Ross Kenzie stated: "Most of our competitors were out of the market at the time. At least we made money available at the time."[2]

Kenzie had been a high-ranking officer of Merrill Lynch, but in 1979 after being passed over for promotion, he left to head the Buffalo Savings Bank. At Merrill Lynch, he had developed a reputation as a hard-nosed executive who had the unfortunate task of firing managers whose performance in the rapidly changing financial services industry was unsatisfactory. Kenzie joined Buffalo Savings Bank with the objective of generating growth by diversifying into real estate and mortgage banking and through the acquisition of other thrifts. A principal limit on his growth plans was the depletion of capital by the continuing losses on outstanding loans. As with other thrifts, Buffalo Savings Bank was being hurt by the imbalance between record high interest rates, which made funds expensive, and the low yield on its long-term loan portfolio.

Although the 900 renegotiable rate mortgages were callable after 5 years, the monthly payment on the mortgages had been calculated on the customary 25- or 30-year basis. Borrowers had been informed of the call provision, and one of the borrowers, Joseph Leto of Tonowanda, remembered noticing the clause when he closed his mortgage.[3] Richard K. Schueckler, vice president in charge of loan servicing, recalled, however, that the bank had also indicated to the borrowers that it had never before called in a mortgage instrument.

One alternative the bank was considering was to offer the 900 borrowers the option of refinancing their mortgages at an interest rate of 14 percent, even though the going rates on new mortgages were 17 to 18.5 percent. Refinancing the mortgages at 14 percent would yield the bank an additional $1 million annually in interest income. The bank, however, was concerned about the impact of the refinancing on the borrowers. For a $30,000 mortgage, the monthly payment with a 30-year term and an 8.5 percent interest rate was approximately $230. At 14 percent, the monthly payment would be $355, while the payment at an 18 percent rate would be $452. Although refinancing the mortgages at 14 percent would impose a significant additional cost on the borrowers, they would still be receiving a substantial benefit relative to the current market rate of interest.

Bank managers who favored calling the mortgages argued that the renegotiable rate mortgages were a form of risk-sharing between the bank and the borrowers and that the borrowers had been informed of this provision. Furthermore, they argued that the borrowers had received a benefit of 2 to 2.5 percent during the past 5 years compared with the market rate at the time the mortgages were extended. In exchange, the borrowers bore some risk that market rates 5 years in the future would exceed 8.5 percent. The fact that the bank was considering offering to renegotiate the mortgages at 3 to 5 percent below current market rates was viewed as a considerable concession.

Opponents of calling the mortgages argued that not only would the borrowers suffer from the higher monthly payments, but the bank might find its reputation impaired by calling the mortgages during a period of extremely high interest rates. After all, the bank's motto was, "You can believe in Buffalo." ■

[1]State usury laws on home mortgages were prohibited by the federal Monetary Control Act enacted in March 1980.
[2]Owner financing of home sales had begun by 1981, and loan contracts often specified balloon payments after a period of 3 to 5 years. Those payments would not start coming due until 1984.
[3]New York law required homebuyers to be represented by an attorney, who in all likelihood would have reviewed the clause with the client.

PREPARATION QUESTIONS

1. What gave rise to this issue?
2. Apply the framework in Figure 2–4 to the issue of whether to call and refinance the mortgages.
3. What is likely to happen if the bank calls the 900 mortgages?
4. What specifically should the bank do about the 900 mortgages?

CHAPTER 3

The News Media and Nonmarket Issues

Introduction

The news media plays an important role in society by providing information to the public about matters affecting their lives and the society in which they live. The news media also plays a role in identifying nonmarket issues, providing information about them, and stimulating nonmarket action that affects their progress through their life cycles. The news media finds business and nonmarket issues of interest, and with stories instantly transmitted around the world by the broadcast media and the Internet, coverage often means that the firm's steps to address an issue are in the eye of the public and under the scrutiny of interest groups, activists, and public officeholders. For example, Phil Knight, chairman and CEO of Nike stated in its 1996 annual report, "Yet no sooner had the great year ended than we were hit by a series of blasts from the media about our practices overseas." Managers thus must understand which issues the media will cover and how it will treat the issues it covers.

The news media plays an essential role in a democracy and thus has a responsibility to provide information in an accurate and unbiased manner so that individuals can formulate their own conclusions about issues. News organizations, however, operate in a world of incentives, including those provided by profits and those associated with career and professional advancement. News organizations also operate under a variety of pressures, such as competition within and among the media. These incentives and pressures complicate the fulfillment of that responsibility. The news media itself is a diverse collection of organizations, including television, radio, newspapers, magazines, journals, and Internet services. The focus here is on the print media and television news.

The Role of the News Media in Nonmarket Issues

In Chapters 1 and 2 the nonmarket environment was characterized in terms of the four I's, and the news media was identified as one of the institutions in whose arena nonmarket issues are addressed. Editors and journalists are the "officeholders" of the institution, even though they are not chosen by the public. In addition to serving as an arena in which nonmarket issues are addressed, the news media plays an important role in identifying nonmarket issues and in placing issues on agendas of firms. Media coverage can

- alert the public, activists, interest groups, and public officeholders to nonmarket issues

- raise moral concerns about the policies and practices of firms
- provide information about the consequences of alternative courses of action
- reduce the costs of nonmarket and collective action
- limit alternatives for addressing nonmarket issues
- serve as a component of a nonmarket strategy by conveying information generated by an interest group

Interest and activist groups, as well as public officeholders, are prepared to act on a variety of issues, and media coverage of an issue can inform them of developments that spur action. An interest group may seize the opportunity created by media coverage of an event to further its cause or interests. Media coverage can also provide a natural opportunity for a politician to advance an issue, represent individuals affected by the issue, or claim credit for addressing it. The news media can also represent certain interests and principles consistent with its perception of its role in society.

The news media can also serve as a vehicle for political entrepreneurship by public officeholders.[1] Many nonmarket entrepreneurs outside of public office also have developed effective strategies for attracting media coverage to call attention to nonmarket issues, influence the public, and stimulate government action. As considered in Chapter 12, environmental groups use the release of the EPA's annual Toxic Substances Inventory to hold press conferences to name the nation's largest polluters and call for more stringent environmental standards. Similarly, Ralph Nader is effective in using media coverage to advance the issues on his agenda, as indicated by the Microsoft example in Chapter 2.

A striking example of the role of the news media in an interest group's strategy is provided by the Natural Resources Defense Council's (NRDC) campaign on Alar, which is a chemical used to make apples ripen more uniformly and stay crisp when stored. In a 1989 policy study, "Intolerable Risk: Pesticides in Our Children's Food," the NRDC argued that Alar led to an increased risk of cancer and called for a ban on its use. To advance its position through the media, the NRDC hired Fenton Communications. After the media campaign, David Fenton described their strategy.[2]

> Our goal was to create so many repetitions of NRDC's message that average American consumers (not just the policy elite in Washington) could not avoid hearing it—from many different media outlets within a short period of time. The idea was for the "story" to achieve a life of its own, and continue for weeks and months to affect policy and consumer habits. Of course this had to be achieved with extremely limited resources....
>
> It was agreed that one week after the study's release, [Meryl] Streep and other prominent citizens would announce the formation of NRDC's new project, Mothers and Others for Pesticide Limits. This group would direct citizen action at changing the pesticide laws, and help consumers lobby for pesticide-free produce at their grocery stores.
>
> The separation of these two events was important in ensuring that the media would have two stories, not one, about this project. Thereby, more repetition of NRDC's message was guaranteed.
>
> As the report was being finalized, Fenton Communications began contacting various media. An agreement was made with *60 Minutes* to "break" the story of the report in late February. Interviews were also arranged several months in advance with major women's magazines like *Family Circle,*

[1]See Cook (1989) and Garber (1990).
[2]*The Wall Street Journal,* October 3, 1989.

> *Women's Day* and *Redbook* (to appear in mid-March). Appearance dates were set with the *Donahue* show, ABC's *Home Show,* double appearances on NBC's *Today Show* and other programs . . .
>
> In addition, we arranged for Meryl Streep and Janet Hathaway of NRDC to grant 16 interviews by satellite with local TV major market anchors. . .
>
> In the ensuing weeks, the controversy kept building. Articles appeared in food sections of newspapers around the country. Columnists and cartoonists took up the story. *McNeil/Lehrer, The New York Times* and *Washington Post* did follow-up stories, as did the three network evening programs and morning shows. Celebrities from the casts of *L.A. Law* and *thirty-something* joined NRDC for a Los Angeles news conference.

This episode illustrates both the responsiveness of the media to an issue such as pesticide use and its central role in stimulating nonmarket action that advances an issue through its life cycle. Not only did the NRDC orchestrate newsworthy events, but it also coordinated them to extend the media attention. In addition to its media strategy, the NRDC organized picketing and applied direct pressure on government.

This episode should not be viewed as indicating that it is easy to use the media in a nonmarket strategy. The news media guards the independence of its editorial judgments and takes care to avoid being used as part of a nonmarket strategy. However, when an issue is of interest to viewers and readers, the news media has incentives to cover it, and that coverage can serve the interests of activists, interest groups, public officeholders, and others. When those parties can make the issue more newsworthy and more interesting to an audience, the news media can become a force in the development and progress of the issue. The Alar episode serves as a reminder of the potential effect of media coverage of an issue and of the power of the media to place issues on a firm's agenda and shape the context in which they are addressed. Addressing the issue, then, is considerably more difficult as indicated in the chapter case *The Alar Episode (A),* even though there was little if any scientific basis for the NRDC's allegations. The chapter case *Veggie Libel Laws* concerns subsequent developments.

Messages and Their Interpretation

Because of the importance of the news media in the nonmarket environment, firms and their managers must anticipate which issues and events will attract media coverage and how the media will treat them. Figure 3-1 illustrates the role of the media in informing the public and in facilitating nonmarket action. Issues and events are observed by the media, which then decides whether to cover them and how to treat those it chooses to cover. Coverage and treatment provide messages and information to which readers and viewers are exposed and on which interest groups, politicians, firms, and others condition their attitudes and actions. The messages and information provided by the news media are filtered and interpreted in a variety of ways by individuals depending on their prior information, beliefs, and preferences.

Even though the interpretation of messages depends on several factors, their impact can be systematic and hence important. In a series of laboratory experiments, Iyengar and Kinder (1987) investigated the agenda-setting role of the news media and the ways in which news stories affect viewers' attitudes toward issues and political leaders. Their research indicated that viewers attach greater importance to an issue after seeing news coverage of it. They also found that news coverage primes viewers by affecting

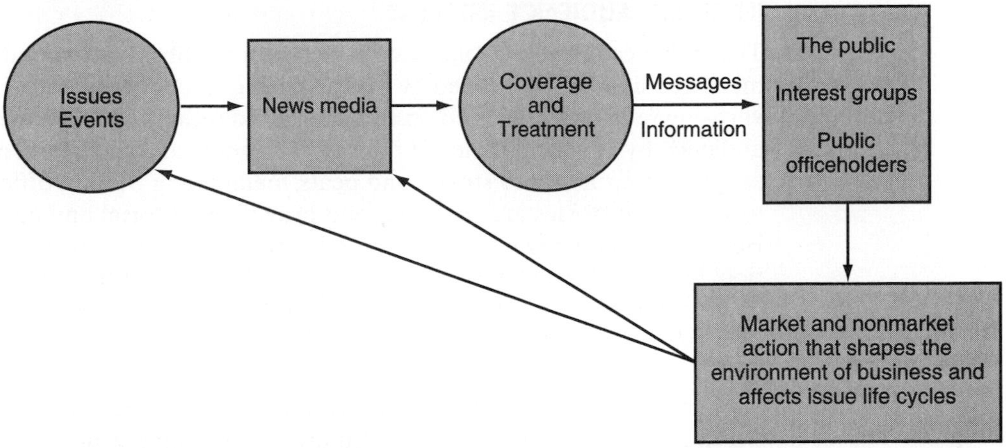

FIGURE 3–1 The News Media and the Environment of Business

"what springs to mind and what is forgotten or ignored."[3] These agenda-setting and priming effects are important both to the development of nonmarket issues and to management's efforts to address them.

The messages and information received by the public, interest groups, and public officeholders can give rise to market and nonmarket action that shapes the environment of business and can affect the progress of issues through their life cycles. As the Alar episode indicates, interest groups may seize opportunities to gain media coverage for their causes and may orchestrate events to generate additional coverage. The result can be a dynamic as illustrated in Figure 3-1 that can have important consequences for a firm and its managers.

A Theory of the News Media Coverage and Treatment

To understand the effect of the news media in nonmarket issues, a theory is needed for the middle of the process shown in Figure 3-1 in which the media observes issues, events, and actions and chooses whether to cover them and how to treat those it covers. The unit of analysis is thus the "issue," and the theory is intended to explain and predict coverage and treatment. Treatment may take several forms:

- a straightforward presentation of facts and description of events
- an interpretation of the facts and events
- an exploration of their potential significance and ramifications
- advocacy of a course of action.

Although the fourth is, in principle, to be restricted to the editorial page, advocacy can occur, as considered later in the chapter.

A variety of explanatory variables could be used in a theory of media coverage and treatment, but in the interest of parsimony only two will be considered—the intrinsic audience interest in the issue and its societal significance as perceived by the news media. As indicated in the previous section, audience interest and societal significance may themselves be influenced by the news media.

[3]See Iyengar and Kinder (1987, p. 114).

INTRINSIC AUDIENCE INTEREST

The audience interest perspective begins with the observation that coverage and treatment decisions are governed by revenue and cost considerations. Subscription and advertising revenues are based on circulation and ratings, and the objective is to attract an audience by covering issues of interest to readers and viewers. Costs include those of assigning journalists to stories and beats, maintaining bureau offices, getting reporters to where the stories are breaking, and providing editorial and administrative support. Because the coverage of issues is costly, the media seeks low-cost sources of information. Firms and interest groups thus often are sources of the information the news media needs to present stories of interest to an audience. Although cost considerations are important, the explanatory power of this perspective derives primarily from the interests of the audience.

If news coverage and treatment respond to and anticipate the audience, predicting which issues the media will cover requires determining which issues are of intrinsic interest to readers and viewers. Similarly, to predict the treatment that an issue will receive it is necessary to determine what attracts and holds their attention. Thus, the principal predictions of the audience theory are that (1) coverage increases with audience interest, and (2) treatment will be chosen to appeal to and retain an audience.

Assessing intrinsic audience interest in issues such as international trade policy, health risks, product safety, employee rights, environmental protection, and employment practices of overseas suppliers generally lies in the realm of judgment rather than measurement. Product safety issues centering on a hazard to consumers attract an instant audience, whereas most international trade issues have limited audience interest due to their complexity and their indirect effect on people. Public opinion polls and surveys help assess audience interest, but survey responses reflect both people's interests and the information they have, and the latter is a function of news coverage and treatment. The theory thus focuses on intrinsic audience interests holding media influence constant.

SOCIETAL SIGNIFICANCE

The societal significance perspective views coverage and treatment as a reflection of the news media's perception of the significance of an issue to society. This perspective reflects the news media's perception of its role in society as protecting democracy by providing the information the citizens need. Veteran journalist Edwin Newman (1984, p. 19) said, "We in the news business help to provide the people with the information they need to frame their attitudes and to make, or at any rate to authorize or ratify, the decisions on which the well-being of the nation rests." Louis H. Young (1978), former editor-in-chief of *Business Week,* stated, "Reporters see themselves as guardians of the public's right to know; the sole custodians of truth; and they see every move they make motivated by the need of the public to know." Applied to business issues, he described an incident involving a company's board of directors meeting and explained, "The magazine's position was—and is—that what the directors ate or drank was their business; but when they considered replacing the chief executive of a company it was the business of stockholders, both present and future." A duty to provide information to the public thus places the news media in a watchdog role and frequently in an adversarial one. Louis Banks, former managing editor of *Fortune* stated, "The editorial mind-set is influenced by the periodic—and important—feats of investigative reporting or crisis coverage that bring out the natural adversarial aspects of the business-media relationship and reassure the media about their watchdog, top-dog role."[4]

[4]*Fortune,* October 14, 1985, p. 207.

The societal significance perspective emphasizes issues that pertain to important strands in the social fabric and to the tensions in those strands. Two similar events will receive quite different coverage if one has a racial dimension and the other does not. Similarly, issues that have a human cause are more likely, under this perspective, to be covered. For example, two similar health risks associated with food products will receive different coverage if one involves a man-made risk and the other a natural risk. Although the risk from Alar may be similar to that from natural chemicals in the food supply, the news media accords more attention to the man-made risk. The societal significance perspective also emphasizes forerunners of changes in the social fabric, particularly when moral concerns are raised. An issue such as the responsibility of U.S. companies for the working conditions in the factories of their suppliers in developing countries is important to the evolving conceptions of corporate responsibility, as Nike has painfully learned. (See the Chapter 4 case *Nike in Southeast Asia.*)

A strong version of the societal significance perspective can be summarized as follows. The news media has a special role in a democracy and is assigned, or has assumed, the duty of serving the people's right to know. This duty is recognized in the First Amendment, which protects the news media in its role of providing the information people need. As a protector of democracy, the media has a duty to inform citizens about issues important to the fabric of society. Moreover, the media has a duty to identify antidemocratic and unjust behavior and to help eliminate it by notifying the public. Consequently, the greater the media's perception of an issue's societal significance, the more likely it is to be covered. Also, the greater the perceived societal significance, the more likely the treatment given it will be characterized by advocacy. Issues high on the social significance dimension include health, safety, environmental protection, individual liberties, discrimination, and social justice.

COMBINING THE PERSPECTIVES

Combining these two perspectives provides a theory of news coverage and treatment. This theory is intended to predict coverage and treatment as a function of intrinsic audience interest and the media's assessment of the societal significance of the issue. In this theory, treatment depends more on societal significance than on audience interest, whereas coverage depends more on audience interest than on societal significance. Both explanatory variables have several important subdimensions that will be developed in more detail in subsequent sections.

Figure 3-2 illustrates the predictions of the theory, which can be refined through additional analysis and detail. In particular, coverage and treatment may differ between the print and broadcast media. Coverage and treatment in *The New York Times* may differ from that in the *New York Post;* coverage and treatment on *Nightline* may differ from that on *60 Minutes.* Moreover, Figure 3-2 provides a snapshot but does not capture the dynamics illustrated in Figure 3-1. Also, over time issues may change their location in the audience interest-societal significance space. Over the past two decades issues involving health risks and environmental protection have moved to the upper right corner.

As Figure 3-2 indicates, the theory predicts that issues low on both the audience interest dimension and the societal significance dimension will receive little coverage. Most routine business news is in this category and at most is covered by the business press. Stories pertaining to economic regulation, such as those found in the public utility industries, are generally relegated to the business sections of newspapers and business magazines. The treatment of these issues will tend to be descriptive, factual, objective, and balanced.

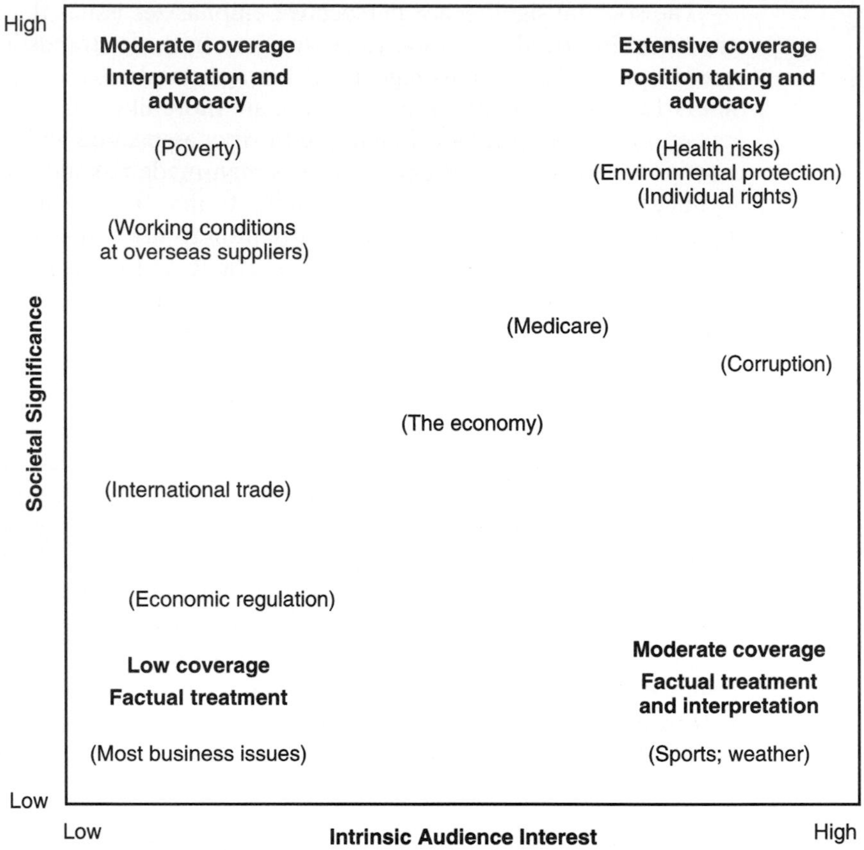

FIGURE 3–2 Theory of Media Coverage and Treatment

Issues that are high on the audience interest dimension but low on the societal significance dimension include the weather, sports, and the closing stock prices on the New York Stock Exchange. These issues receive moderate coverage and are generally treated in a factual and balanced manner and often with interpretation and analysis added.

Issues low on the audience interest dimension but high on the societal significance dimension include poverty, much of politics, and working conditions at the factories of overseas suppliers. Such issues are likely to receive only moderate coverage because of their limited audience interest. Their treatment, however, may involve a degree of position-taking or advocacy. An issue such as working conditions in suppliers' factories in developing countries is a distant issue for most readers and viewers, but because of its high societal significance as perceived by the media it receives considerable coverage. In its role as a protector of the public's right to know, the news media may advocate a course of action. Treatment may characterize the issue, for example, as referring to suppliers' factories as sweatshops or presenting the allegations of activists.

Issues high on both the intrinsic audience interest and societal significance dimensions receive extensive coverage, and their treatment may involve both factual reporting and position-taking and advocacy. These issues include health, the environment, and individual rights. A health risk, and in particular the protection of society from such a risk, is high on both the audience's interest and the societal significance dimensions.

Consequently, the Alar issue received considerable coverage, and its treatment reflected the media's assumed duty to inform and protect the public. The media also covered the events organized by the NRDC because those events made the story more appealing to audiences.

To illustrate the distinctions provided by these dimensions, consider the following two issues: regulation of airline safety by the Federal Aviation Administration (FAA) and deregulation of the electric power industry by the Federal Energy Regulatory Commission (FERC). FAA regulation is directly related to passengers' safety and thus has considerable audience interest. It is also high on the societal significance dimension because of its relationship to health and safety. Safety regulation is certain to receive news coverage and may, depending on the specifics of the issue, receive treatment that emphasizes the need for more stringent regulation. Deregulation of the electric power industry by FERC has a major impact on economic efficiency, but economic deregulation neither commands the same audience interest nor is as high in perceived societal significance. Furthermore, economic deregulation is complex and thus difficult for the media to explain or for readers or viewers to understand. Safety regulation can, however, always be explained in terms of risks and possible threats even if they are difficult to quantify.

As another example, in explaining why the national news media failed to cover the savings and loan crisis when it began to develop in the mid-1980s, Ellen Hume wrote: "It was all too complicated and boring to interest many mainstream journalists. Regulatory changes—such as the accounting tricks and reduced capital requirements that helped paper over the first phase of the savings and loan crisis in the early 1980s—weren't big news . . . When asked why TV hadn't covered the crisis much even after it made headlines in 1988, the president of NBC News, Michael Gartner, observed that the story didn't lend itself to images, and without such images, 'television can't do facts.' "[5] Hume added that as the issue developed, the victims (the depositors) did not complain because their deposits were federally insured. Controversy and conflict were absent, and the appeal of the issue to the media was reduced. Media interest in the issue developed as the magnitude of the crisis became evident and as revelations about malfeasance occurred.

Based on this theory of the news media, two sufficient conditions for coverage of an issue have been identified. One is societal significance and the other is intrinsic audience interest. The treatment an issue receives depends mostly on its societal significance, but features such as visual effects, human interest, conflict, and controversy are also important. The theory is extended along these dimensions in the next section.

Extending the Theory

NEWSWORTHINESS

The newsworthiness characteristics of issues or stories extend the intrinsic audience interest and perceived societal significance dimensions. The more people to whom the issue matters and the more it matters to them, the more newsworthy is the issue. Environmental protection issues matter to many people, so environmental stories have a natural audience. Even an issue remote in its origins and distant in its effects can attract

[5] Ellen Hume, "Why the Press Blew the S & L Scandal," *The New York Times,* May 24, 1990.

interest, as in the case of the destruction of Amazon Basin rain forests. The more proximate the consequences, however, the greater the (at least) local interest. An issue of groundwater contamination in a community will attract a local audience but may not be of enough regional or national interest to warrant more widespread coverage.

An issue is also more newsworthy if it has a degree of immediacy or urgency. The massive television coverage of a natural disaster results in part because it is a breaking story. The risk to life and property makes it urgent. The burning of Amazon Basin rain forests has less urgency, but its link to global warming makes it more immediate than it would otherwise be. A groundwater contamination issue has a degree of urgency if there is a threat to health.

An issue is also more newsworthy if it has a human interest dimension with which the audience can identify. Television often features stories about people and, particularly, victims of injustice, accidents, or natural disasters. A story about groundwater contamination that involves a family exposed to a health hazard is more newsworthy than a story about the groundwater damage to crops.

The way in which a story is presented influences how much it engages an audience's attention. A story is often more interesting if it is told by someone involved in the issue rather than by a correspondent. In an era of electronic channel changers, television producers are reluctant to air a "talking head" segment with a correspondent telling a long and complex story. When the story is told by participants in it, however, the result is often not just an eyewitness account, since they may take the opportunity to express judgments about the issue or advocate action.

An issue will often be more newsworthy if it involves a celebrity. The NRDC was correct in thinking that Meryl Streep would attract coverage for the Alar issue. Similarly, the news media may choose to cover an issue because it is entertaining or may add an entertaining dimension to a story. Particularly for television, an issue is more newsworthy if it has visual appeal, since that attracts and holds viewers.

A story is more newsworthy if it deals with controversy or conflict. An environmental issue will be more newsworthy if it involves an environmental group making allegations that apple growers are creating hazards for an unsuspecting public. A story can be made more newsworthy if it ties to an issue such as health with high intrinsic audience interest. In particular, linking it to the health of children provides not only a human interest dimension but also demonstrates that the news media is fulfilling its role by protecting the public's right to know. A common approach to developing controversy and conflict in a story is to have each side present its version of the story or its position on the issue. This provides balance, but it also dramatizes the conflict.

In contrast, stories about ideas are often difficult to write and present, particularly for a medium such as television. Stories about ideas often provide few opportunities for the media to develop controversy, drama, and human interest or to provide visual appeal. The media thus may not give as much coverage to issues centering on ideas as they might merit in terms of their societal significance. The idea that the dramatic increase in interest rates during the late 1970s and early 1980s had made virtually all savings and loan associations insolvent was not one the media found either attractive or easy to address.

THE AUDIENCE

The issue's audience also affects its treatment. Many nonmarket issues, such as opening a foreign market closed by nontariff barriers or the filing of an antidumping petition against foreign imports, are primarily of interest to those who want business information. The journalist assigned to such a story will often be a specialist in business issues, and the story is likely to be factual and not rely on controversy, conflict, or human interest to make it engaging.

For other nonmarket issues, however, the audience is the broader public, particularly when the media perceives that the issue has high societal significance. Coverage will then extend beyond the business media, and the journalists assigned to the story may be less knowledgeable of and experienced with the issue. To engage the broader public, the story must have a high degree of intrinsic audience interest or else it must be made engaging through visual effects, controversy, conflict, and human interest. This often involves presenting the views of critics as well as with the position of the firms involved. With issues such as the environment, discrimination, and health and safety, coverage is likely to be extensive and the treatment may be styled to engage the broader audience.

THE COST OF COVERAGE

News coverage is also a function of the costs of obtaining information and producing a story. Once journalists are assigned to a story and are on location, the marginal cost of coverage is reduced and the media is more likely to use stories from that source. As Edwin Newman (1984, p. 29) stated, "What is news on television often depends on where your reporters and cameramen are. If you keep people at the White House, you will be tempted to use stories from there, if only for economic reasons, . . . If you send reporters and camera crews on a trip with the secretary of state, you tend to use what they send back. If you staff a story day after day, you will have it on the air day after day."

Both the costs of obtaining information and the budget pressures on most media organizations have forced them to rely increasingly on such low-cost sources of information as interest groups, government agencies, and businesses, rather than developing first-hand sources of information. Because the information provided by these sources often is strategically chosen and presented, journalists may end up reporting what their sources say, or claim, are the facts, rather than gathering those facts directly. Brooks Jackson, a Cable News Network correspondent and former *Wall Street Journal* reporter, observed, "We usually depend on governmental institutions or groups like Common Cause or Ralph Nader or General Motors or somebody to make sense out of all this data for us."[6]

The Nature of the News Media

THE NEWS MEDIA AS A BUSINESS

In the United States, news media organizations are owned by for-profit companies, so a primary objective is profit generation. If it were not, the market for the control of firms would be expected to force attention to profits, as evidenced by the ownership of ABC by Walt Disney, CBS by Westinghouse Electric, and NBC by General Electric. As profit-oriented firms, media companies are interested in attracting readers and viewers, as both subscription and advertising revenue depend on audience size. According to Young (1978, p. 2):

> As more organs of the media are owned by large corporations, whose prime interest is financial, the journalistic principles of a publication can be compromised by—or dissipated in—the business needs. The demand [is] for more circulation, more advertising, and more profit. To achieve these, the media will cater to populist—meaning antibusiness—fears and prejudices,

[6]Quoted in Ellen Hume, "Why the Press Blew the S & L Scandal," *The New York Times,* May 24, 1990.

> entertain instead of enlighten, pander instead of lead. They reduce big issues to oversimplified personality battles, because both people and disputes make good reading and viewing.

This statement is surely too strong, but it indicates the tension between the need to attract an audience and the journalistic standards of the profession.

THE PROFESSION

The media is shaped in part by the people who chose careers in journalism. Journalists are often perceived as more liberal and activist than the public in general. A widely shared perspective among journalists is that they are serving the public by providing the information it needs. Many current journalists joined the profession in the wake of Robert Woodward and Carl Bernstein's triumph in the Watergate affair. Not only had journalists succeeded in uncovering illegal activity, but they contributed to the resignation of a U.S. president.

Writing before Watergate, Epstein (1973, p. 219), who studied the operations of network television news programs, addressed journalists' views of their role and power.

> Privately almost all network correspondents expressed a strong belief in their ability to effect change in public policy through their work, if not as individuals, then certainly as a group. Some considered their self-perceived political powers "frightening" and "awesome," while others merely depicted them as a necessary part of the political process.

As a profession, journalism is governed by standards enforced by the news media companies and by professional associations. Professional standards and editorial controls require that a story be accurate, provide balance and fairness, and present a comprehensive picture of the issue. Accuracy involves not only verifying facts but also ensuring that the story as presented portrays the situation correctly. Balance requires presenting both sides of an issue, which often involves providing an opportunity for representatives of the various sides to present their positions on the issue. Balance thus also develops controversy and emphasizes the conflict among those involved, making the story more attractive to the audience. Editorial standards intended to ensure accuracy, balance, and fairness often stand in the way of advocacy, and, as Epstein indicates in the next section, those standards may be suspended on some issues.

Fairness involves ensuring that the various participants in an issue have an opportunity to present their views and that a person or subject is not presented or treated in an unjust manner. The latter is particularly relevant on those issues high on the societal significance dimension on which the media may take an advocacy position.

Comprehensiveness pertains to presenting the entire issue rather than only a segment of it. The bane of comprehensiveness is the desire of the news media to simplify an issue to make it more understandable and attractive to the audience or to fit it into limited time or space.

DOES THE MEDIA TREAT ISSUES SELECTIVELY?

The media does not cover every issue under the same criteria. Most issues are treated under controls and editorial standards. On some issues, however, the media adopts an advocacy approach. Although the standard of accuracy is not abandoned, the standards of fairness and balance may be suspended on such issues. Epstein (1973, p. 233), states that

> controls tend to be disregarded when executives, producers and correspondents all share the same view and further perceive it to be a view

> accepted by virtually all thoughtful persons. News reports about such subjects as pollution, hunger, health care, racial discrimination, and poverty fall in this category. On such consensus issues, correspondents are expected by executives openly to advocate the eradication of the presumed evil and even put it in terms of a "crusade," as a CBS vice-president suggested with respect to the pollution issue. The subjects that fall within this consensus are clearly demarcated for correspondents; in fact they are usually "cleared" in advance by executives for use in speeches and public appearances by correspondents. At times, however, what are assumed to be commonly held values turn out to be disputed ones in some parts of the country; and when executives are apprised of this (by affiliates and others), the usual "fairness" controls are applied to the subject.

There is certainly consensus in preferring less to more pollution, but often the real issue, as in the case of global warming, is how much reduction in emissions is warranted and how the cost of that reduction will be distributed. On these dimensions, consensus is usually not present and indeed considerable disagreement exists. For example, the UAW and automobile manufacturers prefer lower fuel economy standards than the Sierra Club.

Pollution and environmental protection are not consensus issues, nor are most issues in the nonmarket environment of business. As an example, an article in the *San Francisco Examiner,* headlined "Trendy pollutant—single use cameras," criticized (by quoting environmental activists) both the use of disposable cameras and the industry leaders, Fujifilm and Kodak, for their recycling programs. Kodak, which at the time recovered 50 percent of the cameras through collection facilities in 150 countries, was contacted to provide balance and controversy. Kodak explained that its biggest problem was small photo-finishing shops that claimed that their volume was not sufficient to warrant the inconvenience of recycling the cameras. In a letter to the editor, a Kodak spokesperson, calling the article "surprisingly biased," pointed to achieving 50 percent recycling in just 4 years and asked, "At what point does a company receive credit for environmental responsibility?"[7]

The media may also suspend certain controls based on societal significance, "protection of democracy," or the "people's right to know" considerations. From the media's perspective, issues that are high on this dimension include freedom of speech and of the press, the media's watchdog role, and issues of social justice. This may correspond to a duty assumed by the media to represent those whom they judge are not adequately represented. The media thus seeks to uncover malfeasance and misfeasance on behalf of those who otherwise would be ignorant of these wrongs. On such issues, the media may suspend its editorial controls and advocate a position or a particular resolution of the issue.

BIAS AND ACCURACY

Most nonmarket issues involving business are complex, and the ability to present that complexity and achieve accuracy, balance, comprehensiveness, and fairness differs considerably among media organizations. Some newspapers and magazines can present complex stories in a comprehensive manner and in enough detail to provide accuracy and balance. Television, however, may not be well suited to presenting complex stories, in part because of the brief time that can be allocated to a story. As Epstein (1981, p. 127)

---

[7] *San Francisco Examiner,* September 15, 1994.

stated, "This enforced brevity leaves little room for presenting complex explanations or multifaceted arguments." As importantly, the need to retain viewer interest requires that a story be attractive and entertaining. Furthermore, the desire to develop human interest and conflict in a limited time slot can lead to sacrifices in comprehensiveness and, at times, in accuracy. Qualification and complexity, even when written into a story, may be edited out to provide time for other stories. Many complaints by business executives about television news coverage are due to the simplification needed to shoehorn a story into a 30-second slot. Distortion in a story thus may result from simplification rather than bias.

Because the journalist is writing for the public and not for the protagonists in a story, the subjects of a story frequently desire that the story not appear or that more attention or credence be given to their side. The difference between the objective of providing information to the public and the subject's interest in a favorable portrayal can lead to a perception of bias.

The treatment of issues, and, in particular, whether advocacy journalism is practiced and editorial controls are suspended, not only affects the responses of interest and activist groups, politicians, and individuals but also frames the issue in a manner that can make a response difficult. News coverage of fires due to the use of space heaters may involve the victims telling of their plight and demanding that the manufacturer and the government take action. Given the framing of the issue, manufacturers have considerable difficulty providing information about the costs and benefits of the space heaters, the safety features already incorporated, the possibility that the victims may have misused the heaters, and the measures taken to reduce the likelihood of misuse. The fact that no space heater can be perfectly safe reduces the credibility of such explanations.[8]

Journalists seek professional attainment and reward. A necessary condition for attainment is that a journalist's work be published or aired and have an impact. Journalists thus have a strong incentive to develop and present stories that will pass editorial scrutiny and be sufficiently newsworthy that editors will decide to print or air them. A journalist is trained to present the who, what, where, when, and why of a story. Stories must be read or viewed, however, so journalists also seek to make their stories engaging. These factors can result in inaccuracies, bias, and in some cases fabrication.

In a 3-month period in 1998 the news media was racked by a series of disclosures about the fabrication of stories and gross inaccuracies that raised concerns about the controls exercised by news organizations.

- *The New Republic* fired a highly regarded journalist for having fabricated all or parts of 27 of the 41 articles he had written for the magazine.
- *The Boston Globe,* a unit of *The New York Times,* fired a columnist, a Pulitzer Prize finalist, after she acknowledged fabricating people and quotations in her columns.
- For four consecutive days the *Cincinnati Enquirer,* owned by the Gannett Company, ran an article on its front page and a banner headline "An apology to Chiquita." The apology was for an investigative journalism story on Chiquita Brands's business practices. The *Enquirer* admitted that the journalist who wrote the article had stolen voice mail messages from Chiquita and agreed to pay $10 million to the company. The journalist pleaded guilty to two felony charges.

[8]See the Chapter 11 case *California Space Heaters (A).*

- The star columnist of *The Boston Globe* resigned after editors were unable to find any evidence that two young cancer victims described in a column ever existed. The resignation came eight days after the *Globe* withdrew its demand that the columnist resign because of unattributed quotations used in another column.
- CNN retracted a segment broadcast on its program, *NewsStand: CNN & Time,* which had reported that the U.S. military used lethal nerve gas on American defectors in Laos in 1970. After its senior military analyst resigned in protest, CNN admitted that the evidence did not support the story and apologized. It also fired the producers of the story, and the executive producer of the story resigned. *Time,* which had published the story, also apologized. Ted Turner also personally apologized for CNN's erroneous story.
- Later in 1998 the executive producer of *60 Minutes* apologized on the air for having broadcast a free-lance report on Columbian drug couriers, portions of which had been faked.
- Earlier in 1997 the *San Jose Mercury News* admitted publicly that its award-winning, but highly criticized, story linking the Central Intelligence Agency to the sale of crack cocaine in Los Angeles was, along with its editorial process, flawed. The newspaper admitted that the facts did not support the claimed link.

A similar episode is presented in the Chapter 1 case *GM Like a Rock (A).*

Some news organizations responded to the disclosures by strengthening their internal controls. CNN, for example, established an internal watchdog office, the Journalistic Standards and Practices office. Cost and competitive pressures, however, work against stronger internal controls. Some news organizations, such as *Time,* had earlier shifted some fact-checking responsibilities to their researchers and reporters.

Business criticism of media coverage and treatment of nonmarket issues is due to a variety of considerations. First, no one likes his or her activities to be publicly scrutinized. Second, the desire for balance and the desire to develop controversy to make stories appealing often gives critics of the firm an opportunity to deliver their message to the public. Third, some believe that the media is biased against business and market competition. Fourth, particularly in the case of television, the control of the editing process gives the media the opportunity to select the parts of an interview that make the best story, rather than the parts business prefers to have shown. Fifth, and perhaps the most important, media treatment almost always results in oversimplification and may preclude the presentation of the full justification for a firm's actions.

Business Interactions with the News Media

THE NEED FOR INFORMATION

Because many business issues are newsworthy, the media needs information about those issues. Often only business has the information that can serve as the basis for a story. Firms thus have an opportunity to develop a relationship with news organizations in which they provide the information needed in exchange for stories that will be fair and balanced. Many firms have thus professionalized their interactions with the media by employing public affairs and communications specialists. At the same time, business interactions with the media are also broadening as more managers assume an expanded role in interacting with the media.

MEDIA STRATEGIES

Media strategies are founded on an understanding of the news media and provide the basic approach to interactions with the media and communication with stakeholders and the public. Evans (1987, pp. 84–87) identifies six elements of an effective media strategy:

- The unusual is usual.
- Emphasize the consistency of business and the public interest.
- Remember your audience.
- Communicate through the press.
- The medium is the message.
- Establish credibility—not friendship.

Newsworthy nonmarket issues are more likely to be the extraordinary than the ordinary. Ordinary events and issues are unlikely to be high on the intrinsic audience interest dimension, but extraordinary issues, such as a health risk to children from eating apples, is often likely to be high on both dimensions in Figure 3-2. For most nonmarket issues the interests of a firm are consistent with some aspect of the public interest or at least with the interests of stakeholders. Emphasizing the effects of the issue not on profits but on stakeholders can be effective, as can pointing out that the practice in question is consistent with the public interest.

The relevant audience for a story about a nonmarket issue affects both coverage and treatment, and the firm's interactions with the media should depend on the audience. In interacting with the media the firm is speaking not only with the journalist but more importantly with the audience, and the information should be presented for the understanding of that audience. A firm's message thus should be tailored to whether the audience is knowledgeable about the issue, as in the case of an issue that will only be covered by the business press, or is uninformed and hence likely to interpret the message through generic rather than issue-specific lenses. The messages and how they are presented also depend on the medium. In their efforts to make a story engaging, journalists seek articulate answers and noteworthy quotes from managers, and for television a visually appealing setting or illustrations and examples can be effective in enhancing the firm's message. In interviews, managers should not only answer questions but should also take the opportunity to make affirmative statements to the audience about the firm's position. As considered in more detail below, many firms develop relationships with journalists and media organizations and sustain those relationships through their forthrightness and the credibility of the information they provide.

COVERAGE AND RESPONSES

On many issues—particularly those that may generate nonmarket action—business prefers that no story appear. One natural strategy is thus to not comment to the media in the hope that no story will result. Particularly if it seems likely that the story will appear anyway, the "no comment" strategy can be risky. Presenting the firm's side of the story is often better than having it remain untold. Especially on issues that are high on the societal significance dimension, the media may adopt an advocacy approach, either directly or by airing the allegations of others. Leaving a vacuum that the firm's critics can fill can often be more damaging than having the firm tell its side of the story, even if that story is not compelling. Providing facts and demonstrating concern, even if the facts are not all favorable to the firm, can narrow the space in which other parties can maneuver.

Many firms have concluded that there are some media representatives or programs with which it is better to not talk. Many will not talk with investigative-journalism-cum-entertainment programs because of concerns about how they and their firm will be portrayed. They prefer a statement such as "company X refused to comment" to risking an interview from which the editors will extract 15- to 30-second clips to be interspersed with commentary or interviews with people on the other side of an issue.

DEVELOPING RELATIONSHIPS WITH THE MEDIA

Many firms develop relationships with the news media based on mutual respect and honest and forthright exchange. The development of such a relationship is easier with the business press than with the general media, both because of the business press's greater need for information and because the business press typically assigns journalists to regular beats. The journalist then has an opportunity to develop both expertise and relationships with business managers. This provides the manager with an opportunity to develop a relationship of trust and confidence with the expectation that the journalist will be more knowledgeable about the relevant issues and hence that the resulting stories will be more accurate. If the firm interacts with the media on a regular basis, public affairs specialists may play a role in this relationship. Furthermore, if a journalist has demonstrated an understanding of the firm, the industry, and the issues, the firm may choose to release its information first to him or her as a reward.

Developing relationships with the representatives of the more general news media, particularly television, is more difficult because few journalists are assigned to business beats, and for those journalists without a regular beat the incentive to develop expertise in the field can be low. For example, a journalist assigned to an issue high on the social significance dimension—products with health risks, for instance—may not have expertise on the issue. In such cases it is particularly important for a manager to communicate effectively with the journalist.

MEDIA INTERVIEWS

Because of the importance of the media in nonmarket issues, managers are frequently interviewed by the media and called on to speak to public groups on issues. Media training is customary in many firms, and a communications training and consulting industry has developed to support that training. Many firms also often provide guidelines for their managers in dealing with journalists. The Hewlett Packard Corporation's guidelines for its managers are presented in Figure 3-3.

Perhaps the best advice for media interviews was given by the publisher of a major newspaper. He said that when dealing with the press, there are three cardinal rules. The first is "Tell the truth." The second is "Tell the truth." The third is "Always remember the first two." A pragmatic version of the publisher's cardinal rules was provided by a judge who said, "Always tell the truth—it's easier to remember." Answering truthfully is always a good policy, but simply responding to questions is not. Managers must be prepared to make affirmative points when responding to an interviewer's questions and to seize or create opportunities to make affirmative points.

When asked to appear for a television interview, some business executives request to go on live so that their comments cannot be edited. Stations, however, often will not agree to an unedited interview. The interviewee thus is often advised to answer questions in a manner that makes it difficult to edit. Sometimes a manager may ask the reporter to submit questions in advance, but that request is usually rejected. When agreeing to an interview, some firms find it prudent to audiotape or videotape the interview. Taping the interview provides a record of what transpired and can be useful if a dispute with the media arises. Taping may also remind journalists to be careful about what they write or broadcast. When agreeing to an interview, it is important to recognize that at

HEWLETT PACKARD CORPORATION'S TWELVE GUIDES FOR CONDUCTING A MEDIA INTERVIEW.

- Assume everything you say is "on the record."
- Speak in plain English.
- State your main point or conclusion first. . . .
- If you don't understand a question, say so.
- If presented with a "laundry list" of questions, identify the one question you are responding to before answering it.
- Don't hesitate to repeat an answer.
- Volunteer information to make your points and to give perspective.
- Use anecdotes and illustrations involving people.
- Have fun doing the interview, without being flippant, of course.
- Don't be afraid to admit mistakes.
- Don't expect the editor to clear the story with you before it's published.
- Never, never, never stretch the truth.

FIGURE 3-3 Hewlett Packard Corporation Guidelines

times the media may already have the story in the can and may be seeking an interview to develop balance or controversy.

Strategies for Addressing Media Issues

ANTICIPATABLE ISSUES

When a nonmarket issue can be anticipated, the theory of the news media should be used to assess whether the issue is likely to be covered and, if so, the type of treatment it is likely to receive. The likely treatment provides the basis for the formulation of the firm's media strategy. For those stories that will be covered only by the business press, a firm can hope, and in many cases expect, that the correspondent has a degree of expertise in the subject matter of the story. If, in addition, the issue is low on the societal significance dimension, the firm may need do little more than provide the media with factual information and present its side of the issue.

A broader set of the news media is likely to be attracted to issues that are high on the societal significance dimension, which makes interactions with the media more complex. Such an issue also may attract interest and activist groups. In many cases, those groups can be expected to advance their sides of the issue both in the media and before public institutions. The Alar episode was more orchestrated than most issues, but the point is clear. Interest groups can orchestrate events to advance their causes both in a planned manner and in response to an issue brought to their—and the public's—attention by the media. Indeed, interest groups may seize the opportunity created by a breaking story to advance their agenda.

When media coverage of an issue can be anticipated, the firm has the opportunity to prepare. Preparation includes gathering all the information about the issue, and its context. Preparation also includes assessment of the messages likely to be conveyed and the possible reactions to them. As discussed in the context of Figure 3-1, the messages are a function not only of the coverage and treatment given to the issue but also of the information the audience already has. Different individuals, interest groups, and politicians may evaluate a story in different ways. Some may consider the story in terms of their own self-interest, whereas others may look at it in terms of broader principles.

These varied evaluations can result in market and nonmarket actions that affect the development of the issue and cause change in the firm's environment.

Many firms attempt to educate the media about important issues in their nonmarket environment. Some go further by attempting to communicate directly with the interest groups that are likely to be concerned with issues. To the extent that a firm can anticipate the effects of the story and take measures to deal in advance with the likely repercussions, it is better positioned to participate responsibly as the issue progresses through its life cycle.

The chapter case *Illinois Power Company (A)* addresses the preparation for the media coverage of a story, as well as the aftermath of the story.

UNANTICIPATED EVENTS

Because events such as environmental or injury-causing accidents can occur, firms should have a routine to follow in the event of a crisis or a breaking event. If the issue is one that need not be made public—embezzlement, for example—the first decision is whether to release the information to the news media or attempt to keep it confidential. The latter can be successful in many cases, but leaks occur more often than most managers expect.

If the incident is public, the first step is to gather as much information as possible as quickly as possible. There is little that can damage a firm more than having others uncover information that management itself does not have. One useful precaution is an accurate record-keeping system that, for example, keeps track of the wastes generated by a plant and of where they are disposed. Having the facts readily accessible not only allows the firm to be in the position of being the best source of information for the media, but it also provides a basis on which management can develop a strategy. In the case of an accidental spill of a pollutant, for example, it is also often wise for the firm to speak with a single voice. The appointment of a spokesperson requires that the individual have all the information on the issue so as not to be blindsided. The information also helps the spokesperson anticipate the story's likely development.

The Body Shop example indicates the response to a critical article on the company. These actions resulted in continuing problems with the media and with the public.

Recourse in Disputes with the Media

PRIVATE RECOURSE

The subjects of news coverage at times perceive their treatment to be incomplete, inaccurate, or unfair. Some take actions ranging from writing to the editor to correct inaccuracies to initiating legal action. Firms may also take economic measures against the media by, for example, withdrawing advertising in response to a story that management believes has misrepresented the facts. When neither economic measures nor legal action is warranted as a reaction to an erroneous, inaccurate, or unfair story, it can be useful to bring concerns about it to the attention of the media. Some firms make a practice of notifying editors about their concerns about stories, with the objective of not only improving future stories but also establishing a reputation for a readiness to act. In more egregious cases, companies may take economic measures against the media. The Procter & Gamble example describes one such case.

The news media is governed by professional standards, and journalists and editors develop and maintain reputations for professionalism. Organizations such as the Society of Professional Journalists, Sigma Delta Chi, and the American Society of Newspaper

EXAMPLE

The Body Shop

By 1994 the Body Shop had achieved both financial and social success. Emphasizing cosmetics made from natural ingredients, the company had grown from a single shop to 1,100 stores in 40 countries. Part of its strategy was to do social good at the same time as making profits. It developed a widely publicized "Trade Not Aid" program in which it bought raw materials from indigenous peoples. For example, it purchased blue corn from the Santa Ana Pueblo tribe in New Mexico and nuts from the Kayapo people in Brazil. It also used those programs in its promotional and public relations activities. The Body Shop had become one of the darlings of the social responsibility community, winning praise for its activities and making an international celebrity of its founder, Anita Roddick, who along with her husband, Gordon Roddick, ran the company.

The image they had carefully crafted came under attack when an investigative journalist wrote a critical article attacking the accomplishments of the company.[1] The journal in which it was to appear intended to make a splash and promoted the article in advance of publication. The British and American press picked up the issue and others joined in the criticism of the Body Shop; for example, British labor unions renewed their criticism of the company for its opposition to unionization at its main plant in England. The article detailed alleged mistakes and shortcomings by the company, but the principal message was that the company was not living up to the image its promotional activities had created.

The Roddicks were incensed and leaped into action. They viewed the image they had created in their publicity as an aspiration toward which they worked, and they disputed both the facts and the message of the article and attacked the author. Before the article appeared, Anita Roddick wrote daily to the company's staff, franchisees, and other supporters rejecting the allegations in the article and reassuring them of the company's record. The Body Shop had both its British solicitor and its U.S. law firm write the journal about the author and requested a copy of the article in advance. The letters led the journal to take out libel insurance.[2] After publication of the article, the Body Shop sent out lengthy press releases countering the alleged facts presented in the article and attacking the credibility of the author and the journal editor. The company admitted that its record was not perfect, but argued that it was far better than others in the cosmetics industry and that the company should not be judged against a standard of perfection. The company's press releases were countered by letters and press releases from the author of the article and the journal editor defending the article and the information on which it was based.

The Body Shop also elicited testimonials from its business partners and others sympathetic with the causes it espoused. The Roddicks convinced Ben Cohen, founder of Ben & Jerry's ice cream company, to resign from the advisory board of the journal. Gordon Roddick also wrote to all the advisory board members and sent a 10-page letter to every one of the journal's subscribers defending the company's record and challenging the motives of the journal's editor. Criticism continued, however, as Franklin Research and Development, an investment firm that provides investment advice about socially responsible firms, issued a report critical of the company's record. Franklin, which had previously given its highest social rating to the Body Shop, indicated that its investigation had corroborated some of the information in the article. Franklin also criticized the Body Shop for its attacks on its critics.[3] Franklin's basic criticism was not only that the Body Shop had not lived up to the lofty standards it had set for itself but that it had benefited financially from the image it had promoted. Hence, not living up to that image was of real concern.

To address the substance of the criticism, the Body Shop decided to undergo an independent social audit and publish the audit regardless of its conclusions. The results of that audit are considered in Chapter 20.

---

[1]Jon Entine, "Shattered Image," *Business Ethics,* September–October 1994, pp. 23–28.

[2]The Body Shop had earned a reputation for aggressive actions with respect to the media, and in 1992 had won a libel case against a British television station for a critical documentary.

[3]Franklin Research and Development, "Investing for a Better World," September 15, 1994.

Editors work to foster high professional standards and ethics in journalism. In 1973 the news media established a self-regulatory body, the National News Council, that heard complaints about news coverage, investigated the complaints, and issued reports on them. Its activities, however, were not recognized by prominent news organizations such as *The New York Times* and the *Associated Press,* and its impact was limited. In 1984, the council voted to dissolve.[9] The FCC had required broadcasters to provide time for contrasting views on public issues, but in 1987 it repealed the Fairness Doctrine after concluding that it did not serve the public interest. The principal forms of discipline for the news media are thus professional standards, controls established by media organizations, and lawsuits.

Media organizations take actions to discipline their correspondents, editors, and managers who violate professional standards. Correspondents may be suspended, reassigned, or fired for violations. In the Chapter 1 case *General Motors Like A Rock? (A),* NBC took disciplinary actions when it was revealed that its *Dateline* producers and correspondents had used a model rocket engine to ignite a fire during a test collision of a GM pickup truck. NBC reassigned the correspondent and fired the producer of the *Dateline* segment. The senior producer and the executive producer "resigned," and Michael Gartner, president of NBC News, also "resigned." NBC also hired an ombudsman to supplement its professional standards and to review segments for news programs as well as programs such as *Dateline.*

RECOURSE TO THE LAW: DEFAMATION AND LIBEL

Defamation is a branch of torts pertaining to false statements made to a third party that damage a person's reputation. The category of "person" includes human beings as well as legal entities such as corporations. Defamation takes the form of either libel or slander. Libel pertains to statements that are either written or broadcast, whereas slander pertains to statements that are spoken. A finding of slander requires a showing of actual damages, but a finding of libel generally does not require such a showing. Defamation cases are governed by the common law and state law. Defamation cases generally center on statements made in public, but in *Dun & Bradstreet v. Greenmoss Builders,* 472 U.S. 749 (1985), Greenmoss Builders was awarded $350,000 when Dun & Bradstreet issued an erroneous credit report. Thus, defamation more generally applies to a statement made to a third party.

A defendant in a defamation suit has several possible defenses, which fall into the categories of "truth" and "privilege." A defendant always has the defense that what was said, written, or broadcast was the truth. In some states truth constitutes an absolute defense, whereas in others it may be subject to limitations such as those arising from laws on privacy. For example, in some states it is illegal to disclose that someone has been convicted of a crime or has a disease.

In 1990, 20 Washington State apple growers filed suit against CBS and the NRDC seeking $250 million in damages alleging that the *60 Minutes* segment on Alar had led to a panic among consumers that had cost the state's growers $150 million in sales. A federal district judge in Spokane dismissed the suit because the plaintiffs had not shown that the broadcast was false. The judge stated, "Even if CBS's statements are false, they were about an issue that mattered, cannot be proven as false and therefore must be protected." CBS had argued that its story was based on an EPA report, and the judge stated, "A news reporting service is not a scientific testing lab, and these services

[9] See Schmuhl (1984).

EXAMPLE

Procter & Gamble and Neighbor to Neighbor

Neighbor to Neighbor, an activist group located in San Francisco, opposed U.S. support for the government in El Salvador and called for the end of military aid to that country. The group claimed that coffee growers in El Salvador financed right-wing death squads with moneys obtained from exporting coffee to the United States. From the group's perspective, U.S. coffee companies that imported Salvadoran coffee beans were supporting the death squads.[1]

Neighbor to Neighbor took its message to the American public by placing advertisements in *The New York Times, The New London Day* (Connecticut), and *The Progressive* magazine. The group also advocated a consumer boycott of U.S. coffee brands. The best-selling U.S. brand was Folgers, produced by the Procter & Gamble Company (P&G). To generate support for the boycott, the group produced a 30-second television commercial that it planned to air on several television stations. The commercial, narrated by Edward Asner, named only Folgers and showed an upside-down coffee cup dripping blood.[2] The inscription on the cup read "Seal of Salvadoran Coffee," and Asner read, "The murderous civil war in El Salvador has been supported by billions of American tax dollars and by the sale of Salvadoran coffee ... Boycott Folgers. What it brews is misery and death."[3]

Of the 30 television stations approached by Neighbor to Neighbor, all but two stations rejected the commercial. After reviewing it for taste and content, investigating its content, and obtaining legal advice on the possibility of libel suits, the CBS affiliate WHDH-TV of Boston broadcast the commercial twice in May 1990.[4] Seymour L. Yamoff, president and general manager of WHDH-TV, stated, " 'The information on this particular commercial is correct.... We screen them for accuracy, libel, slander and 'Do they meet a standard of fairness?' " He also stated that the station had never broadcast such "issue advertisements" other than in election campaigns, and he could not recall any such advertisement being aired in Boston during the 20 years he had lived there.

P&G was shocked by the commercial. It purchased coffee from 30 countries, and less than 2 percent of its supply came from El Salvador. P&G was one of the country's largest television advertisers and provided advertising revenue of $1 million annually to WHDH-TV, which represented nearly 2 percent of its advertising revenue. The revenue from broadcasting the Neighbor to Neighbor commercial totaled less than $1,000.[5]

P&G decided to withdraw its advertising from WHDH-TV and threatened to withdraw its advertising from any other station that broadcast the ad.[6] In 1991 P&G announced that it would resume advertising on WHDH-TV after a *Washington Post* reporter, Scott Armstrong, hired by WHDH-TV had conducted a 5-month inquiry into the commercial. In the draft of his report, he concluded "that certain conclusions. . . were not substantiated."[7] "David Mugar, chairman of New England Television Corp., owner of Channel 7, yesterday said that the experience had resulted in a new policy at the station. Any public-issue commercials submitted to the station in the future will be broadcast only after the truth of their claims has been determined," Mugar said.[8] "A Procter & Gamble spokesman, Donald P. Tassone, said 'We were satisfied that WHDH had on further review concluded that certain representations in the

[1]The National Coffee Association of the U.S.A. reported that Salvadoran beans constituted 5 percent of U.S. coffee imports and that about half of Salvadoran coffee exports went to the United States.

[2]The print advertisements had mentioned other coffee brands in addition to Folgers.

[3]*The Boston Globe,* December 12, 1990. A similar commercial calling for a boycott of Hills Brothers Coffee was aired on the West Coast where Hills Brothers had its largest market share.

[4]The other station was a UHF station in Worcester, Massachusetts.

[5]Procter & Gamble had not placed advertising with the Worcester station.

[6]*The Wall Street Journal,* November 8, 1990.

[7]*Boston Globe,* December 12, 1990.

[8]*Boston Globe,* December 12, 1990.

anti-Folgers ad were not substantiated and . . . it was an appropriate time to resume advertising on that station.' "[9] As a result of a peace accord between the government and rebels in El Salvador in March 1992, the boycott was called off.

[9]*Boston Globe,* December 12, 1990.

should be able to rely on a scientific Government report when they are relaying the report's contents."[10]

In the category of privilege, Article I, Section 6 of the Constitution provides an absolute immunity from defamation for legislators speaking on the floor of the Congress and in hearings as well as to participants in judicial proceedings. Senator William Proxmire (D-WI) was found guilty of slander when he made the mistake of announcing his "golden fleece award" off the Senate floor.[11]

A degree of privilege is also provided to the media by the First Amendment, which extends protection but does not provide an absolute defense. In *New York Times v. Sullivan,* 376 U.S. 254 (1964), the Supreme Court delineated a standard of proof required of plaintiffs in a defamation suit.[12] The ruling requires plaintiffs who are "public figures" to show that the statement in question was made with actual malice; that is, either with knowledge that it was false or with "reckless disregard" for whether it was true. Being careless or sloppy with the facts is not sufficient for a finding of libel. In a complex case, the court attempts to balance the rights of the plaintiff with the rights of the media as provided by the First Amendment.

The rationale for the standard enunciated in *Sullivan* is that although individuals retain rights to privacy, they lose a degree of privateness when they participate in "public" activities. The publicness of a plaintiff is not restricted to public officeholders but also pertains to private citizens who voluntarily appear in public. A corporate executive who makes public speeches or testifies in public hearings may be held to be a public figure in a defamation suit. Thus, a corporate plaintiff in a defamation suit may have to meet the standard of proof delineated in *Sullivan.*

To illustrate the application of this standard, in 1981 anchorman Walter Jacobson of CBS's Chicago television station WBBM stated in a commentary that Brown & Williamson Tobacco Corporation was trying to lure young people to its Viceroy cigarette by using a marketing strategy that related the cigarette to "pot, wine, beer, and sex." Jacobson based his commentary on an FTC study that reported that a Brown & Williamson advertising agency had hired a consultant who had proposed such a strategy. The FTC study, however, did not indicate that Brown & Williamson had adopted the consultant's recommendations. Indeed, Jacobson's assistant had told him prior to the broadcast that the company had rejected the proposed strategy. In spite of having been so informed, Jacobson made his commentary. The jury concluded that Jacobson

[10]*The New York Times,* September 15, 1993.

[11]*Hutchinson v. Proxmire,* 443 U.S. 111 (1979). Senator Proxmire regularly made an "award" for the worst federal expenditure.

[12]This case arose when supporters of Martin Luther King placed an advertisement in *The New York Times* describing the activities of the Alabama police. The advertisement contained "several minor inaccuracies and exaggerations" (Schmidt, 1981), and an Alabama jury found that the supporters and the newspaper were guilty of defamation under state law. The Supreme Court viewed a standard requiring complete accuracy as conflicting with the First Amendment's protection of freedom of the press.

made a statement that he knew to be false and held for Brown & Williamson. The jury awarded $3 million in compensatory damages and $2 million in punitive damages against CBS and WBBM and $50,000 in punitive damages against Jacobson. A federal judge reduced the compensatory damages to $1, but the Court of Appeals reinstated $1 million in compensatory damages. The decision was appealed to the Supreme Court, which allowed the Court of Appeals's decision to stand.[13]

A relatively untested aspect of the law pertains to information posted on the Internet. Such posting can be widely disseminated and could form the basis for a defamation lawsuit for the author. On-line services companies could also be the potential subject of a lawsuit if they played a role in maintaining a bulletin board or exercising editorial control over postings or access. The Decency Act of 1996 provides a degree of protection to Internet service providers, but no case has yet reached the Supreme Court to clarify the application of the law.

In a libel suit, the defendant typically makes a motion for summary judgment. If granted, the facts in the case are not disputed, and the case is decided only on questions of the law. The purpose of the motion is to avoid having the case go to a jury trial, as a judge can decide matters of law. The plaintiff typically opposes such a motion unless it would substantially reduce court costs.

Although plaintiffs win some libel suits against the media, the media is generally successful in defending itself given the protection provided by the Constitution and Supreme Court rulings. The news media, however, remains very concerned about libel suits and supports the Libel Resource Center, which works against libel allegations. In some cases, media companies file friend-of-the-court briefs in support of other media defendants.

The law of defamation differs considerably across countries. In the case of the Body Shop, libel cases are easier for plaintiffs to win in the United Kingdom because defendants are not protected by *Sullivan.* Moreover, British law differs from U.S. law in that the loser must pay the winner's legal costs, making lawsuits riskier for both plaintiffs and defendants.

OTHER LAWS

In the 1990s several companies adopted a new approach to recourse through the law. Instead of filing defamation cases the companies filed lawsuits challenging the means by which the news media obtained information for a story. Two producers for ABC News's *Primetime Live* submitted fake resumés to obtain jobs in the meat department of a Food Lion supermarket. The two producers then used hidden cameras to film material for a story about unsanitary food-handling practices. Food Lion sued ABC for fraud, trespass, and breach of company loyalty in using the hidden cameras. A federal jury found ABC News and four ABC producers guilty and assessed compensatory damages of $1,042 and punitive damages of $5.5 million, which were later reduced to $315,000.[14]

In 1998 a federal court jury found *Dateline NBC* guilty of negligence and misrepresentation and ordered NBC to pay $525,000 in damages. The plaintiffs were a Maine trucking company and one of its drivers who had agreed to let an NBC film crew accompany the driver on a cross-country trip. The plaintiffs argued that they had been led

[13]Juries often award large judgments against the news media in libel cases, and judges frequently view the awards as excessive and reduce them.

[14]Roone Arledge, Chairman of ABC News, stated, "But we give undercover work careful consideration before we undertake it. We did it in this case because we felt we had to and because we believed it was legal and ethical." *The New York Times,* August 30, 1997.

to believe that the story would be positive, but instead it focused on safety violations such as the driver driving longer hours than allowed by the law.

Summary

The news media is a source of information for those in the nonmarket environment of business, and it plays an important role in setting a firm's nonmarket issue agenda. It alerts the public, activists, public officeholders, and interest groups to nonmarket issues and to the activities of firms. Those interested in advancing an issue also may attempt to use the media as part of their nonmarket strategies. Although the media guards its independence, it may at times find components of those strategies to be newsworthy, as in the Alar case.

Because the news media plays an important role in the development of nonmarket issues, managers must assess which issues the media is likely to cover and the treatment the issues are likely to receive. The theory of coverage and treatment predicts that the news media will cover issues with a substantial intrinsic audience interest or perceived societal significance. Stories are more likely to be newsworthy if they have broad audience interest, timeliness or immediacy, human interest, controversy and conflict, and, for television, visual appeal. The societal significance dimension corresponds to the media's role as a protector of the public's right to know. In this role, the media may at times engage in advocacy by making judgments or supporting particular policies.

The media needs information for its stories, and on many issues business is the best and lowest-cost source of information. Firms thus have an opportunity to develop relationships with journalists who cover business issues on a regular basis. Managers may be called on to interact with the media, and to prepare for those interactions they need to be fully informed about the issue in question as well as the intended audience.

Business issues are often complex and may be difficult for television and the general media to cover. Although the media applies standards of accuracy, fairness, and balance to a story, it has incentives to make the story appealing to the audience and therefore may overemphasize conflict and controversy. It may also simplify a story to fit a time slot or a space limit. Many of the complaints about news coverage result from oversimplification.

The news media is both a business and a profession. Media companies are motivated by profit considerations, and journalists are motivated by individual incentives for professional recognition and attainment. Journalists are guided by professional standards, but a tension can exist between those standards and corporate and individual incentives. That tension can at times compromise accuracy, fairness, and balance.

The subjects of media stories frequently believe that they were unfairly treated or that a story was inaccurate or incomplete. One recourse is a defamation suit, but such lawsuits are typically costly and difficult to win. The standard under which a case will be judged is important to its eventual outcome. For a "public figure" the standard articulated in *New York Times v. Sullivan* may be applicable. This standard provides considerable protection for the media because a plaintiff must show actual malice and a "reckless disregard" for the truth.

Information is essential for democracy, and the news media is a principal source of information for citizens. Along with this role comes the responsibility to uncover, report, and interpret news and to present it under standards of fairness, accuracy, and balance. The news media is, in principle, not to create news or to conduct trials to determine right and wrong, and drawing conclusions and advocating positions are to be confined to the editorial page.

The news media at times compromises these principles, and so some critics have called for restraints. Despite its lapses and occasional abuses, the news media plays an essential role in a democracy, and the imperfections in the coverage and treatment of stories may be a price worth paying for the benefits it provides. As Thomas Jefferson wrote, "Were it left to me to decide whether we should have a government without newspapers or newspapers without a government, I should not hesitate to prefer the latter."

CASES

The Alar Episode (A)

Alar, which had been licensed for use on apples in 1968, is the brand name for daminozide, a chemical produced by the Uniroyal Chemical Company, a unit of Avery, Incorporated. Alar first became an issue in 1986 when Ralph Nader and several consumer and environmental groups urged the EPA to ban the chemical. In 1985, studies on animals had shown that daminozide and a by-product, UDMH, might cause cancer, but an EPA science advisory panel advised the agency to delay its decision in favor of additional study.

In response to the concerns raised by the activists, 15 food companies announced that they would no longer use apples treated with Alar. Over the next 3 years, Alar use decreased to approximately 5 percent of the apple crop from 40 percent in 1985. As of 1989, sales of Alar were approximately $5 million annually, with approximately half accounted for by exports.

In 1989 the NRDC executed a carefully designed media strategy that alleged a health risk for children who ate apples treated with Alar. In its study of 23 chemicals and pesticides and the diets of preschool children, the NRDC concluded that 0.03 percent of children aged 1 to 5 years would eventually get cancer from pesticides in the food they eat. The NRDC estimated that the risk was 240 times the EPA's acceptable level.[1] Alar was cited as one of the most hazardous of the 23 chemicals. The concern was not only with daminozide itself, but also with UDMH, which is produced from Alar when the chemical is heated during cooking.

After the *60 Minutes* broadcast highlighting the NRDC's allegations, the media leaped on the issue. Thousands of parents protested to their representatives in Washington, and politicians jumped on the bandwagon. Apple growers, supermarkets, producers of apple-based foods, and the producer of Alar came under attack. Even though the EPA estimated that in 1988 only 4 to 8 percent of apples were treated with Alar, parents, politicians, and activists called for apples to be removed from school cafeterias and demanded that they be banned altogether. Congressional hearings were held, and Meryl Streep testified before a Senate committee and also visited the White House to meet with an advisor to President Bush.

The FDA, the EPA, and the Department of Agriculture responded to the Alar scare by issuing a joint statement in March 1989 stating, "There is not an imminent hazard posed to children in the consumption of apples at this time, despite claims to the contrary." The agencies added, "The federal government encourages school systems and others responsible for the diets of children to continue to serve apples and other nutritious fruit to American children."[2] Tests by the Los Angeles Unified School District convinced the district to resume serving fresh apples, apple juice, and several other processed apple products.

Supermarkets were worried by the potential of the scare, and many immediately removed apples from their shelves, pledging to sell only Alar-free apples. In checking supermarkets' compliance with their Alar-free policies, *Consumer Reports* found traces of the chemical in 55 percent of 20 samples of fresh apples tested.[3] It also reported that it tested 50 samples of apple juice and found residues of Alar in three-quarters of the samples. The manufacturers of 26 of the brands claimed not to use Alar-treated apples.[4]

Apple growers claimed that Consumers Union's testing procedure was unapproved and inaccurate. Consumers Union had used a new testing procedure

[1] *The Economist* (March 18, 1989, p. 25) characterized the NRDC's study as follows: "Few paused to assess the science on which the NRDC's report was based. The group took some old toxicology studies that the EPA had rejected in 1985 as flawed, ignored some new ones commissioned by the EPA which showed daminozide as causing only benign tumors in mice (and not rats) only at absurdly high concentrations, did a small survey of how many apples children eat, inserted a factor for the greater vulnerability of children than adults, ignored the fact that 95 percent of apples never have daminozide applied to them, and came out with a figure that one in 4,200 children is likely to get cancer solely because of eating contaminated apples, 100 times the risk the EPA calculates. The EPA says the data were discredited and the logic faulty."

[2] *Peninsula Times Tribune,* Palo Alto, CA, March 17, 1989.

[3] *Consumer Reports,* May 1989, p. 291.

[4] Alar may be absorbed by the tree itself, so it may be possible to find traces of Alar in apples that have not been treated.

capable of detecting concentrations as low as 0.02 parts per million (ppm). The testing equipment used by most apple processors is capable of detecting Alar at a concentration of only 1 ppm. The Processed Apple Institute reported that it found Alar in only 8 of 4,623 samples.

In 1986 Safeway instituted a policy of accepting only Alar-free apples for its supermarkets. Instead of doing the testing itself, however, Safeway relied on its suppliers and buyers to ensure that the apples it sold were Alar-free. In 1988 consumer groups alleged that Safeway continued to sell apples treated with Alar. An independent laboratory, under contract from WMAQ-TV of Chicago, had found traces of the chemical in apples sold in Safeway supermarkets in Los Angeles and Sacramento but not in San Francisco. The highest concentration found was 2.52 ppm. (The EPA limit was 20 ppm for Alar.)

The EPA commissioned additional studies of daminozide, and the "studies showed no strong evidence of carcinogenicity."[5] The concern about UDMH, however, remained. Preliminary results from a study conducted by Uniroyal showed that a high dose of UDMH caused a high incidence of cancer in mice. The EPA believed that a limit lower than 20 ppm was appropriate for UDMH and began the required rule-making process, which takes from 18 to 24 months, that could lead to a ban on Alar. Although the EPA disagreed with the estimation procedures used by the NRDC, it believed that the risks from Alar and UDMH might be high enough to justify banning Alar. ■

[5] *Consumer Reports,* May 1989, p. 289.

PREPARATION QUESTIONS

1. How did the NRDC strategy and the media coverage affect the life cycle of the Alar issue? Which firms have this issue on their nonmarket issue agenda? How important an issue is it?
2. How should the apple industry respond to the campaign against Alar? Should it seek rebuttal time on *60 Minutes?*
3. How should Safeway implement its Alar-free policy?
4. What, if anything, should Uniroyal Chemical Company do about its production of Alar while the EPA considers a ban on its use?

Veggie Libel Wars

The *60 Minutes* episode on Alar in 1989 led to a collapse in apple prices and a loss the industry estimated at $250 million. In addition to the immediate steps taken by the industry and the U.S. government to counteract the scare, the industry filed a libel suit against CBS. In 1993 a federal district judge held for CBS on the grounds that although some studies had shown Alar to be safe, the statements on *60 Minutes* had not been shown to be false (*Auvil v. CBS "60 Minutes,"* 836 F. Supp. 740 [E.D. Wash.]). The decision was upheld by the 9th Circuit Court of Appeals, and the Supreme Court refused to grant certiorari.

Although the industry failed in the courts, the episode generated considerable sympathy for the industry. The American Feed Industry Association (AFIA), a trade association, seized the opportunity and hired a Washington, DC, law firm specializing in food and drug issues to draft a model "food-disparagement bill" for introduction in state legislatures. The model bill would change state libel laws to make false statements against perishable agribusiness products illegal. The model bill provided a cause for action against a party that made "disparaging statements" or disseminated "false information" about the safety of a food product. Steve Kopperud, senior vice president of AFIA, said, "There has been long-standing frustration . . . that an activist organization, for the price of a full-page ad in *USA Today* can say whatever it wishes to scare the public."[1]

[1] Marianne Lavelle, *The National Law Journal,* May 5, 1997.

Several courts have held that on matters of public concern, such as the safety of food, the standard established in *The New York Times v. Sullivan* applied. The model bill set a different standard that could hold plaintiffs libel for false statements they did not know were false. The model bill was based on court decisions on commercial speech in which, for example, a firm could be held liable if it intentionally made disparaging statements about a competitor's product for the purpose of harming its sales. Mr. Kopperud stated that the food disparagement laws were intended "to impose the same kind of burdens of proof you see in commercial speech cases . . . you can't say, 'This sugar pill will cure cancer,' but an activist can say, 'This egg will kill you.' "[2]

By mid-1997, 13 states had enacted versions of the model bill, which have become known as "veggie-libel" laws. For example, in 1995 Texas enacted its "false disparagement of perishable food products" law. Larry Gearhardt of the Ohio Farm Bureau said that Ohio's disparagement law "gives protection to people who could not protect themselves—individual farmers who could be hurt by a disparaging comment."[3]

In addition to the veggie-libel laws, corporations and other interests backed The Advancement of Sound Science Coalition (TASSC), an organization of scientists that opposed advocacy based on what it referred to as "junk science." TASSC supported the inclusion of standards of "sound science" in the veggie-libel laws. The language in most state veggie-libel laws defined "false information" as lacking a foundation in "reasonable and reliable scientific inquiry, facts or data." Steve Milloy, executive director of TASSC said, "Junk science lurks everywhere in the environmental and food science movements, from pesticide warnings to the greenhouse effect . . . Junk science is like obscenity: it is hard to define, but I know it when I see it."[4]

Critics of these laws argued that they placed the burden of proof on defendants to demonstrate conclusive scientific evidence, which they argued was a standard that would stifle free speech. "John Stauber, director of the Madison, Wisconsin-based public-interest group the Center on Media and Democracy, argued, 'Under this definition, it would have been illegal in the 1960s to criticize pesticides such as DDT, which were believed 'safe' for the environment according to data that was then considered 'reasonable' and 'reliable' "[5] Attorney Kevin Isern said, "We're not trying to restrict anybody's free speech, but free speech has to be correct speech. I think there is still a duty on the part of the talk shows to report what the truth is."[6] Sarah Delea, a spokeswoman for the United Fresh Fruit and Vegetable Association said, "We feel these laws serve as a reminder to groups and individuals that they need to stay within legal boundaries when disseminating information. Groups or individuals should not defame a product or the way it is grown/produced without factual, scientific basis in order to further their own agendas and cause unnecessary public fear."[7]

The first test of a veggie-libel law resulted from a segment on the *Oprah Winfrey Show* in April 1996 during the height of the mad cow disease scare in Great Britain. Medical studies suggested, but did not prove, that the Creutzfeldt-Jakob disease in humans, which can destroy the brain, might be contracted from eating beef contaminated by the mad cow disease, bovine spongiform encephalopathy. Studies in Britain suggested that feeding the ground-up remains of dead cattle to other cattle could spread the disease.[8]

In the interview in question, Howard Lyman, head of the Humane Society's "Eating with Conscience" campaign and a former rancher and current antimeat activist, discussed the mad cow disease. Ms. Winfrey asked, "You say this disease could make AIDS look like the common cold?" Mr. Lyman replied, "Absolutely." He explained, "One hundred thousand cows per year in the United States are fine at night, dead in the morning. The majority of those cows are rounded up, ground up, fed back to other cows. If only one of them has mad cow disease, it has the potential to infect thousands." He added that ranchers were turning cattle into "cannibals." At the end of his pitch, Ms. Winfrey said, "It has just stopped me cold from eating another burger." The "Oprah crash" in beef prices began that day and continued for 2 weeks before beginning a recovery.

---

[2]Marianne Lavelle, *The National Law Journal,* May 5, 1997.
[3]*The Columbus Dispatch,* June 29, 1997.
[4]*The Village Voice,* April 29, 1997.
[5]Marianne Lavelle, *The National Law Journal,* May 5, 1997.
[6]*The Independent,* June 10, 1997.
[7]Marianne Lavelle, *The National Law Journal,* May 5, 1997.
[8]In 1997 the Food and Drug Administration banned carcass recycling.

Paul Engler, an Amarillo, Texas, rancher and owner of Cactus Feeders, an operation with revenues of $650 million a year, took action by filing a class action lawsuit in federal district court against Ms. Winfrey, the show's producers, and Mr. Lyman.[9] Mr. Engler alleged that the segment caused beef prices to fall from 62 cents a pound to 55 cents resulting in a loss to him of $6.7 million. Joining Mr. Engler in the lawsuit was Amarillo cattleman Bill O'Brien, owner of Texas Beef. Pickup trucks in Texas began to carry the bumper sticker, "The only mad cow in America is Oprah." ■

[9] *Engler v. Winfrey,* 2-96-cv-233 (N.D. Texas).

PREPARATION QUESTIONS

1. Are veggie-libel laws an appropriate response to the strategies of activists?
2. What standard of proof should be required for a finding of libel? Is the commercial speech standard appropriate?
3. Should Mr. Engler have sued Ms. Winfrey and Mr. Lyman?
4. Is the filing of the lawsuit likely to discourage other activists and media programs from making allegations such as those made by Mr. Lyman on the *Oprah Winfrey Show?*

Illinois Power Company (A)

At 8 A.M. on November 26, 1979, the executives of Illinois Power Company, a medium-size utility headquartered in Decatur, Illinois, met to decide how to respond to a *60 Minutes* program that had been broadcast the night before.[1]

The *60 Minutes* segment had used Illinois Power's Clinton Nuclear Power Plant as an example of severe cost overruns and excessive delays, which the CBS report said were typical of nuclear power plant construction. In late 1979 public interest in the cost and safety of nuclear power was at a peak; the Three Mile Island nuclear accident had occurred in March 1979.

In the late 1970s, *60 Minutes* was among the most popular programs on television and frequently led the list of the most watched television shows. The program, which featured pugnacious reporters Mike Wallace, Dan Rather, Morley Safer, and Harry Reasoner, prided itself on being the advocate of the "average American." Each 1-hour program consisted of three 15- to 18-minute segments or stories. Usually, two of the three weekly stories would focus on individual or bureaucratic malfeasance or misfeasance. The program's producers particularly liked to stage interviews where a camera and one of the star reporters would burst unannounced into the office of the person to be interviewed.

The *60 Minutes* segment on Illinois Power featured interviews with three former Illinois Power employees, who claimed the cost overruns and production delays were due to mismanagement. The company believed that the three employees were using the charges as revenge for alleged mistreatment by the company. One employee had been fired; another resigned over wage increases he found unsatisfactory. The former employee who had suggested that *60 Minutes* do the story on Clinton had been denied permission to appear as an expert witness before state regulatory hearings after it was discovered he had falsified his academic credentials and work experience. Nevertheless, CBS featured him as Illinois Power's "sharpest critic."

More troubling to Illinois Power was that Harry Reasoner, who reported the story on the air, appeared to be misstating several key facts that had been discussed with him and explained at length. The story left the strong impression that Illinois Power was mismanaging the construction of the Clinton Nuclear Power Plant and expected their customers

[1] A transcript of the *60 Minutes* segment is found in CBS News, *60 Minutes Verbatim,* Arno Press, New York, 1980, pp. 149–153.

to pay higher rates to compensate for this mismanagement. Reasoner stated that the nuclear facility would come on line much later and at a much higher cost than Illinois Power was now predicting.

Illinois Power executives felt betrayed. They had welcomed the *60 Minutes* producer, reporter, and camera crews. Illinois Power had taken one precaution, however; it had filmed everything the *60 Minutes* cameras had filmed on Illinois Power property. Company executives believed they could show with these films that Harry Reasoner had deliberately misrepresented the facts in at least three instances.

Company executives were particularly concerned about the impact such a negative report would have on the company's customers ("the residents of one-third of Illinois"), its shareholders, its own employees, and its case for a 14 percent rate increase then before the Illinois Utility Regulatory Commission. What could the company do now to counteract whatever damage had been done?

Among the alternatives suggested were to ignore the whole incident, to sue CBS for damages (it would be necessary to show deliberate misrepresentation), to request equal time under the Fairness Doctrine by petitioning the FCC, and to seek a public judgment against CBS from the National News Council, a self-regulatory group of the media that published its decisions in the *Columbia Journalism Review.* Illinois Power's management wondered which might be the most effective in controlling the damage to the company, or whether the company ought to consider other alternatives. ■

This case was prepared by Kirk O. Hanson, Senior Lecturer in Business Administration, from publicly available sources as a basis for class discussion rather than to illustrate the effective or ineffective handling of an administrative situation.

PREPARATION QUESTIONS

1. Where is this story located in Figure 3–2? What makes it newsworthy?
2. If Illinois Power files a libel suit, under what standard is it likely to be tried? Is Illinois Power likely to win?
3. What should Illinois Power do?

CHAPTER 4

Private Nonmarket Action

Introduction

Private nonmarket action takes place largely outside, but in the shadow of, public institutions. It includes actions ranging from direct pressure on firms, such as boycotts, to attempts to affect public sentiment. Its primary objective is to cause a firm to change its policies or practices. Private nonmarket action arises from self-interest as well as moral concerns. In some cases, it arises from a single individual who becomes concerned with an issue, as in the case of Ralph Nader's campaign against Microsoft discussed in Chapter 2. More often, private nonmarket action originates from interest groups, as when labor unions take nonmarket action to further the interests of their members by, for example, demanding higher wages and improved working conditions in the factories of foreign suppliers of the apparel and footware industries. Private nonmarket action is also led by activist and advocacy groups that serve broader interests as well as the interests of their members. The causes these individuals, interest groups, and activists pursue are important components of the nonmarket environment, and the issues on their agenda are frequently thrust onto the nonmarket issue agendas of firms. Understanding their concerns, organization, and strategies is essential to addressing the issues they advance and the pressures they exert.[1]

These groups are important because they affect the issues, interests, institutions, and information that comprise the nonmarket environment. First, they can identify issues about which management either is unaware or has not understood as important to others. Observant managers will already have identified many of these issues, but in some cases these groups may alert managers to new issues that they will eventually have to address, as they did with ozone depletion and the possible health risks from cellular telephone radiation. Similarly, the actions of Greenpeace calling attention to Shell UK's plan to sink its oil storage platform, *Brent Spar,* in the North Atlantic generated nonmarket action in Germany and elsewhere on the European continent even though the plan had been approved by the government of the United Kingdom. Interest and activist groups thus play an important role in setting the nonmarket issue agenda of firms and in advancing issues through their life cycles. Moreover, the issues they raise and the concerns they express may point in the direction of more effective and responsible management. The chapter case *Denny's and Customer Service (A)* addresses such an issue.

Second, individuals, interest groups, and activists can affect the organization of interests by forming watchdog and advocacy groups and by mobilizing people to work

[1]See Vogel (1978) for an analysis of citizen pressure on corporations.

for causes. These groups have been instrumental in advancing the causes of environmental protection, health and safety protection for consumers, and civil and individual rights. The organizations they form are an important component of the nonmarket environment.

Third, the pressure these groups exert can affect the institutional configuration of the nonmarket environment. Their actions have led to new laws, expanded regulatory authority, court orders, legislative oversight activities, and executive branch initiatives. Activists were the prime movers behind the creation of the Environmental Protection Agency and the Consumer Products Safety Commission, and organized labor worked for the creation of the Occupational Safety and Health Administration. Activists also direct attention to government agencies, seeking to prod them to act on issues. For example, activist groups regularly file petitions with agencies such as the National Highway Traffic Safety Administration (NHTSA) to force them to initiate investigations or enforcement activities. Frequently, they file lawsuits in an attempt to compel agencies to act.

Fourth, individuals, interest groups, and activists provide information to the public and public officeholders. Rachel Carson's *Silent Spring* spurred the environmental movement by calling attention to the harmful effects of DDT. Activists at the Earth Island Institute spurred a public outcry and boycotts of tuna products when they produced a film showing dolphins drowning in nets used to catch tuna.[2] The news media plays a major role in disseminating this information, and an important component of activists' strategies is to attract media coverage, as illustrated by the campaign against the apple-ripening chemical Alar discussed in Chapter 3.

Whether these groups are right in their causes, their actions can damage a firm, its reputation, and its constituents. Some products, rightly or wrongly, have been doomed by the actions of activists. Ralph Nader's attacks on the safety of the General Motors Corvair, for instance, contributed to the car's elimination. Activists have been vocal opponents of agricultural biotechnology, causing delays in new products and increasing costs, as indicated in the Part I integrative case *Calgene, Inc. and Infrastructure Marketing.* The strength of activists can vary across countries. The opposition to agriculture biotechnology has waned in the United States as more products have been brought to market without the harmful effects claimed by some opponents. Opposition to agricultural biotechnology, however, remains stronger in some countries in Europe. For example, a major Swiss pharmaceutical company has located biotechnology units just inside the French border and connected those units by pipeline to its plant just inside Switzerland. In effect, the plant lies on both sides of the border with the biotechnology components located in France.

BOYCOTTS

A frequently used tactic of activist groups is to launch a boycott of a company and its products. Some of these boycotts are more symbolic than real, but many attract considerable media and public attention. Boycotts against companies including General Electric, the Walt Disney Company, Shell, and Mitsubishi have attracted national and international attention.

In 1998 the Walt Disney Company was the subject of several boycotts. The National Hispanic Media Coalition announced a boycott against Disney because of its record in hiring Hispanics. The Southern Baptist Convention organized a boycott to protest

[2]Putnam (1993) provides an analysis of the boycott of H.J. Heinz over the killing of dolphins in conjunction with tuna fishing.

Disney's decision to extend employee benefits to gay and lesbian domestic partners.[3] International labor groups also called for boycotts of Disney toys because of working conditions in the factories of its Asian suppliers. The Texas State Board of Education sold 1.2 million shares in Disney to protest violence and sexually explicit movies produced by its Mirimax Films subsidiary.

Boycotts are not only directed at the general public but also at specific customer groups. In the early 1990s General Electric came under attack for its operation of nuclear weapons facilities. A boycott and other pressures were directed at the company by the United Methodist Church, Physicians for Social Responsibility, and INFACT, an activist group that had led the campaign against Nestlé for its marketing of infant formula in developing countries. INFACT produced a documentary film, *Deadly Deception: General Electric, Nuclear Weapons and the Environment,* that won an Academy Award for best documentary in 1992. The award also provided the filmmaker an opportunity to criticize General Electric in her acceptance speech broadcast worldwide. Physicians for Social Responsibility claimed a more direct effect on General Electric. It claimed that its campaign had caused physicians to buy $43 million of medical equipment, such as magnetic resonance imaging machines, from other suppliers than General Electric. General Electric denied that the boycott had any effect, but in 1993 it sold its aerospace division which included its nuclear weapons facilities.

Even companies such as Levi Strauss that pride themselves on their record of corporate responsibility have been subjected to activist complaints and boycotts. Levi Strauss, for example, has been dogged by protests and picketing by a group of former employees who had been laid off in San Antonio when the company moved some of its production to Latin America.

Do boycotts have an effect on either the performance of firms or on their behavior, policies, or actions? Nearly all companies state that a boycott has not had any significant effect on their performance, yet some customers do stop purchasing a company's products as a result of a boycott. For example, as considered later in the chapter, as a result of a boycott of Mitsubishi organized by the Rainforest Action Network, Circuit City stopped carrying Mitsubishi televisions. The question is thus better posed in terms of how big the effect is on company performance. Evidence is largely anecdotal, but Davidson, Worrell, and El-Jelly (1995) conducted an event study of the performance of the stock prices of companies that were the target of a boycott relative to the stock prices of companies not subject to a boycott. They found that the announcements of 40 boycotts between 1969 and 1991 resulted in a statistically significant decrease in the share prices of their targets. Since the time of their sample period, the number of boycotts has increased significantly.

Which companies are most susceptible to boycotts? Figure 4-1 presents a set of characteristics of companies, their products, and their nonmarket environment. A consumer products company is susceptible because consumers, if motivated to do so, can switch to competing products. This action is easiest when switching costs are low, as in the case of tuna or televisions. A company with a brand name that can be damaged is also susceptible, because customers can punish the company by not buying a different product if the switching costs on one product are high. General Electric experienced this even outside its consumer product lines.

A company whose activities produce externalities such as pollution or a possible health hazard could be subject to protests from those affected or from advocacy groups that support them. Operating in an interest group-rich environment, such as Europe and the United States, provides a ready set of groups that could organize a boycott. Compa-

[3]The Convention also published a book, entitled *Send a Message to Mickey: The ABCs of Making Your Voice Heard at Disney.*

- consumer products
- products with low switching costs
- a brand name that can be damaged
- activities that produce externalities
- operating in an interest group–rich environment
- multinational/global operations—issues can spill over to other units and countries
- operating in developing countries
- decentralized organization, so that external effects are not naturally considered

FIGURE 4–1 Susceptibility to Public Protests and Boycotts

nies with multinational operations also must be attentive to the effects of actions taken in one country on interest groups and activists in other countries. Operations in developing countries may encounter fewer organized interest and activist groups, but groups in developed countries closely monitor activities in developing countries. For example, Shell learned this lesson from the local and international protests against its environmental practices in Nigeria and its decision not to intervene when the Nigerian government executed nine activists who in part were protesting the degradation of their region due to oil production. The organization of a company can also be important. In a highly decentralized company, a subsidiary in one country may not take into account or even be aware of the potential effects of its actions on nonmarket action in other countries. The combination of the direct effect of the boycott and the public attention given to it, frequently under the scrutiny of the media, can make nonmarket action effective.

The characteristics identified in Figure 4-1 can be used in chapter cases *Shell, Brent Spar, and Greenpeace* and *Nike in Southeast Asia* to assess whether the boycotts of Shell and Nike are likely to be successful.

An example of private nonmarket action taken by an interest group and a company's response is provided in the boxed example.

Activist Strategies

Activists choose nonmarket strategies just as firms do. Activism is a means of furthering interests, as when a labor union leads a boycott of a company whose workers it seeks to organize, as in the Pizza Hut example, or pressures companies regarding wages in their suppliers' factories in Asia with the objectives of reducing the competitiveness of imports that threaten union jobs in the United States. For some, activism provides training for political office or for advancement in the network of interest groups participating in public policy processes. For others, an activist group provides a pulpit from which personal preferences and visions can be expressed. Most activists, however, are motivated by concerns about specific issues. Some are concerned about an environmental or health issue, such as Alar, or about the well-being of a group of individuals such as workers in Asian factories producing sneakers. Some are concerned about the ability of others to exercise their rights or pursue their interests. Some advocate specific policies, whereas others see advocacy as a strategic instrument intended to advance a broader social agenda.

Concerns must be turned into action, which requires strategies to advance the issue. These strategies are implemented in institutional arenas ranging from public sentiment to the administrative processes of regulatory agencies. Two basic strategies of activists are applying direct pressure and petitioning public institutions. Pressure is

EXAMPLE

Pizza Hut and Health Insurance Reform

In the summer of 1994 Congress was occupied with Clinton administration health care proposals to change both the health care system and how Americans pay for health insurance. Interest group activity was intense. In July the Health Care Reform Project, an interest group formed by a coalition of organizations led by organized labor, released a report attacking Pizza Hut and McDonald's for providing less health care coverage for their employees in the United States than they did in Germany, Japan, and other countries.[1] To publicize its campaign seeking mandatory employer-provided health insurance and universal coverage, the group held a press conference and placed full-page advertisements in *The New York Times* and the *Washington Post.* The headline read "No Matter How You Slice It.... Pizza Hut Does Not Deliver the Same Health Benefits in America As It Does in Germany and Japan." The group also produced a commercial it planned to show on four New York and Washington television stations. Showing a young man delivering a pizza by bicycle, the commercial said that Pizza Hut provided health coverage for all its employees in Germany and Japan, "but for many workers in America, Pizza Hut pays no health insurance. Zero." Neither the advertisement nor the commercial mentioned McDonald's. The strategy of the interest group was coordinated with one of its allies in Congress, Senator Edward Kennedy (D-MA), chairman of the Senate Labor Committee, who appeared at the news conference and asked, "What do they have against American workers?" He announced plans to hold committee hearings the next week on the issue and asked Pizza Hut and McDonald's to appear.

Under attack, Pizza Hut first addressed the imminent problem of the television commercial. It had its Washington law firm write to each of the television stations pointing out its concerns with the commercial. The letter stated, "If you cause to be broadcast any statement to the effect that Pizza Hut does not offer health care coverage for its employees in the United States, the company will regard that false broadcast as having been made with knowledge of falsity or in reckless disregard of falsity."[2] (See the section "Recourse to the Law" in Chapter 3 for the explanation for this language.) This veiled threat of a libel suit caused the television stations not to broadcast the advertisement.

Pizza Hut then sought to explain more fully the underlying issue and defend its policies. It indicated that health care coverage was not provided for part-time, hourly employees for the first 6 months of employment, although employees could purchase a basic plan for $11 a month. After 6 months, Pizza Hut paid for a modest supplement to that insurance. Pizza Hut had 120,000 employees who work 20 hours a week or less, and most of them had health care coverage through their families. Moreover, few part-time workers remained on the job for 6 months. Pizza Hut also stated that health care coverage was mandatory in Germany and Japan and was one of the reasons a pizza that sold for $11 in the United States sold for $19 in Germany and $25 in Japan. Pizza Hut claimed that the cost of a pizza would increase by 10 percent if the plan supported by the interest group and Senator Kennedy was adopted.

Pizza Hut also had allies in Congress, and its home state senators, Robert Dole (R-KS) and Nancy Kassenbaum (R-KS), defended the company. Speaking on the floor of the Senate, Senator Dole said, "I don't know what company or industry will next be attacked by the White House, the Democratic National Committee or their allies, but from the arguments they use, I know they like their pizzas with a lot of baloney."[3]

Pizza Hut president and CEO, Allan S. Huston, appeared before Senator Kennedy's committee and defended the company's record and practices. Choosing to let Pizza Hut take all the heat, McDonald's declined to appear at the hearing and

[1]Health Care Reform Project, "Do As We Say, Not As We Do," Washington, D.C., July 1994.

[2]*The New York Times,* July 16, 1994.
[3]*The New York Times,* July 24, 1994.

staffers placed a Big Mac, fries, and a soft drink on the table in front of the empty chair provided for its CEO. Senator Kennedy attacked the companies for "an unacceptable double standard."

Shortly afterwards, the health care reform efforts collapsed in disarray and the Health Care Reform Project closed its doors. Although Pizza Hut had incurred only minor damage, the issue of health care coverage for part-time workers was unlikely to go away. The issue had attracted considerable media attention because of the societal significance of health care and the attention being given to health care reform. Moreover, organized labor and other interest and activist groups, as well as some members of Congress, would continue to raise the issue—perhaps with different tactics.

applied by calling attention to the activities of a firm, as in the Pizza Hut example. This may involve attempting to attract the media to the issue, communicating directly to and through community groups, or attempting to reach opinion leaders and public officeholders. The media may be attracted by picketing, demonstrations, or press conferences at which studies are released or allegations made. Some activists have access to a network of organizations through which their concerns can be communicated. Others may enlist the aid of public officeholders, such as Senator Kennedy in the Pizza Hut example, who may be willing to help advance the issue.

Pressure on a firm may be achieved directly through the activities of the activist organization or in a decentralized manner by relying on local organizations. As an example of the latter, the Emergency Planning and Community Right-to-Know Act of 1986 requires the federal government to publish annually the Toxics Release Inventory, which lists the emissions of over 300 possibly hazardous chemicals from every plant in the country. Using data from the Inventory, the Natural Resources Defense Council holds an annual press conference and releases a study of the nation's biggest polluters. The Inventory and the media coverage alert local communities to the emissions in their areas. Local groups, using private nonmarket action, then pressure firms in their areas to reduce their emissions. Partly as a result of these activities, several major companies, including Monsanto, Du Pont, and Dow Chemical, have implemented plans to reduce emissions below the levels required by EPA regulations.

A common strategy of activists and sympathetic government officials thus is to release information to the public so that local activists and interest groups can directly pressure companies. In addition to the Toxics Release Inventory, the government regularly releases mortgage lending data by census tracts and the chemical composition of drinking water. Much of the information is now available on the Internet.

Activist groups also use their standing before courts, legislatures, and administrative organizations to petition, sue, and advocate action. Environmental legislation and certain health and safety legislation, such as the Consumer Products Safety Act, were written to give citizens the right to petition regulatory agencies for action and sue those agencies if they fail to act. In the chapter 1 case *General Motors Like A Rock?(A),* the Center for Auto Safety petitioned NHTSA to recall the General Motors pickup trucks with side-mounted gas tanks. As illustrated in the Pizza Hut example, many activist groups have contacts with legislators and officials in executive branch agencies who can influence agendas.

Access to public institutions is a lever activists often use to encourage firms to bargain. The possibility of taking an issue into the arena of a public institution serves as a threat to be exercised if the firm does not agree to negotiate or is unwilling to agree to a satisfactory resolution of an issue. Even if an issue has little likelihood of succeeding, taking it to the arenas of public institutions may result in delays that can serve the activists' interests. In cases in which government approval is required before a firm can act, as in the case of the marketing of an agricultural biotechnology product or the construction of a plant, petitioning or suing the cognizant agency at a minimum causes delay.

A common strategy of activists is to conduct a policy study or scientific investigation to call attention to an issue. Even when the study or investigation involves only secondary sources, this practice of "advocacy science" can effectively advance the activists' cause. As in the Alar case, the release of a study can attract the media, and hence the public, and give a degree of credibility to the claims of the activists. It can also attract sympathetic legislators, who can respond with statements of support, the introduction of legislation, and hearings at which activists can testify. The study is most effective if it can be coordinated with other events to prolong attention to the issue and provide a series of newsworthy events.

The use of advocacy science is illustrated in the efforts of Monsanto to market the hormone bovine somatotropin (BST), or recombinant bovine growth hormone (rBGH), used to increase milk production by 10 to 20 percent. rBGH was the first commercially important genetically engineered product of the agricultural biotechnology industry, and its developers spent hundreds of millions of dollars to bring it to market. The use of rBGH was approved as safe by the Food and Drug Administration (FDA) in 1985, and final approval for full-scale commercial use was underway in 1990.

In December 1990, the Consumers Union, an organization that adopted activist strategies during the 1980s, released a study of rBGH by its Consumer Policy Institute. The study did not involve any new research but instead reviewed and evaluated publicly available work. It concluded with a call for a reopening of the issue of the safety of rBGH. Dr. Michael K. Hansen, author of the report, stated, "This is a very powerful growth hormone and the Government has not looked at all the potential health effects. . . . They are playing roulette with the nation's milk drinkers."[4] The report warned that Insulinlike Growth-Factor-I, a natural substance that acts with rBGH to increase milk production, might be absorbed into human blood and react with high levels of human growth hormone and pose a health risk. Articles published in the August 1990 editions of the *Journal of the American Medical Association* and *Science,* however, concluded that there was no such risk.

Using the theory of the media presented in Chapter 3, the issue of possible health risks from genetically engineered foods was high on both the audience interest and the societal significance dimensions and invoked controversy. The media thus could be expected to provide coverage. To increase the impact, Consumer's Union released its study 2 days before the opening session of a National Institute of Health conference on the hormone.

Consumers Union pulled out all the stops by attacking rBGH on environmental and economic grounds as well. It argued that because of the federal milk price support system taxpayers would pay another $1.7 billion a year in increased dairy subsidies. The Foundation on Economic Trends, headed by Jeremy Rifkin, a long-time opponent of genetic engineering, also filed a petition with the FDA requesting a full-scale reevaluation of rBGH. The chapter case *Monsanto and the Synthetic Milk Hormone* continues the saga of rBGH.

At times, activist organizations can place erroneous issues on the agenda of firms. Public Citizen, a Nader group, released a 124-page study that reported that five large insurers had failed four tests it had devised and suggested that they might fail in a severe economic downturn. The report received considerable media coverage, but within

[4]*The New York Times,* December 4, 1990.

days Public Citizen began to retract its conclusions. "We have concluded that neither Hartford nor Aetna should have been highlighted [included among the five] in the report."[5] It also wrote to the American International Group (AIG), one of the five listed in the report, stating, "Public Citizen did not suggest, or intend to imply, that AIG's financial condition is such that it is in danger of becoming insolvent, nor did we intend to cast doubt upon AIG's ability to meet its obligations."[6]

Activists also direct pressure at entrepreneurs, owners, and managers in both their personal and professional roles. Attention typically focuses on those who are perceived as influential and possibly influenceable. Pro-choice demonstrators participating in the National Organization of Women's nationwide boycott picketed Domino's Pizza outlets, claiming that the chain opposed abortion rights. Although Domino's Pizza had no policy on abortion, its owner, Thomas S. Monaghan, had made a personal contribution of $50,000 to the Committee to End Tax-Funded Abortions. Because of the protests resulting from his personal contributions, Monaghan said, "I have seriously considered putting Domino's up for sale so that franchises will not be hurt by my actions."[7]

Although some of these actions may be seen as coercive, particularly when an individual is the target, they indicate the range of private nonmarket actions used by interest and activist groups. Thus, individuals as well as firms must anticipate the actions of activist groups and the issues that they may place on the firm's agenda and must be prepared to deal with them.

Figure 4-2 characterizes the strategy used by many activist groups in attempting to advance the issues on their agenda. This characterization is based on the central role of the news media in informing the public about issues, as considered in Chapter 3. The activist group first identifies an issue and selects a target, as in the case of H.J. Heinz, whose Starkist unit was the only U.S.-owned tuna company. When the concern is with the practices of a company, the target and the issue are identified simultaneously, as in the case of General Electric. At this stage the activist group typically attempts to frame the issue by identifying its social significance and the company's role in the issue. The objective is to attract the news media to the issue, and the activist group may orchestrate events to attract the media. The activists also seek to become a low-cost source of information for the journalists by providing commentary on developments and sparking controversy. The news media then makes coverage and treatment decisions based on its perception of the societal significance of the issue and the audience interest in the issue. When media coverage is difficult to attract, some activist groups take out advertisements in newspapers.

The audience interest in an issue is determined by people's sentiments, and those sentiments may be based on moral concerns. The messages provided by the news media and the people's sentiments determine the public's awareness and concern about the issue. In addition, interest groups or other activists may become concerned. The hope of the activists that initiate this process is that people and interest groups will take action in the form of protests, boycotts, and collective action that may also attract the attention of the news media. In addition, government officials may act either in their role as a political entrepreneur or as an institutional officeholder.

The objective of the interest groups is to frame the issue to attract the interest of the public and the news media and induce people and government officeholders to take action that will give the issue a life of its own. The General Electric and Monsanto examples illustrate this.

---

[5]*The Boston Globe,* October 26, 1990.
[6]*The Wall Street Journal,* November 16, 1990.
[7]*The New York Times,* September 12, 1989.

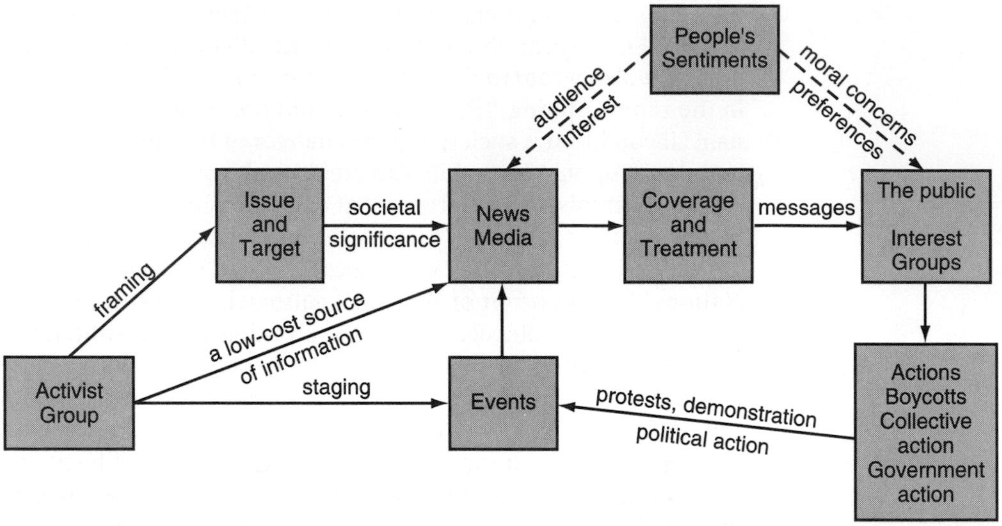

FIGURE 4-2 Activists' Generic Strategy

Activist Organizations

ACTIVIST ORGANIZATIONS AND NETWORKS

The nonmarket environment is populated by hundreds of activist groups, although some of them have only brief periods of activity. Because these groups shape the nonmarket environment of business and the nonmarket agendas of individual firms, managers must be aware of their organization, agenda, and tactics.[8] This section illustrates the scope of these groups and the networks they form with a focus on the Nader organizations, and then the activities of Greenpeace are considered in more detail. These groups may be no more or less important than others, and the focus on them here is intended to be illustrative and not a judgment about their importance.[9]

Ralph Nader was propelled to prominence in 1966 by his allegations about the danger posed by the Corvair and the revelation that GM had hired a private detective to investigate him. He has continued as a prominent activist, advocating a variety of causes associated with consumer safety, the environment, health, and the conduct of government and business. He also is the titular leader of a network of activist organizations, some of which specialize in specific policy domains and others of which attempt to further broader interests. These organizations conduct policy studies, advocate the interests of certain groups, and work to advance their agendas through direct pressure, the media, communication with the public, litigation, and political action. Part of the effectiveness of this group of organizations comes from their association with Nader. His influence is illustrated by his successful efforts in 1988 to block a 51 percent pay raise for members of Congress, federal judges, and other high-ranking federal employees. With a telephone call to a radio talk show in Boston, he initiated a movement that put such pressure on Congress that the pay raise was defeated.

---

[8]Rothenberg (1991) examines agenda setting in the interest group Common Cause.
[9]Mundo (1992) provides an analysis of the history, evolution, organization, and activities of the Sierra Club.

More important than Nader himself is the array of activist groups that he has founded or are linked to him. The Nader organizations include the following nucleus organizations: Center for Study of Responsive Law, U.S. Public Interest Research Group, Corporate Accountability Research Group, and Essential Information.[10] Less directly connected with Nader personally is Public Citizen, which sponsors the Health Research Group, Critical Mass Energy Project, Buyers Up!, Congress Watch, Global Trade Watch, and the Litigation Group. Other organizations include the Aviation Consumer Action Project, Center for Auto Safety, Center for Science in the Public Interest, Clean Water Action Project, Disability Rights Center, National Insurance Consumer Organization, Pension Rights Center, and Telecommunications Research and Action Center. Less directly affiliated with or aided by Nader are the Gray Panthers Project Fund, Citizen Action, Advocates for Highway and Auto Safety, Council for Responsible Genetics, Citizens for Tax Justice, and the National Insurance Consumer Organization.[11]

Another set of activist organizations has been spawned by David Brower, former executive director of the Sierra Club, who founded the Earth Island Institute (EII) in 1982. Organizations founded through EII include the International Rivers Network and Rainforest Action Network. Activist organizations frequently join in coalitions to advance particular issues. For example, the Beyond Beef Coalition, whose agenda is to reduce worldwide beef consumption by the year 2002, counts as its members 33 groups from 16 countries including several from the Nader and Brower networks.

Activist organizations such as these are an important component of the nonmarket environment of many firms and industries. These groups are often staffed by dedicated and ambitious people pursuing a cause they view as just or at least opportune. They are an important source of information for citizens, politicians, and the media. Many are also involved in taking direct action in political arenas and the courts and in shaping public opinion.

GREENPEACE

Greenpeace International is an environmental organization with nearly 3 million members, offices in 32 countries, and a budget of $146 million. Greenpeace began in 1971 with a high-profile effort to stop nuclear testing in the Aleutian Islands, and its most widely-known incident occurred in 1985 when French commandos sunk the Greenpeace ship *Rainbow Warrior* in Aukland Harbor in New Zealand, from which it was attempting to block French nuclear testing. That incident caused membership in the United States to climb to 1.2 million in 1991. Because of Greenpeace's opposition to the Gulf War against Iraq and of the successes of the environmental movement, such as the ban on hunting whales, membership declined to 400,000 in 1997. The loss of membership in the United States forced Greenpeace to close its 10 regional offices and resort to mobile units. It also stopped its canvassing activities for new members, which had been one of its hallmarks. Nevertheless, Greenpeace remains one of the most formidable environmental activist groups, particularly in Europe.

Greenpeace has seven campaigns: climate, toxics, nuclear, ocean, genetic engineering, ocean dumping, and forests. Internally, Greenpeace has two competing factions. The (rubber) suits argue for a continued emphasis on high-profile, sensationalist actions to

---

[10]Griffin (1987) presents Nader's approach of forming public interest groups on college campuses.
[11]This list is based on Internet sites, the *Encyclopedia of Associations*, 24th edition, 1990; "Ralph Nader, Inc.," *Forbes*, September 17, 1990; and "The Resurrection of Ralph Nader," *Fortune*, May 22, 1989.

call attention to issues, whereas other members argue that it should focus on participation in policy processes and finding and promoting alternative solutions to environmental problems. For example, Greenpeace developed a new, environmentally safe cooling system for refrigerators, which it argued should be adopted as an alternative to current HFC-based refrigerators.

In the United States Greenpeace's activities have reflected this tension. In 1997 Greenpeace led a group of 31 environmental and other organizations in opposing the EPA's approval of plants genetically engineered to resist certain pests. It also took out full-page newspaper advertisements criticizing shrimp farming for destroying natural habitats and spreading pesticides and chemical additives. It also conducted a study that claimed that toys made from polyvinyl chloride contained dangerous levels of lead and cadmium. In an effort to stop trawlers from going to sea and to protest overfishing, Greenpeace activists dangled by rope from a bridge in Seattle for 48 hours. The chapter case *Shell, Greenpeace, and Brent Spar* deals with another of Greenpeace's high-profile actions.

Interacting with Interest Groups and Activists

The frameworks developed in the previous chapters may be used to address challenges from interest groups and activists. Management must first assess where the issue is in its life cycle and how rapidly it is progressing. Often the issues generated by activists and interest groups are early in their life cycles, and thus firms have an opportunity to affect their progress, as illustrated in Figure 2–3. The next step involves identifying potentially interested parties and assessing how likely they are to become informed about the issue. As indicated in Figure 4-2, activists may attempt to bring the issue to the attention of the public and government officials through media strategies, and the theory of the news media presented in Chapter 3 can be used to assess how the media may cover and treat an issue. Prediction of the likely consequences of alternative strategies is often difficult when the issue is the subject of media and public attention, and that attention may advance an issue quickly through its life cycle. In the case of a boycott, the firm must predict how many people are likely to become aware of the issue and be sympathetic to the position of the activists. Sympathy, however, does not necessarily translate into action, so the likelihood that individuals will actually respond must be assessed. The Mitsubishi example involves an activist challenge and illustrates the analysis.

STRATEGY AND NEGOTIATIONS

When confronted with private nonmarket action, the natural first reaction is to be defensive. A better first step is to evaluate the claims and demands made by the activists and determine whether they have merit. For example, McDonald's faced a major solid-waste disposal problem, and when invited by the Environmental Defense Fund (EDF) to discuss the problem, it decided to accept. The result was a voluntary working arrangement with the EDF to develop a plan of action that included waste reduction, recycling, and substitute packaging.[12] The arrangement provided McDonald's with insight into the concerns of environmental groups, but more importantly it yielded fresh ideas for addressing the waste disposal problem. It may also have avoided costly litigation by the EDF and other activist groups. Working with the EDF, however, did not ensure that other environmental groups would find the programs sufficient.

[12]See the Chapter 1 case *The Nonmarket Environment of McDonald's* and the discussion in Chapter 12.

EXAMPLE

Mitsubishi and the Logging of Tropical Rain Forests

In May 1993 the Rainforest Action Network (RAN), a network of 30 environmental groups claiming a membership of 40,000, announced a U.S. boycott of the Mitsubishi Corporation, which is Japan's largest timber supply company. RAN claimed that Mitsubishi, both directly and through its Meiwa Trading Company subsidiary, was destroying tropical rainforests in Indonesia, Malaysia, and elsewhere. Hiroshi Saito of Mitsubishi stated that "the allegation is unsubstantiated and misdirected. The Rainforest Action Network grossly overstates the size of our tropical timber business and overlooks our commitment to sustainable development of forest resources."[1] Mitsubishi also stated that its rain forest harvesting worldwide was only 0.04 percent of the total. Michael Masayma, a spokesperson for Mitsubishi said, "We are not doing anything, so there's nothing to correct. Logging doesn't mean deforestation. We are cutting logs, but we are not deforesting."[2] RAN disputed the Mitsubishi statements.

RAN stated that Mitsubishi had been chosen as the target, rather than Marubeni or Mitsui, because it sells branded products in the United States. The boycott was directed at Mitsubishi Electric and Mitsubishi Motors, even though neither company was involved in logging and both were independent companies and not subsidiaries of the Mitsubishi Corporation or its trading company. RAN acknowledged that they were independent corporations but indicated that 11.9 percent of the shares of Mitsubishi Electric and 46.3 percent of Mitsubishi Motors were owned by members of the Mitsubishi *keiretsu.*

RAN employed a variety of boycott tactics. It produced a 14-page case study of Mitsubishi, its rain forest operations, the worldwide pressure being applied to Mitsubishi, and RAN's correspondence with Mitsubishi. It established an 800 number that supporters could call and for $9.75 send telegrams to Mitsubishi, the prime minister of Japan, and the premier of Alberta where Mitsubishi also had timber operations. RAN organized picketing of Mitsubishi automobile distributorships and retailers such as The Good Guys and Circuit City that sold Mitsubishi electronics products. RAN also distributed T-shirts carrying the message, "Save the Rainforest—Boycott Mitsubishi." RAN took out a full-page advertisement in *The New York Times* in the Northeast urging a boycott of Mitsubishi automobiles and televisions as well as Nikon cameras and Kirin beer, which were produced by other members of the Mitsubishi *keiretsu.* RAN also organized demonstrations at automobile shows. At the San Francisco automobile show, 37 protesters were arrested for throwing sawdust and chopsticks at the Mitsubishi cars on display.

On April Fool's Day in 1996 RAN launched a coordinated series of demonstrations in the United States and Japan. Protesters scaled and hung banners from Mitsubishi office buildings in San Francisco, Portland, Oregon, Los Angeles, Seattle, and New York. In Japan, demonstrators gathered outside the Mitsubishi Corporation headquarters to protest its operations in Burma.

Analysis

The key elements of the analysis are the nature of the nonmarket issue, the institutions in whose arenas it will be addressed, the nonmarket issue life cycle, the forces that move an issue through its life cycle, and interactions with activists. The nonmarket issue is Mitsubishi's role in the deforestation of tropical forests. This issue is at the interest group formation stage, since although the issue of deforestation had already been identified, Mitsubishi's role had been highlighted only recently. RAN and other activists were attempting to provide enforcement through direct pressure on Mitsubishi. The institutions involved are the "court of public sentiment" with possible, but unlikely, action by Congress or perhaps U.S. trade negotiators.

The progress of this issue through its life cycle depends on the media attention it attracts, the sustainability of the activists' efforts, the reaction of the general public, the participation of mainline environmental groups, and the attraction of a

[1] *San Francisco Chronicle,* May 11, 1993.
[2] *San Diego Union-Tribune,* July 25, 1993.

political entrepreneur. In terms of the theory of the media in Chapter 3, this issue is not high on the audience interest dimension, and it is only moderately high on the perceived societal significance dimension. The environmental issue is not new nor is it timely. It does not have a strong human interest dimension nor does it have a strong malfeasance dimension. The media is thus likely only to cover new "incidents" and to treat any story with only limited advocacy.

Some mainline environmental groups have deforestation on their agenda, but most use tactics quite different from those of RAN. A political entrepreneur is unlikely to pick up this issue because it does not involve an American company, and there are more proximate environmental issues. It is possible that the deforestation issue may be added to the U.S. trade negotiation agenda, but the issue probably has low priority.

The activists' strategy has three components. One is to put pressure on Japan. Americans sending telegrams to heads of government of Japan and Alberta will have little effect, although Japan is generally nervous about how it is viewed by other countries. The second component involves appealing to the public. This requires either a large budget, which RAN does not have, or substantial coverage by the media, which, as indicated, is unlikely. To encourage local groups to publicize the issue, RAN produced advertisements that they could place in local newspapers. To make the advertisements more relevant to Americans, they highlighted the destruction of forests in Oregon and Washington.

The third and most important component was the boycott. For the boycott to be effective it must affect retailers and that required either broad public awareness or continued demonstrations. Direct pressure from RAN led Circuit City to stop selling Mitsubishi televisions. The key to broader success of the boycott was whether protesters could be mobilized and whether moral concerns would motivate consumers to avoid Mitsubishi products. One ready source of demonstrators is college students, and RAN encouraged campus groups to organize media events and to demonstrate at local auto shows and auto dealerships. RAN told Mitsubishi auto dealers that it would suspend the demonstrations if they would write to Mitsubishi asking the company to change its logging practices. When only 10 percent of the dealerships sent letters, the demonstrations resumed.

Even though RAN's efforts may not have had a major effect on Mitsubishi, the challenge from the activists must be taken seriously. The companies must work with their dealers and retailers to counterbalance the pressure being put on them. The company also may want to meet with the activists to explain the company's policies, to express its concern about deforestation, and to emphasize its policy of sustainable development. A meeting can give the activists a sense of accomplishment and may diminish their fervor, but it could also increase their resolve. A meeting could also be an opportunity to begin negotiations to resolve the issue.

As a precautionary matter it would also be wise for Mitsubishi to present its side of the issue to the cognizant congressional committee members and their staffs and to executive branch agencies. Mitsubishi may also want to meet with newspaper editors and television producers to tell its side of the story.

Determining the most effective strategy requires understanding the nature and strength of activists and interest groups, the concerns that motivate them, the likelihood of media coverage, how much damage they might be able to cause, how central the issue is to their agenda, and whether they are led by professionals or amateurs. Professionals are more difficult to co-opt, but they may be more practical as well. With limited resources activists and interest groups must determine which issues to address, and they may abandon an issue that appears to be unwinnable or requires too much of their available resources.

Some activists are motivated by strongly held beliefs and are highly motivated. Others may believe in the merits of the issue but may not have the energy or the time to take action. In many cases, activists may be motivated by their own self-interest, as is often the case in not-in-my-backyard (NIMBY) movements. Few people want a nuclear power plant, toxic waste facility, incinerator, airport, or prison near their neighborhood. Self-interest is a strong source of motivation and a principal source of private nonmarket action.

Many firms are willing to meet with activist groups to demonstrate their concern about an issue, to explain the steps being taken to address it, or to indicate the difficulties involved in addressing it. Meetings may also help the firm understand the motivations of the activists and how likely they are to persist in their efforts. Meetings can also lead to negotiations to resolve an issue. Negotiations with activists can be voluntary, as in the case of McDonald's decision to join with the EDF to address its solid-waste problems. Often, however, negotiations take place under the shadow of public institutions. Two examples are provided by the negotiations between OnBank and community groups in Syracuse and Mitsubishi and RAN.

EXAMPLE

Negotiating with Activists: OnBank[1]

The issue resulted from the conjunction of two federal laws. In response to charges that some financial institutions used practices that limited lending in inner-city neighborhoods, Congress enacted the Community Reinvestment Act (CRA) in 1977. The CRA requires federally chartered banks and thrifts to lend in the communities in which their depositors live. The Home Mortgage Disclosure Act (HMDA) requires banks and thrifts to report their mortgage lending by census tract. When two banks announce a merger, activist groups frequently seize the opportunity to challenge the merger. The groups assert that the merging banks have not complied with the CRA, and they support that assertion with data on mortgage lending by census track filed in compliance with the HMDA.

In 1992 OnBank announced it would acquire another local bank, Merchants National Bank & Trust. When an inner-city resident's application to refinance his mortgage was rejected by OnBank, he turned to a community organization. The organization examined OnBank's lending record and found that it seldom made loans, it had no branches in the inner city, and it refused to participate in the city's Syracuse Housing Partnership. Merchants, however, had four branches in the inner city, participated in the Housing Partnership, and made significantly more loans in the inner city. Community organizations feared that the acquisition might result in Merchants operating as OnBank did. The community organizations began a letter-writing campaign to state and federal regulators calling attention to OnBank's lending record. OnBank countered with data showing that its record compared favorably with other banks in the state of New York, and it received endorsements from local organizations such as the United Way and the Urban League.

The community organizations gave OnBank a list of 26 concerns and proposed that it and the bank meet. The two sides met to discuss the issues, but the bank was unwilling to conclude an agreement. Meanwhile, OnBank was negotiating with state regulators, and when the state approved the acquisition, the community groups protested and attracted considerable media coverage. The acquisition still required approval by the Federal Reserve Bank, and the protests led to a second meeting at which regulators were present as observers. Little progress was made until the bank agreed to participate in a number of smaller working groups to address specific issues. The smaller groups made rapid progress and with the threat of direct action against the bank and federal approval still pending, the bank and the community organizations reached an agreement to increase lending in the inner city.[2] The threat of direct action against the bank, the required regulatory approval, and the reporting of lending data by census track provided the opportunity to pressure OnBank and obtain lending commitments.

[1]This example is based on an article in *The Wall Street Journal*, September 22, 1992.

[2]This process is repeated throughout the nation, and community organizations have formed an organization, the Association of Community Organizations for Reform Now (ACORN), that helps local organizations intervene in the bank merger approval process.

EXAMPLE

Mitsubishi and RAN

After 2 years of negotiations the Rainforest Action Network and Mitsubishi Electric America and Mitsubishi Motor Sales of America reached an agreement in 1998 ending the 8-year campaign and boycott. The agreement was announced at a press conference at the National Press Club and the three parties hailed it as "landmark." The companies agreed to stop using old-growth forest products and to stop using tree-based products by 2002. The companies also established a "Forest Community Support Program" to fund activities to preserve forests and aid the indigenous cultures that live there. The three parties agreed to establish an "ecological accounting" system to track the environmental improvements.

In full-page newspaper advertisements RAN and Mitsubishi Electric proclaimed, "Before, Rainforest Action Network & Mitsubishi Electric America Were Barely On The Same Planet. Now, They're On The Same Page."[1] Ralph Nader commented, "This agreement . . . is a testament to the efficacy of consumer boycotts!"[2] Neither the boycott nor the settlement reduced Mitsubishi's logging operations, so RAN settled for actions that would reduce the demand for timber. RAN's president stated, "Reduce the use of wood, and it's less profitable to log it."[3]

[1] *The New York Times,* February 22, 1998.
[2] RAN Press Release, February 11, 1998.
[3] *The New York Times,* February 12, 19998.

Summary

Private nonmarket action primarily takes place outside the arenas of public institutions and typically is intended to cause a firm to take actions that it would otherwise not take. Private nonmarket action is often led by activist organizations that attempt to advance issues on their agenda through direct pressure. Activists play an important role in the nonmarket environment because (1) they can alert management to issues of concern to others, (2) they may affect the organization of interests, (3) their actions can lead to changes in the set of institutions in the nonmarket environment, and (4) they may provide information to the public and government officials, often by attracting media coverage.

The nonmarket environment of business is populated by numerous interest groups and activist organizations that both raise concerns about the practices of firms and pressure them to change those practices. These organizations frequently interact with each other, and some form networks such as those associated with Ralph Nader and those that participate in the Rainforest Action Network. Activist organizations employ a variety of strategies to advance the issues on their agenda. One strategy is the direct application of pressure through demonstrations, boycotts, and public attention. The objective is to shine the spotlight of public attention on the firm with the hope that it will cause the firm to change its practices. A second strategy is to use the threat of the involvement of public institutions as a lever to encourage negotiations over the issue or, failing that, to file a formal petition for government action. Both of these strategies may involve advocacy science, policy studies, and media strategies to bring the issue to the attention of a broader public.

The framework presented in Figure 4-2 helps in understanding the strategy of activist organizations and formulating strategies for addressing the issues they identify. In dealing with activist organizations, firms take a variety of approaches. Some ignore the issue and the activists in the hope that their interest will wane or that they will be unable to generate broader support. Many negotiate directly with them as in the case of

OnBank. Others may work with the activists to find a solution to the problems identified, as in the case of McDonald's and EDF. When a firm believes that its practices are appropriate or that the activist group is weak, it may oppose the activists. Most firms, however, prefer to negotiate rather than become engaged in a protracted confrontation that could continue to attract the attention of the media, the public, and government officials. In most cases firms prefer to avoid creating enemies.

CASES

Shell, Greenpeace, and *Brent Spar*

The North Sea was a mature petroleum province where several facilities had already been abandoned or were approaching the end of their useful life. There were about 400 offshore petroleum platforms in the North Sea, about half of which were in the United Kingdom sector. The removal of platforms was governed by a variety of international regulatory principles. According to the guidelines of the International Maritime Organization any installation in shallow waters had to be completely removed and dismantled on land. A substantial portion (about 50 in UK waters) of the current installations, however, were in deeper water, and if approved, could be disposed of at sea. According to the British interpretation of international conventions and guidelines as well as UK legislation, operators had to submit their preferred disposal option, the Best Practical Environmental Option (BPEO), for government approval. Each such case for disposal then was individually considered on its merits. If the platform were disposed at sea, any remains had to be left at least 55 meters below the surface. Proposals had to be well documented and include a review of the options considered. The costs of abandonment were to be borne by the field licensee. Part of the cost (50 to 70 percent) was tax deductible.

ROYAL DUTCH/SHELL

The Royal Dutch/Shell Group of Companies was a multinational holding of service and operating companies engaged in various branches of the oil, natural gas, chemicals, coal, and related businesses throughout the greater part of the world.[1] The parent companies, Royal Dutch Petroleum Co. (domiciled in the Netherlands) and the "Shell" Transport and Trading Co., PLC (domiciled in the United Kingdom), did not themselves engage in operational activities. There were about 295,000 shareholders of Royal Dutch and some 300,000 of Shell Transport. Royal Dutch and Shell Transport owned the shares in the Group Holding Companies, Shell Petroleum NV (the Netherlands), The Shell Petroleum Company Limited (United Kingdom), and Shell Petroleum Inc. (USA). These Group Holding Companies between them held all Group interests in the Operating companies, such as Shell UK or Shell Germany (*Deutsche Shell AG*). The management of each Operating company, although bound by common standards, was fairly independent in its decision making and was responsible for the performance and long-term viability of its own operations. It could, however, draw on the experience and expertise of other operations.

By most international standards Royal Dutch/Shell was one of the most successful companies in the world. It was the largest corporation in Europe and the third largest corporation in the world. In recent years Royal Dutch/Shell was Europe's most profitable company. Since 1992, however, it had been in the process of restructuring. One reason was that its return on capital lagged behind its main competitor Exxon. According to C.A.J. Herkstroeter, president of the Group, the process of restructuring, although encouraging, was not yet satisfactory in terms of return on capital employed. Group companies had about 106,000 employees in 1994 (down from 117,000 in 1993). Its net income in 1994 was 4,070 million pounds (up 36 percent from 1993), the return on capital was 10.4 percent (up from 7.9 percent from 1993), and the debt to capital ratio was 16.7 percent (down from 17.8 percent in 1993).

THE ISSUE—DISPOSAL OF LARGE OFFSHORE PETROLEUM FACILITIES

The *Brent Spar* was a cylindrical buoy, 463 feet high and weighing about 14,500 tons. Between 1976 and 1991 it was used as an oil storage facility and tanker loading buoy for the Brent field (which along with *Brent Spar* was 50 percent owned by Esso AG, a unit of Exxon Corporation). In 1991 a review concluded that the necessary refurbishing of the facility was economically unjustifiable. *Brent Spar* was thus decommissioned in September 1991. Shell UK, one of

[1] Royal Dutch Petroleum Company, *Annual Report,* 1994.

the Operating companies of the Royal Dutch/Shell Group, considered several disposal options. These options were evaluated according to engineering complexity, risk to health and safety of workforce, environmental impact, cost, and acceptability by the British authorities and other officially designated parties. The latter included government bodies such as the Scottish National Heritage and the Joint Nature Conservancy Committee, as well as "legitimate users of the sea" (as specified in the 1987 Petroleum Act), mainly fishermen's associations and British Telecom International.[2]

Two options survived the initial screening process: horizontal onshore dismantling and deepwater disposal. The former consisted of the rotation of the buoy to the horizontal, transport to shore, and onshore dismantling. The latter involved towing the structure to a deepwater disposal site in the North East Atlantic and sinking the platform. The study commissioned by Shell UK concluded that deepwater disposal dominated on the grounds of engineering complexity, risk to health and safety of the workforce, and cost (about 11 million pounds versus 46 million pounds). Both alternatives were acceptable to the other parties consulted.

With respect to possible environmental impacts, the study concluded that both options were equally balanced. Whereas the environmental impact was expected to be minimal for both options, horizontal dismantling (due to its considerably higher engineering complexity) would involve an increased potential for mishaps that, if they were to occur in shallow inshore water, could have a significant impact on other users of the sea. In addition, a research team at the University of Aberdeen recommended deep-sea disposal. Consequently, Shell UK proposed deepwater disposal as its BPEO to the British Department of Energy, the relevant regulatory agency. In mid-February 1995 the British Energy minister, Tim Eggart, announced that Shell's BPEO was accepted. The European governments were informed about the decision and were given 3 months to protest the decision. Although some of the European governments, including Germany, were generally critical of deep-sea dumping, no government officially protested, and so Shell UK scheduled the towing of *Brent Spar* to the disposal site in the North Atlantic for mid-June.

[2]Rudall Blanchard Associates Ltd. (for Shell UK Exploration and Production), *Brent Spar Abandonment BPEO,* December 1994.

GREENPEACE

Founded in 1971 Greenpeace had grown to be the world's largest environmental group. It had about 3.1 million contributors worldwide and a budget of about $140 million. Offices were located in 30 countries with a full-time staff of about 1,200. In addition, Greenpeace owned four ships, a helicopter, and modern communications equipment. It could also draw on a wide network of thousands of volunteers. In 1994 Greenpeace was forced to cut its budget by about 10 percent and dismiss more than 90 staff members due to a drop in contributions due mainly to Greenpeace USA's opposition to the Persian Gulf War. The Greenpeace offices were fairly independent but coordinated their decisions through Greenpeace International, located in Amsterdam. Greenpeace strongholds were in Germany, The Netherlands, and the United States.[3]

One of the largest and most active Greenpeace sections was in Germany. Greenpeace e.V. (Germany) had about 120 full-time staff members, and a budget of roughly $50 million, and could rely on over 500,000 enlisted volunteers.[4] Its German headquarters and the North Sea logistic center were located in Hamburg. Greenpeace enjoyed high acceptance and popularity among the German public and had frequently captured center stage through spectacular actions, which was reflected in its donations that reached a record in 1994. Greenpeace Germany alone contributed over 40 percent of the total budget of Greenpeace International. Recently, Greenpeace Germany had also been active in developing alternative solutions to environmental problems.

One of Greenpeace's principal strategies was to attract the public's attention through high profile, confrontational actions, which were covered by Greenpeace photographers and film crews. "We try to keep it simple," said Steve D'Esposito, an American who was executive director of Greenpeace International. "One, we raise environmental awareness. Two, we want to push the world toward solutions, using the most egregious examples. The whole point is to confront; we try to get in the way. Confrontation is critical to get coverage in the press or to reach the public some other way."[5]

THE *BRENT SPAR* PROTESTS

After being informed about Shell UK's plans concerning *Brent Spar* in summer 1994, Greenpeace

[3]*Frankfurter Allgemeine Zeitung,* June 12, 1995.
[4]Interview with Harald Zindler, Greenpeace Germany, August 11, 1995.
[5]*The New York Times,* July 8, 1995.

commissioned a policy study to consider the arguments for deep-sea disposal. The study concluded that total removal and not deep-sea dumping should be adopted as the BPEO, especially from the viewpoint of the environment.[6] By March, Greenpeace had devised a plan to board the *Brent Spar*. To win public support through television coverage, Greenpeace acquired satellite communications and video equipment.

On April 30, 1995, 14 Greenpeace activists from the UK, the Netherlands, and Germany landed on the *Brent Spar* by boat. They were joined by a group of nine journalists who with Greenpeace filmed the incident and broadcast by satellite. After a 3-week occupation, the group was expelled by Shell. Although the UK media gave little coverage to the Greenpeace campaign in the UK, German television extensively broadcast footage of soaked activists. Harald Zindler, head of the section "Campaigns" of Greenpeace, Germany, who organized the *Brent Spar* landing, recalled: "We were very happy when Shell decided to clear the platform. It portrayed Shell as an unresponsive and inconsiderate big business."[7] In response to the media coverage, expressions of outrage and protest in Germany and The Netherlands grew. Members of all German political parties and the German minister of the environment, Angelika Merkel, condemned Shell's decision to dump the rig in the deep sea. On May 22, the worker representatives on Shell Germany's supervisory board expressed "concern and outrage" at Shell's decision to "turn the sea into a trash pit."[8]

Under pressure, executives of Shell Germany met with Jochen Lorfelder of Greenpeace who argued that 85 percent of German motorists would participate in a boycott. He told Shell that "in the four weeks it would take to tow the *Brent Spar* to its dumping site, Greenpeace would make life a nightmare for Shell." The chairman of Shell Germany explained that Shell UK's studies indicated that deep-sea disposal was the best alternative for the environment. Lorfelder answered, "But Joe Six-Pack won't understand your technical details. All he knows is that if he dumps his can in a lake, he gets fined. So he can't understand how Shell can do this."[9]

On June 7 Greenpeace activists again landed on the *Brent Spar* rig but were soon expelled. The next day the Fourth International North Sea Conference began in Esbjerg, Denmark. One of the main topics was the disposal of petroleum facilities. Germany introduced a proposal that would rule out any disposal at sea of petroleum facilities. Norway, France, and the UK, however, blocked the proposal.[10] In the meantime, calls for an informal boycott of Shell by German motorists were mounting. Proponents included members of all German political parties, unions, motorists' associations, the Protestant Church, and the former chief justice of the German Constitutional Court, Ernst Benda.

In its media campaign, Greenpeace successfully appealed to the German enthusiasm for recycling. In their homes many Germans separated garbage into bags for metal, glass, paper, chemicals, plastic, and organic waste. Harald Zindler pointed out the appeal of Greenpeace's strategy to the general public: "The average citizen thinks: 'Here I am dutifully recycling my garbage, and there comes big business and simply dumps its trash into the ocean.' " Greenpeace always tried to keep its message simple and connect it to the public's everyday experiences and values.

Despite the mounting protests and another attempt by Greenpeace to board the rig, Shell began towing the *Brent Spar* rig to its dumping site on June 11. During the following week the boycott of German Shell gas stations was in full swing. Sales were off 20 to 30 percent[11] and in some areas up to 40 percent.[12] The mayor of Leipzig banned city vehicles from using Shell gasoline. Boycotts also spread to The Netherlands and Denmark. During the G7-summit at Halifax, Canada, German Chancellor Helmut Kohl criticized Shell and the British government for persisting with the proposed deep-sea dumping. Two days later a firebomb exploded at a Shell gas station in Hamburg.

Shell had used high-powered water cannons to keep a Greenpeace helicopter from approaching *Brent Spar*, but on June 16, two Greenpeace activists again succeeded in landing on the rig by arriving before the water cannons had been turned on. They managed to stay on *Brent Spar* while the rig was towed to its chosen disposal site. On June 19, the German Economics minister, Guenther Rexrodt, announced that his ministry, too, would join the boycott. During this period the German public received incon-

[6]Simon Reddy (for Greenpeace International), *No Grounds for Dumping*, April 1995.
[7]Interview, August 11, 1995.
[8]*The Wall Street Journal,* July 7, 1995.
[9]*The Wall Street Journal,* July 7, 1995.

[10]Accepted proposals of this conference were non-binding.
[11]*The Wall Street Journal,* July 7, 1995.
[12]*Wirtschaftswoche,* June 22, 1995.

sistent messages from Shell. Although Shell Germany suggested that the project could be halted, Shell UK refused to stop the towing. Meanwhile in the UK, Prime Minister Major was repeatedly attacked in Parliament but would not reconsider the government's decision to approve Shell's proposal.

SHELL'S CLIMB DOWN

After a meeting of the Royal Dutch/Shell Group's managing directors in The Hague on June 20, Christopher Fay, chairman of Shell UK, announced that Shell would abandon its plans to sink the *Brent Spar* oil rig. Mr. Fay stressed that he still believed that deep-sea disposal offered the best environmental option but admitted that Shell UK had reached an 'untenable position' because of its failure to convince other governments around the North Sea.[13] Shell UK would now attempt to dismantle the platform on land and sought approval from Norwegian authorities to anchor *Brent Spar* temporarily in a fjord on the Norwegian coast.

The decision was received with joy by environmentalists and with an angry response by the British government. John Jennings, chairman of Shell Transport apologized in a letter to British Prime Minister John Major. A variety of public relations experts criticized Shell's handling of the protests and its decision to abandon its original plans. Mike Beard, former president of the Institute of Public Relations commented, "They failed to communicate the benefits of the course they believed to be right; they lost what they believed to be their case; and now they're having to defend something they don't consider to be defensible."[14]

In response, Dick Parker, production director of Shell Expro, defended the company's decision not to involve environmental interest groups like Greenpeace: "Greenpeace does not have formal consultative status under the guidelines set out for an offshore installation proposal. Other bodies who represent a wide range of interests or who are accountable to their members are part of the process, and we consulted them."[15] Following the decision to halt the project, Shell started an advertising campaign admitting mistakes and promising change.

AFTERMATH

In the June 29 issue of *Nature,* two British geologists at the University of London argued that the environmental effects of Shell UK's decision to dump the *Brent Spar* rig in deep sea would "probably be minimal." Indeed, the metals of the *Brent Spar* might even be beneficial to the deep-sea environment. Disposing of the *Brent Spar* on land, on the other hand, could pose greater risks to the environment.[16] Robert Sangeorge of the Switzerland-based Worldwide Fund for Nature said, "Deep-sea disposal seemed the least harmful option." He called the *Brent Spar* episode "a circus and sideshow that distracted from the big environmental issues affecting the world."[17] In response, however, a spokesperson for Shell UK reiterated that the company would stick to its decision to abandon deep-sea disposal.

The *Brent Spar* facility remained anchored in Erfjord, Norway. After an independent Norwegian inspection agency, Det Norske Veritas, had surveyed the contents of the *Brent Spar*, some doubts arose about Greenpeace's estimates of the remaining oil sludge on *Brent Spar*. Shell had previously estimated that the Spar contained about 100 tons of sludge. Greenpeace had estimated an amount of 5,000 tons. On September 5, Greenpeace UK's executive director, Lord Peter Melchett, admitted that the estimates were inaccurate and apologized to Christopher Fay. Shell UK welcomed the apology and announced its intention to include Greenpeace among those to be consulted in its review of options and the development of a new BPEO.[18] ■

[13] *Financial Times,* June 21, 1995.
[14] *Financial Times,* June 23, 1995.
[15] Shell UK (Sarah James, ed.), *Brent Spar,* July 1995.
[16] E.G. Nisbet, and C.M.R. Fowler. "Is Metal Disposal Toxic to Deep Oceans?" *Nature* 375:715, June 29, 1995.
[17] *The Wall Street Journal,* July 7, 1995.
[18] *Financial Times.* September 5–9, 1995.

This case was prepared by Daniel Diermeier from public sources, including materials supplied by the Shell Petroleum Co. Ltd. (London, UK) and Greenpeace e.V. (Hamburg, Germany), as well as an interview with Harald Zindler, head of the section "Campaigns" (*Bereichsleiter Aktionen*) of Greenpeace Germany. Reprinted with permission.

PREPARATION QUESTIONS

1. From Shell UK's perspective, what was the issue in this case and where was it in its issue life cycle?
2. In which institutional arenas was this issue addressed? Which interests were active on this issue?

3. Evaluate Shell UK's decision process in choosing a BPEO. Could it have effectively communicated its rationale for deep-sea disposal to the public? Was Shell UK right in abandoning its initial plan? How should Shell have managed the *Brent Spar* disposal? From the perspective of a major multinational corporation such as Royal Dutch/Shell, what managerial strategy should be adopted to participate in, influence, and prepare for the development of this or similar issues? In what way, if any, might the organizational structure of Shell have contributed to the *Brent Spar* issue? Should the management of issues such as the disposal of the *Brent Spar* platform be centralized?
4. How did Greenpeace view this issue? What were its objectives? Why was it able to win the public opinion war? Could Greenpeace use the estimated costs of deep-sea and on-land disposal to its advantage? Why was Shell unable to explain its position and reasoning to the public?
5. Why did the German government not protest Shell's plan before the boycott? Why did the German government oppose deep-sea dumping? Why did the British government approve Shell's BPEO?
6. What should Shell UK now do about *Brent Spar*?

Nike in Southeast Asia

Phil Knight, chairman of the board and CEO, opened Nike's 1996 annual report with an account of the record revenues of $6.5 billion. One paragraph later, though, he added: "Yet no sooner had the great year ended than we were hit by a series of blasts from the media about our practices overseas." Nike had been widely criticized by labor and human rights groups over the working conditions and wages at its suppliers' factories in Asia. The media followed developments closely as revelations of sweatshops in the United States added to the public interest in Nike. *Doonesbury* likened Nike factories to Dickensian sweatshops.

Sourcing shoes from low-wage countries in Asia had been one of the foundations of the company's strategy. Nike had never owned a factory in Asia; instead the company had contractors with whom they contracted production. Thus, shoes and apparel were manufactured in independently owned and operated factories, and Nike took ownership of the product only when it left the factory. The factories were mostly owned by Korean and Taiwanese companies with whom Nike maintained long-term relationships.

In 1997 Nike bought the bulk of its shoes from China, Vietnam, and Indonesia. As the company's visibility increased, so did the scrutiny of its practices. Nike had to deal with allegations of subcontractors running sweatshops, marked by poor working conditions, worker abuse, and below-subsistence wages. Shoes that sold for up to $140 were manufactured by workers earning about $2 a day in such countries as Vietnam and Indonesia.

Nike had contracts with a dozen factories in Indonesia in 1997, employing around 120,000 people. Both Nike's South Korean and Taiwanese manufacturing partners had come to Indonesia to take advantage of the low labor costs. In Nike audits, several problems with Korean and Taiwanese plant managers had been reported. The workers considered some managers too strict, or even abusive, shouting at or striking workers, or issuing punishments considered excessive for bad work or tardiness. In one case, a worker had to run laps around the factory because the shoes she assembled had defects.[1] Nike insisted that managers who were found to be abusive were transferred or removed. Employees and union activists confirmed that Nike's audits had been effective; at the Nikomas plant, for example, a security guard who hit a worker had been quickly fired by the owners.[2]

Underpayment of wages had led to several cases of unrest at Nike's Indonesian contract factories. In April 1997, workers at the PT HASI staged a mass strike and protest. They demanded to be paid the new basic minimum monthly wage of 172,500 rupiah ($71.37), excluding allowances, that went into effect

[1] "Sweatshops haunt U.S. consumers," *Business Week*, July 29, 1996.
[2] Ibid.

on April 1. A representative of the workers said that the company had included their "attendance" allowance in their basic wage, which meant that their minimum wage had actually stayed at last year's levels. The *Jakarta Post* quoted the personnel manager of the company saying that because of its financial situation it had been given permission by the manpower ministry to delay paying the 1997 minimum wage.

After 10,000 of the 13,000 workers at the factory had marched 6 miles to the district parliament to demand the increase and later in the week had burned cars and ransacked the factory's offices, the company agreed to pay the minimum wage without including allowances for attendance, overtime, transport, holiday pay, and meals.[3] Nike claimed that their contract factories paid more than what most laborers would earn in other jobs. "We turn away more prospective employees than we could hire," Knight commented. "It sounds like a low wage and it is. But it's a wage that's greater than they used to make."[4]

In Vietnam, Nike's footwear plants had been under attack by both workers and media since 1996 when a 29-year-old Korean forewoman at the Sam Yang factory lined up 15 female Vietnamese workers and beat them around the face with an unfinished shoe because she was angered by the quality of their work. Workers staged an immediate strike, and the forewoman was fired the same day. Later, she was found guilty in a Vietnamese court of "humiliating" workers.[5] In another incident a Taiwanese manager from the Pao Chen factory forced 56 slow workers to run laps until a dozen fainted. The manager was sentenced to 6 months in prison for physically abusing workers.[6]

The monthly minimum wage at foreign-owned factories in Vietnam was $45 in 1997, compared with about $20 per month at state-owned factories. The Nike contract factories were believed to pay the minimum wage, but some had been accused of paying the workers less than this in the first 3 months of employment, which was illegal.

When it came to average per-capita incomes, cost of living, and the value of workers' benefits, statements from Nike and claims from human rights groups such as the Vietnam Labor Watch (VLW) differed. Although Nike said that the annual per-capita income in areas where Nike factories were located was $200, VLW claimed it was $925. A *San Jose Mercury News* article found the average to be $446 in the areas where 14 of the 15 factories were located. According to Nike, most workers saved enough of their salary to send money home to their families. VLW interviewed 35 workers, and none said they could save money. The *Mercury News* found that 12 of 24 workers could save money. Nike claimed that workers received free health care, whereas the VLW said workers' health insurance was deducted from their paychecks. The *Mercury News* found that employers, by law, deducted and contributed 1 percent of employees' salaries to government medical insurance.[7]

Nike had its first "Code of Conduct" for its contract factories in 1992, after the initial criticism of their labor practices in Asia. In a Memorandum of Understanding signed by all Nike contractors, the contractors were required to comply with all local government regulations, including those on occupational health and safety. Nike banned the use of forced labor, and required environmental responsibility, nondiscrimination, and equal opportunity practices. The rights of association and collective bargaining were to be guaranteed. Nike's production managers who were stationed at the factories monitored working conditions on a daily basis. Enforcement was not a problem according to Nike; many factories produced exclusively for Nike, which gave the company tremendous leverage. Beginning in 1994 Nike hired the Indonesian office of the international accounting firm Ernst & Young to monitor the plants for worker pay, safety conditions, and attitudes toward the job. The auditors were to pull workers off the assembly line at random and ask them questions that the workers would answer anonymously. In September 1997 Nike severed contracts with four factories in Indonesia which did not pay workers the minimum wage. This was the first time Nike had fired contractors for noncompliance with the code of conduct.

In 1996 Nike established a Labor Practices Department to monitor subcontracted manufacturing facilities and upgrade conditions for factory workers

---

[3] "Workers win pay raise at Nike plant in Indonesia," *The Reuters Asia-Pacific Business Report,* April 23, 1997.

[4] "Protests as Nike CEO addresses Stanford students." *San Francisco Examiner,* April 30, 1997.

[5] "Culture Shock: Korean employers irk Vietnamese workers," *Far Eastern Economic Review,* August 22, 1996.

[6] "Nike aide in Vietnam convicted," *The Wall Street Journal,* June 1997.

[7] "Nike's fancy footwork in Vietnam," *San Jose Mercury News,* June 25, 1997.

around the world. The creation of the department was "a further step in Nike's ongoing commitment to have products made only in the best facilities with the best working conditions in the sports and fitness industry." Specific emphasis would be on Indonesia, China, and Vietnam.[8]

Nike had long promised independent monitoring of its factories, and in February 1997 it hired Andrew Young, civil rights activist and former U.S. ambassador to the United Nations and mayor of Atlanta, to review its labor practices. The appointment received a mixed reception; Nike and Young emphasized his independence, but critics claimed he was hired to promote the company's image.

Young's report, which was released in June 1997, called conditions in its overseas factories comparable with those in U.S. factories. The report stated: "The factories that we visited which produce NIKE goods were clean, organized, adequately ventilated and well lit... I found no evidence or pattern of widespread or systematic abuse or mistreatment of workers in the twelve factories." The Young report did not specifically address the wage issue, which Young considered too complex and beyond the capacity of his firm. Phil Knight said, "We will take action to improve in areas where he suggests we need to improve. For although his overall assessment is that we are doing a good job, good is not the standard Nike seeks in anything we do."[9] When the Young report was announced, Nike took out full-page advertisements in some major papers summarizing the key recommendations from the report.

The report was immediately criticized by human rights and labor groups. Thuyen Nguyen, director of Vietnam Labor Watch, noted that Young only spent ten days visiting factories in China, Vietnam, and Indonesia, his tours were conducted by management, and he talked to workers through Nike interpreters. "Workers are not about to complain in front of the boss, especially in authoritarian countries where workers labeled troublemakers can be fired and jailed," wrote Nguyen.[10] Medea Benson, director of the human rights group Global Exchange, said, "I think it was an extremely shallow report. I was just amazed that he even admitted that he spent three hours in factories using Nike interpreters and then could come and say he did not find systematic abuse."[11]

In a letter to Phil Knight, a coalition of women's groups including the National Organization of Women, the Ms. Foundation for Women, the Black Women's Agenda, and the Coalition of Labor Union Women wrote, "While the women who wear Nike shoes in the United States are encouraged to perform their best, the Indonesian, Vietnamese, and Chinese women making the shoes often suffer from inadequate wages, corporal punishment, forced overtime and/or sexual harassment."[12] Fifty-three members of Congress wrote to Phil Knight accusing Nike of "ruthlessly exploiting" workers. Knight invited the Congress members to visit the factories.

The criticism and actions against Nike also occurred at the local level. Protesters distributed leaflets at a Nike-sponsored event at Stanford University where Phil Knight had obtained his MBA.

Five months after Andrew Young's report, the heat was turned up further when a 1997 audit by Ernst & Young, initially intended for Nike's internal use, was leaked to the media. The report revealed unsafe conditions at the Tae Kwang Vina Industrial Ltd. Factory in Vietnam, including chemical levels 6 to 177 times that allowed by Vietnamese regulations. The audit also stated that dust in the mixing room was 11 times the standard and that a high percent of the employees had respiratory problems. Major problems detailed in the report were the unprotected use of dangerous materials, poor air quality, and overtime-law violations. Over 75 percent of the workers in the factory were said to suffer from respiratory problems. Nike said that the shortcomings in the audit had been addressed.

The publicity surrounding labor practices was worrisome to Nike management. In some regions around the world, surveys showed that the bad publicity had affected consumers' perceptions of Nike. Consumers were used to considering Nike a leader in their field, but here the company was stumbling. Bob Wood, vice president of U.S. marketing, stated: "It's obviously not good. It's something that we're really concerned about, but we haven't noticed any literal decline in demand or sell-through of our products because of it."

Knight admitted that Nike had been ill prepared for the media offensive. "Our communications staff is woefully inadequate to deal with this problem right

[8]"Nike Establishes Labor Practices Department," *Canada NewsWire,* October 3, 1996.
[9]*The New York Times,* June 25, 1997.
[10]"Report on Nike Work Force Glossed Over Issues," Thuyen Nguyen. Letter, *The New York Times,* June 30, 1997.
[11]*The New York Times,* June 25, 1997.
[12]*The New York Times,* October 20, 1997.

now," he explained. "Our Washington, DC, office essentially is one guy, and he's always dealt essentially with the trade, with the quota issues." In 1997 Nike's public relations department had a staff of approximately ten people. According to Knight, "They should probably have fifty people in there, but they have to be the right people, and organized right." Martha Benson, a Nike spokesperson in Asia, explained, "We are about sports, not Manufacturing 101."[13]

[13] *The Wall Street Journal,* September 26, 1997.

Phil Knight could not have been more sure that Nike was a force for positive change in Asia. "Whether you like Nike or don't like Nike, good corporations are the ones that lead these countries out of poverty," he said in an interview. "When we started in Japan, factory labor there was making $4 a day, which is basically what is being paid in Indonesia and being so strongly criticized today. Nobody today is saying, 'The poor old Japanese.' We watched it happen all over again in Taiwan and Korea, and now it's going on in Southeast Asia." ■

PREPARATION QUESTIONS

1. How serious are the criticisms of the practices in the factories of Nike's suppliers in Indonesia and Vietnam? Are Nike's sales likely to be hurt by the criticisms and the actions of activists?
2. How effectively has Nike addressed the sequence of episodes? Was hiring Andrew Young wise?
3. What, if anything, should it do about the wages paid in its suppliers' factories in Asia? Is Phil Knight right in saying that companies like Nike can "lead countries out of poverty"?
4. How should Nike deal with the inevitable continued scrutiny its practices will receive?

Monsanto and the Synthetic Milk Hormone

Bovine somatropin (BST), also known as recombinant bovine growth hormone (rBGH), was developed by Genentech and sold to Monsanto in the early 1980s. Cows treated with BST produce 10 to 20 percent more milk than cows that have not been treated. Monsanto was estimated to have invested between $300 million and $1 billion in BST and worked for over a decade to obtain approval to market it. FDA approval was granted in November 1993, and after Congress imposed a 90-day delay, BST became available for sale in February 1994.

Monsanto's market strategy focused on veterinarians and direct marketing to dairy farmers and involved an educational program and free samples. Using the Posilac brand, Monsanto opened a direct marketing sales office in Memphis and over 2,000 initial orders were received.

Despite the approval to market BST, Monsanto continued to be challenged by activist and interest groups. The activists opposed BST for a variety of reasons. Some, such as the Center of Economic Trends headed by Jeremy Rifkin, a longtime opponent of biotechnology, had been opponents during the approval process. Rifkin had also joined with the Pure Food Campaign to oppose agricultural biotechnology. Other opponents included Mothers and Others for a Livable Planet and the Women's Health Network. Some activists opposed BST because, they said, it made no social contribution other than increasing the production of milk, which would advantage large and harm small producers. Others continued to argue that BST-treated cows could pose as yet unforeseen dangers. The Humane Farming Association conducted an ad campaign with a picture of a glass of milk with the caption "Got Hormones?" They also sought to have public agencies refuse to accept BST-treated products, achieving some success when the Los Angeles County Board of Education agreed not to use milk from BST-treated cows for a year. At a more fundamental level, a significant number of consumers had concerns about milk produced with BST.

The activists also alleged that there was a risk of increased antibiotics in the milk. They claimed that cows treated with BST were more likely to develop mastitus, an inflammation of the udder, that would inevitably be treated with increased dosages of antibiotics. The FDA, however, indicated that every tankful of milk was tested for antibiotics, and if antibiotics were detected, the milk was destroyed and the producer penalized.

Wisconsin, the second largest producer of milk behind California, reflected the conflicting views on BST. Many dairy farmers were beginning to use BST, and with over 30,000 dairy farms in the state their interests loomed large. The association representing dairy farmers declined to take a position on BST because some farmers were using it and others were not. Opposition to BST was led by activists and parents worried about a possible risk to their children.

The post-approval strategy of the activists was to attempt to segment the market by labeling milk as rBGH-free. Even though the concerns of most consumers were likely to dissipate as experience with the milk yielded no health problems, some were likely to continue to refuse products produced from BST-treated cows—to the extent that they knew which products those were. The activists, including Consumers Union, sought FDA-mandated labeling of milk from BST-treated cows. The dairy industry and several states also sought a directive on labeling from the FDA. In November 1993 the FDA had ruled that the milk from BST-treated cows did not require any special labeling because the milk was no different from milk produced without the bioengineered hormone. Having failed with the FDA, the activists urged producers not to use BST and to label their products as BST-free or rBGH-free. The Pure Food Campaign claimed to have persuaded 150 companies to so label their products.

Monsanto opposed the labeling as unfair and misleading, and the FDA issued an interim guidance (without the force of law) that producers were free to label their products as BST-free but that they should add a clarification to prevent the labeling from being false and misleading. The FDA directive stated that producers could not label their products just as "BST-free," because the hormone occurred naturally in all cows. Similarly, labeling it as "rBGH-free" was misleading because that would suggest that the milk was different. The FDA asked producers to add a clarification that "no significant difference has been shown between milk derived from rBST-treated and non-rBST-treated cows." The FDA urged states to monitor the labeling by producers. The FDA also suggested that a producer claiming BST-free products must maintain a verifiable paper trail that demonstrated that milk from cows treated with BST was segregated from milk from cows that were not treated. In May, two major milk marketers, Land O'Lakes and Marigold Foods, announced that they would market new milk brands certified as being rBGH-free.

Several retailers, including Kroger, Southland (7-Eleven stores), and Pathmark Stores, announced that they would not sell milk or dairy products produced from cows treated with BST. One problem, however, was their ability to verify that the milk they purchased was actually produced from BST-free cows. Safeway expressed concern about the difficulty of verifying the production of its suppliers. An inability to enforce a policy posed several problems to a retailer, which could be subjected to charges by activists that it was not maintaining its ban. It only took a couple of dairies producing milk from cows treated with BST and reporting it as BST-free to cause a public relations problem.

Monsanto urged the FDA to issue an additional directive on labeling and to "take immediate steps to stop this false and misleading food labeling and to inform the public and the market place that FDA intends to enforce its interim guidance."[1] Monsanto also sought to enforce the labeling directive. It sent warning letters to several companies stating that their advertisements were not in accord with the FDA's guidance. It also sued two milk producers for telling customers that their cows were not treated with BST. A Monsanto spokesperson explained the actions: "Basically, we are trying to stop unfair competition in the form of false and misleading advertising. We contend that these companies falsely implied to consumers that their products are more wholesome and in other ways superior to products that come from milk from BST-treated cows."[2] In addition, several trade associations including the Grocery Manufacturers of America, the International Dairy Foods Association, and the National Food Processors Association sued the State of Vermont over its soon to be

[1] *The New York Times,* May 18, 1994.
[2] *The New York Times,* March 9, 1994.

implemented labeling law. Cedar Grove Cheese of Plain, Wisconsin, however, had received permission from the state to use a red label on its cheeses stating, "Product Certified rBGH FREE." ■

PREPARATION QUESTIONS

1. How should Monsanto deal with the continuing activist challenges?
2. How important is the labeling issue to Monsanto? Is it appropriate to file a lawsuit against producers over labeling? Should Monsanto file suit against Cedar Grove Cheese?
3. Should Monsanto conduct a public education program to educate consumers about the facts of milk from cows treated with BST?
4. How should a supermarket implement an rBGH-free policy? What risks does it take?
5. What should be Monsanto's nonmarket strategy and how should it be integrated with its market strategy?

Denny's and Customer Service (A)

Early on the morning of April 1, 1993, 21 members of the U.S. Secret Service arrived in Annapolis, Maryland, to prepare for President Bill Clinton's speech at the U.S. Naval Academy later that day. Before setting up security at the academy, the contingent, in full uniform, went to a local Denny's restaurant for breakfast. The group included six African American agents who sat at a table together, and an African American supervisor who, with the white agents, sat at other tables. After all the agents had ordered, the six black agents realized that the white agents and their supervisor had been served while they had not. Agent Robin Thompson went to ask the waitress about the order, and she said it was on its way. He then asked to talk with the manager and was told that the manager was on the phone. (White agents seated at other tables later reported that the waitress rolled her eyes after turning to leave the black agents' table.) After having waited an hour, the agents stood to leave, and only then, they said, were they offered a single tray of food. They refused the food because there was no time to eat. "We had to go to a Roy Rogers (a local fast-food restaurant) and eat in the van," said one of the African American agents. On May 24, 1993, 7 weeks after the incident, the six agents filed a lawsuit seeking unspecified monetary and punitive damages. The suit alleged that their civil rights had been violated because Denny's had denied them service because of their race. "It's a classic case of some kind of bias," Thompson said. The lawsuit immediately attracted nationwide media coverage. On the *CBS Evening News* Dan Rather summarized the incident by saying that the agents "put their lives on the line every day, but they can't get served at a Denny's."

Denny's, a unit of Flagstar, Inc., was a nationwide chain operating 1,487 restaurants throughout the United States. Flagstar was formed in 1989 when Coniston Partners headed a leveraged buyout of TW Services. In 1992 Kohlberg, Kravis, Roberts & Company paid $300 million for a 47 percent interest in the highly leveraged Flagstar, which had interest payments of $900,000 a day. Approximately 70 percent of the Denny's restaurants were owned by Flagstar and the rest were owned by franchisees. In contrast to fast-food chains such as McDonald's and Burger King, Denny's operated sit-down restaurants, so when restaurants become crowded, customers did not wait in lines but instead waited to be seated, order, and be served.

In response to the agents' charges, Flagstar ordered an investigation of the incident. After questioning employees at the restaurant the day after the suit was filed, the company fired the manager of the restaurant for failure to report the episode. Flagstar officials also defended their employees' actions. Steve McManus, a senior vice president who had questioned employees at the Annapolis restaurant, said the delay in the agents' service was caused by the size of their party and the complexity of their orders, which caused a backlog in the kitchen. The black agents were most affected by the delay because their table was the last to order, he said. "It's a service issue, not a discriminatory issue." In response, the agents said a group of white customers entered the restaurant after them, ordered, and was served while they waited. Flagstar CEO Jerome J. Richardson said, "We had one cook, and either two or three servers to serve the entire restaurant. If they say they were discriminated against, I apologize. But in my opinion, there was not an intent to not serve black people."[1]

The Annapolis incident was neither the beginning nor the end of Denny's troubles. "It's 1993 and certain things should not be happening. I just cannot imagine them not wanting to serve those children," said Randy Shepard, director of the all-black Martin Luther King All Children's Choir of Virginia. Shepard was referring to a June 1993 incident in which 70 children and 54 adults of the choir returning home by bus to Raleigh, North Carolina, after weekend performances in the Washington, D.C., area were allegedly refused service at two Denny's restaurants. According to Shepard, the group first went to a Shoney's restaurant off Interstate 95 in Woodbridge, Virginia. "The manager there said he would be glad to accommodate us, but there was only 20 minutes before they closed, and service would take a long time," Shepard said. "He suggested we go to Denny's down the street." The three buses then stopped at a Denny's outside Dale City, Virginia, about 11:00 P.M. Shepard said he entered the restaurant and asked a manager if he could accommodate the group. "He said he couldn't accommodate us because he didn't have the staff and recommended a larger Denny's the next exit down." At the second Denny's, Shepard said the manager met him in the parking lot and also told him he could not accommodate the group. "Some of the children had gone in to use the bathroom, so I went to get them," Shepard said. He added that the restaurant did not seem full, and "they seemed like they had ample enough staff around, and it appeared they had already started clearing tables to serve us." Prince William County Supervisor John Jenkins, whose district includes one of the two Denny's restaurants, commented: "I feel like they ought to close that chain down. They have an interstate service route and ought to have enough help to serve those customers." Jenkins called for a county investigation of the incident.

Denny's officials and employees disputed many of Shepard's claims. "Our restaurant can't handle that kind of crowd—not with just two cooks and four servers. And I'm not prejudiced," said waitress Kimberly Marshall, who was white. However, her husband Dennis Marshall, an African American, said "If you're open for business, you can't say you can't serve that many people. It doesn't make sense to me."[2] Denny's officials said that the first restaurant was full, the second was half full and the bus driver had "indicated the group outside was in a hurry." Furthermore, a company spokesman stated that "in both Denny's restaurants, we offered to serve the large group and indicated there would be a lengthy wait," but the group left before the restaurant could serve them. Denny's officials stated that they were not equipped to serve 130 people with a staff appropriate for the non-peak time of 11:00 P.M. The officials acknowledged that the manager at the first Denny's suggested that the group try the other restaurant, but added that "he offered to phone the other restaurant to make the arrangements." Coleman Sullivan, vice president of communications of Flagstar, said, "It was 11:00 P.M. on a Sunday, and our manager told this bus group it would take a while to serve them. There was no discrimination."[3]

Eighteen months before the Annapolis incident, the Justice Department had initiated an investigation of the Denny's chain in response to complaints from African American customers in California. After the Department of Justice investigation substantiated allegations of bias, Denny's and the Justice Department entered into negotiations to settle the complaints. The complainants also took other action. Their lawyers had earlier established an 800 number to encourage others to report racist episodes so they could qualify a class action suit.[4] On March 24, 1993, a group of 32 African American customers filed a class action civil suit in San Jose alleging several discriminatory practices, including the following:

- A group of 18 African American college students were forced to pay a cover charge of $2 each and pay for their meals

[1] *Newsweek,* July 19, 1993.

[2] *Washington Post,* June 7, 1993.

[3] *Fortune,* July 12, 1993.

[4] By early July they had received over 1,000 calls.

in advance at a Denny's restaurant in San Jose, California, while six white students acquainted with one of the African American students were seated at a nearby table and were not required to pay the cover charge or pay in advance for their meals. According to the company, although several Denny's restaurants had in the past implemented a "late night policy" requiring all groups of 10 people or more to prepay for meals after 10 P.M. as a "security measure" to thwart the rising theft of meals, the policy had "not been enforced in a discriminatory fashion."

- A racially mixed couple, Danny and Susan Thompson, took their three children to a Denny's restaurant in Vallejo, California, to celebrate their daughter Rachel's 13th birthday. According to the lawsuit, Denny's refused to serve Rachel their famous free birthday meal, despite the fact that she had both her baptismal certificate and school identification. "I felt violated, humiliated, and embarrassed, so we didn't eat there. I can't adequately describe the pain that you feel to see this happen to your child," Mrs. Thompson said.
- Denny's allegedly threatened or forcibly removed African American customers from several California restaurants.
- Denny's employed "a general policy of limiting black customers," using the term "blackout" to signal employees when too many blacks were in a restaurant. The suit also alleged that one district manager instructed store managers to "start cracking down and get rid of some of those blackouts." Some Denny's managers asked for prepayment of meals or told blacks that the restaurant would be closing soon.
- When an employee at a Denny's restaurant in San Jose, California, told a manager a customer's eggs needed to be recooked, he was told to "take it to the niggers, and if they have a complaint, tell them to come see me."

The class action suit came only 5 months after a $105 million settlement of an employment discrimination suit against Shoney's, Inc., another leading national restaurant chain, which alleged that the company limited the number of African American employees at each location and restricted them to kitchen jobs by blackening the *o* in the word *Shoney's* on the job application to indicate an applicant was an African American. However, lawyers for Saperstein, Mayeda, Larkin & Goldstein, the law firm which represented the plaintiffs in the Shoney's case and was currently negotiating for the plaintiffs in the Denny's suit, commented that the Denny's case may be more remarkable because it dealt with mistreatment of the most important element of any business, the customer. "These practices evoke the bald racism of the 1950s," the lawyers said in a statement. Former California Supreme Court Justice Cruz Reynoso, who had been recalled by California voters and was now a law professor at the University of California at Los Angeles, said he believed the Denny's case was the first "pattern and practice" racism case in the past 15 or 20 years involving a major public accommodation.

The nature of the service in a restaurant depended on a variety of factors, including Denny's policies, the policies and practices of the restaurant managers, and the individual employees of the restaurant. The problem for Flagstar was twofold. First, although the company encouraged Denny's franchises to end practices that might be discriminatory, there was a limit to the control the company could exercise over the privately owned outlets. Second, the application of existing policies was problematic because policies intended to apply to all customers might instead be applied in a discriminatory fashion at individual locations by individual managers or employees.

While the negotiations with the Department of Justice were underway, Denny's addressed some of the issues by apologizing to customers, firing or transferring "bad-apple" employees, and creating a cultural diversity team. The "late night policy," which had been instituted to prevent diners from walking out without paying, was discontinued at all the chain's restaurants, both company owned and franchised. Mr. Richardson said, "The managers had problems with customers walking out on checks. Some required prepayment, which can be a problem when it's not applied to everyone."[5] In addition, Flagstar initiated meetings with civil rights groups.

Complicating the situation, Mr. Richardson, a former wide receiver for the Baltimore Colts who had built the $3.7 billion company from a single hamburger

[5]*Fortune,* July 12, 1993.

restaurant in Spartansburg, South Carolina, had for 6 years been working to obtain one of the two National Football League franchises to be awarded in the fall of 1993. Denny's and Mr. Richardson had been criticized by the Reverend Jesse Jackson and his son, who headed the Rainbow Coalition. The younger Mr. Jackson had asked in a May 27 press release, "Are we seeing the beginning of a racist sports connection and pattern here?"[6] ■

[6] *The Wall Street Journal,* July 1, 1993.

PREPARATION QUESTIONS

1. What were the causes of the individual incidents at the Denny's restaurants? Were they more than incidents of bad service? What might they reflect? How serious are they?
2. What responsibilities does Flagstar have with regard to the incidents?
3. What roles have the media and plaintiffs' attorneys played in this issue?
4. What should Flagstar do about these incidents and allegations?
5. What policies should it adopt for its restaurants and how should they be implemented? How should it deal with independently owned Denny's restaurants?
6. What should Flagstar do about the lawsuits?

PART I

Integrative Case

Calgene, Inc. and Infrastructure Marketing

As he rushed from the boardroom to his office to speak with the head of the Food and Drug Administration's (FDA) Center for Food Safety and Applied Nutrition (CFSAN), Roger Salquist, chairman and CEO of Calgene, Inc., explained that the company was about to make an important announcement. It planned to issue a press release at the close of business on Monday announcing that it was filing a petition with the FDA for food additive approval for its *kan*^{r} selectable marker gene used in the development of its FLAVR SAVR™ tomato. The tomato would be the first genetically engineered food to be approved for commercial production. Approval of the marker gene as a food additive would clear the way for its use in a variety of products without requiring specific FDA approval for each application. Approval would also help calm fears about genetically engineered foods at a time when activists were fueling those fears.

Calgene was founded in 1980 in Davis, California, based on the belief that genetic engineering could be applied successfully in agriculture. The initial goals were to prove the feasibility and worth of biotechnology applications by improving the yields of large production crops like wheat. Starting with four scientists and four lab assistants, by 1992 Calgene had a team of 135 research scientists and support personnel. Since 1980 Calgene and its research partners had spent $90 million in research and development and had a research and development budget of about $15 million. This investment had resulted in 25 U.S. utility patents, 35 foreign utility patents, and over 179 utility patent applications pendings. In 1992 Calgene's primary corporate partners were Campbell Soup Company (tomatoes), Rhone-Poulenc Agrochemie S.A. (cotton), Procter & Gamble (edible oils), Nippon Steel (industrial oils), and Mobil Oil (biodegradable lubricants). Calgene, however, had never made a profit, having accumulated losses of $83 million.

Calgene's first product, the FLAVR SAVR tomato, contained a gene that inhibited the release of an enzyme that causes a tomato to rot. This allowed the tomato to remain on the vine longer for ripening rather than being picked green and ripened by spraying with ethylene gas, which was the current practice. Calgene's second product was a variety of cotton plant containing its patented BromoTol™ gene that made the plant completely resistant to the herbicide bromoxynil, which was less toxic and more biodegradable than conventional herbicides.[1] The cotton fiber itself was identical to the fiber of conventional cottons. Extensive field tests had been conducted, and in November 1992, Calgene had requested that the United States Department of Agriculture (USDA) deregulate its BromoTol cotton.

Calgene's third product area was rapeseed, which had been genetically engineered to produce canola oil that contains laurate, used in detergents and shampoos. Another variety with a high level of stearate was being developed for use in margarine, shortening, and confectionery products. In addition, Calgene would be the exclusive producer of canola oil for Mobil Oil's biodegradable lubricants. These plant varieties were undergoing field testing at the end of 1992.

---

[1]Bromoxynil is a herbicide produced by Rhone-Poulenc Agrochemie, S. A. of France.

THE FLAVR SAVR TOMATO AND THE PG GENE

Tomatoes naturally produce the enzyme polygalacturonase (PG) which reduces the level of pectin in the fruit, causing them to soften as they ripen. Because soft tomatoes are hard to ship without damage, growers are forced to either pick the fruit while it is still relatively hard and unripened or allow the fruit to ripen longer and risk damage during shipping. One (conceptually) simple solution to the problem was to inhibit the production of PG in the tomato fruit. Tomatoes then could ripen longer on the vine before they were picked, resulting in fruit that both shipped well and had good flavor and color. The FLAVR SAVR bioengineers accomplished this by introducing an antisense, or mirror image version, of the PG-producing gene into a living tomato's DNA. Once there, the antisense gene (also known as the FLAVR SAVR gene), produced an antisense RNA that bound with the PG-producing RNA, inhibiting the RNA from performing its normal functions and reducing the level of pectin in the fruit.[2] (The kan^r selectable marker gene was used to detect the location and presence of the FLAVR SAVR gene.)

CALGENE'S BUSINESS STRATEGY

Roger Salquist joined Calgene in 1983 as vice president of marketing and the next year was named president of Calgene. He shaped its future direction by making product development responsible to research rather than to marketing, allowing the science to drive products. Salquist also forced the scientific staff to prioritize its projects according to business as well as scientific criteria, thereby channeling the scientific undertakings to potentially profitable areas.

In 1986 Calgene decided to build vertically integrated operating businesses in its core crop areas—tomatoes, cotton, and rapeseed oils—to be able to introduce its products decisively in the market. This strategy would provide access to agricultural input markets in which Calgene would sell seed engineered with value-added agronomic traits, as well as to agribusiness output markets in which the company would sell fresh and processed plant products with value-added quality traits, cost of production advantages, or both.

[2]DNA transmits its information through an intermediary RNA (ribonucleic acid).

Salquist recognized that Calgene had to be effective in dealing with regulatory agencies and their approval processes and with public attitudes toward biotechnology. Success with government agencies was a necessary condition for success in the marketplace, and the path to the marketplace ran through the nonmarket environment. Calgene's nonmarket strategy was intended to clear the path for its products, both with the public and the government, as well as to help establish Calgene's reputation as the scientific and commercial product leader in agricultural biotechnology.

Salquist called the nonmarket component of Calgene's business strategy "infrastructure marketing." He recognized that Calgene would have continuing interactions with the government and the public over public policy issues pertaining to agricultural biotechnology. He also recognized that the company's own research projects and products would require government approval and were likely to attract public attention. The public concern about the safety and wisdom of genetic engineering would inevitably generate a wide range of nonmarket activity.

Calgene's market and nonmarket strategies for the FLAVR SAVR tomato are illustrated in Figure I–1.

MARKET STRATEGY

Calgene's market strategy centered on the lengthy and expensive process starting with basic research grounded in genetic engineering and ending with the production and marketing of proprietary products. This product cycle could take as long as a decade and cost tens of millions of dollars. As a start-up company that had not been financed by venture capitalists, Calgene had to raise outside capital frequently, and building investor confidence was essential to Calgene's success. Building confidence required establishing a reputation for operating effectively in its nonmarket environment as well as in its market environment. Indeed, a reputation for dealing effectively with government agencies and Congress, and for handling effectively the challenges posed by the opponents of biotechnology, was an important competency.

One important strategic choice for Calgene was whether to integrate vertically into the marketing of its own products or to sell its products to and through other companies. Calgene decided to market its core crop products directly. It acquired a seed company to market its cotton seed, established a joint venture to refine canola seed, and formed a company to market

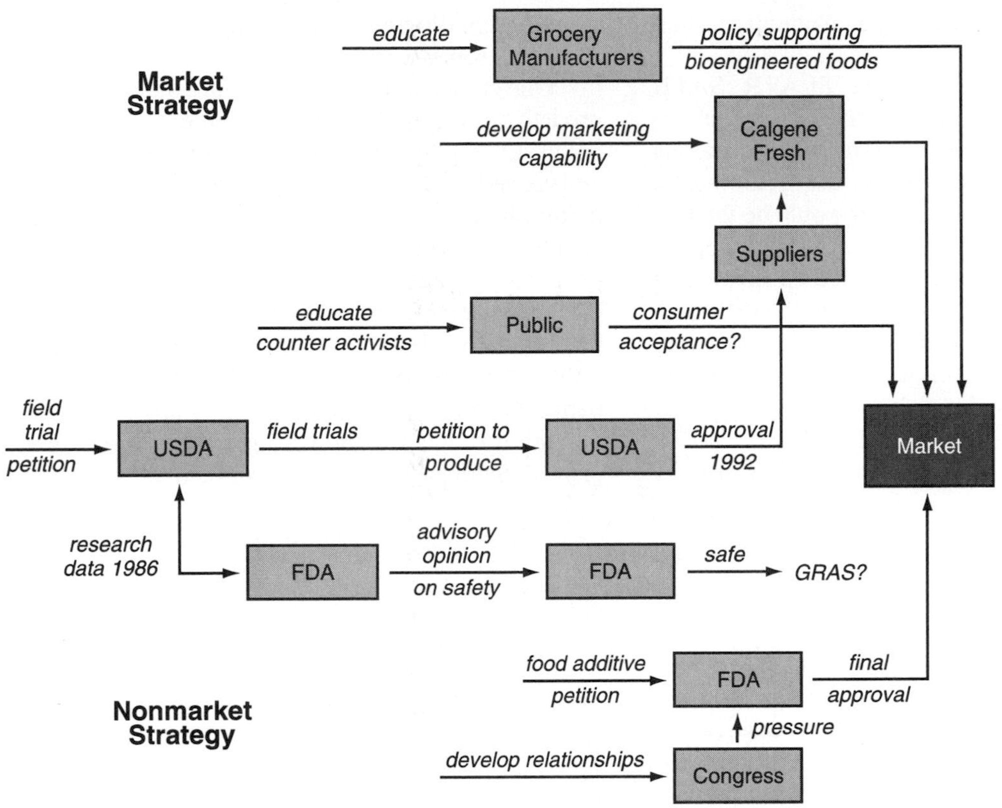

FIGURE I–1 Calgene's FLAVR SAVR Strategy

its tomato. One reason for vertically integrating into processing and marketing was to avoid pressure that could be brought against its customers by the opponents of biotechnology. Calgene worked to secure its customers—such as grocers—to make it less likely that activists would be able to pressure them successfully. The potentially most sensitive customers were those, such as Campbell Soup, with branded products toward which a boycott or adverse publicity could be directed.

The fresh tomato market was $3 billion annually and the processed tomato market was considerably larger. The market strategy for the FLAVR SAVR tomato had a number of components. First, it would be a premium-quality, branded product marketed under the MacGregor's farm stand brand. Second, it would be available year-round. Third, it would be priced at a premium of 200 to 300 percent above the price of regular tomatoes. Fourth, to calm potential fears about a bioengineered tomato and to explain why it was priced at a premium, point-of-purchase labeling information would be provided about biotechnology and the tomato. Fifth, supply would be ensured through contracts with growers. Sixth, Calgene would work with major customer groups to assure them of the safety and quality of the tomato. Seventh, Calgene would work to secure its customers by developing confidence in it and its products. Eighth, the tomato would be test-marketed before proceeding to a national rollout.

INFRASTRUCTURE MARKETING

The principal public institutions in Calgene's nonmarket environment included regulatory agencies (Food and Drug Administration, USDA, Environmental Protection Agency), Congress, and the courts. In addition to the biotechnology companies, the principal organized interests were the activist and interest groups that had biotechnology and agribusiness on their agendas. The principal issues facing Calgene centered on regulatory processes and approval criteria, government policy toward agribusiness and biotechnology, public concerns about biotechnology, and activist pressures directed at specific products, government bodies, and customers.

A new product such as the FLAVR SAVR tomato would cut a path through the nonmarket environment, and Calgene's infrastructure marketing was intended to support progress along that path. Early on, Calgene recognized that it would be the first agricultural biotechnology company to bring crops to the regulatory agencies for testing and approval, and hence the agencies would be developing policy simultaneously with their review of its products. It thus had both a short-run interest in getting its products approved and a longer-run interest in a regulatory policy within which it could work in the future.

The foundation of Calgene's nonmarket strategy was to develop relationships of trust with key members of Congress, the regulatory agencies, the media, and trade groups. Calgene worked to educate the regulatory agencies about biotechnology in general and about the products it was researching. To build confidence, it adopted a policy of full disclosure of its research data. It also provided the data early in the research and product development process rather than all at once at the product approval stage. This strategy also served to establish relationships with agency personnel on which trust could be built.

Calgene focused its infrastructure marketing on Washington. Congress played a central role in agribusiness and biotechnology policy, and Calgene was attentive to its relations with Congress—particularly with the agriculture committees. Its basic strategy was to be a source of information for the committees and to develop a reputation for responsibility so that the committee members and their staffs would turn to Calgene for needed information. To develop its relationships with Congress, Salquist met with members of the agriculture committees at least once a year. His lobbying strategy was to provide information to the members—information relevant to the members' interests. He personally spent time building relationships and lobbying in Washington, since Calgene was too small to afford a Washington office. It employed a veteran lobbyist to complement Salquist's activities and to serve as its eyes and ears in Washington.

Calgene was also involved in issues in judicial arenas. As is frequently the case, some of Calgene's patents had been challenged. ICI Seed of the United Kingdom challenged the patent on the PG gene. Calgene also held a patent on its antisense technology, but Enzo Biochem claimed its patent covered all antisense technology and that Calgene owed it royalties on its tomato.

One component of infrastructure marketing was a proactive position on the environmental movement. Salquist had met with most of the opposition groups, and viewed many of them as seeking an adversarial relationship in part to generate publicity and membership for their groups. He believed in supporting what he referred to as responsible environmental groups.

Calgene's efforts to guide its products through the regulatory processes, and its efforts to address public concerns about genetically engineered foods, benefited other firms, including its competitors, by making it easier for them to get their products approved. Salquist viewed this as positive because the development of a substantial industry would make it easier for all those in the industry. He expressed little concern about the spillover benefits for its competitors because the first-mover advantage in the industry was believed to be substantial.

One advantage of Calgene's leadership in both the science of agricultural biotechnology and regulatory effectiveness was that opportunities were brought to it. In 1992 Calgene licensed trehalose-synthesizing genes from a research team in Norway. These genes converted glucose into trehalose, a simple sugar that had been shown to preserve flavor and texture in frozen, dehydrated, and dried foods.[3] Quadrant Holdings Ltd. of Cambridge, England, had also developed trehalose technology and held several patents covering its food applications. Quadrant recognized that it lacked expertise in moving products through the U.S. regulatory system, and it also recognized Calgene's expertise. Rather than entering the U.S. market itself, Quadrant and Calgene formed a 50-50 joint venture company, to apply Quadrant's patented technologies and the genes Calgene had licensed.

PRODUCTS AND THE NONMARKET ENVIRONMENT

The nature of the product to a large extent determined with which components of its nonmarket environment Calgene interacted, the issues it faced, the regulatory process through which the product had to pass, and the interest groups that would be concerned about it. "The products are really quite distinct, so each one requires a slightly different strategy," said Salquist. "Fresh produce is unique because

---

[3] *Calgene News Release*, November 20, 1992.

it is genetically different from other produce. Calgene's oils will all be processed, and all DNA is thus denatured. There is no evidence that there's anything different about genetically engineered processed oils. But the rapeseed meal will be used in animal feed for cattle and poultry, so there are issues that will undoubtedly arise. In the case of cotton, the fibers, which are the main product, are no different from any other cotton fiber. The gene simply makes the plant immune to a herbicide."

An important part of its market strategy was developing a demand for its products. This was relatively straightforward for its cotton seed, which growers wanted because it would increase productivity by tolerating fewer applications of a more effective and more biodegradable herbicide. In contrast, the FLAVR SAVR tomato would be marketed through grocery stores and supermarkets. To ensure that it would not meet resistance from retailers, Calgene successfully brought together the Industrial Biotechnology Association (IBA) and the Grocery Manufacturers of America (GMA), which adopted a policy supporting genetically engineered products.

THE MEDIA AND PUBLIC RELATIONS

The media had an important role in shaping the environment of agricultural biotechnology. Calgene's fundamental objective was to have an informed national press. Salquist met with most of the journalists covering biotechnology and had a policy of always returning the telephone calls of those whom he viewed as responsible. He also made sure that he gave them something quotable. Many journalists called him for information on the biotechnology industry in addition to information on Calgene. Maintaining relationships with the media also had some unexpected advantages. When environmental activists planned a demonstration at Calgene's headquarters to protest its herbicide-resistant cotton plant, Salquist was alerted to the protest by a reporter. When the protesters arrived, Calgene was ready with a press release presenting its side of the issue, and Salquist was ready to give an interview to the media.

Calgene employed the services of a public relations firm to assist in crisis management and to set up interviews with the press. This firm helped set up interviews on *Money Line,* CNN, and other programs. The environmentalists' demonstration against its herbicide resistant cotton plant led to his appearance on the *Today Show.*

GOVERNMENT REGULATION

Early in his tenure at Calgene, Salquist began to develop relationships with state government. Working with Democratic and Republican leaders in the state assembly. Calgene participated in a study of the adequacy of the state's regulatory system for agricultural biotechnology. The resulting report concluded that the state regulatory system was sufficient. Salquist explained: "We had opened a dialog with [the bipartisan leaders], and they concluded that the economic growth potential was far more important than any theoretical risks."

The same basic approach was used at the federal level. Calgene's regulatory strategy was to develop relationships of trust with the government agencies responsible for product testing and approval. The two principal agencies were the USDA, which had approval authority over plants, and the FDA, which had authority over foods. The EPA also had regulatory authority over pollutants and toxins, such as pesticides and herbicides, that might be used in conjunction with plants.

The objectives of Calgene's regulatory strategy were to move products through the approval process and to avoid unneeded regulation of what Salquist referred to as "imaginary risks." Calgene attempted to make the regulators' job easier by providing all of its test data to the regulators. The implementation of this strategy involved activities at two levels. Salquist interacted with agency and center heads. The Director of Regulatory Affairs and Calgene scientists interacted directly with the regulatory and scientific staff involved in reviewing products and submissions. "We've never had a single rehearsal for our scientists. We've just developed a culture of honesty and openness and told people to go in and tell it like it is. On several occasions our scientists have gone in to make basic science presentations to the regulatory staff to bring them up to speed on the science as well as letting them know where Calgene is in its research," explained Salquist.

ACTIVISTS

The activists and interest groups opposing agricultural biotechnology included its longtime opponents and groups formed recently as genetically engineered products had moved closer to market. The activists' strategy was to raise public concerns about biotechnology and to work to prevent the products from reaching the market. In particular, they wanted cumbersome premarket approval and extensive labeling. The activists also attempted to spread fear on the part of consumers, some of whom were naturally nervous about genetic engineering.

Jeremy Rifkin and his Center for Economic Trends, which had only four employees, had opposed biotechnology for many years. His basic strategy focused on the general public and involved raising concerns about biotechnology and products under development. Rifkin was not a scientists, and part of his strategy was to be available to journalists who wanted a quote to add balance and controversy to a story.[4]

Activists had recently formed the Pure Food Campaign to oppose genetically engineered foods, and the campaign claimed to have attracted over 1,500 chefs. The Campaign argued that premarket approval should be required for genetically engineered foods, including testing for safety before they were allowed to be sold.[5] Rifkin enlisted the support of the Pure Food Campaign saying: "It's been an immense help for us. Chefs see themselves as stewards of the earth. They want healthy cuisine, good tasting food. Green politics and food go hand-in-hand, and food is on the cutting edge of green consciousness. The chefs provide legitimacy."[6] The next phase of Rifkin's strategy was to send "educational materials" to 140,000 school teachers nationwide and urge them to join a boycott.

Rifkin also directed his campaign against the customers for agricultural biotechnology products. Campbell Soup's banner "M'm! M'm! Good!" provided a natural opportunity. Rifkin wrote to Campbell Soup threatening to lead a boycott against it if it did not sever its relationship with Calgene. "Frankly, for us, Campbell is a more important target than Calgene," he said.[7] Campbell Soup replied that it had no plans to use bioengineered foods in its processed food. Campbell's contract research with Calgene had ended in the summer of 1992, and Campbell was evaluating the results. Rifkin announced that he would continue with the planned boycott until Campbell severed all ties with the biotechnology companies with which it had arrangements.

THE FOOD ADDITIVE DECISION

The decision to seek food additive approval of the marker gene was controversial within Calgene. First, it was not clear that approval was required, since under FDA regulations a substance that was generally recognized as safe (GRAS) did not require premarket approval.[8] Since the FDA had already ruled that the FLAVR SAVR was no different than a conventional tomato, it could presumably be declared as GRAS and marketed. Second, the filing could lead to a lengthy approval process that would apply broadly to genetically engineered foods and thus impact the agricultural biotechnology industry. Third, seeking approval as a food additive was exactly what the anti-biotechnology activists wanted. They hoped that requiring approval as a food additive would slow the introduction of bioengineered foods. Any delay in introducing the tomato would be costly because Calgene was already building a marketing organization and had contracted with growers for the first year's supply of tomatoes. Calgene had already submitted extensive test data on the gene, however, and it expected the FDA to make a decision in as few as 4 months.[9] Salquist explained his rationale for the decision: "We have elected to ask the FDA to formally apply the comprehensive standards of food additive review to our *kan*^{r} submission, because of continued misrepresentation of the scope and rigor of FDA review of new food products."[10]

The strategy of seeking food additive approval for its selectable marker gene received predictable reactions. A January 6, 1993, article in *The New York Times* began, "Bowing to pressure from consumer advocates and celebrity chefs, Calgene Inc. said today that it had asked the Food and Drug Administration formally to approve as a food additive a gene implanted in tomatoes to retard spoilage."[11] Other

---

[4]In addition to these groups, the Environmental Defense Fund and the National Wildlife Federation opposed the biotechnology industry. The National Wildlife Federation had produced a report, *Bitter Harvest,* which was critical of the industry.
[5]The FDA does not require a positive demonstration of safety through clinical trials for foods, but instead focuses on whether the food is any different from its natural counterpart. If it is different, the FDA could require food additive approval or could approve the food as equivalent to its natural counterpart.
[6]*The New York Times,* September 30, 1992.
[7]*The New York Times,* January 6, 1993.

[8]GRAS is "[a] designation of regulated food additives the FDA has determined are not harmful. If experts cannot agree whether an additive is safe, it is up to the manufacturer to prove that it is safe." Congressional Quarterly, *Federal Regulatory Directory,* 6th ed., Washington, D.C., 1990, p. 291.
[9]Calgene's research was published in Keith Redenbaugh et al., *Safety Assessment of Genetically Engineered Fruits and Vegetables,* CRC Press, Boca Raton, FL, 1992.
[10]Press Release, Calgene, Inc., January 4, 1993.
[11]*The New York Times* mistakenly referred to the PG gene rather than to the marker gene

observers, however, understood Calgene's submission quite differently: "I consider this shrewd," said James McCamant, editor of the *Agbiotech Stock Letter,* an industry newsletter. ■

This is an abridged version of a case prepared by Professor David P. Baron with the assistance of Justin Adams and Abraham Wu.

PREPARATION QUESTIONS

1. What are the issues, institutions, and interests that constitute Calgene's nonmarket environment and how are they related to its market environment? What role does information play? Identify the path of the FLAVR SAVR tomato through the nonmarket environment.
2. What are Roger Salquist's principal nonmarket activities?
3. How effective is Calgene's infrastructure marketing strategy? What, if anything, should be changed?
4. How well integrated are its market and nonmarket strategies?

PART II

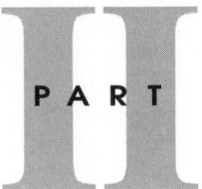

Nonmarket Strategies and Government Institutions

CHAPTER 5

Political Theory and Government Institutions

Introduction

This chapter provides foundations for the study of nonmarket activity that takes place in the context of public institutions. The institutional focus is legislatures, and in particular Congress, as arenas in which the nonmarket strategies of firms and other interests are implemented. Other public institutions, including regulatory agencies, antitrust agencies, and the courts, are considered in Part III of the book, and institutions in China, Japan, and Europe are considered in Part IV.

This chapter is both conceptual and institutional. The conceptual subjects include the role of markets, the relationship between markets and incentives for nonmarket action, collective action and the free-rider problem, social and political dilemmas, and characteristics of majority rule systems. The institutional focus is on the organization of Congress, the legislative process, committees, political behavior, parties, the executive branch, and the courts.

Markets

THE ROLE AND FUNCTIONING OF MARKETS

Markets are the principal institutions through which resources are allocated and firms interact with those in their environment. Goods and services are exchanged voluntarily in markets based on a system of property rights that entitles the participants to the benefits from their exchanges. The basic presumption is thus that market transactions make those who participate in them better off. That is, because they exchange property rights, market participants have incentives to make their transactions purposefully and to their advantage. Some markets may fail to exist and others may fail to perform efficiently because of economies of scale, asymmetric information, and externalities, as considered in Part III.

The focus in this section is on efficient, competitive markets for undifferentiated products in which no participant need take into account the decisions of other market participants. That is, firms take market prices as given and base their decisions on the incentives provided by the opportunity to transact at the market price. Similarly, consumers take the market price as given in making their purchase decisions. The equilibrium market price equates supply and demand, and since the supply function represents the cost of the resources expended to produce the marginal unit exchanged, the market price equals that marginal cost. The market price thus informs buyers and sellers of the cost of society's resources expended in supplying the marginal unit, and the market decisions of consumers and producers determine the allocation of society's resources.

The allocation of resources is evaluated using the concept of Pareto optimality. An allocation is Pareto optimal if there is no other feasible allocation such that all market participants are at least as well off and at least one is strictly better off, evaluated in terms of their preferences. Pareto optimality may be viewed as a necessary condition for market efficiency, and a fundamental theorem of economics is that every competitive market equilibrium is Pareto optimal. Thus, at the equilibrium price there is no additional economic transaction that could make any individual better off without making another worse off.

Pareto optimality pertains only to efficiency and not to the distributive consequences of market competition. An individual with a small endowment of human capital or other resources may fare poorly in a competitive market compared with a better-endowed individual. Similarly, a firm with inefficient production facilities may fare poorly relative to a more efficient firm. The distributive consequences of market competition are a principal source of incentives for nonmarket action, as considered in the following section.

Markets may be imperfectly competitive because of product differentiation, the technological characteristics of production, or barriers to entry that limit the number of firms in the industry. Markets may also be temporally imperfect as the dynamics of innovation and technological change create advantages for some firms and disadvantages for others. Continual technological improvement sustains the advantages garnered by companies such as Intel and Microsoft. In these cases, firms can affect market prices and opportunities, and they will take into account the strategies of other firms in choosing their own strategies. The field of strategic management is concerned with the interactions between the strategies of firms in imperfectly competitive markets.[1]

CONSUMER SURPLUS AND ECONOMIC RENTS

Distributive consequences occur on both the demand and the supply sides of a market. A market, or industry, demand function represents the amount of a good or service consumers are willing to purchase at a given price or, conversely, the amount consumers are willing to pay for an incremental unit of the good. The area labeled *CS* in Figure 5-1 is the surplus, or benefits, that consumers in the aggregate obtain when they purchase a quantity q^o of a good at a price p^o and have willingnesses to pay represented by the height of the demand curve *D*. A decrease in the price would increase the surplus, so consumers have an incentive to engage in both market and nonmarket activity to increase or protect their surplus.[2]

A supply function represents the marginal cost of producing a unit of a good. Supply functions can be short run or long run depending on whether the factors of production are fixed or varied. A long-run supply function reflects the marginal costs of production when all factors of production can be varied in the most efficient manner. A short-run supply function corresponds to a time period for which some factors, such as plant capacity and capital equipment, are fixed and other factors, such as labor and materials, can be varied. If all factors of production are variable and the markets for all factors of production are competitive, marginal and average costs are equal and the long-run supply curve (*LRS*) is horizontal, as illustrated in Figure 5-1. In a market equilibrium then, the price *p* equals marginal (and average) cost, so producers earn only normal profits—profits just sufficient to cover the cost of capital, which is included in the supply function.

---

[1]See Besanko, Dranove, and Shanley (1996), Oster (1994), Porter (1980, 1985), and Saloner, Podolny, and Shepard (2000).

[2]The measurement of changes in consumer surplus as a function of the price is complex because of income effects and because prices of other goods may change. The presentation here abstracts from these considerations.

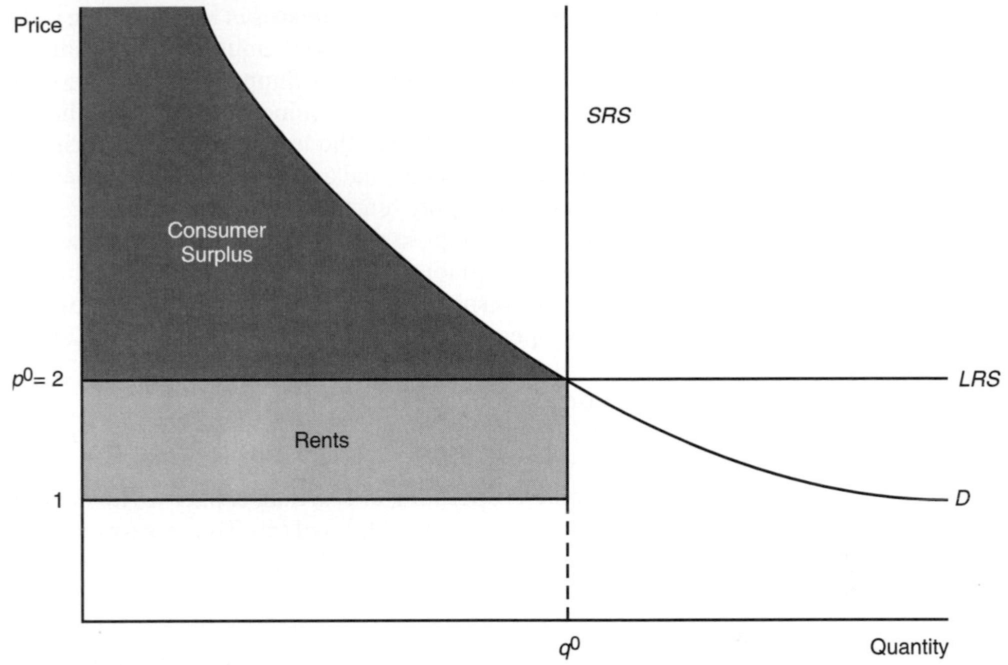

FIGURE 5–1 Long-Run Market Equilibrium

Nonmarket activity takes place in the short run as well as the long run, and firms earn economic rents on their fixed factors of production. An economic rent is the difference between the price at which a unit of production can be sold and the price that is just sufficient to induce the producer to supply that unit.[3] The latter price is given by the height of the short-term supply function, which represents the marginal cost of those factors of production that can be varied. If the costs associated with the fixed factors are sunk, the rents equal the cash flow to the producers. The difference between economic rents and accounting profits is due to depreciation, amortization, and other expenses associated with the fixed factors.

As an example, consider the nonmarket issue of mandating scrubbers for new coal-fired electric power plants to reduce sulfur dioxide emissions, as addressed in the Chapter 6 case *Scrubbers and Environmental Politics.* Since they remove sulfur dioxide from emissions, mandating scrubbers allows high-sulfur eastern coal to be burned in power plants in the East and Midwest. If scrubbers were not mandated, many of those power plants would burn low-sulfur western coal. Mandating scrubbers thus would reduce the demand for low-sulfur coal mined in the West and increase the demand for high-sulfur coal mined in the East. Suppose that in the absence of a mandate the eastern coal industry was in long-run equilibrium. That is, price and output are determined by the intersection of the demand function and the long-run supply function. Suppose that the long-run supply (*LRS*) function is horizontal as illustrated in Figure 5-1. The equilibrium market price is denoted by p^0, and the quantity q^0 produced in equilibrium is equal to the capacity in the industry.

---

[3]In an imperfectly competitive market, rents are defined in an analogous manner. The analysis of the demand side is the same but more complex when, for example, products are differentiated and other dimensions of competition become important. In an imperfectly competitive market, there is no supply curve, and rents are defined in terms of cash flow.

Mandating scrubbers has consequences in both the long run and the short run. Consider first the long run. The eastern coal industry is labor-intensive and has sunk costs in terms of mine shafts and equipment. Suppose the technology in the industry involves only two factor inputs: labor and the mine itself (i.e., the shafts and equipment). Also, suppose that each represents half the total cost. More specifically, assume that it takes $1 of labor to produce 1 ton of coal and it takes $100 to open a mine with a capacity of 100 tons. The long-run supply function is thus located at $2, and $2 is also the industry price p^0 in Figure 5-1. Suppose that the cost of the mine itself is sunk and already paid for but that labor is variable; that is, workers can be laid off or hired if demand decreases or increases, respectively. In the case of a coal company with one mine with 100 tons of capacity, operating at capacity yields revenue of $200 and labor costs of $100. The company thus has a rent, which equals its cash flow, of $100. The rents *R* for the industry are illustrated in Figure 5-1.

To determine the short-run supply function (*SRS*), consider the question, "What price of coal would be required to bring an additional ton of coal into production?" Suppose that the mine is operating at less than capacity. The answer is $1, since only labor has to be hired to produce an additional ton. The short-run marginal cost is thus $1, and this is the short-run supply function for the industry, as illustrated in Figure 5-1. As indicated by the vertical line, an increase in output above the capacity of 100 is impossible in the short run, so the short-run marginal cost becomes infinite. Note that the short run supply function intersects the long-run supply function and the demand function at the long-run equilibrium.

The issue in the scrubbers case resulted from more stringent environmental standards that required reductions in sulfur dioxide emissions. If scrubbers were not mandated, the new environmental standard would shift demand from eastern to western coal. Consider a shift to the left from *D* to D^1 in the demand function for eastern coal due to a required reduction in emissions. As indicated in Figure 5-2, the price falls to

FIGURE 5-2 Market Equilibrium and a Shift in Demand

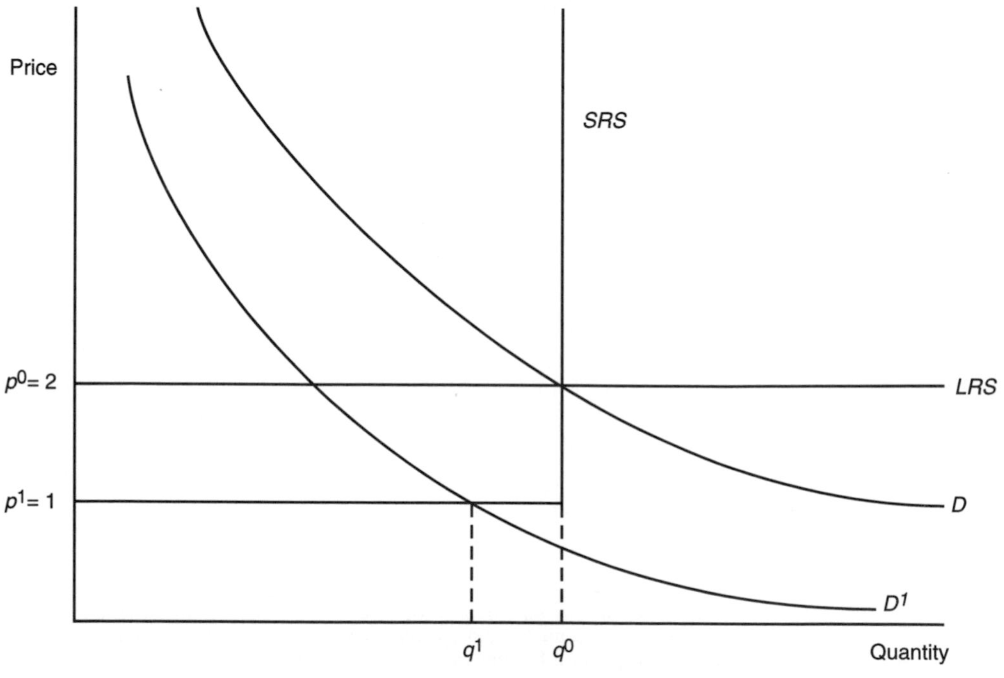

$p^1 = \$1$ and output falls to q^1. Workers are laid off, and coal companies have lost all their rents, because the price of a ton of coal has fallen to the cost of the labor used to produce it. The revenue of a coal company that now produces 80 tons is \$80 and its labor costs are \$80.[4]

If Congress were to mandate scrubbers, the power plants in the East and Midwest would continue to burn eastern coal. Mandating scrubbers thus would prevent a shift in demand from D to D^1 and would preserve the rents being earned by the eastern mines. The incentive to take political action in support of mandating scrubbers arises from preserving these rents. The coal companies have an incentive to seek mandatory scrubbers to prevent the shift in demand and hence retain their rents; and workers, who are represented by the United Mine Workers, have an incentive to retain their jobs.

The Connection between the Market and Nonmarket Environments

THE DEMAND FOR NONMARKET ACTION

This section addresses the relationship between the distributive consequences in the market environment and actions in the nonmarket environment. Interest groups and firms act in the nonmarket environment to affect surpluses and rents. Their actions include lobbying, coalition building, grassroots campaigns, testimony in hearings, and electoral support. These actions affect the outcomes of nonmarket issues, such as whether to mandate scrubbers, which can affect both demand and supply and hence surpluses and rents. In the example considered at the end of the chapter, a number of firms recognized that if daylight-saving time were extended the demand curve for their industries would shift outwards, thereby increasing their rents. Not only would the rents of the firms increase, but the higher output would result in increased employment and higher wages if the labor supply curve were upward-sloping. The rents associated with shifting the demand function provided incentives to firms, labor, and other factors of production to take nonmarket action to obtain an extension of daylight-saving time. The effects on surpluses and rents thus generate a demand for nonmarket action.[5]

A demand for nonmarket action arises not only from the possibility of shifting the demand function outward but also from preventing a shift to the left as in the example in Figure 5-2. Pharmaceutical firms with patented drugs had a demand for nonmarket action to prevent changes in Food and Drug Administration (FDA) regulations to allow generic drugs to be marketed at an earlier date than allowed by existing regulations. A demand for nonmarket action can also arise on the supply side of a market. Pharmaceutical firms worked to accelerate the FDA drug approval process to lower their costs and increase rents. The incentives for nonmarket action thus can come from both the demand and supply sides of a market.

Consumers also have a demand for nonmarket action. Economic theory indicates that protection from imports results in a loss to consumers that exceeds the gains to producers. This, however, does not imply that consumers will take more nonmarket action to oppose protectionism than firms and labor will take to obtain it, since consumers typically have high costs of taking nonmarket action. Because of the costs of nonmarket action, the demand for nonmarket action does not translate directly into realized action.

---

[4]In the long run if demand remained at D^1, mines would be closed, and capacity would be reduced to q^1.

[5]Baron (1997)(1999) provides formal models of the relationship between nonmarket action and rents generated in markets in the contexts of the Chapter 16 case *The Kodak-Fujifilm Trade Dispute* and the Chapter 8 case *CAFE Standards.*

THE COSTS OF NONMARKET ACTION

Pluralist theories predict that common interests, such as those that result from a potential increase in consumer surplus, lead to outcomes consistent with those interests. These demand-side theories draw implications about the outcomes of nonmarket activity directly from the interests of individuals and firms, as measured by surpluses and rents. Olson (1965), however, argued that such theories ignore the costs of undertaking nonmarket and collective action and that those costs are an important determinant of the effectiveness of those with common interests.[6] The higher those costs, the less nonmarket action is taken and therefore the less effective they are in realizing their interests.

Demand-side theory predicts that the greater the demand of those with common interests the more likely they are to prevail in a political arena. Taxpayers have common interests in lower taxes, and consumers have common interests in lower prices. With some exceptions, however, neither taxpayers nor consumers have been particularly effective in legislative politics, in part because their costs of undertaking collective action are high relative to the per capita benefits they would receive.[7] The (per capita) benefits for an individual consumer from eliminating sugar import quotas thus may be outweighed by the costs of taking nonmarket action. Large groups thus may have a high demand for political action, but their costs of taking action can also be high. Therefore, common or aligned interests do not translate directly into political outcomes but instead are mediated by the costs of nonmarket and collective action.

THE FREE-RIDER PROBLEM AND COLLECTIVE ACTION

The costs of nonmarket action can be reduced by joining together in collective action. On many nonmarket issues, a firm's interests are aligned with the interests of other firms, labor, or other groups. With an alignment of interests, collective action is possible. Outcomes of nonmarket issues, however, have an important property that affects the amount of collective action generated. Outcomes have the property of a public good when they pertain to everyone, regardless of whether they took action to realize that outcome. For example, an outcome such as prevention of a shift in demand, as illustrated in Figure 5-2, benefits all firms in the industry regardless of whether they contributed to obtaining that outcome. When the benefits from nonmarket action accrue to those who do not contribute, a free-rider problem is present.[8]

To illustrate this problem, consider the case of an industry such as steel that seeks protection from imports. An individual firm will participate in the collective action if the cost c of its participation is less than the benefits it receives from its effort. Suppose that the action of any one firm yields benefits b to each of the n firms in the industry, for a total benefit of nb. If all n firms contributed to the collective action, the total benefits would be n^2b, which corresponds to the increase in rents in the industry. The benefits to an individual firm would be n^2b divided by n or nb. Consequently, whenever $nb > c$, each firm is better off when all firms participate in the collective action. In this case, it is collectively rational for all firms to contribute to the collective action.

What is collectively rational, however, may not be individually rational. An individual firm has an incentive to participate in the collective action only if the cost c it incurs is less than the benefits it receives from its own participation, and those benefits are only b. Consequently, if $c > b$, an individual firm has no incentive to participate even when its participation produces collective benefits to the industry that exceed its costs

[6]Also, see Moe (1980) and Hardin (1982).
[7]This does not mean that the interests of taxpayers and consumers are not reflected in political outcomes. Their interest can be represented by political officeholders, who can claim credit for having done so.
[8]See Shepsle and Boncheck (1997) for an introduction to collective action.

(i.e., $c < nb$). If $c > b$, the firm thus prefers to free ride on the efforts of the other firms, since doing so saves it the cost c and it loses only the benefits b from its own contribution. Each firm thus has an incentive to free ride, and the possibility of collective action is in doubt. The free-ride problem is present when $b < c < nb$.

The larger the number of potential participants, the more serious is the free-rider problem, and large groups such as consumers and taxpayers have difficulty overcoming the problem. Therefore, large groups must develop means to induce participation. One means of doing so is to provide selective benefits that can be denied to those who do not participate. The largest organized interest group in the United States is the American Association of Retired Persons (AARP), which has a membership of over 30 million. AARP is politically active on a variety of issues of concern to its members, and it attracts members in part by providing selective benefits to them. AARP, for example, offers members discount prices on pharmaceuticals and supplemental health insurance, as well as discounts on travel and accommodations.

Labor unions also face a free-ride problem in obtaining contributions from members to undertake political activities. The unions have solved this collective action problem by obtaining legislation that requires mandatory dues for everyone in a collective bargaining unit, and a portion of those dues is used for political action such as support for candidates in federal and state elections.[9]

In summary, those with aligned interests on an issue have an incentive to take nonmarket action, and the stronger is that incentive the more action will be taken, other things being equal. Other things are not always equal, however. In particular, the costs of taking nonmarket action can exceed the benefits, resulting in no collective action. Interests thus have an incentive to organize to reduce those costs. Large groups have the greatest potential for collective nonmarket action but may be plagued by the free-rider problem. Large groups thus attempt to provide selective benefits to induce participation in collective action. Small groups have lower costs of organizing and often have an easier time punishing or excluding those who do not participate, as considered in the following section. The chapter case *Repeal of the Luxury Tax* provides an opportunity to consider which interests will be active on a nonmarket issue.

Social and Political Dilemmas

As the free-rider problem indicates, certain dilemmas can be difficult to resolve. The characteristic of these dilemmas is that what is individually rational may not be collectively rational. This section examines the nature of these dilemmas and considers how repeated encounters can resolve some of them.

THE PRISONERS' DILEMMA

The prisoners' dilemma is a situation in which each player individually has a dominant strategy, but if each used that strategy, each would be worse off than if they cooperated to their mutual benefit. An example of a prisoners' dilemma is presented in Figure 5-3. Players 1 and 2 each have two possible actions, *A* and *B*, and they each choose their actions simultaneously. The entries in the cells are the benefits to players 1 and 2, respectively. For example, if player 1 chooses *A* and player 2 chooses *B*, then player 1 receives –1 and player 2 receives 4.

[9]Union members can file a statement each year to take back the portion of their dues that would go to political action.

		Player 2	
		A	B
Player 1	A	2,2	−1,3
	B	3,−1	0,0

FIGURE 5-3 A Prisoners' Dilemma

To determine which actions the players will choose, note that for whichever action player 2 were to choose, player 1's benefit from action *B* is higher than that with *A*. That is, if player 2 were to choose *A*, player 1 would receive 2 if she chose *A* and 3 if she chose *B*. Similarly, if player 2 were to choose *B* player 1 would receive –1 if she chose *A* or 0 if she chose *B*. Consequently, *B* is a dominant strategy for player 1 because it yields higher payoffs regardless of the action player 1 takes. The same reasoning implies that *B* is a dominant strategy for player 2. Each player thus chooses *B*. The outcome (0, 0) from these strategies, however, is strictly worse than the outcome (2, 2) if both players were to choose *A*. The dilemma is that it is individually rational for each player to choose *B*, but it is collectively rational for both to play *A*.[10] Individual rationality and collective rationality are thus not the same. As long as this game is played only once and the two players take individual actions, not even communication between the players can resolve the dilemma. Even if the players promise to each take *A*, each has an incentive to deviate and take *B*. Promises are thus likely to be viewed with skepticism.

A variety of business and social situations have the characteristics of a prisoners' dilemma including price wars, defection from certain agreements such as a cartel, the choice of protectionism or free trade by individual countries, the choice of subsidizing or not subsidizing exports, and the overuse of common resources. The free-rider problem is a version of the prisoners' dilemma, where, for example, in Figure 5-3 each player's nonmarket action (*A*) costs $c = 4$ and provides benefits $b = 3$ to each player. The chapter cases, *An Electoral Dilemma (A)(B)*), illustrate a dilemma and one means of addressing it.

DILEMMAS, REPEATED ENCOUNTERS, AND COOPERATION

In markets, participants can write contracts that allow a third party, such as a court, to enforce their promised actions by punishing deviations. In the case of most nonmarket issues, however, third-party enforcement is either impossible or impractical. Agreements in political arenas, for example, typically are not enforceable because political rights cannot be transferred or alienated.

One possibility for resolving dilemmas is cooperation in which each party takes into account not only the consequences of actions for himself or herself but for the other parties as well. Cooperation in this case is mutual altruism. In the context of the prisoners' dilemma in Figure 5-3, cooperation would involve both players recognizing that in the aggregate they are better off by choosing *A* rather than *B*. In this situation, however, there is no compelling reason to believe that the players would actually cooperate. Once they have agreed to do so, it remains a dominant strategy to choose *B*.

---

[10]The prisoners' dilemma received its name from describing the players as prisoners arrested for a crime the police know they committed together. The police, however, only have evidence to convict them on minor charges resulting in a short sentence. The police thus offer each prisoner a deal in which each can provide (B) or not provide (A) evidence against the other prisoner. If a prisoner provides evidence and the other does not, the former prisoner is offered the minimum sentence and the latter is given the maximum sentence. If both provide evidence, both receive the maximum sentence. If neither provides evidence, both sentences are short. It is then a dominant strategy for each to give evidence against the other, resulting in long sentences for each.

That is, once they go to take their individual actions, each recognizes that there is an incentive to defect from the cooperative agreement. Recognizing that player 2 has a dominant strategy of choosing *B,* player 1 is likely to worry about whether player 2 will actually play *A.* Once player 1 harbors some doubt about whether player 2 will choose *A,* the choice of *B* by player 1 becomes even more compelling. Such doubts can lead to the play of *B* by each player.

This reasoning suggests that prisoners' dilemmas are difficult to resolve, yet many are resolved. These resolutions often occur because the prisoners' dilemma is not encountered only once, but instead is repeated. In that case, players have a stake in the future, and the set of strategies that players can employ is much broader. A player can, for example, reward or punish the other player for the choice made in the previous round. A player can adopt a "tit-for-tat" strategy in which she plays *A* in the first round and thereafter plays what the other player played in the previous round. When the game is played repeatedly, the outcome (2, 2) in Figure 5-3 can be attained. These punishment and reward strategies are self-enforcing—they constitute an equilibrium and do not require an agreement enforceable by a third party.[11] The self-enforcement occurs because each player finds it in his or her interest to play *A* in each round, as long as both played *A* in the past. If one chooses *B,* the other can play *B* for a long time as punishment. The long-term loss thus exceeds the short-term gain from playing *B,* and hence each player has an individual incentive to play *A.*[12] In employing these strategies, the players do not include the interests of the other party in their reasoning about how to play, so altruism is not involved. This type of resolution of the prisoners' dilemma is thus noncooperative rather than cooperative.

Behavior such as that generated by repeated play can be facilitated by the creation of an institution to punish deviations from the mutually beneficial actions. The World Trade Organization was created to lower trade barriers for the mutual benefit of its members and is equipped with a dispute resolution and punishment mechanism to deal with deviations from the agreed-to trading rules. Similarly, firms that will repeatedly participate in nonmarket action on a series of issues on which their interests are aligned may be able to solve the free-rider problem by forming an association that can monitor and punish any free riding.

Majority Rule-Based Institutions

PROPERTIES OF MAJORITY RULE

A unanimity rule—a rule that requires the consent of all parties before a decision can be implemented—governs interactions such as market exchange, in which property rights are well defined and in which it is reasonable to allow individuals to make voluntary decisions. In some cases, however, a unanimity rule is either impractical or impossible. For example, if voluntary contributions rather than mandatory taxes were relied on to finance government programs, the free-rider problem would be pervasive. In these situations, the rules used to reach decisions require less than unanimous agreement. Those rules include both the simple majority rule used in committees and New England town meetings and the complex set of rules that govern lawmaking in the federal government.

---

[11]See Dixit and Nalebuff (1991) for a discussion of such strategies in a repeated setting in which information and observability are imperfect.

[12]This reasoning requires that the game be repeated infinitely often, since if it is repeated only a finite number of times, the equilibrium unravels from the last round. That is, in the last round both players have dominant strategies of playing *B,* and given that, each has a dominant strategy of playing *B* in the next-to-last round, and so on.

Although majority-rule institutions have desirable features, they can result in reductions in aggregate well-being and in outcomes that may be contrary to majority preferences. Protection from imports, for example, generally results in higher prices and lower aggregate well-being, as measured by consumers' surplus and producers' rents. Yet the United States continues to protect industries such as textiles, shoes, and sugar. If put to a vote in a public referendum, this protection would likely be rejected by voters because there are many more losers than winners. In majority-rule institutions, however, some industries that can effectively organize collective action have been able to obtain and maintain protection.

ARROW'S IMPOSSIBILITY THEOREM AND POLITICAL INSTITUTIONS

In one of the most important accomplishments in the social sciences, Kenneth Arrow (1963) demonstrated that it is generally impossible to design institutions that aggregate the diverse preferences of individuals in a manner consistent with a set of reasonable conditions. This impossibility theorem has a variety of implications for public institutions and hence for strategies for addressing nonmarket issues.

Arrow asked whether it is possible to design institutions that, using the preferences of individuals, can select social alternatives or public policies in a manner consistent with a minimal set of conditions that any institution should possess. Those institutions include simple majority rule as used in New England town meetings, a strong executive system in which an executive has veto power over a majority-rule legislature, a parliamentary system in which a government continues in office until the next election or until it loses a vote of confidence, or a governance arrangement for a condominium. To simplify the exposition, the institution of simple (50 percent) majority rule will be considered.

Suppose there are three individuals (1, 2, and 3) and three social alternatives (*A, B,* and *C*). Suppose also that the configuration of preference orderings of the individuals is as given in Figure 5-4, where, for example, individual 1 prefers *A* to *B, B* to *C,* and *A* to *C.* When each alternative is paired against each of the other alternatives under majority rule, *A* defeats *B* by a vote of 2 to 1, *B* defeats *C* by a vote of 2 to 1, and *C* defeats *A* by a vote of 2 to 1. Each alternative thus defeats one alternative but is defeated by another. Majority rule thus is incapable of choosing an alternative. That is, majority rule cannot aggregate the preferences of these individuals to select a social alternative.

This paradox, due to Condorcet (1785), illustrates the fundamental problem Arrow examined. Arrow showed that for any institution satisfying certain reasonable conditions there is some configuration of individual preferences such that the institution yields no consistent choice, as in the Condorcet paradox.[13]

Agendas

One implication of Arrow's impossibility theorem is that in an actual institution there may be an opportunity to act strategically to obtain an outcome an individual prefers. For example, with the preferences in Figure 5-4 suppose that individual 1 is an agenda setter and can specify the order in which a legislature will vote on the set of alternatives. Suppose individual 1 sets the agenda in Figure 5-5 in which *A* is first voted against *C* and then the winner is voted against *B.* In their voting, the three individuals will recognize that since in the second stage the winner of the first vote will be voted against *B,* the outcome will be *B* if *C* is the winner of the first vote and will be *A* if the winner of the first vote is *A.* These winners are denoted by the circled alternatives in

[13]Some of Arrow's conditions have been criticized, and several alternative conditions have been proposed; however, they all yield conclusions similar to his impossibility theorem.

1	*2*	*3*
A	*B*	*C*
B	*C*	*A*
C	*A*	*B*

FIGURE 5-4 Condorcet's Paradox

Figure 5-5. Consequently, the first vote is actually a vote between an outcome of *A* and an outcome of *B*. Both individuals 1 and 3 prefer *A* to *B* and thus will vote for *A* on the first vote. Then, on the second vote, 1 and 3 will vote for *A* over *B* yielding *A* as the winner. The agenda setter in this case obtains the alternative that he or she most prefers. It is straightforward to show that the other two possible agendas formed from the three alternatives yield *B* and *C* as the outcomes.

This example should not be interpreted as implying that agenda setters regularly manipulate legislative agenda. An agenda setter who acts against the preferences of a majority can always be replaced. Instead, the example indicates that a simple institutional structure, in this case an agenda, can result in a social choice. That choice, however, depends on which agenda is used, and Arrow's impossibility theorem applies to the choice of an agenda. That is, there is no consistent method for choosing among the three agendas.

THE MEDIAN VOTER THEOREM

The impossibility theorem implies that if there are to be consistent social choices, the social choice problem must satisfy more restrictive conditions than Arrow imposes. An agenda is one such condition, since it imposes a specific order in which votes will be taken. Another condition is when the alternatives can be arrayed on one dimension. For example, the alternatives may be spending on a government program, the stringency of an environmental standard, or the patent duration for pharmaceuticals. If (1) the alternatives are one-dimensional, (2) the decision-making process is open so that all alternatives can be considered, and (3) the preferences of those voting are such that each has a most-preferred alternative or ideal point and prefers alternatives closer to rather than farther away from that ideal point, then the outcome is the median of the ideal points. The median ideal point will receive at least a majority of votes against any alternative to either its left or its right, since including the median, there is a majority of voters on

FIGURE 5-5 A Voting Agenda

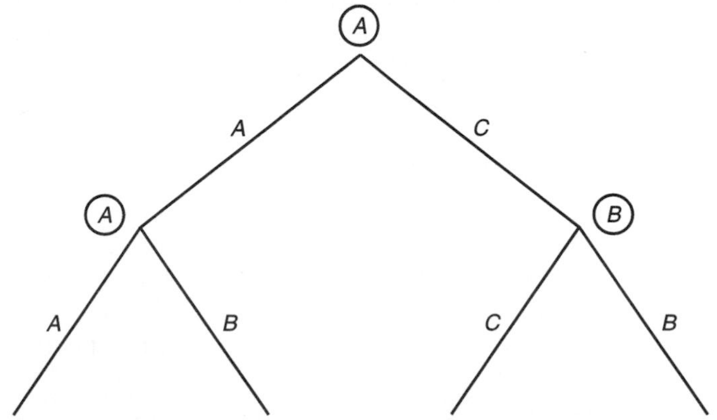

one side or the other that will defeat any other alternative. The logic of this theorem is explored further in the context of the daylight saving time example considered at the end of the chapter.

The median voter theorem is powerful because it is only necessary to know voters' ideal points and not their entire preference ordering. Moreover, if the median ideal point is known, it is not necessary to know the exact location of the other ideal points. Although the median voter theorem does not extend to alternatives in more than one dimension, related results suggest that outcomes are likely to be close to the intersection of the medians on each dimension.

The median voter theorem is a useful tool for analyzing legislative behavior in an open process because if the issue under consideration is one-dimensional and the ideal points of the members of a legislature can be estimated, the outcome can be predicted. Representatives' ideal points are not directly observable, but information on them can be obtained by examining their voting records. Interest groups analyze roll-call votes on issues on their agenda and provide scores for each member of Congress. The League of Conservation Voters provides ratings based on how members of Congress voted on environmental issues. Similarly, Americans for Democratic Action, the Chamber of Commerce, and the American Federation of State, County and Municipal Employees (AFSCME), a union with 1.3 million members, provide ratings based on issues important to them.[14] These ratings are used by analysts as an indicator of the relative location of the ideal points of members of Congress on policy dimensions.[15] The 1996 ratings of these four groups for Senate majority leader Trent Lott (R-MS) and House minority leader Richard Gephardt (D-MO) are:

	LEAGUE OF CONSERVATION VOTERS	AFSCME	CHAMBER OF COMMERCE	AMERICANS FOR DEMOCRATIC ACTION
Lott	0	0	85	5
Gephardt	85	100	27	85

COMMITTEES IN LEGISLATURES

Arrow's impossibility theorem pertains to a situation in which all alternatives are simultaneously compared with, or paired against, all other alternatives. The structure and rules of a political institution can, however, restrict the alternatives that are paired against each other. Legislatures have a committee structure, and each committee can bring to the floor of the legislature only bills in its jurisdiction. Also, amendments may be restricted by the rules under which a legislature operates. In the House of Representatives, a germaneness rule requires amendments to be germane to the policy issue addressed by the bill under consideration. A committee structure and amendment rules can limit the set of alternatives under consideration and yield determinate outcomes, which means that committees play a strategic role in the legislative process and hence are a focus of nonmarket action.

[14]For each member of Congress, the *Almanac of American Politics 1998,* (Barone and Ujifusa, 1997) lists ratings by the following organizations: Consumer Federation of America, League of Conservation Voters, Americans for Democratic Action, Chamber of Commerce, American Federation of State, County and Municipal Employees, Concord Coalition, National Federation of Independent Business, Christian Coalition, National Tax Limitation Committee, American Civil Liberties Union, and American Conservative Union. Each of these groups selects a different set of issues on which to score a member of Congress, so the ratings are not necessarily on comparable issues. Similarly, the issues differ form year to year.

[15]The ratings for the two chambers are not directly comparable because the two chambers do not necessarily have roll-call votes on the same issues.

BARGAINING VERSUS VOTING

Bargaining is used to reach an outcome in situations in which individuals have conflicting interests. When outcomes are governed by a unanimity rule, bargaining is an alternative to arm's-length market transactions. Bargaining, for example, is used in arranging mergers and acquisitions, whereas a tender offer as part of a hostile takeover attempt is an example of an arm's-length transaction. Bargaining also occurs in majority-rule institutions such as legislatures.[16] The instruments of that bargaining may be the trading of a vote on one bill for a vote on another bill or the exchange of favors among legislators. Bargaining takes place within committees, within a chamber, and between chambers. Bargaining also occurs between the Congress and the president, as when reaching a budget agreement. Bargaining is intended to achieve mutual gains relative to what would result in the absence of an agreement. The bargaining outcome reflects the alternatives and opportunities available to the parties and the threats that they may credibly employ. The president has bargaining power on the budget because of the veto.

VOTE TRADING AND PIVOTAL VOTERS

Vote trading involves legislators exchanging support on one bill for support on another. The legislators who are the most willing to trade away their votes on an issue are those who care the least about it. For example, a legislator may be willing to trade a vote on an issue that does not matter to his or her constituents in return for support on an issue that does matter. One political strategy of a firm or interest group, then, is to encourage vote trades. Although one would expect that vote trading would be prevalent in legislatures, there is little systematic evidence demonstrating its presence, suggesting that constituent concerns may be primary on many important issues.

The logic of the constituency connection also implies that attention should be directed not at legislators whose votes are set but instead at pivotal voters who are close to being indifferent among alternatives. Lobbying and other information provision activities as well as vote trading often focus on pivotal voters. In a world with no uncertainty, only enough votes would be obtained in this manner to achieve a minimal majority. The first legislative success of the Clinton administration was the Budget Reconciliation Act of 1993, which passed the House by a vote of 218 to 216 and the Senate by 51 to 50 with Vice President Gore casting the deciding vote. The administration and the Democratic leadership of Congress had made concessions to just enough members to obtain passage. Lobbying, vote trading, and pivotal voters are considered in more detail in Chapters 7 and 8.

Institutions

The institutional features of the U.S. government include a system of checks and balances among the branches of government and a complex process for the enactment, administration, and enforcement of laws. To enact legislation, a majority of those members present in each chamber of Congress must pass the identical bill, and the president must sign it. If he vetoes it, two-thirds of the members of each chamber in Congress may override the veto. The law then may have to withstand legal challenge on constitutional or other grounds.

---

[16]See Baron and Ferejohn (1989) for a theory of bargaining in legislatures.

Once a law is enacted, it must be administered by a regulatory or administrative agency. These agencies operate under procedures specified by the Administrative Procedure Act of 1946 and by their enabling legislation and their own rule making. These procedures require advanced notice of proposed rule making, opportunities for public comment, and in some cases, public hearings. The rulings and decisions of these agencies then may be subject to judicial review. The courts are independent and operate under jurisdictions established in the Constitution, and they are guided by the Constitution, enacted legislation, and precedents established by prior decisions.

Knowledge of the structure and procedures of these institutions is crucial to the development of successful strategies for addressing nonmarket issues in the arenas of government institutions. This section focuses on legislation with an emphasis on Congress and the executive branch. Administrative, regulatory, and judicial institutions are considered in Part III of this book.

CONGRESS

Congress considers a wide variety of nonmarket issues. In addition to enacting legislation, Congress exercises influence over government agencies and bureaus through its oversight activities. In addition, the Senate must confirm presidential appointees to the judiciary, high-ranking executive branch appointments, and ambassadors. Congress is restrained in its activities by the Constitution, by the president's authority to veto legislation, and ultimately by the electorate. In addition to their legislative activities, members of Congress pressure administrative officeholders and interests through hearings and other oversight activities, as illustrated by the hearings held on employee health insurance provided by fast-food restaurant chains considered in Chapter 4. Because of its importance, interest groups direct much of their attention to Congress and its members.

Prior to 1994, a striking characteristic of Congress was the high rate at which incumbents who ran for reelection were successful. In the November 1990 elections only 15 of the 406 House members who ran for reelection were defeated; in the two previous elections, the number was only half as large. Only one incumbent senator was defeated in 1990. This incumbency advantage was due to several factors including franking privileges (allowing free mailings to constituents), name recognition (important because voters are uninformed about issues), seniority on committees (enabling them to provide better constituency services), and the ability to raise campaign funds.

In 1994 a major change in the composition of Congress occurred as a result of voter anger with the Clinton administration and the Democrats, who had controlled both the House and Senate with substantial majorities. Republicans won a majority in both the House of Representatives and the Senate and held that majority through the rest of the decade.

THE ORGANIZATION OF CONGRESS

The Congress is bicameral. The House of Representatives is composed of 435 voting members serving 2-year terms and elected from districts with approximately the same population.[17] The ten largest states account for half the members, whereas Alaska, Delaware, North Dakota, South Dakota, Vermont, and Wyoming have only one representative each. House districts are reapportioned after each census, and as a result of

---

[17]Representatives from the District of Columbia, American Samoa, Guam, Puerto Rico, and the Virgin Islands are members of the House and can vote in committees but not on the floor.

the 1990 census the West and the South gained 19 seats at the expense of the Northeast and the Midwest. The Speaker is the presiding officer of the House and is selected by the majority party and elected by the entire House.

The Senate has two senators from each of the 50 states, each serving a 6-year term. States with a small population thus have relatively more weight in the Senate, and states with large populations have relatively more weight in the House. The vice president presides over the Senate and has a vote when a tie occurs.

The Constitution specifies neither how the chambers are to be organized nor how they are to conduct their business. Over time, they have developed their own formal and informal organizational structures and procedures. The formal organization is detailed in the committee structure and the legislative process. The informal organization is found in the party organization within the chambers. Each party elects a leader, whips, a secretary of the party conference, and heads of policy and steering committees. The primary responsibility of the whips is to generate party discipline on those issues on which the party has taken a position. Although parties and the party organization of Congress are important, members have considerable latitude in their voting, and party discipline is not the rule.

THE LEGISLATIVE PROCESS[18]

Over 4,500 bills were introduced in the House and over 2,200 in the Senate during the 104th Congress (1995–1996), yet the number of laws enacted was about 600.[19] Many bills are introduced with little expectation that they will even be considered, and some are introduced to appeal to interest groups or particular constituents. When submitting a bill a member will often seek cosponsors, but cosponsorship does not commit a member to support the bill if it comes to the floor for a vote. The number of cosponsors also does not necessarily translate into votes because interest group activity often intensifies with the submission of a bill and can result in some members changing their positions. Only members of the Congress may introduce legislation, and the president's legislative proposals are introduced by a member of the president's party.

Figure 5-6 illustrates the legislative process. When a bill is submitted, it is referred to one or more committees. A committee can then consider the bill or take no action on it. A bill is usually considered first by a subcommittee, which, by a majority vote, sends it to the full committee. A subcommittee cannot, however, effectively block a bill that a committee majority wishes to consider because the committee can consider the bill directly. Much of the substantive legislative work is done in committees, including amending and rewriting ("marking up") bills.

When a bill receives a majority vote in committee, it is ready to be scheduled for consideration on the floor of the chamber. In the House the bill first goes to the Rules Committee, which assigns an amendment rule that governs floor consideration. The Rules Committee may assign a restrictive rule, which specifies or restricts the amendments that can be offered, or an open rule, which places no restrictions on the number of amendments that may be offered. Amendments on the floor are subject to a standing rule of the House that prohibits nongermane amendments.[20] Special orders are used to schedule legislation and limit the time allocated to floor debate. Little true debate actually takes place on the floor, and many floor speeches are made to appeal to constituents.

---

[18]Oleszek (1996) provides detailed information on the legislative process and on congressional procedures.
[19]See Ornstein, Mann, and Malbin (1998). Any legislation pending at the end of a Congress dies.
[20]On a majority vote, the House may waive any of its rules.

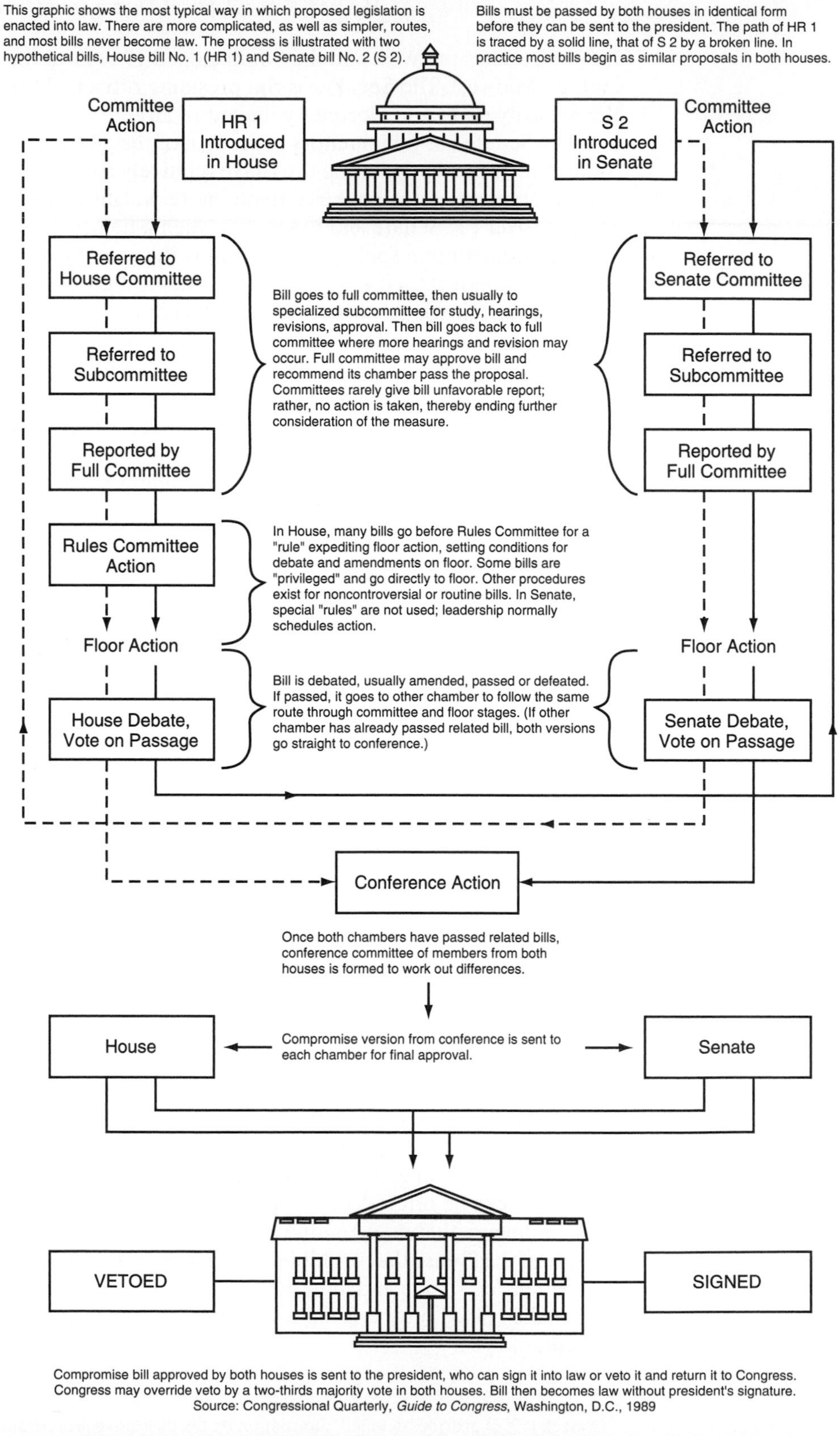
This graphic shows the most typical way in which proposed legislation is enacted into law. There are more complicated, as well as simpler, routes, and most bills never become law. The process is illustrated with two hypothetical bills, House bill No. 1 (HR 1) and Senate bill No. 2 (S 2).
Bills must be passed by both houses in identical form before they can be sent to the president. The path of HR 1 is traced by a solid line, that of S 2 by a broken line. In practice most bills begin as similar proposals in both houses.
Committee Action
HR 1 Introduced in House
S 2 Introduced in Senate
Committee Action
Referred to House Committee
Referred to Subcommittee
Reported by Full Committee
Referred to Senate Committee
Referred to Subcommittee
Reported by Full Committee
Bill goes to full committee, then usually to specialized subcommittee for study, hearings, revisions, approval. Then bill goes back to full committee where more hearings and revision may occur. Full committee may approve bill and recommend its chamber pass the proposal. Committees rarely give bill unfavorable report; rather, no action is taken, thereby ending further consideration of the measure.
Rules Committee Action
In House, many bills go before Rules Committee for a "rule" expediting floor action, setting conditions for debate and amendments on floor. Some bills are "privileged" and go directly to floor. Other procedures exist for noncontroversial or routine bills. In Senate, special "rules" are not used; leadership normally schedules action.
Floor Action
Floor Action
Bill is debated, usually amended, passed or defeated. If passed, it goes to other chamber to follow the same route through committee and floor stages. (If other chamber has already passed related bill, both versions go straight to conference.)
House Debate, Vote on Passage
Senate Debate, Vote on Passage
Conference Action
Once both chambers have passed related bills, conference committee of members from both houses is formed to work out differences.
House
Compromise version from conference is sent to each chamber for final approval.
Senate
VETOED
SIGNED
Compromise bill approved by both houses is sent to the president, who can sign it into law or veto it and return it to Congress. Congress may override veto by a two-thirds majority vote in both houses. Bill then becomes law without president's signature.
Source: Congressional Quarterly, Guide to Congress, Washington, D.C., 1989

FIGURE 5–6 How a Bill Becomes a Law

The legislative process in the Senate is similar to that in the House except that all bills are technically considered on the floor under an open rule. In practice, however, the Senate operates under unanimous consent agreements (UCAs) specifying which amendments may be considered on the floor. These agreements are negotiated under the auspices of the Senate leadership. An objection to a UCA by any senator prevents it from taking effect.

Senate rules allow members to speak on the floor for an unlimited time, and senators opposed to a bill can speak continuously on the floor (a filibuster), thus preventing a vote on a bill. Cloture can be invoked on a vote of 60 senators, preventing any member from speaking for more than an hour and precluding nongermane amendments. The minority party in the Senate frequently uses a filibuster to extract concessions from the majority or at times to kill a bill. A filibuster thus makes it more difficult to change from the status quo.[21]

A majority of the members of the House can bring a bill out of committee to the floor by signing a discharge petition. A senator can introduce any bill as an amendment (called a rider) to any bill being considered on the floor. A committee's ability to prevent legislation from reaching the floor is limited by these procedures.

Before a bill can be enacted, it must be passed by both chambers in identical language. The bills passed by each chamber seldom have the same language or provisions and must be reconciled before they can be sent to the president. Conference committees composed of representatives of each chamber selected by the majority party leadership are usually used to reconcile major legislation.[22] Members of both parties from the committee that reported the bill plus the authors of principal amendments are typically appointed to the conference committee. Conference committees are important because significant changes can result when the bills passed by the two chambers differ considerably. Thus, conference committees are often the focus of considerable political activity, and conference activity is characterized by bargaining. As an indication of the importance attached to conference committees, over 100 members of the House served as conferees on the 1990 amendments to the Clean Air Act. If the conferees from the two chambers agree on common language, the bill is then returned to the floor of each chamber for a final passage vote. If approved by both chambers, it is sent to the president for signature or veto.

A bill passed by Congress becomes law when the president signs it or when Congress overrides a presidential veto on a vote of two-thirds of the members of each chamber. When a bill is passed while Congress is still in session, the president must act on the bill within 10 days or it automatically becomes law. If Congress is no longer in session, the president can choose to not act on the bill, and then it dies.[23] The authority to veto legislation gives the president considerable power.

Because legislation can be stopped at a number of points in the legislative process, it is more difficult to enact legislation than to stop it. To be enacted, a bill must clear a number of hurdles. Committees represent an important hurdle, which gives power to the chairs of the committees. Strong majority preferences of the members of a committee or the parent body can circumvent any hurdle that a chairperson might construct, however.

---

[21]See Krehbiel (1996) for a theory of gridlock and Krehbiel (1998) (1999) for a theory in which filibusters play an important role.

[22]Instead of convening a conference, Congress often uses the procedure of amendments between the chambers to reconcile differences between bills. As in the daylight saving time example, one chamber can simply adopt the language of the other's bill. A bill may go through several iterations of amendments between the chambers before common language is reached. This means of achieving reconciliation typically involves implicit bargaining.

[23]This is referred to as a pocket veto.

COMMITTEES

Much of the work of Congress is done in committees, and each chamber chooses its own committee structure. Since 1946 only one House committee had been eliminated, but in 1995 the Republican majority eliminated three committees and realigned the jurisdictions of several others. The standing committees of the 106th Congress are listed in Figure 5-7. The House has 18 and the Senate has 17 standing committees, each of which has several subcommittees. Each chamber also has select committees, and there are four joint committees.

House of Representatives

Agriculture
Appropriations
Banking and Financial Services
Budget
Commerce
Education and the Workforce
Government Reform and Oversight
House Oversight
International Relations
Judiciary
National Security
Resources
Rules
Science
Small Business
Transportation and Infrastructure
Veterans' Affairs
Ways and Means

Senate

Agriculture, Nutrition and Forestry
Appropriations
Armed Services
Banking, Housing and Urban Affairs
Budget
Commerce, Science and Transportation
Energy and Natural Resources
Environment and Public Works
Finance
Foreign Affairs
Governmental Affairs
Indian Affairs
Judiciary
Labor and Human Resources
Rules and Administration
Small Business
Veterans' Affairs

FIGURE 5-7 Standing Committees of the 106th Congress

Committees have policy jurisdictions, but those jurisdictions can overlap when issues cut across formal boundaries. In the House, for example, an environmental protection issue such as regulation of an agricultural pesticide could be under the jurisdiction of the Agriculture Committee and of committees with environmental jurisdictions. Committees thus often battle over jurisdictions and hence over influence on legislation.

Government expenditures are governed by a complex process requiring both an authorization and an appropriation. The House Agriculture Committee or the National Security Committee may authorize expenditures for an agricultural subsidy program or a new weapons system, but the funds for those programs are provided by the Appropriations Committee. The process is designed to have the authorization committee act first, with the Appropriations Committee then providing funding no greater than the amount authorized. In the 1990s, however, the budget process involved complex bargaining between the president and Congress over both the budget and the funding of individual programs.

Authorization committees have the responsibility for enacting legislation and reauthorizing programs with fixed expiration dates. For example, the charter of the Consumer Products Safety Commission (CPSC) must be reauthorized periodically. When a required process becomes blocked, however, Congress has other means of acting. Conflict over the activities of the CPSC prevented reauthorization legislation for nearly a decade until a bill was finally approved in 1990. In the interim, the CPSC operated under provisions included in appropriations bills. In addition to their legislative roles, authorization committees have oversight responsibilities. Committees attempt to influence the policies of regulatory and administrative agencies, such as the CPSC, by holding hearings and threatening legislative or budgetary action.

Committee membership is proportional to a party's representation in the chamber, and party caucuses assign their members to committees. Newly elected legislators give a ranking of their committee preferences, and the party caucuses do their best to assign members to the committees they have requested. Members of the House generally serve on two standing committees and some also serve on select or joint committees. In the Senate, each member serves on several committees. Members accumulate committee-specific seniority, which is usually not transferable if the member changes committee assignments. Because committee and subcommittee chairs are generally selected according to seniority and because chairpersons have power and influence, members do not frequently change committees. Remaining with the same committee also gives members an incentive and an opportunity to develop expertise in that policy jurisdiction.

The chairs of committees and subcommittees are selected by the majority party, so since 1995 Republicans have held all of them. Approximately half of the House Republicans and virtually all the Senate Republicans are chairs of a committee or subcommittee. Committee chairs are selected by a party caucus and a vote among the committee members, and incumbents generally retain their chairs. Occasionally, however, a chair will be replaced. In 1993 Democrats on the House Appropriations Committee stripped the elderly chairman of both the full committee and the agriculture subcommittee chairs. When they became the majority party in the House in 1995, the Republicans passed over several more senior members in selecting committee chairs. The Republicans also allowed committee chairs to choose the chairs of their subcommittees, and most chose the most senior members.

In 1974 in the wake of Watergate, a large number of new members were elected to the House. They pushed through reforms that gave a degree of autonomy to subcommittees, which previously had been under the control of the committee chair. This decentralization increased the number of powerful positions in the House by a factor of six, significantly changing House activity. As one congressman observed, a system of "wholesale politics" in which strong committee chairs controlled the legislative process was transformed into "retail politics" in which power is diffuse. In addition to their role as the first stage of legislative activity, subcommittees have the opportunity to hold hearings to direct attention to issues, provide interest groups with a forum in which to advance their interests, and pressure those involved in an issue.

COMMITTEE AND INDIVIDUAL POWER

Members develop power based on their committee positions, seniority, expertise, hard work, and ability to form alliances and coalitions. The chair of a committee or subcommittee has a degree of power. The chair can initiate investigations and hold hearings, influence agenda, craft legislative bargains, and trade favors.

One source of committee power is its opportunity to draft, rewrite, and mark up bills. This allows a committee to set the chamber's legislative agenda in its jurisdiction. Without majority support in the full chamber, however, a committee has little ability to move legislation through the chamber. A principal activity of a committee is thus to write legislation that will command majority support. Because most legislation has consequences over several dimensions, a committee may have several different majorities from which it can seek support.

Committee power can also result from its refusal to report a bill for floor consideration. The extent to which committees have this gatekeeping power is a matter of contention, as the parent body has ways to thwart it. In the House, a discharge petition signed by a majority of members brings a bill out of committee to a vote on the floor even though the committee has not reported it. In the Senate there is no germaneness rule, and any member can object to a unanimous consent agreement. Furthermore, a member can offer any bill as an amendment, as in the daylight saving time extension example considered later in this chapter. Nevertheless, committees do gain some leverage because of their opportunity to delay, as well as to draft, legislation.

Expertise is a principal source of power because members of Congress must deal with numerous complex issues, and information on the issues is necessarily imperfect. Members thus seek information from a variety of sources including interest groups, policy analysts, and other members of Congress. A member who develops expertise in a policy domain thus has an opportunity to influence the information that other members have. On floor votes outside their areas of expertise, members will often rely on the advice of another member who has similar preferences and is on the committee bringing the bill to the floor. Expertise also provides an opportunity to form and lead coalitions on legislation. Members may also develop expertise through their knowledge of congressional rules and procedures.

On issues about which information is imperfect, committees play an important role in developing new information and in shaping legislation that serves the interests of the parent body and the committee members.[24] The opportunity to craft bills to serve their own interests provides committee members with an incentive to acquire information and expertise that can be mutually beneficial to their members and to the chamber. Members often obtain information from interest groups, and an information provision strategy can be effective in those policy areas in which information is imperfect.

---

[24]See Gilligan and Krehbiel (1987) and Krehbiel (1991).

BARGAINING IN POLITICAL INSTITUTIONS

Although legislatures take actions under majority rule, bargaining often takes place when disagreements arise among majorities on different dimensions of an issue. Bargaining also characterizes conference committee action, during which House and Senate conferees reconcile differences between the chambers. Congress also has used omnibus legislation, whereby bills from several committees are brought to the floor for a vote in a single package. As an example, the Omnibus Trade and Competitiveness Act of 1988 combined ten Senate bills and seven House bills. On another bill, sections were referred to six different committees. In omnibus legislation a committee may make concessions in its policy jurisdiction in exchange for concessions by other committees on other policy dimensions.

Because Congress is an institution whose members interact repeatedly, legislators can develop long-term patterns of behavior in which the failure to compromise on an issue today may be met with an unwillingness to compromise on future issues. Consequently, the majority and minority parties can establish patterns of behavior that give the minority party opportunities that its minority status does not provide. On committees, for example, the chair often accommodates the interests of the ranking minority member. When bills are considered in committee, the chair has the right to make the first amendment and the ranking minority member has the right to make the second amendment.

DELEGATION

Legislatures delegate the implementation of legislation to agencies, and the nature of that delegation can be important. At times the delegation is designed to favor the interest groups that supported the initial legislation.[25] To promote the development of product safety standards through government regulation, for example, supporters incorporated into the act that established the Consumer Product Safety Commission a provision that allowed anyone to petition for a safety standard for a product. The act also required the CPSC to act on the petition within 6 months.[26] Thus, individuals and interest groups were given an opportunity to set the agenda of the CPSC.

Delegation may also be used for the enforcement of legislation and regulations. Some environmental legislation allows individuals to file suit to enforce compliance by polluters and to retain a portion of the penalties assessed. The Natural Resources Defense Council, for example, used these provisions to generate income for its programs.

Congress also delegates implementation to states. States implement certain provisions of the Clean Air Act, which puts them in potential conflict with the Environmental Protection Agency (EPA). In the case of automobile emissions testing, California refused to enforce the EPA's directive to use centralized testing facilities, forcing negotiations and eventual concessions by the EPA. (See the Chapter 8 case *Envirotest Systems Corporation* (B).)

LEGISLATORS AND THEIR CONSTITUENCIES

Whatever a legislator's personal policy preferences, he or she must be reelected to have a continuing opportunity to realize those preferences. Members thus vote on legislative alternatives based on two considerations—their reelection incentives and their policy

[25] See McCubbins, Noll, and Weingast (1990) for a theory of delegation with this feature.

[26] As considered in more detail in Chapter 11, this opportunity was subsequently eliminated.

preferences.[27] Elected representatives thus are responsive to the preferences of their constituents not only because they have a duty to represent them, but because they want to be reelected. Mayhew (1974) refers to this relationship as the "constituency connection."

A constituency includes voters, volunteers, and providers of campaign resources. A constituency can also include those outside an electoral district whom that member chooses to represent, such as the elderly, environmentalists, labor, or business. The reelection motive gives legislators an incentive to be attentive to the preferences of those likely to vote. It also gives them an incentive to develop a personal constituency by providing services to constituents. The reelection motive also provides an opportunity for interest groups with electorally important resources to attempt to influence the behavior of legislators.

Mayhew characterized members of Congress as exhibiting two types of behavior—*credit claiming* and *blame avoidance.* Credit claiming refers to the practice of claiming credit for legislative or oversight activity that is in the apparent interest of constituents. Because it is difficult for most constituents to know the actual effectiveness, or in some cases even the position, of a legislator, credit claiming may go beyond actual accomplishments. Interest groups, however, monitor the behavior of legislators and often have a good idea of effectiveness and who was working for or against a bill.

Blame avoidance involves distancing oneself from unpopular events, policies, or positions that might provide a platform for an electoral challenge. In an attempt to avoid blame for the savings and loan crisis, several members who had served on the important congressional banking committees chose to leave those committees in 1991. A seat on the House Banking Committee had been attractive in part because the political action committees (PACs) of financial institutions made substantial campaign contributions to committee members. Because of the savings and loan crisis and the associated scandals, however, those contributions became a liability that could be used as a campaign issue by challengers. Of the 51 members who served on the committee in 1990, 16 members did not return to it the following year. One member retired, one resigned after being convicted on criminal charges, two lost reelection bids, four who sought other elective offices were defeated, and eight chose to change to another committee. Most stayed because their seniority on the committee would not transfer to other committees.

COMMITTEE AND PERSONAL STAFFS

Members of Congress each have a personal staff that includes a chief, a press secretary, legislative assistants, and administrative assistants. The senior staff is an important link to members and keeps them informed about legislation, hearings, and other developments. A substantial portion of staff time is also devoted to providing constituents with services such as assisting with lost social security checks, obtaining appointments to military academies, assisting with immigration problems, and interacting with government agencies. The staff also responds to constituents' letters on issues, often acknowledging the receipt of the letter, expressing concern for the issue, and stating that attention is being given to it. From 1960 to 1980, legislators' personal staffs expanded considerably; but since 1980 staff size has been relatively stable.

Committee staffs have shown a similar pattern over the same periods. The committee staff is directed by the chair of the committee and, at quiet times, may serve as

[27]See Fiorina (1989) and Mayhew (1974) for analyses of congressional behavior.

an adjunct to his or her personal staff. The committee staff is important in drafting legislation, marking up bills, and interacting with interest groups. For firms, trade associations, and other interest groups, the staff represents an important source of access to the legislative process and to information about the committee's activities. The majority party is allocated a substantially larger number of committee staff positions than the minority party. In 1995 the Republicans reduced the committee staff in the House by about one-third.

STATE GOVERNMENTS

State governments are granted certain rights by the Constitution, such as the right provided by the 21st Amendment to regulate the use of intoxicating liquors, and the federal government is restricted to matters of interstate and not intrastate commerce. State law tends to govern liability standards, insurance and public utility regulation, occupational licensure, and some aspects of labor and securities law, incorporation law, and commercial law. States also have the authority to levy taxes and make expenditures. State government processes and structures are similar to those at the federal level, although most states elect more of their executive branch officials than is done at the federal level. Also, 23 states have a referendum mechanism by which citizens can exercise direct democracy by enacting legislation or changing the state constitution through referenda. See the Part II integrative case *Proposition 211: Securities Litigation Referendum (A)*.

Because each state can enact its own laws, the multiplicity of state laws is a continuing source of problems for firms. Differences among state regulations and between state and federal regulations force firms to meet a variety of standards, often at considerable expense. Firms and interest groups work in state capitals to address these differing regulations. Firms have also sought uniform federal regulations and standards to replace or preempt different state regulations. For example, in 1994, McDonald's adopted a no-smoking policy at its company-owned restaurants and sought uniform federal regulation banning smoking in restaurants.

PARTIES

Political parties are important in legislative politics, yet legislators have a considerable degree of independence from party positions and their leaders. In Congress, parties attempt to maintain discipline in voting within committees and on the floor. On issues important to their constituents, however, members often depart from the party position. One measure of the degree of party-line voting is the percent of the roll-call votes in which a majority of one party voted contrary to a majority of the other party. In the 104th Congress, approximately 62 percent of the roll-call votes in the Senate and 56 percent of those in the House had this partisan characteristic. As these data indicate, party-line voting is not the rule. The more important an issue is to constituents, the more likely a legislator is to deviate from the party position. Sometimes, though, when the party has taken a position on an issue, stronger constituent pressure may be required to cause members to deviate from that position.

Parties in the United States are relatively weak compared with parties in many other countries, particularly those with a parliamentary system of government. One reason is that in the United States nominations are controlled locally rather than by the national party. In addition, issues important to voters are often local rather than national, which allows members to develop local constituencies to improve their reelection prospects. This personal vote is developed through campaigning, district work, and constituent services. Also, most campaign contributions are made directly to candidates rather than to parties, which gives members a further degree of independence from their party.

THE PRESIDENCY AND THE EXECUTIVE BRANCH

The president has a range of powers—some granted by the Constitution, some delegated by Congress, and some derived from public support.[28] The Constitution assigns to the president the right to veto legislation as well as certain powers in foreign affairs. Congress has delegated to the president the authority to negotiate treaties and trade agreements. The president also has authority in certain administrative areas, as granted by legislation. For example, President Reagan had a substantial impact on regulatory rule making through his executive authority. In 1981 he issued an important executive order requiring a cost-benefit analysis of new regulations proposed by executive branch agencies. When President Clinton took office, he modified the order, requiring a review of costs and benefits only for major regulatory rule making.

The president also appoints, with the consent of the Senate, the heads of cabinet departments, the members of regulatory and other commissions, and the top levels of executive branch agencies. The executive branch thus is responsive to the policy objectives of the president. (Cabinet departments are listed in Figure 5-8.) The executive branch agencies and cabinet departments have influence not only on the administration of policies but also on policy formation through their expertise and their ability to develop policy proposals.

The president submits an annual budget to Congress. Although Congress may make any changes it chooses, the president through pressure, bargaining power, and the veto has considerable influence over the final product. In the last half of the 1990s the budget process has been stymied by conflicting preferences, resulting in intense bargaining between the president and Congress over budget accords.

In reasoning about political behavior, it is important to recognize that the failure to observe certain behavior does not necessarily mean that it is not important. For example,

State
Treasury
Defense
Justice
Interior
Agriculture
Commerce
Labor
Education
Housing and Urban Development
Transportation
Energy
Health and Human Services

FIGURE 5-8 Cabinet Departments

[28]The president can only be removed from office through impeachment by the House and a trial in the Senate. Only Andrew Johnson and Bill Clinton have been impeached, and neither was convicted.

presidents cast relatively few vetoes even when the president and Congress are from different parties. The infrequency of vetoes does not, however, mean that the veto is not an important power. The threat of a veto causes Congress to not pass some legislation that it would otherwise pass and causes it to modify some legislation that it does pass so as to avoid a veto.

One of the most important powers of the president is the authority, with the consent of the Senate, to appoint members of the federal judiciary. In addition to deciding individual cases, the judiciary interprets the Constitution and federal statutes, and the precedents established by its decisions have lasting effects. The Reagan and Bush administrations changed the Supreme Court from one with a liberal and judicial activist orientation to one with a more conservative orientation reflecting judicial restraint.

COURTS

The U.S. judicial system is comprised of federal, state, and local courts.[29] The federal courts include three levels. Cases are tried by U.S. district courts and appeals go to the U.S. Court of Appeals, which consists of 11 circuits plus the District of Columbia circuit. The court of appeals also hears appeals of cases from administrative agencies such as the Federal Trade Commission and the Tax Court. The decisions of a circuit court of appeals apply only to that circuit, but courts in other circuits may be influenced by the reasoning and conclusions of a court in another circuit. The U.S. Court of Appeals for the Federal Circuit hears appeals of cases from specialized courts, such as the U.S. Claims Court and the U.S. Court of International Trade. The Supreme Court hears cases appealed from the courts of appeals, and its decisions apply everywhere in the country. The Supreme Court decides cases involving constitutional issues, as well as cases involving conflicts between laws.

States and their subjurisdictions, such as counties and municipalities, have their own courts systems to administer state law and local ordinances. Most states have trial courts, courts of appeals, and a supreme court. Appeals of decisions by state supreme courts go to the U.S. Supreme Court. In many instances a plaintiff may be able to choose between filing a case in state court or in federal court.

The United States has three basic types of laws. The first are those enacted by Congress, state legislatures, and local government bodies. The second includes rule making and decisions of administrative agencies, frequently involving an administrative law judge, as considered in Chapter 10. The third is the common law, which is law developed from the rulings of courts on cases brought by plaintiffs. The common law consists of the precedents established by those decisions and forms the basis for important branches of the law including the law of torts, as considered in Chapter 11.

Politics and the Public Interest

One approach to understanding political activity is to envision elected officials as serving the public interest by applying a set of normative principles about what is good or right. This "public interest theory" of political behavior has two weaknesses. First, as Arrow's impossibility theorem suggests, there may be no general agreement about which principles to use to identify the public interest and, therefore, which alternatives are in the public interest. Second, much observed political behavior appears to be motivated by private interests rather than by a conception of the public interest, even though that behavior may be cloaked in the rhetoric of the public interest. These observations suggest that the public interest arises not from consensus but from a pluralism of interests

[29] See Bagley (1995) and Carp and Stidham (1991).

and from the competing actions of individuals and the groups they form in the pursuit of outcomes they prefer.

When public policies arise from a pluralism of interests and the political action those interests motivate, the study of individual interests and the manner in which they are transformed into political and collective action, and ultimately into public policy, is fundamental to understanding political and other forms of nonmarket activity. The example analyzed next expands on this perspective.

The Politics of the Extension of Daylight Saving Time

THE NATURE OF POLITICAL EXPLANATIONS

Since the Uniform Time Act was enacted in 1966, daylight saving time began on the last Sunday in April and lasted 6 months until the last Sunday in October.[30] Bills to extend daylight saving time were introduced in Congress beginning in 1976, and the battle for an extension lasted for 10 years, concluding in 1986 with a 3-week extension to the first Sunday in April. The forces that led to the extension are representative of those present in many political issues affecting business.

Two contrasting approaches may be taken to explain the politics of the extension. The public interest perspective predicts that the alternative that best serves that interest will be adopted. In this case, the public interest would select the extension that yielded the greatest differences between aggregate benefits and costs. This perspective was first advanced in 1784 when Benjamin Franklin argued to the French that they could save 96 million candles per year from an extra hour of daylight.[31] During World Wars I and II the United States adopted daylight saving time, and in World War II it lasted for three and a half years. During the oil crisis in 1973 and 1974, the United States extended daylight saving time as a means of saving energy. The waning of the oil crisis and protests from parents who objected to their children having to walk to school in the early morning darkness led to the elimination of the extension. Subsequently, the U.S. Department of Transportation (DOT) estimated that the extension during the oil crisis saved 6 million barrels of oil, and traffic accidents decreased 2 to 3 percent.

A second approach focuses on the political competition resulting from the actions of those whose interests are affected by the length of daylight saving time. For most nonmarket issues it is better to view political action as arising from the impact of alternatives on the interests of individuals, firms, and groups than to view political outcomes as the result of the pursuit of the public interest. This does not mean that public policy analysis has no effect on the outcome of political activity. Often it does. Even in those cases, however, public policy analysis should not be viewed as the determinant of the outcome of political activity. Instead, public policy analysis is better viewed as providing information about the consequences of alternatives.

THE LEGISLATIVE HISTORY OF THE EXTENSION

In 1976 the Senate passed a bill extending daylight saving time to 8 months and 1 week, but the House did not act. In 1981 the House passed a bill providing for a shorter extension, but the Senate did not act. In 1983 the House rejected an extension. Finally, in 1985 the light at the end of the tunnel began to appear. Representative Edward J. Markey (D-MA), chairman of the Subcommittee on Energy Conservation, introduced a bill that would extend daylight saving time from the third Sunday in March to the first

[30]States retain the right to not adopt daylight saving time. These dates were chosen because the weather was generally similar at the beginning and end of the period.
[31]*Fortune,* November 12, 1984, p. 147.

Sunday in November. The Subcommittee approved the bill by voice vote. The Energy and Commerce Committee, however, approved an amendment by Howard C. Nielson (R-UT) that moved the starting date back 2 weeks to the first Sunday in April. Approving the amended bill by voice vote, the committee sent it to the full House, which approved it by a 240 to 157 vote in October 1985.

In July 1985, Senator Slade Gorton (R-WA) introduced a bill extending daylight-saving time, but opposition by senators from rural and Midwestern states led by Senators Wendell Ford (D-KY) and J. James Exon (D-NE) blocked the bill in the Commerce Committee. With the committee gates closed, Senator Gorton introduced his extension bill as a rider to an authorization bill for fire prevention and control programs. The amendment provided the same starting date as the House bill, but to recruit additional votes Gorton removed the 1-week extension in the fall. By a 36 to 58 vote the Senate defeated a motion to table the amendment and then adopted the amendment and the bill by voice vote. The House and Senate thus had both passed extensions of daylight saving time, but the measures were not identical. Rather than convene a conference to reconcile them, the House chose to enact the Senate bill. An authorization bill for fire prevention and control had been working its way through the House, and on June 24, 1986, the House, by unanimous consent, agreed to drop the 1-week extension in November and passed the Senate bill.

THE POLITICS OF DAYLIGHT SAVING TIME

The politics of daylight saving time can be understood as a competition between those interests favoring an extension and those interests opposed to it. Congress was the institutional arena for that competition. Senator Ford characterized the differences in interests as, "Any Kentucky mother who has sent a first-grader out to catch a bus on a dark, misty April morning takes a dim view about. . . electricity that might be saved on the East and West coasts and the number of afternoon tennis games that might be played here in Washington."[32]

The effects of an extension were broadly distributed, and at the beginning of the political competition in 1976 interest groups were poorly organized and their strategies only loosely coordinated. The status quo prevailed. The benefits to a number of groups, including recreation and business interests, were substantial, however, and so interest groups had an incentive to form and take action on the issue.

An extension of daylight saving time affects a wide array of economic activity. As James Benfield, a lobbyist who served as executive director of the Daylight Saving Time Coalition, explained: "Here's a way to increase economic activity by doing nothing more than changing the time on your wrist. . . . We are simply fine-tuning our use of time to adjust for daily life patterns and to translate those patterns into dollars for business."[33] In the context of Figure 5-2, an extension shifts the demand curve outward for a variety of goods. The Barbecue Industry Association estimated that an extension would increase the sales of briquettes by $56 million and starter fluid by $15 million. The Kingsford Company was an active supporter of the extension. Bob Lederer of the American Association of Nurserymen stated: "When daylight saving time comes, people think spring and they start buying plants. And if daylight saving comes earlier, people will buy a lot more plants." [34] The Sporting Goods Manufacturers Association estimated that golfers would spend $7 million more on clubs and balls and would play four

---

[32]*Congressional Quarterly Weekly Report,* May 24, 1986, p. 1177.
[33]*Fortune,* November 12, 1984, p. 150.
[34]*Fortune,* November 12, 1984, pp. 150–151.

million more rounds of golf a year. Expenditures for tennis balls and rackets could increase by $7 million per year. Hardee's estimated that an extension would increase sales by an average of $800 per week per store. The Southland Corporation estimated that daylight saving time could increase sales at its 7-Eleven stores by $30 million annually. Pamela Sederholm, a spokesperson for 7-Eleven, said, "Women shop in daylight hours at a 7-Eleven. They go to supermarkets when it's dark."

Benfield conceived the idea of including Halloween in the extension to bring the candy industry into the political competition.[35] Candy makers were interested in an additional hour of daylight on Halloween because some parents would allow their children to extend their trick-or-treating. Those candy companies were represented by the Chocolate Manufacturers Association, the National Candy Brokers Association, and the National Confectioners Association. Representative Markey said, "This small step could make trick-or-treating for young children a much safer experience."[36] The deletion of the fall extension by Senator Gorton was a substantial blow to the candy interests—as well as to the interests of children.

Firms measure the impact of an extension in terms of their sales and profit. Increased sales, however, also mean that customers benefit. Similarly, increased sales mean an increase in employment. The difference between the benefits to a firm (or its shareholders) and the benefits to customers and employees is less in the magnitude than in the relation between the benefits and the cost of taking political action. Firms have relatively low costs of taking political action and thus may act when groups with higher costs of political action will not act. Customers and future employees typically are widely dispersed and costly to organize, and thus the costs to their taking political action are high. On the daylight saving time issue, they could not be expected to act. Their interests, however, were represented by the political actions of the firms that benefited from an extension. Thus, an important consequence of the participation of firms in political activity is that they often represent the interests of those who might otherwise not be represented because of high organizational costs and their relatively low per capita benefits. Firms regularly inform members of Congress of the jobs and other benefits that accrue to their constituents.

An important factor in political competition is the alignment of interests among dissimilar groups. An interest group with a strong incentive to support the extension of daylight saving time was the RP Foundation Fighting Blindness, which had 400,000 members who suffer from retinitis pigmentosa and other eye diseases that cause night blindness. Although the interests of these individuals were not directly economic, as were those of 7-Eleven and Kingsford, they had an incentive to support an extension just as business interests had. The fact that individuals with night blindness were disadvantaged may, however, be more compelling to some members of Congress than the economic interests of firms, customers, and employees.

On most issues, there are opposing interests, and one political strategy is to provide substitutes to reduce the adverse consequences to those opposed to the issue. The National Association of Broadcasters, for example, opposed the extension. Although most of the 2,450 AM radio stations licensed to operate only in the daytime had a PSA (presunrise authorization) that allowed them to begin broadcasting with reduced power at 6:00 A.M., nearly 450 did not have such an authorization.[37] For many of these stations the most profitable advertising time is the morning commute hours, and profits would be reduced by an extension of daylight saving time that would add an hour of broadcast

[35]He was successful in expanding the coalition from 4 members in 1983 to 16 in 1985.
[36]*Congressional Quarterly Weekly Report,* May 4, 1985, p. 839.
[37]*Congressional Quarterly Weekly Report,* May 24, 1986, p. 1177.

time in the evening and eliminate an hour in the morning. This opposition was relatively easy to accommodate because adjustments in authorizations for AM radio stations were virtually costless to the supporters of the extension. As Benfield argued, the Federal Communications Commission (FCC) could extend the broadcast time in the morning. The amendment offered by Senator Gorton contained a provision allowing the FCC to make appropriate adjustments in broadcasting authorizations.

In other instances there may be no means of satisfying opponents. Some Orthodox Jews opposed the extension because their morning prayers cannot begin earlier than 45 minutes before sunrise, and the length of the prayers might make them late for work. Some Christian fundamentalists opposed the extension because they viewed it as contrary to God's will.

A number of other groups also opposed the extension.[38] Some parents opposed it because their children would have to go to school in the dark. This was, of course, more of a problem on the western edges of time zones.[39] Some farmers objected to the extension, and their interests were represented by a number of members of Congress. Representative Thomas A. Daschle (D-SD) said, "The time shift would hurt farmers, particularly the estimated thirty percent who hold second jobs and who would have less daylight to perform morning chores." Even more important, he said, was a safety threat to "children who would wait in the dark for school buses as early as 6:30 A.M."[40] These interests were represented by organizations such as the PTA and the American Farm Bureau.

THE ROLE OF INFORMATION

One feature of political competition is the provision of information about the consequences of political alternatives. The DOT and the National Safety Council reported that the extension of daylight saving time would not significantly increase the risk to school children. Opponents of the extension attacked DOT's accident data from the 1974–1975 extension and argued that it was insufficient to warrant any conclusion. In 1986 the DOT countered when Secretary Elizabeth H. Dole wrote to Senate Majority Leader Robert Dole (R-KS) stating that its studies concluded that an extension "would reduce traffic deaths nationwide by a minimum of 22, injuries by a minimum of 1,525, and societal costs from auto accidents by a minimum of $28 million [annually]. . . with possible savings being as much as twice as large."[41]

The impact of such facts is difficult to determine, but whatever their significance, politics is not primarily a competition among facts. Politics is better viewed as a competition of interests, and information is important to the extent that it helps identify the relationship between political alternatives and their consequences for those interests.

Information also helped legislators identify the alternative for which to vote. Through the efforts of the Daylight Saving Time Coalition, many legislators recognized the benefits to business and their constituents. Complaints from farmers, parents, and others, particularly on the western edges of time zones, provided information about their preferences and led Representative Daschle and Senators Exon and Ford to oppose an extension.

---

[38]Some opposition defied logic. In 1981 Representative Thomas F. Hartnett (D-SC) asked "how big the mushrooms are going to be with that extra hour of daylight in the evening" (*Fortune,* November 12, 1984, p. 150).

[39]DOT estimated that dawn would be, on average, at 6:48 A.M. but would occur at 7:00 A.M. on the western edges of time zones.

[40]*Congressional Quarterly Weekly Report,* May 4, 1985, p. 839.

[41]*Congressional Quarterly Weekly Report,* May 24, 1986, p. 1177.

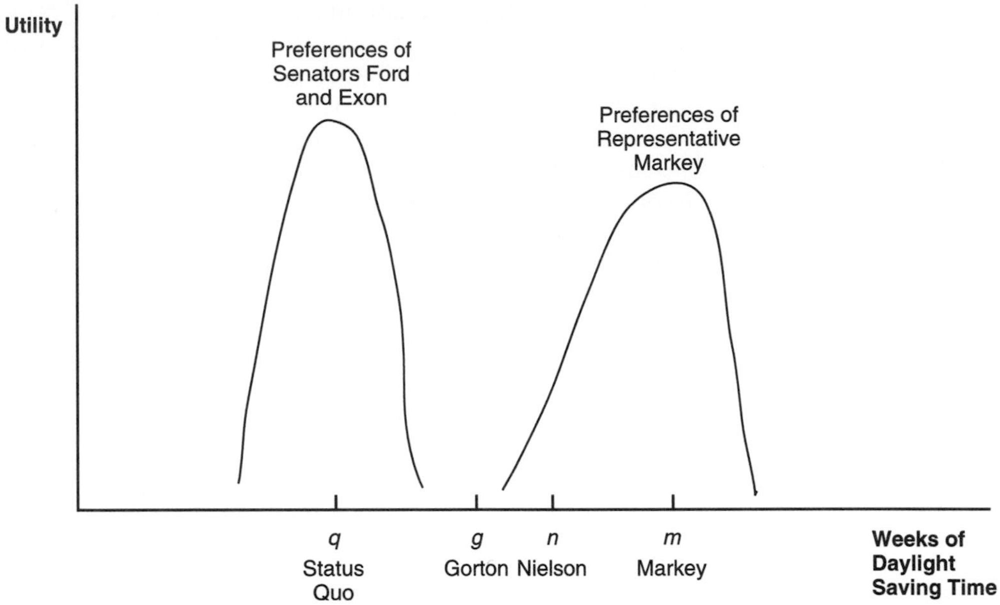

FIGURE 5–9 Median Voter Theorem and Daylight Saving Time

AN ANALYTICAL CHARACTERIZATION OF THE POLITICS OF DAYLIGHT SAVING TIME

The next step in the analysis is to go from interests and interest groups to outcomes. In the case of daylight saving time, the median voter theorem provides that step. The alternatives before Congress can be summarized in terms of the length of daylight saving time, as measured by the number of weeks as constrained by beginning and ending on a Sunday. The principal alternatives in 1986 are displayed in Figure 5-9. The status quo q is farthest to the left, and Representative Markey's bill, denoted by m, is farthest to the right.

Because of the constituency connection, members of Congress are concerned about the interests of their constituents. Particularly in states and districts at western edges of a time zone, pressure from farmers and parents of school-age children outweighed the pressure from the supporters of the extension. Senators Ford and Exon then can be thought of as preferring a length of daylight saving time at, or perhaps to the left of, the status quo. This is illustrated in Figure 5-9 by a preference function with a peak at their most preferred length, their ideal point, and declining the farther an alternative is from that point.[42] Similarly, the preferences of Representative Markey, whose district was on the eastern edge of a time zone, are also illustrated in Figure 5-9. Indeed, each member of Congress can be thought of as having preferences of a similar form.

If the House had only two alternatives, q and m, representatives would simply vote for their preferred alternative. The alternatives were not restricted, however, because the legislative process was open and any number of weeks of daylight saving time could be considered. Legislators could thus introduce alternatives they preferred to either q or m. For example, an alternative to the right of q and to the left of the median would be preferred to q by all those representatives with ideal points to the right of the median plus some of those to the left. It thus would defeat q on a majority vote. Indeed,

[42]Daschle's district was also at the western edge of a time zone, whereas Gorton's was at the eastern edge.

the only alternative that could not be defeated in this manner by some other alternative is the median of the ideal points of the legislators. That is, any other alternative would receive less than half the votes against the median. Hence, the median is the majority rule winner. In the House, Representative Nielson's amendment *n* to the Markey bill may be understood as being closer to the median and was preferred by a majority to both *q* and *m*.

In the Senate Commerce Committee, Senators Ford and Exon were successful in preserving the status quo against Senator Gorton's bill *g*. Senator Gorton, however, was able to attach his bill as a rider to an authorization bill. A majority of the Senate preferred *g* to *q*, as reflected by the 36 to 58 vote defeating the motion to table *g*. The fact that Senator Gorton's proposal provided a week less of daylight saving time than the Nielson amendment may indicate that Gorton believed that *n* was farther from the median of the ideal points in the Senate.

The House and the Senate had thus passed extensions that were preferred to the status quo by a majority in their chambers, but before an extension could become law the two chambers had to reconcile the two bills. Bargaining between the chambers resulted in *g* being enacted.

The chapter case *Summertime in the European Union* examines the daylight saving time issue in the context of the institutions of the European Union.

Summary

Understanding the nonmarket activity that takes place in the arenas of public institutions requires both theories of behavior and knowledge of the structure and procedures of those institutions. Nonmarket activity often arises from the effects of political alternatives on markets. Those alternatives affect rents and surpluses, providing incentives for nonmarket action. Interests, however, do not translate directly into action because of the costs of collective action. In large groups the free-rider problem is likely to be present.

The free-rider problem is a variant of the prisoners' dilemma. The dilemma is that what is individually rational is not collectively rational. Some dilemmas can be resolved through repeated encounters that allow individuals over time to reward and punish each other for their actions. Others are resolved through institutional mechanisms, as illustrated in the chapter case *An Electoral Dilemma (A) (B)*.

Majority rule is an institution for making collective decisions, but, as Arrow demonstrated, a fundamental problem with any collective decision-making institution is that coherent choice is not always possible. If the alternatives are one-dimensional and voters have an ideal alternative and prefer those closer to that ideal point, the median voter theorem predicts that the choice will be the median of the ideal points. The length of daylight saving time is a one-dimensional issue, and the extension can be explained by the median voter theorem. Coherent choice also results because of institutional structures such as agendas, but these institutional structures also create the possibility of strategic behavior on the part of institutional officeholders.

In addition to agendas and committee structures, actual majority-rule institutions such as Congress are structured by procedures that govern amendments, the assignment of bills to committee, and reconciliation between the chambers. The work of Congress largely occurs in its committees which hold hearings, draft and mark up legislation, and conduct oversight activities. Committees have a strategic position in the legislative process, but their ability to thwart the preferences of a majority of the parent body is limited. In the case of the extension of daylight saving time, Senator Gorton was able to circumvent a closed committee gate by attaching his bill as a rider to another bill. Committees have power, however, because of their ability to delay legislation, contribute expertise, and facilitate bargaining that resolves conflicts.

Members of Congress are motivated by reelection considerations, their duty to constituents, and their policy preferences. Reelection is central to the concerns of most members. To improve their reelection prospects they develop personal constituencies and serve the interests of groups that can provide votes and electoral resources. The success of these efforts, in addition to the other advantages of incumbency, is reflected in the incumbency advantage.

The president and the executive branch are important in both legislative and administrative activities. The president uses the power of the veto, public suasion, and executive branch expertise to influence legislation. The president also has a major impact through appointments to the courts, regulatory commissions and agencies, and administrative agencies.

CASES

Summertime in the European Union

Summertime, or daylight saving time, began in Europe in 1916 when Ireland and the United Kingdom set their clocks ahead by an hour in the summer. Italy adopted summertime in 1966, and France introduced it in 1976. The other member states of the European Union (EU) then adopted summertime, with Germany and Denmark the last to adopt it in 1980. Not all the member states, however, had adopted the same beginning and starting dates.

In 1980 the European Union began to harmonize the summertime period, but by the 1990s harmonization had not been accomplished.[1] In the 1990s companies engaged in transportation and communications again sought harmonization of the times across the member states. Opponents, however, viewed this as an opportunity to eliminate summertime.

The European Union encompassed three time zones: Greenwich Mean Time (GMT), GMT + 1 (Central European Time [CET]), and GMT + 2. The countries in the GMT time zone include the United Kingdom, Ireland, France, the Benelux countries, Spain, and Portugal, but during World War II the Germans imposed their time, and after the war France, Belgium, the Netherlands, Luxembourg, and Spain retained GMT + 1. Portugal also adopted GMT + 1. The adoption of summertime by these countries gave them a second hour of summertime for half the year.

Summertime began on the last Sunday of March at 1 A.M. GMT. The sixth EU Directive on summertime extended through 1994 and established that summertime would end on the last day of September on the continent with the UK and Ireland retaining an ending date of the last Sunday of October. In 1994 the EU began consideration of a seventh Directive on summertime.

The principal issue under consideration in the seventh Directive was the ending date for summertime. Recreational and other interest groups supported an ending date of the last Sunday of October, but there was no pan-European confederation supporting the extension.[2] Most business organizations, and particularly the transportation and communications industries, were indifferent to the ending date but supported uniformity across the EU. In the United Kingdom an interest group named Daylight Extra supported an extension on the continent to the last Sunday of October.[3] A European barometer survey of public opinion showed strong public support for an extension.

The possible extension of double summertime in the CET led to opposition by interest groups in several countries and by some pan-European associations of national interest groups. Opposition was concentrated in the countries located in the western part of the European continent and in the southern part, where an extension would mean less daylight. The opposition included GASHE (Groupe d'Action pour une Heure Stable en Europe) with participating associations in Belgium, France, Germany, and Switzerland; COPA (Compagnie d'Organization Professionelle d'Agriculture) representing farmers; and COFACE, a consumer group concerned about children having to go to bed during daylight and get up in the dark. Some of the opposition referred to a "disturbance of the biological rhythm with emphasis on children and elderly people, negative effects on agriculture, and a possible increase in environmental pollution. In addition doubts have been expressed about the real benefits of summertime with particular reference to the energy savings issue, for which it is argued that the savings are not important."[4]

The European Commission, the body that initiates legislation, proposed harmonization to the last Sunday of October beginning in 1997. The harmonization of summertime in the EU was governed by the co-decision procedure established by

[1]Chapter 14 provides information on the institutions of the European Union.

[2]The Belgische Vereniging Pro Zomeruur, composed of hotel and catering interests, supported an extension, for example.

[3]Daylight Extra's principal objective was to move the UK from GMT to CET.

[4]European Commission, "Report on the advantages and disadvantages of summertime," VII-A-2, p. 2.

the Maastricht treaty and incorporated as Article 189a of the EU Treaty.[5] Under this procedure the European Commission prepares a proposal that is then considered by the Council of Ministers and the European Parliament. All laws in the European Union must be enacted by the Council, which has as its members the countries in the EU. Under the co-decision procedure the Council operates under qualified majority; that is, enactment of a law requires 54 of the 76 votes in the Council.[6] A qualified majority in support of a proposal, which can be modified by the Council, results in a "common position." A key feature of the co-decision procedure is that it gives the European Parliament the authority to reject (veto) the common position of the Council. Rejection requires an absolute (50 percent) majority.[7] If the European Parliament does not reject the common position, it becomes law. ■

[5]The co-decision procedure governs the harmonization of regulations for the completion of the single market.
[6]The inclusion of new member states in 1995 changed the qualified majority requirement to 62 of the 87 votes.

[7]If the European Parliament indicates that it intends to reject the Council's proposal, the Council may convene a Conciliation Committee to explore the source of the disagreement. The Conciliation Committee is composed of an equal number of representatives of the Council and the Parliament and seeks to reach a joint text. If a joint text is agreed to, the Council and the Parliament then both must approve it by qualified majority and absolute majority, respectively. If a joint text is not agreed to in the Conciliation Committee, the Council may adopt by qualified majority its initial position. That position is enacted as law unless the Parliament rejects it by an absolute majority. If the Parliament rejects it, the status quo remains in effect.

PREPARATION QUESTION

1. Using a figure similar to Figure 5–9 in the extension of daylight saving time example, what conditions are required for enactment of an extension to the last Sunday of October? Hint: In this framework, the countries represented on the Council correspond to legislators in the U.S. case, and rather than the median legislator being pivotal with simple (50 percent) majority rule, a qualified majority in the Council is required. If a qualified majority in the Council prefers an extension, where must the pivotal voter in the European Parliament be located relative to the preferences of the countries in the Council for the common position to be adopted? Do not consider amendments.

Repeal of the Luxury Tax

In 1990 Congress, with the acquiescence of the Bush administration, enacted legislation that imposed a 10 percent federal luxury tax on the sale of furs and jewelry costing more than $10,000, automobiles costing more than $30,000, boats costing more than $100,000, and aircraft costing more than $250,000 (except for aircraft used at least 80 percent for business). Effective in 1991 the tax was applied to the difference between the price and the tax base, so the tax on a $1,000,000 yacht was $90,000. The luxury tax was a component of the Deficit Reduction Act of 1990 and was viewed not as a significant source of additional revenue but as a symbol that the rich should bear a larger share of the tax burden. The tax yielded $251 million in 1991 and $146 million in the first half of 1992 with the vast majority coming from the sale of automobiles.

As the economy slowed, sales of boats costing at least $100,000 began to decrease, falling from 16,000 in 1987 to 9,100 in 1990. In 1992 after the luxury tax was imposed, only 4,200 boats were sold. Sales of boats 35 feet or longer fell from 1,300 in 1989 to 400 in 1991, with sales revenue falling from $2.5 billion to $800 million. Employment in the industry decreased from 600,000 to 400,000 in 1993. Hatteras Yachts of New Bern, North Carolina, experienced a 50 percent decrease in sales and was forced to layoff 1,000 of its 1,800 employees. Viking Yacht of New Gretna, New Jersey, was forced to cut its workforce to 65 people. Yacht manufacturers from Minnesota, Wisconsin, Maine, Connecticut, and Florida experienced similar declines. As one potential customer who decided to stick with his current yacht rather than purchase a new one said, "I don't care how much you spend for a boat, $190,000 in taxes is ludicrous."[1] Some purchasers of yachts registered their boats in the Bahamas and the Cayman Islands to avoid the luxury and state sales taxes. The National Marine Manufacturers Association and its members blamed the collapse of the market on the luxury tax.

The light aircraft industry was also hard hit, as were the other industries subject to the tax. Jaguar sales fell by 55 percent, and the company went so far as to rebate the luxury tax of over $3,000 to customers.

The luxury tax had been inserted in a large tax bill during conference committee deliberations, and opponents had little opportunity to oppose it. Once in place and its effects were realized, opposition mounted. "The purpose [of the tax] was to tax the rich and their toys," said Republican Senator John H. Chafee of Rhode Island, a big boat-building state. "What it really did was hurt the toymakers."[2] Senator Robert Dole, (R-KS), where light aircraft manufacturers are located, said, "A lot of middle-class people are losing their jobs."[3] Opponents of the tax pressured Congress and the Bush administration, and Senator Dole introduced a bill to repeal the tax. The repeal bill was included in more comprehensive legislation, but Congress was unable to reach agreement on the package. Opponents saw another opportunity in the spring of 1993 as President Clinton pushed for a deficit reduction package that would include increases in personal and corporate income taxes in addition to an energy tax. ■

[1] *Business Week,* August 3, 1993.

[2] *Business Week,* August 3, 1993.

[3] *The Wall Street Journal,* June 12, 1991.

PREPARATION QUESTIONS

1. Use supply and demand analysis to identify the incidence of the luxury tax for the rents of producers and the consumer surplus of customers.
2. Are the consumers or producers of luxury goods more likely to be politically active on this issue? Why?
3. Are the interests of U.S. automobile manufacturers aligned with those of yacht builders?
4. Are the opponents of the luxury tax likely to be successful?

An Electoral Dilemma (A)

Voters may find themselves in a prisoners' dilemma when faced with deciding whether to vote for an incumbent legislator. Incumbency provides several advantages; for example, the seniority that results in good committee assignments can benefit constituents. Other things being equal, then, voters benefit from reelecting their incumbents. Public opinion polls in the 1990s, however, indicated that many voters believed that some of the problems of government were due to incumbents who served their constituents' interests but did not take broader national interests into account. The payoffs to someone who holds this belief might be like those presented in the matrix in Figure 5C-1. The payoffs are higher if a voter in district n votes for the incumbent in her district, but the greater the number of incumbents reelected in other districts the lower the payoffs to the voter. It is thus a dominant strategy for the voter to

FIGURE 5C-1 Reelecting Incumbents: A Prisoner's Dilemma

		Number of Incumbents Reelected in Other Districts					
		0	*1*	*2*	. . .	*n–2*	*n–1*
Voter in District n	***vote for incumbent***	10	8	6	. . .	–14	–16
	vote against incumbent	6	4	2	. . .	–18	–20

vote for the incumbent, and the same is true for voters in every district. All incumbents thus are reelected, yielding a payoff of –16. This outcome, however, is strictly worse for all voters than if they had jointly voted against the incumbents. Voters are thus in a prisoners' dilemma. ■

PREPARATION QUESTION

1. Does repeated play allow voters to work their way out of this dilemma?

An Electoral Dilemma (B)

One means of dealing with a prisoners' dilemma is to use an institution to change the game. Voters in several states approved ballot propositions that limited the number of terms state officeholders could serve. These propositions were intended to reduce the problems associated with incumbency, but while they passed the initiatives, voters also reelected their incumbents. Reelecting incumbents is explained by the prisoners' dilemma in Figure 5C-1, and the success of term limitation propositions is explained by the game in Figure 5C-2.

Consider a voter with the preferences presented in Figure 5C-1. The voter could be either pivotal or not pivotal for the ballot proposition. If not pivotal, one's vote will not affect the outcome on the term limitation proposition, and from Figure 5C-2 the payoff is 6 if the proposition passes or –16 if it fails, regardless of how the nonpivotal voters vote. To simplify the analysis, the proposition is assumed to prohibit any incumbent from serving another term. If the voter is pivotal, the payoffs are 6 if voting for the proposition and –16 if voting against it. The voter thus is at least as well off by voting for the proposition as voting against it, even though the likelihood of being pivotal is very small. The voter thus has both a dominant strategy to vote for the incumbent and a dominant strategy to vote for the term limitation proposition.[1] ■

[1] Although many states have ballot proposition mechanisms, the federal government does not.

FIGURE 5C–2 Term Limitations Proposition

	Voter is		
	Pivotal	***Not Pivotal***	
		Wins	***Loses***
vote for proposition	6	6	–16
vote against proposition	–16	6	–16

CHAPTER 6

Political Analysis for Business

Introduction

This chapter presents a framework for analyzing political and nonmarket action on issues characterized by opposing interests. The framework provides the foundation for strategy formulation and implementation in Chapters 7 and 8, respectively. Although the focus is on the competition among interests in the arenas of public institutions, the approach applies as well to issues involving private collective action as considered in Chapter 4. The approach will be presented in the context of U.S. institutions, but, as indicated in Part IV of the book, it is more broadly applicable. The approach is illustrated using a case involving Boeing and foreign leasing.

From the perspective presented in Chapter 5, public policies result from a pluralism of interests and the political action taken in pursuit of those interests. Consequently, the study of individual interests and the manner in which they are transformed into political action is one foundation for the analysis of nonmarket issues. Political action is transformed into outcomes through public institutions—legislatures, administrative agencies, regulatory agencies, courts, and international accords. These institutions and their characteristics are the other foundation of political analysis. Because these institutions structure the political actions of individuals, firms, and interest groups, the perspective presented here is referred to as *structured pluralism.*

Structured pluralism is illustrated in Figure 6-1 in the context of the issues, interests, institutions, and information that characterize the nonmarket environment. The nonmarket issue is the unit of analysis. The pluralistic private interests affected by the issue take political action based on the likely benefits and costs of those actions, and their actions compete in the arenas of public institutions. The institutions have structures and procedures under which alternatives for resolving the issue are considered by their officeholders. The officeholders themselves have preferences for the consequences of alternatives, and those preferences are derived from their policy interests and, through the constituency connection, the interests of their constituents. Information comes from two sources. First, public policy analysis provides technical information about the consequences of alternatives. Second, private interests provide politically relevant information as well as technical information to institutional officeholders. The outcome of this process is a public policy to address the issue.

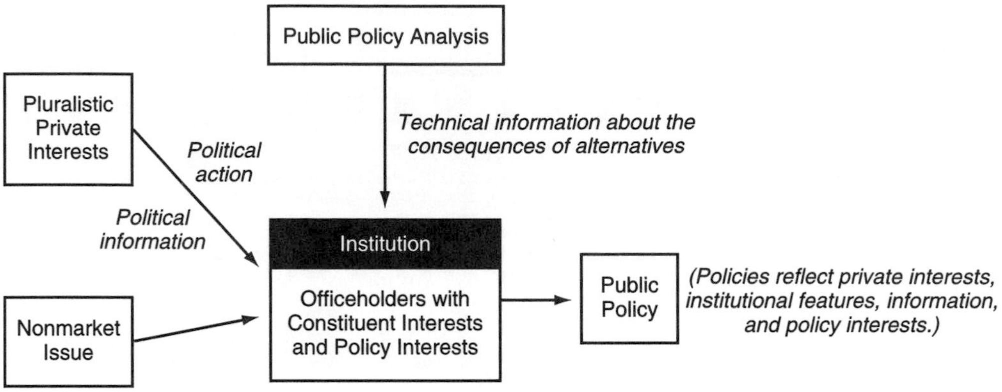

FIGURE 6-1 Structured Pluralism

A Framework for the Analysis of Political and Collective Action

INTERESTS AND INTEREST GROUPS

Because interests and interest groups are at the foundation of political action, the framework begins with an assessment of the interests concerned with an issue. Interests may be assessed on distributive and moral dimensions. Most issues have distributive consequences, as measured by benefits and costs or surpluses and rents. For example, in the daylight saving time extension case analyzed in Chapter 5, convenience stores, sporting goods manufacturers, and the charcoal and barbecue industries identified the effects of an extension on their sales and profits.

Issues may also have moral dimensions. The moral determinants of political action are often more difficult to assess than the distributive consequences, but on some issues they are as important. How individuals with various beliefs about social justice view a political alternative can be assessed, but the more difficult task is determining how many people hold which views about social justice and how likely those individuals are to act in the arenas of public institutions or through private nonmarket action.

Interests, whether distributive or moral in origin, give rise to a demand for political action that can lead an individual, firm, union, nonprofit organization, or activist group to become involved in an issue. Although these interests may act on their own, they also may form interest groups to organize, coordinate, and mobilize the delivery of their political and collective action.

Interest groups form among individuals and organizations with aligned interests. A necessary condition for formation is that the anticipated benefits from collective action exceed the costs of organizing the interest group and of its subsequent actions. Interest groups may organize around a single issue, such as an extension of daylight saving time. High-tech companies, public accounting firms, and other firms formed an ad hoc coalition to lead and coordinate their actions to obtain uniform national standards for securities fraud lawsuits, and their efforts met with success in 1998. Interest groups may also be formed by a political entrepreneur who mobilizes the common interests of dispersed individuals, by a trade association that represents firms in an industry, or by labor unions to represent employees. Once formed, interest groups may join in coalitions to address issues of common interest. Although interest groups join in because of an alignment of interests, they are sustained by the fruits of their efforts.

Interest groups can also have aligned interests that lead them to act in parallel or to coordinate their activities. For example, the Daylight Saving Time Coalition and the RP Foundation Fighting Blindness both worked to extend daylight saving time, although the former represented business interests and the latter represented individuals afflicted with night blindness. Aligned interests also allow specialization. Environmental interest groups engage in a wide variety of political activities, and many focus on particular issues or strategies. The Sierra Club has a broad political agenda, the Wilderness Society focuses on open lands, the Natural Resources Defense Council emphasizes litigation, and Greenpeace emphasizes confrontation in addition to policy advocacy.

In some cases, an interest group may be successful in having the government establish an organization or agency through which its interests can be served. The Small Business Administration, the U.S. Department of Agriculture, and the Export-Import Bank are examples of such agencies. Environmental interest groups repeatedly have sought without success a cabinet department for environmental protection. Members of Congress also interact directly with interest groups and have established means of responding to their interests—the agriculture and small-business committees of both chambers are examples.

The political system also grants rights to individuals and organizations that they can exercise to advance their interests and protect those interests from the collective actions of others. For example, U.S. trade law gives firms, labor unions, and communities rights to seek relief from imports. Similarly, wilderness groups exercise their rights before the courts to block the commercial development of public lands. Whatever their motivation, interest groups have become skillful in exerting pressure on elected and administrative officeholders through direct action, their standing before the courts and regulatory agencies, and their rights to participate in the decision-making processes of public institutions. The chapter case *Tobacco Politics* provides an opportunity to assess the complex act of interests involved in the tobacco issue.

THE AMOUNT OF POLITICAL ACTION

From the perspective of structured pluralism, a principal driver of public policies is the effectiveness of the political action generated by interests. Political action includes activities such as lobbying, grassroots and other forms of constituent pressure, research and testimony, electoral support, and public advocacy. At a conceptual level, the extent of these activities is a function of their costs and the benefits they yield. This is illustrated in Figure 6-2, which presents marginal benefit and marginal cost curves for political action. As indicated in the third panel of the figure, the optimal level of political action maximizes the excess of benefits over costs and is determined by the intersection of the two curves.

The amount of political action generated thus depends on both benefits and costs. If the issue is the extension of daylight saving time, the benefits to firms stem from the increase in demand for their products. The costs of political action are of three types. The first includes the costs associated with organizing for collective action. The second includes the direct costs of undertaking political action, including the cost of lobbying, maintaining a Washington office, and preparing testimony. The third pertains to how effective the political action is, which depends on factors such as the size of the interest group and its resources. The next two sections consider factors affecting the benefits, or demand, and the costs, or supply, of political action.

THE DEMAND FOR POLITICAL ACTION

The demand for political action is derived from the distributive consequences of a political alternative, such as a bill before Congress. For firms, those consequences are reflected in sales, profits, and market value. Employee interests are measured in terms of

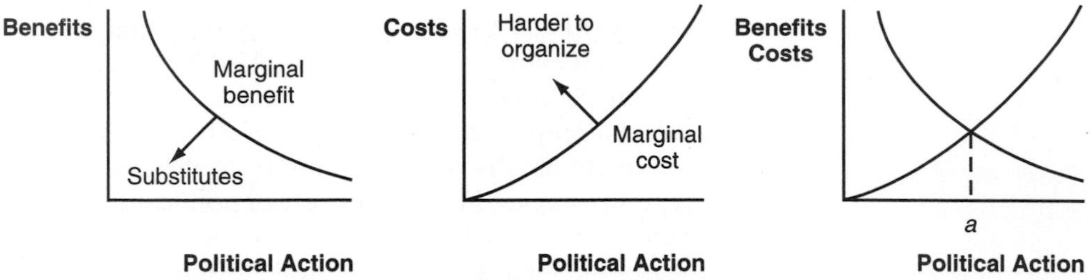

FIGURE 6-2 The Amount of Political Action

jobs and wages. For consumers, the distributive consequences are measured in terms of the prices, qualities, and availability of goods and services.

The demand for political action depends on the magnitude of the benefits it can generate, as reflected in the marginal benefits curve in Figure 6-2. Aggregate benefits are important indicators of the aggregate demand for political action, but in many cases the per capita benefits are a better indicator of the incentive for an individual or a firm to engage in political action. If the benefits are significant and concentrated, the per capita benefits will be high and the potential beneficiaries will have an incentive to act. The members of the Daylight Saving Time Coalition each anticipated substantial benefits from an extension that would shift the demand for their products outward. If the benefits are widely dispersed, however, the per capita benefits can be small, thus providing only a limited incentive for political action. Individual taxpayers, for example, take little political action because the per capita benefits are typically small relative to their cost of political action. In some cases political action can occur even when benefits are not large on a per capita basis. Proposition 13, a public referendum in California that reduced property taxes, resulted from political entrepreneurship that allowed individuals to lower their property taxes by simply casting their votes.

On some issues the benefits from political action can be obtained through other means, referred to as *substitutes.* The benefits from political action are lower when there are other means of generating them, and the closer these substitutes come to replicating the consequences of political action the smaller are the benefits from that political action. Substitutes may be available in the market environment or in the nonmarket environment. On an issue such as unitary taxation—the taxation of corporate profits on a worldwide basis by a state—a foreign electronics firm considering where to locate a new U.S. subsidiary has an incentive to support the repeal of California's unitary taxation law. That firm, however, has available the market substitute of locating its subsidiary in Oregon, which repealed its unitary taxation law. The alternative of avoiding unitary taxation by locating in Oregon reduces the benefits from, and hence lowers the firm's demand for, political action to change the California law.[1] An example of a public substitute is the subsidies paid to U.S.-flagged ships to offset the higher operating costs compared with foreign-flagged ships. U.S. seamen earn between $2,000 and $3,000 a month, whereas foreign seamen earn as little as $300 a month. In addition, U.S.-flagged ships are required to have a crew of 21, whereas many diesel-powered foreign

[1]Under pressure from other countries, California made some revisions in its unitary taxation law. In 1994 the Supreme Court upheld the law.

ships operate with a crew of 14. When the public subsidy for the higher operating costs was eliminated by the Clinton administration in 1994, U.S. shipping companies sought a new subsidy system. When that effort failed, one of the companies immediately exercised its principal market substitute by announcing that it would switch the registry of many of its ships to other flags. In general, the closer the substitutes come to providing the same consequences the lower is the demand for political action. That is, as indicated in Figure 6-2, substitutes shift the marginal benefit curve downward, and closer substitutes shift the curve farther downward.

The benefits from political action also depend on the political action that others take on an issue. A grassroots political campaign in which members of an interest group contact their congressional representatives can be quite effective. If, however, an interest group on the other side of the issue responds by mounting its own grassroots campaign, the benefits will be reduced. Consequently, the assessment of the benefits must take into account the likely actions of other interest groups. In many cases, interests that are aligned can take actions that increase the benefits from the political action of others. In the daylight saving time case, the separate actions of the coalition of businesses and the RP Foundation Fighting Blindness may have increased the effectiveness of each member's political actions.

THE COSTS OF POLITICAL AND COLLECTIVE ACTION

The amount of political action generated depends on cost, or supply, considerations in addition to the benefits. One type of cost is organizational and includes the cost of identifying, contacting, motivating, and organizing the participation of those with aligned interests. If the number of affected individuals or groups is small, the costs of organization are likely to be low. When the number of potential members of an interest group is large, those costs can be high. As indicated in Figure 6-2, the harder a group is to organize the higher is the marginal cost curve. Taxpayers are costly to organize because they are widely dispersed, whereas dairy farmers are relatively easy to organize. The costs of organization can be reduced by associations and standing organizations that represent dispersed interests or specialize in issues around which interests can be organized. Labor unions, the Sierra Club, and business groups such as the National Federation of Independent Business are examples of organizations that reduce the costs of political action for their members.

The organization of interests is also affected by the free-rider problem. If the number of potential members of a group is small, the importance of one additional participant can be significant enough to justify each member's participation. Furthermore, as indicated in Chapter 5, punishment and exclusion are easier to apply when groups are small. If the group is large, a potential participant may conclude that joining in the collective action would have little effect on the outcome and hence may decide to free ride. Free riding shifts the marginal cost curve in Figure 6-2 upward, reducing the political action generated. Organized interest groups attempt to reduce the free-rider problem by bundling together political action and services that benefit potential members. The Sierra Club, for example, publishes a magazine and also organizes trips for its members. The free-rider problem also can be mitigated when interests expect to address a series of nonmarket issues, as participation on today's issue can make it more likely that others will also participate on future issues.

In addition to organizing, interest groups must mobilize their members to deliver collective action and generate political pressure. Members may be mobilized on an ad hoc basis to address a particular issue. They may also be represented by a formal organization that can monitor a series of issues and act when the interests of the group can be served. In addition to this readiness function, formal organizations monitor the progress of issues through their life cycles. Trade and professional associations, the AFL-CIO, the Semiconductor Industry Association, the National Federation of Independent Business, and environmental interest groups provide this function.

THE EFFECTIVENESS OF GROUP ACTION

The effectiveness of the political action of an interest group depends on several factors including the number and resources of its members and their geographic distribution. The constituency connection indicates that the number of members of an interest group, and hence voters, is important to legislators. On an issue affecting a firm, potentially relevant constituents include shareholders, employees, suppliers, distributors, and in some cases customers. There are few U.S. automobile manufacturers, but they employ a large number of people, have extensive dealer organizations, and have many suppliers. The number of members is also important because each can contribute resources. Financial resources fund research, lobbying, legal services, campaign contributions, and the interest group's administrative staff.

Particularly for issues addressed in legislative arenas, the geographic location of interest group members affects the effectiveness of political action. The greater the number of political jurisdictions covered by the group, the more effective are strategies based on the constituency connection. Although small businesses do not have the resources of large businesses, they are politically effective because they are numerous and are located in every political jurisdiction. Automobile assembly plants are concentrated in a relatively small number of states and congressional districts, but the "coverage" of the auto companies' dealer and supplier networks is extensive. The greater the number of districts covered by the members of an interest group, the more effective is its political action. In the context of Figure 6-2 greater effectiveness shifts the marginal cost of political action downward, increasing the amount of political action generated.

This characterization of the supply side of political action predicts that the costs of generating political action are greater when the costs of identifying, organizing, and mobilizing those with similar interests are greater. These costs are also higher when the free-rider problem is more prevalent and fewer means are available to mitigate it. The costs of generating political action are lower as the group's actions are more effective. On a legislative issue, political action is more effective when the resources of the group are greater, the group has more members, and it has more extensive coverage of legislative districts. Any strategy that can reduce the costs of collective action or increase its effectiveness will increase the amount of political action the interest group generates.

THE DISTRIBUTIVE POLITICS SPREADSHEET

The analysis of the demand and supply sides of the political action decision can be summarized in the form of the spreadsheet as presented below in Figure 6-6 for the Boeing case. The distributive politics spreadsheet pertains to a political alternative, such as a bill before Congress, or equivalently to a change from the status quo resulting from the adoption of an alternative. The spreadsheet is organized in terms of the interest groups that would benefit from the political alternative and, hence, support it, and in terms of the interest groups that would be harmed by the alternative and so oppose it. The top panel of the spreadsheet pertains to those interest groups that would benefit from the adoption of the political alternative, in the Boeing case an exemption for job-creating exports, and the bottom panel pertains to the opposing interest groups.

The demand side information summarized in the spreadsheet for each interest includes the available substitutes, the aggregate magnitude of the benefits for the interest group, and the per capita benefits for individual members of the group. The supply side information includes the number of members, their coverage of political jurisdictions, their resources, and the costs of organization. This information provides the basis for a prediction of the amount of effective political action likely to be generated by the interests. This prediction then is used in assessing the likely outcome of the issue and in formulating strategies to affect the outcome.

Institutions are not included in the spreadsheet because they are viewed as arenas in which the political actions of interests are deployed, as indicated in Figure 6-3 considered in the next section. The institutional officeholders who will decide the fate of the political alternative are also not included in the spreadsheet, since they are regarded as part of the institution.

FIGURE 6-3 Political Competition in Institutional Arenas

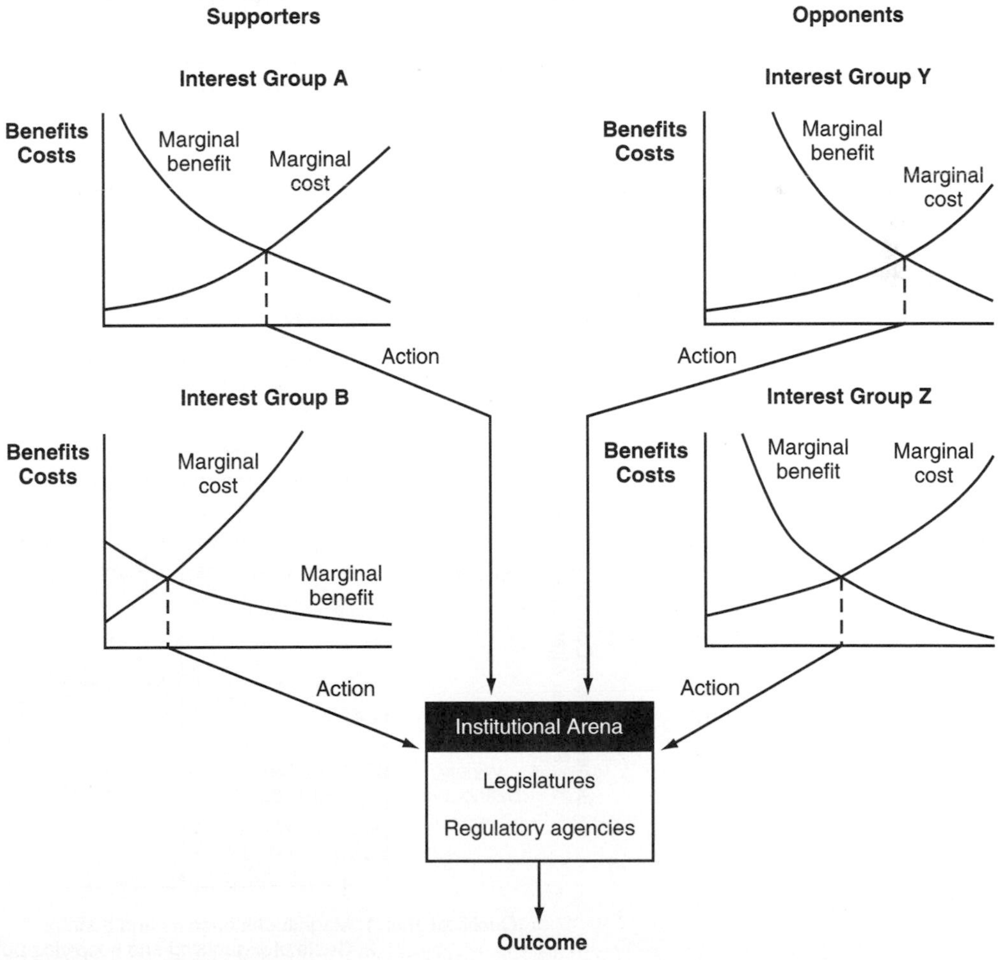

THE NATURE OF POLITICAL COMPETITION

When interests are in opposition, the political actions of interest groups compete in an institutional arena, as illustrated in Figure 6-3. In the figure interest groups A and B would benefit from the adoption of the political alternative. Interest groups Y and Z would be harmed by its adoption and thus have an incentive to oppose it (i.e., they benefit from the rejection of the alternative). The actions of these groups, coupled with the characteristics of the institution, then determine the outcome. The outcome of the political competition may be a win for one side and a loss for the other. In other cases, the outcome may reflect a political equilibrium influenced by all the competing interests. The length of the extension of daylight saving time is an example of such an equilibrium as characterized by the median voter theorem. The ratification of the North American Free Trade Agreement (NAFTA) is an example of a win for business and consumers and a loss for organized labor.

The nature of the political competition on an issue depends on the incidence of the distributive consequences. Building on the work of Lowi (1964), Wilson (1980) categorized the nature of political competition as a function of the relative *concentration* or *dispersion* of the benefits of supporting or opposing an alternative such as a bill before Congress. Although this categorization presented in Figure 6-4 focuses on the nature of the politics and not on the prediction of the outcome, it is a useful perspective for distinguishing among types of political competition.

Wilson's categorization pertains to a political alternative that would change the status quo. If both the benefits from supporting the political alternative and the benefits from opposing it, and hence supporting the status quo, are concentrated, both supporters and opponents have incentives to take political action. If, in addition, their costs of political action are low relative to their benefits, interest groups will be active on both sides of the issue. The resulting political competition, according to Wilson, takes the form of *interest group politics,* and the outcome is largely determined by the relative pressures generated by the interest groups on either side of the issue. Legislation that

FIGURE 6-4 Nature of Political Competition

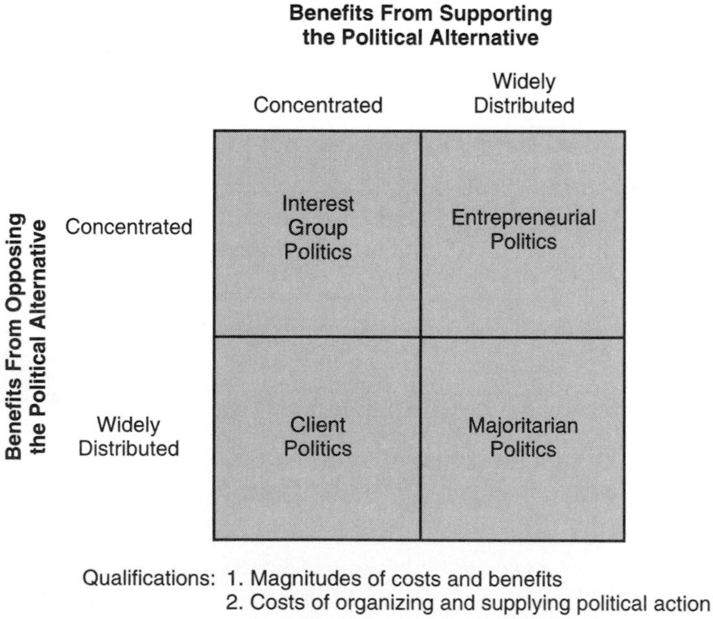

pits business against labor is typically characterized by interest group politics. International trade policy, which often finds exporters opposing firms that compete against imports, is also characterized by interest group politics.

When the benefits from supporting a political alternative are widely distributed, the per capita benefits and the incentives to take political action are likely to be low. Furthermore, if the costs of political action are significant, few will take political action. When this is the case for both those who benefit from and those who oppose the alternative, the politics of the issue is said to be *majoritarian* with the outcome determined by the preferences of the majority of people. The politics of social security are majoritarian in nature because each individual benefits from social security but is taxed to support it, albeit by different amounts.

When the benefits from supporting a political alternative are concentrated and the benefits from opposing it are widely distributed, the supporters have stronger incentives to take political action than do the opponents. The political competition then takes the form of *client politics* with supporters attempting to become the clients of the institutional officeholders who will decide the alternative. In client politics, officeholders can serve their clients without risk of substantial opposition from the other side. Pork barrel programs are characterized by client politics because the benefits are concentrated and the costs are widely distributed among taxpayers. A firm seeking an exemption from a regulation or seeking a subsidy such as for the use of ethanol in oxygenated fuels is likely to be involved in client politics.

When the benefits from supporting a political alternative are widely distributed and the benefits from opposing it are concentrated, the opponents have a stronger incentive to take political action than do its supporters. The location of toxic waste disposal sites and the NIMBY (not-in-my-backyard) movement reflect this distribution of benefits because few communities want a site in their backyard. Wilson refers to this situation as *entrepreneurial politics,* since if the alternative is to be adopted over the status quo, a political entrepreneur is needed to mobilize or represent those with dispersed benefits. A member of Congress, Ralph Nader, or a business leader can be a political entrepreneur.

In terms of the concentration and distribution of benefits, entrepreneurial politics is the opposite side of the coin from client politics. In terms of outcomes, the two differ by whether the alternative or the status quo is favored. In client politics the benefits to the interest groups supporting an alternative are concentrated and those of the opponents are widely distributed, so other things being equal, the alternative is favored over the status quo. In entrepreneurial politics, the consequences to those who would benefit from the alternative are widely distributed, whereas the benefits to the opponents of the alternative are concentrated. This favors the status quo, and for the alternative to be adopted a political entrepreneur is needed to mobilize the interests with widely distributed benefits. When a political entrepreneur is present, the political competition can have the characteristics of both client and entrepreneurial politics.

One strategy of interest groups is to attempt to change the nature of the politics of an issue. The politics of the extension of daylight saving time was basically majoritarian because to some extent everyone would be affected by an extension. Some benefits of an extension were concentrated, however, and those beneficiaries worked to change the politics from majoritarian to client by organizing the businesses that would benefit. The Daylight Saving Time Coalition represented them and reduced the costs of their political action. The opposition to the extension was unable to organize in the same manner and relied on its representatives, such as Senators Exon and Ford, but they were unable to prevail against the better organized interests with concentrated benefits. In this case, the clients prevailed, and Senators Exon and Ford were unsuccessful political entrepreneurs.

INSTITUTIONS AND INSTITUTIONAL OFFICEHOLDERS

Although Wilson's categorization is suggestive of some of the important characteristics of the politics of a nonmarket issue, it does not provide a complete theory of political outcomes on an issue. For example, the effectiveness and skill with which interest groups implement their political strategies can affect the outcome. Outcomes also depend on the institutions that deal with the issue. In addition to the characteristics of legislative institutions considered in Chapter 5, the position taken by a cabinet agency or the president can also be important. The committee structure of a legislature and the location of supporters and opponents on the relevant committees can also affect the outcome. Vote trading and other exchanges of support may also be important.

As portrayed in Figure 6-3, an institution is an arena to which interests direct their political action, and hence the preferences and actions of those who hold offices in the institution can affect the outcome. On some issues, officeholders may be active in support of an interest group or may work to advance their own policy preferences. They may, for example, attempt to influence other officeholders or they may trade their vote on an issue that is of less importance for the vote of another officeholder on a more important issue. Elected officials, however, are constrained by both their duty to represent their constituents and by their desire to be reelected. The constituency connection thus constrains their behavior. One means of determining how legislators are likely to vote on a political alternative is to examine the interests of their constituents and how those interests are affected by the alternative in question. The implications of this constituent connection for strategy formulation are developed further in Chapters 7 and 8.

Moral Determinants of Collective and Political Action

On some issues, moral concerns motivate individuals and activist and interest groups to take political action. Moral considerations are the subject of Part V of this book, and only a brief introduction to the positive application of these concepts is presented here.

Because moral concerns derive from beliefs and values that can differ among individuals, political competition can take place on moral dimensions, as the conflicts regarding abortion and affirmative action illustrate. Just as one would not expect all physicians to perform abortions, neither would one expect all people of goodwill to agree on issues regarding affirmative action, working conditions in the factories of foreign suppliers, or drug testing of employees. The difficulty in predicting when moral concerns will lead to collective and political action arises not only from the differences among individuals but also because the conviction with which those concerns are held can vary.

Managers must understand the moral motivations of individuals and interest groups and the strategies they are likely to employ. A church group concerned about a corporation's marketing activities in developing countries may use a political strategy that is quite different from a group of exporters of capital goods interested in securing a higher lending authorization for the Export-Import Bank. The exporters may use low-profile strategies such as lobbying and coalition building. The church group may initiate shareholder resolutions, pressure institutional investors, adopt media strategies, and demonstrate to attract the attention of government officeholders. These strategies are considered in Chapter 4 in the context of private nonmarket action, and similar strategies can be used in the arenas of public institutions.

Boeing in a Pickle

Beginning in 1962 the investment tax credit provided incentives for capital investment through credits deducted from a firm's tax liability. By the 1980s, however, a number of firms were incurring operating losses and had no tax liability to which the credits could be applied. With the nation in a recession, Congress passed the Economic Recovery Tax Act (ERTA) of 1981 to stimulate economic activity by allowing firms with losses to purchase capital equipment and to "sell" the investment tax credit to a profitable firm that could use the credit to reduce its taxes. Thus, a steel company with operating losses could obtain a new rolling mill by having a lessor take title to the mill and then lease it back to the steel company. The lessor would receive the investment tax credit plus the tax benefits from accelerated depreciation, and the lease payments by the steel company would be lowered by the amount of those benefits.[2] ERTA thus restored the incentives for capital investment of those firms with operating losses.

Many foreign sales were also made under lease arrangements designed to capture the investment tax credit. A U.S. lessor would purchase capital equipment from a U.S. manufacturer, take the investment tax credit and the accelerated depreciation, and lease the equipment to a foreign customer. The tax benefits were then shared among the three participants in the transaction. Commercial aircraft had frequently been sold through these leasing arrangements. Investment tax credits applied to aircraft purchased by a U.S. lessor and leased to a foreign airline if the aircraft were used substantially in regular service to the United States. The "substantially" condition involved a modest number of landings on U.S. territory in a year.

Foreign leasing became an issue because of the way ERTA was written. Its language allowed tax-exempt entities to make the same type of lease arrangements a steel company or a foreign airline could make. In addition, ERTA allowed the sale and leaseback of assets already owned by a firm or a tax-exempt entity. Tax-exempts thus could sell an existing asset to a lessor who would take the tax benefits and lease the asset back to the tax-exempt at a price reflecting the tax benefits.

The number of tax-exempt entities that could benefit from leasing was enormous. Every municipality, museum, school district, college, library, nonprofit corporation, and government entity could use it. The pace of leasing by tax-exempts began to accelerate in 1983, and the federal government became alarmed about the potential loss of tax receipts, particularly because of the record federal budget deficit and the sluggish economy. In addition, several leasing plans attracted media attention. Bennington College announced plans to sell its campus to alumni and then lease it back, with the alumni passing back to the college the tax benefits allowed by ERTA. The Navy began leasing cargo ships instead of purchasing them, with the "purchaser" of the ships taking the investment tax credit and the depreciation benefits and passing back to the Navy a portion of the tax benefits in the form of a price reduction. Transactions such as the Navy's and sale-and-lease back transactions such as that planned by Bennington College were clearly contrary to the intent of ERTA.

The Ways and Means Committee had drafted ERTA, and members of that committee had vested interests in its original intent. Representative J.J. (Jake) Pickle (D-TX), a ranking member of the committee, was determined to eliminate the abuses of ERTA. His idea was that organizations that were exempt from taxes should not receive tax benefits. This was expressed as, "People who don't pay taxes should not get tax breaks."[3] This slogan was quickly interpreted to include foreign lessees, since foreign firms do not pay U.S. taxes.

In May 1983, Representative Pickle introduced a bill, H.R. 3110, that would deny the investment tax credit and accelerated depreciation benefits to tax-exempts and to

---

[2]The economic efficiency rationale for this provision of ERTA was that it would equalize marginal tax rates across firms and thus lessen distortions in the pattern of capital investment. The political pressure from industries unable to use investment tax credits was undoubtedly the impetus for the provision, however.
[3]*Fortune,* September 19, 1983, p. 52.

foreigners who lease assets from U.S. lessors.[4] Hearings before the House Ways and Means Committee were held 2 weeks later, and H.R. 3110 was passed by the committee on July 27. Floor action in the House was scheduled for the end of October. Senators Robert Dole (R-KS) and Howard Metzenbaum (D-OH) introduced a similar bill in the Senate.

At the then-current volume of leasing, the U.S. Department of Treasury estimated that the bill would increase tax receipts by $1.65 billion per year, with foreign leasing accounting for $570 million. Approximately $300 million of the $570 million was attributable to Boeing, which used leasing for nearly half its foreign sales of 747s.[5] The other exporters affected included oil drilling rig manufacturers, producers of containers for ocean shipping, and other aircraft manufacturers.

In 1983, the 747's only competitors were the DC-10 and the Airbus A300. The A300's range did not allow it to make transoceanic flights, so many observers believed that the 747 had little foreign competition for flights to the United States. The DC-10 had a smaller capacity than the 747 but a similar range. McDonnell-Douglas was rumored to be phasing out the DC-10 because of lagging sales.

Boeing maintained that it was locked in a fierce competitive struggle with the highly subsidized Airbus, a consortium of four European companies supported by their home governments. According to Boeing, foreign airlines used their wide-bodied aircraft on many routes that involved a trade-off between long legs and shorter hops. For some foreign airlines, the A300 was a substitute for the 747, according to Boeing. An airline that operated routes in Asia as well as a route to the United States could fly 747s on the U.S. route and A300s on the Asian route, with a series of hops if necessary. Alternatively, it could use 747s on the Asian routes and fly each of them on the U.S. route often enough to qualify for the leasing tax benefits. Thus, elimination of the tax benefits on foreign leasing would result in a loss of U.S. exports, Boeing argued. Critics of foreign leasing, however, maintained that Boeing would not lose sales because it faced no competition. Furthermore, if sales would be lost, then U.S. taxpayers must be subsidizing foreigners. Representative Pickle wanted such subsidization stopped.

One means by which Airbus was subsidized was through government export financing at below-market interest rates. To compound Boeing's problem, the Export-Import Bank (Eximbank) had recently stopped providing subsidized export financing for 747s. This decision reflected the Eximbank's limited lending authorization and its conclusion, strongly denied by Boeing, that the 747 faced no effective competition.[6]

Boeing's competitive position was also adversely affected by the high value of the U.S. dollar. The trade-weighted value of the dollar had fallen from 122.4 at the beginning of the 1970s to 88.1 at the end of the decade. In 1981 the dollar began to rise rapidly and by 1982 it had passed 122 and was still increasing.

Hearings were scheduled before the Senate Finance Committee, chaired by Senator Dole, at the end of September. Neither senator from Washington was a member of the Finance Committee, and Republican Slade Gorton was in his first term in the Sen-

---

[4]Straight-line depreciation would be allowed on foreign leasing.

[5]In 1983 the 747 was the only Boeing aircraft still in production that was certified to cross an ocean. The 767 was not yet certified for transoceanic flights because of the Federal Aviation Administration's (FAA) administrative rule that permitted transoceanic crossings by twin-engine aircraft only if they remained no more than 60 minutes flying time from an acceptable airport. Approval was later granted, allowing the 767 to make transoceanic flights.

[6]The Eximbank had limited lending authority, requiring it to support those exports where its financing would have the greatest incremental effect on exports. See Baron (1983) for an analysis of Eximbank financing.

ate. Longtime Senator Henry Jackson had died in August 1983 and had been replaced by the former Republican governor Daniel Evans, who was in the process of campaigning to retain his seat in the November special election.

Boeing's problem was how to deal with the challenge posed by Representative Pickle's bill.

Analysis of the Case Example

THE NONMARKET ISSUE

The issue of eliminating the tax benefits on leasing by tax-exempt and foreign entities arose suddenly as a result of the rapid increase in leasing by tax-exempts. The potential loss of tax revenue for the federal government was large, and the issue advanced quickly to the legislative stage of its life cycle. Although the politics of the issue were basically distributive, the sale-and-leaseback deals on existing assets by tax-exempts constituted abuse of ERTA's intent because those deals neither created jobs nor stimulated economic growth. The tax abuse coupled with the record federal budget deficit meant that the issue was likely to advance quickly through the subsequent stages of its life cycle. The dilemma for Boeing was that its leasing was threatened by the actions of the tax-exempts.

The following analysis illustrates the approach presented in this chapter.[7] The analysis is intended to develop an understanding of the politics of the issue and the relative strengths of the interests involved. This provides a basis for making judgments about the likely outcomes and therefore about strategy.

DISTRIBUTIVE CONSEQUENCES

The demand for political action depends on the value of the associated tax benefits. The investment tax credit ranged up to 10 percent and represented a cash inflow for the entity holding title to the asset. The value of the accelerated depreciation was the present value of the difference in the tax liability between accelerated and straight-line depreciation. On a sale of a $100 million 747, the tax benefits threatened by Pickle's bill were approximately $20 million, including a $10 million investment tax credit and approximately $10 million due to accelerated depreciation.[8] At a sales rate of ten 747s a year, the tax benefits at stake were approximately $200 million.[9]

Although the magnitude of the tax benefits from foreign leasing are straightforward to estimate, the distribution of those benefits is more complex. A foreign leasing transaction involves three parties: the aircraft manufacturer, the foreign lessee, and the U.S. lessor. The share of the tax benefits captured by each party depends on the competitiveness of the aircraft and leasing industries. The leasing industry includes large banks, some insurance companies, and several leasing companies. Because of the number of potential lessors, competition would be expected to leave them with competitive profits. The benefits thus accrue primarily to the aircraft manufacturer and the foreign airline.[10]

---

[7]The analysis is not a description of Boeing's analysis or reasoning.

[8]Only sales of the 747 are considered here, although the analysis pertains to future sales of the 767 once it became certified for transoceanic flights.

[9]The difference between this figure and the Treasury estimate of $300 million is that the Treasury was reporting the tax collections reflecting the accelerated depreciation during the first years after the sale. The $200 million is a present value that takes into account the lower depreciation in later years.

[10]If the lessors captured the tax benefits, Boeing could establish its own financing subsidiary as McDonnell-Douglas had done. That would permit Boeing to realize the depreciation tax benefits but not the investment tax credit.

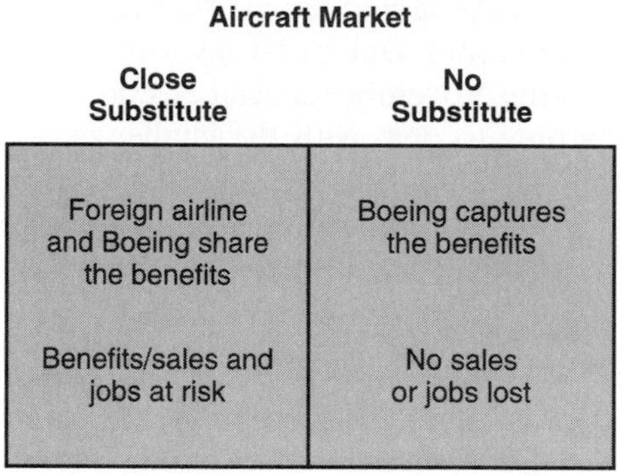

Aircraft Market
Close Substitute
No Substitute
Foreign airline and Boeing share the benefits
Boeing captures the benefits
Benefits/sales and jobs at risk
No sales or jobs lost

FIGURE 6-5 Distributive Consequences of Foreign Leasing for 747s

The distribution of the tax benefits between the manufacturer and the airline depends on whether other aircraft are close substitutes for the 747 for the route configuration of the airline. Indeed, each airline can be thought of as an individual market, and sales are based on negotiations between the airline and aircraft manufacturers. The appendix presents examples illustrating how the tax benefits are distributed, and Figure 6-5 summarizes the analysis. For an airline for which there is no substitute for the 747, Boeing is in the position of a monopolist and captures the tax benefits, as indicated in the right panel of the figure. For example, with foreign leasing Boeing can make the following arrangement for an airline that is willing to pay no more than \$100 million for a 747. Boeing can sell the 747 to a lessor for \$125 million, with the lessor taking the 20 percent tax benefits of \$25 million and leasing the aircraft to the foreign airline at a cost of \$100 million. If the Pickle bill were enacted, Boeing could reduce its price to \$100 million and retain the sale, and no jobs would be lost.

If there were some degree of competition from the A300, the tax benefits from leasing would be shared between the foreign airline and Boeing. If the A300 were a close substitute, the foreign airline might capture all the benefits. In that case, the elimination of the tax benefits would result in the loss of sales and jobs, as indicated in the left panel of the figure. In other cases, Boeing and the airline might each capture a share of the benefits.

The Eximbank apparently concluded that the 747 faced little competition, and hence Boeing captured the bulk of the tax benefits. Representative Pickle and his staff came to the same conclusion. Even if there were a degree of competition, Representative Pickle and the other supporters of the bill had an attractive issue. If there was competition and foreign airlines captured a portion of the benefits, then U.S. taxpayers were subsidizing foreign airlines. If there was little competition and Boeing captured the benefits, U.S. taxpayers were subsidizing a large, profitable firm. Boeing was in a pickle.

Boeing, however, maintained that export leasing allowed it to make sales that would otherwise be lost to Airbus and that Pickle's bill would cost sales and jobs at both Boeing and its suppliers. When it testifies before the Senate Finance Committee, Boeing can expect to be asked why it could not lower its price to retain sales if the tax benefits were eliminated. Boeing can also expect to be asked if the tax benefits on foreign leasing subsidize the foreign airlines that compete with U.S. international airlines.

To assess the impact of the Pickle bill, Boeing must determine if there are any public or private substitutes for the leasing. One obvious private substitute is to lower its price, which to some extent is possible, since Boeing is far down the learning curve on an aircraft that it had been producing for nearly 20 years. The other possible private substitute is to arrange for foreign lessors to make the lease arrangements, taking advantage of their own domestic tax laws. Other countries, however, did not provide investment tax credits, so even if foreign lessors financed Boeing's exports the tax benefits would not be as large. The Eximbank was unlikely to reverse its withdrawal of financing for 747s, so that public substitute was not a realistic alternative. The U.S. government was even less likely to subsidize a profitable corporation.

This analysis suggests that Boeing is likely to be capturing a substantial share of the tax benefits, and if the tax benefits were lost through Pickle's initiative, Boeing would retain the bulk of its sales by reducing its prices, except for some airlines for which the A300 was a close substitute. Boeing thus stood to lose profits but perhaps few sales as a consequence of the Pickle bill—at least that was the conclusion reached by Representative Pickle and the Eximbank.

BOEING'S NONMARKET AGENDA AND OBJECTIVES

Boeing had several issues on its nonmarket issue agenda, including Eximbank policy, U.S. pressure on Airbus and its parent countries, antitrust concerns in the U.S. aircraft industry, the high value of the dollar, the Reagan administration's increased defense spending from which Boeing expected to benefit, and the media and public attention being given to defense contractors. The foreign leasing issue had little direct relationship to these other issues, but the action the company took on the foreign leasing issue could affect its ability to deal with the other issues.

Boeing can pursue the following objectives:

1. Defeat of Pickle's bill
2. An exemption for job-creating leases
3. An exemption for job-creating export leases
4. An exemption for its own leases
5. Grandfathering of its current orders
6. A phaseout of the tax benefits on foreign leasing

The best outcome for Boeing would be the defeat of Pickle's bill, but there is considerable support for the bill, and it is likely to pass in some form.[11] The second objective is consistent with the original intent of ERTA, but a substantial tax loss would remain because tax-exempts would still be able to use leasing for all but sale-and-leaseback deals on existing assets. This objective is unlikely to be achievable. Objective 4 singles out Boeing without any particular justification, and so it, too, is unlikely. Therefore, Boeing's primary objective should be 3, with 5 and 6 as contingent objectives in the event that an exemption for job-creating export leases cannot be obtained. This objective means that the interests of other exporters are aligned with Boeing's interests, whereas the tax-exempts are in the opposition.

THE NATURE OF THE POLITICS

The principal beneficiaries of the Pickle bill are taxpayers and those who would benefit from lower interest rates if the federal budget deficit were reduced.[12] Those benefits are widely distributed and small on a per capita basis. The benefits from opposing Pickle's bill, however, are concentrated among tax-exempts and those exporters of capital goods that use lease financing. In the framework of Wilson's matrix, the politics of Pickle's bill are entrepreneurial, and Pickle is the entrepreneur. This issue is attractive to a politician

---

[11]One indication of this is that the Senate bill was introduced by Senators Dole and Metzenbaum, who are from different parties and have quite different positions on many issues. Their support signals that this is not a partisan bill.

[12]U.S. airlines that compete with foreign airlines would also benefit to the extent that the foreign airlines currently capture some of the tax benefits.

because it involves good government—the elimination of a tax abuse—and the entrepreneur can claim credit for it. Boeing's objective, however, is not to defeat the Pickle bill, which is expected to pass, but instead is to obtain an exemption for job-creating export leasing. The relevant alternative thus is the exemption, and using Wilson's matrix again, Boeing and the other exporters are clients with concentrated benefits from an exemption and widely distributed costs for taxpayers.

Interests and the Demand for Political Action

Boeing accounts for over half the tax benefits associated with foreign leasing, so the other exporters have lower stakes in this issue than Boeing. Employees, suppliers, shareholders, and local communities that depend on the exporters are also at risk to the extent that sales would be lost. The lessors are likely to earn only competitive profits on foreign leasing and so have a weak incentive to take action on the issue.[13] Since a relatively small number of firms is affected, general business associations such as the Chamber of Commerce and the National Association of Manufacturers are unlikely to be active on the issue.

The tax-exempts have a strong demand for political action to oppose the Pickle bill. They also oppose the exemption for export leases because if the exemption fails, Boeing will then be on their side in opposing the Pickle bill. Although the impact on any one tax-exempt is small compared with the impact on Boeing, in the aggregate their demand is great. Many tax-exempts were already squeezed by federal budget reductions and the recession. Furthermore, they have few, if any, substitutes for replacing the tax benefits. Collectively, their demand is high.

The interests of taxpayers are opposed to those of Boeing and the tax-exempts. The benefits to taxpayers from the Pickle bill correspond to the additional tax receipts, which would contribute to lower interest rates and increased economic activity.

The Supply Side

The affected exporters are not only few in number but also are geographically concentrated. Boeing's affected employment, if any, is in the Seattle area. Oil drilling rig exporters are concentrated on the Gulf Coast, and container manufacturers are few in number. The exporters thus have poor coverage of congressional districts, even though they have considerable resources. Boeing, however, has a supplier network whose coverage is extensive, and it could organize its suppliers for political action. Boeing, however, may not want to mobilize its suppliers in a grassroots campaign because the overt use of political pressure by a defense contractor could cause a backlash.

The tax-exempts are numerous, their coverage of congressional districts is virtually complete, and many of their leaders and supporters have access to members of Congress. Although they have few resources, they have the ability to deliver considerable political pressure. To assess their strategy, it is useful to distinguish between those tax-exempts that already have a leasing deal in hand or in the planning stages and those that do not. The benefits of leasing for the latter group are as yet unidentified, so it is difficult to mobilize them for political action. The former group, however, has identifiable benefits and a strong incentive to organize and act.[14] Their benefits, however, can be

[13]No lessor testified in the House hearings on the Pickle bill, although one association of lessors involved primarily in domestic leasing sent a letter that was entered into the hearing record.

[14]Some of the groups testifying were the National Housing Rehabilitation Association; American Federation of State, County, and Municipal Employees; YMCA; National Conference of Black Mayors; Municipal Finance Officers Association; Bennington College; and the Preservation Alliance of Louisville and Jefferson County.

protected by simply grandfathering existing deals. Grandfathering would allow Pickle and Dole to prevent future drains on the Treasury, while dealing with the constituency pressure on them and their colleagues.

Taxpayers are numerous, have complete coverage of congressional districts, and have large resources. They are costly to organize, however, and given their low per capita benefits, cannot be expected to be active on this issue. Their interests are represented by political entrepreneurs such as Representative Pickle.

Boeing's ability to generate effective political action on this issue is limited. It could attempt to mobilize its shareholders, but most are unlikely to write letters to their representatives on an issue such as this. Furthermore, a letter from Boeing stressing the urgency of this issue could cause some of them to sell their shares. Boeing employees have a demand for political action if sales will be lost and their costs of organizing are low. Their coverage of congressional districts, however, is very limited. Consequently, their political action is likely to have only a limited effect, although their unions could represent them. Similarly, the communities potentially affected by the bill are geographically concentrated. Boeing could obtain coverage of congressional districts by mobilizing its suppliers. Their demand for political action varies considerably as a function of their volume of 747 subcontracts, but in all likelihood enough suppliers could be mobilized to supply a moderate amount of political pressure. As a defense contractor, however, Boeing is cautious about taking high-profile actions.

The Distributive Politics Spreadsheet

Figure 6-6 presents a distributive politics spreadsheet summarizing this analysis. The conclusion from this analysis is that the supporters of an exemption for job-creating export leases are unlikely to be able to generate substantial political action. Thus, the likelihood of obtaining an exemption is low. Attention must then be directed to secondary objectives.

INSTITUTIONS AND INSTITUTIONAL OFFICEHOLDERS

Although Congress is the institutional arena in which this issue was contested, the executive branch was also interested in its budget consequences, and a White House working group was meeting to develop measures to curb the use of leasing by tax-exempts. Boeing might have been able to enlist the support of executive branch agencies concerned with exports. The Department of Commerce and the U.S. Trade Representative were potential supporters. The Department of Treasury had stated that the additional tax receipts from eliminating the tax benefits on export leasing were not as important as the exports potentially at risk, but the Treasury could not be expected to make significant efforts on Boeing's behalf.

Boeing's best hope was to have an exemption for job-creating export leases incorporated into the Senate Finance Committee's bill. Success in the Finance Committee would likely mean success on the Senate floor. If the committee did not provide an exemption, the chances of having an exemption amendment adopted on the Senate floor were not good, given the limited coverage of Boeing and its allies. Obtaining an exemption through a floor amendment in the House would be difficult because it would be necessary to obtain an open rule or a modified rule from the Rules Committee to allow the amendment. Ways and Means bills sometimes receive a closed rule, and Representative Pickle would certainly seek one. There was little hope of introducing an amendment in the House.

The likelihood that the Pickle bill would pass in the House meant that if Boeing were successful in obtaining an exemption in the Senate, it would have to preserve that exemption in a conference committee. The contingent objective of grandfathering current

FIGURE 6-6 Distributive Politics Spreadsheet

Alternative being analyzed: Exemption for job-creating exports

Supporting Interests	*Demand Side*			*Supply Side*				*Prediction*
	Benefits from Supporting			*Ability to Generate Political Action*				
Interests	***Substitutes***	***Magnitude***	***Per Capita***	***Numbers***	***Coverage***	***Resources***	***Cost of Organizing***	***Amount of Effective Political Action***
Boeing	lower price							
• shareholders	sell shares	large	small	large	extensive	large	very high	little
• employees	few	large	substantial	large	little	limited	very low	little impact
• suppliers	other business	substantial	moderate	substantial	extensive	moderate	high	moderate
Communities								
• Boeing	few	substantial	considerable	small	little	small	low	little impact
• suppliers	few	moderate	moderate	considerable	extensive	small	high	limited
Oil rig mfgrs.	lower price	moderate	small	few	little	moderate	low	little
Container mfgrs.	lower price	moderate	small	few	little	moderate	low	little
Lessors	other loans	moderate	small	small	little	large	low	little

Opposing Interests	*Demand Side*			*Supply Side*				*Prediction*
	Benefits from Supporting			*Ability to Generate Political Action*				
Interests	***Substitutes***	***Magnitude***	***Per Capita***	***Numbers***	***Coverage***	***Resources***	***Cost of Organizing***	***Amount of Effective Political Action***
Taxpayers	none	large	very small	huge	complete	huge	very high	little
Tax-exempts	none	substantial	substantial	large	extensive	small	low	large

orders might be a reasonable compromise to achieve in conference if the House were unwilling to concede more.

The key institutional actor was Senator Dole. Although Boeing had a major facility in Wichita, much of the work there in 1983 was on defense contracts. The Senator had won with nearly two-thirds of the vote in the last election and was electorally safe. His current policy interest was in reducing the federal deficit, and his personal objectives were to become Senate majority leader and position himself for a possible run for the presidency. To achieve those objectives, he needed to be careful not to offend his Senate colleagues. They were under pressure from their constituents to preserve local leasing deals for tax-exempts in their states. Dole could easily accommodate them and still be fiscally responsible by grandfathering their deals. The bill then would have clear sailing through the Senate.

The final opportunity for Boeing then would be the president. It was unlikely that he would veto this bill, which promoted fiscal responsibility, since he had been berating Congress for its unwillingness to cut spending. If a veto were likely, Congress had ways to protect the bill. One was to consolidate the Pickle bill with other pending tax legislation the president wanted passed. This would insulate the leasing provisions from a veto.

NONMARKET STRATEGY FORMULATION

For a political strategy to be successful on an issue characterized by client politics, the client must demonstrate to enough members of Congress that either their constituents would benefit from an exemption or their own policy interests would be served. Given Pickle's belief (probably shared by Dole) that the 747 faced little competition, it would be difficult to demonstrate either that many jobs would be preserved by an exemption or that the trade deficit would be significantly affected. Indeed, the pressure on Congress came from the tax-exempts, and members were busy working to protect their constituents' deals. A client can also attempt to build a coalition, but in this case there were only a few potential coalition members (the other exporters), and their coverage of congressional districts was very limited.

Boeing's best strategy was to present through lobbying the message that export leases create jobs in a manner consistent with the objectives of ERTA. In doing so it could distinguish between its lease transactions and the sale-and-leaseback transactions that do not create jobs. Boeing could also emphasize its importance in lowering the U.S. trade deficit. The trade deficit, however, was of less concern to members of Congress than the budget deficit. Boeing also could challenge as inflated the Treasury estimate of the increase in tax revenues from eliminating the tax benefits on foreign leases.

Members of Congress were uncertain about Boeing's claims about the effects on sales and jobs, so Boeing could enlist the aid of some of its customers, such as Singapore Airlines, to attest to the impact of this legislation on their orders. In the upcoming hearings, senators were likely to ask if Boeing could not lower its price to retain sales. Although this would lower its profits, few in Congress were concerned about lower profits for a quite profitable company.

Boeing could remind the members of the Finance Committee that it faced unfair competition from a highly subsidized Airbus and that eliminating the tax benefits on foreign leasing would place it at a further disadvantage. This argument, however, had not stopped the Eximbank from ending its financing of 747s. Moreover, Congress prefers to try to stop unfair competition than to subsidize U.S. firms. Furthermore, all U.S. exporters were complaining about losing sales because of the high value of the dollar.

In pursuing its objectives, Boeing can enlist the aid of the congressional delegation from the state of Washington. The House delegation was small, however, and the senators had little seniority. Senator Evans was spending much of his energy campaigning for election in November, and Senator Gorton was in his first term. Neither was on the Senate Finance Committee. Boeing thus had relatively weak representation in Congress, and few other members were likely to view Boeing as their client.

Because of the other issues on its nonmarket issue agenda and because of the sensitivity of overt political activity by a defense contractor, Boeing generally preferred to maintain a low profile. Using suppliers for a grassroots campaign was too high a profile strategy for Boeing on this issue.[15] A grassroots program involving employees or shareholders would also have presented too high a profile and would likely have been insufficient to attain Boeing's primary objective.

Boeing's best political strategies were lobbying and coalition building. Lobbying the Senate Finance Committee was essential. Boeing would be able to address the complexity of the issue in its discussions with key committee members and their staffs. It also could discuss its contingent objectives and the importance of protecting orders already in hand. In its lobbying, Boeing should stress the effect of lost sales on its suppliers and on its own operations and employees. The cost of lobbying is low compared with the potential consequences, and Boeing should use its executives in the lobbying effort and certainly in testifying in hearings.

Boeing could form a coalition with other firms that used leasing to finance exports, or it could coordinate its political activities with them. McDonnell-Douglas, oil drilling rig manufacturers, container manufacturers, engine manufacturers, and a few other exporters had incentives to act, although the aggregate effect on them was smaller than for Boeing. These companies were relatively few in number and had relatively poor coverage of congressional districts, so there was a mismatch between their incentives and their ability to supply political pressure.

Boeing should, of course, modify its market strategy by developing alternative means of financing foreign sales.

THE OUTCOME

The Pickle bill had strong support from members of Congress who wanted to stop the drain on tax revenues, and, as is clear from the previous analysis, exporters were unable to generate substantial political pressure. The bill was eventually incorporated into the Deficit Reduction Act of 1984. The final provisions eliminated the tax benefits for both tax-exempts and foreign leases, but the current projects of many of the tax-exempts were grandfathered. Straight-line depreciation was allowed for foreign leases, but the other tax benefits were phased out over several years. Grandfathering was provided for wide-body aircraft, containers, and drilling rigs. The provision for Boeing read: "The amendments in this section shall not apply with respect to any wide body, 4-engine commercial passenger aircraft used by a foreign person or entity if (i) on or before November 1, 1983 the foreign person or entity entered into a written binding contract to acquire such aircraft, and (ii) such aircraft is placed into service before January 1, 1986." Boeing thus achieved its contingent objectives.

---

[15]Boeing undoubtedly wanted to avoid the media because the political entrepreneur had the better side of this issue. Furthermore, a large, profitable company seeking to preserve tax benefits—or subsidies, as some opponents would surely call them—had the potential for unfavorable news media treatment.

Summary

The analysis of nonmarket and political action has two foundations—interests and institutions. Interests are based on distributive consequences and moral concerns. Distributive consequences can be assessed in terms of the benefits from supporting or opposing an alternative. The moral determinants of political action are based on considerations of well-being, rights, and social justice.

Interests give rise to a demand for political action on an alternative, such as a bill before Congress, and that demand depends on the private and public substitutes available. The incentive to take action depends on the per capita benefits, and if the aggregate benefits are high but the per capita benefits are low, the benefits may be outweighed by the costs.

The costs of political action are of three types. The first is the cost of organizing interests and joining together for collective action. The second is the direct cost of implementing a political strategy. The third is associated with the effectiveness of a given amount of political action. If the number of affected interests is small, the costs of organization are likely to be small. The larger the group the more likely it is to encounter the free-rider problem. The effectiveness of political action depends on the number of people affected, their resources, and their coverage of legislative districts. The paradox of collective action is that while effectiveness increases with the number of interests affected and with their coverage of legislative districts, dispersed groups often have low per capita benefits and high costs of organization, giving them little incentive to take political action.

The analysis of the benefits and costs of taking political action can be summarized in the distributive politics spreadsheet. The chapter case *Scrubbers and Environmental Politics* provides an opportunity to apply political analysis and the distributive politics spreadsheet to a legislative issue.

Interests compete over political alternatives, and the nature of that competition depends on the relative concentration and dispersion of the benefits from supporting and opposing a political alternative. The categories of interest group, client, entrepreneurial, and majoritarian politics characterize the nature of the competition, but the outcome depends on a variety of factors including the characteristics of the institutional arenas in which the competition takes place.

The Boeing case indicates the complexity of even a relatively straightforward issue. It also illustrates the difference between the demand for political action and its supply. Taxpayers have low per capita benefits and high costs of taking political action and thus are represented primarily by political entrepreneurs. The tax-exempts have benefits that exceed their costs, so they were politically active. Boeing and other exporters had a high demand for political action and low costs, but their effectiveness was limited by a lack of coverage of congressional districts. In addition, Boeing had several other issues on its nonmarket agenda. As a defense contractor, it preferred a low-profile strategy to avoid compromising its effectiveness on other issues. Boeing's best political strategy in this case was to lobby using the message that sales and jobs would be lost. The best that Boeing was able to achieve, however, was a phaseout of the benefits and the grandfathering of orders in hand. The chapter case *Pizza Hut and the Legal Drinking Age* concerns a legislative issue that requires similar analysis and strategy formulation.

APPENDIX

The Distributive Consequences of Foreign Leasing

The distribution of the tax benefits depends primarily on the aircraft market as indicated in Figure 6-5. Three examples illustrate the range of distributive consequences that could result depending on the closeness of substitutes for a particular foreign airline.[1] The distributive consequences are bounded by this set of examples. Note that in all of the examples, U.S. taxpayers are providing a subsidy either to Boeing, a foreign airline, or both.

In all of the examples, Boeing's cost of producing a 747, taking everything into consideration, is assumed to be $80 million. That is, it will not make any sale that yields less than $80 million. The lessor is assumed to earn competitive profits, and to simplify the presentation, those profits will be taken to be zero. Similarly, the alternative of Boeing forming its own leasing subsidiary will not be considered.

Example I: An Airline with No Substitute for a 747

Consider a foreign airline with a route structure such that there is no substitute for a 747. Boeing is thus a monopolist with respect to the airline. Assume that if that airline were to purchase a 747, it would pay $100 million. By arranging a lease, Boeing can sell the 747 to a lessor for $125 million. The lessor takes the 10 percent investment tax credit of $12.5 million and the (approximately) 10 percent value of the accelerated depreciation tax benefit or $12.5 million. Thus, the net cost to the lessor is $100 million, so it can lease the 747 for $100 million. In this case, Boeing receives $125 million from the lessor and thus captures the tax benefits of $25 million. U.S. taxpayers thus subsidize Boeing. If the tax benefits on foreign leases were eliminated by the Pickle bill, Boeing would lower its price and sell the 747 to the airline for $100 million. In this example, neither sales nor jobs would be lost as a result of Pickle's bill, but Boeing's profits would be reduced by $25 million.

Example II: A Close Substitute

Suppose that an airline could purchase either 747s or A300s for use on its routes. Also, assume that Airbus would not sell an A300 unless it received more than $64 million. In the absence of lease financing, competition between Boeing and Airbus would drive the price down to slightly less than $80 million, since Boeing can go no lower than $80 million. The sale would go to Airbus.

With foreign lease financing, Boeing could sell the 747 to a lessor for $80 million, and the lessor would receive the investment tax credit of $8 million plus the $8 million tax benefit from the accelerated depreciation. The lessor then could lease the 747 to the airline for $64 million, and the airline would purchase the 747 because Airbus cannot price that low. In this case, foreign leasing generates sales and jobs. U.S. taxpayers, however, are providing a subsidy of $16 million, which is captured entirely by the foreign airline. U.S. taxpayers thus are subsidizing foreigners. Elimination of the tax benefits on foreign leasing in this case would end the subsidization but would result in a loss of the sale and jobs.

Example III: A Close But More Expensive Substitute

Suppose next that Airbus would not sell an A300 for less than $72 million. In the absence of foreign leasing, an airline would buy from Airbus at slightly less than $80 million as in Example II. With the tax benefits on foreign leasing, Boeing could sell a 747 to a lessor for $90 million. The lessor then receives tax benefits of $18 million and leases the 747 to the airline for $72 million. In this case, U.S. taxpayers are providing a subsidy of $18 million. The foreign airline captures $8 million and Boeing captures $10 million. The elimination of the tax benefits on foreign leasing would result in the loss of the sale and jobs.

---

[1]Actual sales arrangements are obviously much more complex than these examples, and sales arrangements with one airline may have implications for the deals that can be made with other airlines.

CASES

Tobacco Politics

The tobacco industry has long been an economic juggernaut. By one estimate, as of 1998, tobacco accounted for 500,000 jobs and generated up to $170 billion in revenue annually in the United States—an amount approximately equal to the gross domestic product of Columbia.[1] Tobacco was grown in 20 states and was one of the most successful cash crops. Renewed efforts by politicians to regulate tobacco were fueled by new reports on the effects of second-hand smoke, such as one claiming that smoking accounted for as many as 400,000 deaths annually.

The federal government's efforts to control tobacco and cigarette advertising can be traced to 1954, when Representative John Dingell (D-MI) proposed a bill banning interstate advertising of tobacco products and alcoholic beverages. Although Representative Dingell's proposal did not succeed, in 1970 President Nixon signed a bill banning cigarette advertising on radio and television. In the 1980s several additional measures were passed that restricted smoking, including banning smoking on domestic airline flights. The 1990s saw further action taken against the tobacco industry, with legislation passed to limit tobacco advertising and banning smoking in federal buildings.

Throughout this period, anti-smoking advocates portrayed the tobacco industry as an all-powerful, evil empire that held lawmakers in its hip pocket. Anti-smoking advertisements in the late 1990s claimed that tobacco companies consciously targeted teenagers in their advertising campaigns in the hopes of recruiting and addicting the nation's youth. The threat to the tobacco industry and its beneficiaries increased significantly in November 1997, when S.1415, the National Tobacco Policy and Youth Smoking Reduction Act, was introduced by Sen. John McCain (R-AZ).

[1]The $170 billion estimate is from Alan Greenblat, "Growing Ranks of Cigarette Tax Critics Invigorate Big Tobacco's Lobbying Effort," *Congressional Quarterly Weekly Report,* May 16, 1998, p. 1306. Bulow and Klemperer (1998), however, report that retail sales of cigarettes were only $50 billion, which suggests that the $170 billion figure includes multiplier effects.

PROVISIONS OF THE ACT

S.1415 was an outgrowth of an agreement reached on June 20, 1997, known as the Tobacco Resolution. The agreement between the major tobacco companies, state attorneys general, and class action lawyers provided the tobacco industry with protection from future punitive damages lawsuits and set caps on damage payments in exchange for a substantial per-pack tax increase and lump-sum damages payments.[2] Overall, the bill would constitute a significant increase in the regulatory role of the federal government with respect to the tobacco industry. As proponents of the bill portrayed it, the bill required tobacco companies to pay $506 billion over 25 years to cover health care expenses related to smoking. The mechanism for funding this transfer was a $1.10 excise tax on the price of each pack of cigarettes. The bill also provided block grants to states to deal with medical costs stemming from tobacco use. In return for the tax increase, the liability of tobacco companies would be capped at $6.5 billion per year.

Besides these monetary and legal provisions, the bill also restricted tobacco advertising and promotion. Tobacco companies would be prohibited from advertising on billboards, in public arenas, and on the Internet. In an attempt to reduce underage smoking, cartoon or human characters such as R.J. Reynolds's "Joe Camel" were to be banned from advertising campaigns. Companies also could not sell items of clothing bearing their brand name, provide gifts to customers, sponsor public events, or pay for product placements in television programs or movies. Advertisements could no longer use phrases such as "low tar" or "light" that would imply that a given cigarette brand was less dangerous than another brand.

Other provisions would affect the regulation and distribution of tobacco. The Federal Drug Administration (FDA) would have the power to regulate nicotine like a drug, including, with the consent

[2]Bulow and Klemperer (1998) provide an excellent overview of the provisions of the resolution.

of Congress, the power to ban it altogether. Retail stores would have to apply for licenses to sell tobacco, and tobacco companies would have to disclose all corporate documents about their product, which would then be placed in a national depository for public use.

INTERESTS

In addition to the tobacco companies, other interests would be affected. Trial lawyers for plaintiffs that had filed individual and class action lawsuits would receive a financial windfall. To avoid the public fallout and demands for accountability associated with the payment of extremely large fees, the bill created a payment mechanism whereby three "arbitrators" representing lawyers and tobacco companies would determine the actual payment figures. In addition, tobacco companies agreed to provide the lawyers, who were instrumental in the agreement, an annuity of up to $500 million a year.[3]

State attorneys general who had filed state lawsuits wanted S.1415 to pass for two reasons. The first was to recover damages associated with smoking that could be used to cover state medicaid expenses. The second and more subtle reason was the expectation of political gains from public sentiment from helping to pass what was being promoted as a major blow against the tobacco industry.

Foremost among the bill's supporters were dozens of anti-smoking groups, including the Coalition for Smoking OR Health, Americans for Nonsmokers' Rights, Action on Smoking and Health (ASH), Airspace, The BADvertising Institute, Smoke*Screen, the National Center for Tobacco-Free Kids, Effective National Action to Control Tobacco (ENACT), the American Heart Association, and the American Lung Association.

Wholesalers would be hurt by the per-pack excise tax provision because of the way in which the tax was to be collected. Wholesalers would have to extend credit to many retailers, and the book value of wholesalers' inventory would be higher resulting in higher insurance costs and "shrinkage" (theft). In estimating the damage at $367 million over 5 years, the American Wholesalers Marketers Association's spokeswoman, Jacqueline Cohen, explained, "Your shrinkage will grow."[4]

[3]Ibid.
[4]Greenblat, ibid.

Cigarette-only stores would benefit under the proposed legislation because they would be exempt from point-of-sale promotional restrictions that would affect other retailers. Some of these stores were "adult bookstores."

Convenience stores would be hurt by the excise tax and the registration requirements. Convenience store cigarette sales accounted for approximately 40 percent of U.S. cigarette sales, and cigarettes alone comprised 20 percent of the average convenience store's total business.[5] A 1997 Department of Agriculture study confirmed the suspicion that many of these stores would most likely not survive price and distribution reforms such as those proposed by S.1415.

The National Association of Convenience Stores, an international trade association, represented almost 3,300 convenience store operators, petroleum marketers, and suppliers, with 63,000 convenience stores around the world. In 1996 the convenience store industry posted $151.9 billion in total sales.[6]

Grocery chains would also be hurt, since tobacco companies currently pay $2 billion annually in slotting fees to obtain prime placement for their products. Grocery retailers were organized in a number of associations, including the Food Marketing Institute (FMI)—a trade organization of over 100 grocers including Giant-Eagle, Dominick's, Piggly-Wiggly, Safeway, and Tom Thumb. The FMI's annual trade show hosted over 35,000 representatives from the supermarket industry. Additionally, the National Grocers Association has a membership of 2,060 and a budget of $5 million. It has food retailer members in 50 states and also includes 60 wholesale food distributors.

The advertising industry would also be affected. By one account, tobacco advertisements and promotions totaled $5 billion, and the provisions of S.1415 chipped away at virtually every advertising approach used by firms.[7] Although print advertisements only generated $20 million in revenue, the prohibition on billboard advertising would eliminate $290 million in revenue. Point-of-purchase displays would also be prohibited and would reduce retailer revenues from

[5]Greenblat, ibid.
[6]http://www.cstorecentral.com/public/nacs/rf05.htm
[7]Greenblat, ibid. Data provided by Bulow and Klemperer (1998), table 10, however, suggests that all tobacco marketing expenses are treated as advertising expenses in the $5 billion figure. Most marketing expenses are promotional allowances such as price cuts for distributors and coupon and retail value-added promotions, neither of which would be prohibited by the bill.

slotting fees. The American Association of Advertising Agencies, with membership of 6 percent of the 13,000 U.S. agencies, accounted for 75 percent of advertising revenue in the United States.[8]

Tobacco farmers naturally opposed S.1415, but a 1997 Department of Agriculture study found that the preponderance of jobs attributed to tobacco were in the retail and wholesale trade—not in farming per se. Furthermore, the bill as drafted was sensitive to farmers' concerns, providing transition payments for farmers. Meanwhile, the foreign market for cigarettes continued to grow.

Concert promoters would be rocked by the expected loss of underwriting which was dependent on prominent displays of advertisements. Likewise, organizers of golf tournaments would be driven to find alternative sources of underwriting revenue, while the net proceeds for tennis promoters would decline.

Not even universities escaped the reach of tobacco politics. By one estimate as many as 70 percent of university portfolios included tobacco stock, and some portfolio managers began to contemplate alternative investment strategies due to heightened public anti-tobacco sentiment and/or reduced profitability of tobacco firms. Harvard and Johns Hopkins had already divested, and Yale's board of trustees considered selling \$16.9 million of tobacco stock from its \$6 billion portfolio. ■

[8]Some legal scholars believed the advertising provisions in S.1415 would be subject to court challenges on grounds of violating the First Amendment.

This case was prepared for class use by Professor Keith Krehbiel and Alan Wiseman using publicly available information.

PREPARATION QUESTIONS

1. For each of the following groups, assess the likelihood that it will engage in nonmarket action on S.1415. Identify the specific cost and/or benefit characteristics underlying your assessment: smokers; tobacco companies; tobacco farmers; trial lawyers; anti-smoking groups; cigarette-only stores; grocery stores; convenience stores; advertising agencies; concert and event promoters; universities.
2. Using the Wilson matrix, what kind of politics best characterizes the activity surrounding McCain's bill?
3. Assess the prospects for coalition formation.
4. What outcome do you predict for the bill and why?

Scrubbers and Environmental Politics

In 1972 the Environmental Protection Agency (EPA) promulgated a "new source performance standard" (NSPS) for new coal-fired power plants, capping sulfur dioxide emissions at 1.2 pounds per million Btus (MBtu) of energy produced. As part of the stationary source emissions control section of the Clean Air Act Amendments of 1977, Congress had the task of implementing the NSPS for these power plants. The issue before Congress was not whether the NSPS would be attained but instead was whether to specify how it would be achieved. More specifically, the issue was whether to require power companies to use a particular technology—a scrubber—to remove sulfur from their emissions.

Coal is produced both in the eastern and the western parts of the United States, but the technologies of extraction and the qualities of the coal differ greatly. Most of the coal in the East (West Virginia, Kentucky, Illinois, Indiana, Pennsylvania) is found in deep seams, requiring shaft mining. Shaft mining is labor intensive, and the coal miners were organized by the United Mine Workers (UMW). The wages earned by UMW members are high, and employee benefits are generous. Much of the coal mined in the East has a high sulfur content of up to 12 pounds per MBtus with an average of approximately 4 pounds. Sulfur dioxide emissions were a principal contributor to acid rain.

In Montana and Wyoming, coal lies just below the surface, and the extraction technology is strip mining, which is capital rather than labor intensive. Western coal is clean, with a sulfur content of approximately 1 pound per MBtus. Miners in the West generally were not unionized, and their wages and benefits were lower than those of the eastern UMW miners. The UMW had tried unsuccessfully to organize the western miners.

The EPA had concluded that scrubbers could remove approximately 90 percent of the sulfur oxides, although this determination was based on engineering data rather than actual applications. A scrubber is a large and very costly system that sprays a water and limestone mixture inside a smokestack, causing a chemical reaction that removes sulfur from the smoke. Sludge is produced by the reaction and is collected at the base of the scrubber, leaving a substantial waste disposal problem. A scrubber may use 400 tons of limestone and thousands of gallons of water a day to remove 200 tons of sulfur dioxide. When they work, scrubbers are effective in sulfur removal but their initial reliability had been low, in part because of the corrosion caused by the chemical reaction and in part because the apparatus could become clogged by the sludge.[1] Scrubbers are thus often shut down while the power plant continues to operate. Not only are they quite expensive to build, they are also costly to operate.

The EPA concluded that the most efficient means—the lowest cost to society—of meeting emissions standards in the Midwest and certain parts of the East would be for new power plants to burn low-sulfur western coal. This would allow emissions standards to be met without having to build and use scrubbers. (Despite the difference in transportation costs, it was less expensive to use western coal in eastern power plants than to use eastern coal and scrubbers.) If scrubbers were mandated, however, it would be more efficient for power plants in the East to burn high-sulfur eastern coal than low-sulfur western coal, since scrubbers would have to be used with either type of coal.[2] Some experts warned, however, that unless significant advances were made in scrubber reliability, emissions in the East would actually be higher with mandated scrubbing and the burning of eastern coal than if scrubbers were not required and western coal were burned.

Environmental groups, which were particularly strong in the West, expressed little concern about the possibility of worsened air quality in the East if scrubbers were mandated and power companies used high-sulfur eastern coal. The western environmentalists were primarily interested in preventing air quality degradation in the West, and they preferred lower emissions in the West than allowed by the 1.2 pounds per Mbtu NSPS. The NSPS standard for the West could be achieved without using scrubbers, but the environmentalists preferred that scrubbers be mandated to reduce emissions below the level allowed by the NSPS. The environmentalists recognized that this would increase the cost of electricity in the West, but their preferences were for cleaner air than required by the EPA's NSPS. ■

[1]By the mid-1980s, scrubber technology had improved significantly.

[2]The effect of the NSPS on eastern coal interests is analyzed in Chapter 5.

PREPARATION QUESTIONS

1. From a social efficiency perspective, should Congress mandate scrubbers?
2. Which interests are affected by this issue? Which are likely to take political action?
3. Are there any opportunities for a coalition to form that would allow its members to achieve their primary objectives?
4. What do you predict Congress will do and why?

Pizza Hut and the Legal Drinking Age

Pizza Hut, a nationwide pizza chain, faced a serious nonmarket threat to a component of its market strategy. The 21st Amendment to the Constitution granted states the right to regulate the sale of alcoholic beverages, including setting the legal drinking age. The National Drinking Age Act adopted in 1984 was intended to induce states to raise their legal drinking age to 21 by making 10 percent of federal funds for highways contingent on their doing so.[1] Most states were expected to raise their legal drinking age. In 1984, twenty states had a legal drinking age below 21.

The problem for Pizza Hut was that many state laws prohibited people younger than the legal drinking age from handling alcoholic beverages or from performing such jobs as serving and cleaning tables in establishments where alcoholic beverages were served. Because 60 percent of the employees in Pizza Hut's 4,000 restaurants were under the age of 21, the implications for Pizza Hut's employment strategy were substantial. The threat was that states might increase their legal drinking age to 21 and not change their labor laws to allow people under 21, who could work under the then-current law, to continue to work in establishments that serve alcoholic beverages. The consequences to Pizza Hut would be either that people under 21 could not work in its restaurants or that it would be forced to stop selling alcoholic beverages. The cost of employing an older workforce would be substantial, but the loss from not selling alcoholic beverages would be greater. ■

[1]In June 1987, the Supreme Court ruled in *South Dakota v. Dole*, 107 S. Ct. 2793 (1987) that the Act was constitutional. The State of Nevada challenged the withholding of federal highway funds, but in February 1990, the Supreme Court let stand an appeals court decision rejecting the challenge.

PREPARATION QUESTIONS

1. What is the nature of the problem the National Drinking Age Act causes for Pizza Hut? What should be Pizza Hut's objectives? What does Pizza Hut have to accomplish to achieve its objectives?
2. Which interests are affected by this issue and are they likely to take political action? Which interests are aligned and which opposed to those of Pizza Hut? With whom, if anyone, should it attempt to form a coalition?
3. What is the nature of the politics of this issue?
4. What strategy should Pizza Hut adopt and how should it be implemented?

CHAPTER 7

Formulating Political Strategies

Introduction

Effective participation in the resolution of nonmarket issues involves identifying alternatives, analyzing their likely consequences, specifying primary and contingent objectives, and formulating and implementing strategies to achieve those objectives. This chapter addresses the strategy process, provides approaches to strategy formulation, and presents examples of political strategies. The integration with market strategies is developed and addressed in the chapter cases. The context is U.S. institutions, but the approach is also applicable to other countries, as indicated in Part III of this book. The effectiveness of various strategies, however, depends on the institutions, the organization of interests, and local standards of responsibility in those countries.

Strategy formulation in the nonmarket environment differs on a number of dimensions from its counterpart in the market environment. First, nonmarket issues attract a broader set of participants than those involved in markets. Second, important components of nonmarket strategies are implemented in public view, which can constrain the actions of firms. Third, the logic of collective and political action is different from the logic of market action. Fourth, in the nonmarket environment issues are not resolved by voluntary agreements as in markets but by government institutions with the power to compel action, regulate, and structure the conditions under which market participants compete. Because governments have these powers, firms and other interests must be sure their strategies are responsible. Using the framework for the analysis of nonmarket issues presented in Figure 2-4 of Chapter 2, political and other nonmarket strategies must be evaluated for responsibility in both the screening and the choice stages.

Responsible Political Action

In the long run, a firm has influence over issues addressed in government institutions to the extent that its interests are aligned with those of citizens. In the short run, however, firms and such other interests as labor unions and activist groups have the ability and the means to alter the outcome of an issue. An important concern about the use of nonmarket strategies thus is the appropriateness of attempting to influence public decisions. In addressing this issue, an analogy to markets is useful. In market competition, a firm that faces weak competition has market power that enables it to restrict output and obtain a price above its cost. Society has two responses to such a situation. First, it may rely on market forces. A high price can attract entrants to the industry and provide incentives for innovation that reduces the market power of the incumbent firm. Second, society may use its constitutional powers to regulate the exercise of that market power or break the firm into smaller units to stimulate competition.

In nonmarket competition, society also has two responses to the exercise of nonmarket power. First, it can rely on competition from interests with opposing preferences to mitigate the influence of both sides. From a pluralist perspective such competition also helps identify appropriate public policies. Participation may be limited, however, because of the free-rider problem and other costs of taking nonmarket action. In some cases, advocacy and watchdog groups can alert the public and government officeholders to the situation, thereby limiting to some extent the exercise of nonmarket power. Second, society can regulate the nonmarket actions of interests or require disclosure of their actions. For example, corporations are prohibited from making contributions to the election campaigns of candidates for federal office.[1] In addition, actions such as hiring a lobbyist and holding *ex parte* meetings with regulators require public disclosure. These responses to the exercise of nonmarket power, however, leave a substantial gray area in which interests must exercise judgment and restraint to ensure that nonmarket strategies are responsible and do not exceed the limits of public acceptability.

CRITICISMS OF BUSINESS POLITICAL ACTIVITY

Business Objectives and the Public Interest

One criticism of political activity by business is that it is contrary to the public interest. What is in the public interest, however, is often the subject of fundamental disagreement. For example, the antidumping laws that impose duties on imported goods sold in an importing country at lower prices than in the exporting country are viewed by many economists and public policy specialists as harmful to consumers and to efficiently operating markets. Yet, antidumping laws have been enacted through legitimate processes not only in the United States but also in most other countries. Firms, labor unions, interest groups, and government agencies use the antidumping laws against foreign imports, even though that may be contrary to some conceptions of the public interest.

From a pluralist perspective, the public interest is identified by the interests of individuals and groups as revealed in the context of political institutions. From this perspective, the public interest is advanced by business participation, since the interests of a firm are ultimately the interests of those who have a stake in its performance, including shareholders, employees, retirees, customers, suppliers, and the communities in which it operates.

Because of the information they can provide, firms have been granted rights to participate in political processes irrespective of the particular interests they represent. In *First National Bank of Boston v. Bellotti,* 435 U.S. 765 (1978), the Supreme Court held that the First Amendment protects the right of corporations to make expenditures and participate in the political competition on a state ballot proposition. The Bank of Boston had challenged a Massachusetts law prohibiting a corporation from making expenditures and contributions to influence the vote on public referenda that did not "materially" affect the corporation. The Supreme Court held that the Bank of Boston's right under the First Amendment derived less from its right to speak than from the public's right to hear what others have to say. The court stated that freedom of speech "embraces at least the liberty to discuss publicly and truthfully all matters of public concern without previous restraint or fear of subsequent punishment. . . ." In addition, the court concluded that a state could not single out a set of entities, such as corporations, because of

[1]As considered in Chapter 8, corporations are allowed to make contributions to political organizations and in some states to candidates' campaigns for state offices.

the interests they represent. The court stated that the prohibition in the Massachusetts law was "an impermissible legislative prohibition of speech based on the identity of the interests that spokesmen may represent in public debate over controversial issues . . . ."

Two years later, the Supreme Court overturned a ruling by the Public Service Commission of New York that had prohibited the Consolidated Edison Company from including messages about public issues in its billing envelopes.[2] The court held that the prohibition was an impermissible restriction on speech. In *Pacific Gas & Electric Co. v. Public Utilities Commission of California,* 475 U.S. 1 (1986), the Supreme Court ruled that a company cannot be compelled to include messages from other groups in its billing envelopes. The California Public Utilities Commission (PUC) had ordered Pacific Gas & Electric to include an insert from a consumer group with its bills. The Supreme Court held that a corporation cannot be forced to associate with ideas to which it objects any more than an individual can be. The majority opinion stated that the PUC order "discriminates on the basis of the viewpoints of the selected speakers and also impermissibly requires appellant to associate with speech with which appellant may disagree . . . that kind of forced response is antithetical to the free discussion that the First Amendment seeks to foster."

The rights accorded corporations by the First Amendment can also override certain restrictions imposed by legislatures. In *Eastern Railroad Conference v. Noerr Motor Freight,* 365 U.S. 127 (1961), the Supreme Court ruled that collective corporate action, such as joint lobbying to influence government, does not violate antitrust laws against collusion because the First Amendment grants the right to petition government. Firms thus have the right to form and participate in coalitions and associations to conduct political activity, provided that the joint organization is not a "sham."[3]

Even though firms have rights to participate in political activity, some forms of participation can be restrained. For example, contributions by corporations to federal election campaigns are prohibited. Furthermore, commercial speech, such as advertising, does not receive the same protection as political speech.

Unwarranted Power

In *Austin v. Michigan Chamber of Commerce,* 494 U.S. 652 (1990), the Supreme Court upheld a Michigan law that prohibited corporations from making independent expenditures on behalf of a candidate.[4] Justice Thurgood Marshall, writing for the majority, referred to "the corrosive and distorting effects of immense aggregations of wealth that are accumulated with the help of the corporate form." In his dissent, Justice Antonin Scalia wrote, "The fact that corporations amass large treasuries is not sufficient justification for the suppression of political speech unless one thinks it would be lawful to prohibit men and women whose net worth is above a certain figure from endorsing political candidates." These opinions reflect disagreement about whether a corporation has the same freedom of speech as a person, and whether wealth and the power it can generate pose a threat to democratic processes.

The criticism that business has unwarranted power also stems from relative considerations. Some interests may not participate because their costs of becoming informed and organizing are too high. Other interests thus are necessarily "overrepresented." Corporate participation in political activities, however, can give voice to people whose interests might otherwise be unrepresented. Just as unions represent their mem-

---

[2]*Consolidated Edison Company v. Public Service Commission of New York,* 199 S.Ct. 2326 (1980).
[3]See also *Mine Workers v. Pennington,* 381 U.SU. 637 (1965) and *California Motor Transport Co. v. Trucking Unlimited,* 404 U.S. 508 (1972). The Noerr-Pennington doctrine may not apply to nongovernmental legislative bodies such as standard setting bodies; see *Allied Tube & Conduit Corp. v. Indian Head,* 486 U.S. 492 (1988).
[4]An independent expenditure is made directly, for example, by taking out an advertisement endorsing a candidate, rather than through a candidate's campaign organization.

bers, corporations give voice to a set of constituencies.[5] Firms represent the interests of their dispersed shareholders and pensioners when they act to increase their market value. Similarly, firms often represent the interests of employees and suppliers in issues affecting sales, and hence employment, and purchases from suppliers. Firms may also represent the interests of customers. An importer that opposes an import quota represents not only its own interests but also those of the consumers who would otherwise have to pay a higher price as a result of the quota.

Often, the political power of business is controlled because it is naturally divided. Business differs from many single-interest groups in that business interests are often fragmented, leaving firms on opposite sides of some issues. U.S. automobile manufacturers may support restrictions on automobile imports, but dealers who sell foreign automobiles oppose them. American exporters interested in opening foreign markets to domestic goods also oppose protectionist measures because they are concerned about retaliation by other countries. In the politics of the investment tax credit in the Tax Reform Act of 1986, capital-intensive industries were opposed by service industries that received little benefit from the credit. Because business interests on many issues are fragmented, so is business power. The chapter case *The Section 936 Tax Credit* illustrates this point.

Business political power is also checked by the power of other interest groups. There are many well-funded environmental interest groups, for example, and they have been quite effective in advancing their agendas in both public and private institutional arenas. Activist groups such as the Nader organizations also serve as a check on business political power. The news media plays an important role in monitoring the political activities of business and other interest groups.

The abstract ability to exercise power is also not the same as its actual use. Business political action committees (PACs) could make their campaign contributions on a partisan basis, but instead they contribute to both Democrats and Republicans. In contrast, labor PACs contribute almost exclusively to Democrats. Business may also exercise restraint on the use of its power. In the example presented in Chapter 6, Boeing did not mobilize its supplier network to oppose restrictions on the tax treatment of leases to foreign customers.

The Possibility of Manipulation

The third criticism of business political activity goes beyond interests and power and focuses on manipulation. Manipulation involves actions based on misrepresentation or that play on ignorance, fear, or biases. In the framework for nonmarket analysis presented in Chapter 2, political strategies with these characteristics are to be rejected in the screening stage. However, not all interest groups reject manipulative strategies, as there can be (at least temporary) advantages to their use.

Although a firm generally has the right to participate in public policy processes, the distinction between participation and the abuse of that right is often a fine one. In 1984 Johnson & Johnson, the maker of Tylenol, the best-selling nonprescription pain reliever in the United States, faced a new competitive challenge when the Food and Drug Administration (FDA) allowed the nonprescription sale of the drug ibuprofen, an anti-arthritis drug previously available only by prescription. Upjohn estimated that within 2 years ibuprofen would garner 10 to 15 percent of the $1.3 billion pain reliever market. Bristol-Myers planned to market Upjohn's ibuprofen under the brand name Nuprin, and American Home Products planned to market its version under the brand name Advil.

---

[5]See Hirschman (1970) for an analysis of the voice issue.

To counter this competitive challenge, Johnson & Johnson filed suit against the FDA challenging the procedures under which it approved the nonprescription sale based on the sufficiency of warnings on ibuprofen labels.[6] The suit alleged that the FDA has authority over the advertising of only prescription drugs, not consumer drugs. Johnson & Johnson also claimed injury by the alleged improper approval, stating that it would have a "direct and immediate impact" on Tylenol sales. Bristol-Myers responded, calling the suit "an arrogant and unconscionable effort by Johnson & Johnson to keep an important new drug off the nonprescription pain-relief market."[7]

By 1989 the tables were turned as American Home Products, which makes Anacin as well as Advil, asked the FDA to require drugs containing acetaminophen to include on their labels a warning about possible kidney damage from extended use.[8] The purpose of the submission was to handicap the market leader, Tylenol, which contains acetaminophen as its principal ingredient. The tables turned further in 1994 as American Home Products filed suit against Syntex and its marketing partner Procter & Gamble, charging that their FDA-approved advertising for their recently approved pain reliever Aleve involved "unwarranted and unsubstantiated claims." Were the Johnson & Johnson and American Home Products actions responsible uses of the companies' standing before the FDA and the courts or did they involve manipulative use of institutional procedures?

Political Strategy Formulation

MANAGERS AND POLITICAL STRATEGIES

Because of the importance of nonmarket issues for the performance of firms, the responsibility for the formulation and implementation of political and nonmarket strategies ultimately rests with management. That responsibility is not necessarily uniformly distributed among the levels of management, however. From the lower levels of an organization, nonmarket and political issues are often seen as regrettable complications that reduce autonomy and complicate performance. The higher managers are in an organization, the more likely they are to understand that the development of these issues can be affected by the firm's participation and the more likely they are to be involved in the formulation and implementation of political strategies.

Most managers are involved in nonmarket issues addressed in government institutions on an episodic rather than a continual basis, and so they need a parsimonious framework for formulating effective and responsible strategies. Much of the task of strategy formulation involves bringing together the approach to political analysis presented in Chapter 6, the institutional knowledge and theories of political behavior presented in Chapter 5, and the characteristics of nonmarket issues developed in Part I of this book. The following sections develop the content of the approach, and the checklist presented in the final section summarizes its components.

As indicated in Figure 7-1, the nonmarket strategy of a firm competes in institutional arenas against the strategies of other interests. Because the resolution of an issue often involves the delegation of administrative responsibility to an agency or a regulatory commission, political strategies focus both on the initial institutional arena in which an issue is addressed and on subsequent delegation to administrative or regula-

---

[6]A 1990 study published in the *Annals of Internal Medicine* reported that ibuprofen could cause kidney failure in individuals who had even minor kidney problems. The editors called for stronger warnings on the label.
[7]The suit failed, and ibuprofen was marketed on a nonprescription basis beginning in 1985.
[8]The basis for the submission was a May 1989 study by the National Institute of Environmental Health Sciences that suggested that daily use of drugs containing acetaminophen for over a year could cause kidney damage. This possibility was confirmed in a study reported in 1994 in the *New England Journal of Medicine*.

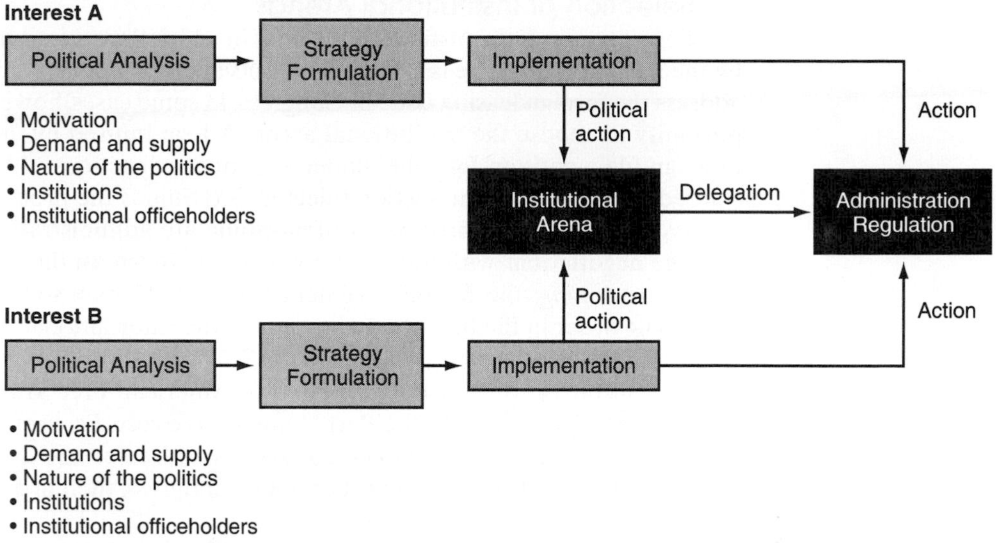

FIGURE 7-1 Approach to Strategy Formulation

tory agencies. These strategies may be in response to a nonmarket issue or may involve initiating an issue, often to affect the firm's market environment. The foundation for those strategies is political analysis.

AN APPROACH TO STRATEGY FORMULATION

Political Analysis

Political analysis involves assessing the characteristics of the issue and where it is in its life cycle, identifying the interests affected by the issue, assessing their motivation, analyzing their likely demand for and supply of political action, assessing the nature of the politics of the issue, identifying the institutional arenas in which the issue will be addressed, assessing institutional characteristics, and identifying the relevant institutional officeholders. If the issue is primarily distributive, the Wilson matrix (Figure 6-4) provides a first step in assessing the nature of the politics. To predict the likely outcome, the demand for and costs of generating political action must be assessed to determine which interests are likely to participate and the amount and effectiveness of the political action they are likely to generate. The distributive politics spreadsheet (Figure 6-6) provides a format for summarizing this analysis. If the issue has moral dimensions, those concerns must be evaluated based on moral principles, and the likelihood of morally motivated political action must be assessed.

Objectives

The specification of objectives is important not only because objectives are the focus of strategies but also because they affect which interests will be aligned with and against a firm. In the Boeing case in Chapter 6, the objective of seeking an exemption for export leasing put it on the opposite side of the issue from the tax-exempts. Contingent objectives must also be specified and pursued in case the primary objectives cannot be achieved. The primary objective may be the defeat of a legislative proposal, but if the proposal is likely to be passed in some form, a more realistic objective is to seek wording that lessens its impact, provides alternative means of compliance, or allows additional time to develop substitutes. Boeing's secondary objectives were to grandfather orders in hand and to obtain a gradual elimination of the tax benefits.

Selection of Institutional Arenas

For most issues, the institutional arenas in which they are addressed are determined by the forces that put the issues on the firm's agenda. Boeing had no alternative but to address the foreign leasing issue in Congress. In some cases, however, a firm has the opportunity to choose the institutional arena. A firm injured by unfair foreign competition can file a petition for relief under a number of sections of U.S. trade law. As considered in Chapter 16, the section selected determines the process and the institutions that will govern it. The processes differ—some are administrative, whereas others encourage negotiations with the other countries involved. In the Chapter 16 case *Cemex and Antidumping,* the Mexican cement producer Cemex sought to overturn an antidumping order in the institutional arenas of the International Trade Commission, the International Trade Administration, the U.S. Court of International Trade, the General Agreement on Tariffs and Trade, the North American Free Trade Agreement, and finally Congress. Similarly, in the Part II integrative case *Proposition 211: Securities Litigation Referendum (A),* high-tech companies addressed the issue of frivolous securities fraud lawsuits first in the courts, then in Congress, then in a state referendum, and finally back in Congress.

Firms may also pursue an objective at either the federal or the state level. When firms seeking protection from hostile takeovers had little success in Congress or with the Securities and Exchange Commission, they turned their attention to the states. For example, Pennsylvania enacted a law that made it more difficult to acquire firms incorporated there. Similarly, business has had little success at the federal level in its attempts to reform the liability system, but it has had some success at the state level.

Political Strategies

Political strategies are the link between objectives and the specific actions taken to achieve them. Because the effectiveness of a strategy depends on the strategies of the other participants in the issue, strategy formulation is not necessarily a linear process but instead may involve a return to the analysis stage. Part of the strategy task thus is to anticipate the strategies of other participants.

The basic principle underlying strategy formulation for issues considered in legislative arenas is that the weight of political action for and against an alternative is an important, but not the sole, determinant of the outcome. Therefore, a strategy should increase the benefits to those with aligned interests and reduce their costs of taking political action. As considered later in the chapter in the context of the rent chain, a firm may reduce the costs of participation for its employees, suppliers, and customers. Conversely, a strategy could reduce the opposing side's incentives or increase its costs of taking political action. Identifying substitutes, for example, can reduce the incentives to oppose the political alternative. The Daylight Saving Time Coalition effectively eliminated opposition by the National Association of Broadcasters by including a provision in the legislation asking the Federal Communications Commission to authorize AM radio stations to begin broadcasting before sunrise. In the Boeing case, opposition from the tax-exempts was reduced by grandfathering those deals already underway.

The political strategies available to firms are the same as those available to other interest groups, but their appropriateness and effectiveness can differ. Activist groups often rely on high-profile campaigns to attract the attention of the media and the public. Such strategies are seldom effective for business and, if undertaken, may embroil the firm in a highly visible controversy that constrains its ability to act on other issues. Thus, the set of effective political strategies for firms is often a subset of the strategies used by other interests.

Political Assets

Firms and interest groups employ political assets in their strategies. Access to institutional officeholders is an important asset to be developed and maintained. Access to members of Congress is a necessary condition for effective lobbying. That access can be based on the constituency connection, campaign contributions, and the provision of reliable information. Some firms obtain access by hiring former government officials or retaining well-connected advisors and consultants. Some firms attempt to develop personal relationships between their managers and influential institutional officeholders.

The reputation of the firm and its top management is also an important asset. The success of the Semiconductor Industry Association has in part been due to the fact that its member firms are at the leading edge of technology and their CEOs are respected entrepreneurs and managers. Reputation also depends on the credibility of the firm and its managers as revealed by how responsible their political actions are. Actions that are deceptive, misleading, or represent an abuse of power can quickly damage a reputation and depreciate its value. Furthermore, interest and activist groups and government officeholders can have long memories.

The theory of collective action identifies the costs of collective action as a significant obstacle to political action, so any means of lowering those costs represents an important political asset. A trade association reduces the costs of collective action, particularly for industries with a substantial number of firms and for issues on which it is important to present a common rather than a fragmented position. When an industry seeks legislation, it is often effective for the firms in the industry to adopt a common position. When an industry seeks to block legislation, a fragmented position may be more effective by revealing a wider set of contentious dimensions and adverse consequences that may result from passage of the legislation.

The Rent Chain

A fundamental political asset is an alignment of the firm's interests with those of the constituents of government officeholders. The value of this asset depends on the number of people affected, their resources, and their coverage of political jurisdictions. A large employment base or an extensive supply or distribution network is a potentially important asset. Its value increases as its coverage of political jurisdictions widens, because that provides a broader base for lobbying and grassroots activities. Automobile dealers represent an important political asset of the automobile industry because they are numerous, have substantial resources, and provide extensive coverage of congressional districts. Similarly, the location of assembly and parts plants in the United States gives Japanese automobile manufacturers a political asset. This type of asset is formalized in the concept of the rent chain.[9]

Porter (1985) introduced the concept of a value chain that identifies the stages of a firm's operations through which it creates value for its owners. Nonmarket strategies are also directed at creating value, and there is an analogous concept for nonmarket strategies. That concept is referred to as a rent chain. Its significance is a basis for influence in the nonmarket environment, particularly in the context of distributive politics. The basic principle is that the greater are the rents affected by a nonmarket issue the greater are the incentives to take nonmarket action to protect or increase those rents.

As indicated in Chapter 5, a rent is a surplus, and for a firm differs from a profit because of sunk costs. Rents are also earned by the factors of production. Employees earn a rent if their wages and benefits are higher than the wages they could earn in alternative employment. When jobs are threatened by a nonmarket alternative, employees thus have an incentive to act to protect their rents. Labor unions are thus one of the

---

[9]This concept is developed in Baron (1995a).

strongest supporters of protectionist measures when the jobs of their members are threatened by imports. Rents can also be earned by distributors, retailers, and customers, and those rents can motivate them to take nonmarket action. Importers of foreign goods, for example, typically oppose protectionist measures. Rents are thus a fundamental source of incentives for nonmarket action.

A firm's rent chain includes those interests that earn rents as a result of the interactions with the firm. When a nonmarket issue, for example, affects the demand for a firm's products, the rents of other components of its rent chain are likely to be affected. Interests are then aligned along the rent chain and hence the potential for collective action is present. Because rents are earned by the factors of production—in supply channels, in the channels of distribution, and by customers—the rent chain is larger than the value chain. The relationship between the rent chain and value chain is illustrated in Figure 7-2. To the extent that jobs, supply contracts, alliance relationships, and communities are affected, the firm has a basis for appealing to political officeholders. Grassroots political strategies are based on these effects, and lobbying also draws strength from the effect of alternatives on the rents of constituents.

The rent chain can have two types of productivity. First, it can provide enfranchisement, giving the firm the right, or opportunity, to participate in public and consultative processes. Many U.S. pharmaceutical firms believed it was important to locate facilities in Japan so that they could better participate in the regulatory and consultative processes that formulate policy and set drug prices. In a country in which market opportunities are controlled by government regulation and where administrative directives are pervasive, the productivity of locating a portion of the rent chain in that country can be high. Second, it can provide the basis for generating nonmarket action through grassroots strategies. The Toshiba case presented later in the chapter includes a grassroots strategy, and these strategies are considered in more detail in Chapter 8.

The rent chain can also be mobilized on issues outside governmental institutions. In 1992 Wal-Mart was the subject of a critical story on NBC's *Dateline,* alleging that some of the company's Asian suppliers used child labor. The story also raised concerns about whether Wal-Mart's Buy America program for sourcing products and creating jobs in the

FIGURE 7-2 The Rent Chain

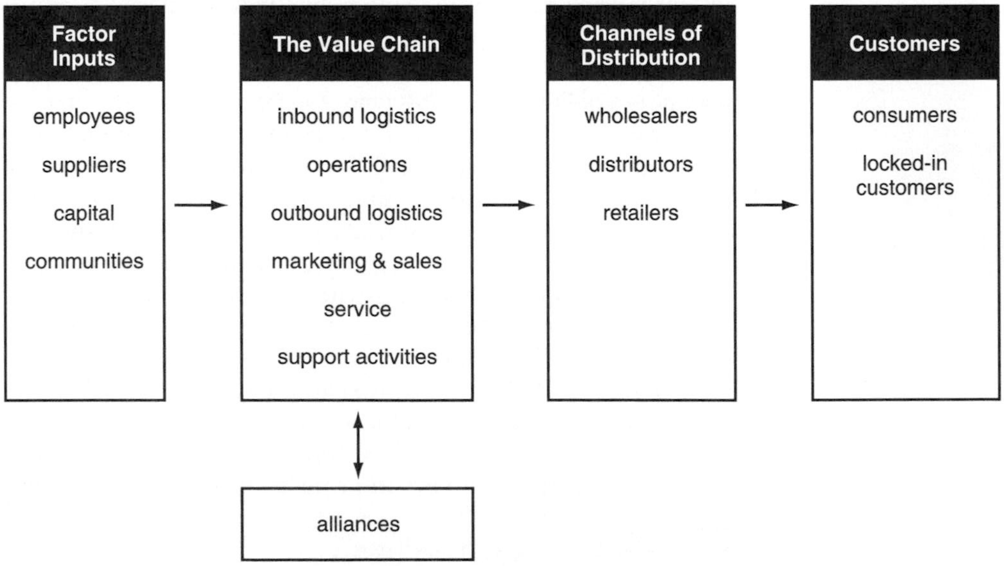

United States was being compromised. In response to the allegations, several of Wal-Mart's suppliers, including large companies such as General Electric Lighting and smaller companies such as Brinkman Corporation and Cheyenne Lamps, took out advertisements in newspapers with headlines, "We Support Wal-Mart's Buy America Program."

Implementation

Implementation pertains to the selection of specific actions and the assignment of tasks to organizational units and individual managers. This can involve undertaking a grassroots strategy, hiring a Washington law firm to provide technical advice on a legislative issue, assigning managers to lobby in Washington, or developing a coalition. The specifics of strategy implementation are considered in Chapter 8.

Strategies are implemented over time, so contingent strategies should be developed. This is particularly important because the political competition on an issue may move from one institutional arena to another. Alternatively, in the context of Figure 7-1, a firm that fails to achieve its objective in a legislature may continue its political activity before the administrative agency to which authority has been delegated. If unsuccessful at that stage, the firm may take the issue to a judicial arena.

Political Strategies

Three broad classes of political strategy are *representational, majority building,* and *informational.* Representational strategies focus on affecting the outcomes of issues based on the consequences of alternatives for constituents and their interests. The Toshiba example, the chapter case *The Section 936 Tax Credit,* and the Chapter 8 cases *Drexel Burnham Lambert and Junk Bond Politics* and *Envirotest Systems Corporation (B)* are examples of representational strategies. These strategies often involve the mobilization of components of the rent chain and may involve grassroots strategies, coalition building, and public advocacy, as considered in Chapter 8. Majority building strategies focus on developing the needed votes in a legislature to enact or defeat a bill. The chapter case *Federal Express (A)* and the Chapter 8 case *CAFE Standards* include majority building strategies. Informational strategies focus on providing information about consequences. Informational strategies can be coupled with representational and majority building strategies as when a firm lobbies to provide information and also organizes a grassroots strategy involving the mobilization of components of the firm's rent chain. Informational strategies are important in the *Drexel Burnham Lambert and Junk Bond Politics* and *CAFE Standards* cases. Many political strategies involve combinations of these strategies as in the chapter case *Echelon and the Home Automation Standard (A)* and the Chapter 8 case *CAFE Standards.* This section presents an example of a representational strategy and then addresses majority building and informational strategies.

A REPRESENTATIONAL STRATEGY: TOSHIBA AND TRADE SANCTIONS

The U.S. Department of Defense observed that Soviet submarines were operating more quietly than in the past, thus making tracking them more difficult. A Pentagon investigation revealed that Soviet propeller technology had improved substantially, possibly due to the sale of highly sophisticated milling equipment to the Soviet Union by the Toshiba Machine Company of Japan. Any such sale would be in violation of the regulations of the Coordinating Committee for Export Controls (COCOM), an international agreement that prohibited the export to communist countries of technology that could improve their military capability.

When a U.S. newspaper reported the Pentagon investigation in March 1987, the Japanese Ministry of International Trade and Industry (MITI) shrugged off the report. U.S. pressure, however, eventually caused MITI to investigate. MITI found that the Toshiba Machine Company had twice sold milling machines to the Soviet Union in violation of both COCOM regulations and Japanese law. This machinery could have enabled the Soviets to improve their propeller technology. Toshiba Machine Company was 50.1 percent owned by the Toshiba Corporation (referred to as Toshiba hereafter), which was reported to be unaware of the illegal sales. The MITI investigation also revealed that Toshiba Machine had falsified export documents to qualify for export licenses and that the trading company Wako Koeki had illegally arranged for computer software for the milling machines to be supplied by Kongsberg Vaapenfabrkik, a government-owned Norwegian defense contractor.

The uproar in the United States was immediate. Several consumer boycotts of Toshiba products were reported, and members of Congress smashed Toshiba products on the lawn of the Capitol. A $1 billion sale of Toshiba laptop computers to the U.S. Department of Defense came under fire. Some U.S. companies canceled purchase agreements with Toshiba, and others were noticeably nervous about dealing with it.

Political entrepreneurs were eager to represent constituents angry over the sale of the milling machines. In mid-June, the House passed a nonbinding resolution calling on the Department of State to seek compensation from Japan for damages. A bill barring Toshiba sales to the Defense Department was introduced, and bills banning all Toshiba imports to the United States for a period of 2 to 5 years were speeding through Congress. Legislatively imposed sanctions seemed a certainty.

Strategy Formulation

Toshiba's problem was characteristic of client-based politics. Because some sanctions seemed inevitable, the relevant status quo was that sanctions would be imposed, and Toshiba's overall objective was to limit them. That is, the benefit Toshiba sought was a reduction in the sanctions it would face. On the other side of the issue, the benefits from opposing a reduction in the sanctions were widely distributed rather than concentrated on identifiable interest groups. Pressure for sanctions came from the public and from members of Congress, who wanted to prevent further illegal sales to the Soviet Union and to claim credit for doing so.

To realize its objective of limiting the sanctions, Toshiba adopted a multifaceted strategy that addressed the threat of sanctions and the concerns the incident had caused. Those facets involved putting its house in order and directly addressing the political issue in the United States.[10] In Japan, Toshiba's strategy had two components. The first was to ensure that no further illegal sales would be made by any of its subsidiaries or affiliated companies. The second was to work with the government to ensure that other Japanese companies would also comply with COCOM regulations.

In the United States, reaction to the sales did not distinguish between the Toshiba Machine Company and the Toshiba Corporation. Toshiba Machine had U.S. sales of only $100 million. Toshiba, with U.S. sales of $2.6 billion, was a much more visible target. One component of Toshiba's strategy was to deflect attention to the Toshiba Machine Company. This involved providing information about the relative independence of Toshiba Machine and the fact that Toshiba had been unaware of the sales. A second component of its strategy was to protect Toshiba Machine's business in the United

[10]The account presented here is based on public sources and does not necessarily reflect the reasoning of Toshiba executives. Instead, the presentation is intended to characterize and analyze Toshiba's strategy and its implementation.

States. The fact that Toshiba Machine had production plants in the United States allowed Toshiba to argue that sanctions could cost jobs. A third component of its strategy was to attempt to place time limits on any sanctions and to allow exceptions for certain exports such as spare parts and specialized products, particularly those used for defense purposes. Furthermore, Toshiba sought to grandfather sales agreements already signed.

Another important component of its strategy was to portray the issue as part of the broader trade negotiations between Japan and the United States. The objective was to imply that any sanctions imposed on Toshiba or Toshiba Machine would "count" toward the trade concessions that Japan would inevitably make as a result of the negotiations. That is, stiff sanctions against Toshiba would make it more difficult for the United States to obtain trade concessions in other sectors.

A variant on the trade policy strategy was to stress that the COCOM regulations were analogous to other export controls intended to limit the flow of high-technology products to the communist bloc. U.S. high-tech firms that were prohibited from sales opportunities by these controls had been working to relax them. Although Toshiba would not be able to join publicly with those firms in their efforts to relax the export controls, it could align with them in its lobbying.

A final component of Toshiba's U.S. strategy was to focus attention on the future rather than on the past. Toshiba emphasized the measures it was taking to ensure that such violations would not happen again.

Strategy Implementation

To implement its strategy, Toshiba took several actions in Japan and the United States. Both Toshiba and the Japanese government acted to put their own houses in order. In an act of contrition, the chairman as well as the president of Toshiba resigned their positions. Toshiba increased by 80 its staff responsible for verifying compliance with export regulations. MITI announced that it would increase its surveillance of exports, strengthen penalties for violations, and contribute more to the support of COCOM's secretariat in Paris. MITI also offered to provide the U.S. Department of Defense with the same milling machines that had been sold to the Soviet Union so that it could develop improved submarine detection devices. The Japanese government hurriedly prepared strengthened laws on COCOM compliance.

Toshiba's strategy in the United States was implemented on a broad scale, reportedly at a cost of $30 million. It took out full-page advertisements apologizing for its actions and pledged not to make any further illegal sales. In other quarters, Toshiba attempted to assure its critics that it was taking steps to prevent further violations.

Toshiba mounted a major lobbying campaign. To obtain access to Congress and the executive branch, it hired several former government officials, including the former chairman of the House Budget Committee, a well-known Republican lawyer who had served in the Nixon administration, a lobbyist who had served in the Nixon White House, and a former deputy U.S. trade representative.

Toshiba also used its rent chain in a grassroots strategy by bringing to Washington the managers of many of its U.S. operations. It also flew a number of its suppliers and customers to Washington to impress on Congress the harm to U.S. interests that harsh sanctions would cause. Toshiba's employment of 4,200 people in the United States provided a link between possible sanctions and constituents' jobs. For example, Toshiba had a microwave oven plant in Tennessee and was able to convince the governor to write to each member of the state's congressional delegation, warning that retaliatory measures directed at Toshiba could have a direct impact on over 600 employees in the state. Even potential employment provided a basis for generating political pressure. The governor of Indiana, who had been working to attract a Toshiba facility to his state, asked the Indiana congressional delegation to oppose sanctions.

Toshiba had little difficulty enlisting the support of its customers, many of whom relied on its products. The Electronic Industries Association argued that over 4,000 jobs held by employees of Toshiba's customers were threatened by the sanctions. Some 40 companies, including Apple Computer and Honeywell—importers of Toshiba printers and semiconductors, respectively—opposed the proposed sanctions. Toshiba suppliers also rallied to its defense. Toshiba was able to enlist other allies as well. In a letter to the House Armed Services committee chairman, an assistant secretary of defense wrote that Japan was "succeeding in punishing the guilty, establishing stronger controls, and funding antisubmarine warfare programs which will help the United States and Japanese navies."[11]

The Outcome

The sanctions eventually imposed against Toshiba were considerably less severe than initially had been expected, and Toshiba's political strategy was given considerable credit for the outcome. The sanctions included a ban on imports by Toshiba Machine and Kongsberg Trade for 3 years and a ban on any sales to the U.S. government for the same period. The parent company in Japan was also banned from sales to the U.S. government for the same period. However, exceptions were provided for products necessary for national security, spare parts, servicing and maintenance, and for those items under contract before June 30, 1987.

MAJORITY BUILDING STRATEGIES

In voting institutions, a majority is required to enact legislation or in the case of a presidential veto, for example, two-thirds of the members of both the House and the Senate are required to overturn the veto and enact a bill. Conversely, to defeat legislation a blocking majority of votes is required, or in the case of a veto one-third of the members of the House or Senate is required. Strategies directed at legislatures focus on building a majority for or against an alternative.[12]

A key component of a majority building strategy is recruiting votes. Votes are recruited by interest groups and by public officeholders. For example, the majority and minority leaders in the House and Senate recruit votes on some legislation by providing favors to legislators. Similarly, the president frequently recruits votes by providing favors to members of Congress. President Clinton used this approach to recruit votes of congressional Democrats for the North American Free Trade Agreement.

Votes may be recruited by interest groups through a variety of means. One is lobbying based on the constituent connection that emphasizes the consequences of a legislative alternative for the constituents of a legislator. Votes can also be recruited through vote trading. A legislator who has strong preferences about the outcome of issue A and does not care about the outcome of issue B may be willing to trade her vote on issue B for a vote on issue A of another legislator who has strong preferences on issue B. Consequently, an interest group with allies in the legislature may be able to enlist them in vote trading.

Votes are also recruited by providing politically valuable support for a legislator. This could involve electoral vote pledges or endorsements by constituency groups such as components of a rent chain. Other means are voter mobilization and supplying volunteers as practiced by labor unions, endorsements and supporting advertisements as used by the Sierra Club and other environmental interest groups, and campaign contributions. There is little evidence that campaign contributions influence congressional

---

[11] *The New York Times,* March 14, 1988.

[12] Baron (1999) introduces the concepts of majority building and vote recruitment strategies for client and interest group politics.

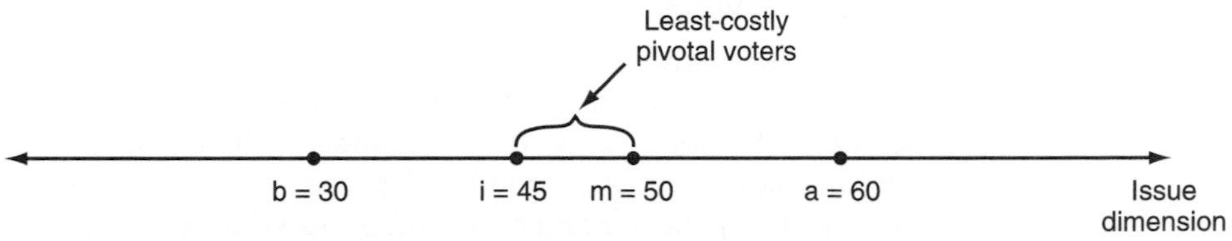

FIGURE 7-3 Majority Building and Pivotal Voters

voting, and the caps on contributions are very low. Campaign contributions are thus better thought of as developing access to members of Congress for the purpose of lobbying, as considered in Chapter 8.

A vote recruitment strategy focuses on pivotal voters—those whose votes can switch the outcome between victory and defeat.[13] To illustrate the concept of pivotal voters in a vote recruitment strategy, consider an issue, such as the extension of daylight-saving time, for which the alternatives can be arrayed on a line as in Figure 5-9. Consider a 101-member legislature that operates under simple (50 percent) majority rule and is considering two alternatives $a = 60$ and $b = 30$, as depicted in Figure 7-3. Also suppose that the preferences of each legislator are represented by the distance of an alternative to her ideal point—the alternative she most prefers.[14] Also, suppose that legislators' ideal points are uniformly distributed along the line in Figure 7-3 with the legislator the farthest to the left having ideal point 0 and the legislator farthest to the right having ideal point 100. The median legislator is denoted by m and has an ideal point at 50. Since alternative a is closer to m than is alternative b, the median voter prefers to vote for a.

Consider a situation of client politics in which an interest group prefers b to a and seeks to build a majority in favor of b by recruiting votes. The first step in a vote recruitment strategy is to identify the pivotal voters. The voter i who is indifferent between a and b has an ideal point at 45, which is the midpoint between a and b, as illustrated in Figure 7-3. In the absence of a political strategy by the interest group, alternative a would be enacted on a vote of 56 to 45, assuming that the indifferent voter $i = 45$ votes with the majority. Consequently, to enact alternative b the interest group and those in the legislature who prefer b to a must recruit six votes. That is, the 45 legislators with ideal points to the left of the midpoint will vote for b regardless of the strategy of the interest group, so only six additional votes are needed to form a majority for b.[15] Any six votes are pivotal, but the interest group prefers to recruit those votes that are least costly. The least-costly votes are of those legislators who only mildly prefer a to b. These are the legislators with ideal points between (and including) 45 and 50. The focus of a vote recruitment strategy is thus on these six legislators.

There is no reason to recruit legislators with ideal points from 51 through 100. First, their votes are not needed to pass b. Second, recruiting their votes would be more difficult to accomplish because they prefer a to b more strongly than the legislators with ideal points between 45 and 50. Using the same logic, recruiting the vote of legislator $m = 50$ is more difficult than recruiting the vote of legislator 45, since m prefers a to b more strongly than does legislator 45. Consequently, greater support or a more valuable vote trade must be provided to m than to 45.

---

[13] The formal theory of vote recruitment in client politics is developed in Snyder (1991).
[14] The preferences of legislators can be assessed based on the characteristics of their constituents and their past voting record using the interest groups ratings discussed in Chapter 5.
[15] If the interest group and its allies in the legislature are uncertain about the preferences of legislation, they may want to recruit more than six votes as insurance.

MULTIPLE PIVOTS

The U.S. legislative process is more complicated than that just considered because it has multiple pivots. First, it is a bicameral system, which requires that the House and Senate both pass a bill in identical language before it can become law. Pivotal voters are thus present in each chamber. Second, senators can filibuster a bill, and cloture—stopping the filibuster and proceeding to a vote—requires a vote of 60 senators. Third, the president can veto a bill, which requires two-thirds of both the House and Senate to overturn the veto and enact the bill.[16] Institutions in other countries also have multiple pivots. In Japan, a two-thirds vote in the lower house of the Diet can enact legislation without approval by the upper house. The Council of Ministers of the European Union operates with qualified majority rule, which requires 62 of the 87 votes to enact legislation.

The chapter case *Federal Express (A)* involves a pivot at the majority needed to overcome a filibuster in the Senate. The Chapter 5 case *Summertime in the European Union* and the Chapter 14 case *The European Union Carbon Tax* involve a pivot at the qualified majority level used in the European Union.

THE NATURE OF THE POLITICS AND POLITICAL STRATEGY

The vote recruitment strategy considered in the context of Figure 7-3 involves only one interest group and thus corresponds to client politics in which opposing interests have low per capita benefits or high costs of taking nonmarket and political action. It may also correspond to the case of interest group politics in which the opposing interest group has already implemented its strategy and the interest group supporting b has the last move. For example, in the chapter case *Federal Express (A)* organized labor deployed its strategy by enlisting its allies in the Senate to undertake a filibuster against a bill sought by Federal Express. Given that organized labor had already deployed its strategy, Federal Express was in the situation depicted in Figure 7-3.

When two competing interest groups are actively choosing their strategies, majority building becomes more complicated. Suppose that one interest group G_a supports the status quo a and another group G_b supports alternative b. Because G_b seeks to overturn the status quo, it naturally moves first. If G_b attempts to build a majority by recruiting votes, the opposing interest group can recruit any majority of votes to preserve the status quo. For example, if in Figure 7-3 G_b were to recruit the votes of legislators 45 through 50, group G_a could counter either by attempting to recruit those same legislators or by attempting to recruit voters to the left of 45 who only mildly prefer b to a. Consequently, group G_b must employ a majority protection strategy that may require recruiting more than the minimal number of pivotal voters. That is, group G_b may have to recruit a supermajority of voters and provide them with sufficient support to protect each majority against the strategy of the opposing interest group.[17]

AGENDA SETTING

If the legislative process is open so that legislators can easily offer amendments and if there is no vote recruitment, the winning alternative is typically centrally-located in terms of the preferences of legislators, as in the daylight saving time example in Chapter 5. That is, in an open process the median voter theorem provides the basic prediction of the outcome. If interests can recruit pivotal voters, the outcome can be moved, as considered in the context of Figure 7-3.

---

[16]Krehbiel (1998)(1999) provides a theory of legislation that considers these pivots.

[17]Groseclose (1995) and Groseclose and Snyder (1996) present a theory of competitive vote recruitment.

If the legislative process is relatively closed, as in the case in which a committee chair chooses the alternative to be considered and the Rules Committee in the House protects it from amendments, strategic agenda setting is possible. For example, in the European Union the Commission is the agenda setter and under some legislative procedures amendments by the European Parliament are difficult to make. The committee in the first example and the Commission in the second are thus strategic agenda setters. The political strategies of interests are often directed to the agenda setter.

Agenda-setting strategies focus first on recruiting the agenda setter and then on the alternative to be placed on the agenda. Consider Figure 7-3, and suppose that the status quo is a. Furthermore, initially assume that there are no interest groups attempting to recruit votes. If the agenda setter has an ideal point at 30, it can place the alternative $c = 41$ on the agenda, and a majority will vote for it against the status quo b. To see this, note that the pivotal voter $m = 50$ just prefers c to a. Consequently, the agenda setter can place $c = 41$ on the agenda, and a majority will vote for it.[18] Consequently, an interest group with an agenda-setter ally with ideal point 30 can obtain $c = 41$ without having to recruit any votes.

The ability of an agenda setter to use the location of the status quo to its advantage is mitigated to the extent that there is vote recruitment competition between interest groups. A strategy that involves agenda setting is thus more likely to be effective in client politics. An agenda-setter's power is also limited by the ability of others to offer amendments or counterproposals. When amendments are freely allowed, the median voter theorem becomes relevant, and in the absence of vote recruitment the outcome can be expected to be centrally located.

INFORMATIONAL STRATEGIES

Information is a politically valuable resource. Information can enable an officeholder to better serve constituents or interest groups or pursue policy interests. Interest groups thus employ informational strategies in an attempt to influence outcomes. Informational strategies are based on the superior information an interest group has about the consequences of alternatives for constituents, for example. Thus, a necessary condition for an informational strategy to be effective is that the interest group be better informed about some aspect of the issue than are public officeholders. Informational strategies are strategic because they typically involve providing information favorable to the firm or interest group. The recipients of the information understand this and take the strategic provision of information into account in updating their beliefs about, for example, the relationship between alternatives and consequences. Even though information may be provided strategically, it can be beneficial to the officeholder.

The strategic provision of information is a, if not the, principal component of lobbying, testimony in legislative or regulatory proceedings, and public advocacy. To implement strategies such as information provision through lobbying, an interest group may invest in obtaining access to a legislator or administrative official. Influence thus often has two stages. The first involves obtaining and maintaining access, and the second involves the strategic provision of information. In public processes such as those of many regulatory agencies, interests have due process rights to participate in the process and provide information. In legislative institutions, however, access is not guaranteed and may have to be developed.

---

[18]Viewing the alternative placed on the agenda as a function of the status quo, note that a more extreme status quo allows the agenda setter to obtain an outcome closer to its ideal point. For example, if the status quo were 70, the agenda setter could place the alternative 31 on the agenda and it would pass. If the status quo were 80, however, the agenda setter would put the alternative 30 on the agenda, as that is its ideal point.

Lobbying involves the strategic provision of two types of information: technical and politically relevant information. Technical information pertains to the consequences of alternatives under consideration. Politically relevant information pertains to the effects of alternatives on the constituents of officeholders. Both technical and politically relevant information may be provided strategically—presented in a manner favorable to the outcome sought by the interest group. This may involve the strategic advocacy of a position by an interest, the choice of methodologies that generate data and conclusions favorable to the interest, or emphasis on favorable, and deemphasis on unfavorable, aspects of an alternative. Some informational strategies are counteractive—that is, they are undertaken to counter the information provided by an opposing interest group.

Information must be credible to have an effect. Credibility can be established in several ways. First, the information may be hard in the sense that when provided with the information, the officeholder can check on its veracity. Second, if it is not hard, information can be credible if a group with interests aligned with those of the officeholder has an incentive to provide it, given that the officeholder will act on it. That is, the officeholder can rely on the information the interest group provides because she knows that the interest group would not provide the information unless it wanted the officeholder to act on it. Third, if the interests of the group and the decision maker are not aligned, the information provided by an interest group can be credible if it is confirmed by information provided by another interest group with different preferences. This confirmatory information need not be identical to that provided by the interest group, but it must corroborate its information. Fourth, an interest may commission a study by an organization that has a degree of independence from the interest and has a reputation to maintain. For example, the Federation of American Health Systems, an association of for-profit hospitals, commissioned a $412,000 study by Project Hope, a health research group, that showed that substantial efficiency gains result when a not-for-profit hospital is acquired by a for-profit hospital. Information, however, can be countered or offset by information presented by opponents. For example, the study commissioned by the Federation was in response to studies released by not-for-profit hospitals showing adverse effects of acquisitions.

The strategic provision of information sometimes involves the biasing of information. This is unacceptable from an ethical perspective and may constitute manipulation. The unethical strategic provision of information is not separated by a bright line from responsible informational strategies; instead there is a substantial gray area. For example, EPA Administrator Carol Browner sought to establish stringent standards on microscopic particles such as soot and dirt in the air, and to achieve her objective the EPA implemented a strategy that emphasized the health risks to children and others. The EPA claimed that the more stringent standards would prevent 20,000 premature deaths annually at an estimated abatement cost of $6 billion. Industry groups, however, estimated the cost at $23 billion. Such differences in estimates are commonplace with both the EPA and the industry groups strategically presenting their sides of the issue. Not only were the EPA's cost estimates challenged, but in April 1997 the EPA was forced to admit that it had made an error and reduced its estimate to 15,000 premature deaths prevented. A scientist and former EPA official working for the Citizens for a Sound Economy Foundation, an industry-backed center opposed to more stringent regulation, had discovered the error. The scientist subsequently estimated that the proposed regulations would prevent fewer than 1,000 premature deaths.[19] Which estimate was closer to the truth is unclear.

---

[19] *San Francisco Chronicle,* May 13, 1997.

Another concern about the strategic provision of information is whether an interest is legally or morally obligated to provide information that it prefers not to disclose. In part the EPA based its stringent airborne soot and dirt standards on a study by Harvard University researchers who found in a longitudinal, epidemiologic study that microscopic particles increased the death rate substantially. The Harvard researchers refused to release the raw data despite requests by governors, EPA officials, and industry groups. Concerns about the scientific basis of the study and the validity of its conclusions were heightened when one of the Harvard researchers participated with the National Resources Defense Council in a news conference on particulate pollution.[20]

Unless there is specific legislation or regulation compelling the provision of information, a company is not obligated to provide unfavorable information about its activities. It would be illegal, however, for a pharmaceutical company to withhold data on the safety of a drug, and it would be immoral, and probably illegal, to make false claims about a product's performance. It is both allowed and commonplace, however, for interests to advocate their side of an issue or to provide estimates based on methodologies likely to provide information favorable to their side. A common example is a trial in which the plaintiff and the defendant provide expert witnesses who reach different conclusions regarding an issue. In executive and legislative institutions, the same type of advocacy takes place, and it is the informational dimension of such advocacy that is the focus here.

PUBLIC OFFICEHOLDERS AS TARGETS OF POLITICAL STRATEGIES

Political strategies are ultimately directed at public officeholders who, often collectively as in a legislature, are the decision makers who determine the outcome of issues. These officeholders have duties to their institution and to their constituents. They also have career interests. Those career interests include reelection, running for higher office, advancement in the bureaucracy, and post-public-service employment. Because of career interests most officeholders are risk averse and wary of taking an action that may limit their advancement or jeopardize their electoral prospects. Officeholders thus generally seek to avoid uncertainty, which can result in a bias toward the status quo.

An interest group that seeks to preserve the status quo can thus adopt a strategy that emphasizes the uncertainty inherent in the issue. This may involve counteractive lobbying that calls into question the information provided by the proponents of change from the status quo. Another strategy that is often effective is to bring new dimensions of the issue to the table. Toshiba, for example, emphasized the importance of its products to U.S. defense contractors. Drexel Burnham Lambert emphasized the importance of junk bond financing to young, high-growth companies that provided much of the new employment in the economy. Through its informational lobbying Boeing attempted to emphasize the uncertainty about the effect of the failure to renew China's MFN status on sales and jobs in the United States, as indicated in the example on the next page.

Conversely, an interest that seeks to change the status quo should focus on reducing uncertainty about the consequences of the change. In the Chapter 5 case *Repeal of the Luxury Tax* yacht builders provided specific information about the loss of jobs caused by the luxury tax. This information must be credible, and its corroboration by other interests contributed to the repeal.

---

[20]*The Wall Street Journal,* April 7, 1997. In an op-ed piece the Mobil Corporation called for a release of the data. (*The Wall Street Journal,* May 23, 1997)

EXAMPLE

China and Most Favored Nation Status

A nonmarket issue that generates intense nonmarket competition is the annual renewal of the most favored nation (MFN) status for China. Also riding in part on this renewal is China's admission into the World Trade Organization (WTO), which the United States had refused to approve because of human rights concerns. In addition to human rights concerns, the disclosures that China had supplied missiles and chemical weapons technology to Iran and that it had attempted to gain influence in the United States through illegal political campaign contributions generated mounting congressional opposition to the renewal of China's MFN status.

In 1997 Boeing, the largest U.S. exporter, was involved in an intense market competition with Airbus, based in France and three other countries, for a $4 billion sale to China. Moreover, China was expected to purchase an estimated $140 billion of aircraft over the next 20 years. In early April at the United Nations human rights conference in Geneva, the United States voted for a resolution to condemn China, whereas France voted against the resolution causing it to fail. With President Chirac of France scheduled to visit China in May, Boeing faced a considerable challenge to obtain the sale.

Larry S. Dickenson, vice president of international sales for Boeing, noted the advantage France had obtained through its vote on the human rights motion: "When President Chirac arrives in Beijing in a few weeks, I am sure he will be rewarded for that stance."[1] When President Chirac arrived in China, the government announced that it would purchase 30 Airbus aircraft valued at $1.5 billion. China's Premier Li Peng explained the decision to buy from Airbus: "They do not attach political strings to cooperation with China. Vice Minister for Foreign Trade Sun Zhenyu said . . . that cancellation of MFN status is 'a double-edged sword that hurts not only China but U.S. middle- and lower-income consumers as well as U.S. investors in China.'"[2]

Boeing and other U.S. firms such as the Ford Motor Company lobbied intensely for renewal of the MFN status for China and for China's admission into the WTO. Representative Todd Tiahrt (R-KS), who had worked for Boeing for 14 years, said he talked with Boeing lobbyists "once a week, sometimes daily. They never fail to bring [MFN] up."[3] After President Chirac's visit, the president of Boeing's commercial aircraft business, Ronald Woodard, said, "The Chinese just bought 30 Airbus planes to reward Europe for not punishing human rights. The Europeans love the fight over MFN."[4]

The information provided by the businesses included the stakes for the companies and their rentholders and their predictions about the broader consequences. Dickenson identified the long-term seriousness of the matter: "If we lose the opportunity to get China into a rule-based organization like the W.T.O. now, it will take us another five years to get back to the spot we're in today."[5] Dickenson added, "I told [Congress] about Airbus, Chirac's visit, what was likely to happen. I told them the realities: that every time there's a blip in U.S.-China relations, it helps our foreign competitors."[6]

Analysis

In this case, Boeing can provide information on (1) the likelihood that sales would be lost, (2) the rents that would be affected if sales were lost, (3) future sales that might be jeopardized, and (4) the effects of the sales on the competitive strength of Airbus and Boeing. Some of this information is soft in the sense that an officeholder is unable to evaluate its accuracy and completeness. In particular, the information in (1), (3), and (4) is to varying degrees soft and difficult to evaluate. Other information, such as that in (2), is hard in the sense that the officeholder can understand the data by inspection; for example, Boeing can identify the aircraft being offered to China, the current subcontractors, and the possible lost sales. In addition to the information being hard or soft, Boeing in

[1] *The New York Times,* April 29, 1997.
[2] *Business Week,* June 16, 1997.
[3] *Business Week,* June 16, 1997.
[4] *Business Week,* June 16, 1997.
[5] *The New York Times,* April 29, 1997.
[6] *The Wall Street Journal,* June 24, 1997.

all likelihood is better informed about (1) through (4) than members of Congress. For example, Boeing is better informed about the likelihood of losing the sale to Airbus than Congress and about the subsequent effects on the competitive strength of the two companies. Because Boeing has superior information, it has an opportunity to provide information strategically. This may involve emphasizing favorable information and remaining silent on unfavorable information. It may also involve emphasizing worst-case scenarios or utilizing data that presents its side of the issue as favorably as possible. In this case, the credibility of Boeing's information can to some extent be verified by the Department of Commerce.

Informational strategies can be integrated with broader nonmarket strategies including the nonmarket strategies of other interests. For example, the major corporations with business at risk in China allocated lobbying responsibilities. Boeing lobbied representatives from Alabama, Kansas, and Washington, and General Motors lobbied representatives from Georgia, Michigan, and Texas. The companies also backed grassroots organizations to support continuation of MFN status. Boeing backed the Kansas Alliance for U.S.-China Trade, which had grown to include 120 member companies that do business with China. Similarly, in California 350 companies participated in the Coalition for U.S.-China Trade.

POLITICAL STRATEGIES IN CLIENT AND INTEREST GROUP POLITICS

The choice of political strategies is related to the nature of the politics of an issue, as characterized in the Wilson matrix presented in Chapter 6. In client politics, the benefits from the political alternative are concentrated on the clients, whereas the benefits from opposing the alternative are widely distributed. Because the opposition is not active in client politics, the client interest group typically adopts a low-profile strategy outside the view of the public.[21] Lobbying and information provision are often the centerpieces of such a strategy. The information is often about the rentholders who would benefit from the alternative sought by the client or about how the alternative would serve the policy interests of the legislator. In a legislative arena the strategy frequently focuses on both majority building and agenda setting with a particular emphasis on congressional committees. Another strategy is to organize and mobilize potential beneficiaries into a coalition that can take coordinated action and improve the coverage of congressional districts. The Daylight Saving Time Coalition's strategy of attracting candy manufacturers by including Halloween in the extension is an example.

The danger in a political strategy in client politics is that opponents in the legislature or watchdog groups will expose the activities of the client. The label often given to client relationships is "special-interest" politics, and many members of Congress seek to avoid being labeled as a participant in such politics. Clients thus often wrap their objectives and messages in broader majoritarian interests.

Interest group politics generally means that the strategies of the opposing sides are more visible. One side often finds it effective to adopt a high-profile strategy, which can force the other side to adopt a similar strategy. A high-profile strategy could include public advocacy, testimony in legislative or regulatory hearings, and grassroots activities. A firm engaged in interest group politics can also utilize client politics strategies, particularly lobbying and coalition building. The formation of the Daylight-Saving Time Coalition was important in achieving an extension that had for many years stalled in Congress. Informal alignments of interests can also be important as in the case of the

[21]Toshiba was in a situation characterized by client politics, but because the issue received considerable attention by the news media, its strategy was more visible.

RP Foundation Fighting Blindness. If a coalition seeks to have new legislation adopted, it should attempt to have its allies in the legislature restrict the abilities of others to amend the proposal in ways that could split the coalition. It is often effective to attempt to incorporate the measure in a larger bill so as to give it a degree of protection. In the chapter case *Federal Express (A),* the company and its allies were successful in having a provision inserted in the bill in conference committee.

Competition between interest groups often gives more power to pivotal legislators requiring more substantial support in majority building strategies. Providing substitutes for opposing interests can be effective in reducing the strength of the opposition and hence conserving resources of the interest group and its allies. In the Boeing and foreign leasing example in Chapter 5, members of Congress who supported the elimination of tax breaks were able to grandfather the deals of tax-exempts that were already in the planning stages. An important component of a political strategy in interest group politics is identifying and proposing compromises. In the foreign leasing case, Boeing was able to attain its secondary objective of preserving its orders in hand and having the tax benefits phased out.

When a firm is on the side of dispersed benefits in entrepreneurial or majoritarian politics, a number of strategies are available. One is to identify pockets of interests that can be organized and mobilized for political action. The basic politics of the extension of daylight saving time were majoritarian, but there were pockets of interests—convenience stores, recreation and sports products firms, candy makers, and nursery firms—that could be organized. This transformed the politics from majoritarian to client politics. A second strategy is to align diverse pockets of interests, as in the case of the Daylight Saving Time Coalition and the RP Foundation Fighting Night Blindness. Another strategy is to seek a political entrepreneur who can either organize those with dispersed benefits or represent them in the political institution. To the extent that a political entrepreneur is able to mobilize dispersed interests, the potential for collective action can be realized. In particular, when interests are not well informed about an issue, a political entrepreneur can alert those interests and provide information on the possible consequences of the issue.

Summary

The checklist presented in Figure 7-4 serves as a summary of the strategy formulation process considered in this chapter. The checklist is not intended to be used in isolation but must be combined with knowledge of the relevant institutions and with methods of analysis. Although the checklist is long, an issue creates a path through it and does not require consideration of every item listed. Many issues, for example, involve only a single institution—Congress or a regulatory agency—and so many of the items in the checklist need not be considered.

Checklist

I. Issue Identification
  A. Significance of the issue
  B. The firm's nonmarket issue agenda—related or competing issues
  C. Location of the issue in its life cycle

II. Nature of the politics of the issue
  A. Distributive politics—Wilson matrix
  B. Moral concerns and motivation

III. Assessment of potential political action
  A. Identification of affected interests
  B. Demand side
    1. Aggregate benefits
    2. Substitutes
    3. Per capita benefits
  C. Supply side (ability to generate political pressure)
    1. Number of people affected
    2. Geographic distribution—coverage of political districts
    3. Resources—financial, volunteers, etc.
    4. Cost of organizing for collective action; free-rider problem
  D. Summary in the distributive politics spreadsheet
  E. Likely objectives, strategies, and effectiveness of affected interests

IV. Institutions and officeholders
  A. Legislatures
    1. Subcommittees, committees and their chairs
    2. Conference committees/amendments between the chambers
  B. Regulatory commissions and administrative agencies
    1. Mandate and procedures
    2. Congressional oversight and judicial review
    3. Commissioners, administrators, and staff
  C. Executive branch
    1. President, Office of the President
    2. Cabinet departments—secretaries, deputies, assistants
    3. Administrators of executive branch agencies
  D. Courts—federal and state

V. Strategy formulation
  A. Objectives—Primary and contingent
  B. Distributive politics and collective action
  C. Political assets and the rent chain
  D. Representational strategies
  E. Majority building, vote recruitment, and agenda-setting strategies
  F. Informational strategies
  G. Is the strategy responsible?
  H. Costs of implementing the strategy

VI. Strategy Implementation (considered in Chapter 8)

FIGURE 7–4 Checklist for Analysis and Strategy Formulation

CASES

Federal Express (A)

Historically, labor relations for the Federal Express Corporation had been governed by the Railway Labor Act (RLA), which required that unions attempting to organize the employees of a company must do so nationally. Federal Express had operated as an "express company" under the RLA. Organized labor, however, had claimed that a bill enacted in 1995 subjected Federal Express to labor organization under a different law, the National Labor Relations Act (NLRA), which allows unions to organize workers locally. Avoiding unionization was a key element of Federal Express's market strategy: Of the 110,000 domestic employees of the company, only its 3,000 pilots were unionized.[1] Because local organization was usually easier for a union than national organization, Federal Express wanted Congress to pass new legislation that would clearly place its labor practices under the RLA.

Federal Express's nonmarket objective was to have a Senate ally attach a relatively small amendment (a "rider") to a much larger bill (a "vehicle"). The legislative vehicle in this instance was the annual authorization bill for the Federal Aviation Administration, which was regarded as a "must-pass" measure.

The substantive aim of the rider was to remove the jurisdictional ambiguity associated with the status quo by clearly making Federal Express's labor relations subject to the RLA.[2] Although minor in comparison with the larger bill, the amendment would have attracted attention and opposition if offered outright on the Senate or House floors, so Federal Express deferred to the judgment of one of its Senate allies who successfully negotiated for insertion of the amendment in the conference committee. When the bill and rider came back to the Senate for a vote on final passage, however, senators who were aligned with organized labor decided to mount a fight. They sought to block the vote on final passage of the conference report (hence the bill) unless and until the rider was dropped. They began a filibuster.

To stop the filibuster (i.e., to invoke cloture) and thereby move to certain passage of the bill and the rider, Federal Express and its supporters in the Senate had to build a majority of at least 60 votes. Suppose that supporters were willing to trade votes or other support of variable value to recruit the needed votes to stop the filibuster. [Refer to the figure on p. 215.] Let the status quo q denote ambiguous labor jurisdiction, and let the conference committee bill b denote unambiguous RLA jurisdiction. Along with the filibuster pivot f (the 41st ideal point) in the Senate, these points are identified in the following figure.

Assume that each senator has a symmetric utility function, so that his or her preference for q or a is determined by the relative distances from his or her ideal point to q and a. For convenience, assume also that the shapes of senators' utility functions are identical and that their ideal points are uniformly distributed (equally spaced) over the line as shown. The median senator's ideal point is shown as m, and Federal Express's allies have ideal points on the right side of the spectrum. Finally, assume that if the support provided or votes traded are sufficiently valuable, a senator will vote for a. Remember, however, that Federal Express supporters do not want to trade more in votes or provide more support than is necessary. ■

---

[1] "This Mr. Smith Gets His Way in Washington," *The New York Times,* October 10, 1996.

[2] Public laws cannot mention private companies explicitly. Therefore, the language that accomplished this task was necessarily opaque. The provision simply inserted the term "express company" into the Railway Labor Act of 1926. The term had been stricken—some claimed accidentally—from the law in 1995 when Congress terminated the Interstate Commerce Commission.

This case was prepared by Professors David Baron and Keith Krehbiel for purposes of illustrating theories of vote recruitment. Although it is based on an actual legislative history, it is not intended to suggest that Federal Express dealt with this nonmarket issue in this manner.

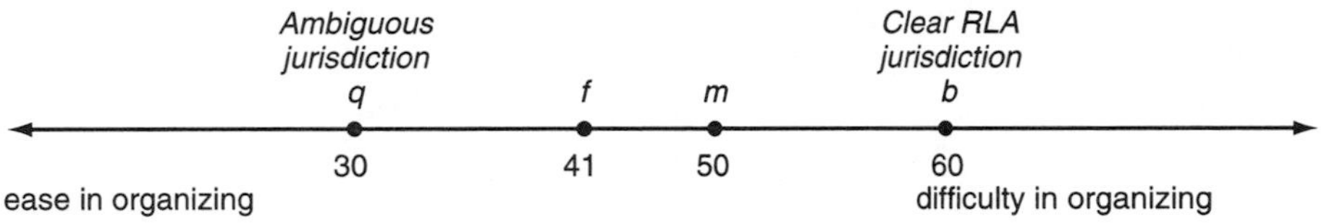

PREPARATION QUESTIONS

1. Which senators will not receive support or vote trades and why not?
2. Which senators will receive support or vote trades and why?
3. Which senator will receive the most valuable support or vote trades and why?
4. Does it make a difference if an opposing group (say, the AFL-CIO) were working to offset the efforts of Federal Express and its legislative allies?

Echelon and the Home Automation Standard (A)

Chris Stanfield, vice president and CFO of the Echelon Corporation, learned much to his surprise that the Federal Communications Commission (FCC) had begun a rule-making proceeding to establish a compatibility standard for the television set, VCR, and cable TV interface that would severely disadvantage Echelon in the home automation market. The FCC's rule-making was mandated by the Cable Television Act of 1992 in response to consumer complaints about difficulties in using advanced features of televisions and in operating VCRs in conjunction with cable television service (e.g., taping one channel while viewing another). The compatibility standard being considered by the FCC was advocated by the manufacturers of televisions and by cable television providers and included a particular communications protocol, referred to as CEBus.™ The proposed CEBus-based standard would change the way consumers interact with their televisions. Televisions would no longer be slaves to the cable box or VCR but instead would serve as the gateway to control systems for other consumer electronic devices. These devices would be connected to the television through a setback box, which would allow the consumer through the television to control other electronic systems in a home, including security systems, timer-operated appliances, heating and cooling systems, and personal computers. The threat to Echelon was that the CEBus protocol conflicted with its LonTalk™ communications protocol, and thus its adoption would severely limit the use of Echelon's control networks in the emerging home automation market. Echelon's objective was not to have its protocol mandated by the FCC but to preserve its opportunities and let the marketplace decide which products, and hence which protocols, would succeed and which would not. The concern was that the FCC would foreclose its opportunities.

COMPANY BACKGROUND

Echelon is a privately held company based in Palo Alto, California, with subsidiaries in London, Paris, Munich, and Tokyo and offices in Amsterdam and Beijing. Its president and CEO since its founding in 1988 has been M. Kenneth Oshman, cofounder and former president of the ROLM Corporation. Echelon was initially backed by venture capital firms, and subsequently others invested in Echelon, including Motorola with a 21 percent stake in the company, Quantum Fund, Detroit Edison, Apple Computer, Bessemer Venture Partners, Davidow Ventures, and 3COM. Echelon held over 50 patents and had hardware licensing agreements with Motorola and Toshiba.

Echelon's primary market is control networks—communications systems that integrate disparate pieces of electronic hardware over some distance. These systems enable administrators to monitor and control remotely the environment under their jurisdiction. Building-wide security systems commonly use such networks, as do automated assembly lines. Hospitals can use control networks for monitoring patients, and home automation can be based on such networks. Demand for control networks had grown rapidly in the last decade, and Echelon expected the market to continue to grow for the foreseeable future.

The analogy between control network architectures and computer operating systems is helpful for understanding Echelon's business. Echelon does not make the actual "nodes" of a control network—thermostats and alarms that actually interact with the physical environment. Like an operating system, control network architecture is the "infrastructure" that ties together the various pieces of hardware and software in the network. Echelon provides "open architecture" systems that allow equipment of different manufacturers to work together. The open architecture also allows systems designers great flexibility in developing a broad array of applications.

Echelon's main product, the LonWorks™ network, is a family of hardware and software systems that provides off-the-shelf foundations for customers to build complete control networks. Since its introduction in 1991, the LonWorks network had been adopted as a standard by several industries. In addition, Echelon had established the LonMark Interoperability Association, which establishes technical guidelines and promotes LonWorks. There were presently over 100 members, from more than 10 countries, including Ameritech, Honeywell, Hewlett Packard, IBM, Microsoft, Motorola, Philips, Toshiba, and Yokogawa.

In 1996 there were over 2,500 developers of LonWorks network technology, accounting for about 2 million installed nodes. Building automation accounted for roughly 30 percent of LonWorks's market. Users of LonWorks included Honeywell's Home and Building Control unit, Schlumberger Industries, Trans-Lite Inc., and NASA. The NASA application demonstrated that in addition to factories, office buildings, hospitals, and homes, satellites could also be monitored using control network technology.

TECHNOLOGY AND COMPATIBILITY

Applications of LonWorks networks fall into four categories: building, home, industrial, and utilities. The home automation category was the application threatened by the FCC's rule making. A home automation network allows a single network to control heating, air conditioning, lighting, watering, energy management, security systems, and consumer electronics devices. LonWorks allows nodes on these systems to be linked using a wide range of network options, from twisted pair to coaxial cable to wireless RF (radio frequency) and IR (infrared). For older homes without preexisting networks, LonWorks includes hardware that uses power lines for communications, thus avoiding costly retrofitting.

Other forms of home control networks are feasible. In particular, the Cable Consumer Equipment Compatibility Advisory Committee (C3AG), a group composed of members of the Electronics Industries Association (EIA) and National Cable Television Association (NCTA), had proposed a Decoder Interface standard to the FCC in August 1994.[1] The EIA's Consumer Electronics Group, which represents a wide spectrum of electronics manufacturers including television manufacturers, favored this standard because it would transform televisions from a commodity product to a high-margin electronic control system.[2] Cable providers favored the standard because it positioned them as the primary providers of the next generation of value-added home electronic services, such as on-line shopping and video entertainment.[3] Although the Decoder Interface standard was aimed primarily at television-related equipment such as cable descramblers and VCRs, it contained the CEBus communications protocol.

Echelon's concern was that the inclusion of the CEBus protocol into the next generation of televisions would effectively establish CEBus as the dominant protocol for home automation services. Indeed, the C3AG proposal to the FCC made explicit

---

[1]The C3AG is not an official advisory group to the FCC but had been working for several years on a standard.

[2]Founded in 1924, the EIA is the principal association of the $381 billion U.S. electronics manufacturing industry. The EIA has a staff of 200, a budget of $26 million, and a new 110,000 square foot office building in Arlington, Virginia. Some of Echelon's investors were also active members of the EIA. For example, Motorola senior vice president John Major was elected EIA treasurer for 1996. The EIA is organized into divisions and groups. The Consumer Electronics Manufacturers Association is one of its principal components, and its members constitute the Consumer Electronics Group. Another association in the EIA is the Telecommunications Industry Association, which includes 600 companies providing telecommunications systems, products, distributions services, and professional services.

[3]The NCTA has 3,073 members, a staff of 92, and a budget of over $5 million. Members include cable operators, cable networks, and suppliers and distributors.

mention of the CEBus protocol as a "home automation standard" for a "wide spectrum of consumer products."[4]

The operating principle behind the CEBus protocol is quite different from that of LonWorks. Its primary technical innovation is to transform televisions from monitors into intelligent devices. Today, many consumers use a cable converter and/or a VCR as an intermediary between the television signal and the physical screen. In effect, televisions are "slaves" of these set-top devices. Televisions with the CEBus-based Decoder Interface, however, would have the ability to communicate with a setback box, which is essentially an elaborate cable converter. Under this system, the user would interact with the television directly, which then gives instructions to the setback box. The setback box could be made to serve as the gateway to the home control network.

In contrast, a LonWorks network places no restriction on the control center of a home control network. In principle, one could use a television with a setback box, a set-top box, a computer, or a custom controller to operate the nodes of the control network. In addition, these nodes could be connected using any means available—wireless or not. The CEBus-based Decoder Interface, however, would specifically require designers to tailor devices to communicate with the setback box and receive only those instructions that could be transmitted through the television. In addition, innovation would be far more centralized with television manufacturers having a favored position if the CEBus protocol were the standard. Wide consumer adoption of home automation technology would then be dependent on a massive replacement of televisions, costing as much as $150 billion.[5] This was the ultimate objective of the television manufacturers. Not only would the CEBus-based Decoder Interface standard handicap Echelon's LonWorks network, but since television life cycles are typically 10 to 15 years, the development of the home control network market itself could slow considerably.

Echelon's problem was that the FCC could preempt the judgment of the marketplace and force standardization around the CEBus protocol. From Echelon's perspective, just as there was no reason for the government to select a standard computer operating system, there was no reason for the FCC to set a standard for home automation networks. A wide variety of companies agreed with this view. For example, home computers are an equally plausible candidate for running control networks, as are set-top boxes. Thus, industry rivals Apple and Intel both opposed a mandated CEBus-based Decoder Interface standard.

THE FCC AND THE CABLE ACT OF 1992

In 1992 the cable industry was under attack by consumers complaining of high prices, abusive market tactics, and problems operating their VCRs and televisions with cable systems. Congress responded with legislation to regulate the industry and addressed the incompatibility problem in Section 17 of the 1992 Cable Act.[6] This section directed the FCC to consult with industry representatives and issue regulations "to ensure compatibility between cable systems and consumer TV receivers and video cassette recorders (VCRs), consistent with the need to prevent theft of cable service."[7] The FCC was to report to Congress in April 1994 with a means for resolving the compatibility issue.

The C3AG had proposed to the FCC the development and adoption of a Decoder Interface connector that would work with an associated setback decoder box and would establish standards ensuring long-term compatibility between cable technologies and consumer equipment.[8] Having received little in the way of objectives, the FCC tentatively endorsed the as yet incomplete standard on April 4, 1994, and gave the C3AG 90 days to submit a completed proposal.[9] In August 1994 the C3AG submitted a

---

[4]EIA submission to FCC, August 15, 1994, p. 8, cited in "Cable Equipment Compatibility Standards." ET Docket 93-7, p. 1.

[5]"Reply Comments of Echelon Corporation." CS Docket No. 95–184, April 17, 1996, p. 8.

---

[6]Cable Television Consumer Protection and Competition Act of 1992, Pub. L. No. 102–385, 106 Stat. 1460, (1992)ξ17, (codified at 47 U.S.C. ξ 544a).

[7]"Implementation of Section 17 of the Cable Television Consumer Protection and Competition Act of 1992, Compatibility Between Cable Systems and Consumer Electronics Equipment," First Report and Order, 9 FCC Rcd 1981 (1981).

[8]"Report to Congress On Means Of Assuring Compatibility Between Cable Systems and Consumer Electronics Equipment." Federal Communications Commission, October 5, 1993.

[9]"Implementation of Section 17 of the Cable Television Consumer Protection and Competition Act of 1992, Compatibility Between Cable Systems and Consumer Electronics Equipment," First Report and Order, 9 FCC Rcd 1981 (1987).

proposal for IS-105, its "interim" Decoder Interface standard. This standard incorporated both a physical interconnection specification as well as the CEBus communications protocol.

THE FCC'S RULE MAKING

Neither Echelon nor its supporters had been heavily involved in the FCC's initial consideration of the Decoder Interface standard, and Echelon had not filed comments for the FCC's May 1994 "First Report and Order" on the implementation of Section 17. Most of the disagreements in the comments filed had pertained to the extent to which third parties could provide the hardware associated with the Decoder Interface. For example, some parties, such as Circuit City Stores of Richmond, Virginia, understandably wanted to prevent cable companies from having a monopoly on the sale of decoder equipment.

The FCC saw Section 17 of the Cable Act as a mandate for using its standard-setting authority to resolve once and for all a host of cable interoperability problems. Part of the disagreement turned on the meaning of the term *interoperability,* as used in the Cable Act. As Glenn Manishin, an experienced technology lawyer and partner in Blumefeld & Cohen, Washington, D.C., pointed out:

> [I]interoperability means different things to different industries. In telecommunications parlance, it generally connotes the ability of systems to communicate and exchange information; in the computer industry, it often has more limited scope, confined largely to the physical interconnectivity of equipment.[10]

From this perspective, the Cable Act required that the FCC regulate interconnectivity, but mandating the CEBus-based Decoder Interface would be a considerable step toward interoperability.

The Consumer Electronics Group of the EIA and the cable industry, however, had bigger objectives than just compatibility among televisions, VCRs, and cable systems. They saw an opportunity to secure an important future market by influencing the FCC's standard setting.

[10]G.B. Manishin. "Learning to (Tele)communicate Together," *Legal Times,* November 6, 1995, p. 45.

ECHELON AND THE FCC

Echelon had been told by an employee of the EIA that there was nothing in the C3AG proposed standard that would affect home automation. However, in late 1994 Chris Stanfield heard that one of the companies supporting the Decoder Interface standard had bragged about the FCC mandating the CEBus protocol. The threat was imminent.

Echelon's first step was to address the standards issue in the arena of the FCC. Echelon was at a disadvantage in the FCC for three reasons. First, it was starting late, since the EIA and NCTA had been working for several years on a compatibility standard. Second, computer companies were not the natural clients of the FCC—the television and cable companies were. Third, Echelon viewed the regulators' mind-sets as quite different from that of high-tech entrepreneurs with regulators preferring certainty and order and entrepreneurs preferring opportunity and the judgment of the marketplace. In November 1994, Echelon initiated a series of *ex parte* meetings with the FCC's Office of Engineering & Technology and Competition Division. The FCC's Office of Engineering and Technology, however, had been working with C3AG, and its influence led the FCC to continue with its rule making and the proposed standard incorporating the CEBus protocol.

ECHELON AND THE COMMUNICATIONS ACT OF 1996

When its attempts to prevent the FCC from mandating CEBus failed, Echelon's only remaining avenue was through Congress. In early 1995 the Republican leadership in Congress was committed to enacting legislation that would reshape the future of telecommunications. The Senate Commerce Committee had recently reported a bill S. 652 that would rewrite the Communications Act of 1934, and the House Commerce Committee was preparing to consider a similar bill H.R. 1555. The CEBus-based Decoder Interface standard had already built a significant constituency of television manufacturers, cable companies, and electronics retailers, so whatever strategy Echelon deployed would meet with considerable resistance. Furthermore, the battle would be a protracted one, since each chamber was expected to pass its own version of the bill, requiring reconciliation of the two versions in a conference committee. ■

This case was prepared by Michael Ting and Erik Johnson under the supervision of Professors David P. Baron, Daniel Kessler, and Keith Krehbiel.

PREPARATION QUESTIONS

1. Why were Echelon's efforts with the FCC unsuccessful?
2. What objectives should Echelon set for its congressional strategy?
3. What strategy should Echelon formulate to achieve its objectives?
4. How should that strategy be implemented; that is, what specifically should Oshman and Stanfield do?
5. How does that implementation relate to the structure of Congress and the legislative process?

The Section 936 Tax Credit

In February 1993, President Bill Clinton, intent on raising new revenue to reduce the mounting federal deficit, proposed as part of his deficit-reduction package a plan to revoke a multibillion dollar tax break for U.S. mainland companies operating in Puerto Rico. The Clinton proposal called for revisions in Section 936 of the Internal Revenue Code, which had been enacted in 1976 with the goal of creating jobs on the island. Section 936 gives mainland U.S. companies exemptions from federal corporate income tax on income received from operations in Puerto Rico, reinvestment on the island of its locally generated profits, and interest on local bank deposits. In addition, dividends paid by a corporation to its U.S. parent are exempt from federal taxes. Thus, a company may set up a manufacturing subsidiary in Puerto Rico, ship products to the mainland, and pay no taxes on the profits or the payment of dividends to the parent.

As a U.S. Commonwealth, Puerto Rico's status closely resembles that of a state in the union. The Commonwealth government controls its schools, police, courts, public works, and internal communications. The U.S. government retains responsibility for diplomatic representations, defense, customs, and international trade. U.S. currency, environmental standards, transportation rules, and energy regulations prevail. Puerto Ricans are not subject to federal taxes, and the island enjoys fiscal autonomy within a customs union allowing free trade anywhere in the world and trade without payment of duty with any other part of the United States. Island residents are U.S. citizens and are represented in Congress by an elected resident commissioner who may vote in House committees but not on the House floor. Historically, elections have been dominated by two political parties: the Popular Democratic Party, which supports retaining Puerto Rico's current Commonwealth status, and the New Progressive Party, which advocates statehood for the island. In November 1992, Dr. Pedro J. Rossello of the New Progressive Party easily defeated the incumbent governor of the Popular Democratic Party.

The population of Puerto Rico included 2.3 million Puerto Ricans living in the United States as well as 3.5 million residents, 60 percent of whom lived below the U.S. poverty line and 18 percent of whom were unemployed. Per capita income was $6,200, the highest in Latin America but still less than half that of Mississippi, the poorest U.S. state.

The Clinton administration proposal called for the provisions of Section 936 to be replaced with a 60 percent wage credit (a tax credit equal to 60 percent of the wages paid by a company to its workers in Puerto Rico) for 1994, which would be phased down 5 percent a year to a floor of 40 percent in 1998. The proposal was estimated to generate $6.7 billion in tax revenue over 5 years. The administration proposal also called for federal taxes on interest earned on corporate Puerto Rican bank deposits, but it would allow a company to offset the additional tax with an interest credit that would effectively exempt from federal taxes $4 billion of the $16 billion then on deposit by U.S. corporations in Puerto Rican banks.

The effects of the proposal would particularly be felt by high value-added companies and companies with capital-intensive production operations. The General Accounting Office reported that the tax breaks earned by chemical and pharmaceutical companies amounted to 212 percent of the wages paid to their Puerto Rican employees. Most of the major pharmaceutical companies had operations in Puerto Rico, and they received tax breaks of $1.146 billion in 1992, which represented 8.2 percent of their corporate net income. Senator David Pryor (R-AR) and other opponents of the tax credit pointed to a study that estimated that 63 percent of the tax benefits (estimated at $2.7 billion a year) went to 60 drug companies, whereas those companies accounted for only 12 percent of the jobs created by the tax credit. The disparity resulted because such pharmaceutical giants as Merck and Pfizer could earn large tax credits by transferring "intangible assets" such as patents to their tax-free Puerto Rican subsidiaries. The opponents also cited a General Accounting Office–U.S. Treasury study that estimated that drug manufacturers in Puerto Rico received nearly $72,000 in annual tax benefits per worker, while paying an average wage of less than $34,000.

Two major groups opposed the Clinton proposal: (1) U.S. corporations, primarily in the pharmaceutical, electrical equipment, and food-processing industries, and (2) many Puerto Ricans living both in the United States and on the island who were concerned about its economic impact. The chief lobbying arm for the U.S. businesses seeking to preserve the tax credit was the 70-member Puerto Rico U.S.A. (PRUSA) Foundation. These and other U.S. companies doing business on the island were also represented by the 1,800-member Puerto Rico Manufacturers Association.

The major argument advanced by groups opposing the Clinton proposal centered on the economic impact of the proposed cuts. Opponents warned that eliminating Section 936 would result in a wholesale exodus of manufacturing operations from the island as well as much of the $16 billion in bank deposits of mainland companies. These losses, they argued, would have three effects. First, most of the 300,000 manufacturing jobs directly or indirectly created by U.S. corporations benefiting under Section 936 would be lost. Second, the Puerto Rican government would lose approximately $500 million in annual revenue (12 percent of its total revenue) currently generated through a "tollgate" tax by which the government taxed profits from operations on the island by up to 10 percent. Third, the loss of U.S. corporate deposits would deprive Puerto Rican banks of the funds they needed to make loans to finance new and expanding businesses, as well as the construction of schools, hospitals, and roads. Together, the critics said, the elimination of Section 936 would have potentially catastrophic consequences for the island and could possibly induce more residents to emigrate to the mainland.

Supporting the Clinton bill were Puerto Ricans who saw the tax credit as an obstacle to future Puerto Rican statehood. They argued that a reduction would both force a restructuring of the economy away from a manufacturing base, which had already lost its growth potential, and increase the likelihood of statehood.[1] This group included influential members of the New Progressive party, which had raised the stakes by scheduling a plebiscite, or vote on statehood, for November 14, 1993.

Section 936 also drew opposition from U.S. labor unions. Although Puerto Rican law specifically prohibited the granting of tax exemptions to companies that take jobs from the mainland, research produced by such groups as the Midwest Center for Labor Research, a nonprofit research organization, estimated that U.S. companies shut down and transferred as many as 11,000 jobs to Puerto Rico. Labor unions argued that the "runaway" of jobs must be stopped.

The Clinton proposal took many companies by surprise. Several companies, particularly in pharmaceuticals, began publicly to oppose the proposal. The early objective of their nonmarket strategy was simple: U.S. companies wanted to shift the focus of the debate from excessive tax benefits to the effects of a tax-credit reduction on the Puerto Rican economy. Lobbyists for the corporations aimed to do two things: convince the new Puerto Rican government to support Section 936 as had the previous government and organize grassroots opposition in Puerto Rico to the Clinton plan.

[1]If Puerto Rico became a state, the Section 936 tax credit would cease, so opponents of statehood used its loss as an argument against statehood.

To convince the Puerto Rican government to become active, U.S. companies represented by PRUSA sent top corporate executives to San Juan in March 1993 to meet with Governor Rossello and convey the message that their companies might be forced to leave the island if the Clinton plan passed intact. Companies also played a major role in organizing and financing La Marcha de las Habichuelas ("the March for the Beans") in San Juan, pouring more than $150,000 into the effort. They helped organize transportation to take employees to the event, posted signs at workplaces to encourage attendance, and fed alarming statistics to local news outlets.[2] The grassroots effort turned out more than 100,000 people in support of Section 936. By May 1993, the Rossello government had backed away from its earlier position of support for the Clinton plan.

Despite these efforts and the dire predictions made by Section 936 supporters, the Clinton plan passed the House in late May 1993. As a concession to organized labor, the bill included an anti-runaway provision that allowed the Treasury Department to deny benefits to companies it determined had fled to the island for tax breaks, while causing layoffs on the mainland.

Companies seeking to preserve the tax provision geared up for the battle in the Senate. Their strategy had three major components: an intensive grassroots campaign, direct lobbying of Congress members whose districts included Puerto Rican voters or were home to Section 936 corporations, and the enlistment of the aid of the congressional Hispanic Caucus.

The grassroots campaign focused on concentrated groups of Puerto Ricans living in Chicago, New York City, and Newark and consisted primarily of advertising and community forums combined with the circulation of petitions. The efforts focused on the annual Puerto Rico Day parade held in New York City on June 13, four days before the first meeting of the Senate Finance Committee on the issue. The groups managed to gather over 400,000 signatures on cards and petitions supporting Section 936. A similar effort at the Chicago Puerto Rican Day parade yielded 50,000 signatures.

Supporters of Section 936 focused their congressional lobbying efforts on Representative Dan Rostenkowski (D-IL), chairman of the House Ways and Means Committee, Senator Daniel Patrick Moynihan (D-NY), chairman of the Senate Finance Committee, and Senator Bill Bradley (D-NJ). They were chosen because of their influential positions and because their districts included a large number of Puerto Rican voters. Moynihan's home state of New York included more than a million Puerto Rican voters who could be influential in his 1994 reelection bid. Moynihan had accepted over $50,000 in campaign contributions from PRUSA during the prior 2-year period. In addition to having a large Puerto Rican constituency, Bradley's home state of New Jersey also housed some of the largest U.S. pharmaceutical companies, which had given $108,000 to his 1990 campaign.

Lobbyists enlisted the aid of members of the House Hispanic Caucus to lobby their Senate colleagues against the Clinton plan. They also met with Clinton in June, a week before the Puerto Rican Day parade, to indicate that their support for Clinton's overall budget plan would depend heavily on the outcome of the Section 936 issue. Lobbyists also sought to highlight the importance of the issue by circulating a 6-minute video of the march in San Juan prepared by the Puerto Rico Manufacturers Association.

The alignment of U.S. companies supporting Section 936 split along capital-intensive versus labor-intensive lines once the House passed the bill. A wage-based credit would favor labor-intensive companies, whereas an income-based credit would favor capital-intensive ones. Bill McLeod, vice president in charge of tax affairs at Allergan, commented on the difference between the two groups: "What's good for the capital-intensive firms is certainly not good for us." Labor-intensive firms, including General Electric, Westinghouse Electric, Storage Technology, PepsiCo, U.S. Surgical, and Allergan, concentrated their efforts on the House version of the credit, working to make it more favorable to labor-intensive companies. Meanwhile, four capital-intensive firms—Pfizer, Merck, American Home Products, and Bristol-Myers Squibb—urged a mix of income-based and wage-based formulas in calculating the credit.

The plan that emerged from the Senate Finance Committee and was passed by the Senate reflected the results of the intensive lobbying effort. It restored $2.7 billion of the original credit and gave corporations a choice between a modification of the House plan and a credit of 60 percent of income in

[2]Industry spokespersons predicted that if the Clinton plan was passed intact, unemployment on the island would rise from 18 to 30 percent, increasing the chance of "political unrest."

1994, decreasing 5 percent a year to 40 percent in 1998 and thereafter. Although the House and Senate bills differed, some change in Section 936 was certain.

Attention turned to the July budget conference, during which House and Senate conferees would try to reconcile the proposals passed by the two chambers. The pro-936 forces increased their lobbying efforts prior to and during the conference. Three Congress members who were of Puerto Rican origin wrote to President Clinton asking for approval of the Senate's Section 936 version with specific improvements that would be "far less disruptive to the island's economy." In consultation with the Rossello government, they proposed that wage credit include fringe benefits and payroll taxes, Puerto Rican income taxes, interest earned on bank deposits, and capital investment in the proposed credit calculation. They also proposed that the income-based credit be maintained at 60 percent of profits through 1998 rather than a gradual reduction to 40 percent. This alternative was estimated to produce \$3 to \$4 billion less in tax revenue than the Clinton plan. Thirteen members of the Hispanic Caucus wrote to Rostenkowski asking him to back the Senate version of the bill.

The efforts had their desired effect. Moynihan, Bradley, and other senators strongly backed the Senate proposal in the conference committee, whereas Rostenkowski, who headed the House conferees, was only lukewarm in his support of the House proposal, thus sending a message that he was amenable to the Senate version. Needing every vote, Clinton announced that he would support a compromise with the Senate plan. The final compromise included something for both capital-intensive and labor-intensive firms, giving corporations a choice between receiving a tax credit for 60 percent of profits in 1994, decreasing 5 points annually to 40 percent in 1998 and thereafter, or a wage-based credit equal to 60 percent of wages paid plus fringe benefits up to 15 percent of the wage base (capped at \$48,960 per employee). The final bill also dropped the runaway jobs provision. Companies could continue to invest their untaxed profits on the island, and the interest on these funds remained tax-free. The compromise was estimated to produce \$3.8 billion in tax revenue over 5 years. ■

This is an abridged version of a case prepared from public sources by Abraham Wu under the supervision of Professor David P. Baron.

PREPARATION QUESTIONS

1. Identify the relevant interests and institutions for the Section 936 issue.
2. What is the nature of the politics of the original Clinton proposal and the Senate proposal?
3. Evaluate the nonmarket strategy employed by the pro-Section 936 interests? Was it responsible?
4. What forces did the outcome reflect and how was it reached?

CHAPTER 8

Implementing Political Strategies

Introduction

The three preceding chapters focused on political theory and institutions, political analysis, and strategy formulation in governmental institutional arenas. Those strategies must be implemented effectively; and conversely, the effectiveness with which strategy alternatives can be implemented affects the choice among them. For example, an informational strategy as considered in the previous chapter requires access to public officeholders, the development of information, and lobbying or perhaps grassroots activities to convey that information. Strategy formulation and implementation thus are necessarily intertwined. This chapter considers the following activities that implement political strategies: (1) lobbying, (2) grassroots activities, (3) coalition building, (4) electoral support, (5) testimony, (6) communication and public advocacy, (7) judicial strategies, and (8) participation on advisory committees.

Nonmarket issues often receive media and public attention, and that attention can shape and accelerate political activity. An important decision in any political strategy is whether a firm's political activity should be high or low profile. A low-profile strategy emphasizes behind-the-scenes activities such as lobbying and is intended to reduce the chances of a reaction from the opposition. Defense contractors, for example, typically employ low-profile strategies. A high-profile strategy involves more visible activities, including grassroots campaigns, news conferences, public advocacy, and broadscale lobbying visible to opposing interests and the public.

Lobbying

Lobbying is a central component of most informational strategies. Lobbying is the personal communication of politically relevant information to public officeholders.[1] That information may be provided to the president, a governor, executive branch officials, members of Congress or state legislatures, their staff, and committee staff. The personal communication of information requires access, and access may be obtained through the constituency connection, campaign contributions, and personal relationships.

The scope of lobbying has broadened considerably over the past two decades. This broadening has had four components. First, managers have become more active

[1] Lobbyists and their clients are listed in *Washington Representatives,* Close, Steele, and Buckner (1993). Foreign companies and countries have become major lobbies in Washington.

participants in lobbying, just as they have become more deeply involved in formulating strategies to address nonmarket issues. Second, the professional lobbying industry has grown substantially as more interests participate in public policy processes. Third, the professional lobbying industry has become increasingly specialized with firms focusing on mobilizing constituents, grassroots lobbying, and research and technical services as well as the more traditional functions of monitoring government activities, providing access, and communicating information. Fourth, on majoritarian issues such as health care policy that affect large numbers of people, communication directly to citizens through the mass media has become more important.

Executives are often effective lobbyists because members of Congress and other government officials want to hear about a firm's concerns from the person in charge. A busy member of Congress will more often meet with a CEO or another high-ranking manager than with a representative of the firm's Washington office. High-level managers have a more detailed knowledge of the firm's activities than other lobbyists can have and thus can be more specific. They also can make commitments that others cannot.

The Nature of Lobbying

Lobbying is a key component of an informational strategy directed at public institutions. In contrast to testimony before congressional committees, lobbying typically takes place behind the scenes. Particularly in Congress, lobbying is important because of the large number of legislative proposals under consideration. Members necessarily know little about many of the proposals, so they have a demand for information. Conversely, in some cases members will check with lobbyists to determine whether the draft language of a bill is acceptable to them, that is, whether they will support or at least not oppose it. This serves as a useful barometer of the political support or opposition a bill is likely to receive.

Lobbying is the strategic provision of information to public officeholders. Lobbying is strategic in the sense of advocating one's position or counteracting the information provided by the other side. Lobbying is also strategic in the sense that it is targeted to influential or pivotal officeholders and timed to the stages of the institutional process governing the issue. Lobbying does not involve threats or coercion and should not involve false information. Crying wolf and making false claims will rarely prove effective in the long run. Members of Congress and their staff have heard such claims before and can have long memories.

TECHNICAL AND POLITICALLY RELEVANT INFORMATION

Lobbying conveys two types of information: technical and politically relevant. Technical information consists of data and predictions about the consequences of alternatives. In the chapter case *CAFE Standards* the automobile companies provided technical information about the cost increase of an automobile if higher fuel economy standards were imposed. The automobile companies also provided technical information about what fuel economy levels were technically achievable, but the credibility of that information was questioned because their statements in the 1970s about technological possibilities were far from actual achievements. Credibility requires an established reputation, self-evident data and analysis, or corroboration by others with different interests. Technical information in this case was corroborated by government agencies, as illustrated in Figure 6-1.

Politically relevant information pertains to the consequences of an alternative for the constituents or the policy interests of a public officeholder. Effective lobbying involves providing information that the officeholder does not already have and is relevant to his or her goals. In the *CAFE Standards* case the automobile companies could provide information on consumer preferences, which to an important extent were for larger, less fuel-efficient vehicles.

The most effective approach in lobbying is to provide politically relevant information about the relationship between alternatives and the legislator's constituents and his or her policy objectives. To support this approach, many firms develop data on their rent chains, including the number of employees and the component and supplies purchases in each congressional district. This allows them to tell members how much business their firm generates in their districts that could be affected by a legislative proposal. The task of the lobbyist is to link the interests of the firm or interest group with those of legislators by providing information about the impact of the legislative alternative on their constituents and the public more broadly.

As an example of politically relevant information, consider the attempt in 1986 to eliminate the tax credit for employing disadvantaged youths. The Treasury had estimated that eliminating the credit would increase tax collections by nearly $500 million a year, helping to reduce the federal budget deficit. One of the largest employers of youth, and thus one of the largest recipients of the tax credit, was the fast-food industry. The lobbying message of Pizza Hut was that the tax credit/employment program served the interests of the constituents of members of Congress and was consistent with the policy objective of providing opportunities for disadvantaged youth. The members of the tax-writing committee understood that Pizza Hut would benefit from retention of the tax credit, but they also understood that Pizza Hut's interests were aligned with those of the disadvantaged. The tax credits were retained.[2]

When lobbying a member of Congress, information should be provided at several levels, as illustrated in Figure 8-1. In the figure the CEO or other high-ranking company officer may directly lobby a senator with access facilitated by a professional lobbyist or government affairs professional. In addition to lobbying at the top, lobbying also takes place at the level of the senator's personal staff and the committee staff. The staff is the eyes and ears of the senator, and providing information to a key staff member may be as important as providing information to the senator. In particular, purely technical information and detailed policy studies are best presented to the staff. In addition, the staff is generally quite knowledgeable and well equipped to evaluate politically relevant information.

The following are principles of effective lobbying:

- Know the institutional arenas in which the issue is addressed (e.g., Congress works through committees).
- Know the officeholder's interests and goals and frame messages appropriately.[3]
- Respect the officeholder and staff; they are in most cases intelligent and savvy.
- Don't just talk. Listen to the officeholder and staff for information about their interests and concerns and for strategic advice about process, other officeholders, etc.

---

[2]The credits came under attack again in 1993. See Chapter 20.

[3]Information on members of Congress and governors is provided in the *Almanac of American Politics,* Barone and Ujufusa (1997), and in *Politics in America,* Congressional Quarterly (1997).

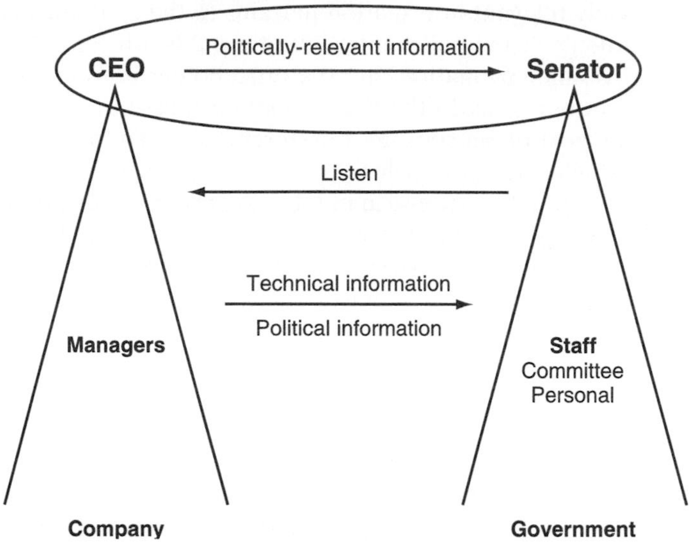

FIGURE 8–1 Multilevel Lobbying

- Make straightfoward presentations. Members of Congress are busy, understand politics well, and can see beyond window dressing. (Managers and professional lobbyists often leave a more detailed written statement with members or their staff.)
- Explore opportunities to build coalitions.
- Explore compromises or concessions that might help resolve officeholders' concerns.
- Time lobbying to the stages of the institutional process.
- Establish access and maintain continuing relationships for future access (e.g., meet with committee staff even if there is no pending legislation).

ACCESS

The congressional decentralization of the early 1970s gave additional powers to subcommittees and increased the number of influential positions substantially, so successful lobbying demands much more than developing relationships with a few powerful committee chairs. A firm that deals with Congress on a variety of issues must maintain access to several committees. Lobbying typically focuses on members who hold strategic positions such as a committee or subcommittee chair and members who may enlist the support of others. On many issues, lobbying executive branch agencies can also be important. The Department of the Treasury, for example, can have a significant effect on the outcome of a tax issue through its expertise in predicting the revenue consequences of tax alternatives. The Department of Commerce is often a willing advocate of business interests. On a trade issue, lobbying may target the Office of the U.S. Trade Representative.

Members of Congress and executive branch officials have only limited time to meet with lobbyists and must allocate access. Those who have access possess an important asset. The key to continued access is the ability to provide politically valuable resources. Those resources may be information about the effects of political alternatives on constituents, technical information linking alternatives to consequences, or information about the support that can be mustered for or against an alternative. Former office-holders are frequently useful in providing contacts and access. Other means of developing access are also available.

Federal Express, which faces a continuing set of issues involving Congress, has developed access through a variety of means. As Doyle Cloud, vice president of regulatory and government affairs explained, "We have issues constantly in Washington that affect our ability to deliver the services our customers demand as efficiently as possible."[4] For all the issues on its agenda, during the first 6 months of 1996, Federal Express spent $1,149,150 on lobbying, including $367,000 on outside law firms. Using outside firms is a common tactic, particularly for their contacts and established relationships with government officials. Federal Express also has on its board of directors Howard H. Baker, Jr., former Republican majority leader in the Senate, and George J. Mitchell, former Democratic majority leader in the Senate. Federal Express also was the fifth largest campaign contributor in the 1995–1996 election cycle, contributing $600,500 through August 30, 1996. Also, on a regular basis Federal Express made its four corporate jets available to members of Congress. Although the members are required to reimburse the company at the equivalent of first-class airfare, the corporate jets provide privacy and convenience to their passengers. In most cases, the flights take members of Congress to fundraising events.[5]

Lobbying takes place at both the state and federal levels. Lobbying expenditures in California totaled $267 million in the 1995–1996 period. The largest expenditures were by governments ($37 million), the health care industry ($31 million), and the finance and insurance industry ($29 million). The largest single spender was the Western States Petroleum Association ($3.9 million).

TIMING

Lobbying should be timed to the stages of the legislative process. In the case of an issue at the subcommittee or committee stage, the appropriate focus is the committee members, particularly the chair and ranking majority and minority members. When legislation is being drafted or rewritten, lobbying often focuses on the committee staff who do the drafting. Because majority rule governs the committee process, lobbying should be directed at those members who are likely to be pivotal. Larry Whitt, vice president for government affairs and public relations at Pizza Hut, explained, "We focus on those on the fence."[6] Lobbying for support on the floor requires a broader effort and again focuses on pivotal members.

On an issue in conference committee, the focus is on the conferees. In the 1986 tax legislation, the House bill provided a 2-year extension of the tax credit for employing disadvantaged youth, whereas the Senate bill provided a 3-year extension. Having been successful in both chambers, Pizza Hut turned its attention to the conference committee. Peyton George, a lobbyist for Pizza Hut, stated, "I've figured out my list of who will be the conferees, and I'm trying to maintain contact with every one of [them]."[7]

---

[4] *The New York Times,* October 12, 1996.

[5] "Mr. Cloud said that during political seasons, Federal Express might fly a group of lawmakers about once a week." *The New York Times,* October 12, 1996.

[6] *Peninsula Times Tribune,* February 23, 1986.

[7] *The Wall Street Journal,* June 25, 1986.

GOVERNMENT ALLIES

The effectiveness of lobbying can be enhanced by developing allies in Congress and enlisting their support. The Semiconductor Industry Association (SIA) encouraged the formation of the Congressional Support Group, a caucus composed of senators and representatives who worked to support the SIA's legislative agenda. Because many SIA members are headquartered in California, the California congressional delegation also represented its interests. Having allies in government can make a difference in the outcome of a political competition on an issue. Not all expressions of support or offers of representation by members of Congress, of course, are credible. For example, in response to constituent or interest group pressure, members of Congress may introduce or cosponsor bills that they know will not pass.

Executive branch officials may also act as allies if doing so will help them further their agency's policy objectives. The Department of Commerce may support a firm seeking to open a foreign market to U.S. goods and may take a position opposing a bill supported by organized labor.

CONTROLS ON LOBBYING

The First Amendment to the Constitution establishes the right to petition the government, so lobbying is a relatively unregulated activity. The principal law regulating lobbying is the Lobbying Act of 1946. The Supreme Court interpreted that act in *United States v. Harriss,* 347 U.S. 612 (1954) as pertaining only to the direct lobbying of Congress by a hired lobbyist. Therefore, activities that involve a firm's own managers and Washington representatives are not considered lobbying under the law. The act also does not cover grassroots political activities.

Recent legislation has focused on the disclosure of lobbying activity. Lobbyists are required to register with the clerk of the House and the secretary of the Senate. They must file quarterly reports listing the issues and bills on which they are lobbying, the positions they support, how long the lobbying is likely to take, and details about how they are financing the effort.

In 1995 on unanimous votes by the House and Senate, Congress passed the Lobbying Disclosure Act that requires lobbyists to report the amount of income they receive as well as their expenditures. The act also requires registration of those who lobby the executive branch and the staffs of Congress members. This provision was estimated to increase the number of registered lobbyists by a factor of 3 to 10 from the 1995 level of 6,000.

Laws as well as House and Senate rules prohibit gifts to members of Congress including dinners and privately paid travel to conventions and events.[8] Laws prohibiting gifts also cover executive branch officials. In 1997 Tyson Foods pleaded guilty to providing the secretary of agriculture in the Clinton administration with $12,000 of illegal gratuities. Tyson paid a criminal fine of $4 million and costs of $2 million.

Even small gifts and gratuities can violate the law. On a trip to Napa Valley to inspect insect damage to grapevine roots, the secretary of agriculture visited the Robert Mondavi winery. The visit to the winery had been arranged by an official of an agricultural cooperative who asked for some wine to put in the secretary's car. The following year during American Wine Appreciation Week, the winery paid for a dinner attended by the secretary. On both occasions a Mondavi official had spoken about the healthful effects of wine and pending government guidelines that would allow mentioning those effects on labels. The secretary had said he would get his department going on the guide-

[8]Senate rules allow gifts or meals up to $50 and up to $100 from any individual.

lines. The $187 for the wine and $207 for the dinner for the secretary and his friend resulted in $150,000 in civil penalties for the winery, including paying for a public education program on bribery and gratuity laws. The secretary was acquitted.

The Ethics in Government Act of 1978 addresses the "revolving door" issue of officials who leave government service and then lobby their former employers.[9] The act restricts the contacts of former executive branch officials and regulators with their former agencies for a 2-year period and former members of Congress and congressional staff from lobbying Congress for 1 year after their terms in office end.[10] The law also prohibits officials who were involved in trade or other negotiations from lobbying their former offices for 1 year.

The interactions of business and other interest groups with regulatory agencies are also limited by *ex parte* restrictions. These requirements typically prohibit meetings with regulatory officials unless all interested parties are notified and have an opportunity to either participate in, or protest, the meeting.

Grassroots Strategies and the Constituent Connection

Grassroots strategies are based on the connection between constituents and their elected representatives.[11] Grassroots campaigns are often a component of a broader strategy and are often tactical in nature. Labor unions, community interest groups, environmental groups, the National Rifle Association, and many other interest groups engage in grassroots political activity intended to demonstrate the breadth, strength, and intensity of their interests on issues.[12] Beginning in the 1980s, several firms and industries adopted this strategy and applied it effectively to issues on their nonmarket agendas. The grassroots campaign by Toshiba (Chapter 7) was effective because it reflected the potential costs to employees, suppliers, and customers. Grassroots strategies have become sufficiently pervasive that a grassroots lobbying industry has developed to organize the campaigns.[13] The industry includes firms that, for example, translate data by postal zip codes into congressional districts. This allows shareholder, retiree, supplier, and customer lists to be organized by district to target members of Congress. In an example presented later in the chapter PacifiCare organized its patients by congressional district.

MOBILIZATION

Members of interest groups and constituents of firms must be mobilized for effective political action, and one role of associations and organized interest groups is this mobilization. Mobilization involves providing information to constituents on the significance of an issue and helping to reduce their costs of participation. Letter-writing campaigns are the least expensive grassroots activity. They are also difficult to implement

---

[9]Not all ex-government employees take jobs in business. Joan Claybrook, former head of the NHTSA, heads Public Citizen, and David Pittle, a former commissioner of the Consumer Products Safety Commission, became the technical director of Consumers Union.
[10]The prohibition extends to 2 years in areas for which they had primary responsibility.
[11]The mobilization of corporate constituents for electoral purposes is difficult and on normative grounds may be objectionable because it could involve an element of coercion. Most firms do not attempt to influence how their constituents vote in elections for public office. On some ballot initiatives and referenda, firms do take a position and urge their employees to vote that position. In the Part II integrative case, *Proposition 211: Securities Litigation Referendum (A),* Silicon Valley firms urged their employees to vote no on the proposition. In the same election in 1996 a number of companies, including Atlantic Richfield, Hewlett Packard, Pacific Gas & Electric, and Southern California Edison, publicly opposed Proposition 209, which would ban affirmative action in public contracts, education, and employment.
[12]See Fowler and Shaiko (1987) for an analysis of the grassroots activities of environmental organizations.
[13]Those who organize grassroots activity are not required to register as lobbyists.

because constituents often are unwilling to spend the time to write a letter or send a telegram. Volume can be generated through the use of preprinted letters or postcards, but recipients know that postcards generally do not reflect the same intensity of preferences as handwritten letters. Although handwritten letters have a greater impact than postcards, there is a trade-off with volume. Some congressional offices sort and count mail by issue and distinguish between letters and postcards. Others, however, just weigh the postcards.

An often more effective means of demonstrating grassroots preferences is to have constituents go to Washington or a state capital to lobby. Labor unions developed this tactic by organizing "bus-ins" in which busloads of union members converged on Washington to lobby and engage in other political activities. "Fly-ins" are the modern counterpart of bus-ins. For example, in many countries U.S. firms participate in the American Chamber of Commerce (ACC). The Asian chapters meet annually to discuss a variety of governmental and nonmarket issues pertaining to international trade policy, government relations, and U.S. policy pertaining to foreign operations. Members of the ACC chapters then conduct a "knock-around" in which they fly to Washington and knock on as many doors as possible to explain their positions on issues.

Grassroots strategies may be directed at public officeholders as in the case of a fly-in or they may be directed at constituents. The former are components of informational strategies and are a form of lobbying. The latter are intended to develop public, and voter, support for or opposition to an issue. As the PacifiCare example indicates, the health care industry has used this strategy effectively. Constituent-based grassroots strategies are frequently accompanied by mass advertising campaigns to inform the public, and officeholders, and to recruit participants, often by giving an 800 number they can call for more information. The Internet is rapidly becoming an important force in generating grassroots activities such as letter-writing to members of Congress. Grassroots activity has also become increasingly specialized. Some political consulting firms now provide "grass-tops" lobbying when they recruit prominent citizens to contact their representative or senator on an issue.

BUSINESS GRASSROOTS CAMPAIGNS

A business grassroots strategy is based on the rent chain and can involve employees, shareholders, retirees whose pensions depend on company performance, franchisees, suppliers, and in some cases customers. Not all constituencies are equally easy to organize and mobilize, however.[14] Shareholders and pensioners may be mobilized to some extent, but alerting them to a potentially serious issue may cause some of them to sell their shares. Retirees whose pensions depend on the market value of the firm are in a position similar to shareholders, although they may have less discretion in selling shares.

To the extent that their interests on an issue are aligned with those of the firm, employees may be relatively easy to include in a grassroots program. Mobilizing constituents can generate criticism, however. In the last days of the Clinton administration's attempt to restructure the U.S. health care system, IBM and General Mills asked their employees to oppose the bills mandating employer-provided health insurance. Some IBM employees complained about the request, and IBM was publicly criticized for breaking its practice of not involving employees in political issues.

[14]See Keim (1985) and Baysinger, Keim, and Zeithmal (1985) for an analysis of corporate grassroots programs.

Suppliers and customers are frequently mobilized when their rents will be affected. The grassroots campaign organized by Toshiba to weaken sanctions resulting from its illegal sales to the Soviet Union relied heavily on its U.S. production base, its suppliers, and its customers. Toshiba's U.S. production provided a link between possible sanctions and jobs at its suppliers. Similarly, Toshiba had little difficulty enlisting the support of its customers, many of whom relied on its products.

THE EFFECTIVENESS OF GRASSROOTS PROGRAMS

The effectiveness of a grassroots program depends on the supply-side factors considered in Chapter 6 as well as on the credibility of the program itself. The larger the number of participants in a grassroots program and the more extensive their coverage of political jurisdictions, the more effective it is likely to be. These factors determine the amount of pressure that can be transmitted through the constituency connection. This pressure, however, must be credible. The following two examples, both of which involve attempts to defeat legislation, illustrate the credibility dimension of a grassroots strategy.

Legislation was introduced in Congress to require financial institutions to withhold taxes on the interest and dividend income of depositors and trust fund beneficiaries. Supporters of the proposal included Treasury officials and members of Congress concerned with the federal budget deficit. In addition to the considerable administrative expense to financial institutions, the legislation would reduce the short-term cash flow to depositors and beneficiaries, who would receive lower quarterly payments as taxes were withheld. The basic structure of the politics of the issue thus was characterized by dispersed benefits for taxpayers, concentrated costs for savers, and concentrated costs for financial institutions. The financial institutions were in a position to mobilize a dispersed constituency of savers to oppose the bill. Their grassroots campaign generated over 22 million letters and postcards, and the interest withholding issue died.

In 1987 the Pharmaceutical Manufacturers Association (PMA) campaigned against the adoption of a catastrophic illness program for the elderly. Pharmaceutical companies were concerned that federal budget pressures would lead to the substitution of generic for brand-name drugs and perhaps to price controls, or reimbursement limits, on drugs. The PMA hired a political consulting firm to conduct a $3 million grassroots campaign opposing the program. Even though the campaign generated over 100,000 contacts between constituents and members of Congress, it was largely ineffective and may have worsened relations between members of Congress and the PMA. As Senator Lloyd Bentsen (D-TX) said, "I know the difference between grassroots and Astroturf."

The PacifiCare example illustrates the range of political activity of a company, including lobbying and grassroots strategies.

Coalition Building

Coalitions are the principal vehicle for forging a majority from a collection of minorities. Business coalitions are of three types: peak organizations, industry associations, and ad hoc coalitions. Peak associations emphasize issues that affect more than one industry, trade associations represent a single industry, and ad hoc coalitions tend to be issue specific. Trade associations and individual firms may also participate in issues addressed by peak organizations and trade associations, respectively.

EXAMPLE

PacifiCare's Political Portfolio

In the second half of the 1990s Health Maintenance Organizations (HMOs) were under attack from patients, doctors, activists, and state and local governments. The health care industry had defeated President Clinton's earlier attempt to restructure the industry, and although HMOs and their managed care providers had been responsible for holding down the cost of health care, complaints mounted from patients who wanted both unrestricted access to care and the lower cost associated with managed care.

Individual HMOs conducted a wide variety of nonmarket activities to avoid more extensive regulation and additional restrictions on their operations. PacifiCare Health Systems with 1997 revenue of $9 billion and profits of $107 million was the fifth largest HMO in the country. It provided managed care for group plans and Medicare beneficiaries in nine states and Guam. As with other health care providers, PacifiCare faced a series of government initiatives to expand the scope of regulation.

To address these challenges, PacifiCare developed a broad political portfolio and an infrastructure to support it.[1] PacifiCare had a vice president for public affairs, a vice president for government affairs, and a senior vice president who had been the head of a state Democratic Party and an unsuccessful senatorial candidate. PacifiCare had no Washington office and relied on the trade association, the American Association of Health Plans, for some lobbying and monitoring work. PacifiCare contributed $900,000 to the association. PacifiCare was also active at the state level and hired a public relations firm to help introduce it to state policymakers.

PacifiCare's PAC, which received contributions from about 250 of its executives, contributed about $100,000 to Republican and Democratic candidates in the 1997–1998 election cycle. This amount, however, represented only a small component of its expenditures. PacifiCare provided almost as much soft money to Democratic and Republican House and Senate reelection organizations, such as the Democratic Senatorial Campaign Committee's Leadership Circle and the National Republican Congressional Committee's Congressional Forum. These contributions provided opportunities to meet with members of Congress and provide information about issues on PacifiCare's agenda. It also contributed $100,000 to the Democratic Leadership Council, composed of pro-business Democrats, and its progressive Policy Institute. PacifiCare also planned to spend $130,000 in 1998 on firms to collect data and prepare research reports for use in its lobbying.[2] It also retained two lobbying firms headed by former Democratic staffers.

To address specific issues such as the Clinton administration's Patient Bill of Rights, PacifiCare contributed to the 1,000-member Health Benefits Coalition which successfully portrayed the administration's campaign as a costly intrusion by government. PacifiCare also used its rent chain by hiring a grassroots lobbying firm, which prepared lists by congressional district of satisfied PacifiCare patients who were willing to write or call members of Congress.

To repair the tarnished image of HMOs, PacifiCare joined with Cigna Corporation, WellPoint Health Networks, and other providers to form the Coalition for Affordable Quality Healthcare. The coalition initially planned to spend $6 million on an advertising campaign. A spokesperson said, "We are concerned we're getting a bad deal with the media and the only way around this anecdote-a-day is to try to appeal directly to the public to make them aware of the benefits of HMOs."[3] The campaign was in response to congressional hearings in which people claimed to have been denied care for serious illnesses.

Despite the low public opinion of HMOs, the industry was able to block the Clinton administration's efforts in 1998. The issue of health care retained considerable popular appeal, however, and PacifiCare and other health care providers would face continuing regulatory efforts at the federal and state levels.

---

[1]This section is based on the article "Capital Clout: A Buyer's Guide," *Fortune,* October 26, 1998, by Jeffrey H. Birnbaum and other public sources.

[2]*Fortune,* October 26, 1998.

[3]*Dallas Morning News,* September 4, 1998.

Many of the most effective coalitions are ad hoc and issue specific. Some alignments of interests are temporary, as in the case of the alignment between the Daylight Saving Time Coalition and the RP Foundation Fighting Blindness considered in Chapter 5. At times, two interest groups may find themselves working on the same side of one issue and opposite sides of another. Automobile manufacturers and the United Auto Workers both worked to limit imports from Japan, but were on opposite sides of the North American Free Trade Agreement issue. Similarly, service industries and capital-intensive industries were on opposite sides of the issue of eliminating the investment tax credit in 1986 but can be on the same side of a labor issue.[15]

PEAK ASSOCIATIONS

Peak, or umbrella, organizations include members from a number of industries and thus represent a range of interests. In the United States these organizations include the Chamber of Commerce, the National Association of Manufacturers, the Business Roundtable, the American Business Conference, the National Federation of Independent Business, and the National Small Business Association, among others. The heterogeneity of the interests of their members limits the political issues on which they act and on some issues may limit the strength of their action. Consequently, individual firms do not rely solely on peak organizations to represent their interests but instead participate in trade associations and often take independent political action.[16]

As an example of an umbrella organization, the U.S. Chamber of Commerce is the oldest general business organization in the United States with 200,000 members and a budget of $72 million. The chamber focuses on such matters as tax, labor, trade, and regulatory issues. An important source of strength for the chamber is its 3,000 state and local chapters, which give it complete coverage of congressional districts. To generate political pressure it has organized over 2,700 Congressional Action committees, composed of local businesspeople who have personal contacts with members of Congress. The chamber has also formed a public interest lobby, Citizen's Choice, that conducts grassroots campaigns. The Chamber's National Chamber Alliance for Politics provides electoral support to candidates in the form of organizational and fund-raising assistance.

The National Federation of Independent Business (NFIB) focuses on the concerns of small business. The influence of small business should not be underestimated. Although individual small businesses may have limited resources, collectively their resources are substantial. The NFIB, for example, has over 500,000 members, which gives it comprehensive coverage of political jurisdictions. It has been effective in lobbying and mobilizing small firms by reducing the cost of their participation in collective action. Small business has been particularly effective in obtaining exemptions from certain regulations. Its effectiveness is strengthened by the access provided by the small-business committees in the House and the Senate.

TRADE ASSOCIATIONS

Trade associations serve a variety of market and nonmarket functions.[17] Market functions include the collection of market and industry statistics, the development of technical standards, and in some cases research. Nonmarket functions center on reducing the cost of supplying political action, particularly by reducing the costs of information acquisition and collective action. Trade associations monitor potential and current

---

[15]See Salisbury (1992) for an analysis of interest group alignments.

[16]Peak organizations are more important in a number of other countries than in the United States. The Keidanren in Japan and the peak organizations in Germany and other European countries are quite influential.

[17]See Lynn and McKeown (1988) for an analysis of trade associations.

EXAMPLE

Calgene and Canola

Calgene, a small agricultural biotechnology company, had developed a strain of rapeseed that produced canola oil—used in a variety of products—and needed to induce farmers in the United States, where rapeseed was not grown, to begin to grow it.[1] One reason farmers did not grow rapeseed was that it was not included in the government's agricultural subsidy system. Calgene initially sought approval for rapeseed to be grown on set-aside land under the USDA's crop stabilization program. That program requires farmers to take land out of production, and since the land was not being used for any other crop, Calgene recognized that farmers would be eager to grow rapeseed rather than let the land remain fallow.

After expending considerable effort lobbying members of Congress without success, Calgene abandoned its focus on set-aside land. It decided instead to seek inclusion of rapeseed in the USDA's commodity support programs by building a coalition to work on behalf of canola oil. Along with companies such as Procter & Gamble, Archer-Daniels-Midland, Cargill, and Kraft, it formed the U.S. Canola Association. In the context of client politics the association was successful in having a bill introduced in Congress to include rapeseed in the commodity support program. To broaden support for inclusion of canola, the bill was written to include sunflower. Support from sunflower growers was important in obtaining inclusion of both canola and sunflower in the commodity support program. The bill was passed as part of a farm bill.

[1]See the Part I integrative case *Calgene, Inc. and Infrastructure Marketing.* Calgene was subsequently acquired by Monsanto.

legislative activity, regulatory rule-making activities, and administrative actions. They also reduce the cost of lobbying, grassroots programs, and other political strategies. Small firms are more likely to rely on trade associations than large firms, as the Calgene and Canola example indicates.

AD HOC COALITIONS

An ad hoc coalition is a group of interests aligned on a specific nonmarket issue. Subsequent to the events in the Part II integrative case *Proposition 211: Securities Litigation Referendum (A),* high-tech companies, public accounting firms, underwriters, and others that had been subject to frivolous securities fraud lawsuits filed in state courts formed the Uniform National Standards Coalition to work for federal legislation requiring security fraud lawsuits to be filed in federal rather than state courts. The coalition was successful with legislation enacted in 1999.

Although interests may be aligned on one issue, they may be opposed on market and on other nonmarket issues. In 1992 British Airlines announced it would invest $750 million in USAir, forming a global alliance. Robert L. Crandall, chairman of American Airlines, criticized the investment on the grounds that the arrangement provided the United Kingdom increased access to the U.S. market, but U.S. airlines would remain restricted in their access to the U.K. market. Crandall was subsequently joined by the CEOs of United Airlines, Delta Airlines, and Federal Express. USAir countered their lobbying with a grassroots letter-writing campaign by its employees, but the relentless lobbying by the four airlines caused British Airlines to cancel the investment and alliance.

The alignment of interests on some issues can be broad. The clean air legislation pending in Congress during the 1980s led to the formation of the Clean Air Working Group, which included 2,000 businesses and trade associations. Aligned with the group were labor unions representing auto, construction, and other workers. This allowed the opponents of stringent legislation to speak from a relatively unified position on the 1990 amendments to the Clean Air Act.

EXAMPLE

Silicon Valley Goes to Washington

As they grew, Silicon Valley companies retained their entrepreneurial characteristics. In particular, their focus on opportunities provided by open markets, rapidly changing technologies, and constant formation of new firms and new markets stood in sharp contrast to the caution, deliberateness, and orientation in Washington. The entrepreneurs' libertarian bent and "bristling self-confidence," as one observer put it, were in sharp contrast to the style in Washington. The companies had a disdain for politics, and their record in Washington increasingly reflected this attitude. Prior to 1996 many companies did not have a lobbyist or a Washington representative. Microsoft, for example, did not hire its first lobbyist until 1996. Many companies did not have a political action committee, and for those that did, many executives refused to contribute.

High-technology industries, including computers, software, Internet service providers, and biotechnology, however, were becoming too important as a source of opportunity, jobs, and growth for the politicians in Washington to ignore. The nonmarket issue agenda began to grow rapidly during the second half of the 1990s. Issues included securities fraud litigation, taxation of electronic commerce on the Internet, increases in visa limits for computer programmers and other specialists, software piracy, export controls of software with sophisticated encryption features, extension of the tax credit for research and development expenditures, privacy of information on the Internet, censorship on the Internet, and on-line child pornography. To advance the export controls and encryption issue, high-tech companies formed an ad hoc coalition, Americans for Computer Privacy, that conducted a television advertising campaign on encryption controls.

Because most nonmarket issues had differing effects on the companies, they often found themselves on different sides of issues, as the Chapter 2 discussion on the nonmarket environment of Microsoft indicates. In 1996 a galvanizing event occurred. California trial lawyers placed on the November ballot an initiative that would make it easier to sue firms for alleged securities fraud. (See the Part II integrative case *Proposition 211: Securities Litigation Referendum (A).*) The Silicon Valley companies viewed the securities fraud lawsuits as extortionary because they were filed whenever a share price fell by 10 percent or more and were intended to extract a settlement from the defendant to avoid a costly court battle. The plaintiffs were not required to have any evidence of fraud but instead hoped to find evidence through the discovery process. Because most of the companies had been sued or recognized that they could be sued at any moment, they found themselves on the same side of the issue.

The following year a group of Silicon Valley executives and venture capitalists gathered to establish a "political relationship" organization named Technology Network (TechNet). TechNet was unique on several dimensions. First, it adopted a very narrow agenda on which its members could agree—education at the state level and federal legislation to take securities fraud cases out of the state courts and into the federal courts. Second, it was explicitly bipartisan striving for balance between Democrats and Republicans. For example, its PAC contributed $25,000 to both the Democratic and Republican gubernatorial candidates in California. Third, TechNet focused on developing relationships between executives and officeholders in Washington and Sacramento. Since members of Congress were eager to learn about high-tech companies, TechNet hosted events for individual members. Those events included "meet and greets," fund-raisers, and small meetings of a dozen or so executives with a senator or Congress member. Vice President Gore was a regular visitor to the Valley, and the meetings arranged by TechNet were referred to as GoreTech. The personal relationships that developed through these gatherings were believed to have been an important factor in the success of the high-tech industry in 1998 on many of its agenda items.

COALITIONS AND CONSENSUS

The heterogeneity or homogeneity of interests not only affects which interests participate in a coalition, but also the bargaining within a coalition. When interests are homogeneous as in the case of the Uniform National Standards Coalition, bargaining is relatively easy because disagreements are likely to be small. When interests are heterogeneous, the bargaining is likely to be more complex and lengthy. The Semiconductor Industry Association (SIA) includes members as diverse as merchant-semiconductor producers such as Intel and Advanced Micro Devices, purchasers of semiconductors such as Hewlett Packard, and firms such as IBM that are both producers and purchasers. The bargaining within the SIA on the issue of Japanese competition and market opening lasted nearly 2 years before an agreement was reached on a position its members could support. The SIA filed a petition for relief under Section 301 of the Trade Act, seeking the opening of the Japanese market to U.S. semiconductors, backed by the threat of U.S. retaliation. This objective appealed both to "free traders" who sought the opening of foreign markets and to those who wanted retaliation against Japan for its trade practices.[18]

On some issues, disagreements among members of a coalition may be unreconcilable. In the Chapter 2 Case *Personal Watercraft aka Jet Skis,* personal watercraft (PWC) manufacturers faced a host of nonmarket issues relating to safety, pollution, noise, and disruption of fishing, canoeing, and other water sports. One strategy used by the PWC manufacturers was to argue that any new regulations on jet skis should also apply to boats. The purpose of this strategy was to force boat manufacturers to oppose any proposed regulations. PWC manufacturers and boat producers belonged to the National Marine Manufacturers Association (NMMA), which worked against the proposed regulations. Genmar, the world's largest independent boat manufacturer, however, objected to being aligned with the PWC manufacturers and quit the NMMA in protest. The Genmar chairman stated, "I am convinced the PWC industry will ultimately force new regulations and restrictions on the boating industry that will cause irreparable damage to us all due to their product's potential dangers and the abuse of our lakes and rivers."[19]

Trade associations are particularly important on those nonmarket issues that have similar impacts on their members. In those cases, a trade association can effectively represent the industry before congressional committees, regulatory agencies, and executive branch agencies. As the jet ski example indicates, however, on matters that affect members quite differently, consensus may not be possible.[20] The pharmaceutical politics example illustrates this in the case of an industry with relatively homogeneous interests.

Testimony

Managers testify before regulatory agencies, congressional committees, administrative agencies, and in courts. In a regulatory setting, testimony is important not only because the information presented can affect regulatory decisions, but also because it creates a record that may serve as a basis for judicial review. Many regulatory rulings

[18]See Yoffie (1988).
[19]Genmar Press Release, November 19, 1997.
[20]For example, in the Part III integrative case *Whirlpool and Energy Efficiency Standards (A),* Whirlpool quit the Association of Home Appliance Manufacturers (AHAM) in 1997 in protest because other refrigerator manufacturers had persuaded AHAM to lobby for a moratorium on compliance with new fuel efficiency standards. Whirlpool had already developed a refrigerator that met the new standards.

EXAMPLE

Pharmaceutical Politics

The Food and Drug Administration (FDA) requires extensive laboratory and clinical testing that may take from 5 to 10 years or more, and many millions of dollars, before a new drug is approved for sale. Since the patent life for a new drug was 17 years, a company with a new drug may have only a few years of protected sales before generic drug manufacturers can introduce a chemically identical drug. Thus, for years the brand-name drug companies had sought a longer patent life for their products. Brand-name drugs had retained some protection because generic drugs had to undergo testing that could take up to 5 years to complete even though they were chemically the same as the already-approved drugs. Furthermore, a federal appeals court had ruled that testing by a generic drug manufacturer could not begin until the patent on the original drug had expired.

In 1984 the Generic Pharmaceutical Industry Association (GPIA) sought legislation requiring the FDA to establish simplified approval procedures for generic drugs, requiring proof only that a generic drug was biochemically identical to an already-approved drug. Legislation to expedite the approval of generic drugs was introduced in both the House and the Senate, and it received considerable support. Changes in the approval process for generic drugs would have a major impact on the pharmaceutical industry because patents on over 150 drugs with sales of $4 billion either had already expired or were about to expire.

The Pharmaceutical Manufacturers Association (PMA), representing the makers of brand-name, patented drugs, opposed the legislation, arguing that the revisions in FDA testing requirements would reduce their incentive to conduct the research necessary to develop new drugs. This, it was argued, would result in fewer drugs being available, which in turn would reduce the level of health care achievable.

The PMA sought outright defeat of the legislation. Once it became apparent that that objective could not be realized, it reached a compromise in negotiations among the GPIA, the chairman of the House Subcommittee on Health and the Environment, and the chairman of the Labor and Human Resources Committee. The compromise would extend patent protection for certain brand-name drugs and speed the approval process for generic drugs.

Consensus on the compromise could not be sustained within the PMA, however. Eleven of the brand-name drug manufacturers were furious with the compromise and succeeded in having the head of the PMA and its chief lobbyist fired. The CEOs of the companies, including American Home Products, Hoffman-LaRoche, and Merck, then lobbied intensely over the next few weeks to strike from the compromise bill the provision that would speed the approval of generic drugs.[1] Their efforts failed, however, and they were only able to obtain a provision pertaining to exclusive-marketing rights for nonpatented drugs.

[1] *Dun's Business Month,* January 1986, p. 36.

are challenged in the courts, and the courts will at times consider both substantive and procedural challenges to a ruling. Testimony thus must not only stand up to cross-examination during the hearing, but it should also provide a foundation for a possible court challenge.

Congressional hearings serve a variety of purposes ranging from issue identification to information provision. A hearing provides an opportunity to present a position that may be backed at times by a policy study conducted by a firm, association, or coalition. Testimony of firms and interest groups, however, is often preceded by lobbying, so for some members of Congress hearings provide little new information.

Hearings are not always held to generate information. Some are held to generate publicity and to mobilize support for a particular position. For example, trial lawyers and consumer groups have opposed revisions in the liability system, and one of their tactics is to bring accident victims to congressional hearings to testify against caps or other limits on liability awards. Hearings can also be managed to promote the side of the issue supported by the chair. Testimony on the chair's side of an issue may be scheduled in the morning so that television stations will be able to prepare the story and edit the tape in time for the evening news. Testimony on the other side may be scheduled for the afternoon, when it is too late for the evening news. By the next day, that testimony is often too old for television. Hearings thus can provide a stage on which a subcommittee or committee chair may play out a story to advance a policy interest or cater to constituents.

Supreme Court Justice Stephen Breyer (1982, pp. 317–340) presented a detailed description of the 1974 overnight hearings on Civil Aeronautics Board regulation of the airline industry. Breyer, who then served on the committee staff, characterized the hearings as "drama" to be orchestrated. In preparation for hearings, the committee staff prepared a script that included an opening statement for the chair and a set of questions to ask each witness. Because the chair already knew much of what the witness would say, the chair was able to direct much of the dialogue. Breyer also discussed the tactics used by members of Congress in their questioning of witnesses. One tactic was to ask a zinger—a question whose only possible answer would support the member's own position. As an example, in the foreign leasing case in Chapter 6, Representative Pickle asked the general manager of Boeing, "Are we not subsidizing the competition of our own foreign carriers?"[21]

Electoral Strategies

Electoral strategies focus on providing electorally important resources to candidates. Unions and some interest groups endorse candidates, provide volunteer workers, staff get-out-the-vote campaigns, and align with political parties. Business, however, tends to concentrate its efforts on campaign contributions. As the PacifiCare example indicates, these campaign contributions are only one component of many companies' political portfolios. This section reviews the legal context for campaign contributions, the pattern of contributions, and the role of contributions in corporate political strategies.

ELECTION FINANCING LAWS

Federal election financing is regulated by the Federal Election Commission (FEC) under the Federal Election Campaign Act (FECA), as amended in 1974. Corporations are prohibited by the Tillman Act of 1907 from making contributions to the federal election campaigns of candidates. Contributions by unions were prohibited in 1943. State campaign contribution laws can vary substantially from federal law. In California, corporations may make direct contributions to state electoral campaigns.

At the federal level, corporations, labor unions, trade and professional associations, and groups of individuals may form multicandidate political action committees, referred to as PACs, for the purpose of soliciting contributions and distributing them to candidates or expending them independently in election campaigns.[22] A major turning point for PAC activity was a 1976 FEC ruling that employees as well as shareholders

---

[21]Hearing, Committee on Ways and Means, House of Representatives, Washington, D.C., June 8, 1983, p. 212.
[22]The FEC designates six categories of PACs: corporate, labor, nonconnected, trade/membership/health, cooperative, and corporation without stock. The organization and operation of PACs are discussed by Handler and Mulkern (1982).

could contribute to corporate PACs. Most contributions to corporate PACs are now made by employees, primarily management, and contributions must be voluntary. The amount a person may contribute to a PAC is not restricted.

Unions collect funds for political contributions through dues, but members cannot be forced to contribute to the union's political activities. The Supreme Court has held that individuals may not be compelled to support political positions they oppose. Applied to unions, this means that members and covered nonmembers can be forced to pay only that fraction of the dues used for collective bargaining purposes.[23]

Campaign financing law distinguishes between expenditures in electoral campaigns and contributions to those campaigns. In *Buckley v. Valeo,* 424 U.S. 1 (1976), the Supreme Court ruled that any limit on campaign expenditures threatens the freedoms of speech and association and thus is a violation of the First Amendment. This decision overturned state laws limiting campaign spending.[24] As a result of this decision, candidates are not restricted in their personal expenditures. In 1984 Jay Rockefeller (D-WV) spent $10.3 million of his own funds, outspending his opponent $12 million to $1.1 million, to win a Senate seat with 52 percent of the vote. In 1994, Michael Huffington spent nearly $28 million of his own funds in his unsuccessful Senate campaign in California.

In contrast to limits on campaign expenditures, limits on contributions to candidates' campaigns have been upheld by the Supreme Court. The court reasoned that such limits represent less of an abridgment of First Amendment rights than limits on expenditures.[25] Contributions to a candidate's campaign are referred to as "hard money" contributions and are strictly limited. Campaign contributions by PACs are limited to $5,000 per candidate per election, but most corporate PACs make contributions well below those limits. In the 1995-1996 election cycle, 1,642 corporate PACs contributed $69.7 million, or $42,000 per PAC. Corporate PACs made 35 percent of total PAC contributions and 9.9 percent of total campaign contributions.[26] Contributions by individuals are limited to $1,000, so contributions to a candidate's primary and general election campaigns can total $2,000 for individuals and $10,000 for PACs. Violations of campaign contributions regulations lead to substantial penalties. A prominent lobbyist was convicted of making illegal campaign contributions to the same secretary of agriculture as mentioned previously and was fined $150,000 and ordered to write an essay on the election laws. The essay was distributed to the members of the American League of Lobbyists.[27]

Individuals, corporations, unions, and other interest groups may make unlimited "soft money" contributions to party committees for party-building activities provided that those funds are not used to urge a vote for or against an individual candidate.[28] Soft money contributions were aggressively solicited by the Democratic and Republican parties beginning in the mid-1990s. Soft money contributions have skyrocketed in part because corporations and unions can make contributions directly from their treasuries, whereas PAC and union contributions to candidates' campaigns must come from the

---

[23]In 1998 the Supreme Court held that federal labor law allows dues collected from nonunion workers in the private sector to be used only for collective bargaining purposes. In 1986 it had made a similar ruling for public employees. In 1991 the Court extended this principle in ruling that public employee union members cannot be forced to support lobbying and other political activities.

[24]In 1998 the Supreme Court declined to review this decision.

[25]Independent expenditures on campaigns were held to be immune to restrictions in *FEC v. National Conservative Political Action Committee,* 470 U.S. 480 (1985), but in *FEC v. Massachusetts Citizens for Life,* 479 U.S. 238 (1986) the Supreme Court stated that restrictions on expenditures by for-profit corporations would be upheld.

[26]See Sabato (1984) for a study of PACs. See Ornstein, Mann, and Malbin (1997) for data on campaign contributions.

[27]*The New York Times,* September 29, 1998.

[28]Interest groups can also make "independent expenditures" in support of or opposition to a candidate. The Christian Coalition and the Sierra Club make such expenditures.

pockets of employees and union members, respectively. Soft money contributions by businesses, unions, environmentalist groups, and individuals are generally structured by the political parties. The Republican and Democratic parties offer donors different levels of access to officeholders depending on the amount of the contribution. As the PacifiCare example indicates, the Democratic and Republican parties and their members have established numerous committees to solicit soft money contributions with the promise of varying degrees of access to officeholders.

There is a fine line between the soft money expenditures by party committees and expenditures on behalf of a candidate. For example, soft money has been used for negative television advertisements mentioning the voting record and policy positions of a candidate. As long as the advertisement does not urge voters to vote for or against the candidate, contributions and expenditures are not restricted. Although disclosure of such expenditures is not required, one study estimated that $260 million was spent in the 1997–1998 election cycle on issue advocacy ads including those about individual candidates.

THE PATTERN OF CAMPAIGN CONTRIBUTIONS

Campaign contributions are an important aspect of electoral politics, if not of corporate political strategies. Sixty percent of hard money campaign contributions to the 1996 federal election campaigns, however, were made by individuals, with PACs contributing only 28 percent.

PAC contributions are primarily made to incumbents, and because a substantial majority of incumbents were Democrats until 1995, a majority of PAC contributions had gone to Democrats. When the Republicans became the majority party in both the House and Senate in 1995, PAC contributions shifted to the Republicans. In the 1996 election cycle Republicans received 53.3 percent of business PAC contributions. Labor PACs contribute almost exclusively to Democrats.[29] The largest PACs are not corporate but are composed of realtors, doctors, lawyers, and agricultural groups.

Hard money contributions to the 1996 congressional campaign totaled $674 million, and soft money contributions as reported by the Center for Responsive Politics were $204 million. In the 1995–1996 election cycle the five largest contributors, including hard and soft money, were Philip Morris, AT&T, the Association of Trial Lawyers, the Teamsters Union, and the Laborers Union.

PURPOSES OF CAMPAIGN CONTRIBUTIONS

Campaign contributions are made for three basic purposes. The first is to improve the chances that the recipient will be elected; the second is to obtain access to present or future officeholders; and the third is to influence legislative voting. Most contributions by individuals are made for the first purpose, as are the contributions by labor PACs. Business, professional, and trade PACs, however, take a more pragmatic approach and tend to make contributions to those most likely to win, largely for the purpose of facilitating access. As former Senator Rudy Boschwitz (R-MN) commented: "All they're [corporate PACs] doing is buying a bunch of access and playing the damn thing like a horse race. They don't do it philosophically. They do it on who's going to win."[30] The role of campaign contributions in providing access was explained in a deposition by former Senator Alan Cranston (D-CA) in the "Keating five" ethics inquiry in 1990: "The only

---

[29]Organized labor also provides substantial in-kind support to Democrats in addition to campaign contributions. Unions provide volunteer workers who staff phone banks, ring doorbells, deliver campaign materials, and help register voters.

[30]*The New York Times,* September 26, 1988.

thing I will grant is that the person who makes a contribution has a better chance to get access than someone who does not. All senators know you may get ten, twenty, thirty, fifty phone calls a day, people trying to reach you, and you cannot answer all those phone calls. So you answer those from those whose names you recognize and who you think you have some obligation to at least hear out."[31]

An access theory of campaign contributions predicts that the more valuable the services the candidate can provide the more an interest group will be willing to contribute to that candidate's campaign. This suggests that access to those members of Congress who hold strategic positions should be more valuable than access to those members who do not. In particular, it suggests that senior members, and particularly the chairs of committees and subcommittees, should receive more contributions than members who are not chairs.[32] The data support this prediction. Similarly, members of the committees that deal with legislation affecting an industry receive substantial contributions from the firms in those industries.

Several studies have investigated whether campaign contributions affect congressional voting, but the studies find little evidence to support such a hypothesis. Studies by Hall and Wayman (1990) and Wu (1994) indicate another purpose of campaign contributions—that of developing allies and encouraging them to work for legislation that the member and the contributor both support. Thus, campaign contributions could affect legislative outcomes by mobilizing congressional effort on behalf of legislation rather than by directly affecting the votes of recipients.

Many firms would like not to make political contributions but believe that they are caught in a prisoners' dilemma. That is, if no other interest group were to make contributions, an interest group that made a contribution would be important to the candidate and might see benefits flow from its contribution. Conversely, if many firms and interest groups contribute, then a noncontributor might be at a disadvantage, possibly suffering a loss of access. Contributing, then, is a dominant strategy, resulting in a situation in which interest groups contribute, even though all would prefer not to contribute.

Communication and Public Advocacy

On some issues, particularly those characterized by majoritarian politics, firms may employ a strategy of communicating directly with the public. The health care industry demonstrated the effectiveness of mass communication with its "Harry and Louise" advertisements, raising alarms about the Clinton administration's plans to restructure the health care industry. The ads turned the public against the administration's plan contributing to its collapse in disarray. As indicated in the PacifiCare example, the industry continued with this approach in its criticism of the Clinton administration's patients' bill of rights.

During the political activity on the Clinton administration's health care restructuring proposal, pharmaceutical firms concerned about possible price controls and mandated rebates adopted a nonmarket strategy that included a communication component. To address the price control issue and the public criticism of the industry, the industry's basic nonmarket strategy was to emphasize the discovery of new drugs and the incentives needed for research and development. A variety of actions were taken. The industry association emphasized the discovery theme and subsequently added

[31] *The New York Times,* November 30, 1990.

[32] See Kroszner and Stratmann (1998) for a study of financial services PACs and their contributions to committees.

"Research" to its name. The Pharmaceutical Research and Manufacturing Association undertook lobbying and public information activities with the message that the discovery of new drugs would be jeopardized by price controls.

Several major pharmaceutical companies also formed a coalition, Rx Partners, that conducted media tours in 65 cities and hosted a series of breakfasts for members of Congress. Individual firms also took actions. Several companies undertook public education campaigns similar to those of Rx Partners. Bristol Myers held 350 meetings with community groups and lobbied extensively in Congress. Several companies conducted advertising campaigns that emphasized the discovery of new drugs. They also stressed the beneficial therapeutic value of existing drugs which, invariably, some member of Congress or a relative had used.

How a message is framed can be important when communicating with the public and government officeholders. An example is provided by the plan developed by AT&T and the FCC to lower long-distance telephone rates toward the cost of service. The reduction was to be accomplished by introducing usage-independent access charges to be paid monthly by residential and business customers for long-distance service. The FCC and AT&T chose the term *access charge* because the monthly charge would cover the costs of the connection, or access, to the interstate telephone network. The reaction to the plan surprised the FCC and AT&T. Customers, consumer groups, and politicians complained about having to pay for access they might not use. The uproar almost resulted in legislation barring the plan. As the FCC scaled back the plan, it renamed the charges "end-user charges." The new term implied "use" and did not serve as a lightning rod. The damage had already been done, however.

Judicial Strategies

Judicial strategies pertain not only to those cases in which a firm finds itself the defendant but also to those in which it initiates legal action as a component of a nonmarket strategy. Judicial strategies are implemented in state and federal courts, which are governed by statutory and common law. Judicial strategies are also implemented in quasi-judicial arenas, such as those of regulatory and administrative agencies, which are governed by administrative law. Judicial strategies are used to enforce rights, obtain damages for breach of contract, and address unfair competitive practices under the antitrust laws. They are also used to deter competitors from taking certain actions and to caution the media or regulatory or administrative agencies. Firms frequently file suits against regulatory agencies, alleging an inadequate basis in the record for their rulemaking. General Motors filed suit against the Department of Transportation because of its preliminary decision to recall GM pickup trucks with side-mounted gas tanks. (See the Chapter 1 case *General Motors Like a Rock? (A).*) The secretary of transportation backed down and did not order a recall. On the other side, environmental and activist groups often file lawsuits against agencies for failure to enforce the laws vigorously.

Judicial action, particularly in the courts, can be costly. The Department of Justice's antitrust suit against AT&T took 8 years before it was settled out of court with the breakup of the Bell system. It is estimated to have cost AT&T $360 million and the government $15 million.[33] Cases in arenas governed by administrative law, such as petitions to the International Trade Commission for relief from injury by imports, often proceed more expeditiously and at lower cost because of legislatively imposed time limits. Al-

[33]Shipper and Jennings (1984, p. 115).

though lawsuits can be extremely costly, awards can also be high. As a fledgling company, MCI successfully sued AT&T on antitrust grounds, and its award was used to finance its expansion. MCI also filed a number of other suits against both AT&T and the FCC seeking the opportunity to provide expanded telecommunications services. The lawsuits helped open the telecommunications market to greater competition.

In 1998 PepsiCo filed an antitrust lawsuit against the Coca-Cola Company alleging that it used exclusionary practices and its dominant position in the fountain-dispensed segment of the soft-drink market. In the past most restaurant chains had avoided carrying Pepsi because PepsiCo owned their competitors Pizza Hut, Taco Bell, and Kentucky Fried Chicken. In 1997, however, PepsiCo spun off its restaurants and began to aggressively pursue the fountain business, which accounts for 27 percent of soft-drink sales. The lawsuit alleged that Coca-Cola's exclusive contracts with independent distributors hindered PepsiCo in its efforts to win the accounts of restaurant chains, since those distributors would not distribute to restaurants that would like to carry Pepsi. Coca-Cola said that the lawsuit "smacks of desperation."

Regulatory and administrative law channels may be used for a variety of purposes including to protect rights, handicap a competitor, or gain a direct advantage. When the FDA attempted to streamline its rules for approving generic drugs, the brand-name pharmaceutical companies filed lawsuits challenging its authority to do so. Thwarted in this administrative channel, the generic drug companies subsequently took their cause to the legislative arena.

Advisory Panels and Committees

The U.S. government sanctions an estimated 1,050 advisory committees and panels. Advisory committees meet a variety of needs of the government as well as of their members. Among other things, they provide the government with expertise. The scientific and economic consequences of proposed policies are often unclear, and the information provided by industry members, scientists, and other professionals can help agencies make better-informed decisions. Advisory committees are also used to assess reactions to policy alternatives. From an agency's perspective, advisory panels also provide a means of building support for its policy objectives. This enhances the power of the agency relative to Congress and other government agencies.

Participation on advisory committees serves several purposes for firms. First, participation can provide information about prospective agency decisions. Second, it may help build a reputation for responsible public participation. Third, it can provide an avenue for putting an issue on an agency's agenda. Fourth, it can provide a means of influencing the agency.

Advisory committees are overseen by the General Services Administration, and balanced representation is required. Nevertheless, advisory committees have been criticized both by members of Congress and by the public because of the possibility of undue influence. In particular, concern has been expressed by such activist groups as Public Citizen about the influence advisory committees give their members.

As an example of the role of advisory committees, the Trade Act of 1974 directed the U.S. Trade Representative (USTR) to form general and sectoral committees that were "representative of industry, labor, or agricultural interests . . ."[34] The advisory committee process provided the USTR with information about the concerns of the interest groups and served to direct political pressure toward the committees and away from

---

[34]Destler (1986, p. 94).

Congress. Each member of a committee also heard the concerns of the others, which served to restrain their expectations about what could be achieved in trade negotiations. Schuler and Rehbein (1998) found that among companies that participated on the advisory committees those with the highest rates of participation tended to be in industries with high ratios of exports to imports. Large companies as well as companies that were defense contractors and were unionized also were active participants.[35]

Organizing for Political Effectiveness

Firms that expect to be involved in issues of a political nature must anticipate rather than simply react to developments. Consequently, they need to organize and prepare for action. It is essential to monitor issues, and for many firms this means full-time representation in Washington and in the capitals of important states. For other firms, associations can be a cost-effective means of providing intelligence, but this may not be sufficient if the firm's interests differ from those that the association represents. Most large firms also have public or government affairs departments that provide expertise and monitor the development of issues. A department may include lawyers, communications experts, former government officials, lobbyists, and analysts.[36]

Washington offices serve as the eyes and ears of firms; provide information on emerging and developing issues; and are a locus of expertise about issues, institutions, and officeholders. Because political issues are often episodic in nature, many firms engage on an occasional basis the services of political consulting firms, Washington law firms, and public relations firms. Similarly, lobbyists may be hired for a specific issue. The size of a firm's permanent staff thus is determined relative to the cost and effectiveness of outside alternatives. Many other firms, including high-tech firms, have shunned Washington offices preferring a lean organization.

Because lobbying is the centerpiece of most firms' participation in political issues, most employ lobbyists who are either political professionals or are managers responsible for presenting the firm's concerns to government officials. Their responsibilities may include maintaining relationships with members of Congress, executive branch officials, and government agencies. Access is a necessary condition for lobbying, so many firms make a practice of maintaining contact with those members of Congress in whose districts they have their operations and with the committees that regularly deal with issues on their nonmarket agendas. Firms also provide training for their managers who become involved in political and collective action issues. That training often emphasizes sensitivity to the possible public reaction to the firm's activities and the development of personal skills for effective participation in public arenas.

Summary

Firms and interest groups have a broad political portfolio. Lobbying is essential in addressing issues in legislative and administrative arenas. Lobbying involves demonstrating to legislators that the interests of their constituents or their own policy interests are aligned with those of the firm and its constituents. Providing politically relevant information to officeholders about the consequences of alternatives is thus at the heart of effective lobbying. Lobbying often focuses on committees and their staffs. Testimony in hearings is related to lobbying and should be coordinated with it. Access to policy mak-

[35]Destler (1986, p. 216).

[36]A detailed description of the organization of a Washington office in the heyday of the politics of the oil industry is provided in the case "Gulf Oil Corporation: Public Affairs and the Washington Office" in Fox (1982, pp. 287–306).

ers is necessary for lobbying. It can be attained through the constituency connection, personal relationships, former government officials, and, in some cases, campaign contributions. Lobbying remains a relatively unregulated activity.

Grassroots strategies are based on the rent chain and are designed to put pressure on legislators through the constituency connection. Firms, associations, and interest groups can organize and mobilize their constituents for grassroots activities, including letter-writing and visiting Washington for personal lobbying. The effectiveness of those activities depends on their credibility as well as on their scale. Grassroots campaigns are often coordinated with public advocacy programs.

Firms participate in peak organizations, trade associations, and ad hoc coalitions. Peak organizations often address general business issues rather than specific industry matters. When issues affect most of their members similarly, peak organizations can be effective. Trade associations are important, particularly for issues that pertain to a specific industry. Ad hoc coalitions address specific issues and often bring together interests that may not be aligned on other issues. When members of a coalition have heterogeneous interests, the maintenance of the coalition requires effort, and its strategies are chosen through internal bargaining. Large firms often supplement coalitional activities with their own individual political strategies.

Electoral strategies of firms primarily involve campaign contributions made through corporate PACs or in the form of soft money from the corporate treasury. These contributions are typically made to obtain access to members of Congress and otherwise seldom play a major role in the strategies of most firms. Some firms also engage in public communication and advocacy intended to inform both the public and those involved in policy-making processes. Judicial strategies are implemented both in the courts and in regulatory arenas governed by administrative law. These strategies can be effective but are often expensive. Firms also participate in government advisory panels that provide expertise to government agencies and information to their participants.

Most large firms are organized to address nonmarket issues in the arenas of political institutions. That organization may involve a Washington office, professional lobbyists, a government affairs department, participation in associations and coalitions, and management training. Many high-tech companies prefer a lean organization and have no Washington office.

The chapter cases, *Drexel Burnham Lambert and Junk Bond Politics, CAFE Standards,* and *Envirotest Systems Corporation (B),* involve issues that require a political strategy and an implementation plan.

CASES

Drexel Burnham Lambert and Junk Bond Politics

In early 1985 Drexel Burnham Lambert faced a political challenge to its lucrative market strategy of using high-yield debt instruments to facilitate acquisitions, restructure firms, and finance growing companies. These debt instruments were popularly called *junk bonds* although Drexel preferred the term *noninvestment grade securities*.

Throughout the 1970s virtually all junk bonds were "fallen angels"—bonds that had been investment grade when issued but had fallen because of the financial difficulties of the issuer. In the late 1970s, Drexel pioneered the use of junk bonds to finance small firms and high-growth firms and to restructure firms through takeovers and leveraged buyouts (LBOs). Takeovers, restructurings, and LBOs provided the bulk of Drexel's profits and the bonuses paid to its employees. The securities issued by the high-growth firms, which had previously had to rely on venture capital and financing by banks and insurance companies, were typically below investment grade because the firms had often only recently gone public or because of the risk associated with their size. The distinctions between these three types of junk bonds—fallen angels, acquisition instruments, and bonds issued by high-growth firms—were not well understood by the public or Congress.

The pace of corporate acquisitions, particularly hostile takeovers, had aroused considerable opposition among many corporate executives. In early 1985, as a result of a variety of forces and with the support of activist groups and some business organizations such as the Business Roundtable, seven bills pertaining to junk bonds were introduced in Congress. Some of the bills would limit the tax deductibility of the interest on junk bonds used in hostile takeover attempts, others would limit the amount of acquisition junk bonds that federally insured institutions could hold, and others would impose a moratorium on hostile takeovers financed with junk bonds. For example, the Securities Safety and Soundness Act would impose a moratorium through December 31, 1985, on those hostile takeovers in which at least 20 percent of the acquisition was financed by junk bonds. The Junk Bond Limitation Act would limit the amount of junk bonds that federally insured financial institutions could hold. As a variety of congressional committees began to consider these bills, the threat to the heart of Drexel's business and its reputation was enormous.

A number of commentators believed that corporations supported the bills because they feared being the targets of hostile takeover attempts. The size of some of the takeover attempts, and the fact that some of them succeeded, sent chills through many an executive suite. Andrew Sigler, CEO of Champion International and chairman of the Corporate Responsibility Task Force of the Business Roundtable, was one of the leading advocates of restrictions on hostile takeovers. He argued for "legislative approaches aimed at curbing the current destructive takeover frenzy and restoring some semblance of sanity to the tender offer process." He warned that increased leverage threatened the future of American corporations.

Those opposing the use of junk bonds also claimed that the acquisitions increased concentration in American industry, threatened local communities, diverted capital from new productive investment, and resulted in layoffs and increased unemployment. Drexel, however, maintained that acquisitions promoted efficiency by replacing ineffective management and that capital was not diverted because it flowed to the shareholders of the acquired firm, who reinvested most of it. Drexel also cited studies by economists showing that, even with the recent spate of acquisitions, industrial concentration had not increased, in part because of the growing number of spin-offs, divestments, and start-ups.

Drexel also pointed out that over 95 percent of U.S. public corporations with assets above $25 million would receive a rating below investment grade from Moody's or Standard & Poor's. Moreover, 12 states had no corporations that would receive an investment grade rating. Furthermore, a Drexel representative said that debt instruments with ratings below investment grade were essential to many of the small, high-growth companies that accounted for a high percentage of the jobs created in the economy.

The investment banking industry was divided on the issue of restrictions on junk bonds. Many of the leading investment banks viewed Drexel, which had the bulk of the junk bond business, with hostility but also with admiration for its rapid growth. Some leading investment banks had refused to use junk bonds, and some refused to participate on the acquisition side of hostile takeovers. Felix G. Rohatyn, a senior partner of Lazard Frères & Company, spoke out against hostile takeovers and the way junk bonds were used to finance them and called for laws to restrict their use. Morgan Stanley commissioned a study showing that the default rate on total debt was 0.08 percent, but the default rate on noninvestment grade debt was 1.52 percent. Drexel refuted those data and cited studies that showed that high-yield bonds outperformed Treasury bills by a wide margin during the late 1970s and the first half of the 1980s.[1]

In April 1985 Drexel was approached by David Aylward, until recently the general counsel of the House Subcommittee on Telecommunications, Consumer Protection and Finance, who proposed forming an association to oppose the bills. The association would solicit contributions of $25,000 each from high-growth companies, ranging from a day care center company to a computer leasing company to a steel company, all of which used high-yield, noninvestment grade bonds to finance their growth. The association would then represent the interests of these and other companies before Congress. Aylward asked for Drexel's assistance in contacting potential members of the association. ■

[1]Frederick H. Joseph, "High-Yield Bonds Aren't Junk," *The Wall Street Journal,* May 31, 1985.

PREPARATION QUESTIONS

1. What are the relevant dimensions of the political threat to Drexel?
2. What is the nature of the politics of the issue and where is it in its life cycle?
3. Which interests are likely to be active on this issue?
4. What political strategy should Drexel adopt and how should it be integrated with its market strategy? How should it be implemented?
5. Should Drexel assist Aylward with the formation of the association he has proposed? What name should be given to it if it were formed? Would the formation of the association be responsible?

Envirotest Systems Corporation (B)

Envirotest's most serious threats came from its nonmarket environment.[1] At the federal level the National Automobile Dealers Association had filed a lawsuit challenging the procedures the Environmental Protection Agency (EPA) used in making its ruling that, in effect, required centralized testing and took from the states the ability to design their own programs.[2] Also, at the federal level the General Accounting Office questioned the efficacy of the EPA's I/M 240 test, and in response the EPA indicated that it would assess alternative tests. Some states objected because the EPA regulations took a command-and-control approach rather than employing performance standards under which states would have flexibility in choosing the program they believed most effectively met their air quality objectives.

Some states had no prior emissions testing program, and others had had such a program—in most cases a decentralized one. In states with no prior emissions testing program, the principal threat came from motorist objections to emissions testing and centralized testing in particular. The EPA estimated that the average cost of a centralized test was $17 and

[1]See The Chapter 2 case *Evirotest Systems Corporation (A).*
[2]The Court of Appeals subsequently rejected the suit and held for the EPA.

ranged from $35 to $70 in a decentralized system, but for a state with no previous testing program, the cost could be a source of complaints.

In addition to the cost of the tests, the failure rate was often set high, and the cost of repairs could be substantial, particularly for older cars. The Colorado Request for Proposals (RFP) specified an initial test failure rate of 30 percent and a retest failure rate of 25 percent, and Pennsylvania also estimated that the failure rate would be 30 percent. In addition, the EPA's enhanced testing requirements included for the first time testing for nitrogen oxide, causing some vehicles that would have passed under the previous decentralized program to fail. Repairs costing as much as $450 could be required, which could force some motorists to scrap their older cars.[3]

Although the centralized test took only 12 minutes, there could at times be significant waits at the testing facility. Motorists would also have longer drives to the facility, since there would be far fewer testing sites under a centralized system. Furthermore, vehicles that failed a test would have to return to be reinspected. Complaints could also arise from testing inaccuracies and errors, although the technology was far more accurate than that used in decentralized systems. Centralized testing facilities would also affect traffic volume near the site, which could result in objections by local residents.

Complaints could also come from unexpected sources. Maine was first to implement an enhanced centralized testing program (provided by Systems Control and not Envirotest) under the EPA mandate, but within months public opposition forced the state to suspend testing for 6 months. Maine had chosen to expand, beyond that required by the EPA, the region in which testing was required, yet citizens complained of unequal treatment since testing was required in some regions and not in others. Motorists also complained about the $24 cost of a test and the possibility of having to spend up to $450 for repairs. Automobile owners also complained because buses and large trucks did not have to be tested. Some implementation mistakes were made as well. Motorists were required to pay in cash, which drew widespread complaints. Also, some of the staff were poorly trained and ineffective in dealing with motorists. The most incendiary event, however, was the governor's decision to allocate pollution credits, earned as a result of the emissions testing program, for the expansion of a plant that had been cited for pollution violations. Some state legislators were furious as were voters, who began a petition drive to repeal the testing program.

In Pennsylvania, which had a decentralized testing program, opposition arose from a variety of sources, including owners of classic cars produced before emissions controls were required. They held a rally on the steps of the state capitol to oppose centralized testing. The centralized testing program became a political football as both gubernatorial candidates accused each other of having imposed the program on the voters.[4] Both pledged to renegotiate with the EPA.Some legislators seized the opportunity to complain that the contract was too lucrative. Calls for rescinding the contract mounted. The state legislature passed a bill to delay implementation of the program, but the retiring governor vetoed it. A special session of the legislature was scheduled for after the November election to vote on overriding the veto. Envirotest threatened to sue the state, seeking damages of $355 million if the state breached its contract. After the election the state legislature easily overrode the veto, and the governor-elect reiterated his campaign pledge to negotiate with the EPA for a program like the one California had negotiated earlier in the year.

In states with decentralized testing programs, a powerful interest group opposing centralized testing was the repair shops that performed testing and repairs. In California there were 9,300 licensed Smog Check shops and 22,000 licensed Smog Check mechanics. The association of repair shops estimated that 1,300 establishments would have to close and 3,000 jobs would be lost as a result of centralized testing. The proponents of centralized testing countered that the higher failure rate with centralized testing would mean more repairs. Furthermore, the centralized testing facilities would create jobs—but not necessarily for the same people who feared that their jobs would be lost.[5]

Carol Browner, administrator of the EPA, argued that not only would centralized testing add jobs, but it would also save Californians money. She said: "Californians today pay much more than other Americans

[3]Most centralized testing programs provide a waiver if the cost of repairs exceeded a figure such as $450.

[4]One candidate had been lieutenant governor when the enabling legislation was passed, and the other had voted for the Clean Air Act when in Congress.

[5]Booz-Allen Hamilton estimated that the net effect would be the addition of 700 jobs. An SRI study estimated an increase of 975 jobs.

for their inspections, about $32 per test. In Maryland, I pay $9 per test every two years. The average cost in test-only states is a bit lower; only $8.50."[6] Despite her threat that the state would lose $600 to $800 million of highway funds, the pressure from the repair shops and others satisfied with the state's current Smog Check program and skeptical of centralized testing caused the state to balk. Reminding Washington of the 54 electoral votes in California and that the presidential election was only a little over 2 years away, both the governor and the state legislature in effect dared the federal government to impose penalties on the state. Willie Brown, the Democrat speaker of the state assembly, said that imposing the EPA's program would be "a fatal step for Bill Clinton's candidacy in 1996." The EPA quickly entered into negotiations with the state and reached a compromise in which the state would retain its current decentralized testing program but would centrally test 15 percent of the vehicles in 1995, increasing to 30 percent in 1996 if the overall program was not sufficiently effective. The state would also experiment with a remote testing program. The two sides would then evaluate the experience with the program and its success.

Observing the experience in California, other states began to balk. Virginia refused to establish a centralized testing program, and the EPA backed away from imposing penalties. Maine suspended its program, and Pennsylvania moved to renegotiate its program. Centralized emissions testing was in jeopardy. ■

[6] *Los Angeles Times,* September 9, 1993.

PREPARATION QUESTIONS

1. What went wrong in the EPA's attempt to implement an enhanced emissions testing program? What types of politics were involved in the emissions testing issue?
2. Is the EPA likely to withhold funds from Pennsylvania?
3. Does Envirotest have any allies in its efforts to have states implement centralized testing programs?
4. What integrated—market and nonmarket—strategy should Envirotest adopt to address the issues in Pennsylvania and California?

CAFE Standards

In the aftermath of the 1973–1974 oil crisis, Congress established a system of Corporate Average Fuel Economy (CAFE) standards for automobiles sold in the United States. The Energy Policy and Conservation Act (EPCA) of 1975 set as a goal the near-doubling by 1985 of the 1975 average miles per gallon (mpg) of 14. The CAFE standards increased to 27.5 mpg in 1985. (The procedure for calculating the CAFE is presented in Appendix A.) By 1985, however, fuel economy was not a major concern to car buyers, who turned to larger—and lower mileage—cars. When U.S. automobile manufacturers began to have difficulty meeting the CAFE standard because of the shift in consumer demand, the Department of Transportation (DOT), using authority assigned to it under EPCA, rolled back the CAFE standard to 26 mpg in 1986. When it took office in 1989, the Bush administration increased the CAFE standard to 27.5 mpg.

The average fuel efficiency of all 1990 model year passenger cars sold in the United States decreased to 28.2 mpg from 28.7 for the 1987 model year, with imported automobiles averaging 29.9 mpg and domestic autos averaging 26.9 mpg in 1990. For 1989 the respective figures were 30.6 mpg and 27.1 mpg. The largest decreases from 1988 to 1990 were recorded by Isuzu, Toyota, and Subaru, each of which decreased by at least 9 percent. Toyota's average for 1990 was 30.5 mpg, which was down from 32.6 in 1989. This backsliding was of concern to environmentalists and others.

Separate CAFEs were computed for U.S. automakers' domestic and imported fleets, and both had to meet the CAFE standard. An automobile was considered domestic if 75 percent of its content by value was U.S. or Canadian. One strategy of a domestic manufacturer to meet the CAFE standard for its domestic fleet was to move fuel-inefficient vehicles into its foreign fleet. Ford planned to purchase enough components from abroad to reduce the domestic content of its Ford LTD Crown Victoria and Mercury Marquis models from 94 to 74 percent. Those autos would then be included in Ford's imported fleet, along with its Korean-made Festiva. Light trucks, which include pickups and recreational and sport utility vehicles, had a separate fuel economy standard, which in 1989 was 20.2 mpg.

Not only did they face the problem of meeting fuel economy standards, but in 1990 U.S. auto manufacturers were experiencing a slump in sales. Moreover, the entry of Japanese automobile companies into the luxury segment of the market threatened their most profitable lines. Nissan's Infiniti and Toyota's Lexus posed a major challenge to U.S. and European luxury cars. The fuel efficiency for the luxury models of Mercedes, BMW, and Infiniti was approximately 22.5 mpg, and Lexus achieved 23.5 mpg. The penalty for not meeting the CAFE standard was $5 per tenth of a mile per automobile, and some companies such as Mercedes-Benz, Jaguar, and Rolls-Royce routinely paid the penalty. In 1988 Mercedes-Benz paid $20.2 million. In addition to the penalty imposed if the fleet average did not reach the CAFE standard, an excise or gas-guzzler tax was imposed on individual models with low mileage. A tax of $500 was imposed on an automobile that did not achieve 22.5 mpg, and it increased to a maximum of $3,850 if the automobile did not achieve 12.5 mpg.

GLOBAL WARMING

In the late 1980s the global warming issue reignited the fuel economy issue. Because the light-duty vehicle fleet accounted for 39 percent of U.S. oil consumption, concerns were raised about the decline in automobile fuel economy. President Bush, who had made a campaign pledge to support the environment and had expressed a concern about global warming, generally supported improved fuel economy.

Concern accelerated in the United States and other countries when Dr. James Hanson, director of NASA's Goddard Institute for Space Studies, declared during a torrid heat wave in 1988 that he was 99 percent certain that global warming had begun. Considerable scientific uncertainty remained, however, about whether global warming was occurring and, if so, how serious a problem it was.

LEGISLATIVE ACTION

In response to concerns about global warming, Senator Richard H. Bryan (D-NV), chair of the Consumer Subcommittee of the Commerce Committee, introduced S. 1224, the Motor Vehicle Fuel Efficiency Act of 1989. The bill would increase the CAFE standard for automobiles from the 1988 actual average by 20 percent for 1995 to 2000 and by 40 percent for 2001 and beyond.[1] The standard for 1995 to 2000 would be bounded by 27.5 mpg at the low end and 40 mpg at the top. After 2001, the lower bound would be 27.5 and the upper 45. Appendix B presents the 1988 CAFE averages by manufacturer and the 1995 and 2001 averages that each manufacturer would have to meet under the bill.

Since the 1970s, the CAFE standards had been uniform; that is, the same standard applied to all automobile manufacturers. The percentage approach in Senator Bryan's bill would impose considerably higher fuel economy standards on Japanese and Korean auto companies than on their U.S. competitors. It would hit the Japanese companies hard, coming just after they had introduced their new luxury models. Senator Bryan's bill would result in a 2001 standard of 45.0 for Toyota and 37.0 for Ford. Only a few of the very smallest cars achieved 40 miles per gallon.

Senator Bryan supported the percentage approach because the imports were "moving aggressively backwards" in fuel economy. The percentage approach was also supported by some environmentalists, who also saw it as preventing the Japanese auto companies from backsliding. Both Ford and Chrysler preferred the percentage approach over uniform standards, while GM continued to oppose any fuel economy standards. The environmentalists were confident. "The car industry is going to fight like hell, but so are we," said Daniel Becker, of the Sierra Club. "And I think Congress is going to conclude they need to tighten up CAFE . . ."[2]

On April 3, 1990, the Senate Commerce Committee passed S. 1224 on a 14 to 4 vote reflecting bipartisan support, despite personal lobbying by Ford Chairman Harold A. Poling. Ford had also hired pro-

---

[1]Light truck standards were not addressed in the Bryan bill.

[2]*The Wall Street Journal,* April 4, 1990.

fessional lobbyists, including William Coleman, former secretary of transportation, and Lloyd Cutler, who had served as White House counsel during the Carter administration. The industry had also generated grassroots pressure by establishing organizations that solicited letters from constituents of key senators. For example, an organization calling itself "Nevadans for Fair Fuel Economy Standards" sent over 10,000 letters to Senator Bryan opposing higher fuel economy standards. Senator Bryan accused the industry of conducting the letter-writing campaign "under false colors." GM spokesman William Noack defended the campaign as "a very straightforward, above-board educational program."

The Bryan bill was scheduled for a final passage vote in the Senate in September. Legislation similar to S. 1224 was under consideration in the House, and a hearing was scheduled for July. The House Commerce Committee was chaired by Representative John Dingell (D-MI), who had close ties to the United Auto Workers and whose district included Ford's headquarters in Dearborn. Representative Dingell had frequently been successful in warding off threats to the auto industry when they jeopardized the interests of union members.

REACTIONS TO S. 1224

The automobile companies were unanimous in their opposition to the magnitude of the increase in the Bryan bill. In their assessment, the bill would require either the downsizing of models and/or major new technological advances. The fuel economy level that could reasonably be attained was the subject of disagreement. Steve Plotkin of the Office of Technology Assessment (OTA) stated:

> I am willing to state a number, 33 miles per gallon by 1995, as a starting point in the complex process of choosing an appropriate fuel economy target for the U.S. fleet. Thirty-three miles per gallon represents OTA's best estimate of the new automobile fleet fuel economy that can be attained.[3]

OTA's assessment was not shared by other agencies. For example, Linda G. Stuntz, deputy undersecretary of the Department of Energy, stated, "The Department of Energy estimates that a reasonable range of model year 1995 fuel economy is 29 to 31 miles per gallon . . ."[4]

Testifying for the Ford Motor Company, Helen O. Petrauskas, vice president for environmental and safety engineering, stated, "While S. 1224 addresses many of the inequities of the present CAFE regulations, the fuel economy standards in S. 1224 are far beyond levels that can reasonably be projected for full line manufacturers."[5]

At one level, the U.S. auto manufacturers opposed the CAFE system itself. Marina N. Whitman, vice president and group executive, stated General Motors's position and linked it to the global warming issue:

> We do not think it is possible . . . to fix the CAFE program. CAFE fails because the law pressures producers to build still more fuel efficient vehicles without creating incentives for consumers to buy them. . . . We believe the use of "command and control" regulatory strategies, such as CAFE, are either ineffective or unnecessarily costly. For this reason, and in considering responses to global warming concerns, we have suggested a comprehensive fee approach be considered. Such a greenhouse or carbon fee merits discussion, since it could be assessed on each primary fuel—that is, coal, oil, natural gas—in proportion to its carbon content per energy unit.[6]

U.S. auto manufacturers argued that the percentage approach placed an equal burden on all manufacturers. R.R. Boltz, Chrysler's vice president for Advanced Product and Operations Planning, stated, "The percentage increase approach is a laudable improvement compared to an absolute CAFE standard because the burden of achieving further fuel economy or fleet fuel economy increases will be distributed equally among all manufacturers."[7]

---

[3]Hearing on the Motor Vehicle Fuel Efficiency Act of 1989, Subcommittee on the Consumer, Committee on Commerce, Science, and Transportation, U.S. Senate, Washington, D.C., September 7, 1989, p. 11.

[4]Hearing, Subcommittee on Energy and Power, Committee on Energy and Commerce, House of Representatives, Washington, D.C., July 13, 1989, p. 3.

[5]Hearing on the Motor Vehicle Fuel Efficiency Act of 1989, Subcommittee on the Consumer, Committee on Commerce, Science, and Transportation, U.S. Senate, Washington, D.C., September 7, 1989, p. 176.

[6]Ibid., p. 145–146.

[7]Ibid., p. 129.

Japanese auto manufacturers argued that their greater fuel efficiency was due only in part to their smaller cars and that a large part resulted from technological advances. Honda said that the 1989 Civic, made in Ohio, was approximately the same size and weight as the 1979 Accord, yet achieved 35 mpg compared with the 1979 model's 28 mpg. The technological advances included turbochargers and multi-valve engines.

Toyota strongly opposed the percentage approach under the banner that "No good deed goes unpunished. . . . The more technologically advanced a manufacturer is at this point in time, the harder it will be to achieve additional increases in fuel economy. That is, if a manufacturer has already made significant commitments to technology, there is little left that will not require either more advanced technology or production of vehicles which will not meet consumer demands. To put it bluntly, this approach penalizes those who are most advanced and benefits those who are not as advanced."[8]

Toyota pointed to another problem with the percentage approach. "The approach proposed in S. 1224 would destroy any incentive a manufacturer might have for exceeding the standard in future years, for fear that their performance might become a new baseline for future legislation. This is a dangerous precedent which would be counterproductive to the task of cleaning the environment, promoting safety, and conserving energy."[9]

Approximately 10,000 U.S. businesses were involved in the sale and service of imported automobiles, employing 300,000 American workers with an annual payroll of $7 billion. The American International Automobile Dealers Association (AIADA) argued that "Driving Japanese firms out of the mid-sized and luxury car markets, as a percentile increase could do, would free domestic manufacturers from price competition in those fields. The additional costs to consumers sure to result from this could be of a magnitude comparable to the expense of the Japanese voluntary restraint agreement, which costs U.S. car buyers as much as $12 billion per year."[10] The Automobile Importers of America added: "[The percentage approach] represents a radical departure from previous legislative and regulatory actions to control the automobile industry. It has always been the practice of the government to set uniform performance standards for all auto makers to meet. This bill would alter this evenhanded approach by varying the difficulty of requirements by manufacturer."[11]

Nissan, which had a 1988 base year CAFE of 30.4 mpg, also argued that the percentage approach would be unfair. "Nissan has already incorporated most of the significant, available fuel economy technologies, so our remaining options for further fuel economy improvements would be (1) downsizing, or (2) incorporating unproven and potentially very costly technology."[12]

Citing data that Ford had increased its imports from 1,300 to 215,000 and GM had increased its imports from zero to 325,000 as the CAFE standard was reduced from 27.5 to 26.0 in 1986, Clarence Ditlow, director of the Center for Auto Safety, stated: "If anything, relaxation of the CAFE standards allows the domestic auto companies to export small car production and United States jobs abroad . . . Unless CAFE standards are increased, the future looks bleak for the American worker."[13] Ditlow's center had proposed to DOT that the CAFE standard be increased to 55 mpg by 2001. Ditlow also questioned the credibility of the U.S. auto industry. He cited 1974 testimony by Ford that the CAFE "proposal would require a Ford product line consisting of either all sub-Pinto-sized vehicles or some mix of vehicles ranging from a sub-sub-compact to perhaps a Maverick."

President Owen Bieber of the United Auto Workers expressed concern about fuel economy and outsourcing:

> The UAW would like to see a revised fuel economy law which guarantees real improvements in fuel efficiency by all companies, which

[8]Hearing on Global Warming and CAFE Standards, Committee on Commerce, Science, and Transportation, U.S. Senate, Washington, D.C., May 2, 1989, p. 306.

[9]Hearing on the Motor Vehicle Fuel Efficiency Act of 1989, Subcommittee on the Consumer, Committee on Commerce, Science, and Transportation, U. S. Senate, Washington D.C., September 7, 1989, p. 147.

[10]Hearing on Global Warming and CAFE Standards, Committee on Commerce, Science, and Transportation, U.S. Senate, Washington, D.C., May 2, 1989, p. 295.

[11]Hearing on the Motor Vehicle Fuel Efficiency Act of 1989, Subcommittee on the Consumer, Committee on Commerce, Science, and Transportation, U. S. Senate, Washington, D.C., September 7, 1989, p. 240.

[12]Hearing on Global Warming and CAFE Standards, Committee on Commerce, Science, and Transportation, U.S. Senate, Washington, D.C., May 2, 1989, p. 329.

[13]Ibid., pp. 264–265.

does not create incentives to source large cars abroad, which provides incentives to build small cars in the U.S. and does not put full-line producers in a position to argue that the law places them at a competitive disadvantage in today's changed market . . . One issue of primary UAW concern which your bill fails to address directly is the continual outsourcing of small cars. While our main concern is the thousands of jobs this trend has cost us over the last ten years, small car outsourcing is more than a jobs issue. It also threatens our automotive base in the long run.[14]

The Energy Conservation Coalition (ECC), representing 19 activist and environmental interest groups, supported the Bryan bill but called for even higher standards. Testifying on S. 1224, Brooks B. Yeagar, vice president for government affairs of the National Audubon Society, announced the ECC's support for the bill but urged "a 65 percent increase in average fuel economy for each manufacturer, or approximately 45 mpg overall for new cars and 35 mpg for new light trucks by the year 2000 . . . " Yeagar also commented on the ECC's concern for the United Auto Workers:

> The United Auto Workers has been a constructive force in the fuel economy discussions over a long period of time, and they are in a tricky position, and I think I would like to say on the part of the environmental community that we are very sympathetic with the problem that they have with outsourcing.
>
> We think that there are ways to solve that and we think, in fact, that a fuel economy bill structured along the lines of yours [Bryan's] can ultimately help with that problem. One way to do that might be to adopt a simple anti-backsliding provision that makes it clear, that makes it impossible for the manufacturers to solve momentary CAFE problems by shifting large cars into the foreign fleet.[15]

An alternative to higher CAFE standards was to increase taxes and let market forces dictate which automobiles would be purchased and produced. The Congressional Budget Office (CBO) studied a "carbon tax," such as GM supported, that would impose an excise tax on carbon fuels. The CBO estimated that to maintain the current level of carbon dioxide (CO_2) emissions, an excise tax of 60 percent of the current price of coal and 8 percent of the current price of gasoline would be required. The CBO also estimated that reducing CO_2 emissions by 20 percent would cost between $800 billion and $3.6 trillion during the next century.

ASSIGNMENT

You are to assume the role of a member on a task force of either the Ford Motor Company or the Nissan Motor Co., Ltd., of Japan. The task force has been formed by the CEO to address the CAFE standards issue. You are not to be constrained by the positions taken so far by Ford or Nissan. Your specific assignment is to (1) formulate an effective and responsible strategy to address the CAFE standards issue, (2) specify how that strategy is to be implemented, and (3) support your proposed strategy and its implementation with an analysis of the politics of the CAFE standards issue. That analysis is intended to provide the CEO with enough information to assess the appropriateness and likely effectiveness of your recommended strategy.

The Ford Motor Company had 366,600 employees, 175,100 of them in the United States. Ford operated 13 plants in North America and had 5,427 dealers. In 1989 Ford sold 6.4 million cars, trucks, and tractors, compared with 6.5 million in 1988. Ford had profits of $3.8 billion on sales of $96.1 billion, compared with profits of $5.3 billion on sales of over $92.4 billion in 1988.

Nissan Motor Co., Ltd., of Japan had three units in the United States. The Nissan Motor Manufacturing Corporation U.S.A. employed 3,300 workers in its plant in Smyrna, Tennessee, which had a production capacity of 240,000 vehicles a year. Nissan Motor Corporation U.S.A., located in Carson, California, was responsible for the distribution of Nissan vehicles in the United States and had 2,140 employees in 13 facilities across the country. Nissan Research and Development Corporation employed 260 people in Farmington Hills, Michigan, and was responsible for the design of vehicles for the U.S. market. Nissan also had 12 other facilities in the United States, employing 1,200 people, and its 1,000 dealers employed 47,000 people. ■

---

[14]Hearing on Motor Vehicle Fuel Efficiency Act of 1989, Subcommittee on the Consumer, Committee on Commerce, Science, and Transportation, U.S. Senate, Washington, D.C., September 7, 1989, pp. 42–43.

[15]Ibid., p. 90.

APPENDIX A

CAFE Formula

The CAFE standard is the number of fleet miles driven divided by the number of gallons of gasoline consumed, under the assumption that all autos are driven the same number of miles and under the same mix of city and highway driving. For example, if a manufacturer produces 200,000 units of model A with an mpg of 25 and 100,000 units of model B with an mpg of 40, the total number of gallons of gasoline consumed if each auto is driven 10,000 miles a year is 105 million gallons. The total miles driven is 3 billion, so the CAFE is

$$\text{CAFE} = \frac{3{,}000{,}000{,}000}{105{,}000{,}000} = 28.57$$

The CAFE formula may also be expressed as

$$\text{CAFE} = \frac{\text{total units produced}}{\dfrac{\text{units of model A}}{\text{model A mpg}} + \dfrac{\text{units of model B}}{\text{model B mpg}}}$$

APPENDIX B

CAFE Standards under S. 1224

COMPANY	*1988 CAFE*	*1995–2000*	*2001–*
BMW	21.6	27.5	30.2
Chrysler (D)	28.4	34.1	39.8
Ford (D)	26.4	31.7	37.0
General Motors (D)	27.6	33.1	38.6
Honda	32.0	38.4	44.8
Hyundai	35.0	40.0	45.0
Isuzu	32.6	39.1	45.0
Jaguar	22.0	27.5	30.8
Mazda	28.7	34.4	40.2
Mercedes-Benz	21.3	27.5	29.8
Mitsubishi	29.8	35.8	41.7
Nissan	30.8	37.0	43.1
Peugeot	23.4	28.1	32.8
Porsche	24.7	29.6	34.6
Saab	26.5	31.8	37.1
Subaru	31.8	38.2	44.5
Toyota	32.6	39.1	45.0
Volkswagen	30.3	36.4	42.4
Volvo	26.0	31.2	36.4

Note: D = Domestic
Source: National Highway Traffic Safety Administration

PART II

Integrative Case

Proposition 211: Securities Litigation Referendum (A)

Our attitude was, 'We don't like the way the political game is played so we're just not going to play it.' But you know what? It's the only game there is. And if you don't play, you get what you deserve. We can't just bury our heads in the sand and assume that what we don't know won't hurt us.

—Tom Proulx[1]

In late July 1996, business leaders in Silicon Valley were anxious. A statewide ballot initiative, Proposition 211, had been certified and placed on California's November 5 ballot. The initiative had been sponsored by attorney Bill Lerach, whose firm, Milberg, Weiss, Bershad, Hynes & Lerach ("the Lerach firm"), had represented plaintiffs in lawsuits against 53 of the top 100 Silicon Valley companies since 1989. A typical lawsuit alleged that a company had committed securities fraud that had harmed shareholders. Executives generally viewed the allegations as without merit and intended to extract a settlement from the company. The trigger for a lawsuit was usually a drop in the company's share price. Said Intel chairman Gordon Moore, "There are only two kinds of companies in Silicon Valley, those that have been sued and those that are going to be sued."[2] Regardless of whether a company had been sued, nearly every Silicon Valley executive recognized the threat of being "Lerach-ed," the term used when a firm was served with such a lawsuit.

Proposition 211 would change state securities laws to make it easier for plaintiffs to prevail in shareholder securities litigation and would heighten liability provisions against a company's directors and officers as well as so-called "aiders and abettors," which could include accountants, underwriters, and other professional services firms.

Tom Proulx, a cofounder of software maker Intuit, was joined by several other business leaders who had volunteered to fight Prop 211—John Doerr, a venture capitalist with Kleiner Perkins Caufield & Byers; John Dean, CEO of Silicon Valley Bank; and

[1] *Los Angeles Times,* November 4, 1996.

[2] Taxpayers Against Frivolous Lawsuits, "License to Destroy" videotape.

John Young, former CEO and chairman of Hewlett Packard. Silicon Valley had developed a reputation for political naiveté, preferring to avoid politics and focus on business and technology. Although Silicon Valley leaders had successfully lobbied some issues in the past, notably issues such as semiconductor trade and stock option accounting, they had never successfully waged a statewide electoral campaign. What strategy would be the most likely to defeat the seasoned political opponent they faced in Bill Lerach and the almost $4 million proponents of the measure had already raised?

BACKGROUND

Shareholders have the right under the Securities Act of 1933 to file suit against public corporations for fraudulent or misleading statements made by management and directors of a company. For example, suppose management announced that it expected continued strong demand for a product line when in fact it knew of underlying factors that might significantly jeopardize sales. When the underlying factors materialized in the form of lower than expected sales, a company's stock price might fall. The drop in the share price could then be cited as damage to the shareholder—a loss of value resulting from the shareholder's purchase of the stock at a price "inflated" by management's fraudulent representations to the shareholders. Lerach had turned this logic around by using a drop in share price to allege fraudulent representations and then using the discovery process to look for evidence to support the allegations.

Prior to 1988, to recover damages shareholders were required to both identify the specific fraudulent information they relied on in making their decisions to purchase the company's stock and to demonstrate that the losses they incurred resulted from their reliance on that information. In 1988, a Supreme Court ruling in *Basic Inc. v. Levinson,* 485 U.S. 224, 108 S.Ct. 978 (1988) changed the reliance requirement by embracing the concept of "fraud on the market." Fraud on the market theory posited that because financial analysts and intermediaries play a crucial role in gathering and interpreting company information, and because in an efficient market this information and its interpretation are incorporated into the price of a traded security, shareholders did not need to demonstrate reliance on specific corporate information to establish fraud. Instead, they could rely on the stock price as an indicator of the impact of such information. Consequently, shareholders could rely on a significant drop in the price of a company's stock as preliminary evidence that fraud had occurred.

Accountants, brokers, and insurers were often named as codefendants in securities class action suits as the so-called aiders and abettors. For example, during the U.S. banking crisis in the early 1990s many large accounting firms were alleged to have conspired with bank management in defrauding bank depositors of their funds. Plaintiffs could recover damages jointly and severally from all codefendants, regardless of the extent of their involvement in the alleged fraud. Thus, if a company became bankrupt or did not have sufficient funds to pay a proposed settlement, the professional services firms became liable for those amounts.

From April 1988 to September 1996, approximately 1,300 shareholder class action lawsuits were filed under Rule 10(b)5 of the Securities Act of 1933.[3] Sometimes lawsuits were filed within hours of a precipitous drop in a stock's price, for example 10 percent or more, regardless of whether the plaintiff had any knowledge or evidence of fraud on the part of management. Shortly after a complaint was filed, a discovery process would begin in which plaintiffs' counsel requested documents and information from the company. Discovery often included depositions of key management personnel.

If management believed the lawsuit was without merit, it would file a motion for dismissal on the basis of insufficient evidence to support plaintiffs' claims. Only about 10 percent of the actions filed were dismissed, however. If the motion were unsuccessful, management could defend the case through trial or settle out of court. This decision relied on several factors including management's and counsel's assessment of the evidence, the cost of defending a case through trial, the likelihood of winning a trial, and potential settlement costs. Many executives preferred settlement to the threat of overly burdensome judgments or the significant cost of discovery and defending through a trial. In one case litigated by Bill Lerach, a verdict of $100 million was ordered against Apple Computer and its officers after 8 years of legal proceedings. Apple appealed and the case was

[3]Investors also have the right to form a "class" of shareholders who have been exposed to allegedly fraudulent information (or, alternatively, the omission of truthful information). The class of shareholders can unite their claim under a single court proceeding and be represented by a single team of attorneys, typically referred to as plaintiffs' counsel.

eventually settled for $16 million. Tom Proulx commented on the decision executives faced in defending against a shareholder suit:

> Someone accuses you of fraud. You know with absolute certainty it's a lie. You want to fight, but then you find out you really don't have the opportunity. You're a dumb businessman if you fight it. No matter how good your case, there's uncertainty in a jury trial. You don't think you're going to lose, but we all know that anything can happen in front of a jury. If you lose, it can mean you're literally out of business. So you settle.[4]

In a study of 952 shareholder suits, 88 percent were settled, whereas only 1 percent were tried (11 percent were dismissed). The average settlement was $7.3 million, and the highest was $250 million. Plaintiffs' counsel typically received one-third of the settlement or the damages ordered by the court.

A lawsuit by one group of shareholders (the group that purchased stock under the allegedly fraudulent conditions) is essentially against another group of shareholders (shareholders that purchased their shares at all other times). Typically, a lawsuit also names as defendants the senior directors and officers who allegedly participated in the fraud. Since companies usually purchase insurance for such claims against their directors and officers, however, payments to the plaintiff class basically represent cash transfers from one group of shareholders to another, less court and attorney costs.

A relatively small number of law firms filed a very high proportion of these class action claims. From 1988 to 1996, three firms were involved in the filing of over 50 percent of the cases, and the Lerach firm was involved in over 30 percent. These firms had developed reputations among some executives as indiscriminate filers of frivolous lawsuits with the objective of extracting a settlement from companies so as to collect attorney's fees. Law firms often competed to be named lead counsel for the class. Some firms were said to have "stables" of "professional plaintiffs" who owned a few shares in several companies and would lend their names to lawsuits—sometimes without their immediate knowledge. The Lerach firm was reported to have represented a single individual in 12 separate class action suits.

[4] *Upside,* November 1996.

INDUSTRY ACTIONS

Growing discontent with the securities litigation process led to pressure from the business community for reforms of the Securities Act of 1933. A loose coalition comprised of groups such as the National Association of Manufacturers, the American Electronics Association, the NASDAQ Stock Market, the American Stock Exchange, the American Business Conference, the National Venture Capital Association, and the Biotechnology Industry Association formed to bring their concerns to the attention of Congress. In early 1994, Senators Christopher Dodd (D-CN) and Pete Domenici (R-NM) introduced a bipartisan bill on shareholder litigation reform, but the 103rd Congress ended without action beyond the committee stage. In the November 1994 elections Republicans gained a majority in both the House and Senate, campaigning on the "Contract with America." One plank of the contract called for shareholder litigation reform.

On February 27, 1995, Representative Thomas Bliley (R-VA), chair of the House Commerce Committee, introduced H.R. 1058, the Private Securities Litigation Reform Act of 1995 (PSLRA). A similar measure was introduced in the Senate. The House bill passed on March 8, and a Senate bill on shareholder litigation reform passed on June 28. The major provisions of the reform were as follows:

- Heightened pleading standards that made it more difficult for plaintiffs to allege securities fraud without having solid information on which to base such a claim
- A stay of discovery while a motion to dismiss was pending
- Designation as the "lead plaintiff" the one with the largest financial interests at stake, giving it the right to control the course of litigation and select the lead counsel for the class (The lead plaintiff would often be an institutional investor, such as a pension fund.)
- Creation of a limited "safe harbor" for the release of forward-looking information about a firm's prospects provided it is accompanied by "meaningful" cautionary language identifying factors that could cause actual results to differ materially from those projected (This provision was intended to prevent companies from being subject to class action litigation simply because their forecasts proved inaccurate.)
- Modification of the "fair share" rule of proportionate liability to limit the exposure of

accountants and underwriters named as codefendants in an action

- A provision to limit attorney's fees to a "reasonable percentage of the amount of recovery awarded the class" as determined by the court

Despite the lobbying efforts by the plaintiffs' bar, by early December the bills received conference committee approval and by votes of 65 to 30 in the Senate and 320 to 102 in the House the bill was sent to President Clinton. The President, citing concerns that the heightened pleadings standards would make it too difficult for defrauded investors to recover losses, vetoed the bill.[5] Three days later both the House (by a margin of 319 to 100) and Senate (by a margin of 68 to 30) had overridden the President's veto, and the PSLRA became law.

STATE VENUES

Although historically the number of securities class action cases filed in state courts was quite low compared with the number of federal cases, the prospective passage of the PSLRA made state courts relatively more attractive. In particular, the new pleadings requirements, safe harbor provisions, discovery stays, and certain other provisions of PSLRA might be avoided in state courts.

As the focus of litigation reform shifted from the federal to the state level, both proponents and opponents were active in California. The first move was made by a group of technology business leaders who sought additional protection for companies from securities litigation. These firms tended to have more volatile stock price behavior than the market as a whole and were targets because the volatility of their stock led to more frequent large stock price changes.[6] Utilizing the California initiative process, an organization calling itself the Alliance to Revitalize California qualified Propositions 201 and 202 for the March 1996 California primary.[7] The Alliance was chaired by Tom Proulx, who had taken leave from Intuit to pursue outside interests. Al Shugart, CEO of disk-drive manufacturer Seagate, was also on the Alliance's board of directors.

Proposition 201 would change state securities laws to require the losing party in any securities class action to pay the winner's attorney's fees and other litigation expenses.[8] By imposing a cost on plaintiffs who file and lose shareholder lawsuits, the measure was expected to discourage lawyers from bringing suits of questionable merit. Proposition 202 would limit attorney's fees in class action and other tort cases with the intent of increasing the incentives for plaintiffs to settle early and avoid the expense of drawn out procedures during which attorney's fees accumulate.

Propositions 201 and 202 were strongly opposed by plaintiffs' counsel. During the final weeks of the campaign, opponents utilized heavy television advertising with messages suggesting that business interests were attempting to build protection that would allow them to defraud investors and reap benefits by exercising personal stock options at prices inflated by their own fraudulent representations. In one television advertisement, the photographic image of Seagate CEO Al Shugart (whose management had been sued under securities laws) was "morphed" into the image of Charles Keating, who several years earlier had been convicted for defrauding bondholders of Lincoln Savings & Loan in a well-publicized case. Proponents of the measures had been less successful than the opponents in raising funds early in the campaign, and when money became available for television advertising only the less desirable media buys were available, such as cable channels and off-peak hours. On March 6, 1996, Prop 201 was defeated by a 59 to 41 percent margin. Prop 202 was more narrowly defeated, 51 to 49 percent.

DRAFTING OF PROPOSITION 211

In May 1995 a group headed by attorney Bill Lerach together with the Consumer Attorneys of California (formerly the California Trial Lawyers Association) drafted the preliminary text of its proposed ballot initiative, the "Pension and Retirement Fund Protection

[5]The plaintiffs' bar and trial lawyers associations were major contributors to the Democratic Party and President Clinton's campaign.

[6]Together, companies from the high-technology and financial services industries were named defendants in 53 percent of securities class action cases and both industries watched litigation reform developments closely.

[7]The process allows any group that succeeds in raising a required number of voter signatures to place a proposed law on the election ballot for voters to decide.

[8]This is similar to the British system for assigning attorney's fees.

Act." The act was drafted in response to Propositions 201 and 202 and to concerns raised by plaintiffs' counsel over proposed federal reforms. Soon after Congress's override of President Clinton's veto of the PSLRA, signature gathering began. The proposed law included the following provisions:

- Removal of "safe-harbor" protection for forward-looking statements by management
- Prohibition of the indemnification of directors and officers (Companies could not make insurance co-payments on behalf of directors and officers for settlements or judgments. This would leave directors and officers personally liable for damages.)
- Authorization of punitive damages, in addition to compensatory damages (Federal law prohibited punitive damages.)
- Authorization of private action against "aiders and abettors," including stock brokers, accounting firms, legal firms, and investor relation firms (Under current law only the Securities and Exchange Commission could bring such actions.)
- Establishment of full joint and several liability
- Elimination of an automatic stay of discovery
- Prohibition of any future regulation of attorney's fees in securities litigation or any other state action

Unlike other state securities laws, the initiative was not expressly limited to securities offers or sales in California. It was envisioned that a company could be sued by injured California residents even if the company was based outside California and conducted the alleged fraud outside the state. While these provisions would be subject to tests of constitutionality, the initiative was potentially applicable to all public corporations in the United States.

In June 1996 the proposition was qualified for the November 1996 ballot and became Proposition 211, popularly known as Prop 211.

PROPONENT'S STRATEGY

The Consumer Attorneys of California (CAOC) had long-established ties with leaders of the Democratic Party, and the Lerach firm in particular was a large donor to the Democratic Party. In the first half of 1996, Lerach and his firm gave over $465,000 to the Democratic National Committee. Lerach personally was the single largest trial-lawyer contributor in the country during the 1989 through 1995 time period, giving over $1.5 million, almost all to Democratic Party causes. A consultant's planning memorandum to leaders of the CAOC indicated that the proponents' strategy would rely heavily on its ties to the Democratic Party. Preliminary polls conducted by the consultants showed over 70 percent of those surveyed supported the measure.

Proponents of Prop 211 also sought the support of two important voter groups: seniors and unions. Both groups had significant assets invested in securities through pension funds and retirement savings plans. Both groups also were well organized politically within the state. Seniors and union members were expected to support Prop 211 because it would give them stronger means of recovering retirement funds lost as a result of fraud on the part of management. An organization known as Citizens for Retirement Protection and Security was formed to support Prop 211. In addition, the Congress of California Seniors endorsed Prop 211 and became a sponsor of the measure and signatory to the arguments that would accompany the proposition on the ballot. Proponents hoped that by bringing together these three politically active constituencies (seniors, unions, and the Democratic Party), voter support would follow.

Proponents of Prop 211 argued that it would benefit Californians by:

- making corporate officers' personal assets available to repay fraud victims
- making all parties fully liable for participating in a fraud
- restoring seniors' legal rights which had been usurped by federal law
- punishing only those executives who committed fraud

To support these messages, campaign literature and publications reminded voters of Charles Keating and the Lincoln Savings scandal, arguing that Prop 211 was necessary to protect future Keating-type victims. In addition, the campaign suggested that fraud among corporations and executives was rampant. A 1990 survey by the National Association of Accountants was cited indicating that 87 percent of corporate executives were willing to commit fraud, and a *San Jose Mercury News* survey was cited indicating that 45 percent of Silicon Valley executives had said their officers, directors, and large investors had violated SEC reporting regulations. Reference was also made to $1.74 billion in payments by Big Six accounting firms to federal government agencies, states, corporations, and individual investors in class action suits in the past 5 years. Jonathan Cunio, a congressional lobbyist for Lerach explained, "This is not just about punishing, this is about deterrence. Generally, in these cases, it is the top executives themselves who are making misrepresentations to the marketplace while pocketing millions of dollar in insider sales."[9] Supporters of the initiative insisted that honest officers and directors had nothing to fear from the initiative.

Responding to criticism that he had sponsored Prop 211 to mitigate the effects of federal reforms on his law practice, Lerach replied, "We have plenty of lawsuits that we are litigating. The reason we are supporting the initiative is that we think it is high time that someone stood up to these big corporations and accounting firms. Is it not better public policy for the state of California to have more protections for victims of fraud?"[10]

Proponents of Prop 211 succeeded in gaining the early support of several seniors and union groups, including the American Association of Retired Persons (AARP), the California State Employees Association, and several regional AFL-CIO councils. Proponents also secured the endorsement of the California Democratic Party.

By June 30, 1996, proponents had spent approximately $3.8 million on their organizational efforts to build support for the measure. No significant paid media campaigns had yet been undertaken. The proponents had retained political and media consulting services from several firms. A leading political consultant was Bill Carrick, who was also a top strategist for the Clinton presidential reelection campaign in California.

OPPONENTS' RESPONSE

In the fall of 1995, when proponents of Prop 211 began the drive to put an initiative before voters, a group calling itself Taxpayers Against Frivolous Lawsuit (TAFL), formed in opposition to the initiative. TAFL was initially led by Kirk West, president of the California Chamber of Commerce, and John Sullivan, president of the Association for California Tort Reform. With substantial financial support from the Big Six accounting firms, TAFL began conducting surveys and initiated campaign planning in December 1995. In a benchmark public opinion survey conducted for TAFL in December, 49 percent of respondents supported Prop 211 with 24 percent opposed and the rest undecided.

After the defeat of Propositions 201 and 202, the opponents' coalition broadened substantially as high-technology business interests became increasingly concerned about the potential impacts of Prop 211. The TAFL steering committee was expanded to include Tom Proulx. TAFL also retained the professional campaign management firm Goddard*Claussen/First Tuesday to help plan, manage, and implement the campaign. In July 1996 John Young, retired president and CEO of Hewlett Packard, was named the national chairman of TAFL. Young was a particularly respected executive among technology business leaders. He said, "Every company in the country lives with the threat of these frivolous lawsuits that serve only to drain the resources for thousands of good jobs. Proposition 211 would impact virtually every public company, not just those in California."[11]

Many executives were concerned about the effect of Prop 211 on the willingness of individuals to serve as directors, since it would make directors personally liable for damages and preclude companies from insuring them. Intel CEO Andy Grove said, "It's a horrendous notion. Boards will either not be able to attract good board members or they have to restructure . . . All is inimical to the interests of shareholders."[12] Separately, he warned, "Passage of Prop 211 would destroy corporate governance as we know it."[13] Venture capitalist John Doerr added,

> Three of the best CEO's I work with are resigning if Prop 211 passes. I can't pay them enough to take on that personal liability. Their vice presidents are resigning. And every one of my partners is resigning from the 40 boards on which we serve that are public. I am worried that if Prop 211 passes, it will be the undoing of

[9] *Wired,* November 1996.
[10] *Chicago Tribune,* June 23, 1996.
[11] *Eye on Global Management,* September 15, 1996.
[12] *Washington Post,* September 24, 1996.
[13] *Forbes,* August 26, 1996.

the risk-taking, reward-gaining entrepreneurial system that we use to build new growth companies.[14]

Citizens for Retirement Protection and Security spokesman Sean Crowley responded to these assertions stating, "That's just a scare tactic to raise money. No director or company officer who is innocent of wrongdoing is at risk. This only punishes those who steal people's retirements savings and pensions."[15] Melvyn Weiss, a partner in the Lerach law firm, suggested, "Corporate America knows that if it beats us, then it is home free to do anything it wants."[16]

PLANNING THE CAMPAIGN

To help create momentum for a successful campaign, leadership of the campaign in Silicon Valley was broadened to include several additional business leaders. John Doerr and John Dean joined Tom Proulx and John Young to lead fundraising and outreach efforts. In late July they met in their Silicon Valley campaign office. With the exception of Tom Proulx's experience in the March campaign, none had previously managed a political campaign. They noted the historic reluctance of the Silicon Valley business community to involve itself in political issues. Many of the business leaders had disdain for the political process, becoming involved only when immediately threatened by potential changes in the political environment. Would business leaders be motivated by the threats posed by Prop 211? Could this motivation be translated into active support for the campaign, financially and politically? How would these efforts be coordinated to present a united coalition to potential endorsers and voters?

As they met, they discussed the challenges before them:

- Proponents were well organized and appeared willing and able to raise significant funds for the campaign—initial estimates based on funds raised in opposition to Proposition 201 and 202 suggested up to $20 million.
- Proponents appeared likely to succeed in gaining the endorsements of seniors and union groups.
- Proponents had several "hot-button" messages that resonated well with potential voters, such as the Charles Keating scandal and the recent bankruptcy of Orange County in southern California.
- The initiative title and summary on the ballot were not viewed by opponents as a fair description of the actual initiative. Voters would need to be educated as to the potential effects of the initiative.[17]
- Opponents ran the risk of being perceived as protecting business interests at the expense of investors and retirees.
- Voters had rejected securities litigation reform sponsored by business interests in the March elections.

Campaign leaders also considered their strategic assets:

- History had shown that a "no" vote was easier to obtain on California ballot measures than a "yes" vote. Moreover, proponents would need to demonstrate to voters that there was a major problem with current securities laws—so dramatic that it required a ballot measure to fix. Preliminary research by opponents suggested this would be difficult.
- According to research studies, trial lawyers were in general not well liked in California. Both the Consumer Attorneys of California and California Trial Lawyers Association were at the very bottom of the credibility scale among nearly 80 individuals and groups in a recent study.

[14] *Financial World,* October 21, 1996.
[15] *San Francisco Chronicle,* September 13, 1996.
[16] *Business Week,* August 26, 1996.

[17] The title and summary are what appear on the ballot itself and in voters' election guides. The title and summary must be approved by the state attorney general. Proponents of Prop 211 had submitted the initiative as the "Retirement Savings and Consumer Protection Act." California Attorney General Dan Lungren, a Republican, changed the initiative title to "Attorney-Client Fee Arrangements. Securities Fraud. Initiative Statute." The summary read: "Prohibits restrictions on attorney-client fee arrangements, except as allowed by laws existing on January 1, 1995. Prohibits deceptive conduct by any person in securities transactions resulting in loss of retirement funds, savings. Imposes civil liability, punitive damages. Fiscal impact: Probably minor net fiscal impact on state and local government." Proponents of Prop 211 lost a suit filed against the state for having made changes in the title and description. Nonetheless, Prop 211 opponents did not view the title or description as accurately describing the intent or potential effects of the initiative.

- Nearly 20 ballot measures had qualified for the November ballot. It was anticipated that voters would experience some confusion, which could encourage "no" votes.
- Opponents' support came from a broad base of industries representing significant financial, information, and communication resources—if they could be tapped.

Campaign leaders needed a strategy built on these assets that would prevail against the proponents of Prop 211. ■

PREPARATION QUESTION

1. What strategy should the campaign leaders adopt and how should it be implemented?

PART III

Government and Markets

CHAPTER 9

Antitrust: Economics, Law, and Politics

Introduction

Antitrust policy is an amalgam of social policy, economics, law, administrative practice, and schools of thought.[1] Antitrust policy had its origins in the populist movement of the 1870s when a number of states enacted statutes to regulate economic activity and control the exercise of economic power. At the federal level, this movement led to the Interstate Commerce Act of 1887, which provided for federal regulation of interstate commerce, and the Sherman Act of 1890, the first federal antitrust statute. These acts resulted from political pressure by farmers and others concerned about railroad cartels, the railroads' pricing practices, and the distribution of power between farmers and railroads. The laws thus represent both social and economic policy.

As social policy, the antitrust laws express concern about concentrations of economic power and the potential for abuse inherent in that concentration. This parallels concern about the concentration of political power and the preference for its dispersion in the electorate and among the institutions of government. Just as the Constitution controls political power through checks and balances among the branches of government and through popular elections, antitrust policy has focused on controlling economic power.

Antitrust policy also reflects economic policy. Antitrust is concerned with the structure of markets, the conduct of market participants, and the resulting performance of those markets. Antitrust economics has both a theoretical and an empirical component. Theory has been an indispensable guide to reasoning about the relationships among structure, conduct, and performance; and empirical research has provided evidence about those relationships.

Antitrust law includes statutes and the court decisions interpreting those statutes. The principal federal statutes are the Sherman Act, the Clayton Act of 1914, and the Federal Trade Commission Act of 1914. These acts are broadly worded, employing such terms as "monopolization," "restraint of trade," and "unfair practices." This has required courts to interpret the acts in the context of the specifics of individual cases.[2] Antitrust law is thus both statutory and interpretive. It is also the subject of politics as interest groups, politicians, and public policy specialists attempt to influence the law.

Although there have been few major changes in the antitrust statutes in recent years, antitrust has not been static. Change results from its administration and enforcement. At the federal level, public enforcement is provided by the Antitrust Division of the U.S. Department of Justice (DOJ) and the Federal Trade Commission (FTC). During the 1980s the DOJ

[1]The antitrust policies of Japan and the European Community are considered in Chapters 13 and 14, respectively.
[2]See Carp and Stidham (1998) for information on the U.S. federal courts.

and the FTC made significant changes in antitrust policy through their merger guidelines, which revised the policies governing federal enforcement. Similarly, enforcement policies on vertical restraints of trade changed considerably. During the 1990s the pace of antitrust enforcement increased substantially. U.S. antitrust laws are enforced less by government, however, than by private litigants—often by one firm filing suit against another. Over 90 percent of the suits filed under the federal antitrust laws are brought by private litigants. Consequently, decisions made by courts on cases brought by private litigants cause antitrust law to evolve, even when there is no legislative or federal enforcement activity.

Much of the recent evolution of antitrust law, and of antitrust policy more broadly, has been the result of changing economic and legal thought about markets, business strategies, and performance. This thought has a coherence and perspective not necessarily found in the historical record of court decisions, and it has shaped a number of recent decisions. Three approaches, or schools of thought, to reasoning about antitrust are considered in this chapter.

The traditional or structural approach focuses on the structure of industries and on conduct that may foreclose opportunities or diminish competition. In the 1970s new understandings of the functioning of markets and the nature of competition were developed by the Chicago school of economics and had a major impact on antitrust enforcement and court decisions.[3] More recently, economists have challenged the conclusions of the Chicago school by considering more closely the consequences of informational asymmetries, network externalities, and strategic interactions among market participants. This perspective has qualified a number of the conclusions of the Chicago school.

These understandings of antitrust's purpose and its appropriate application are particularly important in the United States because of the adversarial nature of judicial proceedings. Both plaintiffs and defendants have incentives to make the best cases they can and to use whatever new understandings support their sides. Consequently, new theories and empirical evidence quickly find their way into court proceedings. Hearing these arguments, judges make decisions which at times are influenced by how compelling the theories are, in addition, of course, to the facts of the case, empirical evidence, and legal precedents. Antitrust law thus is also shaped by economic thought.

Antitrust policy has broad implications for management. Firms must conform to the law, but in many cases and for many practices, there is a considerable gray area in which the requirements of the law are unclear or untested. Similarly, because antitrust law evolves, a practice that once was allowable under the law may no longer be allowable. Other practices which were once illegal may no longer be. Legal counsel is thus essential when issues or practices may have antitrust implications. Managers, however, must have an understanding of antitrust law, enforcement practices, and antitrust thought, since they must recognize when a policy or practice may raise antitrust concerns. The purpose of this chapter is to provide an introduction to antitrust law and an understanding of antitrust thought, the forces that have shaped antitrust policy in recent years, and the forces that may shape its future development.

Antitrust Law and Enforcement

THE ANTITRUST STATUTES

The principal antitrust statutes, excerpts from which are presented in Figure 9-1, have remained largely intact for over 85 years. Section 1 of the Sherman Act pertains to unreasonable restraints of trade with a focus on joint conduct. Section 2 focuses on unilateral conduct and proscribes monopoly and attempts to monopolize. The Sherman

---

[3]Much of the theory was developed by economists and legal scholars at the University of Chicago.

Sherman Act

Section 1. Every contract, combination in the form of trust or otherwise, or conspiracy, in restraint of trade or commerce among the several States, or with foreign nations, is hereby declared to be illegal. . . . Every person who shall make any contract or engage in any combination or conspiracy hereby declared to be illegal shall be deemed guilty of a felony. . . .

Section 2. Every person who shall monopolize, or attempt to monopolize, or combine or conspire with any other person or persons, to monopolize any part of the trade or commerce among the several States, or with foreign nations, shall be deemed guilty of a felony. . . .

Clayton Act

Section 2. (a) That it shall be unlawful for any person engaged in commerce . . . to discriminate in the price between different purchasers . . . where the effect of such discrimination may be substantially to lessen competition or tend to create a monopoly in any line of commerce, or to injure, destroy or prevent competition . . . nothing herein contained shall prevent differentials which make only due allowance for differences in the cost of manufacture, sale, or delivery. . . .

Section 3. That it shall be illegal for any person [to enter an arrangement] . . . on the condition . . . that the lessee or purchaser thereof shall not use or deal in the goods . . . of a competitor or competitors, where the effect . . . may be to substantially lessen the competition or tend to create a monopoly in any line of commerce.

Section 7. That no corporation engaged in commerce shall acquire, directly or indirectly, the whole or any part of the stock or other share capital . . . where in any line of commerce in any section of the country, the effect of such acquisition may be substantially to lessen competition, or tend to create monopoly.*

Federal Trade Commission Act

Section 5. (a)(1) Unfair methods of competition in commerce, and unfair or deceptive acts or practices in commerce, are hereby declared unlawful.**

*As amended by the Celler-Kefauver Act of 1950.

**As amended by the Wheeler-Lea Act of 1938.

FIGURE 9-1 Excerpts from the Antitrust Statutes

Act thus pertains to the reality of monopoly or restraints on trade and to the process of obtaining a monopoly.

The Clayton Act goes further by addressing potentially anticompetitive actions. The Clayton Act contains terms such as "may be" and "tend to," which address monopolization and restraints in their incipiency. The Federal Trade Commission Act goes beyond the other two acts by prohibiting unfair methods of competition and unfair or deceptive acts and practices. The broad language employed leaves considerable room for interpretation and thus a substantial role for the courts.[4]

The Sherman Act does not provide for private lawsuits, but Section 4 of the Clayton Act states "that any person who shall be injured in his business or property by reason of anything forbidden in the antitrust laws may sue therefore in any district court of the United States. . . ." This allows private parties to bring lawsuits for practices that are illegal under either the Sherman Act or the Clayton Act. Section 4 also provides for treble damages. Section 7 of the Clayton Act prohibits mergers that may substantially lessen competition or create a monopoly.

The Robinson-Patman Act of 1934 strengthened Section 2 of the Clayton Act's prohibition of price discrimination. The Robinson-Patman Act was intended to protect small businesses and merchants from their larger competitors, which were able to obtain lower prices on their supplies. Small grocers, for example, sought protection from

[4]See Areeda and Kaplow (1997) for a comprehensive treatment of antitrust law.

supermarkets, which used their greater buying power to obtain lower prices. Critics of the Robinson-Patman Act claim that it causes firms to be wary of price competition, resulting in higher prices for consumers. Proponents, however, contend that it is necessary to prevent small firms from being driven out of business and thereby increasing concentration and lessening competition.

Practices that come under the antitrust laws are classified as *horizontal* or *vertical.* A horizontal practice is one that involves activities in the same industry. A merger, for example, is horizontal if the two firms operate in the same industry. Horizontal arrangements include monopolization, predatory pricing, price fixing, bid rigging, the allocation of customers, and group boycotts. The concern with horizontal arrangements is that they may increase market power, leading to lessened competition and higher prices.

Vertical practices are those involving firms in a supply arrangement or a channel of distribution. Vertical practices include the allocation of territories by a manufacturer among distributors or retailers, refusals to deal, exclusive dealing arrangements, retail price maintenance, reciprocal arrangements, and tying. Vertical practices also include the merger of a manufacturer and a supplier or distributor. Figure 9-2 provides brief definitions of the principal practices of concern under the antitrust laws.

EXAMPLE: MICROSOFT AND MONOPOLY

Monopoly is the subject of Section 2 of the Sherman Act. In *United States v. Aluminum Co. of America,* 148 F2d 416 (2d Cir 1945), Judge Learned Hand stated that the fact of monopoly, and not the abuse of monopoly power, was sufficient and formulated a two-step procedure for deciding monopolization cases under Section 2 of the Sherman Act.[5] The first step is to determine if the defendant has a monopoly, using market shares, for example. The second step is to determine if the monopoly was willfully acquired or the result of "superior skill, foresight and industry."

> [t]he offense of monopoly . . . has two elements: (1) the possession of monopoly power in the relevant market and (2) the willful acquisition or maintenance of that power as distinguished from growth or development as a consequence of a superior product, business acumen, or historical accident.

In 1990 the FTC began an investigation of the competitive practices of the Microsoft Corporation, centering on whether it had gained a monopoly, used anticompetitive practices such as price discounting copies of operating systems sold with personal computers, or had an unfair advantage through the linking of operating systems software with applications software. Some of Microsoft's competitors sought to have the company broken into two parts, one for operating systems and the other for applications. After a 30-month investigation, the FTC deadlocked on a 2-to-2 vote on whether to take action against Microsoft.

The DOJ then decided to undertake its own investigation, and in 1995 reached a consent decree with Microsoft imposing modest changes in its marketing practices, such as requiring Microsoft to allow computer manufacturers to offer their customers a choice of operating systems.[6] The monopolization concerns did not survive the two-step test. Microsoft contended that it did not have "market power in the traditional antitrust sense. Anyone can come in and upset you with better technology." Microsoft also maintained that its marketing practices, such as offering large discounts, were not anticompetitive but were standard practice.[7]

---

[5]Early cases broke up the oil (*Standard Oil Co. v. United States,* 221 U.S. 1 (1911)) and tobacco (*United States v. American Tobacco Co.,* 221 U.S. 106 (1911)) monopolies.
[6]See Gilbert (1999) for an analysis of this case.
[7]A federal judge rejected the consent decree on the grounds that the restrictions placed on Microsoft were insufficient. The DOJ successfully appealed the ruling, and the consent decree was approved.

Horizontal

Horizontal merger—A merger is horizontal if it involves two firms in the same industry. A horizontal merger comes under Section 7 of the Clayton Act and under Section 2 of the Sherman Act, if it would create a monopoly.

Horizontal price fixing (collusion)—Horizontal price fixing includes explicit or implicit agreements to control prices in an industry or with respect to a product. Horizontal price fixing comes under Section 1 of the Sherman Act.

Monopoly—Concerted efforts to monopolize come under the purview of Section 1 of the Sherman Act, and the unilateral attempt to monopolize comes under Section 2 of the Sherman Act.

Price discrimination—Price discrimination involves charging customers different prices that are not justified by cost differences of serving those customers. Price discrimination comes under Section 2 of the Clayton Act, as amended by the Robinson-Patman Act.

Vertical

Boycotts and refusals to deal—A manufacturer refuses to sell to a distributor or a retailer. If two or more parties agree to refuse to deal with another party, it is a boycott. These practices are considered under Section 1 of the Sherman Act.

Exclusive dealing—A manufacturer grants another firm an exclusive right to distribute or market a particular product. Exclusive dealing comes under Section 3 of the Clayton Act.

Exclusive territory—A manufacturer grants an exclusive territory to a seller, and no other seller is permitted to sell in the territory. Exclusive territories come under Section 1 of the Sherman Act.

Resale price maintenance—A manufacturer requires a retailer to sell only at a price at least as high as a price it specifies. Such cases come under Section 1 of the Sherman Act.

Tying—Tying is the practice of bundling one product with another. For example, Mercedes-Benz requires its dealers to carry only Mercedes-Benz parts.* Tying arrangements come under Section 3 of the Clayton Act.

Vertical integration—Vertical integration involves the joining together, in terms of a merger or venture, of firms at various stages of a production process or channel of distribution. A vertical merger comes under Section 7 of the Clayton Act.** A vertical contract that forecloses or restrains competition comes under Section 3 of the Clayton Act.

Conglomerate

Conglomerate merger—A conglomerate merger involves two firms that do not operate in the same industries either as competitors or as part of a channel of distribution or supply. Conglomerate mergers come under Section 7 of the Clayton Act. The concern in the case of a conglomerate merger is the elimination of a potential competitor.***

*The DOJ dropped its antitrust suit against Mercedes-Benz because it concluded that a tying arrangement could only be anti-competitive if it is based on horizontal market power.

**See *Brown Shoe Co. v. U.S.,* 294 (1962), where the Supreme Court invalidated the merger between Brown Shoe and the G. R. Kinney retail chain.

***See *Federal Trade Commission v. Procter & Gamble Co.,* 368 U.S. 568(1967).

FIGURE 9-2 Arrangements and Practices

By 1998 Microsoft had a more dominant presence in the operating system and software markets. As addressed in Chapter 2, issues of monopolization and anticompetitive practices were raised about Microsoft. The chapter case *The Microsoft Antitrust Case* addresses these issues.[8]

[8]Monopolization cases are rarely brought. The most recent case prior to the Microsoft case was against IBM for monopolization of the computer industry. That case was filed on the last day of the Johnson administration in 1969.

EXEMPTIONS

A number of exemptions from the antitrust laws are provided. The Norris-LaGuardia Act of 1932 strengthened the statutory exemption that the Clayton Act provided to unions. The economic activities of labor unions taken in their own interest, such as strikes, are protected.

Exemptions are also provided for agricultural cooperatives and for certain activities of industries such as insurance, which are regulated by government.[9] Exemptions for joint export trading activities are also provided under the Webb-Pomerene Act of 1918 and the Export Trading Company Act of 1982. A partial antitrust exemption was established for joint research and development ventures such as Sematech. Exemptions can also be provided by specific legislation, as in the Soft Drink Interbrand Competition Act considered later in the chapter.

Baseball did not have a statutory exemption from the antitrust laws but was protected by a 1922 Supreme Court decision, which had been upheld in subsequent decisions because the court has believed that it is the role of Congress, not the court, to change the antitrust status of baseball.[10] In 1998 Congress eliminated the antitrust exemption for baseball.

GOVERNMENT ENFORCEMENT OF THE ANTITRUST LAWS

Both the DOJ and the FTC have the authority to enforce the Sherman and Clayton Acts, but only the FTC can enforce the Federal Trade Commission Act.[11] Their dual enforcement responsibilities led the DOJ and the FTC to reach an interagency liaison agreement in 1948. As a result of the agreement, cases are allocated according primarily to industry and secondarily to the nature of the complaint.[12] For example, the DOJ has enforcement responsibility for software and the FTC for semiconductors, so the DOJ has filed the antitrust suits against Microsoft and the FTC filed an antitrust action against Intel. Most enforcement activities are civil rather than criminal, and only the DOJ can bring criminal charges under the antitrust laws. Bringing criminal charges requires a grand jury indictment, and the standards of proof are higher than in a civil case. Three Archer-Daniels-Midland executives were convicted of criminal price fixing in 1998.

In criminal cases, the available penalties are fines and imprisonment. In civil cases, fines can be imposed, contracts dissolved, business units ordered divested, injunctive relief obtained, and consent decrees granted. The courts not only decide cases but also approve consent decrees, such as that which split AT&T into seven regional operating companies and a residual AT&T.[13] The DOJ can enforce the antitrust laws only through lawsuits filed in federal courts, but the FTC has authority to issue orders without court action. The FTC can also seek injunctions in federal court, for example, to block a proposed merger.[14]

---

[9]The exemption for the insurance industry is provided in the McCarron-Ferguson Act, and the exemption for agricultural cooperatives is provided by the Capper-Volstad Act of 1922.
[10]See *Federal Baseball Club of Baltimore v. National League of Professional Baseball Clubs,* 259 U.S.200 (1991), *Toolson v. New York Yankees Inc.,* 346 U.S. 356 (1953), and *Flood v. Kuhn,* 407 U.S. 258 (1972).
[11]Technically the FTC has no authority to enforce the Sherman Act, but in practice it does. The courts have held that practices violating the Sherman Act constitute "unfair" methods of competition under Section 5 of the Federal Trade Commission Act.
[12]See Shugart (1990, p. 947).
[13]A consent decree is an agreement reached by the litigants under the sanction of a court and does not involve a judicial determination, and hence does not signify a violation of the law. A consent decree generally involves restrictions on the actions of the defendant. It binds only the consenting parties and does not set a precedent for the courts.
[14]See Clarkson and Muris (1981) for an analysis of FTC policy and enforcement.

The FTC is an independent commission with five commissioners appointed, subject to Senate confirmation, by the president to 7-year terms. It can initiate its own investigations of practices it believes may violate the antitrust laws. As a consequence of an investigation, the FTC may negotiate a consent decree with a firm. If a firm refuses to agree to a consent decree, the FTC can continue the case through an administrative law procedure. A hearing is held before an administrative law judge, who issues an opinion and recommendations for action. The case is then decided by a majority vote of the commission.[15] As penalties, the FTC can issue cease and desist orders that have the effect of injunctions against the activity in question. If a firm violates an order, the FTC can impose fines. Both the orders issued by the FTC and the court decisions in cases brought by the DOJ can be appealed to the U.S. Court of Appeals.[16]

A consent order typically continues in effect indefinitely and requires the agreement of both parties and the court to lift or modify it.[17] With changing circumstances the order can restrict a firm's market strategy. In 1978 Levi Strauss & Co. entered into a consent order with the FTC to resolve complaints of anticompetitive behavior, including tying. The order effectively prevented the company from operating its own retail stores. The company changed its market strategy to include opening a line of stores, but first it had to obtain a change in the consent order. When the FTC agreed to amend the consent decree in 1994, Levi Strauss announced plans to open 200 retail stores.[18] In 1997 a federal court lifted, effective in 2001, a 1956 consent decree that had restricted IBM's sales and service practices on its mainframe and mid-range computers. The judge concluded that IBM's market power "has substantially diminished."

The 1974 Antitrust Procedures and Penalties Act classified as felonies violations such as price fixing and increased the allowable fines. Fines against corporations can be as high as $10 million per count in criminal cases. Individuals, including managers of corporations, can be fined up to $350,000 and can be imprisoned for up to 3 years. Since 1990 the federal government has been able to collect treble damages. Federal sentencing guidelines enacted in 1991 allow fines to be based on the amount of business affected in addition to other factors. In 1996 Archer-Daniels-Midland was fined $100 million for price fixing of lysine and citric acid, and in 1998 Intermation was fined $110 million for participating in an international cartel that fixed the prices of graphite electrodes.

The Hart-Scott-Rodino Antitrust Improvements Act of 1976 amended Section 7 of the Clayton Act to enhance the enforcement of the antitrust laws pertaining to monopolization and restraint of trade through mergers.[19] Hart-Scott-Rodino requires premerger notification if the acquirer will have a 15 percent stake or a $15 million investment in the acquired firm and the acquirer has either sales or assets of $100 million or the acquired firm has assets of at least $10 million. If the acquired firm is a manufacturer, the asset figure is replaced by sales of $10 million. The amendment requires that firms notify the DOJ and the FTC of their plans to merge. In 1998, 4,728 mergers were reported under Hart-Scott-Rodino. The merger cannot be completed for 30 days, and during this period the agencies can require the firms to submit information about the market effects of their merger. For example, the firms may be required to submit information about their market shares in the market segments in which they both participate. If the DOJ or FTC decides that there are grounds to challenge the merger, it seeks

[15]One difference between the enforcement by the DOJ and the FTC is that the DOJ abandons a case if it loses in court, for example, in an attempt to obtain an injunction to block a merger. If the FTC fails to obtain an injunction, it can use its administrative procedure to pursue the case.
[16]See Weaver (1977) for a study of FTC enforcement policy and Elzinga and Breit (1976) for a study of antitrust penalties.
[17]Consent decrees can have limited duration.
[18]Similarly, in 1994 Eastman Kodak was successful in having 1921 and 1954 consent decrees lifted, providing more flexibility in the marketing of film.
[19]See Federal Trade Commission (1990).

a preliminary injunction against it. In most cases, this convinces the firms to abandon their plans to merge. The chapter case *The Staples-Home Depot Merger?* concerns an FTC action to obtain a preliminary injunction against a merger.[20]

The Robinson-Patman Act prohibits price discrimination that is not justified by cost differences in serving customers. In addition to a cost difference defense, a firm can defend itself by arguing that the price discrimination was necessary to meet competition. The Clayton Act assigns the burden of proof in a price discrimination case to the plaintiff to show that there has been discrimination. Given a prima facie case, the defendant has the burden to show that the discrimination was justified by, for example, cost differences.[21]

The treble damages provision provides a strong incentive to file antitrust suits, and most suits are filed by firms against their competitors. If a suit is filed against a firm by the DOJ, private parties often follow with private suits. A court decision for the government is interpreted by the courts as providing a prima facie case against the defendant, greatly increasing the likelihood that private cases will be decided in favor of the plaintiffs.

During the past 20 years the DOJ and the FTC have effectively stopped enforcing the Robinson-Patman Act because of their view that the act stifles competition. The DOJ and the FTC have also stopped enforcing the prohibition against resale price maintenance, although private enforcement continues. Resale price maintenance pertains to restrictions imposed by manufacturers on the prices that can be charged by retailers. In the 1930s small retailers sought protection from price competition by having manufacturers establish minimum resale prices. States passed "fair trade laws" that required retailers to sell at the prices specified by contracts signed with manufacturers. The Miller-Tydings Act of 1937 allowed states to exempt price maintenance agreements from coverage under Section 1 of the Sherman Act as long as there was competition from other brands. The McGuire Act extended this to nonsigners of resale price contracts. In 1975, Congress repealed the Miller-Tydings and the McGuire Acts and withdrew the states' authority for fair trade laws. Court decisions on resale price maintenance are considered later in the chapter.

The explanation for the lack of government enforcement of the resale price maintenance and price discrimination provisions of the antitrust laws is found in the changing schools of antitrust thought considered later in the chapter. To indicate the type of case to which the DOJ and the FTC object, in the late 1970s Cuisinart was found to have violated the antitrust laws by requiring dealers of its food processors to maintain a minimum retail price. Cuisinart held a dominant share of the market for food processors at the time the suit was filed, but its share was largely due to it having developed the product. Cuisinart had no fundamental horizontal market power, as entry into the food processor market was easy. Furthermore, the high minimum price established by Cuisinart stimulated entry and quickly eroded its market share. Prices fell substantially. The retail price agreement, if it had continued, would likely have had little effect on the market for food processors. To clarify its policy, in 1985 the Antitrust Division of the DOJ issued revised guidelines indicating that it would not investigate vertical accords when a firm has less than a 10 percent market share. A market share above 10 percent could still lead to an investigation.

---

[20]In 1998 the DOJ filed an antitrust lawsuit against Northwest Airlines's acquisition of a controlling interest in Continental Airlines, and instead of requesting a preliminary injunction to block the acquisition, the DOJ agreed to Northwest putting the acquired shares of Continental in a trust for 6 years. The DOJ reasoned that in contrast to a merger which is costly to unwind, a stock acquisition can be easily reversed if the court were to rule against the merger.

[21]A prima facie case is one that needs no further demonstration.

In spite of the lack of enforcement against certain vertical arrangements, federal enforcement of the antitrust laws is active. In the 1990s the FTC became more active in initiating cases on misleading advertising. For example, it charged two manufacturers of athletic shoes with false advertising for labeling their shoes as made in the United States.

During the Clinton administration the pace of federal antitrust enforcement accelerated considerably. In part, this was due to the increase in merger activity. The merger notifications under Hart-Scott-Rodino increased from 1,451 in 1991 to over 4,700 in 1998. The merger boom not only increased the number of potential cases, but the nature of the mergers in 1997 to 1998 was also different from those earlier in the decade. Mergers have increasingly been strategic in nature rather than financially motivated, and a number of the strategic mergers raise horizontal and/or vertical antitrust issues. In 1998 the FTC negotiated 28 consent decrees in merger cases, obtained preliminary injunctions in three cases, and in six cases the parties abandoned the merger. The FTC also brought 13 non-merger cases, which was the highest number in a decade.

The growth in new industries has also generated new antitrust activity. The dietary supplements industry reached $12 billion in sales in 1997, and the FTC turned its attention to the advertising claims made for the supplements. The FTC took legal action against seven supplements manufacturers, sent e-mail warnings to 1,100 Web sites that made "incredible claims," and issued advertising guidelines.[22] In another action the DOJ filed an antitrust case against Visa and MasterCard alleging that the joint ownership of the country's two largest credit card networks by a group of major banks was stifling competition between the two credit cards.

The DOJ also became more active in another area. It filed a price fixing suit against the 23 colleges in the "overlap" group that met annually to exchange financial aid information for admitted undergraduate students. The DOJ reached a consent decree with the eight Ivy League schools, but the Massachusetts Institute of Technology (MIT) decided to go to trial, losing in district court. It appealed the decision and the U.S. Court of Appeals reversed the lower court decision. The DOJ and MIT then reached a settlement in which colleges may discuss general guidelines for financial aid and compare data on financial need but may not exchange information on individual students or their aid packages.[23]

Although the federal antitrust agencies are usually successful in obtaining at least a consent decree in the cases they bring, companies do win cases. In 1994, in a case brought by the DOJ alleging that General Electric had engaged in price fixing for industrial diamonds, the judge ruled that the DOJ had presented insufficient evidence and dismissed the case without requiring the company to present its defense.

PRIVATE ANTITRUST ACTIONS

Most antitrust cases are the result of private lawsuits.[24] The number of private antitrust suits increased from the early 1960s and peaked at over 1,600 in 1977, declining to 570 in 1997. The decline is a function of a variety of factors, including Supreme Court decisions that made it more difficult for some plaintiffs to prevail in cases involving vertical restraints and predatory pricing. Firms also instituted compliance programs that contributed to the decrease.

---

[22] *The Wall Street Journal,* November 18, 1998.

[23] See Bamberger and Carlton (1999). The only schools allowed to participate in the system are those that practice need-blind admissions and provide full-need financial aid.

[24] See White (1988). Viscusi, Vernon, and Harrington (1995, p. 65) report that 93 percent of antitrust lawsuits filed in U.S. courts during the 1970s and 1980s were private.

Most antitrust suits are brought under the Sherman Act, and cases pertaining to vertical arrangements represent a somewhat higher percent of the total than those pertaining to horizontal practices. Of the total cases in their study, Salop and White (1988) found that 36.5 percent were filed by competitors and 27.3 percent by dealers.[25] Of the cases filed before 1980, 71 percent were settled out of court and 11 percent were dismissed. Of the 12 percent of the cases that continued, plaintiffs prevailed in approximately 30 percent. Only 5.4 percent of the cases went to trial.

The treble damages provision of the Clayton Act provides strong incentives to file antitrust suits. Treble damages are understandably controversial. Their proponents argue that they provide an important incentive for private enforcement. Critics contend that treble damages provide an incentive to challenge the practices of competitors, thereby making firms reluctant to compete on a number of dimensions, including price.

Private suits can have significance beyond their impact on the parties involved. When a private antitrust case is tried and appealed, higher court decisions can establish a precedent that is then followed by courts in similar cases. Many of the important interpretations of the antitrust statutes and of the precedents followed by the courts have come from private lawsuits.

PER SE VIOLATIONS AND THE RULE OF REASON

The courts have held that there are some sufficiently egregious acts that on the face of it violate the antitrust laws. These acts are said to be *per se* illegal, and the only defense allowed is that the defendant did not commit the act. The Supreme Court established this rule in *Northern Pacific Railroad Co. v. U.S.*, 356 U.S. 1 (1958) in stating that, "There are certain agreements or practices which because of their pernicious effect on competition and lack of any redeeming virtue are conclusively presumed to be unreasonable and therefore illegal without elaborate inquiry as to the precise harm they have caused or the business excuse for their use."

In contrast, other cases are considered by the courts on the basis of a rule of reason.[26] Under this rule, a restraint of trade, for example, is illegal if it is unreasonable.[27] *Per se* violations are presumed to be unreasonable. The rule of reason was needed because much of the language of the antitrust laws is too sweeping and a literal interpretation would be harmful to competition and efficiency. Section 1 of the Sherman Act, for example, might be interpreted as prohibiting supply contracts because they restrain the opportunities for others. Similarly, combinations such as partnerships might otherwise be held to be in violation of the Sherman Act.

A defendant has two defenses under a rule of reason. The first is the same as under a *per se* rule—the defendant did not commit the act in question. The second is that, although the defendant committed the act, it was not unreasonable to do so. The burden of proof is on the plaintiff to show that it is unreasonable. In evaluating whether an act or a practice is unreasonable, courts look to its purpose and effect. In the case of vertical arrangements, the stimulation of interbrand competition is a purpose the courts recognize. In evaluating the effect of a practice, the courts examine whether it

---

[25]As an example of the specific focus of a private antitrust suit, in 1994 1,346 independent pharmacists filed suits in federal courts in 15 states charging the large pharmaceutical companies with price discrimination because they granted large discounts to hospitals, HMOs, and mail-order drug companies. These discounts were not available to independent pharmacists, which allegedly forced many of them out of business. Four supermarket chains also filed a price discrimination suit against the pharmaceutical companies.

[26]The rule of reason was first articulated by the Supreme Court in *Standard Oil Co. of New Jersey v. United States*, 221 U.S. 1 (1911), which broke up the Standard Oil Trust.

[27]A judicial rule is a standard of interpretation for a law that is ambiguous in the absence of that interpretation.

restrains or promotes competition and whether it is the least restrictive means of achieving the purpose. A court may hold for the plaintiff if either the purpose or the effect is unreasonable.

The courts do not decide which rule is applicable on a case-by-case basis but instead hold that certain practices are *per se* illegal and others are not. Presently, price fixing, output restraints, minimum resale price maintenance, and the allocation of customers among competitors are *per se* violations of the antitrust laws. Some practices that in the past were considered *per se* offenses are now considered under the rule of reason. For example, in 1997 the Supreme Court ruled that maximum price resale maintenance, where a manufacturer sets a maximum price that retailers may charge, is now to be evaluated under a rule of reason rather than being *per se* illegal.[28]

A variety of arrangements and practices have come under the scrutiny of the antitrust laws, as indicated in Figure 9-2. A treatment of each of these requires more space than is available, so the following sections focus instead on antitrust thought and on the application of that thought in the areas of vertical restraints, predatory pricing, collusion, and mergers.

Schools of Antitrust Thought

Antitrust policy, enforcement practices, and court decisions are influenced by the prevailing schools of thought about the purposes of antitrust policy and the likely consequences of specific practices. The traditional or structural school of thought prevailed into the 1970s, when it was confronted with the understandings of the Chicago school of economics and antitrust. The Chicago, or law and economics, school viewed the objectives and principles of antitrust policy quite differently, particularly with regard to vertical arrangements. It has had considerable influence on legal education, the courts, and the enforcement activities of the DOJ and FTC beginning with the Reagan administration. In addition, the courts have adopted many understandings of the Chicago school, and several Chicago school scholars have been appointed to the federal judiciary.

In the 1990s antitrust practice and policy have also been influenced by the work of industrial organization (IO) economists who focused on new considerations such as network externalities and compatibility and on theories of oligopoly that take the strategic interactions among market participants into account. This "new IO" or "post-Chicago" approach challenges some of the understandings of both the structural and the Chicago schools. The new IO approach is at present a collection of theories rather than a unified theory from which broad conclusions can be drawn. Furthermore, courts have only cautiously embraced its theories, in part because of its complexity and the subtle reasoning involved. Nevertheless, it represents an important force in antitrust.

These three approaches agree on many points but differ on several dimensions. Figure 9-3 contrasts the approaches.

THE STRUCTURAL APPROACH

The structural approach views the purpose of antitrust policy as improving economic performance and furthering the social objectives of limiting economic power and of providing fairness to market participants. From this perspective, concentrations of economic power should be checked, just as is political power. Because economic power can result in the unfair treatment of competitors and consumers, government

---

[28]*State Oil Company v. Khan,* 522 U.S. 3; 118 S.Ct. 27 S.

FIGURE 9–3 Structural, Chicago School, New IO Perspectives

Dimension	*Structural View*	*Chicago School*	*New IO*
• Purpose of antitrust policy	Social and political as well as economic objectives.	Economic objectives—efficiency with a focus on prices.	• Economic objectives; static and dynamic efficiency
• View of markets	Markets are fragile and prone to failure.	Markets are resilient; market imperfections can be addressed through incentives.	• Most markets are resilient, but some have imperfections such as network externalities; strategic behavior can limit efficiency
• What is needed	Government to protect society from economic power.	Competition is the best protector of consumers and economic efficiency.	• Competition is the best protector of consumers, but government interventions can be required.
• Perspective on consumers	Need to protect consumers from others and from themselves; e.g., unfair practices.	Consumers are responsible for their own decisions and will protect themselves.	• Consumers can protect themselves when they have choices.
• Requirements for markets to function efficiently	Protect competitors to prevent monopoly; avoid foreclosing opportunities for competitors.	Conditions for perfect competition are sufficient but not necessary.	• Both innovation and competition are required for efficiency
• Relationship between the number of competitors and market performance	More competitors means more competition.	Competition can be effective with only a few competitors.	• Competition can be effective with a small number of competitors
• Entry	High barriers to entry reduce efficiency; potential entry may not limit the power of incumbent firms.	Few barriers to entry; barriers are due to the efficiency of incumbent firms; potential entry limits the economic power of incumbents.	• Barriers to entry can be present; e.g., from the economies of standardization
• Sources of economic power	Market power derives from horizontal power and from vertical arrangements.	Market power can only arise from horizontal power.	• Market power derives from horizontal factors but can be extended through vertical arrangements and strategic behavior
• Collusion	Increases profits, so firms can be expected to collude.	Is difficult for firms to enforce and thus is unlikely.	• Is possible with repeated encounters
• Where is collusion most likely	In concentrated markets.	In industries with government regulation or protection.	• In industries with repeated encounters and easy monitoring, as well as in regulated and protected industries
• Interpretation of the relationship between concentration and profits	Positive correlation indicates that more concentration reduces market efficiency and increases profits.	Positive correlation is more likely due to lower costs of larger firms.	• Positive correlation can be due to lower costs, market power, or strategic opportunities
• Relevant market for antitrust scrutiny should be	Defined narrowly so that pockets of concentration can be detected and addressed.	Defined broadly to include substitutes and imports.	• Define broadly to include substitutes and imports
• Conclusion about antitrust	Proscribe many practices as *per se* offenses.	Judge business practices in terms of their effects on efficiency and prices; use the rule of reason.	• Judge business practices in terms of impact on present and future competition; use rule of reason except for egregious cases such as price fixing
• Values underlying the perspective	Efficiency and fairness; government protection.	Economic efficiency; individual choice and responsibility.	• Economic efficiency; individual and collective responsibility

has a responsibility to protect citizens and society from the presence, and the abuse, of economic power. Antitrust policy and regulation are the principal public instruments for checking that power.

The structural approach to the analysis of economic power takes as its starting point the economic theories of monopoly and perfect competition. Perfect competition serves as the standard for evaluating an industry, and monopoly is its antithesis. Monopolistic pricing can be characterized by the generalized Lerner index given by

$$\frac{p - mc}{p} = \frac{1}{n|\epsilon|},$$

where p is price, mc is marginal cost, n is the number of firms in the industry, and ϵ is the price elasticity of demand.[29] The left side of the index is the percentage markup on price, and for a monopoly ($n = 1$), the markup set by the firm equals one divided by the (absolute value of the) elasticity of demand. As the number of firms increases, the markup decreases as price approaches marginal cost, which is the case of perfect competition. Market power is the ability to command prices above marginal costs and that power is greater the smaller the number of firms in an industry, other things equal. For example, in the chapter case, *The Staples-Office Depot Merger?,* the FTC and the court concluded that prices were higher in markets with only one office supply superstore than with two or three superstores. The structural approach thus views the economic performance in an industry as resulting from the conduct of firms, which is a function of the structure of the industry.

This theory indicates that economic power is a function of the number of firms in the industry or, correspondingly, their market shares. The smaller the number of firms in an industry the more likely they are to collude to raise prices and worsen the performance of markets. The focus of antitrust policy thus should be on the structure of the industry, and industries with substantial concentration—a substantial market share held by a small number of firms—should be regarded with suspicion. The structural approach finds support for this conclusion in empirical studies that show a positive correlation between industry concentration and profitability, as predicted by the Lerner index.

The structural approach thus holds that improving performance by controlling economic power requires dealing with industry structure rather than just with the conduct of market participants. Remedies for antitrust violations, too, should address the structure of the industry. These remedies include breaking up monopolies, ordering the divestiture of business units, requiring tight standards for mergers, and licensing technologies to all who desire to use them. Because a larger number of firms correlates with more competition and lower prices, the more firms in the industry the better. This approach also suggests that to ensure that there are enough firms for vigorous competition it may be desirable to protect firms from their rivals, particularly from predatory behavior or from unfair advantages such as not being able to purchase inputs at low prices (as reflected in the Robinson-Patman Act).

The Lerner index implies that market power arises from horizontal considerations. Market power can also occur from vertical arrangements in channels of distribution, as when a manufacturer requires a distributor or retailer to maintain a minimum price, to carry only the manufacturer's replacement parts, or to sell only within a specified territory. From the perspective of the structural approach, it is important to avoid foreclosing opportunities for competitors, since competition would then be less vigorous. Vertical arrangements thus should be viewed with suspicion because they limit opportunities for competitors and can increase economic power.

---

[29]This relation is derived from a Cournot model of oligopoly.

The economic power of the incumbent firms in an industry can be checked by the threat of entry into the industry. The structural approach, however, is concerned about possible barriers to entry. Barriers to entry are said to include such factors as technological advantages, advertising and brand names, and capital requirements. Because of barriers to entry and economic concentration, the structural approach often views markets as fragile. Government thus has a role in helping markets function more efficiently.

When there are barriers to entry and economic power is concentrated in a relatively small number of firms, incumbent firms may have an opportunity to collude. The structural approach views collusion as more likely the more concentrated the industry. Collusion can take the form of price fixing among firms in an industry or a channel of distribution, as in the case of resale price maintenance. The empirical research reporting a positive correlation between concentration and profitability could reflect this collusion. This provides another rationale for focusing on concentrated markets.

Because economic power harms consumers through higher prices, the structural approach holds that it is important to scrutinize markets narrowly to identify market segments in which economic concentration and power are present. Markets thus should be defined narrowly so that pockets of economic concentration will not be missed. Similarly, it is important to keep market opportunities open. Consequently, restraints of trade and market foreclosures should be limited to those that are absolutely necessary. Antitrust thus should proscribe many practices that foreclose opportunities or restrain competition. Those practices should be *per se* illegal.

In summary, the structural approach is based on the structure-conduct-performance paradigm: Performance follows from conduct which follows from the structure of markets and industries and the economic power resulting from concentration and barriers to entry. Furthermore, collusion is more likely in concentrated industries. Antitrust policy should thus closely scrutinize market structure for economic concentration, market foreclosures, and restraints of trade. A *per se* standard should be applied to many practices, and remedies should be directed at structural factors.

THE CHICAGO SCHOOL

The Chicago school views the objective of antitrust policy as promoting economic efficiency, which may be understood in its simplest form as the maximization of producers' plus consumers' surplus. Since economic efficiency depends on the level of prices, the focus is on the prices that consumers pay. Thus, a price equal to marginal cost is efficient, whether it results from a perfectly competitive market or a monopolistic industry in which price is held down by the threat of entry. The focus of the Chicago school is thus on performance—the prices in markets—and not on the structure of the markets.[30] The Chicago school recognizes the potential for horizontal market power and its abuse but believes that competition, not government, is the best protector of consumers and the best promoter of economic efficiency.

Perfect competition is the ideal, but the conditions for perfect competition—many firms, a homogeneous product, technologies available to all firms, and complete information—are viewed as sufficient but not necessary for economic efficiency. Competition can be efficient even with a few firms in an industry, and given the opportunity, firms will compete vigorously. Profits provide the incentive to compete.

The Chicago school is skeptical about the nature and scope of barriers to entry. Claimed barriers such as advertising, brand-name advantages, and capital requirements are unlikely to be true barriers. Capital markets are viewed as efficient, so investors will provide capital for ventures that have prospects for at least a market rate of return. Any

[30]See Posner (1976) for an analysis of antitrust policy from the Chicago school perspective.

barriers to entry are likely to be due to the cost advantages of incumbent firms, and the inability of a potential entrant to raise capital thus is due to efficiency advantages of incumbent firms. Entry thus may be difficult not because of structural barriers but because of economic efficiency. Indeed, the incumbent firms are those that have survived competition.

The positive correlation between industry concentration and profitability that the structural approach views as reflecting the exercise of economic power could, according to the Chicago school, result from the greater efficiency of those firms that have survived the competitive process. Furthermore, as firms become larger their costs may become lower. Their markups above price thus would be higher but their prices lower than if the firms in the industry were smaller. That is, if as firms become larger their costs decrease and competition is present to force prices down, then consumers benefit. The firms could also benefit because of their lower costs and greater market shares. Consequently, markups and profits can be an increasing function of concentration, yet higher concentration can result in lower prices for consumers.

The Chicago school also holds that collusion among firms is unlikely to be sustainable because of the difficulties in monitoring and enforcing collusive agreements. Colluding firms have a strong incentive to cheat on an agreement by, for example, making secret discounts to customers. A collusive agreement thus may have the structure of a prisoners' dilemma in which each firm finds it in its interest to cheat on the agreement. Unless there is a clear mechanism for monitoring the agreement, collusion is unlikely to be sustained.

From the Chicago school's perspective, collusion is most likely to be sustainable when there is government protection or regulation. In that case, government causes high prices and economic inefficiency. Government regulation that precluded entry into the airline and trucking industries is viewed as having resulted in implicit collusion, with much of the rents captured by labor rather than by firms. Consistent with this perspective, during the Reagan administration the DOJ pressed its antitrust case against AT&T because it believed that regulation was inhibiting competition and technological progress. The DOJ, however, dropped its antitrust case against IBM because whatever market power IBM might have had would soon be dissipated by the rapid technological change in the computer industry.

Because barriers to entry are low and collusion is difficult to sustain, competition—both existing and potential—can be expected. This implies that there are few practices that should be *per se* illegal. Because it is the performance in the market that is important, the rule of reason should be used by courts in judging practices under the antitrust laws. In particular, vertical restraints are harmful only if the firm has horizontal market power, and hence it is horizontal market power that should be assessed for its consequences for performance.

In assessing horizontal power the relevant market should be defined broadly. Both present and potential competition should be considered because either can hold prices down. The relevant market thus includes not only the product in question but also substitutes for that product. The market definition should also include imports as well as domestic products. In the case of capital goods, the relevant market should include the market for used goods. In the case of a commodity such as aluminum, it should include the scrap and recycling markets as well as aluminum produced from bauxite. As an example of this perspective, Eastman Kodak has a 70 percent share of the U.S. color film market, 60 percent of the color paper market, and 70 percent of the wholesale photofinishing market. Its market dominance and anticompetitive practices had twice resulted in antitrust consent decrees. In 1994, however, the courts lifted both consent decrees. The courts concluded that Kodak did not have substantial market power because it had only a 36 percent market share worldwide. The courts concluded that if Kodak were to attempt to exercise market power by restricting output resulting in high prices, imports and private label film would quickly rush into the U.S. market forcing prices down.

In summary, the Chicago school views the objective of antitrust as economic efficiency and competition as the best means of achieving efficiency. Perfect competition is not the only means of achieving that efficiency, however, as competition among a few firms can be sufficient for prices to be driven down. Barriers to entry are seen as low and collusion difficult to sustain, so market forces should correct most attempts to restrain trade. Furthermore, the relation between markups and concentration may be due to costs that decrease with the size of firms rather than due to the exploitation of market power. Because the objective is economic efficiency, the focus of antitrust policy should be on performance, and the market in which that performance is assessed should be viewed broadly.

The Chicago school does not conclude that practices such as vertical arrangements should be legal. Instead, it concludes that vertical arrangements may be pro-competitive rather than anticompetitive. Hence, they should not be *per se* illegal but rather should be considered under a rule of reason. This allows firms to adopt those practices that enhance industry performance but also allows successful prosecution of those practices that harm performance.

THE NEW IO APPROACH

The new IO approach to antitrust is derived from the economics of modern industrial organization. This approach rejects the static equilibrium approach taken by the Chicago school and focuses, for example, on the possibilities for strategic behavior that are present because of repeated interactions among market participants.[31] Even when firms act in a noncooperative manner, implicit collusion can result and can be sustained by expectations that cheating will be met with future punishment by other market participants. Similarly, interactions over time may allow firms to develop a reputation for a particular mode of behavior, such as price cutting in response to new entry into a market, that can deter potential entrants.

The possibilities for such strategic behavior are greater when there is incomplete information about factors important to the strategy choices of firms. A potential entrant may have incomplete information about the costs of incumbent firms and thus may be reluctant to sink costs required for entry, since it could turn out that the incumbent firms actually have cost advantages. Furthermore, incumbent firms may be able to deter entry by signaling that they have low costs even when they have high costs. Moreover, firms may be able to adopt market strategies that raise the costs to competitors, the possibility of which was alleged by the DOJ in blocking the Lockheed Martin and Northrup Grumman merger, as indicated later in the chapter.

The new IO approach is also concerned with the potential for anticompetitive behavior in markets characterized by network externalities and where compatibility is required. For example, the benefits from standardizing software development on a small number of platforms, such as Microsoft's Windows operating system, can result in the development of market power for the suppliers of the platforms. Similarly, network effects are important in businesses ranging from Internet commerce to credit cards to commercial real estate. That is, there are supply-side economies to larger networks, and larger networks are more valuable to customers. This generates incentives to compete to develop the largest network, and the winning competitor then has an "essential facility" and hence market power. Moreover, the owner of an essential facility may be

---

[31]See Holt and Scheffman (1989) for a discussion of this approach and its implications for antitrust.

able to use it to thwart innovation or block alternative technologies that provide potential competition to the facility. Microsoft's concern about potential competition to its dominance of the desktop operating systems from the Internet and Java were alleged by the DOJ to have led it to engage in anticompetitive practices.

As summarized in Figure 9-3 the new IO perspective on antitrust focuses on the objective of static and dynamic efficiency; thus, it is concerned not only about the performance of markets at a point in time but also about innovation and protecting incentives to develop new products and processes. Most markets are viewed as resilient, although some can have imperfections such as network externalities and compatibility requirements. Therefore, although ensuring choice among products and competition are the best protectors of consumers, government intervention may be warranted to ensure that standardization on a particular technology does not lead to market abuse and that incentives and opportunities for innovation are not thwarted. Whereas most markets can be efficient even if there are only a small number of competitors provided that there are low barriers to entry, others may require scrutiny. For example, the efficiencies from standardization can make it virtually impossible for a new firm to enter a market dominated by an incumbent. Easy entry thus cannot be assumed.

The new IO perspective agrees with the Chicago school that market power derives from horizontal considerations but holds that it can be extended through vertical arrangements. For example, in the 1998 antitrust case the government charged that Microsoft attempted to extend its market power to the Internet by bundling its Internet browser with its operating system and giving its browser away for free.

As another example, Toys 'R' Us had a 30 percent market share of the toy retailing market, which is not large enough to allow it to restrict output and drive prices up. The FTC, however, took antitrust action against Toys 'R' Us on the grounds that its horizontal market share was sufficient to exercise power over toy manufacturers. Toys 'R' Us allegedly attempted to persuade toy manufacturers not to sell popular toys to discount warehouses.

The new IO perspective acknowledges that competition with only a few firms can be efficient in a one-time encounter, but it also recognizes that repeated encounters provide an opportunity for implicit collusion. Collusion is more likely the better is the monitoring of the actions of firms. The price fixing cartels in graphite electrodes, citric acid, and lysine are evidence of the ability of firms to collude. The positive empirical relationship between concentration and profits thus could be due to lower costs or to the exercise of market power.

In examining the likelihood of the exercise of market power to reduce static and dynamic efficiency, the new IO perspective agrees with the Chicago school in viewing the market broadly in terms of substitutes. Those substitutes can be actual or potential. For example, the government opposed the merger of SBC and Ameritech, two former Bell operating companies, even though they did not compete in any market. The government argued that although they did not presently compete, with the continued deregulation of the telecommunications industry they were potential future competitors in both the long-distance market and in each other's local service market.

With respect to antitrust enforcement and policy, the new IO perspective concludes that business practices should be evaluated in terms of their effects on static and dynamic efficiency under the rule of reason except in egregious situations such as price fixing. Individuals can protect themselves when choice is available in the market, but government intervention can be warranted when choice and innovation are stifled through the exercise of market power.

The new IO approach thus concludes that there are situations in which firms can employ strategies that are anticompetitive, particularly when the product exhibits network externalities or has compatibility and standardization considerations. The new IO approach has not at this point presented a comprehensive theory of antitrust economics, however. Instead, the approach is a collection of theories about behavior under particular structural and informational conditions.

Examples of the Differences in Antitrust Thought

VERTICAL ARRANGEMENTS

The principal area in which the structural and Chicago schools have differed is in regard to vertical arrangements. These arrangements take a variety of forms, but most involve restrictions imposed by a manufacturer on the sale or distribution of its products. Because most of these arrangements involve the foreclosure of a market opportunity or a restraint of trade, many vertical practices had been held by the courts to be *per se* illegal. Economic understandings developed by the Chicago school, along with a Supreme Court required to interpret laws containing imprecise and general language, changed the law on vertical arrangements. Many of the vertical arrangements that had been *per se* illegal during the 1970s are now considered under a rule of reason. Furthermore, the courts have upheld the use of many of the previously illegal vertical arrangements. These changes have occurred in the absence of new legislation.

Vertical price restrictions had been *per se* illegal since the Supreme Court decision in *Dr. Miles Medical Co. v. John D. Park & Sons,* 220 U.S. 373 (1911).[32] Nonprice vertical restrictions were not *per se* illegal, however, until the decision in *U.S. v. Arnold Schwinn & Co.,* 388 U.S. 365 (1967). In *Schwinn,* the Supreme Court decided that vertical nonprice restrictions on the resale of goods, such as territorial restrictions, restrictions on customers served, refusals to deal, and exclusive dealerships, were *per se* illegal.

The Chicago school found little logic in the court's reasoning because from its perspective a vertical arrangement could be harmful to competition only as a result of horizontal market power. That is, vertical arrangements do not create market power but can reflect market power resulting, for example, from a dominant market position. Indeed, vertical arrangements are generally viewed as tolerable unless there is horizontal market power. When that power is present, vertical arrangements should be judged under the rule of reason.

In reasoning about vertical arrangements, the Chicago school distinguished between interbrand and intrabrand competition. Intrabrand competition refers to competition between sellers of the same brand, as in the case of two Honda dealers competing against each other. Those dealers also compete against the sellers of other makes of automobiles—interbrand competition. If interbrand competition is vigorous so that a manufacturer does not have horizontal market power, restrictions on intrabrand competition will have little impact on the efficiency of the market.

Moreover, vertical arrangements that restrict intrabrand competition can make interbrand competition more efficient by, for example, strengthening dealer networks. Competition among stronger networks holds down prices, and stronger dealer networks can also reduce costs and better serve consumers on the nonprice dimensions of sales. Restrictions on intrabrand competition can also reduce transaction costs in a firm's channels of distribution, as Williamson (1975) has emphasized.

In addition, the Chicago school argued that competition does not take place only on price. Many products require the provision of information to enable consumers to

[32]As indicated previously a 1997 Supreme Court decision held that maximum price restrictions are to be considered under a rule of reason.

make informed choices. Many products must also be supported with service, both at the time of purchase and later. Manufacturers establish dealer networks to provide information and customer service, but the networks are often plagued by the free-rider problem. Customers can visit a dealer to obtain information and then buy from a discount store that offers neither information nor service. Customers then are free riding on the information provided by dealers. This weakens the dealer networks, resulting in less information being provided to consumers, who then may make less-informed decisions, reducing economic efficiency. Indeed, one reason that dealers charge a higher price than discount stores do is that they must have a margin adequate to cover the costs of a well-trained sales staff and a service facility.

In *Continental TV v. GTE Sylvania,* 433 U.S. 36 (1977), the Supreme Court, influenced by this reasoning, changed the precedent established in *Schwinn.* The court held that nonprice vertical restraints should be considered under a rule of reason. GTE Sylvania, a producer of television sets, had experienced declining sales. By the beginning of the 1960s it had only 1 to 2 percent of the U.S. market. Sylvania distributed its television sets through both company-owned and independent distributors which supplied retailers. In an attempt to increase its sales, Sylvania changed its method of distribution by eliminating its distributors and selling directly to franchised retailers. Sylvania also required its retailers to sell only from a specified location. This provision allowed Sylvania to control the number of retail outlets in an area. The objective of the changes was to attract a stronger but smaller group of retailers that would have the incentive to promote Sylvania TV sets. The franchised dealers could sell other brands and were not restricted in the prices they could charge.

The change proved successful. Dealers promoted Sylvania sets, increasing its market share to 5 percent by 1965. In 1965 Sylvania decided to authorize a new retailer in San Francisco. Continental TV, a Sylvania dealer there, protested and asked permission to sell Sylvania TVs in Sacramento. Sylvania refused, and Continental decided to sell them there anyway. Sylvania then refused to sell to Continental. Continental sued, and the federal district court, following *Schwinn,* held in its favor. The Court of Appeals reversed the decision and ordered a retrial on the grounds that it did not believe that *Schwinn* was applicable in this case. Continental appealed, and the Supreme Court took the case as an opportunity to reconsider whether vertical arrangements such as the one in question should be *per se* illegal.

The Supreme Court concluded that "*Per se* rules of illegality are appropriate only when they relate to conduct that is manifestly anticompetitive." As indicated in *Northern Pacific,* such conduct must have a "pernicious effect on competition" and have no "redeeming virtue." In considering whether this was true of the practice in Sylvania, the court found that "The market impact of vertical restrictions is complex because of their potential for a simultaneous reduction in intrabrand competition and stimulation of interbrand competition . . ." The court then held that because of the possibility of the stimulation of interbrand competition a vertical restriction could not be said *a priori* to have a pernicious effect on competition or to have no redeeming virtue. Hence, nonprice vertical arrangements were not *per se* illegal. The court pointed to the possible redeeming virtues stating,

> new manufacturers and manufacturers entering new markets can use the restrictions in order to induce competent and aggressive retailers to make the kind of investment of capital and labor that is often required in the distribution of products unknown to the consumer. Established manufacturers can use them to induce retailers to engage in promotional activities or to provide service and repair facilities necessary to the efficient marketing of their products. Service and repair are vital for many products,

> such as automobiles and major household appliances. The availability and quality of such services affect a manufacturer's good will and the competitiveness of his product. Because of market imperfections such as the so-called "free rider" effect, these services might not be provided by retailers in a purely competitive situation....

The Supreme Court affirmed the decision of the Court of Appeals and thus changed the *per se* rule of illegality for vertical practices to a rule of reason, reversing what had served as law for the previous 10 years. Since *Sylvania,* most nonprice vertical restrictions have been considered under a rule of reason. The new IO perspective generally agrees with this result as now does the structural perspective.

The Supreme Court followed the *Sylvania* decision with two decisions extending the applicability of the rule of reason in nonprice vertical arrangements. In *Monsanto Co. v. Spray-Rite Service Co.,* 465 U.S. 752 (1984), the court held that terminating a price-cutting dealer after complaints from several other dealers was not a *per se* violation. In *Business Electronics Corp. v. Sharp Electronics Corp.,* 485 U.S. 717 (1988), the court held that terminating a dealer relationship because another dealer had complained about its price cutting was not a *per se* violation unless there had been an agreement between the manufacturer and the complaining retailer. The rationale for these decisions was again that the practices could have the redeeming virtue of stimulating interbrand competition and thus should be tried under a rule of reason.

The chapter case *Apple Computer and Mail-Order Sales* raises related issues about nonprice vertical arrangements.

PREDATORY PRICING AND ENTRY DETERRENCE

The traditional perspective on predatory pricing is that a firm may attempt to drive a competitor out of a market by cutting prices below costs. A firm with deep pockets can bear the short-term losses from the price cutting, and once the weaker rival is forced from the market it can set higher prices to recoup its losses. The standard used to determine if a firm is engaging in predatory pricing is whether price is below marginal cost. Marginal cost is not easy for a court to measure, however, so a standard such as average variable cost is often used as the proxy.[33]

The Chicago school's criticism of the traditional view of predatory pricing focuses on its aftermath. Suppose a firm were to engage in predatory pricing and successfully drive a competitor out of the market. Could it then raise its price to a level higher than that prevailing prior to the predation? The answer depends on whether there are barriers to entry in the industry. If there are not, and the Chicago school is skeptical about the presence of barriers to entry, then raising the price will simply attract new entrants. This will force the price down, and the predation will have been for naught. Recognizing this, a firm will not engage in predatory pricing in the first place. In this sense, a market is self-policing.

If there were high barriers to entry, a firm could exercise market power. The principal barrier to entry recognized by the Chicago school is that which results from the sunk costs of incumbent firms. Even those sunk costs, however, are not a long-run deterrent to entry because once an entrant has entered the market, the incumbent firm no longer has a reason to price below long-run costs. Also, if the incumbent firm has sunk costs, then the competitor it is attempting to drive out of the market also is likely to have

[33]See Areeda and Turner (1975).

sunk costs. Prices thus would have to be cut below short-run marginal costs to drive out the competitor.[34]

Even when predatory pricing is possible, it may not be desirable. An industry leader may not have an incentive to engage in predatory pricing, since it would have to incur losses on a much larger volume of sales to drive a smaller competitor from the market. Predation in this case may not be in the interest of an industry leader, even though the industry may have barriers to entry.

The conclusion of the Chicago school is that predation is unlikely to be successful and so it will not be attempted. The price cutting observed in markets thus is likely to be the result of competition rather than of predation. Moreover, applying antitrust law to alleged predation can discourage firms from competing on price, resulting in higher prices.

Research from the new IO perspective, however, casts some doubt on these conclusions. One theory of potential entry is based on the recognition that a potential entrant may not know whether an incumbent firm has a cost advantage. Because of this incomplete information about the incumbent's costs, the incumbent may be able to signal that it has low costs, even though its costs are actually high, by setting a price equal to the average of what a low-cost and a high-cost incumbent firm would choose. This pricing strategy can deter some entry that would be desirable from the perspective of economic efficiency.[35]

Another theory developed from the new IO perspective indicates that an incumbent firm may have an incentive to engage in predatory pricing in one or several geographic or product markets to develop a reputation as a "tough" competitor, thus discouraging entry by new firms.[36] The development of such a reputation hinges on the incomplete information of potential entrants about, for example, the costs of the incumbent firm. A reputation for toughness, then, may deter entry into a market even if no real barriers to entry are present.

Whatever the appropriate economic theory of predatory behavior, antitrust scrutiny of price cutting poses a serious concern. In practice it is difficult to distinguish between vigorous price competition and predatory pricing. Even in a competitive industry, prices will rise and fall in response to shifts in demand, and when entry occurs, prices will adjust as other firms change their outputs or exit the industry. Applying antitrust law in situations in which prices are being cut could stifle price competition. For example, new entrants may adopt a strategy of setting low prices to build market share and utilize their capacity efficiently. Precluding an incumbent firm from responding to those prices would restrain competition and possibly prevent output from being produced at the lowest possible industry cost.

As an example, in 1992 American Airlines revamped its pricing by grouping fares into four classes, and it then cut full-fare prices substantially. Continental and Northwest filed an antitrust suit under the Sherman Act charging that American was trying to drive them out of the market with predatory prices and then use its increased market power to raise prices. The plaintiffs asked for damages of $1 billion, which would be trebled in the event of a guilty verdict. Robert Crandall, CEO of American, said that Continental and Northwest were "hoping to accomplish in the courtroom what they couldn't accomplish in the marketplace." A jury acquitted American.

---

[34]This argument would not hold, however, if an incumbent firm had a cost advantage over a competitor or a potential entrant. The incumbent then could set a price just low enough that the potential entrant would stay out of the market. In this case, the threat of potential entry limits the incumbent firm's ability to increase its price but does not force the price down to the level of costs.

[35]See Milgrom and Roberts (1982a) for a development of this theory.

[36]See Kreps and Wilson (1982) and Milgrom and Roberts (1982b) for a development of this theory.

COLLUSION AND PRICE-FIXING

All schools of thought agree that collusion and horizontal price fixing are anticompetitive, and as indicated, the DOJ has vigorously prosecuted price fixing and bid-rigging cases and obtained criminal convictions and prison sentences for those found guilty. The schools, however, disagree about how likely it is that collusive arrangements can be sustained.

The structural perspective on collusion and price fixing is that firms will collude when possible, and so tight antitrust supervision is necessary. The Chicago school, however, points to historical evidence indicating that cartels break down as a result of cheating by their own members. Furthermore, the larger the number of firms that are required to collude, the more difficult it is to prevent cheating and defection. For collusion to be sustained, the colluders must have a means of detecting cheating, as in the case of bidding on government contracts when the bids are publicly reported.

The new IO approach, however, reaches a different conclusion. Because firms in the same industry will be in competition over time, firms have a broad set of strategies that may sustain implicit collusion even when the detection of cheating is imperfect.[37] A firm that believes that another firm is cheating on an implicit agreement to maintain high prices can punish that firm by lowering its own price. If the second firm is confident that the first indeed has an incentive to punish any perceived cheating, the second firm may have no incentive to cheat. The threat of punishment in repeated encounters thus can in principle enforce high prices even when there is no explicit agreement among firms and no communication between them. Price cutting thus may be a means of punishing deviations from implicit collusion rather than an indication of vigorous competition or predation.

Mergers and Merger Guidelines

Mergers may create horizontal market power or restrain competition in supply or distribution channels. The passage of the Celler-Kefauver Act in 1950 decreased the number of mergers, but when the Reagan administration took office in 1981 it signaled that it did not view mergers with the same hostility as had prior administrations. Indeed, mergers were viewed as potentially beneficial to efficiency and competition. Mergers can yield cost efficiencies and synergies that benefit consumers. Mergers can also remove bad management and eliminate inefficient cross-subsidization of one line of business by another.

To provide guidance to firms about when it was likely to initiate an investigation, the DOJ issued revised merger guidelines in 1982.[38] The FTC issued similar guidelines, and in 1992 the agencies jointly issued updated guidelines.[39] The guidelines reflect both structural and Chicago school perspectives by identifying where market power may be present and whether it can be exercised. The guidelines also reflect the new IO perspective with respect to the dynamics of competition. In contrast to the structural perspective, the guidelines do not assume that market power will be automatically exercised.

The merger guidelines identify collusion as the means to the exercise of market power. Its exercise requires a restriction of output to increase equilibrium prices and profits. The smaller a firm's market share the more it has to restrict output to achieve a given price increase, so unless a firm has a dominant market position, collusion must be the means to the exercise of market power. In accord with the Chicago school's per-

---

[37]See Green and Porter (1984) for a presentation and empirical test of this theory.
[38]See Ordover and Willig (1983) for an evaluation of the DOJ merger guidelines.
[39]Department of Justice and Federal Trade Commission, Horizontal Merger Guidelines, Washington, D.C., April 2, 1992.

spective, the greater the number of firms that would have to collude to restrict output the more likely collusion is to break down. Collusion is easier the more homogeneous the product, since then there is only one dimension of competition that must be monitored under an explicit or implicit collusive arrangement. Collusion is more difficult when substitutes are available in the relevant markets and is easier when repeated encounters provide an opportunity to punish cheating.

In its definition of the relevant market, the DOJ and FTC focus on "economically meaningful" markets. Those are defined in terms of products and geographic areas in which a firm could restrict output and thereby impose a price increase above prevailing levels. To do so, a firm would have to have horizontal market power. Assessing market power involves consideration of substitute products, since an attempt to raise prices may cause consumers to switch to a substitute. It also takes into account imports and the resale market for durable goods. When the DOJ or FTC concludes that market power is present, it also considers whether the acquired firm would fail in the absence of the merger.

To implement this perspective in the case of horizontal mergers, the DOJ and FTC use the Herfindahl-Hirschman index (HHI) to measure concentration in an industry. The HHI is defined as the sum of the squares of the market shares of firms, or

$$HHI = \sum_{i=1}^{n} s_i^2,$$

where n is the number of firms in the industry and s_i is the market share of the ith firm expressed as a percent. The HHI for a perfectly competitive industry is zero and for a monopoly is 10,000. If 2 firms with 10 percent market shares merge, the HHI increases by 200. For an industry with 10 firms with equal market shares, the HHI is 1,000, and for an industry with 2 firms with 30 percent shares and 8 with 5 percent shares, the HHI is 2,000.

The guidelines indicate that the agencies will not challenge a merger in which the postmerger HHI is below 1,000. They are unlikely to challenge a merger in which the postmerger HHI is between 1,000 and 1,800 (six equal-size firms) unless the merger would increase the HHI by more than 100. In the case of an industry with an HHI above 1,800, they are unlikely to investigate if the merger increases the HHI by less than 50 and are likely to investigate if the HHI increases by at least 100. The agencies, however, will take into account other factors that affect market power or its exercise.

The use of the HHI requires identification of the relevant market. One approach to identifying the relevant market is to attempt to identify the scope of substitutes for the product. Another approach is to use data to identify which products compete with which others. This approach was used in the chapter case *The Staples-Office Depot Merger?*

The chapter case *The Staples-Office Depot Merger?* considers an important merger decision centering on the effect of a merger on competition and prices.[40] In this case, using product price data the courts defined the relevant market as office supply superstores, and since there were only three superstores, the HHI was high. Moreover, the HHI would increase substantially if two superstores merged. A merger, however, can result in greater efficiency, and in 1997 the FTC issued a revision to Section 4 of the merger guidelines. While identifying the potential efficiencies from merger, the FTC stated that the efficiencies considered should be net of the efficiencies that would have been realized in the absence of a merger. The FTC also stated that any efficiency claims must be substantiated and verifiable, and that efficiencies would likely carry little weight if the merger were to create a monopoly or near-monopoly. The efficiency considerations played an important role in this case.

---

[40]See also Baker (1997) and Dalkin and Warren-Boulton (1999) for analyses of the Staples-Office Depot case.

In addition to the structural factors involving market concentration, the antitrust agencies may take into account technological change in an industry and the rate of innovation. A large market share by merging companies in an industry that experiences rapid technological change may be of little concern because market share can be won or lost relatively quickly. Similar reasoning led to dropping the government's antitrust suit against IBM.

The antitrust enforcement agencies frequently will negotiate with the merging companies under the "fix it first" approach in which areas of antitrust concern are dealt with prior to the merger being consummated. For example, to preserve competition the DOJ required the $1.75 billion divestment of MCI's Internet business as a condition for approval of its 1998 merger with WorldCom. Similarly, in 1996 the FTC required Ciba-Geigy and Sandoz to sell part of their gene-therapy technology as a condition for their merger to form Novatis.

After the end of the cold war the Department of Defense encouraged U.S. defense contractors to consolidate as a means of lowering costs during a period of reduced military spending. Several mergers resulted, including that of Lockheed and Martin Marietta. In 1997 Lockheed Martin and Northrup Grumman, the second and third largest military contractors, respectively, announced a merger. The DOJ with the support of the Department of Defense challenged the merger on the grounds that it would threaten national defense by limiting competition. For example, the merged company would be a supplier of components for other firms that compete with it, and it could raise the prices for those components to make its rivals less competitive for defense contracts. After months of negotiations attempting to fix the concerns, the two companies abandoned their merger plans.

Antitrust enforcement has also been active in health care industry mergers. The FTC blocked the four largest pharmaceutical wholesalers from merging into two companies. The FTC also blocked several mergers of hospitals in small towns where the merger would have reduced competition substantially, even though cost reductions would be realized through the consolidations.

Nonhorizontal mergers, either vertical or conglomerate, do not affect market concentration and so are not necessarily a threat to competition. Non-horizontal mergers are a concern only to the extent that they have horizontal consequences, such as eliminating a potential entrant. The FTC blocked the merger of SBC and Ameritech because the two companies would be potential competitors once the telecommunications industry has been deregulated. A vertical merger could also serve to create barriers to entry if it forced potential entrants to enter more than one level of the market simultaneously or make entry at one level more difficult.

State Antitrust Enforcement

As the DOJ and FTC became more reluctant to bring to the courts certain types of antitrust cases during the 1980s, state attorneys general became more active in filing antitrust suits under state and federal law.[41] For example, in the first year of the Reagan administration the FTC brought only 41 consumer fraud cases, which was half the number under the Carter administration. (In 1997 the FTC brought 245 consumer fraud cases.) The attorneys general of 19 states joined the DOJ in the chapter case *The Microsoft Antitrust Case.* State attorneys general also negotiated the tobacco settlements in 1997 and 1998. States have also been more active on issues affecting their residents.

[41]See Hayes (1989) for an analysis of state antitrust laws. The FTC at times joins with state attorneys general in the investigation of cases.

For example, in 1998 25 state attorneys general threatened to file an antitrust suit against the major airlines for predation against small airlines with the intent of forcing them out of airports in their states. The attorneys general deferred action awaiting Clinton administration guidelines intended to promote competition.

Compliance

Compliance with the antitrust laws involves both procedures and policy. Firms provide training and guidance to employees who may encounter situations in which antitrust concerns are present. For example, in its Standards of Business Conduct, Hewlett Packard provides guidance on trade practices (vertical arrangements), price discrimination, unfair practices, and competitor relations (horizontal practices).

A firm may find itself in a situation in which a contemplated practice falls in an area in which the antitrust laws and the court decisions interpreting them are unclear or changing. In addition to seeking the advice of counsel, the firm should examine whether the purpose of its proposed practice is anticompetitive. In *Sylvania* the court held that the policy of territorial restrictions served the purpose of stimulating interbrand competition. In such a case, a firm should use the practice that is the least restrictive in achieving the desired purpose. In *Sylvania* the court on retrial acquitted GTE-Sylvania because it concluded that the practice of terminating a dealer who violated its policy was the least restrictive means of achieving the intended purpose of strengthening its dealer network. Hewlett Packard's policy on terminating relationships reflects the decisions in *Sylvania, Monsanto,* and *Sharp* as well as the remaining ambiguity: "Terminating relationships with customers can lead to litigation. It is therefore important that the decision to terminate be made carefully and for valid business reasons. HP's Legal Department should be consulted before terminating any such relationship without the customer's consent. Possible termination of one customer's contract should not be discussed with another customer."[42]

The Politics of Antitrust

Antitrust policy has important distributive as well as efficiency consequences for firms and consumers, so it is the subject of political action.[43] In the 1970s the FTC adopted an aggressive posture and initiated several new investigations, some of which were directed at such politically influential industries as insurance and funeral homes. The political pressure on Congress was such that it passed the Federal Trade Commission Improvements Act of 1980, which reined in the FTC.[44] The framework for political analysis presented in Part II of this book provides the basis for analyzing the politics of antitrust policy.

Most proposed changes in the antitrust laws fail because of the intensity of the ensuing politics and the complexity of the issues. In 1986 the Reagan administration launched legislative initiatives to revise the antitrust laws. It proposed amending Section 7 of the Clayton Act (which deals with mergers) by replacing "may be" and "tend to" with "significant probability." It also proposed relaxing merger standards for firms

---

[42]Hewlett Packard Corporation, "Standards of Business Conduct," Palo Alto, CA, 1989.
[43]See Shugart (1990) for a perspective on antitrust and interest group politics.
[44]See Weingast and Moran (1983), Moe (1985), and Wilson (1989, Chap. 13) for differing perspectives on the relationship between the FTC and Congress.

that had been injured by foreign competition. Because of a concern that private antitrust suits were being used to stifle competition, the administration proposed eliminating treble damages except for price fixing violations. The FTC and the Reagan administration also proposed that the FTC authority over unfair advertising be eliminated, because the term *unfair* was too vague to be enforced. None of these initiatives was successful.

Democrats in Congress have also sought revisions in the antitrust laws, attempting to counter DOJ and FTC decisions to stop bringing suits for certain vertical restraints. They have also attempted to revise the standards established by the Supreme Court in *Monsanto* and *Sharp* involving nonprice vertical arrangements. In 1991, for example, the Senate passed a bill that would make it easier to win suits against retail price maintenance practices. Both activist groups and discounters who had been cut off by manufacturers backed the bill, arguing that consumers were injured by the nonprice arrangements. They were opposed by manufacturers and specialty retailers, who viewed vertical arrangements as promoting interbrand competition. The bill was not enacted.

As mentioned in the previous section, 25 state attorneys general threatened antitrust actions against major airlines for predatory pricing and in addition launched an investigation of the three alliances formed by the six largest airlines.[45] The Clinton administration had proposed guidelines that specified when action would be taken against a major airline for driving a low-cost competitor out of a market by lowering prices substantially and providing more seats on routes. The administration reported that fares for last-minute travel had skyrocketed and that the number of cities served by more than two airlines had fallen by 41 percent in less than 10 years. The airlines countered with a lobbying and public advocacy campaign charging that the Clinton administration was attempting to reregulate the airline industry. One airline hired a former Clinton administration official who argued there was no basis for intervention in the industry. The airlines increased their political contributions by 66 percent in the 1997–1998 election cycle, and backed a bill in Congress that would have delayed for at least a year the implementation of any guidelines. The House Transportation Committee rejected the bill in favor of requiring notification by the Clinton administration before any guidelines were implemented.

The politics of antitrust also manifests itself in legislative action seeking exemptions or providing for affirmative defenses in antitrust suits. As an example, for decades the soft drink industry had been organized around exclusive territories for its distributors. Soft drink manufacturers produced syrup, which was sold to bottlers who were allowed to distribute the soft drink only in a specified geographic area. In July 1971, the FTC issued complaints against seven national-brand soft drink syrup manufacturers, including Coca-Cola, PepsiCo, Seven-Up, and Canada Dry. The complaints charged that exclusive territorial distributorships were illegal vertical restraints of trade. With the strong support of the National Soft Drink Association, in 1972 a bill was introduced in the Senate to permit exclusive territorial arrangements for soft drink manufacturers.

The FTC complaint was resolved in 1978 when the FTC ruled that the exclusive distributorships were anticompetitive. The decision was appealed and was still before the courts when Congress finally acted. After 10 years of effort, the soft drink manufacturers and their bottlers succeeded in December 1980 in obtaining an effective antitrust exemption. The Soft Drink Interbrand Competition Act provided protection from antitrust suits if soft drinks were in "substantial and effective competition." Despite op-

---

[45] *The New York Times,* July 25, 1998.

position by the DOJ, the bill passed the Senate on an 86 to 6 vote, passed the House on a voice vote, and was signed by President Carter.[46]

Summary

The principal antitrust laws are the Sherman Act, the Clayton Act, and the Federal Trade Commission Act. The Sherman Act pertains to monopolization and restraints of trade. The Clayton Act addresses monopolization and restraints of trade in their incipiency and provides the basis for government authority over mergers. The act also restricts price discrimination. The Federal Trade Commission Act prohibits unfair competition and unfair practices.

Both the DOJ and the FTC have enforcement responsibilities for the Sherman and Clayton Acts, but only the FTC can enforce the FTC Act. Considerable enforcement of the antitrust laws occurs through private lawsuits, most of which are filed by one firm against another. Private lawsuits are stimulated by the prospect of treble damages.

Antitrust enforcement and court decisions are influenced by schools of thought about the role of antitrust policy and the likelihood of adverse economic effects from business practices. The structural approach is based on the structure-conduct-performance paradigm and focuses on the structure of industries and on practices that may foreclose opportunities for competitors. The Chicago school focuses on economic efficiency and views markets as both resilient and the consumer's best protection. Both the structural approach and the Chicago school view horizontal market power as a concern but have differed about how likely collusion is and how substantial are barriers to entry. The Chicago school concludes that most practices should be considered under the rule of reason, whereas the structural approach supports a wider range of *per se* illegal practices. The new industrial organization perspective emphasizes the interactions among competitors that can result from repeated interactions and incomplete information. These strategic interactions have the potential to sustain implicit collusion and limit entry into industries. This perspective also focuses on factors such as network externalities and standardization that can provide the basis for anticompetitive practices.

These schools of thought have influenced the thinking of government antitrust officials and judges. In the case of vertical arrangements and maximum price restrictions, the courts reversed earlier decisions in holding that nonprice vertical arrangements are no longer *per se* illegal but are to be considered under a rule of reason. Certain arrangements that enhance interbrand competition but harm intrabrand competition have been held by the courts to be legal under the antitrust laws. The DOJ and FTC have applied revised guidelines to the surveillance of mergers. The guidelines are based both on industry structure and on the likelihood that market power can be exercised.

Antitrust policy has important distributive consequences and so is the subject of considerable political activity. The complexity of the issues, however, makes significant legislative changes in the antitrust laws difficult to achieve.

---

[46]The case *The Malt Beverage Interbrand Competition Act* in Baron (1996) concerns the beer industry's attempt to obtain similar protection.

CASES

Apple Computer and Mail-Order Sales

Apple Computer Corporation of Cupertino, California, started the personal computer industry. At first most of its sales were to hobbyists. As the market began to develop, Apple shifted its emphasis to home computers. By 1981, however, the market changed again as business and professional demand began to grow. The personal computer industry had been born, and in 1981 Apple was the market leader. Apple faced competition from several firms, including Compaq, Radio Shack, Sinclair, and Commodore. IBM was expected to enter the market with its own personal computer in the near future.

The distribution channel had become increasingly important as the market evolved to the personal computer phase. Apple computers were sold primarily through its 1,100 dealers, and dealers sold both over the counter and by mail order. Mail-order sales were generally made to knowledgeable buyers who did not need point-of-purchase information about the selection of a computer and to customers located in areas with no Apple dealers. At the end of 1981, Apple decided to emphasize personal service. It changed its distribution policy, no longer allowing sales that could not be supported with both maintenance and personal service. The policy change meant that telephone and mail-order sales would no longer be permitted. Apple sent out amended contracts to its dealers and included a letter explaining its new policy. In the letter, Apple Vice President Fred Hoar wrote, "Mail-order sales are neither suited to providing the consumer education that emerging markets require, nor are they structured to provide the customer satisfaction that has become associated with the Apple name." Hoar added that no exceptions would be made.

Most Apple dealers reacted favorably to the policy. They faced the problem of customers coming to their stores, obtaining the information needed to make educated choices, and then buying by mail order to save money. The suggested list price for an Apple III computer was $3,495, and Apple dealers could sell it at any price they wished. Some mail-order houses sold it for $2,800. Apple sold the computer to dealers for $2,325 when they made multiple-unit purchases. Edward E. Faber, president of the 182-store ComputerLand system, which sold Apple computers at the suggested list price, welcomed the change in policy. "It's discouraging to do all the presale education and support of a prospective customer, and then have him buy the equipment somewhere else." Faber said that it cost about $150,000 to open a store that provided sales support and maintenance. "If the dealer makes that kind of investment, he must get a return on the sale of the product," he explained. Losing sales to mail-order houses reduced the incentive to provide the service that Apple desired.

Joseph Sidney, owner of Micro Business World of Tarzana, California, said Apple's new policy "stinks" and was "an outright effort to fix prices." He maintained that the mail-order houses adequately educated customers about the choice of a computer and provided sufficient service. Joseph Monroe of Consumer Computers of San Diego said that 75 percent of his $6 million sales were by mail order and Apple's new policy would put him out of business. The mail-order houses argued that Apple was adopting the policy because its dealers were pressuring it to do so.

Mail-order sales of Apple computers were also made by nondealers such as New York's 47th Street Photo, which sold 3,000 Apples a year. Nondealers would not reveal where they obtained their computers, but it was generally understood that they purchased them from Apple dealers who had overpurchased.

One of the most vocal critics of Apple's policy was Francis Ravel, owner of Olympic Sales Company of Los Angeles. "There are about 150 black sheep like us. All we want to do is to buy and sell and be left alone . . . They can't tell us not to ship from our store. Hewlett-Packard wouldn't dare do that." Ravel filed a suit in federal district court in Los Angeles charging that Apple's policy violated federal antitrust law. Ravel asked for a preliminary injunction. Apple described the suit as "completely without merit."

Steve Jobs, cofounder and chairman of Apple, said: "What we're doing is the state of the art in antitrust law. We could go all the way to the Supreme Court." He added: "It's not discounting that bothers us. It's the smile—or rather, the lack of it—on our customer's face when service isn't adequate." ■

PREPARATION QUESTIONS

1. What sections of the antitrust laws pertain to Apple's new policy? What case law is applicable? Is this a *per se* offense or will the case be governed by a rule of reason?
2. On whom is the burden of proof and what does that party have to show?
3. What defense should Apple use?
4. What decision should the court make?

The Staples-Office Depot Merger?

On September 4, 1996, Staples, Inc., the fast-growing No. 2 office supply retailer, agreed to buy Office Depot, Inc., the industry leader, in a transaction valued at $3.36 billion. Staples and Office Depot were among the pioneers that a decade earlier developed the successful concept of office supply superstores. By pursuing aggressive marketing strategies, charging low prices, and leveraging their buying power and efficient mass supply channels to cut costs, the companies created a profitable, rapidly growing industry. Staples had the second largest superstore chain in the United States with approximately 550 stores in 28 states, $3 billion annual revenues, and net income of $74 million. With more than 500 stores in 38 states, Office Depot had the largest sales, approximately $5.3 billion, and net income of $132 million. The only other office supply superstore chain was OfficeMax, Inc.

The companies had identified significant cost reductions as the main reason for the merger. Thomas Stemberg, chairman and CEO of Staples, said, for example, that the two companies bought envelopes from three separate vendors. "We'd entertain proposals from all three," he said, "and we'd say, you can have all of the business or none of it."[1] Stemberg also commented on the combined entity's ability to pass through the savings to customers: "Both Staples and Office Depot were founded a decade ago to bring savings to purchasers of office products. The combined company, with over $10 billion in revenues, will be able to offer even greater value to our customers through increasing operating efficiency and purchasing scale."[2]

The companies, as well as commentators, anticipated from the outset that the transaction would raise antitrust concerns: "The merged organization—with 1,100 stores in 96% of the country's largest metropolitan areas—will reduce the number of distributors for manufacturers, giving them less bargaining power. The deal is also likely to draw close scrutiny from the U.S. antitrust regulators."[3] David Fuente, chairman and CEO of Office Depot, referred to these issues, stressing both that the companies did not compete with each other in many geographical areas, and that the market was much larger than the joint company. Fuente said, "The reality today is that there's very little overlap in our store base and geographical locations, and two or three years from now that might not be the case if both companies continue to grow at the pace that we were predicting."[4] Fuente also stated, "Our new company operates in an office products industry which is very large, highly fragmented and growing rapidly. As a result of this strategic combination, we will be better positioned to participate fully in the enormous growth opportunities that exist in our industry."[5] Juris Pagrabs, vice president of Investor Relations of OfficeMax, the

[1] *The Wall Street Journal,* September 5, 1996.

[2] *Business Wire,* September 4, 1996.
[3] *The Wall Street Journal,* September 5, 1996.
[4] *The Wall Street Journal,* September 5, 1996.
[5] *Business Wire,* September 4, 1996.

third office supply superstore chain, offered a positive view on the announced merger, "We think the merger is quite good for the industry. It's better to have two players instead of three."[6]

The Federal Trade Commission (FTC) did not share this view. The FTC contended that the overall expected effect of the proposed merger on customers would be negative, since it expected the merger to reduce competition significantly in many markets. Underlying this contention was a claim that the expected pass-through to customers of the efficiencies created by the merger would not be large enough to offset the effect of the reduction in competition. The issue, thus, revolved around the assessment of the expected economic consequences of the planned merger. To assess these effects, verbal pronouncements such as "reduction in competition," "respective market," and "efficiencies that pass-through to customers" had to be reduced to quantifiable measures.

THE ANTITRUST REVIEW

Following the procedure required by Hart-Scott-Rodino, Staples and Office Depot filed a Premerger Notification and Report Form with the FTC and the Department of Justice on October 2, 1996. This was followed by a 7-month investigation by the FTC, in which additional information was requested from the companies, hundreds of boxes of documents were examined, depositions were taken of 18 officers and employees of both Staples and Office Depot, and (*ex parte*) discovery of third-party information was made. The FTC voted 4 to 1 to challenge the merger. In an attempt to satisfy the FTC's objections, Staples and Office Depot negotiated a consent decree with the FTC staff that would allow the merger if the companies would sell 63 stores to OfficeMax for $109 million to reduce the concentration in those local markets. The FTC, however, in a shock to the companies, rejected the negotiated consent decree by a vote of 3 to 2, and in a revision of its merger guidelines it expressed skepticism about projected cost efficiencies from mergers that cannot "be verified by reasonable means." The FTC then filed a motion with the District Court of the District of Columbia on April 9, 1997, seeking a preliminary injunction of the merger. The matter thus was for the court to decide.

[6]*The Wall Street Journal,* September 5, 1996.

THE COURT'S REVIEW

In deciding whether to issue a preliminary injunction, the court required the FTC to show (1) that its challenge was *likely* to succeed on the merits after complete consideration of the facts; and (2) that in "balancing the equities," it was of greater harm to let the transaction proceed and later try to reverse it than to enjoin it until the review process reached its final conclusion. Since the preliminary proceedings raised the key issues that would be raised in the complete review process, the hearing on the preliminary injunction would in effect resolve the entire case. The findings of fact by the court are considered to evaluate whether these conditions were satisfied.[7]

LIKELIHOOD OF SUCCESS ON THE MERITS

The Geographic Market

There was no dispute that the appropriate geographic market was 42 metropolitan areas in which Staples and Office Depot competed with each other prior to the merger agreement, as well as several areas in which they planned to begin competing in the near future.

The Product Market

The court defined the product market for antitrust purposes as "the sale of consumable office supplies *through office superstores,*" thereby accepting the FTC's claim that although the products Staples and Office Depot sold had perfect functional substitutes sold by other stores such as Wal-Mart, the market should be viewed as office superstores only. The court based its conclusion on pricing data.

The FTC compared Staples' prices in geographic markets in which Staples was the only office superstore (termed one-firm markets) with markets in which it competed with Office Depot or OfficeMax (two-firm markets), or both (three-firm markets). Prices in one-firm markets were, on average, 13 percent higher than in three-firm markets.[8] Prices were compared at one point in time (January 1997), and they were based on a sample accounting for 90 percent of Staples's sales. Addi-

[7]These findings are based on the public version of the decision. The court examined specific price data submitted by the parties in classified documents. The public version of these documents, as well as the decision, withheld all these data.

[8]These price data had been submitted by the companies.

tional, less comprehensive data showed that average prices were well over 5 percent higher in one-firm markets than in two-firm markets. Based on the merger guidelines, price differences of 5 percent or more were viewed by the court as indirect evidence that office supply superstores were a distinct product market for antitrust purposes. The FTC presented similar evidence regarding Office Depot's prices based on a sample of 500 items (also from January 1997). Prices in Office Depot-only markets were on average well over 5 percent higher than they were in three-firm markets. Additional data showed that on average Office Depot's prices were highest in its one-firm markets and lowest in its three-firm markets.

The FTC also had to determine if the office superstores represented a largely independent market or were part of a much broader office supply market of which the companies had only a 5.5 percent market share. To do this, the FTC considered the cross elasticity of demand between products in the superstore market and their functional substitutes in the broader markets. (The cross elasticity of demand is the percentage change in the demand for one product divided by the percentage change in the price of another product.)

Retail and discount chains other than office superstores carried consumable office supplies (functional substitutes), and the court identified the set of other sellers as Wal-Mart, Kmart, and Target; wholesale clubs such as BJ's and Price Costco; computer and electronic stores such as Computer City and Best Buy; independent retail office supply stores; mail-order firms; and contract stationers. The court reasoned that "these competitors, albeit in different combinations and concentrations, are present in every one of [the superstores' markets]." Despite this fact, Staples and Office Depot were able to charge higher prices in their one-firm markets than they did in their two- and three-firm markets. The court found a lower price sensitivity to the existence of other superstore competitors. For example, Staples maintained a "warehouse-club-only" price zone, which was a zone where it competed with a warehouse club but not with other superstores. The data the FTC presented showed average variation in prices of only 1 to 2 percent between warehouse-club-only zones and one-firm markets; that is, the cross-elasticity of demand was low, suggesting that the stores were not competing in the same market. These findings led the court to conclude that the office superstore market was distinguishable from other markets for consumable office supplies and should thus be considered the product market for antitrust purposes.

Perceptions and Behavior of Market Participants

The court also based its definition of the product market on several additional considerations. First, in all of their internal documents and communications, both Staples and Office Depot viewed the relevant competitive market as comprised of the office superstores only. For example, when determining whether to enter a new metropolitan area, both companies repeatedly referred to markets without office superstores as "non-competitive," regardless of the existence of other sellers of office supplies. Staples used the phrase "office superstore industry" in strategic planning documents. In a monthly report entitled "Competitor Store Opening/Closing Report," which it circulated to its Executive Committee, Office Depot reported all competitor store closings and openings, but the only competitors referred to were Staples and OfficeMax.

Also, both companies price checked the other superstores much more frequently and extensively than they checked other retail outlets. Executives of non-superstore competitors, who were summoned to testify by the FTC were aware of the distinct nature of the superstore market. The court concluded that Staples and Office Depot considered the other superstores as their primary competition.

Cost Differentials

Staples and Office Depot offered two cost differential explanations for the average price differentials between one-, two- and three-firm markets. The first explanation was that there were differences in wages and rents across localities. These differences, however, were not correlated with the price differences across localities, so the court rejected this explanation.

The second explanation was related to differences in advertising and marketing costs. Indeed, these costs were higher, on average, in one-firm markets than in two- and three-firm markets. Yet, the court found that the differences in costs were too small to account for the significant price differentials shown by the FTC. The court rejected the second explanation, as well.

Distinctive Features

The court also distinguished between the superstores and other distribution channels in terms of appearance, physical size, format, variety of items offered, and the type and character of targeted and served customers. The court concluded, ". . . office supply superstores look far different from other sellers of office supplies . . . No one entering a Wal-Mart would mistake it for an office superstore."

THE PROBABLE EFFECT ON COMPETITION

Concentration

Once the relevant product market was defined, the concentration analysis was straightforward. The court examined the concentration within each identified geographic market. The HHIs in many of the geographic markets were at "problematic levels" even before the merger. The least concentrated market had an HHI of 3,597, and the most concentrated had 6,944. In contrast, if the merger were completed, the least concentrated market would have an HHI of 5,003, and many areas would have an HHI of 10,000 (i.e., monopoly). The Merger Guidelines stated that unless mitigated by other factors, an increase in the HHI in excess of 50 in a post-merger, highly concentrated market, raised significant competitive concerns. The average increase in the HHI caused by the Staples-Office Depot merger would have been 2,715 points.

The court also examined concentration statistics. The merged Staples-Office Depot was expected to hold a dominant market share in 42 geographic markets across the country. In 15 markets the combined market share would be 100 percent.

The court's definition of the relevant product market had, in effect, determined the concentration issue. If the product market had been defined more broadly as, for example, "consumable office supplies" or "office supplies," the concentration figures would have been much lower. The product market definition had a similar effect on the consideration of the entry.

Entry

The court assessed the existence and significance of barriers to entry with respect to the relevant market. Staples and Office Depot claimed that the rapid growth in overall office supply sales had encouraged, and would continue to encourage, expansion and entry. They pointed to the fact that all office superstore entrants had entered within the last 11 years, and they also offered testimony regarding the general ability of mass merchandisers of various types to change store configurations and shift shelf space to accommodate new demands. Yet, the FTC showed that new superstore entrants did not survive as self-sustaining businesses. The number of office superstore chains dropped from 23 to 3 over the few years preceding 1997. All but Staples, Office Depot, and OfficeMax had either closed or been acquired. The failed office superstore entrants included large, well-known retailers such as Kmart, Montgomery Ward, Ames, and Zayles.

The court determined that a "new office superstore would need to open a large number of stores nationally to achieve the purchasing and distribution economies of scale enjoyed by the three existing firms." The court thus found that it would be extremely unlikely that a new office superstore would enter the market and thereby lessen the anticompetitive effects of the proposed merger.

The court also concluded that even in one-firm markets no retailer had successfully expanded its consumable office supplies to the extent that it constrained superstore pricing increases to less than 5 percent. Entry into the relevant market was therefore rejected as a factor likely to offset the merger's expected anticompetitive effects.

Efficiencies

Staples and Office Depot submitted an "Efficiencies Analysis" that predicted that the combined business would achieve savings of between \$4.9 and \$6.5 billion over the first 5 years. The companies also claimed that additional dynamic efficiencies would result because the superstores' suppliers would become more efficient as a result of the increase in their sales to the combined business. Staples and Office Depot argued that two-thirds of the cost savings would be passed along to consumers.

The court, however, found these figures to be inflated and unreliable and preferred the evidence and expert testimony the FTC provided. First, the court noted that the estimates provided by the companies exceeded by almost 500 percent the figures that were presented to the two boards of directors in September 1996, when they approved the transaction, and which had been disclosed to the companies' shareholders and the SEC in the Joint Proxy Statement/Prospectus of January 1997. Second, the companies estimated only the overall savings that the merger was expected to yield and did not deduct the savings both companies would generate as stand-alone entities if the merger did not materialize. Third, large parts of the argued savings were unverifiable—the companies' experts could not provide figures and explicit methods of calculation to justify the projections.

The court also found the companies' projected pass-through of savings to customers in the form of lower prices to be unrealistic. The court did not find a convincing argument for the combined business to significantly increase its pass-through rate to two-thirds from the historical pass-through rate of 15 to 17 percent established by the evidence.[9]

Pricing Practices

The court used the historical pass-through rate as an indication of the likely future rate. In a similar manner, as an indication of the likely future behavior and practices of the combined entity, the court used the historical pricing practices of the two companies, which had been established in identifying the relevant product market. This further supported the likely anticompetitive effects of the merger: "The evidence of the defendants' own current pricing practices, for example, shows that an office superstore chain facing no competition from other superstores has the ability to profitably raise prices for consumable office supplies above competitive levels. . . Since prices are significantly lower in markets where Staples and Office Depot compete, eliminating this competition with one another would free the parties to charge higher prices in those markets, especially those in which the combined entity would be the sole office superstore." The court therefore concluded that the FTC had shown that its case was likely to succeed on its merits. The court then considered the equities.

[9]One of the FTC's expert witnesses presented uncontroverted evidence that Staples has historically passed through 15 to 17 percent of firm-specific cost savings in the form of lower prices to consumers.

BALANCE OF EQUITIES

The court concluded that, " 'Unscrambling the eggs' after the fact is not a realistic option in this case." The combined company's post-merger plans included consolidation of warehouse and supply facilities, closing 40 to 70 superstores, changing the name of Office Depot stores to "Staples," renegotiating contracts with manufacturers and suppliers, and consolidating management, which was likely to lead to layoffs of many Office Depot key personnel.

The court then turned to consider the possible private equities. Staples and Office Depot argued that the principal private equity at stake was the loss to Office Depot shareholders, who would likely lose a substantial portion of their investments if the merger were enjoined. While acknowledging this possible harm to Office Depot shareholders "at least in the short term," the court concluded that such private equity alone did not justify a denial of preliminary injunction where the public equity clearly supported it.

The court issued the preliminary injunction requested by the FTC. Shortly thereafter, Staples and Office Depot terminated their merger agreement. ■

PREPARATION QUESTIONS

1. What was the key finding by the court that effectively decided the case for a preliminary injunction?
2. Was the court's analysis of the pricing data appropriate for determining the likely effects of the merger?
3. Could Staples and Office Depot be reasonably expected to pass two-thirds of any cost efficiencies through to consumers?
4. Since Staples and Office Depot and their attorneys understood the antitrust laws and the facts the court would examine, why did they believe that the FTC and the courts would not block the merger?
5. As a commissioner of the FTC how would you have voted on the consent decree negotiated by your staff?

The Microsoft Antitrust Case

> At a 1995 meeting with Intel, Microsoft's Chairman and CEO Bill Gates said, according to an Intel executive, "This antitrust thing will blow over. We haven't changed our business practices at all."

On May 18, 1998, the U.S. Department of Justice (DOJ) together with 19 states filed an antitrust action against Microsoft Corporation in U.S. District Court. The DOJ complaint was filed under Sections 1 and 2 of the Sherman Act (the Act) to restrain anticompetitive conduct by Microsoft, the world's largest supplier of computer software for personal computers (PCs), and to remedy effects of its alleged past unlawful conduct. The complaint alleged that Microsoft "began and continues today, a pattern of anticompetitive practices designed to thwart browser competition on the merits, to deprive customers of choice between alternative browsers, and to exclude Microsoft's Internet browser competitors," most notably Netscape Communications Inc.

The DOJ specifically alleged four violations of the Act:

1. **Microsoft engaged in "unlawful exclusive dealing and other exclusionary agreements"** (Section 1 of the Act). The DOJ contended that Microsoft's agreements requiring other companies not to license, distribute, or promote non-Microsoft products, or to do so only on terms that materially disadvantage such products, and its agreements with PC manufacturers restricting modification or customization of the PC boot-up sequence and screens "unreasonably restrict competition." These agreements allegedly restricted the access of Microsoft's software competitors to significant segments of the market. The DOJ claimed that "the purpose and effect of these agreements are to restrain trade and competition in the Internet browser and PC operating system markets."
2. **Microsoft engaged in "unlawful tying"** (Section 1 of the Act). The DOJ viewed the Windows operating systems and Microsoft's Internet Explorer browser as separate products—since they were sold in different markets, their functions were different, there was separate demand for them, and they were treated by Microsoft and other industry participants as separate products. The DOJ claimed that it was socially "efficient for Microsoft not to tie them and/or to permit [PC manufacturers] to distribute Windows 95 and Windows 98 without Microsoft's Internet browser software." The DOT argued that "Mircosoft had tied and plans again to tie its Internet browser to its separate Windows operating system, which has monopoly power," where the "purpose and the effect of this tying are to prevent customers from choosing among Internet browsers on their merits and to foreclose competing browsers from an important channel of distribution."
3. **Microsoft monopolized the PC operating systems market** (Section 2 of the Act). The DOJ contended that Microsoft "possesses monopoly power in the market for PC operating systems." The DOJ claimed that Microsoft had maintained that power through anticompetitive conduct.
4. **Microsoft attempted to monopolize the Internet** (Section 2 of the Act). The DOJ claimed that Microsoft had targeted software products that had the potential to compete with or facilitate the development of products to compete with its Windows operating system and thereby "erode Microsoft's Windows operating system monopoly." Microsoft allegedly engaged in a "course of conduct, including tying and unreasonably exclusionary agreements," for the purpose of obtaining a "monopoly in the Internet browser market."

In contrast to a private antitrust suit the burden of proof on the plaintiff was lower in a federal suit, since only sanctions to stop abusive practices and not damages were sought. "To do that, the Government must convincingly show 'the power and conditions from which injury can be inferred,' according to Herbert Hovenkamp, a University of Iowa law professor."[1]

THE 1995 CONSENT DECREE

The DOJ also sought to show that Microsoft remained dismissive of a long-running antitrust investigation, even after Microsoft had signed a consent decree with the DOJ in 1995. The DOJ had filed an

[1] *The New York Times,* January 18, 1999.

action against Microsoft under Section 2 of the Sherman Act for "unlawfully maintaining its monopoly in the market for PC operating systems." The complaint alleged, among other things, that Microsoft had engaged in anticompetitive agreements and marketing practices directed at PC manufacturers, and the consent decrees restricted those practices.

In 1997 the DOJ filed a complaint against Microsoft alleging that it had violated the consent decree.[2] In response, Judge Thomas Penfield Jackson, in whose court the 1999 antitrust case was also tried, issued a preliminary injunction requiring Microsoft to offer Windows independently of Internet Explorer. In July 1998 a federal Court of Appeals overturned Judge Jackson's order stating that the courts should not be "second guessing the claimed benefits of a particular product design." Applied to the current antitrust case this ruling could provide a defense to Microsoft if it could demonstrate that consumers benefited from the integration of Internet Explorer and the Windows operating system. The DOJ sought to show that they did not so benefit.

MICROSOFT'S POSITION

Microsoft maintained that because of the nature of the industry it did not have a monopoly in the PC operating systems market nor could it become a monopoly in the Internet browser market, despite its current market shares in these markets. The rapid change in technology and in the business environment did not allow a single company to establish and maintain a monopoly. Microsoft also argued that antitrust law definitions such as monopoly identified by market share did not apply to the software market as they did to traditional markets. Since it could not be categorized as a monopoly, Microsoft contended that its business conduct, even if as depicted by the DOJ, did not amount to unlawful conduct and in fact was common in the industry. Microsoft also rejected many of the DOJ's factual claims regarding its actual conduct and intent. For example, Microsoft argued that Windows and Internet Explorer were integrated to provide consumers with a superior product.

ANTITRUST ECONOMICS OF A DYNAMIC NETWORK INDUSTRY

An industry's economics are key in any antitrust case and in particular in the Microsoft case. First, this was the first major case in which a software maker had been taken to trial for alleged antitrust violations. Terms such as "monopoly power" must be understood in the context of the relevant industry. Second, the DOJ demonstrated at least some of the alleged "course of conduct" factual claims with credible clarity. Therefore, it was likely that the decision, and the expected appeal by the loser, would focus on fundamental economic issues rather than on factual controversies.

The key aspect of the economics of the software market, as viewed by antitrust enforcers, were as follows.[3]

Network Effects in a Dynamic Industry

The term "network" applies to the underlying economics of an industry, not to the hardware or software associated with the product. Network effects, or network externalities, are present when an individual's demand for a product is positively related to the usage of other individuals.[4] Network effects might arise in the context of computer software, for example, because users prefer a word processing program that is also used by others. Network effects can also work through complementary goods. Software developers prefer to write to an operating system used by many people, and conversely the greater the number of popular software applications written for it, the greater the demand for the operating system. Network effects are also present in more traditional industries, but the development of industries such as computers, communications, and software have been driven by network effects.

Network Effects and Standards

Even if there were a dominant firm in an industry, multiple technological standards could exist. However, in industries with network effects consumers have incentives to use products compatible with those used by others. A product or system that has a larger community of users than does

[2]See the discussion in Chapter 2.

[3]The discussion in this section is primarily based on a presentation by Daniel Rubinfeld, Deputy Assistant Attorney General at the Antitrust Division of the U.S. Department of Justice, before the 1998 Spring Symposium of the Software Publishers Association, San Jose, California, March 24, 1998.

[4]See Besanko, Dranove, and Shanley (1996), pp. 554–557 for an introduction to network effects. See also Shapiro and Varian (1999) for a treatment of competitive strategy in information and network industries.

its rivals thus may become the dominant standard even if the products of rivals are not compatible with its own. Such a firm may have incentives to adopt competitive strategies to support a single standard by preventing the products of rivals from achieving compatibility.

Industry standards take many forms, and the existence of an industry standard is neither a necessary nor a sufficient condition for the marketplace to be dominated by a single firm. In some instances, as with the Windows operating system, standards are proprietary and the supporting competitive strategies could make entry more difficult and competition less effective. Even when standards are proprietary, however, competition to become the standard can be intense, and competition among multiple standards can persist when network effects are sufficiently limited, or offsetting factors sufficiently strong, to permit multiple networks to survive in the marketplace.

A Single Industry Standard

In markets characterized by strong network effects where users gain by adopting compatible technologies and where economies of scale in the production of complementary goods are present, a dominant standard could emerge in the market. For example, it could be more efficient to write applications for one rather then multiple operating systems. That network effects make it efficient to have a single standard, however, does not imply that the winning standard must be owned or controlled by a single firm.

Predatory Pricing, Incompatibility, Tying and Leveraging as Anticompetitive Strategies

In dynamic high-technology industries characterized by network effects and incentives to move to a common standard, predatory strategies could be used by a dominant firm to thwart socially efficient entry and innovation. To illustrate such a strategy, suppose a firm is considering innovating in a product market that is complementary to the product controlled by a dominant firm; for example, Netscape developing an Internet browser that is complementary to Microsoft's dominant Windows operating system. A dominant firm could attempt to make the innovations of competitors unprofitable by, for example, making its product incompatible with the innovator's product. It could also discourage efficient innovation by offering at a predatory price a close substitute for the competitor's innovative product. A dominant firm could also integrate its version of the innovator's product with its own dominant product and use its existing channels of distribution (e.g., PC manufacturers that rely on the dominant product) to dominate the market for the innovator's product.

Antitrust enforcers are thus concerned about "leveraging" strategies, including product integration, tying, and bundling. Leveraging occurs when a firm uses its advantage from operating in one market to gain an advantage in another market. Leveraging by dominant firms can be procompetitive or anticompetitive, depending on the circumstances. Procompetitive leveraging can be viewed as a form of vertical integration to increase the efficiency of the firm's distribution system, economize on information costs, or provide benefits to customers. Leveraging can be anticompetitive if it raises rivals' costs of competing in the marketplace or reduces their incentives to innovate.

Tying occurs when a firm conditions the purchase (or license) of one product on the purchase (or license) of another product. Procompetitive reasons for tying include cost savings and quality control (it could be easier to sort out the source of quality problems with a tied sale than if the products were sold separately). Tying could also be an anticompetitive leveraging practice if it foreclosed competition in network markets. For example, a dominant firm with a product protected by intellectual property rights could license its technology only to those firms that agree to also license that firm's complementary product. Moreover, the complementary product could build on the firm's next generation technology. Such a tying arrangement could allow the dominant firm to create a new installed base of users of its next generation technology, which could effectively foreclose opportunities for competing firms to offer their products or to develop competing next generation technologies.

Microsoft argued during the trial that many of its competitors employed strategies similar to its own. Competitive strategies identical to those of a dominant firm are likely to be harmless when used by firms with little or no market power. Moreover, the fact that firms with little market power use the same competitive strategies suggests that there are efficiencies associated with those practices. When used by a firm with substantial market power, however, the efficiency benefits of those strategies could be outweighed by the anticompetitive effects associated with reducing innovation.

Tipping in Dynamic Network Industries

Antitrust enforcers are also concerned when an industry with network effects is subject to tipping. Tipping is a point at which the presence of two incompatible products becomes unstable, with the market tipping in favor of a single product and standard. To which product a market tips depends on users' expectations about the strength of network effects, the likely outcome of market competition, and future technological developments. In markets characterized by tipping, exclusionary practices that deny access to established standards can be effective. In such situations, anticompetitive behavior needs to be addressed quickly, since once the market has tipped, it may be very costly or even undesirable to undo the anticompetitive effects (e.g., to switch locked-in users to another standard or to impose different compatibility requirements).

THE TRIAL

The trial consisted of two phases. The first was a decision by Judge Jackson on the specific allegation made by the DOJ. If Judge Jackson found for the DOJ, the second phase would focus on remedies. The DOJ would propose remedies, but the decision would rest with the court. Whatever the decision as rendered by Judge Jackson, the case was expected to be appealed. A decision by the Court of Appeals could take 2 years. If Microsoft were found guilty, it would face a rash of private lawsuits seeking damages. Several private lawsuits had already been filed, and two were scheduled to go to trial in 1999.

The DOJ's Case

The DOJ's complaint was based on a set of factual claims, which together were intended to establish Microsoft's "unlawful course of conduct."

A Monopoly in PC Operating Systems

- Microsoft possessed monopoly power in the market for PC operating systems (OS). Its Windows operating systems were used on over 80 percent of all Intel-based PCs, the dominant type of PC in the United States. More than 90 percent of all new Intel-based PCs were shipped with a pre-installed version of Windows. PC manufacturers were said to have no commercially reasonable alternative to Microsoft's operating systems for their PCs.
- Barriers to entry in the market for PC operating systems were high. One of the most important barriers stemmed from the network effects and was due to the number of software applications that must run on an operating system to make it attractive to end users. Since end users wanted a large number of applications and most applications were written to run on Windows, it would be prohibitively expensive to create an alternative operating system to run the programs that ran on Windows.
- Consequently, the most significant potential threat to Microsoft's operating system monopoly was not from existing or new operating systems but from new software products that could support, or themselves become, alternative "platforms" to which applications could be written, and which could be used on multiple operating systems.

Microsoft's Course of Conduct

The DOJ alleged and presented evidence to the effect that to protect its Windows monopoly against potential competitive threats and to extend its operating system monopoly into other software markets, Microsoft engaged in a series of anticompetitive activities, including:

- Agreements tying other Microsoft software products to its Windows operating system;
- Exclusionary agreements precluding companies from distributing, promoting, buying, or using products of Microsoft's software competitors or potential competitors; and
- Exclusionary agreements restricting the right of companies to provide services or resources to Microsoft's software competitors or potential competitors.

The Threat of Internet Browsers and Java

Potential competition for Microsoft's Windows operating system monopoly could come from the Internet. The DOJ cited Microsoft's CEO, Bill Gates, as saying in May 1995 that the Internet posed a serious potential threat to Microsoft's Windows operating system. Mr. Gates warned his executives:

> A new competitor 'born' on the Internet is Netscape. Their browser is dominant, with a 70% usage share, allowing them to determine which network extensions will catch on. They are pursing a multi-platform strategy where they move the key API [applications programming interface] into the client to commoditize the underlying operating system.

James Barksdale, president and chairman of Netscape, described a June 1995 meeting with Microsoft as exceptional. He said, "I have never been in a meeting in my 35-year business career in which a competitor had so blatantly implied that we would either stop competing with it or the competitor would kill us."[5]

The DOJ asserted that Internet browsers, and in particular Netscape's Navigator browser, posed a competitive threat to Microsoft's operating system monopoly in two basic ways.

- If application programs could easily be written to run on multiple operating systems, competition in the market for operating systems could be revitalized. The combination of browser technology and a new programming language known as Java held this promise. Applications written in Java, a language developed by Sun Microsystems for writing software that would run on any operating system, threatened one of the key barriers to entry protecting Microsoft's operating system monopoly. Browsers represented the most significant vehicle for the distribution of Java technology to end users. Microsoft recognized that the widespread use of browsers could increase the distribution and use of Java and hence threaten Microsoft's operating system monopoly.

  The DOJ presented documents and e-mail messages indicating that Microsoft regarded Java as a key threat. A Microsoft document said that it was a "strategic objective" for Microsoft to "kill cross-platform Java" by expanding the "polluted Java market"—Microsoft's altered version of Java. A senior Microsoft executive identified Java as "our major threat" in an e-mail sent on July 14, 1997, and added that Netscape's Internet browser was Java's "major distribution vehicle."
- Netscape's browser was itself a "platform" to which many applications were being written and to which more and more applications would be written if it remained successful. Since Netscape's browser could run on any PC operating system, the success of this alternative platform threatened a key barrier to entry.

[5]See Cusumano and Yoffie (1998) for an analysis of Netscape and its competition with Microsoft.

Microsoft's Response to the Threat

Microsoft embarked on an extensive campaign to market and distribute its own browser Internet Explorer (IE). Microsoft executives had described this campaign as a "jihad" to win the "browser war." The DOJ acknowledged that continued competition on the merits between Navigator and Internet Explorer would result in greater innovation and the development of better products at lower prices. According to the DOJ's allegations, however, Microsoft was unwilling to compete on the merits. The DOJ cited Microsoft's Christian Wildfeuer writing in February 1997 that Microsoft concluded that it would "be very hard to increase browser share on the merits of IE 4 alone. It will be more important to leverage the OS asset to make people use IE instead of navigator."

The DOJ claimed that Microsoft thus "began, and continues today, a pattern of anti-competitive practices designed to thwart browser competition on the merits, to deprive customers of a choice between alternative browsers, and to exclude Microsoft's Internet browser competitors. . . Microsoft's conduct with respect to browsers is a prominent and immediate example of the pattern of anti-competitive practices undertaken by Microsoft with the purpose and effect of maintaining its PC operating system monopoly and extending that monopoly to other related markets."

A DOJ economics expert asserted that Microsoft also engaged in predatory pricing by giving away its Internet Explorer browser for free. This was done to thwart the threat posed by its main rivals, Netscape and Sun, in Internet software, even though Microsoft had spent more than $100 million a year since 1995 on browser development.

MICROSOFT'S DEFENSE

Microsoft challenged the government's witnesses and sought to support its fundamental line of argument. Microsoft argued that it did not have monopoly power, that any apparent monopoly power could be quickly dissipated in a dynamic industry, that its behavior and practices were not abusive and were similar to standard practices in the industry, and that consumers were not harmed but instead benefited from its practices. Microsoft argued, for example, that it was not a monopolist, since it faced competition from Sun's Java programming language and from Internet browsers. It also maintained that price discounts to PC makers were not favoritism to reward them for not carrying rival products but instead were related to volume. Microsoft also indicated that 100 million copies of Netscape Navigator had been downloaded in 1998, so the distribution of rival software products and Java-based products was easy. As the defendant Microsoft did not have to prove its arguments but instead needed only to raise substantial doubt about the DOJ's allegations.

Microsoft also argued that if it had monopoly power in operating systems it would have charged a much higher price for Windows. A government witness countered that all that the price charged for Windows indicated was "that Microsoft is not maximizing its shortrun profits." The government witness also testified that it would be difficult to determine the exact standard for concluding that a price for Internet Explorer was predatory, but the fact was that Microsoft charged a "zero price."

Microsoft witnesses argued that the relevant market was not operating systems but was much broader and included the Internet and handheld computers, for neither of which Microsoft had a dominant position. Microsoft executives denied allegations of coercive behavior and argued that consumers benefited from its innovations. Paul Maritz, senior group vice president, testified, "Ironically, the very thing that makes Windows valuable to computer manufacturers, software publishers and customers ... is now under attack in this lawsuit. The popularity of Windows, owing entirely to Microsoft's efforts to innovate, evangelize and license the software cheaply to promote wide distribution, is derided as monopoly."

Much of Microsoft's defense was directed at countering the testimony of government witnesses. A considerable portion of that testimony centered on recollections of and notes taken at private meetings between Microsoft and companies such as Apple, Intel, and Netscape. Microsoft witnesses provided different interpretations of what had transpired at the meetings than had the government's witnesses. Paul Maritz, for example, testified that Microsoft opposed Intel's development of software because that software was second-rate and that Microsoft had withheld software support for Intel's MMX microprocessor because of overzealous intellectual property claims by Intel. Maritz also denied that he had ever told an Intel executive that Microsoft would "cut off Netscape's air supply." He also said that Microsoft's reluctance to continue producing software for Apple's Macintosh was due to concerns that Apple might fold.

Microsoft also denied that its practices had harmed Netscape through exclusive arrangements with and financial incentives to PC makers and Internet service providers. A Microsoft attorney stated, "Whatever those arrangements were, whatever measure of exclusivity they created for a period of time, Netscape was able to gain a substantial number of new users. There was no foreclosure of consumer choice."[6]

Microsoft's direct testimony was attacked effectively by DOJ lead attorney David Boies. *The Wall Street Journal* wrote, "Microsoft's defense is in disarray and its executives and economist have been battered so badly on the witness stand that the judge has questioned key elements of the Redmond, Wash., software giant's case."[7] *The New York Times* referred to the trial as "a humbling courtroom experience" for Microsoft.[8] *Fortune* said, "We're seeing Microsoft's defense go down in flames."[9] Microsoft countered that the DOJ's attacks amounted to showmanship and that the case would be decided on the facts and the law. The DOJ's trial strategy of challenging the credibility of Microsoft's witnesses was not only directed at the decision by Judge Jackson but was also intended to protect the decision from being overturned on appeal on matters of credibility. An appeals court could, of course, overturn a decision based on insufficient evidence or on the law.

One major faux pas for Microsoft occurred in Senior Vice President James Allchin's testimony. Allchin showed a videotape produced by Microsoft that purported to show "performance degradations" in the Windows 98 operating system when

---

6 *The New York Times,* February 28, 1999.
7 *The Wall Street Journal,* February 18, 1999.
8 *The New York Times,* February 28, 1999.
9 *Fortune,* March 1, 1999.

Internet Explorer was removed from the system. The videotape had been produced to challenge the testimony of a government witness that Internet Explorer could be removed from the Windows operating system without any significant performance degradation. Boies challenged the veracity of the videotape, and the government consultants asked to review it noticed that the title bar displayed the words "Internet Explorer" even though the Microsoft narrator said it had been removed. Allchin maintained that the computer shown was the one from which its browser had been removed. Two days later Microsoft admitted that the videotape was prepared in a studio and showed a number of different computers to simulate its claims about performance degradation. Microsoft then prepared a new videotape that observers said showed that the system without Internet Explorer performed well, although applications requiring a browser, of course, did not work.[10]

In another glitch in its defense, an executive of Compaq Computer called by Microsoft admitted under questioning by the DOJ that there was no "commercially viable" alternative to the Windows operating system. The DOJ produced documents from Compaq and depositions of its executives indicating that it may have taken the Netscape Navigator icon off its desktop display and chosen Internet Explorer because of fear of retaliation by Microsoft. Microsoft responded with documentation that AOL had objected to including the Navigator icon on the desktop because it was linked with a competitor of AOL. Microsoft pointed to depositions by Compaq executives stating that Microsoft had never objected to the Navigator icon appearing on the desktop. Microsoft had objected when Compaq planned to delete the Internet Explorer icon.

Also, a Microsoft executive testified that it had not attempted to undermine Java. The DOJ, however, produced a memo from Bill Gates stating that he was "hardcore about NOT supporting" Java. When the executive tried to explain what Gates meant, the judge abruptly cut him off stating that it was abundantly clear what Gates meant.

[10]Another Microsoft executive introduced a videotape that purported to show that it was easy to download Netscape Navigator using a modem. Under questioning by the DOJ the witness admitted that the videotape had omitted several key steps in the downloading process and had used a high-speed LAN connection rather than a modem. The DOJ produced a videotape showing the full set of steps involved in the download, and the Microsoft executive stated that the download took between 45 minutes and an hour with a modem.

Although in its direct testimony Microsoft focused on challenging the government's allegations and evidence, in its rebuttal testimony and closing arguments it could emphasize other arguments. It could argue that it had a right to innovate and that unrestrained innovation benefited consumers. This could be coupled with the identification of the real benefits from its innovations. It could also argue that government-imposed remedies would be worse for consumers than the alleged antitrust violations themselves. For example, any government supervision or regulation of the software industry could stifle innovation and work to the disadvantage of consumers. These arguments could not only be presented in court but could be used in an attempt to influence through political channels any remedies proposed by the DOJ. Such efforts could be directed at both Congress and the White House.

DEVELOPMENTS OUTSIDE THE COURTROOM

Three developments occurred during the trial that lent support to Microsoft's argument that the market was constantly changing and monopoly power was a transient phenomenon at most. A fourth development, Microsoft's record earnings, supported the DOJ's monopoly power claim.

The AOL-Netscape-Sun Alliance

In November 1998 AOL announced that it would acquire Netscape for $4.2 billion and form an alliance with Sun Microsystems. Microsoft asserted that the deal fundamentally changed the industry's landscape and that it therefore was sufficient grounds for the DOJ to drop the lawsuit. DOJ witnesses such as William Harris, chairman and CEO of Intuit Corporation, stated that they did not view the new alliance as an industry shift that diminished Microsoft's dominance. "There's a great deal of merger activity in this industry. Microsoft is rumored to be in discussions for acquisitions. I don't think the AOL-Netscape deal will be the last one we hear of," Harris said. Judge Jackson refused to dismiss the case.

Apple's Revival

Since the 1998 release of the iMac, Apple's new, low-end computer line, Apple's sales and market share increased significantly. Apple computers use Mac-OS, instead of Windows, as their operating system. Microsoft used Apple's comeback to counter the claims that Microsoft had established a monopoly in the operating systems market. DOJ expert witnesses generally dismissed as "marginal" the competitive threat Apple posed to the Windows platform.

The Growing Recognition of Linux

Microsoft lawyers asserted that Linux, a free Unix operating system, posed a potential threat to Windows because several of Microsoft's chief competitors were writing software to run on it. In fact, on March 1, 1999, Oracle, Intel, Dell, and Hewlett Packard all announced substantial investments in Linux, and IBM announced greater offerings of computers using Linux. Although Linux had several million devotees around the world, it held an insignificant share of the operating system market. A DOJ expert witness firmly rejected the proposition that it threatened Windows: "Whatever role Linux may have, it is not expected to constrain the monopoly power of Microsoft... If you truly believe this product is going to constrain Microsoft's market share, then run, don't walk, to your broker and sell Microsoft stock short."

Microsoft's Surging Earnings

In January 1999 Microsoft reported a 75 percent increase in earnings, far exceeding the most optimistic projections of Wall Street analysts. A DOJ lawyer asked Microsoft's economics expert if consistently high profits were an indicator of monopoly power. The witness conceded that persistently high profits suggest "some impediment to competitive alternatives." But, he added, such profits could be due to a very valuable asset, protected by intellectual property rights, like Windows. "You simply cannot infer monopoly power from profits," he said.

REMEDIES

If the court found against Microsoft, the next issue was which remedies to impose. Many companies in the industry, including rivals of Microsoft, were fearful that the cure imposed could be worse than the disease. The principal fear was that some form of government supervision or oversight of the industry would be imposed that would impede innovation and technological change. Although the court would decide on the remedy and Microsoft was expected to appeal any unfavorable decision, the matter of remedies would not be solely a judicial one. Instead, the issue was likely to have a political dimension with industry members as well as politicians lobbying for preferred remedies. Senator Slade Gorton (R-WA) was critical of the DOJ's case, and commentators believed that Vice President Al Gore and the White House would take an interest in the remedy phase of the trial.

Possible remedies were generally classified as behavioral or structural. Behavioral remedies sought to eliminate the abusive and exclusionary practices of Microsoft without altering its control of the Windows operating system. Structural remedies focused on eliminating Microsoft's alleged Windows operating system monopoly either by breaking up the company or by replicating the source of its power through the creation of clones. Behavioral remedies were favored by those who worried that breaking up Microsoft's monopoly could lead to multiple industry standards that would impede the development of software applications. Many commentators and industry members, however, were skeptical that behavioral remedies would be sufficient to curb Microsoft's alleged monopoly power and abusive practices.

Most behavioral remedies under discussion focused on breaking Microsoft's hold on PC manufacturers obtained through licensing agreements for Windows operating system. A number of PC manufacturers had sought more flexible licensing agreements, and under antitrust scrutiny Microsoft had recently granted some leeway. Such remedies could include prohibiting Microsoft from using exclusive contracts that prohibit PC manufacturers from offering other Internet browsers. Another behavioral remedy would be to require Microsoft to publish its "most-favored customer" prices and make those prices available to all PC manufacturers. This would reduce the likelihood that Microsoft could punish a PC manufacturer by not offering it a discount available to other PC manufacturers. Microsoft was said to "take $7.50 off the unit price of Windows if PC makers agree to carry a 'Windows' logo on their machines and submit to certification by Microsoft's labs."[11] More generally the court could impose a pricing "transparency" policy under which Microsoft would set fixed prices for its products. A third behavioral remedy would be to require Microsoft to publish the applications program interfaces, or software hooks, required to write software for the Windows operating system. This would address the alleged strategy of releasing that information in stages or selectively to favored software developers.

Opposition to behavioral remedies not only resulted from skepticism about the effectiveness of such

[11] *The Wall Street Journal,* March 1, 1999.

remedies but also because such remedies would require supervision or regulatory oversight of the industry. Most industry members and economists feared any supervision or oversight of a dynamic industry with rapid product development and obsolescence.

In February 1999 the 1,400 member Information Industry Association (IIA), of which Microsoft was a member, presented a report to the DOJ urging that any remedy imposed on Microsoft not "fracture" the Windows de facto industry standard. The report assessed which possible remedies were workable and evaluated 10 possible remedies, ranging from prohibiting tying to structural remedies including breaking up Microsoft. The report was wary of any remedy that would require government supervision or oversight of the industry. The report urged the DOJ to "seriously consider" structural remedies.[12] The structural remedy preferred by the IIA was to break Microsoft into three stand-alone companies. One would have the Windows operating system including the CE and NT systems.[13] Another would have Microsoft's software business, and the third would have its Internet and electronic commerce businesses.[14]

An alternative structural remedy was to break Microsoft into three to five clones, referred to as "Baby Bills," each of which would have Microsoft's source codes for Windows and its other products. A related proposal was to auction the Windows code and name to several companies. Companies such as Sun Microsystems, Hewlett Packard, and IBM might be expected to bid for the codes. These remedies would introduce competition and break the alleged monopoly power of Microsoft. The IIA report, however, concluded that this type of remedy could be harmful if it led to multiple standards.

[12]The initial draft reportedly recommended structural remedies, but lobbying by Microsoft led to the wording "seriously consider."
[13]See Chapter 2.
[14]Others suggested a breakup with the second and third companies combined into one.

RECESS AND SETTLEMENT NEGOTIATIONS

At the conclusion of direct testimony and cross-examination, Judge Jackson announced a six-week recess after which rebuttal testimony would be offered and closing arguments made. The judge also suggested to the attorneys for the two sides that they consider negotiating a settlement.

For Microsoft a settlement would eliminate the considerable uncertainty about what judgment would be rendered in the case. That uncertainty was likely to continue through the potentially lengthy appeals that were anticipated. A settlement would also avoid any further embarrassments in the remainder of the proceedings.

For the Department of Justice and the 19 state attorneys general a settlement had the advantage of being implemented immediately rather than at the end of the appeals process. In the rapidly changing software and Internet markets a substantial delay could mean that the final judgment would be largely irrelevant. In addition, not settling the case would mean that the DOJ prosecutors would long be out of office, and many of the state attorneys general would have lost an opportunity for credit claiming in their quests for higher office. ■

This case was written by Professor David P. Baron and Chen Lichtenstein from publicly available information from the following sources: court filings made by the U.S. Department of Justice and by the Microsoft Corporation, transcripts of testimonies and related materials posted on the Department of Justice and Microsoft Corporation's Web sites, and court reports. Due to a publication deadline this case was written prior to rebuttal testimony and closing arguments.

PREPARATION QUESTIONS

1. Should the DOJ have brought an antitrust case against Microsoft?
2. Does the evidence indicate that Microsoft violated the Sherman Act?
3. Should Microsoft change its trial strategy to emphasize new arguments?
4. If Judge Jackson were to find against Microsoft, what remedy should the DOJ recommend?
5. Should Microsoft adopt a nonmarket strategy outside the court to influence the choice of a remedy? If so, what should the strategy be and how should it be implemented?
6. Should Microsoft attempt to settle the case out of court? On what terms?

CHAPTER 10

Regulation: Law, Economics, and Politics

Introduction

Regulation is government intervention in economic activity using commands, controls, and incentives. Regulation takes place through a public process that is open and allows participation by interested parties. In contrast to antitrust, regulation is not implemented through judicial institutions but instead by independent commissions and agencies of the executive branch. The courts, however, have played an important role in interpreting regulatory statutes, determining their constitutionality, and ensuring that regulatory decisions satisfy due process requirements.

Regulatory decisions and rule-making proceedings are extremely important to many firms, industries, and interest groups. Kerwin (1994, p. 194) reports a survey of 180 interest groups that found that two-thirds of the groups saw participation in regulatory rule making as at least as important as lobbying Congress and conducting grassroots activists. Nearly two-thirds of the respondents ranked participation in rule making as more important than either campaign contributions or litigation in their nonmarket activities.

Regulation includes a broad set of interventions:

- Controlling prices (electric power, telecommunications, cable television)
- Setting price floors (crops, minimum wages)
- Specifying qualifications (occupational licensure)
- Providing for solvency (financial institutions and insurance)
- Controlling the number of market participants (broadcast licenses and taxi medallions)
- Requiring premarketing approval (toxic chemicals, pharmaceuticals)
- Ensuring product safety (pharmaceuticals, toys, food)
- Mandating product characteristics and technology (automobile safety standards)
- Establishing performance standards (automobile emissions standards)
- Controlling toxic emissions and other pollutants (sulfur dioxide control)
- Allocating public resources (radio spectrum allocations)
- Establishing standards for health and safety (occupational safety)
- Ensuring equal opportunity (banning discrimination in employment)
- Controlling unfair international trade practices (antidumping)

- Providing information (labeling)
- Rationing common pool resources (fisheries)

Because regulation is a broad subject and often specific to particular industries, products, and conditions, the focus of this chapter is on the nature of regulation. Two principal perspectives on regulation are considered—one based on the correction of market imperfections and the other based on the political environment in which regulation is established and practiced. The institutional focus of the chapter is on economic regulation as practiced in industries such as telecommunications, electric power, and transportation. Safety regulation is considered in Chapter 11 in conjunction with the liability system. Environmental protection is considered in Chapter 12. Regulation of international trade is considered in Chapter 16. Regulation of the employment relationship is addressed in Chapter 21.

Periods of Regulatory Change

The United States has experienced four major periods of regulatory change. The first occurred during the populist era of the late 1800s as a result of political action by interest groups. At the state level farmers succeeded in establishing regulatory bodies to control the market power of grain elevators and railroads. This was extended to the federal level with the passage of the Interstate Commerce Act in 1887, which established the Interstate Commerce Commission (ICC) with the authority to regulate railroad rates. In the same tradition, additional legislation was enacted early in the twentieth century to shore up regulatory and antitrust powers that had been narrowly construed by the courts.[1]

The second period was the progressive era and the New Deal. Regulation was extended to labor markets and industries including electric power, food, pharmaceuticals, trucking, air transport, securities, and communications. Much of this regulation was industry specific and focused on pricing, entry, and conditions of service.

The third period, which began in the 1960s and accelerated in the 1970s, brought social regulation. In contrast to the earlier regulation that focused on the economic regulation of industries, social regulation addressed externalities and hazards. Regulation was extended to consumer products, the environment, and the workplace. The new social regulation differed dramatically from that of the prior periods. Instead of being industry specific, the new regulation cut across industries by focusing on dimensions, such as safety, health, and the environment. This changed the nature of the politics of regulation. In the past, the politics had been dominated by industry interests, as when the railroads used ICC regulation to limit competition from the emerging interstate trucking industry. The new social regulation brought to the politics of regulation a new set of interest groups, including safety and health activists and environmentalists.

The fourth period brought economic deregulation to several industries, including electric power, natural gas, telecommunications, air transport, and surface transportation, that were regulated by the agencies established during the first two periods of regulatory expansion. Public policy analysts, regulators, and executive branch officials recognized that regulation, which had been meant to keep prices down, seemed instead to lead to higher costs and higher consumer prices. Beginning in the 1970s several regulatory systems were eliminated, and market forces were used to improve economic

---

[1]See McCraw (1981, 1984) for the history of regulation.

efficiency.[2] In some industries, such as electric power and telecommunications, economic regulation is steadily being replaced by market competition. The deregulation movement has also led to the substitution of marketlike mechanisms, such as auctions and the trading of pollution allowances, for regulatory controls and allocation procedures. On January 1, 1996, the first regulatory agency, the Interstate Commerce Commission, closed its doors.

The past three decades thus have witnessed two quite different regulatory movements. The social regulation that began during the 1960s has expanded at the same time as deregulation has taken place in a number of industries. Although new regulatory agencies have not been created in recent years, the authorities of some existing social regulatory agencies such as the Environmental Protection Agency have been extended. Economic regulation has moved in the other direction as markets and competition have been substituted for government controls. These two movements have come together as marketlike mechanisms have been substituted for some social regulation, as in the case of the trading of sulfur dioxide allowances considered in Chapter 12.

The Constitutional Basis for Regulation

Government regulation can be traced to the 1100s when the English monarchy began to contract with private parties for the provision of services. The monarchy granted rights-of-way to stage lines and in return retained the authority to regulate service and prices. Private property committed to a public use thus became subject to government controls. This contractual relationship between the state and a firm provided the basis for the evolution of regulatory authority through the common law.

The U.S. Constitution provides the authority for regulation but also limits the application of that authority. Section 8 of Article I of the Constitution gives Congress the power "To regulate Commerce . . . among the several States . . ." The Fifth Amendment to the Constitution limits this power by stating, "No person shall be deprived of life, liberty, or property, without due process of law; nor shall private property be taken for public use without just compensation." The Fourteenth Amendment extends the due process protection to actions taken by the states.

Many of the legal principles of regulation in the United States, however, have been based on extensions of the common law. The common law doctrine that private property committed to a public use could be regulated was extended to property that was "affected with a public interest." In *Munn v. Illinois,* 94 U.S. 113 (1877), the Supreme Court upheld an Illinois law regulating the prices charged by grain elevators, which in the state constitution had been declared "public warehouses." The court cited the English common law principle that when "affected with a public interest, [private property] ceases to be *juris privati* only . . . Property does become clothed with a public interest when used in a manner to make it of public consequence, and affect the community at large. When, therefore, one devotes his property to a use in which the public has an interest, he, in effect, grants to the public an interest in that use, and must submit to be controlled by the public for the common good . . ." In this sweeping statement, the court established the government's right to regulate private property. However, it went on to warn: "We know that this is a power which may be abused; but there is no argument against its existence. For protection against abuses by the legislatures the people must resort to the polls, not to the courts." In upholding minimum price regulation of milk sold in grocery stores, the Supreme Court ruled

[2]See Noll and Owen (1983) for an analysis of the political economy of deregulation. They also provide a list of the major deregulation initiatives taken from 1971 through 1982.

in *Nebbia v. New York,* 291 U.S. 502 (1934), that the same principle applies to enterprises that are not affected with a public interest. The scope of the government's right to regulate is thus extremely broad.

The Fifth and Fourteenth amendments, however, place limits on regulation.[3] In *Smith v. Ames,* 169 U.S. 466 (1898), the Supreme Court held that "What a company is entitled to ask is a fair return upon the value of that which it employs for the public convenience."[4] This established the right of public utilities to obtain a fair return on their capital and led to cost-of-service regulation. The due process provisions of the Constitution also are an important factor in structuring the regulatory process and are considered in more detail later in the chapter.

Regulatory Commissions and Agencies

The principal federal regulatory agencies are listed in Figure 10–1. Regulatory agencies are of two basic forms—independent commissions and executive branch agencies. Independent commissions include the Federal Communications Commission, the Federal Trade Commission, the Federal Reserve System, the International Trade Commission, the Federal Energy Regulatory Commission, the Securities and Exchange Commission, the National Labor Relations Board, the Consumer Products Safety Commission, and the Nuclear Regulatory Commission. The Federal Communications Commission, for example, has five commissioners appointed by the president and confirmed by the Senate. They serve 7-year terms and no more than three commissioners may be from the same political party. Most commissions make decisions through majority-rule voting and formal rule-making procedures.

Agencies typically have a single administrator appointed by the president or a cabinet secretary. Most executive branch regulatory agencies are located in a cabinet department, as in the case of the Federal Aviation Administration, the National Highway Traffic Safety Administration, the Occupational Health and Safety Administration, and the Food and Drug Administration. The Environmental Protection Agency is an independent executive branch agency not housed in a cabinet department.[5]

Most states also have regulatory commissions and agencies. Considerable economic activity such as local telephone service and electricity are regulated by the states and not the federal government. Most states also have social regulatory agencies to deal with environmental, occupational safety, and health issues. As indicated in Chapter 12, federal law delegates the implementation of certain federal regulations to the states. States, for example, are responsible for developing implementation plans for achieving clean air standards.

The Nonmarket Environment of Regulatory Agencies

Regulatory agencies operate in a complex environment, and even "independent" regulatory commissions are subject to a variety of influences, as illustrated in Figure 10–2. Commissioners and administrators of regulatory agencies are appointed by the president, and most require Senate confirmation. The appointment of regulators can have

---

[3]The "takings" clause in the Fifth Amendment has been the subject of political and legal activity intended to require public compensation for the loss of value due to regulations such as zoning and environmental protection.

[4]See also *Federal Power Commission et al. v. Hope Natural Gas Co.,* 320 U.S. 591 (1944).

[5]For a description of the regulatory agencies, see Congressional Quarterly (1994).

Federal Reserve System (1913)
Federal Trade Commission (1914)
International Trade Commisson (1916) (formerly the Tariff Commission)—considered in Chapter 16
Federal Energy Regulatory Commission (1930) (formerly the Federal Power Commission)
Food and Drug Administration (1931) [HHS]
Securities and Exchange Commission (1934)
Federal Communications Commission (1934)
National Labor Relations Board (1935) – considered in Chapter 21
Federal Aviation Administration (1948) [DOT]
Federal Maritime Commission [1961]
Equal Employment Opportunity Commission (1965) — considered in Chapter 21
Environmental Protection Agency (1970) — considered in Chapter 12
National Highway Traffic Safety Administration (1970) — considered in Chapter 11
Consumer Product Safety Commission (1972)
Occupational Safety and Health Administration (1973) [DOL]
Nuclear Regulatory Commission (1975) (formerly the Atomic Energy Commission)

Note: The cabinet departments in which agencies are located are shown in brackets.
Source: Congressional Quarterly, *Federal Regulatory Directory,* 7th ed., Washington D.C., 1994.

FIGURE 10–1 Principal Federal Regulatory Agencies and Commissions

an important impact on regulatory policy and practice, as the discussion of the deregulation of the airline industry in Chapter 1 indicates. President Carter sought to deregulate the surface transportation industries. To do so, he needed a majority of pro-deregulation commissioners on the ICC. When his appointment of the chairman gave the pro-deregulation side a four-to-three majority, with four seats vacant, he chose not to fill the vacancies. The ICC then began to deregulate. The executive branch can also influence regulatory commissions through the policy expertise of cabinet agencies. The president thus has a number of instruments to influence regulatory agencies, particularly those in the executive branch.

The president also exercises considerable influence through his ability to direct the review of regulations. President Carter issued an executive order requiring analysis of all new regulations and established the Regulatory Analysis Review Group to review those analyses. Shortly after taking office, President Reagan issued Executive Order 12291, which required that "regulatory action shall not be undertaken unless the potential benefits to society from the regulation outweigh the potential costs to society." The order was associated with the implementation of the Paperwork Reduction Act of 1980 and required regulatory agencies to prepare a Regulatory Impact Analysis for any proposed rule.[6] The Office of Management and Budget (OMB) reviewed the agencies' analyses and could request changes. The order was an important tool in the Reagan and Bush administrations' efforts to limit regulation. It resulted in the delay, revision, and rejection of many regulatory rules. When he took office, President Clinton modified President Reagan's order by restricting the reviews by OMB's Office of Information and Regulatory Affairs to "significant" regulations and by requiring that OMB take into account "qualitative" as well as quantitative measures of costs and benefits.

[6]See Weidenbaum (1990, pp. 216–219).

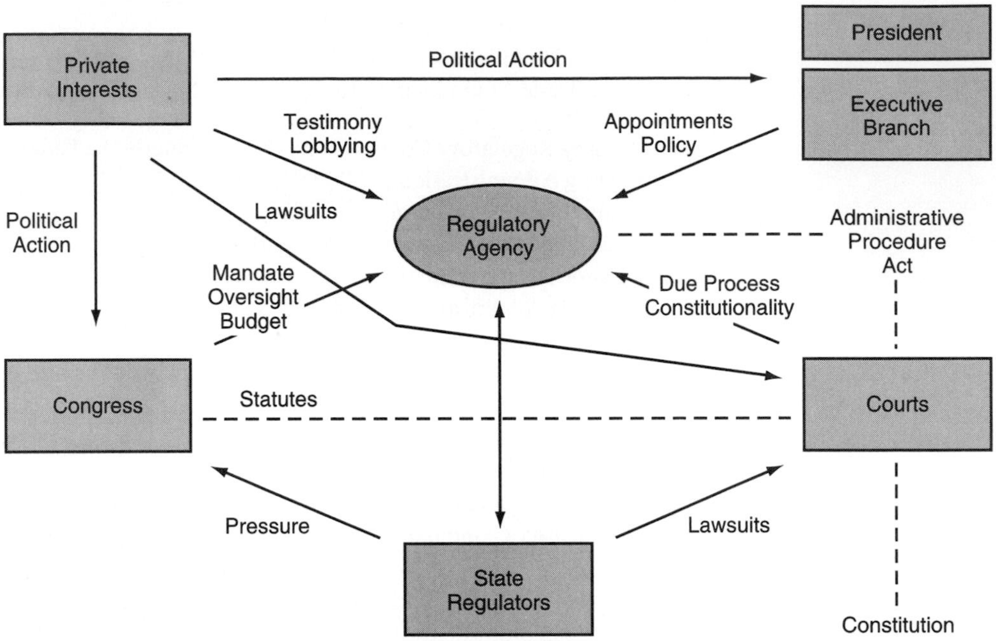

FIGURE 10-2 Influences on Regulatory Agencies

Congress exercises considerable influence over regulatory agencies through its budgetary and oversight responsibilities. Congressional influence also comes from its ability to revise statutes or block changes. The Reagan administration attempted to deregulate in the area of social regulation, but the congressional oversight committees with responsibilities over the regulatory agencies joined with interest groups to oppose those efforts. For example, the Reagan administration sought the elimination of the Consumer Products Safety Commission (CPSC), but Congress refused.

Congress has power over regulatory agencies because it writes their legislative mandates and reauthorizes those agencies whose statutes require it. The CPSC requires reauthorization every 3 years, yet from 1981 to 1990, threatened by a possible presidential veto, Congress could not agree on reauthorization legislation. The difficulty in reauthorization resulted in part because, in contrast to the statutes establishing economic regulation that use broad terms such as "the public interest," the statutes establishing social regulation often have very detailed language. For example, the reauthorization bill passed in 1990 requires the CPSC to establish safety standards for automatic garage door openers.[7] Congress also includes provisions in budget appropriations bills that prevent regulatory agencies from spending any funds on particular programs or regulatory initiatives. For example, in the Part III integrative case *Whirlpool and Energy Efficiency Standards (A): Regulation and Politics,* Congress prohibited the Department of Energy from spending on any new rule making on energy efficiency standards.

Congress and its committees also provide oversight of regulatory agencies and can pressure regulators through oversight hearings in which regulators can be called to task for their actions. Members of Congress also frequently call or write regulatory agencies requesting explanations for agency actions. The agencies always respond.

Some federal regulatory agencies are influenced by state regulatory agencies. The FCC has jurisdiction over interstate telecommunications, and state regulatory commis-

[7] *Congressional Quarterly Weekly Report,* October 27, 1990.

sions have jurisdiction over intrastate telecommunications. The National Association of [state] Regulatory Utility Commissions applies political pressure at the federal level and at times files lawsuits seeking to reverse FCC actions. State commissions also make their interests known to their state's congressional delegation.

Private interests also affect regulatory agencies directly through their participation in hearings and other regulatory proceedings and indirectly through pressure on Congress and the executive branch. Private interests also lobby regulatory agencies, although *ex parte* contracts with regulators must be disclosed in advance. Private interests also often take their cases to the courts. Firms as well as interest groups frequently appeal regulatory decisions. Activists also file suits to force regulators to enforce what the activists see as the agency's mandate.

The courts have a considerable influence on regulation, reviewing action for constitutionality and for consistency with statutes. For example, in the *Illinois Power Company (A)* case in Chapter 3, the state regulatory commission determined how much of the cost of the nuclear power plant was to be included in electricity rates. In this case the commission's decision was appealed. The Court of Appeal's decision was then appealed by all sides in the case: Illinois Power Company, the interest groups representing its customers, and the regulatory commission. As indicated in the following section, the courts also review regulatory actions for due process requirements.

Delegation, Rule Making, Due Process, and Discretion

Regulatory and other administrative agencies operate under a set of procedural and substantive constraints.[8] Article I, Section 1 of the Constitution grants Congress the sole power to legislate. It does not provide for Congress to delegate policy-making powers to agencies. Yet regulatory agencies promulgate rules, establish policies, and resolve disputes. Prior to 1935, courts held that the delegatee was simply making a determination in the implementation of a law enacted by Congress. In 1935 the Supreme Court overturned as unconstitutional two delegation provisions of the National Industrial Recovery Act. Subsequently, the courts have not overturned a congressional delegation.[9] Instead, they sought to ensure that the exercise of any delegated authority was consistent with the constitutional protections of the Fifth and Fourteenth Amendments and the common law doctrine of consistency. In 1999, however, the U.S. Court of Appeals overturned an EPA standard concluding that the EPA had exceeded its authority and that it would have been unconstitutional for Congress to have delegated such broad legislative powers to the EPA. If this decision were upheld on appeal, it could have a major impact on the nature and scope of regulation.

Congress was also concerned about the exercise of agency powers and enacted the Administrative Procedure Act (APA) of 1946 to provide for public notice and comment prior to agency action. Agencies also adopt their own rule-making procedures in a manner consistent with the APA. Under the APA, agencies can use either a formal or an informal rule-making process.[10] The informal model of rule making requires publishing in the *Federal Register* an advance notice of proposed rule making (ANPR) and requesting the submission of comments. The agency may also hold a public hearing on the proposed rule. The agency next reviews the comments received, revises the rule, and publishes it in the *Federal Register* with an effective date at least 30 days in the future.

---

[8]See Kerwin (1994) for an analysis of agency rule making. Magat, Krupnick, and Harrington (1986) and Owen and Braeutigam (1978) consider the administrative processes of regulation.

[9]See Mashaw and Merrill (1985, pp. 2–5).

[10]See Kerwin (1994), Breyer (1982, pp. 378–381), and Howell, Allison, and Henley (1987, pp. 179–188).

Under the formal model, the agency employs a quasi-judicial process involving hearings conducted by an administrative law judge, the presentation of evidence, and the cross-examination of witnesses. A formal record of the proceedings is kept and may be reviewed by the courts, Appearances may be made and testimony given by any interested party. The authorizing statutes of some agencies also prescribe public hearings for certain types of actions. Under this model, the agencies are restricted by *ex parte* rules against having contacts with interested parties outside the proceedings.[11]

The APA grants parties the right to sue for judicial review of an agency action. One basis for that review is the failure to follow the procedures required for an action. This is review under the framework of *procedural due process.* The APA (Section 706(2)(A)) requires that agency actions not be "arbitrary, capricious, an abuse of discretion, or otherwise not in accordance with law." Because of the right to judicial review, agencies are careful to follow procedures and base their decisions on the record.

The courts also review regulatory actions based on *substantive due process.* The basic concern under substantive due process is whether the regulatory action exceeds the scope of the mandate of the regulatory agency.[12] Regulatory decisions thus are required to bear a relationship to a proper public purpose. In *Nebbia,* the Supreme Court stated: "So far as the requirement of due process is concerned, and in the absence of other constitutional restriction, a state is free to adopt whatever economic policy may reasonably be deemed to promote public welfare, and to enforce that policy by legislation adapted to its purpose. . . . If the laws passed are seen to have a reasonable relation to a proper legislative purpose, and are neither arbitrary nor discriminatory, the requirements of due process are satisfied. . . . With the wisdom of the policy adopted, with the adequacy or practicality of the law enacted to forward it, the courts are both incompetent and unauthorized to deal." The courts have traditionally been reluctant to substitute their judgments for those of an agency.[13]

An important procedural due process decision occurred over rule making on automobile safety standards. The National Highway Traffic Safety Administration (NHTSA) began a rule-making proceedings on air bags in 1967; and in 1977, the first year of the Carter administration, it promulgated a rule requiring new automobiles to be equipped with a passive restraint system—either an air bag or automatic seat belts. The Reagan administration opposed the rule, and the new administrator of NHTSA revoked it in October 1981. The revocation was based not on new information but rather on a reevaluation of the previous record. The administrator concluded that because auto manufacturers planned to use seat belt systems that were easily detachable, the benefits from the rule would not justify the costs. The insurance industry, one of the principal interest groups that had worked for the passive restraint rule, filed suit challenging the revocation and the case reached the Supreme Court.[14] The court ruled that the revocation was "arbitrary and capricious" because NHTSA had failed to consider all the available alternatives, such as mandating air bags for all autos.[15] Issues of agency discretion are raised in the chapter case *Sears and the Local Regulation of Advertising.*

Rule making is the most important activity of most regulatory agencies. Agencies must follow the procedures specified in the APA and any procedures specified in their authorizing statutes. Interested parties participate in both formal and infor-

---

[11]See Mashaw and Merrill (1985, pp. 470–476).
[12]See Mashaw and Merrill (1985, pp. 318–385).
[13]See Edley (1990) for a treatment of administrative law and judicial review.
[14]*Motor Vehicles Manufacturers Assn. v. State Farm Insurance Co.,* 463 U.S. 29 (1983).
[15]For the majority, Justice Byron R. White wrote, "We have frequently reiterated that an agency must cogently explain why it has exercised its discretion in a given manner, and we affirm this principle again today." See Mashaw and Merrill (1985, pp. 343–354).

mal rule-making procedures, but they also attempt to influence agency actions outside those procedures. Contacts with firms and other interests are generally required to be disclosed in advance through *ex parte* requirements, which contribute to the relative openness of regulatory processes. Lobbying and other forms of information provision are the principal approaches to influencing agency decisions in addition to participation in formal rule-making procedures. The chapter case *Whirlpool and Energy Efficiency Standards (B): Rule Making* and the Part III integrative case *Whirlpool and Energy Efficiency Standards (A): Regulation and Politics* address regulatory rule is making.

EXAMPLE: THE FCC AND TV, CABLE, AND VCR COMPATIBILITY

In response to consumer complaints about difficulties in operating VCRs and cable receivers in conjunction with a television set (e.g., watching one channel while recording from another), Congress in the Cable Television Act of 1992 directed the Federal Communications Commission (FCC) to issue within a year a standard to ensure compatibility (See the Chapter 7 case *Echelon and the Home Automation Standard (A).*) A committee composed of companies in the electronics and cable television industries proposed a standard that contained a decoder interface that used the CEBus communications protocol. Echelon Corporation, a high-tech electronics company, learned late in the FCC's standard-setting process about the CEBus protocol. CEBus would largely foreclose Echelon's market opportunities in the home automation systems market, since its proprietary communications protocol conflicted with the CEBus protocol. Echelon objected and began to lobby the FCC in an attempt to convince it to adopt an open technology standard that would allow any communications protocol to be used. Echelon was unsuccessful in its efforts.

To understand why Echelon failed with the FCC, consider the issue from the FCC's perspective. The FCC faced congressional pressure to resolve quickly the incompatibility problem, and the committee of cable and television companies had a solution for the FCC's problem. The committee made the FCC's job easier. Moreover, those companies were the natural clients of the FCC and had worked regularly on issues before the FCC. Echelon was not a natural client of the FCC and interacted infrequently with it. Moreover, considering Echelon's objection would only make the FCC's job harder. Had Echelon participated early in the standard-setting process and advocated an open technology, it might have had a better chance at success.

Agencies may at times sidestep rule-making procedures claiming authority outside the APA or that the activity is an extension of a prior rule making. For example, in 1996 the EPA quietly developed a grading system for pollution risks at over 600 plants without going through the notice and comment procedure. When the grades were revealed and errors identified by firms, protests by the firms and 19 state environmental agencies led to the scrapping of the grading system.

Explanations for Regulation

That government has the authority to regulate does not explain where regulation is and is not imposed. Two theories have been offered to explain the locus of regulation. The first is the theory of market imperfections, which predicts that regulation will be instituted to improve economic efficiency by correcting imperfections. The second theory is political and predicts that interest groups seek regulation to serve their interests. The regulation of the prices charged by grain elevators that gave rise to *Munn v. Illinois* reflects the interests of farmers in capturing the rents from the sale of their crops. The same interests were important in the passage of the Interstate Commerce Act. The next section examines six types of market imperfections:[16]

- Natural monopoly
- Externalities
- Public goods
- Asymmetric information
- Moral hazard
- Transactions costs

The following section then considers political explanations for regulation.

Market Imperfections

NATURAL MONOPOLY

A monopoly is natural if one firm can produce a given set of goods or services at lower cost than can any other number of firms. A natural monopoly results when costs are decreasing in the scale of a firm or in the scope of its products or services. The classical theory of natural monopoly predicts that a monopolist will restrict its output resulting in a price above marginal cost. The restriction of output causes economic inefficiency because some consumers who would be willing to pay the cost of the resources expended to satisfy their demand are prevented from doing so by the restricted output. This inefficiency is referred to as a deadweight loss (*DWL*), since an opportunity to achieve benefits is forgone.

The case of a monopoly is illustrated in Figure 10–3, which presents a demand curve (*D*) and the monopolist's average cost (*AC*) and marginal cost (*MC*) curves. The marginal and average cost curves are decreasing because of economies of scale. A monopolist would exercise its market power by restricting its output to the point q_2 at which marginal revenue (not shown) equals marginal cost, resulting in a price p_2 that is above average and marginal costs. The profit of the firm is the difference between the price p_2 and average cost multiplied by the quantity q_2; that is, profit is the area *FAHG*. Consumer surplus is the area under the demand curve above the price p_2. A deadweight loss results because there are consumers who are willing to purchase the product at a price above the marginal cost of producing it. These units are the difference between q_0 and q_2, and the deadweight loss is the shaded area *ABC*. The area *GHBI* represents a pure transfer between the firm and consumers; that is, a gain in consumer surplus and a decrease in profit that would result from lowering the price from p_1 to p_0.

In the case of a natural monopoly, economic theory recommends that government set price equal to marginal cost, or p_0, so that every consumer who is willing to pay the cost of the resources expended in production will purchase the good. In the presence of decreasing costs, however, marginal-cost pricing does not generate sufficient revenue to cover the total cost of the firm. Total costs could be covered by a government subsidy financed by taxes. This alternative is generally opposed, however, because taxes distort the activity on which they are levied and weaken the incentive of the monopoly firm to be responsive to consumer demands. Consequently, regulated prices are either set equal to average costs, denoted p_1 in Figure 10–3, or costs are covered through fixed charges, such as fixed monthly charges.

Before concluding that regulation is warranted under the natural monopoly rationale, two questions must be answered. The first is whether there are any natural monopolies, and if there are, the second is whether significant economic efficiency would be

[16] Breyer (1982, Chap. 1) also discusses the nature of market imperfections.

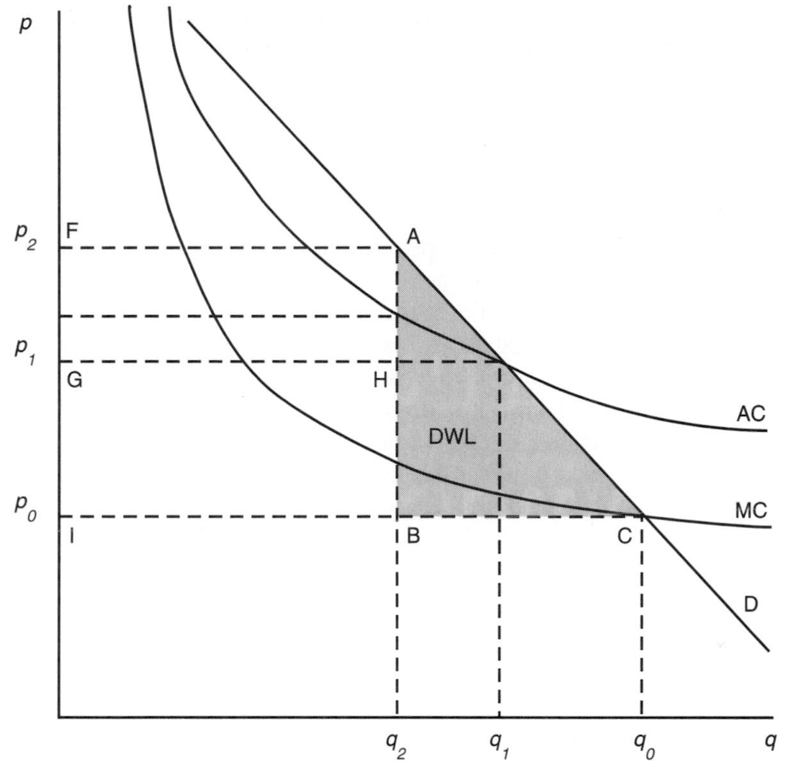

FIGURE 10–3 Monopoly and Deadweight Loss

gained by regulation. Economies of scale and scope certainly exist over some sets of goods and services, but these economies can be exhausted at output levels that allow more than one supplier to persist in the market. Empirical studies indicate, for example, that the large electric power plants in the United States have exhausted the achievable economies of scale. A natural monopoly can also result if having more than one supplier would result in an uneconomical duplication of facilities. Local electricity distribution systems within cities may remain a monopoly to avoid duplicate sets of distribution wires. This rationale does not apply in the telecommunications industry, since cable television and wireless communications systems provide alternatives to the local wire connections. A monopoly could result from network economies and standardization as alleged in the Chapter 9 case *The Microsoft Antitrust Case* with respect to computer operating systems.

If there is a natural monopoly, it does not necessarily follow that there is substantial economic inefficiency. First, if entry into the industry is easy, the threat of potential competition may limit the extent to which an incumbent monopolist will restrict its output. Second, a monopolist may choose to use a nonlinear pricing policy, involving fixed charges and a low unit price; that is a price near p_0, which can both increase profits and benefit consumers. Third, if there are a number of possible suppliers of a monopoly service, competitive bidding for the right to be the monopolist can be used to lower the supply price and increase economic efficiency. (The auctions used in the telecommunications industry are considered later in the chapter.) Similarly, an alternative to the regulation of the electric power industry is for communities to own the local distribution system and bargain with power companies for the supply of electricity.[17] As considered

[17]See Joskow and Schmalensee (1983) and White (1997) for an assessment of the potential for competition in electric power.

in the section on deregulation, industries such as electric power, telecommunications, and natural gas transmissions had been subject to price regulation based on a natural monopoly rationale. Competition, however, is replacing regulation in these industries and not only is improving the efficiency of pricing but is also resulting in lower costs of production.

EXTERNALITIES

Externalities are of two types. A pecuniary externality is present when the actions of one economic agent affect other economic agents through changes in the prices of goods and services. When a firm builds a plant, its demand for labor drives up the wage rate, unless labor is perfectly elastically supplied. This pecuniary externality does not result in economic inefficiency because the wage rate in the labor market is determined by the forces of supply and demand. Similarly, energy-efficiency regulation was not warranted by the high energy prices in the 1970s, since the high prices were the result of market forces although influenced by a cartel that became ineffective over time.[18] Thus, a pecuniary externality does not provide a rationale for regulation.

Even though pecuniary externalities do not result in economic inefficiency, they affect rents and so may stimulate political action. The oil shocks of the 1970s increased prices dramatically, and politicians responded by enacting a complex regulatory system to lower the price of oil and reduce the rents of the owners of U.S. crude oil reserves. The price controls, however, both dampened the incentive to find new domestic crude oil reserves and stimulated the demand for oil, resulting in increased oil imports. The resulting inefficiency was sufficiently costly that crude oil price regulation was eliminated by the early 1980s.[19]

The second type of externality is nonpecuniary and occurs when an action of one economic agent directly affects the preferences or the production opportunities of other economic agents. An individual who drives an automobile generates pollution that is both unhealthy and affects visibility. Similarly, one firm's waste disposal site may pollute another's water supply. These externalities result in the divergence of private costs from social costs. Economic inefficiency results unless agents can "internalize" the external social costs. Externalities provide a rationale for regulation to align private and social costs. Energy-efficiency regulation may be warranted because burning carbon-based fuels to generate electricity causes externalities in the form of pollution and the release of gases that contribute to global warming. Energy-efficiency regulation is, however, only a second-best form of regulation, as considered in Chapter 12 in the context of incentive-based systems for environmental protection.

PUBLIC GOODS

A public good is one whose consumption by one person does not reduce its availability for others. When a person consumes a private good such as an apple, it is not available for consumption by others. When a person consumes a good such as national defense or a radio broadcast, however, the amount of the good available for consumption by others is not diminished. For a private good, economic efficiency requires that the marginal utility from consumption be equal to the price of the good, or, more correctly, that the marginal rate of substitution of one private good for another equals the ratio of their prices. Since a public good is available to all economic agents in a quantity undiminished by their consumption, economic efficiency requires that the sum of the mar-

[18] Energy-efficiency regulation might have been warranted by national security concerns.
[19] See Breyer (1982, pp. 164–171) and Kalt (1983) for analyses of the inefficiency resulting from crude oil price regulation.

ginal utilities of all individuals be equal to the price of the public good.[20] Many public goods are "local" in the sense that due to congestion adding more consumers will at some point diminish the amount of the good available for others.

For some public goods, such as national defense, bridges, and roads, government provision is customary. Public provision, however, does not imply that a good has the characteristics of a public good. Many goods, such as public housing, food stamps, and soil-bank programs, are provided by government for redistribution purposes rather than because they are public goods. Also, public goods can be supplied by the private sector. Radio and television broadcasts are provided by private enterprises subject only to noneconomic regulation. Similarly, the government privatized its Landsat satellite system, which provides data and photographs of the earth's surface.

A fundamental problem with either private or public provision centers on the "revelation of preferences" for public goods. If those who benefit from a public good are asked to pay for a public good based on their valuations for the good, people may understate their valuations and may free ride on the payments of others. Because of the free-rider problem, public provision may be warranted. This, however, does not resolve the problem of determining the public's aggregate valuation of the good and thus whether it should be supplied. If individuals could be excluded from consuming the public good, the revelation and free-rider problems could be resolved—at least in principle. For example, not allowing satellite-dish owners free reception of cable television programming induces customers to pay for the service.[21]

ASYMMETRIC INFORMATION

A fourth type of market imperfection results from asymmetric information. If people have different (private) information at the time they act, markets may not perform efficiently, even when there are advantageous trades that could be made. Akerlof (1970) presented an example of a used car market in which each seller knows the value of the car she wants to sell but the buyers know only the probability distribution of the values of the cars that might be offered for sale. In this market, for each used car there is a potential buyer who is willing to buy it, but a buyer cannot through casual inspection determine the value of any particular used car offered for sale. All he knows is that a car might be a lemon or might be of high quality.

Because of this asymmetry of information, the maximum amount the buyer is willing to pay is the average of the values of those cars that will be offered for sale. Because buyers will only pay the average value, those potential sellers who have high-quality cars find that the amount buyers are willing to pay is less than the value of their cars. They thus will not offer their cars for sale. Buyers recognize this and understand that the only cars that will be offered for sale will be those of low quality. The average value of those low-quality cars is low, however, so buyers will be willing to pay only a low amount. The lower amount buyers are willing to pay again means that the potential sellers of cars at the high end of the remaining range will not offer their cars for sale.

---

[20]In this sense, an externality is also a public good, since the efficient provision of goods involving externalities requires that the sum of the marginal utilities and disutilities from its supply be equated to its marginal cost.

[21]Fire protection has the properties of a local public good and is typically supplied by municipalities and paid for by the taxes of the beneficiaries. It can be provided privately, though, if exclusion can be practiced. Tim Emerson learned this the hard way when his nearly completed house caught fire from a space heater. His house was 5 miles from Taylorville, Illinois, so he called the Taylorville firefighters. They responded to his call. When they got to the house, they asked if the house was covered by the fire protection plan. Emerson, who had not paid the $25 fee, said, "No." The firefighters asked if there was anyone inside; when Emerson replied "No" they drove away, letting the house burn to the ground.

Buyers will then be willing to pay even less for any car offered for sale. The market may collapse with no sales being made. This is clearly inefficient, because for every used car there is a buyer who is willing to buy it if he only knew its true value.

This phenomenon, known as adverse selection, also occurs when sellers have incomplete information about customers. Insurance is, in principle, to provide coverage for individuals with similar risk characteristics. When those characteristics cannot be readily assessed, people with quite different risks are placed in the same pool. The higher risk individuals then have an incentive to buy insurance, which can drive up the price of insurance and cause some low-risk individuals not to buy insurance. Insurance companies respond to this adverse selection by requiring a physical examination for life insurance and basing auto insurance rates on accident and traffic citation histories and on the number of years of driving experience.

When market participants have incomplete information and acquiring information is costly, the mandated provision of information through regulation may be warranted. Regulation may not be warranted in all situations involving asymmetric information, however. Information has value, so there is a demand for it. In the used car example, a potential buyer may take the car to a mechanic for inspection. More generally, individuals may invest in information acquisition or hire agents who are more knowledgeable than they are. On the supply side, manufacturers can offer warranties for their products to signal to consumers that their products are of high quality. Some used car dealers, for example, offer warranties on their cars. Similarly, individuals who trade in the securities or foreign exchange markets have different information, but the market aggregates their information as prices are formed and traders choose their risk-return positions.

Information, however, can remain undersupplied when it is in the self-interest of its possessor not to supply it. Manufacturers are understandably reluctant to release negative information about potential hazards associated with their products because doing so may reduce demand. Consequently, consumers may be poorly informed about hazards. Similarly, an employee may be incompletely informed about possible health and safety hazards in the workplace. In such situations, the liability system, as considered in Chapter 11, is an alternative to regulation.

MORAL HAZARD

Moral hazard refers to behavior induced when people do not bear the full consequences of their actions. In the case of medical care, fully insured individuals have an effectively unlimited demand for medical care, since they bear none of the cost of the care they receive. In addition, individuals may not have the proper incentive to take socially efficient preventive measures because they know that the cost of any illness or accident will be covered by insurance. Similarly, the provision of federally funded flood insurance encourages people to live in areas prone to flooding and can lead to socially inefficient location decisions.

Regulation is one response to moral hazard problems, but regulation can also cause moral hazard problems making the regulation itself less effective. In a controversial article Peltzman (1975) argued that automobile safety regulation induced drivers to take more risks, thus reducing the effectiveness of mandatory safety standards. Peterson and Hoffer (1994) studied data on automobile personal injury and collision insurance claims from 1989 to 1991 and for each model compared data for those vehicles with an airbag to those with no airbag. Their data indicated that the number of accident claims were systematically higher for the identical automobile model with airbags than those without an airbag. The authors concluded that although these results were consistent with Peltzman's moral hazard argument that adding safety features induces drivers to take more risk, they could be due to higher-risk drivers being more likely to choose automobiles with airbags than lower-risk drivers.

Moral hazard can also occur within a firm. To increase the incentives for individuals to report corporate wrong doing, federal laws allow a whistle-blower to receive 10 to 30 percent of any judgment won. In response to such laws, companies have instituted internal disclosure and ethics systems to reduce the likelihood of wrong doing and to encourage the reporting of suspected wrong doing at an early stage. The moral hazard results because the reward provided by the federal law encourages employees to avoid companies' internal control systems, wait for evidence to accumulate, and then go directly to the public authorities. This makes the internal systems less effective in stopping wrong doing.

In industries in which cost-of-service pricing and rate-of-return regulation are used, cost increases are passed on to consumers. The incentive for the firm to hold down costs is thus weakened. This is a form of moral hazard because the firm does not bear the full consequences of the higher costs that result from its own decisions.

The principal means of dealing with moral hazard is to structure incentives so that the induced behavior is taken into account. In the case of medical insurance, copayments can be required and reimbursement limits imposed. Moral hazard can also be addressed by monitoring the behavior of individuals to increase the likelihood that they take proper care. Fines for not wearing a seat belt are an example of monitoring. In cost-of-service regulated industries, the problem of moral hazard is reduced by the delay between the time at which costs increase and the time at which the regulators approve higher prices. Moral hazard is also reduced by breaking the link between cost increases and the prices charged for services, as considered later in the chapter in the context of price cap regulation in the telecommunications industry.

TRANSACTIONS COSTS

Market imperfections can also result from costs associated with making market transactions.[22] To the extent that consumers and producers incur costs in becoming informed about market opportunities and completing market transactions, markets may not perform efficiently. Regulation to reduce those transactions costs then can improve efficiency. In the Part III integrative case, appliance manufacturers sought uniform federal standards to avoid having to produce different models for different states.

A common problem in markets is the incentive for sellers to shirk on the quality of the goods or services they sell. If asymmetric information results when quality can only be observed through use, a seller may have an incentive to shirk. As long as a high-quality good is more costly to produce than a low-quality good and a consumer cannot tell the difference until after it is purchased, a seller may cut back on quality. Understanding this, some consumers may not purchase the product. The consumer and the seller are thus in a one-sided prisoners' dilemma. A consumer could attempt to verify the quality of the product, but the associated costs required to do so may be prohibitive. Sufficiently high transactions costs can result in no transaction being made.

Markets, however, can resolve some of these problems. If consumers can sully the reputation of the firm by informing other consumers that the firm shirked on quality, consumers will not purchase from that firm. Consumers then can follow the strategy of purchasing from the firm as long as its reputation for producing high-quality products is unsullied and not purchasing from it if its reputation is ever sullied. If the potential gain from future sales is sufficiently great, the firm will have an incentive to produce

[22]Transactions costs, defined broadly by Williamson (1975), include the costs of addressing moral hazard problems and opportunistic behavior resulting from incomplete information.

high-quality products.[23] To the extent that there are transactions costs associated with consumers informing each other, this market resolution may be imperfect, however. Information supplied by organizations such as the Consumers Union and the Better Business Bureau economize on those costs. Transactions costs also play a role in the effectiveness of the liability system as considered in Chapter 11.

GOVERNMENT IMPERFECTIONS

Market imperfections in many cases warrant government regulation. In some cases, however, regulation may be a cure that is worse than the disease. Wolf (1979, p. 138) argues that government intervention to deal with a market imperfection or failure may itself be subject to a "nonmarket failure."[24] He argues that the market failure "rationale provides only a necessary, not a sufficient, justification for public policy interventions. Sufficiency requires that specifically identified market failures be compared with potential nonmarket failure associated with the implementation of public policies. . . . The distinctive demand and supply characteristics that give rise to these nonmarket failures include the following: premature but politically effective demands for government action; difficulties of defining and measuring output; lack of a bottom line for evaluating performance; absence of competition; and lack of an effective termination mechanism."

Market imperfections are thus only a necessary condition for regulation to improve economic efficiency. Regulation is not perfect and even well-intentioned regulation can in some instances worsen the performance of markets. In addition, regulation is not always intended to correct market imperfections but instead can be the result of political forces that serve interest groups rather than economic efficiency. The next section considers the political economy of regulation.

The Political Economy of Regulation

One theory of economic regulation is that it is initially imposed to address a market imperfection, but through contact with the firms they regulate, regulators begin to see the firms' problems as their own. Regulation then evolves over time to serve the interests of regulated firms in addition to, or instead of, the goal of economic efficiency.[25] This *capture theory* predicts that regulation initially will be found where there are market imperfections and that over time regulation will evolve to serve interests in the regulated industry.

Observing that much of the economic regulation of industries increased costs and generated rents, Chicago school economists provided a different explanation for where regulation would be expected. Their focus was not on market imperfections as an explanation for economic regulation but on the ability of interest groups to generate rents by obtaining regulation through the supply of political pressure. From this perspective, regulation is demanded by interest groups and supplied through the political process.[26] Regulation thus was not established to address market imperfections and then captured but instead was established in the first place to benefit politically effective interests. Once established, regulation continued to serve those interests. From this *rent-seeking* perspective, the railroads in the nineteenth century sought regulation to support their

[23]See Kreps (1990) for an exposition of this theory.
[24]See also Wolf (1988).
[25]See Bernstein (1955) and Quirk (1981).
[26]See Stigler (1971), Posner (1974), and Peltzman (1976).

cartel agreements, which the railroads were having difficulty enforcing because of cheating on the agreements. Similarly, regulation in the airline and trucking industries was sought in part to serve the interests of incumbent firms by limiting entry and passing on cost increases through higher prices.

Regulation is also supplied in response to the demands of interest groups other than business. This is clear in the context of social regulation where, for example, environmental interest groups successfully overcame agricultural interests in obtaining the regulation of pesticides and where organized labor succeeded in obtaining workplace safety and health regulation. During the early 1990s consumer complaints about basic cable television prices led Congress to establish price regulation over the veto of President Bush.

Firms also frequently seek uniform federal regulations to avoid individual states imposing different regulations that reduce the efficiency gains from the standardization of products and operating procedures. Appliance manufacturers thus sought uniform energy-efficiency standards across the states to avoid having to produce different models for different states. Companies also seek regulation to level the playing field by requiring competitors to meet the same standards they meet. When McDonald's decided to implement a no-smoking policy in its company-owned restaurants, it sought uniform federal regulation to impose a no-smoking policy on all restaurants.

The capture and rent-seeking theories give insufficient attention to market imperfections, as is most apparent in the regulation of externalities such as pollution. These theories also give insufficient attention to the role of institutions in structuring the competition among interest groups, and they lack an account of the organization, strategies, and effectiveness of those interest groups. As indicated in Figure 10–2, regulation takes place in a complex institutional and political environment, and the mandate and procedures of those institutions, as well as the policy objectives of the executive branch, can be important. In the case of the regulation of basic cable television prices, members of Congress saw the issue as sufficiently popular with constituents that it was worthwhile for them to enact regulation in the form of the Cable Television Act of 1992 and claim credit for it.

Regulation, regulatory practices, and regulatory change can be understood through the frameworks presented in Parts I and II of this book combined with the characteristics of the institutional environment, as illustrated in Figure 10–2, and the analysis of market imperfections. Regulation is shaped by market imperfections, institutions, and the political action of private interests resulting from its distributive consequences. The impact of political action on regulatory agencies is direct, as well as indirect through Congress and the executive branch. In addition, regulation has procedural requirements imposed by both legislation and due process rights. The economic efficiency objective of addressing market imperfections also influences the policy-making process, particularly if that objective is embraced by the presidential administration. The civil service personnel of the agencies and the nature of bureaucracy also play a role.[27] Interest group politics represents a strong force for change in some cases and for preservation of the status quo in others.[28] Regulatory change in the telecommunications and electric power industries as considered later in the chapter illustrates the importance of institutions as well as of interests.

---

[27]See Wilson (1989).

[28]See Noll and Owen (1983), Mitnick (1980), Wilson (1980), and Francis (1993) for studies of the politics of regulation.

Regulation is also shaped by the efficiency consequences of policy alternatives and the policy responses to those consequences. The impetus for deregulation in the transportation industries came from information provided by public policy analysts, the staff of the regulatory commissions, and the policy makers in the executive branch.[29] Regulatory policy is thus a function of both interest group actions and institutions and their officeholders.[30]

As an example, one distinctive feature of much of the social regulation enacted over the past 30 years is the regularity of special provisions for small businesses of various sizes. Many regulations provide small businesses with exemptions, streamlined reporting procedures, reduced compliance burdens, smaller penalties, or less stringent standards. Brock and Evans (1986, Table 4.2) list 29 federal regulatory programs that provide "tiers" of regulation based on the size of firms. For example, the Family Leave Act of 1993 exempts firms with fewer than 50 employees. Furthermore, the Regulatory Flexibility Act of 1980 encourages regulators not to burden small businesses unduly.

Small business receives these exceptions in part because the compliance costs, and particularly their administrative components, are disproportionately burdensome for small business. Exceptions, however, can also be viewed as the result of the effective political organization of small businesses. As indicated in Chapter 8, small businesses are numerous, have complete coverage of legislative districts, and in the aggregate have substantial resources. Small business is also well organized for political purposes, with the National Federation of Independent Business and the National Small Business Association having considerable influence in Washington and in state capitols.

REDISTRIBUTION AND CROSS-SUBSIDIZATION

Regulation can also be used to redistribute wealth. Rent control in the housing market is an example, and cable television regulation is another. Regulation can also be used to redistribute income among classes of consumers through cross-subsidization of one customer class by another. Because of distributive concerns, state regulatory agencies have instituted lifeline rates for low-income consumers. In California, lifeline rates for basic telephone services are available to a family of four with a 1990 income of less than $19,200. Lifeline rates require cross-subsidization by other consumers, and some forms of cross-subsidization can have important effects on industry performance and provide an impetus for regulatory change.

Cross-subsidization occurs when one group of customers pays more and another group pays less than the cost of providing their service. Economic inefficiency results on both sides of the cross-subsidization. When a price is too low, some consumers receive a service even though the cost of satisfying their demand is greater than their willingness to pay for it. When a price is too high, some consumers who are willing to pay the cost of the resources required to produce their service are denied the opportunity to do so. An inefficiency occurs in both cases.

Cross-subsidization is a common feature of the regulation of industries. Long-distance and business telephone services have been used to cross-subsidize basic residential service.[31] When airline fares and routes were regulated, long-distance flights cross-subsidized shorter flights, and high-density airline routes cross-subsidized low-density routes. Cross-subsidization is unsustainable when entry is possible and compe-

---

[29]See Derthick and Quirk (1985) for a study of the influence of policy analysts on regulatory policy.

[30]Harris and Milkis (1989) provide an analysis of regulatory change at the FTC and EPA.

[31]In industries such as telecommunications that are characterized by high common costs—costs associated with facilities shared by several services—determining which service is cross-subsidizing another service is difficult.

tition is allowed, since customers who are paying more than the cost of their service have an incentive to seek alternative means of obtaining it. Much of the deregulation movement in the United States has been the result of forces created by cross-subsidization. The entry of MCI into the long-distance telecommunications market occurred because AT&T's long-distance rates were used to cross-subsidize other services. MCI offered services at prices that did not include the cross-subsidization, and customers switched to it.

COST-OF-SERVICE REGULATION

Regulation in the transportation, electric power, natural gas transmission, and telecommunications industries centered on cost-of-service pricing and on who was permitted to provide services. In industries such as airlines and trucking, entry was controlled and industry-wide prices were set and cost increases passed on to consumers in the form of higher prices. This allowed inefficiencies to creep into the industries. Because industry-wide wage increases affected all firms similarly, firms had weak incentives to resist wage demands, since higher wages could be passed along to consumers through the regulatory process. This moral hazard feature of cost-of-service regulation allowed organized labor, such as the Teamsters, to capture substantially higher wages than would otherwise have been possible.[32] When deregulation occurred in those industries and entry was permitted, the rents to labor fell.

In the electric power, natural gas transmission, and telecommunications industries prices were set on a firm-by-firm basis to yield the revenue required to cover the firm's actual costs plus an allowed return on equity capital. Price changes occur only with regulatory approval, and the approval process was similar to formal adjudication. Data and analyses were presented by the firm in support of the price changes, comments were requested from interested parties, hearings were held, witnesses testified and were cross-examined, and the commission issued an order specifying the prices. Much of the contention in this process centered on the rate of return the firm was allowed. In some cases, the emphasis on rate of return caused regulation to focus more on the profits earned by firms than on efficient pricing or cost reductions.

In the telecommunications industry, cost-of-service regulation focused on the rate of return, in part because neither the regulators nor the firms had reliable information about the costs of providing individual services. The cost structure of telecommunications involves large common costs of facilities, such as network and switching equipment, used for a number of services. In addition, there are network externalities that complicate the determination of costs. Finally, the firms' accounting and information systems were not designed to identify costs of individual services, making it virtually impossible to base prices for individual services on actual costs.

This cost-of-service regulatory system has been blamed for inducing high costs and slowing the introduction of new technology. Firms were said to invest in excess capacity and higher-quality equipment than needed because that increased their asset base. Profits were determined by applying the allowed rate of return to the asset base, and when the allowed rate of return was above the cost of capital, higher profits resulted. This also caused other inefficiencies. AT&T was said to have inhibited the rate at which new technology was introduced because it did not want to write off existing assets and lose the return allowed on those assets.

---

[32]See Rose (1987).

Deregulation

TELECOMMUNICATIONS

Over the past 50 years, interstate telecommunications regulation has evolved from the cost-of-service regulation of a monopoly AT&T to reliance on competition with only limited supervision by regulators. Regulation of long-distance service traditionally focused on who was permitted to provide service and what prices could be charged for those services. After World War II a series of technological advances changed the cost structure of the industry with, for example, microwave transmission technology reducing costs dramatically. In the 1950s state police departments and oil and gas pipeline companies requested permission to build communications systems tailored to their specific needs and dedicated to their own use.[33] Entry into the industry had begun.

Technological progress continued, and for several decades both nominal and real prices for telecommunications services decreased. Despite the lower prices, the price structure in telecommunications resulted in considerable inefficiency. Because of the early public policy objective of achieving universal service, the price of basic residential service was kept low and the price of business and long-distance service kept high to cover the revenue shortfall. This cross-subsidization continued as a result of nonmarket pressure from consumers and from politicians who sought to represent consumer interests. Technological change in the form of microwave and satellite systems and electronic switching equipment, however, made it possible for large business customers to bypass the Bell network by establishing their own private telecommunications systems. Bypass was sufficiently attractive that the system of cross-subsidization was in jeopardy.

At the same time, as a result of court orders overturning several FCC decisions, competitors such as MCI and Sprint were allowed to enter increasingly broad segments of the interstate telecommunications market. The break up of the Bell system further complicated the practice of cost-of-service and rate-of-return regulation.[34] The FCC was faced with the problem of restructuring the rates for long distance and local service in light of bypass and competitive pressures. This required increasing the rates for local residential service and lowering the rates for long-distance service. The chapter case *The FCC and International Telephone Charges* presents another instance in which prices required restructuring.

Telecommunications deregulation thus was spurred by technological change and inefficient regulatory policies that provided opportunities for new entrants to offer selected services at prices substantially below regulated rates. In addition, large consumers of telecommunications services had incentives to construct their own telecommunications systems by building their own facilities and using capacity leased from the regulated telephone companies. Technological change essentially eliminated any remaining vestiges of natural monopoly in the industry. For example, local connections could be provided by cable television connections and wireless communications systems in addition to wire. Deregulation proceeded most rapidly at the federal level with more modest steps taken by states, although there was a broad range of incentive plans implemented in the states.

State regulation had been rampant with cross-subsidization with intrastate long-distance service subsidizing local service and business service subsidizing residential service. State deregulation has focused less on cross-subsidization and instead has fo-

---

[33]Pipeline companies already had rights of way and thus could readily construct microwave systems.
[34]See Temin (1987) for a history of the Bell system and its change. See Fisher, McGowan, and Greenwood (1983) for an analysis of the breakup.

cused on incentive regulation intended to provide firms with flexibility to operate more efficiently and to pass on some of the efficiency to customers. Kriedel, Sappington, and Wiseman (1996) reviewed the empirical literature on the consequences of state deregulation efforts. Those efforts in over 30 states included (1) rate case moratoria, whereby a state does not investigate a company's prices or rate of return for a specified number of years; (2) earnings sharing in which a company is freed of rate-of-return regulation but must share with customers some portion of any earnings above a target; (3) revenue sharing in which a company shares revenue but not earnings with customers; (4) price cap regulation in which a price index of services is capped but profits are not regulated; and (5) complete deregulation; for example, with the exception of local service Nebraska has freed telecommunications service from price and earnings regulation. Several other states have retained cost-of-service regulation. Kribel, Sappington, and Wiseman concluded that the evidence on the effects of the regulatory initiatives was mixed; that is, it is "premature to conclude that incentive regulation has been an overwhelming success." They also stated, "There is no evidence that incentive regulation has led to streamlined regulatory proceedings."

At the federal level Congress had attempted for 20 years to amend the Communications Act of 1934, which had remained largely as originally written despite dramatic technological change. Finally, a compromise among the three principal sets of companies—long-distance carriers, regional Bell operating companies, and cable TV providers—was reached in the Telecommunications Act of 1996. The complex act commits to opening both local service and long-distance markets to entry by any firm provided that the entrant's market is open to competition. FCC Chairman Reed Hundt commented, "The halls at the FCC do threaten to buckle under the weight of the advocates pressing their arguments about the meaning of the new law."

Harris and Kraft (1977) examined the act and evaluated the compromises it reflects.[35] A local-service company is permitted to provide long-distance service, which it had been prohibited from providing by the settlement in the AT&T antitrust case, but only if it provides all potential competitors access to its local network. Thus, the quid pro quo for local service companies to be able to provide integrated local and long-distance service is that they open their local service market to competition. Similarly, cable TV companies are to be freed from the price controls imposed in the Cable Television Act of 1992 once the local-service companies are ready to provide video services. Cable TV companies are expected to begin to offer local service as well. Local-service companies are required to provide interconnections to their networks under "most favored nation" conditions under which the most favorable terms offered to any one company must be offered to all companies.

The Telecommunications Act of 1996 is an important step in the transformation of virtually all segments of the telecommunications market from tight regulation to competition. The path to competition, however, will be the subject of continued political action and legal jousting over the interpretation of the act. For example, the act gave the FCC new powers to set pricing standards that would apply within states, but state regulators successfully challenged those powers in a lawsuit that was upheld by the Court of Appeals. The FCC then appealed the case to the Supreme Court. Similarly, AT&T challenged the initial plans of a former Bell operating company to provide long-distance service. Continued legal challenges are likely, but the pace of technological change should lead to increased competition and decreased regulation.

---

[35] They also provide a brief history of deregulation at the federal level.

ELECTRIC POWER

The electric power industry represents approximately 3 percent of U.S. GDP and is nearly the size of the telephone and airline industries combined. Electricity prices vary greatly across the states with an average price in New York of 11.1 and California of 9.1 cents per kilowatt hour at the high end and 3.7 and 4.0 cents per kilowatt hour in Kentucky and Oregon, respectively. The price differences are in large part due to historical factors including the high costs of nuclear power plants still in the rate base.[36] Technological change in electric power has also had an important effect as improvements in gas turbine generators have greatly reduced the economies of scale in the industry. In addition, line losses from electricity transmission have been reduced. These technological changes have made it both feasible and economical to transmit cheap electricity to distant customers. The cost of power in adjacent states has been less than half that in California. This provided incentives for customers in a high-cost state to import electricity from low-cost states. In 1992 Congress passed the Energy Policy Act which required an electric transmission company to "wheel" electricity from a producer in one state through its lines to a customer in a third state. This in effect makes electricity a competitive market. Brokers and trading companies such as Enron now make a market in electricity, where industrial customers buy electricity on the spot market in 15-minute blocks.

White (1997) analyzed the political economy of electric power deregulation across the states. The basic impetus for deregulation and reliance on competition was provided by what White refers to as the "price gap"—the difference between the current regulated price and the price expected to prevail in a competitive market. The actions taken by the states varied considerably, and only the most extensive deregulation effort, that in California, is considered here.

The price gap for California was approximately 50 percent, and industrial customers in the state sought access to cheaper power available just across the border. The opportunity to benefit California customers was constrained by the obligation to cover the costs of the assets of the California electricity producers. If power were imported and the market opened to competition, the California producers would have stranded investments—investments in generating plants that were no longer economical to operate, estimated to be $28 billion.[37] Opening the market would force the California electricity producers to default on their bond obligations. Default could undermine the credit rating of state government forcing it to pay higher interest rates on its bonds, since the investments in generating plants had been made with the approval of state regulators.

The state government essentially struck a bargain in which the likelihood of default was reduced substantially and the market opened to competition in April 1998. Any California customer is now free to purchase electricity from any supplier. An industrial customer or a municipality with its own local distribution system thus could purchase electricity from the lowest bidder. Consumers received an immediate 10 percent reduction in their electricity rates, but those rates were frozen for 4 years to provide income to electricity producers to cover a portion of their stranded investments. That is, costs were expected to fall considerably over the 4 years which with the price freeze would provide earnings to cover a portion of the stranded investments. After 4 years prices will no longer be regulated. Also, state government agencies issued $7.4 billion in bonds the proceeds from which were used to pay off a portion of the stranded invest-

[36]Costs are also high because electric utilities are forced to purchase from independent power producers at high prices fixed by long-term contracts. Most of those contracts were expiring at the end of the 1990s.
[37]Moody's Investor's Service estimated the stranded investment of U.S. electricity producers at $135 billion.

ments. Taking the $7.4 billion off the electricity companies' books allowed the 10 percent price reduction. Consumers, however, were billed for the debt service on the state bonds and thus received little benefit during the 4-year price freeze, scheduled to expire in 2002.[38]

Other states have taken more cautious steps. Federal legislation has been introduced in Congress to allow any customer in the United States to purchase electricity from anyone, but the opposition was substantial. The promise of a competitive market in electricity was nearer but not yet in hand.

AUCTIONS

The FCC has also innovated by substituting auctions for its comparative license award system for allocating the radio spectrum.[39] The FCC had traditionally allocated broadcast licenses, for free, by evaluating applications using a set of noneconomic standards. With the development of cellular telephone technology the FCC had to allocate portions of the radio spectrum for that service, and it initially turned to the same system it used to allocate broadcast licenses.

It became clear, however, that the traditional allocation system was cumbersome and inefficient, and with a major segment of the radio spectrum to be allocated in 1995 for personal communications services, the FCC needed a better mechanism. For decades economists had urged the use of auctions to allocate scarce public resources. Auctions award resources to the highest bidders—the ones with the highest-valued uses for the resource. In a competitive market the highest-valued uses are determined by how effectively the bidders can compete to serve customers. Auctions thus yield economic efficiency; that is, resources (licenses) are allocated to their highest-valued use. Moreover, auctions capture the rents that were previously given as gifts to the selected applicants. The auction for broad band spectrum licenses suitable for personal communications systems held in 1995 attracted 70 bidders and raised $7 billion for the federal Treasury—$7 billion that under the previous system would have been a windfall gain to those receiving licenses.

The FCC continued to use auctions to allocate the radio spectrum. A 1996 auction restricted to small bidders for a 30-MHz block of the broadcast spectrum generated $10.2 billion in proceeds.[40] Cramton (1997) provides a detailed analysis of the first four FCC auctions and concluded that they were well designed and effective in both allocating the spectrum efficiently and in extracting the rents from bidders and for the public treasury.[41]

In the deliberations over the Telecommunications Act of 1996, the broadcast industry defeated an attempt by Republicans to auction the frequencies provided to broadcasters for advanced digital television.

Summary

Government regulation has a long history in the United States, beginning in the populist era, expanding during the New Deal, and taking new directions during the period of social regulation. Although considerable deregulation has occurred particularly at the federal level, there is still considerable economic regulation in many industries.

---

[38]Consumer activists attempted to rescind the California deregulation plan by qualifying a ballot initiative for the November 1998 ballot, but voters rejected it by a 2-to-1 vote.

[39]See Breyer (1982, pp. 71–95) for a description and critique of this system.

[40]Easy credit terms induced aggressive bidding, and one company that had bid $894 million for a license defaulted. The FCC then auctioned those licenses and received higher proceeds.

[41]See the special issue of the *Journal of Economics & Management Strategy,* Fall 1997, for additional analysis of auctions for spectrum allocation.

The government's right to regulate is unquestioned but is limited by due process and the constitutional protections against the taking of property without compensation. Regulation is conducted by commissions and agencies located at both the federal and the state levels. These regulatory bodies are embedded in a complex institutional environment. In addition to their guiding statutes, regulatory agencies are influenced by the executive branch, Congress, private interests, and the courts. The president has considerable influence through both the appointment process and the policies advocated by executive branch agencies. In addition to writing the authorizing statutes for a regulatory agency, Congress controls the agency's budget and has oversight responsibility. Private interests affect the regulatory agency directly through testimony and lobbying and through their influence with Congress and the executive branch. In response to lawsuits filed by private interests, the nature and scope of regulation are also shaped by the courts, which review statutes, policies, and individual regulations.

Regulation is provided in response to both market imperfections and political forces. Market imperfections include natural monopoly, externalities, public goods, asymmetric information, moral hazard, and transactions costs. One role of regulation is to correct these market imperfections, but regulation itself is imperfect and can in some cases be worse than the problem it is intended to cure. In some cases regulation is intended to protect incumbent firms and in other cases to redistribute wealth through cross-subsidization. The political economy perspective on the locus and form of regulation emphasizes the role of private interests in shaping regulation. Institutions and the regulatory agencies themselves have an important impact, and regulators at the federal level have actively worked for deregulation in the airline, electric power, natural gas transmission, surface transportation, and telecommunications industries.

CASES

Whirlpool and Energy Efficiency Standards (B): Rule Making

In 1995 the new Republican majorities in both houses of Congress imposed a 1-year moratorium on new energy-efficiency rule making by the Department of Energy (DOE). This action blocked the refrigerator efficiency rule that had been agreed to just before the November election by a broad coalition of environmentalist, state regulatory officials, and appliance manufacturers and published by DOE as a proposed rule making in July 1995.

In 1996 the political forces that had succeeded in enacting the moratorium renewed their efforts. Some simply wanted to extend the moratorium for another year, but others were more ambitious. For example, Tim Feldman, vice president of government affairs for the National Electrical Manufacturers Association (NEMA), pushed for a more sweeping change in the existing laws on standard setting, saying that current legislation "falls far short of the reforms needed to help industries burdened by the existing regulatory regime."[1] The Association of Home Appliance Manufacturers (AHAM) threatened to push for an extension of the moratorium unless DOE issued a rule that changed its procedure for adopting standards.[2]

The Department of Energy remained a principal target on congressional Republicans' hit list. Some wanted to abolish the department, whereas others took a less harsh stance. Senator Mitch McConnell, for example, again drafted a moratorium amendment, although this time the moratorium would not take effect if DOE committed itself to significant regulatory overhaul.

The Department of Energy was responsive to these political threats. In an effort to encourage industry participation, DOE held a priority-setting meeting on June 14 to determine which appliances would be considered for new standards, assuming that the moratorium was lifted as scheduled in October 1996. Refrigerators were classified as a high-priority appliance and would be among the first in line for standard setting. A month later the DOE issued an interpretive rule in the *Federal Register* that detailed the procedures the department would follow for establishing new standards. The procedures addressed industry concerns by providing for "greatly enhanced opportunities for public input, improved analytical approaches, and encouragement of consensus based standards."[3] The interpretive rule satisfied the main procedural concerns of AHAM, so the stage was set for the adoption and implementation of new standards.

PROPOSALS

Two months before the rule-making moratorium was set to expire, the Department of Energy reopened the comment period, and the basis for comment was the July 1995 proposed rule agreed to by the coalition. Tier 1 of the proposed rule set the energy standard for products manufactured with the soon-to-be-banned HCFC-141b, a foaming agent used in refrigerator insulation. Tier 2 set the standard for products manufactured without HCFC-141b, which would have considerably higher prices. Tier 1 standards were more stringent, calling for an average reduction of 30 percent in energy use. The comparable figure for Tier 2 was 10 percent. From these common characteristics, the DOE identified seven proposals for comment. As summarized in Exhibit 7–1, the proposals differed in terms of when the standards were to be set (immediately or deferred) and when they would take effect. Option 1 was the closest in spirit to the 1994 coalition agreement, whereas Option 4 was DOE's preferred option.

[1]Lisa Behrens, "Appliance Makers May Ask Congress for Another Delay on DOE Standards," *Inside Energy/with Federal Lands.* June 3, 1996.

[2]AHAM's position seems to have been motivated by a relatively small number of member firms that wanted improvements in communication and industry participation in the standard-setting process. Also mentioned was a perceived need for "more pragmatic economic analysis."

[3]*Federal Register,* 61 FR 36974, July 15, 1996.

EXHIBIT 7-1 DOE Proposals

Proposal	*Summary*	*Expected consequences*
1	Adopt the two-tier standard as proposed in July 1995, to become effective in 2000, but phase out the less stringent Tier 2 standard over 6 years.	Advantage in energy savings relative to other proposals, but forces manufacturers to make two significant product design changes within a 3-year period.[5]
2	Promulgate the less stringent Tier 2 standard in 2000, and begin rule making then for a 2005 Tier 1 standard.	Good energy-savings properties depending on the 2000 rule making, but requires two significant product design changes.
3	Promulgate the less stringent Tier 2 standard in 2003, and begin rule making then for tighter standards in 2008.	Low energy savings, but addresses the dual-design-changes problem.
4	Adopt a standard effective in 2003 that is between the Tier 1 and Tier 2 levels, but wait until 1999 to determine the precise level based on information available then.	The final rule would ultimately be based on better information about HCFC-141b substitutes and their costs and benefits. Manufacturers would be certain of the timing of the new standard.
5	Set a single standard between the Tier 1 and Tier 2 standards, effective in 2003.	Avoids the need for 1999 rule making but delays energy-efficiency gains and requires a judgment about HCFC-141b substitutes with minimal information. Requires manufacturers to redesign only once.
6	Specify two separate product classes: One tier for HCFC products and a second tier of non-HCFC insulation products.	Avoids the need for 1999 rule making but requires a judgment about HCFC-141b substitutes with only limited information.
7	Abandon all of the above and start a new rule-making procedure with a wider menu of alternatives.	Rule making would be more complex, consensus would be unlikely and efficiency gains would be lower.

RESPONSES

AHAM was delighted by the so-called preferred Option 4, as was most of the industry. The unspecified nature of the standard until 1999 bought them time during which they could continue to produce and market their existing product lines. Whirlpool's reaction was mixed. It had already developed and marketed a refrigerator that exceeded the 30 percent efficiency gain, whereas its competitors had not. The company was happy to see the resumption of rule making, but its (and the entire appliance industry's) market situation had suffered from price wars in the refrigerator market, leading in some instances to layoffs.[4]

Environmentalists and state regulators were also pleased that rule making was underway, but they worried that DOE would listen too much to the industry or to the wrong people in Congress. The department's preference for Option 4 was cited as evidence that it had been too heavily influenced by the firms it was authorized to regulate.

As required by the Administrative Procedure Act and reinforced by the recent rule adopted pertaining to energy-efficiency standard setting, the DOE invited comments on these proposals. ■

[4]For example, in July 1996 Whirlpool announced that it would lay off 550 to 800 workers from its Evansville, Indiana, plant. "Whirlpool to cut jobs at refrigerator plant," *The Reuters Business Report,* July 17, 1996.

[5]One change in 2000 would be to conform to this rule; the second change would be in 2003 to conform to the EPA's phaseout for HCFC-14lb. Whirlpool, however, disagreed with the assertion that the changes in standards would require two separate production overhauls. Having long known about the future standard changes, Whirlpool had already begun switching over its production line to simultaneously conform to the 2000 and 2003 standards.

PREPARATION QUESTIONS

1. Consider the case from the perspective of a Democrat regulator in the Department of Energy. What are your primary concerns? How should you decide among the options?
2. Which alternative should Whirlpool support? What strategy should it adopt?

Sears and the Local Regulation of Advertising

In 1987 Sears & Roebuck was the nation's largest retailer and third largest advertiser, spending $1.17 billion a year on advertising and promotion. A central component of Sears's advertising strategy was using selective price promotions as a means of attracting shoppers to its 819 retail outlets. Price promotions were effective for a variety of reasons. First, they created a sense of urgency. Second, they were an effective means of competing against discount stores without having to cut all prices. Third, according to Thomas Flynn, a former advertising executive, "These ads create the attitude, 'I'd better check at Sears.' "

To benefit from the scale of its nationwide marketing programs, Sears sought uniformity in its promotion policies, employing a staff of over 100 copywriters, artists, layout experts, and other specialists to prepare advertisements as much as a year before their use. Then, during the year Sears's marketing managers chose which goods would be discounted and by how much. Advertisements such as those in Sunday newspaper supplements, for example, used common advertising styles and were sent to newspapers across the country. Similarly, the same price discount might be offered simultaneously in several parts of the country.

Sears's advertising strategy was complicated by the variety of federal, state, and local regulations governing advertisements. Thomas Morris, vice president of Sears merchandise group, stated that Sears had "people who do nothing but check over all the things that other (Sears advertising) people do to make sure we do nothing to offend a customer, violate our ad policies or Federal Trade Commission rules."

Differences among state and local regulations posed a problem for Sears's national advertising and price promotion policies. Over 20 years ago New York City had enacted a Consumer Protection Law that gave its Department of Consumer Affairs the power to regulate advertising. Over the past 10 years the department had ordered more than 100 merchants to cease certain advertising practices, and in all cases the merchants had complied, some after prodding.

The department found a number of Sears's practices objectionable, including advertising "percent off" prices without indicating the price from which the discount was made. It also objected to advertising stating that the consumer should take advantage of a discounted price by a certain date even though the discounted price would remain in effect beyond that date. Angelo J. Aponte, consumer affairs commissioner for the city, said, "This is the sort of thing you might expect from some small-time schlock operator. It's deceptive to imply this is some special offer when it goes on month after month." For example, for its "Fall Savings Spectacular," Sears added "Hurry! Call by Oct. 24" but on October 25 it ran the same ad with another date. Aponte also objected to advertisements that stated a discount on "selected apparel" without indicating which items were being discounted. "This isn't just a technical violation. Consumers go to Sears thinking they'll get thirty percent off and they're told, 'Oh no, not on this rack. Only on those over there.' "

The department also objected to ads stating that the price for Sears Guardsman Radial Tires was "as low as $34.99," saying that city law required that prices of more expensive items must be published in type "at least as tall and broad as the lowest price stated." Susan Kassapian, a consumer advocate in the department, added, "Sears has the strange idea that they should abide by the lowest common denominator of consumer-protection behavior."[1]

Sears maintained that its advertising was truthful and accurate and that other advertisers used the same practices without the Department of Consumer Affairs objecting. Discussing Sears' tire ads, Stanley Lipnick, an attorney representing the firm, asked, "What about the car ads that say payments are from $95 a month without explaining how much higher they go?" He added that Sears's advertisements were protected by the First Amendment and that New York City was attempting to regulate interstate commerce.

---

[1]In 1983 Sears was successfully sued by the attorney general of California. It was fined $55,000 and agreed to stop "untrue representations" in its advertisements.

After repeated negotiations with the Department of Consumer Affairs, Sears decided to file a lawsuit in federal district court charging that the New York City "regulations are unconstitutional because they prevent us from disseminating accurate information as guaranteed by the first amendment." Sears added, "New York City's Consumer Protection Law brands as deceptive several commonly used advertising claims like 'Save 15% to 30% and more on selected apparel,' and 'prices start as low as $34.99 for our tires.' " Sears stated that "our only alternative was to virtually discontinue advertising in New York City, including national publications and network broadcasts in that market. Since this alternative was unacceptable, we reluctantly brought this action. . . ."

In response, the Department of Consumer Affairs filed suit in state court, seeking fines and a permanent injunction against Sears's "deceptive and/or misleading practices" including its advertising, promotion, and home improvement policies. In the press release announcing the filing of the suit, Aponte stated: "In a discussion recently with Sears' legal representative, I asked whether the company was aware . . . [that] [m]any consumers may be unlikely to rely on Sears' credibility based on its nationwide advertising. I was appalled by the response that 'I don't care what the public thinks.' This single statement for me summed up the company's attitude with regard to the alleged violations and their lack of concern shown by their callous treatment of New York City consumers. . . ." Sears replied that its representative's statement had been taken out of context by Aponte, asserting that its reputation with consumers would not be impaired by its refusal to comply with the Department of Consumer Affairs' orders. W. Stan Knipe of Sears stated, "Our reputation for dealing with the American public is one hundred years old. Our policies haven't changed: The phrase 'Satisfaction Guaranteed or Your Money Back' is still over the door at every store." ■

This case is based on a June 15, 1988, press release "Consumer Affairs Sues Sears" by the Department of Consumer Affairs, a June 15, 1988, press release by Sears, Roebuck & Co., and an article in *The Wall Street Journal,* June 28, 1988.

PREPARATION QUESTIONS

1. Are there market imperfections in the advertising of consumer products? Are they serious?
2. Are the Sears advertisements fraudulent? Are they misleading? Should an advertisement be unambiguous to everyone? To the "lowest common denominator"?
3. Is the department's application of the Consumer Protection Law arbitrary and capricious?
4. Should Sears comply with the Department of Consumers Affairs' wishes?
5. Is it responsible for Sears to refuse to comply with the department's wishes as a means of testing either the Consumer Protection Law's legality or the Department of Consumer Affairs' application of it?

The FCC and International Telephone Rates

A telephone call from the United States to Buenos Aires costs about the same as a telephone call from Los Angeles to New York. Yet, the rates for the two calls could differ by a factor of ten. In addition, the rate for a call from the United States to most other countries was substantially less than the rate for a call in the other direction. A principal cause of the differences was the "settlement rate," also known as the "accounting rate," on which calls were based. Largely because of the settlement rate the average cost of an overseas call was 88 cents a minute compared to 13 cents a minute for a domestic long-distance call in the United States.

For Canada and Germany the settlement rate was 11 cents a minute, and the average cost of a call was 34 and 88 cents a minute, respectively. For India the settlement rate was $1.58, down from $2.70 in 1985. The settlement rate for the Philippines was 50 cents a minute, and the average cost of a call was $1.29. The settlement charges represented a substantial source of revenue for a number of countries. For the Philippines, calls from the United States represented 11 percent of the total revenue of the Philippine telephone company.

Rates for long-distance calls were negotiated between AT&T and other U.S. carriers and the telephone companies in other countries. To promote lower rates and stimulate competition, in 1997 the FCC proposed a unilateral reduction in settlement rates based on the income of the country. The FCC proposal was for benchmark settlement rates in three tiers with a low of 15 cents a minute for high-income countries, a high of 23 cents a minute for poor countries, and the rest of the countries at 19 cents per minute.[1] The FCC proposal would reduce the settlement rate for India from $1.58 to 23 cents. The FCC would direct U.S. carriers to negotiate international call rates based on the benchmark settlement rates. To force the negotiations, the United Kingdom and New Zealand announced that they would publish their settlement rates, joining the United States in making their rates public.

The FCC estimated that the new rates would save U.S. customers $17 billion over the next 6 years. FCC Chairman Reed Hundt said, "We are a nation of immigrants, and we ought to be able to phone home without being E. T. . . . There has been a consensus for a decade that a cartel of companies has jacked up prices to a hideous level."[2]

The settlement rate was also largely responsible for a cash outflow of $5.4 billion from the United States, 70 percent of which represented a subsidy to foreign carriers according to the FCC. The FCC proposal would reduce the outflow to less than $2 billion.

Over 90 countries submitted comments to the FCC on the proposal. John Taylor, director of regulatory affairs of Cable and Wireless PLC of the United Kingdom, said, "Virtually every country was opposed to the FCC's plan, but in terms of retaliation there isn't much you can do."[3] Cable and Wireless owned stakes in the national telephone companies in 30 countries. To mollify other countries, the FCC proposal included five transition stages for lowering the settlement rates.

Earlier in 1997 under the auspices of the World Trade Organization, 69 countries signed an international trade agreement to open domestic telecommunications markets to competition. The European Union planned to open its telecommunications markets to competition on January 1, 1998. ■

[1] The settlement rates for the United Kingdom and Sweden were below the benchmarks.

[2] *The New York Times,* August 8, 1997.

[3] *The Wall Street Journal,* August 8, 1997.

PREPARATION QUESTIONS

1. Should the FCC issue a final rule putting its proposal into effect or should it enter into bilateral or multilateral negotiations with countries over the settlement rates?
2. What posture should AT&T take in the negotiations over new rates with the state telephone companies in the various countries?

CHAPTER 11

Product Safety: Liability and Regulation

Introduction

Safety is a major concern to both the public and firms. Many individuals are increasingly concerned about safety and are careful about the products they use and the foods they eat. Activists have found safety to be an attractive issue because it is universal and important. As the discussion of the automobile industry in Chapter 1 indicates, activists are well organized to bring safety issues before the public and into public institutional arenas. The media and politicians find safety issues to be compelling because they often have a human interest dimension in addition to their societal significance. Safety issues also attract attention because they pertain to fears that most people have about risks to themselves and their property. Safety is thus a particularly salient nonmarket issue.

Safety is also a primary concern for responsible management and occupies a prominent place on the nonmarket agenda of most firms. No firm wants injuries in its workplaces or associated with one of its products, yet preventing all injuries would be prohibitively costly if not impossible. The issue thus is the extent of care to take to reduce the number and severity of injuries. Safety is not only an important nonmarket issue, but it also can affect market strategies. The chapter case *Domino's Delivers (A)* addresses a safety issue associated with a central component of the market strategy of Domino's Pizza.

The principal and most comprehensive source of institutional guidance on safety is the law of torts—particularly products liability. Lawsuits filed by injured persons bring both a specific case and broader issues of responsibility into the institutional arena of the courts. The law of products liability has developed from these cases, and the awards courts make and the costs of litigation and liability insurance provide firms with incentives to take care through the incorporation of safety features, instructions, and warnings.

The law of torts served as the principal source of institutional guidance on safety until the 1970s, when the wave of social regulation led to the creation of regulatory agencies, such as the National Highway Traffic Safety Administration (NHTSA), the Consumer Product Safety Commission (CPSC), and the Occupational Safety and Health Administration (OSHA), to address safety issues. These agencies adopted a command-and-control approach, focusing on specific hazards and mandating controls and safety standards. One rationale for the regulation of safety is that it addresses market imperfections more effectively than can the liability system. The explanation for safety regulation, however, is more complex.

The perspective that the liability system provides incentives for care and that safety regulation corrects market imperfections is based on the social efficiency objective of maximizing the difference between the social benefits of products and the costs of injuries associated with them. Other objectives advocated for product safety policy, however, are simply to reduce the number of injuries and to compensate those who are injured or incur property damage.

These conflicting perspectives on the objectives of product safety policy are not only the purview of the courts and the regulatory agencies but also of legislatures. Business has worked for over two decades for federal products liability legislation that would limit the damages juries could award—particularly punitive damages. They have sought as well to revise the standards on which cases are decided. These efforts to enact significant federal legislation have been blocked by the opposition of safety activists, trial lawyers, and public officeholders who focus on compensation for the injured. Business has had some success in state legislatures, but the differences among state liability laws also cause problems for firms.

This chapter identifies the nature of the product safety issue and considers the guidance that products liability and product safety regulation provide for managers. The next section identifies the product safety problem from the perspective of social efficiency. Principles underpinning the liability system are then considered, followed by an introduction to product liability law. Product safety regulation by the CPSC is considered next. The case of chain saw safety is used to illustrate the liability and regulatory systems.

The Product Safety Problem and Social Efficiency

The product safety problem can be conceptualized as shown in Figure 11-1. The producer makes a number of *ex ante* decisions including product conception, research and development, design, manufacturing, and marketing. Once the product is put on the market, it becomes the property of the consumer. Some consumers may be injured or incur property damage while using the product. From the perspective of social efficiency, decisions by both the producer and consumers should take into account the social cost of possible injuries to persons and property.

In their product selection decisions, consumers should take into account the risk of injury and take appropriate care when using the product. In their *ex ante* decisions firms

FIGURE 11-1 The Product Safety Problem

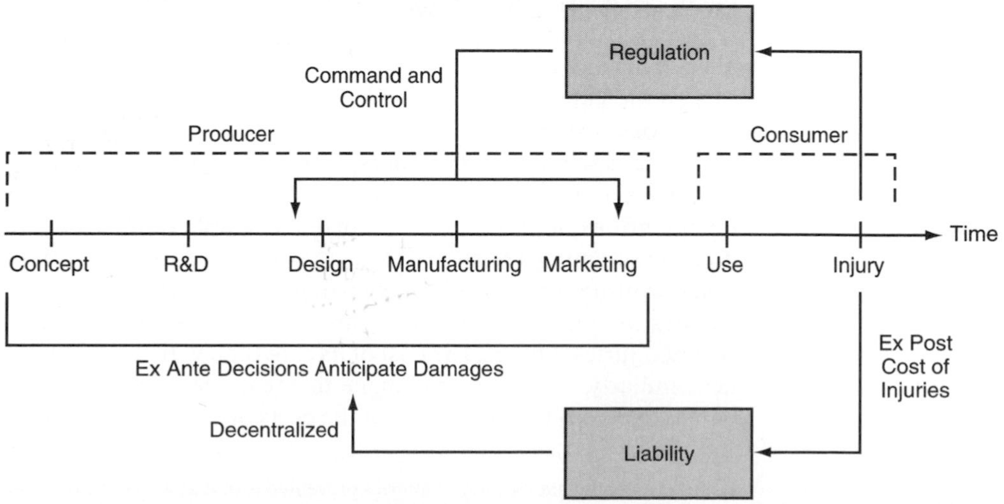

should take into account the *ex post* consequences of the injuries that might result from the use of their products. The likelihood of an injury depends on the product, its design, manufacture, safety features, and the instructions and warnings given. That likelihood also depends on the conditions under which the product is used, the skill and expertise of the user, and the care and precautions taken. The number of injuries thus can be affected by the care taken by the producer and the consumer.

Products also provide benefits, and the benefits must be weighed against the social costs of care and injuries. Making a product safer may reduce the benefits from its use or reduce its performance. Taking care by adding safety features to a chain saw, for instance, reduces the number of injuries but also may decrease its performance by reducing its cutting length and increasing its weight. The higher cost and lower performance can cause some consumers to purchase lower-cost saws with fewer safety features. Similarly, consumers incur costs of taking care in using a chain saw when they purchase goggles, a hard hat, and steel-tipped safety boots. The costs of care thus include the cost of the measures taken by consumers, the cost of the measures taken by the producer, and any resulting loss of benefits because of performance degradation.

Social efficiency requires balancing the costs of injuries and the costs of care. This perspective is illustrated in Figure 11-2, which graphs costs as a function of injuries prevented. The social cost of injuries decreases as more injuries are prevented. If all injuries were prevented, however, the cost of care—the cost of injury avoidance—would be very high. In the case of a chain saw, that could require not producing it. Total social costs thus are the sum of the costs of care and the costs of injuries as illustrated in the figure. The socially efficient number of injuries prevented, or equivalently the optimal amount of care, minimizes total social costs and is determined by a trade-off between the cost of injuries and the cost of preventing them.[1] As shown in the figure, society tolerates some injuries because preventing them is too costly. That is, society prevents those injuries that are not too costly to avoid.

The cost of care curve in Figure 11-2 reflects the most efficient, or least cost, combination of care taken by producers and consumers. Thus, for any given level of injuries prevented, the socially efficient allocation of care between the producer and consumers is that which minimizes the total costs of care. This is referred to as the principle of the least-cost avoider; that is, efficiency requires care by the producer or the consumer or both, depending on which has the lower cost of preventing injury.

The social costs of injuries and the cost of care taken by producers are reflected in the prices consumers pay for products. The higher price required to cover those costs reduces the demand for a product and thus the injuries resulting from it. Consumers will not purchase a product whose price and the associated cost of taking care during use exceed the benefits anticipated from its use. Those who value the product more highly than those costs will purchase it.

From a social efficiency perspective, the objective is to structure the incentives of producers and consumers so that *ex ante* each takes the efficient level of care and that the quantities of products demanded and supplied fully reflect those costs. This can be done by assigning a portion of the *ex post* social costs of injuries to producers and a portion to consumers. A profit-maximizing producer then will choose that level of care that equates the marginal cost of its care with the marginal reduction in the portion of the cost of injuries it bears. The cost of its care then will be reflected in the price of the product. Similarly, consumers will make their care decisions to minimize the sum of the cost of taking care plus the portion of the costs of the injuries assigned to them. Consumers,

[1] The socially efficient number of injuries prevented is that at which the marginal cost of injuries equals the marginal cost of care.

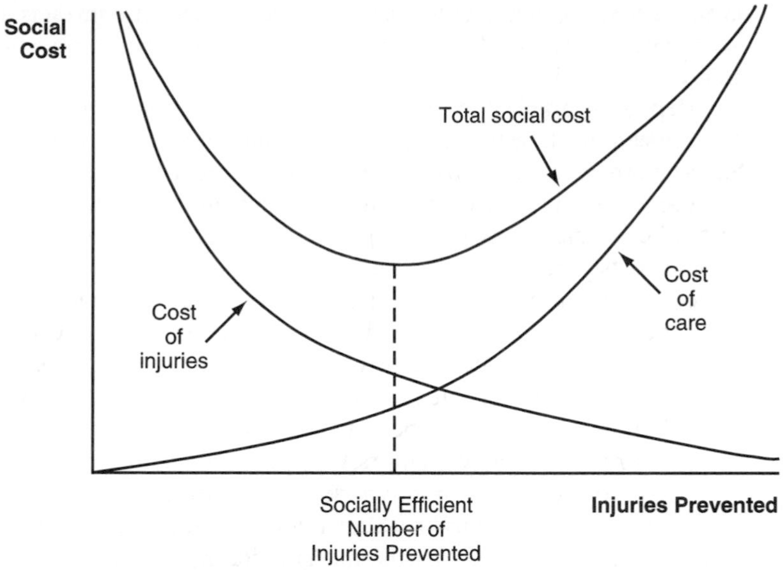

FIGURE 11-2 Social Costs of Injuries Prevented

in principle, equate the marginal cost of their care and the marginal reduction in their costs of injuries. As illustrated in the lower part of Figure 11-1, the institution of liability is intended to assign the *ex post* costs to producers and consumers so that each takes the efficient level of care, which then results in the socially efficient number of injuries prevented as illustrated in Figure 11-2.

In the United States and in many other countries, the institution of liability operates through the courts, which assign shares of the social costs of injuries to consumers and producers through the damages assessed in cases brought by injured consumers. These assignments of costs are intended to induce consumers and producers to take the socially efficient level of care. By aligning private and social costs, the liability system not only provides incentives for the socially efficient level of care, but also allows decentralized decision making on the part of producers and consumers rather than relying on government command and control.

The actual institution of liability, however, differs from this ideal. Distributive considerations also influence court decisions, which can focus on compensating the injured as well as on aligning private and social costs. The distributive consequences of the liability system also motivate political action. Products liability law and measures to reform it are considered in more detail after the Coase theorem and the concepts of liability and property rules are developed.

Entitlements, Liability, and Social Efficiency

THE COASE THEOREM

The Coase (1960) theorem pertains to injuries associated with products and more generally to market imperfections, including externalities, public goods, and natural monopoly. It focuses on the standard of social efficiency and provides a conceptual foundation for both regulation and liability. The theorem does not address other standards, such as distributive objectives and social justice, that could be used in evaluating alternative social arrangements and public policies. The theorem has gained influence in the law through applications to issues such as breach of contracts, pollution control, nuisance law, and torts.[2] Coase's original exposition focused on externalities and that setting will be used here.

Coase observed that an externality is reciprocal in the sense that at least two parties are required. In the case of noise pollution, there would be no externality without the polluter nor in the absence of anyone to hear the noise. In the case of a toxic risk from an oil refinery, an externality exists because of both the refinery and the presence of homes and businesses near it. When an externality is recognized to be reciprocal, it is clear that there is more than one means of achieving social efficiency.

As an example, suppose firm A discharges pollutants into a river whose water is used as an input to a production process by a downstream firm B. (In the context of Figure 11-2, let the horizontal axis represent the amount of pollution abated, the upward sloping curve represent the cost of abatement, and the downward sloping curve represent the harm to B.) In principle, the two firms can voluntarily reach an agreement to internalize the externality. This will be possible whether A has the entitlement to pollute or B has the entitlement to be free from pollution. If A has the entitlement to pollute, B has an incentive to bargain with A to reduce its pollution. B would be willing to pay A to the point at which the marginal damage done to B's production equals the marginal cost of reducing pollution at A, resulting in social efficiency.

If B has the entitlement not to have its production affected by the pollution, A has an incentive to bargain with B to allow A to discharge some amount of pollutants into the river. A is willing to pay B to the point at which the payment would equal the marginal cost of abatement by A. B would require a payment equal to the marginal damage B incurs from the pollution, so the marginal cost of abatement would equal the marginal damage. This assignment of the entitlement also results in the socially efficient level of pollution.

Social efficiency thus is attained if either the upstream firm A has the entitlement to pollute or the downstream firm B has the entitlement not to have its production affected by pollution. The Coase theorem states that, in the absence of transactions costs that would preclude these private agreements, the socially efficient outcome can be realized if the entitlement is assigned to either party. The role of government then is to assign entitlements to the parties and allow them to reach private agreements that internalize the externality. Although social efficiency is attained with either assignment of the entitlement, the assignment affects the distribution of the costs of the externality.

As an example, because of the risks of accidents and toxic discharges, oil refineries have implemented relocation programs in which they purchase homes and small businesses to move people away from their facilities. Exxon, for example, spent $4 million to purchase 110 homes and businesses around its Baton Rouge, Louisiana, refinery. Similar programs by Shell, Dow Chemical, and Georgia Gulf in the same area created safety zones around their plants. From the perspective of the Coase theorem, the entitlements were assigned to the homeowners and the firms bargained to purchase those entitlements, thereby bearing the cost of reducing the risk of harm. These programs thus deal with the externality and accident risks by removing one side of the reciprocal relationship.

ENTITLEMENTS AND THEIR PROTECTION

Calabresi and Melamed (1972) define an entitlement, or right, as the ability of an individual to control a particular resource or to take an action, with the state protecting that control or action from infringement. The nature of the protection given to entitlements

[2] See Polinsky (1989) for an exposition of the role of the Coase theorem in the law.

is important. Calabresi and Melamed distinguish between two types of rules for protecting entitlements—property rules and liability rules.[3]

A property rule prohibits other parties from infringing the entitlement without the consent of the party holding it. Homeowners are protected by a property rule that prohibits a person from either taking their home without consent or forcing them to sell it at a price they deem inadequate. The entitlements of the homeowners around the Louisiana refineries were protected by a property rule, and the homeowners exchanged their entitlements for payments from the oil companies.

A liability rule protects an entitlement in quite a different manner. When an entitlement is protected by a liability rule, a person may infringe the entitlement but must compensate its holder for the objectively assessed loss resulting from that infringement. Although a home is protected by a property rule against infringement by a person, it is protected only by a liability rule against infringement by the state. Eminent domain is a liability rule that permits the state to take a home for a public purpose and requires the state to compensate the owner for its objectively assessed value. Even if owners would prefer to hold out for greater compensation, as would be their right under a property rule, a liability rule does not allow them to do so. A person injured in an accident associated with a product is protected only by a liability rule because individuals are not prohibited from causing accidents. Instead, the producer of a product that causes an injury is required to compensate the victims for some portion of the harm.

The remarkable feature of the Coase theorem is that it establishes that social efficiency is achieved through private agreements when entitlements are protected with either a property rule or a liability rule. As illustrated in the example of the upstream and downstream firms, when an entitlement is protected by a property rule private bargaining leads to social efficiency. If the entitlement is assigned to the downstream firm B and protected instead by a liability rule, the upstream firm A may pollute but must pay the downstream firm for the resulting damage. A will then reduce its discharges to the point at which the marginal cost of its abatement equals the marginal damage, and hence the payment, to B.

Protecting certain entitlements with a liability rule is believed to involve fewer transactions costs than protecting them with a property rule. Consequently, injuries and externalities are governed by liability rules rather than by property rules. The next section addresses the issue of transactions costs and their implications for the use of property and liability rules.

TRANSACTIONS COSTS AND THE LIMITS OF THE COASE THEOREM

The Coase theorem implies that when bargaining between affected parties is possible or compensation for harm can be paid, social efficiency can be achieved even if there is an externality or a risk of injury. Consequently, from the Coasean perspective social efficiency in the case of externalities and injuries is a problem only because of impediments to private bargaining or imperfections in compensation systems. These impediments are referred to as transactions costs because they are associated with the process of arriving at a transaction or agreement.[4] When the parties involved are identifiable

---

[3]Calabresi and Melamed also consider inalienability rules. When an entitlement is protected by an inalienability rule, an individual is not allowed to give up or transfer the entitlement even voluntarily. For example, an individual's entitlement to vote in a public election is governed by an inalienability rule, since a person is not permitted to transfer that entitlement to another person.

[4]See Williamson (1975) for the original presentation of the transaction cost perspective.

and their number is small, transactions costs are likely to be low and private agreements can be made, as in the case of the oil refineries in Louisiana. When the parties are unknown or are great in number, however, private arrangements can be prohibitively costly. When transactions costs are high, social efficiency is unlikely to be achieved through private agreements.

Air pollution caused by cars, for example, must be controlled through government regulation because of the very high transactions costs that would be associated with private bargaining. Millions of drivers generate pollutants, and even more people are affected by that pollution. The costs involved if all these individuals attempted to reach agreements about measures to reduce emissions or the amount of driving allowed would be exorbitant. Similarly, when a product's use involves a risk of injury, consumers could in principle reach agreements with the producer to add safety features. Those agreements would result in the addition of those safety features that reduce the cost of injuries by at least as much as the cost of adding the features. Similarly, every driver could reach an agreement with every other driver and every pedestrian over the compensation to be paid in the event of an accident that resulted in injury. Transactions costs, however, typically prohibit these private arrangements for addressing injuries.

To illustrate the implications of transactions costs, consider the case of a swimming pool in someone's backyard. An externality is present because of the swimming pool and the presence of neighbors. Because the greatest likelihood of injury centers on neighborhood children, they will be the focus. If the swimming pool owner posts a clear and obvious warning not to trespass, anyone who trespasses and is injured in the pool is in some sense "at fault." From the perspective of fault, the swimming pool owner should be protected so that people neither trespass nor use the pool without the owner's consent. The costs of avoiding harm then would be placed on the neighborhood children and their parents. Parents then would take care in supervising their children and take measures such as building a fence around their own yards to prevent their children from going to the pool. Is this assignment likely to result in social efficiency; that is, is it likely to result in actions that minimize the sum of the costs of harm and the costs of the care by the pool owner and the neighbors? No, it is clearly more efficient for the pool owner to build a fence around the pool than for all the neighbors to build fences to keep their children away from the pool. This suggests that the swimming pool owner should be assigned the costs of injuries—be liable for injuries associated with the pool. That assignment would create incentives to build a fence.

THE ASSIGNMENT OF COSTS AND THE CHOICE BETWEEN LIABILITY AND REGULATION

The Coase theorem pertains to situations in which entitlements are clearly assigned and private agreements can be reached without substantial transactions costs. When entitlements are not already well defined or there are transactions costs, the assignment of responsibility for the costs of injuries is a task for government. Calabresi and Melamed provide five principles for the assignment of costs and the choice between the institutions of liability and regulation.

1. The assignment of entitlements should favor knowledgeable choices between social benefits (e.g., preventing injuries) and the social costs of obtaining them.
2. When it is unclear whether the social benefits exceed the social costs, "the cost should be put on the party that is best located to make such a cost-benefit analysis."

3. When there are alternative means of achieving social benefits (or of avoiding social costs), the costs of achieving them (or avoiding social costs from accidents) should be assigned to the party that can do so at the lowest cost.
4. When it is not clear who that party is, "the costs should be put on the party or activity which can with the lowest transactions costs act in the market to correct an error in entitlements by inducing the party who can avoid social costs most cheaply to do so."
5. Given principles one through four, determine if the protection of those assignments with a liability rule or direct government regulation is more likely to lead to social efficiency.

Breyer (1982) gives examples of the application of the Calabresi and Melamed principles to safety and pollution:

> When it is uncertain whether a benefit (such as a lawnmower with a certain risk) is worth the potential costs (such as the harm of related accidents), one should construct liability rules such that the costs (of the harm) are placed on the party best able to weigh the costs against the benefits. This principle is likely to place costs upon the party best able to avoid them, or, where this is unknown, on the party best able to induce others to act more safely. This principle seems to argue for making the lawnmower manufacturer strictly liable if he is best able to weigh the benefits, risks, and avoidance costs involved. Similarly, in the case of pollution, the rule would place liability on the factory owner, for he is in the best position to determine whether it is more efficient to curtail pollution or to compensate the victims of his noisome emissions.

In the case of lawn mower safety, or chain saw safety as considered later in the chapter, the fifth principle pertains to the choices between government regulation, voluntary standards, and reliance on the liability system.

Principles three and four call for placing social costs on those who can most efficiently reduce them or induce others to take care to reduce them. In many cases, this means that the producer and the consumer should each bear some portion of the social costs of injuries, so as to induce each to take the efficient level of care. Some regulators and some activists believe that it is difficult to change people's behavior and so consumers cannot be expected to take appropriate levels of care. They argue that the entire burden should be placed on producers, who can take care through product design and the incorporation of safety features. R. David Pittle, a former CPSC commissioner who has been an advocate of mandatory safety standards for chain saws, said: "Safety campaigns may work to get people to perform a onetime act, like buying a smoke detector. But it is far more cost effective to change a product than to change the long-term behavior of millions of consumers."[5]

Products Liability Law

PRODUCTS LIABILITY CASES

The number of products liability cases increased substantially over the past three decades, although there is some disagreement about whether there has been an "explosion." Dungworth (1988) studied the filings in federal courts and found that the

[5]*The New York Times,* June 18, 1983.

number of cases increased from 1,520 in 1974 to over 12,000 in 1985 and 1986. During this 13-year period, over 85,000 suits were filed against nearly 20,000 defendants. These data reflect several major types of cases. Seventeen defendants accounted for approximately 35 percent of the cases, with three products—asbestos, the Dalkon Shield, and Bendectin—accounting for over 30 percent of the cases. Nearly 21,000 of the suits were on asbestos, leading to the bankruptcy of the Manville Corporation in 1982 as the likely claims exceeded its $1 billion net worth.[6] Another 5,683 suits were filed on the Dalkon Shield and nearly 1,300 on Bendectin, a drug used to treat morning sickness. The pharmaceutical and health care industries accounted for approximately 18 percent of the nonasbestos cases filed. The number of products liability cases filed in federal courts has declined since the 1980s.

Most products liabilities cases are filed in state courts and most are settled out of court. The products liability system, and the tort system in general, involve high transactions costs associated with legal fees and other costs of bringing cases, developing evidence, and providing expert testimony. These high costs provide a strong incentive for plaintiffs and defendants to settle cases before going to trial. The National Center for State Courts' Court Statistics Project (1996) reported that in 1992, 27,568 products liabilities cases were filed in state courts. Only 3.6 percent of those cases were resolved through a trial with the rest settled, dropped, or dismissed. Of those cases that went to trial, plaintiffs won 40 percent.

The size of awards has also increased over time. Although systematic data are difficult to obtain, particularly for state courts, for those products liability cases completing trial in Cook County, Illinois, the average award in constant dollars increased from $265,000 in the 1960 to 1964 period to $828,000 in the 1980 to 1984 period.[7] A more recent study of court decisions in products liability cases for 15 jurisdictions found awards in 1990 to 1994 had increased from the 1985 to 1989 period. Also, the median award differed by a factor of five across the 15 jurisdictions.[8]

Cooter and Ulen (1988) reported that products liability insurance premiums were approximately $3 billion annually in the mid-1980s. In addition, some firms self-insure and others are unable to obtain insurance, so the total cost of products liability cases is considerably higher. The significance of products liability is greater than these costs suggest. Potential liability costs provide incentives for producers to take care in the design, manufacture, and marketing of their products, affecting most aspects of production and sale. The costs of the court cases and insurance are in addition to the costs of the care producers take.

In the late 1980s the trends in verdicts and awards in products liability cases, as well as other injury and malpractice cases, began to change. A 1994 study by Jury Verdict Research reported that of the products liability cases that went to trial, plaintiffs won only 43 percent in 1992 compared with 54 percent in 1987. For consumer products cases, the corresponding figures were 39 percent and 55 percent. Also, over this period the median and mean jury awards were virtually unchanged. These data reflect both the decisions of plaintiffs and defendants to seek settlements rather than go to trial and the actions of juries in those cases that go to trial.

---

[6]As of 1990, 152,000 claims had been filed against Manville, with 22,000 settled at an average award of $42,000. See the report "Understanding Mass Personal Injury Litigation," Institute of Civil Justice, RAND Corporation, Santa Monica, CA, www.rand.org.

[7]The data are from M. Peterson, "Civil Juries in the 1980s: Trends in Jury Trials and Verdicts in California and Cook County," Institute for Civil Justice, RAND Corporation, Santa Monica, CA, 1986. Quoted in Rueter (1988, p. 25).

[8]"Trends in Civil Jury Verdicts: New Data for 15 Jurisdictions," Institute for Civil Justice, RAND Corporation, Santa Monica, CA, www.rand.org.

THE DEVELOPMENT OF PRODUCTS LIABILITY LAW

Products liability is a branch of the law of torts or civil wrongs—wrongs done by one person to another.[9] The law of torts is common law that evolves through decisions made by judges on cases brought by private plaintiffs. Products liability cases that are litigated—particularly those that reach a state or the U.S. Supreme Court—establish legal precedents on which future cases are decided. Those precedents also provide the basis for plaintiffs' and defendants' expectations about likely court decisions in their own cases and so provide the basis for settlements.

The issues brought before the courts change over time and the law evolves to address those changes. Technological progress has changed the nature of many consumer products, particularly as electronics replaced mechanical functions. It is now often more difficult to determine a product's likely hazards through casual inspection. The Calabresi and Melamed principles then suggest shifting the cost of injury prevention toward the producer because the producer is likely to have a lower relative cost of preventing injuries through design and manufacture. The producer is also better placed to take actions in the market, such as providing warnings and instructions, that can induce consumers to take care. Court decisions have followed a similar logic, resulting in new legal standards on which cases are decided.[10]

The law of products liability has evolved considerably since the 1950s, with legal standards originating in the law of contracts evolving into a standard of strict liability under which a producer may be held fully responsible even if it is not at fault and could not have prevented the injury. Some activists and legal scholars have advocated going further to a system of absolute, or total, liability. Under such a system a producer would be held liable for any injury associated with a product. Such a system would be equivalent to a producer attaching an insurance policy, with no deductible or co-payment, to each product it sells.

The law of torts is as complex as its evolution. This section provides an introduction to some of the principal changes and central principles of products liability. One reason for the complexity is that products liability is largely state law, and not all states have adopted the same legal standards. Nearly all states have adopted the standard of strict liability, but some allow certain defenses that others do not allow. Thus, a problem for firms is dealing with dissimilar laws across the states. This has led some business groups and some lawyers to advocate a uniform federal code for products liability.

The law pertaining to product safety developed from the laws of contracts and warranties, which focus on economic well-being. The law of warranties is codified in the Uniform Commercial Code, which has been adopted for commercial transactions by all the states. In addition, the Magnuson-Moss Warranty Act of 1975 regulates the content and clarity of written warranties.

Warranties include those expressly made by the producer and those implied by, for example, the fact that the product was put on the market for sale. Express warranties are made in writing by the producer and, as part of the sales agreement, represent obligations binding on the producer. If the manufacturer states that a chain saw will cut at a particular speed and it does not, the consumer may sue for damages under the law of warranty.

---

[9]See Franklin and Rabin (1987) and Cooter and Ulen (1997) for treatments of the law of torts.

[10]Some legal scholars, such as Posner (1981), argue that social efficiency is the cornerstone of legal justice and that court decisions will in the long run produce a common law that supports efficiency. Rubin (1983) and Priest (1977) have argued that the natural incentives for parties to bring suits when social efficiency gains are potentially realizable will lead to new legal precedents that promote social efficiency.

Implied warranties are not made by producers but are held by the courts to be associated with a product put on the market. Products are held to have an implied warranty of merchantability. A chain saw is supposed to cut wood—if it does not, the consumer may sue. However, a chain saw is not supposed to cut cement blocks or metal pipe. A product also has an implied warranty for fitness for a particular purpose. A food or drink carries an implied warranty of fitness for human consumption.

The legal foundations provided by the law of contracts and warranties were transformed through two steps into the current law of products liability. The first step was a movement away from the rules of contract law by expanding the concept of who has standing to sue whom. In addition, certain principles of tort law were applied to injuries associated with products. The second was the replacement of the standard of negligence by that of strict liability. A negligence standard is still used in many parts of tort law, but the standard of strict liability is used in nearly all jurisdictions in cases of products liability.

At the turn of the century, state laws had generally followed the privity of contract standard, in which a party incurring a loss of property associated with the use of a product could only sue the party from which the product had been purchased. A producer who sold a product through a retailer could not be sued by a consumer because the consumer had privity of contract only with the retailer. In 1916, the State Appeals Court of New York in *MacPherson v. Buick Motor Company,* NY Court of Appeals, 111 N.E. 1050 (1916), held that an injured consumer could sue the manufacturer when the manufacturer had been negligent in failing to detect a defect in a product. The court stated, "If the nature of a thing is such that it is reasonably certain to place life and limb in danger when negligently made, it is then a thing of danger.... If he is negligent, where danger is foreseen, a liability will follow." This decision not only eliminated the privity requirement but also led to injuries associated with products being treated as torts. This began the development of products liability.

The limits of privity of contract were further eroded by a court decision that extended the implied warranty of merchantability to cover an automobile driver, in this case the spouse of the purchaser, who was not in privity with the seller.[11] These two cases extended the reach of tort law to users other than the purchaser and back through the channel of distribution to the manufacturer. In most jurisdictions, a consumer is now able to sue the producer as well as virtually all those in the channel of distribution through which the product passed. In addition, other people, including injured bystanders, can sue the producer for damages.

The *MacPherson* decision applied to cases in which negligence was shown. Negligence is defined as "The omission to do something which a reasonable man, guided by those ordinary considerations which ordinarily regulate human affairs, would do, or the doing of something which a reasonable and prudent man would not do."[12] The second phase of the evolution of products liability was the abandonment of the negligence standard and its replacement by the standard of strict liability in tort. Under a negligence standard, the burden of proof rested with the plaintiff to show that the producer was at fault. Fault was determined by whether the producer had taken due care in the manufacture of the product and whether adequate warnings had been given. Cases often focused on showing that the product had a defect that caused an injury which would not have occurred had the manufacturer exercised due care.

Under strict liability the concept of fault is irrelevant. The courts do not inquire into who was at fault but instead are only concerned with whether the product in question

---

[11] *Henningsen v. Bloomfield Motors,* 32 N.J. 358, 161 A.2d 69 (1960).
[12] *Black's Law Dictionary* (1983, p. 538).

was associated with the injury.[13] The courts also do not allow due care defenses, so a producer may be held liable even if everything possible had been done to prevent the defect that caused the injury.

The transformation to strict liability was the result of a set of cases decided in state courts. In *Escola v. Coca-Cola Bottling Co.,* 24 Cal. 2d 453, 150 P.2d 436 (1944), a case involving a person injured by an exploding Coca-Cola bottle, California Supreme Court Judge Traynor stated in a dissenting opinion: "I believe the manufacturer's negligence should no longer be singled out as the basis of a plaintiff's right to recover in cases like the present one. In my opinion it should now be recognized that a manufacturer incurs an absolute liability when an article that he has placed on the market, knowing that it is to be used without inspection, proves to have a defect that causes injury to human beings." Judge Traynor provided two rationales for his conclusion: one based on *ex ante* social efficiency and one based on which party can best bear the distributive consequences of the injuries. "Even if there is no negligence, however, public policy demands that responsibility be fixed wherever it will most effectively reduce the hazards to life and health inherent in defective products that reach the market. It is evident that the manufacturer can anticipate some hazards and guard against the recurrence of others, as the public cannot. Those who suffer injury from defective products are unprepared to meet its consequences. The cost of an injury and the loss of time or health may be an overwhelming misfortune to the person injured and a needless one, for the risk of injury can be insured by the manufacturer and distributed among the public as a cost of doing business."

Judge Traynor's call for a system of absolute liability has not yet prevailed, but his opinion influenced later court decisions that established the somewhat narrower standard of strict liability. In *Greenman v. Yuba Power Products,* 59 Cal. 2nd 57 (1963), a person injured by a piece of wood when using a shop tool was awarded damages under the principle that "A manufacturer is strictly liable in tort when an article he places on the market, knowing that it is to be used without inspection for defects, proves to have a defect that causes injury to a human being." The explanation given for strict liability was "to insure that the costs of injuries resulting from defective products are borne by the manufacturers that put such products on the market rather than by the injured persons who are powerless to protect themselves." The definition of strict liability is presented in Figure 11-3.

The courts have adopted a broad interpretation of what constitutes a defect in a product. Defects include those that come from manufacturing, as for example, a defective Coca-Cola bottle. Defects can also result from the design of the product. If a shop tool were designed in such a manner that a piece of wood could fly out of it during use, the product may be said to have a defect. Defects also can be associated with the instructions provided with a product, or with the warnings given. Producers thus have a duty to warn. It is often difficult to prove whether a product had a manufacturing defect, so many courts assume that if a person were injured by a product the product was defective.

Design defects include both those that are feasible or knowable and in some cases those that are unknowable—for example, because of the limitations of science at the time the product was manufactured. Manville was held liable for some asbestos-related injuries because of a failure to warn even though the court concluded that the danger was unknown to science at the time and thus the company could not have warned

---

[13]Even direct causation need not be established, as indicated by the DES decision considered later in the chapter.

(1) One who sells any product in a defective condition unreasonably dangerous to the user or consumer or to his property is subject to liability for physical harm thereby caused to ultimate user or consumer, or to his property, if (a) the seller is engaged in the business of selling such a product, and (b) it is expected to and does reach the user or consumer without substantial change in the condition in which it was sold.

(2) The rule in Subsection (1) applies although (a) the seller has exercised all possible care in the preparation and sale of his product, and (b) the user or consumer has not bought the product from or entered into any contractual relation with the seller.

FIGURE 11-3 Strict Liability: Section 402A of the Second Restatement of Torts (1965)

against it.[14] A defense that a firm used the state-of-the-art design may not prevail when a standard of strict liability is applicable.[15] Producers have thus been held liable for injuries from "defects" that were neither knowable nor preventable.

A defect in a warning is complicated because it involves both the warning given by the producer and the consumer's understanding of it. Many firms tailor their warnings to the lowest common denominator, and some have started using pictographs because some consumers cannot read. The adequacy of warnings and instructions is evaluated by the courts.

Warnings about the product's proper and intended use may not protect producers from liability. Intended and proper use is an imprecise concept. Is the intended and proper use of a screwdriver only to turn screws or does it include opening paint cans and serving as a chisel? Because a product such as a screwdriver can be anticipated to be used for a variety of purposes, courts have assigned to producers the duty to anticipate misuse. A manufacturer of a pickup truck, for example, was held liable for an injury caused by a rollover when a user attached a camper that exceeded the truck's stated carrying capacity.[16]

The courts have generally held that producers have a responsibility to anticipate misuse of products and a duty to take care to reduce both the likelihood of misuse and the harm from the misuse that does occur. In 1982, when seven people died after a still-unknown person put cyanide in Tylenol capsules, the families of the victims sued Johnson & Johnson charging that it should have recognized the possibility of tampering with a product it put on the market. Just before going to trial in 1991, Johnson & Johnson settled the cases for an undisclosed sum.

In most jurisdictions, products liability cases are covered by a statute of limitations, which is often 4 years. For capital equipment, a statute of repose serves the same function as a statute of limitations, but the time allowed is much longer.

ALLOWABLE DEFENSES UNDER STRICT LIABILITY

Some defenses are allowed under strict liability, but they vary among the states. In all of these defenses, the burden of proof is on the defendant. The only absolute defense is that the product was not associated with the injury or was not the proximate cause of

[14] *Beshuda v. JohnsManville Prods. Corp.,* 90 N.J. 191, 447 A.2d 539 (1982).

[15] Some states now allow state-of-the-art defenses.

[16] In recent years companies have substantially increased their warnings. After an award to a woman scalded when she spilled a cup of its coffee, McDonald's added the warning on its cup, "Caution: Contents Hot." A manufacturer of a Batman costume warned, "Parents: Please exercise caution. . .cape does not enable user to fly."

the injury. The concept of proximate cause was broadened considerably in the DES case to that of probabilistic causation. A woman whose mother had taken the drug DES during her pregnancy developed cancer over 20 years later.[17] The woman did not know which of several manufacturers had produced the DES her mother had taken, but the court held for her and apportioned damages among the producers according to their market share.[18] By the 1990s, third-generation DES lawsuits were being filed as granddaughters of women who had taken DES sought compensation.

The other defenses are not absolute. One is based on the assumption of risk by the consumer. If a consumer voluntarily and knowingly assumes a risk, a producer may be protected. Such assumptions are routine for surgery and certain medications, but they may provide little protection if the patient did not understand the risk. The burden of proof is on the defendant to prove that the assumption was both voluntary and understood. A producer may also have a defense if the consumer accepted a known and avoidable danger.

As indicated in the statement of strict liability in Figure 11-3, a producer may also have a defense if a product had been altered by someone other than the producer in a manner that caused injury to the plaintiff. A correction of a defect may also provide a degree of protection in some instances.

In some jurisdictions a defense of contributory negligence on the part of the plaintiff is allowed. The burden of proof is on the defendant to show that the plaintiff was negligent in the use of the product; if proven, the defendant may avoid damages or have the assessed damages reduced by the plaintiff's share of responsibility.[19,20] Producers are generally held responsible for anticipating misuse, however.

A producer may be able to use disclaimers to limit liability, but the courts have held some disclaimers to be invalid. The Magnuson-Moss Act prohibits producers from disclaiming express warranties and any implied warranties that go with it. Disclaiming is a concept from contract law and as such is intended to be a factor over which the parties bargain. Otherwise the courts may hold that it is invalid. One type of disclaimer that is upheld by courts is that associated with an assumption of risk in which a consumer voluntarily and knowledgeably agrees to bear the risk. Courts, however, typically examine closely whether the consumer actually understood the disclaimer. Disclaimers that limit the remedies available to parties, such as the right to sue, may not be upheld.

Compliance with government safety standards can in some cases be used as a defense, although such standards may be viewed by the courts as providing only the minimal level of safety. In a potentially important decision in 1993, the Court of Appeals ruled that FDA approval of a medical device and its subsequent monitoring of the device precluded state lawsuits alleging negligence and breach of warranty.[21]

DAMAGES

The principal form of damages awarded in products liability cases is compensatory—compensation for the loss incurred. The determination of compensation is straightforward in the case of property that has a readily established value. In other cases

---

[17]The FDA banned DES in 1971 as a result of an abnormal cancer rate in the daughters of women who had used the drug.

[18]*Sindell v. Abbott Laboratories,* 26 Cal. 3d 588, 607 P. 2d 924 (1980). In 1989 the Supreme Court let stand a New York court verdict holding DES manufacturers liable.

[19]See Cooter and Ulen (1988, pp. 354-360) for an analysis of the efficiency consequences of a contributory negligence defense.

[20]Negligence is not the same as misuse but is better understood as gross misuse.

[21]*King v. Collagen Corp.,* First U.S. Circuit Court of Appeals, No. 921278. The Supreme Court refused to grant *certiorari.*

measurement is more difficult. It is possible to determine the cost of medical care for an injury, but measuring pain and suffering or the loss of a limb or a life is more difficult. Juries do make decisions in such cases, however.

Moreover, lawyers have available detailed data on the damages awarded in personal injury lawsuits. For example, Jury Verdict Research (1997) annually publishes its *Personal Injury Valuation Handbook,* which provides data on awards in a variety of categories such as vehicular liabilities and products liability with breakdowns by type of injury. In 1996 the median and mean jury awards in products liability cases were $773,500 and $3,071,034, respectively. The median jury awards for burns and leg fractures were $891,000 and $500,000, respectively. Most cases do not reach trial, and out-of-court settlements are substantially lower than litigated cases, presumably because stronger cases are more likely to be litigated than weaker cases.

Defendants often complain about the magnitude of some damages awards. A survey by Lawyers Alert reported that the ten largest jury awards in liability cases decided in 1989 totaled $475 million. In 1988, 474 awards of over $1 million were made by juries. The awards reflect the sympathy many jurors feel for accident victims and the deep pockets they see in firms. The awards in many of these cases are reduced by the trial judges or on appeal. Most cases are settled out of court with the settlement amounts not revealed. The largest settlement ever was in 1998 when a class action suit against Dow Corning involving silicone breast implants was settled for $4.5 billion.

In cases in which both the producer and the consumer are responsible for the injury, some courts assess comparative damages. If the consumer is found to be 30 percent responsible for an accident and the producer 70 percent responsible, the producer is assessed damages equal to 70 percent of the consumer's loss.

In most jurisdictions punitive damages can be assessed. The legal standard for imposing punitive damages is higher than that for compensatory damages and generally requires a finding of negligence and fault. This allows defendants to use defenses, such as state-of-the-art design, that may not be allowable under strict liability. Jury Verdict Research reported that in 1995 and 1996 punitive damages were awarded in 12 percent and 6 percent, respectively, of the products liability cases litigated. The median awards were $1.25 million and $2.5 million, respectively. The magnitude of some of the punitive damages awards has attracted considerable attention. In a case in which a Pinto's gas tank caught fire and caused injury, a jury awarded $3.5 million in compensatory damages and $125 million in punitive damages. The judge reduced the punitive damages to $3.5 million.[22] In 1994 the Georgia Court of Appeals struck down the award of $105 million in punitive damages as mentioned in the Chapter 1 case *General Motors Like a Rock (A)?* involving an accidental death in a GM pickup truck with exterior mounted gas tanks.

In 1998 a California jury awarded $760 million in punitive damages to 28 former Lockheed workers exposed to toxic chemicals supplied by five oil and chemical companies. The judge reduced the award to $380 million as fair and reasonable, and the plaintiffs accepted the decision. The defendants planned to appeal.

IMPERFECTIONS IN THE LIABILITY SYSTEM

The products liability system has been criticized on equity, distributive, and efficiency grounds.[23] The equity arguments often express a belief that cases should be decided on the basis of fault and negligence. In particular, firms consider it inequitable to be as-

---

[22]See Cooter and Ulen (1988, pp. 403-407) for an analysis of Pinto cases.
[23]See Viscusi (1991) for an analysis of products liability and recommendations for reform.

sessed damages when there was nothing they could have done to prevent the injury. Objections have been made to the inability to use state-of-the-art design as a defense in cases governed by strict liability. In the absence of a statute of repose for capital equipment, this means that an injured party may be able to sue successfully for an injury caused by a product manufactured many years earlier when technological capabilities were more limited than at present.

The distributive objection is that the awards in many cases are too large and seem to provide a prize, as in a lottery, rather than providing compensation for actual losses. The deep pockets of producers are seen by some jurors as a means of helping those who were unfortunate enough to have been injured. Criticism has centered on damages awarded for pain and suffering, which some argue are often unreasonable and unguided by legal standards. Whether awards are too large is unclear, however, and limits on awards remain the subject of considerable disagreement.

As the Coase theorem indicates, the distributive consequences of a legal standard can be independent of its efficiency consequences. However, liability awards can force firms into bankruptcy or dissuade them from producing certain desirable products. Because a number of pharmaceutical companies had stopped producing certain vaccines as a result of their liability costs, Congress passed the Childhood Vaccine Act of 1986, which established a no-fault compensation system and capped pain and suffering awards. Similarly, there might be no nuclear power plants in the United States were it not for the Price-Anderson Act, which limits liability in the case of an accident. Some critics argue that the development of drugs to treat conditions associated with pregnancy has been chilled by lawsuits such as those involving Bendectin. Congenital abnormalities occur naturally in about 3 percent of newborns, and pharmaceutical companies can face lawsuits if the mother used one of their products.

In addition to concerns about the standards on which cases are decided and awards based, the liability system is costly to operate. Court costs and legal expenses for defendants are high, and under the contingent fee system attorneys for plaintiffs typically receive one-third of any award or settlement. Investigating the facts in a case can also be expensive. Products liability cases are frequently consolidated into class action lawsuits, which generally reduces the costs of litigation. The high cost of taking a case to trial not only encourages settlements but may also encourage frivolous suits that seek to extract a settlement from defendants who wish to avoid legal fees and court costs. The chapter case *Bic Disposable Butane Lighters* provides information on the strategies of trial lawyers in products liability cases.

A particular concern of business is joint and several liability. In a case in which several parties have a role in an injury, such as a manufacturer and a distributor or a manufacturer and a government, all may be held liable. A motorist who hits a pothole, loses control of the car, hits a telephone pole, and is injured may sue both the city government and the telephone company under the principle that the harm to the victim is indivisible.[24] In such a case, the damages awarded are allocated among the defendants in proportion to their responsibility for the injury. Comparative liability is used in all but six states and the District of Columbia. But if one of the defendants is unable to pay its share of the damages, the defendant with "deeper pockets" can be required to pay the entire award. This standard focuses on compensating the injured party rather than on providing appropriate incentives for care.[25]

---

[24]Cooter and Ulen (1988, pp. 408–410).

[25]Some states have limited joint and several liability.

Another criticism is that punitive damages awards are governed neither by statute nor clear constitutional guidelines. Instead, juries are largely free to assess punitive damages as they see fit. The imposition of punitive damages without standards to guide their award has been a source of concern to both firms and jurists. In a concurring opinion, Supreme Court Justices Sandra Day O'Connor and Antonin Scalia, discussing punitive damages, wrote, "The impact of these windfall recoveries is unpredictable and potentially substantial. . . this grant of wholly standardless discretion to determine the severity of punishment appears inconsistent with due process."[26]

Although there are no constitutional limits on punitive damages, in 1996 the Supreme Court threw out as constitutionally excessive a decision against BMW of North America in a case in which a jury awarded $4,000 in compensatory damages and $4 million in punitive damages because the paint on a new car had been retouched. Studies, however, indicate that punitive damages awards on average are less than compensatory damages, and thirty-six states have adopted limits on punitive damages.

From the perspective of producers, damage awards are difficult to predict, complicating the estimation of the *ex post* consequences of their *ex ante* decisions. The insurance system allows firms to insure against that risk, but the insurance system itself is imperfect and costly to operate. Also, many firms are unable to purchase liability insurance. In response, Congress passed the Risk Retention Act of 1981, which allows firms in the same industry to form their own insurance pool.

Another imperfection of the liability system results because consumers generally have imperfect information about risks associated with products. Producers provide information, but a moral hazard problem exists because, as more instructions and warnings are given, consumers may pay less attention to them. In addition, consumers are often poor estimators of risks associated with products.

The standard of strict liability is said by some to assign too much of the cost of injuries to firms and too little to consumers, distorting the incentives for care. This can cause firms to take more care and consumers to take less care than is efficient. Efficiency is improved by allowing a defense of contributory negligence and assigning damages on a comparative basis. In an imperfect world, however, the Calabresi and Melamed principles indicate that liability should be assigned to that party who is best placed to evaluate costs and benefits and to induce the other party to take appropriate care. Producers are generally better placed than consumers for these purposes, so efficiency may be served by assigning liability to producers rather than to consumers.[27]

The chapter case, *California Space Heaters, Inc. (A)* provides an opportunity to consider decisions on safety features in light of the products liability system.

ABSOLUTE LIABILITY

In *Escola,* Judge Traynor argued for a system of absolute liability that goes beyond strict liability by making producers liable for virtually any injury associated with products they offer for sale. Absolute liability is thus strict liability with no allowable defenses other than that the product in question was not associated with the injury. This is equivalent to a requirement that a firm provide complete insurance with its products. The social efficiency argument against a system of absolute liability is that it removes incentives from consumers to take care in the use of products.

---

[26]*Bankers Life & Casualty v. Crenshaw,* 486 U.S. 71 (1988). Quoted in Mahoney and Littlejohn (1989).
[27]See Epstein (1980) for an argument supporting strict liability.

As Cooter and Ulen (1988) suggest, a number of state courts have moved in this direction by reducing the set of allowable defenses under strict liability, including defenses associated with consumer misuse of products and with the voluntary assumption of risk. There are also forces acting in the other direction. For example, in awarding damages some state appellate courts have begun letting juries consider whether a driver injured in an automobile accident was wearing a seat belt.

As the following example indicates, liability cases can result in large settlements even when there is no scientific evidence linking a product to a disease.

EXAMPLE: SILICON BREAST IMPLANTS

In the 1970s and 1980s, 600,000 women received silicon breast implants. In 1982 a woman claimed that she became seriously ill when her breast implants leaked silicon into her body. She sued and received an award of over $1 million. The Dow Corning Company subsequently was sued by 170,000 women, filing bankruptcy in 1995 as a result of a proposed settlement that collapsed shortly thereafter. Three other manufacturers settled the claims against them later in 1995. In 1998 Dow Corning finally reached an agreement with the plaintiffs in which it agreed to pay $3.2 billion over 15 years.

The litigation was coordinated by trial lawyers and was well orchestrated. The trial lawyers hired Fenton Communications to conduct a public relations campaign to highlight the claims of serious illness resulting from the implants.[28] The settlements reached were in spite of consistent scientific evidence that there was no link between the silicon leaks and serious illness. The American College of Rheumatology stated that the scientific evidence was "compelling" that there was no link between implants and systemic disease. The Council on Scientific Affairs of the American Medical Association stated, "to date, there is no conclusive or compelling evidence that relates silicon breast implants to human auto-immune disease." The American Academy of Neurology stated that "existing research shows no link between silicon breast implants and neurological disease." Dr. Marcia Angell, executive editor of the *New England Journal of Medicine* and author of a book on breast implants, said that 15 scientifically valid epidemiological studies had been conducted and none showed any higher rate of illnesses among women with breast implants than women without them. She referred to the systemic diseases reported by women as "coincidental." Dr. David Kessler, who in 1992 as head of the Food and Drug Administration called for a moratorium on the sale of the implants and later became dean of the Yale University School of Medicine, said "There's no evidence that they cause systemic disease."[29]

Citing a Supreme Court decision calling on judges to act as "gatekeepers" to rule out unscientific testimony and speculation in favor of "pertinent evidence based on scientifically valid principles," a federal district court judge hearing implant cases barred plaintiffs' expert witnesses from testifying that the implants can cause systemic diseases.[30] A special panel of independent experts appointed by the judge studied the issue for two years and in December 1998 issued its report concluding that there was no evidence that implants induce systemic diseases. The plaintiffs vowed to continue to press their cases.

---

[28]Fenton Communications was the firm that orchestrated the nonmarket campaign against the apple-ripening chemical Alar considered in Chapter 4.
[29]*The New York Times*, July 11, 1998.
[30]Some women did suffer some scarring and hardening of tissue from leaks.

THE POLITICS OF PRODUCTS LIABILITY

The costs and consequences of liability cases, and the income they provide to trial lawyers, provide strong incentives to take liability issues into the legislation arena. Liability costs not only affect safety decisions, but they also affect the prices of products and in some cases whether products are produced. In part because of soaring liability costs, production in the small aircraft industry fell from 17,811 aircraft in 1978 to 964 in 1993. Cessna Aircraft stopped producing single-engine, piston-powered aircraft in 1986 because of liability costs. The plight of the industry led to enactment of the General Aviation Revitalization Act which prevents lawsuits against manufacturers for accidents associated with aircraft more than 18 years old. When the law went into effect in 1994 Cessna announced that it would produce 2,000 single-engine, piston-powered aircraft a year.

Producers of medical implants such as heart valves have been subject to numerous liability lawsuits. Fearing that they would be included as defendants, the suppliers of biomaterials began to stop supplying implant makers. The amount of biomaterials used in an implant is small and represented little loss of revenue to the suppliers. Implant makers and patient advocacy groups feared that a shortage would develop and worked for federal legislation shielding suppliers from liability. The Biomaterials Access Assurance Act was enacted in 1998.

Business interests have worked for over two decades for federal products liability legislation.[31] With Republican majorities in both houses of Congress as a result of the 1994 elections, business hopes for reform were buoyed. The 60,000-member Association of Trial Lawyers and its consumer advocate allies, such as Public Citizen, renewed their opposition to reforms and geared for another battle. Business also stepped up its efforts at the state level. In 1994, 17 large corporations formed the Civil Justice Reform Group to work for limits on jury awards and to make it more costly for plaintiffs to bring frivolous lawsuits. The American Tort Reform Association, which includes 400 nonprofit organizations, professional societies, trade associations, and businesses, has actively worked for tort reform.

With the new Republican members, the House passed the Common Sense Product Liability and Legal Reform Act, which would have provided major changes in aspects of the liability system. The Senate passed less sweeping legislation, but President Clinton vetoed the final bill in 1996. Efforts to negotiate an acceptable bill continued but in 1998 a compromise bill succumbed to a filibuster by Senate Democrats. The foci of these legislative efforts have been (1) caps on punitive damages for small companies, (2) limits on the liability of wholesalers and retailers in products liability lawsuits unless they altered a product, (3) heightened standards for punitive damages by requiring evidence of "conscious, flagrant disregard" for safety, (4) restrictions on damage awards if the plaintiff misused a product or was under the influence of alcohol or drugs, and (5) a statue of repose of 18 years for durable goods.

In addition to the revisions in products liability law at the federal level, many states have acted to cap and otherwise limit damage awards. Several states have also abolished or otherwise restricted joint and several liability. Cooter and Ulen (1988, pp. 457–461) list actions taken by 31 states but argue that these measures are more in the form of bandaids than the types of revisions needed to improve the efficiency of the liability system. These actions also contribute to the nonuniformity of liability laws across the states. In a study of the effects of changes in state liability laws over the 1970 to 1990 period, Campbell, Kessler, and Shepherd (1998) found that states that decreased their

---

[31]See Cohen (1990) for a review of these legislative efforts.

levels of liability experienced statistically significant higher gains in productivity of approximately 1 to 2 percent. Other studies have indicated that high levels of awards in liability cases reduce innovations.[32]

The future course of products liability will be shaped by the issues brought before the courts and by the tension between the objectives of compensating the injured and attaining social efficiency. The concern with compensating the injured has led not only to higher damage awards but more importantly to a narrowing of the defenses allowed. Some observers believe that this has resulted in too little care by consumers and too much care by producers. The concern for compensating the injured, and in some quarters for punishing producers, however, moves products liability in the direction of absolute liability. More recently, jury awards have leveled off, and juries have been finding for defendants in a higher percentage of the cases. In addition, pressure for reform has resulted in some changes in state laws and some reform at the federal level.

Product Safety Regulation

Federal safety regulation is exercised by the Food and Drug Administration, the Federal Aviation Administration, the Environmental Protection Agency, the National Highway Traffic Safety Administration, the Occupational Safety and Health Administration, the Nuclear Regulatory Commission, the Mine Safety and Health Administration, the Consumer Product Safety Commission(CPSC), as well as other agencies. Safety regulation takes two forms. For some products, such as pharmaceuticals and agricultural biotechnology products, premarket approval is required. For most products, safety regulation is *ex post,* as is products liability, and imposes standards and safety features on products once they have been marketed. In recent years safety regulation has increasingly used informational alternatives to product standards, requiring warnings and labels on products ranging from automobiles to toys.[33]

In addition to their regulatory functions, regulatory agencies provide a degree of confidence to the public that the products they buy are not unreasonably hazardous. Many firms work closely with regulatory agencies on safety problems, seeking cost-effective means of reducing hazards and injuries. In other instances, a firm may oppose a regulatory action. General Motors strenuously opposed the National Highway Traffic Safety Administration's (NHTSA's) attempt to recall its pickup trucks with side-mounted gas tanks, and under threat of continued opposition, NHTSA agreed to a settlement in which the trucks were not recalled.

Safety regulation is often contentious because it imposes direct costs on producers and ultimately on consumers. Social efficiency requires that safety regulation strike an appropriate balance between the benefits from injuries avoided and the costs of avoiding those injuries, as illustrated in Figure 11-2. Safety regulation, however, has often focused on reducing risks using perspectives other than social efficiency. This section illustrates the complexity of safety regulation in the case of the CPSC, and the following section addresses the regulation of a particular product—chain saws.

THE CONSUMER PRODUCTS SAFETY COMMISSION

The CPSC has five commissioners, appointed by the president to 7-year terms. Its regulatory authority comes from the Consumer Product Safety Act (CPSA), the Toy Safety Act, the Child Protection Amendments, the Federal Hazardous Substances

[32]See Viscusi and Moore (1993) and Huber and Litan (1991).
[33]See Magat and Viscusi (1992) for a study of informational approaches to regulation.

Act, the Flammable Fabrics Act, the Refrigerator Safety Act, the Poison Prevention Packaging Act, and the Hazardous Substances Act. The CPSC's basic mandate as stated in the CPSA is "to protect the public against unreasonable risks of injury associated with consumer products." The CPSC's mandate extends to virtually all consumer products except those that come under the jurisdiction of other regulatory agencies, for example, food, tobacco, pharmaceuticals, and automobiles. The CPSC has authority over approximately 15,000 products. The CPSC conducts three types of compliance activities: (1) informing manufacturers of CPSC requirements, (2) maintaining surveillance, and (3) obtaining corrections of violations by (a) working with manufacturers to correct problems, (b) ordering product recalls, and (c) litigating.

The CPSC's authorizing statute reflects the competing pressures from safety activists and business. The statute was written to enable the public to initiate regulatory action and to turn to the courts if the regulators fail to act. The CPSA provided that "Any interested person, including a consumer or consumer organization, may petition the commission to commence a proceeding for the issuance, amendment, or revocation of a consumer product safety rule. . . ." Interested parties, including businesses, also have the right to offer standards to the CPSC. The agency can accept, revise, or reject them. These provisions allow individuals, activists, and business to set a portion of the agenda of the CPSC. The statute also requires the CPSC to act on any petition within 120 days. The complexity of the issues, however, generally forces it to suspend proceedings while it continues its investigation.

In addition to providing access to the public, the statute provides protection for business. To conclude that a product involves an unreasonable risk, the CPSC is directed to take into account the need for the product and the effect of the standard on its performance and cost. The statute also requires the CPSC to minimize the effect of the standard on the industry. These provisions, as well as procedural due process requirements, provide bases for firms to challenge CPSC actions in the courts. Firms have frequently been successful in having the courts overturn CPSC actions.

The CPSC has the authority to set mandatory safety standards, require warnings and information, and approve voluntary standards developed in conjunction with an industry. Despite its broad authority, the CPSC has set only 39 mandatory standards. It has worked with industry in setting 300 voluntary standards, however.[34] In setting safety standards, the CPSC is required to follow procedures similar to those called for in the Administrative Procedure Act. It publishes an advanced notice of proposed rule making (ANPR) in the *Federal Register,* solicits comments, and holds hearings before issuing a standard.

Firms in an industry at times seek product safety standards. The U.S. bicycle industry proposed standards that would have prevented European manufacturers from selling their bicycles in the United States. This was avoided only when U.S. bicycle enthusiasts protested to the CPSC.[35] An industry may also propose a standard to address a market imperfection or to prevent some firms from free riding by producing lower-quality products that result in injuries, harming the industry as a whole by reducing the demand for safe as well as unsafe products.

In addition to setting standards, the CPSC has the authority to use the federal courts to ban an "imminently hazardous consumer product." In 1984, amendments to the Toy Safety

---

[34]Compliance with a mandatory or voluntary standard does not preclude product liability lawsuits, although compliance may help avoid a finding of negligence and the award of punitive damages.
[35]See Cornell, Noll, and Weingast (1976).

Act gave the CPSC the authority to recall unsafe toys. The CPSC has also used its authority to ban several other hazardous products. Most CPSC actions now focus on imminent hazards. The CPSC has a Fast-Track Product Recall Program to help manufacturers implement a recall. In fiscal 1998 the CPSC obtained 120 product recalls of toys and children's products totaling 5.9 million units. In fiscal 1999 the CPSC and Fisher-Price recalled 10 million battery-powered Power Wheels vehicles. While denying any violations, Nieman Marcus agreed to pay a $112,500 fine for selling bathrobes that CPSC alleged violated the Flammable Fabrics Act.

CPSC injury data revealed that in the first 10 months of 1994, 37 children aged from 6 months to 12 years died and 130,300 children 14 years and under were treated at hospital emergency rooms for injuries incurred in conjunction with toys. When the CPSC rejected a proposed labeling rule, safety advocates who had been working for years for improved labeling of toy hazards, turned to Congress, which in 1994 enacted the Child Safety Protection Act. The act was backed by industry, which sought to avoid differing state labeling laws. The law requires warning labels displayed prominently so that they are visible when the toys are on shelves.

One of the CPSC's important regulatory activities is based on Section 15 of the CPSA, which requires firms to report any defect that may pose a substantial product safety hazard. "Substantial" is defined in terms of the pattern of the defect, the exposure of consumers to the product, and the severity of the risk. In 1993, firms made 214 Section 15 reports to the CPSC.[36] The CPSC typically works with the reporting firm to correct the problem. The CPSC has also established an Import Surveillance Program to identify hazards associated with imported products.

The CPSA directs the CPSC "to collect, investigate, and disseminate injury data, and information, relating to the causes and prevention of death, injury, and illness associated with consumer products." The CPSC maintains a National Electronic Injury Surveillance System (NEISS) in which hospitals submit detailed data on injuries reported to their emergency rooms.[37] The CPSC then extrapolates the information to provide estimates of the injuries associated with approximately 1,000 products.[38] For example, the CPSC estimated that 83,000 injuries from in-line skating required emergency room treatment in 1994. The reliability of NEISS data has been questioned at times. Viscusi (1984) concluded that the NEISS-CPSC data were not sufficiently reliable for specific policy formulation or enforcement activity.

NEISS data are useful for spotting problems at an early stage, thereby allowing quick action. In 1990 hospital emergency room data reported to the CPSC revealed that some infants had suffocated in bean bag pillows placed in their cribs. At least 19 babies died from the pillows, and the CPSC acted quickly to recall them. The information received by the CPSC allowed relatively early detection of the hazard and a rapid response. During the 1970s the CPSC's NEISS found that a number of babies had died when they squeezed their bodies between crib slats, became stuck, and choked. The CPSC quickly worked with the industry to establish a standard prescribing narrower spacing between the slats. In 1993 the CPSC recalled 11,000 Playskool portable cribs because the top rails could collapse and suffocate an infant. Some of the cribs were not returned and could not be located, and two children subsequently died in crib collapses. In November 1998 the manufacturer began offering a $120 reward for a returned crib. The information acquisition role of the CPSC is important in identifying imminent

---

[36]Congressional Quarterly (1994, p. 54).

[37]The data do not include the brand of the product causing the injury.

[38]See Viscusi (1984, pp. 48–55) for an analysis of the quality of the NEISS data.

hazards, and its authority to act quickly using recalls and public warnings is an advantage over the liability system.

THE NONMARKET ENVIRONMENT OF THE CPSC

The CPSC's authority to recall and ban unsafe products and set product safety standards makes it potentially one of the most powerful regulatory commissions. The nonmarket environment of the CPSC is complex, however, as indicated in Figure 10-1, and that complexity has made it a relatively weak agency in several ways. First, its task is complex, data are limited, and its authorizing statute has conflicting provisions. Second, it is small and in many areas lacks the technical and scientific expertise to set appropriate standards. Third, it imposes concentrated costs on industries and thus is the focus of considerable political activity.

The CPSC is a small agency with less than 5 percent of the number of employees of the EPA. Its modest capabilities limit its scope and effectiveness. It was designed to be both responsive to activists and yet considerate of the potential burdens that safety regulation can impose on business. Its statutory mandate to protect against "unreasonable risks" is imprecise and a source of contention. The CPSC's early regulatory activities did not explicitly take into account social costs and social benefits, which led the Reagan administration to attempt to eliminate it—an objective shared by some public policy analysts.[39]

The CPSC's activities impose concentrated costs on industries and produce widely distributed safety benefits for consumers. Product safety regulation thus has the structure of entrepreneurial politics. At the end of the 1970s political pressure on the CPSC mounted as it sought to regulate hazards in industries composed of firms with broad coverage of congressional districts. CPSC's program to regulate chronic hazards, such as those associated with the use of formaldehyde in the funeral home and foam insulation industries, led to opposition by those industries.[40] Many business critics argued that the CPSC did not have the scientific expertise to regulate chronic hazards and that the EPA, which has both the expertise and the authority under the Toxic Substances Control Act to regulate hazardous chemicals, was better equipped for that task. Critics also pointed to the CPSC's cumbersome regulatory process, as required under the Administrative Procedure Act, and to the nature of some of the standards it issued. Its product standard for swimming pool slides consisted of required warning labels that included statements such as "Look out for people and objects below," and "Correct belly slide: head up, arms straight ahead, fingers pointing up."[41]

CPSC safety standards have been criticized on several grounds. Its use of design standards necessarily limits the ability of producers to use the least-cost method of achieving a given level of safety. In addition, design standards tend to reduce variety and the range of consumer choice and tend to lock in current technologies, thus limiting innovation. Firms argued that performance, rather than design standards, allow more flexibility for producers and more variety for consumers.

In 1981 under pressure from the Reagan administration, Congress slashed the CPSC's budget, abolished three of its four advisory committees, forced it to revise its

---

[39]See Viscusi (1984).
[40]The CPSC banned urea formaldehyde foam insulation, but in 1983 the U.S. Court of Appeals overturned the ban.
[41]*Fortune,* June 15, 1981.

lawn mower standard, rescinded the right of outside organizations to propose standards to it, and removed its authority to set design standards, requiring it to emphasize performance standards. The legislation also required the CPSC to exhaust all possibilities of arriving at voluntary standards before mandatory standards could be set.[42] The CPSC was required to demonstrate that the benefits from a mandatory standard bear a reasonable relationship to the costs. The 1981 legislation slashed the CPSC budget by 30 percent, and its budget has remained reduced in real terms.

Congress and President Bush recognized that even if they are expensive, safety regulations have considerable popular appeal. After a decade of discord, Congress reauthorized the CPSC legislation in 1990. One of the principal sticking points was a battle between consumer activists and business interests over reporting requirements for product liability cases. The activists sought to strengthen Section 15 by requiring firms to report to the CPSC every products liability suit filed against them and to report it at the time it was filed. Business objected on the grounds that many such suits were frivolous and that the use of filings tended to treat allegations as facts. A compromise was reached in which firms were required to report to the CPSC whenever three cases involving a particular product model are settled in or out of court within a 2-year period.[43] This provision improved the ability to the CPSC to identify dangerous products.

Chain Saw Safety

THE SAFETY ISSUE

A chain saw provides great efficiency in cutting wood, but it is an inherently hazardous product. In 1980 the CPSC estimated that 63,000 injuries associated with chain saws were treated in hospital emergency rooms. Extrapolating from the emergency room data, the CPSC estimated that there were 123,000 medically attended chain saw injuries. The most serious hazard is kickback, which can result in severe injury or death. Kickback involves a violent backward force that causes the saw to move upward toward the user's upper torso and head. Kickback occurs when the chain strikes a knot or other object in the wood, the chain is pinched in the cut, or the upper portion of the tip comes in contact with wood. Although many chain saw injuries are due to improper use, kickback can occur even to an experienced, professional wood cutter. The CPSC estimated that 23 percent of chain saw injuries were the result of kickback.[44]

The CPSC's injury estimates for 1980 were nearly double those of 5 years earlier. The increase in chain saw injuries was largely the result of increased sales and use of the saws in the aftermath of the oil shocks of the 1970s. The increased popularity of wood-burning stoves added to the demand for chain saws. In addition, the mix of saw users changed, with the proportion of casual and inexperienced users increasing substantially. In response to the changing market, producers began producing smaller saws and selling them in discount stores.

In the case of an inherently hazardous product such as a chain saw, firms require guidance about which accident and injury prevention measures to take. The institution of products liability provides guidance for saw design, the incorporation of safety features, and appropriate instructions and warnings. In one liability case, a professional wood cutter who had been working alone was found dead. He had been using a saw

---

[42] *Congressional Quarterly Weekly Report,* August 15, 1981, p. 1479.
[43] Since nearly all products liability cases are settled out of court and settlements typically involve the sealing of the record, the CPSC previously had not had access to most of these data.
[44] Consumer Products Safety Commission (1982).

designed for professionals and presumably had been the victim of kickback. Although the instruction manual had warned about kickback, a court held for the deceased's estate because the warnings should have indicated that kickback could not be avoided and could be fatal. The court held that there was no evidence that the deceased was not using the saw properly, but there was no evidence that he had understood the hazard.[45] As the law firm representing the McCulloch Corporation, a leading chain saw manufacturer, stated, "Companies choosing to market products that are unreasonably unsafe (or that may be found by hindsight not to have been reasonably safe at the time they were produced or sold) will be faced with unusually high product liability insurance costs and also the possibility of very substantial adverse judgments."[46] The incentives provided by strict liability led many manufacturers to incorporate such safety features as chain brakes into their saws. Safety features are expensive, however, and the inexpensive saws sold in discount stores had relatively few safety features.

In 1977 the chain saw safety issue entered the regulatory arena. John Purtle of Batesville, Arkansas, petitioned the CPSC to establish a mandatory safety standard for chain saws.[47] His petition initiated what was to become an 8-year standard-setting effort by the CPSC.

MARKET IMPERFECTIONS

To assess the appropriateness of the institutions of products liability and regulation for addressing the chain saw safety issue, it is useful to examine whether there are market imperfections that warrant regulation. In the absence of market imperfections, the institution of products liability may be sufficient from the perspective of social efficiency. Even if there are market imperfections, the liability system may be a superior institution to regulation. Conversely, the absence of a market imperfection does not mean that regulation will not be imposed. A market imperfection is at best a sufficient condition for regulation but is never a necessary condition, since political choice can impose regulation. Indeed, the CPSC's mandate does not require it to identify a market imperfection before action can be taken. Instead, it need only identify an unreasonable risk and find that the benefits of a safety standard bear a reasonable relationship to the costs imposed by the regulation.

The possible market imperfections associated with chain saws center on asymmetric information, externalities, and moral hazard. Asymmetric information exists when the seller knows of hazards of which the buyer is unaware or does not fully understand. Consumers, for example, may not be aware of hazards such as kickback, and, if they are aware of it, may not understand how to lessen its likelihood or to reduce the severity of injuries through taking care, such as wearing a hard hat. However, producers and consumers may be able to take actions in markets to address the asymmetric information problem.

In the case of chain saws, there are incentives for information provision on both the supply and the demand side of the market. On the supply side, producers have incentives to supply information about hazards and proper use because doing so will reduce the number of injuries and hence liability costs, as McCulloch's law firm indicated. Dealers also have an incentive to supply information on the selection and proper use of a chain saw, and some may provide demonstrations. On the demand side, consumers have incentives to seek information through study and inquiry. When a

---

[45]Manley (1987).

[46]*The Wall Street Journal,* August 23, 1982.

[47]"Chain Saws (A)," Harvard Business School, 9382086, May 1983, p. 3.

chain saw is used on a job, employers have an incentive to provide information and training to employees.

These market responses themselves, however, are imperfect. Chain saw manufacturers may be hesitant to highlight hazards that might reduce demand. Even advertising the safety features of saws could reduce demand by raising concerns among consumers. On the demand side, information has the properties of a public good. It thus may be undersupplied because private providers are unable to capture sufficient returns to cover the costs of supplying the information. Sources such as *Consumer Reports,* however, provide information on performance and safety features. Searching for information is expensive, so consumers may remain inadequately informed. Even though a market imperfection is not completely redressed by these market responses and by the institution of liability, regulation may not be warranted. There are imperfections in government regulation as well as in markets.

Injuries from a chain saw can occur even when a user has complete information and is fully aware of its proper use. One cause is a lack of expertise or skill. Another is misuse, such as boring with the tip of the saw, which can result in kickback or the saw slipping. These causes do not represent market imperfections, however. Some consumers who recognize that they have no expertise will not purchase a chain saw. Some will seek instruction, often from a friend. Some will take safety precautions such as wearing a hard hat, goggles, and safety shoes. Some will carry first-party insurance to compensate themselves and to cover medical costs in the case of an injury. Users will also develop expertise through experience with the saw. Nevertheless, many users will misuse the saw and suffer injuries.

On the supply side of the market, firms recognize that products liability cases are likely to be considered under the standard of strict liability, perhaps with the allowable defenses of contributory negligence or gross misuse. Under strict liability producers are to anticipate misuse by inexpert consumers and so have incentives to provide warnings about hazards and misuse. They also have incentives to add safety features, such as a nose guard over the chain tip to prevent boring.

Even if the user is fully informed, expert, and uses the chain saw properly, however, an injury can result from a pure accident such as kickback. Under strict liability the producer can be held liable for such an injury, so the producer has an incentive to incorporate safety features such as a chain brake, which is tripped when the saw swings upwards. As indicated in Figure 11-2, some accidents and injuries will still occur, even when social efficiency is achieved. Neither the lack of expertise, misuse, nor pure accidents constitute a market imperfection, and all are addressed, albeit imperfectly, by the institution of products liability.

An externality is present to the extent that a user's actions cause injury to others. The standard of strict liability and the elimination of the privity requirement, however, hold the producer liable for injuries to others than the user, so these external consequences are taken into account in products liability. It might be argued that there is another externality because injuries will cause insurance premiums to be higher than they otherwise would be. This, however, is a pecuniary externality, since the price of insurance increases to the level of costs.

Although externalities are likely to be minor in the case of chain saws, a moral hazard problem is present. Moral hazard results when the full benefits from a safety feature or information provided are not realized because they induce offsetting behavior by the user. This has two components, one pertaining to safety and the other to degradation in performance. Because a chain saw has safety features, users may take less care in its use or maintenance. Some users remove nose guards because the guard reduces the length of the cut. Others remove it because they want to use the tip for boring. This is an instance of moral hazard because the full benefits of injury reduction from the safety feature are not realized. The remedy is to make the nose tip non-removable, but that causes difficulties when the chain needs replacing.

Safety features also can reduce the performance of the saw, which not only reduces the benefits from its use but also can increase injuries. Safety features increase the weight of the saw, which contributes to fatigue and may increase the risk of injury. Safety features such as a nose guard can also result in slower cutting, which increases fatigue. Hitting a chain brake causes wear on the chain, which can reduce performance and increase cutting time, thereby lengthening the exposure of the user.

CHANNELS OF DISTRIBUTION AND INFORMATION PROVISION

According to this analysis, asymmetric information and moral hazard are the principal market imperfections, but those imperfections may not be serious. The principal non-regulatory means of responding to such imperfections are safety features and information provision. Much of the information provision takes place in channels of distribution. Chain saws are distributed through (1) servicing dealers that sell higher-priced, higher-performance saws, carry replacement parts, and provide service, (2) non-servicing dealers such as hardware stores, and (3) discount stores. The ability to provide information in the channel of distribution is greatest among servicing dealers and least among discount stores.

The market for chain saws has three segments: professional users, farmers and others who use them regularly, and casual users such as suburban homeowners. The need for information and the likelihood for misuse are undoubtedly greatest among casual users and least among professionals.

Servicing retailers, however, tend to sell to professionals and to those in the middle segment, since their frequent use implies benefits from a higher-performance, higher-priced saw. They are also most likely to need replacement parts and servicing. Casual users who cut firewood once or twice a year typically purchase inexpensive chain saws, often from discount stores. Not only do saws sold in discount stores have fewer safety features than more expensive models, but discount stores are the least able to provide information on saw selection and use. Discount stores also may be least likely to warn of hazards. There is thus a mismatch between the need for information in a market segment and the ability of the channel of distribution to provide that information. Information and safety features are thus less likely to reach those who are most likely to have accidents.

Because information about hazards, proper use, safety features, and user care is likely to be undersupplied in the market, the market imperfection theory of regulation suggests a role for government in providing information. This might, for example, take the form of warning labels, instructions, and a safety informational brochure included in the chain saw box or provided upon request. Because CPSC's mandate is to protect consumers from unreasonable risks, however, it may go further and attempt to reduce injuries through product standards.

THE CONSUMER PRODUCT SAFETY COMMISSION'S STANDARD-SETTING EFFORTS

In response to Purtle's petition, the CPSC initiated an investigation of chain saw safety. The Chain Saw Manufacturers Association (CSMA), which was formed in response to the safety issue, informed the CPSC that it was developing a voluntary standard and had initiated a laboratory study of kickback. The principal scientific uncertainties centered on the physics of kickback torque, which had not yet been studied. At the end of 1979, the CSMA submitted its proposed kickback standard for gasoline-powered chain saws to the American National Standards Institute (ANSI), a private institution that certifies industry standards.

The CPSC, however, published an Advance Notice of Proposed Rulemaking (ANPR) as the first step in the process leading to a mandatory standard. The CSMA opposed mandatory standards and issued a voluntary standard in 1982. The CSMA also argued that manufacturers' voluntary incorporation of safety features had been steadily reducing chain saw accidents. The CPSC continued its standard-setting efforts and also issued a 12-page consumer information guide, "Chain Saw Safety," which provided information on accidents, safety features of saws, user care and precautions, and proper use. The guide stated, "Chain saw kickback can result in death or severe injury."

The battle between the CPSC and the CSMA ended in 1985, as the CPSC withdrew its ANPR and approved a voluntary standard developed through ANSI. The standard was targeted at the models purchased by casual users and applied to all electric chain saws and all gasoline-powered chain saws with an engine displacement of 3.8 cubic inches or less. The saws were required to have a hand guard and two of the following four features: (1) a chain brake, (2) a nose guard, (3) a curved guide bar that reduces kickback, and (4) a low-kickback chain.

In comparing safety regulation with the institution of liability, an important issue is whether the safety features in the voluntary standard would have been adopted anyway because they reduce liability costs. One of the major safety innovations by the industry in the 1980s was a new low-kickback chain designed not to grab when the tip of the saw comes into contact with wood. This considerably reduces the kickback force and the probability of an injury.[48] Moore and Magat (1993) studied the effect of the voluntary standard on the chain saw accident rate and found a significant reduction. The data, however, did not allow distinguishing between the effect of the standard and the reduced use of chain saws.

The chapter case *Bic Disposable Butane Lighters* considers a safety issue addressed in both the institutions of products liability and safety regulation. It also provides an opportunity to consider the safety issue from both the producer's perspective and the perspective of the liability system and the CPSC.

Summary

Accident and death rates in the United States fell during the 1980s. The National Safety Council reported that unintentional fatal injuries decreased from 105,312 in 1979 to 94,500 in 1989 and decreased further to 93,800 in 1997. A variety of factors contributed to the decrease, ranging from campaigns against drunk driving to technological advances such as smoke detectors to a heightened public concern about safety that caused people to take more care in their activities. Institutions also contributed to the decrease with increased liability costs providing incentives for care on the part of producers and with safety features adopted both voluntarily and under government mandate.

The principal institutional sources of guidance on product safety issues are products liability and regulation. Safety regulation is pervasive in some industries, including nuclear power, transportation, and pharmaceuticals, but the safety of most products is not regulated. Even when there is safety regulation and producers satisfy regulatory standards, producers can be held liable for injuries associated with their products. Product safety is generally governed by the legal standard of strict liability,

---

[48]See *Consumer Reports,* May 1990, p. 305.

under which a producer may be held liable even if it has exercised all possible care. The defenses allowed under strict liability vary among the states and include the absence of proximate cause, the assumption of risks, product alteration, disclaiming, and contributory negligence.

The social efficiency role of products liability is to provide incentives to producers and consumers to take appropriate care to avoid those injuries that are not too costly to avoid. The Coase theorem demonstrates that in the absence of transactions costs this can be accomplished by the assignment of an entitlement to either producers or consumers with the entitlement protected by either a property or a liability rule. To economize on transactions costs, a liability rule is used for accidents, injuries, and externalities. The assignment of the entitlement to consumers is generally supported by the Calabresi and Melamed principles. In practice, courts have also assigned the entitlement to consumers to compensate them for the losses they incur. Under strict liability, that compensation can be independent of fault.

Safety regulation addresses market imperfections, but it may also be used simply to reduce the number of injuries. Safety regulation often involves technical and scientific issues, such as the physics of kickback torque, about which little is known. Safety regulation also imposes significant costs on producers and so generates political action to limit those costs. In addition, safety regulation involves a complex regulatory process with participation by a variety of interested parties. Due process and statutory requirements provide opportunities to challenge regulatory decisions in court. The political and legal pressures on the Consumer Products Safety Commission forced it to focus on voluntary industry standards and product recalls and warnings. The CPSC has responsibility for collecting information about injuries and providing information to consumers about hazards and care. The CPSC's information-gathering network and its authority to act in the case of an imminent hazard have enabled it to deal quickly with a number of severe hazards.

Products liability law continues to evolve as courts consider cases involving new issues. This has led to a broadening of the definition of products liability, moving in the direction of a system of absolute liability in which a product carries with it implicit, but complete, insurance. Producers have sought a federal products liability statute that limits liability awards and expands the allowable defenses, but the political competition over this legislation has been intense. Trial lawyers and those concerned about compensation for the injured have defeated the reform attempts at the federal level.

CASES

Domino's Delivers (A)

Thomas S. Monaghan founded Domino's Pizza with the market strategy of delivering hot pizza within 30 minutes. To give credibility to its delivery pledge, Domino's offered not to charge for the pizza if the delivery took longer than 30 minutes. The number of its stores increased from 300 in 1980 to 5,225 worldwide in 1989, and Domino's success was generally credited to its delivery strategy. Some of the Domino's stores were franchised, and some were owned by the company. The revenues of the corporation topped $1 billion in 1988, but profits were only $6.1 million.

By the beginning of the 1990s, competition in the pizza industry was intensifying, particularly among the big three pizza companies. Pizza Hut was the industry leader with 7,500 stores and 1989 sales of $3.8 billion. Little Caesars was third with 2,700 stores and sales of $1.13 billion. These three companies had followed quite different strategies, with Domino's specializing in home delivery, Pizza Hut emphasizing sit-down restaurants, and Little Caesars specializing in carryouts. With opportunities for growth diminishing, the companies went after the market share of the others. Pizza Hut began a delivery service in 1986, and by 1990 had 2,500 delivery units. Pizza Hut offered a 30-minute delivery guarantee in only a few areas, however. Ninety-five percent of Little Caesars's stores remained carryout only, but it had some delivery units and some restaurants. Domino's opened its first Pizzazz restaurant in 1990 and planned to place them in locations such as shopping malls.

The heart of Domino's business and its reputation, however, remained home delivery. That heart had become a serious nonmarket issue. In 1988 Domino's 75,000 drivers were involved in accidents that claimed the lives of 20 people. Critics argued that Domino's policy of offering a refund if delivery was not made within 30 minutes caused drivers to speed, resulting in accidents and deaths.[1] Ron Hingst, a spokesman for Domino's, said, "The speed of our system is in the store, not on the road."[2] Domino's stated that it cooked and boxed its pizza in 12 minutes, leaving 18 minutes for delivery. Hingst added that because there were so many stores, Domino's drivers traveled only short distances for their deliveries. "The hustle ends at the door of the store."[3] Only 5 percent of its pizza was not delivered on time, and the refund was paid by the store not the driver. "The thirty minute rule is not there to penalize the drivers . . . . It's strictly a marketing expense."[4]

Although the refund was paid by the store owner, critics argued that both the owner and the driver had incentives to hurry. Franchisees received a bonus that was calculated on a base that was net of refunds. Also, the faster the deliveries were made the fewer drivers were needed. Drivers' base pay was often the minimum wage plus a mileage allowance, but tips were a function of the number of pizzas they delivered. Critics also claimed that drivers who frequently failed to meet the 30-minute time were given fewer hours of work and those who were fastest were assigned to areas where the tips were expected to be highest.

According to attorney Kenneth R. Behrend, who represented a couple injured when a Domino's delivery car hit their station wagon near a Domino's store, "People are being injured all over the country. . . These drivers are trying to deliver pizza within thirty minutes and sometimes it's not possible. They may run a stop sign, go over speed limits, or make illegal turns."[5] Behrend said, "I want to see the thirty-minute guarantee stopped and my client wants it stopped." He observed that Domino's sponsored a race car at the Indianapolis 500 and that many of the stores displayed a model of the car. "What is the mental attitude they're encouraging?. . . The model of that race car sits in a lot of their stores, encouraging the impression of a race car driver."[6]

---

[1] The refund was reduced to $3 in part because college students had adopted a strategy of giving imprecise directions to get a free pizza.
[2] *Newsweek,* July 10, 1990.
[3] *The New York Times,* August 29, 1990.
[4] *The New York Times,* August 29, 1990.
[5] *The New York Times,* June 17, 1990.
[6] *The New York Times,* June 17, 1990.

As lawsuits began to be filed against Domino's, interest and activist groups took up the issue and media coverage increased. A Pennsylvania judge ordered Domino's to turn over all its accident records and ordered a deposition taken from Monaghan. After 17-year-old Jesse Colson of Indianapolis was killed when the pickup truck he was driving for Domino's skidded on a wet road and hit a utility pole, the Indiana Department of Labor initiated an investigation of whether Domino's delivery policy was contributing to accidents.

The National Safe Workplace Institute announced that it would begin a campaign on college campuses to encourage students not to buy Domino's pizza and not to drive for Domino's. Joseph A. Kinney, director of the institute, estimated that the death rate per Domino's employee was nearly as high as in mining and was nearly twice the rate in construction.[7] "It's a national disgrace," said Kinney. "Kids are paying with their blood for Domino's marketing strategy. We are talking about unnecessary deaths."[8] Hingst said: "Our research says that the majority of the population does not view the delivery policy as a problem. If we were convinced that this guarantee was endangering lives, we would drop it."[9] ■

[7] *The New York Times,* August 29, 1990.
[8] *The New York Times,* August 29, 1990.
[9] *The New York Times,* August 29, 1990.

PREPARATION QUESTIONS

1. Where is this nonmarket issue in its life cycle? What are the forces moving it through its life cycle?
2. How significant is this issue for Domino's and what are its alternatives?
3. What strategy should Domino's adopt to address the delivery safety issue?

California Space Heaters, Inc. (A)

California Space Heaters, Inc. had developed a line of convection kerosene space heaters using a new technology and was making preparations to sell them. For a modest purchase price the heaters could heat a room economically, without requiring a central heating system. A particular advantage of the heaters was that they allowed the consumer to focus the heat where and when it was needed. Because of high energy prices in the early 1980s, the demand for the heaters was expected to be brisk. Demand was anticipated to be particularly strong among low-income consumers and homeowners who had electric heating systems, especially in the East where electricity prices were very high. The heaters would also inevitably be used by people whose electricity had been cut off.

Although the heaters were very economical, there were safety hazards associated with their use, ranging from the risk of fire to adverse health effects from their emissions. The hazards were functions of the heater's design, its maintenance, and the conditions of use, including the fuel used. The company could incorporate a variety of safety features in the heaters, but safer heaters had a significantly higher cost and somewhat lower efficiency, requiring more fuel for the "effective warmth" produced.

For example, the heater could cause a fire if it were placed too near to curtains or furniture. The heaters could be designed so that the temperature could be as low as 320 degrees or as high as 500 degrees. The higher the temperature the more efficient the heating but the greater the fire hazard, and the greater the risk that small children and others could be burned by touching it. The temperature in the heater depended in part on the wick adjustment, which could be controlled manually or by a thermostat. Fires could also occur from "flare up." Should that happen, closing the shutoff valve would extinguish the flame.

Ignition also posed a fire hazard. Electric spark ignition of the wick was safer than match ignition. Fires were a risk each time the fuel tank was refilled, particularly if the unit was already hot. This risk could be reduced by incorporating a removable fuel tank that allowed consumers, if they chose, to fill the tank outside the house. A siphon could also be incorporated into the tank to lessen the risk of spills when using a funnel. Because kerosene expands when warmed, the tank should never be completely filled; instead, some air space should be maintained to allow for expansion. Kerosene itself was difficult to burn without a wick, but if spilled, a carpet or curtains could act as a wick. The units with electric spark ignition—a battery-operated ignition device—could be equipped with an automatic cutoff system that instantly stopped combustion if the heater was tipped over or jarred. These units could also be equipped with a power-loss shutoff system that stopped combustion if the batteries lost power.

In addition to the risk of fire, toxic emissions from the heaters posed a potential hazard because the heaters were not vented to the outside as were central heating systems and fireplaces. Inhaling noxious fumes could be harmful, particularly if substandard kerosene were burned or combustion was incomplete. Kerosene came in two grades: 1K, which had a low sulfur content and was appropriate for the heaters, and 2K, which had a higher sulfur content and was inappropriate. 2K kerosene was the grade used in diesel automobiles and trucks and was available at many gasoline stations, whereas 1K kerosene usually had to be purchased at a hardware or specialty store. Since the two grades of kerosene could not be distinguished without conducting a chemical test, consumers could not easily verify which grade they had purchased and had to rely on the supplier. Gasoline should never be used in the heater, nor should fuel oil, which has a significantly higher sulfur content than kerosene.

Proper ignition involved raising the wick, igniting it, and lowering it until the flame burned cleanly. Some consumers might attempt to regulate the heat by adjusting the height of the wick. If the wick were set too low, combustion was less complete and emissions were increased. A wick stop could be incorporated into the heater to prevent the wick from being lowered too far. Because the heater rested on the floor, it could be difficult to adjust the wick properly, requiring the consumer to bend low to see the flame.

The hazard from improper combustion and the burning of the wrong kerosene centered on carbon monoxide and nitrogen dioxide emissions, which posed particular problems for asthmatics, children, the elderly, and pregnant women. EPA standards for outside air were 9 parts per million (ppm) for carbon monoxide and 0.05 ppm for nitrogen dioxide. U.S. Navy standards for submarines were 15 and 0.5 ppm, respectively, and NASA's standards for the space shuttle were 25 and 0.5 ppm.[1] The company's studies indicated that its heaters would not meet the EPA standards but would meet the Navy and NASA standards by a comfortable margin. The EPA had not issued standards for indoor air nor was it expected to do so within the next several years.

The risk associated with emissions could be reduced by using a kerosene additive that improved clean burning. The wick should be replaced each year, since the cleanliness of the burn depended on its quality. Even if combustion were complete and the proper grade of kerosene were used, however, injury or asphyxiation could occur if the room were inadequately ventilated and the heater consumed too much of the oxygen in the room. A window should be left open to prevent oxygen depletion.

Kerosene heaters using old technologies had been banned by several states and municipalities, but most state legislatures had decided to allow the new-technology heaters because of the savings in fuel costs they provided. No federal safety standards for kerosene heaters had been promulgated but such standards could be forthcoming if injuries resulted from the heaters. The cognizant regulatory agency was the CPSC, but the CPSC had been immobilized recently and was unlikely to mandate standards, at least for several years.

The design alternatives available to California Space Heaters centered on the safety features that could be incorporated into the heaters. Table 11-1 lists the potential hazards and the design steps, beyond the least-expensive model, that the company could take to respond to the hazards. Each safety feature was expected to be effective in reducing the specific hazard. The production process for the heaters involved standard technologies and methods, so the chance of manufacturing defects was slight.

Consumers could also take care to reduce the likelihood of accidents and injury, making sure to always have the room properly ventilated. They could purchase the proper grade of kerosene and could use the "clean burn" additive that sold for $3.99 per 12-ounce bottle. The heater should be cleaned and the wick changed at least at the beginning of each heating season. The consumer should, of course, purchase the appropriate wick.

The least expensive model of kerosene space heater with match ignition could be manufactured for $44 and the standard markup for a discount store was

[1]The EPA standard was set to protect individuals with angina while they exercised.

TABLE 11-1

Heater Hazards and Remedies

Potential Hazard	*Design Remedy*	*Cost*
temperature adjustment	thermostat	$ 7.50
overheating due to flare-up	automatic temperature shutoff	22.00
tank overflow	tank level gauge	3.00
tip-over fire	automatic cutoff	8.00
contact fire	low burn temperature	*
spill during filling	siphon filling system	12.00
ignition fire	electric spark ignition	19.50
	large tank	12.00
fire during refilling	removable tank**	6.00
noxious emissions		
substandard kerosene	none	
incomplete combustion	a) wick stop	6.50
	b) electric wick adjustment	32.00
oxygen depletion	none	—

*Estimated loss in efficiency of $40 per year.
**Only effective if tank is removed and taken outside.

100 percent and slightly higher in an appliance store. With proper use, the least expensive model was safe. The demand for the low-end heaters was expected to be strong and price elastic. At a price of $88 sales could reach 2 million units a year. The safest and most expensive model the company could make would include all the safety features listed in Table 11-1. It could be manufactured for $189. The demand for the safest heater was expected to be limited. The venture capitalist backing the company commented, only partly in jest, that at a price of $378 the only sales would be to rich people for use in their ski cabins.

To indicate the savings attainable by use of the heaters, a marketing analyst compared the cost of heating a house to 68 degrees with heating it to 55 degrees and using a kerosene space heater to bring the living room up to 68 degrees. The estimated savings was $470 a year for a house in New England that used fuel oil; if the house had electric heat, the savings would be $685 a year. Smaller savings could be attained with a portable electric heater, which cost less than a kerosene heater.

The heaters could be marketed through various channels of distribution, ranging from discount stores to appliance stores to heating and air-conditioning shops. Appliance stores might be interested in carrying a full line of heaters, but discount stores were expected only to be interested in the least expensive model. Heating and air-conditioning stores were not expected to keep a stock of the heaters on hand but would order them for customers. Their customers were likely to be interested in the more expensive models.

The company consulted a lawyer who indicated that products liability lawsuits were probable should there be injuries or adverse health consequences associated with the use of the heaters. Strict liability in tort would in all likelihood be the applicable liability standard, so the company would likely be held liable even if an injury were due to foreseeable misuse by a consumer. The costs to the company included the cost of liability insurance, legal and court costs, and the management time devoted to the cases. These costs could be reduced by adding more safety features to the model. The lawyer had investigated the cost of insurance and roughly estimated that insurance costs plus legal fees might be as much as $55 per unit for the lowest priced model and $10 per unit for the safest model given the estimated sales. The lawyer also estimated that the purchasers of the lowest-cost heaters were less likely to file lawsuits in the event of an injury because they were likely to be less familiar with the legal process.

The likelihood of an injury associated with a heater was difficult to estimate, but the company's engineers gave a ballpark estimate of one in a million of a manufacturing defect resulting in a death or a permanent disability from a fire. They estimated that the likelihood of a fire death from misuse was approximately five in one hundred thousand with the least expensive model over the life of the heater and four in a million with the most expensive model. The lawyer asked the engineers for estimates associated with each safety feature, but so far they had provided only two estimates. They estimated that adding electric spark ignition to the least expensive model would reduce the probability of a death by 50 percent, whereas electric wick adjustment would reduce the probability of a death by less than 2.5 percent. ■

PREPARATION QUESTIONS

1. How should California Space Heaters reason about its responsibility for the safety of its heaters and their use?
2. What safety features should be incorporated into the heaters? What criteria should be used for those decisions?
3. What other actions should be taken in the design or marketing of the heaters?
4. How should prices be set; i.e., on what cost basis?

Bic Disposable Butane Lighters

Cynthia Littlejohn was on a camping trip when her Bic disposable butane lighter exploded in her front pocket. Ethel Smith died in July 1985 as a result of the explosion of a Bic butane lighter she was using to light a cigarette. In the Littlejohn lawsuit, the Bic Corporation of Milford, Connecticut, disclosed that over 50 fires had occurred just from lighters carried in left front shirt pockets.[1] In 1986 a jury awarded $3.25 million to Cynthia Littlejohn, and Ethel Smith's husband sued Bic for $11 million. Prior to the Littlejohn suit, Bic had won two cases in Illinois and Michigan. Other suits had been settled out of court with the plaintiffs agreeing not to disclose any information about the settlements.

A products liability suit can be costly to pursue, since it may extend over several years and with appeals, years longer. Most plaintiffs do not have the financial means to pursue such suits, so lawyers take personal injury cases on a contingent fee basis. Under this arrangement, the lawyer bears the costs of a case out of his or her own pocket in exchange for a share, usually one-third, of any court award or settlement. The contingent fee system provides incentives for the attorney to take cases and exert the effort to present the case effectively.

In the case of a product for which there are many injuries, plaintiffs and their attorneys have incentives to share information and coordinate strategies. One strategy is to use one case to pry internal documents from the defendant, so that those documents can be used in other cases. The Association of Trial Lawyers of America assists in the development of networks of lawyers handling similar cases. John Andrews of Tampa, Florida, headed the network of lawyers handling the Bic cases. One purpose of the network was to obtain data on a cross section of cases to develop the basis for a finding of negligence, possibly leading to punitive damages. Andrews gathered data on the cases and helped coordinate strategies on plaintiffs' cases.

A victory for a plaintiff can affect other cases. For cases in the same jurisdiction, the decision in one case can be a precedent for another. A victory may also indicate a line of argument that may increase the likelihood of success in other cases and thus result in more new cases filed. If the Smith estate were to win its case, "there are going to be many more suits filed by smaller attorneys who couldn't afford to file before," said Andrews.[2]

In products liability cases, plaintiffs and defendants typically provide expert witnesses who testify about the design and use of the product. The experts may present analyses of statistical information relating to the frequency and nature of accidents associated with a product. They may also make judgments about product design, engineering, quality control, and instructions and warnings. In a case involving a Bic butane lighter, an expert testified that the design of the Bic lighters was faulty. Small pieces of debris can get under the gas jet, he said, causing butane gas to leak out, so that the lighter does not extinguish when it

---

[1] *The New York Times,* April 10, 1987.

[2] *The Wall Street Journal,* July 5, 1988.

should. He testified that the Bic lighters, unlike other disposable lighters, had no mechanism to prevent debris from entering the valve.[3] " 'We know debris can get in and we know the tell-tale signs when a lighter failed to extinguish, and there just wasn't any evidence that the Littlejohn lighter failed to extinguish,' said Lawrence Broutman, a Chicago plastics expert who testified for Bic after inspecting the Littlejohn lighter."[4]

In the Littlejohn case, evidence was presented indicating that Bic conducted a quality control test in 1983 in which 1.2 percent of the lighters sampled failed to extinguish properly. The resulting "afterburn" was one of the principal causes of injury from butane lighters when the lighter was placed in a pocket or purse. The other principal causes were explosions and leaks that caused flare up. "Bic lawyers and spokesmen said that evidence of this sort has been misinterpreted by plaintiffs' attorneys in the past and would be in the future if it were widely disseminated. The quality audit, for example, was based on Bic's self-imposed standards, which are far tougher than general industry standards, a spokesman said."[5]

" 'These lighters are designed to be thrown away, so they just aren't made very well' said Mel Kardos, the Newtown, PA., lawyer who represented Littlejohn. 'The plastic casing can melt, the canister is easily penetrated, the gas can leak and the whole thing can explode. The old-type refillable lighters were much safer.' "[6] "Richard Custer, who teaches fire protection engineering at Worcester Polytechnic Institute and served as an expert witness for Ms. Littlejohn, suggests that Bic could easily make its lighter safer. 'In this particular lighter, the simplest solution would be to add a cap that drops over the valve when you take your thumb away,' he said."[7]

Other lighters, including Scripto, made by ScriptoTokai of Japan, and Cricket, made by the Swedish Match Corporation, were also associated with injuries, but Bic was the market leader with 58 percent of the market. Scripto said that its lighters were made differently than those of other manufacturers, with a "safety cap and a core made of a self-extinguishing resin that will only melt at 230 degrees centigrade."[8]

[3]*San Jose Mercury News,* April 10, 1987.
[4]*The New York Times,* April 10, 1987.
[5]*The Wall Street Journal,* July 5, 1988.
[6]*The New York Times,* April 10, 1987.
[7]*The New York Times,* April 10, 1987.
[8]*The New York Times,* April 10, 1987.

The CPSC, whose mandate was to protect consumers from "unreasonable risks," also had disposable butane lighters on its agenda. On May 3, 1985, Diane L. Denton, a registered nurse in Louisville, Kentucky, petitioned the CPSC to initiate a rule-making proceeding to establish safety standards for disposable butane lighters. In her petition, she stated: "As a burn nurse the past ten years I have had many occasions to care for children who have been burned due to fireplay. All of these cases are of course sad but over the past two years we are seeing younger children involved in this fireplay. Approximately half of the children we see on our Burn Unit who have been burned by disposable lighters are four years and under."[9]

To obtain data on injuries involving children, the CPSC conducted an investigation of 277 fires in which children had been playing with lighters. The CPSC concluded that:

- Ninety-six percent of the cigarette lighters involved in the incidents were disposable butane models.
- In 90 percent of the incidents, the children who operated the lighters were less than 6 years old, primarily 3 and 4 years old.
- The most common method of operation was with two hands (63 percent of the incidents), using one hand to steady the lighter, and the thumb or index finger of the other hand to roll the wheel and press the fuel lever.
- Many of the children involved in the incidents had had prior experience playing with or operating lighters.

Laboratory examination of 69 lighters, including at least nine different brands, involved in the incidents showed no evidence of malfunction. The average annual cost of deaths, injuries, and property damage from childplay fires was estimated to be about $310 to $375 million (assuming a statistical value of life of $2 million), or about 60 to 75 cents per lighter.[10]

On March 3, 1988, the CPSC published an advance notice of proposed rule making (ANPR) in the *Federal Register.* The ANPR began: "On the basis of currently available information, the Commission has preliminarily determined that unreasonable risks of death and injury may be associated with cig-

[9]Cigarette Lighter Petition, PP 852, November 1987; letter dated April 29, 1985.
[10]Cigarette Lighter Petition, PP 852, November 1987, p. ii.

arette lighters operated by children, and that those risks may be sufficiently severe to warrant issuance of a rule to eliminate or reduce them. The Commission estimates that during the years 1980 through 1985, on average 120 persons have died and 750 persons have been injured each year in fires started by children playing with lighters."[11]

To develop a standard, the CPSC needed a method of evaluating the effectiveness of alternative standards—"to develop a test protocol which would provide a measure of the resistance of a lighter to operation by a child, a contract has been let by the Division of Human Factors in the Directorate for Epidemiology to assess the cognitive and physical abilities of children under five in manipulating disposable butane lighters."[12]

The lighter industry had voluntary product standards formulated through the American Society for Testing and Materials (ASTM), an organization that establishes voluntary standards for products, materials, and processes. The ASTM committee, F15.02 Cigarette Lighters, issued a standard F400 for lighters in the 1970s. The standard had been revised several times, the latest being F400-85. According to the CPSC:

> The standard covers a variety of aspects such as flame height, flame extinction, structural integrity, instructions, and warnings. There are no specific tests in the standard which are intended to provide a measure of the resistance of a lighter by a child.
>
> The standard requires warnings either on the lighters or on the containers. One of these which the standard states shall be emphasized is:—KEEP OUT OF REACH OF CHILDREN.
>
> As far as we know, all major brand lighters sold today in the United States are produced in accordance with the ASTM standard.[13]

The Bic Corporation is a subsidiary of Societé, Bic, S.A., of France, founded by Marcel Bich. In 1986 the Bic Corporation had sales of $267.6 million and profits of $47.9 million, with pretax profits on lighters of $28.5 million. Bic's position on disposable lighter safety was: "Today, to our knowledge, there is no way to manufacture a lighter that works easily for adults and yet foils the advances of children without also destroying the usefulness of the product. . .. It is the very nature of lighters and matches which make them dangerous and demands the utmost in caution from the people who use them. . .. Even a cursory analysis of complaints received by the CPSC reveals that carelessness was the basis for many injuries, rather than a defect in a lighter."[14]

Bruno Bich, president of Bic Corporation, said that he welcomed "an examination of the safety of Bic lighters. We are convinced, based on everything we know today, we can demonstrate that a malfunction of a Bic lighter of the current model has never caused the death of anyone."[15] Bic said that one person had died from a malfunction of a Bic lighter, but the firm had discontinued that model in 1977. Bic had sold 2 billion lighters since they were introduced in 1972, and it said that the number of lawsuits per unit sold had decreased over time. Bic said that it had never had more than 25 suits filed against it in a year; as of 1987, there were 42 cases pending. ■

[11] *Federal Register,* Vol. 53, No. 42, 3, 1988, pp. 6833–6837.
[12] CPSC, Fire and Thermal Burn Hazard Program Staff, "Cigarette Lighter Petition," PP 852, November 1987, p. 5.
[13] CPSC, Fire and Thermal Burn Hazard Program Staff, "Cigarette Lighter Petition," PP 852, November 1987, pp. 45.
[14] *San Jose Mercury News,* April 10, 1987.
[15] *The New York Times,* April 17, 1987.

PREPARATION QUESTIONS

1. From a social efficiency perspective, is the products liability system adequate to address the disposable butane lighter safety issue? Is it equally effective for adults and children?
2. Which legal standard will govern the lighter cases? Does the plaintiff have to prove that the lighter is defective?
3. Is there a market imperfection associated with disposable butane lighters?
4. Should the CPSC set a mandatory standard for disposable butane lighters? How should it determine how safe a lighter should be?
5. Is it likely that political officeholders will take the issue of the safety of disposable butane lighters into the legislative arena?
6. What should Bic do about the disposable butane lighter issue? Should it make changes in the design or marketing of its disposable butane lighter? How should it interact with the CPSC?

CHAPTER 12

Environmental Protection: Economics, Politics, and Management

Introduction

The public, government officials, and business leaders recognize the importance of environmental protection and the benefits it yields. That protection is also expensive. The Environmental Protection Agency (EPA) (1991) estimated that compliance with existing environmental regulation would cost each person in the United States nearly $750 a year in the year 2000—or a total of $185 billion annually, representing 2.8 percent of GDP. Any new programs to meet other environmental goals, such as addressing global warming, would add to that cost. The high cost of environmental protection has raised concerns ranging from who should bear that cost to its effect on the international competitiveness of U.S. firms. It is thus imperative not only that the environment be protected but that it be accomplished as efficiently as possible. Although there is widespread agreement about protecting the environment, there remains considerable disagreement about how much protection is appropriate and about the distribution of the burden of that protection. These disagreements generate the politics of environmental protection.

This chapter focuses on environmental protection and the public and managerial policies for addressing it. The following section considers pollution externalities from the social efficiency perspective introduced in the previous chapter and examines market-like incentive approaches for dealing with environmental externalities. The practice of environmental regulation and its associated politics are then considered. The management of environmental and regulatory issues from a firm's perspective is then addressed.

Socially Efficient Regulation of Pollution Externalities

Social efficiency requires that the polluter and those affected by the pollution externality take into account the damage from the pollution and the social costs of preventing it. Just as it is not socially efficient to prevent all accidents, it is not socially efficient to prevent all pollution. Instead, that pollution which is not too costly to prevent should be prevented, taking into account abatement costs and harm avoided. Pollution control, however, has often taken the form of command-and-control regulation in which regulators order engineering controls, such as scrubbers for electric power plants, or require the best available technology for pollution abatement. This approach deals with the source of the damage, but it addresses neither the benefits of the avoided damage nor the cost of abatement. Command-and-control approaches usually impose uniform controls and standards on dissimilar sources of pollution, resulting in higher-than-efficient abatement costs. For each source of pollution social efficiency requires that costs and benefits be considered and that any reduction in pollution be attained at the least cost. Moreover, the lower the costs of reducing pollution, the larger are the reductions that can be achieved.

Incentive approaches to pollution control allow firms flexibility in achieving environmental objectives and result in social efficiency by aligning the social and private costs of pollution, thereby causing polluters to internalize the externality. These approaches also decentralize pollution-control decisions because the generators of pollution rather than regulators have the responsibility for evaluating alternative emissions control technologies and abatement strategies. Rather than dictating how environmental goals should be achieved, incentive-based approaches impose a cost on pollution-causing activities, leaving it to individual polluters to decide how to respond to those costs. Incentives then drive these decisions toward least-cost solutions and also toward the development of new pollution-control technologies by the private sector.

The control of an externality in a decentralized system has three components. The first is providing polluters with incentives for abatement by assigning to polluters the marginal cost of the harm done by the pollutants they emit. The second is allowing them to respond to those incentives by choosing the most efficient means of abatement. These means include reducing output, installing pollution-control equipment, redesigning products and production processes to reduce the pollutants generated, or reducing the harm from emissions, as when oil refineries create safety zones around their facilities. The third component involves reflecting in the prices of goods and services the social costs of the harm from pollution and the costs of abatement. This allows consumers to take into account the full social cost of the goods they consume.

As the Coase theorem introduced in Chapter 11 indicates, social efficiency can be achieved given any assignment of entitlements. Environmental politics often arises from the existing assignment and its implications on the distribution of the burden of environmental protection. In designing incentive systems such as a tradable permits system the assignment of the permits determines the distributive consequences of the required abatement.

TRADABLE PERMITS SYSTEM

A tradable permits system has been implemented for sulfur dioxide emissions in the United States, and several tradable permits systems are in operation in areas such as Los Angeles. The United States has proposed that a tradable permits system be used worldwide to reduce greenhouse gasses emissions to achieve the goals specified in the Kyoto Protocol on global warming.

A tradable permits system specifies the total amount allowed of emissions of a particular pollutant and issues permits for that amount. For example, a permit could be issued for each pound of sulfur dioxide emissions allowed. Those permits then can be traded among polluters in a market. The Coase theorem applies to this type of system. That is, the permits can be allocated to polluters for no charge or can be auctioned to the highest bidder. With either allocation, social efficiency can be achieved provided that the permits can be traded. The allocation of the permits, however, affects the distribution of

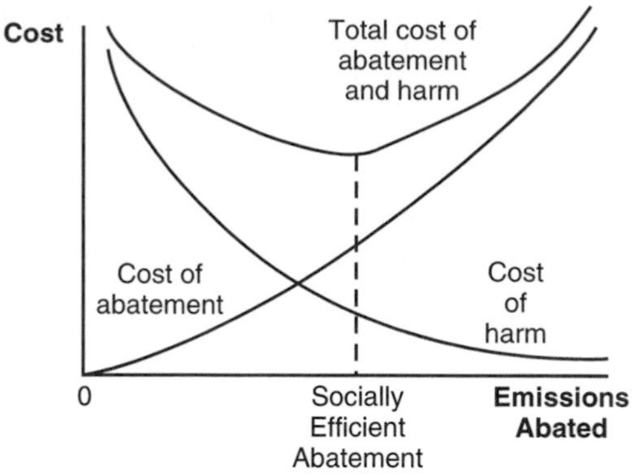

FIGURE 12-1A Socially Efficient Regulation and Total Costs

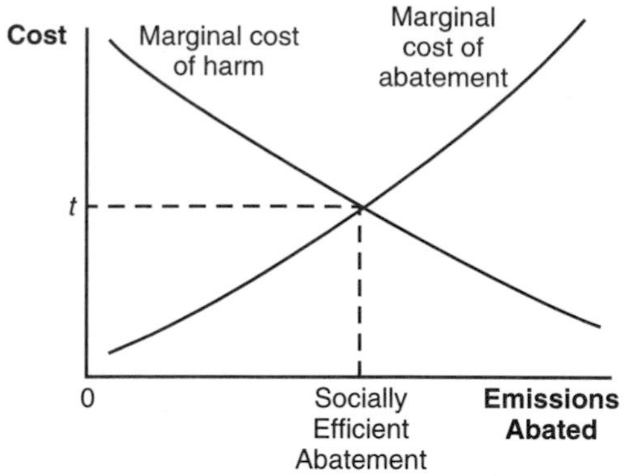

FIGURE 12-1B Socially Efficient Abatement and Marginal Costs

the burden of the emissions reduction and hence motivates distributive politics. The politics of a tradable permits system are considered in the example later in the chapter. The focus in this section is on the social efficiency of a tradable permits system.

A tradable permits system has three components. The first is determining the number of permits to issue. The second is the abatement decisions of individual emitters in response to the price of a permit. The third is the trading of the permits to establish their price. These three components occur simultaneously and an equilibrium results when (1) all advantageous trades have been made, (2) emitters have taken the abatement measures they prefer given the price at which the permits trade, and (3) consumers face prices incorporating the (marginal) costs of abatement and the quantities of products they purchase result in total emissions equal to the permits issued.

The number of permits to issue is that which minimizes the social costs of the harm from the emissions plus the costs of abatement, which is illustrated in Figure 12-1a, where the costs are expressed in terms of the emissions abated. The cost of the harm is decreasing and the cost of abatement is increasing in the amount of emissions abated. Social efficiency requires that the number of permits issued minimize the sum of these costs as illustrated in the figure. Figure 12-1b presents the marginal social costs of harm and the marginal cost of abatement that correspond to the cost curves in Figure 12-1a. At the socially efficient amount of abatement, the two marginal costs are equal.

The number of permits to issue equals the remaining emissions, and trading in a market establishes the price of a permit. Let that price be denoted by t, as illustrated in Figure 12-1b. Consider a firm A whose production process generates one pound of the pollutant per unit of the product produced. Producing a unit of the product thus requires one permit which has a cost t. Instead of purchasing permits, the firm could install pollution equipment or change the design of the product or the production process to reduce the pollution generated. The firm will use these alternatives in the combination that minimizes its cost. Suppose, for example, that the firm can install pollution-control equipment to reduce emissions and that the marginal cost increases with the amount of abatement; for example, a 10 percent reduction costs c, a 20 percent reduction costs $4c$, a 30 percent reduction costs $9c$, a 40 percent reduction costs $16c$, etc. The corresponding marginal cost of abatement function is illustrated in Figure 12-2 . Suppose that t equals $60c$. Then the firm will install pollution-control technology to achieve a 30 percent reduction and will purchase 0.7 permits per unit of output giving it a cost of $9c + 0.7t = 9c + 0.7(60c) = 51c$.[1] Figure 12-2 illustrates the efficient level of abate-

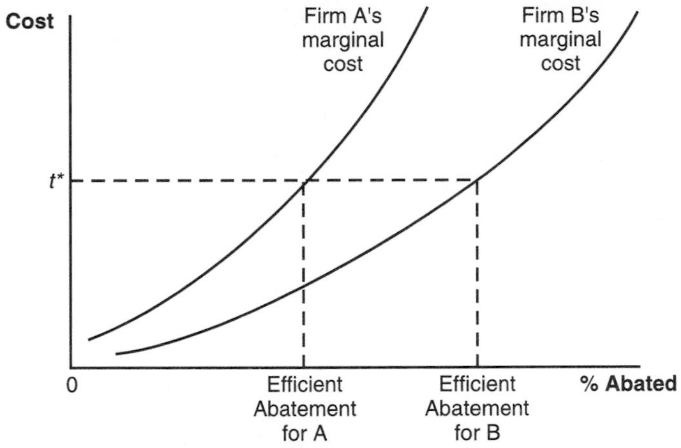

FIGURE 12-2 Abatement Decisions of Firms

ment for firm *A*. The marginal cost of a 30 percent abatement is *t*, the price of a permit. In a similar manner, if the product or the production process could be redesigned to eliminate some of the pollution generated, redesign would be carried out to the point at which the marginal cost of the redesign per unit of pollution eliminated equaled *t*.

Using the same reasoning, a firm *B* that has a lower marginal cost of abatement would abate more than firm *A*, as illustrated in Figure 12-2. Consequently, if the two firms were identical except for their abatement costs, firm *A* would purchase more permits than would firm *B*.

Next consider the market for permits. Suppose that the initial allocation of permits was made to polluters as in the sulfur dioxide permits system discussed later in the chapter. If firms *A* and *B* in Figure 12-2 each had an initial allocation corresponding to the point *x* on the horizontal axis, firm *A* would purchase permits in the market and firm *B* would sell permits. An equilibrium in the market for permits occurs at a price t^* such that no firm prefers to either buy or sell additional permits at that price. This equilibrium has the feature that each firm abates to the point at which its marginal cost of abatement equals the price t^* of a permit, as indicated in Figure 12-2, so all firms have the same marginal cost of abatement in equilibrium. This is the condition for socially efficient abatement decisions.[2]

The final feature of a tradable permits system is for the costs of abatement to be incorporated in the prices of products. As illustrated in Figure 12-3, the marginal costs of abatement are added to the marginal cost of production which shifts upward the supply curve in the industry from *S* to S^*. This reduces the quantity demanded of the product from q to q^* as illustrated in the figure. At the quantity q^* the supply curve S^* is above the supply curve *S* by exactly the price t^* of a permit, which equals the marginal cost of abatement for all firms. In the market equilibrium for the product both consumers and the firms in the industry bear a share of the cost of abatement.

Finally, the equilibria in Figures 12-2 and 12-3 must be consistent with Figure 12-1. That is, the regulator must issue permits that equal the emissions corresponding to the quantity q^* in Figure 12-3 when the firms make abatement decisions as in Figure 12-2.

---

[1]That is, if the firm abated only 20 percent, its costs would be $4c + 0.8t = 4c + 0.8(60c) = 52c$. If it abated by 40 percent, its costs would be $16c + 0.6t = 16c + 0.6(60c) = 52c$. Similarly, if it abated by 10 percent or 50 percent its cost would be $55c$.

[2]The Chapter 19 case *Environmental Justice and Pollution Credits Trading Systems* provides another example of a tradable permits system.

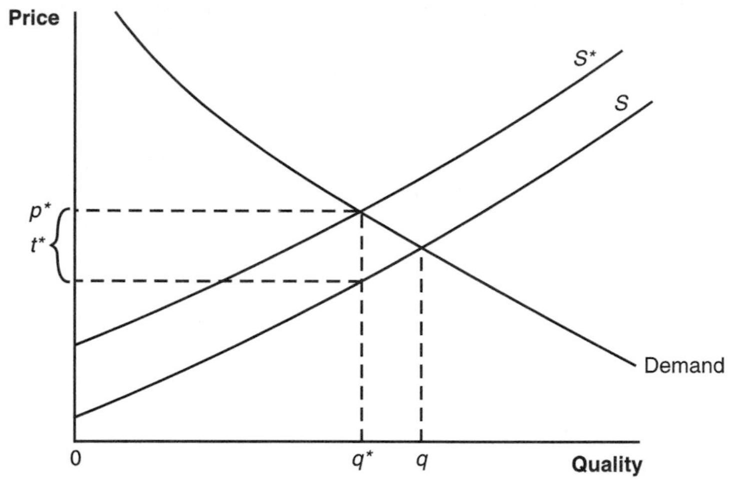

FIGURE 12-3 Product Market Equilibrium

When the price t of a permit in Figure 12-1b is t^*, the equilibrium in the permits market and the product market have the property that the marginal social harm from the emissions and the marginal cost of abatement of each firm equal t^*. This condition is necessary for social efficiency.

A tradable permits system is equivalent to a system in which an emissions tax t^* is imposed on each unit of pollution. The Chapter 14 case *The European Union Carbon Tax* considers such a system.

Tradable permits systems are said to be superior to emissions tax systems because the amount of abatement is known in advance with a permits system, whereas with an emissions tax the amount is only known after firms have responded to the tax. A permits system has another advantage over an emissions tax system in that it allows people with different preferences to express them in the market for permits. If environmentalists have a preference for lower levels of pollution, they can purchase permits and retire them, thereby reducing emissions.[3]

Tradable permits and emissions tax approaches to environmental protection also provide incentives for dynamic efficiency. Firms have incentives to invest in research and development to find more efficient means of reducing their emissions. Similarly, the pollution-control technology industry has an incentive to develop new abatement technologies because firms have a continuing demand for emissions reduction rather than a demand that arises only when more stringent engineering controls are mandated, as in the case of a command-and-control system.

GLOBAL WARMING AND EMISSIONS TRADING SYSTEMS

In November 1998 the Clinton administration signed the 1997 Kyoto Protocol on global warming, which calls for a 7 percent reduction from 1990 levels in U.S. greenhouse gasses emissions by 2010. Approval by two-thirds of the Senate is required for the protocol to be binding on the United States, and the protocol had strong opposition in the

[3]In a related expression of preferences, the Nature Conservancy spent $19 million in 1998 for two large ranches in the San Francisco Bay area totaling 60,000 acres. Shortly thereafter a local radio and television station pioneer donated $70 million to the Trust for Public Land for the purchase of ranches on the California coast.

Senate. In 1997 the Senate adopted a resolution opposing the protocol unless developing countries made firm commitments to reduce their emissions. India and China have been unwilling to do so. The Clinton administration stated that it did not plan to submit the protocol to the Senate until more developing countries had made commitments to reduce their emissions.

The Senate opposition was due to the projected cost of achieving the reduction called for in the protocol. The Clinton administration claimed that the Kyoto agreement would have little effect on costs, but the Department of Energy predicted that gasoline prices would increase by nearly 40 percent and electricity prices between 20 and 86 percent in real terms by 2010. Many U.S. businesses opposed the protocol and had formed the Global Climate Coalition (GCC) to lead the opposition. The coalition included the National Association of Manufacturers, the Chamber of Commerce, and the American Petroleum Institute. The Business Roundtable also opposed the protocol.

By the end of 1998 business opposition to the protocol began to splinter. One reason was the agreement among nations to use an emissions permits trading system to improve the social efficiency of achieving their commitments. The trading system designed by the Environmental Defense Fund would allow countries, firms, and other groups to trade permits. With an emissions permits trading system the cost of achieving commitments could be reduced substantially, since it was generally believed that it would be much less costly for a developing country to reduce, or not increase, its emissions than for a developed country to cut its emissions sharply. A developing country then would sell permits to a developed country. Economist William Nordhaus estimated that an emissions trading system would cut by 85 percent the cost of reducing emissions to 1990 levels. For the United States the cost would be reduced from $582.2 billion to $19.9 billion and for the European Union from $241.4 billion to $8.2 billion.[4]

A number of businesses supported the use of an emissions permits trading system and broke ranks with the opposition. British Petroleum and Shell withdrew from the GCC. Thirteen companies, including Boeing and United Technologies, that participated in the Pew Center for Global Climate Change began promoting the emissions trading system. While retaining its membership in the GCC, General Motors joined 40 other companies and associations in supporting the protocol. Under the sponsorship of the United Nations, the International Emissions Trading Association formed in Geneva and included as members General Motors, British Petroleum, Shell, Texaco, Mobil, and 30 other companies. The emissions trading system not only held promise for reducing the costs of reducing emissions, but it had also served to split the opposition to the protocol.

As the previous section suggests, however, a major issue to be resolved before such a system can be implemented is how the initial allocation of permits will be determined. One estimate placed the value of the permits at $1 trillion, which was certain to generate political competition among nations over the allocation.

Emissions trading systems not only can be used among firms and nations, they can also be used within firms. To address the global warming issue, in 1998 British Petroleum announced a firm commitment to reduce its emissions of greenhouse gasses by 10 percent from 1990 levels. This goal represented a nearly 40 percent reduction compared with the emissions it would have had if no measures were taken. To achieve this goal, British Petroleum worked with the Environmental Defense Fund to develop an internal emissions trading system for the company. A pilot trading program began among 12 of its operating units. British Petroleum's response to the global warming issue is considered in more detail in Chapter 20.

---

[4] *The New York Times,* October 24, 1997.

UNCOMPENSATED DAMAGES

In emissions tax and tradable permits systems, some harm remains at the socially efficient level of pollution. Under regulation, as opposed to the liability system, this harm is uncompensated. As the Coase theorem indicates, social efficiency results under either regulation or a liability system, provided that there are no transactions costs.

The emissions tax collected by the government or the receipts from the auction of permits could be used to compensate those harmed. Paying compensation can result in a moral hazard problem, however. If compensation were available for those disturbed by airport noise, people would be induced to build houses near new airports. Similarly, a moral hazard problem would result if compensation were linked to the amount of the good a consumer purchased. In Figure 12-3, compensation would be equivalent to a refund on the price, which would increase the quantity demanded of the product, which would increase emissions above the socially efficient level. Compensation could be paid as a lump sum that would not affect prices and outputs directly, but measuring the harm to an individual typically is quite difficult. The associated transactions costs of such a compensation system would likely be prohibitive.

Uncompensated harm provides an incentive for political action by those who believe that people harmed by an externality should have their losses redressed. Because compensation cannot be paid, the only way to reduce the remaining harm is to mandate more stringent pollution controls. Uncompensated harm thus provides an incentive for continued political pressure for additional reductions in pollution.

IMPLEMENTING SOCIALLY EFFICIENT REGULATION

A central problem in the implementation of any regulatory approach to the control of externalities is that the regulator usually does not have all the information required to identify the socially efficient policy.[5] Information is likely to be incomplete on the harm from pollution, the industry supply and demand curves, and the costs of abatement. Furthermore, harm can vary considerably with the location of the source of the emissions. Discharges at an upstream point into a river may cause more harm than at a downstream point. In addition, the costs of abatement can vary considerably across emissions sources. These factors complicate any centralized or command-and-control approach to environmental regulation. In contrast, emissions tax and tradable permits systems have the important advantage of allowing firms to make their abatement decisions in a decentralized manner based on their superior information about the costs and effectiveness of abatement alternatives.

Measurement problems also complicate the use of incentive approaches. With a tradable permits system, emissions have to be monitored to ensure that they do not exceed the permits held by the firm. An alternative to controlling emissions through permits is to base them on the output or inputs of the plant. These are second-best means, however, and may distort incentives. A charge on sulfur dioxide emissions, for example, could be assessed on the sulfur content of the coal burned in a power plant. This would provide incentives to use low sulfur coal, to wash the coal before burning to remove sulfur, and to use new technologies such as those funded in the Department of Energy's Clean Coal Technology Program. It would not, however, provide an incentive to install a scrubber if that were the most efficient means of reducing emissions.

One of the explanations for the EPA's use of a command-and-control approach rather than an incentive approach is that with the former it is relatively easy to moni-

---

[5]See Schelling (1983) for an analysis of the complications in implementing market-like mechanisms for pollution control.

tor compliance. Inspectors can readily verify that a firm has installed engineering controls, and the firm can be ordered to maintain records on the percent of the time that the control systems are functioning.

Both emissions tax and tradable permits systems involve complications when abatement costs or damages change. When the change does not affect the socially efficient level of emissions, a tradable permit system has an advantage over an emissions tax system because the price of permits adjusts automatically as producers buy and sell them. To change an emissions tax would require a legislative or regulatory decision, which would likely involve a lengthy process. A permits system avoids the administrative costs of a potentially lengthy regulatory process. If the socially efficient level of emissions changes, however, the number of permits would have to be changed.

In addition to information and measurement problems, some people believe that controlling a social bad, such as pollution, through market-like mechanisms demeans the objectives of environmental protection.[6] Objections have been made that market-like mechanisms amount to a right to pollute—and no one should have such a right.[7] Objections also arise because under incentive approaches some firms will reduce emissions considerably whereas others will reduce them less by buying permits from other firms, for example. Some people who view pollution as a social wrong, rather than as an external cost of production, may believe that all firms should be forced to reduce their emissions by the same amount. The Chapter 19 case *Environmental Justice and Pollution Credits Trading Systems* addresses this issue and the politics it has generated.

The Environmental Protection Agency

The EPA, an independent agency located in the executive branch, is headed by an administrator appointed by the president and confirmed by the Senate.[8] When the Reagan administration attempted to reform the EPA and reduce its size, its efforts were met with a firestorm of criticism from environmentalists, Congress, and the public, leading to the resignation of the administrator and a dozen of her top aides.[9] Since then, presidents have been careful to appoint an administrator who was at least acceptable to environmentalists and their congressional allies. Nevertheless, despite its widespread popular support, the EPA remains a focal point for political activity.

The EPA was created by an executive order of President Nixon in 1970 to bring together in a single agency a number of environmental regulation programs then housed in different federal agencies. Congress quickly passed several measures expanding the new agency's responsibilities.[10] The EPA is now responsible for administering the major acts listed in Figure 12-4. As was characteristic of the new social regulation, the acts were written in the fear that they would not be enforced and that the agencies would be captured by industry. The acts thus are often highly detailed and frequently include timetables intended to force the agency to act.[11] Many of these measures established specific goals for environmental protection without reference to costs. The goals in some cases were unrealistic and served more as symbols of commitment.[12] The Water

[6]Kelman (1981) makes this and related arguments.
[7]See Stewart (1988) for responses to the criticisms of incentive systems for environmental protection.
[8]See Congressional Quarterly (1994) for a description of the EPA and its powers.
[9]See the case "William D. Ruckelhaus and the Environmental Protection Agency: The Second Time Around," S-BPP13, Graduate School of Business, Stanford University, Stanford, CA, 1984, for an account of the administration of the EPA through 1983.
[10]Marcus (1980) discusses the political forces that shaped the EPA in its first decade.
[11]A brief description of most of these acts is provided in Congressional Quarterly (1994).
[12]See Kneese and Schultze (1975) for all early critique of environmental legislation.

Federal Insecticide, Fungicide and Rodenticide Act of 1947 (amended in 1972, 1988)
Clean Air Act of 1963 (amended in 1970, 1977, 1990)
Solid Waste Disposal Act of 1965
Air Quality Act of 1967
National Environmental Policy Act of 1969
Water Quality Improvement Act of 1970
Federal Environmental Pesticide Control Act of 1972
Federal Water Pollution Control Act (Clean Water Act) of 1972 (amended in 1987)
Marine Protection, Research and Sanctuaries Act of 1972
Noise Control Act of 1972
Endangered Species Act of 1973
Safe Drinking Water Act of 1974 (amended in 1997)
Toxic Substances Control Act of 1976 (amended in 1988)
Resource Conservation and Recovery Act of 1976
Clean Water Act of 1977
Comprehensive Environmental Response, Compensation, and Liability Act of 1980 (amended in 1986) [Superfund]
Emergency Planning and Community Right-to-Know Act (1986)
Water Quality Act of 1987
Ocean Pollution Dumping Act of 1990
Pollution Prevention Act of 1990
Oil Pollution Act of 1990
Reclamation Projects Act of 1992
Food Quality Protection Act of 1996

FIGURE 12-4 Principal Environmental Acts

Pollution Control Act of 1972, for example, established the goal of eliminating all discharge of pollutants into navigable waters by 1985.

Reflecting the importance of environmental issues and the public's concern about the environment, Congress has taken a great interest in these issues. In addition to legislation and appropriations for environmental programs, Congress influences EPA policy through the oversight process. Members have sought jurisdiction over EPA programs for their own committees and subcommittees, resulting in multiple and overlapping jurisdictions. Douglas Cottle, EPA administrator during the Carter administration, wrote that at one point the EPA had to "answer to at least 44 Senate and House committees and subcommittees, each exercising jurisdiction over some piece of the agency."[13] The Republican reorganization of Congress in 1995 reduced to some extent the jurisdictional overlap.

Federal environmental regulation is now a major undertaking with a budget of $7.6 billion in 1998 and over 20,000 employees, most of whom are in the EPA. The EPA has responsibility for air and water quality, drinking water safety, waste treatment and disposal, toxic substances, and pesticides. The Department of the Interior has responsibilities for some conservation programs, and the Department of Agriculture has responsibilities for some pesticide control programs.[14]

---

[13]*The New York Times,* April 24, 1983. Quoted in Foreman (1984, p. 197).
[14]Vogel (1986) provides a comparison of U.S. and U.K. environmental policy.

A number of the statutes assign to the states the responsibility for formulating implementation plans for attaining federal environmental standards. Under the Clean Air Act, states develop State Implementation Plans to meet air quality standards. This gives the states a considerable role in environmental protection and regulation. States have their own environmental laws and regulatory agencies as well, and some enforcement is delegated to those agencies.

ENFORCEMENT

The EPA administrative process for enforcement of environmental laws includes the filing of a notice of a complaint and a hearing before an administrative law judge (ALJ). The ALJ's decision can be appealed to the agency's administrator and to the courts. Under some statutes the EPA has the authority to forward cases to the Department of Justice, which can file a civil proceeding in federal district court. Typically, however, the EPA seeks voluntary compliance with environmental standards. Many of the environmental laws also allow suits by private citizens against polluters who violate regulations.

The federal government can seek both civil and criminal convictions of polluters, both of firms and individual managers. In 1997 the EPA referred for prosecution 278 criminal cases and 425 civil cases with total fines of $264.4 million. In the wake of the Alaskan oil spill by the Exxon Valdez, felony and misdemeanor criminal charges were brought against Exxon and the captain of the tanker. The captain was acquitted of three of the four charges, including the felony charges, and convicted on one charge of misdemeanor negligence. In 1991 Exxon agreed to a settlement with the federal and Alaska state governments in which it pleaded guilty to three misdemeanor charges and agreed to pay $1.15 billion in civil and criminal fines and restitution. In 1994 a federal court jury found that Exxon had acted in a negligent and reckless manner and ordered it to pay $5 billion in punitive damages to Alaskans.

STANDARD SETTING AND ENGINEERING CONTROLS

EPA regulation has largely been "command and control," in which uniform rules or standards are ordered and then enforced. This type of regulation is often a blunt instrument, imposing uniform rules on dissimilar situations. For example, uniform stationary-source pollution standards that ignore differences in abatement costs and achievable benefits across emissions sources have created both economic inefficiency and administrative nightmares. As indicated in the Chapter 8 case *Envirotest Systems Corporation (B),* the EPA's centralized auto emissions testing mandate drew opposition for not allowing states to design their own testing program.

The EPA both establishes overall standards, such as for ambient air quality, and specifies engineering controls to reduce emissions. The engineering controls, in order of increasing stringency, are the "best practicable technology," "best conventional technology," "best available technology," and "maximum achievable control technology." The use of engineering controls has been criticized on efficiency grounds, but its advocates believe it is necessary to reduce emissions and force polluters to comply. The Chapter 6 case *Scrubbers and Environmental Politics* illustrates the politics of mandated controls.

One advantage of the standard-setting approach is that it can be used to force the development of new pollution control technologies. Emissions standards for automobiles, for example, were set beyond what available technology could achieve, forcing automakers and suppliers to develop new technologies. These standards have had to be changed at times because of problems in achieving the needed technological advancements, but overall, technology-forcing regulation has been effective in generating new means of reducing auto emissions.

INCENTIVE APPROACHES

In addition to imposing engineering controls and establishing standards, the EPA has increasingly used incentive approaches. One approach used in local air quality regulation under the Clean Air Act is the "bubble" program. Under the command-and-control approach, engineering controls are specified for each individual processing unit in an oil refinery, chemical plant, or steel mill. Under the bubble policy, the EPA sets permitted emissions levels for the entire plant—imagine a bubble around the plant—and allows the producer to achieve those levels in the most efficient manner. The plant, for example, may achieve the needed reduction on a single processing unit or through controls on several units.

Another program to improve the efficiency of the regulation of air quality involves "credits" and "offsets" used in nonattainment areas that do not meet federal air quality standards. For example, under the Clean Air Act Amendments of 1990, the EPA allocates credits to states for implementing enhanced auto emissions testing and maintenance programs.[15] The EPA allocates more credits for centralized testing programs than for decentralized programs because of their greater effectiveness.

Under the offset program, to construct a new plant in a nonattainment area, a firm must reduce pollutants elsewhere in the area by an amount equal to that released by the new plant. The firm can reduce emissions at another of its facilities or may purchase credits from another firm. In 1995 the California Institute of Technology and the Pacific Stock Exchange created an electronic market for trading credits in four Southern California counties. The Regional Clean Air Incentives Market (Reclaim) trades credits in sulfur dioxide, nitrogen oxides, and reactive organic gases.

The EPA does not have the authority to tax pollution, but Congress has taken an interest in pollution taxes. In 1989 a federal law imposed a tax on chlorofluorocarbons (CFCs) as a means of reducing the use of the ozone-depleting chemicals while their production was being phased out. To address the global warming issue, some firms, members of Congress, and environmentalists have urged the use of a broadscale carbon tax on fuels. In 1993 the Clinton administration attempted to have a closely related Btu tax enacted by Congress, but the political pressure from those who would bear the distributive consequences of the tax caused the plan to fail.

SUPERFUND

The EPA administers the Superfund for the cleanup of existing toxic waste disposal sites. Estimates place the number of sites requiring Superfund cleanups as high as 20,000, and cost estimates are as high as $600 billion. The EPA attempts to identify the source of the dumping and to force the source to clean the site. If the EPA does the cleanup, it can go to court to recover the costs. As of 1997 the EPA had completed work on 400 sites, and work was under way on 700 others. The Superfund program has been criticized both for moving too slowly and for spending funds where there was little hope of a successful cleanup. In recent years the pace of cleanup of toxic waste sites has increased. Of the $30 billion spent by business and government on the Superfund program, however, a third is estimated to have gone to lawyers in litigation over who is liable for the costs. Another criticism of the program is that it requires the same cleanup of all sites, regardless of their future use or the costs of cleanup.

In addition to the litigation costs the Superfund has been criticized for its "retrospective liability" feature that requires companies to pay for the cleanup of wastes that

---

[15]See the Chapter 2 case *Envirotest Systems Corporation (A)* and the Chapter 8 case *Envirotest Systems Corporation (B)* for the management and politics of an auto emissions testing program.

had been disposed of legally. The Clinton administration responded to this criticism by proposing to exempt small firms. The criticisms and disagreements over the Superfund have caused its congressional reauthorization to be mired in politics for most of the 1990s. This caused the taxes imposed on firms to fund the program to expire in 1995. The Superfund is now financed by the federal budget.

The Politics of Environmental Protection

Because they are of considerable interest to people, and hence to the media, environmental issues become public quickly and often advance rapidly in their life cycles. Since most of the costs of environmental protection are borne by private parties, government budget considerations have imposed few limits on the advance of environmental issues.[16] The costs of environmental protection are borne by firms, their rentholders, and consumers, and those costs generate opposition to more stringent regulation. Environmental issues thus are the subject of intense political competition, as evidenced by the 1990 amendments to the Clean Air Act, considered later in the chapter, over which Congress struggled for a decade.[17]

Environmental issues are complex, in part because of differing perspectives about the protection of entitlements. From the social efficiency perspective, the entitlement to be free from the hazards of pollution should be protected by a liability rule because the transactions costs associated with a property rule would be prohibitive. Yet many individuals treat the environment and their health as if they were protected by a property rule. They seek to prohibit activities that may pose a risk to their health or to the environment. In one instance, Congress responded to these sentiments by enacting the Delaney amendment, which prohibited the use of any food additive found to be a carcinogen in laboratory animals. Environmental politics—including the NIMBY movement considered in the next section—thus is motivated both by distributive consequences and normative concerns about the protection of the environment and health.

The politics of environmental protection also moves into judicial arenas. The National Resources Defense Council (NRDC) sued the EPA seeking enforcement of the Delaney amendment for pesticides used in the production of foods. As a practical means of dealing with potential risks, the EPA had followed a practice of allowing pesticide use if the risk to human health was "negligible." The courts held for the NRDC, requiring the EPA to enforce the Delaney amendment. This decision required the banning of dozens of widely used pesticides. The court decision added to the pressure for congressional action to repeal the Delaney amendment, which occurred in 1996.

Much remains unknown about environmental hazards and their control, and this scientific uncertainty is a source of contention in environmental politics. For example, the EPA estimated that 8 million homes were contaminated by dangerous levels of radon, a naturally occurring radioactive gas formed as radium decays in the ground. The EPA projected that the exposure to radon over a lifetime may cause 20,000 lung cancer deaths a year. In 1986 the EPA issued an Indoor Radon Health Advisory that said, "Radon causes thousands of deaths each year." Other scientists placed the number of households with radon concentrations at the EPA's action level as low as 100,000. In one

---

[16]Some regulation does have budget effects. For example, municipalities are one of the largest water polluters, and the federal government provides subsidies to municipalities for the construction of water treatment plants. Local governments bear approximately 22 percent of the cost of environmental protection (EPA, 1991).

[17]See Greve and Smith (1992) and Rosenbaum (1995) for treatments of environmental politics.

study, the lung cancer rate of people exposed to radon was found to be no different from that of people who were not exposed.[18] In 1993 the EPA issued voluntary guidelines for new homes and an information pamphlet for homeowners.

The scientific uncertainty about the damage to the environment by pollution and about the risks to people's health provides an opportunity to use advocacy science, which can involve alarmist tactics of proclaiming dangers to health and the environment. The Alar episode considered in Chapter 3 provides an example of the effectiveness of such a strategy. Because the media sees health and environmental risks as having considerable societal significance and audience interest, environmental issues quickly find their way to the public's attention and are frequently contested in full view of the public. These issues often arise from data provided in epidemiological studies. Feinstein (1988) characterized the pattern: "The episodes have now developed a familiar pattern. A report appears in a prominent medical journal; the conclusions receive wide publicity by newspapers, television, and other media; and another common entity of daily life becomes indicated as a menace to health—possibly causing strokes, heart attacks, birth defects, cancer. . . . The reported evidence is almost always a statistical analysis of epidemiological data, and the scientific tactics that produced the evidence are almost always difficult to understand and evaluate." He criticized the studies because "the research methods seldom have the precautions, calibrations, and relative simplicity that are taken for granted in other branches of science."

Another source of contention in environmental politics results from laboratory studies. Such studies of health risks are often conducted on laboratory animals, which are exposed to pollutants at concentrations often orders of magnitude higher than human beings would ever encounter.[19] The laboratory results then must be extrapolated to the size and weight of people. Whether such results bear a reasonable relationship to the health risks to human beings can be a matter of disagreement.

In addition to concerns about hazards, environmental politics is motivated by the distributive consequences of environmental policy, the costs of environmental protection, and the benefits from the reduction in pollution and hazards. (See the Chapter 6 case *Scrubbers and Environmental Politics* and the "Scrubbers and the Clean Air Act Amendments" example in this chapter for the distributive politics of environmental protection.) The immediate costs of reducing pollution are concentrated on the generators of the pollutants. Most environmental protection costs, however, are ultimately borne by consumers in the form of higher prices. The EPA estimated that the price of a new automobile could increase by $600 because of the auto emissions standards contained in the 1990 amendments to the Clean Air Act.

The benefits from environmental protection accrue to people quite broadly, as in the case of the air quality improvements. The basic structure of environmental politics thus is entrepreneurial. The broad public sensitivity to environmental and health issues has meant that there are many political entrepreneurs seeking to represent the dispersed beneficiaries. Particularly when the costs of environmental protection are paid through prices rather than taxes, the government has often been responsive to environmental political entrepreneurship. The growth and sophistication of environmental interest groups, however, have transformed the politics of environmental protection into interest group politics.

There are many national environmental organizations that take political action at the federal, state, and local levels. Environmental groups testify regularly in legislative

---

[18] *The New York Times,* January 8, 1991.

[19] This is often because of the short life span of some laboratory animals and the desire to reduce the cost of experiments and speed the completion of the research.

and regulatory hearings, and some demonstrate to attract media coverage to their side of the issue.[20] Some environmental interest groups such as Earth First, which engaged in tree spiking, and the Earth Libertarian Front, which burned down a Colorado ski resort in 1998, use violence. Environmental groups also monitor the activities of government officials. The League of Conservation Voters annually rates members of Congress based on their votes on a set of environmental bills. The Sierra Club and some other environmental organizations endorse candidates in federal and state elections.

At the federal level, environmentalists had focused primarily on major sources of pollution, often accepting exemptions for small business. The 1990 amendments to the Clean Air Act, however, not only addressed emissions by automobiles and electric power plants but also by dry cleaners, furniture manufacturers, and printers. In spite of their claims of hardship, these firms were required to install costly pollution control systems. Dry cleaners may have to spend between $38,000 to $48,000 per machine. Joe Gerard, vice president of the American Furniture Manufacturers, stated, "What's unnerving for our industry is that the law would affect the application of [wood] finishing materials, and that's what gives us our competitive edge over imports."[21] Linda Greed of the NRDC said: "Everything that comes down the pike, we're told it'll put them out of business. . . . When they come up with the data to show it costs too much, they usually do get some relief. But when it's just arm waving, they don't. We hear it too often to be credible."[22]

The politics of environmental protection also involves the market and nonmarket strategies of individual companies, as indicated in the chapter case *Philips and the Low-Mercury Fluorescent Lamp.* The chapter case *Westlands Water District* considers an environmental issue addressed in a judicial arena.

NIMBY

In 1989 William Ruckelshaus, former EPA administrator and CEO of Browning-Ferris industries, a worldwide waste-disposal company, wrote of the coming solid waste disposal crisis. "More than a third of the nation's landfills will be full within the next decade. New York will exhaust its capacity in nine years, Los Angeles in six, and Philadelphia is out of capacity now, and must engage in continuous negotiations to dispose of its 800,000 tons per year. Why? Nobody wants garbage put down anywhere near where he lives, the 'not-in-my-backyard' syndrome—the dreaded NIMBY."[23] The NIMBY movement focuses on local environmental concerns, particularly as they involve risks to person or property. The movement is often directed toward refuse disposal sites, toxic waste sites, chemical and oil plant emissions, and other facilities that may emit toxics. Hamilton (1993) studied the location decisions and expansion plans of hazardous waste disposal and incineration facilities and found that companies take into account the anticipated opposition by local groups in making their citing decisions for capacity expansion.

At the beginning of the 1990s the NIMBY movement was accelerating and changing the nature of nonmarket action directed at polluters. The National Toxics Campaign, a nonprofit organization that provides assistance to local organizations, reported that the number of community groups contacting it increased from 609 in 1987 to 1,300 in 1989.

---

[20]See the Chapter 4 Case *Shell, Greenpeace, and Brent Spar* for the strategy and tactics of Greenpeace in opposing the at-sea disposal of an oil storage platform.
[21]*The Wall Street Journal,* November 13, 1990. See also the Chapter 16 case *The WTO and the Environment.*
[22]*The Wall Street Journal,* November 13, 1990.
[23]*The Wall Street Journal,* September 5, 1989.

One account put the number of local environmental groups at 7,000.[24] The NIMBY movement has been energized by information provided by the federal government's Toxics Release Inventory (TRI), which provides detailed information on the emissions by 22,000 plants of over 300 chemicals believed to have health consequences.[25]

The TRI is required by the "right-to-know" amendment to a 1985 Superfund reauthorization bill. The amendment was passed by the House on a 212 to 211 vote.[26] This inventory has become the focus of considerable nonmarket activity with some industries seeking to have chemicals they emit dropped from the TRI and industries such as agriculture, forestry, and mining working to preserve their exemptions. Environmentalists have sought to eliminate exemptions and expand the list of chemicals. The release of the TRI has become a strategic event for environmentalists. The NRDC uses the data in the TRI to release the names of the largest emitters of those chemicals listed by the EPA as "probable human carcinogens."

In addition to allowing national organizations such as the NRDC to take action, the TRI facilitates local NIMBY action. The data in the TRI are given for individual plants, so emissions can be identified by individual communities. This allows local citizens to take nonmarket action against the plants. As an example, in 1989 the NRDC released an analysis of the TRI data listing Shendahl of Northfield, Minnesota, as the 45th largest emitter of the 11 chemicals analyzed by the NRDC. Shendahl had been legally emitting 400 tons a year of methylene chloride, a chemical whose emission was unregulated at both the federal and state level. The firm had no visible chemical emissions and had routinely been issued a permit for the discharges.[27]

When residents of Northfield learned of the emissions, their reaction was immediate. Within a week of the revelation, Shendahl announced that it would reduce emissions by 90 percent by 1993 and eliminate them entirely by 2000, switching to flammable solvents. Residents and activists formed Clean Air Northfield to continue the pressure. The activists charged that the company had withheld information on its emissions from the public, knowing that in 1985 the EPA had listed methylene chloride as a probable carcinogen. One activist group sought closure of the plant, but its employees, arguing that it was the largest employer in town, sought an orderly reduction in emissions that would save their jobs. The Amalgamated Clothing and Textile Workers Union, which represented the employees, was concerned that reducing emissions by the planned 90 percent might cause a hazardous accumulation of methylene chloride inside the plant, threatening employees. The union sought and won contract rights to monitor the emissions reduction program. The activists and the union also took action at the state level, persuading the state to include in Shendahl's emissions permit a required 93 percent reduction by 1995. Clean Air Northfield lobbied the state government for the elimination of all methylene chloride emissions by 1995.

EPA Strategy and Activism

With Republican majorities in both houses of Congress beginning in 1995, major new environmental legislation seemed unlikely.[28] Environmentalist and government activists needed a strategy to achieve their objectives without going through Congress or through the traditional procedures required by administrative due process, such as a no-

---

[24] Margaret E. Kriz, "Shades of Green," *National Journal,* July 28, 1990.

[25] Firms are required to notify the federal, state, and local governments of any emissions of the chemicals.

[26] See Hamilton (1997) for a study of the voting on the amendment.

[27] This account is based on an article in *The New York Times,* January 2, 1991.

[28] Some new legislation was enacted. For example, in 1996 Congress enacted the Food Quality Protection Act which among other measures required the testing of all chemicals in food and drinking water for endocrine disruptors that can disrupt reproduction and other bodily processes.

tification and comment period and publication of new regulations in the *Federal Register.* The strategy adopted by the EPA had three principal components. The first was suggested by the success of the Toxics Release Inventory in generating local nonmarket action to force greater reductions in emissions. The Internet provided a powerful new vehicle for disseminating information to local citizens and activist groups. The second component was to focus on possible health risks, rather than environmental protection, associated with pollutants and toxics. The strategy was to emphasize the health risks to children, who were thought to be particularly susceptible to pollutants because their immune systems were not yet fully developed. The third component was to use other laws to expand the scope of the EPA's programs.

The first component of the strategy was implemented in several ways. In 1994 the EPA had added 152 additional chemicals to the TRI. In 1996 it took an additional step in announcing a major expansion in the number of companies to be included in the TRI. The industries added included coal mining, electric utilities, and commercial hazardous-waste treatment facilities, among others. The EPA also quietly launched an internal project to grade the pollution risks at 661 plants and put the information on the Internet. The EPA did not go through the standard public notice and comment process nor did it take the grading project to its Science Advisory Board. When they learned of the EPA project, companies demanded to see the data on which the grading was based. They found serious errors in the data. Some worked with the EPA to correct the errors, and others simply refused to help correct the data, calling the project "irresponsible." Nineteen state environmental agencies also objected to the project, calling it a "premature undertaking of questionable value." Under pressure from companies and states, the EPA shelved its grading project but did put on the Internet detailed records of environmental inspection and infraction reports for 653 industrial facilities. In 1998 the EPA extended the right-to-know initiative to include mercury emissions from coal-fired electric generating plants. EPA Administrator Carol Browner said, "Putting information about toxic chemical pollution directly into the hands of citizens helps them make informed decisions about how to best protect the health of their families and work in their communities to prevent the pollution in the first place."[29]

To implement the second component of the strategy, Browner announced, "From now on, we will take into account the unique vulnerability of children." Browner established an Office of Children's Health Protection in the EPA. She also announced that all new standards would take into account the risks for children. The new emphasis on risks for children also provided a rationale for the review of existing standards, giving the EPA the opportunity to set more stringent standards without new congressional authorization. For example, the standards set under the Clean Air Act, had not been based on the risks to children. Asthma is a chronic childhood illness, and the EPA justified stringent new rules for small particles (dust and soot) and ozone on this basis. The EPA issued new standards for microscopic particles one-thirteenth the diameter of human hair and reduced the standard for ground-level ozone by one-third.[30] Browner said that the particulate rule would reduce premature deaths from lung ailments by 20,000 a year, and the more stringent ozone standard would result in 1.5 million fewer cases of lung disease. In 1999 the court of appeals overturned the small particulate rules on the grounds that the EPA had exceeded its authority and its decision was arbitrary and capricious.

---

[29]EPA press release, November 16, 1998.

[30]The microscopic particulate standard came under heavy criticism from governors and mayors, since the standard would put 74 million people into "non-attainment" areas. In response the EPA relaxed the standard from the proposed 50 micrograms per cubic meter to 65. EPA, "EPA's Updated Clean Air Standards: A Common Sense Primer," September 1997.

A third component of the EPA's environmental strategy was to use the civil rights law to examine the effects of pollution and toxics on minorities and women. President Clinton and Administrator Browner invoked Title VI of the Civil Rights Act of 1964 to launch a program on environmental justice without having to go through Congress for authorization of the new program. The EPA program focused on the disparate effect of toxic waste disposal sites and industrial emissions on minorities and women. Local interest groups also began to file environmental lawsuits under Title VI. The Chapter 19 case *Environmental Justice and Pollution Credits Trading Systems* addresses the ethical and political dimensions of claims about environmental justice.

THE 1990 AMENDMENTS TO THE CLEAN AIR ACT

In contrast to the regulatory statutes for industries such as transportation, electric power, and telecommunications, which were written in general terms and expressed goals often stated in terms of the public interest, the Clean Air Act and its amendments through 1977 totaled 2,500 pages of detailed prescriptions. The act yields widely distributed benefits and imposes concentrated costs on industries such as automobiles and electric power and ultimately results in higher prices for consumers. The act was criticized as unreasonably inefficient and overly burdensome, and the Reagan administration opposed congressional attempts to reauthorize it when it expired in 1983. Congress and the administration were unable to reach agreement on reauthorization, and the act continued in effect through annual congressional extensions.

In 1989 the Bush administration sent Congress a comprehensive bill to address issues such as acid rain and ozone depletion and to improve the efficiency of environmental policy. Congress went considerably beyond the administration's proposal, enacting the 1990 amendments to the Clean Air Act. The amendments cover ambient air quality (smog), motor vehicles, air toxics, and acid rain and include stringent regulations on major sources of air pollutants. Plants are required to use the maximum achievable control technology, which is defined in terms of "the average emissions limitations of the cleanest 12 percent of similar facilities."[31]

On specific issues such as standards for coke ovens of steel plants, environmentalist and industry lobbyists worked within each chamber of Congress to obtain as favorable a regulation as possible. The steel industry was unsuccessful in the House, and in the Senate it was only able to win a postponement in the compliance date, pushing it from 2003 to 2020. In conference, the industry agreed to a bargain in which the 2020 compliance date was retained but an interim standard for 1998 was established.[32] National Steel indicated that it would spend $6 billion by then to meet the standards. David Doninger of the NRDC said, "A generation or more of people will be exposed to very serious cancer risks."[33]

ACID RAIN AND TRADABLE PERMITS

The bulk of the sulfur dioxide and nitrogen oxide emissions that cause acid rain come from coal-fired electric power plants in six states; Indiana, Illinois, West Virginia, Pennsylvania, Ohio, and New York. Although new power plants are subject to New Source Performance Standards (NSPS), existing power plants had not been subject to emission

[31] *Congressional Quarterly Weekly Report,* October 20, 1990, p. 3498.
[32] As an example of the detail in environmental legislation, the amendments instruct the EPA administrator to set emissions standards for coke ovens that include no more than "8 percent leaking doors" and "16 seconds visible emissions per charge." (*Congressional Quarterly Weekly Report,* November 24, 1990, p. 3942.)
[33] *Congressional Quarterly Weekly Report,* October 20, 1990, p. 3498.

limits. These six states, and others as well, had lower electricity prices because their plants did not have to meet stringent controls. Adding a scrubber, for example, can increase the cost of electricity by up to 15 percent. Since the damage from acid rain occurs primarily in Canada and the northeastern states, addressing the acid rain issue involved benefits to one region and costs to another. Bargaining thus focused on both efficiency and the distributive consequences of policy alternatives. The political competition over acid rain had gone on for a decade, culminating with the Clean Air Act Amendments of 1990, which provided for a 10 million pound reduction in sulfur dioxide emissions from the 1980 level and a 2 million pound reduction in nitrogen oxide emissions.

The amendments addressed efficiency through a tradable permits system and the distributive consequences through a number of special provisions. Called "allowances" rather than permits, the system reduced the cost of abatement by allowing electric power companies to use the most efficient means of achieving emissions standards. They could choose low-sulfur coal, methods such as coal washing to remove sulfur before burning, new technologies such as fluidized bed combustion, or a scrubber. More importantly, the system permitted firms to trade allowances in a market, providing incentives for the efficient distribution of abatement among the firms. The tradable permits system was expected to save up to $3 billion per year compared with a uniform command-and-control approach.

In the initial phase of the program the EPA administrator annually allocated allowances to 111 coal-fired power plants in 21 states in the Midwest, South, and East according to formulas specified in the legislation. Unused allowances can be carried forward to the next year and transferred or sold to other companies. Power companies were also allowed to transfer allowances among their own plants. New power plants completed after enactment of the amendments are not allocated any allowances and must purchase them from existing plants. New power plants were already subject to the NSPS of 1.2 pounds of SO_2 per MBtu, so their emissions would be substantially below the emissions limits for existing plants. In 2000 the emissions cap under the Clean Air Act Amendments would be extended to cover all power plants in the continental United States.

Wary of the transferable allowances approach, Congress declared that the allowances were not property rights of the power companies but instead were grants that could be revoked or changed at the discretion of the EPA administrator.[34] The EPA administrator conducts an annual auction of allowances from a reserve formed by taking a percentage of the allowances allocated to the plants.[35]

Joskow, Schmalensee, and Bailey (1998), Schmalensee et al. (1998), and Stavins (1998) have evaluated the market for SO_2 allowances and concluded that by 1994 it was functioning relatively efficiently with the price of an allowance in mid-1997 trading at approximately $100. The market includes several types of trades. Some power companies arrange trades among themselves through bilateral bargaining. Others work through brokers who collect bids and offers and arrange trades among buyers and sellers.[36] Some trades involve swaps in which one company provides to another company allowances for the current year in exchange for allowances after 2000 when allowable emissions levels will be reduced. Trades also take place through the EPA's annual auction.

The distributive consequences of the tradable allowances system depend in large part on how the allowances are allocated. Since regulated electricity prices are cost-of-

---

[34]One reason for not using the term "right" was that some environmentalists criticized transferable allowance systems because they believed that the systems involved trading the right to pollute.

[35]The proceeds are distributed back to the plants from which the allowances were originally obtained.

[36]Three organizations, Cantor Fitzgerald, the Emission Exchange Corporation, and Fieldston, act as brokers and publish price indices on allowance trades.

service based, the full costs of both allowances and abatement are borne by the customers of the electric power plants. If the allowances were auctioned by the EPA, the power companies and their customers in the 21 states would bear the costs of abatement plus the payments for the allowances. Taxpayers across the nation would be the beneficiaries. If the allowances were granted to the power companies, taxpayers would receive nothing, and the power companies and their customers would bear only the costs of abatement. As the Coase theorem indicates, the efficiency consequences of granting or auctioning allowances are identical, and the choice between the two methods is a distributive matter. Granting the allowances produced concentrated benefits in the 21 states and particularly in the six states that emit the most sulfur dioxide. The loss to taxpayers was widely distributed. Client politics prevailed, and the allowances were granted rather than auctioned, resulting in lower costs for the power plants and their customers.

The trading of sulfur dioxide allowances is now extensive, but trading has been criticized by local environmental groups that want lower emissions in their area. In 1991 under pressure from environmentalists and state regulators the Long Island Lighting Company (Lilco) announced that it would no longer sell allowances to power companies in the Midwest and South that are upwind from New York. The higher emissions that result when companies buy allowances, and hence have higher emissions, cause harm to the Adirondacks and Catskills. Since the market for allowances is active and efficient, Lilco's action should have little effect, since the power companies in the Midwest and South will simply buy allowances from other companies.

In 1998 the EPA established an emissions trading system for nitrogen oxide similar to that for sulfur dioxide. The program would reduce by 28 percent the emissions in 22 states and the District of Columbia and would cover coal-fired and oil-fired power plants and industrial boilers. Nitrogen oxide is a major component of smog and can flow to downwind states. The price of an allowance rose from $1,500 in 1998 to $6,000 in early 1999 as companies prepared to meet more stringent nitrogen oxide standards. This increased the marginal generating cost of electricity by more than 50 percent.

Much of the battle over the Clean Air Act amendments was between "clean" and "dirty" states. The clean states wanted credit for their accomplishments and wanted to avoid having to pay the dirty states' cleanup costs. The dirty states are primarily located in the Midwest, and many of them also mine high-sulfur coal. Their representatives in Congress sought both to hold down electricity prices and preserve jobs for miners. The dirty states also sought cost sharing through federal tax subsidies for scrubbers and sought compensation for jobs lost. The following example analyzes the politics of these two issues.

ENVIRONMENTAL POLITICS: SCRUBBERS AND THE CLEAN AIR ACT AMENDMENTS

The NSPS adopted by the EPA in 1972 set allowable emissions standards for all new coal-fired power plants at 1.2 pounds of sulfur per million Btus. As a result, the demand for low-sulfur coal, most of which was mined in Montana and Wyoming, skyrocketed. Coal production in Wyoming increased from less than 10 million tons in 1970 to 171.4 million tons in 1989, surpassing the 158.6 million tons mined in Kentucky and the 151.2 million tons from West Virginia. In 1989 coal accounted for 56 percent of the electricity generated in the United States.

The coal mined in the Powder River Basin of Wyoming contains at most 0.5 percent sulfur, whereas much of the eastern coal has a sulfur content of 4 to 5 percent.[37]

---

[37]Some eastern coal has a low sulfur content.

Much of the eastern coal is extracted in shaft mines, whereas more efficient strip mining is used for western coal. In 1990 the market price for western coal was $5 a ton, and the price of eastern coal was $18 a ton and higher. Eastern coal, however, had a transportation cost advantage for midwestern and eastern power plants. Transportation of western coal to the Midwest and the Southeast could cost $25 a ton, representing over 80 percent of the delivered cost.

Demand for high-sulfur eastern coal had been maintained in part by the Clean Air Act Amendments of 1977, which required scrubbing of flue gases for all new power plants.[38] Existing power plants had not been subject to these regulations, and by 1990 less than one quarter of the coal-fired power plant capacity had scrubbers. The acid rain problem focused attention on those existing power plants that had not installed scrubbers and continued to burn high-sulfur eastern coal. The proposed Clean Air Act amendments threatened the eastern coal industry, but the combination of strong pressure from environmentalists and the Bush administration's commitment made adoption of stringent acid rain provisions likely.

Power plants had three principal means of reducing emissions: using low-sulfur western coal, installing scrubbers, and retrofitting plants with new technology such as fluidized bed combustion. Retrofitting an existing plant was usually expensive, and so many power plants were expected to switch to low-sulfur coal. Thousands of coal miners in the Ohio River Valley and Appalachia were expected to lose their jobs, and a number of small towns that depended on coal mining were expected to be wiped out.

In the Senate, supporters pushed two measures to aid the miners. Senator Robert C. Byrd (D-WV), former majority leader and then-chairman of the Appropriations Committee, offered a bill to provide $500 million in job-loss benefits and retraining programs for displaced miners.[39] The 3-year program would provide 90, 80, and 70 percent of their wages and benefits for 3 years, respectively. In the first year, the average miner would receive $41,000.[40] Senator Byrd called in past IOUs to gain votes, but the Bush administration opposed the measure, and the opposition in the Senate was intense. Senator Phil Gramm (R-TX) said, "People in other states are not going to be treated better than the people in Texas."[41] Bringing one senator from a hospital to the Senate floor, Senator Byrd lost on a 49 to 50 vote as one of his supporters returning from a funeral was delayed by bad weather.

The other measure would provide a 20 percent tax credit for any utility installing a scrubber or other pollution-control device. This would reduce the cost of scrubbing, causing some power plants to choose scrubbing and high-sulfur eastern coal over low-sulfur western coal. Between 3,000 and 5,000 miners' jobs would be saved by the measure, but it was estimated to cost $3.3 billion. The measure was tabled on a 71 to 26 vote.

In the House, representatives from the Midwest were better represented in the Commerce Committee than were midwestern senators on the Energy and Public Works Committee, which had jurisdiction over the bill in the Senate. Supporters of eastern coal sought a subsidy for scrubbers, and representatives from clean states sought special allowances to allow their states to grow without being blocked by emissions limits. After lengthy bargaining in the Commerce Committee a bargain was struck, providing additional allowances to clean states and to plants that installed scrubbers.

The fight for jobloss benefits in the House was led by Representative Bob Wise (D-WV), who was successful in obtaining a 5-year, $250 million program to provide 26 ad-

---

[38]See the Chapter 6 Case *Scrubbers and Environmental Politics.*
[39]His original measure would have provided benefits of $1.6 billion.
[40]*Congressional Quarterly Weekly Report,* March 31, 1990.
[41]*Congressional Quarterly Weekly Report,* March 31, 1990, p. 984.

ditional weeks of unemployment benefits plus retraining.[42] In the conference committee, support for the jobloss benefits was strong, and the Bush administration recognized that it would have to accept some form of benefits for miners. The administration obtained concessions, putting the benefits under an existing retraining program provided by the Economically Dislocated Workers Assistance Act. Authorized funding was left at $250 million.

The supporters of eastern miners were able to incorporate two provisions in the amendments to encourage scrubbing. The acid rain provisions allowed a 2-year extension in achieving emissions standards, but only if the power plant had a scrubber. More importantly, power plants that reduced sulfur dioxide emissions below the NSPS received two allowances per ton of reduction. A total of 3.5 million allowances were earmarked for this during the 1997 to 1999 period.

The failure of the proposed tax subsidy for scrubbers was due to its cost. A subsidy would benefit eastern coal miners and consumers in the states in which the scrubbers would be installed, but these beneficiaries covered only a relatively small number of congressional districts. The tax burden would be widely borne across the country, which usually provides the beneficiaries an advantage in client politics. However, the price tag of up to $1 million per job saved was more than many members of Congress were prepared to accept. The alternative of job-loss benefits for coal miners was an effective substitute that contributed to the failure of the scrubber subsidy measure.

Management of Environmental Protection Issues

The management of environmental issues involves both external and internal activities. Externally, firms and their managers must address a set of issues that arise in their market and nonmarket environments. These issues may be addressed in public institutional arenas such as Congress, state legislatures, courts, and regulatory agencies; or outside those institutions, as with NIMBY activities and direct interactions with environmentalists. The chapter case *Procter & Gamble and Disposable Diapers* brings together a number of these issues.

A significant development began in the 1980s when several firms and moderate environmental groups decided to develop better understandings of each other's concerns. The National Wildlife Federation (NWF) established the Corporate Conservation Council. The council meets quarterly with the NWF to discuss issues such as groundwater protection and hazardous waste reduction. The council issues policy statements on selected issues and presents Environmental Achievement Awards.[43]

The Environmental Defense Fund (EDF) has embraced the objective of efficiency in pollution control and advocates the use of incentive approaches to achieve that end. This earned the EDF a role in the development of the provisions of the Clean Air Act Amendments of 1990 and in designing the emissions permits trading system for achieving the objectives of the Kyoto Protocol on global warming. It also contributed to the relationship developed between EDF and McDonald's considered later in the chapter. As indicated previously, EDF also joined with British Petroleum to develop an internal tradable permits system for CO_2 emissions for the company.

---

[42]This was the first provision since 1978 providing cash payments for workers who lost jobs as a result of new legislation. *Congressional Quarterly Weekly Report,* October 27, 1990.

[43]Policy statements are available from the NWF on the following subjects: groundwater, hazardous waste reduction from industry, conservation of wetlands, and soil conservation. The representatives of the firms on the Council affix their signatures to the policies.

INTERNAL MANAGEMENT ISSUES

Internal management issues involve compliance with environmental regulations, interactions with regulators and environmentalists on compliance matters, preparation for new regulations, and organization for environmental compliance. These require both management and technology. In the case of air and water pollution, technological measures include alternatives ranging from engineering controls to "clean" technologies. The Carrier Corporation, for example, was able to eliminate its degreasing operation in the manufacture of air conditioners through engineering redesign. In the case of toxic and solid wastes, alternatives range from changing disposal methods to reducing the wastes generated.

Commitment of top management is often a necessary condition for the successful management of environmental protection issues. Environmental issues have become so important, pervasive, and costly that high-level attention must be given to them. Some firms have established committees of their boards of directors to assume oversight responsibility on environmental matters. Some CEOs have declared a commitment to environmental protection. When Du Pont Chairman Edgar S. Woolard, Jr., assumed the role of the company's chief environmentalist, the level of awareness rose. Du Pont's vice president for safety, health, and environmental affairs commented on the difference: "I used to have to do a real selling job to line up people. . . . Then suddenly it wasn't just me trying to get the organization to do things, it was Ed. Now they call all the time."[44] Some firms that operate on a decentralized basis have recognized the importance of environmental issues by establishing corporate environmental groups and audit units. IBM, for example, has created the position of vice president for environmental health and safety in its corporate office and given that office responsibility for ensuring compliance with environmental regulations and company policies.

A commitment from top management may be necessary for successful management of environmental matters, but it is not sufficient, since compliance takes place at the level of the individual facility. Furthermore, ideas for waste reduction and pollution control often are generated at the plant level. Management thus must instill the attitude that environmental matters are the responsibility of all employees.

Many firms have extended their internal environmental management programs to include external advice and consultations with local communities. Dow Chemical formed a Corporate Environmental Advisory Council to advise the company on its environmental stewardship policies and programs. Dow also encouraged its plant managers to form community advisory councils to address local issues and assure the community that its activities meet environmental standards. Dow's emphasis is on pollution prevention through the four Rs: reduce, reuse, recycle, and recover. Source reduction is the preferred method followed by recycling and recovery.[45]

Managers must also interact with a host of regulatory officials, ranging from those who grant permits and inspect facilities to those who write implementation regulations. Managers should deal with regulators on the basis of trust and mutual respect but must also be prepared to suggest new means for achieving environmental goals and to oppose rules that may be overly burdensome. Managers should recognize that just as they face competing pressures for profits and for environmental protection, regulators face competing pressures from environmental groups and their political allies and from those who bear the cost of compliance. Recognizing the pressures regulators face can be important in developing workable relationships.

---

[44] *The New York Times,* March 3, 1991.
[45] See Popoff (1992).

In 1996 Intel and the EPA negotiated an innovative program, referred to as Project XL, in which red tape and the regulatory burden were reduced substantially and flexibility in compliance was granted to the company. Intel agreed to recycle most of its water, solid waste, and nonhazardous waste, to reduce the hazardous waste generated at the plant, and to reduce emissions below federal standards. Intel was granted a single permit for the plant rather than having to get a new permit each time it changed its manufacturing processes. Environmental groups criticized the agreement. The NRDC said, "We are disappointed with the environmental performance required by this agreement."[46] Local environmental and labor groups also criticized the agreement charging that it "allows Intel to expose its employees and the communities of Chandler and Phoenix to increased toxic chemical hazards."[47]

MCDONALD'S AND WASTE REDUCTION

McDonald's is the largest restaurant system in the world and one of the world's largest generators of solid waste. For a number of years McDonald's had taken measures to reduce its use of packaging materials. The packaging weight for a Big Mac, fries, and a shake had been reduced from 46 grams in the early 1970s to 25 grams by the 1990s. McDonald's had also conducted a number of waste-reduction experiments, including a test program in 800 restaurants to recycle polystyrene containers. Environmental groups, however, continued to pressure the company to make further reductions in its generation of solid waste.[48] The Citizens' Clearinghouse for Hazardous Waste worked for 3 years to pressure McDonald's to replace its polystyrene clamshell sandwich container. McDonald's replaced the clamshell with paper at the end of 1990.

In 1990 McDonald's decided to work with the EDF on the solid waste reduction issue. EDF had a staff of over 110, including scientists, engineers, economists, and attorneys. It also had both a moderate stance on environmental protection and considerable experience in dealing with solid waste issues. The relationship began when Ed Rensi, president of McDonald's U.S.A., accepted EDF President Fred Krupp's invitation to discuss the waste issue. After a number of joint staff meetings, McDonald's and EDF established a joint task force project to study options for reducing McDonald's solid wastes. The task force studied McDonald's operations and its 39 regional distribution centers and visited suppliers and disposal and recycling facilities. Each EDF member also worked for a day in a McDonald's restaurant to gain an appreciation for its operations.

In April 1991 the task force released its final report, presenting its analysis of the solid waste problem and identifying 40 steps that could reduce McDonald's solid wastes by 80 percent.[49] An important part of the task force study was a detailed investigation of McDonald's solid waste generation. The study revealed, for example, that 79 percent by weight of on-premise waste is generated behind the counter. "'The results of the task force far exceed all of our expectations and original goals,' said Keith Magnuson, McDonald's director of operations development and a task force member. 'We started out to study waste reduction options. Instead, we developed a comprehensive waste reduction plan that is already being implemented.' . . . 'The task force has set forth a long-term

---

[46] *The New York Times,* November 20, 1996.
[47] *The New York Times,* November 20, 1996.
[48] See the Chapter 1 case *The Nonmarket Environment of McDonald's.*
[49] The McDonald's Corporation–Environmental Defense Fund Waste Reduction Task Force report is available on EDF's Web site.

vision bolstered by concrete actions to be taken in the short term,' said Dr. Richard Denison, a senior scientist with EDF and a task force member."[50]

The task force study also resulted in changes in McDonald's decision-making criteria. In its purchasing decisions on disposable packaging, McDonald's had considered three factors: availability, functionality, and cost. As a result of the task force study, it added a fourth: waste reduction.

The recommendations of the task force were in four categories: source reduction, reuse, recycling, and composting. The recommendations included action items to be implemented as soon as possible, testing and evaluation of alternatives, and continued R&D. In source reduction, the action items included using recycled unbleached carry-out bags; testing included eliminating lids on in-store drinks and replacing cardboard french-fry holders with paper bags; and R&D included measures to reduce the use of chlorine-bleached paper. Washable shipping containers were to be used for meat and poultry delivery, refillable coffee mugs were to be tested, and bulk condiment dispensers as replacements for individual packages were to be evaluated. Recycling included the recycling of materials, such as corrugated boxes and food contact paper, and the increased use of recycled materials. Studies of the feasibility of composting were conducted at 10 restaurants. Timetables were established for the action items and for some of the testing and evaluation items. In addition, supplier reviews were conducted, and distribution centers were monitored for compliance.

In addition to the specific measures, the task force emphasized instilling a commitment to waste reduction throughout the McDonald's system. Three-quarters of McDonald's 8,500 U.S. restaurants are owned and operated by independent franchisees. In addition, McDonald's has over 100 packaging suppliers. McDonald's has a tradition of standardization and strict enforcement of policies, so institutionalizing the waste-reduction commitment was not difficult. Overall compliance assurance rests with the Environmental Affairs Department, but the commitment is lodged in all areas of its operations, including suppliers and franchisees. McDonald's senior environmental officer reports directly to the board of directors on progress in implementing the task force recommendations.

KODAK AND THE RECYCLING OF SINGLE-USE CAMERAS

At the beginning of the twentieth century the growth of the Eastman Kodak company was propelled by the success of the Brownie camera. Loaded with a 100-exposure film, the Brownie was returned to Kodak for processing of the film. The camera was then reloaded and resold. In 1987 following the resounding success in Japan of Fuji Film's single-use camera, Kodak introduced the first single-use camera in the United States, followed shortly thereafter by a 35mm version which would become the Fun Saver. The cameras sold for $9 to $15 dollars and were similar to the Brownie. Loaded with a 24-exposure 35mm film, the camera containing the film was returned to a film processor, which removed the film and disposed of the camera. The convenience of the single-use cameras made them a huge commercial success, with over 100 million sold throughout the world in 1993. After their initial success, however, environmentalists and other activists protested the waste involved in disposable cameras.

In 1990 Kodak introduced a closed-loop recycling program intended to reuse virtually the entire camera. The cameras had been designed so that consumers would not

[50]McDonald's Corporation press release, April 16, 1991. In contrast to these statements, the original agreement between Mcdonald's and EDF sought options rather than an action plan and contained language allowing for separate opinions to be issued and for either side to withdraw from the project. No separate opinions resulted.

dispose of them, since consumers cannot remove the film from the camera. The recycling program thus focused on film processors. Processors were paid 5 cents for every camera returned, and Kodak paid the shipping costs. The cameras were received and inspected for reusability by a company employing over 200 physically and mentally challenged workers. Some of the cameras were reloaded and resold up to six times, whereas others were disassembled with some of the parts reused and others processed into new components. By 1994 the recycling rate had reached 50 percent, and 33 million cameras had been recycled. The recycling rate would have been higher, but low-volume film processors did not find it worthwhile to collect and store the cameras. Some low-volume processors simply tossed all reusable cameras into the same recycling box, causing Kodak and Fuji to dispose of the other's reusable cameras. In 1995 the two companies agreed to send the cameras they collect to the other company. By 1997 the Kodak program had resulted in the recycling or reuse of 70 million single-use cameras.

In 1992 Kodak extended its recycling program to include film packages, providing film processors with bins to collect packages, canisters, and plastic spools. Because the film processors did not segregate Kodak materials from those of its competitors, Kodak recycles their wastes as well as its own. By 1997 the metal and plastic materials in 1 billion rolls of film had been recycled.

3M AND POLLUTION PREVENTION PAYS

In 1975, 3M Corporation's board of directors adopted a policy committing the company to respect the environment. 3M identified four goals for its environmental programs. The first was to do "what should be done for environmental protection" even if it compromised economic objectives. The second was to reduce current and future liability. The third was to achieve environmental goals through cost-effective means, and the fourth was to improve the quality of products and production processes.[51]

The policy was implemented through 3M's Pollution Prevention Pays program, which by 1997 had prevented 771,000 tons of pollutants. 3M also reported that the program had saved $810 million. The 3P's program had two principal features. One was to reduce pollution at the source through product reformulation, process modification, equipment redesign, and recycling and reuse of waste materials. The second was the involvement of all 3M employees. Employees were encouraged to propose projects, and recognition was given for significant accomplishments. 3M published "Ideas: A Compendium of 3P Success Stories," in which the idea team was recognized and their solution to a specific problem described.[52] The 3P program received awards from the president's Council on Sustainable Development, the National Wildlife Federation's Corporate Conservation Council, and the World Environment Center.

3M has also established an internal Environmental Management System (EMS) that has been implemented at all its facilities worldwide. EMS is directed at compliance with government regulations and at continuous improvement in reducing emissions. By 1996 fines and notices for emissions violations had decreased substantially, and the number of spills had decreased by 62 percent compared to 1990.

3M's policy of reducing pollutants even when it was not required to do so earned it abatement credits in nonattainment areas that it could either sell or use for new

[51]Bringer and Benforado (1989).
[52]Bringer and Benforado (1989) describe the implementation of the 3P's program.

plants. Three times, though, the firm donated the credits to the local pollution control authority rather than sell them. "Top management felt if we sold credits all we would have done is transfer emissions, not reduce them," said Thomas W. Zosel, one of 3M's environmental specialists. "Making money by selling credits was not the purpose of the program. It was to reduce emissions."[53] 3M did take a tax deduction for the donations.

Some environmentalists remained skeptical, however. "They are good salesmen," said Virginia Yingling, chairman of the Sierra Club's chapter in Minnesota. "They are one of the largest polluters in the state. Our impression is they only make changes when it has a good public relations impact or when it looks like the state may take action."[54]

Summary

Environmental protection has broad support among the public, government officials, and the business community. Environmental protection is costly, however, and the more efficient the approach taken to the reduction of pollution the more reduction can be attained for any given expenditure. Conversely, for a given level of pollution reduction, the approach used to achieve that reduction affects the costs that society must bear. The social efficiency approach to environmental protection seeks to minimize the sum of the harm from pollution and the cost of reducing it.

Approaches for achieving socially efficient environmental protection involve market-like mechanisms that provide incentives for efficiency. An emissions tax system imposes a charge on pollutants emitted, which increases the costs of emissions and provides incentives to reduce them. A tradable permits system limits emissions to the number of permits held by the polluter. A polluter with relatively low costs of reducing emissions has an incentive to reduce emissions by more than its permits require and sell the unused permits to another firm that has higher costs of reducing emissions. Both systems provide the incentives to achieve social efficiency. The EPA has used incentive approaches in its bubble, offset, and credits programs, but the first large-scale system in operation was the transferable allowances program for controlling the sulfur dioxide emissions that cause acid rain. The transferable allowances system substantially reduces pollution control costs, benefiting electric power companies and their customers.

Environmental policies such as the transferable allowances system are the product of a political competition in which distributive consequences and efficiency considerations weigh large. The Clean Air Act amendments of 1990 involved bargaining on several specific measures affecting those distributive consequences. On the acid rain provisions, bargaining occured on the distribution of the allowances and on provisions to protect eastern coal miners.

Environmental issues spark a wide range of nonmarket activity in addition to political action at the federal and state levels. At the local level, environmental groups have been increasingly active in addressing environmental issues. The NIMBY movement has grown and become more effective.

---

[53]*The New York Times,* February 3, 1991.

[54]*The New York Times,* February 3, 1991. Despite its accomplishments, 3M Corporation had been one of the nation's largest polluters, emitting 61.3 million pounds of pollutants into the air in 1988. In the EPA's category of chemicals possibly linked to birth defects, 3M was the largest polluter, releasing 52.8 million pounds. 3M pointed out that the EPAs birth defects classification system was based on limited testing of laboratory animals at high concentrations rather than at the concentrations to which people might be exposed.

Environmental protection and compliance are important aspects of managerial responsibility. Firms and their managers must address a variety of nonmarket issues that involve local and national environmental groups, legislators, and regulators. In recent years, a number of firms and environmental groups have developed relationships that allow them to address issues in a nonconfrontational manner. Some firms have worked directly with environmentalists, as in the case of the McDonald's–Environmental Defense Fund project on reducing the company's solid wastes.

Despite these accomplishments, environmental protection remains a source of contention. Environmental protection issues attract the attention of the public and the media and that attention often focuses more on the risks and damage from pollution than on the costs of pollution control. Furthermore, scientific evidence is often limited, which raises concerns about regulations that impose large costs in response to possibly remote hazards.

CASES

Philips and the Low-Mercury Fluorescent Lamp

In June 1997 the Philips Lighting Company, a division of Philips Electronics North America Corporation, a subsidiary of Philips Electronics N.V., held an unusual news conference in Washington, D.C., to announce that it would share with its competitors its technology for producing fluorescent lamps with low-mercury content. Mercury, which is an essential component of fluorescent lamps, is a highly toxic metal that affects the central nervous system and kidneys and like lead can cause brain damage in children and fetuses.[1] Philips was supported by several environmental interest groups that participated in the news conference and praised Philips's action. Velma Smith, executive director of Friends of the Earth, said, "We thank Philips for, once again, taking a leadership role in an area that will lead to significant, meaningful source reductions of mercury in our environment." Robert K. Musil, Ph.D., executive director of Physicians for Social Responsibility, stated "Residual mercury in the environment poses a clear health risk, especially to pregnant women and young children." Michael Bender, executive director of the Coalition of Lamp Recyclers added, "We strongly support the efforts of Philips to promote lamp recycling, and to keep hazardous fluorescent lamps out of municipal incinerators and landfills." Senator John D. Rockefeller IV (D-WV) also participated in the news conference stating that Philips's development of the low-mercury lamp was "a case history of how the system is supposed to work."

THE MERCURY ISSUE

An EPA-commissioned study identified electric light bulbs as the second largest source (behind batteries) of mercury in the solid waste disposal system. Between 500 and 600 million fluorescent lamps are disposed of each year containing an estimated 34 tons of mercury. Larry Wilton, president and CEO of Philips Lighting, stated, "If all the lamps were replaced with low-mercury types, nine tons of mercury would be removed from the hazardous waste stream annually."

In 1990 the EPA prescribed a stringent Toxicity Characteristic Leaching Procedure (TCLP), which is intended to simulate disposal in a landfill to determine whether mercury leaches out from a fluorescent lamp. A fluorescent bulb that does not pass the TCLP test is classified as hazardous waste under the Resource Conservation and Recovery Act and must be disposed of in an approved hazardous waste facility rather than in a municipal landfill.[2] At the time the TCLP test was introduced, Philips scientists in West Virginia had recently succeeded in removing cadmium from its lamps and had begun working on reducing the mercury content. Philips succeeded in developing a new technology that combines a precise amount of mercury with a chemical buffering mechanism. After considerable testing, in June 1995 Philips introduced its ALTO™ lamp which contains less than 10 milligrams of mercury. Philips's lamp was the only one that had passed at all stages of its life the EPA's TCLP test, allowing the lamp to be disposed of in municipal landfills. Conventional fluorescent lamps must be disposed of in toxic waste facilities. Philips distinguished its Alto lamps with bright green end caps and projected that Alto technology would be used in 80 percent of its bulbs by the end of 1997.

A study by the National Electrical Manufacturers Association revealed that the mercury content of a 4-foot fluorescent lamp had decreased from 45.2 milligrams in 1985 to 38.4 milligrams in 1990 to 22.8 milligrams at the end of 1994. The association estimated that by the year 2000 the content would be below 15 milligrams.

[1]"The presence of mercury is essential for fluorescent lamp operation. Electricity must pass through mercury gas in order to produce the ultraviolet energy that is converted to visible light by the phosphor coating." ("Alto Lamp Technology," Philips Lighting Company.)

[2]Exemptions were provided for homes and businesses, which were classified as "conditionally exempt small-quantity generators" if they disposed of less than 100 kilograms of hazardous waste a month.

RECYCLING

Recycling of electric lamps was spurred by the EPA's 1995 Universal Waste Rule, which provided a platform for states to develop regulations for recycling lamps. By mid-1997, 10 states had adopted such regulations and 17 were in the process of formulating regulations.

Recycling had also been stimulated by the disposal cost of fluorescent lamps. Disposal in a hazardous waste landfill could cost up to $1 for a 4-foot lamp, and recycling costs were between 30 and 50 cents. Mercury Technologies of Minnesota charged hardware stores 55 cents for lamps up to 4 feet and 90 cents for longer lamps. Other estimates, however, placed recycling costs at $2 a lamp. Recycling was estimated to account for approximately 5 percent of the lamps disposed of annually. Philips purchased retorted mercury from recyclers.

THE NONMARKET COMPETITION

Philips's principal competitors in fluorescent lamps were General Electric and Osram Sylvania, a unit of Osram GmbH of Germany. The three companies each had approximately one-third of the market. Although Philips's competitors had recently announced low-mercury lamps, their lamps had not passed the TCLP test at all stages of a lamp's life, which required extensive testing data and several years because the bulbs reach the end of their lives.[3] Philips thus had a considerable competitive advantage relative to its competitors.

In 1995 General Electric and Osram Sylvania went to Congress seeking a "conditional exclusion" from the EPA rules to allow their high-mercury bulbs to be disposed of in state-approved municipal landfills. By 1997 their lobbying was believed to be nearing success as congressional pressure on the EPA had led the agency to reconsider its fluorescent lamp rules. At the news conference, Larry Wilton said, "It's time to play by the rules. Providing an exemption for waste that is defined as hazardous by the Environmental Protection Agency's own standards sends exactly the wrong message. It suggests that uncontrolled release of mercury into the environment is not a problem. And it is a disincentive for manufacturers to produce and market products with low-mercury content. We've met the challenge. Other companies should have no excuse for doing the same." He also said, "There is no need to make high-mercury tubes when America can benefit from low-mercury technology. Exempting traditional high-mercury tubes from hazardous waste rules would send the wrong signal." Senator Rockefeller added, "It would be unfair to penalize a company like Philips that invested and innovated to meet EPA requirements. Now that Philips is sharing its technology, there is no reason to have the EPA set aside or waive the standards." Philips produced most of its fluorescent lamps in West Virginia.

In response to the nonmarket strategy of General Electric and Osram Sylvania, Philips developed a counteractive nonmarket strategy. Its objective was to preserve its current market advantage by blocking the efforts of its competitors to obtain a conditional exclusion. The centerpiece of Philips's strategy was to attempt to switch the institutional arena in which the fluorescent lamp disposal issue was addressed. Rather than leave the issue in the arena of the behind-the-scenes congressional-agency relationship, Philips sought to bring the issue into the arena of public sentiment. Philips's strategy was to make the issue public by drawing the attention of politicians, environmental interest groups, and the public to the disposal issue and the strategy of its competitors. At the news conference Larry Wilton directly addressed the strategies of its competitors, "Two years ago, General Electric and Sylvania went begging to Congress for a special break from this mandate. If they take this route again, and if they succeed, they will have no reason to ever market environmentally responsible, low-mercury fluorescent lamps."

By making the issue public, Philips hoped to have three effects. First, making the issue public made it more difficult for some members of Congress to support the relaxation of the EPA's regulation through the grant of a conditional exclusion. Second, Philips sought to enlist the aid of environmental groups in opposing a relaxation, and the presence of several environmental groups at the news conference was testimony to the success of this aspect of its strategy.[4] For example, Robert Musil of Physicians

[3]Fluorescent lamps sold in the United States had a life of approximately 20,000 hours.

[4]Philips could have contacted the major environmental interest groups on its own, but by making the issue public it brought the issue to local environmental groups and to unorganized components of the public who might become interested in the issue.

for Social Responsibility stated, "EPA's proposed exemption is a setback for pollution prevention and public health." Their involvement and pressure on members of Congress and on the EPA would counteract to some extent the pressure from General Electric and Osram Sylvania and their supporters. The environmental groups also had better means of communicating with components of the public than did Philips. By raising health and safety issues in addition to environmental concerns, some members of the public might choose to act. Third, making the issue public could have a positive impact on its market performance if environmentally-sensitive consumers switched to Philips's low-mercury lamps.

In addition to changing the institutional arena, Philips sought to enlist as allies those in its extended rent chain that benefited from the low-mercury lamps. Those beneficiaries included environmentalists whose objectives were served by Philips's nonmarket strategy. The benefits to its conventional rent chain were attested to by the participation of Senator Rockefeller in the news conference. Philips also sought and received the support of the Coalition of Lamp Recyclers.

Another component of Philips's nonmarket strategy was to reduce the pressure coming from its competitors. One means of doing so was to limit their use of industry associations in their pursuit of a conditional exclusion. The National Electrical Manufacturers Association had lobbied for a conditional exclusion from the EPA for General Electric and Osram Sylvania, but Philips broke ranks and the association went silent. Eric Erdheim, senior manager for government affairs of the association, said, "The position of the industry now is that we have no position."

In addition to making the issue public, Philips also had a regulatory objective. It sought to place fluorescent bulbs under the EPA's 1994 Universal Waste Rule which would simplify reporting requirements but would require continued special handling of fluorescent lamps.

Sharing its technology would weaken Philips's current competitive advantage but perhaps not as much as might be imagined. Philips estimated that it would take its competitors at least 3 years and several million dollars to catch up with its technology. Moreover, General Electric and Philips had a cross-licensing agreement that already gave General Electric access to Philips's low-mercury technology, and Osram Sylvania had recently introduced a low-mercury lamp.

One risk in its strategy was that it would be transparent and characterized as such. *The New York Times* in a June 19, 1997, article referred to Philips's strategy as "enviro-politics" and to the news conference as a "media event." The article characterized its offer to share its technology as "the gimmick of seeming to give away its technology." ■

This case was prepared by Professor David P. Baron from public sources and material provided by Philips Lighting Company.

PREPARATION QUESTIONS

1. How effective is Philips's nonmarket strategy likely to be?
2. Was Philips's nonmarket strategy responsible?
3. Were General Electric and Osram Sylvania acting responsibly in seeking a conditional exclusion?

Procter & Gamble and Disposable Diapers

Disposable diapers have been a great product success. American consumers preferred disposable diapers by at least a 4-to-1 ratio over cloth diapers. With an infant using 7,800 diapers during the first 130 weeks, total disposable diaper use was estimated at 18 billion in 1989. Procter & Gamble (P&G) had approximately half the U.S. disposable diaper market, with its Pampers brand slightly outselling its Luvs brand. Disposable diaper sales in the United States represented nearly $2 billion of P&G's $24 billion in revenue. Kimberly-Clark's Huggies brand had increased its market share substantially at P&G's expense, however, and had over 30 percent of the market.

Disposable diapers offered convenience that appealed to dual-career couples in particular. Priscilla Flattery of the Environmental Protection Agency said, "Disposable diapers are just too convenient and too easy. . . . I've never even bought any cloth diapers."[1] Disposable diapers were also said to be superior because their greater absorbency reduces discomfort and diaper rash.

Disposable diapers had come under attack by environmentalists because of the solid waste disposal issue. A Media General–Associated Press poll found that a ban on disposable diapers was favored by 71 percent of the respondents, and a *Wall Street Journal/NBC News* poll found a ban supported by a 3-to-1 ratio. A Gallup Poll found 43 percent favoring a ban and 38 percent favoring a tax on disposable diapers.[2] Only about 9 percent of households had a diaper-age child.

Disposable diapers represented between 3.6 and 5 billion pounds, or between 1 and 2 percent, of the solid waste disposal in landfills. Calling attention to the contribution of disposable diapers to the solid waste disposal problem, activists both raised awareness among consumers and stimulated political activity to limit the use of disposable diapers.

The disposable diaper issue was on the political agenda in several states, but as of 1990 only Nebraska had enacted a law requiring that by 1993 disposable diapers be "biodegradable." (The biodegradable disposable diapers on the market used corn starch in the plastic, and Nebraska was a leading corn-producing state.) P&G had been successful in defeating bills in California and New York that would have required environmental warning labels on disposable diapers. Wisconsin had proposed a tax on disposable diapers, but Kimberly-Clark, which had operations there, mobilized Wisconsin parents to defeat the bill. Many day care centers would not accept children in cloth diapers, but a law passed in Maine required day care centers to accept them.[3]

As part of its strategy for addressing the disposable diaper issue, P&G produced two six-page pamphlets that it mailed to 14 million households.[4] The pamphlets were titled "Answers to Your Questions about the Environment" and "Diapers and the Environment." The latter, "written in patient, junior-high science text prose, seeks to put the environmental uproar in perspective: 'In repeated studies, experts have discovered diapers make up less than two percent of total solid waste in municipal landfills. This means, in the life of a landfill, diapers represent seven weeks of a 10-year lifetime.' Attached to the brochure: discount coupons for Pampers and Luvs."[5] The brochures stated that disposable diapers kept babies drier than cloth diapers and reduced diaper rash. The brochures also pointed out that cloth diapers harmed the environment.

In the market, some consumers turned to cloth diapers and others to "biodegradable" disposables. The National Association of Diaper Services estimated that 750,000 households used cloth diaper services, representing a 38.5 percent increase over the previous year.[6] In some areas, demand outstripped capacity and waiting lists for diaper service grew rapidly.

P&G expressed confidence about the continued market success of disposable diapers. "'We don't think mothers are willing to give up one of the greatest new products of the postwar era,' said Richard R. Nicolusi, the 42-year-old group vice president in charge of P&G's worldwide paper operations. . . . Why should they?' "[7]

Some consumers responded to environmental concerns, however. Some turned to biodegradable disposable diapers. Disposable diapers were mainly wood pulp with plastic inner and outer wrappers. Biodegradable diapers used plastic mixed with cornstarch. When put in landfills, microorganisms, in principle, would consume the corn starch, causing the plastic to break into small pieces. Those pieces do not decompose, however.

Waste disposal experts pointed out that in most landfills there was not enough moisture or oxygen to allow diapers or other solid waste to decompose. The Environmental Marketing Task Force, formed by the attorneys general of eight states, was investigating the marketing claims of one disposable diaper manufacturer and had earlier sued Mobil Oil, forcing it to withdraw its photodegradable claims for its Hefty brand trash bags. About the biodegradability claims for disposable diapers, Hubert H. Humphrey III, attorney general of Minnesota, said, "We have the possibility of having something that makes the oat bran craze look like a Sunday-school picnic."[8]

---

[1] *The Wall Street Journal,* December 26, 1989.
[2] *Peninsula Times Tribune,* June 14, 1990.
[3] *The Wall Street Journal,* June 15, 1990.
[4] *The New York Times Magazine,* September 23, 1990, p. 27.
[5] *The New York Times Magazine,* September 23, 1990, p. 27.
[6] *Peninsula Times Tribune,* June 14, 1990.
[7] *The New York Times Magazine,* September 23, 1990.
[8] *The New York Times,* February 17, 1990.

P&G joined the biodegradability claim issue. "There simply is no data to support the claim of biodegradability," said Scott Stewart, a Procter & Gamble spokesman. "There's no question that this is a deception to consumers."[9] P&G took its contention to the public in the form of a test advertisement in the *Boston Globe* attacking the biodegradability claims. The ad said, "Almost nothing biodegrades in a landfill. That includes every diaper currently on the shelf. Even the ones calling themselves biodegradable." Neither P&G nor Kimberly-Clark had plans to introduce a "biodegradable" diaper.

Environmentalists were also skeptical of the claims. "Biodegradable plastics are perpetuating the myth that it's okay to produce plastic in great quantity and not worry about its effect on the environment," said Richard Denison, senior scientist for the Environmental Defense Fund.[10] Robert J. Samuelson wrote a column in *Newsweek* about the critics who complained about his declaration that he used disposable diapers for his child. "What my critics really resent is that I've denied their moral superiority. Using cloth diapers is an environmental badge, and I've said the badge isn't worth much."[11]

In response to the biodegradability issue P&G hired Arthur D. Little, Inc. to conduct a study of the overall environmental impact of disposable versus cloth diapers. The study reported that disposables used 25.3 pounds of raw materials and generated 22.18 pounds of solid waste, compared with 3.6 pounds and 0.24 pounds for cloth diapers. Cloth diapers used 144 gallons of water compared with 23.6 gallons for disposables, emitted 0.860 pound of air pollutants versus 0.093 pound for disposables, and produced 0.117 pound of water pollutants compared with 0.012 pound for disposables.[12] The study concluded, "Neither disposable nor reusable diapers are clearly superior in the various resource and environmental impact categories considered in this analysis."[13]

The NRDC was also unable to conclude that disposables were better or worse than cloth diapers. Allen Hershkowitz of the NRDC wrote, "We simply can't say that disposables are terrible and reusable diapers are great for the environment, or vice versa. Whatever the choice, there are environmental costs."[14] He added, "People are wrong to think that simply using cloth diapers puts them on a higher moral plateau."[15] Edward Groth III of the Consumers Union conducted a study similar to that of Arthur D. Little and said, "I came to the same conclusion [NRDC] did, i.e., that there is no clear winner and each poses its own set of environmental problems."[16]

The Arthur D. Little study was criticized for some of its methodological assumptions. "We have a lot of questions about the assumptions in the Little study," said Ann Beaudry, a consultant to National Association of Diaper Services. "The study assumes an average of 1.9 cloth diapers per change compared with 1.0 for disposables. . . .People don't routinely double diaper. Those assumptions can have a big impact on the outcome."[17] Hershkowitz also criticized the study for not taking the pesticides used in cotton fields into account.

"The Environmental Protection Agency has endorsed none of the various comparative studies. The E.P.A. 'generally supports the use of cloth diapers because disposables cause so much solid waste,' said Lynda Wynn, a senior staffer on the Municipal Solid Waste Project at the E.P.A. in Washington. But, Wynn continued, the E.P.A. believes that until a scientifically valid 'product life assessment' methodology is devised, no study can be considered definitive. Toward this end, the E.P.A. will assemble an advisory group of industry representatives, ecologists and government experts to work out methods for evaluating the environmental impact of various types of solid waste."[18]

P&G sought in its strategy to relieve what Chairman Edwin L. Artzt called "the guilt people feel about using products they think contribute to the solid-waste problem."[19] P&G announced that it would spend $20 million on research to develop a disposable diaper that would completely decompose into humus when composted. Artzt said, "We're hoping this will help people really understand the solid-waste issue and convince them that something can be done before we're awash in our own garbage."[20]

---

[9] *The Wall Street Journal,* February 7, 1990.
[10] *The Wall Street Journal,* February 7, 1990.
[11] *Newsweek,* April 16, 1990.
[12] *The New York Times,* July 14, 1990.
[13] *The New York Times,* July 14, 1990.
[14] Quoted in "Diapers: The Sequel," by Robert J. Samuelson, *Newsweek,* April 16, 1990.
[15] *The New York Times,* July 14, 1990.
[16] *The New York Times,* July 14, 1990.
[17] *The New York Times,* July 14, 1990.
[18] *The New York Times Magazine,* September 23, 1990, p. 62.
[19] *Business Week,* October 22, 1990.
[20] *Business Week,* October 22, 1990.

Rather than individual composting, P&G advocated industrial composting. Ten industrial composting plants were in operation in the United States, but they accounted for a negligible share of the solid waste disposed of annually. Environmentalists remained skeptical about composting, observing that most solid waste disposal was done by municipalities, and they were likely to skimp on composting by not sorting the waste enough to produce a product that could be sold.

As part of its study of industrial composting, P&G helped finance a contract between the city of Seattle and Baby Diaper Service Company to recycle disposable diapers. The company collected used disposable diapers from 722 households and 33 day care centers and delivered them to an experimental recycling plant. The plant turned the diapers into paper pulp and recycled plastic. Although the output of the plant was not yet being sold, the pulp could be used by paper mills. "Highgrade pulp is the 'cash crop' of disposable diaper recycling" said Nancy Eddy, a microbiologist for P&G. "Though it can be used for flower pots, garbage bags and a host of other uses, the prices for recycled plastic—when you can sell it at all—are still way below the costs of recovery."[21] ■

[21] *The New York Times Magazine,* September 23, 1990, p. 64.

PREPARATION QUESTIONS

1. Evaluate the components of P&G's strategy for addressing the disposable diaper issue. What is its overall strategy?
2. What is the nature of the politics of disposable diapers? What should P&G do about the politics of disposable diapers?
3. What should P&G do about its diapers? In Europe, P&G marketed a "biodegradable" diaper using cornstarch. Should it introduce that diaper in the United States?

Westlands Water District

Westlands Water District, of Fresno, California, was the largest agricultural water delivery agency in the United States. Part of California's Central Valley Project (CVP), Westlands covered nearly 1,000 square miles of the naturally arid San Juaquin Valley. About 85 percent of CVP water went to farmers, and 15 percent to cities and wildlife. Westlands was organized under state law in 1952 at the request of farmers and landowners who needed a surface water supply to supplement the area's dwindling groundwater supplies. The law provided for the election of a governing board of directors by the landowners in the district, with each landowner voting according to the assessed value of his or her land. The nine-member board oversaw budgetary, fiscal, and operational matters. Westlands' staff was charged with carrying out the policies, rules, and regulations adopted by the board.

Delivery of surface water from the Sierra Nevada Mountains to Westlands farmers began in the 1960s after Westlands secured from the federal government rights to a specified portion of the water. The agricultural consequences included significant increases in acreage, yields, and crop diversity. Because Westlands water was acquired from the federal government and sold to farmers at below-market rates, many California farmers had chosen to grow water-intensive crops (e.g., rice, alfalfa, cotton) in what would otherwise be a virtual desert.[1] By 1992 more than 40 crops valued at over $615 million were produced in the Westlands district alone. Westlands's customers included some of America's wealthiest farmers.

Media accounts often focused on the environmental consequences of Westlands and its customers' water use. For example, selenium-engorged runoff from farms supplied by Westlands had drained into Kesterson Wildlife Refuge, polluting a wetlands retreat for migratory waterfowl and killing thousands of birds since the 1970s. Likewise, Westlands's heavy pumping from the Sacramento River had been a major factor in the collapse of the river's

[1] Central Valley Project farmers paid water prices in the range of $12 to $35 per acre foot. In contrast, during a recent drought the city of Santa Barbara invested in a desalinization plant to help alleviate its shortage at a cost estimated at more than $1,000 per acre foot. Other estimates of water prices in California's urban areas ranged from $400 to $600 per acre foot.

populations of federally protected chinook salmon and delta smelt.

Westlands did not deny that it had some wealthy customers nor that its policies had caused some environmental harm. However, it argued that the most common criticisms were misleading. For instance, as water supplies increased in the 1960s, so did the number of farmers receiving water. Since 1968 the total number of landowners in the district had nearly tripled, whereas the average acreage per farm had been reduced by more than 50 percent. Furthermore, Westlands had expended $8 million since 1986 in an effort to solve drainage problems. These expenditures had funded research on biological processes to remove selenium from drainage water and experimentation with deep-well injection techniques as a potential disposal technology for selenium runoff.

For years Westlands had joined its larger and wealthier agribusiness customers in assorted legal and political strategies aimed at defeating, but settling for diluting, major environmental laws. These included the reauthorization of the Endangered Species Act and the passage of the National Environmental Policy Act (NEPA). Among other things NEPA directed federal agencies to include in any policy recommendation "a finding that the environmental impact of the proposal had been studied and that unavoidable adverse environmental effects were justified by other considerations of national policy." As a practical matter, the stringent requirements for legally acceptable environmental impact statements (EISs) often delayed for years the adoption of policies that involved economic development. ElSs had therefore become powerful legal and political weapons of environmentalists, whereas Westlands (and many other businesses) had consistently opposed EISs in theory and in practice.

In 1992 after years of intense politics, Congress passed another major law affecting California water usage: the Central Valley Project Improvement Act. This law covered a wide range of environmental and agricultural issues, including:

- Prohibiting the renewal of existing long-term water contracts until a comprehensive environmental impact statement was complete
- Making available more water for urban areas and less to the Central Valley
- Instituting a plan to redistribute 600,000 acre feet of federal water from farmers to restore wetlands and fish habitats damaged by irrigation and other farming practices
- Adopting protection, restoration, and enhancement of fish and wildlife resources as a purpose of the CVP; creating a $50 million per year environmental fund to be collected mainly from CVP water and power customers; and prohibiting new contracts entirely until the goal of doubling the number of salmon and striped bass was met

In 1994 Westlands implemented a bold nonmarket strategy in U.S. District Court in Fresno. Before a judge, 19 lawyers, and a handful of farmers, Westlands attorney Toni Birmingham argued that the government—which, under the new law, was to begin redirecting the water to the damaged habitats within weeks—had violated the environmental impact statement requirements of the NEPA. More specifically, Birmingham argued that the ground would sink because farmers would resort to pumping out groundwater to substitute for the lost federal water and that the air in the Central Valley would become dusty because farmers would not have enough water to moisten the ground. Environmentalists were outraged. Asked by the judge whether the public interest was better served by protecting the farmers' environment or that of endangered species, the Westlands attorney said, "Your honor, it is inconceivable that the public interest will not be best served by requiring the government to obey the law."

On April 28, 1994, Judge Oliver W. Wanger ruled in favor of Westlands: The government could not impose new environmental restrictions on farmers' practices because it had not filed an EIS as required by NEPA. Implementation was expected to be delayed for years. A spokesman for Westlands, Don Upton, hailed the ruling: "It's totally in line with federal law." ■

PREPARATION QUESTIONS

1. What is the socially efficient means of allocating water between agriculture and urban areas? How should environmental considerations be taken into account?
2. Is Westlands's nonmarket strategy of turning to the courts after losing in Congress responsible?
3. Is Westlands's demand that an EIS be conducted any different from an environmental group's demand that an EIS be conducted?

PART III

Integrative Case

Whirlpool and Energy Efficiency Standards (A): Regulation and Politics

Differences in interest groups, regulatory institutions, and politics across the states had resulted in a mishmash of state-specific, energy efficiency regulations. This lack of uniformity imposed significant costs on manufacturers, and the costs were largely passed on to consumers. In 1987 the National Appliance Energy Conservation Policy Act was enacted to address this problem by delegating to the Department of Energy the authority to establish uniform national energy efficiency standards. States in effect exchanged some of their standard-setting autonomy for federal uniformity and, presumably, for gains to manufacturers and consumers in the form of lower production costs, lower prices, and lower energy costs. Implicit in the deal was the expectation that the Department of Energy would enact standards in a timely manner and an acceptable form. Standards for refrigerators were established effective in 1990.

PRIVATE REGULATION

In June 1992 a consortium of environmentalists and state utility companies known as SERP (Super-Efficient Refrigerator Program) announced that it would award a $30 million prize to the company that could propose the best design for, and plan to mass market, a super-efficient refrigerator. Entries were to be standard refrigerator size, defrost automatically, use no CFCs (chloroflorocarbons) in the insulation, be moderately priced, yet exceed 1993 government efficiency standards by at least 25 percent. Finally, to receive the prize—or, to SERP sponsors, the "Golden Carrot"—the winner had to sell its refrigerators. The prize was to be used to fund a rebate program in the SERP territories.

One objective of the SERP sponsors was not just to reduce pollution by reducing energy consumption but also to demonstrate that, given appropriate incentives, companies could work with utilities and environmental groups to bring about a "market transformation." That is, the hope was to bring about permanent changes in consumer preferences, product design, and manufacturing infrastructure. Energy efficiency was a key to pollution reduction, and approximately two-thirds of sulfur dioxide emissions and one-third of carbon dioxide emissions resulted from producing electricity. Refrigerators were among the biggest consumers of electricity in the home. If a market transformation could be demonstrated in this industry, then others would follow, the sponsors believed.

SERP attracted over 500 entries from 14 manufacturers. Over a period of months, contestants were first winnowed to 14 semifinalists and then to two finalists: Whirlpool Corporation and Frigidaire Home Products. After thorough consideration of both entries, Whirlpool was selected as the winner in June 1993. Whirlpool was initially secretive about the magnitude of its efficiency gain, but eventually it became public knowledge that the figure was approximately 40 percent.

INDUSTRY LEADERSHIP

Whirlpool had long been an industry leader in energy-efficient appliances, so its success in the SERP competition was not surprising. Similarly, Whirlpool had exercised nonmarket leadership by helping to found the Association of Home Appliance Manufacturers (AHAM). Nevertheless, the company faced a series of significant and interrelated market and nonmarket challenges.

Market Challenges

Whirlpool's SERP refrigerator was not a low-end product. The side-by-side units were expected to be priced at $1,000 to $1,400, which was in the same range as comparable nonenergy-efficient models. Prior to rollout, a Whirlpool spokesperson was optimistic, with qualifications, "We don't anticipate any difficulties selling these because they will be comparably priced." He continued, "The big challenge will be selling them in the non-SERP markets where there is no rebate."

After SERP ran its course, claims about its success were mixed. David Goldstein of the Natural Resources Defense Council, an early and major proponent of SERP, stated, "The ultimate goal was to transform the market so that super-efficient, environmentally friendly models were the only ones to get sold. That has been achieved almost beyond our wildest hopes. . ."[1] A systematic study by an analyst for the Long Island Lighting Company (LILCO) offered a much different assessment:

- Other manufacturers were not building SERP models.
- SERP probably did not influence efficiency levels other than for Whirlpool, since the design changes that had allowed other companies to achieve 15 to 20 percent improvements predated the SERP contest.
- Comparisons of the overall efficiency of refrigerators sold in SERP versus non-SERP markets indicate no difference, in spite of the fact that SERP sales were subsidized by the rebate program in the SERP market.[2]

Perhaps the most telling assessment was that of Whirlpool, whose director of environmental and regulatory programs, Vincent Anderson, said, "We assume MT [market transformation] means a permanent change that exists after the program ceases. Consumer preferences are shifted, manufacturing infrastructure is altered, and undoing this permanent change is not feasible. Based on these assumptions, our experience so far is that SERP is not MT."[3]

Nonmarket Challenges

In early August 1994—approximately a year after Whirlpool was awarded the SERP contract—a large coalition of state agencies, manufacturers, and environmentalists concluded a 2-year series of discussions. In spite of the diversity of interests represented, the parties agreed on a resolution to improve the efficiency of all refrigerators produced in 1999 and thereafter by approximately 30 percent. In 1992 Whirlpool and other members of AHAM had started investigating the feasibility of beginning regulatory negotiations in response to the Department of Energy's forthcoming iteration of energy efficiency standards in 1995.[4] The agreement that emerged from these negotiations was viewed as a significant commitment on the part of manufacturers to increase their production of environmentally friendly appliances. In a November press conference in San Francisco, the agreement was announced with considerable fanfare. Among the par-

[1]Con.WEB, "SERP's Lasting Legacy: Super Efficient Refrigerator Program Ends With Mixed Near-Term Results, Major Long-Term Impacts," July 25, 1997. (Con.WEB is sponsored by several Northwest power companies.)

[2]LILCO had been an enthusiastic member of SERP and thus might have been expected to offer a favorable assessment. The study also pointed out that Whirlpool had decided to drop its line of SERP-clone refrigerators that it had marketed in non-SERP territories. The reason was poor sales attributable in part to the absence of a rebate. (Peter Valcenbach, "Trying Hard to Prove SERP's Market Impact," Association of Energy Services Professionals News.)

[3]"Whirlpool's Viewpoint: Where Do We Go From Here?" www.dnai.com

[4]A new rule pertaining to refrigerator standards took effect in January 1990. Federal law required a 5-year period between the effective starting dates of energy efficiency rules; hence, manufacturers anticipated the next iteration of regulation would occur sometime in 1995 and sought to develop an industry agreement that could be proposed as a possible efficiency rule.

ties who presented the resolution at the press conference were members from AHAM, the National Resource Defense Council (NRDC), and an undersecretary of the Department of Energy (DOE).[5] Secretary of Energy Federico F. Pena extolled the agreement stating, "Not to steal from the President, but we're building a fridge to the future." An aide chimed in that the agreement meant the end of the cold war.[6]

The new standards were estimated by DOE to save the owners of a new refrigerator $20 per year, and DOE stated that the rate of return on the $80 estimated additional cost of a refrigerator would be 20 percent a year. Consumers, however, may have had a different view. "In consumer surveys, energy efficiency consistently ranks behind other factors such as convenience, size, reliability and color. Energy efficiency 'isn't in the top five by a long shot,' says Earl Jones, senior counsel of GE Appliances, a unit of General Electric Co.[7]

Although the unity of the diverse coalition brightened the prospects for rapid rule making, the broader political setting was more complicated. Regulators in the Department of Energy had been appointed by President Clinton, who was pleased with the agreement. In the spring of 1995 the Department of Energy published a proposed rule in the *Federal Register* that replicated the November agreement almost to the letter. The rule would require manufacturers by the year 2000 to produce refrigerators that exceeded 1993 government efficiency standards by 30 percent (SERP's standard was 25 percent). Additionally, other federal regulations required producers to redesign their refrigerators by 2003 to comply with the Clean Air Act that banned the use of HCFC-141b in refrigerators after 2003.[8]

[5]Representatives from the Department of Energy had been present at the meetings that had led up to the industry agreement and had served as regulatory and legal consultants throughout the negotiations. It was generally assumed that following the press conference in November 1994, the resolution would immediately be published in the *Federal Register* as a proposed rule.

[6]*The New York Times,* April 24, 1997.

[7]*The Wall Street Journal,* April 23, 1997.

[8]HCFC-141b was commonly used in foaming insulation in refrigerators. To ease the transition away from HCFC-141b, the rule would allow efficiency standards to drop from a 30 percent improvement over 1993 standards to a 23 percent improvement for refrigerators produced in 2003. These lower standards would stay in place until 2006, at which time all refrigerators would have to conform to the 30 percent improvement standard.

Tensions also existed beneath the surface of the so-called unified coalition, both between environmental and industry groups and potentially within the appliance industry. Whirlpool had not only incurred significant sunk costs in anticipation of the forthcoming 2000 standards but was also an outspoken advocate for achieving the most technologically advanced (yet economically feasible) standards for energy efficiency. Given a product line tailored to meet the forthcoming efficiency standards, Whirlpool was better positioned to reap the benefits of stringent regulation than were other members of AHAM.

An Electoral Shock

In a historic election in November 1994, Republicans took control of both houses of Congress for the first time in 40 years. Most Republicans (and many Democrats who reflected on the election results) were committed to some measure of deregulation. Congress as a whole had just become more sympathetic to those companies that opposed the Department of Energy's standard-setting program.

The Republicans in Congress made several bold moves in their attempt to limit what they viewed as unnecessary government intrusion in the marketplace. Appliance manufacturers rushed in to attempt to forestall, or prevent entirely, rule making on energy efficiency. Heavy lobbying efforts were mounted by almost every signatory of the November agreement. The objective was to persuade legislators to intervene in the rule-making process to prevent the implementation of any new efficiency standards, such as those endorsed just prior to the election. AHAM now claimed that the standards in the coalition agreement were virtually impossible to achieve by the DOE's proposed date. The group also complained about the costs associated with the massive retooling required by 2003 to manufacture products that would comply with the Clean Air Act.

On Capitol Hill

In the House, Congressman Mike Parker (R-MI) was prepared to introduce an amendment to the House Interior Appropriations bill that would cut $12.8 million from the Department of Energy's $16.4 million budget item for standard setting and also expressly prohibit any appropriated funds to be used for energy efficiency standards.[9] The amendment, in

[9]Parker was a Democrat prior to the election. He became a Republican immediately afterwards.

effect, called for a 1-year moratorium on energy efficiency rule making.

In the Senate, Mitch McConnell (R-KY) introduced an amendment to a Senate Appropriations bill that also provided for a 1-year moratorium. Excerpts from Senator McConnell's speech on the Senate floor captured the political winds buffeting the issues Whirlpool confronted:

> If we do not pass this amendment, and the proposed DOE regulations are adopted, consumers will see their range of choices sharply limited—almost to the point of legalized monopoly—and workers could see their plants shut down, almost overnight. . .
>
> Companies that make these basic household appliances are facing enormous costs because of the new standards. Manufacturing processes and product designs will have to be drastically altered. In some cases, entire product lines will simply be abandoned, and the employees who make them will be dumped out on the streets. . .
>
> Consumers who rely on these kinds of basic household appliances will face a drastic reduction in choice, along with steep increases in price, as manufacturers scramble to meet the new standards coming out of Washington.[10]

The Iowa delegation—Senators Tom Harkin (D) and Charles Grassley (R)—echoed McConnell's sentiments. Harkin was especially alarmed by the anticompetitive aspects of the proposed rule.

Interest Group Reactions

The National Association of Regulatory Utility Commissioners (NARUC) decried the proposals for a 1-year moratorium. Endorsing the DOE's proposed rule, the association said that the department's earlier actions had "saved residential consumers about $2 billion in their energy bills. . . net savings are expected to grow to $130 billion over the lifetime of the products covered by these standards.[11]

The California Energy Commission, along with its counterparts in other states, was alarmed and outraged at the proposals for a moratorium. Its officials stated outright what Whirlpool executives believed: that manufacturers had reneged on their commitment, and, likewise, that the federal government was reneging on the deal implicit in the 1987 National Appliance Energy Conservation Policy Act. The commission adopted a resolution supporting the DOE's efforts, arguing that the "efforts in Congress to eliminate or restrict the ability of the U.S. Department of Energy . . . are inconsistent with the agreement underlying California's support for any level of state preemption."[12] If, as seemed increasingly likely, Congress was about to renege on the deal by nullifying the rule-making process, then states would be compelled to seek the return of their rule-making authority. Indeed, California went so far as to begin its own standard-setting procedure for florescent lamp ballasts.

Whirlpool was reeling from the backpedaling in the policy arena. Having invested heavily in what its managers believed was not only a good product but also good public policy, it now faced the prospect of incurring policy-based losses on its investment. Whirlpool was in a good position to refute AHAM's claims about prohibitively high costs, since its prize-winning SERP refrigerator exceeded the 1993 government standards by 40 percent. Mike Thompson, Whirlpool's director of government relations, was quick to wave the green flag, stating that manufacturers had agreed to standards that "would benefit both consumers and the environment" and that the industry had "an ethical obligation to fulfill the terms of the agreement."[13] ■

[10]*Congressional Record,* August 9, 1995, S12023-5. McConnell also quantified the costs of standards for a specific refrigerator company at $187 million in the short term and another $100 million to shut down a facility, and noted that only one manufacturer supported the regulations.

[11]*Ibid.*

[12]Behrens, Lisa. *Inside Energy/with Federal Lands.* "Congress' Action on Appliance Standards May Prompt States to Act," August 14, 1995.

[13]*HFN The Weekly Newspaper for the Home Furnishing Network.* "Whirlpool Standing Alone; Against other industry members who want to oppose federal energy standards for refrigerators," November 6, 1995.

PREPARATION QUESTIONS

1. Did Whirlpool employ an integrated strategy in its decision to enter the SERP contest and/or to develop an energy-efficient line of products? If so, what are the nonmarket components of its strategy? If not, what should have been its nonmarket components?
2. Whirlpool was a founding member of AHAM and had a history of working effectively in and with the organization. What should Whirlpool do about AHAM's stance and activities on rule making and legislation in 1995? (Other regulatory issues on the Department of Energy's agenda include nationwide standards for washing machines—where the company also expected to have a market advantage.)
3. Construct two profiles of legislators: one of which describes the characteristics of the Congress members Whirlpool should contact and the other describes which members it should not bother. Are there any general principles of strategy that emerge from this exercise? If Whirlpool chooses to become active in lobbying Congress, what kind of political allies should it look for and why?
4. Formulate a coordinated nonmarket strategy for Whirlpool in the rule-making and legislative arenas.
5. What is the likely outcome of the moratorium proposal? What regulatory policy will likely be in place, say, by the end of 1997?

PART IV

Global Business and the Nonmarket Environment

CHAPTER 13

The Political Economy of Japan

Introduction

Nonmarket strategies are a function of the characteristics of the market and nonmarket environments, and because those environments can differ among countries, nonmarket strategies must be tailored to individual countries. This chapter provides a framework for nonmarket strategy formulation using as the context the nonmarket environment of Japan. The emphasis is on political economy—the interaction between government and interests—and on strategies for addressing nonmarket issues. Chapters 14 and 15 present similar analyses of the European Union and China, respectively.

Culturally, Japan is relatively homogeneous, which facilitates the structuring of political and social activity. Cultural homogeneity is a consequence of a variety of factors, including Japanese isolation prior to 1853, its resistance to immigration, the absence of fundamental religious differences, relatively small regional differences, and a uniform national education system. This relative homogeneity combines with tradition to generate a system in which consultation and consensus are easier to achieve and sustain than they are in many western nations. Nevertheless, interests are often in conflict, and the willingness to sacrifice for the sake of tradition or for the good of the nation may be diminishing. The pluralism of interests in Japan is sufficiently diverse that those interests are increasingly difficult to bring into agreement, and change is continuous if not always rapid.

A conventional perspective on understanding the market and nonmarket environments in a country is based on cultural and historical explanations for political and social structure. For the purposes of managing in the nonmarket environment and addressing specific nonmarket issues affecting the performance of firms, cultural and historical explanations operate at too aggregate a level to be satisfactory for effective management. On specific issues, interests are the primary driving forces of outcomes, and thus those interests and their actions must be the focus of analysis. Culture and history remain important, but their role is in providing stability to political and social relationships and institutions. Interests and issues change more rapidly than culture and history, and the alignment of interests is specific to the nonmarket issue. The pluralism of interests then implies that the framework of structured pluralism introduced in Chapter 6 is the starting point for understanding the environment of business in a country.[1] That framework—modified to fit Japan—provides a basis for understanding the

[1]Curtis (1975, p. 60–61) provides an early discussion of the pluralism of interests in the business community in Japan. See also Muramatsu and Krauss (1987).

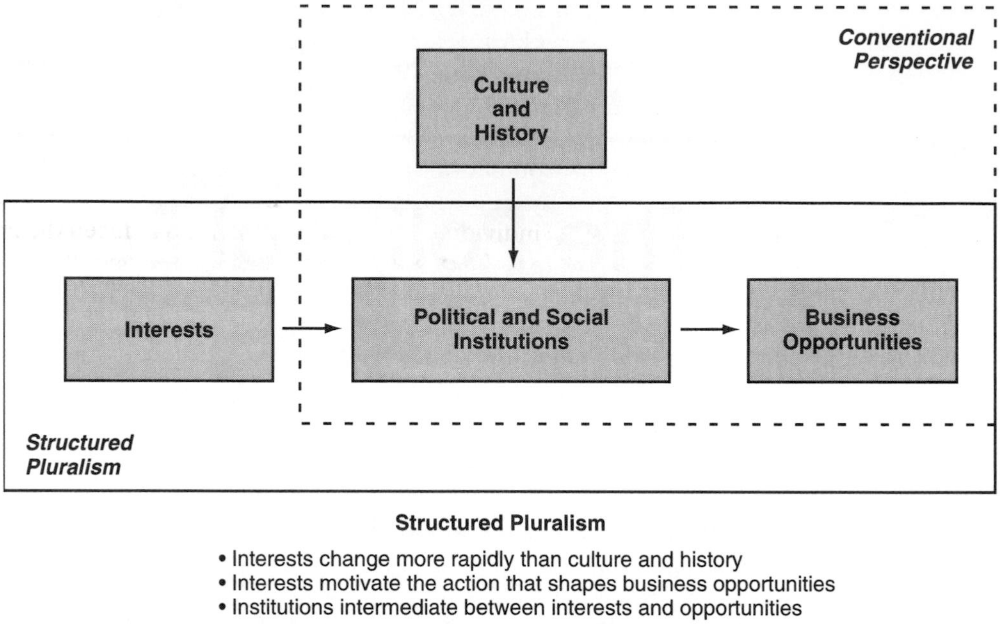
Conventional Perspective
Culture and History
Interests
Political and Social Institutions
Business Opportunities
Structured Pluralism
Structured Pluralism
• Interests change more rapidly than culture and history
• Interests motivate the action that shapes business opportunities
• Institutions intermediate between interests and opportunities

FIGURE 13–1 Structured Pluralism and Culture

Japanese nonmarket environment and how business addresses nonmarket issues in the context of political and social institutions. This perspective is illustrated in Figure 13-1.

The political economy of Japan is complex and requires a more complete treatment than can be given here. The focus thus is on a characterization of the nonmarket environment in terms of the four I's—issues, interests, institutions, and information—and the cultural underpinnings of the interactions between interests and government. The organization of business in Japan differs from that in the United States because of a set of long-term relationships, many of which are supported by patterns of interlocking ownership among firms in a group headed by a major bank or industrial corporation. These *keiretsu* provide benefits for their members, ranging from mutual adjustment to changing circumstances to protection from the market for control. Companies in Japan also develop a set of relationships with political officeholders and the bureaucracy. Some of these relationships are formalized by a system of advisory committees and consultative processes. Others are developed and maintained through political contributions, the hiring of retired bureaucrats, and personal connections. Firms not only develop relationships but also develop the ability to monitor government activities to obtain the information needed to interact effectively with the political parties, the Diet, and the bureaucracy. These relationships provide the foundations for lobbying, electoral, and coalition-building strategies and for their integration with market strategies.

The chapter cases *The Breakup of Nippon Telephone and Telegraph?* and *Toys 'R' Us in Japan (A)* provide opportunities for analysis and strategy formulation in the context of this framework.

Issues

At the end of the 1990s, the principal systemic level issues in the political economy of Japan centered on deregulation of the economy, a massive financial crisis, a stagnant economy, Japan's large trade surplus, and political reform and stability. Japan also faced serious demographic problems. Its population is aging; by 2020, 27.4 percent of the population will be 65 and older. Their retirement and health care costs will have to be borne by a shrinking workforce. Moreover, the birth rate is low, and if it does not increase the population could dwindle from 125 million in 1998 to 55 million in 2100, according to one government forecast.

At the organizational level, issues include the further opening of domestic markets to international competition, the evolution of antitrust policy and more aggressive enforcement, and specific legislative and deregulation measures pertaining to particular industries. At the individual level, managers in Japan faced the challenge of developing strategies to address the proposed measures in the context of a stagnant economy and foreign pressure for more rapid economic reforms.

As an example, the financial services industry in Japan is heavily regulated by the Ministry of Finance (MOF). That industry faces a set of issues arising from within the industry and outside the country. Japan's foreign trade surplus and the difficulty foreign firms have in entering the Japanese market generated continuing pressure for change. Much of the pressure came from the United States and other countries, and the financial services markets were gradually being opened. Some liberalization of the insurance industry, for instance, had resulted from external pressure that caused the governing parties to allow entry into the auto and commercial fire insurance markets. In 1995 Japan and the United States reached an agreement that allowed a broader set of foreign firms to compete for the management of Japan's $1 trillion pension fund market—a market in which only trust banks and insurance companies had been allowed to operate.

Reform in financial services was complicated by a financial crisis that required a massive government bailout. The MOF was blamed for not having dealt with the source of the crisis—speculative real estate investments during the 1980s financed by loans from financial institutions. Moreover, a major scandal involving MOF personnel had undermined its credibility and its ability to implement reforms, such as making the Bank of Japan completely independent of the ministry.

Internally, a major issue facing the financial services industry was the government's huge postal savings system, which was a principal competitor to banks in Japan. The postal savings system offered high interest rates on deposits and low interest rates on loans, providing what was viewed as unfair competition for banks. The postal savings system had $2 trillion in deposits, and $800 billion in insurance policies. The banking industry opposed the postal savings system and urged privatization, but the Ministry of Posts and Telecommunications, which supervised the system, and the postmasters, who generate grassroots pressure against reform, blocked change.

Interests

Interests in Japan are pluralistic, as they are in the United States. In the United States, however, coalitions are fluid and often issue specific, and interactions with the government are often episodic. In Japan, interests are also varied, but coalitions in Japan are less fluid and patterns of interaction with government are structured by formal and informal long-term relationships. If Japanese businesses disagree on a trade issue, they are much more likely to seek consensus within industry and general business associations and with the government and are less likely to contest the issue in public. Business, however, is not a unified interest group in its interactions with government. Its interactions with government are conducted by peak organizations, such as the Keidanren (Federation of Economic Organizations), *keiretsu* (business groups), industry associations, and individual firms. In the business sector, the interlocking ownership in *keiretsu* results in complex aggregations of interests that cannot be as issue specific as they are in the United States.

The interactions among business, the governing political parties, and the bureaucracy are complex and intermediated by a set of formal and informal arrangements. Advisory committees established by government ministries facilitate communication, policy formulation, and consensus between the bureaucracy and interest groups on issues. The career path links between the political parties and the bureaucracy facilitate interactions between them. Many high-ranking bureaucrats take positions in business or seek elected office after they retire, which facilitates the coordination of nonmarket activity.

Japan does not have an encompassing labor organization as do countries such as Sweden and Germany. In Japan, employees of large corporations are unionized, but those unions tend to represent workers at a single enterprise. These enterprise unions are linked in federations and associations, but union members in Japan identify with both their employer and their union.[2] Enterprise unions are not required by law, but evolved in the 1950s as a result of conflict between business and national unions, which had adopted a radical posture. Business defeated the national unions, and most workers organized into enterprise unions and focused on employment-specific matters, although some radical elements remain.

Japan has organized interest and activist groups, but in contrast to the United States they are fewer in number, less active, and more cautious. Dispersed groups, such as consumers and urban residents, are neither well organized nor are they broadly represented. Their direct influence in the nonmarket environment is thus limited, but political parties appeal to their interests to garner electoral support.

Institutions

The Japanese governmental system was modeled after the British parliamentary system, but it has uniquely Japanese characteristics and an overlay of American-style institutions. The country has 47 prefectures, each headed by a governor, and each has its own government—as do cities and municipalities. The powers of the prefecture governments, however, are considerably less extensive than those of state governments in the United States.[3] The principal institutions of Japanese government are the Diet, the bureaucracy, and the electoral and party systems. In addition to its parliamentary structure, Japan has a constitution that guarantees individual rights and a supreme court that has the power to declare laws unconstitutional.

THE DIET (PARLIAMENT)

The government is parliamentary, so the executive and the legislature are aligned. The Diet is composed of two houses with unequal powers.[4] The lower house, the House of Representatives, elects the prime minister and is the more powerful and the focus of most legislative activity. For example, it can enact legislation by a two-thirds vote even if the upper house disapproves it. The upper house, the House of Councilors, also has some powers and can block legislation unless overridden by a two-thirds vote in the lower house. The lower house can vote no confidence in the prime minister, which requires him to either resign or dissolve the lower house and call new elections. The Liberal Democratic Party (LDP) had been in continuous control of the lower house since 1955, but as a result of scandals and its failure to enact electoral reforms, it lost its majority in 1993. Several groups of dissident LDP members split from the party, resulting

[2]In spite of the system of enterprise unions, wages for workers at large companies are negotiated in the annual spring *shunto* that involves federations of unions and the federation of employers.
[3]See Redd (1986).
[4]See Baerwald (1974).

in party fragmentation and shifting government coalitions. The LDP, however, remained the largest party and returned to office shortly thereafter.

The lower house has 500 members. Electoral reform enacted in 1994 replaced the multimember districts by a system in which 300 members are elected from single-member districts and 200 members are elected under a proportional representation system. Elections are scheduled every 4 years, but under the parliamentary system the prime minister may call an early election. The upper house has 252 members who serve 6-year terms, with half elected every 3 years. One hundred "national constituency" members of the upper house are elected at large through a proportional representation system. The rest are elected by prefectures, each of which has at least two seats, so there is an election in every prefecture every 3 years.

In a parliamentary system, a government serves with the consent of the parliament—with the support of a majority of the members of the Diet. A majority party can thus form the government, but in the absence of a majority party, a coalition of parties is required. In forming a coalition government, parties bargain over the allocation of ministries among the parties, the selection of the prime minister, and the principal policies the government will implement.

The government is of the cabinet form, with the cabinet assuming collective responsibility for policy. The cabinet consists of the ministers who head the principal ministries plus the heads of a few other agencies, such as the Economic Planning Agency. The prime minister has few formal powers but plays a number of roles, including convenor of the cabinet, spokesman for the government, and representative of the nation in international affairs. The prime minister does not have formal powers with regard to legislation, as the U.S. president has through the veto. The prime minister consults with the coalition parties and, at times, with opposition leaders, before taking major initiatives. Decisions often await the development of consensus.

The Japanese approach is to achieve consensus within the cabinet before legislation is proposed or major policies adopted. To reach consensus, the government consults with interest groups, the bureaucracy, and on some issues with opposition parties.

The houses of the Diet have a committee structure. The lower house has 19 standing committees, twelve of which correspond to the principal ministries, as indicated in Figure 13-2.[5] In addition to dealing with the budget, the Budget Committee serves as a forum for questioning the cabinet about policies. Diet committees have relatively small staffs, and many staff members are provided by the ministries themselves. Since much of the major legislation is written in the ministries, the Diet committees have traditionally been viewed as relatively weak compared with the bureaucracy. During the past decade, however, the Diet has exercised more power than in the past, and committees have begun to play a more significant role.

POLITICAL PARTIES AND THE ELECTORAL SYSTEM

The 1994 electoral reform could in the long run have an important effect on the number of political parties in Japan and the nature of political competition. Single-member, plurality-winner districts provide incentives for a two-party system so as to avoid wasting votes on third-party candidates.[6] At the end of the 1990s, however, the number and composition of parties were still in flux. Existing parties had splintered, new parties formed and many dissolved, and a variety of coalitions had formed. Several members

---

[5]The upper house has 16 standing committees.

[6]Duverger's (1954) law predicts that single-member districts will result in two-party competition, since with three or more parties some votes will be wasted. A proportional representation system can, in principle, sustain more parties.

Bureaucracy	***LDP***	***Diet***
Ministries	***PARC Divisions***	***Committees***
Agriculture, Forestry, Fisheries	Agriculture, Forestry, Fisheries	Agriculture, Forestry, Fisheries
Construction	Construction	Construction
Education	Educational Affairs	Education
Finance	Finance	Finance
Foreign Affairs	Foreign Affairs	Foreign Affairs
Health and Welfare	Social Affairs	Social and Labor Affairs
Local Autonomy	Local Administration	Local Administration
Internatinal Trade and Industry	Commerce and Industrial	Commerce and Industry
Justice	Judicial Affairs	Judicial Affairs
Labor	Labor	Social and Labor Affairs
Posts and Telecommunications	Communication	Communications
Transport	Transportation	Transport
Defense Agency	Cabinet Affairs	Cabinet
Science and Technology Agency	National Defense	Science and Technology
Economic Planning Agency	Science and Technology	Environment
	Environment	Budget
		Audit
		Rules and Administration
		Discipline

FIGURE 13–2 Parallel Organization

of the LDP had left the party to form new parties, and those parties had formed the opposition. The opposition was motivated by the desire for reforms of the economy and the political system. Thus, both the largest party and the principal opposition party were composed of politicians with the same LDP background. In addition to these parties, Japan has a communist party, a small socialist party, and a party backed by a Buddhist sect. In 1995 in most of the 13 elections for prefecture governor, all parties except the communists backed the same candidate.

Electoral reform was spurred by scandals involving large contributions by businesses to the LDP and other political parties. One of the rationales for establishing single-member districts was to eliminate the competition for votes and funds among members of the same party, which was prevalent in the previous system of multimember districts. The new law provides for public financing of parties based on the number of votes they receive and limits contributions.

Contributions to parties and candidates in Japan are important not only for electoral purposes but also because members of the Diet seek to develop personal relationships with constituents. Among other things this involves holding parties, attending weddings and funerals at which gifts are typically expected, and organizing excursions for constituents.. To maintain constituency support many Diet members have a *koenkai,* a local organization that serves to organize and mobilize support for the member.[7] Because of restrictions on electoral campaigns a *koenkai* is officially a cultural or-

[7]Richardson (1988) reports that 18 percent of the voters in his sample identified themselves as members of a *koenkai.* Often, when a Diet member retires, he turns the *koenkai* over to a family member, which in part accounts for a large number of second-generation members in the Diet.

ganization, and as Reischauer (1988, p. 264–265) indicates, it conducts constituency activities on a year-round basis.

One function of a Diet member is to represent constituents' interests not only in the Diet but also with the bureaucracy. For example, Asao Mihara, an LDP member of the lower house from Fukuoka, "has to spend nearly all his time and most of the funds he can collect from supporters acting as a middleman between his constituents and the central government in Tokyo. This includes submitting petitions to bureaucrats on behalf of local businessmen and steering central government-funded public works projects in the general direction of Fukuoka.[8] This is referred to as a "pipe." Providing a pipe also generates contributions.

Members of the Diet also participate in groups, known as *zoku,* that intermediate between interest groups and the bureaucracy. *Zoku* are important to a ministry because they can represent the ministry's interests when there are interministerial disputes. In exchange for this support, the ministry may serve the interests that provide the political support for the *zoku* and its members. In addition to the *zoku,* Diet members have formed caucuses that support policies that cut across both factions and *zoku.* The principal function of the *zoku,* however, is to represent interest groups. The agriculture *zoku* succeeded in obtaining $60 billion over 6 years for relief for rice farmers who had been hurt by the opening of the Japanese market to imports.

Party Organization

Parties play an important role in governing in a parliamentary system. A majority party resolves internally a variety of matters, including proposed legislation, before it goes to the legislature. Because the LDP has been the major party in Japan, is still the largest party, and its former members are the leaders of the opposition, its structure and functioning will be considered here.

Although it is conservative in its orientation, the LDP is neither strongly ideological nor homogeneous, nor does it have a well-defined legislative program. Instead, its program arises out of the work of the party, the Diet, and the bureaucracy. The LDP is a flexible collection of interests and politicians who have mutual incentives in governing. The LDP is composed of factions. The factions are not ideological but form around leaders and provide a base from which the leader can seek top ministerial positions. Because the size of the factions is important in interparty bargaining and the subsequent distribution of rewards, LDP leaders attempt to increase the size of their factions by attracting junior Diet members to them. For a member of the Diet, a faction provides a vehicle for reaching higher office and a means of participating in legislative activity. LDP members have an incentive to join a faction because the success of the faction and its leader can be important to their personal advancement in the party and in government. Faction leaders are also an important source of campaign funds for members of their faction. The LDP officially dissolved its factions, but the "former factions" still exist.[9]

The LDP has developed an extensive internal decision-making process formalized in the Policy Affairs Research Committee (PARC).[10] PARC has 15 sections, or divisions, whose policy jurisdictions correspond to the ministries and Diet committees as indicated in Figure 13-2.

---

[8] *Far Eastern Economic Review,* March 9, 1989.

[9] In 1998 the leaders of the three largest factions were the former prime ministers Takeshita, Nakasone, and Miyasawa.

[10] See Reischauer (1988, pp. 273–274) and Fukui (1970, pp. 83–89).

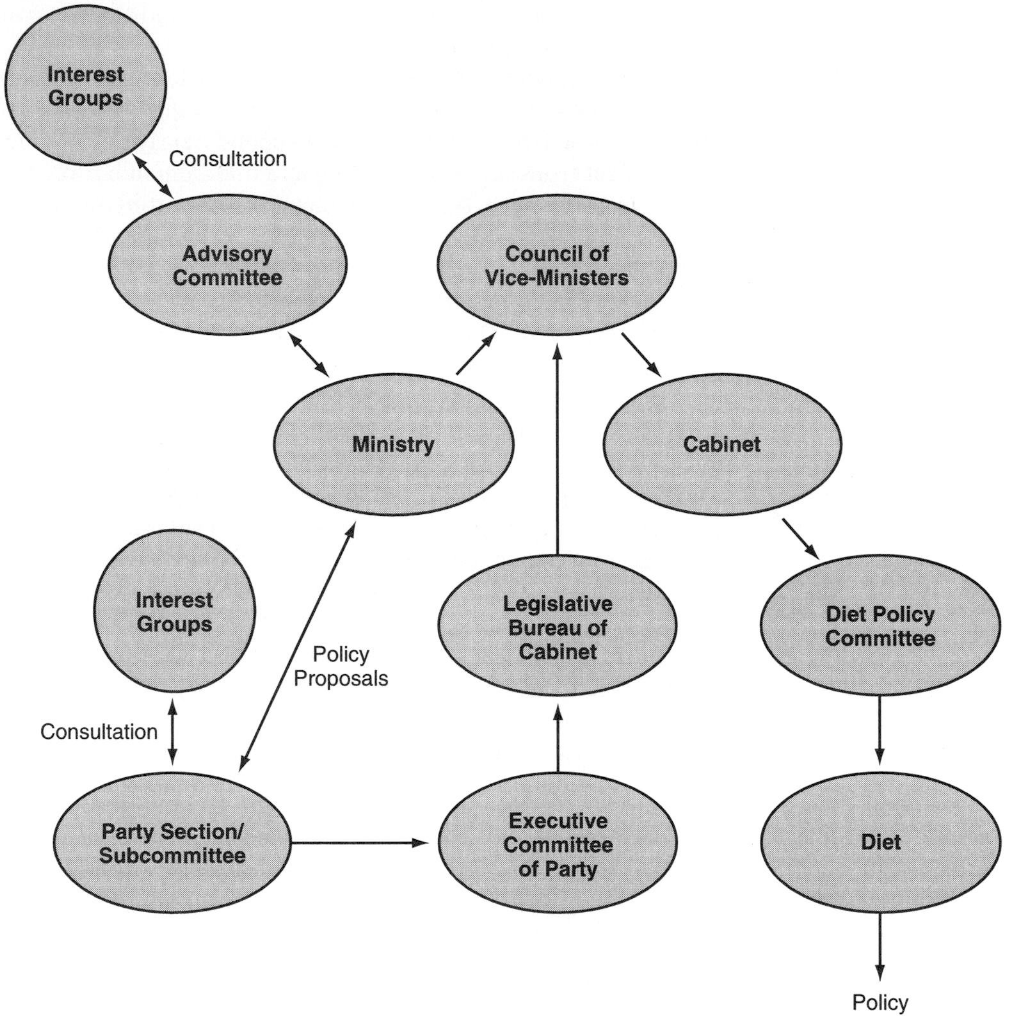

FIGURE 13-3 Policy Formulation and Legislative Process

The Legislative Process

The policy formation and legislative process is illustrated in Figure 13-3. The top portion of the figure represents the bureaucratic portion of the legislative process, as considered later in the chapter. The lower portion represents the component of the process that takes place within the governing coalition. In both portions, interest groups are consulted early in the development of policies. Interest group activity thus begins before the Diet considers legislation.

In the lower portion of the figure, party committees formulate policies and at times draft legislation, although most legislation is written by the bureaucracy. The draft legislation is reviewed by the government's executive committee, which includes representatives of all the parties in the governing coalition. Once the proposal is approved by the executive committee, it is forwarded to the appropriate ministry. Next, it goes to the cabinet; if it is approved there it is submitted to the Diet. Legislation drafted by a ministry passes through a similar process.

By the time a bill is introduced in the Diet consensus has been developed within the policy-making apparatus of the governing parties, support has been obtained from the bureaucracy, and the cabinet has given its approval. Thus, most of the legislative work has been completed before the Diet takes up the bill. In many cases, Diet consideration involves going through the formalities—the outcome has been determined long before a vote is taken. Interest groups thus have a strong incentive to be involved early in this process and to develop relationships with the bureaucracy and the parties to obtain access to the legislative process. Because Diet action comes at the end of the policy-making process, much of the interest group activity and the political competition takes place out of public view.

THE BUREAUCRACY

Structure and Power

The bureaucracy in Japan has traditionally been viewed as the central force in government, and interactions with the bureaucracy are essential to many business activities. Japanese culture confers respect on the bureaucracy, but its status has also been due to its expertise, its dedication to the national interest, the innovativeness and leadership that some ministries have demonstrated, and the economic success Japan had enjoyed. The bureaucracy has also developed exchange relationships with interest groups that give it the political strength needed to develop and administer policies in its jurisdiction. In recent years, however, scandals and poor economic performance have reduced public confidence in the bureaucracy.[11]

As shown in Figure 13-2, Japan has 12 ministries and several agencies. The ministries differ significantly in their functions and their importance. The Ministry of International Trade and Industry (MITI) has a planning and economic rationalization function and is the lead ministry in international trade negotiations.[12] The Ministry of Post and Telecommunications (MPT) has a substantial regulatory role, and the Ministry of Construction plays an important role in the expenditure of government funds. Japan does not have a system of separate regulatory agencies, so the ministries have regulatory as well as policy and administrative responsibilities.

A ministry is generally headed by a politician from one of the government coalition parties and is administered by two vice ministers. The parliamentary, or political, vice minister is a member of the lower house, who typically is rotated through a position in the bureaucracy. The day-to-day affairs of the ministry are supervised by the administrative vice minister, who is a career civil servant.

A ministry has influence as a function of several factors. The two most important are (1) its expertise in resolving problems and devising effective policies and (2) its authority to direct resources or control economic activity through, for example, regulation or the allocation of government funds. One source of power of the bureaucracy is its ability to act without having to have new laws enacted. The ministries have considerable discretion within their jurisdictions and often use administrative guidance to implement

---

[11]As an example of a scandal that reduced the respect for the bureaucracy, to benefit certain pharmaceutical companies the Ministry of Health and Welfare had delayed the introduction of heated blood products that reduce the risk of HIV infection. Hundreds of people unnecessarily contracted AIDS because of the delay.

[12]See Johnson (1982) for an analysis of MITI and industrial policy in Japan. The characterization of "Japan, Inc." and the prominence and foresight often attributed to MITI as an explanation of Japan's economic success may be exaggerated. MITI often has difficulty convincing industries and companies to go along with its policies. Samuels (1987), for example, analyzes MITI's failed attempts to rationalize Japan's oil industry into a vertically integrated, unified industry. Indeed, MITI is often the ministry that must make decisions that benefit one industry and harm another.

their policies. The expertise of the bureaucracy is accentuated because the prime minister, Diet members, and the Diet committees have very small staffs, forcing the politicians to rely on the ministries for information and expertise.

Ministries such as MITI have in some cases been effective in encouraging the development of certain industries, but the power of the ministries is found less in their industrial policies than in their regulatory, licensing, resource allocation, and supervisory functions. Japan has one of the most regulated economies in the world with 11,042 regulations in effect. According to one account there are 10,760 situations in which a government permit is required.[13] Many of the regulatory requirements are nontransparent, causing particular difficulty for foreign and other firms unfamiliar with the system. Shoichiro Toyoda, chairman of Toyota, argued, "Japan must shift from an economy burdened by regulations and bureaucracy to one in which the private sector can operate unfettered. We must also downsize the public sector and create a small, efficient government."[14]

In the mid-1990s the bureaucracy came under criticism from business, the public, and politicians who argued that it was impeding the deregulation needed to improve the efficiency of a number of sectors of the economy in which regulation served to protect firms and impede change. Some reforms have been instituted, but economic activity remains considerably more regulated than in the United States, for example.

Based on interviews with government officials, Okimoto (1988, p. 319) developed the following power ranking of those ministries that interact with business:

- Most powerful (by a wide margin)—MITI; Ministry of Finance
- Very powerful (on local budgetary issues)—Ministry of Local Autonomy
- Powerful (in specific trade issue areas)—Ministry of Agriculture, Forestry, and Fisheries; MPT; Ministry of Health and Welfare
- Fairly influential (in terms of broad involvement)—Ministry of Foreign Affairs
- Weak—Ministry of Labor; Defense Agency; Science and Technology Agency; Economic Planning Agency

Ministries in Japan are considerably more powerful than are the cabinet departments in the United States. One reason is the absence of separate regulatory agencies. The Ministry of Finance, for example, has formal authority over tax collection, the government budget, financial market regulation, tax policy, and the regulation of financial institutions. In the United States these are the responsibility of, respectively, the Internal Revenue Service, the Office of Management and Budget, the Securities and Exchange Commission, the Department of the Treasury, and for financial institutions the Federal Reserve System, the Comptroller of the Currency, the FDIC, and the Office of Thrift Supervision. Although an independent agency, the Bank of Japan (the central bank) is informally controlled by the Ministry of Finance. The administrative vice ministers and senior bureaucrats at a number of agencies, such as the Defense Agency and the Environment Agency, also come from the MOF. As indicated in the next section, the MOF attracts some of the top talent in the nation.

Career Bureaucrats

The bureaucracy attracts some of the best university graduates in Japan, which adds to its expertise and prestige and contributes to its influence. In 1997, 45,000 applicants from universities took the advanced civil service examination for 780 positions in the senior civil service. The ministries then choose from among those successful candidates. The Ministry of Finance chooses first and the Ministry of Home Affairs and MITI choose next. These new bureaucrats become members of the career *gumi,* or career

---

[13] *The New York Times,* November 17, 1996.
[14] *The New York Times,* April 17, 1997.

team. At the Ministry of Finance approximately 800 of the 80,000 employees are career bureaucrats. Graduates of Tokyo University (*Todai*) dominate the highest ranks of the ministries; its graduates held the administrative vice minister post in 11 of the 12 ministries in 1994. In 1994, 90.5 percent and 78 percent of new MOF and MITI classes, respectively, were composed of *Todai* graduates.

The class that enters a ministry constitutes a cohort that moves up, and eventually out of, the ministry hierarchy together.[15] Throughout this process, no member of a cohort will be in a position of hierarchical superiority to another member of the same cohort. Job rotation is an important part of the career path of a bureaucrat, and a shuffle of positions occurs every June. Job rotation develops the breadth and human capital needed for a consensual system in which conflicts are resolved through bargaining and accommodation. It also reduces the likelihood that a bureaucrat will become too closely allied with interest groups that could exert unwarranted influence and divert the ministry from its mission.

The links between ministries and business are facilitated by the *amakudari* ("descent from heaven") system.[16] After 30 years in a ministry, one of the cohort will become a vice minister. During this period others will resign and "descend" to other careers in universities, business, public enterprises, or a government-owned financial institution such as the Export-Import Bank. Others will run for political office; approximately one-third of the LDP Diet members in 1994 were former bureaucrats. Postretirement employment tends to be easiest for bureaucrats from ministries that have regulatory authority over industries, since those industries are most in need of the relationships and information channels that the ex-bureaucrats can provide. The chapter case *The Breakup of Nippon Telephone and Telegraph?* involves a ministry's concern for the placement of its career bureaucrats.

Advisory Committees

The links between the bureaucracy and business are strengthened by over 200 ministerial advisory committees composed of bureaucrats, Diet members, representatives of relevant business and labor organizations, academics, and others. The explicit purpose of the advisory committees is to develop consensus on policies, regulations, or standards before they are proposed as legislation or are implemented by the bureaucracy. The ministries also use advisory committees to persuade business and other interest groups to support—or at least to not oppose—the policy directives the ministry seeks to implement. The advisory committees also serve as communication channels that keep the bureaucracy informed about issues of concern to interest groups and keep the interest groups informed about the activities of the ministry.

The Judicial System and the Antimonopoly Law

The Japanese judicial system is patterned after the civil code systems of continental Europe rather than the adversarial system found in the United States. Japan has no common law but does have antitrust, labor, and securities laws patterned after those in the United States. A striking feature of the Japanese legal system is the reliance on conciliation of disputes. The Japanese people place great value on harmony and the absence of confrontation and conflict. They seek to resolve disputes "within the family" without

---

[15]See Atsuyuki (1988) for a description of a bureaucrat's career. Bronte (1982, p. 137) describes the cohort process in some detail. See "Inside MOF; The Men from the Ministry," *Tokyo Business Today,* January 1995, for a description of the career path in the MOF.

[16]*Amakudari* bureaucrats are to wait 2 years before joining a firm that deals with their ministry, but they can obtain a waiver of the requirement from the National Personnel Authority (*Japan Economic Journal,* May 26, 1990).

recourse to the courts, and hence there is a low demand for the resolution of disputes in the courts. Van Wolfren (1989, p. 214) reported that Japan had one lawyer for every 9,294 citizens, compared with one for every 360 in the United States and one for every 1,486 in Germany.

Japan has an Anti-Monopoly Law (AML), which is enforced by the Fair Trade Commission (FTC).[17] Enforcement is different from that in the United States for cultural reasons, say its proponents—or by intention, say its critics. Frequently, when the FTC concludes that a company has violated the AML, it issues a warning.[18] This administrative sanction is said to be a mark of shame that both causes the practice to end and provides a deterrent to others. Fines are also used, but criminal charges are rarely brought against executives found to have violated the law. The Chapter 16 case *The Kodak-Fujifilm Trade Dispute* raises antitrust as well as trade issues.

Critics contend that the FTC does more to sanction collusion than to deter it. On approval by the appropriate ministry and the FTC, cartels are legal in Japan for the purpose of rationalizing an industry. There are approximately 270 approved cartels, some of which are responses to voluntary restrictions on Japanese imports to the United States. Cartels are believed by many to insulate industries from certain market forces.

Some segments of the construction industry operate under an illegal system of bid rigging, pricefixing, and market allocation known as *dango.* In the *dango* system, construction companies meet in private to decide what bids they will make and which company will win the contract.[19] In 1988 the FTC ruled that 140 construction companies had colluded on bids for work at the U.S. naval base at Yokosuka. The FTC issued a warning but imposed small fines totaling $2 million. The U.S. Department of Justice then hired a Japanese law firm to represent the United States, and within a year 99 construction companies agreed to pay $32.6 million to settle the bid-rigging claims. The settlement represented approximately 25 percent of the value of the contracts in question. Under pressure from within Japan and from the United States, the FTC issued new guidelines for the construction industry defining an additional set of illegal practices.

Cultural Foundations

Japanese culture emphasizes harmony and the role of formal and informal hierarchical relationships, such as that between a superior and a subordinate. At the same time, Japanese business practices emphasize horizontal relationships, flexibility, and consensus. The cultural explanation for these practices lies in part in the importance of groups in Japanese society and the relationship between the individual and the group and between groups and society.

A cultural explanation for the societal value of harmony can be found in the religious tradition in which a person progresses toward a closer relationship with or deeper understanding of the "universe."[20] Work is also a path to a closer or deeper relationship with the universe, which has led to an ethic of diligence and a desire for harmony with other individuals and with groups in the work environment. Employment practices such

---

[17]Private antitrust suits are allowed in Japan but are rarely filed because of limits on discovery, the absence of class actions, high filing costs, and the requirement that the FTC issue a finding of a probable violation before a case can proceed.

[18]See Upham (1987, Ch. 5) for a discussion of litigation and industrial policy.

[19]McMillan (1991) estimates that *dango* increases the price of a public works contract by 16 to 33 percent. In addition, *dango* represents a barrier to trade.

[20]The Confucian support for this perspective is found in the concept of persons having within them a microcosm of the universe that is connected with the outer universe. The Buddhist underpinning of this perspective is the view that all human beings are the same.

as lifelong employment and a seniority system sustain this ethic.[21] A group, including a business group, thus is to be nourished and its members to act in harmony, so that the group can progress thereby allowing its members to progress.[22] Groups balance a need to adapt to their environment, and hence for their members to act in a concerted manner, and a desire for individuals to express their individual intentions and interests. This may require leaders to accommodate their expectations toward their subordinates and may require subordinates to suppress their own interests. Doi (1988, pp. 22–23) argues that this consensus building through accommodation by both leaders and subordinates resolves the fundamental tension in groups. The desire to build consensus for government actions and the extensive consultation processes of the bureaucracy are consistent with this perspective.

Taka (1994) characterizes the social environment in which individuals and groups are located in terms of four concentric circles of "family, fellows, Japan, and the world." Appropriate behavior depends on the principal relationships in each circle. The notion that appropriate behavior differs among the circles, and the relationships in them, derives from early Confucianism, which held that although all persons are equal, a person is "to treat others in proportion to the intimacy of their relations."[23] A fundamental cultural value that characterizes these relationships is *on,* which refers to obligation and its fulfillment. *On,* for example, "is the indebtedness of subordinate to superior for the superior's benevolence in supplying resources to the subordinate."[24] In a fundamental sense, *on* can never be fully repaid and the remaining obligation serves to perpetuate the relationship.

The first circle centers on the *ie,* or family, which is viewed as a group that continues through time. In a business context the second, or "fellows," circle focuses on relationships with friends and colleagues. Viewing a company as analogous to a family, the principal relationship with the work environment is the hierarchical superior-subordinate relationship. This circle also includes the relationships among individual businesses and the ministries relevant to their industry. The fellows circle also includes the businesses in a *keiretsu,* which are expected to contribute to and draw assistance from other fellow members, but each is expected to have a positive balance of benefits over obligations remaining.

Taka characterizes the Japan circle as functioning under the principle of free competition. This is consistent with the notion of *Confucian capitalism,* the term given to the organization of the economy in terms of markets and groups, including *keiretsu,* supply networks, and long-term relationships among companies.[25] The bureaucracy in Japan may also be viewed from this perspective. In Japan a samurai was both a military and a civil officer—a bureaucrat, and Morishima (1988, p. 38) states, "In Confucian political thought, those who play the most important roles in society are the bureaucrats."

In the Japan circle, businesses have mutual interests that are supported by reciprocal behavior, including that with government, to maintain harmony within the country through the accommodation and subordination of interests. This occurs among businesses and business groups (*keiretsu*) in the context of a larger group—the business community—or the business community in relation to government. An economic phenomenon consistent with this value is the rescue of failing firms. When a firm is failing,

[21]A seniority system also is consistent with the Confucian value of respect for elders.
[22]This characterization is based on that provided by Taka (1994).
[23]The five basic Confucian relationships are parent and child, husband and wife, older sibling and younger sibling, friend and friend, and superior and subordinate (ruler and subject). Confucianism is considered in more detail in Chapter 15.
[24]Hamilton and Sanders (1992, p. 24).
[25]Morishima (1988, pp. 3638) addresses the Confucian basis for capitalism.

a group or an industry rescues the firm. The rescuer is not always a Japanese firm—in 1994 creditors asked Ford Motor Company to assume managerial control of the failing Mazda, in which Ford had an ownership share.[26]

The outer, or world, circle requires an outward orientation but order is maintained among those who share the understandings of the inner three circles. Reciprocal relationships are less important in this circle, and business relies more on law to resolve conflicts.

Tying the Components Together: A Framework for Political Exchange

The framework for political exchange brings together the components of government and their interactions with interests. Interests provide the basic incentives for political and collective action, and culture and institutions structure the pursuit of those interests, as indicated in Figure 13-1. The outcome of a political issue affecting business depends on the alignment of interests, the strategies employed by interests, and institutions—the Diet, the governing parties, and the bureaucracy. Because of the powerful bureaucracy and the cultural values of harmony and consensus, political competition is not as freewheeling as in the United States, with much of the action taking place within the governing coalition or in behind-the-scenes consensus-building activities involving the coalition, the bureaucracy, and interest groups. This political action is less visible than it is in the United States.

One path to influence for interests has been through parties and their leaders, but interests have often sought assistance from a broader set of officeholders. *Zoku* and caucuses give Diet members an opportunity to respond to the needs of interest groups. From the perspective of interest groups, *zoku* provide another access point to the government and are an important link between interest groups, the governing parties, and the Diet.

The bureaucracy plays a central role in the maintenance of interest group relationships, and hence ministries to some extent have been politicized. The most politicized ministries are those whose actions have a direct impact on industry, professional groups, and other organized interests through expenditure programs and regulation. Okimoto (1989, p. 324) provides a ranking of ministries in terms of their degree of politicization, which, as he observes, is almost the inverse of their degree of power and prestige:

- Heavily politicized—Construction; MAFF
- Quite politicized—Transportation; Posts and Telecommunications; Health and Welfare; Defense
- Somewhat politicized—Local Autonomy; Finance
- Comparatively nonpoliticized—MITI (excluding the Small and Medium Enterprises Agency); Foreign Affairs; Economic Planning Agency.

POLITICAL EXCHANGE

The interactions between interest groups and the government can be viewed as political exchange in which interest groups provide political support and the government provides programs that benefit them.[27] This takes place through a set of relationships, referred to as an iron triangle, formed by interest groups, political parties, and the bureaucracy. During the 1990s the importance of these iron triangles diminished somewhat, but they remain important for many businesses and interest groups. Okimoto

[26]In 1996 Ford increased its stake in Mazda to 33.4 percent, and a Westerner assumed its presidency.

[27]The bureaucracy plays a role in this exchange, and Aoki (1988) characterizes this as administrative pluralism in which the bureaucracy acts as a referee among competing pluralist interests.

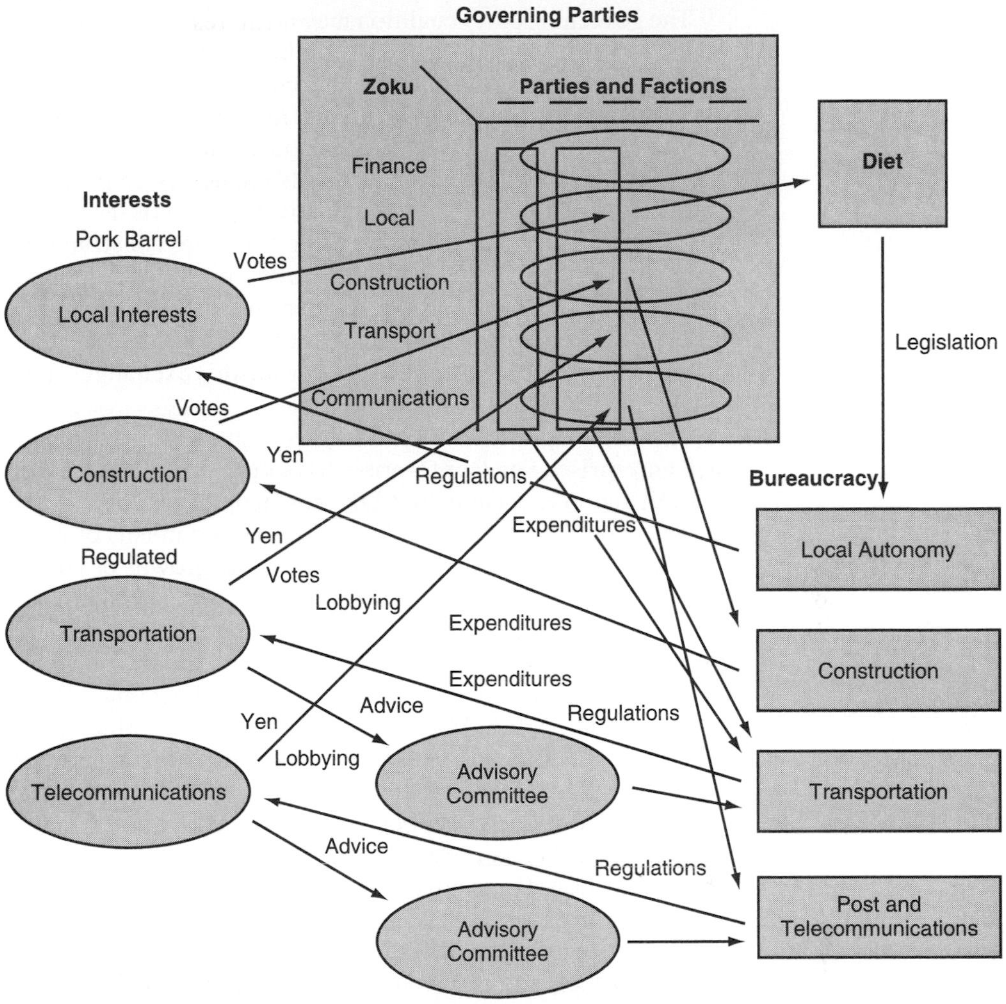

FIGURE 13–4 Reciprocal Exchange

(1989) classifies these exchanges into four categories: (1) clientistic exchange, (2) reciprocal (pork barrel) exchange, (3) untied financial support, and (4) generalized voter support. Only reciprocal exchange is considered here.

Reciprocal Exchange

Reciprocal exchange, illustrated in Figure 13-4, involves government regulatory policies, licensing, and expenditures that benefit particular interest groups that in turn provide support for the governing parties, since the participants recognize that future benefits depend on maintaining the system. Reciprocal patronage also characterizes exchange in regulated industries such as electric power, telecommunications, and transportation. In these sectors, the ministries, which are the regulators, again serve as intermediaries.[28] Expenditure programs primarily affect the construction, transportation, and defense industries. The businesses in these industries are generally not heavily involved in international trade and seek benefits from government programs. In the context of Figure 2-2, the regulation and expenditure programs of these ministries make nonmarket strategies important.

[28]Japan does not have the system of independent regulatory commissions found in the United States.

The governing party coalition may be thought of as a matrix with Diet members belonging to a party, and also possibly to a faction, as well as to a *zoku.,* The points of access for an interest group, then, may be through a party, a *zoku,* or a caucus. The points of access to the bureaucracy include direct relationships and the advisory committee system.

The Ministry of Construction is one of the most important participants in reciprocal patronage. Construction accounts for nearly 15 percent of the GDP, and every project must be licensed by the ministry. Because of the magnitude of the funds allocated by the ministry and its licensing function, construction companies have been strong supporters of the traditional system and are important participants in the *koenkai* of LDP Diet members. As mentioned, the "pipe" funnels government public works programs from Tokyo to a Diet member's district. The Ministry of Construction provides the bureaucratic support for this exchange, and according to Okimoto, is highly politicized.

The nature of political concessions to interest groups is illustrated by the case of small enterprises. Small enterprises have been one of the traditional support groups for the LDP, and in exchange the LDP provided a set of specific benefits, such as preferential tax treatment and favorable regulation, as a means of protecting them. To protect small retailers, the government restricted the growth of large department stores, and this restriction has been in part responsible for Japan's large retail and wholesale sector. To strengthen the reciprocal relationship among small merchants, the bureaucracy, and the LDP, in 1973 the government enacted the Large-Scale Store Regulation Law, which required any store that sought to expand beyond 1,500 square meters to obtain approval from SMEA. When approval was sought, other stores in the neighborhood were consulted. Their protests often delayed an opening for years. In exchange for this regulatory protection, small merchants and wholesalers typically supported the LDP.

When some large stores began to build stores smaller than 1,500 square meters side by side, local retailers pressured municipal and prefecture governments seeking additional protection. Those governments began to enact regulations that placed additional restrictions on large stores. These regulations were "illegal" because they conflicted with the national law, and MITI sought to void them. The municipal and prefecture governments sought and received support from the Ministry of Local Autonomy (MLA), which opposed MITI on this issue. The bureaucratic battle was arbitrated by the Cabinet, which eventually decided in favor of the MLA and the local merchants. Regulations were established requiring that notice be given to the prefecture government of any plan to open a store with more than 500 square meters. These regulations along with subsequent legislation provided a role for local government in the protest process, strengthened the role of the local merchants, and allowed the merchants to appeal decisions to the ministries. The chapter case *Toys 'R' Us in Japan (A)* involves a retailer seeking to enter the Japanese market and facing this set of restrictions and the reciprocal exchange relationship.

Characteristics of Business

THE ORGANIZATION OF BUSINESS

Many of the most prominent Japanese companies are part of a network or group that provides mutual benefits to its members. In the United States, corporations tend to have wholly owned subsidiaries, and cross-shareholding of publicly traded companies is atypical. In Japan, business groups are solidified by interlocking ownership, which serves both to facilitate coordination and insulate the group from outside forces. The groups typically have no more than one firm in any industry, so cooperation and coordination rather than rivalry characterize behavior within a group. Groups compete vigorously against each other, however.

These interlocking networks, referred to as *keiretsu,* are of three types: (1) the three groups, Mitsui, Mitsubishi, and Sumitomo, formed from the prewar, family-controlled *zaibatsu,* (2) groups formed around major banks, and (3) groups formed around major industrial companies. Members of the first two groups are referred to as horizontal *keiretsu,* whereas those in the third are called vertical *keiretsu.*[29] The firms in a *keiretsu* are independently managed, but each *keiretsu* has a "presidents' club" that meets regularly and focuses on group maintenance activities, the exchange of information, and, when necessary, the resolution of conflicts among members.

Ito (1992) indicates that in 1987 six bank-centered groups, the former *zaibatsu* plus three of the groups centered around major city banks, controlled 12.96 percent of the nonfinancial assets in Japan. These six groups also held 24.2 percent of all the shares of the 1,820 companies listed on the Tokyo and Osaka stock exchanges. As Sonji Noguchi, a general manager at the Industrial Bank of Japan (IBJ) (which has the largest shareholdings of any bank) explained: "When we issue stock, friendly companies hold it. When they issue stock, we hold it. . . . If I own 1,000 shares of IBJ, I don't feel I own the company. It's just an investment. It's the relationship."[30]

Figure 13-5 presents the organization of the core Mitsubishi *keiretsu,* which has three lead companies: Mitsubishi Corporation, Mitsubishi Bank, and Mitsubishi Heavy Industries. The companies within the border are the principal members of the group. The presidents of those companies meet on the second Friday of each month at noon to address group maintenance issues. The members of the group are independent companies, although there are some parent-subsidiary relationships as indicated by the arrows. In addition, the group is maintained by a pattern of cross-ownership among the companies. In 1987, 24.69 percent of the shares of Mitsubishi Bank were held by other group members, and Mitsubishi Bank held an average of 3.74 percent of seven other group companies. *Keiretsu* companies owned 28.50 percent of Asahi Glass and 18.77 percent of Kirin Beer, whereas these companies held shares of other group companies.[31] *Keiretsu* companies not only hold shares in each other, but they also lend to each other. The companies typically attempt to purchase from each other, and the presidents drink only Kirin beer at their Friday meetings.

Vertical *keiretsu* are centered around a major manufacturing firm such as Toyota or Matsushita Electric and involve supply and distribution networks. These groups may include wholly-owned subsidiaries, partially owned subsidiaries, and independent suppliers. The form of the relationship varies with some subsidiaries supplying other companies in addition to their parent and the parent purchasing from competitors of a subsidiary. Toyota directly controls 13 suppliers with 1990 ownership shares ranging from 8.9 percent to 49 percent, and another 178 companies, organized into three societies, supply Toyota. Matsushita maintains a distribution network of 25,000 small "National shops" that account for 80 percent of its sales. In 1992 Matsushita restructured its network in response to sales competition from electronics discount stores and pressure from the United States that centered on the alleged barriers to entry said to result from distribution and supply *keiretsu.*

---

[29]Gerlach (1992) provides an analysis of the *keiretsu* and other alliances in Japan and of the implications of these networks for corporate business strategy.
[30]*The New York Times,* June 27, 1989.
[31]See Ito (1992). The non-*zaibatsu* horizontal *keiretsu* tend to have lower cross-shareholdings.

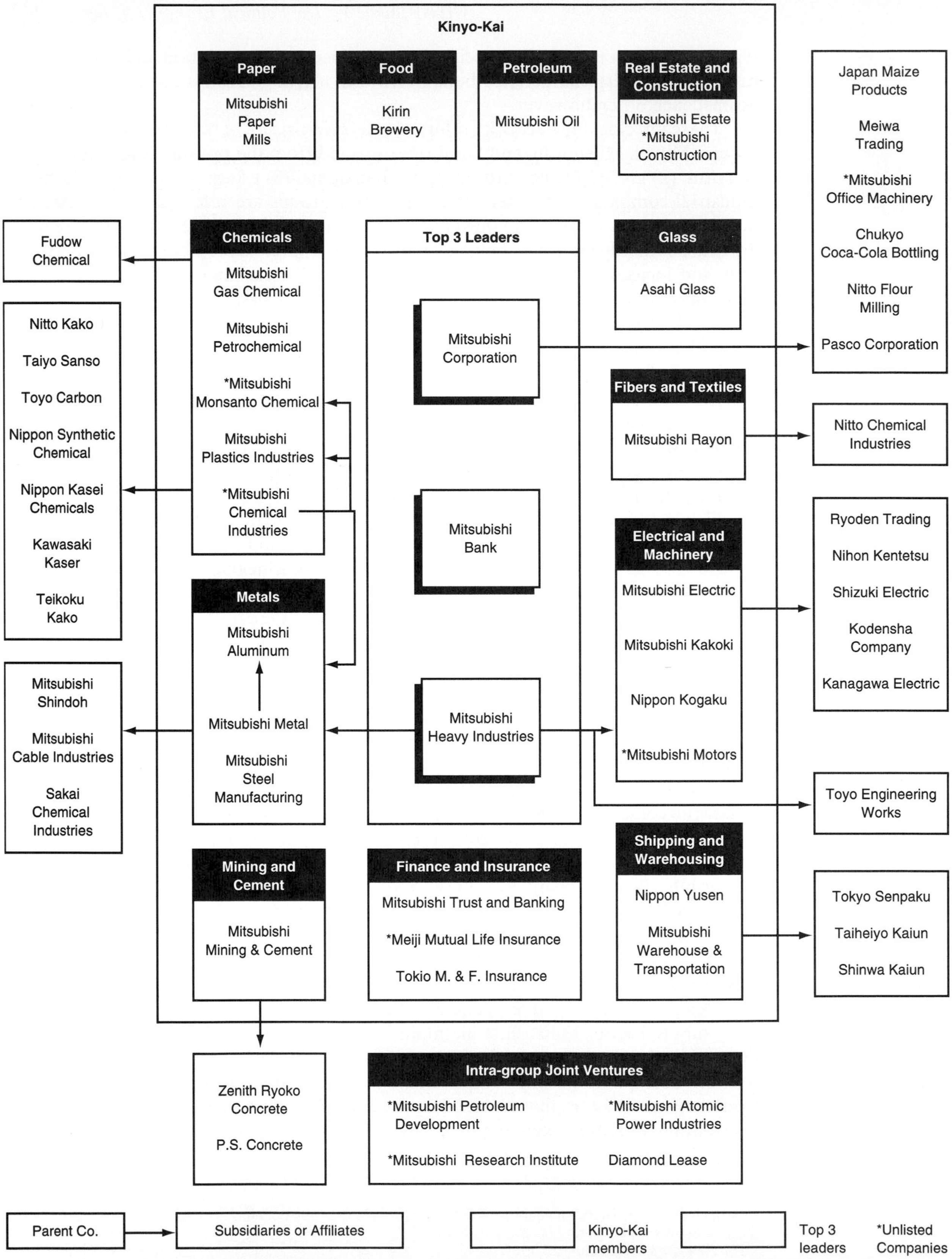

FIGURE 13–5 The Mitsubishi Group

Maintenance of the network relationships in a *keiretsu* may involve sacrifice at times, but the expectation is that future benefits will be received. This system has a variety of consequences for efficiency, risk sharing, and profitability. Networks of implicit, or relational, contracts in Dore's (1983) terminology provide a form of risk sharing in much the same manner as insurance does. When adversity strikes, that adversity is to be shared within the group; when good fortune comes, that, too, is to be shared.

As practiced in Japan, relational contracting is characterized not only by the absence of formal contracts but also by mutual adjustment to changing circumstances. Within a *keiretsu,* long-term supply relationships are frequently augmented by a market allocation system in which suppliers receive fixed percentages of the purchase orders of a company but the quantity purchased varies with the level of demand. The relationship between Nippon Telephone and Telegraph (NTT) and a group of its suppliers had been so stable that the suppliers are referred to as the NTT "family" (See the chapter case *The Breakup of Nippon Telephone and Telegraph?*) Market allocation and long-term relationships make it difficult for new firms, both Japanese and foreign, to enter certain Japanese supply markets.

Implicit contracts also govern the employment relationship in most large firms. The compensation system in Japanese firms typically has three principal components: (1) an annual bonus, (2) pay graduated by seniority, and (3) a contingent retirement payment. Japanese employees receive a significant part of their income in the form of an annual bonus, which can be reduced along with hours worked when the firm has to improve its profits. Consistent with the cultural analogy to a family, most firms base wages on seniority, and because many major firms hire young employees directly from high schools and universities and offer them lifetime employment, workers look forward to a rising income stream.[32] These features of the compensation system provide strong incentives for employees to remain with the firm, and they also align the interests of employees with those of the firm.

Although lifetime employment and seniority systems continue to be used by many major firms, pressure for improved efficiency and lower costs as well as the economic slump in Japan have generated change. Layoffs have occurred and firms have skirted the lifetime employment policies by hiring temporary workers. Compensation systems have also been changed. As Osamu Sakuri, president of the Sumitomo Trust Bank, explained: "Under the lifetime employment system we could not offer appropriately high salaries to obtain top talent. Nor could we hire on a short-term basis."[33] Merit-based, rather than seniority-based, pay is becoming more common, and Fujitsu announced that all employees would be paid based on merit. In addition, companies such as Matsushita are changing their retirement systems by giving employees more control over their retirement programs rather than providing all the funds at the time of retirement. These changes have increased labor mobility.

Business-Government Interactions

THE ORGANIZATION OF BUSINESS FOR POLITICAL ACTION

Mutual gains, such as those from long-term relationships among businesses, also result from relationships with the government. When a Japanese firm faces an issue that involves the government, it has already established relationships that provide it access.

---

[32]Lifetime employment is available, however, to only a small proportion of the workforce. Tachibanaki (1984) estimates that in the late 1970s approximately 9.7 percent of males and less than 2 percent of females had lifetime employment. He argues that this is quite similar to the United States, except that in the United States a much higher percent of young employees engage in job shopping.

[33]Quoted in Mroczkowski and Hanaoka (1989, p. 50).

Japanese firms cultivate relationships with politicians, bureaucrats, and other firms that provide the foundation for participation and influence. Firms establish relationships with important politicians, and most are regular contributors of campaign funds. Firms participate in ministerial advisory committees and develop relationships with the relevant ministries and their career bureaucrats. They may employ *amakudari* bureaucrats or use them as advisors and counselors. Firms develop contacts with the relevant Diet committees and with the *zoku* and caucuses concerned with policy in their industries. Firms also participate in industry associations and *Keidanren* activities and committees. These relationships represent major assets to a company, and considerable effort and resources are expended to maintain them.

These relationships do not guarantee success on nonmarket issues, but they may be necessary for effective participation in the Japanese system. The success of a nonmarket strategy in Japan depends on the strength of the interests and the nature of the exchange relationship between business and government. The opposition to foreign entry into an industry, for example, is naturally weakest for those products that have no Japanese competitor. A company such as McDonald's was able to enter the Japanese market with relative ease because the fast-food market segment was unoccupied. The same was true for Blockbuster. A firm seeking access to an industry in which the relationship between interest groups and the government is characterized by clientistic or reciprocal exchange may, however, find the opposition formidable. In industries such as agriculture and construction, the U.S. government has played a major role in opening the markets. In other cases long-term arrangements through *keiretsu* limit the ability of foreign manufacturers and new Japanese firms to break into some markets. For example, a principal impediment to increased sales by foreign semiconductor manufacturers has been the long-standing supply relationships and market allocation policies of both *keiretsu* and independent firms.[34]

POLITICAL STRATEGIES

The principal political strategies used in Japan are electoral, relationship building, lobbying, and coalition building. Electoral strategies had been a central component of the political strategies of most large firms, and political contributions were a centerpiece of these strategies. These contributions take place in the context of clientistic, reciprocal, and less-structured exchange relationships. Scandals and electoral reforms have reduced their importance, however. Shoichiro Toyoda, chairman of Toyota Motor Corp. and chairman of the Keidanren, stated, "In the future one hopes that public financing and donations from individuals will be sufficient to cover political parties' expenses, but we can't expect to reach that position overnight."[35]

Foreign firms, particularly U.S. firms, may be more hesitant to make campaign contributions in light of the Lockheed scandal, considered in Chapter 22, which involved large, illegal contributions to the office of Prime Minister Tanaka among others. This incident may also have put U.S. firms seeking sales in the Japanese telecommunications market at a disadvantage because Tanaka was subsequently the informal leader of the postal *zoku* that interacted with the Ministry of Posts and Telecommunication (MPT). As Johnson (1989) indicates, Japanese computer manufacturers made daily calls on the postal *zoku,* but U.S. firms were not in a position to influence Tanaka. U.S. firms have also been hesitant to make campaign contributions because of the U.S. Foreign Corrupt Practices Act considered in Chapter 22.

---

[34]Mason (1992) documents the difficulties encountered by firms such as Coca-Cola and Texas Instruments in entering the Japanese market in the early part of the post–World War II period.
[35]*Tokyo Business Today,* September 1994.

Coalition building often takes place through industry associations and peak associations that represent business interests on broad public issues. The principal peak organization is the Keidanren, which includes the 1,200 or so largest firms, both Japanese and foreign, plus the major trade associations. The other three principal peak organizations are the Nickering (Federation of Employers Association), the Japan Chamber of Commerce and Industry, and *Keizai Doyukai* (Japan Committee for Economic Development).[36] The principal business organization for political participation is the Keidanren, which advocates policies that support the general climate for business but typically does not support particular industries or individual companies.[37] The Keidanren's approach is to attempt to build consensus on policies pertaining to issues associated with the economy or business in general. It has supported deregulation and the opening of Japanese markets to imports as a means of improving economic efficiency, reducing its trade surplus, and lessening the pressure from the United States.

RELATIONSHIPS WITH THE BUREAUCRACY

Interactions with ministries and agencies are crucial for many companies because the Japanese economy is heavily regulated, the bureaucracy has considerable discretion under existing laws, and it plays an important role in writing new legislation. These companies develop relationships with the bureaucracy and bureaucrats responsible for their industries. These relationships are reciprocal. Bureaucrats also seek close relations with Japanese companies. Okimoto (1989, p. 158) writes:

> Deputy division directors in MITI's vertical divisions have significant leeway to structure their relationships with corporate executives in ways that fulfill their notion of what their job should entail. Usually, there is a fairly well defined hierarchy of companies with which deputy directors must deal. The three deputy directors of the information industry divisions—Electronic Policy, Data Processing Promotion, and Industrial Electronics—are expected to establish close working relations with representatives from the big, blue-chip electronics corporations that dominate their fields—Hitachi, NEC, Toshiba, Mitsubishi Electronics, and Fujitsu. Working with industrial associations like the Electronics Industry Association of Japan (EIAJ) is also essential, especially when the association is strong or when there are too many large corporations for one or two MITI officials to handle.[38]

As this indicates, companies maintain their own relationships with the bureaucracy, and with parties, and these individual relationships diversify the interactions between business and government.

LOBBYING AND POINTS OF ACCESS

Lobbying is extensive in Japan and involves presenting information and representing interests to the bureaucracy, political party leaders, and the Diet. As shown in Figure 13–3, the policy formulation process begins before legislation is considered by the Diet or actions are taken by a ministry. It is thus essential that a firm or interest group be able to learn when an issue is being considered by a ministry or the policy-making apparatus of the governing parties. This requires developing a variety of relationships and

---

[36]See Lynn and McKeown (1988, pp. 78–81).
[37]The Keidanren does not deal with labor issues, which are the domain of the Nickering.
[38]Okinioto (1989, p. 158).

points of access. Although there are many points of access, because of the close interactions among the governing parties' policy-making apparatus, the bureaucracy, *zoku,* and Diet committees, these points of access are not independent.

The appropriate points of access depend on the issue and the nature of the exchange relationship between business and government. An issue involving telecommunications necessarily involves the MPT and MITI and their advisory committees, but policy committees of the governing parties will also be involved, as will the Diet committees for telecommunications and for commerce and industry. Access to the MPT may be provided both through its advisory committees and by *amakudari* bureaucrats who have maintained personal relationships with current MPT vice ministers and bureau heads. Those high-ranking bureaucrats had been responsible for the careers of those in the junior cohorts who now are in charge of the bureaucracy, so there can be a personal obligation as well as a professional relationship. A number of *amakudari* bureaucrats hold board directorships in firms with which their former ministries had dealt.

The rise of the *zoku,* in terms of both expertise and political power, makes them an important point of access on many issues. Power may be wielded by a politician who holds no government position related to that policy domain. Former Prime Minister Tanaka was the most important politician when NTT was privatized and the telecommunications industry was opened to competition, but he did not hold any formal position in the government other than his seat in the Diet—however, he headed both of the relevant *zoku.*

Access to political parties and members of the Diet is also important, particularly on issues requiring bureaucratic action, since parties can act as intermediaries between firms and ministries. The need for access led many Japanese companies to make campaign contributions to parties and their leaders.

Access is often facilitated by personal contacts between business executives and government officials. Some of these personal relationships reflect family ties that can be important in both politics and business. School ties are also important, and because many top executives and government officials are graduates of the same prestigious Japanese universities, they have a natural point of access. In addition, *amakudari* bureaucrats have by the time of their descent developed extensive personal communications networks called *jinmyaku* that can be valuable to their new employers or clients.

Foreign firms have begun to develop their capacity for lobbying the Japanese government and maintaining ties with the relevant ministries, the governing parties, and the Diet. AT&T hired a former U.S. trade negotiator to be its full-time lobbyist in Tokyo, and Nippon Motorola hired a former U.S. embassy official in Tokyo and a former congressional staffer as full-time lobbyists. Motorola also retains former officials of MITI and MPT as advisors.[39] These two ministries are the most important to the industries in which Motorola is engaged in Japan and were involved in the agreements granting the company access to the cellular telephone market.

In 1994 the American Chamber of Commerce in Japan (ACCJ) began a 3-day series of meetings with key members of the Diet, including the prime minister and cabinet ministers. Rather than focusing on policy issues, the purpose of the meetings was for the U.S. executives from companies such as Boeing and AT&T to develop personal contacts with the Diet members. As the organizer explained, "This is an attempt to go directly to people at the political level who make policy."[40] The ACCJ also monitors the progress on U.S.-Japan trade accords and makes its reports available to Congress and the public.

---

[39]Motorola follows a similar strategy in the United States, where it employs a number of former government officials.

[40]*The Wall Street Journal,* October 19, 1994.

Information

Because legislative activity in Japan is often near completion when a bill is introduced in the Diet and because legislation is written within the bureaucracy and the political parties, information on potential legislative activity is essential for effective participation in the process. Similarly, since bureaucratic decisions are not made in public and regulations and other administrative practices are often nontransparent, advance notice of possible bureaucratic action is necessary. An important activity of business thus is gathering information about government activities, plans, and proposals. Many firms employ *amakudari* bureaucrats to provide them with information; others hire them as advisors. Johnson indicates the scope of the information that Japanese companies routinely develop about the government and its activities.[41]

> The potential lobbyist must know which ministry or ministries has jurisdiction over his or her problem and then find out everything it is possible to know about that organization, including its history, personnel cliques, post retirement patterns, scandals, and so forth. This is precisely the kind of information that any Japanese manufacturer or marketing organization compiles all the time. The major Japanese daily newspapers, for example, routinely print on page 2 details of personnel shifts within the ministries and agencies of the central government. It would be unheard of to read such information in *The New York Times* or the *Washington Post* on, say, the Department of Commerce, but in Tokyo it is important news. The Japanese press reports on who is in charge of what section throughout the Japanese executive branch because its readers need and want that information.

Government officials also need information, and firms are an important source of it. As Homare Takenaka, managing director for external affairs of IBM Japan, explained: "If they think we have good intelligence and information, they rely on us. By doing this we can strengthen and expand our position. . . . I can call on director generals of ministries anytime. I know them personally."[42] Businesses also participate on advisory committees for the purposes of obtaining information and influencing outcomes.

Relationships with Bureaucrats and Politicians

In the context of Figure 2–2, the importance of nonmarket strategies is greater the greater the control of opportunities by government. Extensive regulation and the administrative allocation of government resources such as public works contracts not only makes nonmarket strategies more important but it also creates opportunities and incentives for undue influence.

A common practice among Japanese businesses is extensive, and in many cases lavish, entertaining and gift giving, referred to as *settai,* to politicians and members of the bureaucracy. This practice provides access and is not illegal unless favors are granted to the company. In addition, financial services companies such as brokerage houses are said to provide funds to politicians through investments with assured returns. The extent of these practices and the extent to which favors are granted is not known, but in some sectors of the economy, such as the heavily regulated financial services industry, it is believed to be common. Large banks employ executives, referred to as "MOF-*tan,*" who are responsible for interacting with bureaucrats at the Ministry of Finance. In 1997

[41]See Johnson in Johnson, Tyson, and Zysman (1989, p. 231).
[42]*The Japan Economic Journal,* May 19, 1990.

and 1998 investigations led by a Tokyo prosecutor shed some light on the practices in that industry.

The Ministry of Finance was already reeling from its failure to deal with the nation's banking crises and for having pushed through an increase in the sales tax, which was credited with driving the economy into a sharp recession. Agents from the Tokyo prosecutor's office raided the Ministry of Finance and arrested four bureaucrats, including one member of the career *gumi.* Three of the bureaucrats were accused of accepting entertainment and gifts with values up to $60,000. Two of the bureaucrats were accused of tipping off the MOF-*tans* of "surprise" inspections by the MOF, and the other two were accused of providing favorable treatment and information to companies. A division head of the Bank of Japan was accused of similar practices. The minister and vice minister of finance and the governor of the Bank of Japan resigned to take blame for the incidents, and another bureaucrat under investigation committed suicide. The prosecutor also announced plans to arrest a former MOF bureaucrat and current LDP member of the Diet for having demanded and received guaranteed profits from Nikko Securities on an investment account. He claimed that he was being made a scapegoat; the next day he committed suicide. As a result of the scandal, some banks announced that they were eliminating the position of MOF-*tan.*

COALITION BUILDING

Because of the extensive set of long-term relationships among firms and between business and government in Japan, coalitions in Japan are less fluid and issue specific than in the United States. Thus, many of the interactions with the government take place through standing associations rather than ad hoc coalitions. In Japan, associations are numerous and politically active. Lynn and McKeown (1988) provide an analysis of industry associations in the steel and machine tool industries. The Japan Machine Tool Builders Association represented 112 companies, and the Japan Metal Forming Machine Builders Association represented another 115. The associations address issues of industrial standards and provide information on foreign markets and competitors. These associations are linked through a hierarchical network with other associations, including the Japan Machinery Federation, the Machine Tool and Related Products Committee, and the Japan Society for the Promotion of the Machinery Industry, which funnels subsidies to machinery companies from funds raised through motorcycle and small car racing.[43]

The extent to which companies act on their own outside their industry associations and the Keidanren and whether their participation in *keiretsu* causes them to restrain the pursuit of their own interests are not well documented. Most companies, however, maintain their own relationships with bureaucrats in the relevant ministries and with important politicians in addition to the activities of the associations to which they belong.

AN INCIDENT

Details of corporate political activity are difficult to uncover, but one incident, the Recruit case, reveals its darker side. This incident is considered here not because it is representative of corporate political activity in Japan but because it indicates the importance of government to the success of certain businesses and the steps within and beyond the law to which one firm went. It also suggests the difficulties a new firm has in breaking into the structured relationships between business and government. This case was an important factor in the LDP's loss of control of the government in 1993.

---

[43]Lynn and McKeown (1988, pp. 71–73).

The Recruit Company, founded and chaired by Hiromasa Ezoe, began by publishing a magazine that supplied employment information to Japanese high school and college students. Recruit gave money to officials in the Ministries of Education and Labor in return for lists of students. The students then were employed to distribute the magazines.[44] Recruit was also alleged to have improperly obtained seats on advisory boards that oversaw recruiting regulations.

In another line of business, Recruit established a time-sharing computer network and needed both large-scale computers and special telephone circuits from NTT. Recruit made gifts to NTT officials and gave them stock in a real estate subsidiary, Recruit Cosmos, just before the stock was issued to the public.[45] Recipients of the stock made windfall profits as its price soared when it went public.[46] Recruit also made campaign contributions of $325,000 to the offices of former Prime Minister Nakasone and Finance Minister Kiichi Miyazawa, who became prime minister in 1991.[47] Facing complaints that Japan was boycotting U.S. supercomputers to protect its own development efforts, Prime Minister Nakasone is said to have intervened with NTT chairman Hisashi Shinto to have NTT purchase four Cray supercomputers. Two of those computers were then sold to Recruit for its time-sharing business.[48]

This incident indicates the importance of government bureaucracies in setting the conditions under which businesses can operate. It also indicates that gifts and political contributions have been a part, albeit an illegal or at least a questionable part, of the relationships between business and government. The line between political contributions for the purposes of developing access and relationships with government officials and contributions in exchange for favors, however, is a thin one that most firms are careful not to cross.

Corporate Political Styles

Some U.S. firms have adopted a strategy of acting aggressively, both in Japan and in the United States, to pressure the Japanese government to open its markets to the company's products, whereas other firms have adopted the Japanese style of patience both in markets and in their political and governmental interactions. Two U.S. semiconductor manufacturers, Texas Instruments and Motorola, have production facilities in Japan, and they have followed quite different political strategies. Texas Instruments, which has operated in Japan for nearly 30 years, maintains a low profile. In contrast, Motorola adopted a demonstrative style, skillfully using U.S. trade laws and political sentiment in Washington as levers to open Japanese markets for its telecommunications and semiconductor products. This caused resentment in Japan. Robert Orr, director of government relations for Motorola, explained: "We've got good friends in the U.S. government. And we have good friends in the Japanese government. That's the way it's played.

44Two former deputy ministers were indicted for receiving bribes.

45Gifts of stock are not illegal in Japan as long as there is no favor exchanged for the gift. Stock issued in Japan typically has a very low par value, so the gift appeared small when reported by Recruit.

46Prime Minister Takeshita subsequently resigned after disclosure that his personal secretary of 30 years had accepted shares in Recruit Cosmos on behalf of the prime minister's office. The secretary committed suicide the day after the resignation. Recruit is reported to have made contributions and given stock to 17 politicians. Most of them were in the LDP, but some were in other parties including one who received a 3-year sentence.

47Miyazawa became finance minister again in 1998.

48Shinto resigned from NTT in the wake of revelations that he accepted stock in Recruit Cosmos that yielded a profit of $50,000. According to newspaper accounts, he did not keep the profits but put them into a corporate fund to be used for political contributions and entertainment. In 1990 he was convicted of accepting bribes and given a suspended sentence.

There is resentment because they feel we ignited the trade issue, but it has been here a long, long, long, long time."

Johnson & Johnson has operated in a more traditional style. It had been unable to market Tylenol in Japan because the Ministry of Health and Welfare restricted the dosage of acetaminophen, the active ingredient in Tylenol, to less than half the amount needed to make the pain reliever effective. Instead of taking aggressive action in Washington as Motorola had done, Johnson & Johnson adopted the Japanese style. President Masami Atarashi of Johnson & Johnson Japan attempted to persuade MHW officials to increase the permitted dosage. He explained, "We believe in being an insider, wherever we are."[49]

Figure 2-2 characterizes the importance of nonmarket strategies in terms of the control of opportunities by government. In the heavily regulated sectors of the economy, nonmarket strategies may be essential. In Japan the long-term relationships between firms and government officials impose another dimension of control of opportunities, making market and nonmarket strategies, and their integration, even more important. In conjunction with choosing its strategy, a firm attempting to penetrate the Japanese market must determine whether it should pursue an aggressive strategy or adopt the Japanese style of patience. For a company such as Motorola that required government licenses to sell some of its products in Japan, a strategy of patience may have been infeasible because of the lengthy process required to gain access to the bureaucracy and to markets. The chapter case *Toys 'R' Us in Japan (A)* and the Chapter 16 case *The Kodak-Fujifilm Trade Dispute* provide opportunities to consider strategy formulation in the context of the market and nonmarket environments in Japan.[50]

Ministries may also provide assistance to business through regulation and licensing. When the telecommunication industry was opened to limited entry, the Public Highway Corporation encouraged a group of major companies, including Toyota, Mitsubishi, Mitsui & Company, and Sumitomo Corporation, to form a common carrier in the Tokyo-Nagoya-Osaka corridor. The company, Telway-Japan, was formed shortly before the filing deadline, and one objective of the company was to compete with a joint venture formed by Daini Denden (DDI) and Motorola to provide cellular telephone service.[51] The MPT had the responsibility of deciding which territories Telway-Japan and the Daini Denden-Motorola joint venture could serve. Telway-Japan was allocated the territory constituting the largest potential market for cellular service. The resulting conflict between Motorola and the bureaucracy was a source of considerable discord between the United States and Japan in international trade negotiations. That discord is considered in more detail in Baron (1996).

Summary

The nonmarket environment in a country may be characterized in terms of issues, interests, institutions, and information, and culture and history shape the structure of institutions and the pattern of social interactions. Because of culture and the distinctive characteristics of the nonmarket environments in countries, nonmarket strategies of firms must be tailored to the environment in a country. The framework of structured pluralism provides the foundation for both nonmarket analysis and strategy formulation.

Japan's parliamentary system of government was dominated by the LDP for 38 years, but scandals and defections resulted in a period of party reorganization, consolidation, and intensified competition. The bureaucracy has remained powerful and pro-

---

[49]*Fortune*, September 11, 1989.
[50]See also the Part IV integrative case, *Toys 'R' Us and Globalization*.
[51]Harris (1989, p. 125).

vided stability, but it has been criticized for failing to deregulate the economy more quickly. The parliamentary system results in much of the legislative and policy-making work being done within the ministries and the party structure of the governing coalition. Consensus on policy is sought, although not always attained.

The bureaucracy has multiple roles as policy maker, regulator, and administrator. The ministries differ in the degree of politicization and power. One source of power is their expertise, often supported by a record of past successes. The bureaucracy attracts some of the most able of Japanese college graduates, who enter and remain as a cohort until they retire, and many "descend" to positions in business, politics, or quasi-governmental organizations. Bureaucratic power is also due to regulatory authority and the allocation of public resources. The bureaucracy interacts with interests both directly and through a set of advisory committees that provide a mechanism for sharing information and developing consensus. Much of the important interaction between interest groups and the bureaucracy takes place outside the view of the public.

In Japan, complex networks of political exchange interconnect business and other interest groups with the three principal components of the government: the governing parties, the bureaucracy, and the Diet. The interaction between interests and the government may be understood in the framework of an exchange involving interest groups, political parties, and the bureaucracy. Reciprocal exchange, for example, involves support in exchange for licensing, regulatory, and legislative policies that serve particular interests such as the construction and transportation industries. These interconnections are both formal (party and ministerial advisory committees) and less formal (*zoku*). Some are visible, whereas others, such as the system of political donations and the personal relationships between *amakudari* bureaucrats and those who remain in the ministry, are largely invisible. Participating effectively in this system requires understanding both the pattern of these relationships and Japanese history and culture. Understanding is not enough, however. Firms invest in networks and in personal relationships between their executives and the appropriate members of government. Relationships take time to develop and continuity to sustain, and intermittent government relations are unlikely to be successful.

The principal political strategies of firms in Japan are electoral, lobbying, and coalition building. Electoral strategies have been important, but they provide temptation to engage in corrupt activities. These strategies may diminish in importance as a result of electoral reform and the public financing of elections. Lobbying focuses on the bureaucracy, the governing parties, and Diet members. Access is important, and firms develop relationships with government officials to provide that access. Peak organizations and trade associations are important in business-government relations, and most firms participate in these associations.

In Japan, much of the legislative activity is largely over once a bill is introduced in the Diet. Moreover, economic activity is heavily regulated, and the plans of the ministries can have a major impact on firms. Firms thus develop information about government ministries, Diet activities, and the governing parties' policy processes. Firms often develop close relationships with politicians and bureaucrats. Some engage the services of "advisors" or *amakudari* bureaucrats who both know the organizational and decision-making structure of the ministries and have personal contacts with high-ranking bureaucrats.

CASES

The Breakup of Nippon Telephone and Telegraph?

In 1990 the Japanese government considered breaking up Nippon Telephone and Telegraph (NTT), but postponed a decision until April 1996. During the ensuing 5 years much changed yet much remained the same. The Ministry of Post and Telecommunications (MPT) continued to press for breaking up NTT, and NTT continued to oppose a breakup. As 1996 approached, the political and economic situation remained complex and contentious.

Despite the "privatization" of NTT in 1985, the Ministry of Finance still held 66 percent of NTT's shares. Several planned sales of shares by the MOF had been postponed because of the depressed price of NTT's shares. NTT continued to provide only domestic telecommunications services, and Kokusai Denshin Denwa (KDD) remained the country's dominant international carrier. NTT was prohibited by law from providing international telecommunications services, but it was allowed to invest overseas. NTT had begun investing offshore in 1992, but only 0.3 percent of its assets were outside Japan. NTT did not manufacture telecommunications equipment but instead relied on a set of suppliers with which it maintained long-term relationships. NTT's principal suppliers were Fujitsu, Hitachi, NEC, and Oki, which were referred to as the "NTT family." NTT had begun to purchase from foreign suppliers, but the amounts were a much smaller percent of NTT's total equipment purchases compared with the equipment purchases from foreign suppliers by other Japanese telecommunications companies.

THE TELECOMMUNICATIONS INDUSTRY

On the surface the Japanese telecommunications industry was structurally competitive with over 100 common carriers. In addition to NTT and KDD, there were three domestic long-distance carriers, two international carriers, 32 cellular companies, and 28 personal handheld system providers. As a result of the competition, NTT's long-distance market share had declined to 69 percent, but it still held 99 percent of the local service market and 80 percent of the total domestic telecommunications market.

Most of its competitors were dependent on NTT for access to customers through its local network, and some companies paid up to 50 percent of their revenues to NTT as access charges. Long-distance competitors such as DDI complained that interconnection with NTT required lengthy negotiations. DDI President Yusai Okuyama said, "We have to spend years on interconnection negotiations [with NTT] and that has obstructed the speedy development of our business plan."[1] Jupiter TeleCommunications, a joint venture between Sumitomo Corporation and TeleCommunications International of the United States, sought access to NTT subscribers in its cable franchise area so that it could offer telephone and other services. If approved by NTT, Jupiter would then file for a license with the MPT. In the past NTT had refused to provide interconnections to cable companies.

As a virtual local service monopoly NTT's prices were high. The MPT reported that NTT's basic subscription rate for telephone service had risen by more than 15 percent during the past 10 years, and the initial subscription (hookup) charge of over $700 was four times that in the UK and 13 times the charge in France.[2] Moreover, subscribers had to purchase a long-term telephone bond that helped finance NTT's capital expenditures. NTT's access charges were sufficiently high that they limited entry.

The MPT maintained that not only did NTT's high access charges limit competition, but it also discriminated against competitors in interconnections and obtained commercially sensitive information on competitors through the negotiations on access and interconnection. As an example of the level of cross-subsidization, NTT stated that it planned to reduce the current 340 yen charge for a 3-minute daytime long-distance call to 100 yen in the year 2000.

---

[1] *Financial Times,* August 7, 1996.
[2] *Financial Times,* August 7, 1996.

REGULATION

The MPT had taken some steps to deregulate the long-distance, cellular, and CATV industries, and some politicians and economists believed that further deregulation would stimulate economic activity and create jobs. In 1994 the MPT had allowed customers to own their own cellular terminals, which was credited with spurring growth in cellular telecommunications. This significantly reduced the market shares of existing carriers including NTT and DDI.

BUREAUCRATIC INFLUENCE

Critics of the MPT argued that it had allowed entry into the industry to give it more firms to regulate and more places to which its bureaucrats could descend. Those critics claimed that the MPT's push to break up NTT had the same motivation. As an example of the MPT's strategy for maintaining its influence and providing opportunities for *amakudari* bureaucrats, four members of NTT's board of directors were former MPT officials, including Shigeo Sawada, a former administrative vice minister of the MPT who joined NTT in 1990 as senior vice president, and 18 other former bureaucrats were in NTT-affiliated companies. As another example, the paging industry was divided into 32 regional operators, and according to a senior official at one Tokyo-based paging company, this division was " 'only to give all the regional heads of the ministry places to enjoy their retired life.' "[3] Private companies such as the long-distance and cellular provider DDI also had *amakudari* bureaucrats. DDI President Okuyama was a former MPT administrative vice minister, and three other MPT officials were employed by DDI.

In 1994 the MPT had pushed for Sawada to be appointed president of NTT, but NTT opposed the appointment and supported Junichiro Miyazu, a career NTT employee, for president. A stalemate resulted, and the current president, Masahi Kojima, remained in office. The MPT then turned its attention to preventing NTT from naming Kojima chairman and Miyazu president. The MPT enlisted the aid of the telecommunications *zoku,* members of the Diet who maintained an interest in telecommunications, in support of Sawada, but the financial community preferred Miyazu. Recognizing that Miyazu would likely become president, the MPT then sought to block Kojima from being appointed chairman. It used a 1986 executive directive intended to restrict the influence of *amakudari* bureaucrats in special corporations such as NTT to block the appointment. In 1996 a settlement was reached between NTT and its backers and the MPT and its backers, the telecommunications *zoku,* and politicians. In the settlement Sawada was appointed chairman, Miyazu was appointed president, and Kojima was named special advisor.[4]

THE GOVERNMENT COALITION

After scandals resulted in the resignation of two prime ministers from the opposition parties in 1994, the government was formed by a coalition among the Liberal Democratic Party (LDP), the Social Democratic Party (SDP), and the small New Party Harbinger (Sakigate). To establish the coalition, the president of the SDP was given the position of prime minister. A poor performance in upper house elections and defections from the SDP, however, weakened the prime minister and resulted in a change in the government. Mr. Ryutaro Hashimoto, a long-standing member of the LDP, was elected head of the LDP and became prime minister in 1995. Hashimoto had entered politics at age 25 when he inherited his father's constituency and was elected to the Diet. He joined the Tanaka faction of the LPD and served as Minister of Finance and Minister of International Trade and Industry in previous governments. Hashimoto was popular with the Japanese public in part because he had stood up to the United States in trade negotiations. His popularity gave the LDP hope that it might return to power by winning a majority of the seats in the lower house in the next election to be held by April 1997. The prime minister could dissolve the Diet and call an early election, and the speculation was that Prime Minister Hashimoto would do so.

The Minister of Posts and Telecommunication in Hashimoto's cabinet was Ichiro Hino, a member of the SDP. The SDP was backed by labor unions, including Zen Dentsu which represented 185,000 NTT employees. Zen Dentsu believed that a breakup of NTT would result in a substantial loss of jobs. NTT had already reduced its employment from 314,000 in 1985 to 197,000 in 1994, although some of those job losses represented transfers to affiliated companies.

---

[3] *The Nikkei Weekly,* February 26, 1996.

[4] *Mainichi Daily News,* May 28, 1996.

NTT'S STRATEGY

NTT deployed a well-integrated strategy to avoid a breakup. In its market environment, it announced in September 1995 that it planned to spin off its two software divisions. In the same month it announced that it would open its local service network to competitors. The high access charges, however, would prevent competitors from taking advantage of the opening. NTT subsequently announced that it would reduce its access fees. NTT also announced that it would eliminate 45,000 jobs over the next 5 years to improve its efficiency.[5]

In the nonmarket environment NTT rallied its suppliers and its union. Within the Keidanren, NTT's principal suppliers opposed a breakup, leading the Keidanren to take no position on the issue. Zen Dentsu used its relationships with the SDP to encourage it to oppose a breakup in the cabinet. NTT also argued that size was increasingly important in the global telecommunications industry and that a breakup would threaten its future international competitiveness.

POLICY ANALYSIS

A number of possible ways to break up NTT had been considered. One was to break up NTT geographically into a set of regional companies, but as Japan is approximately the size of California, regional companies might not make economic sense. Another possibility was to break up NTT vertically into a long-distance company and a local service company. A third possibility was to break it into a long-distance company and as many as 11 local service companies.

In late 1995 some policy analysts had come to believe that deregulating the telecommunications industry and allowing increased competition was more important than breaking up NTT. This, however, was contrary to the MPT's plans. Any substantial deregulation would thus have to come from the governing parties through new legislation.

The Keidanren supported deregulation of the Japanese economy, and its Telecommunications Council studied the issue of the breakup of NTT. The council, however, chose to not issue a report due to internal disagreement with NTT's family of suppliers opposing a breakup and NTT's competitors and customers supporting a breakup. A Keidanren spokesperson stated that deregulation should take place before a breakup. The absence of Keidanren support for a breakup weakened the MPT's position.

The National Institute for Research Advancement also studied the issue and concluded that the AT&T breakup model was no longer valid and could weaken research and development and harm rural areas by reducing cross-subsidization. The institute, however, did not make a recommendation.

THE DECISION-MAKING PROCESS

In traditional fashion, the MPT issued a report in 1994 supporting greater competition in telecommunications. An Administrative Reform Council studied the issue and recommended a breakup, but did not specify how it should be done. That decision was referred to the Telecommunications Council, a deliberation council (advisory panel) of the MPT. Deliberation councils rely on the resources of the ministry and have been criticized as supporting the outcome the ministry wanted. The council was asked to make a recommendation regarding a breakup by early 1996.

At the end of February 1996, the Telecommunications Council recommended that by 1999 NTT be split into a long-distance carrier and two local service companies, one serving the western part of Japan including Osaka and one serving the eastern part including Tokyo.[6] In addition, the council recommended that NTT be allowed to provide international services, and KDD and International Digital Communications be allowed to provide domestic services. In an unusual failure of consensus, 3 of 22 members of the Telecommunications Council dissented, arguing that global competition required large companies.

NTT argued that the western region would be unprofitable because it would not serve the main business centers. It projected that the eastern region would have profits of 70 billion yen and the western region a deficit of 80 billion yen. The MPT countered with its own estimates. It forecasted a profit of 217.4 billion yen for the western region.

MITI had traditionally backed NTT because it believed that NTT was Japan's only realistic hope in the international telecommunications industry. MITI believed that it was necessary to preserve NTT's economies of scale and its investments in research and development to ensure its international compet-

---

[5] *The Nikkei Weekly* reported, however, that over half the employees would be loaned to NTT subsidiaries.

[6] Ministry of Post and Telecommunications, "The Status of Nippon Telegraph and Telephone Corporation: Toward the Creation of Dynamism in the Info-Communications Industry," February 29, 1996.

itiveness. Both MITI and the MOF, however, remained largely neutral in the current conflict. ■

PREPARATION QUESTIONS

1. How will the decision regarding breaking up NTT be made? That is, who will have influence in the decision-making and why?
2. How effective is NTT's strategy likely to be?
3. What outcome do you predict and why?

Toys 'Я' Us in Japan (A)

Toys 'Я' Us, the largest discount toy retailer in the world, had fiscal 1989 sales of $4 billion and net income of $238 million. The company operated nearly 500 Toys 'Я' Us and over 100 Kids 'Я' Us stores. By October 1989 Toys 'Я' Us operated over 70 stores in countries other than the United States, including one each in Hong Kong, Malaysia, Singapore, and Taiwan. However, the company had not yet entered the Japanese market.

The opportunities in Japan were substantial. The Japanese toy market was over $5.5 billion, personal income was growing rapidly, and the structure of retailing made the profit potential for discount stores great. One estimate was that over 50 percent of retail sales in Japan was accounted for by shops with one or two employees. Many of these "mom and pop" shops were owned by retirees. The aging of shopowners and their children's reluctance to take over the businesses had resulted in a decline of 9.3 percent in the number of shops from 1982 to 1985 and a 7 percent decline from 1985 to 1988. In spite of the decline, over 1.4 million small shops remained in Japan. These shops represented an important component of the clientistic and reciprocal exchange relationships with the LDP and the bureaucracy. Local merchants also often played an important role in the *koenkai* of many Diet members.

These small shops were an important part of the fabric of Japanese society, but they were also the cap of a very inefficient distribution system. Japan had several more layers to its distribution system than most other countries, and two to three times the number of small shops per capita. This increased costs and prices. The high prices provided an important profit opportunity for an efficient, large-scale retailer such as Toys 'Я' Us.

Chairman Charles P. Lazarus saw a potential for 100 stores in Japan and hoped to open the first Toys 'Я' Us store in Niigata, 160 miles north of Tokyo. Toys 'Я' Us planned to supply the stores directly, bypassing the Japanese distribution system. Approximately 80 percent of the merchandise sold in its Japanese stores would be the same as that sold in the other Toys 'Я' Us stores.

Toys 'Я' Us' market opportunities were controlled by government regulations. As Vice President Michael Goldstein explained: "A lot will depend on whether the Japanese government will relax [its] rules. We think we're going to expand the market there for toys. It'll be good for us, good for our suppliers and will be good for Japan in that we're going to bring a diversity of consumer products for Japanese children."

Entry into the Japanese market was complicated by a variety of factors. The structure of Japanese retailing persisted in part because of the Large-Scale Retail Store Law (LSRSL), which made it difficult to open a large store. Notice had to be given to the Small and Medium-Size Enterprises Agency (SMEA) of MITI to open a store larger than 1,500 square meters.[1] SMEA typically recommended postponing the opening as it sought the advice of a local large-scale retail council. Notice of any store larger than 500 square meters also had to be given to the governor of the prefecture, which had authority similar to MITI's. Two laws enacted in 1977, the Coordinating Sphere of Activities Law and the Small and Medium-Size Business and Cooperative Law, strengthened the position of small enterprises by giving them a stronger voice in the local large-scale retail councils. Those councils sought the advice of the "commercial business arrangement committee," established by the local chamber of commerce. The committee's advice was often reflected in the decision of the governor or minister. Local councils played a role in setting not only store size but also store hours.[2] These laws and the local consultation process provided an opportunity for

[1]Toys 'Я' Us stores are up to four times this size.
[2]Store hours and the number of employees permitted were regulated in the same manner.

local merchants to oppose entry. As Tatsuki Kubo of McDonald's (Japan) explained: "It's a Japanese custom. If a big company wants to move into a local area, the people oppose it."[3]

These laws and the complex approval process did not preclude the opening of large stores, but they could result in long and often prohibitive delays. The laws placed no limit on the length of the consultation period, and there had been delays as long as 10 years. When faced with strong opposition some large-scale retailers had given up, whereas others had chosen to "negotiate" with the local store owners to overcome their opposition.

In spite of these restrictions, some supermarket and department store chains had expanded in Japan. Isao Nakauchi founded the Daiei chain in 1957; by 1988 Daiei had 181 outlets that sold clothing and other merchandise as well as groceries. Nakauchi complained that opening a new store took from 5 to 7 years and that 73 applications had to be filed for 26 permits under 12 laws.

Because of the size of their outlets, companies such as McDonald's and 7-Eleven were often unaffected by the LSRSL.[4] Indeed, McDonald's, led by President Den Fujita, had expanded rapidly and by 1989 had 675 restaurants in Japan. McDonald's Japan was skilled at dealing with the relevant bureaucracy and the local government units whose approval was needed to open a restaurant. McDonald's (Japan) also employed *amakudari* bureaucrats for their relationships with and knowledge of the ministries from which they descended.[5]

In recent years, the approval process had been somewhat streamlined, and in some cases the delays have been reduced to as little as 2 years. Restrictions on store hours and expansion had also been eased. Rumors of the possible entry of Toys 'Я' Us, however, stirred concern in the retail industry. A toy wholesaler in Niigata commented, "This is not just a local problem; Toys 'Я' Us will have a big impact on the entire toy industry. We are opposed to their plan."[6] He said he would be meeting with other members of the industry to formulate a strategy against Toys 'Я' Us. Masao Sakurai, a toy retailer with eight shops in Niigata, predicted, "If Toys 'Я' Us comes in, Japanese shops will be wiped out.[7]

In 1989 MITI issued a report, "Vision of the Japanese Distribution Industry in the 1990s," which criticized the inefficiency in the distribution system and explored possible improvements. One possibility would be to limit the ability of local governments to impose restrictions that favored local retailers. As was frequently the case in Japan, MITI could make some changes through "administrative guidance," although it would have to obtain the consent of the Ministry of Local Autonomy.

Toys 'Я' Us' market strategy was to attempt to bypass the Japanese distribution system by opening large stores and supplying them directly. To implement this strategy, the company faced not only the problem of the LSRSL but also a host of local regulations on retailing. One strategy that Toys 'Я' Us could adopt would be to attempt to place the issue of retailing restrictions on the agenda of the ongoing U.S.-Japan trade negotiations. U.S. Trade Representative Carla Hills was believed to be sympathetic to this issue and might make Toys 'Я' Us a cause célèbre. Toys 'Я' Us also faced the difficult problem of finding store locations because the price of land in Japan had reached astronomical levels. ■

[3] *The Wall Street Journal,* February 7, 1990.
[4] McDonald's Company (Japan) Ltd. is a 50-50 joint venture of the U.S. McDonald's Corporation and Fujita & Company, and 7-Eleven stores are owned by Ito Yokuda, a supermarket and department store chain, which licensed the 7-Eleven name.
[5] *The Japan Economic Journal,* May 26, 1990.
[6] *The Wall Street Journal,* February 7, 1990.
[7] *The Wall Street Journal,* February 7, 1990.

PREPARATION QUESTIONS

1. What does Toys 'Я' Us have to accomplish to enter the Japanese market successfully?
2. In the context of Wilson's matrix in Figure 6–4, what is the nature of the politics of the Toys 'Я' Us entry?
3. Who might serve as an entrepreneur in assisting Toys 'Я' Us in its entry attempt?
4. Which interest groups are likely to be active on this issue? What is the nature of their exchange relationship with the government?
5. What nonmarket strategy should Toys 'Я' Us adopt to deal with the nonmarket issue of entry into the Japanese market? What strategy should it adopt to deal with its market environment, for example, store locations and supply arrangements? How should its market and nonmarket strategies be integrated?

CHAPTER 14

The Political Economy of the European Union

Introduction

The European Union (EU) has taken landmark steps toward economic and political integration. The EU has established a single market with 370 million consumers that allows the free movement of people, goods, services, and capital. It has also established a common currency and an independent central bank and has moved toward greater commonality in defense and foreign policy. The eventual breadth of European integration remains open with over a dozen nations seeking to join the Union. In addition, the eventual depth of that integration, particularly with respect to political union, remains unclear.

The 15 member states in the European Union are Austria, Belgium, Denmark, Finland, France, Germany, Greece, Ireland, Italy, Luxembourg, the Netherlands, Portugal, Spain, Sweden, and the United Kingdom. Norway was approved for membership in the Union, but in 1994 Norwegian voters rejected membership as they had done in 1972. In 2003 the EU is likely to admit five new members, the Czech Republic, Estonia, Hungary, Poland, and Slovenia, and possibly Cyprus. A number of other countries have applied for membership. The member states differ considerably with populations ranging from 400,000 to 80 million, a ratio of more than 2 to 1 in per capita incomes among the members, and unemployment rates ranging from 3 to 18 percent. Yet the member states have made remarkable progress toward economic integration, and the commitment to deeper integration is strong in most of the member states.

This chapter provides a characterization of the nonmarket environment in the European Union using the structured pluralism framework illustrated in Figure 13-1. The nonmarket environment is characterized by the four I's—issues, institutions, interests, and information—however, the culture and history of 15 countries are too complex to address here. Instead, an analysis of the nonmarket environment in Germany is used to illustrate the country-specific factors that are important for operating in individual member states within the Union.

The Union

In the aftermath of World War II Europeans recognized the need to increase trade and encourage political cooperation. In 1951 six nations—Belgium, France, Italy, Luxembourg, the Netherlands, and West Germany—signed the Treaty of Paris, which established the European Coal and Steel Community (ECSC). The ECSC's goal was to improve the efficiency of its member states' coal and steel industries through the reduction of trade barriers.

In 1957 those same nations signed the Treaty of Rome, which provides the basic framework for the European Union of today. The Treaty of Rome established the

European Economic Community (EEC), or the common market, with the objectives of opening domestic markets to the member states and rationalizing their industries.[1] The 1965 Treaty of Brussels represented an important step toward European integration by unifying the administration of the EEC, ECSC, and EURATOM. This provided an administrative structure upon which further steps toward economic and political integration could be built. The European Monetary System was established in 1979 to provide fixed, but adjustable, exchange rate bands for the currencies of the member states. In 1973 Denmark, Ireland, and the United Kingdom joined the EEC. Greece joined in 1981, Portugal and Spain in 1986, and Austria, Finland, and Sweden joined in 1995.

The two most recent major steps toward economic and political union have been the Single European Act and the Maastricht Treaty on European Union, considered next.[2]

THE SINGLE EUROPEAN ACT

Economic growth in the common market was strong during the 1960s, but beginning in the 1970s and particularly in the early 1980s growth dropped markedly, unemployment rolls swelled to over 10 percent, and job creation slowed to a crawl. The slow growth, the high cost of labor, and the difficulties and costs involved in workforce reductions made many firms reluctant to hire. Europeans called their economic disease "Eurosclerosis" and worried that they were losing competitiveness relative to the United States and Japan.

Many business leaders recognized that competitiveness was inhibited by a set of barriers that limited trade and increased costs. Reductions in many barriers had been slow because each state reserved the right to veto changes it believed were contrary to its interests. To document the potential gains from further market integration, the European Commission sponsored the Cecchini study, which concluded that the formation of a single market could increase GDP by 4.3 to 6.4 percent.[3]

The Single European Act (SEA), which amended the Treaty of Rome and took effect in 1987, addressed several impediments to trade and provided measures to facilitate access to national markets.[4] The SEA also increased the power of the EU government relative to the governments of its member states, particularly by limiting the use of a unanimity rule for decision making as allowed in Article 100 of the Treaty of Rome. The act specified the realization of a single market by the beginning of 1993. The program to realize market integration involved the removal of three types of barriers to a single market: physical, technical, and fiscal. The removal of physical barriers pertained to the movement of both goods and people, eliminating customs and other goods inspections, removing restrictions on the entry of people, and allowing individuals to work in any member state.

The EU took two approaches—harmonization and mutual recognition—to the removal of internal barriers to trade. Harmonization refers to the development of a common set of policies for all the member states. Because of the complexity of the bargaining, progress on technical issues such as product standards, product certification, and the licensing of professional services became tediously slow as nationalistic considerations complicated negotiations. To avoid the roadblocks of the past, the principle

---

[1]The six nations also formed the European Atomic Energy Community (EURATOM).
[2]The 1997 Treaty of Amsterdam strengthened the human rights provisions of the EU, committed the EU to take steps to increase employment, adopted the objective of sustainable development, strengthened the Common Foreign and Security Policy, elevated the formal powers of the European Parliament, and prepared for institutional change when new members are admitted.
[3]See Cecchini et al. (1988) and Emerson, et al. (1988).
[4]European Commission (1986). See Overturf (1986) for an analysis of the benefits from economic integration.

of mutual recognition, first articulated by the European Court of Justice in the Cassis de Dijon case, was adopted.[5] The EU states were able to agree on mutual recognition, whereas they had been unable to agree on a common set of standards. The principle of mutual recognition represented a major change in EU policy and increased the speed with which internal barriers were removed.

Fiscal harmonization pertains to tax policy, particularly value-added taxes (VAT), excise and profits taxes, government fiscal policy, and subsidization or "state aids." The member states continue to differ substantially in their tax and other fiscal policies, and those differences can distort trade, the location of facilities, and the movement of people.[6] For example, VAT rates were as high as 38 percent on some goods and as low as zero on others. Furthermore, some countries had multiple tiers of VAT rates, whereas others had a single rate. Progress on fiscal harmonization has been slow.

Harmonization is also the approach taken to the sensitive and important issues of public health, safety, and the environment. The approach has been to reach agreement on a set of basic standards and then allow the individual member states to go beyond those basics as they choose.

THE MAASTRICHT TREATY

In December 1991 in Maastricht, the Netherlands, the member states agreed to the Treaty on Monetary and Political Union. The Maastricht Treaty ran into immediate problems as the United Kingdom opted out of part of it, Denmark first rejected and then narrowly accepted it, and French voters only narrowly approved it.

The treaty established a timetable for a common European currency and an independent European Central Bank.[7] In 1999, 11 member states that had satisfied conditions on inflation rates, government budget deficits, and interest rates formed a monetary union with a common currency—the euro—and a European Central Bank. Denmark, Sweden, and the United Kingdom met the conditions but opted not to join, and Greece had not yet met the conditions. The United Kingdom indicated that it would likely join the monetary union early in the twenty-first century.

Political integration is more difficult to accomplish than monetary union. Some steps toward political union have been taken. All the member states have entered into a protocol to establish a joint social policy. Nine of the member states formed the Western European Union to establish a joint defense policy. Additional proposals include strengthening the European Parliament, establishing a European citizenship, and changing the unanimity rule still in effect for certain decisions.

Whether the full vision of political union will be accomplished remains unclear. Germany has supported a European federal system, but the United Kingdom has balked at political integration that would jeopardize its sovereignty.

Nonmarket Issues

Nonmarket issues in the European Union may be categorized by the level at which they are addressed—the level of the Union itself versus that of a single member state, and whether they are specific to an industry or to an individual firm. At the level of the Union, important issues include further political integration, the administration of competition (antitrust) policy, persistent high unemployment, further reforms of the common

---

[5]In 1979 the court ruled that a German regulation on the alcohol content of liqueurs could not be used to block the sale of the French liqueur Cassis de Dijon.
[6]European Commission (1985, para. 189).
[7]See Committee for the Study of Economic and Monetary Union (1989) and Goodman (1992).

agricultural policy, trade policy, defense, harmonization of fiscal policies, the continued opening to competition of industries such as telecommunications and electric power, and the admission of new members. Some firms are directly involved in issues at the EU level, and more are involved in the issues at the level of member states. For example, Philips Electronics of the Netherlands worked for the creation of a center (JESSI) to conduct research on semiconductors. Much of the nonmarket activity at the level of the Union is conducted by peak associations that represent businesses within the member states. The role of these associations is addressed in more detail later in the chapter.

At the level of the member states, issues involving general policies include the harmonization of pharmaceutical price controls, tax policies to attract business, the convergence of products liability laws, and the opening of government procurement to competition among the member states. Issues also pertain to individual firms including the privatization of government-owned firms and the subsidization of airlines and other firms through state aids. Many of the issues at the level of the member states involve the implementation of EU regulations and directives.

Nonmarket issues at the industry and firm levels are abundant. Two examples at the industry level considered later in the chapter involve pharmaceutical pricing and privacy. The pharmaceutical industry has sought the decontrol of pharmaceutical prices, which have been kept low in countries such as France to relieve the government's health care budget. Much of the nonmarket action at the industry level is conducted by EU-wide associations representing the industry associations in the member states. For example, issues involving the pharmaceutical industry are addressed by the European Federation of Pharmaceutical Industries' Associations. In some cases ad hoc groups of firms from various member states join together to seek support, as when Philips, Siemens, Thomson, and General Electric (U.K.) sought support for the European computer and semiconductor industries.

Many nonmarket issues are firm specific. Many of these result from EU policies and regulations, but some result from actions taken by other firms or by activists. Activist groups, for example, protested a 1994 Benetton advertisement showing a bloody uniform of a fallen Croat soldier in the Yugoslav civil war. The ad was intended as a plea for peace, but Benetton was accused of exploiting the war. The French minister for humanitarian affairs called for a boycott of Benetton and urged people to "pull [Benetton sweaters] off the people who are going to wear them." The chapter case *Benetton, Advertising Protests, and Franchising* addresses this nonmarket issue in more detail.

EXAMPLE: DATA PRIVACY

Differences in cultures and their associated concerns can give rise to nonmarket issues. Many Europeans are quite concerned with privacy issues, and these concerns have led to strong EU measures to protect information about people. These concerns range from information on credit card use to the planting of cookies to track Internet site browsing. Some countries ban telephone marketing and unsolicited sales attempts by e-mail or fax. Germany and the Netherlands, for example, have strong national laws and enforcement agencies governing information. These laws have a potentially important impact on electronic commerce and the Internet. For example, in allowing Citibank (now Citigroup) to offer a credit card in Germany in 1994, the German government obtained the right to supervise the data Citibank stores on cardholders. Inspectors from the Datenschutz regularly visit Citibank's Sioux City, South Dakota, data center "to make sure that the data are being handled according to [German] law."[8] American Ex-

[8]*Business Week,* November 2, 1998.

press reached a similar agreement with several countries. An official with the Data Protection Agency of the Netherlands commented, "We are at the beginning of a new information society, and no one really knows the outcome. But privacy and trust are important parts of this society."[9]

At the EU level the Directive on Data Protection took effect in 1998 and requires that a person grant explicit permission to a company to obtain personal information. Individuals also have the right to inspect any files maintained and to correct any errors. Furthermore, an individual must be notified in advance if any personal information is to be sold. According to a spokesperson for Oracle, "Your business is essentially tubed until you get this resolved. It can be a life-or-death situation for some businesses."[10]

In the United States, the organization TRUSTe has established privacy principles that are adhered to by Web sites that account for a substantial share of Internet traffic. The behavior of Americans on the Internet suggests that many are also concerned about data privacy. Excite reports that 70 percent of Internet users quit a site when asked for personal information. No comprehensive legislation on data privacy has been passed in the United States.

To address the differences in the standards for data privacy between the European Union and the United States, the U.S. Department of Commerce entered into negotiations with the EU seeking a "safe harbor" arrangement under which companies that agreed to follow specific data protection policies would be held harmless by the EU. The EU said it had no current plans to stop data flows or to police the Internet and would decide specific issues on a case-by-case basis. The European activist group Privacy International, however, said it was investigating the practices of 25 companies, including Microsoft and United Airlines, and planned to file lawsuits if it identified any violations of the EU directive. A spokesperson for Time Warner in Brussels observed, "In Europe, people don't trust companies, they trust government. In the U.S., it's the opposite way around: Citizens must be protected from actions of the government."[11]

The Institutions of the European Union

The five principal institutions of the European Union are the European Commission, the Council of Ministers, the European Parliament, the European Court of Justice, and the Economic and Social Committee. Figure 14-1 shows each member country's representation in the first three institutions.

THE EUROPEAN COMMISSION

The European Commission, located in Brussels, is the executive and administrative body of the EU. The commission administers EU policies and enforces the various treaties. It is responsible for monitoring the implementation of EU legislation and ensuring that the member states comply with EU law. The commission is responsible for trade negotiations and policy and manages the EU budget. The commission is the only body with the power to initiate legislation, although as indicated later in the chapter it does not enact it. The European Parliament or the Council of Ministers can also ask the commission to review proposals and consider issues. The European Commission's role

---

[9] *The New York Times,* October 26, 1998.
[10] *San Jose Mercury News,* October 26, 1998.
[11] *Business Week,* November 2, 1998.

Country	*European Commission*	*Council of Ministers**	*European Parliament*
Austria	1	4	21
Belgium	1	5	25
Denmark	1	3	16
Finland	1	3	16
France	2	10	87
Germany	2	10	99
Greece	1	5	25
Ireland	1	3	15
Italy	2	10	87
Luxembourg	1	2	6
Netherlands	1	5	31
Portugal	1	5	25
Spain	2	8	64
Sweden	1	4	22
United Kingdom	2	10	87
Total	20	87	626

*The votes under qualified majority rule.

FIGURE 14-1 Representation by Country in European Union Institutions

in initiating legislation gives it considerable power and makes it a target for lobbying. Moreover, the commission is obligated to consult with interests and to notify the Council of Ministers and the parliament that it has done so. The commission has a relatively small staff (30,000), so it needs information and expertise, and its consultations with interests are a means of obtaining that information.

The commission has 20 commissioners who are obliged to serve the interests of the EU and not their own countries. Commission terms are 5 years, and the commission must be approved by the European parliament. Commissioners are appointed by the individual member states. Each commissioner has responsibility for one or more of the 24 directorate-generals (DGs), and one serves as president. A DG is a bureau with a particular administrative jurisdiction. For example, DG II has responsibilities for economic and financial affairs, DG IV for competition policy, and DG XXIII for telecommunications, the information market, and the exploitation of research. In an unprecedented event all 20 commissioners resigned in 1999 as a result of allegations of corruption and mismanagement and pressure from the European Parliament.

The conflict between national and EU laws creates a tension within the community. EU law takes precedence over national law when a conflict arises, but not all national laws have yet been harmonized with EU law. In a few cases member states have not complied with EU law, and the commission must attempt to obtain compliance.

The commission attempts to operate on a collegial basis, and no public reports of its deliberations or voting are issued. Conflict within the commission, however, can develop over policies, particularly those that have impacts across more than one DG. For example, in 1994 the commissioner for industry proposed the elimination of price controls on pharmaceuticals as a means of encouraging firms to invest more in the development of innovative drugs. The commission, however, rejected this policy in favor of asking the member states to bring their divergent pricing policies into alignment.

THE COUNCIL OF MINISTERS

The Council of Ministers, based in Brussels, is the executive and highest authority of the EU and the only institution that can enact law.[12] In contrast to the European Commission, whose members are obliged to serve the EU, council members are the individual member states. The council consists of one minister from each state, but the nations have different numbers of votes as indicated in Figure 14-1. The presidency rotates among the member nations, and which ministers belong to the council depends on the issue under consideration. On an issue involving economics and finance, the cognizant ministers of the member states meet as the Economic and Financial Affairs Council (ECOFIN). Twice a year, the prime ministers of the member states meet as the European Council.

Associated with the council is the Committee of Permanent Representatives (COREPER), composed of ambassadors, or "permanent representatives," of the member states. COREPER represents the member states before the commission and serves as the secretariat of the Council of Ministers. It prepares the agenda, forms "working parties," and negotiates informal agreements prior to council deliberations. Before the council considers proposals, COREPER appoints an ad hoc working party composed of government officials from the member states. Members of the European Commission may also participate. The working party gives its opinion on a legislative proposal to COREPER. If COREPER agrees with the opinion, it forwards the proposal to the council. COREPER is said to resolve 90 percent of the issues before they come to the council, leaving only the most politically sensitive to the council deliberations. The council operates in private, but beginning in 1995 its votes have been reported publicly.

Council decisions had been governed by a unanimity rule, which gave a veto to the member states. Because this created long delays on some issues, the SEA provided for decisions by majority rule. On most procedural matters the council acts under simple majority rule. Most of its substantive actions, however, require a "qualified" majority of 62 of 87 votes. Decisions involving foreign and security policy, justice and home affairs, and enlargement of the community require unanimity.[13]

The council can take four types of actions, which differ in the extent to which they are binding on the member states.[14]

1. Regulations are legally binding on the member states and are enforced by the commission.
2. Directives are legally binding with respect to the result sought, but national governments are responsible for how the result is achieved.
3. Decisions are legally binding but pertain only to the parties identified in the decision.
4. Recommendations and opinions are not legally binding but may provide guidance and indicate future action on issues.

---

[12]See Hoscheit and Wessels (1988) and Nugent (1994) for an analysis of the Council of Ministers.
[13]Hogan (1991, p. 383).
[14]See Nugent (1994).

EU law becomes effective in a member state when that state accepts it as its law. The Union operates under the principle of "subsidiarity," meaning the intention to accomplish as much as possible at the level of the member states. Article 36 of the Treaty of Rome, however, includes the qualification that the union can act "only if and in so far as the objectives of the proposed action cannot be sufficiently achieved by the member states. . ." This vague qualification has been the source of disagreement about the scope of the EU's actions relative to those of the member states.[15]

THE EUROPEAN PARLIAMENT

The European Parliament (EP) has 626 members directly elected by voters in the member states for 5-year terms. Parliament members organize by parties or political groupings. After the 1994 elections the Socialists had the largest representation, followed by the European People's Party (Christian Democrats). The EP meets in Brussels and Strasbourg.

As the only popularly elected institution in the EU, the European Parliament has powers of "democratic supervision." The EP approves of and can dismiss the European Commission and ask questions of commissioners in writing or during "Question Time" when the EP is in session. Through the co-decision procedure, the EP and the council share legislative authority. Parliament cannot enact laws but plays a role in the legislative process. That role has expanded over time, and the SEA and the Maastricht Treaty gave it new legislative power, as described later in the chapter. Parliament also has budgetary authority.

The EP elects a president, who serves a 2 1/2-year term, and 14 vice presidents. It has 20 committees to which proposals are referred for consideration, and they are a focus of lobbying. Neither the committees nor Parliament has the ability to delay a proposal, since action must be taken within a specified period. The Parliament operates under simple majority rule.

Individual citizens and firms may petition Parliament on issues arising from either EU actions or conflicts between EU law and national laws. Petitions are reviewed by a Petition Committee; if accepted for consideration, the Petition Committee evaluates the position and may hold a hearing. Interest groups often work through their national representatives in the petition process.

THE EUROPEAN COURT OF JUSTICE

The European Court of Justice, located in Luxembourg, is the supreme judicial body of the Union and has the authority to overturn decisions of the Council of Ministers that conflict with the EU treaties.[16] The court has 15 justices—one for each member nation—plus a presidency that rotates among the five largest nations.[17] Although it makes decisions by majority vote, dissenting opinions are not issued. The judges serve 6-year terms and are assisted by nine advocates general who provide independent and impartial opinions. The court hears cases pertaining to the various treaties underlying the EU and other cases involving disputes between the community's institutions. Some of the cases brought to the Court involve complaints by the European Commission against the member states. Actions can also be brought directly to the court by individuals and legal entities of the member states. Although the Court has the final word on

---

[15]The pledge to abide by the principle of subsidiarity was important in obtaining Denmark's support for the Maastricht Treaty.
[16]See Freestone (1983).
[17]Europe also has a Council of Europe that has a European Court, which hears cases under the European Convention on Human Rights.

EU law, treaties give the courts of the member states some responsibilities for implementing EU law. The Court also hears cases from member states when the states' own courts are uncertain about EU law.[18] Because of the Court's workload, the Council of Ministers, under the SEA, established the Court of First Instance (CFI). The CFI applies the law established by the European Court of Justice, and its decisions may be appealed to the higher court.

The European Court of Justice also hears appeals of decisions of the European Commission. For example, cases involving the competitive practices of firms are usually decided by the commission's directorate-general for competition (DG IV). Firms can appeal its decisions and the penalties assessed. As indicated later in the chapter, European airlines appealed the European Commission's decision to allow France to subsidize Air France.

THE ECONOMIC AND SOCIAL COMMITTEE

The Economic and Social Committee (ESC), based in Brussels, is an advisory body whose 222 members represent labor, business, farmers, trades, and other interests. The ESC has nine sections, or committees, which provide forums to express opinions on commission proposals and to suggest changes in them. Interest groups interact with the ESC through the representatives of their home states in the relevant sections. The final opinions of the ESC are important because they reflect the concerns of interest groups.

THE EU LEGISLATIVE PROCESS

The EU has three basic procedures—consultation, co-decision, and assent—for developing directives and regulations.[19] In the consultation procedure which was used for nearly all important issues prior to the SEA, the European Commission, through one of its DGs, formulates a proposal that is sent to the Council of Ministers, which seeks opinions from both the European Parliament and the Economic and Social Committee. The council weighs those opinions and returns the proposal to the commission for revision. The commission then sends the revised proposal to the council, which may amend, approve, or not act on it. If approved, the proposal becomes EU law, and the member states are required to abide by it.

The Single European Act established the assent procedure, which gives the European Parliament a veto over council action. The assent procedure is used for decisions about admission of new member states, international agreements, and the structure of the European Central Bank.

The Maastricht Treaty established the co-decision procedure, and the scope of its use was expanded in the 1997 Treaty of Amsterdam. This procedure, as illustrated in Figure 14-2, gives the European Parliament a greater role and more power relative to the commission and the council. In practice, however, the EP generally goes along with the wishes of the council and commission. This procedure begins as in the consultation procedure, but once the opinions of the European Parliament and the Economic and Social Committee have been obtained, the Council of Ministers develops by qualified majority a "common position" on the proposal. It is then sent to the EP for a second reading. If it approves the proposal, it is enacted. If an absolute majority of the EP votes

---

[18]A major difference between the United States and European countries results from the due process requirements of the U.S. Constitution. As discussed in Chapter 10, due process imposes a complex set of requirements on government processes intended to assure individuals the right to participate in governmental decision-making processes. Unless provided for by specific legislation, the European countries and the EU do not have the same requirements.

[19]See Nugent (1994).

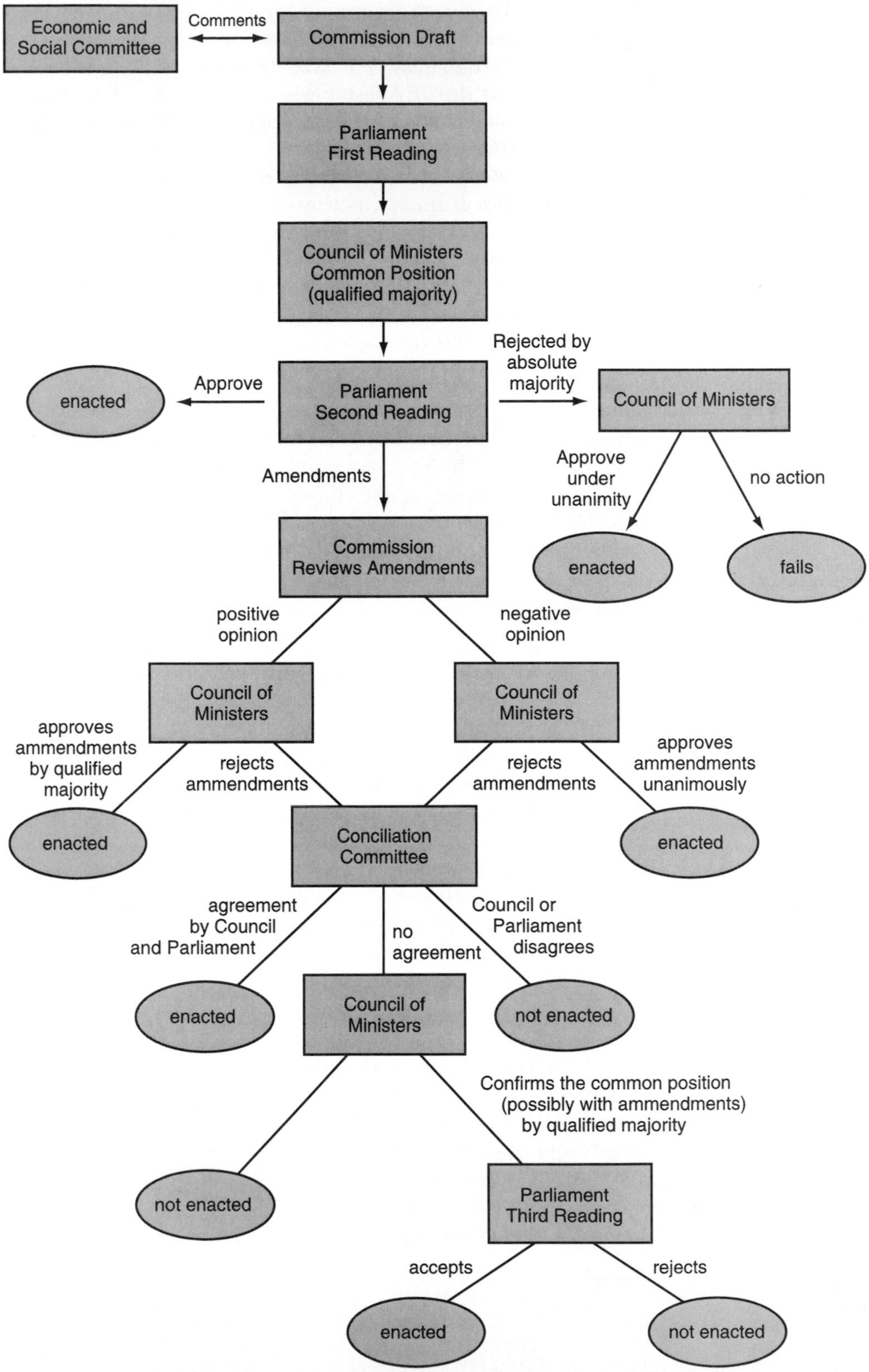

FIGURE 14-2 The European Union Co-Decision Legislative Procedure

against the common position, a unanimous vote of the council is required to enact it. If the EP amends the common position, the proposal goes to the European Commission for review of the amendments. With a positive (negative) opinion by the commission, the council can enact the amended proposal by qualified majority (unanimity). If the council rejects the amendments, a Conciliation Committee composed of members of the council and the EP is formed. If they reach agreement the amended proposal is enacted. If no agreement is reached, the Council of Ministers can confirm by qualified majority the common position with or without some of the amendments, and the common position with council-accepted amendments is enacted if approved by the EP on the third reading.

ECONOMIC AND MONETARY UNION

The European Union's interest in a monetary union officially began in 1989 when the Council of Ministers endorsed a series of steps to realize an Economic and Monetary Union (EMU). The EMU commenced in 1998 with the formation of the European System of Central Banks (ECB) to conduct a single monetary policy for its members. In 1999 the euro became the common currency of the EMU, and its use is being phased in through 2002 when euro notes and coins will replace national currencies.[20] The ECB is an independent central bank patterned after Germany's central bank (the Bundesbank). The stated primary objective of the ECB is "to maintain price stability."

The EU had estimated that the savings on transactions costs associated with currency exchange would be 0.4 percent of GDP. The euro would also become the second most important currency after the U.S. dollar and could provide some benefits to the EU as a reserve currency. Some countries such as Italy saw another advantage in the EMU. It would serve as a commitment device that would provide price stability to which its governments had had difficulty committing.

Not everyone shared the same enthusiasm for the EMU. Feldstein (1997, p. 32–33) warned that the EMU may have costs that outweigh its benefits. He pointed to the loss of flexibility for a country to use discretionary monetary policy to offset temporary shocks to its economy. More generally, he concluded, "My own judgment is that, on balance, a European monetary union would be an economic liability. The gains from reduced transactions costs would be small and might, when looked at from the global point of view, be negative. At the same time, EMU would increase cyclical instability, raising the cyclical unemployment rate. I believe that the EMU would also make it more difficult to reduce structural unemployment and would increase the risk of protectionist policy toward non-EMU countries."

The EMU was put in place by governments that were largely center-right, but by the time the euro became an official currency most of Europe was governed by left parties. Many of their leaders, particularly in Germany and France, argued for a monetary policy that emphasized not only price stability but also economic growth and the creation of jobs. The ECB had been established as independent of the governments of the member states, but the left governments sought to influence the policies of the ECB. The 11 countries participating in the EMU formed the "euro-11" group of finance ministers to discuss ECB policies. The finance ministers of the 11 socialist governments in the EU met at the end of 1998 and called upon the ECB to keep interest rates low to stimulate growth and employment.

---

[20]The European Union had a long history of coordinated exchange rate policies. In the 1970s European countries maintained the "snake" with fixed exchange rates, and subsequently a stable Deutschmark zone developed. Then, the European Monetary System (EMS) was established to band exchange rates together. The EMS also used a weighted average of exchange rates, the ECU, that was a forerunner of the euro.

COMPETITION POLICY

Competition policy includes EU policies involving the structure, conduct, and support of industries, including state aids. Antitrust policy is the centerpiece of competition policy, and this section addresses EU antitrust law and its administration. The member states have their own competition laws. In 1998 France rejected Coca-Cola's planned acquisition of Orangina, after objections by PepsiCo and Orangina employees who feared layoffs.

The basic antitrust law of the EU is found in Articles 85 and 86 of the Treaty of Rome, the principal components of which are presented in Figure 14-3.[21] The articles have two antecedents. The first is the Treaty of Rome goal of market integration. The second is U.S. antitrust law. Articles 85 and 86 correspond to Sections 1 and 2 of the Sherman Act, but EU antitrust law differs substantially from U.S. law. Both aim at promoting competition, but EU law allows defenses, such as economic consequences, not provided for under U.S. law. Hence, EU law does not have *per se* offenses.

As with Section 1 of the Sherman Act, Article 85 refers to group activities that may limit competition or constitute a barrier to trade among member states. Much of the text addresses vertical restraints, which were a particular concern because of the possibility that firms would use such arrangements in their channels of distribution to preserve national markets for themselves. Parts a, b, and c of Article 85, paragraph 1, pertain to vertical arrangements that might foreclose markets, and part d deals with price discrimination among the member states. Part e pertains to tying arrangements or reciprocal deals that might foreclose markets. The feature of Article 85 that distinguishes it most from Section 1 of the Sherman Act is the allowable defenses provided in paragraph 3. A firm may make the affirmative defense that an arrangement improves efficiency. The firm is obligated to use the least restrictive means to achieve that efficiency, and some of the efficiency gains must be passed on to consumers. Paragraph 3 virtually grants block exemptions for a variety of agreements—exclusive distributorships, exclusive purchase arrangements, patent licensing, motor vehicle distribution, specialization, research and development, franchises, and know-how licensing.

Article 86 deals with unilateral actions and differs from Section 2 of the Sherman Act by focusing on the conduct of firms rather than on industry structure. The article is not concerned with how a dominant position was obtained but rather with whether that position is abused. Article 86 thus does not provide a blanket prohibition of monopoly. Its specific provisions apply to unfair practices, monopoly restriction of output, price discrimination, and tying.

Enforcement

Antitrust enforcement is by the DG IV of the European Commission which investigates practices, initiates proceedings, serves as prosecutor, decides cases, and imposes fines. All these activities are within the same bureaucracy, and courts play no role unless there is an appeal of an action. Appeals are heard by the Court of First Instance and then by the European Court of Justice if necessary. Private parties may file complaints with the European Commission, but private lawsuits are not permitted. DG IV is also required to consult with national competition officials before initiating proceedings. Those officials participate in the Advisory Committee on Restrictive Practices and Monopolies.

---

[21] Article 86 is presented in its entirety.

Article 85:

(1) The following practices shall be prohibited as incompatible with the Common Market: all agreements between undertakings and all concerted practices which are liable to affect trade between Member States and which are designed to prevent, restrict or distort competition within the Common Market or which have this effect. This shall, in particular, include:

a) the direct or indirect fixing of purchase or selling prices or of any other trading conditions;

b) the limitation or control of production markets, technical development or investment;

c) market-sharing or the sharing of sources of supply;

d) the application of unequal conditions or parties undertaking equivalent engagements in commercial transactions, thereby placing them at a competitive disadvantage.

e) making the conclusion of a contract subject to the acceptance by the other party to the contract of additional obligations which, by their nature or according to commercial practice, have no connection with the subject of such contract.

(2) Any agreement or decisions prohibited pursuant to this article shall automatically be null and void.

The provisions of paragraph (1) may, however, be declared inapplicable in the case of

-any agreement or type of agreement between undertakings
-any decision or type of agreement between undertakings
-any concerted practice or type of concerted practice

which helps to improve the production or distribution of goods or to promote technical or economic progress, whilst allowing consumers a fair share of the resulting profit and which does not: a) subject the concerns in question to any restrictions which are not indispensable to the achievement of the above objectives; b) enable such concerns to eliminate competition in respect to a substantial part of the goods concerned.

Article 86:

(3) Any improper exploitation by one or more undertakings of a dominant position within the Common Market or within a substantial part of it shall be deemed to be incompatible with the Common Market and shall be prohibited, in so far as trade between Member States could be affected by it. The following practices, in particular, shall be deemed to amount to improper exploitation:

a) the direct or indirect imposition of any unfair purchase or selling prices or of any other unfair trading conditions;

b) the limitation of production, markets or technical development to the prejudice of consumers;

c) the application of unequal conditions to parties undertaking equivalent engagements in commercial transactions, thereby placing them at a commercial disadvantage;

d) making the conclusion of a contract to the acceptance by the other party to the contract of additional obligations which by their nature or according to commercial practice have no connection with the subject of such contract.

FIGURE 14-3 European Union Antitrust Law: Articles 85 and 86 of the Treaty of Rome

The European Commission cannot use structural remedies, such as ordering the divestiture of business units, and is limited to imposing fines. Fines of up to 10 percent of a company's sales may be imposed. In 1994 under Article 85 it imposed fines of 132 million European Currency Units (ECUs) on a cartel of 19 carton-board manufacturers and 248 million ECUs on a cartel of 33 cement producers. Some of the companies filed appeals.[22]

[22] An ECU was a unit of account used by the EU prior to the establishment of the euro. An ECU was equivalent to about $1.20.

Mergers

The Treaty of Rome did not address mergers because they were viewed as a desirable means of enabling small-scale European firms to attain the scale needed to compete globally. In 1989 the Council of Ministers adopted a Merger Control Regulation, assigning the European Commission the responsibility for reviewing large mergers, those in which the combined unit has sales of over 5 billion ECUs and the individual firms had sales of over 250 million ECUs.[23] Thus, two U.S. firms that merge and have operations in the EU with sales of at least 250 million ECUs are subject to review by the commission with regard to their EU operations. Merger review by the commission is based solely on the effect on competition. The member states retain their power to review smaller mergers and can seek permission from the commission to conduct their own review of large mergers. If two-thirds of the revenues of each of two merging firms are from a single member state, that state rather than the commission has authority over the review. This allows a country to permit the merger of two of its major companies.

The European Union has been active in the review of mergers. In 1997 under pressure from the backers of Airbus Industrie and concerned about 20-year sole-supplier contracts signed by Boeing with American, Delta, and Continental Airlines, DG IV threatened to block the planned merger of Boeing and McDonnell Douglas. After intense negotiations between Boeing and DG IV and implicit threats of trade sanctions by the United States, Boeing made concessions sought by DG IV, and the merger was approved. Boeing agreed not to enforce the sole-supplier features of its contracts and to maintain the Douglas Aircraft Company as a separate division.

In 1991 the U.S. Department of Justice (DOJ) and the European Commission signed an agreement to cooperate on antitrust investigations. The DOJ and the commission, acting under a complaint from Novell, Inc., cooperated in the antitrust case against Microsoft (see Chapter 9) with both agencies pressuring the company to enter into a consent decree to change its software licensing practices. In 1998 the EU required the divestiture of all of MCI's Internet assets before approving its merger with WorldCom. As indicated in Chapter 9, U.S. antitrust authorities also required the divestiture.

PRIVATIZATION AND MARKET OPENING

Although the SEA provided the structure for opening national markets to competition, large sectors of the EU economy remained closed, often controlled by state-owned monopolies supported by close relationships with government ministries. The telecommunications and electric power industries, for example, had been controlled by state-owned firms, and the airline industry was cartelized through intergovernmental accords and EU sanction. Many of these firms were inefficient and unprepared to compete in an open market. The pace of market opening had been slow because of political opposition from the state-owned firms, the ministries that supervised them, and the unions representing their workers. The recognition that these industries would eventually be open to competition spurred a number of countries to prepare for competition by privatizing their state-owned firms.[24] This was also spurred by the countries' need for the revenue that privatization would provide and by the encroachment of new market entrants into niches allowed by regulatory loopholes. A large number of companies and financial institutions have been privatized in a broad set of countries.

---

[23]See Fishwick (1993) for an analysis of EU competition policy.
[24]Vickers and Yarrow (1988) provide an economic analysis of privatization.

Both the airline and the telecommunications markets in the EU have been opened to competition. Opening the telecommunications market in 1998 was required by an international trade agreement negotiated under the auspices of the World Trade Organization. To administer the transition to an open market, National Regulatory Authorities were established in the member states, and the European Commission issued guidelines for them. Resistance to the market opening remained strong, however, and some observers believed that it would take 10 years for an open market to be realized. Nevertheless, hundreds of firms entered the market to provide domestic and international voice service.

In 1993 the European Union allowed airlines to serve any city pair across a national border. In 1997 the industry was completely opened to competition even within a country. Market opening led to the creation of many new airlines and expanded services by a number of existing airlines. Fares were driven down and passenger miles grew substantially, increasing the pressure on state-owned airlines for efficiency.

STATE AIDS

One area in which harmonization of laws remains a concern is "state aids" to industry.[25] State aids are subsidies paid by member state governments to industries or government-owned companies. Compared with the United States and Japan, EU states provide considerably more subsidization for their firms. In 1994 the EU member states provided $52 billion in state aids, with Germany providing over $20 billion, representing over 5 percent of its government expenditures. Much of the subsidization has gone to declining industries in an attempt to maintain the rents earned by labor and capital. The European Commission monitors state aids and has directed Italy to obtain a refund for a subsidy given to Fiat and ordered France to stop the large-scale subsidization of Renault.

France has provided large state aid to several of its state-owned companies including the computer maker Machines Bull ($2.1 billion in 1994), banks including Credit Lyonnais and CEPME, Aerospatiale ($341 million in 1994), and Air France ($3.7 billion in 1994). The EU approved these subsidies, but European competitors protested. Some European airlines appealed the subsidization of Air France to the EU courts. The opponents of subsidization argued that the subsidization distorts markets, which was prohibited by the Treaty of Rome, whereas France and the EU maintained that the subsidies were infusions of capital associated with restructurings to provide improved competitiveness. In 1998 the Court of First Instance canceled the EU approval of the $3.7 billion provided to Air France, holding that the commission had provided insufficient justification for the approval.

THE SOCIAL CHARTER AND LABOR MARKETS

The EU has adopted a Social Charter that provides a vision for the free circulation of labor and the rights to fair wages, improvement of living and working conditions, social security, free association and collective bargaining, vocational training and education, equal treatment for men and women, information, consultation and participation for workers, health protection and safety in the workplace, protection for children, adolescents, and the elderly, and protection of the disabled.[26] Translating the vision of the Social Charter into law has been marked by several disagreements between business and labor and the reality of national policy differences.[27]

---

[25]State aids are governed by Article 92 of the Treaty of Rome.
[26]Chamber of Commerce (1989, p. 42).
[27]See Wise and Gibb (1993).

SOCIAL DEMOCRACY AND LABOR

Much of the European labor force is well educated and highly skilled, and labor costs are high. Work weeks are shorter and vacations longer in Europe than they are in the United States and Asia. Bell and Freeman (1994) reported that Americans worked 1,798 hours a year, whereas Germans worked an average of 1,554. Japanese workers averaged over 2,000 hours a year. The short work hours led one German industrial relations manager to observe that "the German worker doesn't work very often, but when he does work, he works very, very hard."[28] France has implemented a program to reduce its workweek to 35 hours by 2000 in an effort to reduce its unemployment rate, which was over 11 percent at the beginning of 1999.

In 1994 the commission issued a White Paper on European Social Policy to guide the formulation of social policy. The SEA and other EU laws reflect the objectives of empowering labor and protecting individuals from risk and hardship through extensive social programs.[29] Most European nations make discharging an employee both difficult and costly. On the supply side generous unemployment benefits and welfare systems reduce the incentive to find a job, and the strong unions make it difficult for wages to fall. A study by William M. Mercer, Inc. found that the cost of dismissing a 45-year-old manager with 20 years experience and a salary of $50,000 ranged from $25,000 or less in Germany, the Netherlands, France, the United Kingdom, and Ireland to $94,000 in Belgium and $130,000 in Italy.[30]

Unemployment rates of over 10 percent have persisted in many European countries during the 1990s, in part because the high cost of discharging a worker makes employers reluctant to hire full-time employees. This has led to a rapid growth in temporary jobs that have provided a degree of flexibility to the labor market. In 1998 the labor minister in France said that "86 percent of new hires are on short-term contracts," most of which extend for 6 months and can be renewed once. Economic growth in the Netherlands far outstripped that in countries such as France and Germany during the 1990s, and unemployment dropped to 4 percent in contrast to 11 percent in Germany and France. The success of the Netherlands was credited to moderate wage growth and allowing labor market flexibility including temporary and part-time work. In addition, the country cut unemployment benefits which increased the incentives to find work. The country also shifted the burden of sick pay from the government to employers, which reduced significantly the number of employees calling in sick. Many of these reforms have come under the leadership of a prime minister who was a former labor leader.

COMPETITION AMONG THE STATES

Although the EU states all recognize the benefits from free trade in a single market, each has an incentive to favor its own citizens, firms, and interests. Consequently, states compete with each other for the location of firms and facilities in their country. Just as states in the United States compete for Japanese and European automobile plants, European states compete for both EU and foreign firms and their facilities. Firms make their location decisions based on a variety of market and nonmarket considerations, including taxes, state aids, and the cost of doing business. In addition to wages, transportation costs, and access to raw materials, costs reflect factors such as work rules, working hours, mandatory social contributions, and regulatory compliance. Ireland, for

---

[28]*The New York Times,* January 25, 1985.
[29]See European Commission (1988).
[30]William M. Mercer, Inc. "Employee Dismissals Costly in Many European Countries," New York, March 2, 1992.

example, cut its corporate tax rate to 10 percent, which has attracted foreign direct investment. The corporate tax rate in the United Kingdom also has proved attractive to companies. Differences in taxes on business have led to calls by some member states for fiscal harmonization.

One form of competition among states is a competition in laxity. Among the EU states, those in northern Europe tend to have stringent environmental laws, whereas those in southern Europe and Ireland have less stringent environmental regulation. One rationale for the EU's attempt to harmonize regulations in the fields of health, safety, and environmental protection is to avoid a situation in which states compete for jobs by providing regulations that could be met at relatively low cost, giving firms locating there a competitive advantage. In 1992 the European Environmental Agency was established with the authority to enforce more stringent, if not uniform, standards on the member states.

As an example of the differences between the northern and southern parts of Europe, in 1998 the EU agreed to ban leaded gasoline by the year 2000, 22 years after the United States banned it. In addition, the sulfur content in gasoline and diesel fuel were to be reduced, and onboard computers will be required to signal if there is a failure in the catalytic converter. The cost increase for a new car was estimated at $300 to $600, and automobile manufacturers invested $65 billion to meet the new standards. The new standards were also estimated to cost oil refineries $35 billion, most of which would be in southern Europe. France, Greece, Portugal, and Spain, which would bear most of the refinery upgrading cost. They were successful in obtaining an interim reduction in sulfur content until the more stringent standard takes effect in 2005.

FORTRESS EUROPE?

The term "Fortress Europe" refers to the concern that although the European Union has reduced internal barriers to trade it has also maintained policies to protect its industries from non-EU competition. These concerns pertain to local content rules and quotas established by a number of member states, as well as measures adopted by the EU itself. For example, the EU restricts imports of steel from Russia, which contributed to a sharp increase in imports of Russian steel to the United States during Russia's financial crisis. The United States also imports more than twice as much from Asia as does the EU despite the EU having a one-third greater population. The Union also has been aggressive in imposing antidumping penalties against U.S. and Asian products, and concerns have been expressed that antidumping policies are being used to protect EU firms.[31]

In 1988 the European Commission stated its basic policy toward non-EU countries: "The Community will respect all international commitments, multilateral and bilateral. However, in areas where international obligations do not presently exist, the EU will not unilaterally extend the benefits of internal liberalization to third countries. Instead, the EU will seek comparable liberalization on the part of its trading partners."[32] The EU thus seeks reciprocity.

Local content rules, coupled with rules or origin, specify that a certain percentage of the value of a product must be produced in the EU to avoid trade instruments, such as tariffs and antidumping provisions, and to qualify for certain preference programs and government procurement programs. Applied to particular industries, these policies can effectively preclude non-EU products, thereby forcing firms to establish production

[31]Bellis (1989) and Schuknecht (1992) provide analyses of the EU's antidumping policies and procedures.
[32]Hufbauer (1990, p. 20).

facilities in the EU. In addition to a 14 percent tariff, the rules governing semiconductor production and screwdriver plants, plants that assembled products in Europe using imported components, effectively forced U.S. and Japanese semiconductor producers to build vertically integrated facilities in the EU.

To protect their domestic industries, various EU states, particularly France, Italy, and Spain, have used quotas that barred most Asian automobile imports. Countries without a domestic auto industry have imposed few restrictions, and Japanese manufacturers have captured up to 40 percent of the market. In Germany, which does not restrict automobile imports, Japanese automobiles have captured approximately one-quarter of the market.[33] France, however, restricted Japanese automobiles to less than 3 percent of its market, Italy to 1.5 percent, and Spain to 1.2 percent. In an accord on a voluntary import restraint system, the EU and Japan agreed to allow the Japanese market share to increase from 11 percent in 1991 to 16 percent in 1999.

Despite some noticeable exceptions most European markets are open to foreign competition. Furthermore, international trade negotiations lead the European Union and other countries toward more open markets.

Interests and Their Organization

Interests are pluralistic in Europe as they are in the United States and other countries, but their organization is different, in part because the governments of the member states are parliamentary. Several European countries, such as Germany and Sweden and others to a lesser extent, have a strong corporatist organization in which interests are represented by national associations that interact directly, and often with formal sanction, with government. The national associations join to form EU-wide associations that implement political strategies directed at the EU institutions. The largest of these associations is the Union of Industrial and Employers Confederations of Europe (UNICE). The European Roundtable of Industrialists represents large companies in Brussels and in the member states. These peak associations take much of the political action that individual firms and ad hoc coalitions take in the United States. Most European firms participate in industry associations that join together in EU-wide, umbrella industry associations. For example, the European Confederation of Retail Trade represents retail interests in the EU, and CEFIC includes as members 15 national associations of chemical companies. A peak organization such as CEFIC represents relatively homogeneous interests, whereas the Confederation of Food and Drink Industries represents relatively heterogeneous interests including soft drinks, beer, beef, and cheese.

Foreign firms are organized in a similar manner. The EU Committee of the American Chamber of Commerce represents over 100 U.S. companies in Brussels and is highly regarded. In addition, several U.S. associations have formed the U.S. Industry Coordinating Group.[34] Some of these associations, such as the Pharmaceutical Research and Manufacturers Association, maintain offices in Brussels.

Unionization in the EU is much more extensive than in the United States, and unions are also organized in national federations and in EU-wide umbrella associations. The unions have considerable power because of the high rate of unionization and also because of their links to political parties, particularly socialist parties which at the beginning of the twenty-first century had formed the governments in most of the EU member states.

---

[33]See Berg (1988), Smith and Venables (1990), and Wells and Rawlinson (1994) for studies of the EU automobile industry and market.

[34]See Calingaert (1993).

Activists and interest groups representing consumers and environmental concerns are active in the EU, particularly in northern Europe. Consumer groups such as Consumentenbond in the Netherlands are linked to consumer groups in other countries. Some interest groups, such as the greens, have formed political parties. Green activists have vigorously opposed biotechnology and have had considerable success in slowing the growth of the industry in Germany. The Chapter 4 case *Shell, Greenpeace, and Brent Spar* concerns an activist protest against a company's actions.

Nonmarket Strategies in the European Union

The EU governmental and political systems and its institutions are evolving along with the relationships among the various states with the Community. The nonmarket strategies for dealing with issues in the EU thus will continue to evolve. Nonmarket strategies are implemented at the levels of the member states and the institutions of the EU. Despite the fact that every state has a form of parliamentary government, the states differ considerably in terms of their governmental institutions, their party organization, and the strength and organization of various interests. Van Schendelen (1993) presents an analysis of interests and lobbying in 12 EU countries, and the focus here is on nonmarket activities and strategies at the level of the Union. Calingaert (1993) provides a description of the organization for political action at the EU level.

In the terminology of Chapter 7, both representational and informational strategies are important in the EU. Representational strategies are based on the constituency for each of the principal EU institutions, as illustrated in Figure 14-4. For example, the constituency of the Council of Ministers is the member states, and hence representational strategies are implemented primarily through the governments of the member states. Because those governments are parliamentary and controlled by the governing coalition, political parties are an important and central focus of these strategies. The patterns of access and influence differ among the member states, and the patterns in Germany are considered later in the chapter. Important points of access to the council are COREPER, and the working groups it forms to address issues.

Lobbying is the principal political activity for implementing both representational and informational strategies in the EU. A lobbyist's strategy is to demonstrate that the interests of a firm or industry are aligned with those of the person or office being lobbied. In the case of the EU, those interests are a mixture of economic efficiency and social objectives at the Union level; sectorial interests in the case of agriculture, steel, or computers; and local interests in the case of some members of the European Parliament

FIGURE 14-4 EU Institutions, Constituencies, and Access

Institution	*Constituency*	*Access*
European Commission	EU-wide constituency—member states, citizens, interests	DGs, commissioners
Council of Ministers	Member states	Member states, political parties, COREPER, working groups
European Parliament	Voters	Committees, political parties, members of Parliament
Economic and Social Committee	Interests	Representatives, Associations

and the Council of Ministers. EU officials face pressures from their home country constituents, from their mandate of economic and political integration, and from the Union's trading partners.

Much of the nonmarket and political action in the EU takes place behind the scenes, and most businesses avoid taking public action that might be subjected to criticism. In addition, because of the pervasive influence of government in most EU countries, firms seldom engage in open confrontation with government, as is more often the case in the United States. Activity often has a longer-term focus, rather than being specific to each nonmarket issue affecting a firm. In addition, in a number of countries business leaders have close personal relationships with government officials. In some countries such as France these relationships may have been formed through attendance at the same *grandes écoles*. In Germany top government officials consult with business leaders because of the status and strength of business in the country.[35]

According to a 1994 study some 3,000 organizations employ 10,000 lobbyists in Brussels, double the number in 1990. In addition, former EU and national government officials have formed lobbying firms to represent interests. EU lobbyists have backgrounds similar to those of lobbyists in the United States. Firms hire former EU officials, trade negotiators, ambassadors, and former officials of national governments as lobbyists. Lobbying services are also provided by law firms and consultants. Firms have been opening offices in Brussels to be close to the EU and to track its activities. Managers frequently participate in lobbying along with heads of industry associations and peak organizations.

Informational strategies center on the strategic provision of information to EU officeholders, and the nature and content of these strategies is the same as characterized in Chapter 7. The key to successful lobbying is the provision of information useful to the institutional officeholders. Successful lobbying requires an understanding of their interests, the relationship between policy alternatives and their consequences, and the procedures and practices of EU institutions. Lobbying also takes place within each member state in attempts to convince politicians and bureaucrats of the importance of the interests affected. Figure 14-4 identifies the points of access.

The form that lobbying takes depends on the institution in question. The European Commission is perhaps the most important body because it is the agenda setter for legislation and it also administers policies. The commission is the focus of interactions and consultations with member governments, and interest groups seeking to influence EU policy and its administration thus lobby the commission extensively. Because the commission has a relatively small staff, it needs and seeks information and expertise for its legislative and regulatory activities. The respect garnered by the American Chamber of Commerce in Brussels is due in part to the detailed information it provides on issues and its accurate representation of American concerns.

Interests may contact the European Commission directly through its DGs, but frequently interests are represented by members of either the European Parliament or the Economic and Social Committee from their home countries. Also, member governments intervene on behalf of interest groups in their own countries. The targets of lobbying are the commissioners and their cabinets. Because commissioners have responsibilities for the DGs, which are the repositories of expertise and deal with the specifics of issues, access to members of the relevant DGs is important. Participation in working parties and advisory committees can be an important means of access as well as a source of information. The commission initiates legislation in the

[35]See Calingaert (1993).

form of drafts that are circulated for comments before the legislative process begins (see Figure 14-2). Lobbying thus begins early in the process and is directed at the formulation of the initial draft as well as to the subsequent legislative process. Affecting the agenda can be an effective means of laying a path to be followed with subsequent lobbying.

Although the Council of Ministers is the final authority on policy and legislation, it is difficult to influence directly because it operates in private. The principal route to influencing the council is through member state governments and their relevant ministries, which then work to influence EU decision making. National interests are also represented by a country's permanent representatives (COREPER) to the Union. COREPER is required by law to consult directly with interests, and industry and labor organizations maintain close contacts with it. COREPER is expected to resolve political issues on behalf of the council. Both individual firms and the associations to which they belong seek to influence the member state governments on their behalf.

As a result of the Maastricht Treaty and the increased use of the co-decision legislative procedure, the European Parliament has become more important. Its constituencies are voters and the political parties that represent them, and the principal points of access are individual members and the EP committees. The EP members are both issue oriented and concerned about the effects of issues on constituents. Members represent a variety of interests and may be willing to act as allies in advancing the interests of firms and industries.

The European Parliament's primary role is in amending commission proposals. Although the EP has committees that formulate amendments, most of the lobbying takes place outside the formal committee structure. In addition, the party organization of the EP means that a path to influence is through the party system in the firm's home country. In practice, the attention given to lobbying the EP is small but growing relative to that given the commission, COREPER, and member state governments.

The custom in Europe has been to use peak organizations, such as UNICE and the Roundtable of European Industrialists, for political and other nonmarket actions. Issues involving the single market and international trade, however, are often industry specific and may affect firms in different ways. Consequently, coalitions are formed that cut across the lines of peak associations. These coalitions may include firms domiciled in different member states acting together on a trade issue or a firm and a union joining together to advance their joint interests.

As an example of an ad hoc coalition formed to address a specific issue, in 1996 the European Parliament proposed amendments to a Commission policy on the media industry. France, backed by socialist members of the EP, pushed for tighter quotas on the foreign content on television and multimedia outlets. According to one report, American companies produced 80 percent of the programming shown on European television. Opposition to the proposed amendments included not only American interests and private broadcasters, but also a broad set of other interests. Advertisers opposed the amendments because they would restrict advertising on home shopping channels. Retailers opposed the amendments because they would restrict the number of hours regular TV channels could devote to teleshopping. The prospect of quotas on Internet content led one Bertelsmann lobbyist to comment, "It's very silly what they want to do. It won't work in an Internet, on-line environment."[36] The chapter case *The European Union Carbon Tax* concerns an issue involving another broad set of interests.

[36]*The Wall Street Journal,* February 12, 1996.

Some firms undertake independent political action or form ad hoc coalitions with other firms to advance their agenda. Philips Electronics has been one of the most active. It was an early advocate of the creation of a single market and also worked to limit competition from outside the EU. For example, it lobbied successfully for protection against Japanese compact disc systems. In addition to its extensive lobbying, Van Schedelen (1993) reports that Philips was successful in "parachuting" one of its technology experts into DG XIII, which is responsible for subsidies for technology programs. By 1990 Philips had obtained R&D subsidies for 150 projects. Philips was also one of the principal forces behind the EU subsidies for the development of a European HDTV system, which ultimately was a failure. Working with the European Information Technology Roundtable, Philips also led the successful effort to obtain $4 billion for semiconductor research.

Philips Chairman Cornelis van der Klugt was personally active, lobbying in Brussels to obtain import protection for Philips's lines of business. He argued that free trade with the EU required "real reciprocity." To protect its VCR business, Philips pushed a 30 percent levy on Japanese and South Korean VCRs through the EU. He worked to have the EU investigate dumping charges against Asian producers of small TVs and compact discs, and to have the semiconductors assembled by Japanese firms in Europe classified as imports so they would be subject to tariffs.[37] An antidumping complaint against six Japanese semiconductor manufacturers led to a 1989 agreement between the EU and Japan that set a price floor on imported semiconductors. Van der Klugt defended his protectionist efforts by saying, "It's not necessary for the Japanese to export unemployment to Europe. We have enough unemployment."[38] At the same time that he worked for protection, van der Klugt pushed the EU to scrap its internal trade barriers as quickly as possible.

Nonmarket issues and strategies are often complicated by national concerns. The EU pharmaceutical industry is far from a single market. Under the principle of subsidiarity the member states are responsible for health care and may institute their own price controls. The European Commission has expressed concern that very stringent price controls are driving pharmaceutical innovation out of the EU.[39] France, for example, requires pharmaceutical companies to sign broad conventions that cover not only prices but also commitments to employment in France and to support of state-owned research institutes. To hold down the cost of its national health care system, prices are set at very low levels. This in part led the three largest French pharmaceutical companies to either merge or spin off their pharmaceutical operations into a jointly owned affiliate. The French Parliament also enacted a law making pharmaceutical companies responsible for any costs above ceilings set by parliament for the national health service. Industry members planned to challenge the new law in France and before the European Commission and the European Court of Justice.[40]

To address concerns about the possible decline of the EU pharmaceutical industry, the European Commission formed a roundtable of industry members, EU officials, and representatives of the governments of the member states. The initial expectation was that the working groups formed by the Roundtable would propose deregulation measures for the industry, but pressure from member states concerned about holding down the cost of health care blocked the deregulation proposals.

---

[37]Upon complaints by Philips and Bang & Olufsen of Denmark, the EU imposed provisional duties of from 6.4 percent to 40 percent on Japanese and South Korean compact disc players. Sony expressed little concern because it planned to supply three-quarters of its European demand from its plant in Colmar, France.
[38]*The New York Times,* June 4, 1989.
[39]European Commission press release, November 25, 1998.
[40]*The Wall Street Journal,* December 7, 1998.

Specific nonmarket issues can also arise in the normal course of EU activities. An example of such a specific issue, a German court decision about wedding dresses that had important implications for franchising, is considered next.

EXAMPLE: PRONUPTIA AND FRANCHISING

In 1984 a German court invalidated a franchise agreement that required a German retailer, Pronuptia, to sell only the wedding dresses of its French franchiser and sell them only in specific territories. The French franchiser appealed the decision to the European Court of Justice. U.S. franchisers saw the decision as crucial to their being able to use U.S.-style franchise arrangements in the EU. They launched a lobbying campaign directed at the European Commission, which was to file an opinion on the case with the Court. The lobbyist engaged by the U.S. franchisers conducted a "teach in" about U.S. franchising practices for officials of DG IV. The commission subsequently argued before the Court that the franchise restrictions were necessary to maintain product quality, among other things. In 1986 the European Court of Justice overruled the German court and upheld the rights of franchisers to restrict the actions of their franchisees on several dimensions.[41]

U.S. franchisers were still concerned that the franchising arrangements allowed by the Court might be challenged under the antitrust provisions in Article 85. Some franchisers, including Pronuptia, sought and received exemptions from the commission. They also encouraged the commission to grant a broader exemption from antitrust rules for franchise arrangements. U.S. interests, including McDonald's, Pizza Hut, Kentucky Fried Chicken, Midas Muffler, Coca-Cola, Holiday Inns, and others, were represented by the International Franchising Association (IFA), which was active in Brussels. The IFA met with a variety of officials including the competition commissioner, who was also lobbied when he visited the United States.

Commenting on his efforts, the lobbyist for the U.S. franchisers said, "The most important lessons we've learned so far are for American interests to get in early; get in a European, not American, way: and demonstrate from the start that American interests are compatible with European interests." From the other side, an official with the commission's competition bureau DG IV said the IFA "made their points forcefully, but also gave us a lot of useful information about how the U.S. system works."[42]

U.S. franchisers obtained "96.5%" of what they sought, but they were not allowed to require franchisees to purchase one brand exclusively. A fast-food chain thus cannot force its franchisees to carry only one soft drink brand.

Germany

Germany is the largest nation in the EU with a population of 80 million and has the largest economy and one of the Union's highest per capita incomes. German automobile, metal-working, chemical, and health care firms are among the world leaders in their industries.[43] German economic activity is marked by ostensible cooperation between business and labor, resulting in a low level of strikes and work interruptions. The burdens of the economic failure of the former East Germany placed a considerable strain on the German economy, however. In addition, a rigid labor system and overregulation contributed to an unemployment rate of 11 percent.

---

[41]*Pronuptia de Paris GmbH v. Pronuptia de Paris Irmgard Schillgalis* (case 161/84), January 28, 1986, Common Market Report (CCH) para. 14,245 (1986). See Rosenthal (1990) for a discussion of this case. Also see Hawk (1988).

[42]*The Wall Street Journal,* May 17, 1989.

[43]Porter (1990) provides an assessment of Germany's competitive advantage and its industrial sectors.

INSTITUTIONS: THE STRUCTURE OF GOVERNMENT

Germany is the only federal republic in the EU and has 16 states (länder). German governmental activity is characterized by extensive consultations intended to allow all interests to present their concerns. The system also has a set of checks and balances that includes an independent judiciary and a bicameral legislature. Governmental structure is specified in the Basic Law. The government is parliamentary and coalition governments are most always formed, so the government reflects a plurality of interests. The president has only minor powers. The government is formed in the parliament, which chooses the chancellor—the executive officer of the nation. The states play an important role in implementing many federal laws.

Germany has an independent judiciary that enforces laws contained in civil and criminal codes. The Federal Court of Justice is the highest court for civil and criminal cases and hears appeals from lower courts. Cases involving constitutional issues are heard by the Federal Constitutional Court.[44]

The lower house of parliament, the Bundestag, elects the chancellor, who forms the cabinet and exercises executive authority. The chancellor can be replaced only on a "positive vote of confidence" in which the Bundestag provides a majority vote for another chancellor. In the early 1980s, the Free Democrats voted with the Social Democrats in the government, but in a conflict over budget and tax policy they switched their support to the Christian Democrats, bringing Helmut Kohl's government to office without an election. The requirement of a positive vote of confidence gives the chancellor and his government a degree of stability and power not found in many parliamentary democracies. The chancellor appoints the cabinet and controls the federal bureaucracy but is careful to give representation to powerful interests through appointments to ministries such as agriculture, labor, economics, and finance.

The federal structure of the German government is reflected in the upper house, the Bundesrat or Federal Council. The Bundesrat is composed of delegates from the states, and small states have disproportionate representation. The Bundesrat has more limited legislative powers than the Bundestag, seldom initiates legislation, and cannot block legislation that is purely within the jurisdiction of the federal government.

All legislation is formally submitted to the Bundesrat before it is introduced in the Bundestag, but the lower house can enact some legislation without the approval of the upper house. All legislation that involves or affects the states, however, requires the Bundesrat's approval. In practice, the Bundesrat considers and approves most legislation except for foreign policy and defense. The Bundestag and the Bundesrat have adopted a cooperative approach to governing and often form joint task forces to consider issues and legislation.

Because of the parliamentary system in which the executive and the majority of the Bundestag are aligned, the Bundestag has less power relative to the bureaucracy than does the Congress relative to the U.S. bureaucracy. The internal organization of the Bundestag includes a committee system, and the bureaucracy has a right to sit on committees and to participate in their deliberations. Because the committee staffs are limited, most of the legislation is drafted in the ministries. The German bureaucracy is generally highly qualified and has considerable discretion in policy making and implementation. Ministries often act as advocates for the interest groups in their policy jurisdictions. Before drafting legislation, the bureaucracy consults with the principal interest groups. Before submitting it to the parliament, the chancellor and the cabinet reach agreement on the draft, and they also consult with important interest groups.

---

[44]Germany's Basic Law serves as its constitution.

Some interest group leaders hold seats in the Bundestag, so officials of business associations, labor unions, and agricultural associations can provide direct representation. Once agreement has been reached, the appropriate minister is often involved in shepherding the legislation through the legislative process. Because the executive and a majority of the legislature are aligned, most of the legislation introduced in this manner is enacted. Most of the legislation introduced by individual members of the Bundestag is defeated.[45]

To obtain seats in the Bundestag, a party must obtain 5 percent of the votes cast or win three districts, which puts small parties at a disadvantage.[46] Germany has four principal political parties, the two largest of which are the Christian Democrats and the Social Democrats.[47] Whichever has more seats in the Bundestag forms a coalition government, which in every postwar government with one exception had included the Free Democrats. A Christian Democrat-Free Democrat coalition formed the government until 1998. The fourth principal party is the Green Party, which first gained representation in parliament in the 1980s. In 1998 the left won the election, and the Social Democrats and Greens formed the government. A fifth party is composed of ex-communists from the former East Germany. The Christian Democrats are basically conservative, and the Social Democrats are to their left. Both favor government social programs, codetermination, and protection for workers. The Social Democrats have close ties to organized labor, and the Christian Democrats draw strength from business and the middle class.

THE POLITICAL ECONOMY OF GERMANY

The German economy is export driven and is dominated by the manufacturing rather than by the services sector. In part, growth in the services sector has been restricted by the tight regulation and the strong role of unions, as described in more detail in the chapter case *Toys 'Я' Us in Germany*.[48] Pressure from foreign competitors has resulted in mergers and restructuring of a number of German firms and a consequent reduction in employment in manufacturing. Germany has an extensive and generous welfare system and correspondingly taxes represent 45 percent of GDP compared with approximately 30 percent in Japan and the United States.

In part, the high German unemployment rate has been due to the generous unemployment benefits and welfare plans, which decrease the incentives to find a job or take a low-paying job. German labor costs are the highest in the world, and with strong unions and employee rights the incentive to create jobs is low. In effect, Germany has chosen a system of high wages, generous welfare benefits, and low job creation. Pressure from foreign competitors and the incentive to seek lower wages by moving production to other countries has forced some unions to allow some flexibility in wages and work rules.

---

[45]See Dalton (1988, p. 297). From 1976 to 1980, 90 percent of the bills introduced by the government were adopted compared with 35 percent of those originating in the Bundestag.

[46]The German electoral system is complex, including a proportional representation system that determines the party composition in the Bundestag and a constituency vote that determines by plurality half the members for the Bundestag. On one German ballot, a voter votes for a candidate, and the candidate with a plurality in each district is elected. On a second ballot, a voter votes for a party under a proportional representation system, and the nationwide percentages of the votes determine the share of the seats each party has in the Bundestag. The number elected on the first ballot for each party is then subtracted from the party's share as determined by the proportional representation ballot. The difference is filled by candidates on lists prepared by the parties in each state. Elections are held every 4 years or earlier if the government resigns.

[47]The Christian Democrats include the Christian Democratic Union and the Christian Social Union, its counterpart in Bavaria. See Klingemann (1987) for a characterization of the policies of the principal parties.

[48]See the Part IV integrative case *Toys 'Я' Us and Globalization* for the company's overall strategy.

Labor Unions and Codetermination

Approximately 40 percent of the German workforce is unionized, and unions have considerable economic and political power.[49] In the postwar period Germany has had a cooperative relationship between labor and management, which has given the nation one of the lowest strike and work stoppage rates in Europe. This cooperative relationship is solidified by company law, which provides for codetermination in which unions have representation on the supervisory boards of firms and also participate at the plant level through works councils.[50] This system has provided Germany with the advantages of economic stability, although labor-management relations have recently come under some pressure.

German unions are typically organized by industry and bargain with associations of employers in those industries. Seventeen German unions engage in collective bargaining. They are members of the federation Deutscher Gewerkschaftsbund (DGB), which exercises relatively tight control over the member unions. Unions and employer associations bargain at the industry level over wages and working conditions, and firms and their work councils bargain over the implementation of the industry agreement. Only the union, and not the works council, can strike, and the conditions under which a strike can be called are limited by law.

At the plant level, workers have both representation and a set of rights to participation.[51] Those participation rights are in the areas of personnel policy, working conditions, and information, requiring notification of business plans that affect workers. Works councils can effectively prohibit weekend and overtime work and have powers over dismissals and reassignments.[52] Works councils use their rights to influence management, and management thus has an interest in accommodating council interests. Management, however, controls most decision making. Some firms have obtained a degree of flexibility in wages and working conditions by negotiating with their local works councils.

The Role of Banks

German banks play a substantial role in financing business and in some cases controlling firms through shareholdings. The five largest banks are reported to own 15 percent of the shares of publicly listed companies. Banks not only own shares, but they vote proxies for other shareholders.

Deutsche Bank is Germany's largest bank and has ownership shares in many major German firms. For example, Deutsche Bank owns a quarter of Daimler-Chrysler, the largest company in Germany. In some cases, companies have cross-shareholdings. For example, Deutsche Bank owns 10 percent of Allianz A.G., Europe's largest insurance company, and Allianz owns 5 percent of Deutsche Bank. As an example of managerial links, the head of Deutsche Bank has also served as chairman of the supervisory board of Daimler-Chrysler. The extent to which the major banks influence the operations and

---

[49]Less than 15 percent of the U.S. workforce is unionized.

[50]Codetermination in Germany takes three forms. In the coal and steel industries, the board of supervisors of firms is composed half of union representatives and half of shareholder representatives, with the chairperson an eleventh and, in principle, neutral member. Unions in those industries thus have considerable power in management, and they have sought unsuccessfully to extend this system to other industries. The second form, established by the 1952/72 Works Constitution Act, gives workers one-third of the seats on the supervisory board of corporations with 500 to 2,000 employees. Workers have no representation on the management board of a firm, however. The third form, established by the 1976 Co-Determination Act, gives equal representation to employees and shareholders, but one of the employee representatives must come from management, which gives shareholders an effective majority. Under this form, employees are represented on the management board by a labor director. See Lane (1989).

[51]See Streeck (1984, Ch. 3).

[52]See Streeck (1984, Ch. 7).

management of the firms in which they have investments varies considerably. If a firm is in trouble, the bank may arrange for a rescue. If the firm is performing well, the banks exercise little control.

To some extent, banks serve as a substitute for a market for control in Germany. Bank representation on supervisory boards serves as a monitor for both owners and lenders, of which the major banks are the largest. The banks may also arrange bailouts, friendly takeovers of firms, or mergers. They also facilitate coordination among firms. How efficient this system is compared with an open market for control is unclear and has been the focus of concern. As capital markets become more global and competition intensifies, the role of German banks is likely to diminish.

INTERESTS AND THEIR ORGANIZATION

Interests in Germany are organized both formally through government sanction and less formally through voluntary associations. Germany, and several other European countries, has a corporatist structure of interest group representation and participation. In a corporatist structure, entities such as unions and business have peak organizations that advise government and negotiate on policy. In Germany, manufacturing enterprises, agricultural interests, service companies, and professionals are organized by law into "chambers," which exercise self-regulatory authority over members and represent their members' interests before the government.

German firms interact with the government principally through associations but also individually. All employers are required to belong to chambers which join together to form peak associations that interact with government on their behalf. The Federation of German Employers' Associations (BDA) is composed of 56 employer associations and represents business on social and labor issues. The Federation of German Industry (BDI), whose members are 39 national federations that include 40,000 businesses and 85 percent of German industry, is more active politically.[53] It provides expert testimony on legislation, lobbies government institutions, and consults with government leaders. The peak business organizations cooperate both formally and informally. Informally, their leaders consult on issues, and formally the BDA and the BDI interact through organizations such as the Joint Committee of German Trade and Industry.

The peak organizations do not attempt to mobilize electoral support but instead focus on influencing policies behind the scenes. Most of their attention is directed at the executive branch. They interact with the chancellor and his staff, the ministries, and the Bundestag on specific legislation.[54]

The DGB is the peak organization for labor and is more cohesive than the peak business organizations. It exercises political power both through the political parties and through its interactions with the executive branch and the Bundestag. Labor has a strong relationship with the Social Democrats and a weaker relationship with the labor wing of the Christian Democrats. Many Social Democrat members of the Bundestag are union members. Much of the focus of the DGB is on the executive branch, however. Labor participates in advisory committees and consults with the ministries on a variety of issues. Whichever parties form the government, the minister of labor is either a union leader or acceptable to the DGB. In the Social Democrat-Green government formed in 1998, the deputy chairman of Germany's largest union IG Metall became minister of labor.

[53]A third, less active, peak organization is the Diet of German Industry and Commerce.
[54]Katzenstein (1989) provides a set of industry studies of the interactions of business, labor, and government in adjusting to changing economic conditions.

The relationships between interest groups and the government are formalized through a system of consultative bodies, which include members of the interest groups as well as elected officials and bureaucrats. These bodies serve many of the same purposes as advisory committees do in Japan, although the bureaucracy may exercise more control in Japan than in Germany. At the federal government level, before a ministry submits a bill for consideration by the Bundestag it is required by law to consult with the peak organizations. Ministries also have a set of advisory committees composed of experts, such as the Council of Economic Experts, that provide advice on economic policy and coordinate government and private sector policies. Most of the activities of the advisory groups and the required consultations take place outside the public's view. Thus, in Germany political pressure is funneled through organized interest groups and a formalized process of consultation. Independent political pressure and grassroots campaigns are less common in Germany than in the United States.

German government is party government, so interest groups and associations also interact directly with the political parties. Election campaigns are largely funded through public funds, however, and private contributions are restricted. Interest groups and individual firms also interact directly with the ministries, providing advice and, at times, political support. Ministries seek to serve interest groups in exchange for their support.

The peak associations play a number of roles including the monitoring of government activities, the funneling of information and expertise from their members to the government, and lobbying. Lobbying is pervasive in German politics, but because of the omnipresence of associations it tends to be collective in its nature. Much of the political influence takes place through the executive branch and the interactions of high-ranking government officials with the leaders of the peak associations. Seventy percent of the BDI's contacts are with the bureaucracy and only 5 percent are with the Bundestag.[55] As a result of the Single Market Act and the increasing importance of the EU government, German associations have increased their presence and lobbying in Brussels.

Germany also has a strong set of activist groups, the most prominent of which is the green movement. Activists employ a range of strategies at both the federal and the state levels. For example, environmental activists have vigorously opposed biotechnology through political action and even by sabotaging experiments. The activists supported stringent regulations on research and other activities and also worked in the state to establish local barriers. Their activities and Germans' fears about genetic engineering caused the German biotechnology industry to operate largely outside the country. In 1994 Germany conformed its law to EU law, and the biotechnology industry began to grow. The Chapter 4 case *Shell, Greenpeace, and Brent Spar* involves a German-led activist group.

Summary

The Single European Act represented a major step toward political and economic integration within the Union. It also increased the political power of the EU institutions relative to the governments of the member states. The Maastricht Treaty provided for a monetary union and for steps toward a political union. It also increased the power of the European Parliament, although that institution remains more of a deliberative body than a full legislature. The principal institutions of the EU remain the European Commission and the Council of Ministers. The Economic and Monetary Union established both a common currency and the European Central Bank among 11 of the member

---

[55]See Kohler-Koch (1993).

states, with others likely to join in the future. Five and perhaps six additional countries are scheduled to join the EU in 2003. Considerable progress has been made in eliminating internal barriers to trade, but several difficult issues, including fiscal harmonization, remain. Rigid labor markets, high wages, benefits, and taxes, and high costs of laying off workers have resulted in an unemployment rate near 10 percent for the EU.

Interests in the EU take action both individually and through associations and peak organizations, which play an important role at the EU level. The pattern of interest group activity and the nature of nonmarket action evolve as firms, unions, and other organizations adapt their strategies to institutional changes. The growth in lobbying is a sign of both the increased importance of the EU government and the stakes involved in its actions. Lobbying is the principal nonmarket strategy for influencing the EU institutions. Since much of the legislative and regulatory activity takes place outside the view of the public, and before the formal procedures begin, it is important to participate both early and continuously in the governmental processes.

Although the power of the EU institutions has increased, the governments of the member nations continue to be the focus of considerable nonmarket activity. Those governments are parliamentary, but differ in their institutional structures and their politics. Unlike the other EU countries, Germany has a federal structure in which its states have representation in the federal government. The organization of interests is characterized by peak associations that are active in political and governmental matters. Individual firms, however, also engage in their own nonmarket activities and are increasingly forming alliances with firms in other EU member states.

CASES

The European Union Carbon Tax

Whether and to what extent global warming was occurring remained the subject of considerable scientific uncertainty, disagreement, and debate during the early 1990s, but the scientific evidence increasingly supported the global warming hypothesis. The principal contributor to global warming was believed to be the burning of carbon-based fuels, principally coal, petroleum, and natural gas.

A European Union (EU) Joint Council of Energy and Environment Ministers declared in 1990 that the member states would by the year 2000 stabilize CO_2 emissions at the 1990 level. Because of projected economic growth, stabilization would require a reduction in emissions of approximately 10 percent from the unstabilized level. Some of the reductions required to stabilize emissions were anticipated to come from improved energy efficiency induced by the current prices of fossil fuels. These "no regrets" conservation measures were estimated to reduce emissions by 5.5 percent by 2000, leaving reductions of 5 percent to be accomplished by other measures. In October 1991 the European Commission issued a draft directive informing the member states of its plans to propose a variety of measures to reduce CO_2 emissions. These measures included R&D programs and a carbon/energy tax to achieve the remaining reduction of 5 percent. The proposed carbon/energy tax was intended to reduce carbon emissions by making fuels, and particularly carbon-based fuels, more costly, and thereby inducing conservation and the substitution of less carbon-intensive fuels.

The European Commission operated under collective responsibility but frequently deferred to the commissioner with policy jurisdiction if the issue was not controversial. This was not an uncontroversial issue. The lead commissioners for this issue were DG XI (environment) and DG XVII (energy). Mr. Carlo Ripa di Meana, EU commissioner for the environment, pushed for a formal proposal by June 1992 in time for the Rio Earth Summit. Mr. Jacques Delors, president of the commission, also supported the tax and the leadership position it would give the European Union in Rio. Mr. Antonio Cardoso e Cunha, EU commissioner for energy, supported the taxes because they would promote energy efficiency.

The European Commission proposal involved specific (per unit) taxes that would impose half the burden on carbon-based fuels and the other half on energy. Because emissions of CO_2 were difficult to measure by source, the taxes would be applied to inputs rather than emissions. The proposed carbon tax would begin at $3 per barrel of oil and increase by $1 a year for the next 7 years, reaching $10 a barrel. (The $10 per barrel tax was equivalent to a tax of $75 per ton of carbon.) An equivalent tax would be applied to coal and natural gas. The energy tax would apply to all energy sources except renewable sources. The energy tax was included to satisfy environmentalists who opposed a pure carbon tax because it would provide incentives for the expansion of nuclear power. Countries such as Germany, Greece, and the United Kingdom, with carbon-intensive energy supplies, also favored an energy tax. The commission estimated that the full tax would increase the price of natural gas for industry by one-third, hard coal by 60 percent, and gasoline by 6 percent.[1]

Two EU member states, Denmark and the Netherlands, and two European Free Trade Association (EFTA) countries, Finland and Sweden, already had imposed a carbon tax.[2] Denmark's carbon tax averaged $16 per ton of carbon for individuals' consumption and $8 per ton for industry. Energy-intensive industries, however, could be granted an exemption of up to 100 percent of the tax. The Netherlands' carbon tax was $12.50 per ton. The tax in Sweden was $62 per ton of carbon, and in Finland the tax was $6.50 per ton.[3]

Neither Japan nor the United States had a carbon tax in 1992. The Japanese government argued that its regulations already set standards that were at least as strong as those the EU carbon tax would

[1] The percent increase for gasoline was low because gasoline was already very heavily taxed.
[2] In 1995 Austria, Finland, and Sweden joined the EU.
[3] See Poterba, (1991, pp. 71–98).

achieve. Presidential candidate Bill Clinton had pledged during his campaign to address the global warming issue using efficient means, including taxes on carbon and/or energy. The Congressional Budget Office estimated that to stabilize CO_2 emissions a tax of $100 per ton of carbon would be required.[4] Representative Pete Stark of California introduced a bill to impose a tax of $15 per ton on coal, $3.25 per barrel of oil, and $0.40 per MCF of natural gas. The European Commission urged the member states to make every effort to ensure that other OECD countries, in particular Japan and the United States, adopted measures similar to its proposed carbon/energy tax.

The carbon/energy tax would affect production and consumption decisions throughout the European Union and would affect the competitiveness of EU businesses, particularly those that use energy-intensive technologies. Mr. Ripa di Meana, however, argued that "This is a chance to update European industry and make it a leader in a green-oriented market." To lessen the impact on the international competitiveness of European companies, the commission proposed to at least partially exempt from the tax industries that employed energy-intensive production processes. The tax would ultimately be borne in large part by individuals and would have the greatest impact on those who used energy, and particularly carbon-based fuels, intensively. Because lower-income individuals spent a higher portion of their income on energy, the tax would be regressive.

A carbon/energy tax would also generate substantial revenue for governments. For example, a tax of $100 per ton of carbon was estimated to generate revenue equal to 1.99 percent of GDP based on consumption in 1988. For France the revenue would be 1.28 percent of GNP and for Germany and the United Kingdom it would be approximately 2.3 percent. The commission suggested that the carbon tax should be "fiscally neutral" for each country, although Mr. Ripa di Meana argued that a portion of the tax revenue should go to developing countries to prevent deforestation. Fiscal neutrality would require that any additional revenue generated by the tax be offset by fiscal incentives or reductions in other taxes. Because the individual member states rather than the European Union would receive the revenue from the tax, each member state would determine its own use of the revenue. Under EU law the member states were responsible for the implementation of the tax.

The EU legislative process required that the imposition of a carbon tax be decided under a unanimity rule. More realistically, some bargaining among the member states would likely be involved with compensation given to certain countries that would otherwise be substantially impacted by the tax. As part of its annual budget, the European Union provided grants of structural funds for economic development to countries and to regions within countries. In 1992 these funds were approximately 19 million ECUs ($25 billion). The budget and thus the amount and allocation of structural funds were decided by a complicated legislative procedure and required decisions on proposals and amendments by qualified majority of the Council of Finance Ministers. In 1992 a qualified majority required 54 of the 76 votes. The number of votes for each member state is presented in Table 14-1.

In December 1991 the EU Joint Council of Environment and Energy Ministers unanimously endorsed the European Commission's draft directive. Denmark, Germany, Italy, Belgium, and the Netherlands came out clearly in favor of the proposal, whereas the poorer southern countries led by Spain, along with Luxembourg, were concerned about how the abatement burden would be divided among the countries. The United Kingdom agreed in principle

TABLE 14-1 Votes of Member States in the Council of Ministers, 1992

Member States	*Votes*
Belgium	5
Denmark	3
France	10
Germany	10
Greece	5
Ireland	3
Italy	10
Luxembourg	2
Netherlands	5
Portugal	5
Spain	8
United Kingdom	10
Total	76

[4]The United States had imposed a tax on CFCs as a means of speeding the elimination of their production. In addition to contributing to ozone depletion, CFCs were greenhouse gases and contributed to global warming.

but was hesitant about the additional taxes. France supported the proposed taxes but wanted to tilt the taxes more toward fossil fuels. Both endorsed the report. A few days later the EU finance ministers took note of the proposal and asked for a detailed study on the practical details of the tax.

THE ECONOMICS OF EMISSIONS CONTROL IN THE EUROPEAN UNION

Before the European Commission presented its proposal for meeting the EU-wide stabilization target, it commissioned a study of the costs and benefits of CO_2 emissions reduction. Although emissions were to be stabilized by the year 2000, the Council of Ministers requested that the study analyze the effects in the year 2010, since the stabilization target was to hold indefinitely and some investments in energy conservation would take several years before they were fully implemented. Table 14-2 outlines the "base-case" scenario that was predicted to occur in 2010 if no EU-wide emissions control took place. Column 1 of Table 14-2 shows 1988 CO_2 emissions for 10 EU countries for comparison purposes (Ireland and Luxembourg are omitted from the analysis because they had the lowest CO_2 emissions in the EU and because important data were not available). Not surprisingly, the largest and wealthiest countries—France, Germany, Italy, and the UK—had the highest levels of CO_2 emissions in 1988. However, the projected growth in emissions for 1988 to 2010 exhibited a very different pattern. The poorest countries—Greece, Portugal, and Spain—were predicted, respectively, to emit 52, 82, and 35 percent more CO_2 by 2010 if no additional measures were taken, compared with declines in emissions in France, Germany, and the UK. The declines were projected to result from increased energy efficiency.[5]

TABLE 14-2 CO_2 Emissions (millions tons) with No Further Abatement: 10 EU Countries

	1988	*projected, 2010*
Belgium	109	110
Denmark	61	60
France	374	370
Germany	718	677
Greece	84	127
Italy	399	489
Netherlands	146	165
Portugal	28	51
Spain	196	265
UK	561	505
Total	2,676	2,819

Source: Coherence (1991), "Cost-effectiveness analysis of CO_2 reduction options," Synthesis report and country reports for the Commission of the European Communities, DG XII, May 1991.

If emissions were to be stabilized in 2000 and beyond, the European Commission had to make a proposal that achieved a 143 million ton reduction in CO_2 by the year 2010. One efficient or cost-minimizing means to obtain this reduction was through a uniform tax on CO_2 emissions in all EU countries. A uniform tax would induce efficient emissions control across countries by giving polluters in each country the incentive to abate up to the point at which the marginal cost of abatement equaled the emissions tax.[6] As a result, the marginal cost of reducing pollution in any one country would equal the marginal cost of reducing pollution in every other country. The tax that achieved the target reduction of 143 million tons of CO_2 was calculated by researchers to be approximately $75/ton of carbon at an exchange rate of $1.30/ECU.[7]

COSTS AND BENEFITS OF A CARBON/ENERGY TAX

The relative impact of a carbon tax would be greatest on the lower-income countries. The tax would reduce their growth rate in addition to imposing high costs of abatement. The countries that would be most severely affected were Greece, Italy, Portugal, and Spain. A reduction in CO_2 emissions by the European Union would constitute a public good for other countries, since all countries would benefit from the reductions. The benefits for individual EU member states would be roughly proportional to their populations.

The effects of the tax on industry were predictable. The trade association Euroelectric, repre-

[5]For example, CO_2 emissions in the United Kingdom in 1992 were below the emissions levels in 1972.

[6]See Chapter 12.

[7]See "Reaching a CO_2-Emission Limitation Agreement for the Community: Implications for Equity and Cost Effectiveness," *European Economy,* Special Edition No. 1, *The Economics of Limiting CO_2 Emissions,* Directorate-General for Economics and Financial Affairs, Commission of the European Communities, 1992.

senting the EU electricity industry, opposed the tax and argued for voluntary conservation measures. Electric power generators—Electrabel (Belgium), Endesa (Spain), PowerGen (United Kingdom), RWE (Germany), Scottish Power (United Kingdom), Union Fenosa (Spain), and VEAG (Germany)—pointed to the uncertain effects of the imposition of a tax and proposed a series of conservation measures as well as the export of energy-efficient technologies to Eastern Europe. In addition to the efforts of the coalition and the trade association, individual power generation companies lobbied to prevent the adoption of the tax.

The European Coal and Steel Council Consultative Committee also opposed the tax and argued for voluntary programs and payments to developing countries to stop deforestation. Opposition also developed within countries. For example, in France 14 major companies, including Electricité de France, Renault, Rhone Polenc, Total, Elf Aquitaine, Pécincy, and Unisor Sacilor, organized "Business for the Environment" to oppose the tax. In exchange, the coalition offered help in cleaning up toxic waste sites.

Chemicals was one of the premier industries in Europe. The industry was energy intensive, and the petrochemical component of the industry used petroleum feedstocks. The global competitiveness of the industry thus would be significantly impacted by the proposed taxes. The industry estimated that the impact of the taxes when fully implemented would be $4.45 billion per year. The chemical industry pointed to the success of voluntary measures undertaken by individual companies. The managing director of Montedison Primary Chemicals stated that since 1974 the European chemicals industry had reduced by 35 percent the energy usage per unit of output and that another 15 percent reduction would be achieved by the year 2000.[8]

As was the case in many European industries, the chemical industry in each country was represented by an association that included most of the companies operating in that country. These national associations acted on behalf of their members within their countries. The associations in the individual countries were organized into the European Chemical Industry Council (CEFIC) that acted at the level of the European Union. As the importance of the European Union governmental institutions had grown, individual companies had begun to take actions independently of their national and pan-European associations. ■

[8] *The Economist,* May 9, 1992.

PREPARATION QUESTIONS

ECONOMICS

1. Identify the efficiency and distributive consequences of a carbon/energy tax.
2. What are the effects of a carbon tax for the global competitiveness of EU companies?

GOVERNMENT

1. What types of politics should be anticipated in the consideration of a carbon/energy tax in the European Union? Which EU institutions will be involved in the decision?
2. What outcome would you expect if the decision on a carbon/energy tax were decided by unanimity and no transfer payments among countries were possible?
3. If structural funds could be provided to countries through the EU budget, what outcome would you expect? Assume for the purposes of this question that the EU makes its decision on structural funds by a qualified majority of the Council of Finance Ministers.

NONMARKET STRATEGY

1. As a European chemicals company dependent on petroleum feedstocks, what effects do you anticipate from the proposed carbon/energy tax?
2. What objectives and strategy should the company adopt to address the carbon/energy tax? How should that strategy be implemented? Which institutions should be targeted?

Benetton, Advertising Protests, and Franchising

Benetton Group SpA of Treviso, Italy, had grown rapidly under its global market strategy of franchising retail outlets for its fashionable clothing lines.

Benetton had worldwide sales of $1.6 billion in 1993, and its sales growth was strong in part because the devaluation of the lira had brought its high labor costs more in line with those of other European countries.

Not only was Benetton well known for its clothing, but it was also well known for its provocative advertising intended to draw attention to social and political issues. President Luciano Benetton explained that the company's advertising continued "to search for new facts and emotions." Benetton produced all of its advertising in-house.

To depict concern over the war in the former Yugoslavia, Benetton obtained from the Red Cross the bloody T-shirt of a slain Croat soldier and a letter from the soldier's father. Benetton used the T-shirt and excerpts from the letter in one of its advertisements, which was published in 110 countries. Oliviero Toscani, creative director of Benetton and the person who took the photograph, commented, "Probably we sell less by doing this, but I believe that a company who has the courage to put its name next to a problem sooner or later will win."[1]

The advertisement caused protests in Europe and the United States. Protests erupted in France, and the French minister for humanitarian affairs publicly denounced the advertisement and Benetton. A Vatican official referred to the advertisement as tantamount to "image terrorism." The mother of a British soldier killed in Bosnia protested the advertisement. Mr. Benetton said he was "very sorry" for the concerns the advertisement had generated. "This is not what a corporate communications campaign should do. It should create interest."[2]

Benetton also produced an advertisement showing a man's arm with the tattoo "H.I.V. Positive." The advertisement generated protests in several European countries. Aides, a group in France that provides support for AIDS victims, sued the French subsidiary of Benetton on the grounds that the advertisement was offensive to AIDS victims. A French court fined the subsidiary $32,000, calling the advertisement "a provocative exploitation of suffering."

The protests were particularly strong in Germany where the advertisement provoked memories of the atrocities of past wars. A Benetton franchisee, Heinz Hartwich, said, "This reminded us of the number they tattooed onto Jews in the concentration camps. How can you combine such horrible tragedy with trying to sell clothes?"[3] German concerns were manifested in direct action against Benetton retailers. As a result of the advertisement Hartwich's store in Kassel was spray painted, glue was put in the door locks, and protesters passed out leaflets in front of his store. Some German consumers boycotted Benetton and sales fell. A 1994 poll taken in Germany found that 84 percent of the people considered Benetton's advertising distasteful.[4]

Hartwich claimed that he had lost $600,000 in sales because of the protests and boycotts, and he tried to sever his franchise agreement with Benetton. He also joined in collective action with 150 other German franchisers. Meeting in 1995, the self-proclaimed "rebels" were joined by several franchisees from France, Italy, Spain, and Sweden who were also concerned about the advertisements and their effects on sales. Several franchisees, including Hartwich, refused to pay for shipments of Benetton clothing.

Benetton argued that the number of units sold in Europe had not fallen and that the franchisees' problems were due to poor management and the European recession. Benetton sued the franchisees for nonpayment.

The attorney representing Hartwich said that he was representing over 50 franchisees and more clients were being added. In addition to claims that the advertisements had injured them, the German franchisees claimed that Benetton was trying to eliminate small retailers and replace them with a smaller number of large stores, some of which would be com-

[1] *San Francisco Chronicle,* February 19, 1994.
[2] *The Wall Street Journal,* March 4, 1994.
[3] *The New York Times,* February 3, 1995.
[4] *The New York Times,* February 3, 1995.

pany owned. Benetton had followed this strategy in the United States and the United Kingdom.

As law suits were filed in other countries, a long and controversial court battle seemed inevitable. ■

PREPARATION QUESTIONS

1. Should the nonmarket reactions to its advertising be of concern to Benetton or is its advertising part of its caché? How should it deal with the protests?
2. Should Benetton have taken legal action against its franchisees?
3. Suppose that Benetton wanted to reduce the number of retailers and replace them with larger, company-owned stores. What means should it use to implement this market strategy? What types of nonmarket responses should it anticipate?

Toys 'Я' Us in Germany

By the mid-1980s, the Toys 'Я' Us strategy of combining discount prices, large stores, and heavy advertising had made it the largest toy retailer in the United States. To continue its growth, it decided to expand internationally. With one of the highest standards of living in the world, Germany offered considerable potential. Although Germany had a relatively open economy, a number of rules, regulations, and traditional relationships presented difficulties for foreign entrants. Entry into retailing, in particular, was more difficult than might have been expected.

Toys 'Я' Us G.m.b.H. was formed in 1986, but as it attempted to enter the German market it encountered several hurdles. In contrast to the United States, a number of European countries had laws favoring employees over consumers. Germany, for example, protected employees in the retail trade by imposing strict rules on store-opening hours, except for gasoline stations and stores in railroad stations and airports. A federal law enacted in 1956 was intended to protect employees from having to work long hours, and it had continuing strong support from the 500,000-member union representing retail, banking, and insurance workers. Union members worked a 37.5-hour week. Many small retailers also supported the law, believing that extended hours would not increase sales enough to warrant the additional cost. Stores were required to close by 6:30 P.M. except on Thursday when they could remain open until 8:30 P.M. The 6:30 P.M. closing time gave employees little time to shop after work. Moreover, stores had to close by 2 P.M. on Saturday and were not allowed to open on Sunday.[1] In addition, in smaller towns many small retailers closed at lunch time.

Other federal laws also imposed some hurdles. Not only were profits taxes the highest in Europe at 50 percent, but Germany also had regulations that were as strict as any in Europe. German labor laws made it difficult to dismiss an employee and gave rights to employees on some policy issues. For example, employees had a say in any legislative effort to revise the store opening laws. In addition, the worker participation requirements in Germany were foreign to an American company and reduced a company's flexibility. Wages and benefits were also very high—German workers typically had 6 weeks of vacation a year and received a thirteenth month of salary as a bonus. German employees were well educated and highly productive, however.

Most German toy retail stores were small, family-owned shops, and many were located in city centers. These retailers were often active members of local organizations. As managing director Arnt Klöser of Toys 'Я' Us G.m.b.H., who had been hired from a leading German department store chain, said, "When you ask a city for a construction permit, the first thing they do is ask the local chamber of commerce and retailers' association what they think of your idea. They always say the same thing: A toy store belongs in the city center, not the meadow on the edge of town."[2] Klöser's strategy was to try to convince the local toy

[1] Stores could remain open until 4 P.M. on the first Saturday of every month and the four Saturdays before Christmas.
[2] *The New York Times*, August 18, 1991.

retailers that Toys ' Я ' Us entry would actually benefit them by expanding the market.

German toy manufacturers also opposed the entry of Toys ' Я ' Us because of concerns about the consequences for their current retail customers. To support local retailers, some manufacturers argued that a self-service retailer such as Toys ' Я ' Us could place children in danger. They said that customers needed the assistance of a *Fachmann* to provide expert advice.

The German Toy Manufacturers Association complained about the Toys ' Я ' Us practice of selling such items as diapers, baby food, clothes, and sporting goods in addition to toys. Some manufacturers went further. The leading manufacturer of model trains, Gebruder Märklin, announced that it would not sell to Toys ' Я ' Us because doing so would damage its image.

Toys ' Я ' Us was willing to commit whatever resources were necessary to enter the German market, but it needed a strategy for dealing with the opposition it faced. ■

This case is based in part on an article in *The New York Times*, August 18, 1991.

PREPARATION QUESTIONS

1. What business strategy—market and nonmarket strategies—should Toys ' Я ' Us adopt to enter the German market successfully? What issues should it address?
2. How should Toys ' Я ' Us deal with the protests of German toy manufacturers and local toy retailers?
3. What should Toys ' Я ' Us do with respect to the government regulation of store hours?

Toys 'Я' Us in Sweden

Operating from its base in the United Kingdom, Toys ' Я ' Us entered Sweden in September 1994, opening stores in Gothenberg, Malmo, and Skarholmen, a suburb of Stockholm.[1] In accord with its policies in other countries, the company required its 110 employees to sign the company handbook, which specified the work rules under which the company operated.

Unions were particularly strong in Sweden with over 90 percent of Swedish employees represented by a union. The Swedish model of labor relations had been an important factor in the country's long record of industrial peace. The Handelsanstallda Forbund, the Retail Workers Union, had signed up a number of workers in Toys ' Я ' Us stores and demanded that the company sign the standard nationwide collective labor agreement. The objective of the collective agreement was to allow organized labor to bring broad pressure on employers as a means of balancing corporate power. " 'In all shops where we have members we want a collective agreement,' said Mr. Bjorn Sjoblom of Handelsanstallda. 'This is quite normal in Sweden. We have not had any problems before with other companies.' "[2]

Toys ' Я ' Us refused to accept the collective agreement but remained willing to negotiate an agreement with the union. "Toys ' Я ' Us does not have any difficulty in accepting an agreement with the union, but considers itself to have the right to participate in negotiations to formulate a firm-adapted agreement,' Sten Yetraeus, attorney with the business law firm Lagerlof & Leman, explained. '[Accepting the collective agreement] would mean that we would be bound to a detailed book of regulations that is the product of many years of negotiations between the Retail Workers and the Retail Employers without us. . . .' " Mr. Yetraeus added.[3] Frank Heskjer, the company's head for Scandinavia, said, "We get by without such agreements in other countries and we'll do the same in Sweden." Retail Workers Union chairman Kenth Pettersson said, "We haven't had a conflict like this for years. Signing

[1]Toys ' Я ' Us became one of the few foreign retail chains operating in Sweden.

[2]*Financial Times*, May 11, 1995.

[3]*Dagens Nyheter*, May 10, 1995.

collective agreements is a virtual formality these days."[4] The Retail Workers Union and its chairman were at the more militant end of the labor spectrum in Sweden.

A government commission failed in its efforts to mediate a settlement, and the first strike by the union in 20 years began. Toys 'Я' Us stated, "[Unions] have forced our employees to strike solely because we will not unconditionally sign a collective agreement." David Rurka, managing director of the company for the United Kingdom and Scandinavia said, "The problem is the culture here. Many of our people don't want to strike. But they say they have fathers or other family members in unions who say they must support the union. The union has motivated the staff with fear and fear alone."[5]

The union provided the strikers with 100 percent pay and took out national advertisements asking the public to support the strike and boycott Toys 'Я' Us stores. The union not only picketed each of the stores but attempted to blockade the stores from supplies. It enlisted the aid of the Transport Workers, and truckers refused to cross the picket lines. The Seamen's Union forced the Swedish flagged carrier Tor Lines to refuse to carry goods from the distribution facility in the United Kingdom to Sweden. The Seamen's Union also announced that it would take actions against Stena Line, Lion Ferry, and SweFerry AB. A Seamen's Union spokesperson said, "A struggle like this is well known within our own union." The expanded actions by the union were in part the result of shoppers who crossed the picket lines to buy low-priced diapers that the union learned were being imported from Denmark. Other unions also announced sympathy measures of support for the Retail Workers Union. For example, the financial sector union refused to handle the Toys 'Я' Us daily receipts.

Toys 'Я' Us provided a wage rate slightly higher than union members earned elsewhere and provided the same insurance. The principal concern, however, was job security. The employee handbook specified performance conditions that could lead to a firing, and one of the strikers explained, "You never felt really secure there, that you can stay." Therese Karlsson, who was let go by the company in Skarholmen during the provisional period, said, "Just prior to [being fired], management said that they were finished making cutbacks in personnel. Those of us who remained could feel secure, and a few were even promised permanent employment. Then they called me at home on a Saturday evening and told me 'you may leave.' "[6] Therese was one of the strikers on the picket line.

The conflict between Toys 'Я' Us and the union also involved other work rule issues. For example, the company handbook stated that employees were forbidden to "speak to or be interviewed by the mass media without special permission in advance from the managing director."[7] Gunnar Jonsson, manager of the Gothenberg store, explained, "Our rules about uniforms, searches at the end of the shift, about not talking to the media and so on do look hard on paper. But all stores demand a neat appearance from their staff, check purses and bags, and so on. Of course our employees may speak with the media—except when it has to do with the internal affairs of the company. . ."[8] Fredrik Larsson, an employee since the store opened, commented, "In my personal opinion, the company's rules don't bother me. I don't see anything against a uniform, and the check that I have to undergo is not insulting, as I see it. After all, it's my own boss who does it. We know each other, and they do it mostly because they have to report to their manager that they have done it."[9]

In response to the strike Toys 'Я' Us halted its planned expansion in Sweden and speculated to the media that it might close its stores and leave the country. The company had planned 15 stores in Sweden employing 500 permanent and 1,000 seasonal workers.

As the strike continued, commentators viewed the conflict between Toys 'Я' Us and the union as a test for the Swedish model of collective bargaining in its new role as a member of the European Union. Peter Skogh, who managed the store in Malmo, said, "We are an international company coming into a new market. Of course we are trying to adapt to the conditions here. But Sweden, in order to survive, must also adapt to the European and international business climate."[10] "One self-employed mother who

[4] *The Reuter Business Report,* May 8, 1995.
[5] *Financial Times,* May 11, 1995.
[6] *Dagens Nyheter,* May 24, 1995.
[7] *Dagens Industri,* May 10, 1995.
[8] *Dagens Nyheter,* May 10, 1995.
[9] *Dagens Nyheter,* May 10, 1995.
[10] *The Guardian,* May 13, 1995.

drove her four children past the pickets said, 'Swedish trade unions are inflexible and only interested in sticking to old principles. Sweden is sick to the back teeth of them.' "[11] Toys 'Я' Us began to receive expressions of support from other companies. ■

[11] *The Guardian,* May 13, 1995.

PREPARATION QUESTIONS

1. Why is Toys 'Я' Us refusing to sign the national labor agreement? Is it wise to refuse?
2. What are the stakes for the Retail Workers Union?
3. What implications does this have for Sweden?
4. What should Toys 'Я' Us do as the strike continues?

CHAPTER 15

China: History, Culture, and Political Economy

Introduction

China is an ancient country that since 1978 has embarked on a remarkable economic path in which foreign direct investment has been encouraged and economic reforms have been frequent if not always successful. Yet, China remains a country under the domination of the Chinese Communist Party (CCP) with little popular participation in political activity and considerable restrictions on human rights. The importance of a country with over 1.2 billion people cannot be underestimated for both foreign businesses and governments, but the absence of democratic institutions and weak legal protections present continuing challenges. Economic reforms have led thousands of companies to set up operations in China and, combined with the liberalization of business opportunities for Chinese citizens, have resulted in spectacular economic growth. Real growth in GDP has averaged nearly 10 percent annually since the open-door policy began in 1978. The Asian economic and financial crisis beginning in 1997, however, posed a particular challenge for China as it attempted to make its state-owned enterprises (SOEs) more efficient and provide greater separation between SOEs and government. This economic liberalization had to be accomplished while preserving the supremacy of the CCP through political authoritarianism.

This chapter provides background on the history and culture of China and briefly characterizes the four I's with an emphasis on government institutions and business issues. The chapter cases provide an opportunity to address particular managerial challenges in the context of China's institutions.

Historical Background[1]

PRE-REPUBLICAN

Ethnic Chinese, also known as Han people, originated in the Yellow River Valley in North-Central China. Organized rural society has existed in this region for well over 10,000 years, and political control was typically divided by rival dynastic kingdoms. Invasion by barbarians resulted in centuries (c. 771–221 B.C.) of political fragmentation,

[1]This section is based on a note prepared by Michael M. Ting under the supervision of Professor David P. Baron. Copyright © 1998 by the Board of Trustees of the Leland Stanford Junior University. All rights reserved. Reproduced with permission.

during which much of China's most impressive philosophy was developed. Three important schools of Chinese philosophical thought emerged in this period: Daoism, Confucianism, and Legalism. Together these laid the basis for much of China's future political thought and made the unification of China a paramount ideal. Confucianism, considered later in the chapter, had a profound impact on the organization of Chinese government, as it advocated the concept of government by meritocracy and thereby provided the intellectual foundation for the imperial bureaucracy.[2]

Many historians regard the victory of the Qin kingdom after a period of prolonged conflicts known as the Warring States Period (403–221 B.C.) as the beginning of China's existence as a unified nation. The resulting state controlled an area roughly half the size of the People's Republic of China today. Technology played a central role in the Qin's success, as it had mastered iron-working in advance of most of its rivals. The Qin Dynasty played an important role in shaping the institutions and practices of imperial China. It eliminated the remnants of China's ancient feudal society and established the beginnings of a central bureaucracy based on Confucian principles. It also standardized the currency, weights, and measures; built some of China's first extensive irrigation projects; introduced a uniform system of writing; and consolidated many of the nation's defensive walls.

Bureaucracy in Imperial China

Despite the immense political changes made by the Qin, China's society and politics were dominated by regional aristocracies for almost another millennium. Each succeeding dynasty, however, expanded and strengthened the bureaucratic system and by the Tang Dynasty (618–907 A.D.) the imperial bureaucracy was considered the preeminent political authority.[3]

Since the Early Han Dynasty (206 B.C.– 8 A.D.), membership in the bureaucracy was attained through highly competitive national examinations that in theory were open to all. The wealth, power, and prestige afforded by passing the examinations were so great that families often invested handsomely in educating their young men. Successful examinees spent their entire youth studying the Confucian classics in preparation for the examinations and were often in their mid-thirties when they passed. The bureaucracy played an important role in ensuring social stability by preventing the rise of rival sources of political power while still permitting the accumulation of family wealth.[4]

Foreign Relations

Imperial China faced external military threats for much of its history. The Ming Dynasty (1368–1644) constructed the Great Wall of China to ward off northern barbarians, but it proved to be a military failure, as it could not stop a Manchurian invasion that resulted in the last dynasty, the Qing (1644–1911). In general, however, the pre-Ming Chinese welcomed foreign commerce. Trade with the Middle East and European nations flourished, and in the early 1400s a fleet of Chinese vessels successfully completed a trade and diplomatic mission to Africa. During the fifteenth century, however, Chinese leaders began to view foreign interaction with a peculiar contempt. Costly border wars and fiscal crises caused the Ming to pull back on their efforts to establish foreign relations and build a navy. Convinced that foreigners could offer little value to China, conservative Confucian scholars of the period increasingly advocated xenophobic foreign policies.[5]

---

[2]See Pye (1978, pp. 32–59; 1985) for an introduction to the early Chinese schools of thought.
[3]See Shue (1988, pp. 84–85) and Moore (1966, p. 164).
[4]Fairbank (1992, pp. 179–182).
[5]Fairbank (1992, 138–140).

Notwithstanding the Qing's hostility, the British, led by the British East India Company, vigorously attempted to maintain trade ties in southern China. With the end of the Napoleonic Wars in 1815, England gradually increased its commercial interest in China. China's defeat in the Opium War at the hands of Britain's vastly superior military technology resulted in the 1842 Treaty of Nanjing. The terms of this treaty were widely regarded as humiliating to the Chinese, as they required massive reparations to Britain, the turnover of Hong Kong, and the opening of five coastal cities to British residents and commerce. Many of the Western powers also insisted on reciprocal "most favored nation" agreements that automatically granted concessions made to one country to every foreign country, thus hastening the pace and extent of concessions.

Collapse of Imperial China

The latter half of the nineteenth century was marked by numerous large-scale revolts that reflected the inability of the Qing to maintain domestic peace and contain foreign influence. The imperial bureaucracy was increasingly perceived as an incompetent and backwards institution, incapable of performing even its traditional duties of maintaining China's important waterways. As the nineteenth century drew to a close, internal calls for reform became increasingly prevalent and indeed the Qing initiated many ambitious reforms. They attempted to copy several Western-style government institutions and abolished the centuries-old examination system in 1905. Their drive toward modernization resulted in the outfitting of a Western-style military and plans for a massive new national rail network.

THE REPUBLICAN ERA

By the first decade of the twentieth century, local warlords had ascended to political prominence in China. Many raised their own armies, collected their own taxes, and showed questionable loyalty to the Qing. In addition, revolutionary societies and fraternities, many loosely organized into a group called the "Revolutionary Alliance," were increasingly active in China's major urban centers. The Revolutionary Alliance, led by Dr. Sun Yat-sen, had relatively strong popular backing, but lacked an army. By early 1912, a large military faction led by former Qing general Yuan Shikai gained the upper hand, and the last Qing abdicated his throne in 1912.

While many credit Sun Yat-sen with the founding of the Republic of China in 1911, China in the 1910s was hardly a coherent political entity. Yuan proved incapable of ruling China, as he insisted on central control over proposed modernizations but lacked substantial authority over local governments. He also actively attempted to undermine his Revolutionary Alliance allies, many of whom had organized themselves into the Guomindang (GMD), or Nationalist Party, under Sun.

Sun's death in 1925 cleared the way for the ascendancy of Chiang Kai-shek as the new GMD leader. Capitalizing on both the strength of his National Revolutionary Army and a wave of nationalist sentiment in the mid-1920s, Chiang launched military offensives in 1926 and 1928 that established a new capital in Nanjing and brought most of China under GMD rule. His sudden success convinced many that the GMD was China's best hope for modernizing its economy and political system. This hope proved to be illusory, however, as the Nanjing leaders lacked sufficient control over many regions to execute their policies. The GMD's support base was primarily urban, but since China's urban-industrial sector was still very small, its resources were limited.

The main unifying force for the GMD was the threat from the Chinese Communist Party (CCP) formed in 1921. Chiang continually harassed the CCP, and in response, several communist uprisings took place, only to be crushed by GMD armies. The CCP did not recover until 1933, by which time it had transformed itself into a rural party largely independent of the international communist party. Headed by Mao Zedong, an early revolutionary leader who had carefully studied the rural economy, the CCP was once again strong enough to be of concern to the GMD. Chiang's continuous attacks drove the CCP to seek a new base in late 1934, and 100,000 soldiers and party members began their famous "Long March."

War and Civil War

In 1937 Japan invaded and Chinese armies were quickly routed by superior Japanese tactics and technology. Chinese resistance to Japan was highly fragmented in spite of the initial promise of a united front between the GMD and CCP. During the war and occupation Mao was able to consolidate his leadership and develop his own distinctive brand of Marxism. As part of his program the CCP began to institute land reform in friendly areas, thus enlisting peasant support and swelling the ranks of CCP troops.

As World War II drew to a close, both sides prepared for a civil war. In 1945 the CCP was stronger than at any point in their history, but its army had little foreign support and was only half the size of Chiang's American-equipped army. American support, however, could not forestall the subsequent rout of the GMD in the 1946 to 1949 civil war. By mid-1949 the communist victory was nearly complete, and on October 1, 1949, Mao proclaimed the founding of the People's Republic of China.

As Chiang's losses mounted in 1948, he transferred the remains of the Republic of China to Taiwan, which as part of the Yalta agreements in World War II had been formally returned to the Republic of China after 50 years of Japanese colonization. The GMD instituted comprehensive land reform and compensated landlords with government bonds. With American economic aid it embarked on vigorous industrialization by attracting foreign investment and targeting export markets.[6]

THE COMMUNIST ERA

Although the communist victory had been complete, Mao and his followers still faced a daunting task that had eluded Chinese rulers for centuries: establishing a state with unquestioned control over the entire nation. The CCP's assumption of power took two distinct tracks. First, in the countryside, it sought to complete the process of land reform that had begun in Northern China earlier in the decade. Because peasants benefiting from land redistribution overwhelmingly outnumbered landlords, the process was quickly and enthusiastically embraced.[7] Second, in keeping with Marxist philosophy, the party sought to control all commerce, but again the magnitude of the task demanded considerable flexibility. Only the largest companies came under state control in the early years, and most urban professionals were allowed to continue working regardless of their political background. Meanwhile governments at all levels gradually asserted control over prices, the banking system, and the allocation of various important goods.

The end of the Korean War allowed policy makers to concentrate on their next task: the transformation of the Chinese economy into a socialist system. Following the early Soviet model, planners in Beijing hoped to stimulate the development of heavy industry by taxing the agricultural sector. They also believed that greater productivity would be best achieved by wiping out the remnants of capitalism and developing huge, self-contained production units in agriculture and industry.

A central feature of the First Five Year Plan was the collectivization of agriculture. Shortly after land reform was completed, the CCP began to organize peasant households into ever-larger cooperative associations. A similar process was underway in the

---

[6]See Deyo (1987) and Haggard (1990) for a comparative perspective on Taiwanese industrial policy.
[7]Vogel (1980, pp. 91–124) discusses policy debates during the early years of land reform.

industrial sector. State takeovers of large enterprises accelerated throughout the 1950s, until only the smallest street merchants were allowed to remain independent. With the aid of Soviet loans, CCP industrial policy emphasized sectors such as steel, petroleum, and chemicals at the expense of consumer goods. In addition to their economic importance, these enterprises also served a vital social role. Labor was furnished through the *danwei* ("work unit") system, under which workers were permanently assigned to enterprises upon completing their education. The *danwei* provided its members with housing, child care, schooling, health care, shops, post offices, and other social services. It was also an instrument of social control. Because there was no welfare system, urban residents had no access to even the most basic social services outside of their *danwei,* and opportunities for changing enterprises were rare.

Convinced that China's lagging production could be blamed not on poor economic reasoning but on a lack of mobilization, the CCP unleashed a flurry of production efforts to spur the economy. Many of these projects launched in the Great Leap Forward in 1958 were at best ill conceived, and at worst destructive.[8] Agricultural cooperatives were rapidly combined into even larger county-size communes, but in 1959 poor weather highlighted the inefficiency of the communes. Production plummeted and China suffered a famine that claimed over 20 million lives through 1962.

The clear failure of the large communes prompted authority to devolve back to smaller production units, so that individual households were once again held responsible for meeting certain production quotas. More importantly, the government legalized private plots, on which peasants were allowed to raise and market their own vegetables and animals while their communes produced grain. On a larger scale, leaders also began to question the Soviet-inspired strategy of developing heavy industry first.

Mao's leftist allies—notably his wife Jiang Qing and army chief Lin Biao—insisted that China's problems were the result of insufficient dedication to the CCP's revolutionary principles. Mao's gambit to reassert power combined this message with his still considerable populist appeal in launching the Great Proletarian Cultural Revolution in 1966. Mao and Lin organized thousands of "Red Guard" units, consisting largely of fanatical students who were directed to purge their jurisdictions of the four "olds"—old ideas, old customs, old cultures, and old habits. Their campaigns destroyed many of China's most valuable cultural artifacts and degenerated into destructive excess and mob rule in the name of Mao. Finally in 1967 the army stepped in to control the chaos, often by imposing martial law. The cultural revolution had decimated much of the party's organization, especially at the provincial and lower levels. It had also elevated the army's status within the party hierarchy.

As a result of the split of the Sino-Soviet alliance in 1958, successive American administrations expressed interest in renewing relations with China, and these efforts culminated in President Nixon's historic visit to China in 1972. As a result of improved relations both nations gained a powerful ally against the Soviet Union.

The Reform Era

The deaths of Mao and foreign minister Zhou Enlai in 1976 led to Deng Xiaoping assuming the leadership of China. Deng's rise occurred during a period of tremendous foreign and domestic ferment. The United States formally switched its recognition of China from Taiwan to the People's Republic on January 1, 1979, after which Deng made historic visits to America and Japan. Inspired by the beginnings of political liberalization many Chinese began to express their bitterness toward the communist party with large posters on various city walls, the most famous of which became known as the

[8]See the chapter case *Wugang and the Reform of State-Owned Enterprises* for a description of one of these projects.

'Democracy Wall' in Beijing. The party, which was ready to commit itself to many reforms, had little intention of sharing its authority, and to emphasize its control, Deng consolidated power.

Deng's economic reforms were headlined by the "Four Modernizations"—agriculture, industry, defense, and science and technology. Recognizing that China needed more exposure to Western products, ideas, and capital, Beijing lifted import restrictions in 1978 under its open-door policy. Four "Special Economic Zones" were opened in Southern China, where foreign investors could take advantage of low-wage labor and preferential tax rates. Small, household-run enterprises were once again legalized. Finally, larger enterprises such as agricultural production teams and many state-owned enterprises were subjected to a new fiscal regime, under which some profits from above-quota production could be retained for the enterprise's use. This exposure to market forces resulted in a dramatic increase in nationwide investment in 1979 and 1980.[9]

A second, more intensive wave of reforms occurred between 1983 and 1985. In the agricultural sector, the government replaced mandatory grain purchases with a contracting system known as the "Household Responsibility System," and prices for many goods were allowed to "float" to market levels. In the cities, state-owned enterprises were given increased discretion over their profits, and individual managers were made more accountable for their performance. Beijing also granted 14 additional coastal cities and Hainan Island a Special Economic Zone status. The sudden changes and influx of wealth, however, created economic and social backlashes. Economic crime and corruption were rampant, and leaders often voiced concerns about excessive Western cultural influence.

Another period of retrenchment occurred in 1986, as restrictions were placed on investments and imports in an attempt to cool the economy. More ominously, however, large-scale social unrest had become evident throughout the country and students and intellectuals grew increasingly disappointed that the nation's rapid economic change was not accompanied by changes in the authoritarian political system. For many students, Hu Yaobang personified many of the disappointments they faced. An outspoken progressive, Hu was forced to resign as party general secretary in January 1987 after other party leaders blamed him for not stopping student protests. His sudden death in 1989 set off a wave of nationwide student demonstrations, the most prominent of which attracted as many as a million demonstrators to Beijing's Tiananmen Square. For weeks, the demonstrators and sympathetic civilians successfully resisted attempts to impose martial law, but in a move that was condemned worldwide, crack army units crushed the protests.

The repercussions of the Tiananmen massacre showed that China's efforts to join the world community were imposing constraints on the CCP and the government. China's desire to realize an international role commensurate with its growing economic strength had generated numerous frictions. Foremost among these were China's foreign economic relations. Both the United States, one of China's largest trading partners, and the GATT/World Trade Organization, which China hoped to join, insisted that China adhere more closely to international norms in its economy.

One foreign policy success was the 1984 agreement with the United Kingdom returning Hong Kong to China in 1997. Under China's "One Country, Two Systems" policy, Hong Kong was to have retained its autonomy, including a separate currency, for 50 years. Shortly before the return, the British government attempted to bolster the colony's legislative body as a popular institution, but Beijing ensured that only its own hand-picked representatives would be permitted to sit. In 1999 Macao was returned to China by Portugal.

---

[9]Harding (1987, Ch. 4).

A potentially more serious sovereignty issue was the status of Taiwan. In their claims to sovereignty over both the mainland and Taiwan, both the CCP and GMD agreed that there was only a single Chinese nation. Because of their disparate political systems, however, movement toward reunification has been virtually nonexistent. Beijing originally proposed the One Country, Two Systems policy for Taiwan, but it was quickly rejected by the GMD government, which refused to unite with a communist regime. Beijing made clear that it would not tolerate a declaration of Taiwanese independence.

Domestic Reform in an Authoritarian Framework

Domestically, China resumed its economic reforms shortly after the furor over Tiananmen subsided. The 1990s saw the increasing autonomy of state-owned enterprises, reforms of the nation's financial system, as well as a fully convertible currency. The government also handled the political transition of Deng's death in 1997 with few problems. The country, however, faced challenges that were as formidable as ever. One of the most urgent was the reform of over 300,000 obsolete state-owned enterprises. Few of these enterprises were profitable because they had functioned too long in the absence of competitive pressures. Many were hopelessly inefficient, saddled with old technology and employing up to 15 million excess workers nationwide. Moreover, these enterprises had accumulated combined debts approaching $120 billion (almost 20 percent of GDP), while absorbing most of China's domestic credit.[10] The problem was tightly linked with a crisis in the national banking system, whose long-standing practice of granting loans on the basis of political connections rather than commercial merit had resulted in high levels of bad debt. Transforming these enterprises into profitable entities would inevitably require the dismantling of the *danwei* system, but there was no social welfare system to replace it.

Beijing also faced a host of long-term economic and political issues. The central government's finances, along with the country's labor and housing markets, all required serious revamping. Corruption and cronyism were prevalent at all levels of government. The growing demand by an increasingly affluent population for energy and consumer goods was exacerbating China's already dire environmental problems. Finally, the CCP faced the daunting task of addressing these issues without once again raising demands for political liberalization.

Confucianism and Social Explanations

An important factor in understanding Chinese social and economic organization is its rich cultural heritage. This section considers Confucianism, which has had a significant influence not only in China but also in several other Asian nations.[11] With its emphasis on hierarchy, deference, moral rectitude and behavioral norms, Confucianism was well suited to the needs of social stability, and indeed many historians have credited China's long existence as a unified nation to its Confucian heritage. Yet the attribution of highly complex social phenomena to a single body of philosophical work would be unwarranted. Over more than 2,000 years of development, a wide variety of theories have worked their way under the Confucian umbrella. Thus, the general framework of Confucian thought displays considerable flexibility. On the one hand, as Confucius might suggest, a degree of modesty is warranted in drawing conclusions about social

---

[10] See Tomlinson (1997) for an example of the privatization of a state-owned enterprise.

[11] This section is adapted from a note prepared by Michael M. Ting under the supervision of Professor David P. Baron.

and economic organization from this highly complex ethical system.[12] On the other hand, attempting to understand Chinese groups, organizations, and behavior without sensitivity to the Confucian heritage would be incomplete at best.

During the political turmoil following the fall of the Zhou Dynasty, Confucius (551–479 B.C.) recorded and organized the extant body of ethical thought and extended it by deemphasizing religious aspects and giving priority to the human condition instead (De Bary, 1991). Under this humanistic reorientation, virtue figured prominently in personal and political affairs, and individuals were to possess virtue and follow rules of behavior just as emperors did. Thus, Confucius was responsible for initiating the central preoccupation of Chinese philosophical thought: moral self-cultivation (Ivanhoe, 1993).

Perhaps the fundamental distinction between Confucianism and many Western systems of thought lies in its orientation toward the fundamental problem of social organization. As Yang (1959, p. 172) explained:

> Self-cultivation, the basic theme of Confucian ethics . . . did not seek a solution to social conflict in defining, limiting, and guaranteeing the rights and interests of the individual or in the balance of power and interests between individuals. It sought the solution from the self-sacrifice of the individual for the preservation of the group.

Confucianism links self-cultivation and social harmony through the development of group relations because it views the family as the ideal setting for moral self-cultivation. According to the *Zhongyong,* "Five Relationships" (*Wu lun*) must be perfected before social harmony is achieved: father and son, husband and wife, sibling and sibling, friend and friend, and ruler and subject. Taking a pragmatic view of human nature, Confucius felt that most people could only achieve perfection in their intra-family relationships. By extension, if virtue and harmony could be found most readily in family relationships, the *process* by which virtue is acquired must be present there as well (Schwartz, 1985, p. 99). As the individuals most responsible for this process, the leaders of such groups—family elders or bureaucrats—were accorded a high degree of deference and respect. Groups were therefore a vital part of the Confucian ethical system, as the individual goal of moral self-cultivation was in some sense an achievement of a larger group, be it a family or a nation.

The objectives of self-cultivation are two interrelated concepts: *ren,* or humanity, and *li,* or propriety. Loosely speaking, the former refers to one's internal discipline, whereas the latter concerns one's social relations. Confucius regarded *ren* as the more fundamental of the two concepts and considered it the ultimate object of moral self-cultivation. In its most abstract sense, the concept refers to the love of all human beings, and all people were thought to have an innate capacity for it.

Li is the external, or social, manifestation of *ren.* Although *li* is most commonly interpreted as "propriety," the term is also synonymous with "ceremony," "ritual," "decorum," and "good form," because it addresses all aspects of human behavior, including personal, familial, social, religious, and political conduct (Tu, 1979, pp. 20–21, 29). The Confucian tradition places a strong emphasis on behavioral minutiae because of its belief that self-cultivation is not a solitary endeavor, but rather occurs in a social context.

---

[12]Although the best exposition of Confucian thought is the *Analects,* over the centuries *Rujia* philosophers added dozens of major variations and extensions to this work. Zhu Xi grouped its existing strands into a two-tiered program of study that is regarded as the Confucian canon. First came the "Four Books": the *Analects, Mencius, Daxue (The Great Learning),* and *Zhongyong (Doctrine of the Mean).* Next were the "Five Classics": *Shujing (Book of History), Liji (Book of Rites), Shijing (Book of Odes), Spring and Autumn Annals,* and *Yijing (Book of Changes).* Thus, while Confucianism lacks a single, comprehensive statement, a commonly accepted body of tenets emerges from these works.

Confucian behavioral norms display a strongly particularistic, as opposed to universal, inclination. In contrast with ethical systems that require equal treatment of all individuals, Confucianism explicitly condoned behavior differentiated on the basis of social relationships. That is, differing standards could be applied to different social relationships, such as within a group to which a person belongs versus with regard to strangers. Appropriate behavior in a group could also differ depending on the person's position. For example, within a family a parent follows a particular form of proper behavior with regard to a child, whereas within a work group the same parent may be in the position of the "child" in relation to his or her employer.

The notion that appropriate behavior is specific to particular social relationships is largely attributable to the group foundations of moral self-cultivation, which forces numerous concessions out of necessity. Self-cultivation ideally encompasses relations with all people, but in practice most individuals can only achieve a limited degree of success in perfecting relationships. A family bond, for instance, creates opportunities for developing *ren* and *li* that may elude those outside the family. Thus, self-cultivation is seen as a process of gradual inclusion, beginning with the individual, then progressing to relations with family, nation, and the world. In this framework, universalism exists as an ideal, but discrimination and favoritism within groups should be expected because Confucians would find the notion of universalistic humanity incoherent without the prior achievement of harmony within smaller groups (Tu, 1979, p. 28).

Another feature of *li* in Confucian ethics is its distinctive conception of reciprocity. Many cultures have some variation of the Golden Rule: "Do unto others as you would have them do unto you." Beginning with the *Analects,* Confucians have devoted a great deal of attention to the idea of *shu,* or consideration. Confucius's classic statement of the rule is:

> Tzu-kung asked saying, Is there any single saying that one can act upon all day and every day? The Master said, Perhaps the saying about consideration: 'Never do to others what you would not like them to do to you.' (*Analects* 15.23)

Numerous variations and extensions on the Golden Rule exist in the Confucian canon. Taken together, they share the characteristic of emphasizing hierarchy. Nivison (1996, p. 73) constructs the following synthesis of the idealized version of *shu*:

> What I do *to* you, if I am in a *superior* position, should be what I would find it acceptable for you to do to me, if our positions were reversed. I should be kind, lenient, considerate . . . What I do *for* you, if I am in an *inferior* position, should be what I would expect you to do for me, if our positions were reversed. I should be "loyal," and so should be strict with myself even when what I am doing might hurt me,. . . .

Western variants of the Golden Rule typically make no allusions to the social status of the actors.

Applications in Society, Politics, and Business

Political Institutions The Confucian ideal of hierarchical relations within the family also extends to the political realm. Whereas family heads could exercise near-absolute authority over other family members, households were expected to defer to the state on nonhousehold matters. The promotion of one's self-interest in society was considered just as inappropriate as a child's selfishness before her parents (Pye, 1985). The analogy helped to justify the Confucians' advocacy of authoritarian rule by a meritocratic elite. It also identified some of the highest political priorities of the state: security, cohesion, loyalty, and stability. Confucius wrote extensively on the behavior expected of a ruler. The following passage touches on some important aspects of a ruler's behavior:

> The Master said, Govern the people by regulations, keep order among them by chastisements, and they will flee from you, and lose all self-respect. Govern them by moral force, keep order among them by ritual and they will keep their self-respect and come to you of their own accord. (*Analects* 2.3)

Confucius saw the ruler as a moral exemplar, but the primary purpose of governing by moral force was not divine reward but the moral development of the people. To achieve this, the ruler could use formal rules or coercion, but setting a virtuous example was both necessary and sufficient for improving society's moral character and inducing social harmony.

One of the most striking differences between Confucian and Western political thought is that the former does not conceive of a role for "civil society," or the collection of intermediate organizations between the family and state (Shils, 1996).[13] Because households were to show the same loyalty to the state that children showed to their parents, allegiance to other organizations had the potential for destabilizing society. Remarkably, imperial Chinese society mirrored these priorities for over two millennia, as merchants never achieved any substantial social status and social advancement was secured exclusively through advancement in the state bureaucracy (Pye, 1985, p. 57). The lack of recognition of legitimate interests outside the state and the deference expected of citizens also rendered Confucianism inconsistent with modern conceptions of democracy.

Firms and Bureaucracies In more modern settings, Confucian paternalism may be seen in the context of other organizations, such as firms and bureaucracies (Abegglen and Stalk, 1985; Dollinger, 1988; Durlabhji, 1990; Taka, 1994). Because of the imperative of maintaining group harmony, decision making is typically achieved through consensus building, although this process requires the cooperation of leaders and subordinates. Leaders must demonstrate decision-making ability commensurate with their position, treat subordinates fairly, and set a good example for all. Personal negotiation may be used to resolve disputes among peers. In return, subordinates are to recognize a leader's authoritarian prerogatives and subsume personal desires to the attainment of group goals. Little emphasis is typically placed on formal rules, and quiet suasion and deference are often sufficient for making decisions and maintaining organizational unity.

This familistic orientation can exert a powerful influence outside the boundaries of formal organizations. Informal personal ties in Chinese society are often referred to as *guanxi.* These relationships may be either vertical (e.g., between teacher and student), or horizontal (e.g., between residents of the same village). *Guanxi* ties create a form of diffuse reciprocity, allowing individuals to exchange favors even years after a formal relationship has been dissolved. Their importance in Chinese society should not be underestimated. Throughout history, decisions ranging from hiring to the sale of scarce goods have gone in favor of those possessing good *guanxi.* Such practices have persisted despite the increased bureaucratization of Chinese society during the communist era. Because these relationships are usually not reflected in formal laws, *guanxi* often makes Chinese organizational behavior appear as nontransparent and at times resembles cronyism to outsiders. The strength of such ties in China has frequently frustrated West-

[13]Gold (1996) argues that large family networks serve as the functional equivalent of civil society.

erners, who are more accustomed to legally circumscribed contracts or quid pro quo arrangements (Pye, 1988).

The importance of *guanxi* is such that individuals must concern themselves with acquiring it. Some ties arise in the course of normal social interaction, for instance through school or family. Others must be cultivated directly through the giving of gifts and favors, for which an elaborate set of norms has evolved. Gift giving in China frequently serves the instrumental goal of initiating a relationship. Whereas gifts may sometimes be used to secure specific favors, the diffuse nature of *guanxi* requires that exchanges occur in private some time before the desired favor to avoid the public appearance of a quid pro quo (Yang, 1994, p. 144).

Confucianism's strong focus on group cohesion and solidarity has implications for other relationships. Because intra-group relations are so important, relationships by subordinates within a group with individuals outside the group are often frowned upon. Such relationships are the responsibility of the group leader, who may require the outsiders to acknowledge his or her moral authority (Pye, 1985, p. 63). As a result, outsiders hoping to influence a group must simultaneously respect the group leader's appearance of control while also exerting effort toward establishing trustworthiness and becoming more of an insider. The latter likely entails a significant investment in the establishment of *guanxi* relationships prior to the execution of any significant interaction.

Business Relationships Confucianism has often been linked with the development and operation of capitalism in China and other Asian countries.[14] In particular, the Chinese tendency toward small, family-owned businesses that operate within tight networks shows many traces of the Confucian heritage (Hamilton, 1996). The high status associated with public office, which required tremendous investment in education, and the traditional practice of dividing inheritances equally among children mitigated the concentration of wealth in large firms.[15] Instead, wealthy merchant families would establish multiple small businesses that could be distributed evenly to the next generation. These multiple businesses relied on sometimes vast *guanxi* networks to conduct their affairs. The success of such businesses depended critically on the level of trust, and *guanxi*-based ties proved to be extremely successful in this regard.[16] Over the past century, during which Chinese have migrated throughout the Pacific Rim, these ties have proven to be invaluable to the success of Chinese business communities throughout the region. In China's reform era, they have also been credited with aiding overseas Chinese who have sought to do business in China.[17]

Commercial and political success were closely linked in imperial China, as successful businessmen could more easily afford to invest in education, and bureaucrats used their political influence to favor family businesses. Thus, relationships between large businesses and government have traditionally been close, often to the point of inappropriateness by Western standards. *Guanxi*-based influence networks remain pervasive throughout Asia, and while they can play an important role in facilitating business, today they are increasingly criticized for inducing favoritism and poor

---

[14]See Weidenbaum (1996).

[15]By contrast, *primogeniture,* or the granting of the entire inheritance to the first son, was practiced in Japan, where it encouraged the concentration of capital.

[16]See Redding (1996) for a discussion and comparison of trust networks in other cultures.

[17]Phil Kelly, head of Dell Asia Pacific explained why Dell believed that direct sales of computers would be successful in China where traditionally people like to see and feel a product before they buy it. "The most important thing in China is *guanxi,* or relationships. That's what Dell is all about. It's taking the middle person out so that a customer can deal with the father rather than the son." *Fortune,* August 17, 1998.

economic decisions by political institutions. The state banking system in China, for instance, faces a bad debt crisis as a result of loans given on the basis of cronyism instead of merit.

The Nonmarket Environment and the Four I's

The framework of structured pluralism illustrated in Figure 13-1 is relevant to China but the importance of the components differs from that in other countries. With regard to culture and history, China has a long history as a relatively unified nation, but it has no democratic tradition. Instead, institutions have been dominated by the bureaucracy and in the postwar period by the Chinese Communist Party. Culturally, China has a rich tradition, and only one aspect of that culture, Confucianism, has been considered here. This section briefly considers the other components of the structured pluralism perspective, the four I's—issues, interests, institutions, and information—and pertains only to the communist period.

A host of contentious market and nonmarket issues faced business and government in China at the end of the 1990s. Internally, China had the problem of reforming or closing a large number of inefficient state-owned enterprises (SOEs), as considered later in the chapter. Many of the SOEs had close ties to the CCP and the ministries that controlled them. International trade issues had blocked China's membership in the World Trade Organization, although the United States and most other countries continued to accord most favored nation status on China. Trade issues focused on commercial piracy, quotas on imports, and restrictions on entry to many markets. A variety of human rights complaints had been lodged with China, ranging from the absence of civil rights to the use of prison labor and the enforcement of the one-child-per-family law. Nonmarket issues also stemmed from the weak protection of intellectual and other property rights in China and the widespread corruption stemming in part from the government's involvement in businesses. Smuggling had also become a major problem and led the CCP to attempt to sever the People's Liberation Army from its business activities.

Interests in China are pluralistic, but because of the domination of the CCP there is little interest group activity in China and collective action is rare. Moreover, independent labor unions are not permitted. Instead, interests manifest themselves through client politics narrowly tailored to specific interests. This implies that interests do not drive outcomes in the same manner as in a democracy such as Japan, the member states of the European Union, or the United States. The government, however, is sensitive to the possibility of popular unrest and attempts to anticipate problems.

The institutions in China are dominated by the CCP and include a strong and encompassing bureaucracy and a relatively weak legislature and judiciary. Despite the tight political control exercised by the CCP, China has devolved considerable authority to the provinces and local governments.

Information is important in China in part because of the presence of a dominant political party and a hierarchical government. It is also important because government rules and regulations are not transparent and can be changed without due process or electoral sanction. This situation is exacerbated by the dominance of a closed political party in both business and the administration of laws. The set of *guanxi* relationships between business and government makes information both important and difficult to obtain.

INSTITUTIONS AND GOVERNMENT

China's government is characterized by intimate ties between the Chinese Communist Party (CCP) and state institutions. In practice a government body wields power to the extent that its leadership is influential within the CCP. The constitution of the PRC places the party in the highest position of authority and requires that government policies and civil liberties conform to its direction. As a result, the informal configuration of power within the party leadership is usually more informative than the government's organization charts for determining where policies are made.

Since the ascendance of Deng Xiaoping, three general trends have become evident. First, political power has steadily devolved to local governments, thus shifting the locus of a considerable body of policy making away from Beijing. Second, the relationship between party and state has been weakened by new restrictions on joint appointments in the leaderships of both bodies. This has been coupled with significant advances in administrative law and an increasing professionalization of the bureaucracy. Third, although their influence remains small, democratic procedures, such as elections to local People's Congresses, that were once considered mere formalities have become increasingly important.

Party Organization

The CCP claims to represent the Chinese working people and is the highest source of political power in China. Moreover, the People's Liberation Army, which has historically been closely linked with the CCP, is sworn to defend the party rather than the state. In 1997 CCP membership stood at 58 million or less than 5 percent of the population. At the local level, the party is represented in virtually all significant societal organizations, including townships, factories, and rural collectives. At higher levels, party organizations mirror the hierarchy of the national government. Decisions at all levels are made by a process known as *democratic centralism,* whereby party units may set their own policies in a democratic manner, but may not contradict the directives of a higher level. This system of representation and centralization of authority guarantees significant party influence over potentially all aspects of political and economic activity.

National Party Congress Nominally the highest authority of the CCP, Party Congresses meet every 5 years. The 15th Party Congress in 1997 had 2,047 delegates, elected from local party organizations, the central party, and the military. Because meetings are brief (usually a few days) and the number of delegates is large, the Congress usually does little more than rubber-stamp the decisions of its delegated bodies.

Central Committee When the Party Congress is not in session, authority passes to the Central Committee, which convenes at least twice annually. The Central Committee is elected by the National Party Congress, but until 1987 ballots were not secret and the number of candidates did not exceed the number of seats. Members represent the central party, local party organizations, the government, and the military. The committee makes decisions by majority rule, and has veto authority over many party decisions. Many of Deng's reforms catered to local governments to avoid a Central Committee veto.[18] The Central Committee also supervises many of the party's internal functions, such as propaganda and organization.

Politburo The Politburo is responsible for the ongoing administration of the party. This body meets regularly and makes decisions by majority rule. It holds a veto over many of the decisions of the Standing Committee and supervises the policy branches of the party organization (e.g., military, foreign affairs, finance). Much of the Politburo's authority comes from its personnel powers.

---

[18]Shirk (1993, Ch. 4).

Standing Committee of the Politburo In the mid-1990s, the Standing Committee consisted of seven members. This group handles the day-to-day affairs of the party and like other CCP bodies makes decisions by majority rule. Much of its leverage comes from its ability to convene Politburo meetings and set their agendas.[19]

The CCP and Policy Making

The prevalence of majority rule in CCP decision making may seem surprising, but in accordance with the principles of democratic centralism, the procedure is taken seriously. However, CCP decision making has an authoritarian character because delegated groups such as the Standing Committee of the Politburo exercise tremendous agenda control over their parent groups. The CCP's appointments process also contributes to intra-party unity. Because career advancement within the party is typically achieved through patronage, intra-party factions tend to be highly cohesive.

As a given policy's importance increases, the number of veto bodies it must pass through also increases. For example, Five-Year Plans must be approved all the way down through the National Party Congress. Because the Congress and the Central Committee are composed of very diverse groups (including geographically based representatives), major policies must satisfy some particularistic interests.

Virtually all high-ranking party officials belong to an "entrance" (*kou*) that covers a major policy area. The most important *kous,* such as Party Affairs and Military Affairs, are led by members of the Standing Committee of the Politburo, while Politburo members lead less important or subordinate *kous. Kous* often form the basis of intra-party factions, and their members typically hold positions both within the party leadership as well as the state institutions that carry out the policies associated with the *kou.*[20]

STATE INSTITUTIONS

The Legislative Branch

The National People's Congress (NPC) is both the highest legislative body and formally the highest institution of the central state. One of its duties is the election of a premier, who serves as the PRC's head of state. The premier, however, has only limited formal authority. The PRC constitution grants the NPC authority to pass legislation and to appoint and remove most executive branch officials. Membership selection has a reciprocal character similar to that of the upper echelons of the CCP: The plenum elects a Standing Committee which in turn selects representatives to the plenum. The NPC's 3,000 delegates are elected to 5-year terms, but the plenum meets for only 2 weeks annually, leaving most day-to-day activities to the 135-member Standing Committee. Representation is both geographical and functional (or corporatist). Large social interests such as the People's Liberation Army, ethnic minority groups, and peasants, among others, are granted fixed proportions of representatives. Non-CCP members account for 20 to 30 percent of NPC delegates.

Historically, the divergence between the NPC's formal and actual powers has been large, due to the domination by the CCP elite of all aspects of statecraft. Since the early 1980s, however, the NPC has with increasing frequency defeated or forced the rewriting of bills submitted by the State Council. Additionally, the NPC has established specialized committees, such as an environmental committee founded in 1990, that have given it some leverage in policy debates.[21] Public appreciation for this trend is evidenced by the growing volume of constituent letters written to NPC delegates.[22]

---

[19]Christiansen and Rai (1996, pp. 110–111).
[20]See Lieberthal (1995).
[21]Christiansen and Rai (1996, pp. 106–107).
[22]See Pei (1997).

The Executive Branch

China's paramount executive body is the State Council, which is headed by the president and serves as China's cabinet. The president is in effect chosen by the CCP leaders and in 1999 was Jiang Zemin, who was also the head of the CCP. The State Council is composed of about 100 people, including the president, several vice presidents, and ministers and vice ministers of all major ministries and commissions. Like most deliberative groups in Chinese government, much of the State Council's day-to-day responsibilities are delegated to a Standing Committee. This committee consists of about 15 of the council's highest-ranking members and meets roughly every 2 weeks.

The State Council presides over dozens of commissions, which coordinate policies functionally across specific ministries. Commissions correspond roughly to departments in the U.S. executive branch; the National Defense Commission, for example, is analogous to the Department of Defense. Sometimes referred to as the "little State Council," the State Planning Commission (SPC) is perhaps the most powerful commission in the PRC. As its name suggests, the SPC is charged with overseeing China's vast planned economy, and the magnitude of that task has resulted in SPC alumni being well represented in the Politburo. The recent decline of the planned sector relative to the private sector has reduced the SPC's authority, and the State Council's current formal delineation of its responsibilities reflects this. Nevertheless, the commission's ability to formulate plans; set macroeconomic targets and prices; regulate finance, credit, and currencies; and approve major capital construction projects makes it extremely powerful.[23]

Below the commissions stand the provinces and ministries. Each of the 22 provinces holds ministerial rank, as do some of China's largest cities (Beijing, Tianjin, Shanghai, and Chongqing). Ministries have more specific jurisdictions than commissions and often find themselves subject to oversight from many commissions. An important exception is the Ministry of Finance, which is the most powerful ministry and informally holds commission rank in the State Council hierarchy. Ministers are typically high-ranking party officials, and departments within ministries are staffed by contingents of party cadres to ensure compliance with CCP directives.

Each national-level commission or ministry is the head of a hierarchy, or *xitong,* of local offices that performs the same role for the corresponding local government. A *xitong* generally is under the informal control of a *kou.* A provincial government's Education Commission is therefore a branch of the State Education Commission. *Xitongs* are known for protecting institutional turf; very little information is shared across hierarchies, and the incentives for vertical integration are strong. Many *xitongs* own companies and operate colleges to satisfy funding and personnel needs. In response, the reform-era CCP leadership has become increasingly active in reorganizing and abolishing ministries, as well as strengthening interdepartmental professional organizations. For example, the Ministry of Power and Water Conservancy was broken up to fragment opposition to the Three Gorges Dam project.[24]

The Judicial Branch

China has no tradition of an independent judiciary, and its highest court, the Supreme People's Court, has long been little more than a reflection of the CCP. There is no judicial review process in China. Likewise, the Supreme People's Procurator has little ability to pursue cases on its own initiative. Nevertheless, the emphasis of Deng's reforms on a stable and predictable legal environment has resulted in a small but

[23]See Wang and Fewsmith (1995) for a discussion of the SPC's political strategies.
[24]Christiansen and Rai (1996, pp. 111–114).

growing role for the national judiciary. Citizens have increasingly turned to the courts to resolve disputes.

PROVINCIAL AND LOCAL GOVERNMENTS

The governments and party organizations at the provincial, county, and city levels essentially mirror those at the national level. The highest state institution at each level is the People's Congress, a legislative body that has formal, but often weak, authority over the executive branch, the People's Government. Many representatives to People's Congresses are elected by popular vote at the county and township levels. The general devolution of fiscal authority to the provinces (as well as lower levels of the state hierarchy) has made local governments more attractive as targets of interest group activity.

Most provinces share their revenues with the central government according to a fixed formula that is renegotiated periodically. These formulas typically allow the provinces to keep a certain proportion of the earnings of provincial enterprises. Across China, lower levels of government also work under similar financial arrangements. As a result, local governments exercise a large amount of budget and taxation authority and are frequently the locus of bargaining with private interests. Village governments, for example, can offer a prospective enterprise favorable tax treatment in exchange for taking on extra workers to alleviate local unemployment.[25]

Business: State-Owned Enterprises, International Trade, and Investment

STATE-OWNED ENTERPRISES

The state-owned enterprise (SOE) is a unique entity that represents the single most important type of company in China. Most of China's largest firms are SOEs, and these enterprises employed over 100 million people and accounted for 34 percent of industrial output in 1994, down from 55 percent in 1990 as other types of firms have steadily gained influence in the economy. Private enterprises have flourished in the reform era, though their role in industrial production remains small. In between the SOEs and private enterprises are the urban collectives, which employed 33 million in 1994. Large urban collectives resemble SOEs in most respects, whereas small ones are run as local profit-sharing firms. Finally, joint ventures between SOEs and private or foreign firms are increasingly common. SOEs technically do not exist in rural areas, where private and collective firms have thrived in response to agricultural policy liberalization and a general lack of regulation. Although they tend to be individually quite small, rural enterprises were estimated to employ well over 100 million in 1994.

The labor policies of the SOEs were the heart of the socialist economic system and gave them a distinctive dual purpose. In addition to production, SOEs are the primary providers of social services in the urban economy. Enterprises provided virtually all the major social services required by employees, their families, and retirees. Moreover, because many goods such as housing and food staples were rationed, workers could only receive necessities through enterprise-issued coupons. This set of services essentially served as China's social welfare system and became known as the "iron rice bowl."

National plans promulgated by the State Planning Commission specified prices and production targets for national-level SOEs as well as for each province. The social welfare role of SOEs made it difficult for managers to dismiss poorly performing employees. The economic role of the SOEs was also flawed. In their rush to develop industry,

[25]Christiansen and Rai (1996, pp. 232–233).

planners set artificially low prices for inputs, including investment capital, and artificially high prices for outputs. In effect, agriculture subsidized industry, but instead of spurring industrial development, the subsidy became a permanent entitlement to the SOEs.[26] As a result, SOEs were inefficient and had little incentive to invest and innovate.

Since the late 1970s, SOE reform has been a constant priority for Chinese leaders. Managers have been given more authority to evaluate employees, and the emergence of the private sector has allowed many SOEs to shed some excess labor.[27] Enterprises were also permitted to retain profits, which are taxed by the state. The deregulation of prices and increasing competition from private, foreign, and rural industries have also increasingly exposed SOEs to market discipline.

Despite these changes, much of the system, and its dual role and chronic inefficiencies, remained intact in the late 1990s. SOEs are increasingly losing money and underutilizing capacity. The Chinese government has ceased using its budget to subsidize SOEs, but in its place the state-run banks have made "policy loans" to many of the SOEs. These, however, are more in the form of subsidy than loans, and expectations are that the loans will never be repaid. These loans have in large part been the cause of the insolvency of the state banks. The government plans to keep many of the larger and more competitive SOEs, but the remainder will be sold, merged, privatized, or closed. The chapter case *Wugang and the Reform of State-Owned Enterprises* provides an example of the reform challenge.

INTERNATIONAL TRADE

In the pre-reform era trade increased substantially, but trade policies remained essentially the same. All trade had to be approved by the Ministry of Foreign Economic Relations and Trade (MOFERT), and imported items were marketed directly by the cognizant state-owned firm. Deng's reforms and the open-door policy allowed China a wide range of international finance arrangements, including direct loans, export credits, and development assistance from foreign governments. In 1980 it joined the International Monetary Fund and World Bank, which gave it access to loans and other development aid.

During the 1980s MOFERT's institutional monopoly was broken, and much of its authority was delegated to provincial and municipal governments, other ministries, and state-owned enterprises. In many cases these entities were also allowed to "profit" from the trade. This devolution of authority substantially lowered the obstacles faced by foreign importers and exporters, who could now negotiate with local officials instead of working through a large, monopolistic national bureaucracy.

Trade policy became one of the primary concerns of China's international relations in the 1990s. The PRC's application for membership in the World Trade Organization (WTO) has become a protracted and contentious issue. Many advanced industrialized nations, particularly the United States, insisted that China open its markets further to foreign businesses as a condition for membership. Beijing has resisted many market-opening initiatives because of worries about social instability caused by workers laid off from uncompetitive state-owned enterprises.

The United States is China's second-largest trading partner (after Japan, now that Hong Kong is part of China). The large U.S. trade deficit with China has aroused animosity from some American policy makers and drawn attention to PRC trade practices,

---

[26]Christiansen and Rai (1996, p. 199). This phenomenon is commonly known as "price scissors," or the "scissor's gap."
[27]See Groves et al. (1994, 1995) for studies of incentives and the managerial labor market in SOEs.

including inadequate protection of intellectual property rights.[28] U.S. concerns over Chinese domestic policies and human rights abuses have also regularly raised the issue of whether to continue granting most favored nation (MFN) status to the PRC. (See the Chapter 7 example of China and the MFN.)

FOREIGN DIRECT INVESTMENT

Joint Venture Policy

One cornerstone of Deng's liberalizations was the Central Committee's July 1979 decision to establish four "Special Economic Zones" (SEZs).[29] As a result of this liberalization, foreign direct investment (FDI) and joint ventures in the PRC skyrocketed, with over 100,000 in operation in the mid-1990s.

Among the several forms of joint ventures, the most important is the *equity joint venture* (EJV). EJVs are limited liability companies in which the Chinese and foreign partners both manage day-to-day operations and divide the risk in direct proportion to their capital contributions to the project. Foreign contributions between 25 and 99 percent are allowed, but until recently board chairpersons were required to be Chinese.[30] EJVs have always been the most common type of joint venture, accounting in 1995 for 60 percent of China's FDI agreements.

Two other forms of FDI have also seen widespread use. *Contractual* (or *cooperative*) *joint ventures* (CJVs) divide risks by contract rather than by capital contribution. These arrangements permit greater flexibility for parties in allocating responsibilities. Such ventures are often riskier, however, because China's legal system is not well equipped to deal with contractual disputes between partners. CJVs were once quite popular but have recently declined in importance. By 1995 they accounted for 13 percent of FDI agreements and 20 percent of invested capital. Nevertheless, this ownership structure remains quite common, as the number of annual agreements increased from 794 to 4,787 during the 1986 to 1995 period.

The final joint venture type is the *wholly foreign-owned enterprise* (WFOE). These give the foreign firm the greatest control and the greatest risk. Until 1988 WFOEs were not particularly popular because foreign firms were often unwilling to undertake the risk in an uncertain legal environment. Additionally, WFOEs generally faced higher tax rates and stricter regulations. The 1990 Law on Wholly Foreign-Owned Enterprises in China prohibited them from operating in markets such as media, insurance, and communications and restricted their activities in public utilities and real estate. Article 3 of the law permits WFOEs if they (a) are technologically advanced and (b) export most of their production. Large Western firms such as Motorola, 3M, and Shell have entered China as WFOEs because these provide the best protection from being forced to share sensitive technology.[31] Beijing has realized that the autonomy offered to such enterprises is necessary for attracting export-oriented, high-technology firms that can help to develop the Chinese economy, and as a result WFOEs have become the fastest-growing segment of the FDI market. Whereas in 1986 there were only 18 agreements accounting for less than 1 percent of FDI, by 1995 the 11,761 WFOE agreements accounted for 32 percent of agreements and 27 percent of invested capital.

China maintained a state monopoly on fixed-line telephone systems and banned foreign participation. To enter this market, Sprint formed a Chinese joint venture with

---

[28] United States estimates of the trade deficit are larger because American statistics include exports that are routed through Hong Kong.
[29] Grub and Lin (1991, p. 65).
[30] Pearson (1991, Ch. 3–4).
[31] Grub and Lin (1991, Ch. 4–5, Appendix 3).

a local company, and then that Chinese company formed a joint venture with a state-owned company to provide a fixed-line system. This in effect put Sprint in the local telephone business. In 1998 the Chinese government, however, banned this type of Chinese-Chinese-foreign joint venture jeopardizing Sprint's $30 million investment.

Government Institutions Involved in Joint Ventures

Foreign companies wishing to invest in the PRC must deal with progressively higher levels of government as the size of the project increases. The largest projects must receive national-level approval from the Leading Group on Foreign Investment (LGFI), a State Council body that creates FDI legislation and coordinates the foreign investment policies of 11 national ministries. Additionally, state-run corporations, such as the China International Trust and Investment Corporation and other trust and investment corporations, play important roles through financial guarantees, financing, and currency swaps.

Local governments, both provincial and city, have parallel institutions (Foreign Economic Relations and Trade Commissions, or FERTCs) that have varying degrees of authority in approving projects. The largest cities such as Beijing and Shanghai, which hold provincial rank in the national hierarchy, can approve projects up to $30 million on their own, and after the 1983 Implementing Regulations small cities were allowed to approve projects valued at less than $5 million.[32] Like the LGFI and its associated agencies, FERTCs examine proposals for legality and feasibility as well as conformance with policies of the local government's other agencies. FERTCs are still responsible for most of the day-to-day regulation of joint ventures in their geographical jurisdiction, regardless of their size.[33]

Continuing Issues

HUMAN RIGHTS AND POLITICAL REFORM

The issue of human rights in China became internationalized in the 1990s. Foreign governments, especially that of the United States, as well as human rights groups have increasingly targeted China as a major abuser of human rights. International concern has focused on four areas.[34] First, China's criminal justice system is said to allow arbitrary imposition of the death penalty, the torture of prisoners, detention without trial, and the use of prison labor in industrial production. Second, China has been accused of persecution of ethnic (primarily Tibetan) and religious (primarily Christian) minorities. Third, Beijing has little tolerance for political dissidents and holds many political prisoners. Finally, the condition of Chinese women has deteriorated despite the advances in gender equality made during the communist era. Beijing has often dismissed these complaints as interference in domestic affairs and has also argued that the nation's main priority for the foreseeable future should be economic development. The chapter case *Fresenius Medical Care in China* addresses the issue of the harvesting of human organs from prisoners in China, and the Chapter 22 case *Levi Strauss in China* addresses concerns about the one-child-per-family policy and other human rights issues.

Several long-standing practices continue to provoke complaints and pose problems for companies. To control its population growth, China instituted a one-child-per-family policy and placed responsibility for administering the policy on employers and local government. To have a child, an employee of an SOE must obtain permission in

---

[32]Pearson (1991, p. 109).
[33]Grub and Lin (1991, Ch. 6).
[34]See Levine (1996) for a summary of human rights concerns in China. The U.S. State Department's *Annual Country Reports on Human Rights Practices* identifies specific abuses and discusses trends in their occurrence.

advance from the company's family planning office as well as from the neighborhood family planning committee. A childless woman, who became pregnant when her contraceptives failed and wanted to have the child but had not received prior approval, was ordered by local authorities to either have an abortion or quit her job. She had the child anyway, and her employer refused to pay the medical expenses for the birth and fined her nearly one-third of her annual wages.[35] The Bejing Family Planning Regulations provided for a considerably smaller fine, and the woman and her husband sued, but lost in court. The fact that such cases are now being taken to the courts is notable.

In 1997 the U.S. Department of State prepared a report on the persecution of Christians in 78 countries and criticized China for the suppression of religious freedom. A year later Chinese police cracked down on "house churches" run by evangelical Protestants who refused to register with the government and to worship in state-sponsored churches.

In exchange for not sponsoring a motion condemning China at the U.N. Human Rights Commission meeting in 1998, China agreed to sign the International Covenant on Civil and Political rights and to release the imprisoned leader of the Tiananmen Square democracy demonstrations. Signing the covenant spurred another democracy effort in 1998. Although some elections have been held at the local level, the CCP has maintained itself as the sole political party in China. When a group of democracy supporters formed the China Democratic Party in November 1998, the government arrested party leaders, including three of the most prominent dissidents remaining in the country. The first to be tried was sentenced to 13 years in prison, and two others were sentenced to 11 and 13 years.

Despite the human rights abuses and political restrictions, Chinese citizens enjoy greater freedoms than at any time since the communists gained control of the country. Much of the improvement has resulted from growing economic prosperity that has given people the means to exercise more control over their lives. In addition, the accumulation of personal property has led people to attempt to protect it, resulting in greater use of the courts. Moreover, with the widespread use of computers, faxes, and mobile telephones, information is more readily available and actions can be coordinated. This will inevitably lead to pressure for greater freedoms and a more responsive government, but democracy is not on the immediate horizon.

Piracy of Intellectual Property

A major concern of foreign businesses is the piracy of intellectual property. Copies of compact discs and videotapes often appear on Chinese street corners before they are available in stores in the United States. Chinese joint venture partners have set up competing companies with technology taken from their foreign partners.[36] Many foreign joint venture partners have complained to their home countries and have begun to take their cases to China's courts.

In some cases the piracy appears to be legal. For example, patents and proprietary pharmaceutical formulas receive administrative protection in China, but first there is an open and lengthy public comment period in which drug patents are available for inspection. Chinese pharmaceutical companies inspect the patent and immediately file for permission to produce and market the drug. If the application is approved before the patent becomes protected, the local company can sell its knockoff drug. For example, a Chinese pharmaceutical company received approval to produce Eli Lilly's Prozac before the patent had been protected. The company beat Eli Lilly to market with its

---

[35] *The New York Times,* April 27, 1998.
[36] See *Business Week,* October 6, 1997, for examples.

drug. Eli Lilly sued in court, but lost at the lower court level. The deputy director of the Chinese company said, "Eli Lilly's effort against us can't possibly lead to any positive result, as any resolution must have a legal basis. And everything we have done is in perfect conformity with the law."[37]

International Trade

China has opened its markets to foreign direct investment, but much of its economy remains closed to imports. It maintains quotas on a number of goods and limits entry into service industries. It also has high tariffs and a variety of other nontariff barriers such as mandatory inspections that restrict imports. These policies and practices have caused countries including the United States to block China's entry into the World Trade Organization. In addition, China has run a large trade surplus particularly with the United States reaching nearly $50 billion. The trade surplus, human rights violations, and specific practices such as piracy of intellectual property have resulted in several trade disputes between the two countries. The importance of a market with over 1.2 billion people and its rapid economic growth, however, provides strong incentives to normalize trade relations with China. The Clinton administration sought to reach an agreement to support WTO membership in exchange for tariff reductions.

The People's Liberation Army Enterprises

In the face of cutbacks in military spending during the 1980s, President Deng Xiaoping encouraged the People's Liberation Army (PLA) to establish businesses to provide it with earnings to offset the budget cuts. By the end of the 1990s the PLA operated an estimated 15,000 businesses providing several billions of dollars annually to the PLA. The PLA was also heavily involved in smuggling, particularly through naval ports, which allowed it to bring in large items such as automobiles and steel. China was estimated to lose $10 billion a year in tariff revenues due to smuggling. More than 100,000 automobiles were believed to have been smuggled into the country in 1997. In addition to widespread smuggling, which was blamed for causing deflation in China, corruption was widespread in China. Transparency International ranked China as 52nd among 85 countries in its corruption perception index.

In 1998 President Jiang Zemin, who as head of the CCP's Central Military Command is the Commander in Chief of the PLA, ordered the military to cease commercial activity and focus on military preparedness. Given the decentralized nature of the PLAs business activity, unwinding the businesses will be difficult and with opposition from military officers may be impossible.

Commitment

One concern in a nondemocratic country such as China is commitment to policies. In democracies changes in policy are often difficult to achieve because of institutional checks and balances and the effects of changes on future elections. In a country in which the only political party dominates all the government institutions including the military, policies can be quickly changed. In the last months of 1998, for example, China acted to shore up its weakening domestic economy. It ordered its state-owned telecommunications companies to buy domestic rather than imported equipment. It also put off indefinitely its stated intention to break up its national telecommunications monopoly China Telecom, and, as indicated, prohibited Chinese-Chinese-foreign joint ventures such as that which had allowed Sprint to invest in the telecommunications industry. Although China had promised not to devalue its currency to compete with the devaluations of

---

[37] *The Wall Street Journal,* March 25, 1998.

other Asian countries, it authorized rebates of export taxes on goods that competed with those of its neighbors. To curb deflation China imposed price floors in 21 industries in an attempt to stabilize the industries. Smuggling and overcapacity were blamed for the deflation. For example, the State Economic and Trade Commission imposed minimum prices on the 13 largest automobile manufacturers in China. The U.S. undersecretary of commerce commented, "The list of [trade] barriers is just getting bigger and we're not crossing anything off the list . . ."[38] The chapter case *Direct Marketing in China* concerns companies attempting to deal with a sudden policy change.

Summary

China presents tremendous business opportunities yet poses a host of problems particularly in the nonmarket environment. China does not have a democratic tradition, and its Confucian heritage provides a degree of deference for hierarchical authority. It also has a long history as a unified nation and a willingness to assert and defend its independence. China is building a modern economy which requires foreign direct investment and reform of its state-owned enterprises. Economic progress enables people to have better control over their lives and generates pressure for political and economic liberalization. China, however, is a communist state with the Chinese Communist Party dominating government at every level. Political competition is not tolerated and human rights are restricted. The government is thus not responsive to interests in the same sense as it is in a Western democracy. In some ways this simplifies the nonmarket environment, because of the lack of activist and organized interest groups that monitor business activity. The government, however, is sensitive to the possibility of popular dissent arising from economic dislocations. Despite the limitations, Chinese citizens enjoy greater economic prosperity and liberty than any time in the postwar period.

The nonmarket environment is complex not only because of the government and party involvement in business but also because of foreign policy issues pertaining to human rights, trade policy, and civil liberties. The nonmarket environment is structured by the hierarchical nature of government which persists despite the devolution of authority to provincial and local governments. Since the government is not checked by opposition parties, elections, or interest or activist groups, some policies can be changed quickly, raising concerns about the credibility of commitments. Furthermore, the judicial system does not provide the same protection as is available in other countries. The importance of *guanxi* networks not only between companies but also between business and government can complicate strategies of those companies new to China. The strategies available to companies are largely restricted to lobbying and negotiating with the relevant government entity and seeking assistance from a company's home country. Joint ventures with domestic companies, most of which are enterprises owned by national, provincial, or local government units, can also provide the *guanxi* networks and access needed to address nonmarket issues. Joint ventures, however, pose their own set of problems.

[38] *The New York Times,* September 23, 1998.

CASES

Wugang and the Reform of State-Owned Enterprises

The Wuhan Iron and Steel Company, also known as Wugang, illustrates the nature of Chinese state-owned enterprises (SOEs) and the problems surrounding their reform.[1] Located in the large industrial city of Wuhan nearly 400 miles up the Yangtze River from Shanghai, Wugang was the first of many massive ironworks built after the Chinese revolution. The $2 billion enterprise has many of the characteristics of a medium-size city. The facility occupies 6.5 square miles and employs 120,000 workers. Most of the employees, plus their families and 30,000 retirees, live in company-provided housing. The company also operates 31 schools, three polytechnic institutes, three universities, and two hospitals.

Built with Soviet technology, Wugang opened in September 1958 at the beginning of Mao's "Great Leap Forward," a crash effort that was to have brought China's industrial output up to par with Western Europe. As a national-level SOE, all inputs and outputs were determined by economic plans. The State Planning Commission and Ministry of Metallurgical Industry specified its prices and production targets, and the Labor Administration Bureau assigned workers to the plant, most of whom were guaranteed by the *danwei* system to remain there for life. Like other national-level SOEs, Wugang played a crucial dual role in the socialist economy. In addition to industrial production, Wugang was the exclusive provider of housing, food, medicine, and other social services to its employees, their families, and retirees. This system, known as the "iron rice bowl," resulted in a high level of vertical integration within the enterprise.

The Chinese steel industry began with high expectations, but three factors combined to undermine its productivity during the 1960s and 1970s. First, the social welfare role of the enterprise robbed its management of labor flexibility. In the 1960s, SOEs generally became overstaffed as central planners reacted to the oversupply of urban youths by assigning them to SOEs, and managers were unable to dismiss poorly performing employees. Second, in their rush to industrialize, planners had set artificially low prices for inputs and artificially high prices for outputs, effectively creating an industry-wide subsidy that resulted in inefficiency and low incentives to invest and innovate. Individual plant managers also had little discretion in investments because profits were taxed at high rates and redistributed by government authorities.[2] Finally, the international isolation that China faced between 1960 and 1980 had cut off foreign investment, technology, and expertise, as well as potential export markets.

By the end of the 1990s the steel industry employed two million workers and accounted for 3 percent of China's industrial output by value. Wugang was one of the nation's four largest steel companies, with an annual production capacity of six million tons. These four facilities accounted for about a third of China's steel production in 1996.[3] After the Baoshan Iron and Steel Corporation (Baogang), Wugang was the second-most profitable steel company in China, earning an $84 million profit in 1996. Although this was expected to drop to $24 million in 1997, Wugang's performance had been fairly good compared with most SOEs. By comparison, Angang, China's largest steel firm, was suffering huge losses. Wugang's primary asset was its specialization in high value-added products. The company manufactured extra-wide and heavy carbon structural plate, alloy

[1]Based in part on R. Tomlinson, "A Chinese Giant Forges a Capitalist Soul," *Fortune* (September 29, 1997), pp. 184–192.

[2]Because prices were centrally planned, profits were in some sense illusory. A ministry in charge of an industry could redistribute funds from profitable to unprofitable enterprises, and it could also require expenditures on items not directly related to the enterprise's production (for instance, social services).

[3]These four companies each produced over 5 million tons per year. There were also 25 companies that produced between 1 and 5 million tons annually. Because many smaller companies were expected to close as a result of restructuring, the four largest SOEs were expected to account for 40 percent of total production by 2005. Sources: *South China Morning Post,* September 19, 1997, and *China Economic Review,* April 1998.

structural plate, low-alloy high strength plate, boiler and vessel plate, ship and offshore oil platform plate, and mould-making plate. It was also the only Chinese supplier of international-quality, cold rolled silicon steel sheets—a highly ductile type of plate. Its production processes had received certification from numerous international bodies, and its quality assurance system met ISO 9000 standards. Yet the firm faced serious challenges. Wugang's productivity, measured by tons of output per employee, was less than a fifth of those of the leading Asian firms.[4] Steel prices in China were declining, partially in response to imports from the former Soviet republics and South Korea, whose currency suffered a steep devaluation in 1997. At the same time, the cost of domestic inputs, such as energy and transportation, had risen substantially in 1997.

SOE REFORM: NATIONAL AND LOCAL STRATEGIES

As China's economic reforms progressed in the 1990s, the leadership in Beijing realized that despite their valuable social welfare role, SOEs were increasingly becoming an obstacle to the creation of a modern economy. The SOE sector employed 100 million people and accounted for nearly half of China's industrial output in the early 1990s, yet few enterprises were profitable, and even successful SOEs were often hopelessly inefficient by international standards. Since the inception of market-based reforms in the 1970s, Beijing had cautiously increased the discretion of SOE managers while also increasing their exposure to market forces. However, party leaders at the Fifteenth Party Congress of September 1997 agreed that more radical reforms would be necessary to prevent the financial collapse of such a large part of the Chinese economy.

While the Congress did not specify many details, it intended to privatize the vast majority of the over 300,000 SOEs by selling shares in the companies. These changes were expected to affect over 10,000 of the 13,000 largest SOEs, but Beijing would continue to own and support many of the largest enterprises, such as Wugang. There were three principal reasons for continuing to support large SOEs. First, since privatization was expected to result in widespread plant closings and layoffs, Beijing wanted to avoid widespread social unrest. Because of the SOE system, China had never developed a social welfare system, and despite a few pilot programs for worker retraining and social pensions, a comprehensive safety net was still years away. Second, Beijing hoped that its larger enterprises could duplicate the past success of large, government-favored industrial conglomerates such as the South Korean *chaebol.* This analogy proved worrisome as it had become increasingly evident that the *chaebol* were responsible in part for serious structural deficiencies in Korea's economy. Finally, the retention of some central control was necessary to placate conservatives within the party.[5]

Unfortunately for Wugang's president, Liu Benren, continued government intervention deprived him of the autonomy to undertake cost-cutting methods that were commonly available to firms in other countries. Liu had little authority to reduce his vastly oversized labor force because the Wuhan government would not permit the city's largest corporate employer to add to the growing unemployment problem. Like other official unemployment statistics across China, Wuhan's unemployment rate was modest, but unofficially was estimated to be as high as 26 percent. Many of the company's activities remained constrained by Beijing, even though in early 1998 steel was removed from the list of products subject to state-planned production targets. As part of the program adopted by the Fifteenth Party Congress, Beijing aided Wugang by facilitating its effort to go public and list its stock on domestic stock exchanges, but it also required the company to merge with smaller steel companies as a condition for doing so.[6] Wugang complied by announcing a merger with two smaller firms, the Daye Steel Group and the Ercheng Iron & Steel Group, in November 1997.[7] In 1998 it acquired the financially troubled Xiangfan Iron and Steel Group.

Liu was able to take some initiatives on his own to address these problems. For a number of years, he had pursued a foreign listing on the Hong Kong Stock Exchange. Despite the fact that the company was only listing its relatively profitable, cold rolled silicon steel unit, the offering was continually delayed due to lack of investor interest in the weak Chinese steel market as well as to the Asian financial

[4] *China Economic Review,* April 1998.

[5] *The New York Times,* September 12, 1997, and *Business Week,* September 29, 1997.

[6] *South China Morning Post,* September 19, 1997.

[7] *South China Morning Post,* November 26, 1997.

crisis.[8] The $200 million listing, underwritten by Merrill Lynch, was finally approved in February 1998, but postponed indefinitely two months later due to poor investor response.[9] Beijing was partly responsible for the failure. One reason for the lack of interest was a Chinese law prohibiting companies from pricing shares below the company's net asset value per share.[10]

Wugang's failure in the stock market had not prevented it from exploring other avenues. Liu had aggressively invested in new technology, adding billions of dollars worth of American and Austrian equipment since 1993. With the improved physical plant, the company hoped to increase capacity to 8 million tons by 2000 and expand sales to foreign markets, which accounted for 800,000 tons of its output in 1997. In March 1998 Wugang proposed a merger with Baogang in the hopes of creating a single advanced, profitable entity that would reduce overproduction in the Chinese steel market.[11] The combined entity would have been one of the world's 10 largest steel firms, but concerns were raised about the efficiency gains from merging facilities 400 miles apart.[12]

Because of the economic crises in Asia and Russia, China was flooded with cheap steel imports. In response, Wugang initiated antidumping proceedings against Russian silicon steel plate exporters with the Ministry of Foreign Trade and Economic Cooperation.[13] The flood of imports along with overcapacity in China continued to drive steel prices down, and the government responded by banning the construction of any new steel plants until 2000.

The company also sought support for more radical reforms from the government. With the support of the State Council, it secured permission to pare its workforce and reduce its dependence on subsidiary workshops that were not part of its core steel business. These "ancillary companies" would be forced to seek outside customers and turn a profit independently of Wugang. Liu hoped that after this process was completed, Wugang would be a leaner, more focused company of only 27,000 employees.[14] This reorganization had helped some of the company's former subunits, such as the Metal Structures Company, which manufactured boilers and furnaces, to become profitable. However, in many cases it had only shifted the tension between social welfare and company efficiency from Wugang to its former subsidiaries.

Some analysts were cautiously optimistic about Wugang's long-term prospects. Part of this optimism, however, stemmed from the strong support the enterprise had received from Beijing. The favorable restructuring plan and technological investments were facilitated by Beijing's unwillingness to allow Wugang—considered one of China's most prestigious steel firms—to fail. It was a measure of the magnitude of the challenges faced by all SOEs that Wugang's viability seemed so uncertain despite this support. ■

[8] *South China Morning Post,* October 21, 1997, and *South China Morning Post,* March 19, 1998.
[9] *South China Morning Post,* February 21, 1998.
[10] *South China Morning Post,* April 1, 1998.
[11] *The New York Times,* March 12, 1998.
[12] *The Wall Street Journal,* March 11, 1998.
[13] *South China Morning Post,* July 14, 1998.
[14] Employment across the industry was scheduled to drop to 500,000 by 2000 and 300,000 by 2005, though many reductions would be achieved through reorganizations. *China Economic Review,* April 1998.

PREPARATION QUESTIONS

1. What social and institutional factors limit Liu Benren's efforts to reform Wugang?
2. What should Wugang do about its social services responsibilities?
3. Should Liu Benren seek complete independence from the Chinese government?

Direct Marketing in China

With over 1.2 billion people China represented an extremely attractive market for direct marketers such as Amway, Avon Products, Mary Kay Cosmetics, Sara Lee, and Tupperware. Also, in the 1990s the restructuring of state-owned enterprises had reduced workforces, providing an ample supply of people interested in becoming direct marketers, many of whom made door-to-door sales calls. With the Asian and Russian financial crises beginning in 1997 the supply of potential direct sales personnel increased further. Amway began sales in China in 1995, and by 1997 it had 70,000 independent sales agents in China producing revenue of $178 million.[1] Avon's revenue in China was $75 million.

Companies such as Amway and Avon operated by enlisting independent sales agents who bought product from the company and sold it door-to-door. The companies operated distributions centers and provided training for their sales agents in both sales techniques and in the company's culture, which emphasized empowerment. Amway had a policy of buying back all unsold product, providing a full refund.

The success of U.S. direct sales companies led to a boom in home-grown direct sales companies selling everything from foot massagers to water beds to elixirs. By 1998 some 20 million Chinese were estimated to be working in direct marketing.[2] It was said that 50,000 people had come to Wuhan seeking jobs selling Xingtian Company's foot massaging machine. Some of these companies operated pyramid and Ponzi schemes in which they profited by recruiting sellers and selling them products rather than making sure that products were being purchased by consumers. Other companies duped unsuspecting consumers. In a front-page article the *China Daily* said that these companies "have been behaving badly, getting involved in underworld crimes and preying on innocent people through their superstitions."

On April 21, 1998, the State Council published a directive banning all direct sales in the country. The directive stated, "Criminals have used direct selling to set up sects and cults, spread superstition and carry out illegal activities, affecting the country's social stability." The directive expressed concern about the massive sales meetings of direct sellers in which they clap and chant to build enthusiasm. The directive also stated that direct selling had attracted people, including teachers, members of the military, and officials of the Chinese Communist Party, who were legally prohibited from such sales activity. The *People's Daily,* the official newspaper of the Chinese Communist Party, justified the State Council's decision: "Due to immature market conditions, inadequate legislation and immature consumer psychology, direct sales have proved unsuitable for China and thus must be resolutely banned." The newspaper also referred to "excessive hugging" at the mass sales meeting held by the direct selling companies.

The State Administration for Industry and Commerce, which was responsible for the distribution industry, asked local officials to enforce the ban and to avoid civil disorder. Its director Wang Zhongfu said, "It's necessary to stop the operation of pyramid sales since it has begun to hurt social stability and economic development."[3] Government officials said that if the U.S. direct selling companies established normal retail shops they could stay.

This was not the first time China had addressed direct marketing. In 1995 it had suspended all direct sales activity for several months over concerns about the "revival meeting atmosphere" used by some of the companies. Avon was forced to change its credo from "God first" to "Faith first."

Once the State Council had banned direct selling, many independent sales representatives were left with goods they could not sell. Protests occurred when they were unable to obtain refunds from companies. According to press reports, 10,000 disgruntled door-to-door salesmen came to the town of Zhangjiajie seeking refunds from a company that made foot massagers, but it had closed its doors. " 'It has left me worse that bankrupt,' says Chen, an unemployed steelworker, who has been left with 60 mechanized foot masseurs and, now barred from selling them, losses of roughly $4,830."[4] Riots broke out leaving four people dead and 100 injured.

---

[1] Amway had 667,000 independent sales representatives worldwide.

[2] In the United States 8.5 million people were engaged in direct marketing.

[3] China Business Information Network, May 12, 1998.

[4] *The Financial Times,* May 5, 1998.

The directive issued by the State Council came as U.S. Trade Representative Charlene Barshefsky was in Beijing making preparations for President Bill Clinton's upcoming state visit to China. In a news conference in Beijing she stated, "The ban has effectively shut down the legitimate operations of these and other U.S. companies in China. These companies have invested over $120 million in China and provide income to more that 2 million Chinese." She added, "It is a serious matter when the [Chinese] government simply bans the legitimate business of foreign-invested companies. . . . [the ban] goes well beyond China's legitimate need to pursue consumer protection." Wu Yi, China's minister for trade and foreign investment, also told her that the direct selling companies were breaking the rule that requires them to sell only goods manufactured in China.

Steve Van Andel, chairman of Amway Asia Pacific, said, "We understand and respect the Chinese government's decision to take additional steps to protect consumers from illegal scams, which have become a more serious social problem in recent months. . . . We have invested over $100 million in China over the past five years and we continue to believe in the long-term business opportunities of this enormous market. . . . While management of Amway China has established strong government relations and is hopeful that discussions with government officials will be successful, it is too early to project the short term and long term impact of the directive on our business."[5] Amway and other direct marketers began to evaluate alternatives for restructuring the way they conducted their sales activities.

Richard Holwill, Amway's director of international relations, said, "We're frustrated that this sledgehammer approach gets rid of ours as well as the ones they're really trying to get rid of. 'Shut it down and sort it our later' seems to be the attitude."[6] Holwill also stated, "We don't want to be part of the problem, we want to be part of the solution." Holwill served as co-chairman of the Asia Task Force of the U.S. Chamber of Commerce and discussed the ban in testimony before the House Ways and Means Committee in June during hearings on renewal of most favored nation status for China. ■

[5] Amway press release, April 21, 1998.
[6] *Los Angeles Times,* April 24, 1998.

PREPARATION QUESTIONS

1. How might the U.S. direct sales companies restructure their sales activities to satisfy the concerns of the Chinese government? Should they establish retail stores?
2. Should U.S. direct marketers form a coalition or act independently to address this challenge?
3. Should the U.S. companies attempt to enlist the aid of the U.S. government?
4. What nonmarket strategy should the U.S. companies adopt?

Fresenius Medical Care in China

Fresenius Medical Care with headquarters in Bad Homburg, Germany, was established in 1996 through the combination of the Dialysis Systems Division of Fresenius AG, a major German pharmaceutical and medical systems producer and distributor, and National Medical Care, a subsidiary of W.R. Grace. Fresenius Medical Care provided dialysis and renal services, dialysis products, and home care. In 1997 it had revenue of $3.3 billion, compared with $3.1 billion in 1996, and profits were $90 million. Fresenius Medical Care's core businesses were dialysis care and sales of dialysis products. Worldwide in 1996 there were 765,000 dialysis patients, representing a total market of $29 billion for dialysis treatment and products. Fresenius Medical Products treated 53,400 patients in the United States and 13,800 outside the United States.

"As a result of our focused acquisition programs in the U.S., Europe and Latin America we dramatically improved our strategic position during the last year, and enhanced our continued leadership of the dialysis care industry," said CEO Udo Werlé. Fresenius Medical Care operated or supplied products in 100 countries and worked to strengthen its market position in the rapidly growing Asian-Pacific and Latin American markets by establishing additional subsidiaries and joint ventures. Fresenius Medical Care viewed Southeast Asia as its next major market for investment. China represented a major market opportunity, and Fresenius had a foothold through a joint venture, the Guangzhou Nanfang NMC Hemodialysis Center, established in 1994 between National Medical Care and a military hospital complex in Guangzhou.

Advanced chronic kidney failure is the irreversible loss of kidney function and requires either regular dialysis treatment or a kidney transplant. Dialysis must be continued indefinitely, whereas a transplant is typically a permanent solution. In the United States in 1995, 200,000 patients received regular dialysis treatment, but only 12,000 received kidney transplants. In the absence of a transplant, dialysis was required for the rest of the patient's life. Dialysis had two modes: hemodialysis and peritoneal dialysis. Hemodialysis involved taking the blood outside the body and through a filter or dialyzer to remove waste products and excess water and then returning the blood to the patient. The treatments lasted 3 to 6 hours each, and three treatments a week were typically required. The treatment was often exhausting and difficult. Peritoneal dialysis used a surgically implanted catheter through which a sterile solution was introduced and used the peritoneal, the membrane in the abdominal cavity covering the intestinal organs, as the dialysis membrane. Peritoneal dialysis involved less disruption of daily life than hemodialysis but required a patient to have some residual renal function. Only 15 percent of the worldwide patient population used peritoneal dialysis.

Human rights groups and activists had regularly charged that China sold human organs harvested from executed prisoners, many of whom were sentenced to death for political crimes or for theft or corruption. In fall 1997 ABC *Primetime Live* broadcast a report that a Chinese doctor was advertising human organs in a Chinese language newspaper in New York with a price of $30,000 for a kidney. The organs were believed to be harvested from executed prisoners. The report included the story of a woman from Thailand who had received a kidney transplant at the military hospital and had received kidney dialysis at the Nanfang dialysis facility.

In February 1998 in New York the FBI arrested two Chinese government officials who were attempting to sell human organs harvested from executed prisoners. The FBI sting was arranged by Harry Wu, a controversial Chinese dissident living in the United States, who had previously exposed a number of human rights violations. In February 1998 the German magazine *Stern* published an article consistent with the information in the *Primetime Live* report. The Chinese embassy in Washington issued a statement that organs were rarely harvested from executed prisoners and only with their written consent.

Fresenius Medical Care's Nanfang facility was operated by Chinese doctors, and Fresenius had one employee in Hong Kong who monitored the facility. The Nanfang dialysis center was located adjacent to a military organ transplant hospital, and Fresenius's investigation revealed that foreign patients were receiving dialysis treatment at Nanfang for relatively short periods. Patients awaiting transplants required ongoing dialysis. *Stern* quoted a Thai kidney specialist to the effect that no consent forms existed and that prisoners were "simply shot in the head and then disemboweled." *Stern* quoted another Thai kidney specialist that "There would be no kidney transplants in Nanfang Hospital without Fresenius." *Stern* also had information on patients in Asia and the United States who were notified about upcoming executions so that they could travel to China. *Stern* referred to this as "patient tourism" and reported that the going price for a kidney transplant was $40,000. ■

PREPARATION QUESTIONS

1. What should Fresenius Medical Care do with regard to the ABC and *Stern* reports?
2. Suppose that the reports were true. What should Fresenius Medical Care do?
3. Should Fresenius Medical Care and Fresenius AG sell medical equipment and supplies to the transplant hospital complex in Guangzhou?

CHAPTER 16

The Political Economy of International Trade Policy

Introduction

International trade policy is the result of economic and political forces. The principal economic force is the gains from trade made possible by comparative advantage, which provides the economic rationale for a policy of free trade. The principal political force is the rents and surpluses that firms, consumers, employees, and suppliers can capture through trade policy. The present and potential recipients have incentives to exercise their political rights by developing nonmarket strategies to protect and increase their rents and surpluses.

At least since the Smoot-Hawley Act of 1930, which raised tariffs dramatically and contributed to the depth and duration of the depression, the United States and other developed countries have supported reductions in tariffs and other barriers to international trade. In the aftermath of World War II, the reductions in trade barriers were largely the result of U.S. hegemony. As other countries recovered from the war and the U.S. share of international trade declined, the principal mechanism for reductions in trade barriers has been multilateral trade negotiations, many of which were conducted in the context of the General Agreement on Tariffs and Trade (GATT). In 1995 the World Trade Organization (WTO) supplanted GATT and broadened the coverage of multilateral agreements and provided a continuing forum for addressing trade issues and resolving disputes among nations. In addition, a number of regional trade agreements, such as the North American Free Trade Agreement (NAFTA) and the treaties that produced the European Union, have reduced barriers and increased trade. The United States and other countries have also concluded bilateral agreements to spur trade in industries such as air transportation. The result has been a steady, if not uniform, reduction in trade barriers, and the resulting increase in international trade has been dramatic.

International trade policy is an important factor controlling the opportunities of and threats to firms. In the context of Figure 2-2, trade policy can foreclose markets to a firm, which provides an incentive to take political action to reduce specific trade barriers in a country or an industry. Trade policy can also distort competition by giving firms in one country an advantage in export markets through export subsidies, domestic subsidies, or other less direct forms of support. Similarly, trade policy can protect an industry from foreign competition through the imposition of tariffs and of nontariff barriers such as quotas and other restraints.

Trade policy consists of both agreements among countries, domestic laws pertaining to international trade, and procedures for administering those laws and resolving disputes. International trade agreements are the result of bargaining among countries, but the positions from which countries bargain depend on domestic economic considerations and, hence, on domestic politics. The interaction between international trade policy and domestic politics is illustrated in Figure 16-1. The international negotiations, shown at the top of the figure, and the agreements reached, shown at the bottom, determine the basic ground rules for the export and import practices of firms. The competition between imports and domestic production and the opportunities to trade in world markets have distributive consequences that provide incentives for interests—firms, employees, suppliers, and consumers—to seek support for exports and/or protection from imports. The opportunities to engage in domestic politics and the rights granted under domestic trade laws allow interests to affect trade policy directly as well as indirectly through the bargaining positions of their governments in bilateral and multilateral negotiations. Trade policy thus depends not only on government action but also on the market and nonmarket strategies of private interests. Conversely, international trade policy has important consequences for the market and nonmarket environments of business and for the opportunities and threats in those environments.

This chapter addresses the political economy of international trade policy, its connection to domestic politics, and the role of business and other interests in those politics. The perspective taken is that the system depicted in Figure 16-1 is animated by the incentives generated in domestic and international markets, and that those incentives give rise to nonmarket strategies, implemented in both domestic and international institutional arenas, that shape trade policy. The chapter also considers the principal international trade agreements that result from the strategies of governments and private interests and provide the starting point for future strategies. The international trade policy of the United States is also considered as is a set of trade disputes and ongoing issues.

FIGURE 16-1 International Trade Policy Process

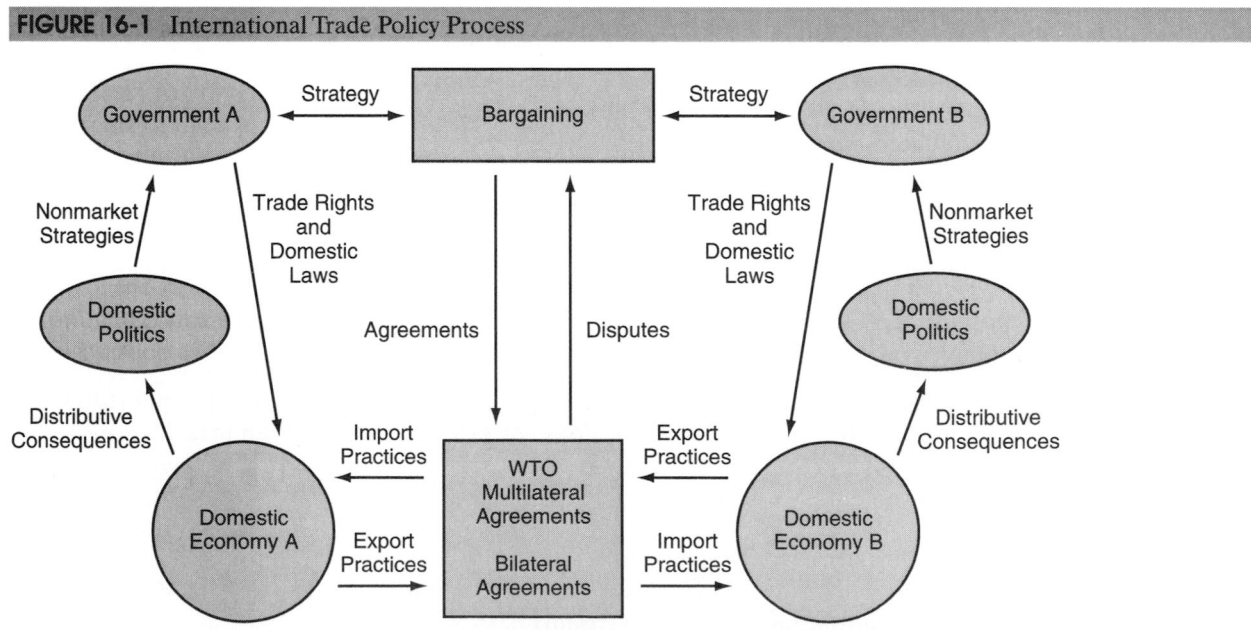

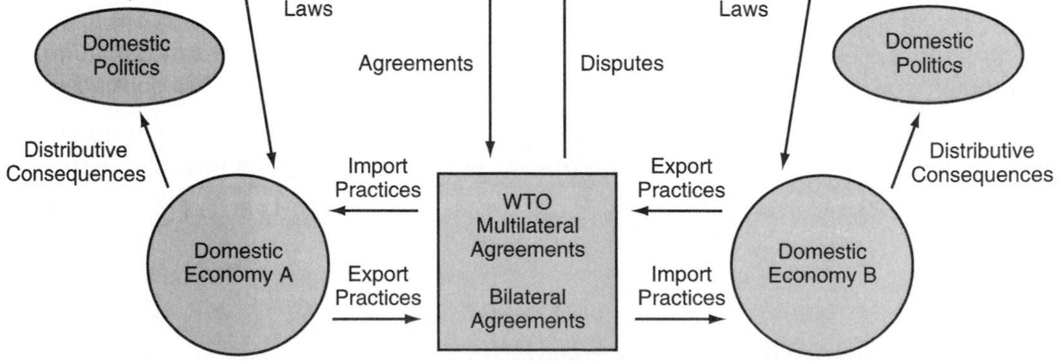

The Economics of International Trade

COMPETITIVE THEORY

The competitive theory of international trade is based on the gains from trade. Those gains are evident in the case of a country that cannot produce a product that its citizens wish to consume. Gains from trade are also evident when one country can produce one product more efficiently than another country, and the latter country can produce another product more efficiently than can the former country. There are also gains from trade when one country is absolutely more efficient than the other in the production of both products. That is, even though a country has an absolute disadvantage, gains from trade can be achieved if it produces the good for which it has the smaller disadvantage and the other country produces the good for which it has the greater advantage. This result, known as the *law of comparative advantage,* provides the basic rationale for the principle of free trade—that is, all countries can gain from trade.

The law of comparative advantage can be demonstrated when two countries either determine the level of their trade through bargaining or trade in a competitive market. Consider two countries, each of which can produce two goods, A and B. The production possibilities of each country are characterized by its resources and the technology it uses to produce the goods. To simplify the analysis, assume that each country has one resource: 12 units of labor. Country I has a technology that requires two units of labor to produce a unit of A and requires one unit of labor to produce a unit of B. Country II can produce a unit of A with one unit of labor and can produce a unit of B with two units of labor. These production possibilities are illustrated in Figure 16–2. As the figure illustrates, Country I is more efficient in the production of good B, and Country II is more efficient in the production of good A.

In the absence of trade, the consumption possibilities of each country are its own production possibilities. That is, Country I can produce and consume 12 units of B and none of A, 6 units of A and none of B, or any linear combination of those two outputs. Each country will produce and consume at the point on its production possibility frontier that yields the greatest aggregate well-being of its citizens. To be precise, suppose that the preferences of citizens in each country are identical and that the representation

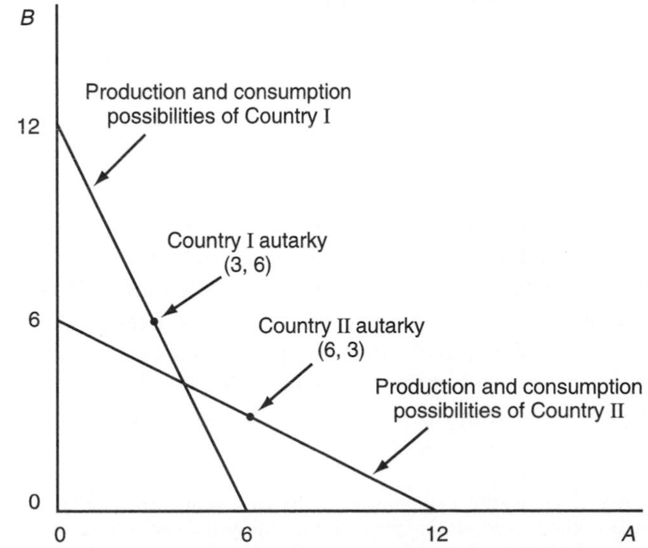

FIGURE 16-2 Production and Consumption Possibilities—Autarky

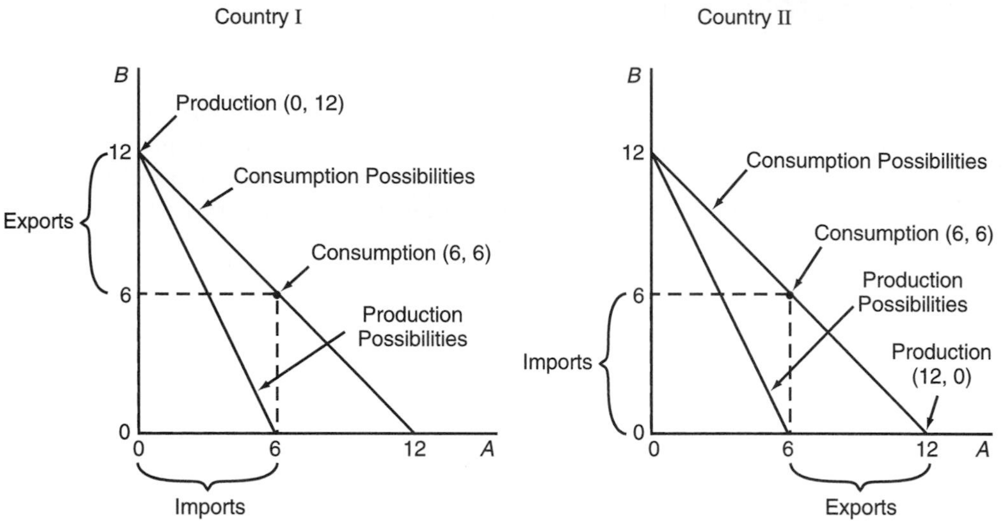

FIGURE 16-3 Production and Consumption Possibilities with Trade

of those preferences by a utility function is given by the product of the quantities consumed of the two goods. The best combination of consumption is an equal amount of each of the goods, but in the absence of trade, referred to as autarky, Country I can do no better than to produce and consume 3 units of A and 6 units of B. Analogously, Country II will produce and consume 6 units of A and 3 units of B. These autarky points are indicated in Figure 16-2 and correspond to utility levels of 18 for each country.

Trade benefits a country by allowing consumption to diverge from production. To illustrate this, Figure 16-3 presents the production possibilities of Countries I and II and their consumption possibilities when they are able to trade. Gains from trade are possible because trade expands the consumption possibilities of each country beyond those of its own production. That is, both countries can benefit if Country I produces more of good B, for which it has an advantage, and Country II produces more of good A, for which it has an advantage. In this example, Country I will specialize in producing 12 units of good B and none of good A, whereas Country II will produce 12 units of A and none of B. Country I then will export 6 units of B and import 6 units of A. Country II's imports and exports will be the opposite of those of Country I. With the trades indicated in the figures, the resulting consumption in each country is 6 units of A and 6 units of B. The utility levels are 36 for each country, so both are better off than under autarky.[1] Open economies and free trade thus allow gains to both countries.

This example has illustrated the gains from trade for the case in which Country I is more efficient in the production of good B and Country II is more efficient in the production of good A. Even if Country I is absolutely more efficient in the production of both goods, there are gains from trade. To illustrate this result, suppose that Country I's technology is as shown but Country II's technology requires 3 units of labor to produce one unit of A and 4 units of labor to produce one unit of B. Under autarky, Country II

[1]This outcome is a competitive equilibrium in the sense that each country, taking prices as given, produces the quantities of the two goods that maximize its utility, and each country consumes the quantities it prefers given the prices for the goods. In this example, the price, or rate of exchange, is one unit of A per unit of B. The value of imports thus equals the value of exports for each country.

would produce 2 units of A and 1.5 units of B for a utility of 3. Both countries can gain, however, if, for example, Country II produces 4 units of A and no units of B and Country I produces 2 units of A and 8 units of B. Country II then can trade 2 units of A to Country I for 3 units of B.[2] The utilities of the two countries are then 20 and 6, respectively, compared with 18 and 3 in the absence of trade. This gain is possible because Country II is relatively more efficient in the production of good A than is Country I. That is, the ratio of the number of units of labor required to produce a unit of A and a unit of B is 3/4 = 0.75 for Country II, whereas the corresponding ratio for Country I is 2/1=2. Country II thus has a comparative advantage in the production of A even though it has an absolute disadvantage in the production of both goods. Because of this comparative advantage, trade benefits both countries.

The law of comparative advantage also holds if there are differences in the relative prices of untraded factor inputs such as labor. That is, if one country has lower wage rates than another, gains can be achieved from trade. The high-wage country can gain by importing labor-intensive goods from the low-wage country and allocating its high-cost labor to the production of goods for which it has a comparative advantage. Consequently, a country such as the United States, with high labor costs, and a country such as China, with low labor costs, can gain by China's producing labor-intensive textiles and apparel for export to the United States and the United States producing capital-intensive machinery for export to China. The United States, however, has for decades restricted textile and apparel imports to protect employment in its domestic industries. The economic theory of comparative advantage thus is not a sufficient theory to explain the trade policies of countries. That is, politics can intervene in international trade as illustrated in Figure 16-1. The political dimensions of international trade and trade policy are considered in more detail in a later section.

STRATEGIC TRADE THEORY

The economic theory of international trade and comparative advantage were developed based on the assumptions of perfectly competitive markets. Information is assumed to be complete, consumers and producers act as price takers, goods are assumed to be undifferentiated, and production is characterized by constant returns to scale or by decreasing returns to scale with costless entry and exit. From these assumptions, powerful theories such as the law of comparative advantage demonstrate the gains from trade among open economies. The theory also implies that intervention by governments in domestic or international markets will reduce aggregate welfare. Competitive theory thus provides a compelling rationale for free trade, and the role of government is then to join in international efforts to reduce tariff and nontariff barriers to trade.

Economists have also considered whether a nation can gain from a strategic trade policy, that is, intervention to protect domestic industries, subsidize exports, or stimulate demand for domestic goods.[3] These interventions can only be beneficial for a country if one or more of the conditions for perfect competition is not satisfied. Theories of strategic trade policy thus are set in the context of imperfect competition resulting either from barriers to entry that limit the number of producers or from characteristics of production that result in decreasing average costs, such as economies of scale and scope.

As an example, consider the case of an undifferentiated good that is produced by only two firms, one domestic and the other foreign. Suppose they engage in Cournot

---

[2]Other mutually beneficial trades are also possible. For example, Country II could trade 2 units of A for 2 units of B.

[3]For a nontechnical exposition of these theories, see Krugman (1986, 1990).

competition in which each firm chooses the quantity it will produce and then sells that quantity in the market. If a government intervenes by subsidizing the output of its domestic firm, that firm's marginal cost will be reduced. This has two effects. First, the lower marginal cost induces the firm to expand its output. Second, as it expands its output, the foreign firm will react by reducing its output. This then allows the subsidized domestic firm to increase its output even more. This second effect is said to be strategic because the subsidization has altered the strategic relationship between the two firms by lowering the cost of one firm. In the new equilibrium, the subsidized firm makes greater profits than it did in the absence of the subsidy. Even taking into account the size of the subsidy, subsidization can increase the aggregate consumers' plus producers' surplus of the subsidizing country.[4] The European subsidization of Airbus Industrie may be an example of this strategy. Although the subsidization of domestic firms in certain industries could increase well-being, it often does not. For example, the subsidization of European Union agricultural exports has resulted in large losses in economic efficiency.

The gains from strategic trade practices can turn to losses if other governments retaliate. If one country adopts a strategic trade policy, other countries can retaliate either by adopting the same policy or by taking measures to offset the effect of the other country's strategy. The strategic situation between countries thus may have the structure of a prisoners' dilemma. If each country could engage in either strategic trade policy or free trade, each may have a dominant strategy of engaging in strategic trade policy. This is collectively irrational, however, because they could both benefit if they both refrained from adopting a strategic trade policy. For example, the United States retaliated against the European Union's subsidization of agricultural exports with its own export subsidies, resulting in large losses to both. To resolve the dilemma, countries negotiate agreements prohibiting such policies and establish institutions to enforce the agreements. This approach, represented by GATT and its successor, the World Trade Organization, is favored by most countries. Before considering international trade agreements, the nature of the politics of international trade is considered.

The Political Economy of International Trade Policy

THE DUAL NATURE OF THE POLITICS OF INTERNATIONAL TRADE

As shown in Figure 16-1, the politics of international trade policy are driven by domestic politics, which in turn is animated by the interactions between international trade and the domestic economy. Trade policy has differentiated distributive consequences with some interests benefiting from trade liberalization and others harmed by it. Trade politics thus has two components—measures to liberalize trade and measures to support those domestic interests that are harmed by liberalization.

According to the typology of political competition presented in Figure 6-4, the politics of international trade policy is at one level majoritarian. That is, everyone is affected by the prices of goods in domestic markets, by export opportunities, and by demand and supply adjustments to changes in trade policies and exchange rates. Because liberalized trade policy is beneficial in the aggregate, the majority of people favor reductions in tariff and nontariff barriers. The benefits, however, are often widely distributed, so preferences for trade liberalization must be transformed into policy. In the

---

[4]Indeed, worldwide aggregate surplus is increased because the total quantity produced, given the subsidization, is greater than it would be without the subsidy. This results because the subsidization leads to a price that is closer to marginal cost. These conclusions, however, are not completely robust and may be reversed if firms compete in a manner different from that assumed in Cournot competition.

United States, as in most countries, the politics of trade liberalization are basically entrepreneurial, with Congress delegating the role of entrepreneur to the president. Congress is willing to delegate because the aggregate benefits of trade liberalization exceed the aggregate costs, and the benefits are sufficiently widely distributed that leadership must be exercised.

The distributive consequences of a liberalized trade policy, however, are not uniform. Instead, it has concentrated effects on particular interests, and those interests have an incentive to take political action to enhance the benefits they receive or to reduce the costs they bear.[5] In the case of policies that reduce domestic barriers to trade and thereby stimulate imports, the benefits typically are distributed broadly among consumers, whereas the costs are concentrated on import-competing industries. When import-competing industries have sunk resources, their rents can be large, providing strong incentives to seek protection. Protectionism is thus characterized by client politics. In most countries, interests, including companies, unions, and industries, can seek protection and relief from injury due to imports. For example, countries have antidumping laws that allow domestic firms to petition to have duties placed on imports sold at "less than fair value."

The benefits from protection are concentrated on those interests that compete against imports, whereas the costs of protection are widely distributed among consumers and other users of the protected goods. Although consumers are harmed by these policies, the harm is typically small on a per capita basis, and hence consumers seldom take political action to oppose protection. Importers, however, are often harmed, and hence can oppose protectionism. In the case of steel imports to the United States, steel companies and the United Steel Workers sought protection from imports, but General Motors and Caterpillar opposed it because it would raise the price of steel. Interest group politics can thus develop. Interest group politics can also occur between import-competing industries and exporters as in the case of the ratification of broad trade liberalizations, such as the NAFTA, that require reciprocity.

The nature of the politics of international trade policy is summarized in Figure 16-4. In the aggregate, trade policy is characterized by majoritarian politics. At a disaggregated level, the nature of the politics depends on the specific policy alternative in question. Trade liberalization and market opening are basically characterized by entrepreneurial politics. Protectionism involves client politics, since the benefits from supporting protectionism are concentrated and the benefits from opposing it are widely distributed. Protectionist policies may generate retaliation and market opening policies may require reciprocity, so the number of interest groups involved can expand. The politics of protectionism and the politics of market opening thus can lead to interest group politics.

ASYMMETRIES IN THE POLITICS

Although trade policy liberalization creates opportunities for exporters and threats for import-competing firms, the domestic politics of international trade are asymmetric due to the magnitude and concentration of the consequences of trade liberalization. The differences in magnitude stem from sunk resources and the rents on those resources. Consider the case of a firm that would construct a new plant dedicated to exports, provided that foreign barriers to trade were lowered. The incentive to undertake political action to open the foreign market depends on the profit it can earn, which is given by the export revenue less the full cost of the resources required to produce the exports. For an

---

[5]Magee, Brock, and Young (1989) provide a theory of rent-seeking to explain aspects of international trade policy.

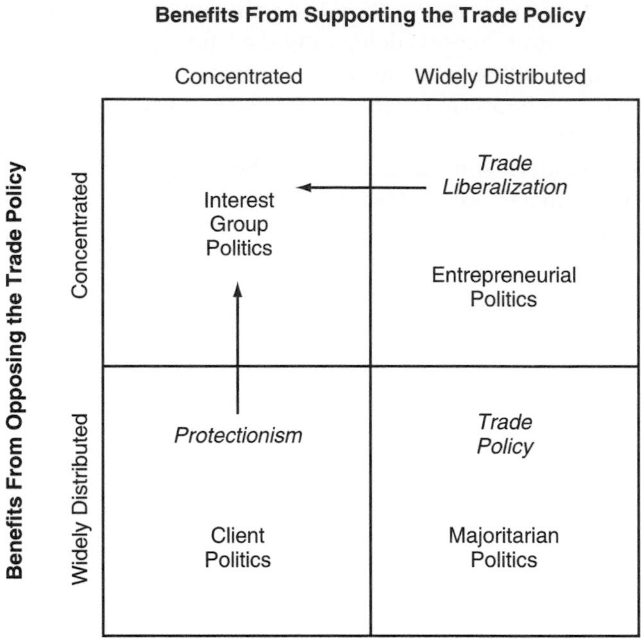

FIGURE 16-4 The Politics of International Trade Policy

exporting industry, profit is the area between the price and the long-run supply curve. In contrast, domestic firms faced with import competition typically have resources that are already sunk. Because of sunk resources the short-run supply curve is below the long-run curve as illustrated in Figure 5-1, so the firm earns rents on its sunk resources. When there are sunk resources, the import-competing industry has more to lose than the exporting industry has to gain, so the incentives for protection can be stronger than the incentives for market opening.

To illustrate the effect of the concentration of costs and benefits, consider the case of labor. Trade liberalization creates new jobs in exporting industries, but at the time at which the trade policy is chosen those new jobs are not yet identified, let alone filled. Those jobs might be filled by many people, and hence the probability that any one person would obtain one of the new jobs is small. The incentive for any individual to take political action thus is small. As the managing director of one of the largest U.S. investment banks commented on labor's concerns about NAFTA, "The jobs that will be lost are identifiable; the jobs that will be created are as yet unidentified." Cisco Systems projected that its increased exports to Mexico would create 200 additional U.S. jobs at its suppliers, but who would hold those jobs was as yet unidentified. Thus, Cisco had clear incentives to support NAFTA, but those unidentified individuals who would in the future hold those new jobs could not support it.

In contrast, jobs threatened by imports are already both identified and occupied. Frequently workers are earning rents in those jobs; that is, their wages are higher than the wages they could obtain elsewhere. Rents are thus concentrated on identified individuals, and their incentives to oppose trade liberalization and seek protection from imports can be strong. This is the case for organized labor, where, for example, the wages of United Automobile Workers (UAW) members are higher than the wages most of them could earn in other employment. Not surprisingly, the UAW has been a leading proponent of protection for the U.S. auto industry. Organized labor vigorously, but unsuccessfully, opposed NAFTA and the Uruguay Round GATT accord that established the WTO.

Multinational firms often have mixed incentives. As with any import-competing firm earning rents, a multinational firm would benefit from protection of its domestic markets. A multinational firm also would benefit from opening foreign markets for its products. The simultaneous protection of domestic markets and the opening of foreign markets is not sustainable, however, since protectionism can generate retaliation by other countries and market opening may require reciprocity. Consequently, most multinational firms support free trade because of the aggregate gains from trade and because free trade allows them to pursue their competitive advantages.

International Trade Agreements

THE GENERAL AGREEMENT ON TARIFFS AND TRADE AND THE WORLD TRADE ORGANIZATION

At the conclusion of World War II, a group of countries led by the United States established the International Trade Organization (ITO). They hoped the ITO would allow them to avoid the disastrous trade policies that had contributed to the depression and the pressures for war. When the U.S. Senate did not provide the two-thirds majority to ratify the organization's treaty, the ITO disbanded. However, a set of principles for international trade in goods had been drafted in conjunction with the ITO, and in 1948, 23 countries formalized those principles as the GATT General Agreement. Seven subsequent rounds of multilateral trade negotiations among the signatories have resulted in major reductions in tariffs and nontariff barriers to trade.

The focus of international trade policy through the 1960s was on tariffs. Because tariffs limit the gains from trade, the United States and other countries sought in the Kennedy Round (1964–1967) of GATT negotiations to reduce tariffs on a more or less uniform basis among all signatories. The result was an average reduction of 36 percent in tariffs, and the volume of international trade increased substantially as a consequence.

After reducing tariffs to the point at which they no longer constituted a major barrier to trade, the focus of GATT turned in the Tokyo Round (1974–1979) to nontariff barriers to trade. Nontariff barriers are more complex and difficult to address and are often deeply rooted in both domestic politics and business practices that protect rents and surpluses threatened by imports.[6] Trade in agricultural products, for example, has been distorted by a variety of policies such as import quotas, domestic subsidies, and export subsidies. Although the Tokyo Round focused on nontariff barriers, it also resulted in an average reduction of 34 percent in tariffs. As a result of the Tokyo Round agreements, the average tariff in developed countries was 6.3 percent. Thirty-two percent of U.S. imports were duty-free, and the average duty on the rest was 5.5 percent.[7]

The Tokyo Round left several sectors such as agriculture unaddressed, and several others, such as trade in services, subsequently became more salient. The Uruguay Round (1986–1993) was intended to improve GATT provisions on trade in goods and expand the multilateral trade agreements to include trade in services, agriculture, intellectual property protection, government procurement, and other issues. After nearly 8 years of negotiations an agreement was concluded that made major improvements in international trade policies and, in addition, reduced tariffs by 38 percent to an average of 3.9 percent in developed countries. To encompass this broader set of agreements, the World Trade Organization (WTO) was established. The GATT agreement remained in effect and was incorporated into the WTO agreements.

---

[6]Grieco (1990) provides an analysis of the compliance with the Tokyo Round nontariff barrier agreements.
[7]See Lande and Van Grasstek (1986, p. 4).

Despite the broad set of agreements, several difficult issues remained unresolved for future multilateral trade negotiations. Congressional approval of the Uruguay Round and WTO agreements stipulated that Congress was to review participation in the WTO every 5 years and allowed the United States to withdraw if its interests were threatened. Withdrawal is highly unlikely.

The WTO has 132 countries as members, and over 30 others including China and Russia have applied for membership. The WTO has three principal roles. First, it provides a system of agreements that helps trade move freely. Second, it provides a forum for trade negotiations such as the telecommunications agreement achieved in 1996. Third, it provides a dispute settlement mechanism to resolve trade disputes in a timely manner.

The central principle of the WTO agreements is embodied in the most favored nation (MFN) requirement that each signatory accord all the other signatories the most favorable terms for trade provided to any country; that is, trade policies are to be nondiscriminatory.[8] A second principle is national treatment; thus, domestic and foreign goods are to be treated the same. For example, Canada imposed higher postage rates on U.S. magazines than for Canadian magazines, and a WTO dispute resolution panel held that the Canadian practice violated the national treatment principle.

GATT covers a variety of practices and policies governing trade in goods.[9] Article VI covers antidumping and countervailing duties and requires both a finding of less than fair value sales or subsidization, respectively, and a finding of material injury. Article XI sets a framework for the elimination of quantitative restrictions on trade, but Article XVIII allows exceptions for the balance of payments problems of developing countries. Article XIX allows for temporary escape clause relief. Article XVI is the subsidies code, and Articles XX and XXI provide exceptions to the free trade provisions of the other articles. For example, a country may impose trade restrictions if they are required by national security considerations.[10]

GENERAL AGREEMENT OF TRADE IN SERVICES (GATS)

U.S. service industries had complained that their international expansion was hindered by the protection many countries provided for their domestic industries. The effort to reduce barriers to trade in services was led by a number of executives, including James Robinson, chairman of American Express, who for years personally campaigned to open foreign markets. In 1982 the Coalition of Service Industries (CSI) was formed and was successful in including trade in services in the Uruguay Round agenda. It participated in the negotiations under the leadership of Citicorp Chairman John Reed.

The result was the General Agreement on Trade in Services (GATS), which covers all services and provides for MFN and national treatment. The agreement also requires countries to make transparent all regulations and conditions of service. Since the services markets of many countries were largely closed to foreign firms, GATS allowed countries temporarily not to apply MFN treatment.

---

[8]Exceptions to the equal treatment principle include colonial preference arrangements in effect when GATT was established, preferences for developing countries, and certain multilateral agreements such as the Multi-Fiber Arrangement.

[9]Prior to 1995 GATT was not a single agreement but instead a set of agreements, each of which countries could choose to sign. For example, GATT includes a subsidies code intended to limit the domestic subsidization of export industries, but the signatories were largely the members of the Organization for Economic Cooperation and Development (OECD). The OECD is an association of 29 industrial democracies.

[10]With the exception of Article II, these articles have counterparts in U.S. trade law.

Two services, telecommunications and finance, posed particular problems because of government ownership of firms and heavy regulation. The Uruguay Round and GATS agreements were signed while negotiations on telecommunications and financial services continued. In 1997 over 68 countries agreed to open their telecommunications to various degrees. Later in 1997, 102 countries reached agreement to open banking, insurance, investments, and other financial services to international competition. Some countries, however, limited foreign ownership stakes in their financial services companies. Many service-related issues remained unresolved, however, and a new round of negotiations was scheduled for 2000 to address subsidization, government procurement, licensing, and technical standards.

TRADE-RELATED ASPECTS OF INTELLECTUAL PROPERTY RIGHTS (TRIPS)

Intellectual property rights include copyrights, patents, trademarks, brand names and logos, industrial designs, semiconductor circuit designs, and trade secrets. Such rights allow individuals and firms to receive the benefits of their efforts in creating new concepts and products, and infringement of these rights reduces the incentives to create. TRIPS provides broad protection and is included in the WTO dispute settlement system, allowing trade sanctions to be imposed in the event of violations. Because many countries had weak domestic laws for protecting intellectual property rights, developing countries were given 5 years to comply and the least developed countries were given 11 years.

AGRICULTURE

Agriculture has been the sector with the greatest distortions in trade. A 1988 OECD report concluded that farm subsidies and import controls cost consumers and taxpayers $270 billion a year. Of that amount, the European Union accounted for $97.5 billion, the United States $67.2 billion, and Japan $57.8 billion. The principal roadblock to an agreement on agricultural trade was the European Union's Common Agriculture Policy (CAP).[11] CAP is intended to maintain farmers' incomes and does so by establishing prices high enough to yield a reasonable income for high-cost farms. The high prices, however, induced efficient farms to expand their output, resulting in huge crop surpluses, some of which have been exported at subsidized prices. The EU's export subsidization resulted in retaliatory subsidization of agricultural exports by the United States.

The Uruguay Round produced an important agreement to reduce tariffs, domestic support, and export subsidies in agriculture. By 2000 developed countries were to reduce their tariffs by an average of 36 percent with a minimum reduction of 15 percent. Domestic support was to be reduced by 20 percent and export subsidies by 36 percent. The reductions required for developing countries were lower, and they were given until 2004 to comply. Because many countries used quotas to restrict imports, the agreement adopted a "tariffs only" policy in which quotas were replaced by equivalent tariffs, which were then subjected to the required reductions. The agreement on agriculture also addressed health and safety issues. It required that regulations be based on science

---

[11]The politics of the CAP are clientistic with agricultural interests receiving large and concentrated benefits and consumers (through high prices) and taxpayers (through the purchase of crop surpluses) bearing broadly distributed costs. Agricultural interest groups lobby at the EU level through the peak association COPA, which submits its opinion on agricultural prices and policies directly to the European Commission. COPA also lobbies the members of the European Parliament and the members of Economic and Social Committee (ESC). National agricultural associations lobby their home country representatives on both the European Parliament and the ESC. They are active in domestic politics and attempt to affect the policies that will be represented by their ministers of agriculture.

and that they "be applied only to the extent necessary to protect human, animal, or plant life of health." The agreement, however, left several remaining issues, and a new round of negotiations on agriculture was scheduled for 1999.

GOVERNMENT PROCUREMENT

The Uruguay Round negotiators reached a new Government Procurement Agreement (GPA) that extended the existing agreement to include construction and services and some procurement by subcentral governments and government-owned firms. The GPA is a "pluralateral" agreement among a subset of WTO countries. Developing countries were given special conditions. In a bilateral agreement with the EU, the procurement of 15 U.S. states and seven major cities were opened to EU firms in exchange for opening the EU's $28 billion heavy electric equipment market.

ANTIDUMPING

The Kennedy Round of GATT negotiations concluded in 1967 incorporated provisions in Article VI allowing domestic laws to include antidumping measures. From the perspective of economic theory dumping occurs when a company sells a good at a price below the cost of producing it. Antidumping, however, pertains to sales at "less than fair value" that materially injure domestic industries and allows a duty on imports intended to bring their price up to fair value. Antidumping provisions are thus intended to provide for "fair trade" rather than free or efficient trade. Antidumping provisions have been criticized as being protectionist, because they can result in the imposition of duties on imports even when prices are above costs. Antidumping basically compares the price of a product in the exporting country with the price at which it is imported, so antidumping actually applies more to price discrimination than to dumping. The chapter case *Cemex and Antidumping* centers on this issue. The Uruguay Round agreement standardized the procedures for calculating the dumping duty and for conducting investigations. It also imposed a 5-year limit on any antidumping duty, unless ending the duty would result in material injury.

Antidumping had been used almost exclusively by developed countries with the number of actions initiated averaging about 200 a year in the early 1990s. The number of actions initiated by developed nations decreased to 120 in 1997. Since 1985 developing countries have become active in using antidumping and by 1997 they initiated more actions than developed countries. Despite the use of antidumping to protect import-competing industries, most countries prefer to retain the provisions as a safety valve to relieve pressure for broader protectionist measures.

DISPUTE SETTLEMENT

Under GATT, disputes between countries could be brought before a panel that investigated and issued a recommendation. The recommendation became binding, however, only if all countries agreed to it, and countries including the United States frequently withheld their consent. A major achievement of the Uruguay Round was to establish the WTO Dispute Settlement Body (DSB) to hear disputes and issue binding orders to resolve them.[12] The Dispute Settlement Body (DSB) encourages the parties to resolve disputes through negotiation and compromise, but if that is unsuccessful, a country may request that a special panel be established to hear the dispute. The entire process, from the filing of the initial complaint to the issuance of a final report by the panel, is to be completed within 1 year, and any appeal is to be resolved in 3 months.

---

[12]The DSB is not an organization but instead is the General Council of the WTO. It is better thought of as a procedure for resolving disputes.

If the DSB finds against a practice of a country, the country is required to correct the fault. Failure to comply can be brought to the attention of the DSB, which can authorize the petitioner to impose trade sanctions against the violator. Thus, countries need not change their laws to comply with the decision of the DSB, but if they fail to do so, sanctions can be authorized by the WTO. The United States and most countries have complied with the decisions of the DSB.

The first case decided by the DSB involved a complaint by Venezuela, later joined by Brazil, that rules issued by the U.S. Environmental Protection Agency (EPA) for reformulated gasoline violated the WTO national treatment principle. The EPA had written its rules based on data that were readily available for U.S. refiners. Because foreign refiners had not kept the same data, the EPA required them to meet a more stringent standard. The DSB decided in favor of Venezuela, and the United States complied by rewriting the EPA rules to provide for national treatment.

Some disputes are directed at specific protectionist practices. The European Union (EU) maintains a set of preferences for the overseas territories and the former colonies of its member states. The United States and Latin American countries filed a complaint against EU rules issued in 1994 for bananas from the overseas territories and former colonies, particularly in Africa.[13] Banana exports from Honduras to the EU fell by 90 percent as a result of the rule, which protected a large number of jobs in countries such as the Ivory Coast. The DSB decided against the EU and rejected an appeal. The EU then revised its rule under contentious internal bargaining, pitting Germany and other countries that opposed the preferences against France and other countries that favored them. The United States and Latin American countries, however, contended that the revised rule did little to remove the barriers to Latin American banana imports. The United States proposed that the new rule be taken to the WTO for an expedited DSB process, but the EU refused. When the DSB failed to authorize sanctions by the required deadline, the United States announced 100 percent punitive tariffs against $500 million of imports of wine, cheese, and other products. The DSB subsequently reached a decision authorizing the United States to impose punitive tariffs on $191 million of imports.

A more controversial case was brought by the United States against the European Union on its ban of beef treated with growth-enhancing hormones. The European ban did not violate the national treatment principle, because it applied to any hormone-treated beef, nor was it intended to protect European beef producers. Instead, the ban was enacted because of consumer concerns about chemicals in their foods. The DSB concluded that there was no scientific basis for concluding that the hormone-treated beef might be a health hazard. The EU, however, was given a period of time to conduct its own safety tests on the hormone-treated beef. After two years of inaction by the EU, the United States announced 100 percent punitive tariffs on $200 million of imports of European goods. After allowing the EU an opportunity to comply with the WTO ruling, the punitive tariffs took effect in 1999. This case is potentially important because it may preclude countries from responding to consumer preferences whatever their basis might be.

The WTO agreements have also sparked controversy with respect to environmental protection. A U.S. law banned the sale in the United States of shrimp caught with nets from which sea turtles were unable to escape. The DSB upheld a complaint by India, Malaysia, Pakistan, and Thailand against the U.S. law on the grounds that the WTO agreements did not permit discrimination against products on the basis of how they are produced. Prior to the establishment of the WTO, a GATT panel had on the

---

[13]The United States was a petitioner because Chiquita Brands and Dole Food Company export Latin American bananas to the EU.

same grounds decided that the U.S. Marine Mammal Protection Act ban of tuna caught in purse sein nets in which dolphins could become caught and drown violated GATT. In the case of the dolphin decision, the United States withheld its consent and the panel decision did not take effect. Under the WTO DSB procedures, the sea turtle decision was binding. Environmental issues such as these and health issues such as the EU ban on hormone-treated beef have spurred calls for a new round of WTO negotiations. The chapter case *The WTO and the Environment* concerns some of these issues.

THE NEXT ROUND?

The Uruguay Round and follow-up agreements have generally been successful, and the WTO dispute settlement process has been effective. Nevertheless, several issues remain unresolved particularly in services, government procurement, and intellectual property rights. In addition, other issues have been identified as a result of disputes brought before the DSB. Moreover, several emerging issues have developed since the conclusion of the Uruguay Round. Both the European Union and the United States have called for a new comprehensive round of multilateral trade negotiations to begin in 2000 within the framework of the WTO. The agenda may include competition (antitrust) policy, environmental protection, health, labor and working conditions, foreign direct investment, and electronic commerce. Even the inclusion of some of these issues on the agenda is contentious. For example, the United States has opposed any measure that would weaken its enforcement of its antitrust laws, whereas the European Union wants negotiations on competition policy.

OTHER TRADE AGREEMENTS

A number of regional free trade agreements have been concluded, and those regions have broadened the set of countries participating. The largest of these free trade areas are the European Union and NAFTA. In addition, 34 Western Hemisphere countries agreed to establish the Free Trade Area of the Americas by 2005. In Latin America there are four regional trading areas: the Central American Common Market, the Andean Community, Caricom, and Mercosur. Mercosur includes Argentina, Bolivia, Brazil, Chile, Paraguay, and Uruguay with 210 million people.

In 1994 the 16 countries participating in the Asia-Pacific Economic Cooperation (APEC) forum agreed to work toward removing all barriers to trade by the year 2020. The developed countries in APEC established a goal of eliminating trade barriers by 2010. The first substantive APEC trade agreement would have reduced tariffs on $1.5 trillion of goods, but in 1998 Japan rejected the agreement because it would reduce tariffs on fish and forest products.

In addition to WTO trade agreements, a large number of bilateral and multilateral agreements are in force. For example, the United States has worked to deregulate international air transportation, which had been governed by a cartel supported by countries with state-owned airlines. The U.S. strategy has been to negotiate with other countries bilateral agreements deregulating air fares and schedules. This has increased competition and brought prices down, although restrictions remain in some markets because landing slots are limited and not allowed to be traded. For example, in 1998 the United States concluded bilateral agreements with France and Germany but had not yet successfully concluded negotiations with the United Kingdom because of disagreements about landing rights at Heathrow Airport.

U.S. Trade Policy

THE STRUCTURE OF U.S. TRADE POLICY

Article 1, Section 8 of the Constitution gives Congress the power "to regulate commerce with foreign nations" and to "lay and collect duties." In 1934 in the aftermath of the disastrous Smoot-Hawley tariff, Congress, through the Reciprocal Trade Agreement Act, delegated to the president the authority to negotiate trade agreements with other nations. The authority for U.S. trade negotiations has remained largely with the president, and most presidents have supported liberalized trade. The Office of the U.S. Trade Representative (USTR), located in the Executive Office of the President, serves as the president's representative in trade negotiations. The United States has supported trade liberalization through the multilateral policies embodied in the World Trade Organization (WTO), regional free trade agreements including NAFTA and the Asia-Pacific Economic Cooperation (APEC) forum, and bilateral arrangements such as those promoting competition in international air transport. In the late 1980s, Congress began to assert its constitutional authority. The USTR is now required to consult with Congress on both trade policy and specific actions that implement that policy.[14] Being closer to constituents than is the president, members of Congress have been concerned with protecting their constituents' interests. The result has been a series of amendments to the trade laws that make it easier for industries both to obtain protection and to initiate action to open foreign markets to their products. The U.S. trade laws establish rights that private parties may exercise to further their interests, so U.S. trade actions have both public and private initiation.

The politics of international trade takes place in four institutional arenas—cabinet departments, regulatory agencies, Congress, and the Office of the President. The administration of trade policy has been placed with executive branch agencies, primarily the Departments of the Treasury, State, and Commerce. The International Trade Agency (ITA) of the Department of Commerce and the International Trade Commission (ITC), an independent regulatory commission, have administrative responsibilities for certain sections of U.S. trade law. Cabinet departments participate in international trade policy, both administratively and politically, and regularly conduct policy research, provide congressional testimony, lobby for their policy objectives and the interests they represent, and interact with other countries.

U.S. TRADE LAW AND ITS ADMINISTRATION

The major components of U.S. trade law are embodied in the Trade Act of 1974 and the Tariff Act of 1930. The principal sections and their purposes are identified here, and more detail is provided in the appendix at the end of the chapter.[15]

- Section 201 (the escape clause) provides for relief for domestic industries injured by imports.
- Section 301 (presidential retaliation) provides for action against countries that restrict imports of U.S. goods or subsidize exports to the United States.
- Section 731 (antidumping) provides authority for the imposition of duties on goods imported to the United States at a price that is less than fair value (LTFV).

---

[14]See O'Halloran (1994) for a study of the development of U.S. trade policy and the choice of trade institutions.

[15]See Trebilock and York (1990) for studies of the administration of trade laws in a number of countries.

- Section 303 (countervailing duties) provides authority for the imposition of duties against those countries that subsidize their domestic industries.
- Section 337 (intellectual property) allows retaliation against countries that violate U.S. patents, copyrights, or protected trade secrets.
- Trade Adjustment Assistance provides funds for those injured by imports.

These sections establish rights that private interests may exercise directly or indirectly through political channels. For example, firms, unions, and other interests may file antidumping petitions that initiate a complex administrative process that can result in duties assessed on imports sold at LTFV. The complaints filed by private interests are considered by the ITA and the ITC; and in Section 201 and 301 cases, the president has final authority. Decisions can be appealed to the U.S. Court of International Trade and the Court of Appeals, and many of the decisions are appealed. The chapter case *Cemex and Antidumping* provides details on the ITC and ITA administration of an antidumping case and considers a firm's market and nonmarket strategies for addressing the dumping complaint.

The Political Economy of Protectionism

FORMAL POLICIES

The politics of protectionism is clientistic as illustrated in Figure 16-4, and in the case of such issues as the Uruguay Round accord and NAFTA, the politics of protectionism is embedded in majoritarian politics. This section is concerned with nonmajoritarian issues in which private parties pursue their interests through political and administrative channels. Although official U.S. trade policy has promoted free and fair trade, the client politics arising from import competition has been important since the eighteenth century. Protection may extend indefinitely, have a specified duration, or be extendable. Protection for coastal shipping has continued since 1789, but most of the recent protectionist measures are intended to be temporary, giving industry time to improve its competitiveness.

Protection applies to two kinds of conditions. The first involves a predatory trade practice, such as export subsidization or dumping, where a foreign firm sells in the United States at a price below its cost. The second involves relative efficiency—when foreign firms are more efficient than U.S. firms and sell in the United States at prices above their costs yet below the prices of domestic goods. Economic efficiency calls for blocking predatory practices only when they can lead to long-run inefficiency and allowing nonpredatory imports. The political process, however, has not drawn the same line as economists have and instead focuses on fair trade and protection from injury.

Predatory and discriminatory trade practices are addressed by the antidumping provisions of Section 731 and by provisions for retaliation against export subsidization under Section 303. From 1990 through 1997, 198 countervailing duty reviews were completed under Section 303, and 668 antidumping reviews were completed under Section 731, although few of the latter cases involved predatory practices. The United States also has established sector-specific retaliation mechanisms to respond to subsidization by other countries. A 1985 act provides for subsidization of exports of agricultural commodities through the Export Enhancement Program in retaliation for agriculture export subsidization by the European Union.[16] This retaliatory program

[16]Althought the program is directed at the EU, it affects countries such as Australia that do not subsidize their agricultural exports. In response to complaints by Australia and other countries, the procedure for determining whether subsidies will be provided must include consideration of the effects on those countries.

was important in the Uruguay Round negotiations on trade in agriculture, which resulted in an agreement to reduce export subsidies and other distortions to trade.

The relative inefficiency of domestic industries is addressed in four ways. First, those injured may be compensated under the Trade Adjustment Assistance Act. Trade adjustment assistance, discussed in the appendix, is intended to help the domestic industry adjust to changes in relative efficiency in a manner that moves it in the direction of greater efficiency. Trade adjustment assistance also compensates those who lose rents, thereby reducing their political opposition to liberalized trade. The assistance is generally restricted to workers and has focused on retraining programs. Trade adjustment assistance has been provided sparingly because of concerns that it might become an entitlement for workers or used as a pork barrel program. For example, laid-off workers are eligible for special retraining programs, relocation payments, and an additional year of unemployment benefits under the NAFTA Transitional Adjustment Assistance Program. The program has been criticized for providing benefits when layoffs were not caused by NAFTA.[17]

Second, relief can be granted under Section 201 in the form of tariffs, import quotas, the suspension of previously granted trade concessions, or other forms of retaliation. Relief under Section 201 is infrequently requested and seldom granted.

Third, relief is granted under Section 731 when a petitioner's dumping complaint is affirmed by the ITC and the ITA. A finding of dumping requires only that the imported good is sold at LTFV and that the petitioner has been materially injured by the imports. Antidumping thus is not restricted to predatory practices but instead can be used to protect import-competing firms from imports.

Fourth, protection is provided by measures ranging from special duties to voluntary agreements to limit imports. The United States imposes a 2.5 percent duty on passenger cars but imposes a 25 percent duty on light trucks. For 10 years, quotas were imposed on steel imports from 29 countries, limiting imports to no more than 21 percent of the domestic market. The quotas protected the U.S. steel industry, but they also served as retaliation for the subsidization of steel producers by countries including France, Italy, Spain, Portugal, Britain, and Brazil. The Bush administration did not renew the quotas, and the industry responded by filing antidumping and countervailing duty petitions against steel producers in 20 countries. In 1993 the Department of Commerce imposed duties averaging 27 percent on steel imports. The ITC subsequently found injury in only 32 of the 74 cases, however. Upon announcement of the ITC decisions, the market value of U.S. steel companies fell by $1.1 billion, and the price of USX (U.S. Steel) shares fell 13 percent.

The Cost of Protectionism

Ultimately, the cost of protectionism is borne by consumers. Hufbauer and Elliott (1994) estimated that in 1990 special trade protection cost consumers over $70 billion, or approximately $280 per capita. U.S. producers were estimated to have captured approximately 45 percent of that amount as additional rents. Of the 21 cases of protection they studied, the annual cost per job saved ranged from $3,000 to $256,000, with an average of $54,000 for the 192,000 jobs saved by the protection. Over 152,000 of those jobs were in the apparel industry, and the cost to consumers per job was over $50,000. Hufbauer, Berliner, and Elliott (1986) estimate that in the early 1980s the voluntary export restrictions (VER) on Japanese automobiles resulted in a 4.4 percent increase in automobile prices in the United States and an increase in employment of 55,000 jobs, at a

---

[17] *The Wall Street Journal,* June 30, 1997.

cost to the economy of $105,000 per job saved in 1984. As a result of the VER, domestic producers captured rents of $2.6 billion per year, and foreign producers captured rents of $2.2 billion.

Although consumers bear the cost of protectionism, they are difficult and costly to organize, and individual consumers are likely to find it rational to remain inactive on protection issues. Furthermore, organized consumer groups have largely been inactive in cases involving protection of domestic industries. This leaves the political arena open to domestic industries, with political opposition coming primarily from importers, U.S. exporters, and those government agencies that are oriented toward free trade and economic efficiency. The president also generally opposes major protectionist initiatives as do members of Congress who support market competition. Most protectionism initiatives are thus specific to well-organized client groups.

CHANNELS OF PROTECTION

Firms, labor unions, and industries can seek protection from imports through political and/or administrative channels. The political channel is through Congress and is directed either at specific legislation, such as a quota on sugar imports, or at the criteria used in the administrative channel. In addition to enacting new legislation, the political channel represents a threat that may strengthen the U.S. bargaining position with other countries. The protection obtained by an industry through the political channel depends on its ability to generate political pressure, as considered in Chapter 6, and on the opposing pressure. Industries such as automobiles, steel, dairy farming, sugar, and textiles with large numbers of employees have been able to generate considerable political pressure.

An administrative channel involves regulatory and executive branch agencies and is accessed by a petition filed pursuant to the U.S. trade laws. Much of the administration of trade policy is delegated to the ITC, the ITA, and the president. In the chapter case *Cemex and Antidumping,* U.S. cement producers filed an antidumping petition against Mexican cement imports. The administrative process imposes a series of hurdles through which a case must pass before relief is granted, and a petition may fail at any of several points in the process. In some cases, the threat of action is used to negotiate a voluntary settlement of the complaint.

EXAMPLE: STEEL IMPORTS AND THE NONMARKET CAMPAIGN

Overcapacity in the steel industry worldwide caused employment in the U.S. steel industry to drop by 325,000 during the 1980s, much of it at the hands of imported steel. Employment at Bethlehem Steel fell from 130,000 in the 1960s to 16,400 in 1998. To improve its competitiveness, the industry invested $50 billion in modernization and new technology. By the second half of the 1990s the U.S. industry had returned to health and prices and profits were up. The situation changed quickly, however, in 1997 as a result of the financial and economic crises in Asia and Russia and to a lesser extent in Latin America. Steel imports increased dramatically as foreign producers looked for markets for their excess capacity, and the robust U.S. economy with open markets was by far the most attractive opportunity. The imports drove prices down sharply and resulted in layoffs and the bankruptcy of one small steel company. The price of hot rolled steel fell by 18 percent in 1998 to the lowest level during the 1990s.

In response, the United Steel Workers (USW) and 12 leading steel producers joined in a broad client-politics nonmarket strategy to limit what they viewed as unfairly dumped steel. Curtis Barnette, CEO of Bethlehem Steel, said, "We're sometimes viewed as protectionist and rust belt in our thinking when we are a high-tech, low-cost, world-class industry. We believe in open markets. But when the rules are breached, they should be enforced. . ."[18] Barnette was referring to U.S. laws against unfair competition resulting from dumping and the subsidization of foreign producers. To implement its nonmarket strategy the industry established the "Stand Up For Steel" campaign to bring the issue to the attention of the public, Congress, and the president.

In June, four producers of stainless steel and the United Steel Workers filed antidumping petitions against eight countries and countervailing duty petitions against Belgium, France, Italy, and South Korea for subsidizing their steel makers. Stainless-sheet steel prices had fallen from $2,700 a metric ton in 1996 to $1,800 in 1998. Industry profits on stainless-sheet steel fell from $466 million in 1995 to $141 million in 1997. In September the industry had filed antidumping and countervailing duty petitions against Brazil, Japan, and Russia for dumping hot rolled steel and against Brazil for subsidizing its steel producers. The industry was preparing additional petitions for other steel products. With the downturn in the U.S. industry reflected in the layoffs and lower prices and profits in the industry, the material injury standard was expected to be met. To speed the process of review of the petitions, the industry argued for an expedited procedure.

In addition to pursuing its case in administrative channels, the industry pursued relief through political channels deploying a political strategy intended to pressure the U.S. government to act. The industry lobbied Congress, and in October the House passed a nonbinding resolution calling for a ban on steel imports for a year. The industry also succeeded in inserting a provision in an appropriations bill requiring the Clinton administration to produce a plan for aiding the industry by January 5, 1999. Barnette and others lobbied in the Senate and convinced the Senate Steel Caucus to call on the administration to restrict imports.

The Stand Up For Steel campaign spent $3 million on a public advocacy campaign, including full-page newspaper advertisements presenting a letter calling on President Clinton to act.[19] George Becker, president of the USW, said, "We're fighting for the heartland of America. All the blood is gone from our industry; we can't bleed anymore."[20]

The industry also met with the secretaries of the Commerce and Treasury, and the Commerce Department agreed to expedite its petitions. The ITA found in favor of the steel industry and announced duties ranging from 3.44 percent to 67.68 percent. Later Becker, Barnette, and Paul Wilhelm, CEO of U.S. Steel, met with the president, vice president, the secretaries of State and Commerce, and the USTR.[21] The industry also sent a message to the president and the Democratic Party. In the 1997–1998 election cycle the USW and the steel companies provided $1.2 million in campaign contributions, most of which came from the USW, with over 80 percent going to Democrats. More importantly, the USW had been very effective in "get out the vote" efforts on behalf of Democrats. The president and vice president were not only concerned with rewarding their important political backers but also feared having unemployed steel workers when the year 2000 elections arrived. Vice President Gore warned a group of European top executives that "the United States cannot be the importer of only resort" for nations in crisis.[22]

The campaign by the steel industry was not unopposed. Steel purchasers argued that any restraints on steel imports would result in higher prices for consumers. Both

---

[18] *The New York Times,* December 10, 1998.
[19] *The New York Times,* September 10, 1998.
[20] *The New York Times,* December 10, 1998.
[21] *The Wall Street Journal,* November 6, 1998.
[22] *The New York Times,* November 11, 1998.

General Motors and Caterpillar criticized the antidumping and countervailing duty petitions. Caterpillar stated, "We strongly object to suggestions that steel trade should be subject to 'special' protection. The quotas used to protect the steel industry in each of the last four decades hurt American industries that use steel and rewarded foreign steel traders with a guaranteed share of a restricted market."[23]

The Clinton administration considered a variety of responses for its January 5 deadline. One possibility was to negotiate a voluntary export agreement with the steel exporting countries. Another was to provide temporary relief under Section 201. A third was to let the administrative processes run their course.

The Political Economy of Market Opening

Market opening occurs through majoritarian policies such as those embodied in the WTO and NAFTA and through entrepreneurial politics, with the president attempting through multilateral and bilateral negotiations to reduce foreign tariff and nontariff barriers to trade. In some cases, market opening is characterized by client politics as interest groups pressure the government to take action to open specific foreign markets. This section considers the political economy of NAFTA, market opening and client politics, and market opening under the threat of retaliation.

THE NORTH AMERICAN FREE TRADE AGREEMENT

The North American Free Trade Agreement established, subject to certain exceptions, free trade among Canada, Mexico, and the United States. NAFTA was an expansion of the United States–Canada Free Trade Agreement that had been in effect since 1988 and adopted many of the features of that agreement. NAFTA is a free trade agreement and not a market integration agreement as is the Single Market Act in the European Union. The agreement thus does not cover the movement of people or the harmonization of domestic laws.

NAFTA provides for the elimination of tariff and nontariff barriers over a 10-year period, although some barriers are to be phased out over 15 years. To the extent that external trade barriers remain in effect, the elimination of trade barriers within North America also gives foreign firms an incentive to locate operations in the NAFTA countries. For example, because of both nonmarket and market factors, Japanese automobile manufacturers have incentives to shift light-truck production to North America. The principal nonmarket factor is the 25 percent U.S. tariff on imports from outside the NAFTA countries. The principal market factor is the lower wages in Mexico.

The free trade agreement does not eliminate all barriers to trade. For example, Canada retains the right to protect and favor "cultural industries" and has taken measures to restrict U.S. publications and television programming. The automobile industry is the largest trader in the region, and NAFTA requires a 62.5 percent "regional value content" on automobiles and other light vehicles to qualify for duty-free treatment. A Japanese light-truck manufacturer thus must have 62.5 percent North American content to avoid the 25 percent tariff.

The elimination of tariff and nontariff barriers does not mean that trade disputes disappear. NAFTA leaves domestic trade laws in place, so antidumping and countervailing duty cases continue. For example, in 1994 Mexico imposed antidumping duties of up to 78 percent on steel plate and other steel imports from the United States. The Canada-U.S. bilateral free trade agreement established a dispute settlement mechanism

[23] *The New York Times,* December 10, 1998.

to avoid use of the courts. NAFTA incorporated this feature by establishing a trilateral Trade Commission, composed of cabinet level officials, to hear complaints and resolve disputes on issues such as the application of antidumping laws.

Despite the expected economic gains, political opposition to the agreement was strong in Canada and the United States. In the United States, opposition was led by organized labor, environmentalists, and populists, who feared the loss of jobs to Mexico. To overcome the opposition, the Bush administration, which negotiated the agreement, and the Clinton administration, which obtained congressional passage, made a number of deals and provided safeguards to obtain the needed votes. Nevertheless, 60 percent of the House Democrats voted against the agreement, and it passed as a result of strong Republican support.

The politics of NAFTA were similar to those of other trade liberalization measures. The weight of majoritarian interests was in favor of liberalized trade, and pockets of interests that stood to lose rents provided the opposition. Without concession those interests and the client politics they generated might have defeated the agreement. Three types of measures were taken to reduce opposition. First, NAFTA included transition provisions for a gradual phaseout of trade barriers to give industries time to adjust. Moreover, to reduce opposition from agricultural interests that feared a flood of low-priced Mexican produce, NAFTA included safeguards that would take effect if there were large surges of imports that depressed agricultural prices. Second, to obtain congressional votes, the Clinton administration made a number of side deals outside the trade area, including approval of public works projects in members' districts. Third, side agreements were concluded to reduce the opposition of environmental interest groups concerned about higher pollution as production expanded in Mexico and of organized labor that feared that high-paying jobs would be lost to Mexico.

NAFTA established the Commission on Environmental Cooperation and the Commission on Labor Cooperation to monitor environmental and labor developments, promote compliance, receive complaints, and resolve disputes. The first petition on environmental protection was filed in 1998 by local environmental groups in Mexico and the United States. In 1998 the Canadian office of the USW filed a complaint against Mexico for failure to protect the rights of Mexican workers to choose which union represented them. The U.S. Department of Labor filed a supporting complaint to be addressed by the labor ministries of the three countries. To address environmental concerns, Mexico and the United States also established the North American Development Bank to fund environmental projects along their 2,000 mile border. The bank had limited resources, however, and did not fund its first project until 1998.

MARKET OPENING AND CLIENT POLITICS

In the mid-1980s the U.S. position as the world leader in the semiconductor industry was challenged by Japanese producers that had made major inroads in the U.S. and other markets. The Semiconductor Industry Association (SIA) argued internally over nonmarket measures to address the Japanese challenge. Motorola advocated a tariff on imports, but the SIA members who were users of semiconductors opposed a tariff because it would raise prices. U.S. semiconductor manufacturers then filed an antidumping petition to prevent LTFV imports. The SIA members subsequently filed a Section 301 petition to pry open the Japanese market to foreign-made semiconductors. Pressure from the United States and the threat of success in the administrative channels resulted in an agreement in which Japanese semiconductor manufacturers pledged not to sell in the United States at less than fair value, to open the Japanese market, and to increase the market share of foreign semiconductors to 20 percent by 1991. The semiconductor agreement was generally viewed as having been successful in opening the Japanese market and has been renewed several times. The chapter case *The Kodak-Fujifilm Trade Dispute* concerns another market-opening initiative using a Section 301 petition.

MARKET OPENING UNDER THE THREAT OF RETALIATION

The most effective means of addressing foreign barriers to trade is through negotiations, but retaliation and its threat can provide leverage in the negotiations. Interest groups such as the SIA had taken actions under Section 301, but the pace of negotiations often had been slow and presidents were hesitant to retaliate. When action was taken, it often proved ineffective. The administration's reluctance to provide relief to domestic industries and to retaliate against other countries increased interest group pressure on Congress. Increasingly frustrated by what it viewed as inadequate action and by a process that placed much of the power in the hands of the president, Congress sought to increase its influence over both the relief and the retaliation processes. In 1988 Congress enacted the Omnibus Trade and Competitiveness Act, which established a mechanism for retaliation under a strengthened Section 301, referred to as "Super 301." This provided interest groups with an additional mechanism to open foreign markets and represented the most politicized of the administrative channels.

Super 301 provided for mandatory sanctions against countries that engaged in unfair trade practices that injured U.S. industries. The first step in the Super 301 process was the annual publication by the USTR of the National Trade Estimate Report (NTER). The report listed the countries with which the United States had a large trade deficit and the policies and practices that inhibited U.S. exports. The USTR then submitted a report identifying "priority countries" and "priority practices" and initiated an investigation of every priority practice and priority country. The 1998 NTER covered practices of 47 nations plus the European Union (EU). The section on the EU was 29 pages. If no satisfactory agreement was reached, the USTR determined whether the practice was unfair. Retaliation was then automatic and could result in withdrawal from trade agreements and the imposition of duties of up to 100 percent. The principal objective of Super 301, however, was to spur negotiations. The threat of mandatory retaliation under Super 301 contributed to an agreement under which Japan pledged to open its markets for wood products, communications satellites, and supercomputers.

Super 301 was harshly criticized by other countries, and both the European Union and Japan retaliated by issuing reports identifying specific U.S. tariff and nontariff barriers. Authorization for Super 301 expired at the end of 1990, but frustrated by the slow progress in bilateral trade negotiations with Japan, President Clinton issued an executive order reinstating a revised version of Super 301. The new Super 301 designates priority practices, but not priority countries, and lengthens the time period for the USTR to negotiate agreements. Sanctions are not mandatory.

Summary

The gains from trade identified by the law of comparative advantage provide strong incentives to reduce trade barriers. Under certain conditions, however, a nation can benefit from a strategic trade policy that restricts imports or subsidizes exports. Under such situations, countries may be in a prisoners' dilemma in which each has an incentive to adopt a strategic trade policy, but all are worse off when they do so. International trade agreements are intended to avoid these dilemmas and allow the gains from trade to be realized.

International trade policy is driven by economic incentives but governed by the politics that stem from those incentives. The politics of international trade are basically majoritarian, but because of rents associated with sunk resources the politics of protectionism is often strong. Protectionism is characterized by client politics, whereas the politics of trade liberalization is entrepreneurial. In the United States the president usually advocates trade liberalization, and protectionism manifests itself primarily in Congress.

Multilateral trade liberalization policies are incorporated in the agreements that govern trade and dispute resolution. The WTO agreements cover trade in goods, services, and agricultural products and provide for intellectual property protection. Several regional free trade agreements, including NAFTA and the European Union, have been established that eliminate internal barriers to trade but pose the potential for maintaining external barriers.

The political economy of international trade is best understood by focusing on domestic politics and the negotiations among countries on trade policy. Trade negotiations among nations reflect the desire to promote free trade while avoiding injury to domestic interests. The political forces supporting protectionism are naturally strong because of the rents that accrue to sunk resources, but in the long run the gains from trade are greater than the rents that would be dissipated by trade liberalization.

The United States has generally supported free trade, yet it provides both administrative and political channels for relief of industries injured by imports. Because protectionism is costly to an economy, the administrative channel has been designed to provide easy access but to make relief relatively hard to obtain. Success for an industry seeking relief in the political channel requires an ability to generate political pressure, and this requires numbers, resources, and coverage of political districts.

The Part IV integrative case *Toys 'Я' Us and Globalization* considers in the context of international trade policy the strategy of a firm seeking to take its domestic market strategy to other countries.

APPENDIX

U.S. Trade Law

U.S. trade law is embodied in the Tariff Act of 1930 and the Trade Act of 1974, as amended. This appendix reviews the principal sections of that law.

Section 201—The Escape Clause

Trade agreements can result in injury to industries, and the United States has long recognized a need to provide relief when it is politically important to do so. Yet trade agreements are beneficial, so violations must not be so easy to obtain as to make the agreements meaningless. The escape clause has been one response to the twin objectives of providing relief while preserving the benefits of liberalized trade.

At the insistence of the United States, the escape clause was incorporated into GATT in 1947 as Article XIX, and a domestic version of the escape clause has been incorporated into every U.S. trade law since then.[1] Relief may be provided in the form of tariffs, import quotas, or assistance in the form of direct compensation. An industry must show that it has incurred a "serious" injury, but the injury does not have to be the result of unfair practices. The Omnibus Trade and Competitiveness Act of 1988 encourages injured industries to make a "positive adjustment" to import competition. An escape clause case can be filed by a private party or the government. In an escape clause case, the ITC makes a finding and may recommend specific relief. The final decision on any relief rests with the president. Escape clause cases are rarely filed because of the difficulty in satisfying the conditions for an ITC decision and the reluctance of presidents to provide relief.

Section 301—Presidential Retaliation

Section 301, as amended by the Trade and Tariff Act of 1984, provides for retaliation by the president against countries that fail to remove trade barriers or that through government policies give their own firms a competitive advantage. An action may be initiated by a petition from a private party or by the president. The administration of Section 301 is the responsibility of the USTR, who has the authority to negotiate with other countries for the removal of the barriers or practices cited. If the negotiations are unsuccessful, the president may take direct action. Few Section 301 cases are filed by private parties, and most investigations are initiated by the USTR. Nearly all cases are resolved by negotiations, but the United States has occasionally imposed retaliation. For example, in 1987 President Reagan imposed duties on a set of Japanese imports in retaliation for Japan's alleged failure to implement the bilateral semiconductor agreement.

Section 731—Antidumping

Dumping involves the sale of a product at a price below that charged in other countries and is viewed as an unfair trade practice. The statutory test of whether a product has been dumped involves a comparison between its price and either the "fair value" of the product or the price at which it is sold in the exporting country. Sales at less than fair value (LTFV) can be subject to a duty equal to the difference between the fair value and the sales price.

The antidumping provisions are invoked either by a petition from a private party to the ITC or, independently, by the ITA. The ITA is responsible for determining whether goods are being dumped and, if so, how large the dumping margin is. When the agency finds that a product is being dumped, the petition is sent to the ITC, which determines whether the dumping has caused injury. The ITC must find that material injury has resulted before duties can be imposed.[2] If the ITC concludes that there was no injury, the case is dismissed. If it finds material injury the case is returned to the ITA, which has the authority to negotiate a settlement or impose duties on the imports in question. Approximately half of the antidumping cases are decided in favor of the petitioner.

Section 303—Countervailing Duties

Countervailing duties are intended to offset the effect of foreign subsidization of exporters or domestic producers. The duties counter, and the threat of their use forestalls, subsidization. The duties are viewed as providing fairness for U.S. firms. Counter-

[1] See Borrus and Goldstein (1987) for a history of the escape clause in international agreements.

[2] A tie vote results in a finding for the petitioner.

vailing duty cases are administered under the same process as antidumping cases. Findings of both subsidization and injury are required before duties can be imposed.

Section 337—Intellectual Property

Section 337 of the Trade Act of 1930 deals with violations of U.S. intellectual property rights, which include those protected by patents, copyrights, trademarks, or laws pertaining to trade secrets. The ITC has administrative responsibility for complaints, and settlements are encouraged. If no settlement is reached, the good in question can be banned from the United States. In 1990 the ITC for the first time concluded that a petitioner had violated the duty of candor and issued a public reprimand of the petitioner.[3]

Trade Adjustment Assistance

Trade Adjustment Assistance (TAA) requires presidential approval and provides direct compensation and assistance to those injured by imports. Relief has primarily taken the form of retraining workers for jobs in other industries. TAA was begun in 1962, expanded in 1964, and expanded again in the Trade Act of 1974. The expansion in 1974 both relaxed the eligibility requirements and extended the benefits, making communities and firms eligible for low-cost loans. With the expansion of international trade and the congressional extension of the assistance program, the number of cases increased from an average of 20 a year prior to the 1974 Trade Act to an average of 1,000 a year, with over 2,000 filed each of the last 2 years of the Carter administration. By 1980 the annual cost of TAA had reached $1.6 billion, and the Reagan administration reined in what it perceived to be a welfare program. Congress finds trade adjustment assistance attractive, however, and expanded eligibility in the Omnibus Trade and Competitiveness Act of 1988. Trade adjustment assistance is used sparingly, however, because of concern that it could become an entitlement to displaced workers.

[3]ITC (1990).

CASES

The WTO and the Environment

National environmental protection policies often conflict with international trade policies and agreements. Two types of concerns have been raised. One was that countries might use environmental regulations as an instrument of protectionism to exclude imports. For example, the U.S. measures to protect sea turtles could be the result of pressure from the U.S. shrimp fishing and farming industries. To avoid such situations, WTO rules prohibited discrimination against a product (shrimp) based on how it was produced. The other type of concern was that different environmental compliance costs would affect the location of economic activity. Environmentalists argued that liberalized trade would cause firms to locate in countries with lax environmental regulations or enforcement. Many companies were concerned that high compliance costs in countries with stringent environmental regulations would result in a competitive disadvantage for firms located there. A number of countries, including several in Europe, subsidized the environmental compliance costs of their firms. This subsidization was said to create an unfair competitive advantage.

The view that fair trade should cover environmental policies as well as tariff and nontariff barriers made these issues candidates for the next round of international trade negotiations. The preamble to the World Trade Organization (WTO) agreement acknowledged the importance of environmental objectives and pledged that its members would develop a program to ensure that environmental considerations were taken into account by the world trading system. Environmentalists had worked for participation rights for nongovernmental organizations (NGOs) in the WTO to give them a forum to raise environmental issues, but WTO members overwhelmingly rejected the participation of NGOs.

In the case of the U.S. law intended to protect the sea turtle from shrimp fishers, the United States had for many years required its shrimp fishers to have turtle-excluder devices (TEDs) in their nets to prevent drowning. The U.S. law banned imports of shrimp caught with nets without TEDs. Thailand had a law requiring TEDs in the trawler nets used by its fishermen, but it joined in the WTO petition against the U.S. law "as a matter of principle."

The WTO explained its reasoning in environmental protection cases: "If the U.S. arguments were accepted, then any country could ban imports of a product from another country merely because the exporting country has different environmental, health, or social policies from its own. This would create a virtually open-ended route for any country to apply trade restrictions unilaterally—and to do so not just to enforce its own laws domestically, but to impose its own standards on other countries. The door would be opened to a possible flood of protectionist abuses."[1]

The guiding WTO rule was Article XX of GATT which provided that a law had to be "relating to the conservation of an exhaustible natural resource," but it could not result in "arbitrary or unjustifiable discrimination" among countries. The WTO Appellate Body of the DSB held that sea turtles were an exhaustible natural resource but that how shrimp were caught was a means of production which was not an allowable basis for discrimination.

The shrimp-sea turtle decision provoked heated reaction among environmental interest groups. Some such as the National Wildlife Federation called for measures to protect the sea turtle. Others such as the Sierra Club saw the WTO decision as an example of the impact of international trade agreements on a broader political agenda.

The National Wildlife Federation called for the United States to lead multilateral negotiations to protect sea turtles and to refuse to change the U.S. law in spite of the WTO decision. It also urged reform of the WTO so that good-faith laws to protect the environment would not be rejected when they inhibited trade.

---

[1]The WTO made this statement in explaining an earlier case involving the rejection of a U.S. law to protect dolphins caught in nets used in tuna fishing.

The Sierra Club was more strident. It criticized the Clinton administration for failing to fulfill its 1994 promise to use the WTO's Committee on Trade and Environment to address conflicts between trade and environmental objectives. More broadly, the Sierra Club criticized the Clinton administration's unwillingness to change the WTO. It stated, "We are also disappointed by your administration's apparent unwillingness to use this opportunity to publicly acknowledge the inherent weakness in WTO rules and procedures. WTO trade rules fail to adequately consider social and environmental priorities. . . ."[2]

The Sierra Club also criticized the WTO initiative on investment:

> Under Clinton Administration trade policy, we are literally trading away our environment for corporate profits. Protections for safe food, clean air, and wildlife are under attack as 'trade barriers.' More and more polluting US factories crowd Mexico's northern border zone despite clean-up promises under NAFTA, a tragic example of how overseas investors often evade their environmental responsibilities.
>
> NOW the corporate lobbyists have dreamed up the most dangerous trade agreement yet—the Multilateral Agreement on Investment (MAI). The MAI was designed to protect corporate property rights worldwide, but it would stifle environmental protection across America and around the world unless we stop it.[3]

The use of environmental regulation as a nontariff barrier to trade could take other forms as well. Germany and other members of the European Union had complained about a Danish regulation prohibiting the sale of beer in nonrefillable containers. The European Court of Justice ruled that Denmark had the right to establish such a regulation. Environmental pressures stemming from the global warming issue focused on conserving forests, but Japan complained that potential bans on log exports from Indonesia, Malaysia, the Philippines, and the United States would constitute unfair trade. Japan imported virtually all its timber. Several countries feared that the European Union and the United States would use their environmental regulations to bar agricultural imports that have traces of pesticides that were allowed by GATT but not by EU or U.S. laws.

"'Right now, we have no machinery for making any kind of judgments about the linkages between trade and the environment,' said David Woods, head of information at GATT's headquarters in Geneva. . . Stewart J. Hudson, legislative representative for international programs at the National Wildlife Federation, acknowledged that anti-pollution and health safeguards 'offer a creative way to protect jobs,' adding that in any new GATT rule-making exercise it would be 'hard to ferret out the protectionist from the conservationist impulse.' But in spite of this, he stressed that 'the environmental concerns are no less valid.'"[4]

At the signing of the Uruguay Round accord in 1994 Vice President Gore called for the WTO to begin debate on the effects of expanded international trade. He called for the protection of natural resources in developing as well as developed countries. Chaudhry Ahmad Mukhtar, Pakistan's minister of commerce, objected, calling it "a new brand of protectionism under the guise of protection of the environment . . . in developing countries."[5]

Daniel Esty (1994), a former official of the EPA, called for the creation of a Global Environmental Organization (GEO) that would be separate from the WTO and would serve as an authoritative body to measure the costs of environmental damage. The GEO would also serve as the arbitrator of disputes arising from differences in regulations among countries. According to Esty, "With a properly defined mandate, such a body could reconcile trade and environmental disputes with the GATT, advance environmental cost internalization, facilitate international environmental agreements—including the creation of baseline environmental standards—and coordinate funding for developing-country efforts to upgrade their environmental programs." President Clinton had stopped short of proposing a formal organization to address trade and the environment but had called for an "eminent persons group" to advise governments and the WTO. ■

[2]www.sierraclub.org
[3]www.sierraclub.org

[4]*The New York Times*, February 11, 1991.
[5]*The New York Times*, April 15,1994.

PREPARATION QUESTIONS

1. What should be on the U.S. environmental agenda for the next round of trade negotiations?
2. What position should businesses take on environmental issues and international trade?
3. How should the environmental impacts of trade policy be taken into account?
4. Should NGOs be given rights to participate in WTO debates and negotiations?
5. Is a GEO likely to be established in the near future?

Cemex and Antidumping

Lorenzo Zambrano was accustomed to making tough decisions. During his 6-year tenure as chief executive officer of Cementos Mexicanos, S.A. (Cemex), he had transformed Cemex from a small Mexican cement manufacturer to an industry superpower. In the fall of 1990, however, Zambrano faced perhaps his most difficult challenge. In August the U.S. International Trade Commission ruled that Cemex had unfairly depressed cement prices in the southern and southwestern United States by dumping cement and cement clinker. As a result, a duty of 58 percent was levied on all subsequent Cemex imports into the region. The ruling threatened Cemex's expansion and its access to the lucrative U.S. markets and required a strategy to address the threat.

In early 1989 cement producers in the southern portion of the United States were concerned about the erosion of their domestic market share due to increased imports from Mexico. Imports of gray portland cement and cement clinker, two principal cement products, had been increasing steadily over the previous 5 years. At the same time the lackluster performance of the economy in the region, and in particular the depressed level of new construction, was reducing the demand for cement.

Historically, the cement industry was a very regionalized business with high overland transportation costs preventing the commodity from freely flowing between regional markets. This insulation helped cement producers ride out hard times in the highly cyclical industry. Throughout the 1980s, however, Mexican cement producers were able to transport their products across the border and still remain competitive on price, sometimes undercutting domestic producers. The majority of Mexican cement imported into the United States came from one producer, Cemex.

U.S. cement companies in the South and Southwest realized that imports from Cemex and other Mexican companies presented a threat to their profitability and perhaps to their survival. They believed that with high transportation costs, Mexican producers must be selling their cement at less than fair value, which would constitute dumping under section 731 of the Tariff Act of 1930, as amended by the Trade Agreements Act of 1979. Cement producers in Arizona, New Mexico, Texas, and Florida filed an antidumping petition claiming that Cemex and the Mexican cement industry were dumping cement and clinker in their markets.

THE MEXICAN CEMENT INDUSTRY

Portland cement was used predominantly in the production of concrete, and cement clinker was the primary component in the production of portland cement. Demand for cement was cyclical and followed the general economic climate, demographic trends, and construction expenditures. In Mexico approximately 60 percent of cement expenditures were in residential construction, 20 percent in public works, and 20 percent in commercial construction.

A principal input to cement production was oil, with energy costs accounting for 40 to 50 percent of cement production expenses. Mexican cement firms had benefited from governmental policies. Mexico's vast oil resources allowed it to implement targeted domestic industrial policies, and in 1986 the government provided its domestic producers with oil for as little as $4 a barrel, compared with a weighted-average world price ranging from $14 to $16 a barrel.[1] In 1990 oil prices were raised to world levels.

---

[1] "Cement Makers Fight, Yet Buy From, Importers," *Business Marketing,* August 1986, and "Energy Statistics Sourcebook," 1987.

The Mexican cement industry was dominated by Cemex, which by the early 1990s was the largest cement company in North America and the fourth largest in the world. By the end of 1991 its capacity had grown to 24 million tons, which was 63 percent of Mexican capacity. Cemex's primary Mexican competitor was Grupo Cementos Apasco, S.A. de C.V. (Apasco), which was 60 percent owned by Holderbank Financère Glaris Ltd. (Holderbank), a Swiss company that is the largest cement company in the world. Apasco had 17 percent of the Mexican market in 1991. The next largest competitor was Cruz Azul, which had 13 percent of the market.

Part of Cemex's rapid growth had come through acquisitions. Cemex had spent nearly $1 billion on acquisitions acquiring Cementos Anahuac, then Mexico's third largest cement producer, in 1987 and in 1989 acquiring Empresas Tolteca, Mexico's second largest producer and Cemex's chief competitor. Geographic diversification in addition to locating plants close to major markets rationalized production. Cemex also spent $950 million on new plant and environmental control equipment. This made the plants more energy efficient, raised labor productivity, and added 4.8 million tons of new capacity. Another $330 million was spent to develop international operations, including U.S. distribution facilities in Arizona, Texas, and California. Cemex subsequently acquired for $1.8 billion the two largest Spanish cement producers giving it a presence in the European Union.

In 1991 Cemex's sales were approximately $1.7 billion with exports accounting for 15 percent of the total. The combination of its plant modernization and capital expenditure programs and its management and engineering know-how had given Cemex a very low cost structure. Cemex had outstanding plant management practices and had been able to reduce plant downtime substantially, which increased its effective capacity and reduced its costs.

Cemex had high brand loyalty in Mexico. In most countries, cement was a commodity primarily purchased by industrial and commercial buyers. In Mexico, however, about 78 percent of cement sold was through retailers in bags under brand names. In 1991 Cemex's bagged cement was sold through 4,500 exclusive retail distributors. Cemex provided technical and marketing assistance to its dealers and maintained long-term relationships with them.

Cemex had several plants located close to the U.S. border. Cemex's headquarters in Monterrey was only 130 miles from Texas, and the rapid economic growth in Mexico along the U.S. border provided an attractive location for new cement plants. Since cement production involved economies of scale, large plants were desirable, leaving some capacity for exports to the United States.

THE U.S. CEMENT INDUSTRY

As in Mexico, the U.S. industry was highly cyclical, depending on the general state of the economy and the construction industry in particular. Because of high overland transportation costs 95 percent of all gray portland cement shipments were made to customers located within 300 miles of the production site.

The U.S. industry was not nearly as concentrated as the Mexican industry. The leading U.S. cement producer in 1990 was Holnam Inc., which was owned by Holderbank and had 11.8 percent of the domestic market.[2] Holnam was followed by Lafarge Corp. (6.7 percent), Southdown Inc. (6.1 percent), Lone Star Industries (5.5 percent), Ash Grove Cement Co. (4.9 percent), and numerous other companies, at least five of which each had a domestic market share of over 3 percent. By 1989, 60 percent of the U.S. cement companies were owned by foreign companies, mostly European with some Japanese ownership. For example, Lafarge was owned by Lafarge Coppée of France, which was the world's second largest cement producer.

Cement imports accounted for 22 percent of the approximately 90 million tons of annual U.S. cement consumption, and imports had somewhat higher shares in the southern tier states. The Portland Cement Association estimated that in 1986 U.S. producers bought and resold approximately two-thirds of the cement imported into the country. The rationale provided by U.S. producers was that imports were priced very low, and since cement was a commodity, they were forced to serve their customers from the lowest-cost source.

The U.S. construction industry was weak at the end of the 1980s. The growth of the U.S. cement market was 1.3 percent in 1989 and 2.9 percent in 1990, whereas the growth rates of the Mexican cement market for the same years were 3.7 percent and 7.3 percent, respectively. In the southern and southwestern United States in particular, the success of Mexican cement importers contrasted sharply with the

[2]Holman was formed by the merger of Dundee Cement and Ideal Basic.

decline of local cement firms. In 1988, Mexican imports accounted for 14 percent of the Arizona-New Mexico-Texas market and 22 percent of the Florida market. In addition, since 1983 seven domestic cement plants had closed in the Arizona-New Mexico-Texas region and two had closed in Florida.

Domestic firms believed that Mexican firms were dumping cement in the United States by selling their exports at less than fair value (LTFV). The antidumping petitioners included two unions and eight companies, which formed the Ad Hoc Committee of AZ-NM TX-FL Producers of Gray Portland Cement, which was led by Southdown, the largest U.S.-owned cement manufacturer. "Our investigation to date . . . convinces us that the Mexicans' success in U.S. markets is due to dumping and not to any other factor," stated Clarence Comer, chief executive of Houston-based Southdown and chairman of the committee.[3]

The petitioners claimed that they had been materially injured by Mexican cement producers. The petition alleged that the dumping of cement depressed prices in the United States, caused investors to abandon the industry, and threatened their markets, production, and jobs. Comer summarized the allegation: "U.S. cement producers should not have to accept declining returns, declining employment, and declining capital investment. We should not have to cede U.S. markets and U.S. jobs to unfairly priced imports from Mexico. If we lose out to fair competition from Mexico, so be it."[4] Comer surmised that additional injury to the cement industry in the southern and southwestern United States was imminent. "Mexican producers continue to build export oriented capacity aimed at American markets."[5]

The petitioners also outlined two principal reasons the U.S. cement producers were vulnerable to imports from Mexico. First, because cement was a commodity, a small price change could result in large shifts in market shares. Thus, even a small price difference would cause a large loss of volume for domestic producers if they did not meet the lower import price. Second, dumped cement imports displaced domestic production ton for ton because aggregate demand for cement was derived from the demand for construction, and cement represented a small share of construction costs. Consequently, the aggregate demand for cement did not vary appreciably with price, so the lower prices of imports did not create additional demand.[6]

A similar but unsuccessful antidumping petition had been filed in 1986 by all U.S. cement producers against Mexico, Colombia, Venezuela, France, Greece, Japan, South Korea, and Spain.[7] In that case, the International Trade Commission (ITC) determined that there was no material injury to the U.S. cement industry because it had begun its recovery from the recession. The 1989 case, however, differed from the 1986 case in three key respects: the petition was more narrowly focused; demand for cement in Arizona, New Mexico, and Texas was depressed; and Mexican imports were rising while U.S. cement prices were falling.

U.S. ANTIDUMPING LAW

The antidumping laws codified in Section 731 allow either a private party or the International Trade Administration (ITA), an arm of the Department of Commerce (DOC), to file a petition for redress. The executive branch agencies charged with the administration of trade law in dumping cases are the ITC and the ITA. The ITC conducts a preliminary investigation to determine if there is a "reasonable indication" of material injury, or the threat of such injury, to the industry. Typically, the investigation covers the previous 3 years of activity. If no indication of injury is found, the petition is dismissed.

With a positive preliminary determination from the ITC, the ITA investigates whether there is a "reasonable likelihood" that imports are being sold at LTFV and calculates a preliminary estimate of the dumping margin. If there is an affirmative finding that a reasonable likelihood exists, the importer is required to make a cash deposit or post a bond or other security to guarantee the potential dumping liability. Upon concluding its investigation, the ITA announces its final determination of whether dumping was found. A positive finding includes the final estimate of the margin of dumping. A negative finding results in the petition being dismissed.

Following an affirmative finding by the ITA, the ITC begins the industry analysis stage. Here, the ITC

[3]"U.S. Cement Companies Charge Mexican Producers With Dumping Cement in U.S. Markets," *Business Wire,* September 27, 1989.
[4]*Ibid.*
[5]*Ibid.*

[6]*Ibid.*
[7]In contrast to shipping by land, shipping by sea is low cost.

investigates whether the imports in question cause or threaten to cause injury to the domestic industry. Unless the ITC finds material injury to the industry, the case is dismissed. If the ITC finds material injury, the case returns to the ITA for the negotiation of settlements and/or the imposition of duties.

THE ITC AND ITA DETERMINATIONS

To find material injury or the threat of material injury, the ITC must first determine the "like product" and the "domestic industry." The petitioners and respondents agreed that gray portland cement and cement clinker comprised a single like product. On November 8, 1989, the ITC issued a unanimous affirmative preliminary determination in favor of the petitioners. The DOC then formally notified the Mexican cement producers that they had to submit to and fully cooperate with an administrative review if they wished to continue exporting to the United States. Questionnaires sent to Cemex requested general information on Cemex's strategy, production capacity, and number of plants. They also requested specific information on the Mexican and U.S. markets, including Cemex's costs, prices, pricing policies, market share, and customer information for the different markets.

The ITA concluded that Type II gray portland cement was the "like product" and that the bulk cement market was the relevant market for the basis of comparison. To test for dumping or the selling of a product at LTFV, the ITA considered the weighted-average price (for all the different plants from which U.S. sales were made) of the product as sold by the foreign firm to the first unrelated party in the importing country. This price was then compared with the price at which the same or a similar product was sold in the home country. Since data for the price comparisons were limited, the ITA "constructed" prices at the mill gate using an administrative provision in its procedures that subtracts transportation and other costs. The price comparison thus was of mill net prices, determined by taking the sale price and deducting all costs other than those incurred in the mill. Dumping would be found if the price at which a ton of cement left the mill to a U.S. customer was greater than the price at which a ton of cement left the gate to a Mexican customer. The dumping margin was then the average of all the margins for those comparison sales for which dumping was found. Exhibit 16-1 presents a sample calculation.

EXHIBIT 16-1 Example of the Antidumping Margin

	Matched Pair of Sales In	
	Mexico	***United States***
Price	$85	$80
Transportation to terminal	10	30
Customs	0	2
Terminal and distribution	11	7
Other expenses	12	10
Mill Net Price	$52	$31
Dumping margin = 100(52–31)/31 = 68%		

The ITA set the dumping margin for Cemex at 58.38 percent and for Apasco, Cementos Hidalgo, and all others at 53.26 percent, 3.69 percent, and 58.05 percent, respectively. Thus, if the ITC were to find injury, Cemex would be assessed a duty of 58 percent of the dollar value of each ton of cement leaving the mill for the U.S. market.

To determine whether there was "material injury" or the "threat of material injury" from imports of Mexican cement, the ITC assessed the effects of Mexican cement imports on U.S. prices, production, capacity, capacity utilization, shipments, inventories, employment, wages, financial performance, capital investments, and research and development expenditures. The data showed that from 1986 to 1989 the total quantity of cement shipped by U.S. producers had increased by 4.7 percent but declining prices caused the total value to decrease by 3.7 percent. Capacity for cement and clinker production changed little, and capacity utilization decreased slightly. Additionally, the employment, wages, and hours of production and related workers fell by 19 percent, 13.8 percent, and 14 percent, respectively. Productivity rose by 23 percent. The financial performance of southern tier producers deteriorated, as gross profit fell by 18.1 percent and operating income dropped by 36.7 percent. Some firms had curtailed planned investment. The data also indicated that the volume of Mexican imports had increased 24 percent.

Consequently, in August 1990 the ITC issued an affirmative final determination in favor of the petitioners. To continue importing cement and clinker after August 30, 1990, Mexican importers were required to tender cash deposits to the U.S. Customs Service equal to the estimated dumping margins. For Cemex and Apasco, those margins were 58 percent and 53 percent of their mill net prices, respectively. The antidumping order had a 10-year sunset provision, so the duties would remain in effect until the year 2000 unless the dumping were to cease. As a result of the duties, all the Mexican producers except Cemex left the U.S. market.

CEMEX'S STRATEGY

From the beginning of the process, Cemex complied fully with requests for data. Cemex also opened its operations to the DOC as much as possible to expedite the administrative process and to demonstrate that the company was confident that it would prevail.

Cemex assigned the dumping issue top priority and created a new department with full support to oversee the implementation of a multipronged strategy to address the issue. First, a U.S. law firm specializing in dumping cases was hired to provide advice. Second, Cemex sought to use the media in Mexico to build support and call the attention of the Mexican people to the alleged "unfair" treatment. Cemex also sought coverage from the U.S. media, including *The Wall Street Journal,* to educate the American people about Cemex and its overall strategy and performance both in Mexico and in the United States. Third, a presentation was made to the Mexican Commerce Department to demonstrate the importance of the petition and the effect it would have on Cemex and Mexico. The goal was to obtain the Mexican government's support against the U.S. action. The Mexican government, however, was concerned about possibly jeopardizing the ongoing North American Free Trade Agreement (NAFTA) negotiations and decided not to pressure the U.S. DOC.

The opportunity for lobbying in Washington was limited because the issue was in the jurisdiction of regulatory rather than legislative institutions. As a result, little lobbying was done, although certain political leaders (including senators and governors in states where Cemex had operations) were contacted to explain the antidumping petition and Cemex's position.

Cemex believed that in reaching their conclusion that dumping had occurred the U.S. agencies had ignored Cemex's actual price and shipping costs. For example, Cemex sold its cement in the United States at market prices, but nearly a third of that went to the cost of transporting the cement from its plants south of the border. Zambrano noted that the ITC deducted the transportation costs and thus concluded there was dumping, since cement was then selling in Mexico for a higher price.[8]

Cemex argued that the antidumping petition was nothing more than an attempt by its competitors to halt its expansion in the United States. "Some of our competitors thought we were a rather weak neighbor," stated Zambrano. "And it just so happens that we grew, and they didn't like it."[9]

The ITC ruling had potentially devastating ramifications for Cemex's expansion drive into the U.S. market, and Zambrano implemented an integrated strategy, combining both market and nonmarket components. The market component consisted of a revamped short-term business strategy to reduce the duty assessed. The nonmarket component focused on reducing the duty and reversing the ruling. It was designed to seek redress through three institutional arenas: administrative, judicial, and international.

CEMEX'S MARKET STRATEGY[10]

First, Zambrano decided to reduce Cemex's exports to the United States. In late 1990 he foresaw a reduction for the year of 30 percent. Additionally, Cemex's home market had become much more attractive, since Mexico had initiated a number of public works projects that caused demand for cement to grow by about 10 percent.

Second, the 58 percent duty made shipments unprofitable in states where cement prices were low, so Zambrano decided to withdraw completely from some U.S. states and focus only on those with higher prices. Cemex abandoned Florida outright after the ITC ruling and was content with breaking even in the higher-priced markets. Selling only in regions with high prices had the advantage of reducing the difference between U.S. and Mexican mill net prices, which would result in a lower dumping margin at the next annual review.

Third, Cemex decided to maintain a substantial Type II (bulk) cement market in Mexico so that the ITA would compare the product sold in the U.S. market with the Mexican Type II (bulk) cement market. Cemex wanted to avoid the ITA concluding that the like product was its branded bagged cement

[8]"Cement Wars," *Forbes,* October 1, 1990.
[9]Ibid.
[10]Ibid.

in Mexico, which would substantially increase the dumping margin.

CEMEX'S NONMARKET STRATEGY

As part of its nonmarket strategy Cemex requested administrative reviews of the duty, and in the first review the petitioners alleged that Cemex had created a fictitious bulk market in its home country to reduce or eliminate the duties. The ITA found that no fictitious market had been created, and as a result of Cemex's new market strategy of limiting exports to regions with high prices, the duty was reduced to 30.74 percent.

Zambrano also attempted to have the ITC's ruling reversed in the judicial arena. Cemex appealed the ITC determination of material injury to the U.S. Court of International Trade (CIT), arguing that the ITC had not followed proper procedures. The CIT rejected Cemex's argument, and Cemex appealed, using the same argument, to the U.S. Court of Appeals, but was also unsuccessful. Cemex appealed to the CIT the duties imposed by the ITA, arguing that the ITA had followed neither statutory requirements nor precedents in determining the dumping margin. The CIT, however, ruled that the overall weight of precedent was in favor of the approach used in the Cemex case. The CIT upheld the dumping duty.

After the failures in the U.S. judicial arenas, the Mexican government petitioned the General Agreement on Tariffs and Trade (GATT) requesting that a panel be established to review the antidumping dispute. In July 1992 the GATT panel found that the United States had improperly imposed duties on the Mexican cement industry and recommended that $30 million in duties already collected be returned. The order to refund duties was rarely made by GATT, so the decision was considered severe. The panel did not address whether the Mexican companies had sold at less than fair value. Rather, the panel concluded that the U.S. Department of Commerce had not verified that the ad hoc committee of petitioners that brought the action was sufficiently representative of the industry. The committee represented only 61.7 percent of all U.S. cement producers in the region, but under GATT antidumping rules, the petitioner in a regional dispute must represent all or almost all of the production in the region.

Since all GATT member nations had to adopt the panel's recommendation for it to take effect, any single member could effectively block action. Concluding that the basis for the GATT panel's determination was contrary to U.S. law, the United States withheld its approval and the duties and findings imposed under U.S. trade law remained in effect.

Frustrated by the U.S. rejection of the GATT panel's decision, Cemex faced four immediate problems. First, the antidumping duty remained in effect on Cemex's remaining exports to the United States, and the U.S. producers were sure to continue to argue at every administrative review that the bulk cement market in Mexico was fictitious and that bagged rather than bulk cement was the relevant like product. This posed the threat of an even higher duty. Second, Cemex had some stranded assets in terminal and distribution facilities in the United States. Third, the reduction in exports to the United States left Cemex with excess capacity in Mexico. Fortunately, domestic demand for cement had grown. Fourth, Cemex had to decide what to do about the U.S. market.

U.S. demand continued to exceed domestic capacity creating a demand for imports. Cemex could import cement from Spain, but this left the risk of another antidumping petition. Cemex could also directly invest in the United States by building new plants. This would meet some of the shortfall in domestic supply and reduce the need for imports. Cemex could also attempt to purchase existing capacity from a U.S. producer. This would be advantageous if Cemex were confident that it could operate the plants more efficiently than the seller. Purchasing capacity would not reduce the demand for imports, leaving export opportunities if the antidumping problem could somehow be resolved. ■

This case was written by Justin Adams under the supervision of Professor David P. Baron. It draws upon two previous case studies, "Cemex and Mexican Cement Imports," by Darryl E. Walsh, and "Cemex vs. U.S. Sunbelt Competitors," by Juan Prestarno, as well as "Gray Portland Cement and Cement Clinker from Mexico," Determination of the ITC in Investigation No. 731–TA-461 (Preliminary) and (Final).

PREPARATION QUESTIONS

1. Why might the price of cement be higher in Mexico than in the United States?
2. Is the dumping of cement likely to be harmful to the U.S. economy?
3. What was the motivation of the U.S. producers in filing the antidumping petition? Is this protectionism?
4. Evaluate Cemex's strategy for addressing the antidumping ruling. How well were its market and nonmarket components integrated?
5. After the U.S. withheld its approval of the GATT decision, what should Cemex do about the four problems?

The Kodak-Fujifilm Trade Dispute

The Eastman Kodak Company (Kodak) and Fuji Photo Film Co. (Fujifilm) are the dominant companies in their domestic markets and the worldwide leaders in film and photographic paper. Each had approximately 70 percent of its home market, and outside Japan and the United States Kodak had 36 percent of the market, and Fujifilm had 33 percent. Kodak had long been the worldwide market leader, but in the past few decades Fujifilm had achieved major gains in market share as Kodak struggled to overcome a series of strategic mistakes outside its core lines of business. Fujifilm's dominance of the Japanese market provided it with a profit base for its expansion in the Asian, U.S., and European markets. Digital imaging technology represented a major opportunity, but it also posed a substantial threat to the core businesses of both companies.[1]

Fujifilm and Kodak had been intense rivals for nearly 50 years, but the rivalry took a different direction in May 1995 as Kodak filed a Section 301 petition under U.S. trade law, supported by a 252-page report, charging that Japanese market practices, aided by government policies, prevented Kodak from capturing more than 7 to 10 percent of the Japanese market.[2] Kodak charged that the principal impediment was Fujifilm's exclusive distribution arrangements with the four principal wholesalers for color film and photographic paper and that the Japanese antitrust authority, the Japan Fair Trade Commission (JFTC), was tolerating pervasive anticompetitive practices. Kodak claimed that Fujifilm controlled the four primary wholesalers that in turn controlled 70 percent of the color film market, resulting in Kodak film being available in only 15 percent of the retail outlets in Japan.[3]

In a 588-page rebuttal, Fujifilm denied both allegations and asserted that both companies had a home country advantage that had given them dominant positions in their home markets.[4] Fujifilm argued that Kodak's market share in Japan was due to consumer preferences and a series of strategic mistakes by Kodak regarding distribution and the introduction of new products. It also charged that Kodak dominated the U.S. market as a result of practices that were more egregious than those alleged to be used by Fujifilm in Japan. The conflict between the two companies turned acrimonious as George Fisher, CEO of Kodak, vowed to press on with the Section 301 petition, and Fujifilm President Minoru Ohinishi called Kodak's allegations a violation of business ethics and said that Kodak "shamelessly made false allegations" against Fujifilm.[5]

Section 301 petitions typically led to negotiations between the countries involved, but the Minister of International Trade and Industry (MITI) vowed that Japan would not cooperate with the

[1] Digital technology was expected to have at least three effects. First, while it would generate new sales, it would also cannibalize the sales of traditional film and photographic paper. Second, it would accelerate the rate of technological progress in the photographic supplies industry. Third, the development of new technology required substantial funds.

[2] Dewey Ballantine for Eastman Kodak Company, "Privatizing Protection: Japanese Market Barriers in Consumer Photographic Film and Consumer Photographic Paper," Memorandum in Support of a Petition Filed Pursuant to Section 301 of the Trade Act of 1974, As Amended, Rochester, NY and Washington, D.C., May 1995. (Referred to as Kodak, hereafter.)

[3] Those retail outlets accounted for approximately 30 percent of film sales in Japan.

[4] Fujifilm, "Rewriting History: Kodak's Revisionist Account of the Japanese Consumer Photographic Market," Tokyo and New York, July 31, 1995. (Referred to as Fujifilm, hereafter.)

[5] This case does not attempt to assess the merits of the arguments of Kodak and Fujifilm.

U.S. investigation of the allegations made by Kodak. In a news conference in Tokyo in July, Kodak's Ira Wolf said "to expect a long, drawn-out series of government-level negotiations between Japan and the United States. . . ."[6] He added, "We understand the risks inherent in going ahead with a 301 case, especially given the feelings of the average Japanese consumer about 301. But we decided there was no alternative. . . . The Office of the Trade and Investment Ombudsman [Japan] is too weak and Geneva-based World Trade Organization does not cover competition policy."[7]

THE FUJI PHOTO FILM CO., LTD.

In 1994 Fujifilm had sales of ¥1.067 trillion and net income of ¥63.771 billion. Sales peaked in 1992 at ¥1.142 trillion, and profits peaked at ¥94.778 billion in 1991. In response to its weaker economic performance and the appreciation of the yen, Fujifilm had embarked on a strategy of "localizing production." For example, in 1995 in Greenwood, South Carolina, where it had videotape and presensitized plate manufacturing facilities, Fujifilm opened a plant to produce one-time use cameras. Kodak had filed an antidumping petition against Japanese producers of color photographic paper, and in 1994 Fujifilm and Konica agreed to raise their prices for imports into the United States. Fujifilm then decided to build a color photographic paper plant in South Carolina, which was scheduled to open in 1997.

THE EASTMAN KODAK COMPANY

The Eastman Kodak Company was a global producer of consumer, professional, and business imaging products. Kodak had been besieged by bad investments and burdened by high costs and had been criticized for not having done enough to counter the growth of Fujifilm from a modest domestic company to a powerful, worldwide competitor. In response to sluggish economic performance, in 1993 Kodak's board of directors fired the CEO and recruited George Fisher, chairman of Motorola, to be CEO. Mr. Fisher's aggressive management style contrasted with Kodak's customary style and pace. He embarked on a restructuring program that included cost reduction programs, head count reductions, and the sale of its clinical diagnostics business, home products division, and pharmaceuticals business. As a result of the restructuring and new leadership, Kodak hoped that its troubles were behind it and that it was prepared to strengthen its leadership in the imaging industry.

Fisher focused Kodak on a single line of business—imaging—and began to invest heavily in digital imaging capability. He also assessed Kodak's worldwide position in all the markets in which it operated. The market that stood out was Japan. Kodak had a high share of the professional market and in sensitized plates, X-ray film, and movie film, but its share of the consumer film market stood at 8 percent with its share of the photographic paper market only slightly higher.

Fisher decided to adopt a new strategy for the Japanese market. That strategy had four components. The first was to achieve and maintain product leadership through innovation, including the more rapid introduction of new products. Kodak also planned to advertise heavily in its role as official sponsor of the winter Olympics to be held in Nagano. The second was to leverage its brand name by, for example, supplying co-branded film. The third was to build a more effective organization in Japan. For example, Kodak opened a new distribution facility that significantly improved efficiency. Kodak also hired as its director of Japan relations Ira Wolf, who had headed the USTR's Japan office and had negotiated frequently with Japan. Kodak also appointed a Japanese president of Kodak (Japan). The fourth component was to obtain greater access to the market. Fisher hired the Washington office of the law firm Dewey Ballantine to conduct a study of the Japanese market.

THE JAPANESE MARKET

The Japanese film and photographic paper market was the third largest in the world with sales of $9 billion, close behind the markets in the United States and Europe. In film Fujifilm's only domestic competitor was Konica, and its only other major competitors were Kodak and Agfa.

During the past decade three major developments had affected the Japanese film market. In 1986 Fujifilm introduced the first one-time use camera, and Kodak followed with its own one-time use camera 2 years later. By 1992 one-time use cameras had captured 16 percent of the Japanese film market. In

[6] *Daily Yomiuri,* July 27, 1995.
[7] *Kyodo News Service,* July 26, 1995.

1989 Fujifilm introduced a new high-resolution ISO 400 film, and 2 years later Kodak introduced its own high-resolution ISO 400 film. The market share of ISO 400 film climbed from less than 10 percent in 1989 to 47.5 percent in 1994, with the market share of ISO 100 film falling from 90 percent to 47.5 percent. Kodak's sales were largely unaffected by the introduction of the new film, as the shift was primarily Fujifilm customers switching from ISO 100 to the higher-priced ISO 400 film. Finally, the expansion of retail store chains, supermarket chains, and discount houses had increased their share of film sales to 30 percent, whereas the share held by small camera stores, photo shops, and kiosks had decreased to 50 percent. Kodak had a 25 percent share of the discount house and retail chain segment of the market in the major cities but only a very small share of the market served by small retailers.

LIBERALIZATION COUNTERMEASURES

Direct investment in many industries was prohibited after World War II, but when Japan joined the OECD in 1964 it was required to eliminate its restrictions on foreign investment. The photographic supplies industry was one of the last to be liberalized, and Fujifilm was able to capture most of the growth in the market during this period. The 1964 GATT Kennedy Round agreement required reductions in tariffs, but it was not until 1971 that the tariffs on color film and color paper were reduced to 26 percent. The 1979 Tokyo Round of GATT negotiations required countries to reduce nontariff barriers to trade in addition to tariffs.[8] According to Kodak, the tariffs and slow liberalization were one component of a set of "liberalization countermeasures" instituted by the Ministry of International Trade and Industry (MITI). Makoto Yokota, deputy director of MITI's chemical products division, explained, "We were afraid that Kodak would use its own capital structure to control the market with huge incentives like low prices, or attach some kind of gift to the films, and then, after ruling the market, they would raise the price. There was this worry, so we issued guidelines so that the competition would be fair."[9]

KODAK IN JAPAN

Kodak entered the Japanese market in 1889 and, operating through the Japanese distribution system, developed a substantial business. After World War II the Japanese government restricted the entry of foreign firms by limiting direct investment and by imposing tariffs and quotas on imports. In 1960 Kodak was told by the Japanese government that it would be required to import through a single importer, forcing Kodak to stop supplying wholesalers directly. Kodak chose the trading company Nagase & Co.

Kodak was frequently criticized for its reliance on Nagase. Abegglen and Stalk commented, "Nor does [Kodak] have control over its sales in Japan. It continues to sell through an agent, maintaining a liaison office with no direct sales force or sales management, and only indirect influence on pricing and promotion."[10] According to Huddleston, "One simply has to control the distribution to control one's destiny. This was Kodak's problem."[11]

In 1984 Kodak revised its strategy for the Japanese market, sending American managers to run its business in Japan. It formed a joint venture in Japan to take over Nagase's Kodak division, and Kodak's shares were listed on the Tokyo stock exchange.[12] Because Japanese consumers preferred a sharper image to the softer image preferred by American consumers, Kodak reformulated its film for the Japanese market, introducing its Ektar 100 film for that market. Kodak also developed and introduced other new products for the Japanese market and advertised heavily in Japan, including sponsoring athletic events. Kodak took its campaign to the skies where its blimp, carrying the figure of a carp, which is a symbol of strength, dueled with Fuji's blimp.

Kodak imported all its consumer film and photographic paper in Japan. Because of economies of scale in film production and low transportation costs, it was efficient to manufacture in a relatively small number of locations. A modern machine that pro-

---

[8]In 1995 Japan had no tariffs on imported film, whereas the U.S. tariff on imported color film was 3.7 percent. In 1995 Japan was the only industrialized country without a tariff on color film and photographic paper.

[9]*The New York Times,* July 5, 1995.

[10]Abegglen, James C. and George Stalk, *Kaisha, The Japanese Corporation* (New York: Basic Books, 1985), p. 240.

[11]Huddleston, Jackson N., *Gaijan Kaisha: Running a Foreign Business in Japan* (Armonk, NY: M.E. Sharpe, 1990), p. 218.

[12]The acquisition of Nagase is discussed in Albert Sieg, *The Tokyo Chronicles* (Essex Junction, VT: Oliver Wight Publications), pp. 101–108.

duces both film and photographic paper was nearly 1,000 feet long and 100 feet high.

Kodak invested $750 million in Japan and built its own distribution system with over 3,000 employees by 1992; yet its market share remained under 10 percent. Kodak believed that its sales were limited by the tight control Fuji held over the distribution system for film and photographic paper. It had thought that aggressive advertising, a strengthened sales organization, and price discounting would penetrate the Japanese market. By the 1990s, however, it was clear that its efforts were bearing little fruit.

THE DISTRIBUTION SYSTEM

The Japanese retail and wholesale sectors differed substantially from those of most other developed economies. Japan had substantially more retail establishments per capita, and to service them the Japanese distribution system had more layers than found in other developed countries. For many products, the distribution system included primary wholesalers that sold to secondary wholesalers that in some cases sold to tertiary wholesalers, which then supplied the retailers. Manufacturers maintained close, long-term relationships with distributors, including making equity investments in them. Their relationships were said to result in implicit agreements to maintain prices. Ito referred to this pricing practice as *tatene,* or suggested pricing,[13]

> which means that the manufacturer sets the price at each level of wholesale and at retail .... Retailers go along with this rigid pricing structure in part because of a carrot and in part because of a stick. The carrot is that manufacturers agree to buy back all unsold inventory at the price retailers bought it for and pay rebates based on the volume sold. They also pick up promotional expenses, provide employees and accept IOUs from retailers. The stick is that retailers who object to this system find themselves subject to boycotts.[14]

THE DISTRIBUTION SYSTEM FOR PHOTOGRAPHIC FILM AND PAPER

Kodak maintained that the photographic film distribution system in Japan was dominated by four primary wholesalers—Asanuma, Misuzu, Kashimura, and Ohmiya. In the immediate postwar period they carried competing products such as Konica and Kodak film. Fujifilm, however, formed exclusive distribution arrangements under which the four wholesalers became "special contract agents" or *tokuyakuten.* Asanuma carried Fujifilm and Nikon products, and Fujifilm accounted for between 40 percent and 80 percent of the revenues of the other three. Fujifilm owned 17.8 percent of Misuzu and 15 percent of Kashimura. The *tokuyakuten* supplied Fuji film directly to large retail customers and to 300 secondary wholesalers which in turn supplied 280,000 retail outlets. Figure 16-5 illustrates the structure of the distribution system.

Kodak argued that the distribution system was an "essential facility" for reaching the market segment consisting of the 280,000 smaller photo shops, kiosks, and retail outlets. In addition to the exclusive arrangements with the four primary wholesalers, control was said to be exercised through formal means including rebates used throughout the tiers of the distribution system, shareholdings of some wholesalers, and the holding by Fujifilm of security deposits made by wholesalers. Control was also said to be exercised through long-term relationships among Fujifilm, wholesalers, and retailers, as well as through their dependence on Fujifilm for most of their revenue. For fear of upsetting Fujifilm, wholesalers and retailers were said to be reluctant to discount prices of Fuji film or to sell Kodak film at significant discount from the price of Fuji film. Kodak alleged that the *tokuyakuten* maintained tight control over many retailers by threatening to cut them off from supplies if they did not comply with a wholesaler's directive. In addition, associations of retailers and wholesalers participated in the enforcement of fair trade codes, which Kodak maintained discouraged non-price promotions as well as price discounting.

Kodak argued that the *tokuyakuten* were controlled through a rebate system constructed to promote the sale of Fuji film and discourage the sale of competitors' film. In addition to the rebates, the profit of the *tokuyakuten* depended on the price Fuji charged for film. According to Kodak, the price and the rebates were set so that the *tokuyakuten* were

[13] Ito, Takatoshi, *The Japanese Economy* (Cambridge, Mass.: MIT Press), 1992. *Tatene* is defined as "a price to be used as a standard in sales transaction," *Iwanami Japanese Dictionary,* vol. 4, p. 609.

[14] "Adam Smith in Tokyo," *Financial World,* 4 January 1994, p. 22. Quoted in Kodak, *op cit.,* p. 49.

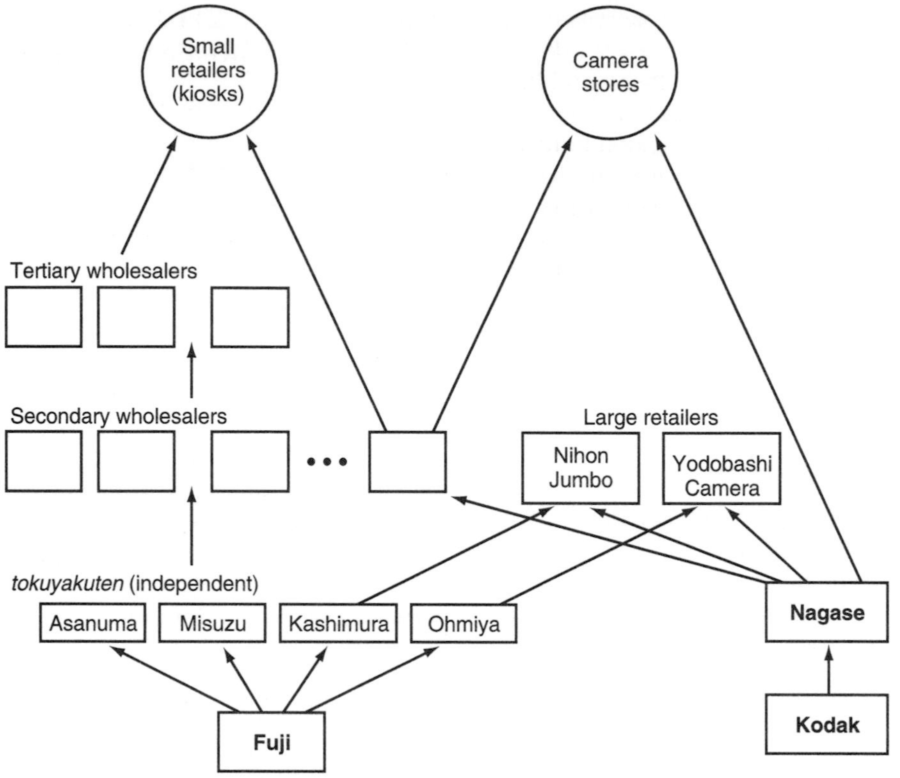

FIGURE 16-5 The Japanese Film Distribution System

only marginally profitable and hence dependent on year-end rebates.

Fujifilm called Kodak's assertions about its rebates "a fantasy" and stated that it did not rely on rebates. In 1991 Fujifilm revised its rebate system for the *tokuyakuten* and the progressivity was less than 0.6 percent. Fujifilm also provided rebates to retailers, but after 1990 it offered retailers rebates only to increase their sales of higher valued products, and these rebates were not progressive. The primary wholesalers also provided rebates to retailers and secondary wholesalers. The Nihon Jumbo company, an independent processor operating through 40,000 outlets, reported that Fujifilm had replaced its retail rebates with supplementary payments to share promotional expenses.

Small retailers were important in Japan, and Kodak had had difficulty selling to them. Fujifilm argued that the small retailers (e.g., kiosks) only had space to display one brand, and since consumers preferred Fuji film, the small retailers chose that brand. Carrying one brand also reduced the administrative costs of the small retailers. Kiosks accounted for approximately 10 percent of film sales in Japan.

Albert Sieg, president of Eastman Kodak (Japan), characterized the significance of the kiosks:[15]

> In fact, these tiny outlets are often replenished a number of times throughout the day by small trucks or motorbikes that deliver "just-in-time inventory": a small number of magazines, packs of cigarettes, pieces of candy, and say ten rolls of film. Fuji film, that is, and that was the rub for us, especially the kiosks . . . we spoke with many kiosk people who informed us that they had no objection to selling Kodak film but that they could sell only what the "guy on the motorcycle brings us. We don't want to upset that system in any way."

Walter Stork, president of Agfa-Gevaert Japan, commented on the difficulty of competing with a distribution system organized in this manner: "When

[15]Sieg, *op cit.*, pp. 156–157.

you have one film maker that is so strong it has 70 percent of the market, the consumer tends to identify film with that brand. Getting consumers to think of another brand when buying film requires tremendous investment in advertising. However, consumer recognition is only part of the battle. Unless retailers are willing to stock the film so that consumers can buy it, expensive advertising is wasted. . . . As soon as competitors found our products on the shelves, they would come and move it to the corner."[16] In 1993 Agfa revised its strategy and began supplying private-label film to Daiei, Japan's largest retail chain; Lawson, an affiliated convenience chain; Shashimya-san 45; and Yodobashi Camera, a discount chain. Agfa's market share increase from 1 percent to 5 percent in 1994, but its share withered thereafter. In February 1995 Kodak began supplying at a 30 to 40 percent discount a private-label brand "CO-OP" to the Japanese Consumer Cooperative, which had 2,500 retail stores. The introduction of private-label film contributed to an estimated 10 to 15 percent retail price decline during 1994 and early 1995. Later in 1995 Kodak introduced co-branded film, which carried both the Kodak name and the retailer's name. The market for private-label and co-branded film was believed to be quite limited, however.

In addition to the vertical arrangements in the distribution system, Kodak argued that the wholesalers and retailers were organized horizontally through associations that served to limit competition. Fujifilm, Konica, and two producers of photographic paper constituted the *Kanzai Kogyokai* (Photo Sensitized Materials Manufacturing Association), which exchanged trade data. The retailers affiliated with Fujifilm and Konica constituted the *Zenren* (All Japan Federation of Photo Dealers), which Kodak maintained served to discourage price competition.[17] Kodak reported that "In 1995, when Kodak began selling film under private label with the Cooperative Stores the Zenren decided that 'we will ask them to consider our position.' "[18] The 19 principal wholesalers, including the *tokuyakuten,* constituted the *Shashoren,* and the *Zenraboren* was composed of the color finishing laboratories, including discounters and Kodak-affiliated laboratories. In 1982 these associations and the Camera Manufacturers Association joined to form the *Kosei Torihiki Suishin Kyogikai* (Fair Trade Promotion Council) to promulgate fair competition codes for industry members as a means of limiting certain types of promotional activities. These codes had been approved by the JFTC under the authority of the Premiums Law.

ANTITRUST ISSUES

Japan's Anti-Monopoly Law (AML) was enforced by the JFTC, an Extra Ministerial Agency attached to the office of the prime minister. In practice, it is an independent commission.[19] Japanese antitrust law was in many ways similar to that in the United States, but it was more oriented toward enabling fair competition that was not destructive or excessive. Consequently, Japanese antitrust enforcement tended to focus on establishing guidelines for the practices of industry members. This could involve approving policies promulgated by industry members and delegating to the industry their enforcement, as in the case of the Fair Trade Promotion Council. The JFTC had rule-making authority to approve retail price maintenance cartels and to define unfair business practices. It also had quasi-judicial powers to enforce the AML through consent agreements and civil and criminal penalties.

The JFTC emphasized stopping illegal practices rather than punishing those involved as a means of deterrence. This led to relatively few formal cases.[20] When it found practices inconsistent with the AML, it typically asked the parties involved to cease the practices. Because of its dominant market position, the JFTC had classified Fujifilm as an "influential company" and monitored the film market for anticompetitive practices. Fujifilm had a code of practices intended to ensure that it did not violate the AML.[21]

Private parties with a permanent establishment in Japan could file antitrust suits under the AML, but such suits were rare for several reasons. First, no private party had ever won an antitrust suit. Second, for a private antitrust suit to be successful, the JFTC

[16] *Finanical Times,* June 1, 1995.

[17] Fujifilm reported that *Zenren* has only 7,000 members of the 280,000 film retailers. Fujifilm, *op cit.,* Appendix, p. 23, rejected the assertion that *Zenren* was a force for horizontal price stabilization.

[18] Kodak, *op cit.,* p. 45. See also Fujifilm, *op cit.,* Appendix, p. 25.

[19] See Iyori, Hiroshi, and Akinori Uesuji, *The Antimonopoly Law in Japan* (New York: Federal Legal Publications), 1983.

[20] Until 1991 there had been only one criminal prosecution under the AML.

[21] Fujifilm, Legal Department, "Antimonopoly Law Don'ts," July 1992, Fuijfilm, *op cit.,* Exhibit 15.

must find that there had been a probable violation of the AML before the suit can proceed. Third, the filing fee for antitrust laws was one percent of the claimed damages, which discouraged suits. Fourth, discovery was limited in the Japanese legal system, making it difficult for plaintiffs to substantiate charges. Fifth, the Japanese legal system did not provide for class action suits.

As a result of the Structural Impediments Initiative trade negotiations, the Japanese government agreed to adopt several new measures to strengthen its antitrust policies and enforcement activities. One such measure was the promulgation by the JFTC in 1991 of Antimonopoly Act Guidelines Concerning Distribution Systems and Business Practices. The guidelines for the distribution system pertained to "resale price maintenance, vertical non-price restraints, providing rebates and allowances, interference in distributors' management, and abuse of dominant bargaining position by retailers."[22] The guidelines prohibited manufacturers and distributors from threatening to cut off the supply of products if distributors or retailers, for example, dealt in imported products. The guidelines also prohibited a manufacturer or wholesalers from refusing to supply products to a distributor that discounted prices and from joining with manufacturers or other distributors to refuse to supply products to new entrants. As a result of his analysis of the 1991 guidelines, Richards concluded, however, that "the nature of the Japanese legal system and the Japanese marketplace will prevent the new measures from making significant changes in the Japanese marketplace. Furthermore, it is highly questionable whether stricter antitrust enforcement measures, in general, will do anything to significantly change the Japanese marketplace."[23]

The JFTC had the authority to set Fair Competition Codes as drafted by Fair Trade Councils and enforced by the JFTC and Prefecture Governors and monitored by the industry.[24] These codes were authorized under Article 10 of the Law Against Unjustifiable Premiums and Misleading Representations (Premiums Law). The Premiums Law governed the use of promotional contributions and misrepresentations (e.g., misleading practices). Retailers and wholesalers were involved in enforcing the codes, such as those of the Fair Trade Promotion Council. Kodak argued that the Premium Law allowed wholesalers and retailers to limit both price and non-price competition.

Kodak concluded that the JFTC was part of the problem. "The JFTC was itself actively engaged in, and had extended its legal authority to, a systematic campaign to stamp out a broad range of innocuous discount and promotional activity. In effect, the JFTC itself had become part of the problem."[25]

THE TRADE COMPLAINT

The Dewey Ballantine study of the Japanese market was headed by Alan W. Wolff, a former deputy USTR who was one of the nation's leading trade lawyers.[26] The completion of the study coincided with tense negotiations between Japan and the United States on access to the Japanese automobile and parts markets. In May 1995 President Clinton had announced 100 percent punitive tariffs on Japanese luxury car imports, and many observers believed that the threat of punitive measures was credible.

Later that month Kodak filed its petition pursuant to Section 301 of the Trade Act of 1974. The petition alleged that "The Government of Japan has also engaged in 'unreasonable' tolerance of systematic anticompetitive practices which restrict the sale of U.S. consumer film and paper in Japan. The Fuji distribution system and its associated conduct are inconsistent with at least Articles 3, 8(1), and 19 of the AML [Anti-Monopoly Law]. The Japanese government tolerated the anticompetitive practices systematically by not vigorously enforcing the AML, by aggressively supporting the so-called industry 'Fair Competition Codes,'. . ."[27] Kodak concluded that "Japanese market barriers in [color film and photographic paper] have cost Kodak an estimated $5.6 billion in foregone export sales since the mid-1970s, have enabled Fuji to amass a cash surplus of $10 billion in its home market sanctuary, have fostered dumping in the U.S. market, and are fundamentally altering the global competitive balance between the two companies."[28] The Section 301 petition was a key

[22]Richards, Jonathon D. 1993. "Japan Fair Trade Commission Guidelines Concerning Distribution System and Business Practices: An Illustration of Why Antitrust Law is a Weak Solution to U.S. Trade Problems with Japan," *Wisconsin Law Review,* 921–960; p. 942.
[23]Richards, *op cit.,* p. 947.
[24]The Fair Competition Code on Camera Related Products apparently did not specifically cover film, but in practice it appeared to do so.

[25]Kodak, *op cit.*, p. 135.
[26]Mr. Wolff is the subject of an article "Wolff at the Door," by Ben Wildavsky, *Natinal Journal,* August 5, 1995, pp. 1994–1997.
[27]Kodak, *op cit.*, p. 19–20.
[28]Kodak, *op cit.*, p. i.

element of the market access component of Kodak's Japan strategy, but Kodak also hoped to pry open the distribution system by inducing secondary wholesalers and perhaps one of the *tokuyakuten* to carry its products.[29]

In filing a Section 301 petition, Kodak chose a relatively political channel for market opening, but it believed that without a formal petition its complaints would not receive attention. In conjunction with the release of the Dewey Ballantine study and the filing of the Section 301 petition, Kodak and Dewey Ballantine conducted a high-profile public relations and lobbying campaign designed to build public and political support for its action. Fisher and Wolff held press conferences and lobbied in Washington. In a major coup for Kodak, *The New York Times* in an editorial entitled "Tokyo's Trade Hypocrisy" stated, "The upshot is that Kodak's sales are limited despite the high quality and competitive prices of its products. Japanese officials blatantly violated bilateral commerce accords, international trade accords and Japan's own antitrust laws to keep Fuji atop the market."[30] Kodak also lobbied in Congress, and Fisher obtained a letter of support from Senate Majority Leader Robert Dole.[31] Fisher explained, "I've never lost to a good Japanese company in my life. . . . When you are sitting down with less than 10% market share and in the rest of the world you're sitting around 40% or higher, something is funny some place."[32]

Kodak's nonmarket strategy was presaged by the nonmarket strategies of Motorola and the Semiconductor Industry Association (SIA). In 1983 when he represented the SIA, Alan Wolff pioneered the strategy of preparing a detailed industry study in support of a Section 301 petition. While at Motorola George Fisher had been involved in trade disputes with Japan, as Motorola sought to unlock the Japanese markets for its pagers, semiconductors, and cellular telephone equipment using the power of the U.S. government. Fisher was the head of Motorola's pager division and was able to enlist the aid of the U.S. government in opening the Japanese market to Motorola pagers, and he was later involved in the cellular telephone dispute.[33]

Motorola's strategy had two objectives. One was to obtain access to the potentially lucrative Japanese market. The other was to make certain that its Japanese competitors did not have a protected sanctuary from which they could generate profits to fund their worldwide competition and expansion. Motorola Chairman Robert W. Galvin referred to this as the "Principle of Sanctuary."[34]

> You cannot allow any competitor to have sanctuary in his or her native market and be allowed to roam in your market in a way that would both cultivate customers and undermine your strengths. Simply put, you must find your way effectively into his native sanctuary. . . . We simply knew we could not leave Japanese competitors the isolation in Japan, while they prospected in our home market.

Mr. Fisher said, "While Fuji competes with Kodak on a global basis, it makes virtually all of its profits in Japan, using those proceeds to finance low-price sales outside Japan."[35] He also said, "The Japan market, a large percentage, maybe 70%, is closed to us. And as a result, Fuji is allowed to have a profit sanctuary and amass a great deal of money, which they use to buy market share in Europe and in the United States."[36]

Mr. Fisher added, "All we are seeking is the opportunity to compete in an open market. We want resolution, not retaliation. Nor do we want market share targets. We want an end to illegal market barriers. . . . Kodak sells world class products. If given the chance, we believe that our products can compete successfully in any market. We have not had that chance in Japan."[37] Alan Wolff explained, "This is not a spat between the companies. There is illegal activity taking place—it is not an industry-to-industry matter but a U.S. government concern over whether the government of Japan is behaving properly, reasonably."[38]

---

[29]For example, in 1995 Oriental, one of the producers and distributors of color photograhpic paper, began to distribute Kodak paper.

[30]*The New York Times,* June 1, 1995. The editorial also stated, "To be fair, the Fuji has not had the opporturnity to respond fully to charges. But Kodak's case will be tough to refute." Bill Barringer, counsel to Fujifilm, was astounded by the *Times* editorial. "It's incredible to me that *The Times* did that. Any lawyer can put together a petition that makes their case look good. How can you write an editorial like that before getting the facts from the other side?" (*National Journal,* August 5, 1995, p. 1995.)

[31]As Wolff characterized the perspective in the *National Law Journal* in 1987, "In a large trade case, the interaction of legislative activity, litigation and public policy-making in the executive branch can provide the solution. It's absolutely necessary to lobby."

[32]*The Wall Street Journal,* May 19, 1995.

[33]See Baron (1996), pp. 492-493, 505-575 for a discussion of the cellular telephone dispute.

[34]Robert W. Galvin. "International Business and the Changing Nature of Global Competition,"Miami University, Oxford, OH, October 1992.

[35]*International Trade Reporter,* BNA Inc., June 7, 1995.

[36]*Moneyline,* August 2, 1995.

[37]Eastman Kodak Company press release, July 27, 1995.

[38]*The Christian Science Monitor,* August 2, 1995.

FUJIFILM'S RESPONSE

Immediately upon Kodak's filing of the Section 301 petition, Fujifilm responded by sending to the media and to the South Carolina congressional delegation a 16-page letter rejecting Kodak's allegations. Fujifilm hired the U.S. law firm Wilkie Farr & Gallagher to prepare a rebuttal and hired Edelman Communications to handle the public relations associated with the response. Its 588-page rebuttal to Kodak's claims was issued on July 31, 1995.

Fujifilm was infuriated by Kodak's filing and its timing. President Minouri Ohnishi characterized Kodak's actions as:[39]

> Kodak has violated all the standards of business ethics. It has shamelessly made false allegations against Fujifilm in a self-serving attempt to use political pressure to accomplish what its own lack of managerial effort and failed marketing strategies have not been able to accomplish. What is most troubling about Kodak's action is not that it attempts to tarnish Fujifilm with false allegations of anticompetitive practices, but that it attempts to exploit growing tensions between the U.S. and Japan on trade issues to the detriment of a crucial bilateral relationship.... Kodak's management, however, seems to view the bilateral tensions as an opportunity for Kodak to gain through the political process what it has been unable to gain through the competitive process.

Fujifilm argued that the Section 301 petition was without merit and that such petitions must be addressed to present and not past practices; "any alleged violations [of treaties] ended some 20 years ago."[40] Moreover, Fujifilm argued that Kodak should exhaust domestic remedies in Japan before resorting to a Section 301 petition. Fujifilm stated that Kodak,

1. has never complained to the Japan Fair Trade Commission (JFTC) about Fujifilm's alleged anticompetitive practices;
2. has never taken its case to the Office of Trade and Investments, an ombudsman system created to mediate market opening disputes; and
3. has made no attempt to introduce the issue onto the agenda of the U.S.-Japanese bilateral negotiations under the Framework Agreement.

Kodak maintained that the four *tokuyakuten* were an "essential facility" for penetrating the Japanese color film market. Bill Barringer, senior partner of Wilkie Farr & Gallagher, stated that there were three primary ways Kodak could increase its market share in Japan—by competing on price, through innovation, and with massive advertising. Barringer said that Kodak failed on all three accounts.

- Price—With the exception of a brief period in the early 1980s, Kodak has maintained a relatively small discount off of Fujifilm's prices. It has never seriously attempted to gain market share by pricing aggressively relative to Fujifilm, and Kodak executives have been quoted as saying that they have no intention of doing so in the future.
- Innovation— Fujifilm has consistently beaten Kodak to market with new and popular products. When Fujifilm introduced the first one-time use camera and high-resolution ISO 400 film in Japan, it took Kodak more than 2 years to introduce similar products. These products account for almost two-thirds of the total color film market in Japan.
- Advertising—In relative terms, Kodak has not spent enough on advertising in Japan, a prerequisite for improving brand awareness and capturing additional market share. Kodak makes much of the fact that it spent 5.3 billion yen on advertising between 1986 and 1988. However, over the same period Konica spent 8 times this amount on advertising, and Fujifilm spent 10 times this amount.

Kodak countered that it had been an innovator in the Japanese market, introducing "Ektar 1000 film, the Weekend 35 single-use camera, and the Panorama single-use camera-all tailored for Japanese consumers. Recently, Kodak's Snap Kids EX has won favorable reviews from the Japanese press."[41] Kodak also said that when it had sharply discounted prices, many of the retailers refused to pass along the discounts to consumers for fear of upsetting Fujifilm. Kodak provided

[39]Fuji Photo Film Co. press release, Toyko, July 31, 1995.

[40]Wilkie Farr & Gallagher, "Comments of Fujifilm Regarding Legal Issues," filed in conjunction with USTR Docket No. 301-99, August 8, 1995, p. 2.

[41]Eastman Kodak, "Kodak Answers: Counter Points to Fuji's Assertions Regarding Kodak's Market Access Case," Rochester, NY, July 24, 1995.

data indicating that it had lowered its wholesale price of ISO 400 film by over 50 percent since 1986, but retailers continued to price its film in the same proportion to the price of Fuji film during that period.

FUJIFILM'S ALLEGATIONS ABOUT THE U.S. MARKET

In its rebuttal Fujifilm argued that Kodak's practices and dominance of the U.S. market were worse than Kodak's allegations about the Japanese market and Fujifilm's practices. The U.S. market differed in several ways from the Japanese market. First, retail chains, such as Wal-Mart, K-Mart, Eckerd Drugs, Walgreens, and Rite Aide, accounted for a large share of film sales, whereas in Japan chains accounted for only a third of sales. Second, the chains bargained with and sought bids from film suppliers for exclusive supply of photographic paper and for placement of film in checkout lanes and other high-traffic areas. Third, manufacturers supplied the chains and other retailers directly without going through wholesalers.

Decades earlier Kodak's anticompetitive practices had resulted in two antitrust consent decrees, but those decrees were lifted by the courts in 1994. The standard used in the United States in cases alleging horizontal market power was whether a restriction in output would result in higher prices. In judging this issue, the courts looked to the availability of substitutes, including imports, that could offset any reduction in output. Antitrust authorities also looked to the relevant market. In lifting the two consent decrees, the court agreed with Kodak that the relevant market was worldwide and that given Kodak's 40 percent market share, it did not have the market power to restrict output and force prices higher. The court concluded that imports and private-label film would rush in to offset any restriction of output by Kodak.

Fujifilm maintained that if this standard were applied to Japan a court would conclude that it did not exercise market power in Japan. Kodak contended, however, that imports and private-label film could not reach most of the retail outlets because Fujifilm had locked up the distribution system, which was the only means of reaching those outlets.

Fujifilm stated that Kodak had exclusive arrangements for color film with several major retail chains including Eckerd Drugs, Caldor, Publix Supermarkets, Bradlees, K-Mart, the Army and Air Force Exchange Service, and several major theme parks. Kodak's exclusive contracts with retailers were alleged to have been won through bids providing lump-sum, up-front payments. Kodak was reported to have paid K-Mart $25 million up front to win all its photofinishing.[42] Competitors such as Fujifilm, with smaller market shares, argued that they could not match such payments. In 1996, however, Fujifilm outbid Kodak for a 10-year exclusive contract with Wal-Mart for the supply of photographic paper.

George Fisher responded to Fujifilm's allegations stating, "For Fuji or the Japanese government to claim that what Kodak faces in Japan is the 'Mirror image' of what Fuji faces in the United States is absurd. What Fuji is trying to do is take the focus off the facts."[43] ■

[42]Fujifilm, *op cit.*, p. 253.
[43]*The Wall Street Journal,* July 31 1995.

This case was prepared by Professor David P. Baron from public sources, including materials supplied by the Eastman Kodak Company and Fuji Photo Film Co. (Ltd.). This case focuses on consumer film and not on photographic paper.

PREPARATION QUESTIONS

1. Why is the Japanese market so important to Kodak? Does Fujifilm have a profit sanctuary? Where is it?
2. Assess Kodak's market strategy in Japan prior to George Fisher becoming CEO. What were the causes of Kodak's problems in the Japanese market?
3. Evaluate Kodak's market and nonmarket alternatives for penetrating the Japanese market.
4. How well integrated were Kodak's market and nonmarket strategies? What other steps, if any, should Fisher take? In its discussions with the USTR, what specific concessions should Kodak press for?
5. Assess Fujifilm's strategy in response to the petition.
6. Was Kodak acting responsibly in filing a Section 301 petition?

PART IV

Integrative Case

Toys 'Я' Us and Globalization

Charles Lazarus began his career working in his father's used bicycle shop. He subsequently started selling children's furniture out of the shop, and when customers kept asking if he carried toys, he added some toys in addition to the children's furniture. He soon recognized, however, that he was not getting any repeat business. "Furniture lasts forever," Lazarus pointed out. "But toys," he continued with a laugh, "toys are great because they have built-in obsolescence. Kids break them."[1]

Lazarus was intrigued by the success of self-service supermarkets and conceived the idea of selling toys in a similar manner. He opened his first Toys 'Я' Us store in 1957 using shopping carts, a large selection, and low prices. Because toy sales were highly seasonal, he advertised to build a year-round demand. To raise funds for expansion, in 1966 he sold the company to Interstate Stores, a retailing conglomerate, for $7.5 million. Lazarus retained operating control, and when Interstate went bankrupt, the court made him the president. After selling off the other Interstate assets, in 1978 he renamed the company Toys 'Я' Us and launched a rapid expansion program. Toy industry analysts had estimated that over the next 10 years industry-wide sales of toys by specialty retailers would increase to $2.4 billion. Over that period, the sales of Toys 'Я' Us alone increased by over ten-fold reaching $4 billion in (fiscal) 1989, including clothing sales at Kids 'Я' Us stores. Profits were $268 million. Because of his vision and the company's tremendous success, Lazarus was widely viewed as a retailing genius.

The Toys 'Я' Us market strategy was built on three principles: price, selection, and stock. The original idea was to sell at discount prices in stores with supermarket-style service and limited sales staff. It soon became clear that consumers wanted one-stop shopping, leading to larger stores, more varieties of items, and a broad range of goods including items such as disposable diapers. Toys 'Я' Us then began to stock an average of 18,000 items in its stores. The key, of course, as Lazarus explained, was "to pick the right toy at the right time—the toys that sell. We're very much like the fashion industry. Customer tastes are very fickle, and you have to move quickly when they change. Otherwise, you'll be out of business. It's that simple."[2] The third principle was to have the goods on hand, so Toys 'Я' Us operated a sophisticated inventory tracking and supply system designed to avoid stock outs. The company used electronic point-of-purchase sales terminals in each store, which are linked to its central computers in its headquarters.

To supplement these principles, Toys 'Я' Us relied on advertising to get consumers to purchase toys

[1] *Solutions,* March/April, 1988.

[2] *Solutions,* March/April, 1988.

year-round, which both increased demand and reduced seasonality. It also maintained a money-back guarantee policy under which a customer could return any item for any reason. In the United States, the location of stores was crucial. Toys 'Я' Us preferred locations with ample and adjacent parking, so that customers could go out the door of the store and directly to their cars.[3] Toys 'Я' Us also sought to keep its stores open 7 days a week, 365 days a year, where local ordinances permitted it. Toys 'Я' Us owned all its stores so as to maintain standardization and control.

GLOBALIZATION

By 1984 Toys 'Я' Us operated 169 stores in over 40 states and had revenue of $1.3 billion and profits of $92 million. Although it operated only within the United States, it had developed a worldwide supply system, purchasing toys from around the world. East Asia represented the largest source of supply.

The company's initial international steps were cautious. It opened its first store outside the United States in Canada and then opened a store in England. Lazarus explained that "the Canadians seemed to be much like ourselves, and [our approach] seemed to work pretty well. And we went to England." Toys 'Я' Us continued to expand in Canada and the United Kingdom.

Its other early international steps were serendipitous. Toys 'Я' Us had been approached by Jopie Ong, director of Singapore's Metro retail group, which wanted a franchise to open a store in Singapore. The Toys 'Я' Us policy was not to use franchisees, and hence it rejected the request. Ong persisted, however, and was eventually able to persuade the company to form a joint venture. Toys 'Я' Us–Metro opened its first Singapore store in 1984.

Its entry into Hong Kong was also serendipitous. Joseph Baczko, president of the Toys 'Я' Us international division, had met Victor Fung when they were both at Harvard. When Fung became chairman of Li & Fung Ltd., a Hong Kong trading company, the two companies were natural partners. The Toys 'Я' Us–Li & Fung joint venture was formed and opened a store in Hong Kong in 1985. The success of its stores in Singapore and Hong Kong led Toys 'Я' Us to develop a globalization strategy. Lazarus explained that the company was "interglobal." "Our registers in Hong Kong take eight currencies. . . .They just punch in what kind of currency you're giving them. It's a really international kind of thing. You have to see it to believe it." The company also preferred to hire locals as store and country managers.

Toys 'Я' Us viewed opportunity in a country as stemming from a large population and high income. Those factors "combined with the lack of any dominant toy retail competition in Europe and Asia, afford Toys 'Я' Us with an ideal climate for aggressive international expansion. . . ."[4] As Lazarus put it, "We can go anywhere there are supermarkets and kids because we are, after all, a supermarket for kids."[5]

Each country posed different hurdles, however. Some were market based and others were nonmarket. For example, in Japan less than 5 percent of the $5 billion toy market was accounted for by imported toys. Domestic toy manufacturers had a lock on the distribution system that supplied the thousands of small toy stores that accounted for virtually all the toy sales in the country. Retail stores in Japan were generally small, in part because of laws that made it difficult to obtain approval for large stores of the scale that Toys 'Я' Us operated. In Europe, Toys 'Я' Us faced the prospect of having to buy from national distribution systems, which limited its ability to realize scale economies in its supply system. In Germany, Toys 'Я' Us faced opposition from toy manufacturers, restrictions on store opening hours, and labor representation issues. A number of Asian countries had restrictions on foreign investment that made it difficult to open stores. Taiwan had tariffs as high as 55 percent on some items. Furthermore, although Taiwan had a large toy manufacturing sector, the factories were located in duty-free zones and produced for export. If those toys were sold in Taiwan, import duties and a value-added tax were added, typically making the toys more expensive in Taiwan than in other countries.

Assignment

This case focuses on integrated market and nonmarket strategies in the context of the political

[3]This is the same principle used by supermarkets.

[4]Toys 'Я' Us, "Annual report," 1991, p. 7.
[5]*Soultions,* March/April 1988.

economy of international trade policy and of Japan and the European Community. The case is to be used in conjunction with the Chapter 13 case *Toys 'Я' Us in Japan (A)* and the Chapter 14 cases *Toys 'Я' Us in Germany* and *Toys 'Я' Us in Sweden.* The focus is its strategy to expand globally in light of the challenges it faced. ■

PREPARATION QUESTIONS

1. What is the Toys 'Я' Us market strategy?
2. In what kinds of national markets are its opportunities the most attractive? Which companies are its natural competitors? Are any of them global?
3. What nonmarket forces potentially impede the success of its market strategy?
4. What overall market and nonmarket strategies should Toys 'Я' Us develop and how should those components be integrated?
5. What specific strategy should it adopt to gain entry to the Japanese market?
6. What specific strategy should it adopt to enter the German market successfully?
7. What should it do about the situation in Sweden?

PART V

Ethics and Responsibility

CHAPTER 17

Corporate Social Responsibility

Introduction

Through their market activities firms contribute to social well-being by serving consumer demands, providing jobs, innovating, and paying taxes that fund public programs. Through their nonmarket activities firms act to shape their nonmarket environment by, for example, supporting free trade and socially efficient approaches to environmental protection and product and employee safety. Firms also give representation to stakeholders who might not otherwise be represented in public processes. Although some market and nonmarket activities may at times raise concerns, business remains the principal engine for improving social well-being.

Many firms go beyond what is required by their market and nonmarket environments and attempt to serve directly the needs of their stakeholders or, more broadly, of society. For these firms, successful performance involves not only compliance with the law and public policies but also requires fulfilling broader responsibilities. Firms make charitable contributions, provide direct assistance to community organizations, support schools, provide employee and community education programs, establish programs to aid the disadvantaged, and take measures beyond those required by law to protect the environment and the safety of employees and customers. Firms vary considerably in the scope of these activities, however. That scope depends on their conceptions of the role of business in society and of corporate social responsibility.[1]

Social responsibility is neither necessary nor sufficient for successful financial performance. Many people argue that selling cigarettes is socially irresponsible, yet cigarette manufacturers have been highly profitable and have used their profits to acquire a number of well-known firms. Conversely, in its approach to the cause of social responsibility Control Data experimented with a variety of innovative, but costly, social projects that largely failed and contributed to a major restructuring of the firm.[2]

---

[1]Perspectives on the social responsibility issue are provided by, among others, Carroll (1981), Engle (1979), Goodpaster (1983), Haas (1981), Jones (1980), Keim and Meiners (1978), Post (1978), and Preston and Post (1975).

[2]Control Data's founder and long-time chairman and CEO William C. Norris proclaimed the company's mission as "addressing society's major unmet needs as profitable business opportunities." During the 1970s and early 1980s, Control Data undertook projects that included a computerized educational system called Plato; the Wheels Program, which provided low-cost auto financing for ex-convicts; countertrade with Eastern European countries; research on a technology for growing vegetables in water in greenhouses; assistance to small farmers to improve their efficiency; a windmill farm in Hawaii; and instruction in Ojibwa to Chippewa Indians. Control Data also instituted a no-layoff policy for full-time employees, which it was forced to violate because of its deteriorating performance.

Furthermore, there is no systematic empirical analysis on the relationship between dimensions of performance, such as competitiveness and profitability, and actions taken in the cause of social responsibility. Even if there were an empirical correlation, the direction of causality would have to be established. That is, does socially responsible behavior lead to superior performance or does superior performance allow a firm the luxury of taking socially responsible actions?[3]

The previous chapters provide a basis for addressing issues in the market and nonmarket environments, but the focus was primarily on the nonmarket challenges that various interests directed at firms. Social responsibility focuses less on pressures from interests and more on normative principles that identify duties based on conceptions of well-being, rights, and justice. This chapter examines the role of business in society and considers several conceptions of the responsibilities of business. The content of social responsibility is developed in the following chapters in terms of ethical systems and their application in management, and Chapter 20 addresses the implementation of concepts of corporate responsibility.

This chapter distinguishes between socially responsible policies and policies that simply represent sound business practice. Attention to customer preferences is sound business practice and requires no justification other than the remuneration it provides. Similarly, creating a culture that builds mutual commitment between the firm and its employees requires no justification beyond the benefits it provides. In contrast, responding to a community need for low-income housing is beyond the normal scope of sound business practice. The strategic use of corporate social responsibility to increase profits thus should be distinguished from morally motivated actions.

The motives for taking an action are also important for distinguishing between socially responsible actions and actions that are forced on the firm by its environment. Negotiating with an interest group to minimize the damage it could impose should be distinguished from an action taken voluntarily by a firm. The following example poses the question of which actions are socially responsible and which are responses to nonmarket pressure.

EXAMPLE: TUNA AND DOLPHINS

Environmental and animal rights groups protested the use of purse seine nets to catch yellowfin tuna in the Eastern Pacific fishery. In the Eastern Pacific, tuna swim underneath dolphins, and fishing boats cast their nets around the dolphins knowing that the tuna will be caught. Environmental groups estimated that more than 100,000 dolphins a year were being caught in the nets and drowned. August Felando, president of the American Tuna Boat Association in San Diego, however, argued that the 30-vessel U.S. fleet accounted for the deaths of only 12,643 dolphins in 1989, compared with the U.S. limit of 20,500 established by the Marine Mammal Protection Act of 1972. He added that the number had been decreasing because U.S. fishermen had become skilled in freeing the dolphins from the nets. All U.S. tuna boats carried U.S. observers to monitor fishing practices. The United States also attempted to enforce its regulations on foreign boats, with 30 percent of foreign tuna boats, mostly from Latin America, also carrying U.S. observers.

---

[3]Ulmann (1985) and McGuire, Sundgren, and Schneeweis (1988) review the research on the relationship between economic performance and corporate social responsibility. The research is generally inconclusive. McGuire, Sundgren, and Schneeweis suggest that "It may be more fruitful to consider financial performance as a variable causing social responsibility than the reverse."

On April 12, 1990, H.J. Heinz President Arthur O'Reilly announced that its Starkist Seafood Company would only purchase "dolphin-safe" tuna and would no longer use tuna caught in purse seine nets.[4] StarKist planned to market its tuna under a "dolphin-safe" label. Heinz and other tuna companies had been under pressure for some time. The "save the dolphins" project had been working to convince tuna companies to change their practices and had led a national boycott of yellowfin tuna products. The Humane Society, Greenpeace, the Earth Island Institute (EII), and the Dolphin Coalition were also pressuring the tuna companies. The key event in the boycott campaign was a videotape taken by a biologist who had signed on as a crew member on a tuna boat. The videotape showed dolphins drowning in purse seine nets. The videotape was broadcast by the national television networks, and suddenly the public became involved in the issue. EII, which had helped organize the boycott of Starkist, took out newspaper advertisements calling on Heinz to stop the "dolphin massacre." Some consumers responded, school children boycotted tuna, and the boycott even found its way into movies such as *Lethal Weapon 2.* Politicians also became interested in the issue, introducing legislation to require "dolphin unsafe" labels on cans containing tuna caught with purse seine nets. O'Reilly said that his children had asked him to stop killing dolphins.

In 1988 Hobee's restaurants, a popular and growing chain, switched from yellowfin to Tongol tuna, which is not caught in a manner that contributes to dolphin deaths. In early 1990 the ten Hobee's restaurants in the San Francisco Bay area began a boycott of all tuna products. Hobee's replaced many of its tuna items with chicken, placed pamphlets on each table explaining its policy, and provided training to its servers so that they could provide more information on the subject if asked. Hobee's also began a boycott of all Heinz products, substituting other brands for such staples as Heinz ketchup.[5] The boycott sent a signal to Heinz.

Is Hobee's or Heinz, or both, acting in a socially responsible manner? This question will be addressed later in the chapter, after the role of business in society and alternative conceptions of social responsibility have been considered.

The Role of Business in Society

THE EFFICIENCY PERSPECTIVE

The classical view of the role of business in society is based on the economic principle that the efficient use of scarce resources is essential to human well-being and that the free enterprise system is the best means of achieving that well-being. Particularly in a period of rapid technological progress, innovation, and the globalization of markets, efficiency and competitiveness are necessary for improvements in the social well-being—or even its maintenance. The best means of achieving economic efficiency is through the incentives provided by the institution of private property, as implemented through the corporate form, with markets as the institution for organizing economic

---

[4]O'Reilly's announcement is included in the film "Where Have All the Dolphins Gone?" produced by the Marine Mammal Fund and the American Society for the Prevention of Cruelty to Animals and narrated by George C. Scott and Charles Coburn. Shortly thereafter, Bumble Bee Seafoods and Van Camp Seafood Company, producer of Chicken of the Sea brand tuna, announced that they would do likewise. Bumble Bee was owned by Unicord of Thailand, and Van Camp was owned by the Mam Trust of Indonesia.

[5]Hobee's lifted its ban on other Heinz products after the April 12 announcement, but it continued its boycott of StarKist tuna, awaiting the implementation of Heinz' program.

activity. The failure of the economies of the former Soviet Union and Eastern Europe and the increased reliance on markets rather than government allocation of resources demonstrate that private enterprise and the reliance on markets are the keys to economic growth and well-being. The extensive privatization of government-owned corporations in both developed and developing countries reflects this conclusion.

As Adam Smith (1776) concluded, the surest way to achieve well-being is to place esources in the hands of individuals and allow them to compete in markets in response to consumer demand. Not only are markets the best means of directing scarce resources to society's needs, but they are also a source of protection for consumers who can turn to other suppliers if they become dissatisfied with a product or service. Markets also allow decentralized decisions and encourage innovation. Smith concluded that it was better to rely on the profit incentives that private ownership provides than to rely on goodwill:

> It is not from the benevolence of the butcher, the brewer, or the baker, that we expect our dinner, but from their regard to their own self-interest. We address ourselves, not to their humanity but to their self-love, and never talk to them of their own necessities but of their advantages.

The corporate form is important to efficiency because share ownership and the limited liability of owners provide a means by which ownership and management can be separated. This allows a person working in one field to provide capital for enterprises in other fields. The capital market then coordinates the allocation of capital resources between investors and business opportunities. Management then acts as an agent of the owners—the providers of capital—and serves their interests by maximizing the value of the resources they provide. When markets are competitive, value maximization by firms results in economic efficiency and maximizes aggregate well-being.

From this perspective, the role of business in society is to generate well-being through economic efficiency. Private ownership, the corporate form, and markets are the principal institutions for organizing economic activity. The maximization of market value—or long-term profit maximization—is the objective that provides the strongest incentives, and competition directs those incentives toward efficiency.

CONCERNS ABOUT THE EFFICIENCY PERSPECTIVE

The efficiency perspective leaves unresolved a number of issues about the role of business in society. First, market imperfections as considered in Part III can cause a divergence between private and social costs and warrant a role for government institutions such as regulation and antitrust. Institutions such as incentive-based regulation and the liability system are intended to address these inefficiencies and direct economic activity toward efficiency.

Second, the reliance on private ownership and markets as the means of generating well-being is justified by the moral philosophy of utilitarianism. Other conceptions of morality, such as those based on rights and justice, are also important. They may call for limitations on private property and ownership, the restructuring of incentives, and government intervention for purposes other than the correction of market imperfections. For example, principles of distributive justice may warrant the redistribution of wealth and income to those who are less advantaged, and fundamental rights may require that the fair equality of opportunity be provided in society.

Third, just as markets can be imperfect, so too can government. Government may be ineffective in satisfying needs and assuring rights, and thus some critics of the efficiency perspective argue that business has an affirmative duty to address needs unfulfilled by government.

MARKET CAPITALISM AND MANAGERIAL CAPITALISM

The corporate form involves a separation of management from ownership. Although this separation is essential for the efficient allocation of capital, it also gives managers a degree of discretion to pursue interests as they define them rather than those of owners.[6] The separation of ownership from management and the resulting realm of managerial discretion means that Adam Smith's market capitalism—the reliance on markets to direct the allocation of resources—coexists with managerial capitalism—the reliance on managers for the allocation of resources.[7]

The market for the control of firms provides one means of aligning the interests of managers with those of owners. Managers who do not serve the interests of shareholders can be replaced, either directly by the board of directors or through a takeover or proxy contest. Some corporations, however, are protected from the market for control by anti-takeover charter provisions and poison pills. The alignment of the interests of managers with those of owners then must come from the incentives provided by managerial compensation systems such as bonuses and stock options.

In principle, managerial capitalism could be more efficient than market capitalism. It allows the accumulation of resources through retained earnings and their allocation within the firm without having to incur the transactions costs of continually raising funds in the capital markets. It may also have advantages if management has information whose value would be dissipated if disclosed in the context of raising capital. Managerial capitalism, however, can result in inefficiency when the incentives of management are not structured properly. For example, some firms cross-subsidize losses in one line of business with profits from another line of business. The more open are domestic and international markets, the stronger is competition, and the less restricted is the market for control, the more imperative are efficiency and competitiveness, leaving less discretion to managers.

THE SOCIAL RESPONSIBILITY PERSPECTIVE

The social responsibility perspective focuses on roles for business identified by concerns that extend beyond economic efficiency. Those roles may stem from societal needs not otherwise adequately addressed or from the consequences of market imperfections such as externalities. They may also stem from concerns that government is either unable or unwilling to address. For example, some companies have voluntarily instituted programs to reduce carbon dioxide emissions in response to global warming. Social responsibility thus arises from the needs and legitimate concerns of individuals. From this perspective, business must evaluate those needs and concerns to determine the extent of its responsibilities.

Business leaders advocate corporate social responsibility for a variety of reasons. Some argue that there are societal objectives that can only be achieved through direct corporate action. Business, for example, may be more efficient than government or educational institutions at training workers for certain jobs. Other business leaders call both for restraint on the pursuit of efficiency and profits and for self-regulation in the hope that it will forestall additional government intervention and regulation. These calls are viewed by some as a necessary response to pressures arising in the nonmarket environment, which if ignored could lead to more serious threats to the free enterprise system. Some calls for corporate social responsibility are directed to the public with the

---

[6]Berle and Means (1932) first called attention to the issue of the separation of ownership and control and to its implications. Fama and Jensen (1983) provide a contractual perspective on the issue.
[7]See Chandler (1977) and Chandler and Tedlow (1985).

intent of increasing public support for business. Some who call for corporate social responsibility believe that unless business uses the rhetoric of social responsibility, more onerous intervention by government will result. That intervention could not only harm their interests but would also impair efficiency, competitiveness, and the well-being of society.

Conceptions of the Social Responsibility of Business

THE LAW

Any conception of the social responsibility of business must include compliance with just laws. Both civil and criminal law apply to firms and their managers. Criminal prosecution can occur under the antitrust laws, securities and exchange laws (as with insider trading), certain environmental laws, the Racketeer Influenced and Corrupt Organizations (RICO) Act, and many others. Individual managers and corporations are also subject to fines and can be liable for damages under both statutory and common law. These laws proscribe actions that legislatures and/or the courts have held to be socially unacceptable.[8] Actions not explicitly proscribed by law also may be socially unacceptable based on moral principles.

In addition to proscribing actions, the law assigns certain duties to firms and managers. For example, the Americans with Disabilities Act considered in Chapter 21 assigns an extensive set of duties to firms to provide for the disabled in the workplace. Such duties are not necessarily the limits of social responsibility. As considered later in this chapter and in subsequent chapters, duties also arise from moral considerations. The law thus is an essential guide for responsible management, but reliance solely on the law may not be sufficient.

The nature and extent of corporate social responsibilities is considered next, using the perspectives of Milton Friedman and the Business Roundtable. Friedman may be thought of as an advocate of market capitalism, whereas the Business Roundtable reflects the perspective of managerial capitalism.

CORPORATE SOCIAL RESPONSIBILITY AS PROFIT MAXIMIZATION

Friedman (1970) argues that the responsibility of business is "to conduct the business in accordance with [owners'] desires, which generally will be to make as much money as possible while conforming to the basic rules of society, both those embodied in law and those embodied in ethical custom." The objective of a corporation thus is the maximization of its profits, or market value, subject to the constraints represented by the rules of society. Friedman concludes that those who argue that a "corporate executive has a 'social responsibility' . . . must mean that he is to act in some way that is not in the interest of his employers"; that is, the shareholders.

He argues further that corporate executives who serve some social purpose act as civil servants imposing taxes and making expenditures. They act as if "political mechanisms, not market mechanisms, are the appropriate way to determine the allocation of scarce resources to alternative uses." According to Friedman, that amounts to socialism rather than capitalism. Furthermore, calls for a broader social responsibility may, in Friedman's view, actually promote that which corporations seek to avoid. That is, by

---

[8]See Foote (1984) for an analysis of the implications of several changes in the law.

calling for the adoption of objectives other than profit maximization, managers are advocating the use of the political process to direct the allocation of corporate resources. It is these calls for social responsibility that Friedman believes will weaken the free enterprise system and the well-being that flows from it.

From Friedman's perspective, a corporation is a voluntary association of individuals who have joined together for a mutual purpose. That purpose may be the generation of profits in which they will share or the achievement of some social or nonprofit objective. In the case of a for-profit corporation, shareholders have a property right to its assets and to the return on its assets. As indicated in Figure 17-1, as owners shareholders are principals and have the right to the surplus earned by the corporation. The corporation is managed by agents—the managers—who are to operate it in the best interests of the principals. In a complete capital market, shareholders will be unanimous in preferring that the firm be operated to maximize its market value. If one shareholder prefers to donate all his returns to charity and another prefers to spend all her returns on consumption, both will prefer that the firm be operated to make those returns as great as possible. If management does not maximize the value of the firm, the market for control will replace that management—if shareholders have not already done so.

From this perspective, the corporation engages in voluntary transactions with both providers of resources and customers. As Figure 17-1 indicates, labor and resource markets intermediate between resource providers and the corporation, and product and services markets intermediate between customers and the corporation. If markets are competitive, value maximization by the firm will be consistent with economic efficiency and the greatest aggregate well-being for society.

According to Friedman, then, the responsibility of managers acting as agents of their employers, the owners of the firm, is to increase market value by engaging in open and free competition. In that competition, firms are to engage in voluntary exchanges with others, while abiding by the law and ethical custom.

The Role of Government

In a fundamental sense, it is impossible to have a conception of the responsibilities of business without having a conception of the responsibilities of government. In Friedman's view, government is to impose taxes and determine expenditures, and the judiciary is to mediate disputes and interpret the law. The government may also equate social and private costs. For example, when there are market imperfections, private costs may diverge from social costs. At a conceptual level, private and social costs can be

FIGURE 17-1 Friedman's Conception of a Corporation

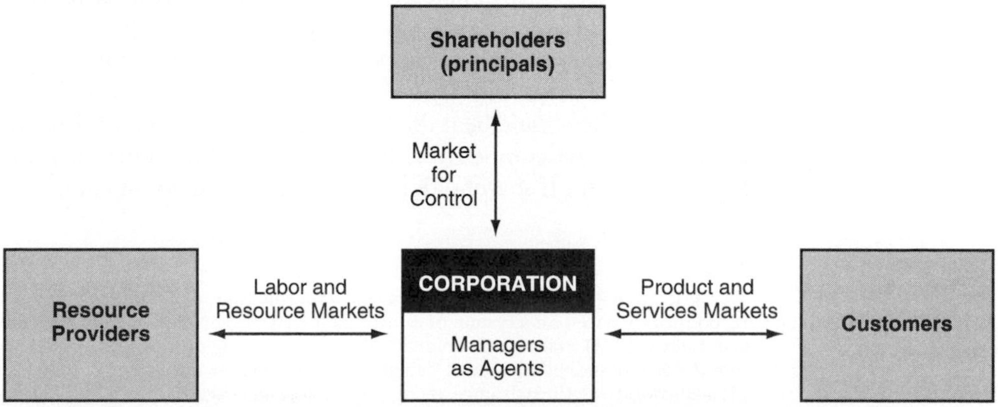

aligned through the assignment of rights coupled with private bargaining, as in the Coase theorem considered in Chapter 11. Also, the government may equate private and social costs through market-like mechanisms such as emissions charges or tradable allowances for pollution control, as considered in Chapter 12. These functions are reserved for government and its coercive powers, which are limited by a system of checks and balances, individual rights, and the popular election of representatives. According to Friedman, a call for corporate social responsibility "amounts to an assertion that those who favor the taxes and expenditures in question have failed to persuade a majority of their fellow citizens to be of like mind and that they are seeking to attain by undemocratic procedures what they cannot attain by democratic procedures." Friedman, however, does not indicate whether and to what extent firms should participate in political processes to influence government policies.

Philosophical Underpinnings

The view of a corporation as a voluntary association of individuals that maximizes the value of their property is supported by Friedman not only because of its economic efficiency consequences but also because it is consistent with a philosophy of individual liberty and responsibility. From this perspective, society, which is a collection of individuals with differing interests, can be free only if its citizens can own private property and voluntarily transact in markets with minimal interference from government. Since individual liberty and voluntary actions take priority over government direction, resource allocation is to take place through markets rather than through a political process.[9] In this philosophy, competition not only promotes efficiency but also limits people's ability to coerce others by providing alternatives in the marketplace.

The Social Responsibility Label

A firm operating under this perspective may act directly to benefit others. A value-maximizing firm may make philanthropic contributions because it increases public support for business and strengthens the firm's community, thereby helping it to attract and retain employees. A firm may institute worker participation programs to improve productivity and lower costs by enhancing satisfaction. A firm may design high-quality products and inform consumers of their safety and performance features because doing so reduces liability costs and increases profits. According to Friedman, when such actions increase the market value of the firm, they should not be given the label of social responsibility. Social responsibility must have a cost to the firm and its shareholders or else it is simply another component of a strategy of value maximization.

From Friedman's perspective, corporate social responsibility that differs from value maximization can have only two interpretations—either managers are to act as principals rather than as agents or a political process is to be used by the firm to make decisions. If social responsibility is different from value maximization, then managers must determine who should bear the cost of that responsibility. When the markets in which the firm operates are competitive, the costs of social responsibility must ultimately be borne by shareholders. If shareholders prefer that a firm not maximize its value, it may become

---

[9]See Friedman (1962, Chapter 8). The moral underpinnings of Friedman's conception of corporate social responsibility based on a system of individual liberty and property rights are similar to those of individualism. Lukes (1973) characterizes individualism as consisting of four elements: (1) accepting the intrinsic *moral worth* of individual human beings, (2) advocating the *autonomy* of individual thought and action, (3) acknowledging the existence and importance of individual *privacy,* and (4) expressing *self-development* or self-regulation as a desirable goal.

the target of a takeover attempt by investors who would operate it to maximize its value. In principle, unless it is restricted, the market for control would drive the firm toward value maximization. This market is considered in more detail later in the chapter.

THE BUSINESS ROUNDTABLE STATEMENT ON SOCIAL RESPONSIBILITY

The Business Roundtable was founded in 1972 to "examine public issues that affect the economy and develop positions which seek to reflect sound economic and social principles."[10] In 1981 one of its task forces issued a "Statement on Corporate Responsibility." This statement reflects a constituency perspective and states that business is to "serve the public interest as well as private profit." The Roundtable states that "some leading managers . . . believe that by giving enlightened consideration to balancing the legitimate claims of all its constituents, a corporation will best serve the interest of its shareholders."

The Roundtable's basic view of the firm is illustrated in Figure 17-2. The Roundtable identifies seven constituencies: customers, employees, financiers, suppliers, communities, society at large, and shareholders. "Responsibility to all these constituencies in total constitutes responsibility to society, making the corporation both an economically and socially viable entity." The corporation thus is an entity whose existence depends on society's support. That is, a corporation is a legal entity granted certain privileges, including limited liability, indefinite life, and special tax treatment such as depreciation allowances. In exchange for these privileges, the corporation has a responsibility to the society that granted them.

According to the Roundtable, customers have "a primary claim for corporate attention," so in Figure 17-2 they are represented separately as the providers of revenue for the firm. Shareholders also "have a special relationship to the corporation" but are viewed as "providers of risk capital" rather than as principals, as Friedman views them. The Roundtable goes further and criticizes institutional investors because "a high proportion of [shareholders] is made up of institutionally-grouped and often unidentified short-term buyers most interested in near term gain. This has affected their role among business constituencies." Ownership is never mentioned in the Roundtable statement,

FIGURE 17-2 The Business Roundtable View of a Corporation

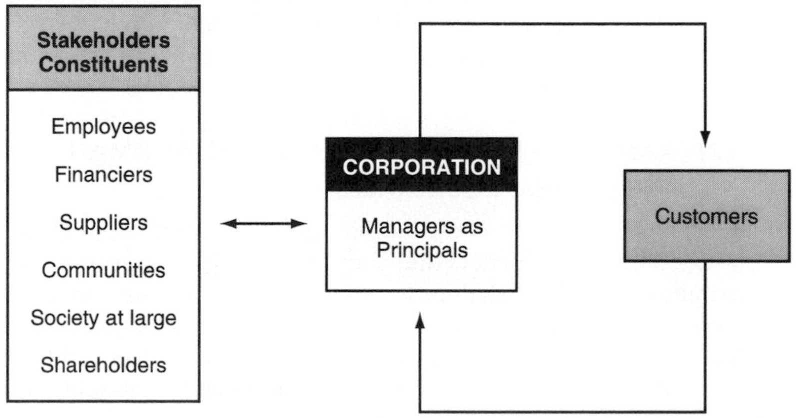

[10]See Business Roundtable (1981).

which suggests that the corporation exists as a legal entity with shareholders in the role of providers of risk capital. In contrast to Friedman's perspective, the principals in the Roundtable's view are management.

The objective of a corporation is not as clearly identified in the Roundtable statement as it is in Friedman's theory. Instead, managerial decision making involves "weighing the impacts of decisions and balancing different constituent interests . . . " The statement adds, "The shareholder must receive a good return but the legitimate concerns of other constituencies also must have the appropriate attention." Although the terms "legitimate" and "good" are not defined, this balancing is presumably different from value maximization. Management is to ensure that the corporation remains viable, but beyond a reasonable return all constituents can have a claim to its resources and returns. The Roundtable statement intentionally provides little guidance about how a corporation makes tradeoffs between the interests of various constituencies, since that is the responsibility of managers as principals.[11] As Vogel (1991, p. 114) notes, part of the "universal appeal of the concept of corporate social responsibility rests on the concept's ambiguity," allowing management to formulate more specific objectives.

Although the Roundtable argues that the legitimate concerns of constituents are to be taken into account, it does not want those constituents to participate in managerial decision making. Although "[i]t is important that all sides be heard . . . " management is to give attention to constituents' interests, and management is to decide whether and how much to respond to those interests. The relationship to constituents, or stakeholders, is considered in more detail in a later section.

According to MacAvoy (1981), the Roundtable's concern for constituents "implies that the large corporation is a political entity subject to the votes of interest groups, rather than an economic organization subject to the market test for efficient use of resources." He continued, "Political interests should not be served from corporate investment returns. If the stockholder wishes to support the local schools, or solutions to international problems, then he or she should do so with his or her own dividends." If managers operate their firms otherwise, they are acting as "politicians of the Roundtable," according to MacAvoy.

In its statement "Corporate Governance and American Competitiveness," the Business Roundtable (1990, p. 5) states, "It is important that all stakeholder interests be considered, but impossible to assure that all will be satisfied because competing claims may be mutually conflicting." The Roundtable argues that corporate governance differs from political governance on several dimensions, including the speed and boldness with which businesses must act and the means through which shareholders can influence the course of management. Governance and shareholder relationships are considered later in the chapter.

AN EXAMPLE OF THE DIFFERENCE BETWEEN FRIEDMAN AND THE BUSINESS ROUNDTABLE

Corporate charitable contributions are tax deductible; dividends paid to shareholders are taxable. Shareholders thus should prefer that the corporation make charitable contributions on their behalf rather than pay those amounts as dividends and letting shareholders make their own contributions with after-tax dollars. Corporations, however, make charitable contributions for a variety of reasons in addition to the preferences of their shareholders.[12] Some contribute out of an investment motive—for example, they

---

[11]The absence of specifics increased the support for the statement among members of the task force.

[12]See Useem (1988) for a study of corporate contributions.

give to organizations in the communities in which they operate. This strengthens the communities, making them more attractive to employees, improving employee satisfaction, and making recruitment of employees easier. Some make contributions in response to pressure from interest groups.

Decisions about the allocation of a firm's charitable contributions typically are made by management—or by the officers of the firm's foundation if the firm uses that vehicle for its contributions. According to Warren Buffett, chairman of Berkshire Hathaway Corporation, "What bothers me is the way gifts tend to be based more on who does the asking and how corporate peers are responding than on an objective evaluation of the donee's activities."[13] In 1981 Buffett initiated a program that recognized that charitable contributions are made with shareholders' property and thus that shareholders should designate the recipients. Shareholders were given a long list of donees and an amount per share they could designate to them.

Few corporations follow this practice, some citing the administrative cost and the possibility that contributions would be made to controversial organizations or that too much would be given to religious organizations. Responding to the arguments that administrative costs would make such a program prohibitively costly, Friedman argued: "Why is this any more difficult than sending out dividends or proxies? It's absolutely wrong for companies to distribute stockholders' dollars in a way that appeals just to the bureaucrats who run the company."[14]

THE STAKEHOLDER CONCEPT

As the Business Roundtable emphasizes, a firm interacts with a number of constituencies, including employees, suppliers, customers, the communities in which its facilities are located, and the public in general. To the extent that these constituencies have an interest, or "stake," in their relationship with the firm, they may be referred to as stakeholders.[15]

A stakeholder relationship centers on an exchange, as when an employee provides labor services to a firm in exchange for wages. Both parties presumably benefit from the continuation of such an exchange relationship. Employees who have developed firm-specific human capital may earn a higher wage with their current employers than if they reentered the labor market.[16] Similarly, the firm may benefit to the extent that wages are less than the value of employees' contributions plus the costs of finding and training replacements. Both the firm and the employees then have incentives to take into account the interests on the other side of the relationship.

The Business Roundtable's conception of corporate social responsibility identifies a set of stakeholders whose interests are to be taken into account. This conception leaves open the issue of whether responsibility extends to the stakeholders of its stakeholders and to social problems beyond the stakeholder relationships. The chapter case *Advanced Technology Laboratories, Inc.* raises these issues. These issues are considered in more detail in Chapters 21 and 22 and in the Part V integrative case, *Levi Strauss & Co. Global Sourcing Guidelines,* the chapter 22 case *University Games, Inc.* and the Chapter 20 case *Levi Strauss & Co. Terms of Engagement Audits*.

---

[13] *The Wall Street Journal,* April 26, 1983.
[14] *The Wall Street Journal,* April 2, 1983.
[15] See Freeman (1984) for an examination of stakeholder concepts and business strategy and Pfeffer and Salancik (1978) and Thompson (1967) for organizational perspectives.
[16] The magnitude of a stake is determined relative to the opportunities the stakeholder has through alternative relationships. For example, the stake of a supplier is the profits or rents earned on the resources committed to the relationship relative to the opportunity cost of those resources.

Strategic Uses of Corporate Social Responsibility

Some firms use corporate social responsibility for strategic purposes. From a defensive perspective, some firms act to reduce the likelihood that stakeholders will damage the firm. Stakeholder groups are capable of damaging the firm through actions taken in markets or in the nonmarket environment. Customers may stop buying a product such as canned tuna; customers, employees or communities may sue to block the closing of a plant; and consumer and environmental interest groups may intervene in regulatory proceedings.

Policies that respond to the interests of stakeholders or interest groups can also build support in the market and the nonmarket environments. Firms may develop loyal customers, suppliers, and local communities whose support they can call on if they need to expand their facilities or influence government policy. For example, a firm may cooperate with stakeholder groups to attain greater efficiency through worker involvement programs or to seek political support in the form of tax incentives or protection from imports. Furthermore, if the firm has invested in its relationships with stakeholders and understands the nature and extent of their interests, it may be able to negotiate more effectively with them.

Consideration of stakeholder interests is important because implicit contracts, understandings, and expectations can at times be more efficient than explicit bargaining and contracting. This may involve the granting and honoring of trust and the creation of realistic expectations about how issues not covered by explicit agreements, such as labor contracts, will be addressed. To the extent that employees, customers, suppliers, and communities understand their mutual interests in the continuation of their relationships, all parties can benefit.

Policies such as allowing employees on company time to volunteer in community organizations can also improve employee morale and may be rewarded through higher productivity, lower turnover, or lower wage rates. Similarly, charitable contributions to local organizations can strengthen a community and improve employee satisfaction and morale as well as attracting better employees.

Company policies that embrace principles of responsibility based on moral standards can also reduce the likelihood that an employee will violate a law or a widely shared ethical principle. This can reduce the likelihood of a challenge from the nonmarket environment and may better position the firm in that environment.

Policy positions regarding dolphin-safe tuna, environmental protection, or a commitment to particular principles may also affect consumer demand for a firm's products or services. Consumers may prefer products produced from recycled materials or produced by a company with a reputation for environmentally friendly policies. This effect would likely be stronger for consumer products than for industrial products. With the deregulation of electricity markets that allows consumers to choose their source of power generation, consumers can choose power from sustainable sources such as wind or solar. The issue, then is whether consumers would be willing to pay the higher price for power from sustainable sources.

Responsible policies may also provide better access to government institutions and their officeholders. This may increase the effectiveness of lobbying and other political strategies, which can result in more favorable government policies or decisions.

Responsible policies may also result in activists having greater trust in the firm. This may provide an opportunity to communicate with them in the event of an emerging nonmarket issue. If the activists are willing to listen to the firm's position, that may allow the firm to get its message out in a less hostile environment. There may be additional benefits to interacting with activists. For example, an oil company that had developed a relationship with Greenpeace in the wake of the *Brent Spar* episode learned about a planned Greenpeace action against one of its facilities and was prepared to respond when it occurred.

Adopting socially responsible policies can also carry risks. For such policies to be sustainable the firm must meet the expectations it creates through its policies, and if those policies establish high standards, the firm can be held accountable for them. Levi Strauss & Co. has set high standards and has successfully sustained those standards for decades. In 1997 when it was forced to lay off over 6,000 employees in the United States because of a falling market share for its jeans, the company was obliged by its reputation to provide very generous severance packages for the employees who lost their jobs.

Reputations for socially responsible behavior can also be dissipated. The Body Shop had promoted its cosmetics business using its policies of protecting the environment and aiding indigenous peoples through purchases of natural ingredients from them. As discussed in Chapter 3 and developed further in Chapter 20, the Body Shop came under attack from critics who argued that it had not met the standards it set for itself.

In 1995 the Shell Oil company was a highly respected global company with an enviable environmental record and reputation. Within 6 months, however, its reputation had taken a battering. Its attempt to sink the *Brent Spar* platform in the North Sea generated a storm of protest by individuals and governments in northern Europe. Its reputation also suffered from its role in environmental damage in Nigeria and its rejection of demands by human rights groups to intervene with the Nigerian government to stop the execution of nine dissidents from the region in which Shell and its Nigerian government partner produced crude oil.

The strategic use of corporate social responsibility, either offensively or defensively, for the purpose of increasing a firm's market value would be viewed by Friedman as just another strategy to add value to the firm. If a policy reduced the value of the firm but increased the benefits to a stakeholder group, Friedman would view that as contrary to the role of business in society. From the Business Roundtable's perspective the strategic use of social responsibility would be viewed as responsible behavior, since it takes into account the interests of stakeholders. The next section provides examples to provide additional insight into the concept of corporate social responsibility.

Examples of Corporate Social Responsibility?

UNOCAL CORPORATION AND THE DIRTY CAR BOUNTY

Air quality in the Los Angeles basin has been among the worst in the nation, and stringent measures were being prepared to address the problem. Proposals included restricting driving and shutting down factories when air quality reached potentially hazardous levels. Some firms began to take steps on their own to address the problem.

Unocal announced a novel program in which it offered to pay $700 cash for 7,000 pre-1971 automobiles, which would then be scrapped.[17] The scrap value of the cars was estimated to be $10 to $20, and their market value was believed to be considerably lower than $700.[18] In addition, Unocal offered to provide free tune-ups for pre-1975 cars. The cost of the program was estimated to be nearly $10 million. Unocal Chairman and CEO Richard J. Stegemeier explained: "Sixty percent of smog comes from mobile sources, cars and trucks. Thirty percent is coming from pre-1975 automobiles. If you want to

[17]The 7,000 represented approximately 1.7 percent of the old cars in the Los Angeles area.

[18]Because of the attractiveness of the offer and its desire to focus on the Los Angeles basin, Unocal restricted the offer to autos registered in the area for at least the prior 6 months.

make a big impact in a hurry, this is by far the quickest and most cost-effective way."[19] Although the impact on air quality depends on which modes of transportation replace the old cars, Unocal estimated that emissions of pollutants would be reduced by 6 million pounds a year.[20] Within months, more than 10,000 car owners had applied to the program. Unocal also encouraged other companies to participate in the program. In July 1990 Ford announced that it would buy 1,000 old automobiles in the Los Angeles area and would offer the sellers an additional $700 rebate on the purchase of a new Ford.

The fact that the South Coast Air Resources Board subsequently adopted an old car scrap plan suggests that the Unocal's innovation benefited society.[21] Unocal also benefited from the program. Goodwill was generated, and it earned emissions credits for reducing pollutants. The program relieved pressure on environmental issues.

ARCO AND GASOLINE PRICE RESTRAINTS

After Iraq invaded Kuwait in 1990, crude oil prices doubled, and the price increase was quickly reflected in higher gasoline prices. Three hours before President Bush asked oil companies "to do their fair share to limit their price increases," ARCO announced that it would freeze prices for gasoline, diesel, and aviation fuel in the five western states in which it operated. Within 10 days ARCO was forced to withdraw its freeze on diesel and aviation fuel because prices had increased so steeply that ARCO's supplies were running out. The company, however, increased its wholesale gasoline price by only four cents a gallon, whereas gasoline on the spot market had increased by 20 cents a gallon. Demand was so strong that despite daily deliveries many ARCO stations ran out of gasoline every day for hours at a time. Within 2 weeks ARCO ended the freeze.

From the perspective of economic efficiency, a price below cost encourages consumption and dampens the incentives for exploration. The oil price controls imposed during the 1970s were estimated to have cost the United States billions of dollars a year by discouraging production, encouraging higher consumption, and strengthening the OPEC cartel. To promote economic efficiency and avoid taking advantage of a price increase resulting from a crisis, ARCO could have priced at market levels and given the additional profits to charity.

Some analysts speculated that ARCO's freeze was politically motivated to increase its standing at a time when it was engaged in a campaign to open the Arctic National Wildlife Refuge to oil exploration. Others viewed it as lessening the calls for oil price controls or a windfall profits tax, both of which had been imposed in the 1970s. Others pointed to the personal relationship between President Bush and ARCO's chairman, who had contributed $100,000 to the Republican Party in 1988.

MALDEN MILLS INDUSTRIES

In the 1980s employees at Malden Mills Industries discovered how to combine synthetic yarns to produce cloth with textured faces. The new fabric, sold as Polartec, was featured in outerwear marketed by companies such as Patagonia, Lands End, and L. L. Bean. The success of Polartec was interrupted when a devastating fire destroyed the Polartex production facilities at Malden's mill in Lawrence, Massachusetts. Aaron Feuerstein, owner of Malden Mills, pledged to get Polartec production restarted as soon as possible and

---

[19]*The New York Times*, April 27, 1990.
[20]Cars built before 1975, when catalytic converters were required on new automobiles, emit 50 grams of carbon monoxide per mile driven on average, whereas post-1975 models emit 20.7 grams per mile. Cars too old to have catalytic converters also emit many more hydrocarbons and nitrogen oxides than newer models.
[21]Unocal sought to build goodwill by producing television commercials showing the crushing of old automobiles under its program.

quickly purchased new production equipment set up in a warehouse while the mill buildings were reconstructed. Feuerstein decided to rebuild in Lawrence rather than move production to a less expensive location. He also rebuilt the mill's facilities in the original nineteenth-century style, including expensive details and finishings. He also pledged to reemploy all the mills' workers and to pay the 1,380 laid-off workers full wages for 90 days while the Polartec facilities were being rebuilt. Feuerstein explained, "I feel that I am a symbol of the movement against downsizing and layoffs that will ultimately produce an answer. People see me as a turning of the tide."[22]

The Polartec facilities were back in operation in 6 months, but shortly thereafter Malden Mills announced that it would not recall 450 workers in its flock division because rebuilding those facilities was more costly and would take much longer than initially anticipated. A company spokesperson stated, "We have to be profitable in the long run. But with Aaron we don't have to be two percentage points more profitable than the next guy. We are going to end up keeping more people than we would need if we were to run with flat-out efficiency."[23]

AETNA AND HOUSING REHABILITATION

In 1982 Aetna Life & Casualty was one of the largest insurers in the United States, and Chairman John H. Filer was a public advocate of corporate social responsibility. The insurance industry had been stung by allegations that it had engaged in a practice, referred to as "redlining," in which banks and insurance companies were said to refuse to lend or issue insurance to individuals living in certain geographic areas, often inner-city neighborhoods. In response to the concern that inner-city neighborhoods were being neglected, Aetna, in conjunction with neighborhood activist groups, undertook a National Demonstration Urban Neighborhood Investment Program. President William O. Bailey explained that Aetna "believes neighborhood revitalization to be good business.... The purpose of the demonstration program was to provide financial and technical support to the leading role taken by grassroots neighborhood organizations in implementing a housing development program in their communities."

According to Aetna, the "demonstration program was undergirded by two key contextual themes. The first reflects a choice between two positions, one espoused by Milton Friedman, that 'the only business of business is business,' and the other by Kenneth Dayton, that 'the purpose of business is to serve society.' It is apparent that the intention... is to make Aetna a corporation that is sensitive and responsive to societal issues, and by so doing, improve Aetna's business success and the environment in which it works."[24]

Aetna's approach was to become directly involved in neighborhood projects by providing management assistance and financing. During the first 2 years of the program, Aetna committed over $11 million of mortgage financing to the rehabilitation of 900 housing units in five neighborhoods. The company also provided direct grants of $425,000 to neighborhood groups. Aetna's experience with the projects was mixed, and its provision of management assistance embroiled the company in at least one neighborhood squabble. Eventually, however, the company extended the program to include 12 neighborhood groups in 11 cities. The demonstration project resulted in 129 loans totaling nearly $30 million for the construction and renovation of 1,950 housing units.

---

[22]*The New York Times,* July 4, 1996.
[23]*The New York Times,* July 4, 1996.
[24]See Aetna Life and Casuality (1982), p. 3.

Three of the neighborhood groups experienced difficulties and some restructuring of projects was required, but no defaults or foreclosures resulted, according to Aetna. Although Aetna declared the demonstration program a success, it ended the program.

SOUTH SHORE BANK AND COMMUNITY DEVELOPMENT

In contrast to Aetna's direct involvement in the rehabilitation of housing, several corporations, foundations, and other organizations, including the Ford Foundation, Allstate Insurance, and the Episcopal Church, formed the Shorebank Corporation to purchase the South Shore Bank in 1973. The coalition's objective was for the bank to participate with neighborhood groups in the renewal of local communities in Chicago. The bank also opened branches in the Austin neighborhood. Over 90 percent of the residents in the South Shore and Austin communities were minority group members, and the housing stock was primarily apartment buildings.

Working with neighborhood groups, by 1992 South Shore Bank has been involved in the rehabilitation of over 3,000 housing units and had over $162 million in loans outstanding. Its return on equity was nearly ten percent. In recent years, it has emphasized lending to small commercial establishments that might not qualify for regular bank loans. South Shore Bank helped form banks and development corporations in Cleveland, the Upper Peninsula of Michigan, and Washington's Willapa Bay. Similar organizations were started in other communities.

South Shore Bank was the inspiration for the federal government's Community Development Financial Institution (CDFI) program to provide credit to people who do not have access to conventional financing. The program administered by the Treasury Department provides subsidized financing and grants to CDFIs that finance housing and businesses in poor areas. By 1998 approximately 350 CDFIs were in operation with lending capacity of over $2 billion.

Social Responsibility: Motives and Causality

In reasoning about whether actions, such as those in the previous examples, constitute corporate social responsibility, it is useful to assess both consequences and motives. The consequences can be assessed in terms of benefits and the costs. The motives depend on whether the action was taken in response to the needs and interests of constituents or in response to the damage they can do to the firm. Motive is important because a firm that acts as a result of pressure from activists, interest groups, stakeholders, or the government is not necessarily socially responsible. When the motive for an action is to limit the damage to a firm, it is necessary to look beyond consequences to motives. These two dimensions, consequences and motives, provide the basis for a typology for the concept of corporate social responsibility.

To illustrate the issue of motive, Heinz's decision to not purchase tuna caught in purse seine nets served the interests of various constituencies. Moreover, given the pressure in its nonmarket environment, shareholders were likely better off than they would have been had Heinz continued to resist the pressure. Both shareholders and external interests thus benefited from the decision. The motive, however, was likely to have been to reduce the actual and potential damage.

Pressure can be accompanied by information. As considered in Chapter 4, activists and other critics of business activity can identify issues or concerns about which management had been unaware. In the Heinz case, the company undoubtedly was aware of the fishing practices in the Eastern Pacific and the number of dolphins being killed. The company also understood the widespread concern about the issue once the videotape was broadcast in March 1988. That Heinz did not announce a change in its policy for 2 years and not until it had become a boycott target suggests that it was responding to pressure and not to new information.[25]

In contrast, Hobee's restaurants did not act in response to pressure. Its actions benefited those seeking to protect dolphins and may have had costs to Hobee's owners. The motive for the actions was likely to have been to follow an ethical principle. The motive for Hobee's actions thus differs from that of Heinz's, and a typology of social responsibility should distinguish between their actions.

As an initial step in the development of a typology, the consequences of an action can be classified in terms of shareholder interests, or private profit, and societal interests. The term "societal interests" refers to the aggregate interests of "society," including shareholders. These two dimensions are intended to correspond to the Business Roundtable's statement that business is to "serve the public interest as well as private profit."

Friedman's perspective on corporate social responsibility is based on an alignment of the interests of shareholders with those of society. That is, in a world in which markets are competitive and in which private bargaining and government-structured incentives are used to internalize externalities, the interests of shareholders are aligned with those of society. An action that benefits shareholders thus benefits society as well. Friedman would not refer to such actions as corporate social responsibility, however. If shareholders, acting as principals, were to direct the firm to take an action that benefited society at their expense, Friedman would call it individual, rather than corporate, social responsibility.

To the extent, however, that markets are not competitive, that transactions costs impede bargaining, and that government policies do not align private and social costs, shareholders' interests can diverge from society's interests. Then, corporate social responsibility, as the Business Roundtable perceives it, would require the firm to take an action if stakeholders' interests would be served even if shareholders would be worse off. The limits to this principle come from the need for the firm to earn a "reasonable return." Similarly, actions that would harm stakeholder interests would be taken only when they are necessary to allow the firm to earn a reasonable return.

In a typology, the actions of firms must be assessed relative to the relevant status quo, which is the situation at the time the firm takes the action. It thus includes whatever pressure is being exerted on the firm, as in the Heinz case. Consider first the case in which a firm faces pressure from constituent or interest groups as represented by the panel on the left in Figure 17-3. The firm may take an action which, in contrast to fighting the pressure, benefits both society and shareholders. The Heinz case is in this category, and the Aetna case may be as well if the primary motive was to respond to the pressure stemming from the redlining issue.

Responding to pressure may not always be in society's interests, however, as in the case in which a pressure group engages in extortion. If the firm paid the extortion, it could be better off than if it did not pay it, but society would surely be worse off if extortion were rewarded. Payments demanded by foreign government officials for the exercise of their duties is such an example, as considered in Chapter 22.

---

[25]In an interview in the film referenced in footnote 4, O'Reilly said: "I think it would be a poor chief executive officer that was not attentive to his customers . . . because of the affection children have for Flipper . . . there was a growing barrage of criticism, well-orchestrated, which I think served to convey a growing sentiment among school children that the previous fishing methods were no longer acceptable."

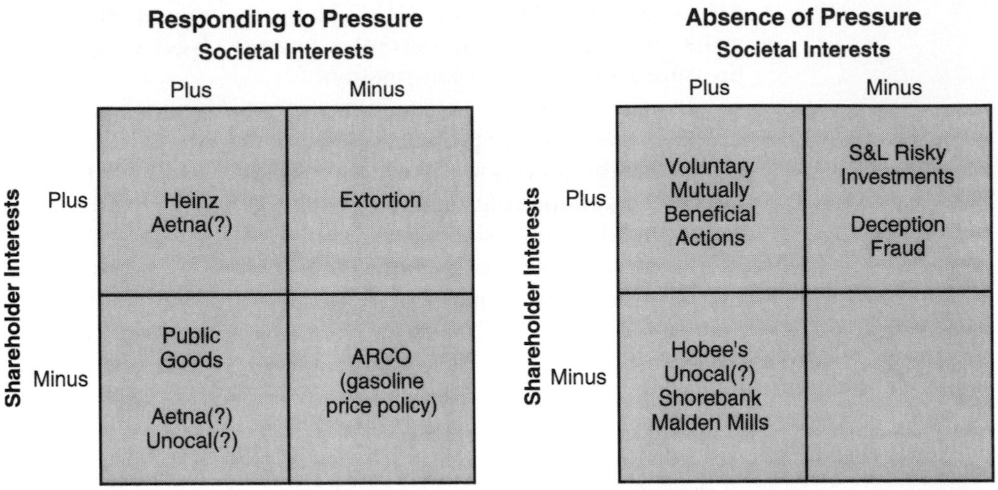

FIGURE 17-3 A Typology for Corporate Social Responsibility

An example of an action that benefits stakeholders but can make shareholders worse off is the provision of a public good when the provider is unable to capture benefits sufficient to cover the cost of its provision. The Unocal old-car program represents a public good. Unocal identified an innovative alternative to more costly measures of reducing automobile emissions. The program has been adopted elsewhere by private parties and by governments and has become a serious instrument in pollution control programs.[26]

Actions that make society worse off and decrease shareholders' returns should be rare, although ARCO's decision to freeze gasoline prices may be an example of such an action. If ARCO had continued to hold its price for gasoline below the market price, shareholders would be worse off, as would society because gasoline would be priced below its opportunity cost.

The right panel of Figure 17-3 pertains to cases in which there is no pressure on the firm, so the motive is not to avoid damage. The strategic use of corporate social responsibility is in this category. As indicated, the Business Roundtable might refer to such actions as socially responsible, but Friedman would not. Actions that benefit constituents but harm shareholder returns may include Hobee's decisions to not purchase tuna caught in purse seine nets and to change its menu items accordingly. Although privately owned and not accountable to shareholders, Malden Mills's commitment to its employees places it in this category. Shorebank is also in this category because its founders did not receive a return for their original contributions. Charitable contributions made in the absence of pressure thus are in this category. Aetna may also be in this category. The provision of a public good when there is no compelling pressure to do so is in this category. Unocal's purchase of "dirty" cars would also be in this cell, if it were not under pressure for emissions reductions.

In the upper-right cell are actions that benefit shareholder interests and harm society—for example, the high-risk investments made by savings and loan associations in the 1980s in an attempt to regain solvency. Actions involving deception and fraud and the violation of environmental standards also are in this category.

---

[26]See, however, the Chapter 19 case *Environmental Justice and Pollution Credits Trading Systems.*

In addition to distinguishing between consequences and motives, it is important to assess the direction of causality; that is, whether policies of corporate social responsibility contribute to improved economic performance or whether successful economic performance allows firms to afford socially responsible activities. For firms such as Levi Strauss & Co., Ben and Jerry's, Cummins Engine, Johnson & Johnson, and Malden Mills, concepts of corporate social responsibility are ingrained in the companies' operating principles and practices and are said by the companies to contribute to successful economic performance, or at least are so integrated with market activities that the direction of causality is difficult to identify.[27] Other companies, particularly small businesses early in their development, emphasize economic performance, and if they succeed, may implement programs in the social responsibility domain. Programs implementing conceptions of social responsibility and ethics are considered in Chapter 20.

Consideration of motives and causality is useful for clarifying the corporate social responsibility issue, but there are additional aspects of the issue. In particular, the typology emphasizes consequences and gives inadequate attention to considerations such as liberties and rights, which are viewed in an instrumental manner. These moral dimensions, as considered in subsequent chapters, provide an additional basis for guiding and evaluating corporate actions.

The chapter cases *Western National Bank* and *Headquarters Relocation: Kimberly-Clark and the State of Wisconsin* provide opportunities to consider specific decisions involving consequences and motives.

Corporate Governance

CONSTITUENT REPRESENTATION?

If corporations are to take into account stakeholder and broader public interests as the Business Roundtable suggests, activists argue that stakeholders should be represented in corporate decision-making processes. One approach would be to allow them to participate in corporate decision making at the board of directors level, with board members selected by and representing the principal constituencies. During the Carter administration activists supported an unsuccessful legislative effort, referred to as the "corporate democracy act," that would have required board representation of stakeholder groups.

Most firms oppose board representation of constituent groups. The Business Roundtable (1990, p. 18) stated: "We reject the notion of so-called constituency directors. Individual directors responsible to particular claimant groups would introduce into the board a divisive and adversary atmosphere which would obstruct the effective performance of the enterprise. Moreover, the notion that the board as a whole has a direct responsibility to groups other than share owners would mean that there was no clear measure of board performance."[28] The Roundtable prefers that managers consider the interests of constituents rather than allowing them to participate in decision making. A few firms have included union leaders on their boards, but some union leaders subsequently resigned because of concerns about their independence being compromised. In other countries such as Germany, for example, legislation gives labor representation on

---

[27]Levi Strauss & Co. and Malden Mills are privately owned, and Ben & Jerry's is 42 percent owned by its founders.

[28]This statement was written by a different task force from the one that wrote the statement on social responsibility.

supervisory boards and for large companies on the management board. As the result of the merger, the United Automobile Workers union received a seat on the management board of Daimler-Chrysler.

SOCIAL ACCOUNTABILITY

Accountability continues to be an issue for firms that seek to be socially responsible. Some have experimented with "social audits" of their efforts, and some have published reports on their activities. The call for social audits faded in the 1980s as the impact of such reports was questioned, but in the mid-1990s they began to receive increased attention. As indicated in Chapter 3, the Body Shop decided to have an independent social audit conducted as a means of quelling criticisms that its practices fell short of its pronouncements. This social audit is considered in Chapter 20.

Accountability not only involves firms reporting to constituents but also involves external monitoring and evaluation of activities by activist and interest groups. A number of "socially responsible" mutual funds have been established and refuse to hold shares in cigarette companies, weapons manufacturers, or firms that damage the environment. Also several organizations provide institutions, such as universities and pension funds, with evaluations of the social performance of firms. As an example of these evaluations, in 1990 Franklin Research & Development provided evaluations of firms on seven dimensions of performance: South Africa, employee relations, environment, citizenship, energy, product, and weapons. In 1994 Franklin withdrew its highest rating for the Body Shop.

THE DUTIES OF BOARDS OF DIRECTORS

Corporations are "managed under the direction" of their board of directors, and board members have fiduciary responsibilities to shareholders and to society. The legal obligations of directors generally fall into categories referred to as the duty of loyalty and the duty of care. The duty of loyalty pertains to conflicts of interest and requires that directors serve the interests of the corporation and its shareholders. According to Clark (1985, p. 73), "Case law on manager's fiduciary duty of care can fairly be read to say that the manager has an affirmative, open-ended duty to maximize the beneficiaries' wealth . . . " The duty of care requires directors to take care in their direction of the corporation under the "prudent person" standard and to make informed decisions. (Officers of the corporation have the same duty.) Directors are not expected to participate in the day-to-day management of the corporation.

The courts judge the discharge of the obligations of directors according to a common law standard referred to as the "business judgment rule." Under this standard, actions taken by the board are not generally subject to judicial review if they are taken in accord with the duty of loyalty and the duty of care. The business judgment rule is based on the view that courts have no special expertise in second-guessing business decisions, and that business decision making would be unduly hampered if it were subject to judicial review. Furthermore, the courts are likely to be less effective in monitoring managerial decisions than is the market for control.[29]

If directors do not exercise due care, they may be held liable.[30] In *Smith v. Van Gorkom* (1985), 488 A.2d 858 (Del.), the Delaware Supreme Court held that the directors of Trans Union Corporation were grossly negligent, and hence not protected by the business judgment rule, since they failed to independently value the firm in a leveraged buyout. A subsequent case, *Hanson Trust PLC v. ML SCM Acquisition* (1986), 781 F.2d 264 (2nd Cir. 1986), established that being adequately informed is not sufficient to be

---

[29]See Easterbrook and Fishel (1981).
[30]See Bagley (1995), Chapter 21.

protected by the business judgment rule. Directors must be well informed when they make decisions. Consequently, boards now seek the advice of independent experts in any valuation decision and in many other decisions as well. Reliance on experts is not sufficient, however, and directors are required to inquire into the content and quality of the reports given by management. The *Van Gorkom* and *Hanson* decisions caused the cost of directors and officers insurance to increase sharply.

The duty of care supports Friedman's position and the strategic use of corporate social responsibility. The business judgment rule, however, means that management and the board of directors have a substantial range of discretion in deciding the extent of that responsibility. For example, Ben & Jerry's donates 7.5 percent of its pretax profits to charities and pays a premium for milk from dairy farmers who pledge not to use the bio-engineered hormone rBGH. The company also negotiated a settlement with the State of Illinois allowing it to state its policy on its ice cream containers along with the statement, "The FDA has said no significant difference has been shown and no test can now distinguish between milk from rBGH treated and untreated cows." Ben & Jerry's also did not enter the Japanese market after a leading Japanese company offered to distribute the product. CEO Robert Holland, Jr., explained, "The only clear reason to take the opportunity was to make money."[31]

In addition to legal requirements, boards have a number of specific roles and functions. The Business Roundtable (1997, pp. 4–5) identified five principal functions of the board:

(i) Select, regularly evaluate and, if necessary, replace the chief executive officer, determine management compensation, and review succession planning.
(ii) Review and, where appropriate, approve the major strategies and financial and other objectives, and plans of the corporation.
(iii) Advise management on significant issues facing the corporation.
(iv) Oversee processes for evaluating the adequacy of internal controls, risk management, financial reporting and compliance, and satisfy itself as to the adequacy of such processes.
(v) Nominate directors and ensure that the structure and practices of the board provide for sound corporate governance.

The Roundtable also argued that board attention should focus on strategic decisions and the social impacts of corporate decisions, although it drew considerably narrower boundaries on social responsibility than did the task force statement on corporate social responsibility.

The Roundtable recommended a board composed of "a substantial majority of . . . outside (nonmanagement directors)." It also recommended inclusion of more women and minorities on boards. Not all managers agreed with this viewpoint. In response to an unsigned form letter from a nun asking that Cypress Semiconductor appoint women and minorities to its board, outspoken CEO T. J. Rodgers replied and sent a copy of his letter to all Cypress shareholders. Rodgers wrote, "Choosing a Board of Directors based on race and gender is a lousy way to run a company. Cypress will never do it." He adds for good measure that "bowing" to "special-interest groups is an immoral way to run a company . . . "[32]

The Roundtable also stated that "it is highly desirable for a board to have a central core of experienced business executives." Many corporations assign only nonmanagement directors to the audit, compensation, and nominating committees of their boards to ensure that the shareholders' interests are being served by management.

---

[31]Holland resigned less than 2 years after being recruited, reportedly because of disagreements with the company's founders over policies.
[32]*The Wall Street Journal,* July 15, 1996.

The Investor Responsibility Research Center (IRRC) (1993) surveyed institutional investors regarding their voting on corporate governance issues. A majority of the 85 institutional investors, which manage nearly half a trillion dollars of investments, responded that they routinely vote for shareholder proposals for a board with a majority of independent directors, a compensation committee composed entirely of outside directors, an independent nominating committee, and the annual election of directors.[33] A 1996 study by Korn/Ferry International reported that 36 percent of the largest industrial companies surveyed had a "lead director," 98 percent regularly evaluated the performance of a CEO, and 73 percent had outside directors meet without the CEO. Institutional investors clearly cast their votes for market capitalism.

Concerns about managerial capitalism and the objectives that management pursues have resulted in direct pressure from institutional investors for a more independent board of directors. The nation's largest fund, the California Public Employees Pension Fund (CalPERS), for example, put pressure on firms to have more independent boards and improve their financial performance. CalPERS went directly to their outside board members, bypassing management. TIAA-CREF, a $113 billion pension fund for teachers and professors, joined with CalPERS seeking changes in boards of directors of companies such as Heinz, arguing that the board was not sufficiently independent. By 1994 outside directors were a majority on the boards of 86 percent of U.S. corporations and 91 percent of financial institutions.

In 1994 General Motors took an important step that may be a precursor to the future structure and activities of boards of directors. It issued 28 guidelines on corporate governance issues. The guidelines give greater power to the board, rather than de facto to management, in nominating new directors, require a review of each director's continuation every 5 years, and provide for an annual board review of the performance of the CEO. With respect to board structure, the guidelines establish a "lead" outside director who conducts three yearly executive sessions of outside directors. The outside directors are also given access to GM's management rather than having to make inquiries through the CEO. These guidelines increase both the powers and responsibilities of outside directors.

THE MARKET FOR CONTROL

The market for control supervises the actions of management and directors through mergers, acquisitions, hostile takeovers, and proxy contests and thereby disciplines management and provides it with incentives to serve shareholder interests.[34] However, many managers prefer to be insulated from the market for control, arguing that they are best able to chart the firm's course.[35] Investors often disagree and favor the discipline of the market to the discretion of management; that is, they prefer market capitalism to managerial capitalism. For example, through a series of acquisitions, United Airlines, which was renamed Allegis, included in its system Hertz Rent-A-Car, Westin Hotels, and Hilton International. Pressure on Allegis for better financial performance caused its board of directors to replace its CEO. Under new management Allegis was broken up, with UAL, Inc. the surviving entity. In his letter to shareholders, the new chairman and CEO wrote: "My objective . . . has been . . . enhancing near-term stockholder values and the goal of permitting United Airlines to operate successfully and gain in value in the future in a very competitive environment. . . . We have determined

[33]The other institutional investors generally vote on a case-by-case basis.
[34]See Weston, Chung, Hoag (1990) for a comprehensive treatment of the market for control.
[35]See Coffee, Lowenstein, Rose-Ackerman (1988).

to proceed immediately with the sale of all of our non-airline businesses—Hertz, Westin, and Hilton International—and to distribute the net proceeds from those sales to stockholders."[36]

Institutional investors are an increasingly important force in the market for control. During the 1970s and most of the 1980s, institutional investors were relatively passive and seldom attempted to influence the management of the firms whose shares they held. Shareholder resolutions tended to focus on issues such as operating in South Africa, and institutional investors seldom initiated resolutions. Most institutions voted with management on proxy issues. With institutions holding over 50 percent of the shares of U.S. corporations, compared with slightly over 20 percent in 1970, institutional investors have been crucial in forcing management changes in companies such as General Motors and Eastman Kodak. Pension funds, such as CalPERS, in particular have been concerned about the return on their investments and have increasingly opposed management on proxy challenges, anti-takeover charter amendments, and shareholder resolutions directed at forcing management to improve profitability. In addition, the Department of Labor has instructed pension fund managers to vote on proxy issues in the best interests of their beneficiaries.[37] In 1992 the Securities and Exchange Commission issued rules giving shareholders new powers, such as calling special meetings and maintaining confidentiality on proxy measures, that make it easier to take collective action against management.

Under pressure from a number of corporations and organized labor, Pennsylvania enacted an anti-takeover law intended to protect its firms and the jobs they provide in the state.[38] This event provided evidence on both the market for control and managerial responses to the protection of firms and their management. A unique feature of this law was that it provided corporations with a window during which they could opt out of one or more of its protective provisions. The capital market reaction to the law occurred soon after the bill was introduced in the state legislature. The price of a market basket of 60 companies incorporated in Pennsylvania fell over 5 percent relative to the Corporate Standard & Poor's 500 index. As the likelihood that the bill would pass increased, the gap increased as well—by January 1990, when the state senate passed the bill, the gap was 6.9 percent.[39] Given that some firms were expected to opt out of the law, the decrease for those that were expected to be covered was considerably higher.

Summary

The role of business in society and the extent of its social responsibilities remain subjects of disagreement. The duties of care and loyalty and the business judgment rule leave considerable discretion to directors and so to management, but management is not free to rely on its personal preferences for charting the paths of the firms they control. Management and directors face continuing pressure for improved financial performance, which limits management's discretion to pursue social objectives.

In assessing what constitutes corporate social responsibility, it is important to consider the motive for an action and whether it was taken based on principle or in response to pressure. Actions taken to benefit shareholders by responding to pressure that can damage the firm differ from actions taken in response to the needs of constituents or to moral principles. Moreover, using the interests of constituents or moral

[36]April 25, 1987, letter to Allegis Corporation stockholders from Frank A. Olson.

[37]The Department of Labor has regulatory authority under the Employee Retirement Income Security Act of 1974.

[38]The legislation was spurred by the attempted takeover of Armstrong World Industries by the Belzberg family of Canada.

[39]See Karpoff and Malatesta (1989).

arguments to justify actions taken independently of those considerations is not social responsibility. That is, it is necessary to look behind the rhetoric of social responsibility to its content and motives.

The relationship between social responsibility and economic performance remains unclear, but several leading companies argue that the two can, and do, go hand in hand. Even Friedman's dictum to maximize market value is subject to the limits of the law and ethical custom, both of which leave a gray area between what is clearly responsible and what is clearly irresponsible. On such issues managers obtain guidance from two principal sources. The first is government, which proscribes as well as prescribes certain actions and provides incentives to adopt certain types of policies. The tax deductibility of philanthropic contributions and the tax advantages provided for hiring disadvantaged youths are examples of such incentives. The second source of guidance is ethics. Ethical principles provide a basis for reasoning about and evaluating actions and policies. The content of social responsibility ultimately is found in those principles and their moral foundations. Moral foundations, however, do not always provide unambiguous prescriptions nor are the prescriptions provided by different ethical frameworks necessarily the same. The following chapters develop these frameworks and consider applications within the scope of the social responsibility debate.

CASES

Advanced Technology Laboratories, Inc.

Advanced Technology Laboratories, Inc. (ATL), with worldwide headquarters in Bothell, Washington, and European headquarters in Munich, Germany, is a leader in digital diagnostic ultrasound technology and equipment. "Ultrasound is a noninvasive technology that uses high frequency sound waves to image the body's soft tissues, organs and fetal anatomy and to display blood flow in real time."[1] ATL's ultrasound systems are used by cardiologists, radiologists, vascular surgeons, obstetricians, and gynecologists. Applications of ultrasound technology in gynecology included diagnosis of ovarian cysts, endometrial hyperplasia, endometrium, and ovarian flow.

ATL ultrasound systems were sold in 100 countries to village clinics and world-renowned medical research centers. The worldwide ultrasound market was estimated at $2.5 billion. In 1996 ATL earned $21.8 million on sales of $419 million. Its competitors include such companies as General Electric and Siemens.

ATL's principal subsidiaries were located in OECD countries as well as in Argentina and India. In other countries ATL sold its systems through agents. Demand in the United States was sluggish, and ATL's worldwide competitors had introduced new products during the past 2 years. ATL looked to developing countries for growth.

The most attractive growth opportunities were in large countries with high growth rates of spending for medical care and health services. India with a population of 800 million and a forecasted growth rate of 15 to 20 percent a year for medical devices represented a particularly attractive market. ATL India, located in Madras, was responsible for sales in India and Nepal. China with a population of 1.2 billion also represented an attractive market, and the installed base of ultrasound equipment was lower than in India. In 1997 ATL formed ATL China, where it had sold ultrasound systems since 1978. ATL also had a technology transfer agreement with the Shantou Institute of Ultrasonic Instruments.

In 1997 ATL introduced its HDI 1000 system which replaced 50 percent of the hardware components with multitasking software, making digital ultrasound technology available at a substantially lower cost. ATL's Handheld Systems Business Division had also developed its FirstSight™ digital imaging technology that would bring "highly portable, handheld ultrasound devices . . . [with] the immediacy and efficacy of ultrasound to the examining table, the bedside and the field." ATL Chairman and CEO Dennis C. Fill said, "We believe that in the next few years these handheld ultrasound devices could have the same impact on patient care as the stethoscope and have the potential to create entirely new markets across many medical disciplines."[2]

In certain cultures some parents value sons more than daughters. In the 1990s ultrasound devices became an effective means of allowing parents to engage in sex selection. Ultrasound was capable of identifying the sex of a fetus as early as 16 weeks, and local ultrasound clinics began to spring up throughout a number of Asian countries. A study by the Indian government revealed that for every 1,000 baby boys born, only 929 baby girls were born. A study reported that of the 8,000 abortions performed at one Bombay hospital, all but one were female fetuses.

One explanation for the preference for boys was given in a *CNN World News* story. "Sons are favored in India because it is they who are expected to carry on the family name and take care of the parents in their old age. Daughters are seen as a liability, and an expensive one at that. Families pay small fortunes in dowries to get their daughters married. . . . For those Indians too poor to afford tests, there is a grimmer option. Skakuntala admits to killing her newborn daughter several years ago. She already had two girls and didn't want another. 'We were poor,' she says. 'I put my sari over her face and she stopped breathing. It was the only thing to do.' "[3] CNN also reported that 25 percent of the girls born in India do not reach the age of 25, and in some families boys are given disproportionate shares of food, medical care, and education.

In 1994 India responded to the practice of using ultrasound to identify the sex and abort female fetuses

[1]ATL Web site: www.atl.com.

[2]ATL Web site atl.com.

[3]*CNN World News,* September 17, 1995.

by enacting the Pre-Natal Diagnostic Techniques (Regulation and Prevention of Misuses) Act. The law limited the use of ultrasound to women who were at high risk due to age or other factors and banned abortions of female fetuses identified by either amniocentesis or ultrasound. However, the use of ultrasound combined with abortion for purposes of sex selection continued unabated. According to *The New York Times,* "[f]or an investment amounting to a few thousand dollars, a mobile clinic operator can reap a small fortune from rural women, many of whom have never used a telephone or watched a television. Charges for the test can run as low as 150 rupees in poorer regions, about $5 . . ."[4] The same report noted that the law did not include registration of ultrasound machines, so it was virtually impossible to control their use in mobile clinics.

Gender selection was also practiced in several other Asian countries, including China. The natural ratio of boys to girls at birth worldwide was 105 to 100, but in China it was 114 to 100 and was considerably higher in some rural districts.[5] Chinese law prohibited gender selection through abortion, infanticide, and child abandonment.

Sex selection was widely criticized. The United Nations International Conference on Population and Development opposed sex selection. In the United States the President's Commission for the Study of Ethical Problems in Medicine and Biomedical and Behavioral Research strongly opposed the practice, as did the American College of Obstetricians and Gynecologists' Committee on Ethics. The Ethics Committee of the American Society for Reproductive Medicine argued that doctors should use "moral suasion" to convince couples to avoid sex selection.

In 1995 the Canadian minister of health ordered Canadian doctors to cease providing sex selection services for nonmedical purposes, and the British Columbia College of Physicians and Surgeons issued guidelines urging doctors and sonographers not to reveal the sex of fetuses. Vancouver, which has a substantial population of Asian-Canadians, was concerned about people going to the United States for fetal sex identification and returning to Canada for an abortion paid for by the government. Dr. Dalip Sandhu said, "I tell them it's a sin. But they're not here to ask for my opinion. They want the information. They don't get it from me. It doesn't mean it stops them."[6] Shashi Assanand, director of the Lower Mainland Multicultural Family Support Services Centre in Vancouver blamed the dowry system. "Besides paying for a lavish wedding, the bride's family is expected to buy her a complete wardrobe and jewelry, as well as clothes and jewelry for the new son-in-law's family, with whom their daughter will be living. 'That's the minimum,' says Assanand. Those who can afford more are expected to give their new in-laws 'cash, furniture, appliances, a car and even property.' "[7]

Another group concerned with sex selection and women's issues was the Women's Environment and Development Organization (WEDO). WEDO and other women's groups were concerned about what was becoming known as the "missing women" of Asia.[8] ■

[4]John F. Burns, *The New York Times,* August 27, 1994, section 1, p. 5.
[5]The ratio in South Korea was 114 to 100 and in Taiwan was 110 to 100.
[6]*Chicago Tribune,* August 3, 1997.
[7]*Chicago Tribune,* August 3, 1997.
[8]See also *The Endangered Sex: Neglect of Female Children in Rural North India,* by Barbara Miller, 1997.

PREPARATION QUESTIONS

1. Identify the moral concerns in using ultrasound for sex selection.
2. What possible reactions might ATL encounter on this issue?
3. Does ATL have any responsibility regarding the use of its products in sex selection?
4. Should ATL introduce its FirstSight™ handheld product in India?
5. Develop a strategy for ATL with respect to the issues discussed in the case. Be sure to include specific steps you would take to implement your strategy.

Headquarters Relocation: Kimberly-Clark and the State of Wisconsin

Over 100 years ago, J. Alfred Kimberly and three friends founded the Kimberly-Clark Corporation in the small town of Neenah, nestled in the Fox River Valley of Wisconsin. Kimberly-Clark has since become the largest U.S. maker of consumer paper products and the largest corporation headquartered in Wisconsin. Its Kleenex tissues, Kotex tampons, Huggies diapers, and other consumer products generated sales of $2.96 billion and net profits of $197 million in 1982, placing it 134th and 74th on the respective *Fortune* 500 lists. In 1982 net income was down nearly 4 percent, and Kimberly-Clark placed only 248th on the *Fortune* 500 list in total return to investors. In the first quarter of 1983 net income declined another nine percent even though sales had risen ten percent.

Kimberly-Clark's chairman and chief executive officer, Darwin E. Smith, had become concerned about the climate for business in the state of Wisconsin. For 80 years Wisconsin had had a reputation as a progressive state in the LaFollette tradition and had been a leader in innovative state regulation of business and in the provision of public services. In part it was the consequences of this tradition that concerned Smith and caused him to consider moving Kimberly-Clark's headquarters from Wisconsin. Kimberly-Clark employed approximately 2,300 people at its headquarters and employed a total of 4,700 in Wisconsin.

One concern about the business climate in Wisconsin was the regulatory burden. Smith noted that Kimberly-Clark was currently building a plant in Conway, Arkansas, that it had wanted to build in Wisconsin. A construction permit had taken only 8 weeks to obtain in Arkansas, and Smith said, "In Wisconsin, we were told, it would take eleven months to get a commitment to do anything."

Of greater concern to Smith were the high taxes on both corporate profits and personal income. The Wisconsin Taxpayers Alliance reported that in 1981 Wisconsin had the fifth highest per capita state tax load—$352 per person compared with the national average of $181. This difference was made more significant by the fact that wage rates in Wisconsin were substantially lower than in a number of the other high tax rate states, including California, Massachusetts, and New York. In addition, to balance the budget Wisconsin was expected to pass a $738 million tax increase, primarily in the form of a ten percent surcharge on corporate and personal income taxes.

Smith was also concerned about the direction and policies of the newly elected state government. The new governor, Anthony Earl, was a liberal Democrat who had been the secretary of the state's Department of Natural Resources and was believed by the business community in Wisconsin to be unfamiliar with the problems facing business. Governor Earl had proposed boosting the minimum tax rate from 3.4 to 3.6 percent and the maximum rate from 10 to 10.5 percent. In addition, the state legislature had taken actions that indicated possible future threats to business. In 1983 the Democratic majority leader of the state senate had introduced a bill to impose a 3-year moratorium on home-mortgage foreclosures. Although that bill was narrowly defeated, it was widely believed to be indicative of the sentiments of a large segment of the state legislature. In a 1982 study, Alexander Grant & Company, a Chicago accounting firm, had ranked Wisconsin as having the twelfth worst business climate among the 48 contiguous states. According to the state's Bureau of Business Information Services, in the past 5 years 19 companies had moved out of Wisconsin. As State Senator Michael Ellis of Neenah said, "If Kimberly-Clark leaves, it acts as a signal to all business in the state that better times can be had outside of Wisconsin. It would be the start of the exodus from Wisconsin."[1]

An additional problem centered on the difficulty in recruiting professional and managerial talent to Wisconsin. As Smith said: "When you see our present highly talented employees and the younger generation that's coming up behind them—highly trained, highly skilled, technical people on the leading edge of know-how—they're the type of people that we've got to pay a great deal of money to. And

[1] *The Northwestern,* April 29, 1983.

why do they want to come to the state of Wisconsin when they see a tax rate, already at ten percent, put on their salaries and talk about going to 11 1/2. It's a question of recruiting and keeping good people. And I regret to tell—those of you who live in Wisconsin—that we've found it much easier to find skilled, highly trained people to live in other states than in Wisconsin."[2]

Rumors had begun to circulate about possible offers from Georgia and Texas to locate the headquarters in one of those states. In addition to what was perceived to be a more favorable business climate, Georgia had a corporate tax rate of six percent compared with Wisconsin's 7.9 percent, and its maximum personal income tax rate was six percent on all income above $10,000 compared with ten percent on income above $51,600 in Wisconsin. In 1981 Wisconsin had the seventeenth highest state and local property taxes, with an average of $41.78 per $1,000 of personal income, whereas Georgia was thirty-seventh with an average of $27.36. Georgia was believed to be a natural location for a paper products company because of the importance of the timber and wood products industry in the state. The nation's largest timber and wood products company, Georgia-Pacific, was headquartered in Atlanta and was the state's second-largest corporation after Coca-Cola. Many other timber, paper, and wood products companies also had operations in Georgia. During the past 10 years Kimberly-Clark had divested itself of significant timberland in Wisconsin and other Great Lakes states to concentrate its resources in the South and in Canada.

In 1980 Kimberly-Clark had established operations near Atlanta in Roswell, Georgia, and by 1983 had invested $34 million in office and research and development facilities, employing nearly 600 people. W. L. "Pug" Mabry, mayor of Roswell, stated, "We would certainly invite them to move their headquarters to Roswell," but he added, "to my knowledge K-C has never indicated to the city that it intends to move its headquarters here."[3] The city had been accommodating when Kimberly-Clark first began to build there. Rumors of a move to the Atlanta area were fueled by the application of a subsidiary of K-C Aviation to provide commercial service between Appleton (serving Neenah) and Chicago and Atlanta.

Smith's announcement became *the* news item in Wisconsin, but Governor Earl said "that the Kimberly-Clark story has gotten all out of proportion." The governor emphasized the positive aspects of Wisconsin, including the high quality of its public services and the recently adopted tax exemption for equipment and machinery. He said that Wisconsin did not compare badly with other states when all factors were considered, although he added that he would like to see an improvement in "the relatively poor perception some legislators have of business and some businesses have of legislators. Some businesses think lawmakers are only interested in raising taxes and setting onerous regulations. Lawmakers sometimes think businesses only want to make excess profits."

Governor Earl and Smith agreed to meet to discuss their concerns and scheduled a luncheon meeting in Kimberly-Clark's headquarters in Neenah.

Assignment

This assignment provides for a simulation of a fictitious discussion between a board committee of Kimberly-Clark and a working group from the state government. In preparation for the meeting with the governor, the Public Interest Committee of the Kimberly-Clark Board of Directors convened to discuss the possible headquarters location. A staff memorandum requested by Smith laid out several positions that might be taken in the discussion. One alternative was to commit the firm now to moving and announce it to the governor at the meeting as a fait accompli. This alternative had the advantage of terminating what might otherwise be a lengthy series of discussions with state officials. This alternative would necessitate expediting negotiations with Georgia or Texas officials, but they were likely to be receptive because of the importance of the relocation. A second alternative was to decide now to move the headquarters but not tell Governor Earl until the negotiations there had been completed. The advantage of this alternative was that it would not tip Kimberly-Clark's hand and hence would give the company more bargaining power with the states to which it might relocate. A variant of these two alternatives was to move only the portion of its headquarters most plagued by the difficulty of attracting and retaining managerial talent, leaving the lower-level staff in Neenah. A third alternative was to use the meeting with the governor to bargain for tax concessions. If they were granted, the company might

---

[2]Comments at the Kimberly-Clark annual meeting, April 28, 1983, Appleton, Wisconsin.
[3]*Post-Crescent,* May 15, 1983.

remain in Wisconsin. A fourth alternative was to seek a pledge from the governor to reduce taxes and lessen the regulatory burden on business in the state. A fifth possibility was to take Mr. Smith's concerns about the business climate to the people of Wisconsin in a mass media campaign that would inform them of the problems of doing business in the state and urge them to pressure the governor and their state legislators.

Governor Earl also assembled a working group, including the state treasurer, the state secretary of Employment and Labor, the chairman of the Wisconsin Chamber of Commerce, and the chairman of the State Federation of Labor, who was also the president of the United Auto Workers of Wisconsin, to prepare the state's position and meet with Kimberly-Clark.

The following small group assignments are fictitious and are identified to provide structure to the discussion.

Role Information: Kimberly-Clark's Public Interest Committee

Darwin E. Smith, Chairman and CEO. You are known to be seriously considering moving the headquarters, but you have not yet made a final decision.

President and COO. You are concerned about the profitability of the company and its need to raise capital to support new product development, test marketing, and nationwide marketing campaigns for new products. You were born and raised in Neenah and joined Kimberly-Clark after graduation from the University of Wisconsin.

Vice President of Personnel. You have been plagued by the difficulty in recruiting highly-talented MBAs and other executives.

President of a large Wisconsin-based foundation that supports medical research. You are very concerned about the long-term "health" of the state.

Partner, Morgan Stanley & Company. You have warned Smith about the financial community's concern with the company's performance.

Role Information: Governor's Working Group

The governor recognized that steps could be taken to improve the business climate in Wisconsin, but he was also aware that he had been elected to serve broader constituent interests.

Anthony Earl, Governor. You are very concerned by Kimberly-Clark's possible move. Your objective is to persuade Smith to not move the headquarters, or, failing that, to delay the move for as long as possible.

Treasurer. Your concern is with the financial health of the state and the need to generate tax receipts to pay for the services the Earl administration wants to provide.

Secretary of Employment and Labor. You are concerned about the state's ability to attract new industry to reduce unemployment. Unemployment, having fallen from 12 percent in February to 9.3 percent now, was a major concern because of the hardship on the unemployed and the resulting burden on the state budget.

Chairman, Wisconsin Chamber of Commerce. You have repeatedly warned the governor and the legislature about the business climate in the state. You have privately proposed that the state should commission a consulting firm to do a study of the business climate in Wisconsin and how it could be improved.

Chairman, State Federation of Labor and President, United Auto Workers of Wisconsin. You are concerned about the flight of jobs from the state and have suggested to leaders of the state legislature that it consider adopting a strict plant closing law. ■

Western National Bank

Since 1950 the federally chartered Western National Bank had maintained a branch in East Palo Alto, California, a small community made up largely of low-income individuals, most of whom were members of minority groups. The branch had about 1,100 checking accounts, almost all of which were personal as opposed to business accounts. The branch had very few savings accounts. Activity at the branch was low and centered mainly around the cashing of checks at the beginning of the month. The branch had never been more than marginally profitable and was not earning an adequate return on Western's investment.

In 1981 the Bank of America closed its branch in East Palo Alto, and in April 1985 Glendale Federal Savings closed its branch there, leaving Western as the only remaining bank. The newly formed East Palo Alto Citizens for Fair Banking claimed that the closures discriminated against the community.

The Western branch made loans for the purchase of motor vehicles but did not process home loans, since all mortgage applications were handled at the regional office in San Jose. Western made few mortgage loans in East Palo Alto because most residents had weak credit ratings, which made them ineligible under the bank's standards. Furthermore, most of the residents lived in rental housing, so the demand for mortgage lending was low. A number of owners of small apartment units had begun to convert to condominiums as a means of avoiding the risk of rent control, however, so the demand for the financing of condominium purchases had increased. The bank viewed these mortgage opportunities as unattractive because of economic and political risks. The political risks had increased since East Palo Alto incorporated as a city in 1983. The pace of political activity and community action had increased as a consequence of incorporation. The Stanford University Law School had recently opened a clinical law project in East Palo Alto as a means of helping the community and its residents. The budget problems of the new town were severe, however, and prevented it from controlling its rising crime rate.

Western had kept the branch open in recent years primarily because it provided a community service, but competitive pressures had caused it to begin to close "nonperforming" branches. In June 1985 Western's regional office staff evaluated the prospects for the East Palo Alto branch and concluded that there was little likelihood that the branch could be brought up to the performing standard.

The regional manager for Western had the authority either to close the branch or leave it open. If the branch were to close, the bank's ATM would also have to be removed because transferring money to the machine would become a security risk. ■

PREPARATION QUESTIONS

1. Given the two alternatives of closing the branch or leaving it open, which should the regional manager choose? Which would you choose and why would you choose it? How would you explain that decision to your superiors?
2. If you decide to leave the branch open, identify the principles that led you to that decision. If you decide to close it, explain why and identify the likely ramifications and their implications for Western.

CHAPTER 18

Ethical Systems: Utilitarianism and Management

Introduction

Ethics is the study of moral judgments about the rightness of actions and rules of behavior. At the systemic level, ethics is intended to contribute to mutually beneficial modes of conduct as an alternative to government prescription and enforcement. At the organizational level, ethics is a guide to managerial decision making and policy formulation. At the individual level, ethics provides a basis for justifying one's actions, evaluating the actions of others, and reasoning about moral dilemmas.

This and the following chapter address the role of ethics in management and provide an overview of three principal ethical systems. The objective is to increase moral sensitivity and encourage reasoning based on ethical principles and moral standards. To accomplish this, it is necessary to consider issues from the perspectives of several ethical systems. The systems considered here are utilitarianism, moral rules and rights, and a framework for justice. These systems correspond to basic ethical intuitions about the good and the right and provide guidance to firms and managers in the formulation of policies and the evaluation of alternative strategies.

Ethics and its application in management constitute a broad and deep subject. The approach taken here is to address the subject in a series of steps. This and the following chapter address the role of ethics in management, introduce the three ethical systems, and consider reasoning about nonmarket issues based on those systems. Chapter 20 then focuses on implementation issues, and the following two chapters address ethical issues that arise in the employment relationship and in international business. The chapter cases provide opportunities to reason from the perspectives of ethical systems and to apply ethical principles and methods to managerial problems.

Ethics has several managerial functions. As a normative approach, ethics provides principles for evaluating alternatives and formulating policies. In the context of the framework for nonmarket analysis presented in Chapter 2 and Figure 2-4, ethics in its normative role is used in both the choice and the screening stages. At the choice stage, ethics provides a basis for evaluating whether claims have moral standing and thus whether they are to be respected in the firm's actions. In the screening stage, ethics provides the underpinnings for policies that guide managers in determining which alternatives should be screened out and which should be considered further. Ethics also provides a basis both for assessing whether moral consensus is present and for justifying a firm's actions to stakeholders and the public.

Ethics is also an important component of the positive analysis of nonmarket issues. Individuals, activists, interest groups, and government officeholders can be motivated by moral concerns about a firm's actions. In the analysis stage of the framework in Figure 2-4, ethics contributes to the prediction of morally motivated nonmarket action. Because individuals have a range of ethical intuitions and concerns, it is necessary to view issues from the perspectives of several ethical systems. In its normative and positive roles, ethics thus provides a basis for analysis and for the formulation of strategies to address nonmarket issues and the nonmarket actions associated with them.

Ethics thus has a number of applied roles in management. First, it provides a basis for decision making and policy formulation. Managers must address a variety of complex issues, and ethics provides guidance about how to take into account the interests, rights, and liberties of those affected by business decisions. Ethics also provides a basis for evaluating the moral claims made by individuals and groups in the nonmarket environment. Second, ethics provides a means of justifying decisions to various constituencies, government officials, and the public. Third, ethics provides a basis for predicting whether individuals and groups will be motivated to act on an issue. Managers must be sensitive to the moral determinants of nonmarket action and, in addition to evaluating moral claims, understand how that action can affect the firm and shape its nonmarket environment.

What Ethics Is and Is Not

Ethics is a systematic approach to moral judgments based on reason, analysis, synthesis, and reflection. Ethics addresses matters of importance to human well-being, autonomy, and liberty. Ethics is based on moral standards that are independent of the declarations of governments or other authoritative bodies. Moral standards are impartial, take precedence over self-interest, and are to apply to everyone; that is, they are to be universal.[1] Ethics thus is the discipline concerned with judgments based on moral standards and the reasoning therefrom.

The issues considered in this and subsequent chapters involve significant moral concerns not easily resolved through approaches that are independent of moral standards. The focus thus is not on simple temptation. There are many managerial situations in which an action is contrary to the law, a well-established company policy, or widely accepted ethical principles, yet managers may be tempted to take the action because they, or the firm, may benefit from it. Since what is good or right is evident in these situations, they have only limited interest from the perspective of ethics. Addressing the issue of temptation remains important, however. One responsibility of management is to develop procedures to reduce the temptation that often arises, for example, from how performance is compensated. Approaches to reducing temptation and guiding managers through situations in which temptation may arise are considered in Chapters 20 and 22.

Ethics is also not the simple reliance on values or the search for value consensus. Values are expressions of desired outcomes or behavior. As a shortcut to ethical reasoning, individuals often rely on their values to guide their personal behavior. Values, however, differ among individuals, and there is little justification for concluding that because a majority has value X and a minority has value Y, value X should prevail. Furthermore, for an organization, policies must be both general and consistent and cannot be dictated by the personal values of whoever happens to occupy a particular managerial position at a particular point in time. Although statements of values by a firm, as

[1]Moral claims are distinguished from prudential claims, which are based on considerations of self-interest.

considered in Chapter 20, are a useful guide for managers in the screening stage of the framework illustrated in Figure 2-4, managers must be able to reason from principles about new issues and situations and must evaluate whether current policies continue to be appropriate. Values are not a sufficient basis for ethical analysis and reasoning by management.

The focus is also not on issues involving direct mutual advantage because such issues generally do not require ethical analysis. Every sale a firm makes benefits it and its customer. In the absence of external consequences, the transaction is generally free from moral objection. Mutual advantage may also control temptation. A consulting or investment banking firm often has an opportunity to serve its own rather than its clients' interests. To attract future clients, however, the firm has an incentive to establish a reputation for effectively serving client interests. Honoring expectations in such cases can be explained by self-interest independently of moral standards.

Moral philosophers search for ethical systems that can withstand both philosophical criticism and the test of practical application. The result has been an array of ethical systems rather than consensus on a single system. On some issues, decision alternatives may be consistent with one ethical system and inconsistent with others. Random drug testing of employees may increase social benefits and reduce social costs, and hence pass a utilitarian standard, yet it may violate an individual's right to privacy. Similarly, an absolute right to privacy would be unjust if it prevented drug testing of employees whose responsibilities affect public safety.

Business Ethics

Business ethics is the application of ethical principles to issues that arise in the conduct of business activity. There is no separate discipline of business ethics. As opposed to personal ethics, where an individual is a principal in the sense of Chapter 17, business ethics pertains to situations in which individuals are in an organizational position and act as agents of the company and its owners. Business ethics also differs from personal ethics in the sense that in the former a manager has accepted the responsibilities of the position occupied, whereas with the latter the responsibilities are to family and those—friends and communities—that the individual chooses. The set of issues also differs from those one encounters in one's personal life. In an organizational setting an individual may have obligations, such as preventing sexual harassment or meeting fiduciary duties, that one may not have encountered in one's personal life. Moreover, in one's personal life an individual may be able to focus on the virtuous life in an Aristotelian sense or a life of propriety in a Confucian sense. In an organization role, however, a manager must reason about situations in which virtue is not always present, conceptions of what is good or right differ among individuals, or interests are in conflict. Consequently, the focus here is on philosophical ethical systems and their application to moral issues that arise in business.

The approach taken does not promote a particular moral vision nor use ethics to mold consensus on a particular set of standards. In the case of "hard" issues such as drug testing of employees, reasonable people of goodwill may disagree on the appropriate actions. The objective thus is to present ethical systems and methods of reasoning that deepen one's understanding of a situation, identify relevant moral concerns, and provide a means of evaluating actions and policies. Even though many managerial actions are based on ethical intuition rather than on explicit reasoning from ethical principles, that intuition can often be sharpened and deepened by ethical analysis, and consistency can be improved.

One reason for considering several ethical systems is that doing so helps sensitize managers to the variety of moral concerns that may be raised about an issue. Considering a variety of systems also aids managers in reasoning about those concerns based on moral standards that give rise to those concerns. In particular, in addressing nonmarket issues it is important to understand and evaluate moral concerns from the perspectives that others may hold. To illustrate the notion of sensitivity to moral concerns involved in nonmarket issues, consider the issue of integrity tests.

ISSUE: INTEGRITY TESTS

In 1988 a federal law took effect prohibiting the use of pre-hiring polygraph tests, which had been given to approximately two million current and prospective employees annually.[2] The law also placed certain restrictions on the use of polygraph tests for employees suspected of violating laws or company policies. In response to the ban on pre-hiring polygraph tests, employers began to substitute more extensive background checks and to use written "integrity tests." Integrity tests are paper-and-pencil examinations intended to identify individuals with desirable or undesirable traits.[3] Examples of questions on the tests include, "Do you think a person should be fired by a company if it is found that he helped the employees cheat the company out of overtime once in a while?" and "If you found $100 that was lost by a bank truck on the street yesterday, would you turn the money over to the bank, even though you knew for sure that there was no reward?"[4] Firms use these tests, along with information on a potential employee's ability, education, and experience, to screen for integrity and potential loyalty to the firm. Some firms have found the tests to be quite useful in identifying individuals who may be a problem on the job.

Integrity tests raise several ethical concerns. From the perspective of costs and benefits, integrity tests can produce benefits to the extent that they help better match potential employees to the jobs in which they will be most productive. The tests may yield substantial benefits for some jobs and few benefits for others, however. Firms thus must decide for which positions the tests provide benefits that exceed the costs.

Integrity tests also raise a number of concerns about rights. Integrity tests may represent an invasion of privacy if the questions are personal. The tests also raise concerns about arbitrary treatment to the extent to which the tests are imperfect measures and hence may misclassify individuals. Employers, however, have a right to hire whomever they prefer as long as they do not engage in illegal discrimination, and they may use relevant means of making hiring decisions. The tests also raise justice considerations because they may deny opportunity to those who, for whatever reason, do not perform well on such tests. Justice considerations may also be involved if the tests put at a disadvantage individuals with past experiences that cause them to perform poorly on the test.

The remainder of this chapter addresses the methodology of ethics and presents an overview of utilitarianism, which provides a basis for the evaluation of issues such as the use of integrity tests. The issue of integrity tests is addressed again in the next chapter from the perspective of moral rights and justice. The Chapter 20 case *Genetic Testing* raises related issues.

Ethics and Private Interests

Ethical patterns of behavior allow society to realize the benefits from social interactions and enable individuals as autonomous ends to realize their own interests. Ethical be-

---

[2]Exemptions from the law are provided for security guards and jobs that involve health and safety. Pharmaceutical companies are also exempt, as is government.

[3]See Sackett and Harris (1984).

[4]The questions are from the Integrity Attitude Scale published by Reid Psychological Systems. (*The New York Times,* November 28, 1997.)

havior does not always make an individual or a firm better off, however. A policy of refusing to make payments to government officials can result in costly delays or the loss of sales in some countries. Furthermore, ethical behavior may not be self-evident to others, and even if it is, it may not be rewarded. A policy of hiring veterans or the disabled may be right from an ethical perspective but may not be the most profitable. Ethical behavior thus can conflict with profit objectives or with an individual's self-interest, since ethical principles prescribe behavior based on considerations that take precedence over self-interest. This is perhaps clearest in a utilitarian framework in which a person's own interests are given no greater consideration than the interests of any other person. Good ethics is thus not always profitable for an individual or a firm; however, good ethics is good for society and is a requirement of good management.

Although good ethics may not always be profitable, unethical behavior can result in substantial losses, as evidenced by the experience of firms involved in the investment banking scandals of the late 1980s. Unethical actions by a firm can also worsen the environment for all firms by causing the public to become suspicious of business and its motives. This can increase the likelihood of government regulation. In the long run, harmony between business and society requires behavior consistent with the principles embodied in the social contract under which business operates. Business and its management thus are evaluated not only in terms of financial performance but also in terms of moral standards and ethical principles.

Ethics, Politics, and Change

Ethics involves a disciplinary inquiry into whether a proposition has moral status. Propositions may be classified as claimed or granted, where a granted proposition is one that has been established by an authoritative body such as government or by ethical consensus. Claims are often made that a proposition has moral status. Frequently, these claims are intended to increase the likelihood that the proposition will be granted by government. For example, in some areas delivery services are plagued by robberies and threats to the safety of delivery personnel. As a result of reports from drivers concerned about their safety, a Federal Express district manager suspended after-dark pickups in Gary, Indiana. Similarly, a Domino's Pizza franchisee refused to deliver in certain high-risk areas in Miami. The proposition then is that delivery services may not refuse to serve parts of their normal service area, even if the motive is to avoid possible harm to delivery personnel. Ethics is used by the supporters of the proposition to argue that it is unjust and discriminatory not to deliver to a person who happens to reside in, for example, a high-crime area. The use of ethics to establish moral status of a proposition is illustrated by the horizontal arrows in Figure 18-1, which classifies propositions as claimed and granted and according to their moral status.[5]

Politics may be interpreted as the vertical status of propositions in the context of Figure 18-1. Most politics centers on private interests and is advanced in the absence of arguments about moral status, as illustrated by the three arrows in the left column of the figure. Some politics focuses on propositions with established moral status, as indicated by the arrow in the right column. For example, the policies restricting deliveries were rescinded after vocal protest by the mayor of Gary and under court order by a U.S. district court judge. San Francisco passed an ordinance making it illegal to refuse to deliver in parts of the regular service area of a restaurant.

Change thus can come from both ethics and politics. The Chapter 20 case *Pollution Credits Trading Systems and Environmental Justice* focuses on a possible change advanced by the ethics and politics of the proposition that less-advantaged persons,

[5]This figure is due to Keith Krehbiel.

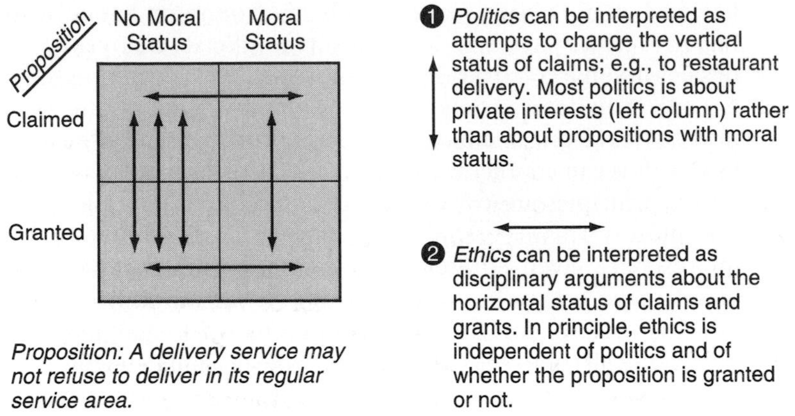
Proposition
No Moral Status
Moral Status
Claimed
Granted
Proposition: A delivery service may not refuse to deliver in its regular service area.
1 Politics can be interpreted as attempts to change the vertical status of claims; e.g., to restaurant delivery. Most politics is about private interests (left column) rather than about propositions with moral status.
2 Ethics can be interpreted as disciplinary arguments about the horizontal status of claims and grants. In principle, ethics is independent of politics and of whether the proposition is granted or not.

FIGURE 18-1 Ethics, Politics, and Change

including minorities and women, are adversely affected by certain environmental protection policies.

Casuistry

Ethics is principled reasoning and is to be distinguished from casuistry, which is an approach to moral practice that seeks to balance competing considerations by making exceptions to principles in particular cases. Casuistry is an ancient approach that reemerged during the Reformation as the argument that different principles are applicable to different situations. Casuistry was attacked by Pascal, who argued that although they may have been well intentioned, casuist methods were flawed and the results therefore questionable. Casuistry has been characterized as a false art of making exceptions in particular situations, resulting in the violation of underlying principles.[6] This approach is contrary to the ethical systems considered here, which are intended to apply universally. Thus, the familiar saying that "a diplomat is a person who lies abroad for the benefit of his country" may characterize politics but not ethics.

The following example is intended to illustrate casuist reasoning.

EXAMPLE: SAVING THE DIVISION

The Leyden Corporation is a small manufacturer of household appliances, including blenders, food processors, mixers, and coffee makers. Competition had intensified in all its lines of business, particularly as companies in the newly industrialized countries of Asia entered its markets. In 1997 Leyden incurred a loss of $1.2 million, and the first half of 1998 was worse. Leyden saw little opportunity to turn the situation around.

The most serious problem was with its line of blenders, which because of low-priced imports had experienced decreasing sales and was losing nearly $2 million a year. The blender division had done all it could to reduce costs, including freezing wage rates for the past year. If the profitability of the division could not be improved, Leyden's only alternative would be to close its plant. The general manager of the blender division formulated a plan that he believed would save the plant for a few years to buy time in the hope that something favorable, such as a change in exchange rates, might occur.

---

[6]See Jonsen and Toulmin (1988) for a history of casuistry and for its defense as a practical ethics.

The general manager's plan involved cutting the quality of the blenders but continuing to market them as before. The plan was to use a lower-quality motor and cheaper internal materials, which together would reduce costs by nearly 14 percent. This would enable the plant to remain open—as long as volume could be maintained. Although the blenders would not be as durable, a consumer would have no way of knowing that fact at the time of purchase. To ensure that buyers and consumers would not soon detect the lower quality, the general manager proposed charging the same price, advertising and marketing the blenders as before, and making certain that the new blenders had the same external appearance as the current ones. The general manager was confident that neither retailers nor customers would soon detect the changes.

The general manager reasoned that the plan would benefit employees and shareholders, and Leyden could be said to have a social responsibility to both groups. Consumers would be worse off compared to their expectations, but employees were a more immediate constituency, and consumers would still be getting a serviceable blender. From the point of view of responsibility to constituents, the general manager concluded that the plan should be implemented.

This reasoning is an example of casuistry. That is, the reasoning proceeds from a concept of responsibility to the particulars of a case without reliance on principles. From a utilitarian perspective, selling a lower-quality product as if it were a higher-quality product reduces aggregate well-being because some consumers would make choices they would not make if they knew of the change. From the perspective of moral rules, the plan involves deception, which is difficult to support in any ethical system. Furthermore, it treats consumers as a means of saving the division. From a justice perspective, the company is unjustly taking advantage of them.

The casuist approach is dangerous precisely because it shortcuts the application of principles in favor of conceptions of responsibility that may be inconsistent with moral standards. Furthermore, those conceptions can be a disguise for the self-interest of the decision maker. Several factors indicate when casuistry is being practiced. It is often present in situations in which the action the manager wants to take is identified by self-interest, the firm's interest, or constituents' interests. Casuistry may also be present when managers find themselves searching for a justification for the actions they wish to take based on self-interest. Casuistry may also be present when a manager tries to rationalize around principles to benefit some constituency group. The Chapter 20 case *Delta Instruments, Inc.* raises issues of responsibility and principles.

The Methodology of Ethical Analysis

The appropriate methodology of ethical analysis is illustrated in the left panel of Figure 18-2. It involves the identification of decision alternatives, evaluation of those alternatives in terms of ethical principles and moral standards, and choice based on those evaluations. Ethical analysis is intended to be applied early rather than late in the managerial decision-making process. As illustrated in the right panel of Figure 18-2, ethics that serves only to explain already-chosen actions is inappropriate. It encourages managers to choose actions that serve their and their firms' interests and then to search among the various ethical systems to find one that comes closest to justifying the already-chosen action. This does not mean, of course, that when correctly applied, ethics should not be used to justify the action taken. That justification, however, should be consistent with the motivation and the basis for the action.

Figure 18-3 provides more detail on the methodology of ethics. The methodology begins with the identification of the facts about the issue, because if the facts are incorrectly understood even a correct analysis can result in an inappropriate decision. Along with the facts, the moral concerns associated with the issue must be identified. They may involve concerns about distribution, rights and liberties, and fairness for those involved.

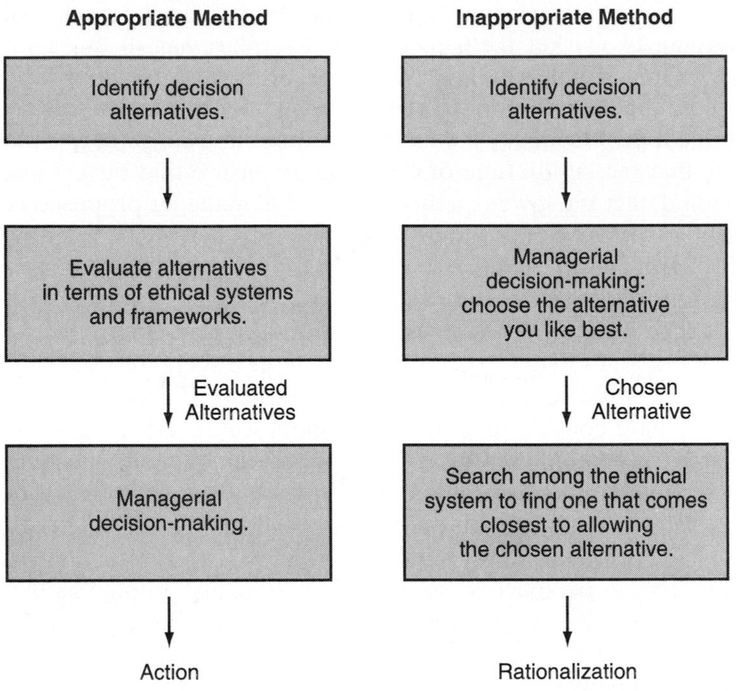

FIGURE 18-2 Appropriate and Inappropriate Methods of Applied Ethics

Management also must identify alternatives for addressing the issue, and creativity must be used in generating alternatives.

Once the facts have been discerned, moral concerns identified, and alternatives generated, ethical principles and moral standards are used to analyze those alternatives. Analysis involves reasoning that is logical, systematic, consistent, and reflective. The re-

FIGURE 18-3 Process of Ethical Analysis

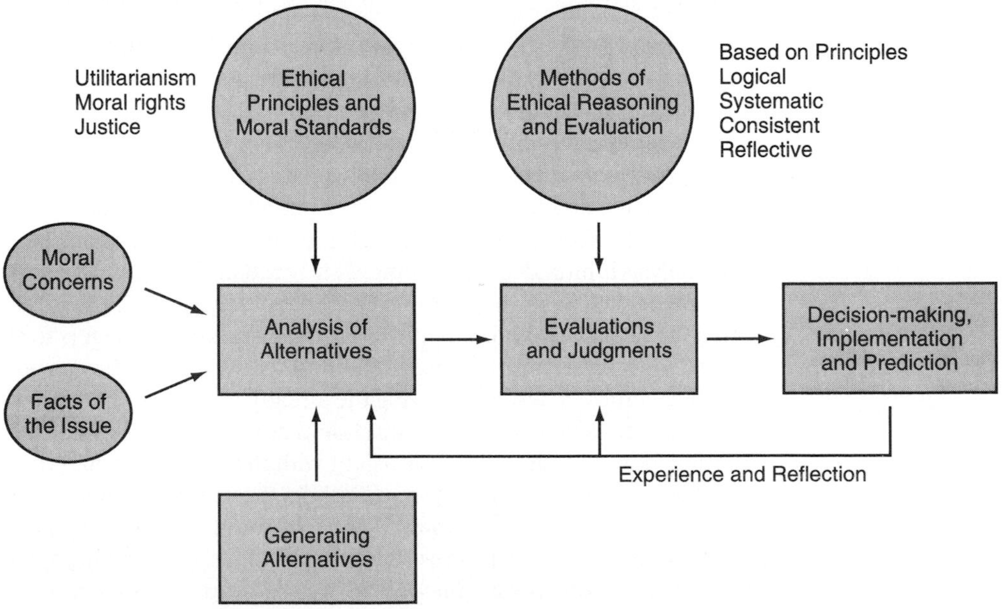

sults are judgments about whether the alternatives are consistent with ethical principles and moral standards. When ethics is directed at decision making, the final stage involves choice and implementation. When ethics is used for positive purposes, the final stage involves predicting whether objections to a decision are likely and whether nonmarket action can be expected. Finally, experience and reflection provide lessons for refining the methods of analysis and evaluation.

The Relationships Among Moral Philosophy, Ethics, and Political Philosophy

Figure 18-4 illustrates the relationship between moral philosophy and ethics. Moral philosophy is concerned with deducing moral principles and standards from axioms or self-evident principles. The self-evident principle that what matters is human well-being is the basis for utilitarianism. From that principle, the standard of maximizing aggregate well-being is deduced. The action that maximizes aggregate well-being then has moral standing because it yields the greatest good. As considered in Chapter 19, Kant's categorical imperative provides the basis for deducing the principles of universalizability and reversibility, which in turn provide a basis for identifying individual rights. The choice of a social contract from behind a veil of ignorance about a person's position in society provides the basis for identifying liberties and responsibilities, such as a right to maximal liberty consistent with equal liberty for all, as considered in Chapter 19.

As indicated in Figure 18-4, ethics is concerned with analysis and reasoning based on principles and standards. This reasoning may be directed toward the design of society's institutions, such as the public education and justice systems, the identification of specific rights, and the identification of appropriate behavior. The analysis and reasoning may also be directed at determining which actions provide the greatest aggregate well-being or at assessing whether a right of privacy takes precedence over other rights.

FIGURE 18-4 Relationship between Moral Philosophy and Ethics

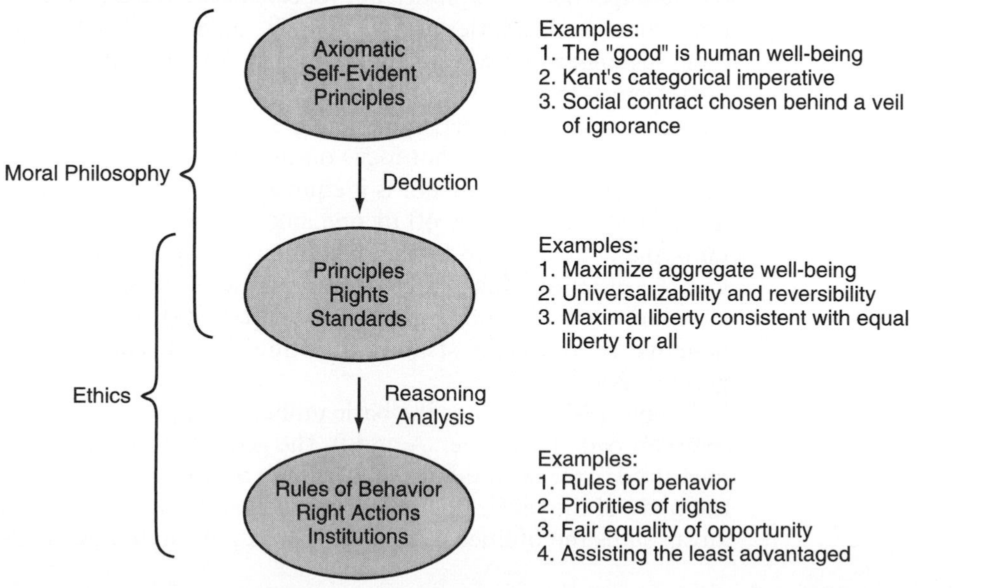

Political philosophy is related to ethics and moral philosophy but focuses on the interactions among individuals and the institutions that intermediate those interactions. Political philosophy naturally focuses on conceptions of the state, the manner in which the state may grant and limit liberties and ensure justice, and the extent to which markets and other institutions are used to intermediate voluntary actions.

Moral and political philosophy come together when they provide principles to govern the interactions among individuals. Utilitarianism provides a basis for a political philosophy in which the choice between private institutions, such as markets, and public institutions, such as government, is made according to which maximizes aggregate well-being.

Utilitarianism: A Consequentalist System

Utilitarianism has a rich history with its origins in the work of Jeremy Bentham (1789), who argued for a calculus of pain and pleasure, and then of John Stuart Mill (1861). The moral standing of utilitarianism, however, is better understood in more recent expressions to which the criticisms applied to hedonism are less applicable. Utilitarianism is better understood as a particular form of a consequentialist moral philosophy.

In a consequentialist system, an alternative is moral if it produces better consequences for human well-being than any other alternative. Utilitarianism is a particular consequentialist system that holds that consequences are to be evaluated in terms of the preferences of individuals and that those preferences are to be aggregated. Aggregation is required because an action may make some individuals better off and others worse off. The notion of human well-being and the need to consider the consequences for all persons correspond to a fundamental ethical intuition.

As an example, since the oil crisis of 1973 the United States had a national speed limit of 55 miles per hour. As oil prices dropped and Americans increased their driving, the pressure for higher speed limits mounted. In 1995 Congress abolished the federal speed limit, and by 1998 all but one state had increased their speed limits. Some increased their speed limit to 70 on certain stretches of interstate highways, and Montana had no daytime speed limit. Although not yet conclusive, the data indicate that the higher speed limits increased fatalities and injuries. The higher speed limits also saved motorists and their passengers many hours of travel time. The overwhelming revealed preference for higher speed limits suggests that the benefits from the time saved outweighed the costs. As one motorist said referring to the greater risks, "I'll take that tradeoff."

Utilitarianism does not focus on the numbers of people who are better or worse off because of an action, nor is it equivalent to a vote among alternatives. If an action makes 100 people worse off by one unit each and makes one person better off by 101 units, the action should be taken. Utilitarianism is also not "the greatest good for the greatest number." That statement is ambiguous because, as the example indicates, one alternative could produce the greatest good yet another alternative could produce benefits for the greatest number. Utilitarianism chooses the action that yields the greatest good.

Table 18-1 illustrates the basic utilitarian approach. A decision maker is to choose between two alternatives, A and B. The good for each of the four members of society, measured in terms of their preferences or utilities for the consequences, is presented in the body of the table. The aggregate good is the sum of those utilities; that is, utilitarianism sums the utilities of the individuals. Alternative A yields an aggregate utility of

TABLE 18-1 Utilitarianism Example

	Utility from Alternative	
Individual	**A**	**B**
1	**3**	**3**
2	**3**	**5**
3 (the decision maker)	**3**	**2**
4	**2**	**4**
aggregate utility	**11**	**14**

11, whereas action B yields a greater aggregate utility of 14. Utilitarianism identifies action B as the moral action, since it yields the greater good.

UTILITARIANISM AND SELF-INTEREST

Utilitarianism is nearly the antithesis of self-interest because one's own interests are to be given no more consideration than those of any other person. That is, decisions are to be impartial. The interests considered thus are not just those of the decision maker but those of everyone affected by the action. In this sense utilitarianism is impartial, since the decision maker's interests are given the same weight as the interests of the other persons affected by the decision. In Table 18-1 individual 3 is worse off with action B than with A, but as a utilitarian decision maker, 3 has a moral duty to choose B over A. Note also that as utilitarians each of the four individuals is to choose alternative B. That is, utilitarianism is universal.

Utilitarianism coincides with self-interest only when social consequences are perfectly aligned with private consequences. For example, if one firm signs a contract with another to supply a product, both firms presumably are better off as a result of the transaction. From a utilitarian perspective the transaction is morally good provided there are no externalities associated with the supply arrangement. Moreover, as long as both parties agree to the contract, the price at which the product is exchanged is irrelevant. That is, if the value of the product to the buyer is 20 and the cost to the supplier is 15, the transaction results in a net benefit of 5 regardless of the price. The price paid is a pure transfer between the buyer and the seller, and the transfer nets to zero in the utilitarian calculus.

UTILITARIANISM, DISTRIBUTION, AND ALTRUISM

Utilitarianism aggregates individuals' well-being as evaluated in terms of their preferences, and hence each person's preferences are given equal weight. In this sense utilitarianism does not take into account the distribution of utility across individuals. In the example in Table 18-1 the distribution of utility is more equal with alternative A than with alternative B, but since utilitarianism is only concerned with aggregate well-being or utility, it does not matter how that utility is distributed across individuals. Alternative B yields the greater aggregate utility and hence is the moral choice.

Although utilitarianism aggregates the preferences of individuals, it need not give equal weight to everyone's well-being if individuals have altruistic preferences. That is, if some individuals have altruistic preferences for the well-being of others as well as their own well-being, the well-being of those others receives greater weight. For example, if a rich person has altruistic preferences for the well-being of the poor, utilitarianism gives greater weight to the well-being of the poor than to that of the rich person.

The rich person's preferences for the poor cannot be arbitrary but instead must be those on which the rich person is willing to act. The rich person may redistribute some of her wealth or contribute time to the well-being of the poor. In evaluating two alternative government programs designed to benefit the poor, it is the preferences on which the rich person is personally willing to act that are counted. Thus, a person concerned for the well-being of the poor is not able to assign an arbitrary weight to their well-being. That rich person may, however, attempt to persuade others also to be altruistic or may engage in political activity to compel others to benefit the poor. If the taxes paid distort incentives and thus reduce economic efficiency, the cost of those distortions must be taken into account in evaluating the programs to benefit the poor.

SUMMARY

Utilitarianism is thus a moral philosophy that holds that:

- the moral good of an action is judged in terms of its consequences;
- consequences are evaluated in terms of human well-being;
- human well-being is evaluated in terms of individual preferences; and
- the rightness of an action is judged by the aggregate well-being, or good, it yields.

Moreover, utilitarianism is the antithesis of self-interest, and the two are consistent only if all the consequences of an individual's actions are internalized.

Applied Utilitarianism—Cost-Benefit Analysis

One applied version of utilitarianism is the concept of a social welfare function in the field of economics. A social welfare function is based on individual preferences as represented by the individual's utility function. Those utility functions are then summed and, in principle, could be used to evaluate public policies, including welfare and workfare, alternative tax systems, liability rules, and environmental protection policies, as well as private decisions. Arrow's impossibility theorem, however, demonstrates that there is no means of aggregating individual preferences in a consistent manner for all conceivable preferences individuals may have.[7] Despite its problems, the social welfare approach forms the basis for cost-benefit analysis in which consequences are evaluated in terms of individuals' revealed preferences. Cost-benefit analysis is an application of a utilitarian moral philosophy.

One role of government is to provide institutions that align private and social benefits and costs. This then allows individuals to evaluate actions in terms of their own preferences rather than having to take into account the consequences for all others affected by their actions. Many of society's institutions are based on this principle and are designed to internalize social costs and align the interests of firms and individuals with the aggregate interests of society.

The institutions of private property and markets provide one means of alignment, since a voluntary transaction, such as the supply arrangement discussed previously, makes both the buyer and seller better off. A transaction that constitutes a Pareto improvement—makes at least one person better off and no one worse off—thus is morally good from a utilitarian perspective. In the case of environmental protection, pollution credit trading systems or emissions fees as considered in Chapter 12 provide incentives to pollution emitters to reduce their emissions. The law of torts considered in Chapter 11 is an institution that assigns the social costs of accidents to individuals and firms. The chapter case *Living Benefits* considers a market that arose in response to a demand for

---

[7]See Chapter 5.

flexibility in the use of life insurance benefits. When such institutions are in place and markets are competitive, the maximization of profit by a firm results in the greatest aggregate well-being, that is, the greatest difference between social benefits and social costs. This alignment of private interests and social interests forms one basis for Milton Friedman's view that the social responsibility of business is to maximize profits, as considered in Chapter 17.

UTILITARIAN DUTY AND THE CALABRESI AND MELAMED PRINCIPLES

In an imperfect world in which transactions costs and market imperfections impede the efficiency of institutions intended to align private and social interests, an individual or a firm cannot rely solely on its own incentives. One means of reasoning from a utilitarian perspective in such situations is based on the Calabresi and Melamed principles presented in Chapter 11, which provide a test for whether a decision maker has a moral duty to take a particular action. Those principles are intended to identify which party is in the best position to determine whether the benefits of an action outweigh its costs, which party is in the best position to induce others to take actions that yield benefits that exceed the costs, and which party is in the best position to induce others to act to correct a misassignment of entitlements. That party then has a duty to act.

For example, the appropriate level of safety to incorporate into a product depends on the safety features the manufacturer could incorporate and on the care taken by the user of the product. To determine if the manufacturer or the user has the duty to add safety features or take care, respectively, the Calabresi and Melamed principles provide the following tests:

1. Assign the duty to the party—the manufacturer or the user—that can best achieve improvements in the difference between aggregate benefits and costs.
2. If it is not clear which party that is, the duty should be assigned to the party that is in the best position to assess the aggregate benefits and costs.
3. If that is unclear (and hence a mistake in the assignment of duty could be made), assign the duty to the party that can at the lowest cost induce the other party to take actions to improve the difference between aggregate benefits and aggregate costs.

For example, in the case of product safety the duty is usually assigned to the manufacturer who is in the better position to assess aggregate costs and benefits and to reduce accidents through the incorporation of safety features. Moreover, the manufacturer is usually well positioned to provide instructions and warnings to induce the consumer to take care. Furthermore, the application of the Calabresi and Melamed principles to product safety as considered in Chapter 11 indicates that a manufacturer has a duty to anticipate carelessness and even misuse of a product by a consumer.

Act and Rule Utilitarianism

Utilitarianism may be applied in two forms, "act utilitarianism" and "rule utilitarianism."[8] Act utilitarianism focuses on the consequences of a particular action in a particular situation and prescribes the action that yields the greatest difference between benefits and costs for everyone affected by that action. Rule utilitarianism focuses on a general rule of behavior to be followed by all individuals in all similar situations. A moral rule is then the one that does best in terms of its consequences for everyone affected in those situations. A moral action is then that which is consistent with the moral

[8]See Brandt (1959) (1979) for this distinction.

rule appropriate for the particular situation. Rule utilitarianism is viewed by its advocates as providing a set of rules for guiding the behavior of all individuals in society in a mutually advantageous manner. Act utilitarianism focuses on individual actions and cannot explain what the overall consequences would be for society if everyone were to act in that manner.

To illustrate the substantive and methodological distinctions between act and rule utilitarianism, suppose that in a particular situation deceiving rather than dealing with a person honestly would yield benefits that exceed the costs. Under act utilitarianism, deception is a morally justified action in this situation. If the general rule of behavior, however, were, "People may deceive others when it is beneficial to do so," relying on the word of others would be problematic. Aggregate well-being then would presumably be lower, and mutually advantageous reliance on the word of others would require costly enforcement mechanisms. A rule such as "Always deal with people in an honest and forthright manner" would yield greater aggregate well-being and thus have moral standing. Moreover, act utilitarianism can deteriorate into self-interest, since it focuses on an individual's action in a specific situation rather than on general rules of behavior that everyone is to follow.

The weakness of rule utilitarianism, however, is precisely the strength of act utilitarianism. If deception in a particular situation X yields benefits that exceed the costs, the following modification of the rule would yield greater aggregate well-being: "Always deal with people in an honest and forthright manner except in situation X in which deception is permitted." Amending the rule to allow an exception for a particular situation clearly improves the utilitarian calculus and hence is a morally superior rule. Then, any exception that yields benefits in excess of its costs will also yield a morally superior rule. Rule utilitarianism then degenerates into act utilitarianism.[9]

One response of a rule utilitarian is that utilitarian methods are necessarily applied in an imperfect world in which some facts are missing, information is incomplete, and not all consequences can be foreseen, let alone evaluated. In such a world, it is better to evaluate general rules of behavior to guide individuals in society rather than to apply utilitarian methods separately to each action and to each situation.[10]

Rule utilitarianism also encourages individuals to think about whether they would like everyone to follow the same rule of behavior in all similar situations. That is, the focus of act utilitarianism on the evaluation of specific actions can place an individual on the slippery slope leading toward evaluating actions based on self-interest rather than the consequences for all affected. Rule utilitarianism thus is the preferred form of utilitarianism.

Rule utilitarianism also encourages an individual to think beyond the specific situation to a more general set of situations with similar characteristics. As an example, in the late 1980s American Airlines and United Airlines became concerned about the changes in medical standards adopted by the new federal air surgeon, an officer of the Federal Aviation Administration (FAA). The federal air surgeon has responsibility for granting medical waivers, referred to as "special issuances," that allowed reinstatement of pilots who had had their certification suspended. One pilot who had blacked out in the cockpit had been granted a special issuance, as had a pilot who had had bypass surgery. An airline was not required to allow a pilot with a special issuance to fly, and American and United had kept their pilots grounded until receiving clearance from their own chief medical officer. The moral question was whether the airlines should take any action with regard to the policies being followed by the federal air surgeon. Since

[9]See Lyons (1965).
[10]See Hardin (1988).

the airlines could ground their pilots with special issuances that were questioned by their own medical officers, the airlines were not concerned about their own pilots. The broader concern was with general aviation pilots and other airlines that might not be aware of the change in the standards. American and United extrapolated their own situations to the broader population of pilots and airlines—they considered a general rule and concluded that they had a duty to make their concerns public. The airlines went to the FAA and to the congressional committee with oversight responsibilities for the FAA, which held hearings leading to a review of the medical standards being used.

SIMULTANEOUS CHOICE BY SEVERAL INDIVIDUALS

The distinction between act and rule utilitarianism can be clarified by considering situations that depend on actions taken by more than one person.[11] When consequences are jointly determined, utilitarian analysis is more complicated. In act utilitarianism an individual chooses the action that maximizes aggregate well-being taking the behavior of others as given. In rule utilitarianism an individual chooses not only one's own behavior but also simultaneously a rule to govern the behavior of all individuals. In so doing the individual is choosing a rule of behavior to be followed by everyone, so it is universal. Moreover, that rule is mutually advantageous for society. In addition, all persons would choose the same rule, since each maximizes aggregate well-being. Each individual thus is not only choosing in an impartial manner but also chooses the same rule, so there is unanimity.[12]

As an example of the application of rule utilitarianism, consider two individuals who each must decide whether to act honestly or dishonestly. Table 18-2 presents their utilities as a function of the actions each takes, where the first entry in each cell is the utility of person 1 and the second is the utility of 2. Acting honestly is better for individual 1 if and only if individual 2 acts honestly, but acting dishonestly is better for 2 regardless of whether 1 acts honestly or dishonestly. As rule utilitarians each individual is to choose between two alternative rules: (A) Always act honestly and (B) Always act dishonestly.[13] Rule A yields aggregate utility of 17, whereas rule B yields aggregate utility of 11. As rule utilitarians both individuals would choose rule A, so they are unanimous in their choice.

Act utilitarianism takes the other individual's action as given in choosing an action. In the example in Table 18-2 if 2 were to act dishonestly, as an act utilitarian individual 1 would act dishonestly, which yields aggregate utility of 11 instead of 10. If 2 were to act honestly, 1 would act honestly. Individual 2 would reason in an identical manner, acting honestly if 1 were to act honestly, and acting dishonestly if 1 were to act dishonestly.

TABLE 18-2 Rule Utilitarianism

		Individual 2	
		honest	dishonest
Individual 1	honest	10,7	2,8
	dishonest	7,2	4,7

[11]See Harsanyi (1982, p. 57) for this characterization and also Harsanyi (1977).

[12]As developed further in the next chapter, such a rule meets the two higher-order moral standards—universalizability and unanimous choice from behind a veil of ignorance—that give it moral standing.

[13]Note that there are other possible rules, such as, "Individual 1 is to act honestly and individual 2 dishonestly." The two rules A and B are considered because they are symmetric.

Which actions would be taken thus depends on what the other individual can be expected to do. Suppose that 1 suspects that individual 2 might not be a utilitarian but instead could be motivated solely by self-interest. If 1 harbors such suspicions, the better action could be to act dishonestly. That is, if 2 were indeed motivated by self-interest, it would act dishonestly, since that is a dominant strategy; that is, acting dishonestly is better for 2 regardless of how 1 acts. If instead 2 were an act utilitarian but believed that 1 was suspicious and might believe that 2 were self-interested, then 2 would act dishonestly. In this case incomplete information about the type of the other individual could cause act utilitarianism to degenerate into both being dishonest.

Decision Making in the Face of a Moral Transgression

Next consider the case in which 1 is a rule utilitarian and 2 is known to be self-interested and hence will act dishonestly. Is 1 morally justified in acting dishonestly? The answer at one level is no because the moral rule is for both to act honestly. It is 2 who is acting immorally. Under act utilitarianism 1 is morally right to act dishonestly, since doing so is justified by avoiding even a worse outcome with an aggregate utility of 10. Rule utilitarianism, however, indicates that it is right for 1 to act honestly. In Chapter 22 a policy of the Cummins Engine Company to address such situations is considered.

Utilitarianism and Rights

Rights may be classified as intrinsic or instrumental. Intrinsic rights are to be respected because they have moral standing independently of the consequences they yield. Instrumental rights are to be respected because they lead to desirable consequences. Instrumental rights are justified in a consequentialist system, such as utilitarianism, because in a wide variety of settings their existence results in benefits that exceed the associated costs. Property rights are an example of instrumental rights, since they facilitate beneficial economic transactions. Utilitarianism thus provides a means of evaluating instrumental rights but does not provide a basis for evaluating intrinsic rights, which must be justified by other considerations as addressed in Chapter 19. The chapter case *Sex-Differentiated Retirement Benefits* considers issues of efficiency and rights.

Criticisms of Utilitarianism

One criticism of consequentialist systems is that they do not give adequate attention to intrinsic rights and liberties, which are said to have fundamental importance. A related criticism is that consequentialist systems treat all things alike in their calculus. Thus, aspirations, wants, needs, liberties, and opportunities appear to be accorded equal status. As Sen (1987, pp. 74–76) argues, however, consequences must remain an essential focus even of an ethical system that considers intrinsically important concepts.

Another concern with utilitarianism pertains to the duty to take a particular action. If there is only one person who can take the action, the assignment is clear. In some cases, however, there may be more than one person who could take the utilitarian action. One resolution is that the duty should be assigned collectively to all those who could take the action, but that leaves a collective choice problem that could be difficult to resolve. If there are costs associated with taking the action, the utilitarian resolution of the collective choice problem is that the person with the lowest cost should be assigned the duty. In some cases the assignment may be either to a firm or to the government. For example, in the case of permanent layoffs, the duty to retrain laid-off employees could rest with the employer, the government, or the employees. The duty to retrain workers has primarily been assumed by the individuals themselves and by government, whereas many companies have assumed the responsibility for upgrading the education and skills of their employees.

Utilitarianism is also criticized for its focus on human well-being. Critics claim that it should be expanded to include the well-being of other living creatures such as animals and trees and inanimate objects such as rocks and soil. This claim is the subject of much disagreement, but if the claim were accepted, the approach to taking these broader considerations into effect would be similar to how altruism is taken into account. Since the good is to be measured in terms of the preferences of individuals, the preferences of those individuals concerned with animate and inanimate objects would be taken into account, but only to the extent that they would act on those preferences on their own. Some go farther and argue that in the realms of conservation and the protection of nature what matters is not the pleasure that individuals obtain from an undisturbed mountain lake. Instead, the claim is that the well-being of the lake itself is to be taken into account.

A difficulty in the application of a utilitarian system centers on whether well-being can be evaluated from observed actions; that is, from revealed preferences. If people choose to indulge in a habit such as smoking or take actions such as hang gliding that can reduce their life expectancy, is that a benefit or a cost? If preferences are revealed by actions, the indulgence presumably has benefits that outweigh the costs of the reduced life expectancy. In a government cost-benefit analysis, however, the reduced life expectancy counts as a social cost, and the benefits of the indulgence are generally not counted. A related issue is whether observed data, such as wage differentials, can be used to measure certain social costs. For example, are the wage premiums paid for dangerous construction work an appropriate measure of the social costs of the accidents and deaths associated with that work? One answer is that workers have chosen those jobs in exchange for higher wages, and those choices reveal their trade-off of wages for risks. Another answer is that workers took those jobs because they had few attractive alternatives.

Another criticism is that an individual's or a firm's actions often do not directly determine the consequences.[14] Instead, consequences are often determined jointly through the actions of several, or many, persons, as in the discussion of the example in Table 18-2. Hence, the link between actions and consequences involves strategic interactions, as in the case of a prisoners' dilemma or a free-rider problem. Assigning duties and responsibilities in strategic situations can be a complicated task.

A fundamental problem with utilitarian analysis is the difficulty, if not the impossibility, of making interpersonal comparisons of preferences. The preferences considered in the discipline of economics are ordinal in the sense that they only indicate how an individual orders one set of consequence relative to another. Those preferences do not reflect intensity, so interpersonal comparisons are problematic unless some common measure of intensity can be devised.[15] The Pareto criterion avoids interpersonal comparisons, since it requires only that a rule not make anyone worse off and make at least one person better off. A rule that produces a Pareto improvement thus has a strong claim to moral standing in a consequentialist ethical system.

In spite of the difficulties in making interpersonal comparisons of preferences, utilitarianism frequently is applied to public policies by measuring benefits and costs in monetary units. Measurement may involve a direct estimate of how much individuals are willing to pay, or accept, for one outcome rather than another. Indirect estimates—using wage differentials to evaluate the cost of job hazards or housing price

[14]See Hardin (1988).

[15]Harsanyi (1982) argues that the problem of interpersonal comparisons of preferences can be overcome by applying a similarity postulate that holds that after allowing for differences in tastes, individuals can be viewed as reacting similarly when choosing among alternatives.

differentials as a function of the distance from an airport to estimate the cost of noise pollution—are also possible. Because of the difficulties in making interpersonal comparisons, cost-benefit calculations are often only one of several considerations used in public policy analysis.

Utilitarianism In Application

CATEGORIES OF SITUATIONS

In applying utilitarianism it is useful to distinguish between two categories of situations. The first includes those in which institutions are in place to align the interests of the decision maker with the aggregate well-being of society. The second includes those in which institutions are either not in place or imperfectly align private and social interests.

In the first category of situations, actions taken in the interests of the firm are also in the interests of society, so the firm can act based on its own interests. If a firm manufactures and sells a product that is hazardous when misused, and if misuse can be anticipated, the firm's decisions about safety features under a utilitarian standard can be made as considered in Chapter 11. The firm can choose safety features based on their cost and the anticipated reductions in liability awards and legal costs. Even though these costs are not perfect measures of social costs, they represent the guidance of an institution, the law of torts, that has evolved over time in response to those social costs. The law of torts is thus an institution consistent with utilitarianism.

Similarly, if markets are competitive, a decision regarding closing a plant can be made on the basis of profitability. If the plant's costs are too high for it to be competitive, economic theory recommends that the resources used in that plant be reallocated to higher-valued uses. Furthermore, the government has established a set of institutions, such as unemployment insurance and job training programs, to deal with unemployment and reemployment. Decisions based on profitability then serve society's long-term interest in the efficient use of resources—although in some cases they do so only imperfectly. This does not mean, however, that the firm cannot take measures to ease the transition for its former employees nor that other ethical considerations such as rights and justice are not relevant.

The second category of situations includes those in which institutions are not in place to align the interests of the firm and society. In those situations, utilitarian analysis must be applied directly. Many government agencies conduct cost-benefit analyses to provide information to policy makers, and firms also conduct cost-benefit analyses, as the chapter case *Pricing the Norplant® System* indicates. These analyses are not always without controversy, however.[16]

As an example, after an airline crash in 1989, safety activists led a movement to require the use of infant safety seats in aircraft. Children under the age of 2 years had been permitted to travel on airlines without tickets if they were held by a parent. Safety activists advocated that parents be required to purchase a ticket for the child and use an infant safety seat. The Federal Aviation Administration (FAA) conducted a cost-benefit analysis of the safety seat issue and concluded that requiring the use of safety seats would actually increase injuries and fatalities. The FAA estimated that the seats would save one infant's life over a decade. Requiring infant safety seats, however, would increase the cost of air travel for families, causing some to substitute driving for flying. Since driving is considerably more dangerous than flying, deaths and injuries would in-

---

[16]See also the Chapter 4 case *Shell, Greenpeace, and Brent Spar* in which Shell conducted a form of consequentialist analysis on alternatives for the disposal of an oil platform.

crease. The FAA's estimate was nine additional highway fatalities, 52 serious injuries, and 2,300 minor injuries. The methods and conclusions of the FAA study were criticized on several dimensions including the estimated cost increase for air travel for families. Others attacked the conclusion itself. Representative Jim Lightfoot (R-IA) stated, "What's your child worth? Is it worth the price of an airline ticket?"[17]

METHODOLOGY

The framework for the application of utilitarianism is illustrated in Figure 18-3. It begins with the identification of the facts of the situation. As applied in the form of social cost-benefit analysis, the methodology then involves the following steps:

1. Identify the alternatives—rules of behavior and actions.
2. For each alternative, identify the set of consequences for all persons affected.
3. Determine which of the consequences are social costs and which are social benefits.
4. Evaluate and estimate the social costs and benefits.
5. Choose the action or rule that yields the greatest net social benefits.

The objective of a complete utilitarian analysis is to arrive at the optimal decision in step 5. A more modest objective is to encourage managers to think broadly, rather than narrowly, about the consequences of their actions. Even if a complete analysis cannot be conducted because, for example, of measurement and information problems, completing the first three steps can deepen the understanding of the issue and provide a sounder foundation for the application of ethical intuition and judgment. In particular, those steps encourage managers to consider the consequences of alternatives for all those affected.

Difficulties in the Implementation of Utilitarian Analysis

The three principal difficulties in the implementation of utilitarian analysis are determining what is a social cost or a social benefit, evaluating and measuring costs and benefits, and obtaining the needed information.

IDENTIFYING SOCIAL COSTS AND BENEFITS

In principle, what is a social cost or benefit is determined by a person's preferences. In assessing preferences, economists look at what individuals reveal through their actions rather than what they say. That is, rather than asking people how costly is noise pollution, economists estimate the price differentials of homes on airline flight paths.[18] If individuals voluntarily choose to ride motorcycles without wearing helmets, then, in the utilitarian calculus, the benefits outweigh the costs to them. In the case of substance abuse, however, addiction makes choice less than voluntary, and hence revealed preferences are not a satisfactory indicator of preferences. That is, social costs and benefits cannot be identified by revealed preferences unless choices are voluntary.

Since utilitarianism considers the consequences for everyone, certain consequences net to zero. If a social cost must be borne by someone, from an aggregate perspective it may not matter whether person A, person B, a firm, or government bears it. Hence, in Chapter 11, the focus of the analysis of the liability system was on efficiency rather than on the distributive consequences. Similarly, in the tradable allowances system for controlling sulfur dioxide emissions from power plants considered in Chapter 12, it does not matter from a utilitarian perspective whether the allowances are given free to power

---

[17] *Washington Post,* July 13, 1990.
[18] This approach takes into account the location decisions of people who have various tolerances for noise.

plants or auctioned. It does matter, however, whether the FCC auctions licenses to use the radio spectrum rather than awarding them based on noneconomic criteria, since an auction allocates them to their highest valued use. Auctioning licenses also redistributes wealth from broadcast companies to the government and hence to the public.

THE MEASUREMENT PROBLEM

Most applications of utilitarian analysis involve difficult measurement and estimation problems. Social costs and benefits typically are measured in monetary units based on the amount a person would accept in exchange for a beneficial consequence or would forgo to avoid an adverse consequence. Consequences are thus measured in terms of their monetary equivalents. The methods of measuring monetary equivalents in cost-benefit analysis in the public sector serve as guides for the conduct of utilitarian analysis. These methods are presented in Boardman (1996), Gramlich (1998), and Linneman (1980); and Moore and Magat (1996, 1997) present detailed cost-benefit analyses of product safety standards.

Some consequences, including the effects on sales and the costs of manufacturing, are readily estimated from a firm's own data. Other consequences, such as personal injuries and environmental damage, are more difficult to evaluate. Assigning a value to a life or a limb is difficult at best. Increasing the speed limit results in more deaths and injuries, but the public's revealed preferences were clear, indicating that the costs were exceeded by the benefits. The liability system makes explicit judgments about the value of a life or a limb. A firm that regularly faces injury claims, such as a chain saw maker or an automobile manufacturer, can develop a reasonably good estimate of the awards that juries make. In addition, insurance companies provide information on awards, both directly through their studies of claims data and indirectly through the premiums they set. In spite of these measures, there is frequently considerable room for disagreement about the appropriate measures of the cost of personal injuries and environmental damage.

An alternative to a cost-benefit analysis of cases involving hazards is a cost-risk analysis or a comparative risk analysis. Cost-risk analysis focuses on the costs required to reduce risks (e.g., to avoid the loss of a life) and compares the case in question with other cases. In evaluating the use of infant safety seats, the FAA estimated the lives that would be saved by the seats and the lives that would be lost because more families would drive rather than fly. The decision was then clear. In the chapter case *Pricing the Norplant® System,* instead of attempting to measure social benefits, Wyeth-Ayerst Laboratories examined the relative effectiveness of its product compared with others on the market.

THE INFORMATION PROBLEM

A serious problem in the managerial application of utilitarianism is obtaining the information required to evaluate the consequences for all those affected, either directly or indirectly. In the case of an action that only affects the firm and its immediate stakeholders, the required information may be available. If the action affects others or if the effects are indirect, as when intermediated by markets or other institutions, or when consequences depend also on the actions of the other parties, the information problem can be more serious.

The information problem is also more serious in the application of rule utilitarianism because the rule is intended to be applicable to many decision makers and many similar situations. Obtaining information about those other situations may be difficult, and any analysis requires assumptions. For example, in addressing a pollution issue not covered by environmental regulations, or in considering whether to go beyond the requirements of the law, a firm will have reasonably good information about its own abatement costs but will have considerably worse information about the costs of other firms' compliance. Those costs are likely to be a function of the age of their plants, the likely exposure of people and property, and the current level of ambient pollution, among other factors. To the extent that these vary significantly among firms, the evaluation of a general rule is difficult.

One response to the information problem is extrapolation. If other firms are facing the same issue and if a firm is reasonably representative of the others, it may be possible to extrapolate to the broader class of firms based on one firm's own information. If the issue is the potential radiation hazards to employees who use video display tubes or chronic health problems, such as carpal tunnel syndrome resulting from repetitive tasks, the experiences of most firms and their employees are likely to be similar. On such issues, extrapolation may be straightforward. The case of American Airlines and United Airlines and the special issuances is an example of this approach.

Even if measurement and information problems are insurmountable, identifying the consequences and conducting an informal analysis can be worthwhile. To illustrate the analysis at this level, several examples are presented. These examples will also be considered in Chapter 19 from rights and justice perspectives.

EXAMPLE: CORPORATE SOCIAL RESPONSIBILITY?

The headquarters and largest plant of a medium-size machine tool company are located on a wooded tract at one end of which is a marsh fed by an underground spring. The marsh attracts a wide variety of birds, including ducks, herons, egrets, wood ibis, and kingfishers. Muskrats, beavers, and water moccasins also make the marsh their home. One of the company's employees, an avid bird-watcher, proposed that the company make a number of improvements to the marsh and open it to the public so they can enjoy the birds and other wildlife.

Management asked one of its engineers to conduct a quick study of the proposal. The engineer concluded that a road and a parking lot would have to be constructed to provide access to the marsh. County regulations also required that rest rooms be constructed. Access to the marsh itself would require a trail from the parking lot that would lead to wooden slat walkways and viewing platforms. The engineer was unsure whether the visitors would disturb the wildlife by leaving the walkways. If that were to happen, an employee would have to be stationed at the marsh to remind visitors to stay within the designated areas. New fencing would be required to keep visitors away from the company's plant.

The engineer estimated the cost of construction at $650,000 for the improvements plus an annual maintenance cost of $75,000. Approximately $50,000 a year would be required to equip and station an employee at the marsh, if that became necessary. Management had no idea how many people might visit the marsh, but the bird-watcher claimed it would attract considerable interest. The company concluded that charging admission would not be cost effective because it would require an additional employee.

The company itself would not benefit from opening the marsh, since it produced industrial products and promoting its image by advertising about the refuge would not affect its sales. There might be a positive effect on employee morale and loyalty, but the personnel manager observed that most employees were more interested in hunting wildlife than watching it.

The company asked the county if it were interested in developing the marsh along the lines of the company's initial feasibility study, but the county responded that although it would be willing to accept the land as a gift, its budget could not accommodate the required improvements or maintenance. The company also talked with the Audubon Society, but the state chapter did not have the funds to operate the refuge. The company thus had to decide whether to go ahead with the development of the refuge on its own.

In this case, act and rule utilitarianism are essentially the same because the company's situation is likely to be representative of that of other firms facing the same type of decision. In the absence of transactions costs, the issue would be resolved as suggested by the Coase theorem.[19] The potential beneficiaries would simply gather, determine the value of the refuge to themselves, and then decide whether to buy the land and develop it. The transactions costs associated with identifying the potential beneficiaries, the problem of determining their valuations, the free-rider problem, and bargaining costs likely preclude this resolution of the issue.

Because of imperfect information, the benefits from opening the marsh to visitors remained uncertain. A form of break-even analysis could be helpful, however. If the refuge were open 250 days a year and were visited by 50 people per day on average, the annualized cost to the company would be approximately $11 per visit, determined by dividing the 12,500 annual visits into the annualized cost of $140,000 (equal to the $75,000 plus the construction cost annualized at a discount rate of 10 percent). If the worst-case scenario were that visitors would come primarily on weekends and average only 10 visits a day, or 2,500 visits a year, the annual cost per visit would be $56. If an employee had to be stationed at the refuge, the respective costs per visit would increase to $15 and $76. These figures could be reduced somewhat by closing the refuge during periods of anticipated low usage. The potential benefits to visitors were unknown to management, but some information could be obtained by examining the prices charged at other wildlife refuges and sanctuaries.

The right action from the perspective of utilitarianism is to build the refuge if and only if the expected benefits exceed the company's costs. In this case, the company had reasonably good estimates of the costs but only limited information on the benefits. Even the lowest cost estimate of $11 a visit was considerably higher than charged at Audubon Society refuges, which to some degree reflects the preferences of those who visit wildlife refuges. Developing the refuge thus likely fails the utilitarian test.

EXAMPLE: INTEGRITY TESTS

From the perspective of rule utilitarianism, the use of integrity tests is warranted if it improves economic efficiency by better matching prospective employees to jobs. Integrity can be particularly important for jobs that involve security, as in defense industries; jobs that involve access to confidential information, such as that pertaining to clients; or jobs in which an employee is entrusted with resources, as with accountants, couriers, and bank tellers. Integrity tests may also contribute to efficiency if they enable employers to select employees who are more likely to fit with the firm's culture. For these purposes, an integrity test may be one of several sources of information, including personal interviews and reference checks. Such tests can also be advantageous competitively. W. Thomas Van Etten, senior vice president of Sun Bank in Miami, commented on his bank's use of an integrity test, a background check, and urinalysis for prospective employees, "People with a substance-abuse or integrity problem are more likely to look for work with our competitors who don't take as close a look as we do."[20]

If integrity tests are used for these purposes and if they are shown to be reasonably reliable, they seem to pass the cost-benefit test and, if so, are morally good from the perspective of utilitarianism. In Chapter 19, integrity tests are considered from rights and justice perspectives.

EXAMPLE: INSURANCE SCREENING FOR PRE-EXISTING CONDITIONS

To determine eligibility for individual life insurance policies, the insurance industry uses medical examinations to screen for such preexisting health problems as a heart condi-

[19]See Chapter 11 for the Coase theorem.
[20]*The New York Times,* October 1, 1989.

tion or a stroke.[21] Once people have a life-threatening condition, they have an incentive to purchase life insurance to provide for dependents or others. Screening is intended to prevent someone from purchasing a large policy once his or her health is impaired. This provides incentives for people to purchase insurance *ex ante* rather than *ex post.*

The ethical issue is whether people with preexisting conditions should be able to purchase insurance *ex post* in a pool with those with no preexisting conditions. The rule to be evaluated is:

> Screening is permitted for preexisting conditions as a requirement for eligibility to purchase an individual life insurance policy.

If this rule were not followed, insurance companies would have to increase the price of insurance to cover the higher expected payments to beneficiaries. The higher price would cause some individuals without preexisting conditions not to purchase insurance. This is an instance of adverse selection in which those with higher risks choose to buy life insurance, which increases the price of insurance, and causes others who would have purchased insurance at the lower price not to do so. If enough people with preexisting conditions buy life insurance, the price could ratchet up to the point at which those without preexisting conditions would drop out of the market. Those with preexisting conditions would then be alone in the pool, and the price would reflect the risks of their conditions. At that price, purchasing insurance could well not be attractive to anyone.

Not screening for preexisting conditions thus would result in lower aggregate well-being because insurance would not be available to those who otherwise would be willing to pay for it. Utilitarian analysis thus supports a rule permitting screening for preexisting conditions. This analysis may be questioned from the perspective of moral concerns other than those taken into account by utilitarianism. Those concerns are considered in Chapter 19.

EXAMPLE: REDLINING

An action that may be moral from the perspective of one framework may not be moral from the perspectives of another ethical framework. A significant problem in the insurance and banking industries arises from imperfect information about risks. The costs of investigating and assessing risks are often high, and risk assessment is itself imperfect. The collateral for a mortgage on a home or a small commercial establishment serves as a means of reducing the risk to the lender, but the value of the collateral depends on property values in the area in which the property is located.

Insurance companies have similar difficulties assessing property and casualty risks on homes or automobiles when the risks depend on location and on precautions taken by owners. For example, even if an applicant takes every measure of care, the likelihood that an automobile will be stolen or vandalized is higher in some neighborhoods than in others. When prices are required to be uniform over broad geographic areas, policies written on high-risk areas can result in losses for insurance companies.

To deal with the costs of risk assessment and evaluation, differential risks, and uncertain collateral, some financial institutions and insurance companies identified high-risk regions of cities and refused to lend or write policies in those regions. This practice, referred to as redlining, might have been efficient, and hence ethical from a utilitarian perspective, if the costs of risk and credit evaluation and the likelihood that a loan or policy

---

[21]Group life insurance plans, such as those provided by an employer, typically do not require screening for preexisting conditions, but group policies are experience-rated and premiums are adjusted annually. In contrast, premiums for an individual life insurance policy are fixed at the time of purchase.

[22]Similar practices exist in a number of other industries, as indicated by the discussion above of delivery services.

application would be rejected on its merits were high. That is, if the average cost of credit evaluation were high and demographic data indicated that most residents in an area would not purchase insurance or qualify for a mortgage, it could be efficient for the insurance company or financial institution not to consider applications from the area.[22]

Redlining may be ethical from the perspective of costs and benefits, but from other ethical perspectives it is unethical. Redlining is said to be unjust to the extent that it denies opportunity to those who would qualify for loans, insurance, or receive deliveries but who do not have the opportunity to do so because they reside in a redlined area. Redlining is also said to result in de facto discrimination against minorities and the poor to the extent that they are overrepresented in high-risk areas. Rights and justice frameworks thus bring important considerations to bear on issues such as redlining and have resulted in laws prohibiting the practice. The redlining issue illustrates that a practice could be ethical from the perspective of one system but unethical from the perspective of another.

Summary

Ethics is intended to provide mutually beneficial rules of behavior without requiring government prescription and enforcement. Some of those rules are incorporated into constitutions and legislation, but ethics extends beyond the law to provide guidance to people in their behavior and to firms in their formulation of policies.

Ethical standards are impartial and are to be applied universally, as opposed to casuistry which holds that those with responsibilities may violate ethical standards so as to fulfill their social responsibilities. Ethical standards generally differ from self-interest and may be the antithesis of self-interest. For example, utilitarianism holds that every individual's well-being is given equal weight. If one has altruistic preferences for the well-being of others, those preferences must be those that the individual is willing to act upon.

Utilitarianism is a consequentialist ethical system that defines the good in terms of human well-being and evaluates that well-being in terms of the preferences of individuals. Utilitarianism then sums those preferences to obtain a measure of aggregate well-being and identifies the right action in terms of the greatest good. Utilitarianism's practical usefulness is in providing a system for evaluating actions that make some individuals better off and others worse off.

The two forms of utilitarianism are act and rule utilitarianism. Act utilitarianism focuses on an individual action taking the actions of others as given. Rule utilitarianism focuses on rules that all individuals in similar situations are to follow in similar situations. Act utilitarianism is criticized for allowing exceptions to general rules of behavior, which can then degenerate into self-interest. Rule utilitarianism seeks rules of behavior that apply universally to all individuals. When consequences are a function of the action of more than one individual, rule utilitarianism considers the actions of all individuals simultaneously.

An applied form of utilitarianism is benefit-cost analysis that evaluates actions and rules in terms of the willingness of individuals to pay for alternative consequences. The application of utilitarianism, however, involves three principal problems: (1) determining what counts as a benefit and a cost, (2) making interpersonal comparisons among individuals, and (3) conducting analysis with imperfect information about consequences and preferences. Utilitarian principles are applied in the form of cost-benefit analysis, but often, critics say, it fails to account for other important considerations. For example, utilitarianism considers rights only in their instrumental role of producing well-being.

CASES

Living Benefits

Herman H. Silverman, a high school English teacher, recently started a part-time business called Beat the Grim Reaper International, Inc. Silverman's company—and rival upstarts—bought the beneficiary rights to the life insurance policies of the terminally ill, principally people with acquired immune deficiency syndrome (AIDS), but some cancer patients as well.[1] Silverman was sanguine about his new enterprise: "I don't think there's anything as guaranteed as this is in terms of getting a return."

The following examples clarify the contractual arrangements surrounding what have come to be known generically as living benefits or viatical settlements. One of Mr. Silverman's new competitors, Living Benefits, Inc., purchased a $100,000 insurance policy for $53,000 from a 34-year-old Boston real estate salesman with AIDS. For 65 cents on the dollar, the company also purchased a $250,000 policy from a 59-year-old San Diego man with cancer. As the new legal beneficiary, Living Benefits pays the premiums on the policies and will receive all the proceeds upon their deaths. In the meantime, the former policyholders receive $53,000 and $162,500, respectively, for use in their final years.

The benefits provided by these entrepreneurial enterprises did not go unnoticed by major public insurance companies. Robert Waldron, spokesman for the American Council of Life Insurance, said, "We recognize there's a desperate need. The high cost of dying just goes up every year." Indeed, the cost of prolonged illness frequently caused terminally ill individuals to stop their insurance premium payments before their deaths, causing their policies to lapse.[2] "As long as they're going soon anyway," added Silverman, "there's a service that I can provide for people who want to have their money right now." Living Benefits customers were favorably disposed toward the provision of these services. "I think it's a great idea," said the salesman from Boston. "It benefits the person who is suffering." Likewise, the San Diego man dying of cancer was spending some of the proceeds to build a new house for his wife. "It's like having your cake and eating it too," he said. "As far as I'm concerned, I'm going to keep living."

The process of contracting for living benefits was somewhat more complicated than these examples might suggest. Applicants for living benefits from Beat the Grim Reaper typically must endure an 8-week information-gathering process that begins with a four-page questionnaire. Next, the applicant's medical and insurance records are transmitted to Grim Reaper. Grim Reaper employs a staff of consulting physicians who meet with the applicant's attending physicians to determine the applicant's life expectancy.[3] Grim Reaper then offers the applicant a price for the policy. The price is based on the applicant's life expectancy, the face value of the policy, the premiums required to maintain an active policy, and interest rates.[4] Upon receipt of a waiver form signed by the beneficiary, the policy and the proceeds of the sale are placed in escrow. Shortly thereafter, funds are transferred to the applicant. Grim Reaper has a policy of offering its services only to those with a "pronounced financial need."

A range of objections—emotional and moral—have been raised to the provision of living benefits. Some observers claimed that this growing industry was exploiting the impaired judgment of the terminally ill and, in the process, trampling on the rights of the would-be beneficiaries. The president of Living Benefits, Rob T. Worley, conceded that some public reactions were negative: "We've had a few people that say this is ghoulish." Mr. Waldron of the American Council of Life Insurance took the argument a step farther: "This gives a third party who's

---

[1]AIDS groups have a well-developed national information network that tells members of the existence of such firms. Silverman also advertised in the classified section of a New York-based gay news magazine.

[2]A living-benefits spokesperson claimed that well over 50 percent of those who die with AIDS let their life insurance policies lapse prior to death.

[3]Grim Reaper regarded medical forecasts of life expectance of greater than 18 months as unreliable and, therefore, did not purchase a policy unless the applicant was judged to have less than 18 months to live.

[4]Regression models were used in these calculations.

not family an economic interest in a policyholder's death. As a concept, that is dangerous."

Nevertheless, living benefits arrangements were increasingly common. Indeed, the life insurance industry had started offering its own version of living benefits. One major public insurance company announced a plan that would let its policyholders with 6 months or less to live get the bulk of their life insurance proceeds before they die. Others had taken steps toward providing living benefits to their policyholders, but usually allowed policyholders to withdraw no more than half the policy's face value, and then often only in monthly installments.

As CEO of Prudential Insurance Co., you are uncertain whether you should offer your customers this kind of piece of the rock. Based on current information, three policy options were available. One was not to provide living benefits, no matter what your competitors, public or private, do. Another was to seek regulation by state insurance commissions to ban the provision of living benefits by third parties such as Grim Reaper and Living Benefits. A third policy option was to provide living benefits to your policyholders, knowing that with your superior databases and experience you could provide these services more efficiently than the small firms can—and also knowing that as a major firm in the insurance industry your participation would receive widespread attention. ■

PREPARATION QUESTIONS

1. Should living benefits be allowed? What guidance does a utilitarian system provide?
2. Is act or rule utilitarianism appropriate for formulating a policy for Prudential?
3. If living benefits are allowed, should purchasers be allowed to package policies and resell them as is done with mortgages?
4. Should a company be allowed to operate solely as a broker matching sellers and investors? Is this making a market in death?
5. What should Prudential do and why?

Sex-Differentiated Retirement Benefits

Nathalie Norris was surprised to learn that the $320.11 monthly annuity check she would receive from her employer, the state of Arizona, when she reached the retirement age of 65 was less than the $354.87 a month a man who retired at the same age and had contributed the same amount would receive. The present values of the annuities for men and women were the same, but the monthly payments were lower for women because they had a longer life expectancy than men.

To challenge this differentiation, Norris filed a lawsuit alleging that the retirement plan illegally discriminated against women because it paid women a lower monthly annuity. In 1983 in a 5-to-4 decision the Supreme Court upheld the lower court ruling that sex-differentiated annuities are in violation of Title VII of the Civil Rights Act of 1964, which prohibits sex discrimination in benefit and retirement programs offered by employers.[1]

More than 100 years earlier the insurance industry stopped basing insurance contracts on race, and in 1978 the Supreme Court, in *City of Los Angeles v. Manhart,* 435 U.S. 702 (1978), ruled that requiring women to contribute more per month than men were required to contribute to their pension plans was illegal sex discrimination under Title VII. The Norris case raised strong sentiments throughout the country, with women's activist groups supporting the case and the insurance industry opposing it. In his 1983 State of the Union address, President Ronald Reagan

[1] *Arizona Governing Committee for Tax Deferred Compensation Plans v. Norris,* 468 US 1073 (1983).

called for an end to discrimination by sex in insurance and retirement plans.

The argument in favor of banning sex discrimination was summarized by Daniel Seligman: "We [as a society] agree that women as a class live longer than men. However, we do not agree that an individual woman should be treated as a member of the class when it comes to writing insurance; she may, after all, die tomorrow, while a man her age may live for decades. Indeed treating people as a member of a class, rather than as individuals, is precisely what we mean by discrimination—and is precisely what was forbidden by the Civil Rights Act, at least with respect to classes involving race, color, religion, national origin, or sex."[2] Justice Thurgood Marshall, in the majority opinion, stated, "The use of sex-segregated actuarial tables to calculate retirement benefits violates Title VII whether or not the tables reflect an accurate prediction of the longevity of women as a class, for under the statute 'even a true generalization about [a] class' cannot justify class-based treatment."

The basic argument in favor of a system in which annuities are differentiated by sex is that the differentiation in annuities is not based on prejudice but rather on actuarial data for an identifiable group of individuals. Furthermore, requiring that men and women receive the same monthly annuity payments would constitute unfair treatment of men. On average, men would be subsidizing women, since women on average live longer than they do and therefore would have greater expected compensation than men if the monthly annuity payments were the same. For example, annuities for participants in TIAA-CREF, the retirement fund used by most colleges and universities, were decreased by 8 percent for men and increased by 8 percent for women. If the previous actuarial tables had been "accurate," the redistribution from male to female participants as a result of the Supreme Court decision was 8 percent.

Life expectancy data clearly indicate that as a class women live considerably longer than men. Women born in 1981 are estimated to have a life expectancy of 78.3 years, whereas the corresponding figure for men is 70.7 years. When they reach 60, women have a life expectancy of 22.1 additional years versus 17.1 for men, and women at the retirement age of 65 have a life expectancy of 4 years longer than men. Sex-differentiated annuity programs are based on these differences in life expectancy. Given the same total contribution to a retirement program, benefit programs provided a smaller monthly annuity payment to women so that men and women would receive annuities with the same expected present value.

One response of employers to the Supreme Court decision was to eliminate the annuity option. This was the response of the state of Arizona when it lost the lower court suit filed by Nathalie Norris. Many private corporations had already dropped their annuity plans, but an estimated 450,000 pension plans covering 25 million employees, mostly in the public and nonprofit sectors, were affected by the decision. When annuity plans are dropped, upon retirement employees receive a lump-sum payment equal to the accumulated value of their and their employer's contributions, rather than a monthly annuity payment. Individuals are then free to do whatever they wish with the proceeds. Male and female employees who contributed the same amount would thus receive the same amount and would not be restricted in how they used those funds during their retirement. ■

[2]*Fortune,* February 21, 1983.

PREPARATION QUESTIONS

1. Are sex-differentiated retirement benefits economically inefficient? Do they pass a utilitarian standard?
2. Is discrimination per se unacceptable or is only unfair discrimination or discrimination based on prejudice unacceptable?
3. If discrimination in annuity payments based on gender is prohibited in employer-sponsored retirement programs, should a similar prohibition be imposed on the private annuity market? That is, if individuals receive a lump-sum payment at the time of their retirement, many will prefer to purchase an annuity rather than make their own investment decisions. While annuities purchased by individuals are not covered by the Civil Rights Act, an extension of a prohibition of sex-differentiated retirement plans to the private annuity market might be logical.
4. If the prohibition were extended to the private annuity market, the response of individuals would have to be considered. For example, men might prefer not to purchase annuities, because

if they did, they as a class would be subsidizing women as a class, who would receive greater expected payments per dollar paid for an annuity. Men would thus be expected to set up their own "annuity equivalents" through the purchase of securities that provide desired patterns of returns. The securities market would be expected to provide securities that would enable the purchaser to create such annuity-equivalent patterns of payments. This would tend to result in an annuity market in which women pay the expected cost of an annuity for the class composed of women. The *de facto* result thus could be the situation challenged in Norris's suit. Should such annuity equivalents be prohibited?

5. As an employer that had been using sex-differentiated actuarial tables, should monthly annuity payments be equalized, should annuities be dropped as an alternative for employees, or should some other alternative be considered?

Pricing the Norplant® System

Toward the end of the summer of 1993, Wyeth-Ayerst Laboratories, a unit of the American Home Products Corporation, was enjoying the continuing success of its contraceptive, the Norplant System. Introduced in 1991 in the United States, 1992 revenues from the Norplant System were $105 million, which exceeded projections by nearly 100 percent. Executives at Wyeth-Ayerst expected annual sales of the Norplant System to stabilize just below $165 million for the near term. Given the current hostile political and regulatory environment faced by the pharmaceutical industry, this success was indeed welcomed.

The Norplant System is a progestin (levonorgestrel) encased in six permeable polymer capsules (Silastic). The capsules, which are inserted in a woman's upper arm, continuously release the progestin into the bloodstream for 5 years. The progestin alters the chemical balance of a woman's own progesterone levels. This alteration prevents ovulation, decreases circulating sperm concentrations, and creates within the uterus an environment hostile for pregnancy.

The popularity of the Norplant System was not surprising. It exhibited several advantages over alternative forms of contraception. For instance, clinical studies indicated that the Norplant System was a highly effective contraceptive method.[1] The average pregnancy rate for women using the system over the entire 5-year period was less than 1 percent, and the first-year pregnancy rate was less than 0.2 percent. In contrast, the first-year pregnancy rate was 3 percent for oral contraceptives and intrauterine devices (IUDs), 18 percent for diaphragms, and 0.4 percent for tubal ligation. The Norplant System had a strong record of safe use, having been used by 500,000 women worldwide for the past 20 years. Clinical tests of the Norplant System were conducted on over 55,000 women in 46 countries prior to introduction in the United States.[2] The Norplant System also required no effort to use and was easily reversible. The Norplant System did, however, require surgical implantation and removal and provided no protection from sexually transmitted diseases.

PRICING THE NORPLANT SYSTEM

The Norplant System was developed jointly by Wyeth-Ayerst and the Population Council, a nonprofit organization. In the development of the Norplant System, the Population Council received $10 million in grants from the federal government and private philanthropic organizations. The system uses Wyeth-Ayerst's hormone levonorgestrel, which was licensed by Wyeth-Ayerst from its developer. Wyeth-Ayerst held the exclusive right to produce and distribute the Norplant System and could set the price of the Norplant System. It paid the Population Council a royalty of no more than five percent of the sales price.

In its process of establishing a price for the Norplant System, Wyeth-Ayerst first conducted a study of the relative costs and benefits of alternative contraceptive methods. The direct costs to consumers included the financial costs of the contraceptive (i.e.,

[1] Population Council. *Norplant®: A Summary of Scientific Data.* New York, January 1989.

[2] Sivin, I. "International Experience with Norplant® and Norplant®-2 Contraceptives." *Studies in Family Planning,* 1988: pp. 1981–1994.

average retail price), any additional costs related to the use of the contraceptive (i.e., fitting a diaphragm and spermicidal cream; inserting an IUD, insertion and removal of the Norplant System), additional physician follow-up visits (i.e., checkup and monitoring, recuperation, or development of side effects and complications), and the convenience and ease of use (i.e., the need to take oral contraceptives daily). The indirect costs included the need for medical treatment of the side effects resulting from contraceptive use (i.e., medical treatment of hypertension caused by oral contraceptives), the possibility of hospitalization due to side effects (i.e., cost of hospitalization for treatment of pelvic inflammatory disease), supplies used to treat side effects (i.e., the costs of the prescription and nonprescription drugs and supplies needed post vasectomy), the loss of productivity due to side effects (i.e., absenteeism during recuperation), and the costs of contraceptive failure (i.e., the medical costs of abortion or delivery). Certain indirect benefits (i.e., the fact that oral contraceptives reduced the risk of ovarian and endometrial cancers) were also considered. Based on these studies and using the actual average retail price of other contraceptive methods, Wyeth-Ayerst concluded that even at an initial price of $600, the annual expected costs of the Norplant System would be five percent less than the IUD, 31 percent less than oral contraceptives, and 50 percent less than diaphragms. The annual expected costs of the Norplant System at an initial price of $600 were, however, eight percent higher than tubal ligation and 375 percent higher than vasectomy.

Apart from scientific studies on the relative benefits of the Norplant System, Wyeth-Ayerst also had to consider the market for contraceptive devices in the United States. Marketing studies indicated that women perceived a benefit from the Norplant System that justified high initial retail prices in the $400 to $600 range. The scientific and practical advantages of the Norplant System were evident to potential consumers.

Two important features of the market complicated Wyeth-Ayerst's pricing decision, however. First, a significant percentage of all contraceptives were distributed through not-for-profit family planning clinics. These clinics financed their purchases of contraceptives and provided compensation to health professionals through grants from governments and philanthropic organizations. These clinics, which were usually strapped for funds, often enjoyed discounts from pharmaceutical manufacturers. For instance, Wyeth-Ayerst deeply discounted the price it charged these clinics for oral contraceptives. Such clinics would expect similar discounts on the Norplant System. Second, most contraceptives distributed in the United States were financed by third-party payers such as insurance companies, state, county, and city governments, and health maintenance organizations. In a world of rapidly escalating health care costs, these third-party payers were not simply price takers but, instead, engaged in tough negotiations with pharmaceutical companies to obtain as low as possible a price on drugs. The discounted prices that some pharmaceutical companies offered family planning clinics were often used as targets in negotiations by third-party payers. Any discounts to family planning clinics would almost certainly be sought by the medical insurers and government agencies.

The other consideration in the pricing of the Norplant System was costs. The actual costs of producing the Norplant System were quite small, less than $50 per unit including the insertion kit. An additional cost was the training of doctors and other health professionals in the insertion and use of the Norplant System. Wyeth-Ayerst estimated that these costs would be approximately $15 million annually. The other relevant cost was that of liability, since lawsuits follow from the use of virtually all contraceptive systems.

Under these circumstances Wyeth-Ayerst adopted a uniform price of $350 for the introduction of Norplant. This price included the six progestin capsules and the disposable kit required for insertion. The patient also must pay a doctor for the insertion and removal of Norplant. No discounts were given to family planning clinics or third-party payers. Wyeth-Ayerst, however, helped establish and fund the Norplant Foundation to distribute the Norplant System free of charge to indigent patients.

PUBLIC REACTION TO THE PRICING OF THE NORPLANT SYSTEM

Although commercial success of the Norplant System heartened Wyeth-Ayerst executives, public reaction to its pricing decision was not positive. Health professionals in family planning establishments criticized the pricing of the Norplant System on several grounds. Critics pointed to the $23 price per unit in bulk shipments of the Norplant System to developing countries (without the insertion kit) to highlight the glaring difference between the costs of production and average retail price of the Norplant System in the United States.[3] Wyeth-Ayerst, critics charged, was price-gouging American consumers. Whereas executives said that the success of the system indicated that it was priced fairly, critics countered that the pricing reflected the monopoly Wyeth-Ayerst enjoyed to supply the Norplant System.[4] This monopoly position was particularly troublesome for critics, who charged that the bulk of the development cost of the Norplant System was provided by public funds through the activities of the Population Council.

Critics also charged Wyeth-Ayerst with betrayal and creating a "financial nightmare" for family planning clinics. Many family planning officials believed that they were instrumental in gaining approval for the Norplant System in the United States. However, as a result of Wyeth-Ayerst's pricing decision, they claimed, their budgets had been ruptured. For example, the director of a family planning unit in a major hospital said that shortly after the introduction of the Norplant System, 500 women applied for treatment. The costs of supplying the system to all these women would have been $175,000, but the clinic's yearly budget for all contraceptives was $20,000. "All of the income for Norplant goes right to the drug company," said Mr. Salo of Planned Parenthood in San Diego. "We don't charge a margin on it. We lose money on each patient that we serve because Medicaid doesn't reimburse the full cost. Staff members have had to forgo raises, and plans for outreach have been shelved as a result," he said.

Critics were also concerned about the implications of Wyeth-Ayerst's pricing of the Norplant System for the pricing of other advances in women's health care products scheduled for introduction in the coming years. For example, Upjohn, Inc. recently introduced a new contraceptive, Depo-Provera, which was priced much higher in the United States than it was overseas; and some were concerned about the pricing of RU-486, the so-called abortion pill, scheduled to begin clinical tests in the United States the following year. "Are we going to see RU-486 come into this country at a price that makes it no cheaper than getting a first trimester abortion?" asked Mr. Kring, vice chairman and treasurer of the Norplant Foundation. "It's a trend that scares me to death—that people are making huge profits in women's health care."

The pricing of the Norplant System also attracted the attention of lawmakers. Representative Ron Wyden (D-OR), a senior member of the Subcommittee on Health and the Environment of the House Energy and Commerce Committee, vowed to hold hearings on Wyeth-Ayerst's pricing decision this fall. "You have a situation where clearly Americans are being charged more," said Representative Wyden. "We have a chance to expose these kinds of pricing practices and create a more competitive price."

The Assignment

The Executive Committee on Pricing for Wyeth-Ayerst hastily gathered for a meeting. The members were concerned with the public criticisms directed at the pricing of the Norplant System and about the unfolding political threats. The committee, composed of the top executives of Wyeth-Ayerst, knew that a good deal of their time over the coming months would be spent on this issue.

They were also concerned with a more general issue that had become increasingly important as the health industry came under closer public scrutiny. The issue revolved around the pricing of proprietary medicines. What factors or principles should guide the Pricing Committee's decisions? Up to this point, the Pricing Committee's primary consideration was the relative quality and costs of available substitutes. In the view of the committee, if Wyeth-Ayerst could provide a better product at or below the costs of existing medicines, everyone would be better off. This focus had led to the comparison of the Norplant System with oral contraceptives in determining the $350 price. But were other factors important as well? For instance, would the pricing of the Norplant System continue to be a public issue or would the issue dissipate with time? Did Wyeth-Ayerst's responsibilities extend beyond providing a more effective contraceptive at a price below those of available substitutes? Should the fact that contraceptives are

[3]Wyeth-Ayerst pointed out that these units were produced by a Danish manufacturer that held the exclusive right to distribute the Norplant System in certain African countries.

[4]Pharmaceutical prices generally involved a large markup above costs, since the prices of successful pharmaceuticals must cover the research and development costs of both successful and unsuccessful attempts to discover new drugs. This also explained in part why prices of pharmaceuticals were higher in the United States and in other countries that have a pharmaceutical industry engaged in research and development than prices in countries that do not have a research-and-development-intensive pharmaceutical industry.

primarily a women's health care product have a bearing on the price it charged?

Should the fact that family planning clinics play an important role in the distribution of contraceptives to poor women be a factor? Should the fact that the Norplant System was deeply discounted in developing countries play a role in determining the prices charged in the United States? Should the fact that Wyeth-Ayerst discounts oral contraceptives to family planning clinics impact the decision of whether to discount the Norplant System to the poor? What should Wyeth-Ayerst do with respect to the family planning clinics?

The Pricing Committee has asked you to provide specific criteria for pricing proprietary medicines and to apply them to the pricing of the Norplant System. That is, you are to come up with a number that you would have adopted for the price of the Norplant System if it had been your decision to make. The Pricing Committee has asked you for an oral and written presentation of clarity sufficient to implement your proposed criteria. To help your analysis, the committee has set the following set of parameters:

1. The variable costs of the Norplant System (including insertion kit) is $50 per unit. This figure includes all production and delivery costs as well as the expected costs of products liability claims. This cost also includes the royalties Wyeth-Ayerst pays the developer of levonorgestrel and the Population Council.
2. Wyeth-Ayerst employs 2,700 staff, executives, health care professionals, and salespeople, who educate health professionals on the insertion and use of the Norplant System. To this point, Wyeth-Ayerst has trained over 28,000 doctors on the use of the Norplant System. With benefits, the average annual cost per employee is roughly $65,000. The Norplant System is expected to generate nearly 6 percent of Wyeth-Ayerst's total revenues of $2.8 billion. If the total labor costs were amortized to each of Wyeth-Ayerst's products based on their contribution to revenues, nearly $11 million in annual labor costs would be assigned to the sale of the Norplant System.
3. Wyeth-Ayerst allocates approximately $5 million annually for the advertising and promotion of the Norplant System.

This case was prepared by Thomas Gilligan from materials and information contained in *The Wall Street Journal,* August 30, 1993, and the article "Contraceptive Pharmaco-Economics: A Cost Effectiveness Analysis of the Norplant® System (levonorgestrel implants)," *Medical Interface,* a publication of the Medicom International, pp. 4–8.

CHAPTER 19

Ethical Systems: Rights and Justice

Introduction

Consequentialist ethical systems such as utilitarianism focus on the good and evaluate the good in terms of individuals' preferences, which are given equal weight in evaluating aggregate well-being. Rights established under a consequentialist system are instrumental, since their justification is in terms of the consequences they yield. Some moral philosophies hold instead that there are certain rights and liberties justified by considerations independent of their consequences. Basic liberties such as freedom of speech and rights such as equal employment opportunity are fundamental concepts that express considerations of freedom, autonomy, and basic equality. Other moral philosophies emphasize justice, which requires comparisons of the situations of individuals. For example, in the integrity tests example considered in Chapter 18, issues can be raised about the possible violation of rights to privacy and of the fairness to individuals who for some reason do not perform well on such tests. This chapter considers ethical systems that emphasize considerations of rights and justice.

Classification of Ethical Systems

Ethical systems are classified as teleological or deontological. Teleological, or consequentialist, systems define the rightness of an action in terms of the good it yields. Deontological ethical systems hold that moral right takes precedence over the good and can be judged by considerations independent of, or in addition to, consequences.[1] From a deontological perspective, the objective is to deduce from fundamental axioms principles that have moral standing and to identify rights and rules of behavior that correspond to those principles. Those rights and rules of behavior are intrinsic. The principal deontological system considered here is Kant's theory of moral rules. Rawls's theory of justice brings together elements of deontological and consequentialist considerations and prioritizes the two.

As illustrated in Figure 19-1, both teleological and deontological systems are ultimately concerned with the evaluation of actions. Teleological systems approach this task by examining the relationship between actions and consequences. Deontological systems approach this task by examining the relationship between actions and the reasons or motives for taking those actions. In a teleological system, consequences are evaluated in terms of a value theory that is a part of the particular system. Utilitarianism,

[1]The root of deontology is *deon,* which means obligatory; to bind, or must.

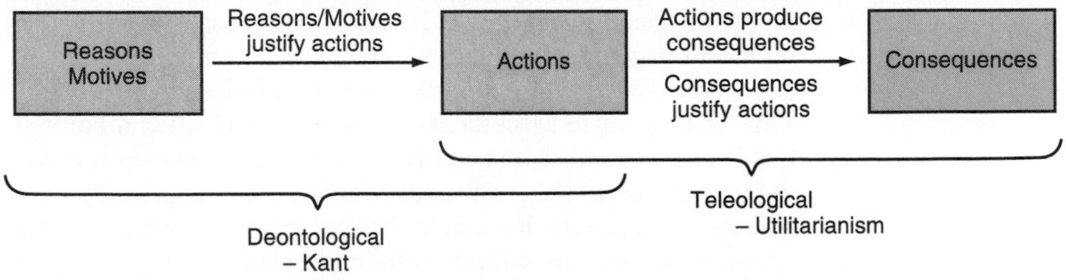

FIGURE 19-1 Teleological and Deontological Ethical Systems

for example, is based on a value theory defined in terms of individual preferences and their aggregation.

In deontological systems, the motive or reason for taking an action, or abiding by a principle, is required to have moral standing. A principle, for example, could be "respect each person's liberty by treating each person as he or she has freely consented to be treated." The reason to abide by a principle then is that individuals are willing to have everyone abide by it and are willing to have the principle applied to themselves.

Teleological and deontological systems are sufficiently different in their nature and structure that they do not necessarily yield the same evaluations of actions. Because no ethical system is immune to criticism, the objective is not to determine which ethical system is the most appropriate but instead is to understand the guidance that each provides.

Classes of Rights

Rights may be derived from moral principles or may be established through political choice. Rights established by political choice and embedded in laws often reflect moral principles. The U.S. Constitution identifies individual liberties, such as the freedom of speech, and rights to political participation. Rights are also established through legislation, such as the Civil Rights Act of 1964, which prohibits discrimination on the basis of race, color, religion, sex, or national origin. Legislation has also established entitlements, such as the right of the poor to receive medical care under Medicaid. Rights are also established by private agreements, such as contracts, that specify mutual obligations and expectations enforceable by the courts. Rights may also be established by implicit contracts such as those associated with the employment policies of a firm.

Rights are often categorized as negative or positive. Reflecting the intellectual tradition at the time it was written, the U.S. Constitution primarily establishes negative rights that impose duties on people and the state not to interfere with the actions of an individual. Freedom of speech and assembly are negative rights because they prohibit others from restraining those activities. A property right is also a negative right because other individuals are prohibited from compelling the holder to take an action with respect to that property. Positive rights impose affirmative duties on others to take particular actions. An individual, for example, has a positive legal right to some amount of public education and to a minimum level of public assistance. Some individuals argue that people should have positive "economic rights" to food, housing, and medical care. Others believe, as in the case of economic rights, that positive rights have lower standing than negative rights because positive rights impose duties that necessarily limit the liberty and autonomy of others.

An important difference between rights established by the state and those based on moral principles is that the former can be enforced, whereas for moral rights there is no enforcement mechanism other than individual sanction. Rights granted by the state or by private agreements are generally specific; if ambiguity exists, an authoritative body such as a court clarifies the right. For example, to set premiums for identifiable categories of risk, insurance companies ask applicants whether they smoke. To discourage lying, courts have held that policyholders who have not told the truth on their applications may not collect on their policies.[2]

Rights and entitlements evolve over time as a consequence of technological developments, demographic change, and changes in preferences. Rights may also evolve because of changing perceptions about the appropriate extent of liberties, the dimensions of justice, or the relative importance of rights. Rights also change as a consequence of interest group pressures acting through the institutions of government and public sentiment.

The evolution of the rights of university students provides an example. In the 1960s many universities followed the principle of in loco parentis, under which the distribution of rights between the university and the student was analogous to that between a parent and a child. The distribution of rights has evolved to the point at which enrollment now carries with it a well-defined set of rights and access to quasi-judicial mechanisms intended to ensure fair treatment.

Rent control is an example of a right resulting from collective action by interest groups. Rent control, such as on apartments, is a means of redistributing wealth from one group to another. If apartment renters and those who support their interests have sufficient political power, they may be able to institute rent control as a means of benefiting themselves at the expense of landlords. Rent control on apartments also harms those people who will be unable to find rental housing in the future, because rent control decreases the construction of apartments and spurs the conversion of apartments to condominiums.

Kantian Maxims or Moral Rules

For Kant (1785, 1797) the foundations of a theory of morality are freedom and rationality. The expression of freedom is found in the concept of individual autonomy, and the requirement of rationality is found in the relationship between free will and maxims that govern actions. These maxims, or rules, are derived independently of their consequences by reasoning about the implications of freedom of the will. That is, maxims are evaluated based on the reasons or motives for them. The resulting maxims are thus impartial and universal—the person is to will universal rules. The purpose of the maxims is to allow individuals to judge their actions, and the actions of others, from the point of view of those maxims. As indicated in Figure 19-1, Kant's system is based on the motive, or mental disposition, and the reason for the action. Kant thus emphasizes the "right" over the "good."

Because individuals are rational and each deduces maxims from a conception of freedom and autonomy that resides in everyone, Kant argues that all individuals will deduce the same maxims. Reasoning in Kant's system is to be based on a fundamental axiom known as the categorical imperative.[3] The categorical imperative serves two basic functions. First, it provides a basis for determining moral rules. Second, it prescribes

---

[2]In January 1991, the Third Circuit Court of Appeals so ruled.

[3]The term *categorical* means that the imperative is not conditioned on any purpose other than the imperative itself. Kant (1785, p. 26) wrote, "It is not concerned with the matter of the action and its intended result, but rather with the form of the action and the principle from which it follows: what is essentially good in the action consists in the mental disposition, let the consequences be what they may."

that individuals are to act in accord with those rules. Kant provides several formulations of the categorical imperative, but they basically hold that individuals are to be treated as autonomous, as ends rather than solely as means, and are to act based on a reason that each would will to be universal. Kant's basic formulation of the categorical imperative is:[4]

> Act according to the maxim that you would will to be a universal rule.

According to Kant (1785, p. 39), "All rational beings stand under the law that each of them should treat himself and all others never merely as means but always at the same time as an end in himself." Morality for Kant then is the condition in which each individual can be an end, and ethics "is conceived as the law of one's own will, ..." (1797, p. 47). This yields a second formulation of the categorical imperative:

> Treat individuals always as autonomous ends, and so never solely as means.

This does not mean that a person cannot be treated as a means, for example, a means of production, but that person is also to be treated as an end with the autonomy to choose. An employee can thus be required to meet the standards for a particular job but should have the right to qualify for better jobs.

The strength of Kant's conception of morality is that it focuses on motives or reasons for acting that are universal—apply to everyone—and thus are reversible—apply to oneself. The categorical imperative thus embodies two standards for the evaluation of maxims—*universalizability* and *reversibility.* Universalizability may be thought of as, "Would I want everyone to behave according to that rule?" Reversibility may be thought of as "Would I want that rule applied to me?"[5] For example, if the rule under evaluation is "discrimination based on height is not allowed," reversibility requires that others not discriminate based on my height. Universalizability requires that I would will a society in which no one discriminates against others on the basis of their height. The third standard for evaluating a candidate for status as a maxim or moral rule is, "Does it treat people always as ends and never solely as means, respecting their autonomy to choose?"

Example: Living Benefits

The Chapter 18 case *Living Benefits* focuses on the moral issue of living benefits or viatical settlements: whether it is right for companies to buy the life insurance policies of terminally ill individuals at a substantial discount from the face value of the policy. The magnitude of the discount depends on the estimated life expectancy of the individual, the risk the company bears in holding the policy and paying the premium, and the competitiveness of the market for such policies. To assess whether such a practice is moral from a rights perspective, consider the maxim, "People may make viatical settlements." The categorical imperative asks whether this maxim treats people as autonomous ends and never solely as means. The policyholders are treated as a means to a profit for the companies that buy the policies, but they also act autonomously in the sense that they can choose whether to sell their policy. That they have a free choice between holding and selling their policies means that they are treated as ends. As long as their capacity to choose is not impaired, viatical settlements seem to satisfy this formulation of the categorical imperative. The other formulation of the categorical imperative is whether one would will the maxim to be a universal rule. Since all individuals reason rationally from the same concept of freedom and autonomy, Kant would conclude

---

[4]This formulation applies to a broad class of rules including some that could be conceived but never acted upon, so the categorical imperative is sharpened to pertain to rules that could be acted upon.
[5]Reversibility is implied by universalizability, but it is useful to state it separately as a reminder.

that they would will it to be universal. Whether all individuals would in fact reason in the same manner is difficult to assess, as considered in the section on criticisms of moral rights.

THE RELATIONSHIP BETWEEN MAXIMS AND RIGHTS

Kant's system is expressed in terms of maxims, which individuals have a moral duty to respect. That duty establishes moral rights. Those moral rights are intrinsic, since they are derived from the categorical imperative and not from other considerations such as consequences. To illustrate the relationship between maxims, rights, and duties, consider the maxim, "A firm must sell its product to anyone who wants it, regardless of the price they are willing to pay."[6] This maxim violates the categorical imperative of treating individuals, in this case the owners of the firm, as autonomous ends, since they would be treated as means when forced to sell the product regardless of whether they wanted to sell it.

Consider next the maxim, "A firm must sell its product to anyone who is willing to pay the price set by the firm." This maxim satisfies the categorical imperative of treating everyone as autonomous and as ends and satisfies universalizability. Hence, it is a moral rule. This rule then has implications for rights and duties. First, it establishes property rights as moral rights. Second, it does not allow the firm to distinguish, or discriminate, among buyers based on any considerations other than their willingness to pay. This establishes a right not to be discriminated against and a corresponding duty not to discriminate on irrelevant considerations in making sales.

Consider next the maxim, "A firm must sell its product to anyone who is willing to pay the cost of producing it." This rule violates the categorical imperative by not treating the owners of the firm as autonomous ends and respecting their liberty. The regulation of a natural monopoly by setting price equal to cost thus would not be permitted in a Kantian system unless the firm were compensated sufficiently so that it would freely choose to set that price.

Rights consistent with Kant's system include the freedom of speech and conscience, since otherwise a person would not be an autonomous end. Rights also include political equality and the right to vote. Kantian rights require the opportunity to exercise individual autonomy, which includes the right not to be discriminated against on dimensions irrelevant to those opportunities.

The categorical imperative draws a line between the right of opportunity and nondiscrimination and the claim that individuals should be provided with the means to pursue opportunity and thus that others have a duty to provide those means. This claim may treat the recipients as ends and respect their autonomy and freedom, but it does not so treat those who have the duty since it uses them as means for serving others. Consequently, economic rights, such as rights to food or housing, are not consistent with Kant's ethical system. Kant's system and Nozick's system allow the voluntary provision of the means to individuals, whereas Rawls's system of justice requires, as considered later in the chapter, the fair equality of opportunity where fairness requires that individuals have the means to realize opportunities.

As another example of Kant's framework, consider the nature of the relationship between an employer and an employee. In the nineteenth century, the employment relationship was governed by the "at-will" legal doctrine derived from the theory of free contract under which either party was free to terminate the relationship whenever it chose. The Kantian right to be treated as an end rather than solely as a means suggests that even though both human beings and machines are factors of production, human beings differ from machines in that they are to be treated as ends. The employer's right

---

[6]This example was suggested by Daniel Diermeier.

to free contract and to dismiss an employee at will thus may be limited by an employee's right to be discharged only for cause. The maxim thus is, "An employer may dismiss an employee only based on considerations relevant to his or her performance on the job." A corresponding duty is associated with any right, and in this case the duty is assigned to the employer. What constitutes "relevant to his or her performance" remains a matter of disagreement, particularly as it pertains to issues such as the testing of employees. Rights in the employment relationship are considered in Chapter 21, and the chapter case *Genetic Testing in the Workplace* raises employment testing issues.[7]

INTRINSIC AND INSTRUMENTAL RIGHTS

Rights may be instrumental or intrinsic. Instrumental rights are to be respected because they contribute to achieving better consequences, by, for example, enabling individuals to pursue their interests. Contract rights are instrumental because they facilitate mutually beneficial economic transactions by ensuring reliance on the delivery of goods and services. Rent control redistributes wealth between landlords and tenants by granting tenants of certain buildings the rights to enforce rent ceilings. Claims that individuals have economic rights to housing or food are claims about instrumental rights intended to enable people to act as autonomous individuals and exercise their liberties and pursue their opportunities.

Intrinsic rights are to be respected in and of themselves and do not require any justification in terms of consequences or other considerations. Intrinsic rights are derived from fundamental moral concepts such as autonomy and liberty, as in Kant's system. Examples of intrinsic rights are freedom of speech, equal opportunity, and certain aspects of privacy. Some rights, such as property rights, are intrinsic when viewed from the perspective of autonomy and liberty and instrumental when evaluated in terms of the consequences they yield. These rights may be stated in constitutions and laws, but intrinsic rights are to be respected independently of formal institutions. Claims are easily made about the extent and scope of intrinsic rights, and formal institutions are often relied upon to resolve conflicting claims. The extent of a right to privacy in the employment relationship remains a subject of competing claims, as indicated in the analysis of the integrity tests example considered later in the chapter.

To illustrate the distinction between instrumental and intrinsic rights, a consequentialist example presented in Figures 19-2 and 19-3 will be used. These figures depict the possible combinations of utility for two individuals, 1 and 2, as a function of the activities in which they may engage given society's institutions. That is, each point in the oblong shapes—the utility possibility sets—corresponds to the utilities the individuals could attain if they acted to serve their own interests, given the opportunities and incentives provided by a particular configuration of institutions. The institutions might correspond to various assignments of rights, the tax and transfer payment systems, the laws of torts and contracts, and public education. A point in the figure reflects the incentives provided by those institutions, so if the tax system dampens incentives for capital formation, aggregate output and the utility of both individuals could be lower than if stronger incentives were provided.

An instrumental right, such as the system of property rights enforced by the powers of the state, affects the shape and size of the utility possibility set. For example, the dotted line might correspond to the set of institutions in communist countries such as the former Soviet Union and the nations of Eastern Europe under its control. The economies of those countries failed because the institutions of centralized state planning resulted in both insufficient capital formation and weak incentives for effort. The

[7]Kupfer (1993) provides an ethical analysis of genetic testing.

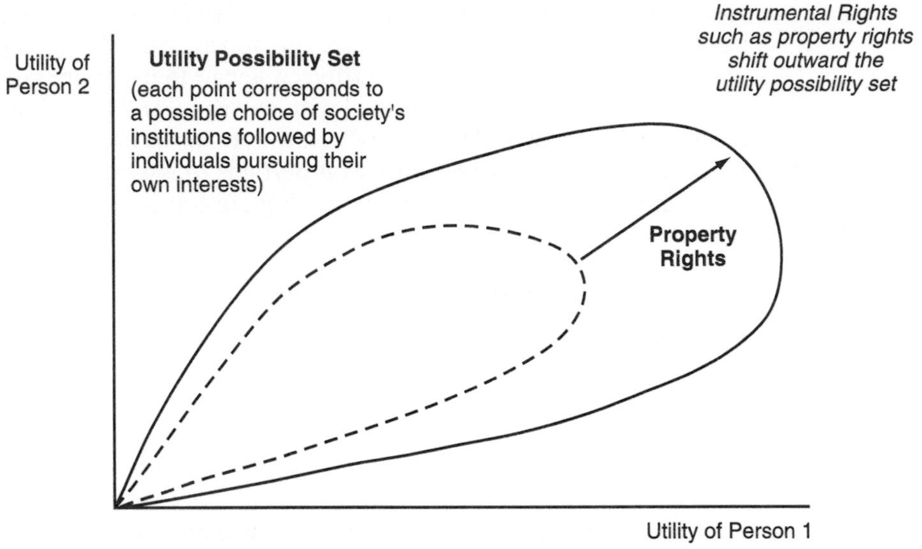
Utility of Person 2
Utility Possibility Set
(each point corresponds to a possible choice of society's institutions followed by individuals pursuing their own interests)
Instrumental Rights such as property rights shift outward the utility possibility set
Property Rights
Utility of Person 1

FIGURE 19-2 Instrumental Rights and Consequences

institution of property rights in which individuals keep the fruits of their efforts provides strong incentives for effort and capital formation and expands the utility possibility set as illustrated in Figure 19-2. The privatization of companies in the former communist nations and in many other countries is one manifestation of this recognition.

Intrinsic rights impose duties on individuals to respect those rights. Viewed from a Kantian perspective, property rights allow individuals to act as autonomous ends, and hence they have moral standing as intrinsic rights. In the context of Figure 19-2, the duty to respect those rights prevents others from moving from the larger to the smaller utility possibility set. Similarly, an intrinsic right to equal opportunity can increase the size of the utility possibility set. An intrinsic right to equal opportunity, however, is not established with reference to its effect on consequences but instead is established from fundamental axioms as in the Kantian system.

FIGURE 19-3 Intrinsic Rights and Consequences

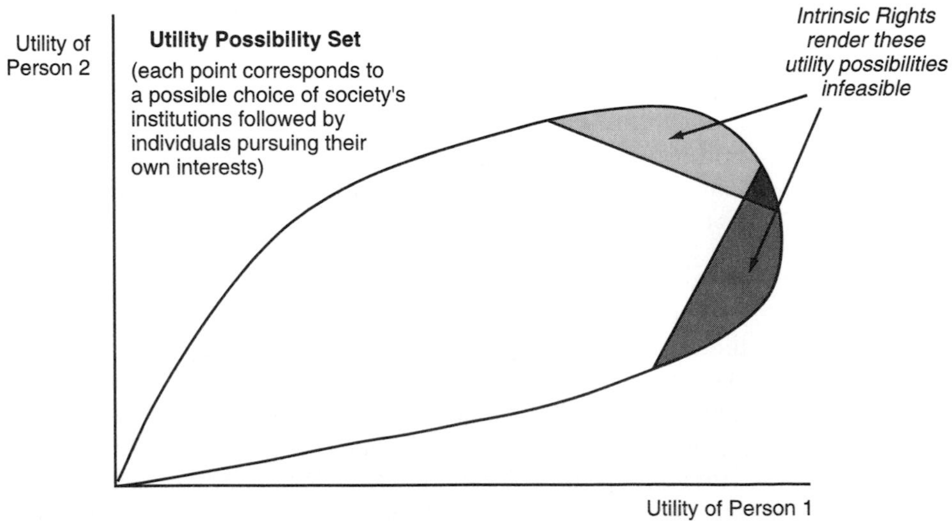
Utility of Person 2
Utility Possibility Set
(each point corresponds to a possible choice of society's institutions followed by individuals pursuing their own interests)
Intrinsic Rights render these utility possibilities infeasible
Utility of Person 1

Other intrinsic rights, however, may restrict the utility possibility set as illustrated in Figure 19-3. The claimed intrinsic right to privacy or to safety in the workplace may limit the possible levels of utility attained in a society. That is, intrinsic rights can constrain the set of available alternatives, and from a consequentialist perspective this can make at least some, and perhaps all, individuals worse off. A right to privacy, for example, could be argued to prohibit genetic testing in the workplace, making it more difficult to move genetically susceptible individuals away from possible exposure to harmful chemicals.

CRITICISMS OF KANTIAN RIGHTS

The criticisms of Kant's ethical system include both those that pertain to deontological systems in general and those specific to his system. The fundamental criticism of deontological systems is that they fail to explain why a principle or right should be respected. When one attempts to do so, one is often led to justifying it in terms of the extent to which it protects or promotes human interests. For example, why is treating individuals as ends important if it is not to give them the opportunity to pursue their interests? Thus, critics contend that consequences rather than motives actually underlie the moral standing of these principles.

More specific criticisms of rights-based ethical systems are that they may not (1) be sufficiently precise to identify where the corresponding duty lies, (2) indicate the priority when one right conflicts with another, and (3) indicate when—if ever—it would be acceptable to violate a right. With respect to the first criticism, every right is accompanied by an associated duty, but who is to bear the burden of that duty is not always clear. Some negative rights, such as the right of free speech, presumably impose a duty on all. In the case of a claimed positive right, such as a right to medical care, however, the duty may fall on the individual, relatives, an employer, government, or private charities. In such circumstances, legislation is often required to clarify where the duty lies. Legislation, however, reflects interests, and hence preferences and consequences.

The second criticism is that Kant's system does not clearly indicate whether or when one right has priority over another. The prioritization of rights is considered later in the chapter in some detail, so only the basic issue will be raised here. The categorical imperative requires that individuals be treated as free and autonomous and so always as an end and never solely as a means. A right to privacy seems essential if a person is to be treated as an end, as does the right of free contract. Yet, in an employment relationship into which an employee and an employer freely enter, should an employer have the right as a condition of employment to require job applicants to take integrity tests or drug tests or not to smoke?

The third criticism centers on whether there are any circumstances in which it would be acceptable to violate a rule or right. When rights are in conflict with each other, it may be necessary to violate one to respect another. A violation of a right for whatever reason is a moral wrong, but the seriousness of the violation must be considered. In the language of justice theory, the issue is when it is acceptable to violate one right to avoid a more serious violation of another right or a violation of a more important right.

In spite of these criticisms of the foundations of rights and maxims, individual rights are a fundamental component of ethical intuition. Rights are embedded in constitutions, legislation, and moral understandings. The duties corresponding to legal and moral rights provide fundamental constraints on the actions of managers and on the policies of firms. The practical difficulties with the application of rights-based ethical systems pertain to the evaluation of claims about rights, the priority of various rights, and the relationship between rights and other concerns such as well-being and justice. The next section addresses these difficulties in the context of applied rights analysis.

Applied Rights Analysis

In the context of managerial decision making, rights have two effects. First, as illustrated in Figure 19-3, they rule out certain alternatives, such as those that would violate constitutionally protected rights or moral principles. Second, a right may carry an affirmative duty that requires a firm to take particular actions. For example, the equal employment opportunity laws prohibit discrimination, whereas affirmative action regulations impose affirmative duties on employers to redress the effects of past discrimination and provide opportunity. The second effect is addressed in Chapter 21 in the context of equal employment opportunity, affirmative action, and the Americans with Disabilities Act. The focus here is on rights that rule out decision alternatives.

CLAIMED AND GRANTED RIGHTS

The framework for nonmarket analysis and strategy formulation summarized in Figure 2-4 of Chapter 2 distinguishes between claimed and granted rights. A granted right is established by moral consensus or by the state and is accompanied by a clear assignment of the corresponding duty. If the duty has not been clearly assigned, moral consensus is absent, or if the state has not spoken, the right in question is claimed. Individuals claim rights and make demands on others by asserting moral justification, but others may view those claims as morally unjustified. To address nonmarket issues in which rights are claimed, managers must be able to evaluate the contesting arguments. To illustrate the evaluation of a claimed right, consider the claim that the poor have, or should have, entitlements different from those of other people.

In *Kadrmas v. Dickinson Public Schools*, 487 U.S. 450 (1988), the Supreme Court affirmed its 1973 ruling that the equal protection clause of the Constitution does not give special protection due to income. Plaintiff Kadrmas challenged a North Dakota law that allowed school districts to charge a fee for school bus service. The Dickinson School provided bus service for rural students, picking them up at their doors, but charged them $97 per year for the service. The Kadrmas's income was close to the "officially defined poverty level," and Kadrmas refused to pay the fee. The school bus then no longer stopped for Sarita Kadrmas. Since the Kadrmases lived 16 miles from the school, they had to incur an additional expense for Sarita's transportation. They sued, and the case reached the Supreme Court. For the majority in a 5-to-4 decision, Justice Sandra Day O'Connor wrote,

> The Constitution does not require that such [school bus] service be provided at all, and it is difficult to imagine why choosing to offer the service should entail a constitutional obligation to offer it for free. . . . We have previously rejected the suggestion that statutes having different effects on the wealthy and the poor should on that account alone be subjected to strict equal protection. . . . Nor have we accepted the proposition that education is a 'fundamental right,' like equality of the franchise, which should trigger strict government scrutiny when government interferes with an individual's access to it.[8]

The majority's opinion thus distinguishes the constitutional grant of equal protection from the claim that individuals should be relieved of certain economic burdens. Managers must make similar judgments about rights, and a method for the analysis of claimed rights is presented next.

---

[8] *United States LAW WEEK*, (56), 6-21-88, 4777–4783, p. 4780.

A METHOD FOR RIGHTS ANALYSIS

Rights analysis has two principal components. The first is determining whether a claimed right has moral standing. The second is determining how conflicts among rights are to be resolved. The methodology of rights analysis is as follows:

1. Identify the rights claimed and their claimed moral bases.
2. Determine which claimed rights satisfy moral standards; for example, Kantian standards.
3. Identify the actions consistent with the protection or promotion of the rights.
4. Identify conflicts among rights. If there are none, those claimed rights with moral standing are to be respected.
5. If there are conflicts among rights with moral standing, investigate the importance of the interests those rights are intended to protect or promote.
6. Prioritize the rights based on the importance of those interests and determine the extent to which each is constrained by the others.
7. Choose the action that does best in terms of the priorities established.

The following two examples introduced in Chapter 18 illustrate the first four steps in the methodology; then the issues of conflicts among rights and prioritization are addressed.

Example: Corporate Social Responsibility?

In this example presented in Chapter 18, there is no moral right of the public or bird-watchers to have wildlife refuges provided for their enjoyment. Their enjoyment reflects a preference rather than a right, and from a rights perspective no duty falls on the firm to satisfy such preferences. If potential visitors wish to have the refuge developed, they can exercise their autonomy either by offering to purchase the marsh or, through political action, attempt to have the government acquire and develop it.

The only right present in this case is the company's right to use its property as it chooses. From the perspective of the law, this property right is inviolate except from eminent domain and government regulation. From a moral rights perspective the firm should build the refuge only if its owners freely choose to do so, since property rights are intrinsic and have moral standing in the Kantian system.

Example: Insurance Screening for Preexisting Conditions

The reasoning in the Kadrmas decision suggests that individuals have no granted right to life insurance nor to purchase insurance at a particular price. Insurance companies thus need not provide insurance to everyone or anyone. When life insurance is offered, however, screening for preexisting conditions is claimed to be discriminatory and an invasion of privacy. In most jurisdictions, an insurance company has a granted right to screen for preexisting conditions and to deny or at least limit coverage.[9] That right can be withdrawn or limited through government action, but in the absence of restrictions most insurance companies screen for preexisting conditions based on efficiency, or utilitarian, considerations. Claims about privacy and discrimination, however, warrant examination because if they have moral standing in this situation, then legal and moral rights would be in conflict.

[9]The grant may extend considerably beyond screening. In 1990 a federal district court judge dismissed a suit filed by an employee with AIDS who had charged that it was illegal for a firm that self-insured to limit medical coverage for AIDS. The judge held that the firm had complied with the requirements of the Employee Retirement Income Security Act (ERISA) by notifying employees that its medical plan could be revised on an annual basis. The Court of Appeals rejected the plaintiff's appeal, and in 1992 the Supreme Court let that decision stand.

Conflicts among Rights

Rights can be in conflict, and those conflicts may mean that there is no alternative that satisfies all the claims. This section presents an approach to addressing conflicts by examining the interests the rights are intended to protect or promote and by prioritizing those rights based on the importance of those interests. This approach thus adds considerations of consequences to the deontological ethical system of Kantian rules.

RIGHTS AND INTERESTS

Because moral and legal rights can be in conflict in managerial settings, they must be prioritized. Priorities are established by the institutions of society and by moral principles. The Constitution establishes certain priorities. For example, one has a right in one's home to prohibit others from trespassing for commercial purposes. However, one does not have the same right when its exercise denies others the opportunity to exercise their rights of free speech or religion. Consequently, home owners may not have the right to call on the state to prevent people from knocking on their doors to distribute religious materials.

In the case of moral rights, or rights more generally, one approach to reasoning about, if not resolving, conflicts is to inquire into the importance of the interests they are intended to promote or protect. Rights established by deontological systems are intrinsic, however, and are justified independently of the interests to which they contribute. By inquiring into the importance of interests, rights are necessarily treated as instrumental and consequences must be considered. Nevertheless, the approach of inquiring into interests is a practical method for resolving conflicts in managerial applications and is consistent with ethical intuition.

To illustrate the inquiry into the interests a claimed right is intended to promote, in his dissent in *Kadrmas* Justice Thurgood Marshall stated his view of the constitutional basis for a right:

> The statute at issue here burdens a poor person's interest in an education. The extraordinary nature of this interest cannot be denied. By denying equal opportunity to exactly those who need it most, the law not only militates against the ability of each poor child to advance herself, but also increases the likelihood of the creation of a discrete and permanent underclass. Such a statute is difficult to reconcile with the framework of equality embodied in the Equal Protection Clause.
>
> As I have stated on prior occasions, proper analysis of equal protection claims depends . . . upon identifying and carefully analyzing the real interests at stake.[10]

Justice Marshall thus turned to the interests of the individual in attempting to determine the priority of the claimed right to free school bus service. Justice O'Connor, in contrast, focused on whether a right has been granted rather than on the interests affected.

PRIORITIZATION

The approach to analyzing conflicts among rights, as summarized in the framework in Figure 19-4 for the case of integrity tests, begins with an identification of a right, an assessment of whether it is claimed or granted, and its bases. The possible bases for a right are moral and legal, where the latter includes the Constitution, legislation, and contracts. A granted right is established by the state, by another individual or entity, or by moral consensus and

[10]*California Reporter,* 829 (1987), p. 4782.

has a clearly assigned duty. A claimed right either does not have a clearly assigned corresponding duty or has not been established by either a grant or moral consensus.

These first three steps identify rights and their status, but in the case of conflicts, priorities must be assessed. Some priorities are clear. Constitutional rights take precedence over legislatively granted rights, particularly because many constitutional rights also have a moral justification. Those rights that are both granted and have a moral basis often have priority over claims that have a disputed moral basis. More difficult are cases in which a granted right is in conflict with a claimed right that is said to be justified by moral standards.

To assess priorities in such a case, the interests that those rights are to protect and promote are examined. Those interests may range from the opportunity to pursue one's well-being to personal privacy, which has a moral basis in the right of conscience in a Kantian framework. The interests identified are intended to be basic, as in Justice Marshall's identification of the importance of education to opportunity. Once the interests have been identified, the rights that further those interests are to be assigned priority. At this point individuals may have differing assessments of priorities, but the assignment of priority is intended to be impartial and based on the importance of the interest and not on the personal preferences of the person conducting the analysis. The final column in Figure 19-4 identifies the actions that are consistent with a right.

The result of the analysis may be that there is no action that does not violate some right with legal or moral standing. Any action thus will result in a moral violation, and the prioritization identifies the seriousness of a violation. Given the assessment of priorities, the managerial task is to determine which actions come the closest to meeting the priorities.

EXAMPLE: INTEGRITY TESTS

Integrity tests are currently legal under federal law and under the laws of at least 49 states, so the focus is on claimed moral rights. The rights claimed are the prospective employees' right to privacy, their right not to be subject to arbitrary treatment as a consequence of an inaccurate test, and the employer's right to choose standards for hiring employees, as long as those methods do not discriminate on an illegal basis. Since these rights are in conflict, it is necessary to evaluate and prioritize them.

FIGURE 19-4 Applied Rights Analysis: Integrity Tests

			Addressing Conflicts		
Right	*Claimed/ Granted*	*Bases*[*]	*Intrests the Right Protects*	*Priority*	*Actions Consistent with the Right*
Privacy	Claimed	Moral	Liberty Human dignity	1[†] 2[††]	Limited use of tests
Free from arbitrary treatment	Claimed	Moral	Fair opportunity to pursue interests	2	Test verified Professional interpretation of results
To hire	Granted	Moral/ Legal	Autonomy of employer Economic efficiency	3[†] 2[††]	Test where honesty is important to job performance

[*]moral, legal (constitutional, statutory, common law)
[†]for jobs where the efficiency interest is not compelling
[††]for jobs where the efficiency interest is compelling

As they apply to integrity tests, the rights of prospective employees are claimed rather than granted. Neither of the employees' rights is explicitly established by law, although the law clearly pertains to each. The bases for the rights are indicated in Figure 19-4. The right to privacy is granted by legislation as it pertains to certain types of tests, such as polygraphs, but it is claimed as it pertains to integrity tests. Congress might in the future extend the right of privacy to integrity tests, but it has not done so. A right to privacy that prohibits integrity testing is thus claimed.

The right to be free from arbitrary treatment is based on the claim that the tests may misclassify individuals because of inaccuracies. The firm's right to select among prospective employees, as long as it does not illegally discriminate, is granted and has both a moral and a legal basis. The moral basis derives from the autonomy of the employer and the liberty to enter into contracts.

To investigate priorities, the interests that the rights are intended to promote or protect must be identified. The claimed right to privacy is intended to promote liberty and individuals' opportunities to pursue their own interests. The claimed right to be free from arbitrary treatment protects the opportunity to qualify for positions. The employer's right to choose standards for hiring is, as an instrumental right, intended to promote economic efficiency by allowing employers to match prospective employees to jobs and firms.

In addressing the conflicts among these rights, intrinsic rights should have priority, because in a deontological system the right takes precedence over the good. The right not to be subjected to arbitrary treatment seems paramount in this case. In the rightmost column in Figure 19-4 the actions consistent with this right center on ensuring accuracy in testing. In 1991 the American Psychological Association issued a report concluding that "the preponderance of the evidence" indicates that integrity tests can be useful, but it expressed concerns about some of the tests, the claims made for them, and their use in the absence of supervision by a qualified psychologist. Given these concerns, the tests should be carefully evaluated and supervised by trained personnel. Furthermore, because of possible inaccuracies, passing an integrity test should not be a necessary condition for employment, but could serve as one of several factors considered.

With respect to privacy, the fundamental issue is whether it is morally acceptable to base employment and job assignments on psychological and personal considerations. Integrity and other forms of psychological tests are said to invade privacy by asking questions that are too personal and not closely linked to job requirements. Such questions might pertain to lifestyle and off-the-job activities. Privacy can be limited when there is a compelling reason, however.

The employer's rights to select employees on nondiscriminatory grounds is intended to respect autonomy and enhance the good of economic efficiency. In a deontological framework, the former right may be limited if otherwise the liberties or rights of individuals would be limited. The good of economic efficiency is clearly important, but the right that promotes it is instrumental. Furthermore, deontological systems can require the sacrifice of efficiency for the respect of rights, as illustrated in Figure 19-3. The actions consistent with this right thus might be to test prospective employees and use the test results, assuming a reasonably accurate test, in hiring and in job assignment decisions depending on how compelling is the interest; that is, how important integrity and loyalty are for a particular position. A position such as security guard, bank teller, or purchasing agent might warrant an integrity test, whereas a custodial position might not.

Although there is ambiguity in the application of rights-based systems in this case, the freedom from arbitrary treatment and the right of privacy seem to have priority. This conclusion is tempered in the case of jobs for which the traits these tests can measure can substantially affect efficiency or compromise the interests or property of the employer.

Consequently, necessary conditions for their use are that the tests be reasonably accurate and administered by qualified individuals, that they be limited to jobs for which the tested traits are important to the interests of the firm, and that they be only one of several factors considered in employment decisions.[11] The chapter case *Genetic Testing in the Workplace* raises similar considerations about rights and their priorities.

Neoclassical Liberalism

Liberalism emphasizes the liberty of individuals and is concerned with the relationships between liberty and morality and between that liberty and the state.[12] The former pertains to which rules or rights have moral standing, whereas the latter pertains to how individual liberty should be limited by the liberty of others and by the institutions individuals establish to govern their interactions. Liberal theory has a rich intellectual tradition including Hobbes (1651) and Locke (1690), but only a relatively recent version of that theory, that of Nozick (1974), will be considered here. Nozick's theory is considered because it stakes out a position for a minimal state and because it provides a conception of rights and justice that is quite different from that of Kant and Rawls.

As with Kant, Nozick attempts to deduce principles that define the scope of autonomy and liberty and then to derive a principle of justice. His starting point is the self-evident principle of relying on an individual's free consent to any restrictions on personal liberty. Nozick derives his system based on the side constraint that "no moral balancing act can take place among us; there is no moral outweighing of one of our lives by others so as to lead to greater overall social good. There is no justified sacrifice of some of us for others" (p. 33). In Nozick's view, this side constraint ensures that individuals will be treated as ends—as the categorical imperative requires—and not as means. This is a stronger version of the categorical imperative than Kant employs, because Kant recognizes that individuals may be treated as means as long as they are also treated as ends.

Nozick recognizes that in the exercise of their own rights individuals may coerce or violate the rights of others, so individuals will form a voluntary association to enforce rights jointly. That association is then one to which all individuals have unanimously and freely consented and is the only entity that is allowed to use force to prevent violations of rights and liberties. That association may be viewed as a state, and the activities it is empowered to undertake have moral standing because its establishment satisfies the categorical imperative.

Nozick concludes that the state would have minimal powers, limited to "protecting its citizens against violence, theft, and fraud, and to the enforcement of contracts . . . " (p. 26). Individuals thus have the negative right not to be coerced by others, and the state has the duty to enforce that right.

The fundamental principle of consent also provides Nozick's conception of distributive justice, which pertains to an individual's entitlement to goods and to the corresponding duty of others to satisfy that entitlement. Because any concept of distributive justice must be based on voluntary consent, Nozick's conclusion is that what is just is whatever is the result of the voluntary actions of individuals. His maxim (p. 160) is expressed as, "From each as they choose, to each as they are chosen."

---

[11]Dalton and Metzger (1993) reach a different conclusion based on concerns about the accuracy of the tests.

[12]The term *liberal* is generally used in the United States to refer to positions that are to the left on a ideological dimension in which individual responsibilities and limited government are on the right and collectivist responsibilities and larger government are on the left. In many countries, liberalism refers to positions on the right of this dimension.

Nozick's theory has been criticized for its sole reliance on free consent. One line of criticism is based on utilitarian perspective that actions should be evaluated in terms of their consequences. Another line of criticism is that his theory ignores the situation of those who are poorly off because of their initial endowments of abilities and resources. More importantly for applied purposes, Nozick's conception of a minimal state seems far removed from modern society. It does, however, provide a basis for the respect for and extension of liberties.

Categories of Justice Theories

Theories of justice add a comparative dimension to moral standards. They are concerned with how different individuals stand relative to each other on dimensions including, but not limited to, rights, liberties, and consequences. Rawls's theory of justice as fairness, for example, concludes that equality of moral and political rights is required but that economic rewards and burdens can be distributed unequally.

The three principal categories of justice theories are (1) distributive, (2) compensatory, and (3) retributive. Distributive justice is concerned with providing incentives to contribute to the well-being of society and with providing a fair and just distribution of the rewards of those contributions. Compensatory justice is concerned with principles for determining how individuals should be compensated for the harm done by others. Retributive justice is concerned with punishment for actions contrary to societal well-being or to a moral rule. Retributive justice may be used to deter actions. Only distributive and compensatory justice are considered here.

DISTRIBUTIVE JUSTICE

Distributive justice is concerned with the distribution of the rewards and burdens of social interaction. A distributive standard is necessarily comparative, since it identifies how those rewards and burdens are assigned to individuals with particular attributes or in particular situations. Tax policy, for example, assigns the tax burden based on income, asset holdings, and consumption. Distributive justice thus is concerned with which attributes are relevant for particular issues, such as the distribution of income, wealth, opportunity, rights, and duties. Just as rights can rule out certain decision alternatives as illustrated in Figure 19-3, justice principles can also rule out alternatives. They also can impose duties to ensure that the distribution of rewards and burdens is just.

The basic comparative principle of distributive justice is that "Equals should be treated equally and unequals, unequally." Velasquez (1992, p. 91) elaborates by stating the principle,

> Individuals who are similar in all respects relevant to the kind of treatment in question should be given similar benefits and burdens, even if they are dissimilar in other irrelevant respects; and individuals who are dissimilar in a relevant respect ought to be treated dissimilarly, in proportion to their dissimilarity.

This principle implies that individuals should receive different pay if their productivity is different but should receive the same pay if their productivity is the same even though they differ in terms of irrelevant factors such as race or gender.

Distributive justice has a variety of conceptions. Egalitarianism requires the equal distribution of the rewards and burdens of society. This concept is typically rejected because an equal distribution of rewards distorts the incentives to produce those rewards. That is, at some point the more equally a society attempts to divide its pie the smaller the pie will be. Rawls's theory of justice as fairness concerns distributing the rewards

TABLE 19-1 Utilitarianism, Egalitarianism, and Rawlsian Justice

	Utility		
Individual	***Utilitarianism***	***Egalitarianism***	***Rawlsian Justice***
1	10	3	6
2	6	3	5
3	2	3	4
Aggregate utility	18	9	15

and burdens of society in a manner that is fair yet gives attention to incentives to increase the size of the pie.

To illustrate the differences, consider the example in Table 19-1 of a three-person society in which individual 1 has greater ability than individual 2 who has greater ability than individual 3. The society has three possible systems of organizing the interactions of its members. A utilitarian system has the strongest incentives for individuals to use their abilities to pursue their interests, resulting in greater aggregate utility than the other systems. The distribution across individuals, however, could be unequal as indicated in the utilitarianism column of the table. Compared with the utilitarian system, an egalitarian system would redistribute aggregate utility equally among the three individuals. To accomplish this, incentives would have to be distorted by, for example, taxing the more able and productive, which in the example reduces aggregate utility from 18 to 9. In contrast, Rawls's conception of justice requires making the least advantaged individual, who in this society is individual 3, as well off as possible. In doing so Rawls seeks to preserve incentives and to allow individuals to use their abilities to pursue their interests, so utility can be unequally distributed. Aggregate utility is lower than that under utilitarianism since utility is redistributed in favor of individual 3, but it is greater than under egalitarianism since individuals have stronger incentives to pursue their interests and utilize their abilities.

COMPENSATORY JUSTICE

Compensatory justice is concerned with whether and how a person should be compensated for an injustice. Compensatory justice has fairness and restitution as its goals. If a person injures another accidentally, the institutions of society may be designed to compensate the injured. The principal institutions through which compensation for accidents is provided are the liability, workers' compensation, and insurance systems. Compensation in these cases serves two objectives. First, it provides restitution. Second, it provides incentives to reduce injuries and social costs by imposing the burden on the party that caused the accident. If the institution of compensation is not well designed, however, it can result in a moral hazard problem that generates social costs by distorting incentives for care. In such a case, the benefits of compensation must be weighed against the consequences of the distortions of economic incentives the compensation causes. For example, the provision of government-backed flood insurance can result in more home building in flood-prone areas than would be warranted by economic efficiency considerations. There is, however, no necessary requirement for a direct link between the compensation and the incentives, as evidenced by no-fault insurance and workers' compensation systems.

Because of past injustices from discrimination in hiring and promotion practices, the courts ruled that compensation was owed to minority group members as a class, rather than just to the identifiable victims of discrimination. Rawls's principle of fair equality of opportunity provides a different justification for this ruling by focusing not on the nature of past injustices but on ensuring that all individuals have fair equality of opportunity. This requires not only the absence of discrimination, but also the fair opportunity for all to qualify for positions and pursue their interests. From this perspective, measures to ensure opportunities are warranted even if they extend beyond the set of actual victims of past discrimination. These issues are addressed more extensively in Chapter 21.

INJUSTICE

A general principle advanced in conceptions of justice is that an injustice is morally tolerated only if it is necessary to avoid a greater injustice. Such a principle requires an ordering of injustices. Gert (1988, pp. 110–111) offers a standard for when a violation of a moral rule is justified.

> A violation can be justified by providing reasons which would result in either some impartial rational persons advocating that that kind of violation be publicly allowed or less frequently, all impartial rational persons advocating that such a violation be publicly allowed.

Gert thus requires that the violator have reasons for the violation and that an impartial observer understand those reasons and be willing to have that form of violation publicly allowed. An injustice may be met by retribution or compensation.

An applied version of Gert's principle is the public disclosure test: "If I disclosed publicly that I had taken an action that violated a moral standard and explained my reasons for doing so, would the public understand and approve of my action?" One such explanation would be that a greater injustice was avoided. Since the public disclosure test is intended to be a hypothetical and reflective question to be answered by the person contemplating the action, it is important that the test not turn into a rationalization of a violation in the absence of avoiding a greater injustice. For this reason the public disclosure feature of the test is crucial.

This principle will be applied in Chapter 22 to the issue of whether avoiding a greater injustice justifies making improper payments demanded as a condition for a sale. In the chapter case *Genetic Testing in the Workplace* a central issue is whether the injustice of the invasion of privacy through genetic testing is warranted to avoid the greater injustice of a person incurring serious physical harm from exposure in the workplace. The chapter case *Delta Instruments, Inc.* raises justice issues in the wake of a moral wrong.

Rawls's Theory of Justice

THE FRAMEWORK FOR JUSTICE AS FAIRNESS

Rawls (1971) presents a theory of distributive justice set in the tradition of the social contract theory of Locke (1698), Rousseau (1762), and Kant. Rawls argues for the priority of the right over the good, but he is less concerned with developing maxims for judging the reasons or motives that individuals have for their actions than with developing principles to guide the design of society's institutions. According to Rawls (1971, p. 7), "the primary subject of justice is . . . the way in which the major social institutions distribute fundamental rights and duties and determine the division of advantages from social cooperation . . . the legal protection of freedom of thought and liberty of conscience, competitive markets, private property in the means of production, and the monogamous family are examples of major social institutions."

Because any contemporaneous choice of principles by individuals would be based at least in part on who those individuals are and what roles they have in society, Rawls concludes that just principles are those that would be "chosen behind a veil

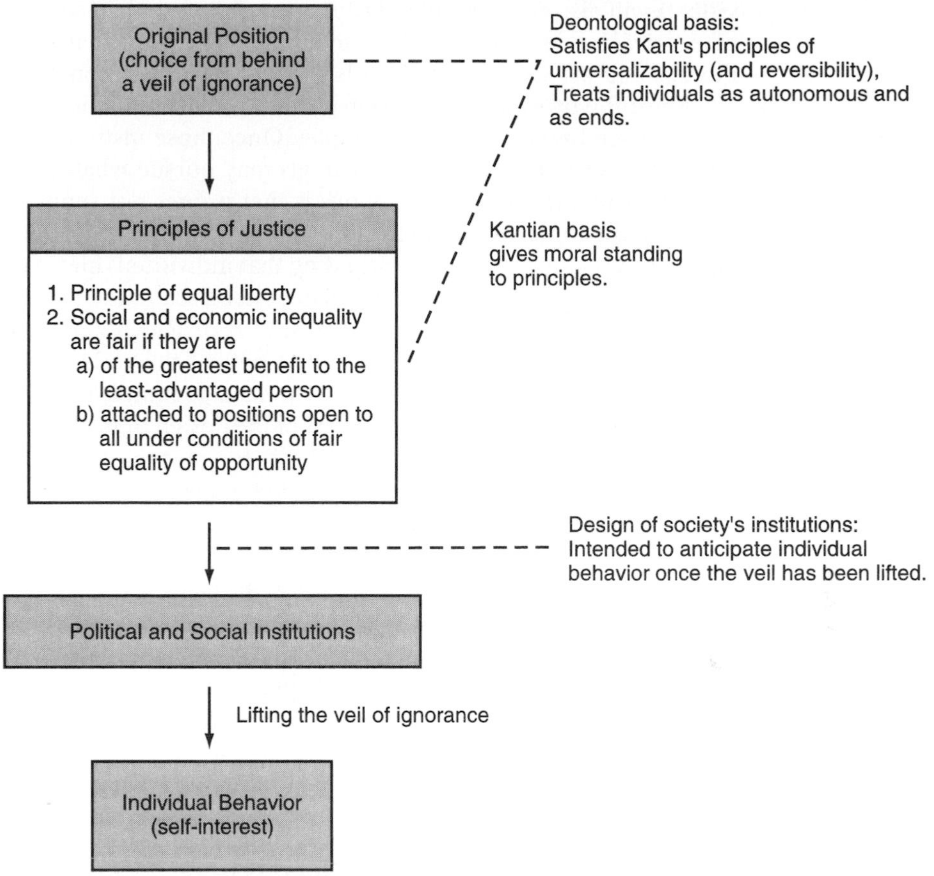

FIGURE 19-5 Rawls's Contractarian Framework

of ignorance" from an "original position" in which one does not know one's personal characteristics and the place one will subsequently have in society. In this original position each individual is equal to every other individual, and the principles chosen will have moral standing, it is argued, because they are deduced from an impartial method of choice in which no one has an advantage.[13]

Rawls's contractarian method is illustrated in Figure 19-5. In the original position, individuals do not know which abilities they will have, which positions in society they will occupy, or what their tastes will be. What they do know is that there is a set of possible abilities, tastes, and positions they might be fortunate or unfortunate enough to have once the veil of ignorance has been lifted. They also know the laws of the natural sciences and the understandings gained from the social sciences, so they can predict the behavior that will result once society's institutions are in place and the veil has been lifted. Since in the original position all individuals are equal and the principles they will choose will apply to everyone and so to themselves, the original position satisfies the Kantian standards of universalizability and unanimity. From the original position, indi-

[13]One concern with deducing maxims in Kant's framework is that individuals, knowing their present positions in society, might not reason in an impartial manner. Kant argues that the sense of freedom and autonomy in everyone leads everyone to reason impartially and to will the same maxims, resulting in unanimity. Rawls seeks to ensure impartiality and unanimity through the device of the original position.

viduals will also treat people always as ends rather than solely as means. Since Kant's categorical imperative is satisfied, the principles chosen in the original position will have moral standing, according to Rawls.[14] Those principles constitute the social contract.

Once the principles have been chosen, society's political and social institutions are to be chosen based on those principles. Once those institutions are in place, the veil of ignorance is to be lifted and individuals may pursue whatever interests they have. An important feature of Rawls's theory is that it does not suppose that once the veil has been lifted people will necessarily behave according to a set of rules that take precedence over self-interest. Understanding that individuals may pursue their own interests, he focuses on the role of institutions in guiding the pursuit of those interests in a mutually advantageous manner. The central task of Rawls's method then is to determine which institutions would be chosen from behind the veil of ignorance.

The relevance of Rawls's system for management is found both in the principles of justice he identifies and in the concept of the design of institutions consistent with those principles. The principles provide a basis for reasoning about issues with moral concerns. The formulation of policies to guide managers in dealing with such issues corresponds to the design of Rawls's institutions. These policies are used in the screening stage of the framework for nonmarket analysis and strategy formulation introduced in Chapter 2 and summarized in Figure 2-4. In the case of integrity tests, for example, the principles provide a basis for reasoning about whether such tests involve an unjustified intrusion on the liberties of prospective employees, whether they distort opportunities, and whether they have desirable distributive consequences.

THE PRINCIPLES OF JUSTICE

Rawls argues that individuals would adopt two principles as a basis for justice as fairness:

> First: each person is to have an equal right to the most extensive basic liberty compatible with similar liberty for others.
> Second: social and economic inequalities are to be arranged so that they are both (a) to the greatest benefit of the least advantaged and (b) attached to positions and offices open to all under conditions of fair equality of opportunity.[15]

The first principle is referred to as "the equal liberty principle," part (a) of the second as the "difference principle," and part (b) as the "fair equality of opportunity principle." Rawls's principles may be thought of as incorporating both deontological considerations (in the form of liberties, rights, and opportunities) and considerations of well-being (in terms of the benefits to the least advantaged).

Rawls argues that the principle of equal liberty has precedence over the fair equality of opportunity principle, which has precedence over the difference principle. By the first precedence, Rawls means "that liberty can be restricted only for the sake of liberty itself." The second precedence means that the difference principle is to be applied only after conditions ensuring the fair equality of opportunity are in place. In Rawls's system, no trade-off is permitted between basic liberties and social and economic gains. Rawls thus concludes that society's institutions should be characterized by political equality but that social and economic inequalities can be tolerated as long as they are arranged in accord with the principle of fair equality of opportunity and the difference principle.

---

[14]See Rawls (1980) for a further analysis of the Kantian construction.
[15]Rawls (1971, pp. 60, 83). A more extensive statement of the principles is given on pages 302–303.

The equal liberty principle pertains to liberties such as the freedom of conscience and speech, the right to vote, the right to be eligible for office, freedom of assembly, freedom from arbitrary arrest, and the right to hold property. Such liberties can be limited only as necessary to maintain conditions of reasoned discourse and public order. For example, rules of recognition and procedure may be instituted to allow everyone to speak in a manner that allows that speech to be heard. With respect to political liberties, Rawls argues that there must be limits on "the scope of majority rule," such as the limits specified in the Constitution and in the Bill of Rights.

Fair equality of opportunity is necessary to allow individuals to realize the worth of their liberty, and it requires that positions in society be open to all and that all individuals have a fair opportunity to quality for those positions. When fair equality of opportunity has been assured, the difference principle requires that the least advantaged individuals receive assistance to allow them to realize the worth of their liberty through the pursuit of their interests. The second principle thus is comparative and may require, for example, special provisions for the physically disabled that provide them access to public facilities and to the same employment opportunities open to others. Rawls further argues that policies that improve the well-being of the least-advantaged individual would also improve the well-being of most, if not all, of the disadvantaged because their positions are "closely-knit." Thus, a policy that benefits the least advantaged also benefits many others.

To apply the difference principle, Rawls faces the task of determining who are the least-advantaged persons. This involves making comparisons among individuals, but as indicated in the discussion of utilitarianism in Chapter 19, such interpersonal comparisons are problematic. Rawls attempts to avoid this problem by identifying a set of "primary goods" that all individuals are said to require to be able to pursue their interests, whatever those interests might be. The primary goods are divided into broad categories—rights and liberties, opportunities and powers, and income and wealth. Rawls argues that an index of these primary goods be used to assess the well-being of individuals. This allows for interpersonal comparisons. The difference principle thus takes well-being into account.

THE ROLE OF INCENTIVES

From Rawls's perspective, the institutions of society should allow one individual to be better off than another if that were necessary to make the least-advantaged person better off. This is illustrated in Table 19-1 where the Rawlsian choice results in lower aggregate utility than utilitarianism, but makes the least-advantaged person better off than under the other two social arrangements. The Rawlsian choice also allows more-advantaged persons to pursue their interests resulting in greater aggregate well-being than the egalitarian choice. Rawls, however, is concerned with the well-being of the least advantaged rather than aggregate well-being.

The role of incentives and the comparison between the utilitarian, egalitarian, and Rawlsian systems are also illustrated in Figure 19-6, where the utility possibility set corresponds to institutions that satisfy the equal liberty and fair equality of opportunity principles. In Figure 19-6, individual 1 is more advantaged than individual 2, since more of the alternatives result in a higher utility for 1 than for 2. Egalitarianism requires that the institutions be chosen to attain point A, which yields the greatest utility of both individuals subject to the restriction that both are equally well-off. The difference principle states that it is just to move from A to B, even though individual 1 does relatively better than 2, since the less-advantaged 2 is made as well-off as possible at B. Institutions that would allow C to be attained, however, are unjust, since moving from B to C

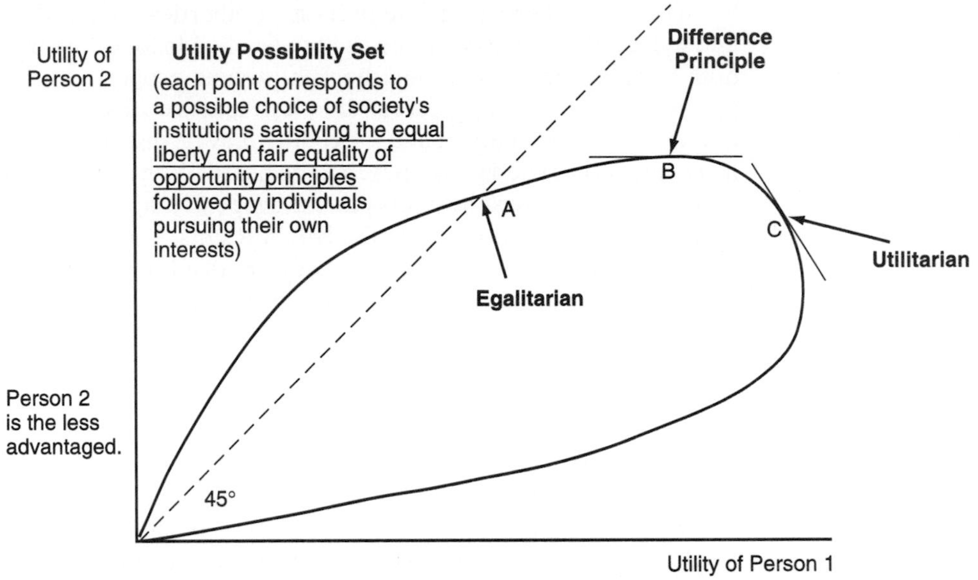

FIGURE 19-6 Difference Principle, Utilitarianism, Egalitarianism

reduces the well-being of the less-advantaged person even though the well-being of 1 increases by more than the well-being of 2 decreases. A utilitarian system that weights the well-being of both individuals equally would choose institutions that allow the attainment of point C.[16]

Rawls thus supports economic efficiency and the role of incentives and markets in attaining that efficiency. But his system of justice supports the market system only in so far as it serves the well-being of the least advantaged. Economic efficiency and aggregate well-being thus can be sacrificed if that improves the situation of the least advantaged.

Example: Living Benefits

Is the purchase of life insurance policies from the terminally ill, as considered in the Chapter 18 case *Living Benefits,* consistent with Rawls's theory of justice? With respect to the principle of equal liberty, no liberties are infringed by the purchases, since a person can freely choose to sell a policy or retain it.[17] Indeed, purchasing policies better enables the terminally ill to realize the worth of their liberty by providing funds for their use. Similarly, the purchases do not infringe the fair equality of opportunity, and if anything they expand the opportunities available to the terminally ill. The terminally ill can be regarded as the least advantaged, and allowing purchases of life insurance policies makes them better off. From a deontological perspective, the purchases allow the terminally ill to better realize the worth of their liberty, and from a consequentialist perspective the terminally ill can attain better consequences. The difference principle is thus satisfied. Under Rawls's theory the purchase of life insurance policies by the terminally ill is just and would be allowed in a choice from behind a veil of ignorance.

---

[16]Rawls's difference principle requires that the choice of social institutions be Pareto optimal. That is, any choice of institutions that yields a point in the interior of the utility possibility set in Figure 19-1 can be improved upon to make both persons better off.

[17]As in the analysis of living benefits from the perspective of Kantian rights, the person must be competent to make a free choice.

DUTY IN RAWLS'S THEORY

The assignment of duty in Rawls's theory of justice is part of the choice of political and social institutions based on the principles of justice. Duty may be assigned to government, individuals, and organizations such as firms. All have a duty to respect and promote the basic liberties identified by the principle of equal liberty. The duty to respect and ensure fair equality of opportunity is generally assigned to government and employers. Offices and positions are to be open to all, and employers may be assigned the duty to ensure that their employment practices provide all qualified individuals with the opportunity to be considered. The duty can extend further by requiring employers to take positive measures to ensure that employees have the means to qualify. The Chapter 18 case *Sex Differentiated Retirement Benefits* addresses the related issue of the equal treatment of men and women.

The duty to attend to the interests of the least advantaged under the difference principle should be assigned so that incentives are not distorted to the point that they jeopardize capital formation, investment, and the creation of jobs. In the terminology of economics, incentives should be preserved so that society remains on the frontier of the utility possibility set in Figure 19-6. Thus, the party that is best positioned to attend to the interests of the least advantaged, and to do so efficiently, should be assigned the duty. That duty is generally assigned to government. Assigning that duty directly to individuals would violate the equal liberty principle, so individuals may through their voluntary choice contribute time and money to charitable and related activities. Firms as the property of owners may also contribute to such activities on the same grounds. Some duties to attend to the interests of the least advantaged are assigned to firms in the case of injured workers, but most of the duty rests with government and the free consent of individuals.

CRITICISMS OF RAWLS'S THEORY

Some critics, such as Shapiro (1986), raise concerns about the original position and about what individuals are assumed to know in that position. In the original position, individuals are assumed to understand that the nature of people is such that they will pursue their own interests. A person thus is not assumed to act in a purely altruistic or egalitarian manner. Rawls recognizes this form of criticism by noting that his theory of justice is as much a political as a moral philosophy.[18]

Another form of criticism centers on whether all individuals in the original position would choose the same principles and, if so, whether they would choose Rawls's principles rather than some other principles.[19] For example, if the first principle is to take precedence over the second, then the "most extensive basic liberty compatible with similar liberty for others" could be viewed as implying the neoclassical liberalism principle of a minimal role for government. Rawls, however, concludes that the role of government should be extensive.

Another criticism centers on Rawls's conclusion that in the original position, once liberties and equal opportunity have been assured, society would choose institutions that would provide the maximum benefit to the least-advantaged person. Some have argued that people would not choose such a principle, because the chance of any one person being the least disadvantaged is minuscule. Harsanyi (1982), for example, argues

---

[18]See Rawls (1993) for a modification of his theory in light of the criticisms it received.

[19]The same criticisms may be made about Kant's system. Brandt (1979) argues that individuals could well choose a variety of different principles. Gauthier (1986) provides a moral theory that addresses the issue of compliance with the initial choice. Binmore (1994) provides a strategic theory with a framework similar to Rawls's.

that people would choose a principle corresponding to average rule utilitarianism, since that maximizes the expected well-being of everyone from behind the veil of ignorance. Rawls's use of primary goods as a means of assessing the advantages of individuals is also subject to the same criticisms as are interpersonal comparisons of utility.

As with utilitarianism and rights theories, a conceptual and applied difficulty in justice theories pertains to how duty is to be assigned. The issues pertaining to basic liberties are similar to those previously addressed, and the assignment of the burden of assuring fair equality of opportunity and improving the position of the least advantaged raises issues similar to those addressed in Chapter 18 in the context of utilitarianism. On some matters such as opportunity in employment, the duty naturally falls to the employer. Similarly, the duty to assure fair equality of opportunity and nondiscrimination in housing falls on landlords. But, the duty to provide Rawls's primary goods, such as a minimum standard of living, so that individuals have a fair opportunity to realize the worth of their liberty is a collective responsibility. As such, the assignment rests primarily with government. Nozick would argue that it rests instead with the free choice of individuals who may, if they so choose, contribute to the well-being of others. Private charity is one reflection of this principle.

Nozick (1974) observes that Rawls's theory pertains to a "time slice" in which the allocation of rewards and burdens of society must necessarily be judged by "end results" and independently of history. He argues that how individuals arrived at the current point in time is important from a moral perspective. For example, if an injustice were done to a person in the past, it would be necessary to examine the subsequent chain of events to determine what compensation, if any, were warranted. If people had made voluntary choices that worked to their disadvantage, however, is there a duty to compensate? Nozick also argues that Rawls's system of justice is necessarily patterned according to characteristics of individuals or their situations, as required in the application of the difference principle. Whatever form of patterning is used, Nozick argues, it must interfere with basic liberties.[20] This, he argues, means that no actions can satisfy both the equal liberty principle and the difference principle.

Although Rawls's theory has been criticized on a variety of dimensions, it remains an important philosophical work and provides a useful framework for reasoning about managerial problems. His theory brings together several considerations, including liberties, opportunities, and consequences, that ethical intuition recognizes as important. It also provides a degree of prioritization that can be used to structure analysis. The chapter case *Environmental Justice and Pollution Credits Trading Systems* provides an opportunity to reason about a managerial policy from Rawls's perspective.

THE APPLICATION OF THE PRINCIPLES OF JUSTICE

Although Rawls's system of justice is as much a political as a moral philosophy and is thus directed at the design of institutions more than at the evaluation of actions, it provides a set of considerations helpful to managers who must establish policies. Company policies are the managerial analogues of Rawls's institutions.

Because of its close relationship to Kantian rights, the application of Rawls's principle of equal liberty involves the same considerations found in rights analysis. This section thus focuses on fair equality of opportunity and the difference principle.

The principle of fair equality of opportunity is most directly applicable to policies associated with the employment relationship, as considered in Chapter 21. That principle includes considerations such as those in Title VII of the Civil Rights Act of 1964,

[20]See Nozick (pp. 160-164).

which prohibits discrimination in employment. Rawls's principle, however, goes beyond the prohibition of discrimination and requires the "fair equality" of opportunity. Fair equality requires not only that positions be open to all, but that individuals have the means to attempt to qualify for them. Justice Marshall's arguments in *Kadrmas* are consistent with this principle. Affirmative action programs, as considered in more detail in Chapter 21, may be viewed as one implementation of this principle.

The difference principle is applicable once liberties and fair equality of opportunity have been assured. That principle calls for affirmative consideration of those who are the least advantaged or who would be put in such a position by policies or actions. As Rawls argues, the position of the least-advantaged person is closely linked to the positions of other disadvantaged persons. The difference principle provides a justification, for example, for special programs that make facilities accessible to the disabled and provide opportunities for disadvantaged youths. It also provides a justification for policies that respond to the needs of laid-off employees and the communities in which they live.

The managerial application of Rawls's framework involves the successive elimination of policy alternatives by using first the equal liberty principle and then the fair equality of opportunity principle. The remaining alternatives are then evaluated for fairness, and the choice among those remaining alternatives is based on the difference principle. The methodology for the application of Rawls's framework may be summarized as follows:

1. Identify the liberties and rights involved.
2. The principle of equal liberty: Evaluate alternative policies in terms of how extensive are the corresponding liberties and rights of individuals consistent with equal liberties and rights for all. Prioritize rights and liberties when conflicts arise. Eliminate alternatives that limit liberties for reasons other than assuring other liberties and rights.
3. The principle of fair equality of opportunity: Identify the opportunities associated with each remaining alternative, and evaluate those alternatives in terms of how extensive the corresponding opportunities are. Eliminate alternatives that limit opportunities.
4. For the remaining alternatives, evaluate their fairness implications for those affected, with a focus on the least-advantaged individuals.
5. Choose among the remaining policies based on the difference principle by favoring policies that benefit the least advantaged even if they reduce aggregate well-being.

In applying this methodology it is important to remember that a departure from equal liberty cannot be justified by greater advantage in social or economic matters for any individual.

Example: Corporate Social Responsibility?

Rawls's principles of justice provide no compelling justification for the development of the wildlife refuge. No basic liberties are involved, and the principle of fair equality of opportunity seems inapplicable, since no position nor primary good that provides the means for individuals to realize their interests is involved. The difference principle also seems inapplicable, since developing the refuge cannot reasonably be viewed as affecting the least-advantaged persons. Those individuals would presumably be better off if the funds were used for education, housing, or medical care. Furthermore, to arrange society's institutions so that every individual were compelled to act on the difference principle at all times would violate the principle of equal liberty. The action of opening the refuge thus seems to be in the domain governed by property rights and free choice.

Example: Integrity Tests

Much of the rights analysis of integrity tests is relevant to the perspective of justice as well, so the focus here is on the difference principle and fair equality of opportunity. One concern with an integrity test is whether it puts those who are already disadvantaged at a further disadvantage. If they are already disadvantaged for a reason that would be revealed by the integrity test and result in a "failure" on the test, an objection on justice grounds could be raised. Similarly, if the test systematically affects the opportunities of individuals with particular attributes that are irrelevant to job performance, the test would be unjust. Such concerns are reflected in laws in a number of states that prohibit employers from inquiring about criminal records of job applicants or about their lifestyles. The more compelling are the firm's interests and the more important are the tested traits for a particular position, the more likely they are to be justified, however. Justice principles require that the tests not adversely affect individuals on irrelevant grounds, but otherwise may be used if they enable the firm to improve its performance.

Example: Insurance Screening for Preexisting Conditions

If screening for preexisting conditions for life insurance purposes is not a violation of the principle of equal liberty or the principle of fair equality of opportunity, it may conflict with the difference principle. Treatment of diseases such as AIDS can be very expensive, and to the extent that that cost is borne by the victim and the victim's family it can represent a heavy if not insurmountable burden. To the extent that the cost of treatment substantially disadvantages some persons, the difference principle requires that institutions be designed to relieve at least some of that burden. Rawls then asks to which institution the duty should be assigned. The institution of life insurance seems less appropriate than the use of public funds, since adverse selection by those with preexisting conditions could substantially reduce the efficiency of the life insurance system.

Higher Order Standards for Evaluating Ethical Systems

The ethical systems based on utilitarian, rights, and justice considerations use two general standards for determining which principles or rules have moral standing. The first is universalizability (which implies reversibility). A principle or rule has moral standing if one would be willing to have everyone, including one's self, behave in accord with it. This standard, however, does not necessarily imply that everyone would choose the same set of principles or rules. The second standard—unanimous choice as from behind a veil of ignorance—is intended to focus on those principles and rules that everyone would choose to have everyone abide. The notion of reasoning about principles from behind a veil of ignorance is important, because ethical principles are to be impartial and not based on the actual position a person occupies in society.

Rule utilitarianism and the rules derived from it have moral standing because each individual chooses a rule to be followed by everyone and, since each individual is maximizing aggregate well-being, each would choose the same rule. That is, the principle of maximizing aggregate well-being is universalizable, since one would will that everyone abide by it. The principle would be chosen unanimously from behind a veil of ignorance, since the maximal utility yields the greatest utility for people once the veil has been lifted.

Rawls's principles of equal liberty and fair equality of opportunity meet both the standards of universalizability and unanimous choice from behind a veil of ignorance. Rawls's difference principle clearly meets the first standard, since an individual could well be willing to have everyone abide by it. It is not at all clear, however, that from behind a veil of ignorance everyone would choose the difference principle and not some other principle such as the utilitarian principal of maximizing aggregate social well-being.

Kantian rules meet both standards. The categorical imperative implies that rules will be universal. The view that every individual is rational and deduces maxims from a conception of freedom and autonomy that resides in everyone means that each will choose the same rule, so unanimity results. Kant's view of rationality and a common conception of freedom and autonomy serve as a veil of ignorance because reasoning and choice are impartial.

In business applications these two higher order standards provide a basis for evaluating alternative policies and provide guidelines for managers to follow in the context of nonmarket analysis and strategy formulation. These standards are used in Chapter 20 to evaluate the principles developed by Levi Strauss & Co. and Cummins Engine to guide their managers.

Summary

Rights and justice considerations are important ethical concepts that form part of one's basic ethical intuition. Rights may be classified as intrinsic or instrumental. Intrinsic rights are justified independently of consequences by their consistency with conceptions of liberty and autonomy. Instrumental rights have moral standing because they lead to higher levels of well-being. Instrumental rights are an important component of teleological systems, which judge the good in terms of consequences. Intrinsic rights are a central component of deontological ethical systems, which are based on considerations other than, or in addition to, consequences.

Kant's theory of moral rules is based on the categorical imperative, which holds that individuals are to be treated always as ends and never solely as means, and that rules of behavior are to be universal and reversible. Moral rules identify intrinsic rights of individuals and the corresponding duties to respect those rights. Moral rights are held to take precedence over considerations of well-being, but the ethical intuition that well-being is also important is strong.

Justice theories add an explicit comparative dimension to deontological systems. The three principal categories of justice theories are distributive, compensatory, and retributive. Distributive theories focus on the distribution of the rewards and burdens of social interactions. Compensatory theories are concerned with compensating for injustice. Retributive theories focus on punishment for moral wrongs. An injustice is a moral violation and is tolerated only if it is necessary to avoid a greater injustice.

Rawls provides a theory of justice as fairness that incorporates the Kantian framework and focuses on both liberties, rights, and the comparative treatment of individuals. Rawls's theory prescribes that individuals are to be treated equally with respect to basic liberties but that individuals may be treated unequally in terms of rewards and burdens as long as the inequality satisfies conditions of fairness as embodied in the difference principle and in the principle of fair equality of opportunity. Rawls argues that liberties have first priority, and when they are assured, the provision of fair equality of opportunity is required. The difference principle, which requires that institutions and policies be designed to benefit the least advantaged, is then applied.

Higher order standards are used to evaluate moral rules and principles. One such standard is universalizability, which requires that an individual would will that everyone follow the rule or abide by the principle. The second standard is unanimity, which requires that everyone would choose that rule or principle. Reasoning about which rules and principles would be unanimously supported is intended to be based on Kant's conceptions of autonomy, freedom, and rationality and is to take place behind a veil of ignorance.

Managers must make decisions in situations in which there are competing moral claims that require judgments about the effects of decisions on individuals, the prioritization of rights, and concerns for the distributive effects on individuals. An understanding of ethical systems and ethical reasoning and a sensitivity to the ethical dimensions of issues are important for managers for several reasons. First, sensitivity to the ethical dimensions of issues and the use of ethical frameworks can help managers avoid wrongs that may otherwise result from a narrow focus on the firm's interests. Second, sensitivity to the moral concerns that others may have about the policies and practices of the firm can enable management to anticipate nonmarket actions and pressures. Third, managers will be more likely to make decisions that serve the long-run interests of society and ultimately of business itself. Fourth, the content of corporate social responsibility is to be found in the principles and standards of ethical systems, as considered in Chapter 20.

CASES

Delta Instruments, Inc.

Delta Instruments, Inc. was founded in 1973 to produce a unique, patented mechanical pressure gauge for industrial and military use. The gauge design provided a very accurate, long-life instrument that was extremely rugged and could be used in high vibration, pulsation, or corrosive service. Industrial applications were typically in the process industries, including power plants, refineries, and chemical plants. Military applications were quite broad, with the U.S. Navy the largest user (e.g., on aircraft-servicing nitrogen carts, diving chambers, and magazine sprinkler systems). Delta made no other products in significant volume.

Delta's total annual revenues were approximately $4.5 million. The firm employed 65 people in a single office-factory in Southern California. Approximately 45 employees worked in the factory. Delta had a three-person quality control department and a two-person engineering department. Delta was wholly owned by Jack Armstrong, who was actively involved in Delta's day-to-day operations.

Since its inception, Delta had supplied the government both directly and through prime contractors. Currently, Delta sold about $250,000 per year of military-specified gauges to various government prime contractors and about $200,000 per year directly to 10 to 15 government agencies or facilities. The Defense General Supply Center (DGSC) was the largest customer. Government sales, both direct and subcontract, were approximately 10 percent of Delta's total revenues. The direct contracts with the government were each usually small (under $50,000) and were often for standard Delta products.

Late in 1989 the DGSC awarded 19 contracts to Delta, worth $876,142, for the production of pressure gauges built to unique and rigorous specifications. Both Armstrong and the director of engineering concurred that although the gauge specifications were among the most difficult Delta had ever encountered, the specifications could be met. As was typical, each contract required that prototype gauges be tested to ensure compliance with required specifications and that the results of these preliminary tests be reported to the DGSC in the form of a First Article Test Report (FATR). Approximately 90 percent of the testing was to be conducted by independent testing laboratories with the remaining 10 percent being done by Delta. According to normal procedure, the testing laboratories were to submit their findings to Delta, which would add its findings to complete the FATRs and then submit them to the DGSC.

By July 1990 Delta had purchased the materials needed for production and had begun the first article testing on prototype gauges for 6 of the 19 contracts. After five of the six FATRs had been submitted to DGSC, Delta's presubmission review of the sixth FATR revealed several anomalous data points. (For instance, an entry that should have read 90 was reported as 9). Further inspection by the junior engineer and the quality control director revealed that the original reports furnished by an outside laboratory differed from the copied reports included in the FATR submitted by Delta. When confronted with this inconsistency, the director of engineering, who was responsible for compiling the FATRs, admitted that he had altered the outside laboratory data included in the sixth FATR by using liquid paper whitener, changing the data, and then reproducing the page to mask the change. The effect of these alterations suggested that the prototype gauge produced under the sixth contract had passed the testing when, in fact, it had failed.

Following this discovery, Delta began an internal investigation of the five previously submitted FATRs. It found that three of the five reports also contained alterations of the data and the test results of outside testing laboratories. In general, these alterations overstated the performance of the tested gauges and claimed compliance with contract specifications even though no such compliance had actually been found. In a subsequent interview with Armstrong, the director of engineering stated that he had altered FATR data on "one or more reports," had acted alone, had not been asked to falsify data by anyone, and that these were the only test data he had ever altered at Delta. Both the quality control director and the junior engineer claimed no knowledge of this or any other incident of data falsification having previously occurred at Delta.

No gauges had yet been produced or delivered to the DGSC. Delta had received no payments, nor had any been requested. Moreover, the problems found in the prototype gauges were correctable and compliance with the original contract specifications achievable. Indeed, there appeared to be some method behind the director of engineering's madness. The data alterations reflected the anticipated performance of the gauges. The opinions of Armstrong, the quality control manager, and other engineers at Delta confirmed that the performance anticipated by the director of engineering would indeed be met when the problems in the prototypes were addressed.

Armstrong was shocked and embarrassed by this incident. Delta had an immaculate reputation based chiefly on the quality of its products and the integrity of its organization. For nearly two decades, no other incident had the potential of impugning Delta's reputation. Furthermore, there had never been any contract disputes with the U.S. government. There also had been no contracts terminated for default. Moreover, the corporate culture at Delta embodied many of Armstrong's most deeply held values, including openness, honesty, and professionalism. Armstrong was proud of his company's record and its culture and was anxious to preserve Delta's reputation. But how? Should he forget about the already submitted FATRs and strive to bring the gauges into compliance with the reported data? Should he simply withdraw the submitted FATRs, citing "technical difficulties" or "administrative errors," and resubmit the FATRs when the gauges performed as required? (An attorney claimed that both of these options were arguably within Armstrong's legal rights.) Or should he inform the DGSC of the inaccuracies in the FATRs, as well as the source of these errors?

Armstrong also felt a strong obligation to fairness in the treatment of the director of engineering. This obligation was enhanced by the fact that the director was a long-time friend, who often had accompanied Mr. Armstrong on skiing and fishing vacations. Moreover, he had recently developed a heart condition that required extensive, and sometimes expensive, medical treatments. Termination would deprive him of his medical insurance coverage and benefits. The director of engineering was an affable man, highly regarded and well liked by other Delta employees. ■

PREPARATION QUESTION

1. Armstrong wanted to do the right thing, but what was right in this case?

Genetic Testing in the Workplace

Companies and their employees have an important interest in reducing health risks in the workplace. One approach to doing so is to alter production processes and the workplace to reduce hazards. For some companies, this can be quite expensive. Another approach is to choose the workforce to minimize the risk. This may be done through evaluating workers' qualifications and experience. It may also be done by determining workers' susceptibility to certain diseases that could result from exposure in the workplace. Genetic testing is one means of determining susceptibility to certain hazards and can be done from a sample of blood or other bodily fluid. Such tests are generally accurate, and although they can be expensive, they offer a basis on which to select and assign workers to minimize the risks from exposure to certain health hazards and the possible tragedy of chronic or terminal diseases.

One genetic test is for G-6-PD (glucose-6-phosphate dehydrogenase) deficiency. G-6-PD is an enzyme required for the stability of red blood cells. "Those with the deficiency are highly susceptible to having their red-blood-cell membranes destroyed by certain drugs or other oxidizing agents. It is especially a problem for blacks and some Mediterranean people."[1] The G-6-PD deficiency is carried by a sex-linked recessive gene, and approximately 100 million males worldwide are estimated to have the deficiency.

Another genetic test is for alpha-1-antitrypsin (AAT) deficiency, which results in susceptibility to

[1] *The Wall Street Journal,* February 24, 1986.

respiratory irritants such as those found in many workplaces. Treatment of the deficiency involves intravenous injections of AAT on a frequent basis.

Genetic testing can be used for either screening or monitoring purposes. In screening, genetic testing can be used to select among job applicants for positions that may involve a potential health hazard. Screening can also be used in assigning current employees to jobs so as to minimize risks. Genetic testing can also be used to identify susceptible individuals who can take precautions to protect themselves or be moved to other jobs with less exposure to possible irritants.

Genetic testing can also be used to monitor groups of employees over time to determine if they experience chromosome damage due to exposure in the workplace. This could be important for employees who work with lead, beryllium, and other potentially toxic metals and chemicals.

In addition to providing information that could be used to reduce risks, some companies believed that genetic testing might give them a degree of protection from liability if a worker chose to stay in a job after being notified that he or she was genetically susceptible to a disease that could be triggered by exposure in the workplace.

With the advances in genetic mapping achieved by the Human Genome Project the possibilities for more accurate and extensive genetic testing were seemingly unlimited. ■

PREPARATION QUESTIONS

1. Consider the use of genetic testing for screening job applicants, for assigning current employees to jobs, and for monitoring employees for genetic damage from exposure in the workplace. Which rights might be said to be violated by either the use or the prohibition of the use of genetic testing for these purposes? How do you prioritize those rights?
2. Is genetic testing in the workplace warranted from a utilitarian perspective; that is, by the potential benefits it can yield? What ethical concerns does it involve?
3. Is there a risk that an individual found to have a genetic abnormality might be subject to unfair discrimination? Who should be informed of the results of a genetic test?
4. Are there other moral considerations relevant to genetic testing in the workplace?
5. Is the use of genetic testing for monitoring more or less appropriate than its use for screening purposes?
6. Organized labor and some activists oppose genetic testing on the grounds that the employer should ensure a safe workplace. Does an employer have a moral duty to reduce risks in the workplace to the point at which any qualified person regardless of his or her susceptibility can safely occupy the position?
7. If an employee with full understanding of his or her genetic susceptibility chooses (because, for example, of higher pay) to work in an area in which exposure is possible, should the employer be absolved of liability for subsequent illnesses due to the exposure?
8. Should there be a rule prohibiting the use of genetic information in determining eligibility for insurance or for setting premiums? Does basing insurance decisions on genetic characteristics differ from basing insurance decisions on preexisting health conditions?
9. Consider the case of a company with a production process that requires the processing of a metal, such as beryllium, that can be toxic to employees. The company has installed dust collection and ventilation equipment, and the workplace meets all government safety requirements by a substantial margin. Nevertheless, an individual with a particular genetic deficiency can develop chronic and serious long-term illnesses from exposure to the metal. At an annualized cost of $1 million the company could install additional equipment that would reduce by half the risk to an employee with the genetic deficiency, but illness could still occur. The company could also screen job applicants for the metals-processing unit for the genetic deficiency and not hire those who have the deficiency. The cost of the screening would be approximately 10 percent of the cost of the additional equipment and would reduce the risk of disease by 90 percent. The company also has the alternative of replacing 80 percent of the workers in the metals-processing unit with sophisticated and expensive robotic equipment at a net annualized cost of $3 million (net of the savings in labor costs). This would result in the layoff of 48 employees. What should the company do?

Environmental Justice and Pollution Credits Trading Systems

As executive vice president for West Coast operations of Westco Oil Company, Jeremy Bentley was proud of the environmental accomplishments of his company in California. Emissions at the company's Long Beach refinery had been reduced and oil spills at its marine terminal in El Segundo had been reduced dramatically.

Jeremy was aware of the Environmental Protection Agency's environmental justice campaign and supported its concern about the siting of facilities, such as hazardous waste disposal sites, in areas in which minorities and the poor were overrepresented. He was shocked, however, when he was confronted by novel initiatives by the environmental justice movement. Not only were the arguments made by the activists novel, but they struck at the heart of the evolving system of pollution control being implemented in the Los Angeles area and elsewhere in the United States. That system emphasized attaining environmental goals using the least costly means of abatement. Attaining the goals at least cost to society required that greater reductions in emissions be made at facilities with low costs of abatement and smaller reductions at facilities with high costs of abatement.

To implement this system the South Coast Air Quality Management Board (AQMD) had established a pollution credits trading program that allowed abaters to earn credits for emissions reductions and to sell those credits to emitters of pollution that had higher costs of abatement. As indicated in more detail below, the trading of credits reduced the aggregate costs of attaining environmental goals. The AQMD had supported the development of markets in credits. Under one program approved by the AQMD, automobile scrap yards would buy old, high-pollution automobiles for $600 to $700 and receive a credit that they could sell either to the AQMD, a company, or an environmental group. If a company purchased a credit, it would not have to reduce its emissions by as much as it would otherwise have to reduce them. Under Jeremy's leadership Westco had participated in the AQMD program and purchased credits that it used at its marine terminal. Jeremy had also purchased credits though other programs and had used those credits at its Long Beach refinery.

Environmental justice and pollution credits trading systems collided in July 1997 in Southern California as environmental groups and advocates for low-income groups, led by the interest group Communities for a Better Environment, filed lawsuits seeking to force the EPA to rescind the authority granted to the AQMD and the California Air Resources Board to operate a pollution credits trading system. One focus of the lawsuits was the pollution credits trading system and the purchase and scrapping of old, high-pollution automobiles. One lawsuit filed by Communities for a Better Environment against five oil companies including Westco alleged that residents in San Pedro and El Segundo had been exposed to harmful hydrocarbon emissions because the companies violated the federal Clean Air Act by failing to reduce emissions at their marine terminals. Instead, the companies had earned pollution credits by purchasing and scrapping 7,400 old cars as allowed under the AQMD program. Westco had been one of the leading purchasers of the credits.

Unocal, which had initiated the program to purchase and scrap high-pollution cars, operated a subsidiary, Eco-Scrap, that purchased old cars for companies that wanted to earn pollution credits. Spokesman Barry Lane said, "We still believe that the emission control program is of great value, it makes good sense."[1]

In another lawsuit, the Center on Race, Poverty and the Environment and the National Association for the Advancement of Colored People joined Communities for a Better Environment in alleging that the pollution credits trading system violated the civil rights of minorities by subjecting communities in which they are disproportionately represented to high levels of health-threatening pollutants. The lawsuit cited Title VI of the Civil Rights Act of 1964, which prohibits discrimination, such as against minorities and women, in programs and activities receiving federal funds.

In conjunction with the filing of the lawsuits, the activist and advocacy groups held a press conference at which local residents told of the harmful effects of

[1] *Los Angeles Times,* July 23, 1997.

the pollutants. Fifth-grader Laurie Johnson, who was on medical leave from Wilmington Park Elementary School, reported that she and other children at the school had health problems attributable to the emissions. She said, "It's time for our corporate neighbors to be responsible and give us a hand."[2] The 69-year-old Lily Camarillo, who lived near a Texaco refinery, said, "I've raised several kids there, lost three others and you wouldn't believe the problems we've had. Headaches, sick stomachs; my daughter has leukemia."[3]

Richard Drury, attorney for Communities for a Better Environment, turned the pollution credits trading system principle on its head by arguing that it exposed residents to the equivalent of "thousands of cars idling at each marine terminal." He also said, "It's a good thing to get old cars off the road; they cause a lot of pollution. But you don't trade the health of workers and the residents who live near those facilities in exchange for that."[4] Later on CNN he said, "If you have enough money, you can buy enough pollution credits and pump out as much pollution as you want to. That's going to create toxic hot-spots."[5]

AQMD spokesman Tom Eichorn stated, "These people think they're being affected by air pollution problems . . . our job is to respond to their complaints." But, he added that the agency did not believe that emissions were higher than before the pollution credits trading system was instituted.[6] Barry Wallerstein of AQMD said, "The preliminary analysis by our legal department indicates that we're in full compliance with federal law."[7] "James Lents, the AQMD's outgoing executive officer, said he believes that the agency is not violating civil rights because toxic hot spots around industries are reduced under a separate rule, which prohibits fumes that pose a risk exceeding 100 cases of cancer among every million people exposed. However, that standard is less stringent than environmentalists and some health officials have wanted. AQMD board members, skeptical of the cancer danger posed by the [hydrocarbon] fumes, set the scaled-back standard in 1994."[8]

Faced with moral accusations, lawsuits, and community pressure, Jeremy had to decide what to do. First he wanted to evaluate the moral claims being made by the activists and residents. Then, he would have to assess whether their claims, if morally supported, warranted a change in Westco's environmental protection programs. Jeremy also wondered whether he should meet with the residents or the activists to see if there was a common ground from which they could work to resolve the issues.

ENVIRONMENTAL JUSTICE

The environmental justice campaign began with concerns raised by activists that the poor and minorities were disproportionately affected by pollution. Since housing prices were naturally lower near industrial areas, low-income individuals tended to disproportionately locate in those areas. Concern for their well-being centered not only on issues of poverty and opportunity but also on the effects of pollution on their health. In 1992 the EPA issued a report raising the environmental justice issue, and when President Clinton appointed Carol Browner, an environmentalist who had worked for Vice President Al Gore, she initiated an environmental justice program. In 1994 President Clinton issued an executive order directing federal agencies to ensure that public health and environmental programs were nondiscriminatory and provided environmental justice. The president referred to Title VI of the Civil Rights Act in his order.

Many environmental interest groups and activists opposed the use of pollution credits trading systems. Some were suspicious of using incentive systems to control a social bad such as pollution. Some preferred uniform command-and-control regulations that forced a direct abatement requirement on all pollution sources and hence would result in a similar reduction in pollution in every locale rather than different levels of abatement across locales, depending on where the pollution credits were used. More fundamentally, however, most of the activists preferred lower emissions than mandated by legislation and EPA regulations.

As some commentators observed, with the mainstream environmental groups "under the thumb of Vice President Al Gore, their political patron," the cause of environmental justice has been led by some of the smaller and newer environmental interest groups.[9] In the 1990s those groups emphasized the twin themes of health, particularly for those at risk, and of environmental justice. These groups argued

[2]Copley News Service, July 23, 1997.
[3]Copley News Service, July 23, 1997.
[4]*All Things Considered,* National Public Radio, July 24, 1997.
[5]*CNN Today,* August 1, 1997.
[6]Copley News Service, July 23, 1997.
[7]*CNN Today,* August 1, 1997.
[8]*Los Angeles Times,* July 23, 1997.
[9]*In These Times,* July 28, 1997.

that pollution control policies should take into account the special interests of low-income people who disproportionately live and work in areas of high pollution. President Clinton and Vice President Gore embraced both the concept of environmental justice and the use of pollution credits trading systems.

In 1997 the U.S. Court of Appeals gave individuals the right to challenge state environmental permits on the grounds of a disparate effect on low-income and minority groups. The Supreme Court, however, chose to review the decision.

As the EPA began to announce its implementation plans, the environmental justice movement met with increasing opposition as business groups and members of Congress became concerned about the objectives of the movement and the consequences of such a policy. The U.S. Chamber of Commerce and the National Black Chamber of Commerce led a campaign to revoke the EPA's environmental justice program.[10] "We fully support the U.S. Chamber's efforts to repeal the EPA's misguided policy," Black Chamber President Harry Alford said. "This represents the beginning of a close working relationship between the U.S. Chamber and our organization to support black businesses around the country."[11] "It's an economics problem; it isn't race," Alford said. "If you're going to dump trash, you're going to dump it on land that's cheap. We feel the EPA is exploiting the Civil Rights Act and exploiting the black communities in an attempt to gather a vocal constituency in its ever-growing fight against big business."[12]

Alford was particularly concerned about the policy driving jobs away from the areas in which minorities live. Alford pointed to the case of a permit sought by Shintech, a Japanese-owned company, to build a $700 million polyvinyl chloride plant in Louisiana's St. James Parish. Local activists had protested the plant, even though it would bring badly needed jobs to the parish. Alford and others also argued that the EPA's environmental justice program would hinder attempts by cities to attract businesses to so-called "brownfields," some half a million abandoned industrial sites most of which are located in inner-city areas. The U.S. Conference of Mayors spoke out against the EPA's environmental justice program, urging the EPA to develop a new policy that would encourage rather than hinder brownfield developments.

Congress also took an interest in the EPA program. The House Appropriations Committee inserted language in the EPA's fiscal 1999 appropriation barring it from taking any new civil rights actions under the program. The House Commerce Committee launched an investigation into the EPA's environmental justice program.

In a challenge to President Clinton, Carlos Porras, director of Communities for a Better Environment for Southern California, said, "[Environmental justice] is a defining issue for the president's administration. This has national significance and we're very interested to see where the Clinton administration draws the line."[13]

POLLUTION CREDITS TRADING SYSTEMS

For decades economists and business leaders had advocated the use of pollution credits trading systems to achieve environmental objectives at the least cost to society. Pollution credits trading systems had been implemented in the Midwest and Northeast for sulfur dioxide and nitrogen oxides, and several systems were in place in Southern California to control a number of pollutants. Many other states were considering using similar systems, and with the recent promulgation of costly new federal regulations regarding microscopic airborne particulates, additional states and regions were expected to consider these systems.

To illustrate the difference between pollution credits trading systems and the traditional command-and-control approach, consider an environmental objective of reducing emissions of hydrocarbons by 50 percent in the oil industry in the Los Angeles basin. Under a command-and-control system all pollution sources would be required to reduce their emissions by 50 percent. In a pollution credits trading system the 50 percent reduction would be achieved by requiring a source to hold a permit for each pound of hydrocarbons emitted. Permits would then be issued equal to 50 percent of the pre-reduction emissions. For example, one permit could be issued for each pound of hydrocarbon emissions allowed with the

[10]The National Black Chamber of Commerce has 180 chapters representing 62,000 black-owned businesses.
[11]*Washington Times,* July 20, 1998.
[12]*The National Journal,* July 11, 1998.

[13]*Los Angeles Times,* July 23, 1997.

permits allocated among the emitters according to some baseline such as their pre-reduction emissions.[14] Then, an emitter with low costs of abatement that reduces its emissions below the number of permits it was allocated could sell its excess permits, or credits, to an emitter with high costs of abatement, which would reduce its emissions by less than 50 percent. Thus, low-cost abaters would reduce their emissions by more than high-cost abaters, allowing the environmental objective to be achieved at the lowest total cost. In characterizing pollution credits trading systems, David Roe, a senior attorney for the Environmental Defense Fund, said, "What this allows for the first time is that companies that have the technical ability to go beyond the law in reducing their emissions have a reason to do it."[15]

As an example, consider a region with three pollution sources *a, b,* and *c* in locations *A, B,* and *C,* respectively. Suppose the sources each have been emitting 200 pounds of hydrocarbons and that the new environmental objective is to cut emissions by 50 percent to 300 pounds in total. Also assume that each source is allocated 100 permits. Suppose that the costs of abatement for each source are as given in Table 19-2.

For example, if source *a* were to abate 100 pounds, its cost would be $10, and if it were to abate 200 pounds, the cost would be $20. The corresponding costs for source *c* are $20 and $35, respectively. If under a command-and-control system each source were to reduce its emissions by 100 pounds, the total cost of the 300 pounds of abatement would be 10 + 15 + 20 = $45.

TABLE 19-2

	Costs of Abatement by Source ($)		
Pounds of Abatement Per Source	***a***	***b***	***c***
100	10	15	20
200	20	30	35

The environmental objective of 300 pounds can, however, be attained for $35 if *a* reduces its emissions by 200 pounds (at a cost of $20) and *b* reduces its emissions by 100 pounds ($15). Source *a* would then have zero emissions, *b* would have emissions of 100, and *c* would have emissions of 200.

For this outcome to be realized, source *c* either must reduce its emissions by 100 or under a pollution credits trading system purchase 100 credits. By purchasing the 100 credits, *c* would avoid a cost of $20, and by reducing its emissions by 200 rather than 100 pounds *a* incurs a cost of only $10. Since *c* is willing to pay up to $20 for 100 credits and *a* requires only $10 of compensation to reduce its emissions from 100 to 0 pounds, the two sources can reach an agreement. Thus, source *a* reduces its emissions by 200 pounds, source *b* reduces its emissions by 100 pounds, and source *c* purchases 100 credits from *a* rather than reducing its emissions. The equilibrium price for a credit is $15, since if *a* were to attempt to sell credits for more than $15, *b* would offer to sell credits for slightly less. Then, the competition between *a* and *b* would drive the price down to $15. Similarly, if the price were less than $15, *b* would offer to buy credits from *a.* Then *b* and *c* would compete for the credits driving the price up to $15. The distribution of the cost of achieving the environmental objective with a price of $15 is then $5, $15, and $15, respectively, for sources *a, b,* and *c.*

In designing a pollution credits trading system, an important factor is the geographic region the system will cover. The basic principle is that the region include those affected by the emissions, as in the Los Angeles basin. Then, the focus is on the aggregate reduction in emissions in that region rather than in specific locations. In the example, a reduction of 200 pounds was achieved by source *a* and 100 pounds at *b.* The result can also be stated in terms of the remaining emissions, which are 0, 100, and 200 pounds in locations A, B, and C, respectively. ■

[14]The permits need not be issued to the emitters. To whom they are issued is a distributive and not an efficiency issue. In the sulfur dioxide trading system for electric power plant emissions, the permits were allocated to the electric utilities.
[15]*The Wall Street Journal,* July 24, 1997.

PREPARATION QUESTIONS

1. Evaluate a pollution credits trading system from the perspective of utilitarianism.
2. Are the claims of the neighbors and activist groups actually claims about a Kantian right to have one's health protected from pollution?
3. Compare command-and-control and pollution credits trading approaches in terms of Nozick's imperative of free consent.
4. Evaluate the claims of the activist and advocacy groups based on Rawls's principles of justice. Is the AQMD's "separate rule" for hot spots an appropriate response to justice concerns?
5. Do oil companies have a duty to reduce their emissions at their marine terminals and refineries even though doing so would reduce the efficiency of the pollution credits trading system?
6. What should Jeremy Bentley do and why? Should he voluntarily stop purchasing credits? Should he meet with the residents and activists?

CHAPTER 20

Implementing Ethics Systems

Introduction

Ethical systems have both positive and normative applications. In positive applications ethics contributes to the explanation and prediction of nonmarket behavior. Its principal role is in assessing the moral determinants of nonmarket action; that is, in assessing the motivation of individuals and groups as a function of their moral evaluations of an issue.

The normative application of ethics includes the formulation of policies to be used in the screening stage of the framework for nonmarket analysis summarized in Figure 2-4 of Chapter 2. In the choice stage, ethics provides the basis for evaluating moral claims and for choosing among policy alternatives. Because all employees of a firm are expected to abide by its policies, those policies must be implemented in a manner that ensures that real people in real situations will be able to act in accord with them.

Implementation requires measures ranging from developing and supporting personal integrity to providing guidance for the types of situations likely to be encountered. For example, Boeing uses a training program entitled "Questions of Integrity: The Boeing Ethics Challenge." The program includes 54 situations that provide a basis for discussion among employees. Implementation in the screening stage of Figure 2-4 requires a clear statement of the firm's policies so that employees can follow the rules and can reason based on principles when they encounter new situations. Implementation may also involve compliance and audit programs capable of detecting violations and ensuring that standards are met. Compliance may involve institutional features such as an audit committee, an ombudsman, or a corporate ethics officer or department. Because structural approaches can be bureaucratic, less formal approaches emphasizing personal commitment and integrity are commonly used.

This chapter focuses on the managerial implementation of ethical principles and conceptions of corporate social responsibility. An example is presented next to illustrate the basic approach to implementing the framework presented in Figure 2-4. The chapter also addresses tensions in the application of ethical principles, including issues of individual responsibility, paternalism, and the extent to which self-restraint should be exercised in corporate political activity. Sources of unethical behavior, the normative implementation of ethics, and company ethics codes are then considered.

EXAMPLE: LEVI STRAUSS & CO. AND GLOBAL SOURCING

Levi Strauss & Co. is a privately owned firm that has integrated core values into its internal policies and earned a reputation for adherence to ethical principles and concern for the interests of its stakeholders.[1] In the 1980s the company made two important

[1] This example is based on Baron (1995b).

market decisions: to broaden its product lines, particularly into casual wear, and to expand internationally in both the markets in which it sells and in its sourcing of products. The expansion of its markets and product lines, sales growth in the United States, and pressure for low-cost sources of supply resulted in a rapid expansion in the number of its suppliers. Levi Strauss soon found that a high percent of its garments were no longer being produced in its own facilities but instead by over 700 foreign suppliers.

The company became concerned about whether its suppliers met the safety and other standards it maintained in its own production facilities. In addition, Levi Strauss was concerned about possible damage to its brand name resulting from conditions in and the potential for incidents at its suppliers' facilities. The company had concerns pertaining to child labor, prison labor, plant safety, and environmental protection. The company also had concerns about the human rights conditions in several countries in which its suppliers were located. The Levi Strauss market strategy of expanding its markets and sourcing globally had generated a set of complex issues with ethical dimensions. Its problem was how to bring its supplier relationships into congruence with its ethical principles and core values.

Levi Strauss formed a task force to develop two policies to guide its managers: Terms of Engagement for suppliers and Guidelines for Country Selection for determining in which countries it would do business. The former focused on working conditions in suppliers' facilities and covered dimensions such as safety, working hours, discrimination, child labor, dormitories for workers, and environmental protection. The latter focused on human rights concerns, political stability, the safety of company employees, and legal protection for trademarks and commercial interests. The development of its policies is addressed in more detail in the Part V integrative case *Levi Strauss & Co. Global Sourcing Guidelines.*

These policies affected its market strategy in several ways. First, the company terminated its arrangements with suppliers in Burma because of widespread human rights violations. Also due to human rights concerns, it decided to withdraw from China over several years. Not only did the China decision eliminate a low-cost, high-quality source of supply, it also precluded Levi Strauss from investing in its own facilities in China. (The China decision is addressed in the Chapter 22 case *Levi Strauss & Co. in China.*) Second, the Terms of Engagement policy was implemented by audit teams that annually visit each supplier and provide a detailed assessment of the conditions at the supplier's facilities. This implementation process is considered in the chapter 20 case *Levi Strauss & Co. Terms of Engagement Audits.*

The process used by Levi Strauss to develop the guidelines can be characterized in the framework of Figure 2-4. The top panel of Figure 20-1 represents the development of policies to guide its managers, and the bottom panel represents the application to two issues: (1) whether to source in China and (2) how to address a safety issue in suppliers' factories. Referring to the top panel, Levi Strauss developed policies pertaining to suppliers and countries and considered alternatives ranging from complete withdrawal from countries to requiring suppliers to meet U.S. building codes. Screening involved the application of fundamental ethical principles in addition to its business objectives. Analysis involved the application of its "principled reasoning approach," considered later in this chapter, in which stakeholder interests are explicitly taken into account. The third stage involved the formulation of recommendations and the choice among them. Choice also involved decisions about how broad the policies should be—should they cover effluents from washing operations—and how far down the supply chain they should go. Do the policies extend to fabric producers or only to cutting and sewing operations? The results of this process were the Country Selection and Terms of Engage-

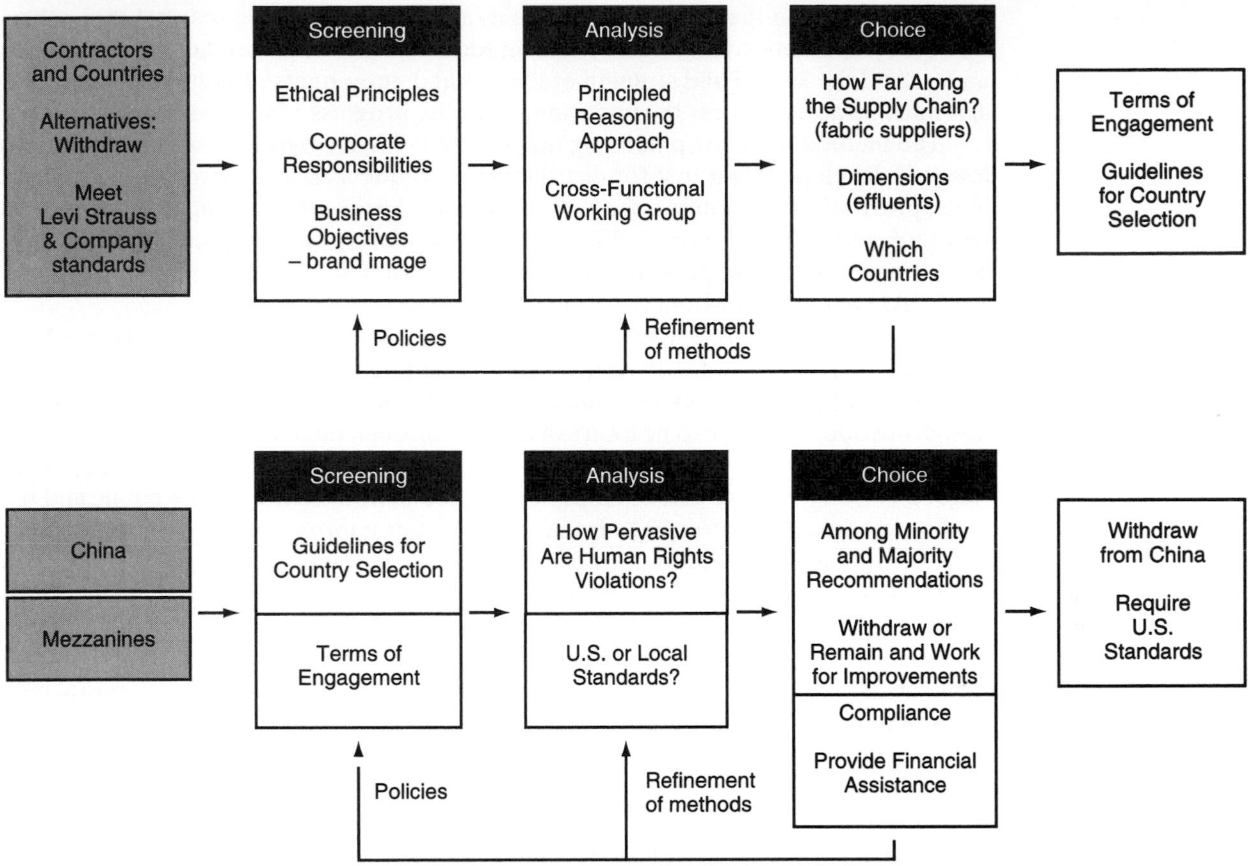

FIGURE 20-1 Levi Strauss & Co. Global Sourcing Guidelines

ment policies that now guide managers in their decision making about contractor practices and involvement in countries. (The Terms of Engagement are presented in this chapter, and the Country Selection guidelines are presented in Chapter 22.)

The bottom panel illustrates the application of the process to specific decisions on doing business in China and safety concerns about interior mezzanines in suppliers' factories in the Caribbean. The screening stage involved the application of the two policies, and analysis centered on the impact of alternatives on stakeholders as well as on specific concerns, such as how pervasive the human rights violations in China were and whether U.S. safety standards should be applied in the case of the mezzanines. Choices then were made between withdrawal and constructive engagement in the case of China and about who should pay for the safety improvements in the case of the mezzanines.

Moral Determinants of Nonmarket Action

The framework for the analysis of nonmarket and collective action presented in Chapter 6 is based on two principal sources of motivation—distributive consequences and moral concerns. Although nonmarket behavior is often motivated by self-interest, on many issues it is motivated by moral concerns. A broad set of activists, advocacy groups, public interest centers, religious groups, civil rights organizations, community groups, and politicians use the language of morality to advance their causes, mobilize others who are sympathetic to their causes, and set social and political agendas. Managers must understand the source and strength of the moral determinants of nonmarket behavior and must be able to assess the implications for the progress of issues in their life cycle.

The methodology for predicting nonmarket behavior based on moral concerns is less well developed than that for distributive consequences. Furthermore, as indicated in the previous two chapters, unanimity about moral principles cannot be assumed. The task thus is to predict the types of issues on which morally-based action is likely. An approach to prediction is presented next, and then the Chapter 2 case *Buffalo Savings Bank (A)* is used to illustrate the approach.

The first step involves assessing the range of moral concerns individuals may have about an issue. Since moral concerns are not the same as self-interest, individuals who are not directly affected by an issue may be motivated to act on a nonmarket issue. These individuals may become aware of an issue through media coverage, as considered in Chapter 3. Activist groups and the networks of interest and community groups considered in Chapter 4 are also an important source of information to the public and the media, and they often attempt to frame issues in moral terms.

The next step is to determine how individuals and groups are likely to evaluate an issue, situation, or action. Since individuals use a variety of moral standards, managers should examine the issue from utilitarian, rights, and justice perspectives. That is, managers should assume the perspective of those in the firm's environment and evaluate the issue as they might. The objective of this step is to identify the range of moral concerns that may be raised about an issue.

As with nonmarket behavior motivated by distributive consequences, the link between moral concerns and action is mediated by the cost of taking individual and collective action. These costs are difficult to assess, but it is clear that there are some individuals who have a high degree of commitment and low costs of acting based on moral concerns. The likelihood of collective action then is governed by the same factors considered in Chapter 6. The costs of nonmarket and collective action are lower when people with similar moral perspectives are involved. The impact increases with the number of individuals, their resources in terms of dollars, time, and energy, and the effectiveness of the strategies they employ.

An important factor in collective action is the extent to which the initial actions of those motivated by moral concerns will strike a responsive chord among the public or attract the attention of politicians. In assessing the likelihood of striking a responsive chord, it is useful to consider the claims and arguments made in attempting to attract broader support. Even when motivation is based on distributive consequences and self-interest, moral claims and arguments may, of course, be used to advance a cause.

The final step is to predict the likely individual and collective action. This involves an assessment of how many people may act and how their moral concerns may affect the behavior of institutional officeholders. Little systematic evidence is available on how many individuals participate in nonmarket activity as a function of moral concerns, so experience is important in assessing morally motivated behavior.

EXAMPLE: *BUFFALO SAVINGS BANK (A)* REVISITED

In the *Buffalo Savings Bank (A)* case in Chapter 2, the bank called the mortgages and offered to refinance them at an interest rate of 14 percent. The mortgage holders immediately took collective action to oppose the call. The bank quickly backed down, leaving the mortgages in effect at the original interest rate, even though in all likelihood it had the legal right to call the loans.

From a positive perspective, collective action should have been anticipated. Mortgage holders were motivated by self-interest as well as by a sense of indignation. The self-interest was clear, but the calling of the mortgages struck a broader chord as the national and local media took an interest in the issue. As considered in Chapter 3, the issue was high on the societal significance dimension because of its moral dimensions.

To assess the moral dimensions, note that the increased mortgage payments represented a transfer from mortgage holders to the bank and its depositors.[2] Consequently, even though the self-interest of the mortgage holders was affected, a utilitarian evaluation of the increase is neutral. From a rights perspective, the bank's contractual rights are clear, but some mortgage holders may not have understood the call provision. Even if they had fully understood the call provision 5 years earlier, they would in all likelihood have accepted the mortgage terms because the interest rate was significantly below the market rate. Moreover, even if no rights were violated, mortgage holders could claim a violation or express indignation because they simply had not understood. Some mortgage holders could be expected to justify their indignation to the public through the media and appeal for sympathy and support by claiming that their rights were violated.

The principal moral concern, however, was justice. The monthly payments of the 900 mortgage holders would have increased by a substantial percentage, whereas depositors would each benefit by only a small amount. The economy in Buffalo was depressed in 1981, so the increase would likely constitute a real hardship for some mortgage holders. Some might have been unable to make the higher payments, forcing the bank to foreclose. These justice or fairness concerns struck a responsive chord with the media and the public.

An important component of the positive analysis is assessing whether others would view calling the mortgages as wrong. The media facilitated communication by the mortgage holders to the public, and some in the public were sympathetic to the fairness of the situation, if not to the other moral claims. The mortgage holders picketed the bank and appealed to local government officials. The potential impacts on future depositors and on the regulatory climate of the bank, plus possible political reactions, led it to rescind the call.

Tensions in the Implementation of Ethical Principles

INDIVIDUAL ACTIONS AND RESPONSIBILITY FOR THEIR CONSEQUENCES

Responsibility for one's own actions is part of the American tradition. Placing responsibility on the individual creates incentives for care in choosing actions and draws attention to the burdens one places on others. Managerial decisions based on the assumption of individual responsibility can result in unwelcome consequences, however. This section addresses the issue of individual responsibility and provides background for the *Circle K Corporation and Employee Health Care Costs (A)* chapter case. The case and this section are not intended to establish the extent of individual responsibility. Instead, the objective is to remind managers to be sensitive to how others evaluate actions that management believes are consistent with ethical standards.

---

[2]The bank was a mutual savings bank, so the depositiors were the "owners."

In contrast to pure accidents and other acts of nature, many individual actions, and the burdens they impose, are neither random nor unavoidable. Some individuals engage in hang gliding, mountain climbing, or recreational flying. Others abuse substances, become overweight, or smoke. The former group of actions, most people would agree, are voluntarily taken. Consensus regarding the second group is less clear. Some view cigarette smoking as a voluntary action, as indicated by the large number of people who permanently quit smoking. Others view smoking as a function of societal forces and the enticement of cigarette advertising. From their perspective, it is society, and not the individual, who is responsible.[3]

Whatever their source or cause, actions such as these often impose burdens on others who do not choose to bear them. Substance abuse results in billions of dollars of medical care costs, lost workdays, and illegal activities including automobile accidents, crime, and property damage. Cigarette smoking and the poor physical condition that comes from a lack of exercise can result in high medical care costs. Recreational flying or hang gliding can create burdens, at a minimum, through medical costs.

The burdens of these activities are borne by the individuals undertaking them, by society collectively through government institutions such as the welfare system, or through institutions such as insurance and private charity. In the case of substance abuse, the individual abuser certainly bears some of the costs, but a portion is also imposed on others. An employer-provided group insurance policy is one mechanism by which the medical care costs of a substance abuser are covered. Group policies are experience rated, so the costs are ultimately borne by the employer and employees. The relevant normative issues center on whether it is just to impose burdens on others and whether it is acceptable for an employer to exclude coverage for the burdens imposed by certain actions, some of which may be voluntary.

The more general issue is whether firms should be responsible for the lifestyle choices of their employees and whether they should be able to discriminate among employees on dimensions such as whether they smoke, drink alcoholic beverages, or engage in hazardous activities. Some firms, for example, have instituted no-smoking policies under which job applicants are rejected if they smoke. The issue of lifestyle discrimination has received increased attention, and the chapter case *Circle K Corporation and Employee Health Care Costs (A)* raises one such issue.

PATERNALISM

Paternalism refers to actions taken to benefit a person without that person's consent. In any ethical system emphasizing individual autonomy and liberty, consent is essential for an action or a rule to have moral standing. Paternalism is also objectionable to the extent that it denies individuals the opportunity to make choices that would further their interests. Gert (1988, pp. 286–287) provides a definition of paternalism:

> One is acting paternalistically toward a person if and only if (one's behavior correctly indicates that one believes that):
> 1. one's action benefits that person,
> 2. one's action involves violating a moral rule with regard to that person,
> 3. one's action does not have that person's past, present, or immediately forthcoming consent, and
> 4. that person is competent to give consent (simple or valid) to the violation.

---

[3]DeGeorge (1982, pp. 194–197) provides an ethical analysis of the regulation of advertising and its relationship to paternalism.

Actions taken on behalf of others are often justified by claims that if those others had the information that the action taker has, consent would have been granted. According to Gert's definition, an action taken to benefit a person who has incomplete information about a situation is not paternalistic if the person would grant consent once the action has been explained and the information presented. Incomplete information is thus a necessary, but not a sufficient, condition for an action not to be paternalistic.

It may be difficult, however, to know whether consent would be granted if the individual were informed. In the context of corporate social responsibility, firms take a variety of actions to benefit their constituencies. A firm may bargain with HMOs over the price for health care services, and the firm's bargaining power can lower the cost to both employees and the firm. In such a case, it is in the interests of both employees and shareholders to have the firm represent them. Consent would surely be given.

In contrast, few companies endorse candidates for public office. Voting is an exercise of individual autonomy, and individuals have the right not to be forced to associate with ideas, positions, or candidates with which they disagree. Consent by individuals to the endorsement of candidates by their employer likely would not be granted. Labor unions, however, regularly endorse candidates for office without the consent of their members. Labor unions differ from firms in an important dimension, however, since union members have the right to elect their leaders.

POLITICAL ACTION AND RESTRAINT

In the United States, individuals, corporations, interest groups, foreign governments, and others have broad granted rights to engage in political activity. Firms as well as other interests, however, must decide whether and to what extent they should restrain the exercise of those rights.[4] From the perspective of moral rights, that exercise should not be restrained unless doing so would result in broader rights for everyone or in a greater equality of rights. On an issue such as the antitrust exemption sought by the soft drink industry discussed in Chapter 9, the right of bottlers to seek the exemption is clear, even if it would benefit bottlers to the detriment of consumers and society.

In some cases, the political actions of business serve to uphold laws. The California constitution requires that a ballot proposition be limited to a single issue. When Proposition 105 was approved by the voters, the Chemical Specialties Manufacturers Association and the California Chamber of Commerce filed suit on the grounds that the proposition covered many different issues. The proposition pertained to the disclosure of toxic substances, apartheid, nursing home standards, the state election process, and protection for senior citizens against fraud. The court invalidated the proposition on the grounds that it was overly broad.

If a political alternative would result in a reduction in aggregate well-being, as is likely in the case of the antitrust exemption sought by the soft drink industry, a utilitarian standard calls for restraint. More generally, utilitarianism views political rights as instrumental and calls for their exercise only to maximize aggregate well-being. Even if the exercise of political rights is based on self-interest, the political competition among interests may work in the direction of maximizing aggregate well-being. The intense political competition over the ratification of NAFTA is one such example.

Political rights are not allocated in proportion to the stakes in an issue, however, so the exercise of political rights would not necessarily be expected to maximize aggregate well-being. Also, political rights do not translate directly into political action because of differential costs of taking political action. Nevertheless, political rights are granted with few restrictions and with no duty to observe a particular ethical standard.

---

[4]Reich (1998) offers a perspective on political restraint.

Pizza Hut's lobbying to retain the targeted-jobs tax credit for the employment of low-income youths was discussed in Chapter 8. In August 1993 the inspector general of the Department of Labor (1993) released the results of a study of the program's impact indicating that instead of enhancing the employment prospects of those taking the subsidized jobs, the jobs "often appeared to be one more low-skilled, low-wage job in a succession of similar jobs in a worker's employment history." The recipients of the $2,400 tax credit were primarily large corporations in the fast-food and retail industries that had high turnover in low-wage jobs. Furthermore, the companies surveyed reported that they would have hired 95 percent of the people even without the tax credit. The program, estimated to cost $282 million in 1994, was described as the "most wasteful of all programs, the kind where the federal government gets involved when people would have done something anyway."[5]

In light of this study, should Pizza Hut support this program or should it support its elimination? Certainly, a company has the right to accept tax credits offered by the government and has the political right to lobby the government in support of the tax credits with the objective of increasing its profits. The program was established with the understanding that the tax credit would apply to jobs that would have been filled anyway, so Pizza Hut was acting in accord with the law. Moreover, its support was consistent with the intent of the government, since the Clinton administration had proposed making the program permanent rather than requiring annual congressional authorizations. The intent of the program was to provide incremental employment to low-income youth, so the issue of responsibility was whether Pizza Hut should take the credit only for individuals who would not otherwise have been hired in the absence of the subsidy.

Lobbying and other political activities by business and other interest groups are an integral component of the democratic process in a pluralistic society. In participating in this process firms not only represent the interests of their owners but also can give voice to stakeholders and others who would not otherwise participate in the process because of the costs of individual and collective action. Participation by firms and other interest groups, however, must be guided by both the law and ethical principles.

Lobbying is the strategic advocacy of a position, and as in a court of law most lobbyists advocate a position and rely on the other side to present its case. Advocacy must be guided by principles, however, including avoiding false statements—for example, denying that tobacco can be addictive. This may require advocating actions that may be contrary to the firm's immediate interests when such actions are clearly warranted by ethical consensus.[6] For example, once the National Academy of Sciences issued its report concluding that CFCs damage the ozone layer, Du Pont decided to stop CFC production even earlier than called for by the government. British Petroleum viewed the growing scientific consensus on global warming as sufficient to warrant actions to reduce its CO_2 emissions and promote sustainable energy sources such as solar power. Similarly, the coalition of Silicon Valley businesses that opposed Proposition 211, which would have made it easier for law firms to extract settlements from companies with volatile stock prices, acted in the interests of aggregate well-being by allowing more information on company prospects to flow to the capital markets and by avoiding costly, frivolous lawsuits.

Since political rights are granted, the issue of political restraint often focuses on actions that may be deceptive. As an illustration of the type of actions that raise concerns, firms and interest groups frequently support grassroots organizations that lobby, support candidates for office, and campaign on public referenda. On the issue of fuel economy standards for automobiles, General Motors sponsored an organization called

---

[5]*The Wall Street Journal,* August 24, 1993.

[6]See Hamilton and Hoch (1997) and Weber (1996).

Nevadans for Fair Fuel Economy Standards, which sent 10,000 letters to Senator Richard Bryan (D-NV) opposing his bill to raise CAFE standards. Senator Bryan accused the industry of conducting the letter-writing campaign "under false colors." GM spokesman William Noack defended the campaign as "a very straightforward, aboveboard educational program."[7] If Senator Bryan was correct in his assessment that the letter writers did not understand what they were writing about, the campaign was unwarranted because it treated the letter writers as means and not also as ends. Moreover, such campaigns impose a negative externality in that they make it more difficult for knowledgeable letter writers to be heard.

Corporate Social Responsibility Revisited

The social responsibility of business to its various constituencies and to society is found in ethical principles and reasoning based on those principles. The reliance on principles not only encourages managers to reflect on company policies and their own actions but it also reduces the likelihood that they will reason in a casuist manner.

The reliance on principles, however, may not be sufficient to identify the appropriate concept of corporate responsibility. Ethical systems are not sufficiently precise to determine whether corporations should contribute zero, two, or five percent of their pretax profits to charity. A system of justice might imply that some portion of profits be used for charitable purposes, whereas a rights-based system that emphasizes maximal liberty would hold that the firm's owners as principals should choose whether and how much to contribute. On some issues there may be differences between actions consistent with a utilitarian standard and actions consistent with rights or justice standards. From the perspective of utilitarianism, an integrity test is appropriate for a job if the benefits it yields are greater than its costs. An ethical system that holds that individuals have rights to privacy and freedom from arbitrary treatment, however, suggests that the use of the tests should be limited. The challenge for responsible management is to formulate policies that strike an appropriate balance between these important considerations.

The implementation of ethical systems and conceptions of corporate responsibility frequently involve the provision of public goods. An educational program a firm provides for its own employees may be justified by higher productivity and improved profitability. Motorola instituted an extensive educational program for its employees aimed at developing basic skills and providing remedial education. With the increased use of automated equipment and robots, the skill requirements of many production jobs had changed dramatically. Employees were required to monitor controls, determine whether required tolerances were being achieved, read graphs, and take independent action when needed. Rather than dismiss employees who lacked the required skills, Motorola chose to invest in its employees by providing them with on-site educational programs in English and basic mathematics. Such a program served both the firm's interests and those of its employees.

A firm that provides an educational program for a community in which it operates, however, has no realistic expectation that it will be able to appropriate sufficient benefits to cover the cost of the program. The American Express Company was dissatisfied with the quality of the pool of high school graduates and decided to establish a program to prepare students for positions in financial services. It helped establish programs in seven New York City high schools and encouraged the participation of other firms. By

---

[7] *The Wall Street Journal,* April 4, 1990.

1989 over 150 firms were participating, including providing summer jobs to the students. Although some of the students took jobs with the participating companies after graduation, over 90 percent chose instead to attend college.

Corporate Social Responsibility and Ethics in Practice

BRITISH PETROLEUM AND GLOBAL WARMING

Much uncertainty remains about the actuality, magnitude, and causes of global warming, but a growing scientific consensus has been building around the twin themes that temperatures have been rising and that human activity is in part responsible for that warming. The 1997 Kyoto Protocol that established country goals for reductions in CO_2 emissions reflected the developing consensus.

Most businesses, and particularly those in the energy industries, opposed taking measures to address global warming until the scientific evidence was clear. In 1997 Lee Raymond, chairman of Exxon, expressed the view that costly actions should not be taken until the scientific evidence was more conclusive.

As a result of the *Brent Spar* episode and the criticism of Shell for its activities in Nigeria, British Petroleum (BP) had begun a dialogue with environmental interest groups including Greenpeace, the Environmental Defense Fund, and the World Resources Institute.[8] In addition, BP reviewed the scientific evidence on global warming and the policy alternatives for addressing it. The company, led by CEO Sir John Browne, decided that action was called for. Breaking ranks with the oil industry in 1997, Browne stated in an address at Stanford University,

> The time to consider the policy dimensions of climate change is not when the link between greenhouse gasses and climate change is conclusively proven—but when the possibility cannot be discounted and is taken seriously by the society of which we are part.
>
> We in BP have reached that point. It is an important moment for us. We must now focus on what can and what should be done not because we can be certain climate change is happening but because the possibility cannot be ignored.[9]

BP announced five specific steps it was taking: (1) monitoring and controlling its emissions of carbon dioxide, including that generated in production and through flaring of natural gas in conjunction with oil production; (2) supporting scientific research on climate change; (3) transferring technology and participation in programs of reforestation and forest conservation; (4) developing and extending its reach in solar energy; and (5) participating in the public policy debate on answers to global climate change. BP set a 2010 goal of cutting greenhouse gas emissions by 10 percent of its 1990 levels, representing a 55 percent reduction compared with the projected emissions levels if no steps were taken. The company pledged to make the reductions "in transparent ways so the reduction can be measured and verified by outside observers."

BP also participated in the World Business Council on Sustainable Development, and Browne and other business leaders met with President Clinton to discuss measures to deal with global warming. BP also joined with the Environmental Defense Fund and other companies to develop an emissions trading system for greenhouse gasses. BP joined The Nature Conservancy, American Electric Power, the U.S. and Bolivian gov-

---

[8]See the Chapter 4 case *Shell, Greenpeace, and Brent Spar.*

[9]Browne, John. 1997. "Speech at Stanford University, 19 May, 1997." *Review: The BP quarterly technology magazine,* July/August: pp. 11–13.

ernments, and a local conservation group to conserve a tropical forest in Bolivia. Flaring, the burning of natural gas generated in conjunction with crude oil production, is a major source of carbon dioxide emissions, and BP had dramatically reduced flaring in its Norwegian operations. The company pledged to eliminate all flaring. BP already produced solar panels in Australia, Spain, and Saudi Arabia, and had a dozen plants in construction including one in California. BP also served as the chair of the International Climate Change Partnership.

Browne also spoke at a Greenpeace convention and continued a dialogue with leaders of environmental groups. Chris Rose, deputy executive director of Greenpeace's environmental activities said, "Compared to other oil companies, BP was the first major to come out in favor of policies to reduce CO_2 emissions. I guess you can say on a scale of good to bad, they, and the Shell Oil Company, are the good guys in this industry."[10] In August 1997 Greenpeace landed two protesters on a leased oil exploration rig under tow to a new exploration area in the North Sea. BP took a kind and gentle approach to the protest, including posting a watchman to look after the safety of the protesters and offering them showers on a BP ship. BP also sued Greenpeace for the additional lease costs caused by the delay in towing the rig to the exploration site. Under the threat of a costly legal judgment, Greenpeace withdrew its protesters and agreed not to take any unlawful actions.[11] Matthew Spencer of Greenpeace said that BP has "made a valiant attempt to put a green sheen on his organization. Inevitably, if you scratch the surface, you find an aggressive company looking for new oil reserves."[12]

STATEMENTS OF COMMITMENT AND EXPECTATIONS

A number of companies specifically identify the set of responsibilities they assume and state those responsibilities in mission and vision statements as both a form of commitment and an agenda for managerial action. One of the oldest of these statements is Johnson & Johnson's *Our Credo,* first issued in 1948, which identifies a set of responsibilities and forms the basis for the expectations of its constituents.

In accord with *Our Credo,* in 1979 Johnson & Johnson implemented a program to reduce its workplace injuries and accidents with the goal of an injury-free work environment. As a result of both capital expenditures and safety programs, the company reduced its lost workday incidence rate from 1.81 in 1981 to 0.14 by 1989.

The safety program established goals in the following areas: injury prevention and loss control, environmental surveillance and control, medical surveillance and examination, work-related injury and illness management, and disease intervention and associated employee assistance programs. In addition to complying with regulations, operating units were to "Establish health and safety guidelines where Credo commitments, scientific principles or regulatory inadequacies dictate." The operating companies of Johnson & Johnson were then evaluated on their safety records.

The safety program included a requirement that the head of the unit in which a serious, lost workday accident occurred file a report on the accident within 24 hours. The unit head then must travel to company headquarters to report in person to the operating board on the steps being taken to prevent similar accidents in the future.[13] The purpose of the report is informational and is directed at measures that can be taken to reduce future accidents.

---

[10] *The New York Times,* December 12, 1997.
[11] "British Petroleum (C): Social responsibility, " S-IB-16C, Graduate School of Business, Stanford University, May 1998.
[12] *The Wall Street Journal,* August 12, 1998.
[13] Forty of these reports were required in 1989, and a smaller number were required in 1990.

EXAMPLE

Johnson & Johnson's Our Credo

We believe our first responsibility is to the doctors, nurses and patients, to mothers and fathers and all others who use our products and services. In meeting their needs everything we do must be of high quality. We must constantly strive to reduce our costs in order to maintain reasonable prices. Customers' orders must be serviced promptly and accurately. Our suppliers and distributors must have an opportunity to make a fair profit.

We are responsible to our employees, the men and women who work with us throughout the world. Everyone must be considered as an individual. We must respect their dignity and recognize their merit. They must have a sense of security in their jobs. Compensation must be fair and adequate, and working conditions clean, orderly and safe. We must be mindful of ways to help our employees fulfill their family responsibilities. Employees must feel free to make suggestions and complaints. There must be equal opportunity for employment, development and advancement for those qualified. We must provide competent management, and their actions must be just and ethical.

We are responsible to the communities in which we live and work and to the world community as well. We must be good citizens—support good works and charities and bear our fair share of taxes. We must encourage civic improvements and better health and education. We must maintain in good order the property we are privileged to use, protecting the environment and natural resources.

Our final responsibility is to our stockholders. Business must make a sound profit. We must experiment with new ideas. Research must be carried on, innovative programs developed and mistakes paid for. New equipment must be purchased, new facilities provided and new products launched. Reserves must be created to provide for adverse times. When we operate according to these principles, the stockholders should realize a fair return.

CORE PRINCIPLES AND THEIR EVOLUTION

Johnson & Johnson's *Our Credo* identifies commitments to a set of constituents and is revised periodically as the set of relevant issues in those relationships evolves. Revisions are based on a set of core principles that provides consistency over time. The relationship between core principles and current policies and practices can be illustrated in the context of Hewlett Packard's *The HP Way.* It consists of three components: organizational values, corporate objectives, and strategies and practices. As indicated in Figure 20-2, organizational values serve as the core principles that guide the strategies and practices of the company as it strives to achieve its objectives.[14] HP's core principles and values developed in 1957 are unchanging. The organizational objectives are revised when necessary but only infrequently. The strategies and practices are revised frequently as a function of the salient issues and conditions in the market and nonmarket environments. HP's organizational values are the following:

- We have trust and respect for individuals.
- We focus on a high level of achievement and contribution.
- We conduct our business with uncompromising integrity.
- We achieve our common objectives through teamwork
- We encourage flexibility and innovation.

---

[14]This figure is due to Kirk Hanson.

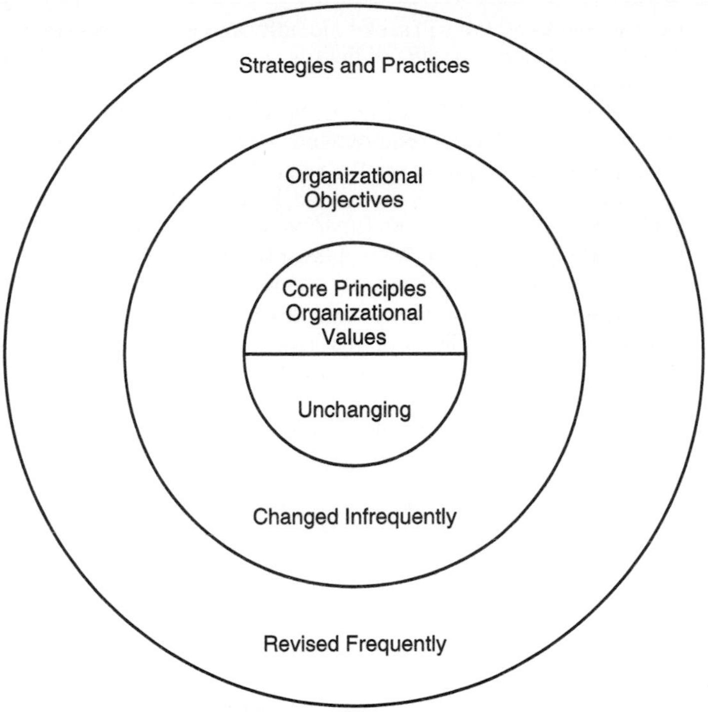

FIGURE 20-2 Principles, Objectives, and Strategies

Its corporate objectives pertain to profit, customers, fields of interest, growth, its people, management, and citizenship. Its strategies and practices include an open-door policy, open communication, management by objectives, and management by wandering around.

Statements such as *Our Credo* and *The HP Way* serve as commitments to stakeholders and other constituents, and also communicate to employees a set of principles and values that they can follow in their jobs. A more specific application of this approach is presented next.

LEVI STRAUSS & CO. BUSINESS PARTNER TERMS OF ENGAGEMENT

To govern its relationships with its suppliers and to ensure that fundamental standards are maintained in its suppliers' operations, Levi Strauss formulated its Business Partners Terms of Engagement, presented in Figure 20-3, to address issues substantially under the control of a supplier. Those issues not under the control of a supplier are covered by its Guidelines for Country Selection, presented in Chapter 22. The development of these policies is addressed in the Part V integrative case *Levi Strauss & Co. Global Sourcing Guidelines.*

To some extent the Terms of Engagement apply American standards to other countries, but they also attempt to strike a balance with the culture and norms of countries. For example, wage rates and working hours vary by country and can be very different from those in developed countries. Similarly, in the United States 14-year-old children are not allowed to work full time, but in an impoverished country their working may be a necessity for a family.

1. **Ethical Standards:** We will seek to identify and utilize business partners who aspire as individuals and in the conduct of their business to a set of ethical standards not incompatible with our own.
2. **Legal Requirements:** We expect our business partners to be law abiding as individuals and to comply with legal requirements relevant to the conduct of their business.
3. **Environmental Requirements:** We will only do business with partners who share our commitment to the environment and who conduct their business in a way that is consistent with Levi Strauss & Co.'s Environmental Philosophy and Guiding Principles.
4. **Community Involvement:** We will favor business partners who share our commitment to contribute to improving community conditions.
5. **Employment Practices:** We will only do business with partners whose workers are in all cases present voluntarily, not put at risk of physical harm, fairly compensated, allowed the right of free association and not exploited in any way. In addition, the following specific guidelines will be followed.
   - Wages and Benefits: We will only do business with partners who provide wages and benefits that comply with any applicable law or match the prevailing local manufacturing or finishing industry practices. We will also favor business partners who share our commitment to contribute to the betterment of community conditions.
   - Working Hours: While permitting flexibility in scheduling, we will identify prevailing local work hours and seek business partners who do not exceed them except for appropriately compensated overtime. While we favor partners who utilize less than sixty-hour work weeks, we will not use contractors who, on a regularly scheduled basis, require in excess of a sixty-hour week. Employees should be allowed one day off in seven days.
   - Child Labor: Use of child labor is not permissible. "Child" is defined as less than 14 years of age or younger than the compulsory age to be in school. We will not utilize partners who use child labor in any of their facilities. We support the development of legitimate workplace apprenticeship programs for the educational benefit of younger people.
   - Prison Labor/Forced Labor: We will not knowingly utilize prison or forced labor in contracting or subcontracting relationships in the manufacture of our products. We will not knowingly utilize or purchase materials from a business partner utilizing prison or forced labor.
   - Health & Safety: We will only utilize business partners who provide workers with a safe and healthy work environment. Business partners who provide residential facilities for their workers must provide safe and healthy facilities.
   - Discrimination: While we recognize and respect cultural differences, we believe that workers should be employed on the basis of their ability to do the job, rather than on the basis of personal characteristics or beliefs. We will favor business partners who share this value.
   - Disciplinary Practices: We will not utilize business partners who use corporal punishment or other forms of mental or physical coercion.

Source: Reprinted by permission of Levi Strauss & Co.

FIGURE 20-3 Business Partner Terms of Engagement

To realize the worth of these principles, Levi Strauss implemented a supplier audit process in which each supplier is visited annually by a team that inspects its working conditions and practices. In the first round of audits conducted in 1993, 70 percent of the suppliers met the standards, 25 percent needed improvements, and in 5 percent of the cases the supplier was discontinued. The chapter case *Levi Strauss & Co. Terms of Engagement Audits* illustrates the audit process.

PROCESS

Policies such as the Terms of Engagement are developed through the process outlined in Figure 20-1. The core of Levi Strauss & Co.'s process was its "principled reasoning approach." This approach is described in the Part V integrative case *Levi Strauss & Co. Global Sourcing Guidelines,* and its purpose is "to protect against self-deception, self-interest, and expediency and to ensure consistency and fairness in decision making."[15] The process consists of six steps: (1) identification of the problem, (2) identification of the relevant principles, (3) identification of the relevant stakeholders, (4) identification and evaluation of alternatives for addressing the problem, (5) assessment of the consequences of the alternatives and choice among those alternatives, and (6) implementation. The process is intended to be iterative rather than linear, so for example, the assessment of the consequences of alternatives may result in a better understanding of the dimensions of the problem, thus returning the process to step (1).

MAINTAINING A CULTURE

In a 1990 interview Robert Haas, CEO of Levi Strauss & Co., described its approach to unavoidable layoffs.

> "How are we going to treat people who are displaced by technology, by changes in production sources, or by market changes?" We are committed to making the transition as successful as possible and to minimizing uprooting and dislocation. We give more advance notice than is required by law. We provide more severance than is typical in our industry, so the effect of displacement is cushioned. We extend health care benefits. We also support job-training programs and other local initiatives to help our former employees find new jobs. And in the community itself, which has been depending on us as a major employer, we continue for a time to fund community organizations and social causes that we've been involved with, . . .
>
> One of the most frequent things I hear is: "When the next downturn in the business happens, is top management going to remain committed to [these principles]?" The only answer to that one is, "Test us." . . . I have no doubts about what management's commitment is.[16]

By 1997 the market share of Levi's jeans in the United States had fallen from 48 percent in 1990 to 32 percent. After much deliberation and procrastination, the company had no alternative than to close plants. It announced that it would close 11 of its 37 plants in the United States and Canada, cutting its North American workforce by 34 percent or 6,935 people. To ease the transition for the employees Levi Strauss & Co. committed $200 million or over $31,000 per employee, for employees earning between the minimum wage of $5.15 per hour to $12 per hour. The company paid the employees for 8 months even though they were required to work only until the goods on the factory floor were completed. The laid-off employees were paid regardless of whether they found another job during the 8 months, and they received a $500 bonus when they found a new job. The company also paid their health benefits for 18 months, provided incentives to take early retirement, and provided $6,000 for each employee for use in education, moving, or job

[15]"Ethical Practices" Statement, Levi Strauss & Co., Human Resources Department, October 1991.
[16]Howard, Robert. 1990. "Values Make the Company: An Interview with Robert Haas," *Harvard Business Review* (September-October): pp. 133–144.

training.[17] In addition, the Levi Strauss Foundation provided $8 million to the communities in which plants were closed. At a substantial cost Levi Strauss & Co. had kept its commitment to itself and to its employees.

THE BODY SHOP AND THE SOCIAL AUDIT

By 1998 the Body Shop International PLC had grown from a single shop in Brighton, England, to over 1,500 stores in 47 countries. Founder Anita Roddick had propelled the growth of the Body Shop by positioning the company as an ethical and socially responsible merchandiser of cosmetics with environmentally friendly products and practices. The Body Shop developed a widely publicized Trade Not Aid program in which it sourced raw materials from indigenous peoples, purchasing, for example, blue corn from the Santa Ana Pueblo tribe in New Mexico and nuts from the Kayapo Indians in Brazil. In its promotional and public relations activities, the company used these programs, along with other policies such as not testing its cosmetics on animals and pledging to "use our purchasing power to stop suppliers' animal testing." For example, Anita Roddick appeared in an American Express advertisement touting its program of buying ingredients from developing countries. These programs brought the Body Shop rapid growth, as consumers supported its messages. The economic and social success of the company made an international celebrity of Anita Roddick, who used her podium to campaign for a variety of causes such as saving whales. To protest Shell Oil Company's failure to halt human rights abuses by the Nigerian government, she erected a large electronic sign across from a Shell service station reading STEER CLEAR OF SHELL—BOYCOTT NOW. The Body Shop also carried is campaigns into its stores.

In 1994 the Body Shop was criticized by a journalist in the magazine *Business Ethics*.[18] The criticism centered not on whether the Body Shop's record was better than that of other companies but instead on whether the company was living up to its lofty pronouncements. A company that had used its ethical and environmental policies to promote its business was required to meet a higher standard than other companies. The Body Shop and Anita Roddick aggressively attacked their critics, but when the concerns did not subside, the company commissioned a social audit of its policies and accomplishments. The report concluded that "The Body Shop has been an important and powerful example to many other businesses and to consumers that it is possible to serve both social as well as economic goals. It has also pioneered many social innovations that have stimulated others to try similar efforts. The company's impact as an exemplary business, however, has at times been weakened by some of the behaviors noted in this report."[19]

The audit evaluated the Body Shop's social performance on the following dimensions: company values and mission; relations with shareholders, customers, employees, franchisees, suppliers, community, and the trading with communities in need; concern for the environment; and contributions to social change. The audit gave high marks to the company's values, mission, and contributions to social change and the lowest mark to its reactions to criticisms. The audit also indicated several areas in which the company had not lived up to its proclamations. The company purchased only £2.25 million from communities in need, and the audit pointed to conflicts with its trading partners, in-

---

[17] *The New York Times,* November 4, 1997.
[18] See Chapter 3.
[19] Hanson, Kirk O. "Social Evaluation: The Body Shop International 1995," The Body Shop International PLC, Watersmead, England, 1996.

cluding the Kayapo Indians. The report stated, "In this area more than any other, the company's performance lags behind what has been implied by its past promotions."[20]

CODES OF CONDUCT

Ethical principles and company policies are implemented by individuals who may differ in their ethical beliefs, their ability to reason from ethical principles, and their moral fortitude. Firms thus provide guidance to their employees in the conduct of their duties. This guidance often is codified in a statement of principles and/or a detailed set of practices to which employees can refer when confronted with particular issues.[21] These statements include the requirements established by laws, prescriptions of behavior that go beyond the law, tests to determine whether an action should be taken, and, in some cases, principles from which the employee is to reason about a situation.

The Business Roundtable (1988, pp. 5–6) identified a set of topics covered by company codes of ethics and standards of conduct.

- Fundamental Honesty and Adherence to the Law
- Product Safety and Quality
- Health and Safety in the Workplace
- Conflicts of Interest
- Employment Practices
- Fairness in Selling/Marketing Practices
- Financial Reporting
- Supplier Relationships
- Pricing, Billing, and Contracting
- Trading in Securities/Using Inside Information
- Payments to Obtain Business/Foreign Corrupt Practices Act
- Acquiring and Using Information about Others
- Security
- Political Activities
- Protection of the Environment
- Intellectual Property/Proprietary Information

COMPETITIVE AND PROPRIETARY INFORMATION

Practices specified in a code of conduct are often directed at situations particular to the industries in which the firm operates. In an industry characterized by a high level of research and development, rapid technological progress, and intense competition, market and competitor intelligence activities can be important. A temptation in such situations is to obtain information that may have intellectual property protection. Hewlett Packard's policy on this issue is as follows:

> HP must be well informed of competitive developments and is entitled to review all pertinent public information concerning competitive products (e.g., published specifications and prices and trade journal articles). However, HP may not attempt through improper means to acquire a competitor's trade secrets or other proprietary or confidential information, including information as to facilities, manufacturing capacity, technical developments or customers. Improper means include industrial espionage, inducing a

---

[20]In 1998 poor business performance of the company led Anita Roddick to give up her position of CEO, becoming cochairman of the board along with her husband.

[21]See Brooks (1989), Falsey (1989), Gorlin (1990), and Matthews (1987) for data on company codes.

> competitor's present or former personnel to disclose confidential information, and any other means that are not open and aboveboard. HP must not use consultants to acquire information by improper methods.[22]

Competitive situations may also involve the temptation to obtain business by demeaning competitors rather than by promoting the virtues of a firm's own products. Hewlett Packard's policy is: "It is HP's policy to emphasize the quality of its products and to abstain from making disparaging comments or casting doubt on competitors or their products. If statements (oral or written) are made concerning a competitor or its products, they must be fair, factual and complete."

PRINCIPLES AND REASONING

The content of company codes depends on the set of issues employees are likely to encounter and the approach the individual company takes. The Cummins Engine Company has long had a reputation for its policies of corporate social responsibility, which are based on ethical constructs that provide both consistency and a basis from which employees can reason. Cummins's basic principle is a version of the Golden Rule:

> For Cummins, ethics rests on a fundamental belief in people's dignity and decency. Our most basic ethical standard is to show respect for those whose lives we affect and to treat them as we would expect them to treat us if our positions were reversed. This kind of respect implies that we must:
>
> 1. Obey the law.
> 2. Be honest—present the facts fairly and accurately.
> 3. Be fair—give everyone appropriate consideration.
> 4. Be concerned—care about how Cummins's actions affect others and try to make those effects as beneficial as possible.
> 5. Be courageous—treat others with respect even when it means losing business. It seldom does. Over the long haul, people trust and respect this kind of behavior and wish more of our institutions embodied it.

An application of Cummins's fundamental principle is presented in Chapter 22 in the context of questionable foreign payments. That application is important because it provided a basis from which employees can reason about a situation based on moral principles.

The implementation of Cummins's principles is to be guided by the following standards:

> 1. Cummins Engine Company, Inc. competes on a straight commercial basis; if something more is required, the Company is not interested.
> 2. Cummins employees do nothing in search of business that they should not reveal willingly and publicly to any other member of the Cummins family or to any government official in any land.
> 3. Cummins neither practices nor condones any activity that will not stand the most rigorous public ethical examination.
> 4. If an employee has any doubt about the appropriateness or morality of any act, it should not be done. If an employee believes that there is a conflict between what his or her supervisors expect and what corporate ethical standards require, the employee should raise the issue with the Corporate Responsibility Department. The Company is prepared to help any employee resolve a moral dilemma and to ensure that no employee is put at a career disadvantage because of his or her

[22]Hewlett Packard Corporation, "Standards of Business Conduct," Palo Alto, CA, 1989.

> willingness to raise a question about a corporate practice or unwillingness to pursue a course of action which seems inappropriate or morally dubious.[23]

The fourth point is particularly important because it identifies what the employee is to do in case of doubt. It also places the burden on the company to protect the employee in the fulfillment of his or her responsibility to raise concerns about its issues and practices.

Although company codes are often presented as statements of ethics, some are intended to build a common approach to issues or to specify particular behavior. To the extent that a code is concerned with establishing a culture, a community, or a mode of behavior to achieve company objectives, it is an instrument in attaining improved performance. Hewlett Packard states that *The HP Way* "will provide HP with the competitive edge in our global environment." In 1999 Hewlett Packard split into two companies to pursue more effectively opportunities in different lines of business.

ETHICS PROGRAMS

Upon revelation of illegal and unethical practices at General Dynamic's Electric Boat and Pomona divisions in 1985, Secretary of the Navy John Lehman ordered General Dynamics to institute a set of contract compliance measures and "to establish and enforce a rigorous code of ethics for all General Dynamics officers and employees with mandatory sanctions for violations." When asked which measure was the most important, Secretary Lehman answered: "Well, I think the code of ethics, because I think that the others are merely manifestations of an approach, an attitude, that has pervaded their doing business with the government. . . . It isn't the problem of one or two individuals doing the wrong things. It is a pervasive record of corporate policy that we want changed."[24]

In the wake of additional defense contracting scandals, the President's Blue Ribbon Commission on Defense Management recommended that defense contractors institute ethics programs. The commission concluded that self-regulation by defense contractors, rather than mandated requirements, was sufficient to achieve the objectives, and contractors were "asked" to pledge to develop codes of ethics. The defense contractors who agreed to the policies specified by the President's Blue Ribbon Commission (1986, p. 4) pledged to take the following measures to implement those policies:

- have and adhere to written codes of conduct;
- train their employees in such codes;
- encourage employees to report violations of such codes, without fear of retribution;
- monitor compliance with laws incident to defense procurement;
- adopt procedures for voluntary disclosure of violations and for necessary corrective action;
- share with other firms their methods for and experience in implementing such principles, through annual participation in an industry-wide "Best Practices Forum"; and
- have outside or non-employee members of their boards of directors review compliance.

---

[23]Cummins Practices, October 1, 1980.

[24]"The Ethics Program 1985/1986," General Dynamics Corporation, 1986.

To implement the ethics codes, contractors developed companywide instructional and training programs to ensure that the policies were understood by all employees. All 103,000 General Dynamics employees participated in the training program.[25]

COMPLIANCE

The Blue Ribbon Commission viewed a compliance system as an integral part of a corporate ethics program. Compliance with company practices involves a commitment by management—particularly top management. Compliance also involves a structure, including systems of internal auditing, and may also involve a committee of the board of directors charged with oversight of the practices of the company. Such a committee often consists of independent directors. Personal commitment is often formalized by the requirement that managers annually sign a pledge of compliance with company policies. The final component of a compliance program is a disciplinary system to address violations.

Employees at General Dynamics were required to sign a card that read: "I have received and read the General Dynamics Standards of Business Ethics and Conduct. I understand that these Standards represent the policies of General Dynamics." General Dynamics identified the following set of disciplinary measures that may be taken in the case of violations of its code: "A warning; A reprimand (will be noted in individual's permanent personnel record); Probation; Demotion; Temporary suspension; Discharge; Required reimbursement of losses or damages; Referral for criminal prosecution or civil action."[26]

In 1991 the United States Sentencing Commission issued the Federal Sentencing Guidelines that governs fines for corporations that break laws. The Guidelines provide for varying levels of fines depending on whether the firm had instituted organizational procedures for prevention of crimes and compliance with laws and standards. Fines can range, for example, from five percent of the damage to customers if a company has a complete compliance program to 400 percent if a company has no program and the crime involved top management.[27] Paine (1994, p. 109) summarizes the components of a compliance program as identified in the sentencing guidelines:

> Managers must establish compliance standards and procedures; designate high-level personnel to oversee compliance; avoid delegating discretionary authority to those likely to act unlawfully; effectively communicate the company's standards and procedures through training or publications; take reasonable steps to achieve compliance through audits, monitoring processes, and a system for employees to report criminal misconduct without fear of retribution; consistently enforce standards through appropriate disciplinary measures; respond appropriately when offenses are detected; and, finally, take reasonable steps to prevent the occurrence of similar offenses in the future.

The Sentencing Guidelines has led many companies to institute compliance programs, and by 1998 over 500 had established positions of ethics officers. Ethics is an integral part of any compliance program, but compliance with company codes can at times be in conflict with bottom-line pressures. More importantly, the law is not a sufficient guide for ethical practices. Ethics includes compliance with laws, but there is often a large gray area between what is legal and what is clearly ethical. Moreover, companies may assume duties and responsibilities that extend beyond the requirements of the law. Ethical principles as identified in Chapters 18 and 19 help guide actions in the gray areas and identify responsibilities, as the examples in this chapter illustrate.

---

[25]See Barker (1993) for an evaluation of the ethics program at General Dynamics.
[26]General Dynamics, "Standards of Business Ethics and Conduct," p. 19.
[27]See the example in Paine (1994).

EXAMPLES OF IMPLEMENTED POLICIES

Community Involvement in Silicon Valley

Many Silicon Valley companies are in industries characterized by rapid technological change, growth, and contraction. Survival and risk are the centerpieces of management attention for many small firms, and change is the routine for large firms. A frequently heard comment has been that these companies were too harried to be involved in community assistance programs. A study released in November 1994 compared to national statistics the involvement of 61 firms employing 140,000 people in the Silicon Valley.[28] The study found that large Silicon Valley corporations were somewhat more philanthropic and small corporations somewhat less so than the national average.

More importantly, the study identified an "entrepreneurial style" of community involvement that, for example, included reliance on individual employees as volunteers rather than on corporate staff programs. The study also provided a model community involvement program consisting of 16 elements, which included:

- Community involvement is explicitly stated as a corporate goal or value.
- The company regularly evaluates its community involvement efforts and communicates about them to its own organization and to the public.
- The company makes use of in-kind donations to leverage its contributions to the local community.
- The company encourages and provides incentives for employee volunteering.
- The company takes leadership in selected community projects where it can make a difference.
- The company partners with other organizations to get things done in the community.

A 1998 follow-up study of 57 companies found that community involvement programs, philanthropic contributions, and volunteer programs had grown substantially.[29] The companies' philanthropic contributions exceeded national averages for similar companies and focused more on education. The rationale given by corporations for their involvement typically centered on business reasons, including productivity gains from better community services such as education and health care and improved employee morale.

AIDS in the Workplace

The issue of AIDS in the workplace is complicated and involves a range of ethical considerations. Levi Strauss & Co. was one of the first firms to develop a far-reaching program to address those considerations. Since the company is privately held and controlled by the Haas family, its policy perhaps more closely reflects the preferences of its owners than might be the case for other firms. The company began to address the AIDS issue in 1982 when some of its employees asked permission to distribute AIDS literature in the lobby of the company's headquarters. To avoid stigmatizing those employees, Robert D. Haas, currently president and CEO, and other top managers joined them in distributing the literature.

Levi Strauss prohibits discrimination against employees with AIDS but does not have a separate AIDS policy. Employees with AIDS are treated in the same manner as

---

[28]American Leadership Forum–Silicon Valley Forum and the Community Foundation of Santa Clara County, "Corporate Community Involvement in Silicon Valley," by Kirk O. Hanson, Peter D. Hero, and James L. Koch, November 1994.
[29]American Leadership Forum–Silicon Valley Chapter and Community Foundation Silicon Valley, "Corporate Community Involvement in Silicon Valley 1994–1997, Kirk O. Hansen, Alison Davis, Julie Juergens, and Steve Wilbur, June 1998.

any other employee with a life-threatening condition, such as cancer or heart disease, that is not transmitted in the normal course of work activity.[30] This includes full eligibility for medical benefits and life insurance and the right to work as long as it is medically advisable. The company uses flexible work schedules and provides part-time work to allow the employee to continue to work.

Levi Strauss also provides medical coverage and care for the terminally ill. This includes continued hospitalization coverage, home health care, and hospice care. For the critically ill, a one-to-one case management approach is used to coordinate benefits and services. The company thus has assumed responsibility for the medical care of its employees with life-threatening diseases.

The company protects employees' confidentiality and conducts education programs required of all employees to address concerns about AIDS in the workplace. The education programs not only allay fears in the workforce but also create an environment in which ill employees can work with dignity and security. According to Haas, "You have to keep at it, but once people have HIV education, [AIDS] just settles down as an issue in the workplace. It's very moving, in fact, to see the way people respond to a co-worker who has been afflicted by HIV."[31]

To address the AIDS in the workplace issue more generally, Levi Strauss hosted a conference on AIDS in the workplace, attended by representatives of 150 companies. Levi Strauss also serves as a resource for other companies and as a model for the programs of several other firms.

Sources of Unethical Behavior

Unethical behavior can arise from a number of factors, some of which are idiosyncratic to the particular individuals involved and others of which are functions of the managerial setting or the policies of the firm itself. Codes of conduct provide useful guidance, but they are insufficient to prevent unethical behavior and promote ethical behavior. If the culture in the organization encourages or condones questionable behavior or if incentive systems place self-interest before all else, ethical behavior will primarily rest on the personal integrity of employees. Personal integrity may be sufficient for most, but perhaps not all, employees, and for most, but perhaps not all, issues.[32]

Personal weakness and temptation are sources of unethical behavior in business, as well as in other contexts. This may include situations in which an individual understands what is right but does not have the fortitude to take the right action, perhaps because it involves a degree of personal risk. In that case, the policies of the firm should be reexamined to lessen the personal risk associated with taking the right action. This may require revisions in incentive structures so that employees do not find themselves in positions in which their performance will be evaluated poorly as a consequence, for example, of a lost sale that could only have been obtained through an unethical act. Cummins's fourth standard is one means of addressing this problem. The Sentencing Guidelines also recommend not delegating authority to individuals or positions when temptation may be strong or personal integrity weak.

The structure of both explicit and implicit incentives within a firm can be an important obstacle to ethical behavior. In 1990 Eastern Airlines and nine of its mainte-

---

[30]The Americans With Disabilities Act of 1990 subsequently prohibited discrimination against employees with AIDS.

[31]*Business Week,* February 1, 1993.

[32]See Sonnenfeld and Lawrence (1978) for an analysis of the causes of price fixing in the folding carton industry.

nance supervisors were indicted for failing to perform required maintenance and falsifying maintenance records.[33] To improve its on-time performance, Eastern had instituted an incentive system for maintenance supervisors in which bonuses were paid for good on-time performance. Supervisors whose on-time and flight cancellation record was poor were transferred or in some cases fired. Not only did the supervisors face incentives and pressure from upper management, but the unions, which were incensed by layoffs and management's demands for wage reductions, often blocked supervisors' efforts to improve on-time performance. Under pressure from both sides, maintenance supervisors began to falsify records for maintenance that was not performed. The situation deteriorated to the point at which some pilots refused to fly aircraft that had accumulated maintenance problems. Believing that the complaints were part of the unions' struggle with management, Eastern executives reportedly continued to pressure the supervisors.

In 1992 charges were brought against Sears for alleged widespread practices of recommending unneeded repairs, such as brake repairs and front-wheel alignments, in its auto centers. Service advisors reportedly recommended the repairs to earn higher commissions, and in settlements of charges in 41 states and 19 class action lawsuits, Sears agreed to eliminate commissions for its service advisors. After a corporate restructuring in 1993, the position of service advisor was eliminated and replaced by the position of service consultant, who was paid on a commission basis. The position of service consultant differed significantly from that of service advisor, however, because the consultants could not recommend repairs, whereas the advisors inspected cars and identified needed repairs. Repairs are now recommended only by mechanics, who do not receive commissions. Nevertheless, when its new system was announced, Sears received increased scrutiny by state attorneys general.

The problem of temptation can be exacerbated by several factors. First, if there is a belief that others are acting in an unethical manner or are succumbing to temptation, an individual may have more difficulty resisting temptation. This is particularly true if employees find themselves in a prisoners' dilemma in which each has a dominant strategy of succumbing to temptation. For example, if a partnership will go to the associate with the highest billings, the competing associates may be induced to take unwarranted actions. What is required is a promotion system that considers factors in addition to billings. Second, succumbing to temptation is more likely if the prevailing attitude in the firm involves either shortcutting ethical analysis or using standards that allow casuistry to be practiced. For example, the balancing of responsibilities can induce managers to underemphasize rights and principles of justice in favor of lessening constituent pressure.

Unethical behavior can also result from too narrow a focus on the duties imposed by the law. The law identifies actions that an individual or firm should not take, but the set of lawful actions may be considerably larger than the set of ethical actions. The law thus provides minimum restraints on behavior. Another cause of unethical behavior is reliance on an ethical framework that gives insufficient attention to important considerations. Reliance on utilitarian reasoning that ignores intrinsic rights can result in actions that violate ethical standards that at least some individuals hold to be important. For this reason, each of the three ethical systems addressed in the previous two chapters should be considered.

The chapter case *Honda and Excess Demand* deals with a situation conducive to unethical behavior.

---

[33]The FAA had frequently cited Eastern for maintenance, safety, and record-keeping violations and fined it $12 million between 1987 and 1989.

Summary

A useful test in situations with ethical dimensions is to reflect on whether the action can be explained both to others in the firm and to the public. This public disclosure test has two purposes. First, it forces the manager to articulate the reasons or basis for the action. This should involve an articulation of the reasoning used in arriving at the decision rather than a search among ethical systems for arguments that come closest to justifying the action the manager prefers to take on other grounds. Second, it requires the manager to reflect on how others will evaluate the action. This does not mean that the action is to be subject to a vote among constituents. Instead, it focuses attention on the moral evaluations that others may have of the action. This can be useful for both positive and normative purposes.

Reliance on the personal integrity of employees is rarely sufficient to ensure ethical behavior, and employees should not be left to operate in an ethical vacuum. A commitment by top management is essential, and part of top management's responsibilities is to establish an environment in which ethical action is encouraged, supported, and rewarded. This requires formal and informal communication about exemplary conduct and leadership by deed as well as by word.

Statements of corporate responsibility, policies, and codes of conduct can be useful guides for employees. These should identify principles, provide specific guidance for situations that are likely to arise, and indicate how to reason about situations and issues. A code should indicate what an individual is to do when uncertain about which action is right. A compliance system is an important component of the application of ethics and should be designed to give top management confidence that unethical actions will be revealed. A process that encourages and does not unduly punish self-disclosure can be an important component of a compliance system.

Temptation and pressure are principal causes of unethical behavior. Performance standards should be realistically attainable through means consistent with ethical standards. Incentive systems should be structured in a manner that encourages rather than hinders ethical conduct. In many firms, the selection, retention, and promotion of employees depend on the individual's record of conduct and integrity in addition to more traditional measures of performance.

CASES

Circle K Corporation and Employee Health Care Costs (A)

Employee health insurance is a major cost for most employers, and many companies have taken steps to contain those costs. Some have limited coverage for retirees, others required a waiting period before coverage begins, and others excluded coverage for preexisting conditions.

Health care costs of the Circle K Corporation of Phoenix, Arizona, nearly doubled during 1986 and 1987. Circle K, the second-largest convenience store chain in the United States, had approximately 26,000 employees, all of whom were nonunion. Circle K had 4,097 locations in 27 states in the South, West, and Midwest. It marketed gasoline, groceries, fast food, doughnuts, and video cassettes, with gasoline accounting for approximately 30 percent of its revenues. In 1987 Circle K earned $49 million on sales of $2.3 billion.

As indicated by the opening statement in its annual report, 1987 was a difficult year for Circle K.

> Fiscal 1987 was probably the most competitive twelve-month period your company has experienced in the last five years. We achieved additional growth in revenues despite a dismal economy in the Central Texas and Louisiana Gulf Coast areas, an unexpected upheaval in the gasoline business early in the year and increased competition from established convenience store operators and from gasoline marketing companies as they expanded their operations in the convenience store industry.

Due to the nature of its business, Circle K's employee turnover rate was 170 percent a year. Because Circle K hired so many people each year, some employees "are shopping us for insurance coverage," according to Charles Shoumaker, vice president of human resources. In addition, Shoumaker stated, "[The high turnover rate] means we have a higher chance of hiring someone with AIDS."[1] Nearly 4 percent of Circle K's health care costs went for the treatment of AIDS, whereas, according to Shoumaker, the corresponding figures for other companies were 1 to 2 percent.

As a result of its soaring health care costs, in 1987 Chairman Karl Eller asked Shoumaker to consider "all the different angles" to contain its health care costs. As a result, a number of changes were made in its coverage. Restrictions were placed on elective surgery, and new employees were not covered until they had worked for Circle K for 6 months. In addition, Circle K no longer covered medical care for "personal lifestyle decisions" of employees.

Employees were notified of the changes in a letter signed by President and CEO Robert M. Reade. The letter stated:

> The company is concerned about certain personal life-style decisions regarding the use of alcohol, drugs, self-inflicted wounds and sickness due to acquired immune deficiency syndrome. We believe that these personal life-style decisions could seriously impact other participants' health care costs. Employees who are proven to suffer illness and accidents that result from the use of alcohol, drugs, self-inflicted wounds and AIDS, proven not to be contracted from blood transfusion, will not be eligible to receive company health care coverage in those circumstances. . . . Health care costs have almost doubled over the past two years. Hopefully, all the changes made in our health programs will result in controlling medical expenses while continuing to provide our employees with adequate health benefits.[2]

Shoumaker explained, "We felt we had to take certain steps to help contain our medical costs, and we felt that this was one thing we could do." He added, "There are certain lifestyle decisions that we are just not going to assure the results of."[3] Although the letter did not so indicate, Circle K later stated that current employees would be grandfathered, so

[1] *The Wall Street Journal,* August 18, 1988.

[2] *The New York Times,* August 6, 1988.

[3] *The New York Times,* August 6, 1988.

the revisions would apply only to employees hired after January 1, 1988.

Circle K self-insured and paid its employees' medical bills directly rather than through an insurance company. Nearly 8,000 Circle K employees participated in the program. Self-insurance programs were governed by the Employee Retirement Income Security Act of 1974 and regulated by the Department of Labor. The revisions in Circle K's policy were believed to be consistent with existing laws. Similarly, the company's policy was not subject to the state of Arizona's insurance laws. Circle K checked with a prominent Phoenix law firm, which gave it a go-ahead. According to a Circle K spokesman, "The plan was thoroughly researched before it was promulgated and it is legal." " 'I'm not aware of anything in the law that would prohibit [Circle K] from doing this,' said a supervisor in the Los Angeles office of the U.S. Labor Department's pension and welfare benefit administration."[4] Health care insurance frequently excluded coverage for preexisting conditions and often excluded certain kinds of care, including psychiatric, dental, and nursing. Health care insurance typically had exclusions for suicides but often covered AIDS and provided some treatment for substance abuse. ■

[4] *The Wall Street Journal,* August 5, 1988.

PREPARATION QUESTIONS

POSITIVE ANALYSIS

1. Does Circle K's policy involve moral concerns that are likely to motivate nonmarket behavior? Are there organized interest groups that are likely to be concerned about Circle K's policy? Is this policy likely to be of interest to the news media?
2. Is Circle K likely to encounter any difficulties in implementing its policy? For example, how would it determine the cause of an employee's injury or illness? How would it determine whether AIDS was contracted through a blood transfusion? What would the verification process involve?

NORMATIVE ANALYSIS

1. Is Circle K's policy ethical? Under which ethical frameworks would it be considered ethical? Under which ethical frameworks would it be considered unethical?

Honda and Excess Demand

In the early 1980s Japanese automobile models were among the best sellers in the United States. As a result of this success in the U.S. market, General Motors, Ford, Chrysler, and the United Automobile Workers sought protection from imports. The result was a voluntary export restraint (VER) by Japan that sharply reduced the exports of Japanese automobiles to the United States. The VER and the continued popularity of Japanese automobiles resulted in excess demand with some car buyers willing to pay several thousand dollars more than the sticker price.

Honda automobiles were among the most successful in the U.S. market with the Accord becoming the leading seller. The excess demand for Hondas provided an opportunity for Honda dealers. Some decided to charge a premium, referred to as the dealer's markup, or add low-cost options at inflated prices. One Honda dealer was able to sell a $12,000 Honda Prelude for $5,000 above the list price.

The opportunity to sell Hondas at a premium created strong incentives for dealers to obtain larger allocations of cars from Honda. Some executives and managers of Honda also saw an opportunity for gain. A number were envious that their $50,000 salary paled in comparison to the gross profits of as much as $2,000,000 for a dealer.

Some Honda managers demanded gifts and payments from dealers before allocating them vehicles, and some dealers offered gifts and cash payments to Honda marketing zone managers to obtain more cars. Some dealers even secretly offered free ownership shares in their dealerships to Honda managers as a way to increase their allocations.

In 1986 as Honda was launching its Acura line, Richard Nault applied for an Acura dealership in Manchester, New Hampshire. Honda, however, awarded Nault a dealership in Concord, 15 miles from Manchester. Nault and his partner invested $2.2 million in a new facility, and Nault claimed that Honda had promised him 150 cars on opening and 75 cars a month but actually provided him with only 20 cars initially and 24 a month. Moreover, too many of the cars were high-priced Legends rather than the faster-selling Integras. During the first 10 months of 1988, Nault's dealership lost $466,527, and Nault moved his Acura dealership into his adjacent Lincoln-Mercury dealership. Shortly thereafter Honda canceled its dealership agreement with Nault on the grounds that he was operating in a substandard facility and that the dealership was undercapitalized. Nault tried to persuade Honda to buy back the abandoned Acura facility, but Honda refused.

Nault charged that his woes were the result of Honda's favoritism of a rival dealer, Thomas Bohlander, in Nashua, New Hampshire. Nault claimed that Honda provided him with more cars than Nault was allocated and that Honda delayed opening a dealership in Manchester to aid Bohlander.

The alleged favoritism appeared to have deeper roots. Bohlander "acknowledged that in November 1986 he provided David L. Pedersen, a Honda assistant zone manager, a 1987 Acura Integra as a gift. He said he also paid $17,197 in tuition to Gannon College in Erie, Pennsylvania, where Mr. Pedersen's son was a student. Bohlander testified that the gifts were for friendship, not for the allocation of cars."[1] Bohlander also said that Pedersen had called him twice and asked him to lie about the payment to Gannon College.

The Bohlander incident was not an isolated instance. Damien C. Budnick, a former district sales manager "testified that in the mid-1980s he delivered $100,000 in cash from a Honda dealer in Cocoa Beach, Fla. to Mr. Pedersen, then an assistant zone manager in Georgia." "Picking up a payoff and giving it to a superior, Budnick testified, was known as 'Passing the football.' He said that he had knowledge that those footballs—usually $100,000—were passed to Jack Billmyer and Jim Cardiges, both former Honda vice-presidents, and former regional sales manager John Conway. 'That dealer (who paid a bribe) had a direct line to top management,' and could bypass district managers, said Budnick."[2]

A former Honda dealer Edward M. Mixon testified that he promised a Honda zone manager ten percent of his proposed new dealership "because he had been helpful to me in the past."[3] A Honda dealer in Concord, California, alleged that a competing dealer in Walnut Creek had given a Honda executive vice president a ten percent ownership share of his dealership. Tom Roulette, who operated a Honda dealership in Painesville, Ohio, said that he had been told by Honda managers that he had to "play the game." He provided cash and gifts to Honda managers. "On some Christmases he received a list specifying what executives expected from Santa. One year, he recalls, he sent his wife to buy a watch costing more that $2,000 for the wife of a Honda Executive."[4] "These guys were so cocky, they'd come in, put their feet upon my desk, and tell me what I had to give them," Roulette said. ■

[1] *The New York Times,* May 2, 1993.

[2] *Boston Herald,* March 2, 1993.

[3] *The New York Times,* May 2, 1993. The dealership was never opened.

[4] *The New York Times,* May 2, 1993.

This case was prepared from public sources by Professor David P. Baron.

PREPARATION QUESTIONS

1. What led to these practices?
2. Should Honda's top management have anticipated these types of practices?
3. Should there be limits on gifts provided by dealers to a Honda manager?
4. How can Honda's top management prevent this type of practice from developing in the future?
5. What should a Honda dealer do if a zone manager demanded a gift or cash in exchange for a larger allocation of cars?

Levi Strauss & Co. Terms of Engagement Audits

Implementation of Levi Strauss & Co.'s (LS&CO.'s) Business Partners Terms of Engagement component of its Global Sourcing Guidelines required the development of procedures and standards for evaluating contractor compliance.[1] It also meant that inspections and audits of each of its contractors' facilities had to be conducted and that LS&CO.'s personnel had to be trained to conduct the audits. LS&CO. developed a standard audit form, but the responsibility for the audits was delegated to each of the organizations in its global sourcing system. The auditors gathered in Puebla, Mexico, in 1993 in LS&CO.'s first global sourcing audit conference.

LS&CO.'s CCAM (Caribbean, Central America, and Mexico) unit was responsible for the supply of apparel from its region for the U.S. market. Responsibility for the implementation of CCAM's audit procedures was assigned to Roberto Ortega, engineering manager of its El Paso, Texas, facility. In addition to the standard audit form, Ortega developed a comprehensive facilities profile booklet, providing for the collection of information on and evaluation of facilities and practices. The audit form covered the following categories: employment practices (wages and benefits, working hours, child labor, prison labor/forced labor, disciplinary practices, employment practices—and general), the environment, health and safety, legal requirements (e.g., lawsuits outstanding against the contractor), ethical standards, and worker dormitories and overnight facilities.

The inspections and audits were conducted by LS&CO. personnel from the cognizant office, and many of the audits were conducted by personnel from the El Paso office. The audit team for a number of the facilities consisted of Ortega and an industrial engineer in his group. The audits began in February 1993, and each involved an 8-hour visit to the facility. Travel time to the facilities was often substantial, and additional time was spent in El Paso completing the forms, assessing the data, and providing an overall evaluation of the contractor and its facilities.

The audits identified a potentially hazardous deficiency resulting from the construction of interior mezzanines in the factories of 13 contractors—two in Costa Rica, nine in the Dominican Republic, one in Honduras, and one in Mexico. In a number of countries, local building codes covered the factory building itself but not its interior. To create additional space, factory owners had constructed interior mezzanines extending from the walls of the building and supported by trusses and columns. Some of the mezzanines were constructed of concrete, whereas others were constructed of timber. The mezzanines were used for sewing and other operations as well as for storage. One was used as a cafeteria. Some were in new, prefabricated buildings and others were in older buildings. The audit teams had concerns not only about the structural integrity of the mezzanines, but also about egress, ventilation, fire and smoke alarms, and the absence of fire retardant materials in floor coverings.

An important issue was the standards the contractors would be required to meet. Ortega concluded that where local building codes were available, it was sufficient to meet those codes. If the mezzanines were not covered by a building code, Ortega reasoned that if LS&CO.'s own facilities were required to meet U.S. building codes, its contractors should have to meet those standards as well. (The buildings themselves were all covered by codes and were evaluated by LS&CO. on the basis of whether they were "safe to work in.") Ortega decided to deal first with the potentially hazardous mezzanines and then to develop a policy for the buildings themselves.

Some of the concerns, such as adequate means of egress, were relatively easy for the audit team to identify. Others, such as the structural integrity of the mezzanines, required expertise not available within LS&CO., and Ortega hired a consulting engineering firm to conduct a structural review of the mezzanines. The review involved an on-site inspection, a review of engineering records for the factory and the mezzanines, and an analysis of the structural members constituting the mezzanine. The review compared the stress loads on the members with the 1991 U.S. Uniform Building Code. In most cases, the struc-

---

[1]See the Part V integrative case *Levi Strauss & Co. Global Sourcing Guidelines.*

tural members carried a higher load than either the standard of 75 pounds per square foot (psf) for light manufacturing or 50 psf for office space. At some factories in which the mezzanine was used for storage, the problem could be resolved by not stacking containers as high as they were being stacked. In other cases, compliance with the code required structural changes, including adding columns at the truss midspans.

Once the consulting engineers had completed their reports and the audits were finished, Ortega telephoned and wrote to the contractors, enclosing the Terms of Engagement (in Spanish) and the consulting engineers' report. In his letter he stated, "We would appreciate your response on the findings of the analysis as well as your thoughts on a plan of action you would like to take to rectify the situation upon review of the analysis."

The responses of the contractors varied. Two contractors in the Dominican Republic decided not to comply and were discontinued by LS&CO. In the interim three other contractors in the Dominican Republic and one in Costa Rica had been discontinued because of low demand. The others indicated that they would comply and were given time to remedy the deficiencies. Some undertook the corrective measures on their own account. Others pleaded that they did not have the financial resources to make the improvements and needed assistance from LS&CO. LS&CO. had no policy with respect to financial assistance.

Once the contractors reported completion of the corrections, Ortega and the consulting engineers planned to revisit the facilities to verify that the corrections have been made. ■

This is an abridged version of a case prepared by Professor David P. Baron. Roberto Ortega and Elissa Sheridan provided invaluable assistance and insight.

PREPARATION QUESTIONS

1. Should LS&CO. be concerned with and take measures to remedy the deficiencies in the mezzanines? Does the volume of business the contractor does with LS&CO. matter?
2. Was Ortega right in requiring the mezzanines to meet the U.S. Uniform Building Code? Should LS&CO. require the factory buildings to meet the U.S. Uniform Building Code?
3. Should LS&CO. provide financial assistance to the contractors for the corrections?

CHAPTER 21

Ethical Issues in the Employment Relationship

Introduction

Employees are the most important resource of most firms, so the management of the employment relationship is crucial to superior performance. Management involves developing loyalty and motivation as well as compensation, training, employment security, benefits, and employee rights policies. The employment relationship also involves a range of ethical issues centering on rights and opportunities, efficiency, and fairness. Because of these issues the employment relationship is heavily regulated under a number of statutes and by precedents established by the courts. The set of issues that management must address continues to evolve, with issues such as unionization diminishing in importance, and issues such as providing equal opportunity and affirmative action having been institutionalized in most firms. Issues with increasing saliency include opportunity in the upper ranks of management, preference and reverse discrimination, sexual harassment, diversity, privacy, and accommodating work, family, and lifestyle choices. This chapter focuses on selected issues in the employment relationship that have ethical dimensions. The specific issues addressed include employment rights, equal employment opportunity, affirmative action, reverse discrimination, sexual harassment, diversity, organized labor, drug testing, and whistle-blowing.

Employment Rights

THE EVOLUTION OF EMPLOYMENT RIGHTS

The employment relationship continues to evolve, refining the rights of employees and the duties of employers. This section reviews some of the developments in the legal interpretation of the employment relationship, some of the forces underlying those developments, and their implications for management. When the United States was largely an agrarian society, people relied on the land for a living. Ownership of land provided employment, and since that ownership was protected by a property rule, employment was in effect protected by a property rule. The evolution to an industrial society led to a reliance on an employer for a job. Most jobs were protected only by the labor market and the goodwill of the employer.

The rise of labor unions established employment rights through contracts with employers, but since less than 14 percent of the U.S. workforce is now unionized, that protection is not extensive. Some upper-level managers have employment contracts, but most employees and their jobs are protected by the opportunities available in the labor market, common law, and the employment practices of firms. Court decisions and legislation have clarified the rights of an employee to, and in, an existing job and have defined the allowable bases for dismissal. An employee's rights can be addressed in the context of jobs that will continue if the employee is dismissed and in the context of jobs that are eliminated.[1] Discrimination in hiring and employment are discussed in a later section.

EMPLOYEE RIGHTS IN CONTINUING JOBS

The employment relationship had been governed by the "at-will" doctrine that treated the employment relationship as a voluntary contract and hence terminable by either party at will. This doctrine has undergone considerable change through legislation and court rulings. One of the earliest changes was the result of labor legislation that prevented employers from dismissing employees if the intent were to prevent unionization. The civil rights and equal employment opportunity laws protect employees against discrimination on the basis of "race, color, religion, sex or national origin." Several well-publicized cases involving employees who were dismissed so that their employer could avoid incurring their pension liability led to the Employment Retirement Income Security Act of 1974, which established regulations governing employer-provided pension plans.

Much of the change in the at-will doctrine, however, occurred through the evolution of the common law, largely in state courts. Court decisions initially focused on abusive discharge or wrongful termination and subsequently broadened those concepts. These rulings gave rise to the concept of discharge "for cause" and established the tort of wrongful discharge under which an employer may be liable for compensatory and possibly punitive damages. These rulings apply not only to employees who have a contractual agreement with an employer or who are protected by equal opportunity laws, but also to employees to whom informal promises have been made by employers during recruitment or who are covered by company policies as stated in employee handbooks.

Courts have found that these informal promises or statements of employment policy can constitute an enforceable implied contract, establishing rights and imposing duties. In *Touissaint v. Blue Cross & Blue Shield,* 408 Mich. 579 (1980), a case involving termination without cause, the Michigan Supreme Court ruled:

> If there is in effect a policy to dismiss for cause only, the employer may not depart from that policy at whim simply because he was under no obligation to institute the policy in the first place. Having announced the policy, presumably with a view to obtaining the benefit of improved employee attitudes and behavior and improved quality of the work force, the employer may not treat its promise as illusory.

The courts have also been active in defining specific rights of employees. In *Perks v. Firestone,* 611 F.2d 1363 (3d Cir. 1979), the court ruled that an employee could not be dismissed because of refusal to take a polygraph test when a state law barred employers from requiring such tests. A number of states subsequently passed legislation prohibiting the use of polygraph tests as a condition of employment; and a federal ban on polygraph tests, with a few job categories exempted, was enacted in 1988.

---

[1]See Ewing (1983) and Werhane (1985, 1988) for more extended treatments of employee rights.

Courts have also protected certain basic liberties in the employment relationship. In *Holodnak v. Avco,* 423 US 892 (1975), Holodnak was dismissed because he had written a newsletter in which he attacked both Avco and the union to which he belonged. A U.S. district court judge concluded that Holodnak's right of free speech had been infringed by Avco and that "Against Holodnak's interest in having his say, Avco's interest in maintaining efficiency in production is insufficient."[2] In this case, a basic liberty was held to have priority over the employer's economic interest.

Firms affect the extent of rights in and to a job by the way they structure their employment relationship. In response to the pattern of court decisions, some firms require new employees to sign disclaimers stating that they understand that they may be discharged at will. Some firms have expunged any suggestions that jobs or a person's employment are permanent. Written statements are not sufficient, however, since courts may uphold oral promises of employment even if those promises are later contradicted by written policies.

The law governing employee rights in a job continues to evolve, and the trajectory has been to extend those rights in a number of directions. The courts have focused both on fairness considerations and on implied obligations. In addition to legal standards, moral standards govern the employment relationship. Those standards pertain to rights and justice considerations, aspects of which are considered in the following sections.

EMPLOYEE RIGHTS WHEN JOBS ARE BEING ELIMINATED

Firms eliminate positions for a variety of reasons. Product demand may decline, resulting in a lower demand for labor. Technological advances may dictate the substitution of capital for labor. Reorganizations and restructuring can lead to the elimination of jobs. A firm may eliminate jobs in one country and move them to another country to benefit from lower wages or tax advantages. Downsizing and organizational change such as flattening an organization can eliminate positions.

Although the courts have reallocated rights from employers to employees in cases in which a job is to continue, state legislatures and Congress have been reluctant to establish employee rights as they pertain to job eliminations. Although the courts have been concerned with the fairness and due process rights of employees, legislatures have been cautious about diminishing the efficiency and competitiveness of the firms located in their states. In addition, states are reluctant to pass plant-closing laws that would reduce the incentive for new plants to locate there. Congress has also been reluctant to act because of the effect on the economic efficiency and competitiveness of U.S. firms in world markets. Instead, Congress has provided direct assistance to workers who have lost their jobs as a consequence of structural change in the economy. The assistance includes extended unemployment benefits, aid provided under the Trade Adjustment Assistance Act, and retraining programs.

In 1988 Congress passed the Worker Adjustment and Retraining Notification (WARN) Act and the Economic Dislocation and Worker Adjustment Assistance (EDWAA) Act to provide employees with advance notification of layoffs and readjustment services in the event of a layoff. WARN requires employers with 100 or more employees to provide 60 days advance notice of plant closings or layoffs, but small firms are exempted, so fewer than 50 percent of private sector employees are covered. Furthermore, exemptions are granted if there has been a major loss of orders or if the firm is "faltering." WARN has had little impact on the number of plant closings. EDWAA is intended to reduce transactions costs, relocation expenses, and training costs by making services available prior to the actual layoffs.

---

[2]Quoted in Ewing (1983, p. 356).

Layoffs and plant closings are often unavoidable, and should be managed with respect for employees' rights, both legal and moral. For example, many firms reduce their workforce by providing incentive payments to employees to retire, which is an acknowledgment that employees have rights to their jobs. Early retirement programs that make uniform offers, perhaps graduated by length of service, are subject to adverse selection, however. Employees with the highest ability may have the best employment opportunities elsewhere and thus may be disproportionately represented among those who accept the early retirement offer, leaving the firm with its less productive employees.

Equal Employment Opportunity

Equal employment opportunity is a principle supported by virtually all ethical systems. Its legal manifestation is Title VII of the Civil Rights Act of 1964, which prohibits discrimination on the basis of "race, color, sex, religion, or national origin." Title VII applies to employers engaged in interstate commerce with at least 15 employees. Most states have similar laws applicable to businesses operating within their state.

Concern about illegal discrimination in the employment relationship now focuses less on intentional discrimination and more on employment practices and policies that, while appearing neutral with respect to an identifiable group, have a disparate impact on the members of that group. An employment policy that is neutral with respect to race, for example, has a disparate impact if a lower proportion of minorities than whites are hired. Employers then must establish that the policy is required by business necessity—a bona fide occupational qualification (BFOQ). The concept of a disparate impact is broad and applies to hiring, promotion, and compensation. More subtly, it may also apply to grooming rules, physical requirements, language requirements, and information about an individual's past, such as an illness, criminal conviction, or a past substance abuse problem. The disparate impact applies to any identifiable group protected by Title VII. Other laws have applied the same principles to other attributes, including age, disability, and pregnancy. A number of the relevant laws are reviewed in the appendix to this chapter.

Title VII is administered by the Equal Employment Opportunity Commission (EEOC), an independent administrative commission with five members appointed by the president. The EEOC can act on its own or in response to a complaint filed by an individual. In addition, the EEOC has rule-making authority over compliance with Title VII and may file suit in federal court if conciliation fails. An individual may also file suit in federal court once the EEOC has attempted to resolve the issue. Because most states have laws similar to Title VII, the EEOC allows state agencies to handle many of these cases.[3]

The remedies available to the EEOC or a court under Title VII include injunctions and mandated changes in practices. The complainant may be awarded reinstatement, promotion, payment of back wages, attorney fees, or other awards. As an example, in 1993 Commonwealth Edison agreed to a $3.3 million settlement of an EEOC complaint, providing $3 million to women allegedly discriminated against in applications for meter reading jobs and $300,000 for a training program to prepare women for nuclear power plant operating positions. In 1993 Shoney's Inc. agreed to a $105 million settlement in a case alleging discrimination against African Americans. Shoney's also agreed

[3]See Howell, Allison, and Henley (1987, p. 505).

to institute an aggressive affirmative action program with a 10-year goal of 20 to 23 percent African American managers and assistant managers in its 754 company-owned restaurants. The Chapter 4 case *Denny's and Customer Service (A)* addresses another discrimination case outside the employment relationship.

In 1996 Texaco settled a racial discrimination lawsuit for $176.1 million and agreed to establish an "equality and tolerance task force." The task force was composed of three members named by Texaco, three named by the plaintiffs, and one member selected by both sides. The task force was to help set personnel policies, and its recommendations must be implemented unless Texaco can convince the judge supervising the settlement that the recommendations are infeasible or unsound. Texaco also settled a complaint with the EEOC, allowing it to scrutinize Texaco's hiring and promotion policies for 5 years.

An employer has several defenses in a Title VII case. One is that of "business necessity," such as testing individuals for job-relevant skills. A second defense against a disparate impact charge is that of a BFOQ, but the EEOC and courts have interpreted this quite narrowly. A BFOQ defense pertains only to discrimination based on sex, religion, and national origin under Title VII and age under the Age Discrimination in Employment Act of 1967. Racial discrimination is never justified by a BFOQ. Third, seniority systems are not covered by Title VII, so a plaintiff must show intent of discrimination rather than a disparate impact. Seniority systems have been held to be protected against Title VII complaints that they perpetuate the effects of discrimination.[4]

As an example of a BFOQ, in *Murname v. American Airlines, Inc.,* 667 F.2D 98 (1981), the Court of Appeals upheld American Airline's policy of not hiring anyone over the age of 40 as a flight officer. A district court had found that "the best experience an American Captain can have is acquired by flying American aircraft in American's three cockpit positions." The Court of Appeals viewed the age limit as a BFOQ on the following rationale: "Since it takes at least ten to fifteen years to progress from Flight Officer to Co-pilot to Captain, if appellant were hired as Flight Officer in his forties he would probably not become Captain until his late fifties. The Federal Aviation Administration itself requires retirement at age 60, so that he would be able to serve only briefly as an American Captain before he had to retire."[5] The chapter case *American Airlines and Weight Standards* raises issues about job qualifications.

The ban on discrimination provided by Title VII generally overrides other important considerations. In 1991 the Supreme Court in *Automobile Workers v. Johnson Controls,* 499 U.S. 187, 111 S.Ct. 1196 (1991), invalidated Johnson Controls's fetal protection policy, which prohibited women, but not men, up to age 70 from working in its battery operations. The policy applied to all women, including those who have had surgery that prevented them from becoming pregnant. Johnson Controls instituted its fetal protection policy because battery production involves lead, and lead particles in the air can cause birth defects. The court held that "the absence of a malevolent motive does not convert a facially discriminatory policy into a neutral policy. . . . Johnson Controls' professed moral and ethical concerns about the welfare of the next generation do not suffice to establish a BFOQ of female sterility. Decisions about the welfare of future children must be left to the parents who conceive, bear, support, and raise them rather than to the employers who hire those parents."

---

[4]See *International Brotherhood of Teamsters v. United States,* 431 U.S. 324 (1977), *American Tobacco Company v. Patterson,* 452 U.S. 937 (1982), and *Firefighters Local Union No. 1784 and Memphis Fire Department v. Carl W. Stotts et al.,* 467 U.S. 561 (1984).

[5]In 1991 the Supreme Court let stand a federal Court of Appeals decision upholding the FAA's right to establish a mandatory retirement age of 60 for commercial airline pilots.

In addition to Title VII, the Civil Rights Act of 1866, codified as Section 1981 of Title 42 of the United States Code, provides protection against discrimination based on race. Section 1981 states that "all persons . . . have the same right to make and enforce contracts . . . as enjoyed by white persons." Since employment is viewed as a contract, Section 1981 covers the employment relationship. Protection from discrimination applies not only to minorities but to majorities as well. In *McDonald v. Santa Fe Trail Transportation Co.,* 427 U.S. 274 (1976), the Supreme Court held that Section 1981 protects whites from discrimination.

In 1968 the Supreme Court held that Congress enacted the Civil Rights Act of 1866 pursuant to the 13th Amendment, which abolished slavery, rather than pursuant to the equal protection clause of the 14th Amendment. This meant that the act applies not only to government actions but also to private actions.[6] This considerably expanded the scope of application of Section 1981 and had a number of significant implications beyond those of Title VII. First, unlike Title VII, the act has no statute of limitations. Second, the act imposes no limit on the awards that the courts may make, including compensatory and punitive damages. Third, the act applies more broadly than Title VII, since it covers all employers whereas Title VII covers only those with at least 15 employees. Fourth, an individual can file a lawsuit directly without having to go first to the EEOC.

The Age Discrimination in Employment Act prohibits discrimination in all aspects of employment against individuals 40 years or older by employers with at least 20 employees. The provisions of seniority systems are exempted, and BFOQ defenses are allowed. Age discrimination cases are frequently filed when employees are laid off. In the first 6 months of 1992 over 22,000 age discrimination complaints were filed with the EEOC. The Older Workers' Benefit Protection Act of 1990 allows employers to compensate employees in layoffs if they sign a waiver not to sue for age discrimination.

THE BURDEN OF PROOF

Although there is widespread agreement that discrimination is morally wrong and should be illegal, establishing a rule for determining whether an employer has discriminated in an employment decision is difficult. In addition, the nature and magnitudes of the awards to individuals who have been discriminated against are the subject of controversy. Some argue that only compensatory damages are appropriate, whereas others argue that punitive damages, with or without limit, should be awarded as well.

Title VII bars discrimination in employment but is silent about how a finding of discrimination is to be made. In *Griggs v. Duke Power,* 401 U.S. 424 (1971), the Supreme Court held that an employment policy that is "fair in form, but discriminatory in operation" is in violation of Title VII. Duke Power had required a high school diploma for employment, but its policy had a disparate impact on African Americans, who were less likely than white applicants to have graduated from high school.

Griggs also established that the burden of proof rests on the employee or the EEOC to show that the policy in question has a disparate impact on a protected class.[7] If that is shown, a *prima facie* case of illegality has been established. The burden is then on the employer to establish that the policy in question is a business necessity. The employer must demonstrate that a particular job requires a high school degree, that an employment test actually tests knowledge or skills needed on the job, or that physical requirements are necessary for a job.

---

[6]See Howell, Allison, and Henley (1987, p. 538).

[7]See also *McDonnell Douglas Corp. v. Green,* 411 U.S. 792 (1973) and *Texas Department of Community Affairs v. Burdine,* 447 U.S. 920 (1981).

In 1989 the Supreme Court reversed an earlier Court's assignment of the burden of proof. In *Wards Cove Packing Co. v. Antonio,* 490 U.S. 642 (1989), the court held that the plaintiff had the burden to show that the employer's policy was not justified by the job. This decision placed a considerable burden on plaintiffs because of the cost and difficulty required to show that the policy was not justified.[8]

The Bush administration and Congress negotiated a compromise and the Civil Rights Act of 1991 was enacted, amending several civil rights laws and overturning several recent Supreme Court decisions.[9] It reversed *Wards Cove* by placing the burden on the employer to show that a practice was a business necessity. The act also allowed punitive damages for intentional discrimination on the basis of sex, religion, national origin, or disability.[10] The act also overturned a 1989 Supreme Court decision that had restricted Section 1981 to hiring decisions. Section 1981 as amended now covers hiring, working conditions, promotion, and termination.

Affirmative Action

Affirmative action is a conscious attempt to realize equal opportunity. It includes steps to remedy the effects of past discrimination and may involve preferential treatment for individuals in protected classes. The EEOC oversees affirmative action plans and issues guidelines for their design. Affirmative action requires that employers adopt recruiting policies that ensure that minorities and women are included in the pool of candidates and that all those who meet the qualifications, or are qualifiable, are given fair consideration. To ensure that employers follow these affirmative action principles, demographics are used to indicate characteristics of the pool of potential candidates and to set goals for the hiring of minorities and women if they are underrepresented in a firm's workforce.

To ensure compliance with the principles of affirmative action, President Lyndon Johnson issued Executive Order 11246, which requires every federal contractor and subcontractor with at least 50 employees and a contract of at least $50,000 to develop explicit policies containing quantitative goals. Over 10,000 firms, as well as universities and nonprofit organizations, are covered by this requirement. Compliance may require changes in recruitment, hiring, or promotion policies, additional training programs, and the establishment of explicit goals. Affirmative action plans have been adopted more broadly than required by law and have become part of the social fabric of most companies.

Two ethical bases for affirmative action are compensatory justice and fair equality of opportunity. Compensatory justice is intended to compensate individuals for injustices and, in the context of affirmative action, applies to both individuals and protected classes. From this perspective, compensation for the actual victims of illegal discrimination is justified. Compensation may also be justified for classes, even though the individuals receiving the compensation have not themselves been the subject of discrimination. The rationale for compensation for a class is that their "starting position" has been adversely affected by past discrimination.[11] This is consistent with the ethical principle of fair equality of opportunity, which holds that individuals are to have a fair

---

[8] A business justification is an easier standard for defendants to prove than a business necessity.

[9] Consideration of the bill was complicated by the revelation that the Department of Labor had been promoting "race norming." The department had encouraged state employment agencies and some federal agencies to use an alternative scoring procedure on its General Aptitude Test Battery. Since minority applicants scored lower than whites on the test, the department provided the agencies with adjustments that made the curves for all races the same. Race norming was being used in 38 states.

[10] The Civil Rights Act of 1866 only allowed punitive damages for racial discrimination.

[11] Groarke (1990) offers a moral justification for compensation and restitution.

chance to qualify for positions and pursue their interests. If individuals are at a disadvantage because of their education, training, or other conditions important for qualification, justice considerations may call for providing them the means to pursue opportunities.

Seniority in labor union contracts serves as a basis for promotion and determining who retains a job when there is a reduction in the workforce. Courts have upheld the use of seniority for such decisions and have held it to be a fundamental component of employee rights. In some cases, seniority rights may take precedence over affirmative action programs. The Civil Rights Act of 1991 permits challenges to seniority systems that are intentionally discriminatory.

PREFERENCE AND REVERSE DISCRIMINATION

Affirmative action is not immune to ethical criticism. Criticism centers on who is to bear the burden of the compensation and how the opportunities of others are to be altered to provide opportunity to those who have been disadvantaged. One means of compensation that generates relatively little opposition is providing additional education and training.

In some situations, such as in training programs and promotions, providing compensation to one individual, or to a class of individuals, adversely affects other identifiable individuals. In some cases, the courts have upheld a right not to be the subject of reverse discrimination because of preferential treatment given to others.[12] Section 703(j) of Title VII states: "Nothing contained in this title shall be interpreted to require any employer . . . to grant preferential treatment to any individual or to any group because of race, color, religion, sex, or national origin . . . on account of an imbalance . . . to the total number or percentage of persons . . . employed . . . in comparison with the total number of persons of such race, color, religion, sex, or national origin . . . in the available work force. . . ."

An important attribute of many of the affirmative action programs that have withstood court scrutiny is that they are voluntarily agreed to. The court, however, may block a program that constitutes a permanent obstacle or barrier to those bearing the burden of an affirmative action program. In *Regents of University of California v. Bakke,* 438 U.S. 265, the Supreme Court struck down a voluntary policy that established a quota for minority admissions to a medical school because it precluded the admission of a qualified white male. In contrast, in *United Steelworkers of America v. Weber,* 443 U.S. 193 (1979), the court upheld a voluntary agreement between an employer and a union that established numerical goals for minority inclusion in a company training program. The court ruled that the agreement did not constitute discrimination against a white male with more seniority who was denied inclusion, since the goals were temporary and did not constitute an absolute barrier to his subsequent inclusion in the program or to promotion.

In 1993 the Court of Appeals overturned a Department of Agriculture decision denying a white applicant's attempt to buy a farm under a federal program to help socially disadvantaged people. The court held that the application was denied "solely on skin color" and that the applicant could be entitled to damages. The Clinton administration chose not to appeal the decision. In 1989 a New Jersey school board laid off a white teacher rather than an African American teacher expressly for the purpose of promoting diversity. The white teacher complained to the EEOC of illegal discrimination and later filed a lawsuit seeking reinstatement and lost wages. The white teacher

---

[12]See Newton (1973) and Wasserstrom (1978) for perspectives on this issue.

won at the district court and Court of Appeals level. To avoid having the case reach the Supreme Court where an unfavorable ruling would set a national precedent, the Black Leadership Forum, an umbrella group that includes the NAACP Legal Defense and Education Fund and the National Urban League, took the unusual step of paying $300,000 to the white teacher to settle the case.[13] These decisions are consistent with the pattern of court decisions suggesting that the law is best served when it is color blind.

In contrast to the language of Title VII, the federal government has a variety of programs that explicitly take race or sex into account. These include minority preference programs for broadcasting licenses, small business loans, college scholarships, and highway construction and defense contracts.[14] For example, federal law specified that ten percent of the contract dollars on federally aided road projects be set aside for minorities. In 1988 Congress included women under the same program. On federal highway contracts a company qualified as "disadvantaged" is given up to a ten percent price advantage over other firms.[15] Federal set-aside programs awarded $10.6 billion of contracts under the disadvantaged criteria, which automatically includes any minority- or woman-owned company.[16] A Small Business Administration program known as "8 (a)" awarded $6.4 billion in contracts in 1996 to 6,115 companies, all but 27 of which were minority owned. Under this program Asian American contractors increased their share of contracts to 23.7 percent in 1996 compared with 10.5 percent in 1986, whereas African American contractors' share fell from 50.5 percent to 36.7 percent over the same period.

When Adarand Constructors lost a contract to a minority-owned firm even though it had the lowest bid, it sued the federal government arguing that its right to equal protection under the Fifth Amendment had been violated. In 1995 the Supreme Court in *Adarand Constructors v. Peña,* 515 U.S. 200 (1995), held in favor of Adarand, thereby forcing changes in federal set-aside programs. Responding to the interests of important constituencies of the Democratic Party, the Clinton administration sought to comply with the Court decision by allowing up to a ten percent price advantage when there was an "underutilization" of qualified minority businesses. Also, the administration broadened the 8 (a) program to include companies headed by "socially disadvantaged" persons, which under the law automatically includes minorities.

The courts had upheld preference programs when they served a compelling interest. As an example of a compelling interest, in 1990 the Supreme Court in *Metro Broadcasting v. F.C.C.,* 110 SCt 2997 (1990), upheld an FCC policy that gave preference to minorities seeking to acquire a broadcasting license. The Court held that the FCC policy was important to the interest of providing a diversity of viewpoints and programming on the airways.[17] In 1998, however, a federal appeals court held that the *Adarand* decision implied a higher standard of scrutiny and concluded that the FCC policy was important but not compelling. Although the FCC policy was invalidated, many broadcasters vowed to continue voluntarily to follow the FCC guidelines.[18]

---

[13]A court of appeals decision serves as a precedent for the circuit of that court, whereas a decision by the Supreme Court serves as a nationwide precedent.
[14]See Lodge (1990, pp. 409–421) for a description of a minority procurement program.
[15]That is, if a non-disadvantaged firm bids $100 on a contract and a disadvantaged firm bids $109, the contract is awarded to the disadvantaged firm at the bid of $109.
[16]Only the Department of Transportation includes women in its preference program.
[17] See Spitzer (1991) for an analysis of the justifications for minority preference in broadcasting. In 1992 the U.S. Court of Appeals ruled that the FCC policy giving preference to women constituted illegal discrimination against men.
[18]In 1995 Congress repealed a law that gave a tax break to broadcasters that sold a station to a minority-owned firm.

Preferences have also been addressed in state ballot measures through which legislation can be enacted directly by voters thus bypassing the state legislature. In 1996 California voters approved with 54 percent of the vote a measure that would ban preferences based on the categories identified in Title VII. The initiative was upheld by the U.S. Court of Appeals, and the Supreme Court let the decision stand. In 1998 voters in Washington State approved a similar ballot measure. These measures do not affect private affirmative action and preference programs.

Affirmative action and preference programs are likely to continue to receive scrutiny by the courts and be the subject of legislative action and state ballot measures. Although court scrutiny of government affirmative action and preference programs is likely to continue, the affirmative action programs of most companies are likely to remain intact since they are by now a part of the fabric of those companies. The objectives of many of those programs are as yet unrealized, however. In addition to issues pertaining to employees, affirmative action may be extended to other constituencies. Many firms have a considerable underrepresentation of minorities and women among their distributors, franchisees, and agents, and civil rights advocates have been working to extend affirmative action goals to these positions.

Americans with Disabilities Act

The Americans with Disabilities Act (ADA) of 1990 bans discrimination on the basis of disability in virtually all aspects of the employment relationship for employers with 15 or more employees.[19] Disability is broadly defined to include "a physical or mental impairment that substantially limits one or more of that person's major life activities." Substance abuse is not considered a disability, but a person who no longer abuses substances and has completed a rehabilitation program can be considered disabled. AIDS is considered by the courts as a handicap under the 1973 Vocational Rehabilitation Act and hence represents a disability. An employer may select employees using only criterion that are job related and required by job necessity. For example, Target Stores discontinued the use of a psychological test when the ADA was enacted.[20]

Between 1993 and 1996 the ADA resulted in 72,687 complaints by employees and job applicants and has been a source of considerable management uncertainty. Determining what exactly constitutes a disability under the ADA has been left to the EEOC and the courts. For example, in 1997 the EEOC issued guidelines that defined mental illness as a disability. Employers are not required to lower their performance standards but must make reasonable accommodation through work schedules and changes in the physical workplace for employees with emotional or psychological problems. In the case of a woman with HIV but no symptoms who had chosen not to have children for fear of passing on the virus, the Supreme Court ruled in 1998 that she was covered by the ADA because reproduction was a major life activity that was limited. The implications of this decision for other disabilities were unclear, but some have argued that the decision would expand coverage to people with diabetes, infertility, drug and alcohol addiction, and the homeless who have addiction problems.

---

[19]Another important component of the ADA is the requirement that business, including retail stores and restaurants, provide "reasonable accommodations" for the disabled.
[20]See Bagley (1995, Ch. 13) for an extended treatment of the ADA.

Sexual Harassment

Sexual harassment is prohibited by Title VII. Harassment may be physical, verbal, or written and may include offensive language, unwanted sexual advances, or demeaning comments. Seeking sexual favors constitutes illegal sexual harassment if it involves a relationship of authority or power, such as the supervisor-subordinate relationship. The favors must be unwelcomed and viewed by the employee as probably required by the employer or supervisor. An employee who is the subject of sexual harassment may file an action with the EEOC under Title VII. The number of sexual harassment claims filed with the EEOC nearly doubled between 1991 and 1993, reaching 11,908 in 1993.

"Title VII does not proscribe all conduct of a sexual nature in the workplace. Thus it is crucial to clearly define sexual harassment: only unwelcome sexual conduct that is a term or condition of employment constitutes a violation."[21] Sexual harassment can be of one of two types: quid pro quo and hostile environment. The former occurs when "submission to or rejection of such conduct by an individual is used as the basis for employment decisions." The latter occurs when the sexual conduct in question "unreasonably interferes with an individual's job performance" or establishes an "intimidating, hostile, or offensive working environment."[22,23] The Supreme Court in *Mertior Savings Bank v. Vinson,* 477 U.S. 57 (1986), held that a hostile environment represents illegal discrimination under Title VII. Bagley (1995, p. 413) presents conditions for establishing a sexual harassment claim. See Figure 21-1.

Sexual harassment is at its foundation a moral problem, and Title VII makes it also a legal problem.[24] In the employment relationship the responsibility for preventing sexual harassment is assigned to the employer, which may be held liable even if it has a policy prohibiting harassment. That is, the employer is responsible for the violation of its policies by one employee against another. In addition to having a specific policy, the employer is required to educate its employees, deter harassing actions, and take precautions to avoid a hostile work environment. For example, many employers established internal complaint mechanisms that allow an employee to go to a person not involved in the incident in question. Such mechanisms often also include a procedure to investigate complaints and resolve them without going to court. Well-publicized sexual harassment episodes at Mitsubishi Motors Corporation's assembly plant in Illinois and at Astra USA, a unit of Astra AB of Sweden, as well as allegations against Supreme Court Justice Clarence Thomas and President Bill Clinton, suggest that sexual harassment may be widespread and not easy to eradicate.

The legal standards for sexual harassment cases were clarified in two 1998 Supreme Court decisions.[25] The Court held that a person need not suffer a tangible job detriment, such as the loss of a promotion, to bring a sexual harassment case. A company, however, can prevail if it has an anti-sexual harassment policy and an effective internal complaint system that the employee failed to use. The chapter case *Advanced Technology, Inc. (ATI)* includes a sexual harassment issue.

---

[21]Employment Practices, Commerce Clearing House, Inc., 1990, p. 6921.
[22]Employment Practices, Commerce Clearing House, Inc., 1990, p. 6922.
[23]The EEOC Policy Guidance, N-915.050, issued on March 19, 1990, states that "Where unwelcome sexual conduct by a supervisor has created a hostile environment, an employer will be directly liable if it knew or should have known of that conduct. . . . The EEOC will generally find apparent authority for hostile environment sex harassment by a supervisor where an employer has not established a policy against sex harassment and does not have a complaint procedure for sex harassment victims."
[24]See Wells and Kracher (1993) for an analysis of sexual harassment in the context of Rawls's theory of justice and Feary (1994) for another moral critique.
[25]*Burlington Industries Inc. v. Ellerth,* No. 97-569 and *Faragher v. City of Boca Raton,* No. 97-282.

Unwelcome sexual advances, requests for sexual favors, and other verbal or physical conduct of a sexual nature constitute sexual harassment when:

1. An individual's employment depends on the submission to such conduct;
2. Submission to or rejection of such conduct is used as the basis of employment decisions; and
3. Such conduct unreasonably interferes with the individual's work performance or creates an intimidating, hostile or offensive working environment.

In order to establish a *prima facie* claim of sexual harassment under Title VII, it must be shown that:

1. the employee belongs to a protected group;
2. the employee faced unwelcome harassment;
3. the harassment was based upon sex;
4. the harassment affected a term, condition or privilege of employment; and
5. the harassment's severity or pervasiveness implied employer responsibility.

Source: Reprinted by permission from page 413 of *Managers and the Legal Environment: Strategies for the 21st Century,* Second Edition, by Constance E. Bagley; Copyright © 1995 by West Publishing Company. All rights reserved.

FIGURE 21-1 Elements of a Sexual Harassment Claim

Diversity

The Bureau of Labor Statistics estimated that in the year 2000 white males will constitute 39 percent of the workforce, down from 49 percent in 1976. White males were estimated to represent only 20 percent of those entering the workplace by the year 2000. These demographic changes increase the importance of developing an employment relationship and a culture within the firm that accommodates diversity and draws strength from it. Moral standards, including treating individuals as ends and never solely as means, require that individuals not be compelled to comply with unitary modes of behavior that are inessential to job performance. Instead, understanding, tolerance, and respect for diversity should characterize future developments in the employment relationship.

Some companies have undertaken diversity training programs. These programs require top management support and must be carefully designed and implemented, since a backlash is possible among employees. Mobley and Payne (1992) list a dozen potential problems in diversity training programs. Henderson (1994) provides recommendations for the design of successful programs and for effective communication on cultural diversity issues.

Government statistics indicate that the percentage of management positions held by women increased from 9 percent to 33 percent and by minorities increased from 2 percent to 12 percent from 1966 to 1995. The representation of women and minorities among top management has remained relatively low, however. A study of 200 large companies by *The Wall Street Journal* (March 29, 1994) found that 25 percent of the jobs the EEOC classifies as "officials and managers," a broad category, were held by women in 1992. A number of companies have implemented aggressive programs that have resulted in higher representation. The percentages of women and minorities in management positions at Bank of America increased from 34 percent to 43 percent and 15 percent to 19 percent, respectively, from 1991 to 1996.[26]

[26] *The New York Times,* November 20, 1996.

In 1998 women held 11.1 percent of the seats on the board of directors of the Fortune 500 companies, but 71 of the companies had no women directors. This has given rise to the term *glass ceiling,* which refers to being able to see, but not reach, top management positions due to patterns of subtle discrimination. Congress passed the Glass Ceiling Act as Title II in the Civil Rights Act of 1991 in an attempt to eliminate artificial barriers to advancement.[27]

Women in Management

Many women managers face a set of challenges in addition to those posed by discrimination, sexual harassment, and glass ceilings. In the workplace, women managers are often expected to serve as exemplary role models, mentors to younger women managers, and representatives of women in general. Many women also face the curse of affirmative action—the suspicion that their advancement was due in part to their gender. Many women also face challenges due to family responsibilities and wonder whether they will be able to compete against men who have wives who take care of the children and manage the household.

Companies have adopted a variety of programs to accommodate the responsibilities of women and other employees. An increasing number of companies allow employees time for child and elder care, and many credit job flexibility and work-family policies for improving employee morale and job retention. The Family Medical Leave Act allows parents to take as much as 12 weeks of unpaid leave to care for children. Job sharing, telecommuting, part-time work, and flextime programs provide degrees of flexibility, but whether taking advantage of opportunities such as job sharing and part-time work limit one's chances for advancement remains a concern—among men as well as women.

Because statistics have shown that women are more likely than men to leave jobs, or interrupt their careers, Schwartz (1989) argued that women are more costly employees than men. She recommended that firms establish "career primacy" and "career and family oriented" tracks into which women can self-select. This recommendation was strongly criticized on a number of grounds, such as that it forces an unnecessary choice. An alternative is for firms to establish multiple paths to more responsible positions, including top management. Nevertheless, some women managers are reluctant to avail themselves of the programs companies offer for fear that they will find themselves on a mommy track—the term given by critics to Schwartz's recommendation. Schwartz observed that "women can't have it all. They have to make tradeoffs."[28] A responsibility of employers is at least to make those tradeoffs, if necessary, at least possible.

An increasing number of successful women managers have left large companies to start their own businesses. In 1996 women owned 5.9 million, or over one-third, of small businesses. This represented a 43 percent increase from 1987, compared with a 26 percent increase in small businesses. Women are starting small businesses at twice the rate of men, and ten percent of U.S. employees work for a woman-owned company, according to the National Foundation for Women Business Owners. Many of the issues involving women and management extend beyond ethical considerations in the employment relationship and relate to individual career choices and management styles. The chapter case *Advanced Technology, Inc. (*ATI) addresses a number of these issues.

---

[27]See Bagley (1995, p. 426).
[28]*The New York Times,* March 28, 1993.

Company Programs

Some firms have established extensive programs intended to attract and retain minorities and women. Corning Incorporated, a family-controlled firm located in the small town of Corning in rural western New York State, had been relatively successful in attracting African Americans but had a poor retention record.[29] The company decided that it had to do more. It abandoned the concept of a melting pot in favor of the concept of having a mix of employees and drawing strength from diversity. Corning established Quality Improvement Teams (QIT) to identify issues, make recommendations, and monitor progress. The Black Progress QIT established goals that have led to programs on career plans, recruiting, internship, "pre-review black employee Performance Reviews," and awareness training. The Women's QIT was charged with helping "Corning become free of gender constraints." Corning also established "Valuing Diversity" programs with titles such as "Men and Women as Colleagues," "Black Employees Workshop," and "Supervisor of Black Employees Workshop."

Another step was to make the town of Corning more attractive to African Americans. The company arranged for the local cable TV network to carry a black radio station and the Black Entertainment Network and helped to attract African American teachers, barbers, and hair stylists. Corning also recruited at as many predominantly black colleges as it did Ivy League schools. Corning established the Corning Black Engineering Scholarship and Training program and provided internships for college students to encourage them to continue with their science and engineering studies.

In 1994 Bank America began a diversity program that established "diversity-awareness workshops, a large-scale internal communications program with frequent articles on diversity in internal publications, formal networks for minorities and women to encourage them to discuss common problems and develop diversity-related events in their communities, and business school scholarships for minorities."[30] Bank America also established an on-line resumé system through which managers can search broadly within the company for people to fill job openings. This system was intended to break the old-boy network. The percent of women in senior management positions increased to 25 percent in 1996 from 18 percent in 1994 and minorities increased to 11 percent from 9 percent.

Johnson & Johnson instituted a comprehensive plan to assist its employees in balancing work and family responsibilities. These programs include:

- A supervisor/manager training program so that supervisors and employees are able to "work out reasonable and appropriate solutions to address specific business and family needs."
- Family care leave allowing up to 1 year of unpaid leave for care of a newborn or adopted child and guaranteed employment upon return.
- Family care paid leave for emergency care for a family member.
- Child care facilities at its headquarters and at one other location.
- A resource and referral program to assist employees in finding child and elder care services.
- A 24-hour crisis management and services system.
- Adoption services, including reimbursement for up to $2,000 of expense.
- Assistance for employees in relocation planning.
- Flexible time and work location arrangements.

---

[29] *The New York Times,* October 4, 1990.
[30] *The New York Times,* November 20, 1996.

- A flexible benefits program.
- Tuition payment programs for employees and low-interest loans for their children's college education.[31]

Organized Labor

Labor unions are an important feature of the employment relationship in many industries. However, union membership as a percent of the workforce has declined dramatically as a result of the growth and decline of industries and falling unionization within some industries. By 1997 only 14.1 percent of the employees belonged to a union, down from 20.1 percent in 1983. Only 11.8 percent of private sector employees belong to unions, whereas 37.7 percent of government employees belong to a union.[32] Membership in the United Auto Workers union fell from 1.5 million members in 1979 to 850,000 in 1994. The shift in economic activity from manufacturing to services reduced union membership, but workers have also increasingly rejected attempts at unionization. Beginning in 1997 organized labor became more aggressive in attempting to recruit new members, with a number of unions allocating a greater share of their budgets to organizing campaigns. Despite some success the growth in the economy caused union representation to decline.

The principal U.S. labor laws include the National Labor Relations Act (NLRA) of 1935, the Taft-Hartley Amendments of 1947, and the Landrum-Griffin Amendment of 1959. Among other provisions, the NLRA requires employers to bargain with unions and established the National Labor Relations Board to administer the NLRA. As a result of the NLRA and other forces, union membership increased five-fold from 1935 to 1947.

Enacted in response to the perceived abuse of union power, the Taft-Hartley Act prohibited certain practices of unions, banned the closed shop, and gave the president the power to seek an injunction to block a strike for 80 days.[33] In response to concerns about corruption in some unions, the Landrum-Griffin Amendment established rights of union members and regulated the election of union officers. A major defeat for organized labor has been its inability to persuade Congress to enact the Common Situs Picketing bill, which has been strongly opposed by business.

One role of unions has been to protect the rights of employees. As discussed earlier in this chapter, however, employee rights have been established independently of collective bargaining agreements. This has reduced the value of unions to employees and is part of the explanation for the decline of unionization in the United States.

As courts continue to establish rights to fair treatment and in jobs, and as employers respond to the needs of their employees, organized labor may emphasize its other roles as a bargaining agent and as a participant in the public policy process. Hirschman (1970) and Freeman and Medoff (1979) argue that unions give voice to employees in both political arenas and the employment relationship. Labor's political power, however, has decreased with the decline in membership, and labor's ability to vote as a block has been limited by the independence shown by some union members. Organized labor has had some successes, however, as shown by the Occupational Safety and Health Act, which requires employers to meet a wide array of safety standards and allows employees to file suits to force compliance. Unions also played a major role in obtaining an increase in the minimum wage in 1996 and in "get-out-the-vote" campaigns in 1998.

---

[31]The program is described in Johnson & Johnson brochures "Balancing Work and Family," "Elder Care Program," and "Child Care Program."

[32]Bureau of Labor Statistics, *Employment and Earnings,* Washington, D.C., January 1994.

[33]A closed shop arrangement requires an employer to hire only union members. A union shop arrangement allows an employer to hire nonunion members, but employees must join the union within a specified period.

As discussed in Chapter 8, in 1988 the Supreme Court ruled that union members cannot be forced to contribute to a union's political activities. In practice, union members must formally request the return of the portion of their dues used for political purposes. In the second half of the 1990s business and conservative groups supported ballot propositions and bills in state legislatures in a number of states to prohibit unions from spending a member's dues for political activity without explicit authorization by the member. Four states already had such "worker protection" laws, and unions spent $8 million in 1998 in defeating a ballot initiative in California. While the unions' efforts were largely successful, they reduced the funds available to unions to support political candidates.

The other principal role of unions is to increase the bargaining power of employees relative to their employers. The NLRA allows monopolization on the employee side of the employment relationship, and the resulting power has helped many unions garner high wages and favorable work rules. However, markets limit the gains that unions can obtain. To avoid unions, many firms moved facilities to the South, where the rate of unionization has been lower than in the North. Also, the increase in international competition and the growth in U.S. imports has dampened demand in many unionized industries, particularly in manufacturing. High wages coupled with inefficient production facilities and work rules led to the downsizing of firms, wage concessions, the elimination of some restrictive work rules, and large reductions in workforces. The increase in international competition has led some unions to emphasize job protection and income security instead of wage increases. In 1998 General Motors sought to outsource more of its parts supply, and to protect its jobs the UAW struck for 6 weeks idling 160,000 workers. The strike was successful, but GM subsequently announced that it planned to spin off its Delphi parts division.

Organized labor has been a vociferous political opponent of liberalized international trade, as considered in Chapter 16. Organized labor opposed both the North American Free Trade Agreement (NAFTA) and the Uruguay Round of the General Agreement on Tariffs and Trade (GATT) agreement. Although it won some concessions on NAFTA through side agreements, its efforts to protect its members' jobs and wages were soundly rejected. Organized labor has also opposed fast-track provisions intended to make congressional ratification of trade agreements easier.

Union power would be expected to be greatest in those industries that are most insulated from competition. In the post–World War II period, several industries, including trucking and airlines, were regulated in a manner that made entry very difficult. Furthermore, cost-based regulatory pricing rules allowed industries to pass on cost increases through higher prices. With entry into the industry effectively blocked, wage increases and inefficiencies were quickly passed on to customers. Rose (1985, 1987) estimated the impact of deregulation on the wages of union members in the trucking industry and found that the pre-deregulation premium of 50 percent was reduced to less than 30 percent when entry was allowed. Union employment in the industry also fell dramatically. Increased competition, both domestic and foreign, thus limits union bargaining power.

Unions' bargaining power has also been reduced by the increasing use of temporary and permanent replacement workers during strikes. One of the principal political objectives of organized labor and its congressional allies is a law prohibiting the hiring of permanent replacement workers during a strike.[34] With the advent of the Clinton

---

[34]As an example, in 1992 14,000 UAW workers struck Caterpillar, but when the company advertised for permanent replacement workers and hundreds of people responded to the ads, the strike quickly collapsed. The 1992 strike was over the terms of a new contract, for which the hiring of permanent replacement workers is allowed under the law. In 1994 the UAW adopted a new tactic in striking Caterpillar on the grounds of unfair labor practices, since permanent replacements cannot be hired during such a strike. Caterpillar's response was to continue to operate and to encourage strikers to cross the picket lines. Caterpillar ultimately prevailed.

administration, organized labor along with a coalition of civil rights groups, women's groups, and religious leaders backed legislation to ban permanent replacement workers. Despite their efforts and the support of the Clinton administration, the bill succumbed to a filibuster in 1994. With the Republican majorities in both houses of Congress beginning in 1995, there was little likelihood of such a bill being enacted. Seeking the support of organized labor, President Clinton issued an executive order barring firms that hire permanent replacement workers from holding federal contracts. The order was overturned by the courts. Republicans in Congress subsequently pushed legislation to counter labor's recruiting tactics. One bill would allow employers to fire "salts"—union organizers who obtain jobs at different construction work sites for the purpose of recruiting more union members.

Privacy and Drug Testing

The right to privacy is at the center of both public and political debate on issues ranging from abortion to roadside sobriety checkpoints to testing for HIV. In the employment relationship, privacy pertains to issues such as whether employers can inspect the contents of an employee's locker, whether workplace surveillance of employees is permitted, whether supervisors can listen in on telephone order takers to determine how they handle customer calls, and whether employees can be tested for substance abuse. The principal subject of this section is testing for substance abuse in the workplace.

A moral basis for a right to privacy derives from the Kantian categorical imperative that individuals are to be treated always as ends and never solely as means. Freedom and autonomy are restricted when privacy is violated. This right, however, can conflict with other rights, such as the right to safety and an employer's right to establish the conditions of employment. In addition, other ethical systems, such as utilitarianism, identify important interests that may justify limits on a right to privacy, as when public safety may be jeopardized.

The legal basis for a right to privacy is provided by the Fourth Amendment which states: "The right of the people to be secure in their persons, houses, papers, and effects, against unreasonable searches and seizures, shall not be violated. . . ." This prohibition is generally held to pertain to the actions of the federal government. A right of privacy, however, is not absolute even for government actions and must be evaluated relative to other rights with which it may conflict. The courts have upheld some federal drug testing programs, such as required for federal employees in such sensitive positions as safety inspectors, customs inspectors, and air traffic controllers. Pursuant to the order, the Federal Aviation Administration (1989) issued guidelines for antidrug programs for airlines, including both drug testing and the establishment of employee assistance programs.[35] The drug testing program may include six types of testing—pre-employment testing, periodic testing, random testing, post-accident testing, reasonable-cause testing, and return-to-duty testing. In 1995, six million additional workers were required to undergo periodic testing. The ADA explicitly excludes drug testing from its restrictions on pre-employment screening.

---

[35]In response to an incident in which airline pilots were observed drinking alcoholic beverages prior to a flight, the Department of Transportation in 1992 expanded drug and alcohol testing to seven million transportation workers.

These federal programs have generally withstood court scrutiny.[36] In 1989 in *Skinner v. Railway Labor Executives' Association,* 489 U.S. 602 (1989), the Supreme Court reviewed a ruling by the Federal Railroad Administration requiring train crews to be tested for substance abuse after accidents. The court held that such tests were an acceptable intrusion on the employee's privacy because of a compelling public safety interest. Similarly, in 1989 the court held that customs inspectors could be tested for substance abuse because of the sensitive nature of their jobs. The Supreme Court ruled in *Consolidated Rail Corporation v. Railway Labor Executives' Association,* 491 U.S. 299 (1989), that railroads and airlines may test employees for drugs if their labor agreements permit them to do so.[37]

These cases have clarified the federal government's use of drug testing, but the law pertaining to drug testing by private businesses is less clear. A number of states have enacted laws on drug testing, and those laws vary considerably across the states. In 1990 the California Supreme Court ruled that a Southern Pacific employee who refused a random drug test could not be fired because of her refusal. The court held that Southern Pacific had shown no "compelling interest" that would warrant invasion of the employee's right to privacy as provided in the California Constitution. In 1994, however, the California Supreme Court upheld the NCAA's drug testing program and rejected the compelling interest standard in favor of a "balancing test" in which "legitimate, countervailing" interests are weighed.[38] Some state laws allow testing only if employers have suspicions that an employee may be under the influence of drugs.

The consequences of substance abuse to individuals, employers, and the nation is substantial. A U.S. Department of Labor survey indicated that 20 percent of employers test for drugs. Drug use as estimated by the National Institute on Drug Abuse (NIDA) had declined substantially since 1979, and data indicate that only 3 percent of random drug tests are positive.[39] A 1994 study by the American Management Association found that 87 percent of the 680 companies surveyed had a drug testing program. Drug testing programs can be costly, and a number of companies have discontinued them. Some now rely on more thorough pre-employment screening and on post-accident testing.

Testing is only one component of a substance abuse program. Two other principal components are assistance and education.[40] The Drug-Free Workplace Act of 1988 requires businesses with federal grants or contracts to institute workplace practices and educational programs about drug abuse. Businesses are required to notify employees that drug use and possession are prohibited in the workplace and to establish an awareness program. The act also makes employment conditional on compliance with the employer's drug-free workplace policy and requires an employee convicted of a criminal drug violation to notify the employer and the federal agency that issued the grant or contract.

The design of substance abuse testing programs has come under ethical scrutiny. One guide to the design of a drug testing program for a private firm is to draw an analogy to the relationship between the government and its citizens and the relationship

[36]See Cozzetto and Padeliski (1997) for privacy in the workplace issues pertaining to public employees.
[37]The relevant labor law is the Railway Labor Act, which allows employers to set working conditions.
[38]State constitutions and laws vary widely on the right to privacy and the right of employers to test.
[39]See Bahls (1998).
[40]The availability of an employee assistance program varies considerably across employers, particularly by size of firm. A 1988 Bureau of Labor Statistics survey of employers with a total of 84.9 million employees found that most firms with 5,000 or more employees had such a program, whereas most small firms did not. Of the 31 million employees of firms with fewer than 50 employees, fewer than 3 million were covered by a drug abuse assistance program.

between an employer and its employees. The Fourth Amendment limits intrusion by the government. Reasoning by analogy, some argue that the right of privacy, particularly as it pertains to the testing of employees, should also be respected and protected. This implies that testing for substance abuse should be restricted to those jobs that affect an important interest. This may involve jobs affecting public safety, the safety of other employees, security, or jobs entrusted with company resources.

Another perspective focuses on enhancing overall productivity. Substance abuse can decrease productivity, thereby increasing costs and the prices of goods and services. From a utilitarian perspective employees should not abuse substances on the job or in a manner that affects their productivity. Furthermore, the employment relationship is analogous to a contractual relationship, and employers have a right to prescribe the conditions of employment and to screen prospective employees.[41] Critics contend, however, that productivity improvements do not justify violations of a right to privacy and that drug tests police lifestyles and personal activities off the job. Random drug testing is more intrusive, it is argued, than are scheduled or preannounced tests.

Critics of employee drug testing programs contend that the programs are unethical because they do not test the employees' abilities to perform their jobs. In response to this criticism and the consequences of employees who work under the influence of substances, a number of companies have focused on "performance testing" or "fitness-for-duty" testing for certain jobs, such as truck driver and machinery operator.[42] These computer-based tests are intended to measure neuromuscular functioning and require, for example, that the employee match objects on a computer screen or keep a randomly moving pointer on the center of the screen. If an employee fails the test, the employer can investigate further.

Whistle-Blowing

Whistle-blowing refers to actions taken by employees in response to their employer's activities. The form of whistle-blowing considered here involves going public with allegations of wrongdoing or unethical practices.

Whistle-blowing about illegal acts is protected by the courts. In the case of the dismissal of an employee who blew the whistle on overcharging by a bank, the West Virginia Supreme Court of Appeals in *Harless v. First National Bank in Fairmont,* 162 WVa 116 (1982), ruled that although employment at will was an established rule, "There is a growing trend that recognizes that an employer may subject himself to liability if he fires an employee who is employed at will if the employee can show that the firing was motivated by an intention to contravene some substantial public policy."[43] In this case, the individual's right to free speech took precedent over the employer's right to dismissal at will. Similarly, in *Tameny v. Atlantic Richfield Company,* 27 Cal. 3d 167 (1980), the Supreme Court of California held that,

> An employer's authority over its employee does not include the right to demand that the employee commit a criminal act to further its interests, and an employer may not coerce compliance with such unlawful directions by discharging an employee who refuses to follow such an order. An employer engaging in such

[41]See the Chapter 19 case *Genetic Testing in the Workplace* for other dimensions of employee testing.
[42]Such testing may be subject to bargaining with unions.
[43]Quoted in Ewing (1983, p. 359).

> conduct violates a basic duty imposed by law upon all employers, and thus an employee who has suffered damages as a result of such discharge may maintain a tort action for wrongful discharge against the employer.

In addition, federal legislation such as the Mine Safety and Health Act, the Toxic Substances Control Act, the Occupational Safety and Health Act, the Clean Air Act Amendments, and the Water Pollution Control Act protects employees when they report a violation of a law or regulation by their employer. The Whistleblower Protection Act of 1989 protects whistle-blowers from wrongful discharge, and many states have statutes that protect public and private sector employees.

Whistle-blowing on firms supplying the federal government is encouraged by the financial incentives provided by the False Claims Act, enacted during the Civil War to encourage citizens to help the government eliminate fraud. The law allows private citizens to file *qui tam* suits on behalf of the government.[44] In 1986 the law was amended to provide for treble damages and to allow the Department of Justice (DOJ) to participate in the suit. The citizen receives from 15 to 25 percent of damages awarded, with a percentage of up to 30 percent if the DOJ elects not to participate in the case. Over 700 whistle-blowing lawsuits were brought from 1986 through 1994, and 360 were filed in 1996. In a $150 million settlement between United Technologies and the federal government in 1994, the former vice president for finance received 15 percent, or $22.5 million, for exposing alleged improper billing practices. Only 11 percent of the False Claims Act cases, however, resulted in recovery of damages by the government.

Whistle-blowing is directed at stopping serious harm by providing information to the public and to authorities. It is important to distinguish between exposing violations of illegal or unethical practices and going public on issues of personal preference. Exposing illegal and clearly unethical practices should be encouraged and supported. As Westin (1981, pp. 66–67) points out, however, some individuals may go public with a concern about a social responsibility issue that is a matter of management discretion or involves a judgment, such as what constitutes an unreasonable risk of injury. Furthermore, a disgruntled employee may use whistle-blowing to avoid disciplinary action or to retaliate against an employer. In such cases, disciplinary measures or dismissal of the employee may be warranted. Several companies have employment policies that require such disputes to be resolved by arbitration, and the courts have generally supported arbitration as a means of reducing their case load. Arbitration has several advantages for firms over litigation. First, arbitration often prevents an employee from going public with allegations. Second, arbitration can be substantially less costly than litigation. Third, arbitrators seldom award punitive damages.

The managerial issues pertaining to whistle-blowing center on when it is appropriate for an employee to blow the whistle and which policies an employer should institute to address instances of whistle-blowing.[45] Most firms prefer to establish policies that encourage employees to bring matters of concern to the attention of management without penalty, so that they can be evaluated and addressed internally. The False Claims Act, however, creates a moral hazard problem (see Chapter 10) because it encourages

---

[44]In 1997 a federal district court judge ruled that the False Claims Act was unconstitutional because under the separation of powers only the Executive Branch and not Congress has the power to assign the right to prosecute fraud cases. This case has not yet been resolved at the appellate level.

[45]See Miceli and Near (1992).

employees to go public when they believe that a monetary award can be obtained. As an example, the DOJ asked the courts to reduce a whistle-blowing award to an employee, who had "manipulated" the law by delaying his case for 4 years in the hope of obtaining a larger reward. In the case, General Electric claimed that the "bounty" provided by the False Claims Act caused the employee to avoid the company's internal control systems. The DOJ stated that the employee "actively concealed the fraud from other employees and lied to General Electric on forms that asked employees whether they knew of any wrongdoing." The judge reduced the award but not by as much as requested by the DOJ.

De George (1982b) provides three necessary conditions for an employee to be morally justified in whistle-blowing.[46]

1. The firm, through its product or policy, will do serious and considerable harm to the public, whether in the person of the user of its product, an innocent bystander, or the general public.
2. Once an employee identifies a serious threat to the user of a product or to the general public, he or she should report it to his or her immediate superior and make his or her moral concern known. Unless he or she does so, the act of whistle-blowing is not clearly justified.
3. If one's immediate superior does nothing effective about the concern or complaint, the employee should exhaust the internal procedures and possibilities within the firm. This usually will involve taking the matter up the managerial ladder, and if necessary—and possible—to the board of directors.

The first condition is effectively a utilitarian standard and places the responsibility on the employee to assess the likely public benefits from whistle-blowing. It also provides a basis for the employer to assess whether the employee's action is warranted. Since whistle-blowing can be costly to the firm and often to the employee, the second condition requires that the individual bring the matter to the attention of management. If this does not resolve it, the third condition requires the employee to bring it to those higher in the organization. If this fails to resolve the matter, the individual is morally justified in going to the public, according to De George's framework.

Summary

Employees have legal rights in jobs that are continuing and in jobs that are being eliminated. Those rights are established by contract, such as that entered into by a firm and a labor union; by legislation as in the case of the NLRA; and by the common law. The courts have substantially revised the at-will doctrine through the extension of rights that require cause for dismissal. Firms are generally free to lay off workers and close plants, although advance notice may be required. Firms have voluntarily established rights for their employees through explicit employment policies and practices and through grievance procedures. Labor agreements established through collective bargaining are also a source of employee rights. Although the percent of the workforce that is unionized has decreased substantially over the past several decades, labor unions remain important in many industries.

Equal employment opportunity is a moral right and is also a legal right for employees of all except very small firms. Its transformation into a legal right has involved a number of complicated issues about standards, the assignment of the burden of proof,

[46]See also De George (1982a, pp. 157–164) and Bowie (1982, 140–148).

and admissible defenses. The courts have held that unintentional discrimination resulting from practices that have a disparate impact on a protected class is covered under Title VII. The burden of proof is on the employer to show that its practices are necessary.

Affirmative action is intended to remedy the effects of past discrimination through hiring, promotion, and other policies that involve specific goals and practices. The courts have limited the scope of affirmative action policies that grant preferences prohibited by Title VII. Almost all employers, however, have affirmative action policies, and most are committed to hiring and promoting women and minorities. Nevertheless, women and minorities are underrepresented in upper management, and a challenge for firms is to remove invisible barriers to advancement and create a climate in which diversity is valued and flourishes. Increasingly, firms are developing policies that allow employees to balance family and work responsibilities.

A number of issues, such as privacy and substance abuse, arising in the employment relationship require policies that balance the rights of employees and the interests of employers and the public. Employers also have the responsibility of encouraging employees to bring to their attention practices, such as sexual harassment and unethical or illegal activities, and to protect the employees when they do so. Whistle-blowing by employees on illegal activities is protected by law.

APPENDIX

The Principal Equal Opportunity Laws

The *Equal Pay Act of 1963,* an amendment to the 1938 Fair Labor Standards Act, was the first law establishing the principle of "equal pay for equal work," specifying that men and women performing functions that require "equal skill, effort, and responsibility under similar working conditions" in the same facility be paid at the same rate. Amended in 1972 and 1974 to include academic, executive, and professional jobs, the Equal Pay Act does not outlaw pay differentials based on factors other than sex, such as seniority, merit, or quantity and quality of output.

The *Civil Rights Act of 1964* addresses discrimination in housing and access to public facilities. Title VII pertains to employment. This is the fundamental EEO law, making discrimination on the basis of race, color, sex, religion, or national origin illegal for employers, labor unions, and employment agencies. The act outlaws discrimination in all aspects of employment—hiring, firing, compensation, and any other "terms, conditions, or privileges" associated with employment. It is also illegal to discriminate or retaliate against an employee who has filed a complaint. Title VII established the Equal Employment Opportunity Commission (EEOC) to develop guidelines for implementing Title VII and to hear complaints and conduct investigations into alleged employment discrimination.

Executive Orders Nos. 11246 and 11375, issued by President Lyndon Johnson in 1965 and 1967, apply to government contractors. Together they use the federal government's purchasing power to require affirmative action plans for any employer who receives more than $10,000 in federal government contracts. This includes banks that receive federal deposits and universities and nonprofit organizations that receive grants or payments, as well as private firms that bid on contracts to provide goods or services. The executive orders go further than Title VII by requiring that employers not only eliminate discriminatory practices but take positive action to remedy the effects of past discrimination. Employers with more than $50,000 of federal government business and at least 50 employees must submit written affirmative action plans for hiring and promoting women and minorities. Enforcement powers have been consolidated in the Office of Federal Contract Compliance Programs (OFCCP). OFCCP issues regulations, handles complaints, and reviews federal contractors' compliance. Firms that do not comply risk losing the right to compete for federal contracts, a penalty called debarment. Under revised Order 4, issued by the OFCCP, contractors may be excused from not achieving goals set in their affirmative action plans if they can demonstrate that they made "good-faith efforts" to meet them.

The *Age Discrimination in Employment Act (ADEA) of 1967,* amended in 1978, prohibits discrimination on the basis of age against employees or applicants from 40 to 70 years old. It outlaws involuntary retirement before age 65 for top-level executives or policy makers. Employees in all other positions cannot be forced to retire against their will before they are 70. This law applies to all firms with 20 or more employees, except where state law sets a higher age limit on, or altogether prohibits, mandatory retirement. The ADEA also applies to hiring and promotion decisions. There is no affirmative action requirement based on age.

The *Equal Employment Opportunity Act of 1972* gave the EEOC power to intervene, investigate, conciliate complaints, and file lawsuits on behalf of individuals or groups allegedly injured by employment discrimination prohibited under Title VII. If conciliation fails or if the EEOC finds a systematic pattern of discrimination in policies and practices, the public or private employer (with 15 or more employees) can be sued. This act also set up mechanisms to facilitate coordination among the various state and federal agencies that handle EEO complaints and greatly strengthened EEO enforcement.

The *Rehabilitation Act of 1973* extended the executive orders issued by President Johnson to cover employment of the disabled. Like the earlier law, it requires any government contractor with more than 50 employees and $50,000 in contracts to submit a written affirmative action plan for hiring and promoting disabled employees. Disability under this law is defined very broadly as occurring when a person has, is perceived as having, or possesses a record of having, a physical or mental impairment that limits one or more major life activities. Alcoholism and drug abuse are not considered disabilities for purposes of this law, but many other common problems may be. The law can cover people with little or no visible evidence of their disabilities—those who have diabetes, heart conditions, back problems, learning disabilities, hearing trouble, or allergies, to name a few. The employer must make a good-faith effort to hire and promote disabled people for jobs they are capable of performing with reasonable accommodation to their disabilities. Accommodation may mean modifying the worksite, altering aspects of the job, or providing aids to overcome the individual's limitations.

The *Pregnancy Discrimination Act (PDA) of 1978* expands the definition of sex discrimination under Title VII to include basing employment decisions on "pregnancy, childbirth, or related medical conditions." The major application of the PDA has been to require employers to treat pregnancy like other temporary, non-job-related disabilities under their leave policies and benefit plans that apply to nonpregnant employees faced with a temporary disability. The only valid criterion for employment decisions about a pregnant employee is the individual's ability to work.

The *Americans with Disabilities Act (ADA) of 1990* bars discrimination on the basis of disability in employment, public accommodations, and services. The ADA requires employers to make "reasonable accommodation" for their disabled employees. Retailers are also required to make reasonable modifications to accommodate disabled customers. Employers and merchants who can demonstrate that the required changes are unduly expensive or disruptive can be exempted. Whatever penalties are available to remedy discrimination in employment on the basis of race, color, sex, religion, and national origin also apply to discrimination against the disabled.

The *Civil Rights Act of 1991* overturns portions of several Supreme Court decisions that had made it more difficult for plaintiffs to win discrimination suits. Once the plaintiff has shown a disparate effect, the burden of proof is placed on the defendant as in *Griggs* to show that a practice is a business necessity. The act also for the first time incorporated into legislation the business necessity condition by requiring the employer to show that practices are "job-related for the position in question and consistent with business necessity." The act extends the right of plaintiffs to sue for actual and punitive damages for intentional discrimination on the basis of sex, religion, national origin, and disability, as allowed on the basis of race by the Civil Rights Act of 1866. ■

This appendix is an updated version of "The Manager's Introduction to Equal Employment Opportunity & Affirmation Action," prepared by Cynthia M. Ulman, Graduate School of Business, Stanford University, 1983.

CASES

American Airlines and Weight Standards

The American Airlines Flight Attendant Weight Program stated that a "firm, trim silhouette, free of bulges, rolls or paunches, is necessary for an alert, efficient image." American maintained that its grooming policy was required to convey to the public the image the airline desired. American's policy was a result of a 1977 court-ordered settlement of a suit brought by flight attendants.[1] The settlement prohibited American from using an arbitrary weight policy but allowed the airline to set a deadline for meeting weight standards for employees who returned from any leave. For example, women on maternity leave had to lose excess weight within 6 weeks. Active flight attendants who exceeded the weight limit were required to lose 1.5 pounds a week and were given three chances to meet the limit. If an employee failed to meet the weight limit, suspension or termination could result.

The weight limits used by American were based on the 1959 Metropolitan Life Insurance Company tables. The airline used the tables for small and medium frames for women and the large-frame table for men. At American the maximum weight was 129 pounds for a 25-year-old, 5-foot 5-inch woman, whereas at United the limit was 137 pounds and at Delta was 138 pounds. Continental had no predetermined limit. A 5-foot 5-inch man had a weight limit of 145 pounds at American. In contrast to other airlines, American did not adjust its weight requirements for age. For a 5-foot-5 inch woman, the American limit remained at 129 pounds, whereas the United limit increased to 146 pounds at age 55. Delta's limit increased to 142 pounds.

The Association of Professional Flight Attendants represented 13,500 American employees, 90 percent of whom were women. The union opposed the weight policy and chose to address the issue in the arenas of public sentiment and the courts rather than through contract negotiations. The union used billboard advertisements and luggage tags that read "Weigh my performance, not my body."

The union also filed suit in federal court alleging that the weight policy discriminated on the basis of sex and age. One allegation was that the use of the small-frame and medium-frame weight tables for women and large-frame range for men discriminated against women. The suit also alleged that not adjusting the weight limit as a function of age was discriminatory because as women age they gain weight. The union also alleged that the failure to increase the limit with age was directed at getting rid of older employees who had higher wages. The union's Tommie Huttow-Blake said, "The company tries to say it's a bona fide occupational qualification. But that's baloney. These appearance standards have nothing to do with proficiency."[2] American's attorney Maureen F. Moore said, "The policy is intended to make flight attendants 'presentable' to the public, but is not discriminatory because weight requirements apply to both male and female attendants."[3]

A week after the union filed its suit, the Equal Employment Opportunity Commission filed a class action lawsuit charging that the weight policy discriminated against women over 40 years of age. ■

---

[1]Earlier, airlines had restricted the position of flight attendant to single women 32 years old or younger and had specific, detailed grooming requirements. Court rulings in the late 1960s prohibited the age and no-marriage provisions. The courts banned such policies in 1971.

[2]*The Wall Street Journal,* April 10, 1990.
[3]*Peninsula Times Tribune,* April 10, 1990.

PREPARATION QUESTIONS

1. Is American's weight policy discriminatory? On what basis? What burden of proof is placed on the plaintiffs?
2. If the plaintiffs satisfy that burden, what burden of proof is placed on American?
3. Should American change its policy or contest the lawsuits?

Beards

Pseudofolliculitis barbae, or PFB, is a skin condition caused by tightly curled facial bristles which, when sharpened by shaving, can reenter the skin and cause inflammation, infections, and scars. The most straightforward means of dealing with the condition is to grow a beard, since as the hair grows it pulls the tip from the skin. Nearly 90 percent of African American men have this condition in some degree, and according to dermatologists perhaps 30 percent have it so severely that they should not shave. Some members of other races also have the condition but in much smaller percentages.

Donald Boyd, an officer with the University of Maryland-Baltimore Department of Security, was forced to resign after he developed a severe case of PFB and grew a beard in violation of the department's clean-shaven policy. When the case was brought before the Maryland Commission on Human Relations in 1990, the hearing examiner ruled that the clean-shaven policy had a "disproportionate impact" on African American men, since it "falls more harshly on one group than others and cannot be justified by business necessity. . . . No testimony was introduced that would indicate that the wearing of a beard by a police officer results in that officer being unable to perform his police duties."[1]

Chief John J. Collins of the Department of Security said, "I'm more comfortable if I don't have to shave also, but I've been trained to be clean shaven to go to work. This is really a case of a disgruntled employee taking an extremist position and trying to dress it up in racial overtones. There are white officers who have similar conditions, like acne that's so inflamed they can't put their hats on, but they are committed to the job and they put more effort into keeping their conditions under control. We've had other blacks who have problems shaving. They'll use creams, take a few day's sick leave, and come back."[2]

The military had a clean-shaven policy, but because of complaints during the Vietnam War, the Army, Navy, and Air Force allowed a one-quarter inch beard. "Dr. Richard B. Odom, chief dermatologist at the University of California at San Francisco, said that as a white physician who was part of an Army committee that developed new guidelines concerning the condition, he often felt that blacks were discriminated against because they were not allowed to grow beards when medically warranted."[3] " 'If you are part of a decision-making group [setting a shaving policy] and you don't have the problem, you don't understand how it makes you uncomfortable,' said Dr. Lucius C. Earl 3d, a black dermatologist in Chicago who wore a beard for many years until the condition wore off as it sometimes does."[4]

In the 1970s the Fourth Circuit Court of Appeals rejected a claim of racial discrimination as a result of the clean-shaven policy of a supermarket chain. The court found that the chain had shown that the appearance of cleanliness was a business necessity for a supermarket. The Supreme Court refused to hear the case on appeal.

A variety of organizations, including police departments, airlines, fast-food chains, and a number of other companies, had policies that required employees to be clean shaven, and some employers had a policy of assigning bearded men to jobs that did not involve contact with the public. Domino's Pizza Corporation was one of the companies that had a clean-shaven policy for all its employees who deal with the public.

Domino's Pizza's clean-shaven policy for deliverers was challenged in federal court by Lanston J. Bradley of Omaha, Nebraska, who argued that it violated federal civil rights laws by having a disparate impact on blacks because they were disproportionately afflicted with PFB. Mr. Bradley stated, "I thought it was discriminatory, because it cuts down chances for black men to do that kind of work if there is a rule against beards. Also, I have been through the military, where I had gotten a shaving waiver, so I knew having a beard would not impact on my ability to do the job. It's a matter of principle for me."[5] ■

[1] *The New York Times,* July 15, 1990.
[2] *The New York Times,* July 15, 1990.
[3] *The New York Times,* July 17, 1990.
[4] *The New York Times,* July 17, 1990.
[5] *The New York Times,* November 3, 1993.

PREPARATION QUESTIONS

1. Should any grooming policy that has a disproportionate effect on a protected group be illegal?
2. Is a clean-shaven policy a business necessity for Domino's Pizza?
3. Does such a policy constitute illegal or unethical discrimination?
4. In light of the ruling by the Maryland Commission on Human Relations and the lawsuit by Mr. Bradley, should Domino's change its policy?

Advanced Technology, Inc. (ATI)

Celine Lange, president of Advanced Technology, Inc.'s software division, walked out of ATI's headquarters in Santa Clara, California, on Friday evening. After a long day at work, she had to pick up her 10-year-old son from baseball practice. As Lange was driving north on Route 101, a call came through on her car phone. It was Bill Montgomery, chairman and CEO of ATI, calling to move their Monday morning meeting forward to 8:00 A.M.

As Lange hung up the phone, her mind raced over several important topics she planned to discuss with Montgomery. She sighed as she thought about the short- and long-term implications these issues had for her career and those of many others at ATI. She realized that part of her Saturday would be spent at the office outlining her recommendations to be fully prepared for Monday morning's meeting.

NETWORK PLUS

After graduating from Stanford University's Graduate School of Business in 1975, Lange had worked for a large computer manufacturer. As one of the few women in a male-dominated environment, she felt her potential for advancement was limited and soon began thinking about starting her own business. In 1983 she founded a software company, Network Plus, just as computer networks were developing. The company began with five employees working at Lange's home. Through 11 years of technical excellence and hard work, Lange had led Network Plus to sales of $370 million and profits of $41 million in 1993, with 1,480 employees worldwide. Her determination and innovative approach kept the company on the forefront of networking technology.

In a recent issue of *Inc.* magazine, Lange was noted for her "participatory management style and progressive human resource practices." She was one of the first Silicon Valley CEO's to institute job sharing, extended parental leave, telecommuting, and 360-degree reviews.[1] In a predominately male field, Lange had attracted a number of talented female engineers and programmers, achieving almost equal representation of women and men on Network Plus's professional staff.

In September 1993, Lange and her board of directors agreed to sell Network Plus, then a public company, to ATI in a stock exchange valued at $925 million, 12 percent of ATI's market value. With the acquisition, ATI, a prominent personal computer and advanced workstation company, became a $6.8 billion business with $342 million in profits. While the acquisition brought financial independence to Lange, she decided to accept a position as head of ATI's software division to see her vision of networking in the twenty-first century to completion. At the age of 44, Lange also had the ambition to lead a large computer company. When Montgomery initiated discussions about the acquisition of Network Plus, he had indicated that if Lange joined ATI, she would be well positioned for the CEO position when he retired in 5 years.

THE PROMOTION

As Lange reflected on her busy afternoon, she recalled her discussion with Catherine Moore, a marketing director in the personal computer division. Moore had initiated the meeting to receive some career guidance from Lange. Moore was frustrated by her lack of advancement and felt that she had been placed on a "mommy track." She had recently been

[1]360-degree reviews are an evaluation process in which information is gathered from subordinates, peers, and superiors.

passed over for a promotion to vice president of marketing. Lange was struck by Moore's words: "It's not just that I didn't get this promotion. Many other women at ATI complain of similar obstacles. Something has to be done. We're hoping that you will be able to initiate changes which improve the situation."

The position had gone instead to Don Baxter, another marketing director, who had been with ATI for 7 years. Although Moore agreed that Baxter was talented, she nonetheless felt his promotion illustrated the strength of the "old boy network." Moore had been with the firm 3 years longer than Baxter and had even helped to hire and train him. Baxter quickly gained the favor of upper management through a particularly successful product launch of ATI's first 386 personal computer. Recently, he had contributed to a five percent increase in market share by expanding ATI's sales in several key industries.

Moore was also highly regarded by management and had been on the fast track in the marketing department before taking an extended 6-month maternity leave. She had created a winning marketing strategy for ATI's entry into notebook computers. But ever since Moore had returned from maternity leave almost a year ago, some of her coworkers had the impression that she was no longer committed to her job. Whereas the norm in the office was to work past 7 P.M., she tried to leave promptly at 5 P.M. She avoided breakfast meetings, which were common at ATI, and appeared reluctant to travel.

Having been appointed by Montgomery last February to head a committee focused on ATI's promotion and review process, Lange was already aware of Moore's situation and might be in a position to help. As Lange understood it, the decision to promote Baxter over Moore had been made by the president of the division, based on recent feedback from Moore's coworkers and concern about her performance potential.

Lange was concerned that Moore might leave the firm, or even consider taking legal action. Over lunch, Lange had heard that the vice president for marketing in the services division was planning to leave ATI next month. The services division specialized in network integration for the financial industry. Lately, the top people in marketing in the services division had been spending at least 2 days a week on the East Coast, where the financial industry was concentrated. Lange doubted that Moore would be happy with these travel requirements. Lange also knew that management at ATI would fear that offering a promotion to Moore would set a precedent for shorter hours and lighter travel requirements. Historically, ATI tended to promote those who combined top performance with visible dedication to the firm. Lange herself wondered whether promoting Moore would lower the morale of her coworkers and subordinates who had complained about her work ethic.

Lange had to decide whether to recommend Moore for this position before her meeting with Montgomery. She wondered whether this might be a good opportunity to introduce policies that would ease the transition for employees returning from parental leave and would ensure objective promotion criteria that did not indirectly discriminate against women.

COMMUNICATION STYLE

At last Wednesday's executive committee meeting, the 5-year strategic plan was reviewed. Throughout the meeting, Lange had tried to express opinions about her area of expertise—the integration of networking software with advanced workstations. She was frustrated because her peers did not seem to value her opinions. Every time she spoke she was interrupted. Soon after she made a suggestion that appeared to be ignored, someone would rephrase her idea and suddenly everyone took note. This problem seemed to be an ongoing one for her with this group. Lange was the youngest member of the executive committee, and the others seemed not to take her seriously. She had tried to gain credibility over the past 4 months, but still felt that her power and influence with the executive committee did not reflect her position within the firm.

She was disappointed that ATI executive committee meetings were run in an aggressive manner, which she found to be overbearing. Although Lange had never considered herself shy or reticent, she was uncomfortable in this combative setting. She was also concerned that by being aggressive—shouting and swearing with the men—her behavior would be interpreted negatively and she would be labeled a "bitch." However, by not promoting her ideas in a way that matched her colleagues' forceful manner, she feared she would continue to be overlooked and that her influence at ATI would be undermined.

At this coming Wednesday's meeting, Lange was scheduled to present formally her $20 million product expansion plans for the software division. This amount was critical for her division and would account for ATI's biggest product development expense of the year. Because she was asking for more than her "fair share" of the budget, she realized there probably would be some opposition. The other division heads could oppose her plans because the allocation might take away from investments in their divisions. Over the weekend, she needed to devise a way to get buy-in on her expansion plans from the executive committee.

SEXUAL HARASSMENT

Earlier in the day Montgomery had called Lange into his office to discuss an important matter. He told her that Denise Sanchez, director of sales administration in the personal computer division, had formally complained of sexual harassment by Jim Callahan, president of the division. According to Sanchez, Callahan had accompanied her on a business trip to one of ATI's largest customer sites. After dinner one evening, Callahan had called Sanchez and two sales managers into his hotel room to plan for the next day's customer visit. After meeting for over an hour, the sales managers left, but as Sanchez was at the door, Callahan asked for her opinion on one more matter. She felt very uncomfortable alone in the hotel room with Callahan and suggested instead that they continue their discussions the next morning over breakfast. However, Callahan insisted that they should discuss it that night. As they sat down again, Callahan asked Sanchez if she would like a drink. He proceeded to talk with her about her family, hobbies, and career aspirations. He never mentioned the next day's customer visit. After several polite attempts at leaving, Sanchez finally departed abruptly.

According to Montgomery, Callahan denied any wrongdoing and explained that in fact he had been trying to learn more about Sanchez in order to provide informal career advice. She was one of the few senior women working for him, and he felt he had a responsibility to act as her mentor, particularly since he had heard complaints from women that no one helped to guide them through the unwritten rules of the organization. Callahan had explained to Montgomery that he had only the best of intentions in dealing with Sanchez.

Although Montgomery initially believed Callahan, the personnel guidelines dictated that the matter be investigated further. Callahan and Sanchez's stories were quite different. For example, Sanchez claimed that she told Callahan that she was uncomfortable being alone in the hotel room with him, but Callahan denied that Sanchez expressed anything of the sort. Montgomery was worried that a pattern was emerging, since a similar incident involving Callahan had been rumored in 1992. Montgomery was also aware that Sanchez had brought formal complaints against two other individuals in the past, neither of which was substantiated.

Montgomery asked Lange to join the committee reviewing the complaint. Lange's initial reaction was to avoid joining the committee because there was already some tension between her and Callahan. Callahan seemed to fear Lange gaining power at ATI. With an active role in the fact-finding, Lange was afraid she would appear to be trying to sabotage Callahan's career.

Lange believed that Montgomery had asked her to join the committee primarily because she was the top woman at ATI. She resented this burden and realized that she could easily be labeled negatively by other top players at the firm as a result. However, she was also afraid that if she refused, the information gathering would not be handled in a complete and sensitive manner. She worried that avoiding a role in the process would send a signal to Montgomery and others in the firm that she did not consider sexual harassment to be an important issue.

CLASH

The ring of the car phone suddenly interrupted Lange's thoughts. Ruth Goldberg, ATI's executive vice president of human resources, was calling to request a meeting Monday afternoon. Monday was already going to be busy for Lange, but Goldberg was insistent that the family leave question needed to be settled immediately.

Although most of Network Plus and ATI's human resource policies had been integrated at the time of the acquisition, issues surrounding family leave remained unresolved. Currently, in compliance with the Family and Medical Leave Act of 1993, ATI offered up to 12 weeks of unpaid leave. Although employees could take additional time off, their position was not guaranteed upon returning. Network Plus had a much more liberal family leave policy. Employees were allowed up to 6 weeks paid leave, and an additional 18 weeks of unpaid leave could be taken with a comparable position guaranteed upon their return. At the beginning of any paid or unpaid leave, employees must exhaust their sick leave and annual leave as part of that particular family leave.

In general, Goldberg had been hesitant to recognize women's concerns in the workplace, and she felt strongly that Network Plus's family leave policies were too expensive and impractical for the larger organization. Based on preliminary estimates, Goldberg had calculated the total cost to ATI for matching Network Plus's policies at $2.5 million per year. This expense seemed outrageous to Goldberg. She was adamant that the cost was unreasonable for ATI and wanted the software division to conform to ATI's policies.

From Lange's perspective, Goldberg seemed to have enjoyed her position as the only high-ranking female at ATI. Goldberg had been with ATI since its inception in 1965 and was proud to have made it in a "man's world." With Lange on the scene, Goldberg seemed concerned that her power might be usurped. Goldberg had sacrificed a lot to reach her current position and felt no need to make it easier for other women. Throughout her tenure at ATI, Goldberg had been approached by female employees seeking informal career advice and guidance. As the only senior woman at ATI, Goldberg had been overwhelmed by these requests and typically was unsympathetic.

Lange was not sure what approach to take. She felt strongly that the family leave policy should not be taken from her employees who had counted on it. Lange was personally committed to this issue as part of her original vision for Network Plus and did not want to take a step backward, but she was unsure how she could justify its expense. ■

This case is excerpted from the case *Advanced Technology Incorporated, S-W-1,* prepared by Julia B. Bates and Robin G. Joy under the supervision of Constance E. Bagley, senior lecturer of law and management, Stanford University Graduate School of Business, as a basis for class discussion rather than to illustrate either effective or ineffective handling of an administrative situation. The authors gratefully acknowledge the contributions of Dr. Dan R. E. Thomas, president of FOCUS.

PREPARATION QUESTIONS

1. What should Lange do about the possible promotion of Catherine Moore?
2. What should she do about Montgomery's request that she join the committee to investigate the sexual harassment allegation by Denise Sanchez?
3. What should she do about the family leave policy?
4. How should she deal with the communication style problems she has encountered in the executive committee meetings?

CHAPTER 22

Ethical Issues in International Business

Introduction

Ethical issues abound within a country, but they take on added dimensions when a firm operates across national and cultural borders. Countries differ in the institutions that govern their political and economic activity as well as in their customs and culture. Just as there are differences in institutions, there are differences in the issues and practices in their nonmarket environments.

Countries also differ in their capacities to address issues of social and ethical concern. The capacities of many countries are limited by poverty, corruption, and political turmoil. Furthermore, their legal, health care, educational, and social services capabilities are often constrained by limited resources. World Bank (1997) data reported that from 1980 to 1995 per capita real gross domestic product (GDP) in many countries in sub-Saharan Africa decreased substantially from an already impoverished level.[1] For example, the Central African Republic and the Cameroons experienced 13.4 percent and 18.3 percent decreases, respectively. Although autocratic, one-man rule and Marxist policies have been replaced by democracy and private ownership in a number of countries, the base from which they are beginning presents enormous challenges.

In contrast to the differences among countries, ethical systems are intended to be universal; but with such substantial differences among countries, additional complications arise in applying ethics in international settings. For example, are the costs and benefits resulting from an action such as environmental protection in a high-income country the same as the costs and benefits of the same action taken in a low-income country? Is the harm from an injury to a person in a low-income country the same as in a high-income country? Should a firm maintain the same safety and environmental standards in all countries? Do and should individuals in all countries have the same rights? Should practices that are morally unacceptable in one country be acceptable in other countries where they are legal? At a more general level, are the Western ethical systems considered in the previous chapters applicable in countries that do not have the Western intellectual and moral traditions?

Rather than attempt to address the broad range of ethical issues that arise in international business, emphasis here is on four specific issues—culture and moral standards, human rights, operating in a developing country, and questionable foreign payments made to secure sales—and on the use of one set of standards in developed countries and

[1]In contrast, per capita real GDP increased by 26.4 percent in the United States and 127.7 percent in Singapore.

a different set of standards in developing countries, as illustrated by the example of cigarette marketing. These issues are developed further in the chapter cases. Before addressing these issues, international law and institutions are considered.

International Law and Institutions

Interactions between nations and foreign firms are governed by the laws of the host nation and by international law. International law consists of national laws that pertain to foreign persons, entities, and other nations; intergovernmental treaties and agreements; rulings by international courts; and actions of international bodies such as the United Nations and the Organization of American States.[2]

National laws include laws pertaining to international trade; official boycotts such as that against Cuba; the Foreign Corrupt Practices Act (FCPA), and required government approval for the acquisition by a foreign firm of a U.S. firm essential to national defense. Treaties and agreements include the North American Free Trade Agreement, the International Monetary Fund, the Treaty of Rome, the Geneva convention, the Kyoto Treaty on global warming, reciprocal tax agreements, and accords on technical standards. International court rulings include those of the World Court and the European Court of Justice, and the World Trade Organization's dispute resolution mechanism. Actions of international bodies include the United Nations (UN) response to Iraq's invasion of Kuwait, the Law of the Sea, and the UN Convention on Contracts for the International Sale of Goods.

International agreements also provide frameworks within which continuing problems can be addressed. The 1985 Vienna Convention for the Protection of the Ozone Layer provided a framework for addressing ozone depletion and global warming.[3] The 1987 Montreal Protocol on Substances that Deplete the Ozone Layer resulted from this framework and committed the signators to reduce CFCs to 50 percent of 1986 consumption. This reduction was judged insufficient, and the 1989 Helsinki Declaration committed the parties to eliminate all CFC production as soon as possible and no later than 2000.

The international law pertaining to global warming began with United Nations action in 1988 and the 1989 Hague Declaration calling for the establishment of the UN Framework Convention on Climate Change. The convention covers greenhouse gasses not covered by the Montreal Protocol. The convention established a Conference of Nations as well as a secretariat and two advisory committees and committed the parties to concluding a more specific agreement by 1997. The result was the Kyoto Treaty on global warming.

International law differs from domestic law because sanctions may not be credible and enforcement is often left to individual nations. Some sanctions, such as the economic and military sanctions imposed on Iraq for the invasion of Kuwait and others imposed because of international trade violations, have been shown to be credible. Many elements of international law, however, are respected not because of possible sanctions but because of mutual interests in preserving those laws. For example, the Dispute Resolution Body of the World Trade Organization (WTO) rules on trade disputes, but it has no real enforcement powers. It can only authorize a country to retaliate against another country that refuses to halt the trade violation. Nevertheless, the United States has complied with all WTO decisions.

---

[2]See Shaw (1997) for a treatment of international law.

[3]See Shaw (1997, pp. 610–614).

Firms that operate internationally are subject to the laws of both their home country and their host countries, and at times those laws may be inconsistent. Practice and law are also often in conflict, as in the case of questionable foreign payments. The FCPA prohibits practices that are not uncommon in some countries. Because of the demands for payments, a number of companies have adopted codes of conduct that go beyond the requirements of the law. Increasing and persistent corruption and pressure from the United States and other countries resulted in an international agreement to prohibit certain types of bribery.

Practices within a country pose both legal and ethical concerns. In some countries corruption is a fact (although not an inevitable fact) of life in many sectors of business activity.[4] In the mid-1980s Indonesia concluded that corruption and bribery in its ports were impeding economic growth by delaying imports and exports, at times for substantial periods. One report placed the amount of bribes at $200 million annually. To address the problem, the government ordered half the 13,000 employees in the Customs and Excise Service not to report to work. They continued to be paid their full wages, receive benefits, and even promotions, but they were not in a position to extract payments from importers and exporters.[5] A number of countries, including Indonesia, have hired foreign firms to operate their customs service. Similarly, in an unannounced move one night in 1991, Mexico fired all of its customs inspectors working at the U.S. border and replaced them with new inspectors who had been secretly trained by the government. The chapter case *Complications in Marnera* addresses management issues in a country with significant corruption.

Cultural Relativism

In 1991 the Coalition for Justice in the Maquiladoras launched a campaign to improve conditions in the 2,000 U.S. plants located in the area near the U.S. border from Tijuana to Matamoros, Mexico. The coalition argued that although the firms met local standards in Mexico, they should meet the same health, safety, and environmental standards they meet in the United States. "Moral behavior knows no borders. What would be wrong in the United States is wrong in Mexico," said Sister Susan Mika of the Interfaith Center on Corporate Responsibility. Sister Mika expresses the view that moral standards are universal and that the standards in developed countries are the ones that should apply universally. The former is a rejection of cultural relativism, whereas the latter is a claim about particular standards. Costs and benefits in the two countries differ, as is evident in the differences in wage rates and environmental protection. A utilitarian or cost-benefit perspective thus could lead to different standards in Mexico and the United States. Differences also could be expected in terms of distributive justice as a result of the differences in standards of living between the countries.

Ethics, however, requires that firms, as well as individuals, not simply accept existing customs or prevailing practices. Instead, firms and their managers are to evaluate issues of importance in terms of principles and standards that are to be universal.[6] Some cultural differences, such as in the institutions of political representation in democracies, are easily accepted. For example, a democracy with a strong executive and a system of checks and balances as in the United States is morally no better or worse than a parliamentary democracy. Some differences, such as the status of women in some fun-

---

[4]See Palmier (1989) for examples.

[5]*Far Eastern Economic Review,* June 6, 1990.

[6]See Donaldson (1989, Ch. 2) and Freeman and Gilbert (1988, Ch. 2) for analyses and rejections of cultural relativism. Brandt (1959) provides an extended evaluation of ethical relativism.

damentalist Islamic societies, are not easily tolerated. Some differences, such as the suppression of political liberties and human rights in countries such as Myramar (Burma) and North Korea, are not tolerated but are difficult to change.

Sen (1997) argues that generalizations about countries and cultures "hide more than they reveal." He advocates the simultaneous recognition of:

- the significance of cultural variation
- the need to avoid cultural stereotypes and sweeping generalizations
- the importance of taking a dynamic rather than a static view of cultures
- the necessity of recognizing heterogeneity within given communities

In considering the relevance of differences in cultures and in the positions of peoples and nations in their development, it is useful to identify the two extremes of *cultural relativism* and *cultural imperialism* and to recognize that there is a considerable distance between the two. In its strongest version, cultural relativism holds that appropriate behavior in a country or culture is determined by its laws and customs.[7] That is, what is moral is defined by the customs within an individual country; when in Rome, do as the Romans do. If corruption is widespread in a country, then a firm should accept the functioning system and act as domestic firms do. At some level cultural differences surely are important, and it is clear that moral standards differ among cultures. Ethical principles, however, are to be universal rather than culturally determined.

Cultural imperialism in its strongest form means that a firm maintains the standards of its home country and judges others by those standards.[8] Cultural imperialism is limited by laws of the host country, but this perspective is generally intended to apply to situations in which the customs and laws in a host country allow practices that would not be acceptable in the firm's home country.

Donaldson (1996, p. 49) argues that "Cultural relativism is morally blind. There are fundamental values that cross cultures, and companies must uphold them." He also cautions, "At the other end of the spectrum from cultural relativism is ethical imperialism, which directs people to do everywhere exactly as they do at home." In rejecting the latter perspective, Donaldson cites the instance of a U.S. company that caught one of its employees in China stealing and turned the employee in to the authorities—who had the employee executed.

Donaldson (1996) identifies two fundamental conflicts between moral absolutes and local traditions and context. The first is a "conflict of relative development," which requires firms to recognize that countries and their peoples may differ in their capabilities due to their stage of economic development. He advocates that the following question be used to guide practices, "Would the practice be acceptable at home if my country were in a similar stage of economic development?" Levi Strauss & Co., for example, accepts suppliers that pay the prevailing wage and employ children as young as 14, when that is consistent with host country laws. A firm may thus be justified in paying the prevailing wage rate in a country, but should it maintain the prevailing safety standards? One answer to this question is whether the prevailing safety standards are unreasonable to the point of jeopardizing a person's human dignity by failing to treat the person as an end as well as a means.

The second conflict is a "conflict of cultural tradition." In many cases, this conflict is more difficult to resolve. Donaldson (1996, p. 60) argues, "Managers should deem a

---

[7]See Bowie (1990).

[8]De George (1993) argues for an intermediate position in which the goal is not a set of ethical principles on which agreement is unlikely but rather is a set of international guidelines for business practice on which everyone can agree.

practice permissible only if they can answer no to both of the following questions: Is it possible to conduct business successfully in the host country without undertaking the practice? And is the practice a violation of a core human value?" For example, the arbitrary firing of employees is unlikely to be necessary to operate successfully and is a violation of basic principles. A company thus would not be justified in acting in this manner. Bribery and extortion, however, are sufficiently pervasive in some countries that they might be required at times to operate successfully. A company thus could be justified in providing bribes in certain circumstances, as indicated below in the context of questionable foreign payments. Levi Strauss & Co. goes further in asking whether it should do business in a country where the answer is persistently "no" to the first question and "yes" to the second question. The company refuses to do business in Myramar.

Donaldson (1996, pp. 61–62) argues that three general principles should guide businesses:

1. Respect for core human values [human dignity, respect for basic rights, and good citizenship], which determine the absolute moral threshold for all business activities.
2. Respect for local traditions.
3. The belief that context matters when deciding what is right and wrong.

He also offers five guidelines for "ethical leadership": (1) Treat corporate values and formal standards of conduct as absolutes.[9] (2) Design and implement conditions of engagement for suppliers and customers. (3) Allow foreign business units to help formulate ethical standards and interpret ethical issues. (4) In host countries, support efforts to decrease institutional corruption. (5) Exercise moral imagination.

As an example of moral imagination, Levi Strauss faced a dilemma in Bangladesh. It learned that one of its suppliers was employing children younger than 14 years of age. The income earned by the children was important to their often impoverished families, yet their working deprived them of the opportunity to attend school. Faced with this dilemma Levi Strauss convinced the supplier to pay the children their wages and benefits while they attended school and to guarantee that they could return to their jobs once they completed their schooling.[10] Levi Strauss paid for their tuition, books, and school uniforms.

As indicated in Chapters 18 and 19, ethical frameworks can differ in terms of how the good and the right are conceived, their methods of analysis, and their prescriptions. These differences, coupled with the differences among countries, suggest that at least some differences in practices and standards should be tolerated. Yet there are universal principles that are sufficiently important that firms should work toward their achievement. Donaldson (1989, pp. 81–86) proposes that respect for and promotion of rights should be universal and that all nations, firms, and individuals have a duty to respect a certain minimal set of rights. Those rights are the following:

1. Freedom of physical movement
2. Ownership of property
3. Freedom from torture
4. Fair trial
5. Nondiscriminatory treatment (freedom from discrimination on the basis of such characteristics as race and/or sex)
6. Physical security

---

[9]For example, do not make exceptions to standards to improve one's business prospects.
[10]See "Third-World Families at Work: Child Labor or Child Care?" *Harvard Business Review,* January-February, 1993.

7. Speech and association
8. Minimal education
9. Political participation
10. Subsistence

Using a distinction suggested by Shue (1980), Donaldson argues that firms have a duty not to deprive individuals of any of these rights and an affirmative duty to help protect individuals from being deprived of any of the last six rights. He also argues that the rights to nondiscriminatory treatment, political participation, and ownership of property are subject to cultural interpretation. One might disagree about which rights should be included in this set, but the concept that respect for and promotion of certain rights constitutes minimal acceptable behavior is important. The next section considers one company's attempt to address human rights issues through the choice of the countries in which it operates.

Human Rights and Justice

Some ethical issues are not a result of the actions of individuals and firms, but instead are the result of the policies of countries. Particularly in the case of countries that are not democracies, the policies of a country can raise ethical concerns pertaining to human rights and justice. In some countries, firms may be required to implement aspects of these policies. For example, in China firms have responsibilities for enforcing aspects of the government's one-child-per-family law. Many people view this policy as violating basic human rights, such as those spelled out in the Universal Declaration of Human Rights proclaimed by the United Nations in 1948 and endorsed by many countries.

Because of concerns about human rights in the countries in which their suppliers are located, several firms including Levi Strauss & Co. and Reebok have formulated human rights statements pertaining to their business partners. Reebok's "Human Rights Production Standards" covers the following subjects: nondiscrimination, working hours/overtime, fair wages, child labor, freedom of association, and a safe and healthy work environment.

Whereas Reebok applies its standards at the level of its business partner, Levi Strauss also applies its standards at the country level. It concluded that it should not do business with even an exemplary contractor if the policies of its home country resulted in pervasive violations of human rights. The development of its Guidelines for Country Selection is considered in the Part V integrative case *Levi Strauss & Co. Global Sourcing Guidelines* and these guidelines are presented in Figure 22-1 for use in conjunction with the chapter case *Levi Strauss & Co. in China.*

To implement the guidelines, Levi Strauss established an internal country review process that utilized information from a variety of public sources, such as the United Nations and the U.S. Department of State, as well as its own independent assessments. The review process led the company to withdraw immediately from Myramar and to announce that it would withdraw over several years from China. The company also immediately canceled all contracts in China in which prison labor was used, since the prisoners could have been convicted for political reasons.

The Levi Strauss Terms of Engagement policy (Chapter 20) and Guidelines for Country Selection illustrate the relationship between core principles and policies. On one hand, if the human rights conditions in China were to improve substantially, the company could reverse its decision to withdraw, as it did in 1998. On the other hand, its commitment to safety, health, and working conditions standards is irreversible, given the Levi Strauss core principles. The chapter case *University Games, Inc.* addresses related issues facing a small business with limited resources.

The following country selection criteria address issues which we believe are beyond the ability of the individual business partner to control.

1. *Brand Image*

We will not initiate or renew contractual relationships in countries where sourcing would have an adverse effect on our global brand image.

2. *Health & Safety*

We will not initiate or renew contractual relationships in locations where there is evidence that Company employees or representatives would be exposed to unreasonable risk.

3. *Human Rights*

We should not initiate or renew contractual relationships in countries where there are pervasive violations of basic human rights.

4. *Legal Requirements*

We will not initiate or renew contractual relationships in countries where the legal environment creates unreasonable risk to our trademarks or to other important commercial interests or seriously impedes our ability to implement these guidelines.

5. *Political or Social Stability*

We will not initiate or renew contractual relationships in countries where political or social turmoil unreasonably threatens our commercial interests.

Source: Reprinted by permission of Levi Strauss & Co.

FIGURE 22-1 Levi Strauss & Co. Guidelines for Country Selection

SLAVE LABOR IN SAIPAN?

Shortly after their approval, the Global Sourcing Guidelines underwent their first significant challenge. The issue involved a contractor based in the U.S. Territory of Saipan, who worked for a number of apparel firms, including Levi Strauss, Liz Claiborne, and Eddie Bauer. Levi Strauss learned in late 1991 that the contractor was in legal trouble, and one of its vice presidents met with the contractor in San Francisco. He asked blunt questions about the contractor's legal problems, but the contractor assured him that there were only routine problems and that he need not be concerned.

In early 1992 the NBC affiliate in Washington, D.C., broadcast a story about the Saipan contractor, alleging that he was using Chinese workers as "slave labor" and that the merchandise they produced was mislabeled as "Made in the U.S.A." In reality, products produced in Saipan are required to carry that label. The slave labor allegation, however, was more serious. It centered on the common practice in Saipan of bringing young women from China to work in the factories for a few years and then returning them to China. The young women were eager to come because the wages were high compared with wages in China. The story also reported that the contractor was about to plead no contest to a felony charge involving the denial to workers of compensation totaling several million dollars.

Two days after the story broke and a day after it made the national news, Levi Strauss executives met to conduct their own investigation of the Saipan facilities. A small group of senior executives decided to visit the factory and found it to be an excellent facility—better than some in the United States. The dormitories where the workers were housed were substandard, but Levi Strauss concluded that the allegations of slave labor were unwarranted. What was clear, however, was that the contractor had consistently misled Levi Strauss about its dealings. The recently approved Global Sourcing

Guidelines called for business partners with ethical standards consistent with the company's standards. Consequently, Levi Strauss canceled its contract with the Saipan contractor and paid several hundred thousand dollars in contract penalties to do so.

To Levi Strauss executives, the Saipan incident indicated why guidelines were needed. They would protect the company's integrity and commercial success by preventing it from sourcing with contractors with questionable policies.

Operating in Developing Countries

The institutions found in developed countries are not always present in developing countries to provide guidance to firms and their managers. Issues are also more complex when people do not have the means to protect their rights and advance their interests. Poverty, illiteracy, lack of education, and inadequate health care create situations in which individuals cannot be expected to make the same decisions that would be made in a developed country. Furthermore, their governments may not have the means to provide the needed information, guidance, or regulation found in developed countries.

In developed countries, for example, the liability system assigns the social cost of injuries to producers and consumers, thereby creating incentives for care and the reduction of hazards. Regulation establishes safety standards and requires information and warnings about hazards. If these institutions are not present or function imperfectly in a developing country, business is without a principal source of guidance. In such cases, the temptation may be to do whatever maximizes profits given the existing institutions. The consequences, however, may not be acceptable. It could lead to the exploitation of the ignorant and disadvantaged or the exposure of consumers or workers to hazards that they may not reasonably be able to avoid.

In such situations, ethical principles can provide guidance. To understand how a firm might reason in situations in which institutions are imperfect, consider the case of a safety decision about a product marketed in a low-income country. Suppose that the product is safe under proper use but that misuse can result in injury. Many of the people who are likely to buy the product are impoverished and have a minimal formal education. There is no functioning liability system, and regulatory agencies are overburdened and cannot be expected to address the safety issue. The firm and its managers must provide their own guidance on appropriate action.

From a utilitarian perspective, the Calabresi and Melamed principles considered in Chapters 11 and 18 provide a basis for reasoning about the appropriate level of safety and how the product should be marketed. Those principles are intended to be applied in situations in which institutions are imperfect, entitlements and their protection are unclear, and transactions costs prohibit bargaining to resolve the issue. The principles first ask who is best placed to make a cost-benefit analysis of the product and its safety features. In a developed country, the answer is typically that the government is best placed to do so, as reflected in the institutions of liability and regulation. In the absence of those institutions, the responsibility falls on the firm and consumers. In a low-income country, many consumers are poorly placed to evaluate the hazards and exercise proper care. The firm thus has the moral responsibility to make the evaluation.

The Calabresi and Melamed principles also ask which party is in the best position to induce others to take actions that will improve the difference between social benefits and costs. Consumers are certainly not in that position. The firm may be able to induce consumers to use the product properly and to take steps through product design to reduce the hazards from anticipated misuse. The former, for example, might require instructions presented in pictures as well as in words. In addition, marketing might be targeted to those market segments in which the product is most likely to be used properly. Similarly, distribution of the product might be restricted to outlets in which instruction in proper use can be given. In a number of countries, however, these measures may not be sufficient.

The firm then is faced with the prospect of anticipatable misuse. Depending on the product in question, design and safety features may be effective means of reducing hazards, but there are no institutions of liability and regulation to provide information on which safety features to incorporate. The firm then is left with the issue of determining if the social costs of an injury in Bangladesh are the same as in Germany. Compensation for injuries is not the same even among developed countries, and the disparity between developed and developing countries can be considerable. The Calabresi and Melamed principles are incapable of resolving this issue, and utilitarianism evaluates alternatives using the preferences of those affected. This suggests using the trade-offs made in the country between safety and other consequences such as the benefits of the product.

Firms may also be guided by principles of rights and justice. When misuse of a product can be anticipated, marketing to those who are likely to misuse it may constitute deception. This would violate moral rules focusing on treating individuals as ends whose ability to choose should be developed rather than their ignorance exploited. Advertising is often viewed as a culprit in such situations. Hazards that are involuntarily assumed are also objectionable from a rights perspective.

Donaldson (1989, p. 116) addresses the issue of risks in developing countries and proposes a modification of Rawls's second principle to guide decisions about risks. He argues that the "difference principle would need to be adjusted to include freedom from risk as one of the primary goods normally covered by the principle." From this perspective safety should be assumed for all individuals, which suggests that higher standards than those in developing countries should be used.

In low-income countries the marketing and promotion of certain products are claimed by critics to pose an unjustified economic burden on individuals. Distributive justice principles call for relieving the economic burdens of the poor rather than contributing to those burdens. For example, critics argue that the promotion and advertising of cigarettes in developing countries poses not only a health hazard but is also an economic burden on the poor. The chapter case *Marketing Infant Formula in Developing Countries* raises several of these issues.[11]

SWEATSHOPS

In the mid-1990s concern developed in the United States about "sweatshops" that supplied U.S. sporting goods and apparel companies. The issue was propelled by poignant stories of poverty and abuse, and by nonmarket action by labor unions, human rights groups, and activists, as well as pressure from the Department of Labor. The pressure reached a crescendo when abuses at a Nike supplier in Vietnam were reported.[12] (See the Chapter 4 case *Nike in Southeast Asia.*) To improve practices in suppliers' facilities, President Clinton appointed an 18-member White House Apparel Industry Partnership, which included Nike, Reebok, L.L. Bean, Liz Claiborne, unions, human rights groups, and interest group and activist representatives. The task force was charged with

[11]See Clement (1978), Dobbing (1988), McComas, Fookes, and Taucher (1982), and Molander (1980, pp. 264–283) for discussions of Nestle's marketing of infant formula in developing countries.

[12]One result was the 1997 enactment of the Sanders Amendment, which bans the import of foreign products produced with forced child labor.

producing a code and enforcement mechanism to achieve standards including a 60-hour workweek, a minimum employment age of 14, and wage guidelines. The task force, however, became embroiled in strong disagreements about implementation details.

The Union of Needletrade, Industrial, and Textile Employees and activists sought a majority on the governing board of the Fair Labor Association, the organization created by the 18-member partnership to audit compliance with the standards. The companies were worried that the independent groups that conducted the auditing of contractors' facilities would find that some companies met the standards and others did not, giving the former group a public relations advantage over the others. The companies were successful in having the board have 50-50 representation of companies and the other groups. The other sources of disagreement proved to be more difficult, and the task force failed to reach an accord by the deadline. The two sides disagreed on the percent of supplier facilities to be inspected each year, and the labor and human rights groups pressed for a Labor Department study of "living wages," rather than the prevailing wages, for suppliers' employees. The labor and human rights groups also sought a provision directed at China requiring that workers have the right to form unions and engage in collective bargaining. Such a requirement could force companies not to source products in China. Company representatives suggested that the motivation behind these two provisions was protection of union jobs in the United States.

With the partnership deadlocked a group of the members including Liz Claiborne, Nike, and Reebok reached an agreement on standards including a 60 hour work week, a ban on employing children under the age of 15 unless the country explicitly allowed 14-year olds to work, and a requirement to pay the official minimum wage or the prevailing market wage if higher. The agreement also required independent monitoring of suppliers' compliance with the standards. Two members of the partnership, the Needletrades Union and an activist group, rejected the agreement. The U.S. Secretary of Labor praised the agreement, "It is workable for business and creates a credible system that will let consumers know the garments they buy are not produced by exploited workers."[13]

This approach is to be contrasted with the approach taken by Levi Strauss & Co. as discussed in Chapter 20, the chapter case *Levi Strauss & Co. in China,* and the Part V integrative case *Levi Strauss & Co. Global Sourcing Guidelines.* In 1998 Levi Strauss & Co. in a pilot program had independent third parties evaluate the implementation of its Terms of Engagement policy for its suppliers. Five NGOs evaluated implementation at the facilities of four suppliers in the Dominican Republic and produced a set of recommendations for improving implementation. The recommendations primarily focused on training, standardization of evaluation tools and processes, and involving workers more in implementation.[14]

INTERNATIONAL CODES

In 1994 a group of business leaders and academics gathered to identify a set of transcultural values. The resulting Caux Round Table *Principles of Business* set forth both obligations and values derived from the western concept of human dignity and the Japanese concept of *kyosei,* or acting for the common good.[15] According to the Caux Round Table, "*kyosei* means living and working together for the common good—enabling cooperation and mutual prosperity to coexist with healthy and fair competition.

---

[13]*The New York Times,* November 5, 1998.

[14]Levi Strauss & Co., "An Independent Evaluation of Levi Strauss & Co.'s Code of Conduct Process: A Pilot Program in the Dominican Republic," San Francisco, CA, August 1998.

[15]See Skelly (1995) and Kung (1997, pp. 24–25).

'Human dignity' refers to the sacredness or value of each person as an end, not simply as a means to the fulfillment of other's purposes or even majority prescription." The concept of *kyosei* can be understood in the traditional eastern focus on groups beginning with the family and extending outward to the work unit and nation. The concept of human dignity is based on Kant's categorical imperative.

The *Principles for Business* includes a set of "general principles" and a set of "stakeholder principles" identifying responsibilities to customers, employees, owners/investors, suppliers, competitors, and communities. These responsibilities are similar to those espoused by the advocates of corporate social responsibility. The general principles represent an attempt to identify a set of values that can be respected across western and eastern cultures, and they have a strong communitarian flavor. The seven principles are as follows:

1. *The Responsibilities of Business: Beyond Shareholders Toward Stakeholders* ... Businesses have a role to play in improving the lives of all their customers, employees, and shareholders by sharing with them the wealth they have created....
2. *The Economic and Social Impact of Business: Toward Innovation, Justice, and World Community* ... Business also should contribute to human rights, education, welfare, and vitalization of the countries in which they operate. Business should contribute to economic and social development not only in the countries in which they operate, but also in the world community at large, ...
3. *Business Behavior: Beyond the Letter of the Law Toward a Spirit of Trust* ... businesses should recognize that sincerity, candor, truthfulness, the keeping of promises, and transparency contribute not only to their own credibility and stability, but also to the smoothness and efficiency of business transactions, ...
4. *Respect for Rules* ... business should respect international and domestic rules. In addition, they should recognize that some behavior, although legal, may still have adverse consequences.
5. *Support for Multilateral Trade* Businesses ... should cooperate in efforts to promote the progressive and judicious liberalization of trade, and to relax those domestic measures that unreasonably hinder global commerce, while giving due respect to national policy objectives.
6. *Respect for the Environment* A business should protect, and where possible, improve the environment, promote sustainable development, and prevent the wasteful use of natural resources.
7. *Avoidance of Illicit Operations* A business should not participate in or condone bribery, money laundering, or other corrupt practices: indeed, it should seek cooperation with others to eliminate them....

Questionable Foreign Payments

In a number of countries, the exchange of gifts and favors is customary, and in some cases favors may extend into the domain of unethical conduct. In a country in which small payments to low-level government employees are necessary to clear administrative hurdles, a firm may be justified in making the payments to avoid a greater injustice. When those payments are recurring and pervasive, however, the question of which is the greater injustice remains. A firm may decide to forgo sales if those sales necessitate a serious violation of ethical principles.

When corruption is pervasive, a company may decide to withdraw from a country. A Unilever executive explained the company's decision to leave Bulgaria: "It was impossible for us to do business without getting involved in corruption. So we took the logical step and accepted the consequences. That meant packing our bags.[16]

QUESTIONABLE PAYMENTS AND ETHICAL PRINCIPLES

In 1975 the disclosure that the Lockheed Corporation had made payments of over $12 million to Japanese business executives and government officials to secure a sale of commercial aircraft led to revelations that over 450 U.S. companies had made similar payments totaling more than $300 million worldwide. The questionable foreign payments ranged from outright bribes to obtain sales to extortion payments made to customs officials to avoid delays in the clearance of imports. In response, Congress passed the Foreign Corrupt Practices Act (FCPA) of 1977.

Some payments were made because firms, or their sales representatives, had reason to believe that competitors were offering payments to a customer. In an industry or a country in which such payments are common, a firm may be unable to change the practice, and the payments can be self-perpetuating.[17] This, however, does not provide a moral justification for the practice and change can occur.[18] In Italy corruption and bribery were widespread and involved many of the country's most prominent companies, business executives, and leaders of the major political parties. Revelations about the scope of the corruption resulted in widespread moral condemnation and led to prosecutions, a major restructuring of the electoral system, the formation of new parties, and changes in government.

In a situation in which payments are either demanded or likely to be required to obtain a sale, firms and their managers have two sources of guidance—one is ethics and the other is laws such as the FCPA. Ethical evaluation will be considered first, and then the law will be presented and interpreted. Corporate codes of conduct will then be considered. The ethical analysis focuses on bribery and the question of when, if ever, a firm is morally justified in making such a payment.

A bribe is a payment to an individual in an organization intended to influence that person's exercise of his or her responsibilities; that is, a bribe is intended to corrupt the behavior of the recipient. Bribery is ethically objectionable on a number of grounds. From a utilitarian perspective, bribery distorts markets and hence efficiency. That is, when bribes replace value and merit as the basis for decisions, competition cannot be as efficient. From a rights perspective, bribery distorts the fair opportunity to compete on value and merit in markets. Furthermore, bribes induce the recipients to violate a duty to the principals who employ them.

More fundamentally, the bases for Kant's moral rules are violated. First, a rule under which bribes are paid is not universalizable because there is little reason to believe that individuals would will a competition in bribes rather than a competition without bribes. Second, bribery is not reversible. A firm would not want its own purchasing agents to make their decisions based on the bribes they receive.

With respect to justice, bribes paid to government officials undermine the impartiality of government and hence the equality of political rights. In terms of the fair equality of opportunity, a bribe exploits the position a person occupies in the recipient organization. Also, people who might seek that position may not be equally informed about the bribery associated with it, so the position is not open to everyone under the

---

[16]*The Wall Street Journal,* February 16, 1999.

[17]See Carson (1987) and Philips (1984) for perspectives on bribery.

[18]Klitgaard (1988) discusses the steps taken by the U.S. Army to overcome corruption in the construction and supply industries in Korea in the 1970s.

information that its holder may receive such payments. Furthermore, the recipient may receive too much, having done nothing to deserve it. Bribes would also not be expected to benefit the least advantaged, even indirectly.

The remaining issue is whether bribes are justified if there is a greater injustice that can be avoided. This issue is considered next in the context of the Lockheed case.

THE LOCKHEED CASE

The Lockheed case is described by Vice Chairman A. Carl Kotchian (1977), who authorized the payments in Japan. The $12 million payments in question represented less than 3 percent of the revenue on the L-1011 aircraft sold to All Nippon Airlines (ANA). The payments were made to the office of the prime minister, to seven other politicians and government officials, and to the president of ANA. The payments were not illegal under U.S. law at the time, and such payments were not unknown in the aircraft industry.[19] However, the payments were in violation of Japanese law, and if Kotchian had been unsure of their legality in Japan, he could have contacted a Japanese lawyer or the commercial attaché at the U.S. embassy. In Japan it is customary to give gifts, but an individual payment of $1.7 million cannot be viewed as a gift nor as a routine political contribution.[20] Similarly, a payment of $50,000 per aircraft to the president of ANA could not be viewed as a part of the functioning system and represented the exploitation of his position in the company.

Mr. Kotchian offered several justifications for making the payments.[21] He argued that the payments were "worthwhile from Lockheed's standpoint" because "they would provide Lockheed workers with jobs, and thus redound to the benefit of their dependents, their communities, and stockholders of the corporation."[22] As considered in Chapter 18, this is casuist reasoning in that an unethical action is claimed to be justified by the benefits it provides stakeholders. From a utilitarian perspective, the benefits to Lockheed's stakeholders are likely to be little different from the benefits to Boeing's or McDonnell Douglas's constituents if they were to obtain the sale. Furthermore, markets in which a competition in bribes takes place will not function as efficiently as when decisions are made on the basis of merit and value.

The ethical reasoning about this case depends on whether in the absence of payments ANA would have selected Lockheed aircraft. If ANA would have selected another aircraft supplier, Lockheed's payments would be an explicit bribe, which cannot be ethically justified. Lockheed could have reduced the price of the aircraft, in which case the benefit would accrue to ANA and not to its officers and government officials.

A second possibility is that ANA would have purchased the L-1011 even if the payments were not made. The ethical issue then is whether Lockheed would be justified in making the payments, which, under this supposition, would be a response to extortion,

---

[19]Lockheed's subsequent legal problems in the United States were due to a failure to disclose the payments as required by U.S. law. Lockheed later disclosed other payments made to secure sales, including a commission paid to Prince Bernard of the Netherlands. See Hay and Gray (1981, pp. 134–138) for a discussion of some of the Lockheed payments. In 1982, the Boeing Company pleaded guilty and paid a $400,000 fine for 40 counts of failure to disclose to the Export-Import Bank that it had paid "irregular commissions" to agents involved in foreign sales. (The Export-Import Bank requires such disclosure on any sales it finances.) In 1981 the McDonnell Douglas Corporation pleaded guilty to fraud and false statements and paid fines of over $1.2 million.

[20]It might also be argued that the payments were justified because they were a part of the functioning system in the aircraft industry. This, however, is not a moral justification, even if the competitive situation demands payments.

[21]See Drucker (1981) for another evaluation of this case.

[22]Kotchian (1977, p. 12).

as Kotchian claimed it was. He wrote: "From a purely ethical and moral standpoint I would have declined such a request [for payments]. However, in that case, I would most certainly have sacrificed commercial success."[23] Extortion involves the use of coercion to extract a payment. Such a payment would be morally justified in the case of ransom paid in a kidnapping, for example. The difference between a ransom payment and the payments that Lockheed made, however, is that if after the fact Lockheed had publicly revealed the payments, the public would have reacted quite differently than it would in the case of a ransom payment. The Lockheed payments thus do not pass Gert's injustice test (Chapter 19) or the "public disclosure" test discussed in Chapter 19. Gert's test for when an injustice is warranted to avoid a greater injustice requires that a rational observer would understand the reason for the action. That test would surely not be met. That is, Lockheed would have had difficulty justifying the payments to the Japanese and American publics.

A third possibility is that the payments were required to match payments offered by other aircraft manufacturers. This situation is considered next.

A UTILITARIAN ANALYSIS OF BRIBERY

From a utilitarian perspective bribery is bad because it distorts economic transactions away from those that produce the greatest well-being. To illustrate this, consider the following example involving two companies A and B seeking a contract for a sale to country C. Company A's product is likely better for C than is the product of company B and in the absence of bribes would likely be selected by C. If no bribes are offered, the expected utilities of A and B and country C are 4, 2, and 14, respectively. For example, suppose that the profit on the sale will be $6 million, and in the absence of bribery the likelihood that A will be selected is two-thirds and the likelihood that B will be selected is one-third.

Consider the possibility that the government officials responsible for selecting the contract can be bribed. If one company offers a bribe and the other does not, its probability of winning the contract becomes one. Bribery involves transactions costs because both parties must conceal the payments and take other measures to justify the selection. Suppose that the utilities if A does not bribe whereas B does bribe are 0, 5, and 9, respectively.[24] The utilities if A does not bribe and B does are 5, 0, and 11. If both companies make bribe payments, the utilities are 2, 1, and 12. These utilities are presented in Table 22-1.

Under rule utilitarianism each of the three parties chooses actions for A and B simultaneously based on the greatest aggregate utility. The aggregate utilities are presented in Table 22-2. The moral rule thus is that both A and B not bribe.

Since bribery is common if not widespread, a natural question is whether a counteracting bribe is ethically justified. From the perspective of rule utilitarianism, the answer is "no." From an act utilitarianism perspective, however, the question is posed as "Should A offer a bribe if B is offering a bribe?" From Table 22-2, if B is offering a bribe, A should offer a bribe because that results in an aggregate utility of 15 compared with 14 if it does not offer a bribe. Such reasoning can perpetuate bribery and is inappropriate.[25]

---

[23]Kotchian (1977, p. 12).

[24]Recall that B's product is worse for C than is A's product so C's utility if B is selected is lower than if A is selected.

[25]The same question can be posed regarding whether B should offer a bribe if A is offering a bribe. The answer is no, since the aggregate utility with only A bribing is 16, whereas if both offer bribes, it is 15.

TABLE 22-1 Utilities of A, B, and C

		Company B	
		Not Bribe	*Bribe*
Company A	*Not Bribe*	(4, 2, 14)	(0, 5, 9)
	Bribe	(5, 0, 11)	(2, 1, 12)

Another test is whether a matching bribe is justified to avoid a greater injustice. The test provided in Chapter 19 is: "A violation of a moral rule [offering a bribe] can be justified by providing reasons which would result in either some impartial rational persons advocating that that kind of violation be publicly allowed, or less frequently, all impartial persons advocating that such a violation be publicly allowed." A more applied version of the test is: "If I disclosed publicly that I had taken the action would the public understand and approve of my action?"

In the case of bribes, if one can show that the payment is extortion, the public is likely to approve of it. If the payment is to induce the recipient to take an action that the recipient has a duty to take and that does not affect the outcome of the business transaction, the public is likely to approve of the payment. If one is offering a bribe unilaterally, the public surely would not approve. If one can show that the payment matches a payment that a competitor is offering, would the public approve? In some countries the answer would be "yes." In the United States the FCPA requires the answer "no." That is, pay no bribes but instead work to convince others not to offer or accept bribes.

A practical problem in applying the injustice standard is how to show that a competitor is offering a bribe. Both the offeror and the recipient have strong incentives to deny it, which is one reason bribery is difficult to eradicate.

Another reason not to pay bribes in situations in which there will be repeated encounters was provided by an executive of a global company. He said, "If you pay once, you pay forever."

THE FOREIGN CORRUPT PRACTICES ACT

In the Lockheed case the payments were made both through an official agent, the Marubeni Trading Company, and a confidential consultant. In conducting business in foreign countries, it is often advisable to retain the services of a national who is familiar with the system in that country and has contacts that will, at a minimum, save time in arranging appointments and may help speed contracts through the host country's institutional structure. These agents are often compensated on a fee or commission basis, and the disposition of those monies may be known only to them. If a portion of the commissions might be passed on to influence the actions of customers or government officials, the firm may be contributing to a corrupt act. Ethically, the firm has an obligation

TABLE 22-2 Aggregate Utility

		Company B	
		Not Bribe	*Bribe*
Company A	*Not Bribe*	20	14
	Bribe	16	15

to instruct its agent about which practices are acceptable and which are unacceptable. Moreover, the firm has a duty to monitor the activities of its agents. The FCPA addresses these issues, among others.[26]

The FCPA makes bribery of foreign officials, political parties, and candidates for office a criminal offense. It provides for a fine of up to $1 million for the company and up to $10,000 and imprisonment for not more than 5 years for an individual making a payment or offer covered by the act. It assigns the burden of knowing whether illegal payments are being made to the company and imposes detailed record-keeping requirements. Under the FCPA, it is unlawful for a company subject to the Securities Exchange Act of 1934 to make any "offer, payment, promise to pay, or authorization of the payment of any money, or offer, gift, promise to give, or authorization of anything to (1) any foreign official for purposes of (A) influencing any act or decision of such foreign official . . . (B) inducing such foreign official to use his influence with a foreign government or instrumentality thereof . . . in order to assist . . . in obtaining or retaining business. . . ." The term *foreign official* "does not include any employee of a foreign government or any department, agency, or instrumentality thereof whose duties are essentially ministerial or clerical." The FCPA thus allows "facilitating payments" to low-level government employees. It also does not prohibit payments to private businesses.

The use of intermediaries or third parties is also covered. In its original language, the act pertained to "any person, while knowing or having reason to know "about a payment for the purposes listed above. After the first few years of experience with the FCPA, however, a poll of 1,200 large businesses indicated that substantial sales had been lost in countries in which bribery was a common practice.[27] Although U.S. firms indicated that they supported the FCPA, 68 percent of the respondents stated that the record-keeping burden should be reduced and that the law should be more specific about who in a foreign country can receive payments and for what purposes.

The Omnibus Trade and Competitiveness Act of 1988 amended the FCPA in several ways. First, it altered the language about the use of third parties or intermediaries by eliminating the phrase "or having reason to know." Second, a payment to a foreign individual became illegal under the act if it is illegal in the foreign country. Third, if a payment were legal in the foreign country, the defendant in an action brought under the act could use that legality as a defense. Fourth, the language of the act was clarified to indicate that payments that secure performance of routine government actions, such as signing customs documents and unloading or loading cargoes, are not illegal. Fifth, the amendments provided firms with a number of affirmative defenses, including consistency with host country laws and legitimate business expenses.

COMPANY CODES

Most firms have policies or codes to ensure compliance with the FCPA and to clarify when foreign payments can be made and how they are to be accounted for. The three principal purposes of these codes are to provide guidance to employees, to make it easier for them to say "no" to requests for payment, and to discourage requests for payments from the firm and its representatives.

The extent to which a firm encounters demands for payments and is tempted to make them depends on its lines of business, the countries in which it does business, and its organization. Some industries and some countries are characterized by a functioning system in which bribery and facilitating payments are common. A firm's lines of business and the countries in which it operates thus affect the scope of the problems it faces. That

---

[26]See Pastin and Hooker (1988) and Alpern (1988) for ethical analyses of the FCPA.
[27]*Business Week,* September 19, 1983.

scope is also affected by the organizational structure of the firm. Firms may conduct their foreign business through a wholly-owned subsidiary, a joint venture, a sales office that manages local dealers and distributors, or agents with whom the firm deals at arms length. Controlling and monitoring payments generally become more difficult and making questionable payments becomes easier the more independent is the intermediary.

Company codes typically state the principal features of the FCPA; require that the representative of the firm know the local laws and the functioning system in the country; distinguish between gratuities, facilitating payments, and bribes; and specify record-keeping and reporting requirements. A code may also provide guidance for handling a request for a payment and indicate to whom an employee is to turn if a payment's propriety is in question. Firms have also established auditing procedures to detect illegal payments. In many firms, managers and sales representatives are required to pledge to abide by the FCPA and company guidelines.

As an example of the content of a code, Hewlett Packard's Standards of Business Conduct includes the following policy for "Foreign Sales Representatives, Agents and Consultants":

> Commission or fee arrangements shall be made only under written agreement with firms or persons serving as bona fide commercial sales representatives, agents or consultants. Any commission or fee for assistance in securing orders or for services must be reasonable and consistent with normal practice for the industry, the products involved, and the services to be rendered. Such arrangements shall not be entered into with any firm in which a government official or employee has an interest unless permitted by law and with the prior written approval of HPs General Counsel. Payments shall not be made in cash.[28]

These policies not only provide guidance to managers and sales representatives, but they also establish a basis for a response when a government official or a customer demands a payment. A response that "company policy does not permit it" may, in some cases, lead to the demand being retracted. Furthermore, knowledge that the firm does not make such payments may eventually decrease the number of requests. For this to be effective, however, the firm must establish a reputation for not responding to such demands.

CUMMINS PRACTICE

The Cummins Engine Company's policy about questionable foreign payments is striking in its articulation of a principle for reasoning about whether a payment should be made in a particular instance. Cummins states its "Primary Ethical Guide":

> The key element which distinguishes ethically unacceptable payments is the corruption of [a] relationship of trust. When a company pays an agent of a buyer in order to influence that agent's purchasing decision, and when that payment is not known to the buyer, the company corrupts a relationship of trust between buyer and agent. The buyer's expectation that his agent will act with only the buyer's interest in mind is betrayed. Similarly, when a company pays a government agent in order to influence that agent's official decisions, the company corrupts a relationship of trust between the public and that official. The corruption of such a relationship of trust not only violates fundamental principles of fair dealing but also hampers efficient economic development and undermines social cohesion.[29]

---

[28] Hewlett Packard Corporation, "Standards of Business Conduct," Palo Alto, CA, 1989.
[29] Cummins Practices, October 1, 1980.

Using the concept of higher order standards introduced in Chapter 19, Cummins's guide meets both the Kantian standard and the standard of rule utilitarianism. It treats the buyer as an autonomous end, and the rule of not corrupting a relationship of trust is one that people would will to be universal. From the perspective of rule utilitarianism the guide supports efficiency by requiring competition to be on a commercial basis rather than on bribes.

Figure 22-2 displays the framework of this principle. In contrast to Kotchian's analysis, which focuses on the consequences to the firm from making the payment, Cummins's principle focuses on the buyer and its agent. That agent is in a relationship of trust with its principal. (Shareholders are the principals of private firms, and citizens may be regarded as the principals of a government agency.) In this relationship, the agent is to serve the interests of the principal, and accepting a bribe sacrifices the interests of the principal for the interests of the agent. Cummins applies this reasoning in the tests that an employee is to use in determining if a payment is unacceptable. "Does this payment undermine a relationship of trust? What expectations does the principal have of his agent in the particular transaction at issue? Is the payment known to the principal or is it not?"

Payments are allowable under Cummins's principle only if three conditions are met: "a. The payment is required to induce the official to perform a routine act which he is already under a duty to perform . . . b. The payment is consistent with local practice. If the payment is consistent with local practice, it is reasonable to assume that it is consistent with public expectations of official behavior, and c. There is no reasonable alternative available for obtaining the official act or service at issue."

Although the phrase "reasonable alternative" is not precise, condition c. requires the company to consider such possibilities as reducing the price or expediting delivery to obtain the sale. Reducing the price to make the sale, rather than paying a bribe, causes the benefit to go to the principal rather than the agent, which is consistent with the relationship of trust. The relevant test is the requirement that the Cummins employee determine whether the principal knows of the payment, since then the principal can determine where the benefit should reside.

In cases in which the employee is uncertain whether a payment is allowable, Cummins states, "Where there is a question as to the propriety of a particular payment in view of the foregoing standards, the payment should not be made." To encourage compliance, Cummins also assures that "no employee is put at a career disadvantage because of his or her willingness to raise a question about a corporate practice or unwillingness to pursue a course of action which seems inappropriate or morally dubious." Cummins also provides its version of the public disclosure test: "Cummins employees do nothing in search of business that they should not reveal willingly and publicly to any other member of the Cummins family or to any government official in any land."

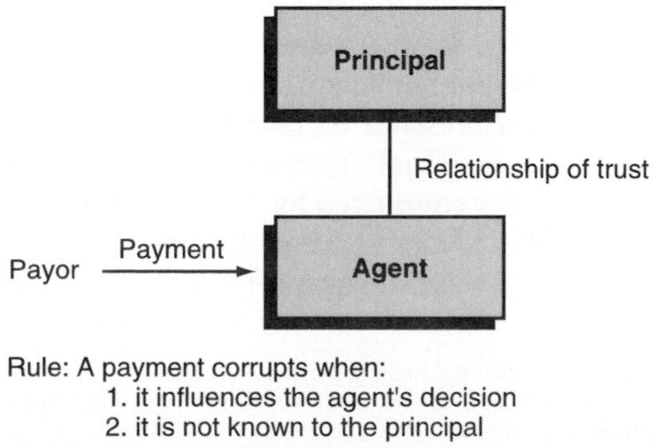

FIGURE 22-2 Cummins Engine Company: Questionable Foreign Payments and the Relationship of Trust

In addition to providing principles on which to reason and standards for assessing when a payment is allowable, Cummins's standards go beyond the FCPA by prohibiting corrupt payments to private, as well as to public, buyers. Recognizing that in some countries payments that do not satisfy its three standards could be necessary to do business, Cummins states that it will "accept the loss of business." If the pattern of acceptable payments continues, Cummins states that it will bring the matter to the attention of the host government to determine how the government wants the matter to be handled. If the demands for payments persist, Cummins is prepared to forgo the business. The chapter case *Complications in Marnera* raises a number of similar issues.

THE OECD CONVENTION ON COMBATING BRIBERY

For over two decades the Foreign Corrupt Practices Act stood alone among the developed countries with its imposition of both criminal penalties and stringent requirements for reporting and monitoring. The United States estimated that its companies lost billions of dollars a year in sales because of bribes paid by companies from other countries. In France, Germany, and most other European countries, bribes and other payments to foreign officials were tax deductible if required to secure a sale. With the growth in foreign direct investment in developing countries and increased trade, the scale of corruption expanded, and more countries became concerned about both the effect of corruption not only on business activity but also on the countries that received the payments. Pressure from the United States and other countries and from organizations such as Transparency International, an NGO founded in 1993 in Berlin by a former World Bank official, led to negotiations within the OECD.[30] The result was the 1997 Convention on Combating Bribery of Foreign Officials in International Business Transactions, signed by the 29 OECD member countries plus Argentina, Brazil, Bulgaria, Chile, and the Slovak Republic.

The Convention took effect in 1999 and makes the act of bribery and the making of other forms of illicit payments to foreign government officials a criminal offense, whether paid directly or indirectly "in order to obtain or retain business or other improper advantage in the conduct of international business."[31] Small "facilitation" payments that are not made "to obtain or retain business" are not viewed as an offense. A foreign government official is defined to include not only those holding elective or appointive office, but also officials of public agencies and public enterprises at least 50 percent owned by the government. The Convention also imposes record-keeping obligations on businesses, so that payments can be identified.

The bargaining on the Convention indicated the complexity of the issue. Since in many developing countries the government owns or controls many companies, the United States argued and eventually was successful in including government-controlled companies under the Convention. The United States also successfully obtained inclusion of elected members of parliament in the category of government officials, over the objections of Austria, Germany, and Finland which allowed payments to their members of parliament provided the payments were not to influence votes. The United States lost, however, in its attempt to include payments to political parties as an offense.

One source of pressure on countries to curb bribes is the annual publication of Transparency International's Corruption Perception Index (CPI). The CPI is developed from annual surveys conducted by six organizations plus data compiled from Internet services. According to its chairman, "Transparency International is not saying in this index that one country is more corrupt than another. We are reporting how business peo-

---

[30]Transparency International has chapters in 60 countries.

[31]The Convention pertains to "active corruption" committed by the offeror of a bribe rather than to "passive corruption" committed by the recipient of the bribe.

ple, political analysts, and the general public around the globe perceive levels of corruption in different countries." In the 1998 CPI for 85 countries, the five with the best ratings were Denmark, Finland, Sweden, New Zealand, and Iceland, and the five with the lowest ratings were Cameroon, Paraguay, Honduras, Tanzania, and Nigeria. The United States was rated 17 and China 52. Among large countries with populations over 30 million the United Kingdom was highest, ranked at 11 with Germany at 15.

Summary

Countries differ considerably in terms of their history, culture, resources, and institutions, yet fundamental ethical principles are intended to be universal rather than culture specific. Cultural relativism, in which one relies solely on host country laws and practices, is inappropriate, yet differences among countries cannot be ignored. The principles underpinning utilitarianism, rights theories, and theories of justice are useful guides for operating across borders and provide minimal constraints on behavior. The application of these principles, however, leaves unresolved issues about trade-offs among costs and benefits, how duties to ensure rights are assigned, and how justice considerations are to be taken into account.

Guidance for managers is provided by international, host country, and home country law and by ethical principles. International law has force, yet its enforcement is often irregular and its application to moral issues is often limited to general, rather than specific, statements. Host country law is an important guide, and when those laws meet universal standards they are to be respected. If they do not meet those standards, firms must develop policies based on principles. Firms also must determine whether they will apply the same standards to their operations in all countries or adapt their policies and practices to each host country. This is a particular challenge in low-income countries that do not have the capacity to regulate and enforce standards or in which the people prefer economic development to maintaining the standards maintained by high-income countries.

In some countries practices may violate fundamental principles, and those practices may be pervasive. Bribery and other forms of illicit payments are common in some countries. The FCPA and the OECD Convention provide guidance, assign duties, and impose penalties for violations. However, laws leave a variety of issues, such as payments to private companies, unaddressed. In such cases, principles in addition to host country practices can provide guidance. Utilitarianism concludes that bribery is morally wrong. Some managers argue that bribes are required because they are extorted by government officials or match bribes offered by competitors. In such cases, the injustice standard is applicable and requires that the manager ask whether, if the payment were publicly disclosed, the publics in the host and home country would agree that it should have been made.

The approach of Cummins Engine is useful for guiding managers in their reasoning about such issues, even if one does not reach the same conclusions as that company reaches. That approach involves a statement of principles, a method for reasoning from those principles to the specifics of a situation, standards that managers are to apply, and protection for individuals who raise such issues within the firm.

The range of ethical issues that arise in multinational operations is much broader than those in a firm's home country, and in developing countries the institutions found in developed countries may be missing or function imperfectly. Furthermore, the facts of the situations encountered internationally may be more difficult to uncover. These factors complicate the application of ethical principles and leave managers with the difficult task of formulating policies guided by a combination of law, ethical principles, and culture.

CASES

Complications in Marnera

Pat Liu and her team of engineers from the Bolton Engineering and Construction Company would be spending the next 6 months in Marnera while the government selected the contractor to develop a copper and gold mine in a remote part of the country. The project was likely to produce revenue of nearly $200 million over the next 7 years. Bolton had just completed a successful mining project in a neighboring country, and Liu believed that Bolton was best qualified for the job because of that experience. This project was particularly important because Bolton wanted to avoid laying off the engineers who had been working on the project in the neighboring country. Bolton had a modest local operation in Marnera, but Liu was the ranking Bolton official and would be in charge over the next 6 months. If Bolton were to win the contract, she would have responsibility for the project.

Upon arriving at the airport in Marnera, Liu and her team encountered an immediate problem. Each member of the team carried a top-of-the-line laptop computer, and in a traveling case they had brought along three spares in case a computer were to develop problems due to the high humidity in Marnera. The customs official inspecting their bags expressed concern that Liu might try to sell the computers in Marnera. Selling the computers would violate import laws that required a license and customs duty for the sale of imported computers. Liu explained that the computers were for backup and would be used only by Bolton employees. The customs inspector remained concerned, however, and said that he would have to impound all their computers until either Bolton obtained a license and paid the customs duty or a hearing on the matter could be scheduled. The customs official said that he realized that they needed their computers and that the process of obtaining a license and paying the duty would take only a few weeks. A local Bolton employee who had met Liu and her party at the airport asked whether it would be possible for the customs inspector to take care of the matter if Bolton would entrust the customs fee to him. The customs official nodded. Needing the computers Liu decided to give the fee to the customs official, who stamped their customs declarations allowing the team and their computers to enter the country.

Shortly thereafter Liu encountered the tax system in Marnera. The tax laws were clear, but their interpretation and enforcement were a different matter. For corporations the typical approach was for the National Tax Service (NTS) to send a company a bill for its taxes. The tax bill was an estimate based on previous years or on estimates of what the company might have earned. The tax bill was understood by those familiar with the system as an invitation to negotiate with the NTS over the actual payment. Companies typically engaged the services of a licensed tax accountant or attorney to conduct the negotiations on their behalf. Bolton decided to seek the advice of a highly regarded and well-connected local attorney, who indicated that for a fee of 2 million richas he could take care of the matter and negotiate a quite reasonable tax bill. Liu expressed surprise at the size of the fee, and the attorney explained that much of the 2 million richas was for expenses that would be incurred during the negotiations with the NTS. The attorney said that this was the standard practice in Marnera and that the fee was tax deductible. The attorney also explained to Liu that if she did not hire someone to handle the negotiations, Bolton would undoubtedly be assessed a final tax bill at least as high as the initial bill. He said that the NTS inspectors had a variety of means to increase tax bills, the easiest of which was to disqualify certain costs as non-tax-deductible. Liu thanked the attorney for his advice and told him that she would get back to him within the week. Concerned about how the 2 million richas would be used, Liu decided to call the commercial attaché at the U.S. embassy whom she had met at a social event. The commercial attaché assured Liu that hiring an attorney to negotiate a company's tax bill was customary in Marnera. When Liu asked what the fee would be used for, the attaché avoided the question. Liu had to decide whether to hire the attorney or prepare Bolton's own tax statement.

In making final preparations for her presentation to the Ministry of Mining, Liu was surprised to learn from the managing director of Bolton's Marnera office that the bidding process had been changed. Instead of evaluating the bids directly, the Ministry would first select a preferred bidder based on its assessment of the technological capabilities of the bidders, their expressed willingness to utilize local suppliers, costs, and intangible factors. Then the Ministry would solicit final bids with the preferred bidder having the right to make the last bid—a right of first refusal. If the preferred bidder matched the highest bid of other contractors, it would be awarded the contract. If it did not match the highest bid, the selection process would be reopened.

One factor important in the cost of completing the project was the level of safety to provide for workers. Bolton could maintain U.S. safety standards and procedures or it could use the prevailing practices in Marnera. With U.S. safety standards and procedures, the pace of work would be slower, requiring the hiring of more workers to complete the project on time. This could add five percent to the cost of the project. Much of the work involved in bringing in roads, power, and water to the mine site, as well as the work on the mine itself, was hazardous, and accidents could be expected. Following the prevailing practices would result in more accidents, and in Marnera there was neither a system of workers' compensation nor a functioning liability system that would allow injured workers to sue for damages. Instead, the local custom was that if an employee were injured on the job and unable to work, that employee's job would be given to another family member so that the family would be supported. Two questions entered Liu's mind. First, what was the right decision regarding safety? Second, if the right decision were to use U.S. standards, would Bolton be at a competitive disadvantage relative to its competitors?

Before leaving for Marnera Liu had been warned that one of Bolton's European competitors would undoubtedly offer payments directly to the top officials at the Ministry of Mining. Such payments were prohibited by U.S. law and by the recently negotiated OECD Recommendation on Bribery in International Business Transactions, and nations were to bring their domestic laws into harmony with the OECD Recommendation.[1] A number of countries still had laws that allowed their companies to make such payments if necessary to obtain business, and the payments were tax deductible. Some countries were expected to move slowly in changing their laws. Then, the matter of enforcement remained.

As a precaution Liu wondered if she should engage the services of the local attorney to represent the company before the Ministry. She was particularly concerned about the effect that losing the bid would have on the employees of Bolton, many of whom would lose their jobs if she failed to get this contract. "It would be unfair if we lose this contract to one of our rivals because of questionable payments," she thought.

Thinking ahead to the possibility of Bolton being selected as the preferred bidder, Liu wondered how high competitors might bid. She mused that it would be fortunate if they confined their aggressiveness to the competition for selection as the preferred bidder.

In anticipation of the competition for the mining project, the managing director of Bolton's Marnera operations had been developing a relationship with the vice minister of Mining. He had recently attended a reception at the vice minister's home and had brought his wife and children expensive gifts. The vice minister had mentioned that he was hoping to send his eldest son to a university in England, but the cost seemed prohibitive. ■

[1]The OECD does not have legislative or enforcement authority. Legislation and enforcement are the responsibility of the member nations.

PREPARATION QUESTIONS

1. How should Liu reason about these situations from the perspective of utilitarianism? What other considerations are relevant?
2. Should Liu have made the payment to the customs official?
3. Should Liu engage the services of the tax attorney to deal with the tax matter?
4. What should Liu do about the safety issue?
5. What, if anything, should Liu do given the likelihood that the European company would offer a payment? Consider the issue from the perspectives of act and rule utilitarianism.
6. What should Liu do if Bolton were selected as the preferred bidder?

Marketing Infant Formula in Developing Countries

In 1972 the United Nations Protein Advisory Committee reported on the dilemma faced by developing countries as they tried to promote breastfeeding while making infant formula available for infants whose mothers could not lactate or chose not to nurse. Infant formula is a nutritious product that provides the needed protein that is often deficient in the diet of infants in low-income countries. Some form of infant food is necessary for infants whose mothers are unable to lactate and do not have access to a wet nurse. A supplement food is also necessary once infants reach the age of 4 to 8 months. Traditional infant food, or home brews, as well as infant formula, can be used, but as Dobbing (1988) notes, "Traditional supplementary feeds are almost invariably nutritionally inadequate as well as contaminated ... such feeds ... include rice cooked in broth or mixed with bananas, or rice previously chewed by the mother and fed directly from her mouth into the baby's (Thailand and Bangladesh . . .), sugar, sweet beverages or raw milk (Zaire . . .), and bush tea (Jamaica . . .), as well as home-made paps in many parts of the world, and gruels made from local grain, for example in parts of West Africa."

In contrast to traditional supplements, infant formula is nutritious and, when properly prepared, contributes to infant health and well-being. Proper preparation requires boiling the water mixed with the powdered formula, mixing the proper amount with the water, sterilizing the nipple and the bottle, and, if more than one serving is prepared, refrigerating the remainder. In some countries, many low income people have neither access to treated water nor the means to prepare or store the formula properly. Poverty may lead to dilution of the formula and hence to malnutrition, and boiling the water, sterilization, and refrigeration may not be feasible. When prepared improperly, the use of infant formula can result in persistent diarrhea and marasmus. Traditional supplements can result in similar problems.

Breastfeeding has a variety of advantages over other infant foods. First, unless the mother herself is malnourished, breast milk is nutritious. Second, it is essentially costless. Third, breast milk contains the mother's antibodies, which protect infants against disease. Fourth, breastfeeding contributes to wider spacing between babies. Estimates indicate that 90 to 95 percent of mothers are able to breastfeed. However, many women in developing countries, as in developed countries, view the use of infant formula as "modern." In testimony before a Senate committee Professor Derrick Jelliffe said, "We have calculated that if breast-feeding could be reinstated in developing countries, very probably—and this, of course, is based on available figures, but partly a guesstimate—some 10 million babies would be saved from diarrhea disease and marasmus each year."

During the 1970s and early 1980s proponents of breastfeeding and critics of the use of infant formula in developing countries argued that the marketing practices of the infant formula manufacturers led to malnutrition rather than to improved nutrition.[1] The critics cited a variety of marketing practices that induced mothers to stop breastfeeding and inevitably led to malnutrition, disease, and, in some cases, death. Mass advertising was said to induce mothers to stop breastfeeding, often in the name of modernity.

Labels on the infant formula packages typically showed chubby, healthy Caucasian babies. Some advertisements conveyed the impression that infant formula was superior to breastfeeding.

Some infant formula manufacturers routinely provided free samples to mothers, at times in the clinic or hospital in which they gave birth. (It is virtually impossible for a mother to resume breastfeeding if she stops for even a few days.) Free samples were given to clinics and hospitals for those infants whose mothers could not breastfeed. Samples were also given to mothers who could breastfeed but did not want to. Many mothers did not have access to a clinic or a hospital, however, and some manufacturers employed uniformed "milk nurses" who visited mothers in their homes to provide information about

[1]Critics organized a boycott of Nestlé, S.A., the Swiss company which had nearly a 50 percent market share worldwide. See the cases Nestlé Boycott (A)-(E), S-BPP-5 through S-BPP-5F, Stanford University, Stanford, CA, 1981.

infant care and feeding and to promote infant formula. The sales forces of the infant formula companies focused on doctors, clinics, and hospitals, as well as retail outlets. Donations of product and money were made to doctors' associations and hospitals. Sales representatives were often paid on a commission basis. ■

This case is based on materials presented in Dobbings (1988).

PREPARATION QUESTIONS

1. Who is responsible for the proper use of infant formula?
2. Are the infant formula manufacturers doing anything wrong in their marketing of infant formula in the developing countries? Whose standards should be used to determine what "wrong" means?
3. How should an infant formula company market its product in developing countries? Which principles should guide its marketing?
4. Should the availability of infant formula be restricted? If so, how?
5. Are there other products or marketing practices in developing countries about which similar objections might be raised?

Levi Strauss & Co. in China

Since 1986 Levi Strauss & Co. (LS&CO.) had sourced garments for the U.S. market from independent contractors in China. It also had been evaluating joint venture opportunities in China, and early in 1992 after several years of study, it decided to forego direct investment because of concerns about China's one-child-per-family law and to await the development of its global sourcing guidelines.[1]

Later in the year when it had completed its Business Partner Terms of Engagement and Guidelines for Country Selection policies, LS&CO. began the task of determining whether the practices of its contractors and their countries conformed with the newly developed policies.[2] LS&CO. conducted an assessment of each country that had possible human rights issues addressed by the new Guidelines for Country Selection. Two Asian countries, Burma and the People's Republic of China, both had clear human rights violations. The task for LS&CO. was to determine if those violations were pervasive. Of the two cases, Burma proved to be the easier. The company's assessment team determined that there were "pervasive human rights violations" in Burma, and, in late 1992 LS&CO. decided to phase out, over the course of 3 months, its sourcing in the country.

In the case of China the issues were more difficult. LS&CO. purchased more than ten times the volume from Chinese contractors than from their Burmese counterparts, and the low labor costs made expansion of sourcing in China attractive. China also represented a huge market opportunity. Yet the human rights violations and the risk of political instability stood in conflict with LS&CO.'s Guidelines. In late 1992 the company formed a task force to study the China issue in more detail. The 12-member China Policy Group (CPG) was tasked with determining the company's future presence in China, including both direct investment and sourcing.

The application of ethical principles, as embodied in the guidelines, to a business decision, however, involved a number of complex issues and conflicting concerns. On the one hand, LS&CO. was already sourcing in China, and there were two main reasons why it should increase or at least maintain its presence in China. First, labor costs in China were low relative to those in other countries, and plans for 1993 called for a large increase in direct sourcing. LS&CO. also purchased several million yards of fabric in China or enough material for about four million

---

[1]See the Part V integrative case *Levi Strauss & Co. Global Sourcing Guidelines.*

[2]Contractor audits are the subject of the Chapter 20 case *Levi Strauss & Co. Terms of Engagement Audits.*

garments. Some of the fabric was purchased directly, and the rest was purchased indirectly through contractors in other Asian countries such as the Philippines, Indonesia, and Sri Lanka. In addition, eight of LS&CO.'s domestic contractors sourced in China. Second, a presence in China would allow LS&CO. to position itself favorably in an emerging market with vast business and profit potential.

On the other hand, the newly written guidelines required it to withdraw from a country with pervasive human rights violations. In addition, some LS&CO. executives were concerned that its brand image might be damaged if the company continued to do business in a country with a questionable human rights record. When the CPG was formed, U.S. trade policy was under review with the focus on human rights concerns. At stake was China's most favored nation (MFN) trade status, which allowed the country to export goods to the United States at the lowest possible tariffs.

THE PROBLEM

LS&CO. faced both market and nonmarket issues with regard to China. On the market side, increased production costs from moving sourcing and processing operations to another country would reduce its competitiveness and profits. Labor costs to make a pair of pants amounted to approximately $6 in China versus $8 in Taiwan and $10 in Indonesia, but those costs represented only a portion of the total cost of the garment. Other factors such as quality, the cost of rework and repair, the reliability of delivery, the flexibility of the contractors, the lead times required to get the goods delivered, and the management time required were all integral to determining the true cost per garment. These factors varied considerably from country to country, so the cost advantage from contracting in China was difficult to measure. The cost difference to produce a garment elsewhere was significant, however, and the cost difference translated into five to six times that amount at retail. By these estimates the cost to the company of moving its sourcing from China to another country could amount to a significant increase in cost. Although moving its sourcing out of China would increase costs, LS&CO. also had to consider the possible negative effects on its brand image of doing business in a country with a questionable human rights record. The increased labor costs might well be balanced, or even overshadowed, by the benefits from avoiding damage to its reputation and brand image. Needless to say, the potential damage was difficult to quantify.

On the nonmarket side, two issues emerged. First, the CPG had to assess the pervasiveness of the human rights violations by assessing whether a great majority of the people were affected, how severe the violations were, how many types of violations there were, whether there was a trend toward improvement or worsening, and what the government was doing to improve the situation. The second nonmarket issue facing the group was the hardship withdrawing from China would cause its contractors—for policies they did not directly control and likely could not influence. The alternative was for LS&CO. to remain in China and work to improve human rights there.

The human rights violations that concerned LS&CO. could be broadly divided into two categories: the general human rights climate in the country and specific concerns pertaining to the workplace. In 1992, 3 years after Tiananmen Square, the human rights climate in China had not improved substantially. The Chinese government still restricted political rights and arrested citizens for the practice of religion. In the workplace, the most pressing issues were the use of prison labor, restrictions on freedom of association, and the moral and ethical issues associated with China's controversial one-child-per-family law. The one-child-per-family law, instituted in 1979 in response to soaring population growth, provided rewards and penalties to induce couples to limit their families to one child. The law received particular attention from the CPG for two reasons. First, employers in China were, through direct pressure on workers, the primary enforcers of the law. Employers could be asked to require women employees to report on their birth control practices and be monitored at company clinics. A company might also be required to impose fines on or fire a woman who refused to have an abortion. Second, many of the complaints by U.S. and international human rights organizations over the past decade had focused on the one-child campaign. These complaints centered around allegations of coercion in enforcing the policy, including forced abortions and involuntary sterilizations, even though China's official policy neither authorized nor condoned such practices.

RECOMMENDATIONS AND THE DECISION

The CPG identified five options, ranging from the extremes of investing and sourcing in China irrespective of human rights conditions to an immediate withdrawal from all business ties with that country. In between, the group considered policies that would maintain a company presence in China but also work toward improving human rights conditions. The arguments for and against each approach centered around the same basic themes: compliance with the Guidelines for Country Selection, short- and long-term costs resulting from transferring the China operations to other countries, protection of its brand names, and opportunities to gain experience and build consumer loyalty in an emerging market. By February 1993 the group had split into two sides, one supporting each of the two remaining options.

The majority wanted, under certain conditions, to continue to source finished products and purchase raw materials in China. Those conditions were: first, the suppliers complied with the Terms of Engagement normally applied to global sourcing; and second, sourcing and fabric purchases were done in compliance with a set of conditions under which it would maintain its presence in China for the purpose of promoting human rights. This option reflected the belief that promoting human rights in China rather than withdrawing was more in keeping with the spirit of its new guidelines. The majority's recommendation included such items as the hiring of a full-time person to promote human rights improvement, a ban on political activity in the workplace, education and training in company ethics and values for workers, and a nondiscrimination hiring clause. The recommendations also called for the company to "organize its enterprise so as to ensure that management cannot be compelled to administer the punitive provisions (e.g., economic rewards for compliance and penalties for noncompliance) of China's one-child policy directly." Similarly, the majority pledged LS&CO. to "come to the aid of any employee penalized for the exercise of human rights," for example, by being an advocate for the employee. Finally, it called for LS&CO. to support organizations outside China working to advance human rights in the country and to reevaluate on a regular basis the human rights conditions in the country.

The minority held that LS&CO. should neither invest directly nor source in China. The minority cited the Guidelines for Country Selection in concluding that the company should withdraw from China. One minority member believed that LS&CO.'s presence in China was contrary to the values of the company and that under its guidelines it was compelled not to do business in a country with pervasive human rights abuses. Another member's view was more pragmatic. He was more concerned about whether operating in any country with pervasive violations of basic human rights would harm LS&CO.'s corporate reputation and brand image. The two joined in drafting the minority opinion.

Both the majority and minority recommendations were presented to LS&CO.'s senior management in early 1993. CEO Robert Haas accepted the minority recommendation to withdraw gradually from its Chinese sourcing contracts and postpone any direct investment in the country. In a letter to company employees, Haas explained that he concluded that the minority recommendation was more appropriate because "we have always been willing to hold ourselves to a higher standard than the general business community, and that is a source of pride for employees and shareholders, . . . In countries that do not offer protection of basic legal and human rights, we potentially expose our employees who live and work there to unacceptable risks; we put our commercial interests and business reputation at risk; and we subject the company to a claim of legitimizing and supporting governments whose practices are condemned." ■

This case was prepared by Abraham Wu under the supervision of Professor David P. Baron. Information for the case was gathered primarily through interviews with company officials and staff and from company documents. Robert Dunn, Peter Jacobi, Iain Lyon, and Elissa Sheridan provided invaluable assistance and insight.

PREPARATION QUESTIONS

1. Is LS&CO.'s brand image at risk because of human rights violations? Is its reputation at risk?
2. Evaluate the rationales of the majority and minority for their recommendations.
3. Did LS&CO. make the right decision? Why or why not?
4. If the majority opinion had prevailed, how far should LS&CO. have gone in seeking to advance human rights in China?
5. Should LS&CO. extend its policy to the suppliers of its domestic-based contractors?

University Games, Inc.

Bob Moog, president and founder of University Games, Inc. of Burlingame, California, returned from a 3-day trip to Chang Mai, Thailand, in January 1993. Bob received his MBA from the Graduate School of Business at Stanford in 1984 where he had been an informal student leader and creator of pranks, mischief, and camaraderie. After graduation he founded University Games to develop and market board games. By 1993 the company had U.S. sales of $8.5 million and worldwide sales of over $10 million. Not only was Bob the president of University Games, he was also the inventor of most of its proprietary board games. In addition to developing its own game themes, University Games licensed themes, such as Dick Tracy and Carmen Sandiego. University Games contracted out all the production of its games, and most of its sales were made through independent agents and representatives.

University Games had recently acquired exclusive U.S. rights to a line of wooden puzzles under the Rain Tree label. The puzzles were produced in a factory in northern Thailand from a dark wood that gave them an attractive appearance. To obtain a higher margin, the puzzles were sold in specialty stores and not in discount stores. The puzzles were expected to produce revenue of nearly $700,000 in 1993. Moog planned to expand the line and had recently hired an outstanding new manager for the Rain Tree product line.

The factory was owned by a Thai, who had received an engineering degree in the United States. After returning to Thailand he established a woodworking shop and began to create his own puzzles that he sold locally. After struggling for many years, he began to achieve success when his puzzles were introduced in the United States. The factory's shipments increased rapidly from 500,000 baht in 1987 to 27 million baht in 1992 (25 baht to the dollar). He was particularly proud of being able to provide employment for over 300 people.

Moog's visit to the factory had two purposes. One was to discuss supply arrangements for the expansion of the product line and the production of other wooden game products that University Games was developing. The second purpose was to inspect the working conditions at the factory.

Although the working conditions were said to be good by the standards of northern Thailand, Moog described them as "pre-industrial revolution." The production process began with large pieces of wood being dried in kilns. Then, a group of men and boys sawed, drilled, and carved the dried wood in an open Quonset hut. The men were barefooted, and safety conditions were virtually nonexistent. For example, the men frequently used machetes to cut wood they held between their legs. Although the wood shop was cleaned and mopped every night, by 10:00 A.M. the men were covered with sawdust. About half of them wore bandannas across their noses and mouths to avoid inhaling the dust.

Inside the main building of the factory, 50 to 60 young girls worked in the paint shop handpainting the wooden pieces. The girls sat in circles on the floor, talking and painting and seemed to be having a good time. There were a few older women supervisors, but generally the employees seemed to work with little supervision. The factory owner was a tough employer who occasionally would fire employees who did not produce acceptable quality products, even though at times it may not have been the fault of employees, who sometimes did not know the standards they were expected to meet. He explained, "I don't give them a lot of chances."

The workers were thin but seemed to be in good health and quite happy. They worked 10 hours a day, 6 days a week, and had a 45-minute lunch break and three 20-minute breaks a day. They earned approximately $100 a month. In addition, many of the employees lived free of charge in a 3-year-old dormitory located on the factory premises. The factory owner believed that his was the only factory in Northern Thailand with a dormitory for its employees. The rooms in the dormitory were like those in a college dormitory and housed four to a room. The bathrooms in the dormitory were adequate, and the residents had access to a kitchen. The factory owner also provided food, which he sold to the employees.

In addition to employing over 300 people, the factory owner contracted out some work to local villages. In effect, he staffed the factory for the base work load and subcontracted the extra work to the villages. In the villages people lived in houses built of wood or concrete block with thatched roofs. The houses had electricity and some had running water.

Work at the factory seemed very inefficient. Sawdust covered much of the production floor and also covered the puzzle pieces waiting to be assembled. When workers cleaned the pieces to prepare them for painting, assembly, or shipping, some were damaged and had to be scrapped. In the paint shop, the girls wanted to sit in circles so they could talk as they worked. Rather than specializing, each girl performed each of the tasks. For example, instead of one girl painting only the yellow dots on each of the pieces, each painted a yellow dot, a red dot, a blue dot, and a green dot on each piece. One obstacle to improving productivity in the factory was the difficulty in getting the girls to work in a line or even to work at assembly and painting tables. Two years earlier the owner had put work tables in the paint shop, but as soon as he would leave the shop, the girls would either sit on the tables or push them aside and sit on the floor in circles to work. They preferred the social interaction to the higher wages that would accompany higher productivity.

Moog was concerned about the conditions at the factory and wondered what he could and should do about them. Although University Games was a small company, it was one of only two customers of the factory and accounted for 25 percent of its shipments. When Moog discussed the working conditions with the factory owner, it was clear that the owner was proud of what he had accomplished and did not want any meddling. When Moog asked about the conditions under which the wooden pieces were produced in the villages, the factory owner said: "I don't get involved in how the villages do the work for me, and you shouldn't get involved in how I do the work for you. All you should care about is do I get it done on time and do I get it done to the quality you want." Bob responded: "Look, if I were one of a hundred customers, I might agree with you. You are my only supplier for these puzzles, and I am one of two customers you have and I represent 25 percent of your sales. We have to work together on this." Moog was also concerned about the impact of any higher costs on his company's profits, since his shareholders were pressing for higher profits. ■

PREPARATION QUESTIONS

1. How should Moog reason about his responsibility, if any, with respect to the factory in Thailand? Which practices should concern him?
2. What specifically should he do? Prepare a policy and plan of action.
3. How should he interact with the factory owner?

PART V

Integrative Case

Levi Strauss & Co. Global Sourcing Guidelines

By the 1990s Levi Strauss & Co. (LS&CO.) had become the world's largest brand-name apparel manufacturer. Much of its success was attributable to its successful decisions to go global in the mid-1960s and to add new lines of casual garments to its traditional line of jeans. The rapid sales growth of casual products, as well as the cost competitiveness of the casual apparel industry, resulted in a change in LS&CO.'s sourcing mix. By 1991 it had almost 700 outside contractors, mostly in Asia and Latin America. This change presented a dilemma to Peter Jacobi, LS&CO.'s president for global sourcing, and other senior management. Its relationship with its foreign suppliers had focused on quality and delivery and not with the full range of issues addressed in its owned-and-operated facilities. LS&CO. executives feared that the company's brand image and its reputation for high ethical standards could be hurt by its contractors' business practices.

COMPANY BACKGROUND AND ETHICAL CONDUCT

In 1850 in San Francisco Levi Strauss started supplying gold miners in Northern California with dry goods supplied by his brothers on the East Coast. In 1873 he and Jacob Davis, a tailor to whom he sold canvas and denim, began to sell blue denim pants with patented brass rivets on the stress-bearing pockets. The basic jeans (style 501) were LS&CO.'s mainstay product for more than a century.

In the 1960s LS&CO. began to add other products to its original jeans line, including fashion wear, accessories, and youth wear. By 1993 it was the world's largest brand-name apparel manufacturer with sales of $5.9 billion. It designed, manufactured, and marketed apparel for men, women, and children, including jeans, slacks, shirts, jackets, skirts, and fleece. Most products were marketed under the LEVI'S and DOCKERS trademarks and sold throughout most of the world.

Since its founding, LS&CO. has been led by Levi Strauss and his descendants. The company was owned by the descendants of Levi Strauss and employees until 1971, when the company went public to finance its rapid domestic and international growth. Family members retained control of approximately 50 percent of the outstanding stock, however. In 1985 the company returned to private ownership through a leveraged buyout. The company was acquired by Levi Strauss Associates, Inc., a holding company created by members of the Haas family and LS&CO. executives solely for the purpose of regaining control of the company. In 1992 the board of directors of Levi Strauss Associates included five family members.

LS&CO. was widely recognized for the ethical conduct of its business. The company's emphasis on ethics began with Levi Strauss and had continued with both his descendants and company employees. The company had a Code of Ethics as well as a set of Ethical Principles by which employees were to conduct themselves. The code stated that the company's ethical values were based on four elements:

- a commitment to commercial success in terms broader than merely financial measures
- a respect for our employees, suppliers, customers, consumers and stockholders
- a commitment to conduct which is not only legal but fair and morally correct in a fundamental sense
- avoidance of not only real, but the appearance of conflict of interest

From these elements derived the principles the company strove to follow: honesty, promise keeping, fairness, respect for others, compassion, and integrity.

CONSEQUENCES OF THE CHANGES IN MARKET STRATEGY

Peter Jacobi took over as president for global sourcing (for the U.S. market) in 1988 and had responsibility for all owned-and-operated facilities as well as contracting both in the United States and overseas. Jacobi was surprised by two facts. The first was the extent to which the sourcing mix had changed from just a few years earlier. Through the 1970s, LS&CO. obtained all of its fabric for domestic production from major U.S. textile producers, and manufacturing was done in owned-and-operated facilities, supplemented by two independent contractors that produced solely for LS&CO. and by a number of other U.S. contractors when needed.

In the 1980s LS&CO. expanded its product line to casual clothing under the DOCKERS trademark. The DOCKERS product line was one of the most rapidly growing and successful lines in the U.S. apparel industry. Although jeans and jeans-related products still accounted for approximately 72 percent of the company's total worldwide sales, casual products had been an increasingly important source of revenue in the U.S. market.

As a result of its global business strategy, its sourcing network expanded rapidly, particularly for its casual lines. Overseas contractors were very cost competitive for casual clothing. Indeed, a large and increasing share of clothing sold in the United States was produced in Asia and Latin America. Between 1991 and 1992 the share of LS&CO. garments produced by independent contractors and sold in the United States jumped from 35 to 54 percent.

The second surprise for Jacobi was some of the business practices of the overseas contractors. The growth in sourcing abroad meant that relationships with contractors were not as close as when LS&CO. along with a small and stable set of suppliers accounted for most of its production. In many cases, the company was unaware of its contractors' policies regarding working conditions, health and safety, human rights, and environmental protection.

Jacobi and other senior executives began touring overseas factories in 1990. They found that contractors were largely driven by pressure, both subtle and overt, to reduce costs. Many of these contractors supplied other apparel companies in addition to LS&CO., and because the apparel industry was highly competitive, contractors with the lowest costs were the most attractive. Some apparel firms used the threat of switching suppliers to compel contractors to reduce costs.

More importantly, Jacobi found that the common understanding among the contractors was to reduce costs by any means—and this often meant at the expense of workers. For example, a prominent contractor in Costa Rica had a policy of firing women once they married. The contractor's rationale was that the women would eventually become pregnant and he would have to pay for the baby and other expenses thereby adding to his costs.[1]

Jacobi concluded that the local LS&CO. managers were evaluating contractor practices by comparing them with local practices rather than with its fundamental principles. Although the local practices might be appropriate from some perspectives, Jacobi asked, "What would this look like if the '60 Minutes' camera showed up at the [factory] door?" Regardless if LS&CO. owned the factories, he believed that the company would be held accountable by the public for whatever occurred there.

Bob Dunn, vice president for corporate affairs, had similar misgivings. Information was now global, so anything happening anywhere in the world could be available instantly everywhere. Thus, whatever activities LS&CO. undertook anywhere in the world could potentially be open to public scrutiny.

This had potential significance for the company's brand image. The LEVI'S brand was one of the company's most valuable assets. Consumers associated positive American images with it, like the freedom and individualism of the Old West. LS&CO. believed that consumers purchased its products for

[1]Jacobi convinced the contractor to eliminate this policy.

reasons above and beyond quality and styling, and activities associated with the company could hurt its reputation and tarnish its brand image.

DEVELOPMENT OF THE GLOBAL SOURCING GUIDELINES

In the summer of 1991 senior management convened the Sourcing Guidelines Working Group (SGWG) to formulate a policy for guiding the company's relationships with its foreign suppliers. LS&CO. was lauded for its policy of corporate social responsibility, and the company wanted everything it did to be consistent with that policy. The company recognized that the "product is more than the product." The product was also the LEVI'S brand, and consumers' feelings toward the brand could be affected by business practices and corporate reputation.

Principled Reasoning Approach[2]

To aid in formulating ethical policies, LS&CO. had developed a process referred to as the Principled Reasoning Approach (PRA). The PRA was designed "... to protect against self-deception, self-interest, and expediency and to ensure consistency and fairness in decision making" where ethical considerations were involved.[3] It served as the SGWG's framework for formulating the Global Sourcing Guidelines. The PRA consisted of six steps: the problem, the principles, the stakeholders, the solution, the consequences, and the implementation. All steps had to be undertaken, but the process was flexible in that no particular order was prescribed. Steps could be repeated and reevaluated on the basis of new information.

The SGWG developed two separate problem statements. First, "What requirements should we have for business partners associated with manufacturing/finishing Levi Strauss & Co. branded products?" Second, "Under what conditions would Levi Strauss & Co., a global company, not consider sourcing in any country?" The SGWG also had to decide what "partners" meant. Did it include subcontractors as well as contractors? And how far down the supply chain should it apply?

The SGWG had to determine which ethical principles were relevant to the problem. The Ethical Principles outlined by LS&CO. (honesty, promise keeping, fairness, respect for others, compassion, and integrity) formed the basis for all company decision making and thus were included. Additional principles could be added, however, and the SGWG chose five: corporate social responsibility, strategic global leadership, loyalty, commercial success, and respect for cultural diversity.

A stakeholder was defined as any person, group, or entity significantly or materially impacted by the issue under consideration. The SGWG first had to identify relevant stakeholders, both internal and external to the company. Stakeholders were intermittently interviewed by SGWG members, throughout the process, and the SGWG assessed the extent to which each stakeholder group should be considered in the decision-making process.

The SGWG identified a different set of stakeholders for each of its two problem statements. For business partners terms, the list of stakeholders internal to LS&CO. consisted of employees making sourcing decisions, the merchandising group, shareholders, top management, employees of owned-and-operated plants, licensees and affiliates, global sourcing personnel, and all LS&CO. employees in general. The set of stakeholders external to the company included outside contractors (owners and management), their employees, plant communities and local governments, suppliers, public interest organizations (e.g., unions, church groups, environmental groups), and the environment. For country selection, the SGWG chose the same internal stakeholders, although it deleted global sourcing personnel and added operations support employees (who travel to countries for inspections, evaluations, mill visits, etc.). Stakeholders external to LS&CO. remained the same except that citizens of the contractor country replaced public interest groups.

The SGWG then developed alternative solutions to the two problems it had posed and tested those solutions against the ethical principles to screen out options inconsistent with the principles. Regarding business partner requirements, the SGWG tried to resolve two conflicting and fundamental demands. One was the need to specify at least minimal standards for its business partners, for instance, in hiring practices and workplace health and safety. The other was the recognition of the diversity of ethical and cultural systems around the world. Attempting to mandate something akin to U.S. standards for the rest of the world would have been both unworkable and unwise. The SGWG sought to strike a balance.

Country selection raised difficult questions for the SGWG because the concept was revolutionary. People generally understood that if a contractor did some-

---

[2]Much of this section is based on SGWG meeting notes.

[3]"Ethical Practices" Statement, October 1991, Levi Staraus & Co. Human Resources Department.

thing egregious the relationship would be severed, but it was unclear at first how this could be applied to a country. The SGWG easily agreed that LS&CO. should not be involved in a country if it could not protect its trademark or if being there could damage its brand image. Likewise, stability issues and safety of its employees were straightforward to address.

Human rights issues, however, were very controversial. The SGWG researched the issues, and after consulting the Universal Declaration on Human Rights (written in 1948 by the United Nations and ratified by countries around the world) and data from the U.S. State Department and various human rights groups, the group was able to reach a consensus. It decided to use the Universal Declaration as the definition of human rights and concluded that the company should not source in countries with "pervasive" violations of those basic human rights.

The SGWG began examining the consequences of its Global Sourcing Guidelines once it had agreed on working drafts for each component. For example, it discussed how the severing of relationships with contractors having substandard employment practices could cost innocent workers their jobs when those contractors were dependent on LS&CO. for work. Additionally, human rights violations in a country could lead to the loss of contractors who were committed to LS&CO. The SGWG had to weigh these negative consequences against the positive consequences, such as a protected brand image and the honoring of its corporate social responsibility.

To implement its solution, the SGWG concluded it would have to conduct periodic audits of its partners. For the country selection criteria, the SGWG had to determine who would make selection decisions and on what criteria.

In February 1992 the completed Global Sourcing Guidelines were presented to top management, which ratified them later that month. The Terms of Engagement are presented in Figure 20-3 and the Guidelines for Country Selection are presented in Figure 22-1.

IMPLEMENTATION OF THE GLOBAL SOURCING GUIDELINES

Development of Business Partner Audits

When the Global Sourcing Guidelines were promulgated and the first stages of implementation began in March 1992, the SGWG had not yet developed formal procedures for company audits. The incident in Saipan (Chapter 22) served as a catalyst for the development of an audit instrument. The company's sourcing groups recognized that there were vulnerabilities with regard to their contractors, and they took an aggressive approach to the Global Sourcing Guidelines to prevent serious embarrassment or damage to the brand.

The first round of audits covered sewing and finishing contractors. Prior to the initial audits, LS&CO. sent every contractor a copy of the guidelines with letters explaining what they meant and why they were important. It reassured contractors by having auditors meet with them to discuss any misgivings. A handful of contractors protested, but as Bob Dunn stated, "That's as clear a signal as you could want that they're not going to be the kind of people we'd want to deal with anyway."

Many contractors welcomed the audits. Some had worked with LS&CO. in the past to improve their quality and efficiency. They had found that meeting the company's strict quality standards opened doors to more work from other companies: if they could meet LS&CO.'s standards, they could work for anyone in the industry. These contractors believed that accommodating the Global Sourcing Guidelines would bring similar benefits.

In the initial round of audits, 70 percent of the contractors were found to be in compliance with the guidelines, 25 percent were found to need some improvements, and the other 5 percent were dropped. (Contractor audits are the subject of the Chapter 20 case *Levi Strauss & Co. Terms of Engagement Audits.*)

Country Audits

Beginning in the spring of 1992 more than 50 countries in which LS&CO. did business were evaluated. Like the implementation of the Terms of Engagement, the company had to develop audit procedures for countries. Corporate affairs executives decided that country audits would focus on two principal criteria: political and social stability and human rights. LS&CO. wanted to ensure that company personnel and assets were not threatened by instability. Additionally, the standard of pervasive human rights violations required a definition of "pervasive." To assess whether there were pervasive violations, corporate affairs analyzed countries comparatively, using data from the U.S. State Department and human rights organizations. Not all countries received the same attention in their evaluations, with countries having questionable human rights practices or political instability receiving closer scrutiny. Countries with good records were examined less critically.

Burma was the first country to be evaluated, and it was the most clear-cut. Sourcing was suspended in Burma due to pervasive violations of basic human rights. Colombia, Guatemala, Indonesia, and Sri Lanka, where there were questionable human rights practices, were all approved for sourcing after the evaluations. Human rights assessments were also completed for countries where LS&CO. investment might occur in the future. Sourcing was suspended in Peru due to political instability. (The decision process of reviewing LS&CO.'s participation in China is considered in the Chapter 22 case *Levi Strauss & Co. in China.*)

Working to Improve Contractor Practices

The nature and magnitude of the improvements required varied greatly across contractors and countries. In some cases, LS&CO. required upgrades of the facilities. In Mexico, for instance, a contractor was found to have a fire hazard because its factory had only one entrance and exit. In the Dominican Republic a factory had installed potentially hazardous plywood mezzanines to accommodate more workers. Some contractors needed more sanitary rest rooms, as well as first-aid kits and fire extinguishers. In other cases, LS&CO. required contractors' business practices to change. In Bangladesh, two contractors were found to employ child labor. About 5 percent of the employees at these factories were under the age of 14.[4]

As a rule LS&CO. would not pay for the improvements at its contractors' facilities. At the same time, it recognized the burdens it imposed on its contractors. Expenditures by contractors to accommodate LS&CO. affected their cost-competitiveness and thus their attractiveness to other apparel manufacturers as well. For some contractors for whom it was their primary customer, LS&CO. believed it had certain special responsibilities. Jacobi noted, "The challenge for us, and I really mean this, is not to exploit that relationship, since you can exploit it when you become such a huge part of his [a contractor's] business that he loses all leverage." Thus, LS&CO. would often negotiate joint solutions with its contractors. It used three types of solutions: acceptance of higher contractor prices, loans to contractors, and guarantees of specific levels of purchases so that a contractor could be assured that its investment would be worthwhile.

Inevitably, the Global Sourcing Guidelines would translate into higher production costs, and this could put LS&CO. at a cost disadvantage relative to its competitors. LS&CO. had not put some products on the market that it otherwise would have, and it had lost some business as well as profit margin. For example, Burma was the company's largest and cheapest source for casual shorts, and transferring the work to other countries resulted in an increase in production costs.

LS&CO. officials believed, however, that looking only at direct costs did not show the entire picture. ". . . [T]hat doesn't tell you anything about the quality of the pants, the cost of rework and repair, the reliability of delivery, the flexibility of the contractor, the lead times required to get those goods delivered, and how much management time is required to supervise," stated Bob Dunn. Jacobi said, "The concept of what I call 'island hopping'—which means that you move from contractor to contractor to contractor based on cost—really at the end of the day is very inefficient and very unproductive cost-wise."

LS&CO. executives envisioned the need for closer relationships with suppliers. They found that when contractors needed to make significant changes or investments in their businesses, some sort of substantial long-term relationship was required. To develop these relationships, supply had to be distributed among a smaller set of contractors so that contractors felt a sense of investment in LS&CO., as it felt in them. Jacobi said, "My hope would be that the best relationships are those where there is mutual trust, where the working relationship between the local LS&CO. people and the local contractor is such that a contract isn't needed." This would return Levi Strauss & Co. to the same types of relationships it had with its U.S. contractors prior to developing its global sourcing network. ■

[4]See Chapter 22.

This is an abridged version of a case written by Justin Adams under the supervision of Professor David P. Baron. Information was gathered primarily through interviews with company officers and staff and from company documents and annual reports. Robert Dunn, Peter Jacobi, Iain Lyon, and Elissa Sheridan provided invaluable assistance and insight.

PREPARATION QUESTIONS

1. Should LS&CO. assume responsibility for its contractors' practices? Does doing so represent paternalism?
2. What costs do the Global Sourcing Guidelines impose on LS&CO.? How far down the supply chain should the guidelines be applied?
3. Evaluate the appropriateness of the Terms of Engagement and Guidelines for Country Selection. Do they go too far? What, if anything, should be added?
4. Evaluate LS&CO.'s approach to implementing its policies.
5. Do your answers depend on the fact that the company is privately owned and family controlled? Should a publicly owned firm adopt LS&CO.'s Global Sourcing Guidelines?

References

Abegglen, James C., and George Stalk, Jr. (1985). *Kaisha, the Japanese Corporation.* New York: Basic Books.

Adams, William C., Dennis J. Smith, Alison Salzman, Ralph Crossen, Scott Hieber, Tom Naccarato, William Vantine, and Nina Weisbroth. (1986). Before and After *The Day After:* The Unexpected Results of a Televised Drama. *Political Communication and Persuasion, 3,* 191–213. Reprinted in Garber (1990), 54–65.

Aetna Life & Casualty. (1982, November). A Neighborhood Reinvestment Program, Hartford, CN.

Akerlof, George A. (1970, August). The Market for 'Lemons': Qualitative Uncertainty and the Market Mechanism. *Quarterly Journal of Economics, 84,* 488–500.

Almond, Gabriel A., and G. Bingham Powell, Jr. (Eds.). (1988). *Comparative Politics Today: A World View.* Glenview, IL: Scott Foresman.

Alpern, Kenneth D. (1988). Moral Dimensions of the Foreign Corrupt Practices Act: Comments on Pastin and Hooker. In Donaldson and Werhane, 54–59.

Alt, James A., and Kenneth Shepsle (Eds.). (1990). *Perspectives on Positive Political Economy.* Cambridge, UK: Cambridge University Press.

Aoki, Masahiko (Ed.). (1984). *The Economic Analysis of the Japanese Firm.* Amsterdam, The Netherlands: North Holland.

Areeda, Phillip, and Louis Kaplow. (1988). *Antitrust Analysis: Problems, Text, and Cases* (4th ed.). Boston: Little, Brown.

______. (1997). *Antitrust Analysis* (5th ed.). New York: Aspen Law and Business.

Areeda, Phillip, and Donald Turner. (1975, February). Predatory Pricing and Related Practices under Section 2 of the Sherman Act. *Harvard Law Review, 88,* 697–733.

Arrow, Kenneth A. (1963). *Social Choice and Individual Values* (2nd ed.). New York: Wiley.

Atsuyuki, Suzuta. (1978). The Way of the Bureaucrat. *Japan Echo, 5,*(3), 42–53. Reprinted in Okimoto and Rohlen (1988), 196–203.

Baerwald, Hans H. (1974). *Japan's Parliament: An Introduction.* London, UK: Cambridge University Press.

Bagley, Constance E. (1995). *Managers and the Legal Environment: Strategies for the 21st Century* (2nd ed.). St. Paul, MN: West Publishing Co.

Bahls, Jane Easter. (1998). Dealing with Drugs: Keep It Legal. *HRMagazine* (March), 104–116.

Baker, Jonathan B. (1997). Econometric Analysis in *FTC v. Staples,* Federal Trade Commission, Washington, DC.

Baldwin, Robert E., and Michael O. Moore. (1991). Political Aspects of the Administration of the Trade Remedy Laws. In Boltuck and Litan, 253–287.

Bamberger, Gustavo E., and Dennis W. Carlton. (1999). Antitrust and Higher Education: MIT Financial Aid (1993). In John E. Kwoka, Jr. and Lawrence J. White, *The Antitrust Revolution: Economics, Competition, and Policy.* (pp. 264–285) New York: Oxford University Press.

Barker, Richard A. (1993). An Evaluation of the Ethics Program at General Dynamics. *Journal of Business Ethics, 12,* 165–177.

Baron, David P. (1983). *The Export-Import Bank: An Economic Analysis.* New York: Academic Press.

______. (1995a). The Nonmarket Strategy System. *Sloan Management Review, 37,*(Fall), 73–85.

______. (1995b). Integrated Strategy: Market and Nonmarket Components. *California Management Review, 37*(Winter), 47–65.

______. (1996). *Business and Its Environment* (2d ed.). Upper Saddle River, NJ: Prentice Hall.

______. (1997a). Integrated Strategy in International Trade Disputes: The Kodak-Fujifilm Case. *Journal of Economics and Management Strategy, 6*(Summer), 291–346.

______. (1997b). Integrated Strategy, Trade Policy, and Global Competition. *California Management Review, 39*(Winter), 145–169.

______. (1999). Integrated Market and Nonmarket Strategies in Client and Interest Group Politics. *Business and Politics, 1*(April).

Baron, David P., and John A. Ferejohn. (1989). Bargaining in Legislatures. *American Political Science Review, 83*(December), 1181–1206.

Barone, Michael, and Grant Ujifusa. (1997). *The Almanac of American Politics 1997–1998,* Washington, DC: National Journal.

Bartlett, Christopher A., and Sumantra Goshal. (1989). *Managing Across Borders: The Transnational Solution.* Boston, MA.: Harvard Business School Press.

Baysinger, Barry D., Gerald D. Keim, and Carl P. Zeithaml. (1985). An Empirical Evaluation of the Potential for Including Shareholders in Corporate Constituency Programs. *Academy of Management Journal, 28,* 180–200.

Bell, Linda, and Richard Freeman. (1994). Why Do Americans and Germans Work Different Hours, Working Paper No. 4808, National Bureau of Economic Research, Cambridge, CA.

Bellis, Jean-Francois. (1989). The EEC Antidumping System. In Jackson and Vermulst, *Antidumping Law and Practice: A Comparative Study.* (pp. 41–97).

Bentham, Jeremy. (1988). *An Introduction to the Principles of Morals and Legislation* (1789). Buffalo, NY: Prometheus Books.

Berg, Hartmut. (1988). Motor-Cars: Between Growth and Protectionism. In H. W. DeJong (Ed.), *The Structure of European Industry.* (pp. 245–267).

Berle, Adolph A., and Gardiner C. Means. (1932). *The Modern Corporation and Private Property.* Reprint Buffalo, NY: W. S. Wein, 1982.

Bernstein, Marver H. (1955). *Regulation by Independent Commission.* Princeton, NJ: Princeton University Press.

Besanko, David, David Dranove, and Mark Shanley. (1996). *The Economics of Strategy.* New York: Wiley.

Black, Henry C. (1983). *Black's Law Dictionary* (abridged 5th ed.). St. Paul: West Publishing Co.

Blanpain, Roger. (1983). *The OECD Guidelines for Multinational Enterprises and Labor Relations.* Deventer, Netherlands: Kluwer.

Boltuck, Richard and Robert E. Litan. (Eds.) (1991). *Down in the Dumps: Administration of the Unfair Trade Laws.* Washington, DC: Brookings.

Bork, Robert H. (1978). *The Antitrust Paradox: A Policy at War with Itself.* New York: Basic Books.

Borrus, Michael, and Judith Goldstein. (1987). United States Trade Protectionism: Institutions, Norms, and Practices. *Northwestern Journal of International Law & Business, 8* (Fall), 328–364.

Bowie, Norman E. (1982). *Business Ethics.* Englewood Cliffs, NJ: Prentice Hall.

______. (1990). Business Ethics and Cultural Relativism. In Peter Madsen and Jay M. Shafritz (Eds.), *Essentials of Business Ethics.* (pp. 366–382) New York: Penguin Books.

Bradshaw, Thorton, and David Vogel. (1981). *Corporations and Their Critics.* New York: McGraw-Hill.

Brander, James A. (1986). Rationales for Strategic Trade and Industrial Policy. In Paul R. Krugman, 4(Ed.), *Strategic Trade Policy and the New International Economics* (pp. 23–46).

Brandt, Richard B. (1959). *Ethical Theory.* Englewood Cliffs, NJ: Prentice Hall.

______. (1979). *A Theory of the Good and the Right.* Oxford, UK: Claredon Press.

Breyer, Stephen. (1982). *Regulation and Its Reform.* Cambridge, MA: Harvard University Press.

Bringer, Robert P., and David M. Benforado. (1989). Pollution Prevention as Corporate Policy: A Look at the 3M Experience. *The Environmental Professional, 11,* 117–126.

Brock, William A., and David S. Evans. (1986). *The Economics of Small Business.* New York: Holmes and Meyer.

Bronte, Stephen. (1982). *Japanese Finance: Markets and Institutions.* London, UK: Euromoney Publications.

Brooks, Leonard J. (1989). Corporate Codes of Ethics. *Journal of Business Ethics, 8,* 117–129.

Budge, Ian, David Robertson, and Derek Heal. (Eds.) (1987). *Ideology, Strategy, and Party Change: Spatial Analyses of Post-War Election Programmes in Nineteen Democracies.* Cambridge, UK: Cambridge University Press.

Bulow, Jeremy, and Paul Klemperer. (1998). The Tobacco Deal. *Brookings Papers on Economic Activity.* Washington DC: Brookings.

Business Roundtable. The Role and Composition of the Board of Directors of the Large Publicity Owned Corporation. New York, 1978.

______. Statement on Corporate Responsibility. New York, October 1981.

______. Corporate Governance and American Competitiveness. New York, 1990.

______. Statement on Corporate Governance, New York, September 1997.

Calabresi, Guido, and Douglas A. Melamed. (1972). Property Rules, Liability Rules and Inalienability: One View of the Cathedral. *Harvard Law Review, 85,* 1089–1128.

Calingaert, Michael. (1993). Government-Business Relations in the European Community. *California Management Review* (Winter), 118–133.

Campbell, Thomas J., Daniel P. Kessler, and George B. Shepherd. (1998). The Link Between Liability Reforms and Productivity: Some Empirical Evidence. *Brookings Papers in Economic Activity: Microeconomics,* Washington, DC: Brookings.

Carp, Robert A., and Ronald Stidham. (1998). *The Federal Courts* (3d ed.). Washington, DC: CQ Press.

Carroll, Archie B. (1981). *Business & Society: Managing Corporate Social Performance.* Boston: Little, Brown.

Carson, Thomas L. (1987). Bribery and Implicit Agreements: A Reply to Philips. *Journal of Business Ethics, 6,* 123–125. Reprinted in Newton and Ford (1990), 291–294.

CBS News. (1980). *60 Minutes Verbatim.* (pp. 149–153). New York: Arno Press.

Cecchini, Paolo, with Michel Catinat and Alexis Jacquemin. (1988). *The European Challenge 1992: The Benefits of a Single Market.* Aldershot, UK: Wildwood.

Chamber of Commerce (U.S.). (1989). *Europe 1992: A Practical Guide for American Business.* Washington, DC.

Chandler, Alfred D. (1977). *The Visible Hand.* Cambridge, MA: Harvard University Press.

Chandler, Alfred D., and Richard S. Tedlow (1985). *The Coming of Managerial Capitalism: A Casebook on the History of American Economic Institutions.* Homewood, IL: Richard D. Irwin.

Christiansen, Flemming, and Shirin M. Rai. (1996). *Chinese Politics and Society: An Introduction.* New York: Prentice Hall.

Clark, Robert C. (1985). Agency Costs versus Fiduciary Duties. In John W. Pratt and Richard J. Zeckhauser (Eds.), *Principals and Agents: The Structure of Business.* (pp. 55–79). Boston, MA: Harvard Business School.

Clarkson, Kenneth W., and Timothy J. Muris (Eds.). (1981). *The Federal Trade Commission Since 1970.* Cambridge, UK: Cambridge University Press.

Clement, Doug. (1978, March). Infant Formula Malnutrition: Threat to the Third World. *The Christian Century.* Reprinted in Newton and Ford (1990), 150–158.

Close, Arthur C., J. Valerie Steel, and Michael E. Buckner (Eds.). (1993). *Washington Representatives 1993.* Washington, DC: Columbia Books.

Coase, Ronald H. (1960). The Problem of Social Cost. *The Journal of Law and Economics, 3* (October), 1–44.

Coffee, John C., Jr., Louis Lowenstein, and Susan Rose-Ackerman. (1988). *Knights, Raiders & Targets: The Impact of the Hostile Takeover.* New York: Oxford University Press.

Cohen, Henry. (1990, November) Products Liability: A Legal Overview. Washington, DC: Congressional Research Service, Library of Congress.

Committee for the Study of Economic and Monetary Union. (1989). Report of Economic and Monetary Union in the European Community. Brussels, Belgium.

Condorcet, Marquis de. (1785). Essai sur l'Application de l'Analyse a la Probabilité des Decisions Rendues a la Pluralite des Voix. New York: Chelsea, 1972.

Congressional Quarterly. (1990). *Politics in America.* Washington, DC: CQ Press.

______. (1994). *Federal Regulatory Directory* (7th ed.). Washington, DC: CQ Press.

______. (1997). *Politics in America: The 104th Congress.* Washington, DC: CQ Press.

Consumer Products Safety Commission. (1982, September). Chain Saw Safety. Washington, DC.

Cook, Timothy E. (1989). *Making Laws & Making News: Media Strategies in the U.S. House of Representatives.* Washington, DC: Brookings Institution.

Cooter, Robert, and Thomas Ulen. (1988). *Law and Economics.* Glenview, IL: Scott, Foresman.

______. (1997). *Law and Economics* (2d ed.). Reading, MA: Addison-Wesley.

Cornell, Nina, Roger Noll, and Barry Weingast. (1976). Safety Regulation. In Henry Owen and Charles Schultze, *Setting National Priorities: The Next Ten Years.*

Cozzetto, Don A., and Theodore B. Pedeliski. (1997). Privacy and the Workplace: Technology and Public Employment. *Public Personnel Management, 26,* (Winter), 515–527.

Cramton, Peter. (1997). The FCC Spectrum Auctions: An Early Assessment. *Journal of Economics & Management Strategy, 6*(Fall), 431–495.

Crombez, Christophe C.M.G.M. (1996). Legislative Procedures in the European Community. *British Journal of Political Science, 26,* 199–228.

Cummins Engine Company. (1980, October). *Cummins Practice.* Columbus, IN.

Curtis, Gerald L. (1975). Big Business and Political Influence. In D. Vogel, *Modern Japanese Organization and Decision-Making* (pp. 33–70).

Cusamano, Michael A. and David B. Yoffie. 1998. *Competing on Internet Time: Lessons from Netscape and Its Battle with Microsoft.* New York: The Free Press.

Dalkir, Serdar, and Frederick R. Warren-Boulton. (1999). Prices, Market Definition, and the Effects of Merger: Staples-Office Depot (1997). In J. E. Kwoka and L. J. White, 143–164.

Dalton, Dan R., and Michael B. Metzger. (1993). "Integrity Testing" for Personnel Selection: An Unsparing Perspective. *Journal of Business Ethics, 12,* 147–156.

Dalton, Russell J. (1988). Politics in West Germany. In G. A. Almond and G. B. Powell, *Comparative Politics Today: A World View.* (pp. 257–308).

Davidson, Wallace N., Dan L. Worrell, and Abuzar El-Jelly. (1995). Influencing Managers to Change Unpopular Corporate Behavior Through Boycotts and Divestitures. *Business & Society, 34,* (August), 171–196.

De Bary, William T. (1991). *The Trouble with Confucianism.* Cambridge: Harvard University Press.

De George, Richard T. (1982a). *Business Ethics.* New York: Macmillan.

______. (1982b). Whistle Blowing as Morally Justified. In DeGeorge. Reprinted in L. H. Newton and M. M. Ford (1990) (pp. 60–64).

_____. (1993). International Business Ethics. *Business Ethics Quarterly* (4), 1–9.

DeJong, H. W., (Ed.) 1988. *The Structure of European Industry.* Dordrecht, the Netherlands: Kluwer.

Department of Labor, Office of Inspector General. (1993). Targeted Jobs Tax Credit Program, State of Alabama, October 1, 1990–September 30, 1991. Washington, DC.

Derthick, Martha, and Paul J. Quirk. (1985). *The Politics of Deregulation.* Washington, DC: Brookings Institution.

Destler, I. M. (1986). *American Trade Politics: System Under Stress.* Washington, DC: Institute for International Economics.

Destler, I. M. and John S. Odell. (1987). *Anti-Protection: Changing Forces in United States Trade Politics.* Policy Analyses in International Economics 21, Institute for International Economics, Washington, DC.

Deyo, Frederic C. (Ed.). (1987). *The Political Economy of the New Asian Industrialism.* Ithaca, NY: Cornell University Press.

Dixit, Avinash, and Barry Nalebuff. (1991). *Thinking Strategically.* New York: Norton.

Dobbing, John (Ed.). (1988). *Infant Feeding: Anatomy of a Controversy 1973–1984.* Berlin, Germany: Springer-Verlag.

Doi, Takeo. (1988). Dependency in Human Relationships. In D. I. Okimoto and T. P. Rohlen, 20–25.

Dollinger, Marc J. (1988). Confucian Ethics and Japanese Management Practices. *Journal of Business Ethics, 7,* 575–584.

Donaldson, Thomas. (1989). *The Ethics of International Business.* Oxford, UK: Oxford University Press.

______. (1996). Values in Tension: Ethics Away From Home. *Harvard Business Review* (September–October), 48–49, 52–56, 58, 60, 62.

Donaldson, Thomas, and Patricia H. Werhane. (1988). *Ethical Issues in Business: A Philosophical Approach*(3d ed.). Englewood Cliffs, NJ: Prentice Hall.

Dore, Ronald. (1983). Goodwill and the Spirit of Market Capitalism. *British Journal of Sociology, 34,* (4), 459–481. Reprinted in D. I. Okimoto and T. P. Rohlen (1988), pp. 90–99.

Dornbusch, Rudiger, and James M. Poterba. (Eds.) (1991). *Global Warming: Economic Policy Responses.* Cambridge, MA: MIT Press.

Drucker, Peter B. (1981). What is 'Business Ethics'? *The Public Interest, 63,* (Spring), 18–36.

Dungworth, Terence. (1988). Product Liability and the Business Sector: Litigation Trends in the Federal Courts. RAND Corporation, Santa Monica, CA: Institute for Civil Justice.

Durlabhji, Subhash. (1990). The Influence of Confucianism and Zen on the Japanese Organization. *Akron Business and Economic Review, 21,* (2), 31–45.

Duverger, Maurice. (1954). *Political Parties: Their Organization and Activity in the Modern State,* translated by Barbara and Robert North. New York: Wiley.

Eads, George C., and Michael Fix. (Eds.) (1984). *The Reagan Regulatory Strategy: An Assessment.* Washington DC: Urban Institute Press.

Easterbrook, Frank H., and Daniel R. Fischel. (1981). The Proper Role of a Target's Management in Responding to a Tender Offer. *Harvard Law Review* (April), 1161–1204.

Edley, Christopher F., Jr. (1990). *Administrative Law.* New Haven, CN: Yale University Press.

Elzinga, Kenneth G., and William Briet. (1976). *The Antitrust Penalties: A Study in Law and Economics.* New Haven, CN: Yale University Press.

Engle, David L. (1979). An Approach to Corporate Social Responsibility. *Stanford Law Review, 32* (November), 1–98.

Environmental Protection Agency. (1991). *Environmental Investments: The Cost of a Clean Environment.* Washington, DC: Island Press.

Epstein, Edward Jay. (1973). *News from Nowhere.* New York: Random House.

______. (1981). The Selection of Reality. In Elie Abel (Ed.), *What's News* (pp. 119–132). San Francisco: Institute for Contemporary Studies.

Epstein, Richard A. (1980). *A Theory of Strict Liability.* San Francisco: Cato Institute.

Esty, Daniel C. (1994). *Greening the GATT: Trade, Environment, and the Future.* Washington, DC: Institute for International Economics.

European Commission. (1988). Social Dimensions of the Internal Market. Commission Working Paper, SEC (88) 1148, Brussels, Belgium.

Evans, Fred J. (1987). *Managing the Media.* New York: Quorum Books.

Ewing, David W. (1983). *Do It My Way Or You're Fired.* New York: Wiley.

______. (1989). *Justice on the Job: Resolving Grievances in the Nonunion Workplace.* Boston, MA: Harvard Business School Press.

Fairbank, John K. (1992). *China: A New History.* Cambridge: Harvard University Press.

Falsey, Thomas A. (1989). *Corporate Philosophies and Mission Statements.* New York: Quorum Books.

Fama, Eugene F., and Michael C. Jensen. (1983). Separation of Ownership and Control. *Journal of Law & Economics, 26* (June), 301–325.

Feary, Vaughana Macy. (1994). Sexual Harassment: Why the Corporate World Still Doesn't 'Get' It. *Journal of Business Ethics, 13,* 649–662.

Federal Aviation Administration, Department of Transportation. Advisory Circular: Guidelines for Developing an Anti-Drug Plan for Aviation Personnel, Washington, DC, March 16, 1989.

Federal Trade Commission. (1990). The Hart-Scott-Rodino Antitrust Improvements Act of 1976. Washington, DC.

Feldstein, Martin. (1997). The Political Economy of the European Economic and Monetary Union: Political Sources of an Economic Liability. *Journal of Economic Perspectives, 11*(Fall), 23–42.

Feinstein, Alvan R. (1988). Scientific Standards in Epidemiologic Studies of the Menace of Daily Life. *Science, 242*(December), 1257–1263.

Fiorina, Morris P. (1989). *Congress: Keystone of the Washington Establishment* (2d ed.). New Haven, CN: Yale University Press.

Fisher, Franklin M., John J. McGowan, and Joen E. Greenwood. (1983). *Folded, Spindled, and Mutilated: Economic Analysis of U.S. v. IBM.* Cambridge, MA: MIT Press.

Fishwick, Frank. (1993). *Making Sense of Competition Policy.* London, UK: Kogan Page.

Foote, Susan Bartlett. (1984). Corporate Responsibility in a Changing Legal Environment. *California Management Review, 26,*(Spring), 217–228.

Foreman, Christopher H., Jr. (1984). Congress and Social Regulation in the Reagan Era. In George C. Eads and Michael Fix (Eds.), *The Reagan Regulatory Strategy: An Assessment.*.

Fowler, Linda L., and Ronald G. Shaiko. (1987). The Grass Roots Connection: Environmental Activists and Senate Roll Calls. *American Journal of Political Science, 31* (August), 484–510.

Fox, J. Ronald. (1982). *Managing Business-Government Relations: Cases and Notes on Business-Government Problems.* Homewood, IL: Richard D. Irwin.

Francis, John. (1993). *The Politics of Regulation: A Comparative Perspective.* Oxford, UK: Blackwell.

Franklin, Marc A., and Robert L. Rabin. (1987). *Cases and Materials on Tort Law and Alternatives* (4th ed.). Mineola, NY: Foundation Press.

Freeman, Richard B., and James L. Medoff. (1979). The Two Faces of Unionism. *The Public Interest* (Fall), 69–93.

Freeman, R. Edward. (1984). *Strategic Management: A Stakeholder Approach.* Boston: Pitman.

Freeman, R. Edward, and Daniel R. Gilbert, Jr. (1988). *Corporate Strategy and the Search for Ethics.* Englewood Cliffs, NJ: Prentice Hall.

Freestone, David. (1983). The European Court of Justice. In J. Lodge, *Institutions and Policies of the European Community.*

Friedman, Milton. (1962). *Capitalism and Freedom.* Chicago: University of Chicago Press.

______. (1970, September 13). The Social Responsibility of Business is to Increase its Profits. *New York Times Magazine,* pp. 32–33, 122, 126.

Fukui, Haruhiro. (1970). *Party in Power.* Berkeley, CA: University of California Press.

Gale, Jeffrey, and Rogene A. Buchholz. (1987). The Political Pursuit of Competitive Advantage: What Business Can Gain from Government. In A. A. Marcus, A. M. Kaufman, and D. R. Bean, 31–42.

Galvin, Robert W. (1992, October). International Business and the Changing Nature of Global Competition. Oxford, OH: Miami University.

Garber, Doris A.(Ed.). (1990). *Media Power in Politics* (2d ed.). Washington, DC: CQ Press.

Garrett, Geoffrey. (1993). The Politics of Maastricht. *Economics and Politics,* 5:102–124.

General Dynamics Corporation. General Dynamics Standards of Business Ethics and Conduct, St. Louis, Missouri.

______. The Ethics Program 1985/1986, St. Louis, Missouri.

Gerlach, Michael L. (1992). *Alliance Capitalism: The Social Organization of Japanese Business.* Berkeley, CA: University of California Press.

______. (1987). Business Alliances and the Strategy of the Japanese Firm. *California Management Review, 30* (1), 126–142.

Gert, Bernard. (1988). *Morality: A New Justification of the Moral Rules.* New York: Oxford University Press.

Gilbert, Richard J. (1999). Networks, Standards, and the Use of Market Dominance: Microsoft (1995). In John E. Kwoka, Jr. and Lawrence J. White, *The Antitrust Revolution: Economics, Competition, and Policy.* (pp. 409–429) New York: Oxford University Press.

Gilligan, Thomas W., and Keith Krehbiel. (1987). Collective Decision-Making and Standing Committees: An Informational Rationale for Restrictive Amendment Procedures. *Journal of Law, Economics, and Organization, 3* (Fall), 287–335.

Goldstein, Judith. (1988). Ideas, Institutions, and American Trade Policy. *International Organization, 42,* (Winter), 179–217.

Goodman, John B. (1992). *Monetary Sovereignty: The Politics of Central Banking in Western Europe.* Ithaca, NY: Cornell University Press.

Goodpaster, Kenneth E. (1983). The Concept of Corporate Responsibility. *Journal of Business Ethics, 2,* 1–22.

Gorlin, Rena A. (1990) *Codes of Professional Responsibility* (2d ed.). Washington, DC: Bureau of National Affairs.

Gramlich, Edward M. (1998). *A Guide to Benefit-Cost Analysis* (2d ed.). Prospect Heights, IL: Waveland Press.

Green, Edward, and Robert Porter. (1984). Noncooperative Collusion under Imperfect Price Information. *Econometrica, 52,* 87–100.

Greve, Michael S., and Fred L. Smith, Jr. (1992). *Environmental Politics: Public Costs, Private Politics.* New York: Praeger.

Grieco, Joseph. (1990). *Cooperation Among Nations.* Ithaca, NY: Cornell University Press.

Griffin, Kelley. (1987). *Ralph Nader Presents More Action for a Change.* New York: Dembner Books.

Groarke, Leo. (1990). Affirmative Action as a Form of Restitution. *Journal of Business Ethics, 9,* 207–213.

Groseclose, Timothy. (1996). An Examination of the Market for Favors and Votes in Congress. *Economic Inquiry, 34*(April), 1–21.

Groseclose, Timothy, and James M. Snyder, Jr. (1996). Buying Supermajorities. *American Political Science Review, 90*(June), 303–315.

Groves, Theodore, Yongmiao Hong, John McMillan, and Barry Naughton. (1994). Autonomy and Incentives in Chinese State Enterprises. *Quarterly Journal of Economics, 109*(February), 183–209.

______. (1995). China's Evolving Managerial Labor Market. *Journal of Political Economy, 103*(August), 873–892.

Grub, Phillip D., and Jian Hai Lin. (1991). *Foreign Direct Investment in China.* New York: Quorum Books.

Haas, Walter A., Jr. (1981). Corporate Social Responsibility: A New Term for an Old Concept with New Significance. In T. Bradshaw and D. Vogel, *Corporations and Their Critics.*

Haggard, Stephen. (1990). *Pathways from the Periphery: The Politics of Growth in the Newly Industrializing Countries.* Ithaca, NY: Cornell University Press.

Hall, Richard L., and Frank W. Wayman. (1990). Buying Time: Moneyed Interests and the Mobilization of Bias in Congressional Committees. *American Political Science Review, 84,* 707–820.

Hamilton, Gary G. (1996). Overseas Chinese Capitalism. In W. M. Tu (Ed.), *Confucian Traditions in East Asian Modernity.* Cambridge, MA: Harvard University Press.

Hamilton, J. Brooke, III, and David Hoch. (1997). Ethical Standards for Business Lobbying: Some Practical Suggestions. *Business Ethics Quarterly, 7,* 117–129.

Hamilton, James T. (1993). Politics and Social Costs: Estimating the Impact of Collective Action on Hazardous Waste Facilities. *RAND Journal of Economics,* 24 (Spring), 101–125.

______. (1997). Taxes, Torts, and the Toxics Release Inventory: Congressional Voting on Instruments to Control Pollution. *Economic Inquiry, 35* (October), 745–762.

______. (1998). *Channeling Violence: The Economic Market for Violent Television Programming.* Princeton, NJ: Princeton University Press.

Hamilton, V. Lee, and Joseph Sanders. (1992). *Everyday Justice: Responsibility and the Individual in Japan and the United States.* New Haven, CT: Yale University Press.

Handler, Edward, and John R. Mulkern. (1982). *Business and Politics.* Lexington, MA: Lexington Books.

Hardin, Russell. (1982). *Collective Action, Resources for the Future.* Baltimore, MD: Johns Hopkins University Press.

______. (1988). *Morality within the Limits of Reason.* Chicago, IL: University of Chicago Press.

Harding, Harry. (1987). *Chinas Second Revolution: Reform After Mao.* Washington, DC: Brookings Institute.

Harris, Richard A., and Sidney M. Milkis. (1989). *The Politics of Regulatory Change: A Tale of Two Agencies.* Oxford, UK: Oxford University Press.

Harris, Robert G., and C. Jeffrey Kraft. (1997). Meddling Through: Regulating Local Telephone Competition in the United States. *Journal of Economic Perspectives, 11*(Summer), 93–112.

Harsanyi, John C. (1997). Rule Utilitarianism and Decision Theory. *Erkenntnis, 11,* 25–53.

______. (1982). Morality and the Theory of Rational Behavior. In A. Sen and B. Williams, *Utilitarianism and Beyond* (pp. 39–62).

Hawk, Barry E. (1988). The American Antitrust Revolution: Lessons for the EEC? *European Competition Law Review, 9,* 53–87.

Hay, Robert D., and Edmund R. Gray. (1981). *Business & Society: Cases and Text.* Cincinnati, OH: Southwestern.

Hayes, William J., Jr. (1989). *State Antitrust Laws.* Washington, DC: Bureau of National Affairs.

Henderson, George. (1994). *Cultural Diversity in the Workplace: Issues and Strategies.* Westport, CT: Quorum Books.

Hewlett-Packard Company. (1989). Standards of Business Conduct. Palo Alto, CA.

______. (1984). How to Deal With the Press. Palo Alto, CA.

Hirschman, Albert O. (1970). *Exit, Voice, and Loyalty.* Cambridge, MA: Harvard University Press.

Hobbes, Thomas. (1651). *Leviathan.* Edited by C. B. Macpherson. London, UK: Pelican Books. 1968.

Hogan, James. (1991). *The European Marketplace.* London, UK: Macmillan.

Holt, Charles A., and David T. Scheffman. (1989). Strategic Business Behavior and Antitrust. In R. J. Larner and J. W. Meehan, *Economics and Antitrust Policy* (pp. 39–82).

Hoscheit, J.M., and W. Wessels (Eds.). (1988). *The European Council 1974–1986: Evaluation and Prospects.* European Institute of Public Administration.

Howell, Rate A., John R. Allison, and N. T. Henley. (1987). *The Legal Environment of Business.* Chicago: Dryden Press.

Huber, Peter, and Robert E. Litan (Eds.). (1991). *The Liability Maze: The Impact of Liability Law on Safety and Innovation.* Washington, DC: Brookings.

Hufbauer, Gary C., (Ed.). (1990). *Europe 1992: An American Perspective.* Washington, DC: Brookings.

Hufbauer, Gary C., Diane T. Berliner, and Kimberly Ann Elliot. (1986). *Trade Protection in the United States: 31 Case Studies.* Washington, DC: Institute for International Economics.

Hufbauer, Gary C., and Kimberly A. Elliott. (1994). *Measuring the Costs of Protection in the United States.* Washington, DC: Institute for International Economics.

Hufbauer, Gary C., and Jeffrey J. Schott. (1993). *NAFTA: An Assessment.* (rev. ed.). Washington, DC: Institute for International Economics.

Inoguchi, Takashi, and Daniel I. Okimoto (Eds.). (1988). *The Political Economy of Japan: Volume 2, The Changing International Context.* Stanford, CA: Stanford University Press.

International Trade Commission. (1990). *1990 Annual Report.* Washington, DC.

Investor Responsibility Research Center. (1993). Voting by Institutional Investors on Corporate Governance Issues. Washington, DC.

Ito, Takatoshi. (1992). *The Japanese Economy.* Cambridge, MA: MIT Press.

Ivanhoe, Philip J. (1993). *Confucian Moral Self Cultivation.* New York: Peter Lang.

Iyengar, Shanto, and Donald R. Kinder. (1987). *News That Matters.* Chicago: University of Chicago Press.

Johnson, Chalmers. (1982). *MITI and the Japanese Miracle: The Growth of Industrial Policy, 1925–1975.* Stanford, CA: Stanford University Press.

______. (1989). MITI, MPT, and the Telecom Wars: How Japan Makes Policy for High Technology. In C. Johnson, L. D. Tyson, and J. Zysman, *Politics and Productivity: The Real Story of Why Japan Works* (pp. 177–240).

Johnson, Chalmers, Laura D'Andrea Tyson, and John Zysman. (1989). *Politics and Productivity: The Real Story of Why Japan Works.* Cambridge, MA: Ballinger.

Jones, Thomas M. (1980). Corporate Social Responsibility Revisited, Redefined. *California Management Review, 22,*(Spring), 59–67.

Jonsen, Albert R., and Stephen Toulmin. (1988). *The Abuse of Casuistry.* Berkeley, CA: University of California Press.

Joskow, Paul L., and Richard Schmalensee. (1983). *Markets for Power: An Analysis of Electric Utility Deregulation.* Cambridge, MA: MIT Press.

______. (1998). The Political Economy of Market-Based Environmental Policy: The U.S. Acid Rain Program. *Journal of Law and Economics, 41* (April), 37–84.

Joskow, Paul L., Richard Schmalensee, and Elizabeth M. Bailey. (1998). The Market for Sulfur Dioxide Emissions. *American Economic Review, 88*(September), 669–685.

Jury Verdict Research. (1997). Personal Injury Valuation Handbook: Current Award Trends in Personal Injury, 1997 Edition. LRP Publications.

Kahn, Alfred. (1970). *The Economics of Regulation: Principles and Institutions, Volumes I and II.* New York: Wiley.

Kalt, Joseph P. (1981). *The Economics and Politics of Oil Price Regulation.* Cambridge, MA: MIT Press.

Kant, Immanuel. (1785). *Ethical Philosophy, (a) Grounding for the Metaphysics of Morals;* (1785) *(b) The Metaphysical Principles of Virtue* (1797). Translation by James W. Ellington, introduction by Warner A. Wick. Indianapolis, IN: Hackett. 1983.

Karpoff, Jonathan M., and Paul H. Malatesta. (1989). The Wealth Effects of Second-Generation State Take-over Legislation. *Journal of Financial Economics, 25,* 291–322.

Katzenstein, Peter J. (Ed.). (1989). *Industry and Politics in West Germany: Toward the Third Republic.* Ithaca, NY: Cornell University Press.

Keim, Gerald D. (1985). Corporate Grassroots Programs in the 1980s. *California Management Review, 28*(Fall), 110–123.

Keim, Gerald D., and Roger E. Meiners. (1978). Corporate Social Responsibility: Private Means for Public Wants? *Policy Review, 5*(Summer), 79–95.

Kelman, Steven. (1981). *What Price Incentives? Economists and the Environment.* Boston: Auburn House.

Kerwin, Cornelius M. (1994). *Rulemaking: How Government Agencies Write Law and Make Policy.* Washington, DC: CQ Press.

Kester, W. Carl. (1991). *Japanese Takeovers: The Global Competition for Corporate Control.* Boston: Harvard Business School Press.

Klingemann, Hans-Dieter. (1987). Electoral Programmes in West Germany 1949–1980: Explorations in the Nature of Political Controversy. In I. Budge, D. Robertson, and D. Hearl, *Ideology, Strategy and Party Change: Spatial Analysis of Post-War Election Programmes in 19 Democracies* (pp. 294–323).

Klitgaard, Robert. (1988). *Controlling Corruption.* Berkeley, CA: University of California Press.

Kneese, Alvin V., and Charles L. Schultze. (1975). *Pollution, Prices, and Public Policy.* Washington, DC: Brookings Institution.

Kotchian, A. Carl. (1977, July 9). The Payoff: Lockheed's 70-Day Mission to Tokyo. *Saturday Review,* pp. 5–12.

Krehbiel, Keith. (1991). *Information and Legislative Organization.* Ann Arbor: University of Michigan Press.

______. (1996). Institutional and Partisan Sources of Gridlock: A Theory of Divided and Unified Government. *Journal of Theoretical Politics, 8,* 7–40.

______. (1998). *Pivotal Politics: A Theory of U.S. Lawmaking.* Chicago, IL: University of Chicago Press.

______. (1999). Pivotal Politics: A Refinement of Nonmarket Analysis for Voting Institutions. *Business and Politics,* 1(April).

Kreps, David M. (1990). Corporate Culture and Economic Theory. In J. A. Alt and K. Shepsle, *Perspectives on Positive Political Economy* (pp. 90–143).

Kreps, David M., and Robert Wilson. (1982). Reputation and Imperfect Information. *Journal of Economic Theory, 27,* 253–279.

Kridel, Donald J., David E. M. Sappington, and Dennis L. Weisman. (1996). The Effects of Incentive Regulation in the Telecommunications Industry: A Survey. *Journal of Regulatory Economics, 9,* 269–306.

Kroszner, Randall S., and Thomas Stratmann. (1998). Interest Group Competition and the Organization of Congress: Theory and Evidence from Financial Services Political Action Committees. *American Economic Review* 88 (December) 1163–1187.

Krugman, Paul (Ed.). (1986). *Strategic Trade Policy and the New International Economics.* Cambridge, MA: MIT Press.

Krugman, Paul R. (1990). *Rethinking International Trade.* Cambridge, MA: MIT Press.

Küng, Hans. (1997). A Global Ethic in an Age of Globalization. *Business Ethics Quarterly, 7,* 17–32.

Kupfer, Joseph. (1993). The Ethics of Genetic Screening in the Workplace. *Business Ethics Quarterly, 3,* 17–25.

Kwoka, John E., Jr., and Lawrence J. White (Eds.). (1999). *The Antitrust Revolution: Economics, Competition, and Policy.* Oxford, UK: Oxford University Press.

Lande, Stephen L., and Craig Vangrasstek. (1986). *The Trade and Tariff Act of 1984: Trade Policy in the Reagan Administration.* Lexington, MA: Lexington Books.

Larner, Robert J., and James W. Meehan, Jr. (Eds.). (1989). *Economics and Antitrust Policy.* New York: Quorum.

Lieberthal, Kenneth. (1995). *Governing China.* New York: W. W. Norton.

Linn, Scott C., and John J. McConnell. (1983). An Empirical Investigation of the Impact of 'Antitakeover' Amendments on Common Stock Prices. *Journal of Financial Economics, 11,* 361–400.

Linneman, Peter. (1980). The Effects of Consumer Safety Standards: The 1973 Mattress Flamability Standard. *Journal of Law and Economics, 23*(October), 461–479.

Littlejohn, Stephen E. (1986). Competition and Cooperation: New Trends in Corporate Public Issue Identification and Resolution. *California Management Review, 29*(Fall), 109–123.

Locke, John. (1700). *The Works of John Locke.* Westport, CN: Greenwood. 1989.

Lodge, George Cabot. (1990). *Comparative Business-Government Relations.* Englewood Cliffs, NJ: Prentice Hall.

Lodge, Juliet (Ed.). (1983). *Institutions and Policies of the European Community.* New York: St. Martin's Press.

Lowi, Theodore J. (1964). American Business, Public Policy, Case-Studies, and Political Theory. *World Politics, 16*(July), 677–693.

Lukes, Steven. (1973). *Individualism.* Oxford: Basil Blackwell.

Lynn, Leonard H., and Timothy J. McKeown. (1988). *Organizing Business: Trade Associations in America and Japan.* Washington, DC: American Enterprise Institute.

Lyons, David. (1965). *The Forms and Limits of Utilitarianism.* Oxford, UK: Oxford University Press.

MacAvoy, Paul W. (1981, December 20). The Business Lobby's Wrong Business. *The New York Times.*

Magat, Wesley A., Alan J. Krupnick, and Winston Harrington. (1986). *Rules in the Making: A Statistical Analysis of Regulatory Agency Behavior.* Washington, DC: Resources for the Future.

Magat, Wesley A., and W. Kip Viscusi. (1992). *Informational Approaches to Regulation.* Cambridge, MA: MIT Press.

Magee, Stephen P., William A. Brock, and Leslie Young. (1989). *Black Hole Tariffs and Endogenous Policy Theory: Political Economy in General Equilibrium.* Cambridge, UK: Cambridge University Press.

Mahoney, Richard J., and Stephen E. Littlejohn. (1989). Innovation on Trial: Punitive Damages Versus New Products. *Science, 15* (December), 1398.

Maheshwari, Shriram. (1987). *The Higher Civil Service in Japan.* New Delhi, India: Allied Publishers.

Malatesta, Paul H., and Ralph A. Walking. (1988). Poison Pill Securities: Stockholder Wealth, Profitability, and Ownership Structure. *Journal of Financial Economics, 20,* 347–376.

Manley, Marisa. (1987). Product Liability: You're More Exposed Than You Think. *Harvard Business Review,* September-October, 28–30, 34, 36, 40.

Marcus, Alfred A. (1980). *Promise and Performance: Choosing and Implementing Environmental Policy.* Westport, CN: Greenwood Press.

Marcus, Alfred A., Allen M. Kaufman, and David R. Beam (Eds.). (1987). *Business Strategy and Public Policy.* New York: Quorum Books.

Mashaw, Jerry L., and Richard A. Merrill. (1985). *Administrative Law: The American Public Law System: Cases and Materials* (2d ed.). St. Paul, MN: West Publishing Co.

Mason, Mark. (1992). *Access Denied?: American Multinationals and Japan, 1899–1980.* Cambridge, MA: Harvard University Press.

Matthews, Marilyn C. (1987). Codes of Ethics: Organizational Behaviour and Misbehaviour. In *Research in Corporate Social Performance* (vol. 9) (pp. 107–130). Greenwich, CN: JAI Press.

Mayhew, David. (1974). *Congress: The Electoral Connection.* New Haven, CT: Yale University Press.

McComas, Maggie, Geoffrey Fookes, and George Taucher. (1982). The Dilemma of Third World Nutrition. Nestle S.A., Geneva.

McCraw, Thomas K. (Ed.). (1981). *Regulation in Perspective: Historical Essays.* Boston: Harvard Business School.

McCubbins, Mathew, Roger Noll, and Barry Weingast. (1987). Administrative Procedures as Instruments of Political Control. *Journal of Law, Economics and Organizations, 3,* 243–277.

McDonald's Corporation-Environmental Defense Fund, Waste Reduction Task Force, "Final Report," April 1991.

McGuire, Jean B., Alison Sundgren, and Thomas Schneeweis. (1988). Corporate Social Responsibility and Firm Financial Performance. *Academy of Management Journal, 31,* 854–872.

McMillan, John. (1991). DANGO: Japan's Price-Fixing Conspiracies. *Economics and Politics, 3,*(November), 201–218.

Miceli, M. P., and J. P. Near. (1992). *Blowing the Whistle: The Organizational and Legal Implications for Companies and Employees.* New York: Lexington Books.

Milgrom, Paul, and John D. Roberts. (1982). Limit Pricing and Entry Under Incomplete Information. *Econometrica, 50,* 443–459.

Mill, John Stuart. (1859). *On Liberty* (Edited by David Spitz). New York: Norton. 1975.

______. (1861). *Utilitarianism.* In Alan Ryan (Ed.), *Utilitarianism and Other Essays: J. S. Mill and Jeremy Bentham.* New York: Penguin Books. 1987.

Moe, Terry M. (1980). *The Organization of Interests.* Chicago: University of Chicago Press.

______. (1985). Congressional Control of the Bureaucracy: An Assessment of the Positive Theory of "Congressional Dominance." Paper presented at the American Political Science Association annual meeting.

Molander, Earl A. (1980). *Responsive Capitalism: Case Studies in Corporate Social Conduct.* New York: McGraw-Hill.

Moore, Barrington. (1966). *Social Origins of Dictatorship and Democracy.* Boston: Beacon Press.

Moore, Michael J., and Wesley A. Magat. (1993). The Efficacy of Voluntary Safety Standards: Lessons from Chain Saws and All-Terrain Vehicles. Working paper, Duke University, Durham, NC.

Morishima, Michio. (1988). Confucianism as a Basis for Capitalism. In D. I. Okimoto and T. P. Rohlen, 36–38.

Mundo, Philip A. (1992). *Interest Groups: Cases and Characteristics.* Chicago: Nelson-Hall Publishers.

National Center for State Courts, Court Statistics Project. (1996). Examining the Work of State Courts.

Natural Resources Defense Council. (1989). Intolerable Risk: Pesticides in Our Children's Food. Washington, DC, February 27.

Newman, Edwin. (1984). A Journalist's Responsibility. In R. Schumhl. *The Responsibilities of Journalism,* pp. 19–38.

Newton, Lisa H. (1990). Reverse Discrimination as Unjustified. *Ethics, 83*(July). Reprinted in L. H. Newton and M. M. Ford (1990), pp. 94–98.

Newton, Lisa H., and Maureen M. Ford (Eds.). (1990). *Taking Sides: Clashing Views on Controversial Issues in Business Ethics and Society.* Guilford, CN: Dushkin.

Nivison, David S. (1996). *The Ways of Confucianism.* Chicago: Open Court.

Noll, Roger G., and Bruce M. Owen. (1983). *The Political Economy of Deregulation: Interest Groups in the Regulatory Process.* Washington, DC: American Enterprise Institute.

Nozick, Robert. (1974). *Anarchy, State, and Utopia.* New York: Basic Books.

Nugent, Neill. (1994). *The Government and Politics of the European Union.* Durham, NC: Duke University Press.

O'Halloran, Sharyn. (1994). *Politics, Process, and American Foreign Policy.* Ann Arbor: University of Michigan Press.

Okimoto, Daniel I. (1988). The Liberal-Democratic Party's "Grand Coalition." In D. I. Okimoto and T. P. Rohlen, *Inside the Japanese System: Readings in Contemporary Society and Political Economy* (pp. 179–180).

______. (1988). Political Inclusivity: The Domestic Structure of Trade. In T. Inoguchi and D. I. Okimoto, *The Political Economy of Japan: Volume 2, The Changing International Context,* 305–344.

______. (1989). *Between MITI and the Market: Japanese Industrial Policy for High Technology.* Stanford, CA: Stanford University Press.

______. (1988). Political Inclusivity: The Domestic Structure of Trade. In T. Inoguchi and D. I. Okimoto, *The Political Economy of Japan: Volume 2. The Changing International Context,* pp. 305–344.

Okimoto, Daniel I., and Thomas P. Rohlen (Eds.). (1988). *Inside the Japanese System: Readings on Contemporary Society and Political Economy.* Stanford, CA: Stanford University Press.

Oleszek, Walter J. (1996). *Congressional Procedures and the Policy Process.* (4th ed.). Washington, DC: CQ Press.

Olson, Mancur J. (1965). *The Logic of Collective Action.* Cambridge, MA: Harvard University Press.

Ordover, Janusz A., and Robert D. Willig. (1983). The 1982 Department of Justice Merger Guidelines: An Economic Assessment. *California Law Review, 71,* 535–574.

Ornstein, Norman J., Thomas E. Mann, and Michael J. Malbin. (1997). *Vital Statistics on Congress.* Washington, DC: American Enterprise Institute.

Oster, Sharon M. (1994). *Modern Competitive Analysis* (2d ed.). Oxford, UK: Oxford University Press.

Overturf, Stephen F. (1986). *The Economic Principles of European Integration.* New York: Praeger.

Owen, Bruce M., and Ronald Braeutigam. (1978). *The Regulation Game: Strategic Use of the Administrative Process.* Cambridge, MA: Balinger.

Owen, Henry, and Charles Schulze (Eds.). (1976). *Setting National Priorities: The Next Ten Years.* Washington, DC: Brookings.

Paine, Lynn Sharp. (1994). Managing for Organizational Integrity. *Harvard Business Review,* (March–April), 106–117.

Palmier, Leslie. (1989). Corruption in the West Pacific. *The Pacific Review, 2,* (1), 23.

Pascale, Richard, and Thomas P. Rohlen. (1983, Summer). The Mazda Turnaround. *Journal of Japanese Studies, 9* (2), 219–263. Reprinted in D. I. Okimoto and T. P. Rohlen (1988), pp. 149–169.

Pastin, Mark, and Michael Hooker. (1988). Ethics and the Foreign Corrupt Practices Act. In T. Donaldson and P. H. Werhane, 48–53.

Pearson, Margaret. M. (1991). *Joint Ventures in the Peoples Republic of China.* Princeton: Princeton University Press.

Pei, M. (1997). Racing Against Time: Institutional Decay and Renewal in China. In William A. Joseph (Ed.), *China Briefing 1995–1996.* Armonk, NY: M. E. Sharpe.

Peltzman, Sam. (1975). The Effects of Automobile Safety Regulation. *Journal of Political Economy, 83*(August), 677–725.

______. (1976). Toward a More General Theory of Regulation. *Journal of Law and Economics, 19,* 211–240.

Peoples, James. (1998). Deregulation and the Labor Market. *Journal of Economic Perspectives, 12*(Summer), 111–130.

Peterson, Steven P., and George E. Hoffer. (1994). The Impact of Airbag Adoption on Relative Personal Injury and Absolute Collision Insurance Claims. *Journal of Consumer Research, 20,* (March), 657–662.

Pfeffer, Jeffrey, and Gerald Salanic. (1978). *The External Control of Organizations.* New York: Harper and Row.

Philips, Michael. (1984). Bribery. *Ethics, 94(July).* Reprinted in L. H. Newton and M. M. Ford (1990), pp. 280–290.

Polinsky, A. Mitchell. (1989). *An Introduction to Law and Economics* (2d ed.). Boston: Little, Brown.

Popoff, Frank P. (1992). Going Beyond Pollution Prevention. In Business: Championing the Global Environment, Report Number 995, The Conference Board, New York.

Porter, Michael E. (1980). *Competitive Strategy: Techniques for Analyzing Industries and Competitions.* New York: Free Press.

______. (1985). *Competitive Advantage.* New York: Free Press.

______. (1990). *The Competitive Advantage of Nations.* New York: Free Press.

Posner, Richard A. (1974). Theories of Economic Regulation. *Bell Journal of Economics, 5*(Autumn), 335–358.

______. (1976). *Antitrust Law: An Economic Perspective.* Chicago: University of Chicago Press.

______. (1981). *The Economics of Justice.* Cambridge, MA: Harvard University Press.

Post, James E. (1978). *Corporate Behavior and Social Change.* Reston, VA: Reston Publishing.

Poterba, James M. (1991). Tax Policy to Combat Global Warming: On Designing a Carbon Tax. In Rudiger Dornbusch and James M. Poterba (Eds.), *Global Warming: Economic Policy Responses* (pp. 71–98).

Prahalad, C. K., and Gary Hamel. (1990). The Core Competencies of the Corporation. *Harvard Business Review,* (May–June), 79–91.

President's Blue Ribbon Commission on Defense Management. (1986). *A Formula For Action.* Washington, DC.

Preston, Lee E., and James E. Post. (1975). *Private Management and Public Policy.* Englewood Cliffs, NJ: Prentice Hall.

Priest, George L. (1977). The Common Law Process and the Selection of Efficient Rules. *Journal of Legal Studies, 6*(January), 65–82.

Putnam, Todd. (1993). Boycotts Are Busting Out All Over. *Business and Society Review,* 47–51.

Pye, Lucian W. (1978). *China: An Introduction.* Boston: Little, Brown.

______. (1985). *Asian Power and Politics: The Cultural Dimensions of Authority.* Boston: Little, Brown.

Pye, Lucian W. (1988). *The Mandarin and the Cadre: China's Political Cultures.* Ann Arbor: University of Michigan Press.

Quirk, Paul J. (1981). *Industry Influence in Federal Regulatory Agencies.* Princeton, NJ: Princeton University Press.

Rawls, John. (1971). *A Theory of Justice.* Cambridge, MA: Belknap Press.

______. (1980). Kantian Constructivism in Moral Theory. *The Journal of Philosophy, 9*(September), 515–572.

______. (1993). *Political Liberalism.* New York: Columbia University Press,:

Redding, S. Gordon. (1996). Societal Transformation and the Contribution of Authority Relations and Cooperative Norms in Overseas Chinese Business. In Wei-ming Tu (Ed.), *Confucian Traditions in East Asian Modernity.* Cambridge: Harvard University Press.

Reed, Steven R. (1986). *Japanese Prefectures and Policymaking.* Pittsburgh, PA: University of Pittsburgh Press.

Reich, Robert B. (1998). The New Meaning of Corporate Social Responsibility. *California Management Review, 40*(Winter), 8–17.

Reischauer, Edwin O. (1988). *The Japanese Today: Change and Continuity.* Cambridge, MA: Belknap Press.

Richardson, Bradley M. (1988). Constituency Candidates Versus Parties in Japanese Voting Behavior. *American Political Science Review, 82*(September), 695–718.

Roetz, Heiner. (1993). *Confucian Ethics of the Axial Age.* Albany, NY: State University of New York Press.

Rose, Nancy L. (1985). The Incidence of Regulatory Rents in the Motor Carrier Industry. *Rand Journal of Economics, 16*(Autumn), 299–318.

______. (1987). Labor Rent Sharing and Regulation: Evidence from the Trucking Industry. *Journal of Political Economy, 95*(December), 1146–1178.

Rosenbaum, Walter A. (1995). *Environmental Politics and Policy* (3d ed.). Washington, DC: Congressional Quarterly.

Rothenberg, Lawrence S. (1991). Agenda Setting at Common Cause. In Allan J. Cigler and Burdett A. Loomis, *Interest Group Politics* (3d ed.), (pp. 131–149). Washington, DC: Congressional Quarterly.

Rousseau, Jean Jacques. (1762). *Of the Social Contract.* New York: Harper and Row. 1984.

Rubin, Paul H. (1983). *Business Firms and the Common Law: The Evolution of Efficient Rules.* New York: Praeger.

Rueter, Paul. (1988). The Economic Consequences of Expanded Corporate Liability. Santa Monica, CA: Institute for Civil Justice, RAND Corporation.

Rumelt, Richard. (1984). Towards a Strategic Theory of the Firm. In R. Lamb, *Competitive Strategic Management.* Englewood Cliffs, NJ, Prentice Hall.

Sabato, Larry J. (1984). *PAC Power: Inside the World of Political Action Committees.* New York: Norton.

Sackett, P. R., and M. M. Harris. (1984). Honesty Testing for Personnel Selection: A Review and Critique. *Personnel Psychology, 37,* 221–245.

Salisbury, Robert H. (1992). *Interests and Institutions.* Pittsburgh: University of Pittsburgh Press.

Saloner, Garth, Andrea Shepard, and Joel M. Podolny. (2000). *Strategic Management,* forthcoming.

Salop, Steven C., and Lawrence J. White. (1988). Private Antitrust Litigation: An Introduction and Framework. In L. J. White, *Private Antitrust Litigation: New Evidence, New Learning.*

Samuels, Richard J. (1987). *The Business of the Japanese State: Energy Markets in Comparative and Historical Perspective.* Ithaca, NY: Cornell University Press.

Sazanami, Yoko, Shujiro Urata, and Hiroki Kawai. (1994). *Measuring the Costs of Protection in Japan.* Washington, DC: Institute for International Economics.

Schelling, Thomas C. (1983a). Prices as Regulatory Instruments. In Schelling, *Incentives for Environmental Protection.*

Schelling, Thomas C. (Ed.). (1983b). *Incentives for Environmental Protection.* Cambridge, MA: MIT Press.

Schmalensee, Richard, Paul L. Joskow, A. Denny Ellerman, Juan Pablo Montero, and Elizabeth M. Bailey. (1998). An Interim Evaluation of Sulfur Dioxide Emissions Trading. *Journal of Economic Perspectives,* 12(Summer), 53–68.

Schmidt, Benno C., Jr. (1981). The First Amendment and the Press. In Elie Abel (Ed.), *What's News* (pp. 57–80). San Francisco: Institute for Contemporary Studies.

Schmuhl, Robert (Ed.). (1984). *The Responsibilities of Journalism.* Notre Dame, IN: University of Notre Dame Press.

Schuknecht, Ludger. (1992). *Trade Protection in the European Community.* Chur, Switzerland: Harwood Academic.

Schuler, Douglas A., and Kathleen Rehbein. (1998). Uncovering the Dimensionality of Corporate Political Involvement. Working paper. Houston, TX: Rice University.

Schwartz, Benjamin I. (1985). *The World of Thought in Ancient China.* Cambridge: Harvard University Press.

Schwartz, Carol A., and Rebecca L. Turner (Eds.). (1993). *Encyclopedia of Associations, 1994* (28th ed.). Detroit: Gale Research.

Schwartz, Felice N. (1989). Management Women and the New Facts of Life. *Harvard Business Review,* (January–February), 65–76.

Sen, Amartya. (1987). *On Ethics & Economics.* Oxford, UK: Basil Blackwell.

______. (1997). Economics, Business Principles and Moral Sentiments. *Business Ethics Quarterly, 7,* 5–15.

Sen, Amartya, and Bernard Williams (Eds.). (1982). *Utilitarianism and Beyond.* Cambridge, UK: Cambridge University Press.

Shapiro, Carl and Hal R. Varian. 1999. *Information Rules: A Strategic Guide to the Network Economy.* Boston, MA: Harvard University Press.

Shapiro, Ian. (1986). *The Evolution of Rights in Liberal Theory.* Cambridge, UK: Cambridge University Press.

Shaw, Malcolm W. (1997). *International Law* (4th ed.). Cambridge, UK: Cambridge University Press.

Shepsle, Kenneth A., and Mark S. Bonchek. (1997). *Analyzing Politics: Rationality, Behavior, and Institutions.* New York: Norton.

Shils, Edward. (1996). Reflections on Civil Society and Civility in the Chinese Intellectual Tradition. In Weiming Tu (Ed.), *Confucian Traditions in East Asian Modernity.* Cambridge: Harvard University Press.

Shipper, Frank, and Marianne M. Jennings. (1984). *Business Strategy for the Political Arena.* Westport, CN: Quorum Books.

Shirk, Susan L. (1993). *The Political Logic of Economic Reform in China.* Berkeley: University of California Press.

Shue, Henry. (1980). *Basic Rights: Subsistence, Affluence, and U.S. Foreign Power.* Princeton, NJ: Princeton University Press.

Shue, Vivienne. (1988). *The Reach of the State.* Stanford: Stanford University Press.

Shugart, William F., II. (1990). *Antitrust Policy and Interest-Group Politics.* New York: Quorum Books.

Sigman, Betsy Ann, and Susan-Kathryn McDonald. (1987). The Issues Manager as Public Opinion and Policy Analyst. In A. A. Marcus, A. M. Kaufman, and D. R. Beam, (pp. 164–194).

Skelly, Joe. (1995). The Rise of International Ethics: The Caux Round Table *Principles for Business. Business Ethics,* (March–April Supplement), 2–5.

Smith, Adam. (1776). *An Inquiry into the Nature and Causes of The Wealth of Nations* (Edited by R. H. Campbell and A. S. Skinner). Oxford, UK: Clarendon Press. 1995.

Smith, Alasdair, and Anthony J. Venables. (1990). Automobiles. In G. C. Hufbauer, *Europe 1992: An American Perspective* (pp. 119–158).

Snyder, James. (1991). On Buying Legislatures. *Economics and Politics, 3*(July), 93–109.

______. (1990). Campaign Contributions as Investments: The U.S. House of Representatives 1980–1986. *Journal of Political Economy, 98,* 1195–1227.

Sonnenfeld, Jeffrey, and Paul R. Lawrence. (1978). Why Do Companies Succumb to Price Fixing? *Harvard Business Review, 56*(July–August), 145–157.

Spitzer, Matthew L. (1991). Justifying Minority Preferences in Broadcasting. *Southern California Law Review, 293,* 334–336.

Stavins, Robert N. (1998). What Can We Learn from the Grand Policy Experiment? Lessons from SO_2 Allowance Trading. *Economic Perspectives,* 12(Summer), 69–88.

Steidlmeier, Paul. (1997). Business Ethics and Politics in China. *Business Ethics Quarterly, 7,* 131–143.

Stewart, Richard B. (1988). Controlling Environmental Risks through Economic Incentives. *Columbia Journal of Environmental Law, 13,* 153–169.

Stigler, George. (1971). The Theory of Economic Regulation. *Bell Journal of Regulation, 2*(Spring), 3–21.

Streeck, Wolfgang. (1984). *Industrial Relations in West Germany.* New York: St. Martin's Press.

Tachibanaki, Toshiaki. (1984). Labor Mobility and Job Tenure. In M. Aoki, *The Economic Analysis of the Japanese Firm* (pp. 77–102).

Taka, Iwao. (1994). Business Ethics: A Japanese View. *Business Ethics Quarterly, 4,* 53–78.

Taylor, Stan A. (1989). Tobacco and Economic Growth in Developing Nations. *Business in the Contemporary World* (Winter). Reprinted in L. H. Newton and M. M. Ford (1990), pp. 298–308.

Temin, Peter, with Louis Galambos. (1987). *The Fall of the Bell System.* Cambridge, UK: Cambridge University Press.

Thompson, James. (1967). *Organizations in Action.* New York: McGraw-Hill.

Tobacco Company Representatives. (1989). Letters to the Editor: The Tobacco Controversy. *Business in the Contemporary World* (Winter). Reprinted in L. H. Newton and M. M. Ford (1990), pp. 309–313.

Trebilcock, Michael J., and Robert C. York. (1990). *Fair Exchange: Reforming Trade Remedy Laws.* Toronto, Canada: C. D. Howe Institute.

Tu, Wei-ming. (1979). *Humanity and Self-Cultivation.* Berkeley: University of California Press.

Ulmann, A. (1985). Data in Search of a Theory: A Critical Examination of the Relationship among Social Performance, Social Disclosure, and Economic Performance. *Academy of Management Review, 10,* 540–577.

United States Trade Representative. (1993). Trade Agreements Resulting from the Uruguay Round of Multilateral Trade Negotiations. Washington, DC, December 15.

______. (1994). Final Act Embodying the Results of the Uruguay Round of Multilateral Trade Negotiations (Version of 15 December 1993). Washington, DC: U.S. Government Printing Office.

Upham, Frank K. (1987). *Law and Social Change in Postwar Japan,* Cambridge, MA: Harvard University Press.

Useem, Michael. (1988). Market and Institutional Factors in Corporate Contributions. *California Management Review, 30* (Winter), 77–88.

Vagelos, P. Roy. (1991). Are Prescription Drug Prices High? *Science, 252,* 1080–1084.

Valeo, Francis R., and Charles E. Morrison (Eds.). (1983). *The Japanese Diet and the U.S. Congress.* Boulder, CO: Westview Press.

Van Schendelen, M. P. C. M. (1993). The Netherlands: Lobby It Yourself. In M. P. C. M. Van Schendelen (Ed.), *National Public and Private EC Lobbying.* Hants, UK: Aldershot.

van Wolferen, Karel. (1989). *The Enigma of Japanese Power.* New York: Alfred A. Knopf.

Velasquez, Manuel G. (1988). *Business Ethics: Concepts and Cases* (2d ed.). Englewood Cliffs, NJ: Prentice Hall.

Vickers, John, and George Yarrow. (1988). *Privatization: An Economic Analysis.* Cambridge, MA: MIT Press.

Viscusi, W. Kip. (1984). *Regulating Consumer Product Safety.* Washington, DC: American Enterprise Institute.

______. (1991). *Reforming Products Liability.* Cambridge, MA: Harvard University Press.

Viscusi, W. Kip, and Michael J. Moore. (1993). Product Liability, Research and Development, and Innovation. *Journal of Political Economy, 101,* 161–184.

Viscusi, W. Kip, John M. Vernon, and Joseph E. Harrington, Jr. (1995). *Economics of Regulation and Antitrust* (2d ed.). Cambridge, MA: MIT Press.

Vogel, David. (1978). *Lobbying the Corporation: Citizen Challenges to Business Authority.* New York: Basic Books.

______. (1986). *National Styles of Regulation: Environmental Policy in Great Britain and the United States.* Ithaca, NY: Cornell University Press.

______. (1991). Business Ethics: New Perspectives on Old Problems. *California Business Review, 33*(Summer), 101–117.

Vogel, Ezra F. (Ed.). (1975). *Modern Japanese Organization and Decision-Making.* Berkeley, CA: University of California Press.

Vogel, Ezra F. (1980). *Canton Under Communism.* Cambridge: Harvard University Press.

Wang, L., and Joseph Fewsmith. (1995). Bulwark of the Planned Economy: The Structure and Role of the State Planning Commission. In Carol L. Hamrin and Suisheng Zhao (Eds.), *Decision-Making in Deng's China.* Armonk, NY: M. E. Sharpe.

Wartick, Steven L., and Robert E. Rude. (1986). Issues Management: Corporate Fad or Corporate Function. *California Management Review, 29*(Fall), 124–140.

Wasserstrom, Richard. (1978). A Defense of Programs of Preferential Treatment. *National Forum: The Phi Kappa Phi Journal, 58*(Winter), 15–18.

Weaver, Suzanne. (1977). *Decision to Prosecute: Organization and Public Policy in the Antitrust Division.* Cambridge, MA: MIT Press.

Weber, Leonard J. (1996). Citizenship and Democracy: The Ethics of Corporate Lobbying. *Business Ethics Quarterly, 6* (April), 253–259.

Weidenbaum, Murray L. (1990). *Business, Government, and the Public* (4th ed.). Englewood Cliffs, NJ: Prentice Hall.

______. (1996). The Chinese Family Business Enterprise. *California Management Review, 38* (Summer), 141–156.

Weingast, Barry M., and Mark Moran. (1983). Bureaucratic Discretion or Congressional Control? Regulatory Policymaking by the Federal Trade Commission. *Journal of Political Economy, 91*(October), 765–800.

Wells, Deborah L., and Beverly J. Kracher. (1993). Justice, Sexual Harassment, and the Reasonable Victim Standard. *Journal of Business Ethics, 12,* 423–431.

Wells, Peter, and Michael Rawlinson. (1994). *The New European Automobile Market.* London, UK: St. Martin's Press.

Werhane, Patricia H. (1985). *Persons, Rights, and Corporations.* Englewood Cliffs, NJ: Prentice Hall.

______. (1988). Employment at Will and Due Process: Contrary Employment Practices. In T. Donaldson and P. H. Werhane, 313–319.

Westin, Alan F. (1981). *Whistle Blowing: Loyalty and Dissent in the Corporation.* New York: McGraw-Hill.

Weston, J. Fred, Kwand S. Chung, and Susan E. Hoag. (1990). *Mergers, Restructuring, and Corporate Control.* Englewood Cliffs, NJ: Prentice Hall.

White, Lawrence J. (Ed.). (1988). *Private Antitrust Litigation: New Evidence, New Learning.* Cambridge, MA: MIT Press.

White, Matthew W. (1997). Power Struggles: Explaining Deregulatory Reforms in Electricity Markets. *Brookings Papers on Economic Activity: Microeconomics,* 201–250.

Williams, Jeffrey R. (1992). How Sustainable Is Your Competitive Advantage. *California Management Review,* (Spring), 29–51.

Williamson, Oliver E. (1975). *Markets and Hierarchies: Analysis and Antitrust Implieations.* New York: The Free Press.

Wilson, James Q. (1980). *The Politics of Regulation.* New York: Basic Books.

______. (1989). *Bureaucracy: What Government Agencies Do and Why They Do It.* New York: Basic Books.

Wise, Mark, and Richard Gibb. (1993). *Single Market to Social Europe.* Essex, UK: Longman Scientific & Technical.

Wolf, Charles, Jr. (1979). A Theory of Nonmarket Failure. *Journal of Law and Economics, 22* (April), 107–139.

______. (1988). *Markets or Governments.* Cambridge, MA: MIT Press.

World Bank. (1997). World Development Indicators. Washington, DC.

Wu, Abraham H. (1994). Contributions, Lobbying, and Participation. Working paper. Stanford, CA: Stanford University.

Yang, C. K. (1959). *Chinese Communist Society: The Family and the Village.* Cambridge: MIT Press.

Yoffie, David B. (1983). *Power and Protectionism: Strategies of the Newly Industrializing Countries.* New York: Columbia University Press.

______. (1988a). How an Industry Builds Political Advantage. *Harvard Business Review,* (May–June), 82–89.

______. (1988b). Motorola and Japan and Motorola and Japan: Supplements I, II, III, 0-388-057, 0-388-058, 9-388-059. Boston, MA: Harvard Business School.

Yoffie, David B., and Benjamin Gomez-Casseres. (1994). *International Trade and Competition* (2d ed.). New York: McGraw-Hill.

Young, Lewis H. (1978, September 21). Business and the Media: The Failure to Understand How the Other Operates. Speech delivered at the ITT Key Issues Lecture Series, Columbia, Missouri.

Youngblood, Stuart A., and Gary L. Tidwell. (1981). Termination at Will: Some Changes in the Wind. *Personnel* (May–June), 22–33.

Index

A

B

C

D

E

F

H

I

M

O

P

Q

R

T

U

V

W

Z